Why Do You Need this New Edition?

If you're wondering why you should buy this new edition of *Understanding Psychology*, here are 7 good reasons!

1. There are more than 400 **NEW references** for this edition, of which 330 are from 2009–2011. Morris/Maisto provide a thorough review of introductory psychology, and the authors are very careful to include only recent research that has been supported by enough studies to qualify it as "accepted" by the psychological science community. Examples of new topics in the Tenth Edition include coverage of the insula (a brain region linked to emotion and desire), the effect of colors on behavior, sensitivity to sound in people who are blind, the impact of sleep deprivation on attention and memory, gender differences in sexuality across cultures, the influence of violent video games on aggressive behavior, adolescent cognitive development and legal responsibility, dramatic increases in well-being after age 50, long-term effects of stress on families, neurosurgical techniques, and how social psychological principles can be used to enhance environmental sustainability.

2. **Updated examples** throughout, particularly in the areas of culture and diversity. For example, new material on the importance of recognizing diverse forms of leadership in a global economy, new information on how culture influences our memory for music and the ability to detect subtle variations in music, an updated consideration of cultural differences in ways of thinking, and new material on gender differences in sexuality and the facial expression of emotion across cultures.

3. Instructors and students often complain of the growing "encyclopedic" books in introductory psychology. Through judicious editing by the authors, all the new content in the **Tenth Edition does not increase page count**.

4. The **visual content** of the book has been **thoroughly updated**, with some new chapter-opening photos and many new in-text photos throughout.

5. **Updated cross-references to MyPsychLab have been** integrated into the text and highlight the best videos, podcasts, and simulations that can be found in MyPsychLab. The icons are not exhaustive; many more resources are available than those highlighted in the book, but the icons do draw attention to some of the most high-interest materials available at www.mypsychlab.com.

6. **Updated Interactive PowerPoint Slides** built around the text learning objectives draw students into the lecture and provide wonderful interactive activities, visuals, and videos directly in the slides.

7. **Revised easily navigated eBook** with highlighting and note-taking features and powerful embedded media including simulations, podcasts, video clips, and an interactive timeline. The online media for *Understanding Psychology*, Tenth Edition, includes the new MyPsychLab video series, a 17 part series filmed in 2010 in high definition covering all of the major topics of the introductory psychology course, available only from Pearson.

PEARSON

UNDERSTANDING PSYCHOLOGY

TENTH EDITION

CHARLES G. MORRIS

ALBERT A. MAISTO

DSM
5

PEARSON

Boston Columbus Indianapolis New York San Francisco Upper Saddle River
Amsterdam Cape Town Dubai London Madrid Milan Munich Paris Montréal Toronto
Delhi Mexico City São Paulo Sydney Hong Kong Seoul Singapore Taipei Tokyo

Editorial Director: Craig Campanella

Editor in Chief: Jessica Mosher

Executive Editor: Stephen Frail

Editorial Project Manager: Judy Casillo

Editorial Assistant: Madelyn Schricker

Director of Marketing: Brandy Dawson

Marketing Manager: Brigeth Rivera

Marketing Assistant: Jessica Warren

Managing Editor: Maureen Richardson

Project Manager: Sherry Lewis

Operations Manager: Mary Fischer

Operations Specialist: Diane Peirano

Design Director: Leslie Osher

Designer: Ximena Tamvakopoulos

Cover Photo: Glow Images, Axiom Photographic

Full-Service Project Management: GEX Publishing Services

Composition: GEX Publishing Services

Printer/Binder: Courier, Kendallville, IN

Cover Printer: Courier, Kendallville, IN

Text Font: Minion Pro Regular 10/12

Credits and acknowledgments borrowed from other sources and reproduced, with permission, in this textbook appear on appropriate page within text (or on pages CR-1–CR-2).

Cataloging-in-Publication Data is on file at the Library of Congress

10 9 8 7 6 5 4 3 2

ISBN-10: 0-205-98618-8

ISBN-13: 978-0-205-98618-7

Brief Contents

Contents

8 _Motivation and Emotion_   258

9 _Life-Span Development_   292

10 _Personality_   332

Preface

With each new edition, we strive to make the text as current as possible, and continuously improve the book based on suggestions from the professors and students who use the current edition. At the same time, our original goals for this book remain the same. We wanted to present a scientific, accurate, and thorough overview of the essential concepts of psychology; to use engaging language that students can easily comprehend; to be current without being trendy; and to write clearly and accessibly about psychology and its concrete, real-life applications—without being condescending to the introductory-level student.

CONTINUED FOCUS ON BASIC UNIFYING CONCEPTS

In this new edition, we continue to focus on three unifying, basic concepts, which have been woven throughout every edition of our texts:

1. **Psychology is a science that is rapidly evolving.** From the thousands of articles that have appeared during the past several years, we selected more than 400 new references for this edition, of which 330 are from 2009–2011. Examples of new topics that did not appear at all in the previous edition include the impact of colors on behavior, sensitivity to sound in people who are blind, the impact of sleep deprivation on attention and memory, gender differences in sexuality across cultures, the influence of violent video games on aggressive behavior, adolescent cognitive development and legal responsibility, dramatic increases in well-being after age 50, long-term effects of stress on families, neurosurgical techniques and how social psychological principles can be used to enhance environmental sustainability.
2. **Human behavior and thought are diverse, varied, and affected by culture.** We have continued to give close attention to diversity. For example, in Chapter 6, we added new information on how culture influences our memory for music and the ability to detect subtle variations in music. In Chapter 7, we updated the discussion of cultural differences in ways of thinking and gender differences in cognitive skills. In Chapter 8, we added new material on gender differences in sexuality across cultures and added new material on the facial expression of emotion across cultures. In Chapter 9, new material was added on cultures that are death-affirming. In Chapter 11, we significantly revised and updated the discussion of gender differences in coping with stress. In Chapter 13, we provided new information on the importance of client diversity and treatment.
3. **The study of psychology involves active thinking, questioning, and problem solving.** We retained all the "Thinking Critically About" exercises. The topics encourage the reader to engage in genuine critical thinking by questioning the methods used to gather data, considering possible alternative explanations for findings, and imagining further research that might shed additional light on the phenomenon under study.

CONTINUING ATTENTION TO ENDURING ISSUES

We believe that an important part of active learning is for students to recognize recurring themes that run through the material they are reading. In Chapter 1, we introduce a set of five **Enduring Issues** that cut across and unite all subfields of psychology (see pages 6–7):

- **Person–Situation:** To what extent is behavior caused by processes that occur inside the person, such as thoughts, emotions, and genes? In contrast, to what extent is behavior caused or triggered by factors outside the person, such as incentives, cues in the environment, and the presence of other people?
- **Nature–Nurture:** Is the person we become a product of innate, inborn tendencies, or a reflection of experience and upbringing?

- **Stability–Change:** Are the characteristics we develop in childhood more or less permanent and fixed, or do we change in predictable (and unpredictable) ways over the course of our lives?
- **Diversity–Universality:** Because we are all human, each person is like every other person. But in some respects, each person is only like certain other people. And in other respects, each of us is like no other person. Thus, anywhere humans exist there will be both similarity and diversity.
- **Mind–Body:** How are mind and body connected? Many psychologists are fascinated by the relationship between what we experience, such as thoughts and feelings, and biological processes, such as activity in the nervous system.

These five issues represent enduring themes in the history of psychology. Depending on the events and intellectual climate of a given time period, one or another of these issues has assumed special prominence. For example, the role of genetics (heredity) is receiving much greater attention today than it has in the past. Diversity is also an issue of much greater concern, as is the role of biological processes.

Throughout this book, we will highlight the importance of these matters. Each chapter opens with a section highlighting the enduring issues to be encountered in that chapter. Several times in each chapter we will call the reader's attention to the way in which the topic under consideration—whether it be new discoveries about communication within the nervous system, research into how we learn, or the reason that people abuse drugs—reflects one of these issues. In this way, we will show the surprising unity and coherence of the diverse and exciting science of psychology.

Learning Objectives

The chapter learning objectives were carefully written to cover the content of each chapter and to ensure that students who master the objectives will indeed have a thorough grasp of the material. The objectives also help to organize the supplementary material, allowing for easy customization by instructors.

Opening Vignettes

Each chapter of our text begins with an opening vignette. Reviewers have often commented on how useful it is to have the vignette woven throughout the chapter to help students understand and apply information.

* ☀️┤Explore on **MyPsychLab**

((•● ((•●┤Listen on **MyPsychLab**

↻➤ ↻➤┤**Simulate** on **MyPsychLab**

👁 👁┤Watch on **MyPsychLab**

✔•┤**Study** and **Review** on **MyPsychLab**

MyPsychLab Integration

Throughout the text, you will find marginal icons that link to important videos, simulations, podcasts, and activities you can find on MyPsychLab. There are many more resources on MyPsychLab than those highlighted in the text, but the icons draw attention to some of the most high-interest materials.

NEW TO THIS EDITION

As authors and teachers, we are especially mindful of concerns about the rising cost of textbooks. One way to reduce costs is to reduce the length of a textbook. Since we reduced the length of the previous edition of *Understanding Psychology* by 10%, further reductions in length without reducing the coverage of the field turned out to be a real challenge. We started by making judicious editorial changes literally sentence by sentence. We also examined every reference to determine whether it is necessary and current. At the same time, we updated the content of the text and added new material throughout. We also set out to refresh the visual content of the textbook with some new chapter-opening photos and many new marginal photos throughout.

In addition to streamlining content, updating references and learning objectives, and adding numerous new photographs and figures, the following list highlights some of the most significant chapter-by-chapter changes.

CHAPTER 1 The Science of Psychology

- New material on the standards that apply to the use of animals in research
- New coverage of the history of psychology from the Greek philosophers to the 1880s
- New resources provided for information on careers in psychology
- Updated the topic of the complex relationship between genetics and environment
- Updated and extensively revised the discussion of evolutionary psychology
- 29 new references

CHAPTER 2 The Biological Basis of Behavior

- New coverage of the neurotransmitters GABA, Glutamate, and Glycene
- New information on neural plasticity
- New information on the insula and the ways in which this brain structure may be involved in the conscious expression of emotion and desire
- Expanded discussion of the role of testosterone in aggression and other behaviors
- Expanded discussion of fetal nerve cell transplants
- Expanded discussion of the ways in which handedness is expressed in non-human primates
- 56 new references

CHAPTER 3 Sensation and Perception

- New material on the effect of colors on behavior
- New discussion of hearing loss among teenagers
- New material on touch and communication of emotions
- New information on sensitivity to sound in people who are blind
- Extensive revision of section on visual adaptation
- Extensive revision of material on the gate control theory of pain perception
- 19 new references

CHAPTER 4 States of Consciousness

- New information on the use of sleeping pills
- New information on the impact of sleep deprivation on air traffic controllers
- New material on the ways in which campus alcohol policies can reduce binge drinking
- New information on caffeinated alcoholic beverages and energy drinks
- New material on nicotine's role as a potential "gateway" drug
- New material on the association between marijuana usage and reductions in white matter of the frontal lobes
- Updated all figures and references to the prevalence of using various drugs, alcohol consumption, fatalities in alcohol-related traffic accidents, as well as data on the consequences of drug use and abuse
- Significant updating and expansion of the discussion on biological and environmental factors that contribute to addiction
- 48 new sources

CHAPTER 5 Learning

- New material on superstitions and their effect on behavior
- Updated information on the long-term effects of rewarding behavior
- Significant updating, new material, and editing on cognitive learning in non-humans
- 10 new references

CHAPTER 6 Memory

- New material on the role episodic memories play in anticipating and envisioning future possibilities
- New material on how memories are stored in the brain
- New material on the role of sleep in improving procedural and emotional memory
- New material on how sleep deprivation may interfere with long-term potentiation
- New information on how culture influences our memory for music and the ability to detect subtle variations in music
- New material on the risk of fabricating false memories among individuals who spontaneously recover memories
- 36 new references

CHAPTER 7 Cognition and Mental Abilities

- New discussion of neural mechanisms that underlie creative thinking
- Updated discussion of cultural differences in ways of thinking
- Updated coverage of animal cognition
- Updated coverage of WAIS and WISC tests
- Updated discussion of long-term effects of Head Start
- Updated and revised discussion of gender differences in cognitive skills
- 28 new references

CHAPTER 8 Motivation and Emotion

- New material on role of advertising as it contributes to the drive for sweetened beverages
- New material on the brain structures involved in hunger drive
- New material on treatment for anorexia and bulimia
- New material on gender differences in sexuality across cultures
- New material on the nature versus nurture issue as it applies to sexual orientation
- New material on aggression and evolutionary psychology
- New material on the influence of violent video games on aggressive behavior
- New material on how oxytocin and dopamine are related to social bonding
- New material on facial expressions of emotions across cultures
- New material on mimicry in conversation and how it can diminish the ability to detect deception communication
- Updated aggressive behavior statistics
- 44 new references

CHAPTER 9 Life-Span Development

- New material on adolescent cognitive development and legal responsibility
- New, up-to-date coverage of bilingualism
- New material on technology's effect on social relationships in adolescence
- New information on the impact of divorce on children
- New information on dramatic increases in well-being after age 50
- New information on cultures that are death-affirming
- Updated information about partnerships in adulthood
- Updated information on women in the workplace
- Updated information on life expectancy
- 30 new references

CHAPTER 10 Personality

- New material on recent psychoanalytic theories and gender
- New research on the relationship between components of the Big Five Personality traits and job performance
- New subsection on how the Big Five are represented in the brain
- New mention of MMPI-2 in forensic evaluations
- Revised information on impact of Freud's theory
- 14 new references

CHAPTER 11 Stress and Health Psychology

- New chapter-opening vignette
- New figure on sources of stress 2007–2010
- New information on long-term effects of stress on families
- New information on hardiness and resilience
- New information about discrimination as a source of life-long stress
- New information about the effectiveness of counseling Type A people to reduce CHD
- New information about chronic stress and the immune system
- New information about long-lasting effects of stress
- Up-to-date information on stress in American families in 2010
- Significant revision of and new information about gender differences in coping with stress
- Up-to-date information on unemployment as a source of stress
- 28 new references

CHAPTER 12 Psychological Disorders

- New information on the estimated rate of schizophrenia across cultures and gender
- New material on the complex role of genetics in schizophrenia
- New information on the estimated prevalence of ADHD among US children
- New material on the role of the prefrontal cortex in ADHD
- New material from neuroimaging on the role of the frontal lobes, the amygdala, and the cerebellum in the development of autism
- New material on the possible role of maternal antibodies contributing to the development of autism
- 26 new references

CHAPTER 13 Therapies

- New information on telehealth
- New information on insurance companies' encouraging brief therapy
- "Psychosurgery" renamed "Neurosurgery" and thoroughly updated to include newer techniques
- New information on cost savings possible with early intervention with children
- New information on the importance of client diversity and treatment
- Additional information on varieties of person-centered therapy
- 17 new references

CHAPTER 14 Social Psychology

- New material from neuroscience examining the brain mechanisms that underlie the formation of a first impression
- New information on how repeated exposure enhances familiarity and liking

- New material from social neuroscience examining the brain mechanisms underlying the perception of attractive people
- New material on the role of the prefrontal cortex on the adaptive and self-monitoring aspects of attitudes
- New material from social neuroscience examining the brain mechanisms involved in Asch's classic conformity experiment
- New material on the importance of recognizing diverse forms of leadership in a global economy
- New Applying Psychology box on how principles learned from social psychology (i.e. social norms, persuasion, and social influence) can be used to enhance environmental sustainability
- Updated material on factors influencing the bystander effect
- Additional information on female leadership
- 24 new references

TEACHING AND LEARNING PACKAGE

It is increasingly true today that, as valuable as a good textbook is, it is one element of a comprehensive learning package. We have made every effort to provide high-quality instructor and student supplements that will save instructors preparation time and will enhance the classroom experience. **For access to all instructor supplements for Morris/Maisto, *Understanding Psychology*, Tenth Edition, and any other Pearson text, instructors can simply go to** the Pearson Instructor Resource Center at **http://www.pearsonhighered.com/irc** and follow the directions to register (or log on if you already have registered).

After logging on, the supplements for this text are accessed by using the "Browse by discipline" field at the top left of the screen. Select "Psychology," followed by "Introductory Psychology." Then click on the book cover for Morris/Maisto, *Understanding Psychology*, Tenth Edition in the list on the screen. Click on the "Resources" tab at the center of the next screen. A list of all of the supplements will appear under that tab. Under the description of each supplement is a link that allows instructors to download and save these resources to their own computers.

Hard copies of the supplements can be requested through your Pearson sales representative. If you do not know your sales representative, go to **http://www.pearsonhighered. com/replocator/** and follow the directions to locate your sales representative.

For technical support for any of your Pearson products, you and your students can contact **http://247.pearsoned.com.**

NOTE: The Morris/Maisto *Understanding Psychology*, Tenth Edition textbook is available in these formats:

Paperback (ISBN 0-205-84596-7)

Hardcover (ISBN 0-205-84616-5)

Books á la Carte (ISBN 0-205-84721-8)

CourseSmart e-Textbook subscription (http://www.coursesmart.com)

Test Item File One of the most respected test banks on the market today, this test file contains more than 4,000 multiple-choice, true/false, and essay questions. An additional feature of the test bank is the inclusion of rationales for the correct answer in the *conceptual* and *applied* multiple-choice questions. The rationales help instructors reviewing the content to further evaluate the questions they are choosing for their tests and give instructors the option to use the rationales as an answer key for their students. The Test Item File also provides a chapter-by-chapter "Total Assessment Guide" that arranges all questions in an easy-to-use reference grid. The TIF is available for download from the Instructor's Resource Center at http://www.pearsonhighered.com/irc or from the Instructor's DVD (ISBN 020584832X).

BlackBoard Test Item File and WebCT Test Item File: For instructors who only need the test item file for their learning management system, we offer the complete test item file in BlackBoard and WebCT format. Go to Instructor's Resource Center at **http://www.pearsonhighered.com/irc.**

MyTest The tenth edition test item file comes with Pearson MyTest, a powerful assessment generation program that helps instructors easily create and print quizzes and exams. Questions and tests can be authored online, providing instructors with ultimate flexibility to manage assessments efficiently any time, anywhere! Instructors can readily access existing questions and edit, create, and store using simple drag-and-drop and Word-like controls. A textbook page number is provided for each question, and each question maps to the text's major section. MyTest is available at **http://pearsonhighered.com/irc** with additional information at **http://www.PearsonMyTest.com.**

Interactive PowerPoint Slides: Available on the Instructor's Resource DVD (ISBN 020584832X). Bring the Morris/Maisto design right into the classroom, drawing students into the lecture and providing wonderful interactive activities, visuals, and videos. The slides are built around the text learning objectives and offer multiple pathways or links between content areas. Icons integrated throughout the slides indicate interactive exercises, simulations, and activities that can be accessed directly from the slides if instructors want to use these resources in the classroom.

Standard Lecture PowerPoint slides are also available on the Instructor Resource DVD (ISBN 020584832X) and online at **http://www.pearsonhighered.com/irc**, with a more traditional format with excerpts of the text material, photos, and artwork.

Classroom Response System (CRS) PowerPoint Slides: These slides are not only intended to be the basis for class lectures but also for class discussions. The incorporation of the CRS questions into each chapter slideshow facilitates the use of "clickers"—small hardware devices similar to remote controls, which process student responses to questions and interpret and display results in real time. CRS questions are a great means to engage students in learning and precipitate contemplation of text concepts. The slides are available for download at **http://www.pearsonhighered.com/irc.**

NEW MyPsychLab Video Series (17 episodes): This new video series offers instructors and students the most current and cutting-edge introductory psychology video content available anywhere. These exclusive videos take the viewer into today's research laboratories, inside the body and brain via breathtaking animations, and onto the street for real-world applications. Guided by the Design, Development and Review team, a diverse group of introductory psychology instructors, this comprehensive series features 17 half-hour episodes organized around the major topics covered in the introductory psychology course syllabus. For maximum flexibility, each half-hour episode features several brief clips that bring psychology to life:

- *The Big Picture* introduces the topic of the episode and provides the hook to draw students fully into the topic.
- *The Basics* uses the power of video to present foundational topics, especially those that students find difficult to understand.
- *Special Topics* delves deeper into high-interest and cutting-edge topics, showing research in action.
- *In the Real World* focuses on applications of psychological research.
- *What's i n It for Me?* These clips show students the relevance of psychological research to their own lives.

Available in MyPsychLab and also on DVD to adopters of Pearson psychology text-books (ISBN 0205035817).

Instructor's Resource Manual: Available for download from the Instructor's Resource Center at **http://www.pearsonhighered.com/irc** or on the Instructor's Resource DVD (ISBN 020584832X). In this abundant collection of resources, for each chapter, you'll find activities, exercises, assignments, handouts, and demos for in-class use, as well as guidelines for integrating the many Morris media resources into your classroom and syllabus. The material for each chapter is organized in an easy-to-use Chapter Lecture Outline. This resource saves prep work and helps you make maximum use of your classroom time. A unique hyper-linking system allows for easy reviewing of relevant sections and resources.

Instructor's DVD (ISBN 020584832X): Bringing all of the tenth edition's instructor resources together in one place, the Instructor's Resource DVD offers both versions of the PowerPoint presentations, the electronic files for the Instructor's Resource Manual materials, and the Test Item File to help you customize your lecture notes. (Note that these resources can also be downloaded from the Instructor Resource Center online by following the directions at **http://www.pearsonhighered.com/irc.**)

Study Guide for *Understanding Psychology*, Tenth Edition, (ISBN 020584311): The tenth edition study guide contains material to help reinforce students' understanding of the concepts covered in the text. Each chapter provides an overview to introduce students to the chapter; learning objective exercises to test students' understanding of the main themes; and multiple-choice pre- and posttests for gauging students' progress. Contact your local Pearson Education sales representative for a package ISBN of the text and study guide.

MyPsychLab

New MyPsychLab for *Understanding Psychology*, Tenth Edition

Personalize Learning With MyPsychLab

*   The **new MyPsychLab** delivers proven results in helping students succeed, provides engaging experiences that personalize learning, and comes from a trusted partner with educational expertise and a deep commitment to helping students and instructors achieve their goals.

    New MyPsychLab Video Series: New, exclusive 30-minute video segments for every chapter take the viewer from the research laboratory to inside the brain to out on the street for real-world applications.

*   The **new Experiments** application allows students to experience psychology. Students do experiments online to reinforce what they are learning in class and reading about in the book.

*   The **Pearson eText** lets students access their textbook anytime, anywhere, and any way they want—including listening online or downloading to an iPad.

*   A **personalized study plan** for each student, based on Bloom's Taxonomy, arranges content from less complex thinking—such as remembering and understanding—to more complex critical thinking—such as applying and analyzing. This layered approach promotes better critical-thinking skills and helps students succeed in the course and beyond.

*   **Assessment** tied to every video, application, and chapter enables both instructors and students to track progress and get immediate feedback. With results feeding into a powerful grade book, the assessment program helps instructors identify student challenges early—and find the best resources with which to help students.

*   An **assignment calendar** allows instructors to assign graded activities, with specific deadlines, and measure student progress.

*   New **MyClassPrep** collects the very best class presentation resources in one convenient online destination, so instructors can keep students engaged throughout every class.

MyPsychLab for BlackBoard and MyPsychLab for WebCT: The customized BlackBoard cartridge and WebCT epack include the complete Test Item File, chapter Learning Objectives, Glossary Flashcards, Chapter Summaries, a link to MyPsychLab, and Chapter Exams. Ask your Pearson representative about custom offerings for other learning management systems.

CourseSmart (http://www.coursesmart.com): CourseSmart Textbooks Online is an exciting new choice for students looking to save money. As an alternative to purchasing the print textbook, students can subscribe to the same content online and save up to 50% off the suggested list price of the print text. With a CourseSmart eTextbook, students can search the text, make notes online, print out reading assignments that incorporate lecture notes, and bookmark important passages for later review. For more information, or to subscribe to the CourseSmart eTextbook, visit www.coursesmart.com.

Other Texts That Might Interest You

Contact your Pearson Education representative to package any of the following supplementary texts with *Understanding Psychology*, Tenth Edition (Note: a package ISBN is required for your bookstore order):

Current Directions in Introductory Psychology, **Second Edition (ISBN 0137143508):** The second edition of this reader includes more than 20 articles that have been carefully selected for the undergraduate audience and taken from the very accessible *Current Directions in Psychological Science* journal. These timely, cutting-edge articles allow instructors to bring their students real-world perspective—from a reliable source—about today's most current and pressing issues in introductory psychology.

Forty Studies That Changed Psychology, **Sixth Edition (ISBN 013603599X) by Roger Hock (Mendocino College):** Presenting the seminal research studies that have shaped modern psychological study, this brief supplement provides an overview of the environment that gave rise to each study, its experimental design, its findings, and its impact on current thinking in the discipline.

The Psychology Major: Careers and Strategies for Success, **Fourth Edition (ISBN 0205684688) by R. Eric Landrum (Boise State University) and Stephen Davis (Morningside College):** This paperback text provides valuable information about career options available to psychology majors as well as tips for improving academic performance and a guide to the APA style of research reporting.

College Teaching Tips, **Second Edition (ISBN 020580960X):** This guide by Fred W. Whitford (Montana State University) helps new instructors or graduate teaching assistants manage the myriad complex tasks required to teach an introductory course effectively. The author has used his own teaching experiences over the past 25 years to help illustrate some of the types of problems that a new instructor may expect to face.

ACKNOWLEDGMENTS

We are grateful for the assistance we received from those who reviewed the previous editions and suggested improvements for this edition. Their thoughtful comments helped greatly to identify areas in need of special attention.

Eileen Achorn, *University of Texas–San Antonio*
Jackie Adamson, *Del Mar College*
Cheryl Bluestone, *Queensborough Community College*
Dixon A. Bramblett, *Lindenwood University*
Janet Cathey-Pugh, *Wallace Community College Selma*
Kelly Charlton, *University of North Carolina, Pembroke*
Christie Chung, *Mills College*

Stephen M. Colarelli, *Central Michigan University*
David Copeland, *University of Southern Mississippi*
Orlando Correa, *Harford Community College*
Layton Seth Curl, PhD, *Metropolitan State College of Denver*
Jim Dalton, *Sanford-Brown College*
Daniel Dickman, *Ivy Tech*
Michael Durnam, *Montana State University, Bozeman*
Joy Easton, *DeVry University*
Judith Easton, *Austin Community College*
Tom Frangicetto, *Northampton Community College*
Christian Fossa-Anderson, *DeVry University South Florida*
Lisa Fozio-Thielk, *Waubonsee Community College*
Joe Grisham, *Indian River Community College*
Dr. B. Hannon, *University of Texas, San Antonio*
Stephanie Hargrave, *Friends University*
Jack Harnett, *Virginia Commonwealth University*
Deborah Horn, *Blinn College*
Sonya Hutchinson, *Stillman College*
Jason Kaufman, PhD, *Inver Hills Community College*
Heather Lacost, *Waubonsee Community College*
Joseph Lao, *Borough of Manhattan Community College*
John Lindsay, *Georgia College and State University*
Brian Littleton, *Kalamazoo Valley Community College*
Nicholas Lynchard, *SUNY Ulster*
Gregory G. Manley, PhD, *University of Texas–San Antonio*
James Meyers, *Columbia Southern University*
Dr. Dan Muhwezi, *Butler County Community College*
Nathan Munn, *The University of Montana-Helena*
Kaneez Naseem, *Monroe College*
Dina Neal, *Vernon College*
Katy Neidhardt, *Cuesta Community College and California Polytechnic State University*
Jennifer Peluso, *Mercer University*
Terry Pettijohn, *Ohio State University*
William Premo, *Minnesota School of Business*
Leslie Reeder, *Wallace Community College*
Dr. Sharon Sawatzky, *Butler County Community College*
Harold Souheaver, *East Arkansas Community College*
Dr. Gary J. Springer, *Texas State University, San Marcos*
Krishna S. Stillanos, *Oakland Community College–Highland Lakes*
Karen Tinsley, *Guilford College*
Carolyn Tremblay, *Orlando Culinary Academy*
Blaine Weller, *Baker College*
Fred Whitford, *Montana State University*

We continue to be immensely grateful to our outstanding colleagues at Pearson, without whose assistance this book simply would not exist. Stephen Frail, Executive Editor, provided valuable advice and counsel from start to finish. Editorial Assistant, Maddy Schricker, superbly handled the many administrative details that inevitably arise as a book evolves. Judy Casillo, Managing Editor–Editorial, was once again an invaluable colleague who worked with us day-by-day (and occasionally hour-by-hour!) to help bring this revision in on schedule. The production of the tenth edition was expertly managed by Maureen Richardson and Sherry Lewis. Leslie Osher and Ximena Tamvakopoulos provided a terrific design for both the interior and the cover. Finally, our continuing thanks to the Pearson sales staff for their enthusiastic support of our text and for the excellent service they provide to our adopters.

Charles G. Morris
Albert A. Maisto

UNDERSTANDING PSYCHOLOGY

1

The Science of Psychology

OVERVIEW

Vernita Lee was 18 and unmarried in 1954 when she gave birth to a daughter in her mother's rundown Mississippi farmhouse. The baby's father, Vernon, was not seriously involved with Vernita, who continued to live with her mother, Hattie Mae. Four years later Vernita moved to Milwaukee, where she heard that young Black women could earn good money working as maids. Her daughter remained with Hattie Mae, helping to tend the pigs and chickens and hauling water from the well to the house. Without neighborhood friends to play with, the child entertained herself by talking to the animals, delighting in making speeches to the cows. Extremely gifted in language and encouraged by her grandmother, who highly valued education, she learned to read and write at the age of 3. Because of her remarkable ability to memorize passages from the Bible, she soon began delivering inspirational speeches in church, earning her the nickname "Little Preacher."

But the precocious child's life took a turn for the worse when she went to Milwaukee to live with her mother in a shabby rooming house. Vernita did not share Hattie Mae's devotion to education and she belittled her daughter's deep love of books. Neglected and often inadequately supervised, the girl was raped by a 19-year-old cousin when she was only 9 years old. Terrified, she kept her dark secret, only to become sexually abused by a procession of other men. Soon she blamed herself for what was happening to her. She also began to lie, steal, and run away. Vernita tried but failed to have her placed in a home for delinquent teenagers. Instead, the now pregnant 14-year-old girl went to live with her father, Vernon, in Nashville, Tennessee.

After the baby was born prematurely and died soon after birth, Vernon was able to provide his troubled daughter with the love, stability, and discipline she needed to turn her life around. He and his wife Zelma encouraged her to study hard and cultivate her talent for public speaking. Winning a speech contest earned her a 4-year scholarship to college. Other contest victories followed, capturing the attention of staff at a local radio station, who offered her a job as a newscaster even before she had graduated from high school. In college, CBS in Nashville hired her to anchor the evening news. She eventually moved to Chicago, where she began hosting a popular TV talk show. Audiences loved her personal touch and the way she often shared her innermost thoughts and feelings. Within a year the show had a new name. Rather than "A.M. Chicago," now it was "The Oprah Winfrey Show."

WHAT IS PSYCHOLOGY?

"Most psychologists study mental and emotional problems and work as psychotherapists." Is this statement true or false?

Why have we chosen the story of Oprah Winfrey to introduce you to the subject of psychology? It is because this story raises so many fascinating questions about human beings. What motivates a person to persevere against all odds and overcome enormous challenges? Do certain personality traits give such people unusual resilience to hardship? Or could anyone, investing enough effort, accomplish what Oprah has done? Many people in Oprah's situation would have succumbed to depression and given up trying to achieve. Why does this happen to some people but not others?

These are the same kinds of questions that psychologists also ask. Psychology is not confined to investigating abnormal behavior, as many people mistakenly assume. **Psychology** is the scientific study of behavior and mental processes in all their many facets. As such, viewed from a wealth of different perspectives, it encompasses every aspect of human thoughts, feelings, and actions. 👁

The Fields of Psychology

One way to grasp the breadth and depth of topics in psychology is to look at the major subfields within it. These are shown in **Table 1–1.** As you can see, psychology is not so much a single, unified field of study as it is an umbrella concept for a loose amalgamation of different subfields. Here, we introduce you to seven of the largest subfields in psychology.

Developmental Psychology *Developmental psychologists* study all aspects of human growth and change—physical, mental, social, and emotional—from the prenatal period through old age. Most specialize in a particular stage of human development.

◁┈┈ **LEARNING OBJECTIVES**

- Define *psychology* and describe some of the major subfields within psychology.
- Describe the five enduring issues that cut across the subfields of psychology.
- Explain what psychology has in common with other sciences, how psychologists use the scientific method, and the difference between theories and hypotheses.
- Apply critical thinking to an article in a magazine or newspaper.

👁─**Watch** the **Video** The Big Picture: Asking the Tough Questions on **MyPsychLab**

psychology The scientific study of behavior and mental processes.

TABLE 1–1   American Psychological Association Divisions (2011)

The two major organizations of psychologists in the United States are the American Psychological Association (APA), founded over 100 years ago, and the Association for Psychological Science (APS), founded in 1988. Members of both groups work in a wide variety of areas. The following list of divisions of the APA reflects the enormous diversity of the field of psychology.

Division*

1. Society for General Psychology
2. Society for the Teaching of Psychology
3. Experimental Psychology
5. Evaluation, Measurement, and Statistics
6. Behavioral Neuroscience and Comparative Psychology
7. Developmental Psychology
8. Society for Personality and Social Psychology
9. Society for the Psychological Study of Social Issues (SPSSI)
10. Psychology and the Arts
12. Society of Clinical Psychology
13. Society of Consulting Psychology
14. Society for Industrial and Organizational Psychology
15. Educational Psychology
16. School Psychology
17. Counseling Psychology
18. Psychologists in Public Service
19. Military Psychology
20. Adult Development and Aging
21. Applied Experimental and Engineering Psychology
22. Rehabilitation Psychology
23. Society for Consumer Psychology
24. Theoretical and Philosophical Psychology
25. Behavior Analysis
26. History of Psychology
27. Society for Community Research and Action: Division of Community Psychology
28. Psychopharmacology and Substance Abuse
29. Psychotherapy

30. Society of Psychological Hypnosis
31. State Psychological Association Affairs
32. Humanistic Psychology
33. Mental Retardation and Developmental Disabilities
34. Population and Environmental Psychology
35. Society for the Psychology of Women
36. Psychology of Religion
37. Child, Youth, and Family Services
38. Health Psychology
39. Psychoanalysis
40. Clinical Neuropsychology
41. American Psychology—Law Society
42. Psychologists in Independent Practice
43. Family Psychology
44. Society for the Psychological Study of Lesbian, Gay, and Bisexual Issues
45. Society for the Psychological Study of Ethnic Minority Issues
46. Media Psychology
47. Exercise and Sport Psychology
48. Society for the Study of Peace, Conflict, and Violence: Peace Psychology Division
49. Group Psychology and Group Psychotherapy
50. Addictions
51. Society for the Psychological Study of Men and Masculinity
52. International Psychology
53. Society of Clinical Child and Adolescent Psychology
54. Society of Pediatric Psychology
56. American Society for the Advancement of Pharmacotherapy
56. Trauma Psychology

*There are no divisions 4 or 11.

For information on a division, e-mail the APA at division@apa.org, or locate them on the Internet at www.apa.org/about/division.html

Source: American Psychological Association (2011). Divisions of the American Psychological Association from www.apa.org/about/division/index.aspx

Child psychologists focus on infants and children, concerning themselves with such issues as whether babies are born with distinct temperaments and at what age sex differences in behavior emerge. *Adolescent psychologists* look largely at how puberty affects a range of developmental phenomena, from relationships with peers and parents to the search for a personal identity. Finally, *life-span psychologists* focus on the challenges and changes of adulthood, from marrying and having children to facing the transitions related to aging and eventual death.

Physiological Psychology *Physiological psychologists* investigate the biological basis of human behavior, thoughts, and emotions. Among these, *neuropsychologists* are interested in the workings of the brain and nervous system. Their colleagues known as *biological psychologists* study the body's biochemistry and the ways that hormones, psychoactive medications, and "social drugs" affect us. *Behavioral geneticists* add yet another dimension: They explore the impact of heredity on both normal and abnormal behavior.

Experimental Psychology *Experimental psychologists* conduct research on basic psychological processes, including learning, memory, sensation, perception, thinking, motivation, and emotion.

Personality Psychology *Personality psychologists* study the differences among individuals in such traits as sociability, conscientiousness, emotional stability, self-esteem, agreeableness, aggressive inclinations, and openness to new experiences.

Clinical and Counseling Psychology When asked to describe a psychologist, most people think of a therapist who sees troubled people in an office, clinic, or hospital. This popular view is half correct. About 50% of psychologists specialize in clinical or counseling psychology, both of which seek to help people deal more successfully with their lives. *Clinical psychologists* are interested primarily in the diagnosis, causes, and treatment of psychological disorders, such as depression or acute anxiety. *Counseling psychologists,* in contrast, are concerned mainly with the everyday problems of adjustment that most of us face at some point in life, such as making a difficult career choice or coping with a troubled relationship. Clinical and counseling psychologists often divide their time between treating people and conducting research on the causes of psychological disorders and the effectiveness of different types of therapy.

Social Psychology *Social psychologists* believe that our thoughts, feelings, and behaviors are all greatly influenced by other people and the social situations in which we find ourselves. Social psychology is the scientific study of how these social influences are exerted and the effects they have.

Industrial and Organizational (I/O) Psychology *Industrial and organizational (I/O) psychologists* apply the principles of psychology to the workplace. They are concerned with such practical issues as selecting and training personnel and improving productivity and working conditions.

An overview of these major fields of psychology is presented in the following **Summary Table**.

How does Oprah Winfrey's life illustrate key points in psychology?

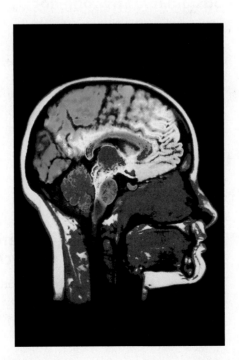

Recent advances in neuroimaging techniques enable physiological psychologists to investigate how specific regions of the brain are involved in complex behaviors and mental processes.

SUMMARY TABLE	THE FIELDS OF PSYCHOLOGY
Field of Psychology	**Description**
Developmental Psychology	The study of how people grow and change physically, cognitively, emotionally, and socially, from the prenatal period through death. Subfields include: *child, adolescent,* and *life-span* psychology.
Physiological Psychology	Investigates the biological basis of behavior. Subfields include *neuroscience, biological psychology,* and *behavior genetics.*
Experimental Psychology	Investigates basic psychological processes such as sensation and perception, memory, intelligence, learning, and motivation.
Personality Psychology	Studies the differences between individuals on such traits as sociability, emotional stability, conscientiousness, and self-esteem.
Clinical and Counseling Psychology	Applies the principles of psychology to mental health and adjustment. *Clinical psychology* focuses on the diagnosis and treatment of mental disorders while *counseling psychology* is more concerned with "normal" adjustment issues such as making difficult choices or coping with a troubled relationship.
Social Psychology	Explores how society influences thoughts, feelings and behavior.
Industrial and Organizational (I/O) Psychology	Applies the principles of psychology to the workplace.

APPLYING PSYCHOLOGY

Psychology's Contribution to a Sustainable Environment

Alan Kazdin, president of the American Psychological Association in 2008, has made the argument that the great variety of specialty areas in psychology is actually "an enormous strength" (Kazdin, 2009, p. 339). Psychologists, because of their diversity, are uniquely positioned to investigate and understand complex social problems such as terrorism, climate change, disasters, health care, crime and fostering a sustainable environment. Those problems share a number of characteristics, among them the fact that previously tried strategies are not likely to be effective. They call for new ways of thinking about and solving problems. Chapter 14's APPLYING PSYCHOLOGY box, "Conserving the Environment," describes specific examples of ways in which psychology can be applied to help conserve the environment.

ENDURING ISSUES

Given this broad range of careers and interests, what unifies the field of psychology?

What do psychologists who study organizations, psychological disorders, memory and cognition, behavioral genetics, or changes across the life span have in common? All psychologists share a common interest in five enduring issues that override their areas of specialization and cut to the core of what it means to be human. ∎

Person–Situation To what extent is behavior caused by such internal processes as thoughts, emotions, motives, attitudes, values, personality, and genes? In contrast, to what extent is behavior caused by such external factors as incentives, environmental cues, and the presence of other people? Put another way, are we masters of our fate or victims of circumstances? We will encounter these questions most directly in our consideration of behavior genetics, learning, emotion and motivation, personality, and social psychology.

Nature–Nurture To what extent are we a product of innate, inborn tendencies, and to what extent are we a reflection of experiences and upbringing? This is the famous "nature versus nurture" debate. For decades, psychologists have argued about the relative influence of heredity (genes) versus environment (experience) on thought and behavior. More recently, psychologists have begun studying the extent to which genetic differences only appear in specific environments, and the extent to which certain experiences only affect people with particular genetic predispositions (Champagne, 2009). This complex issue surfaces most clearly in our discussions of behavior genetics, intelligence, development, personality, and abnormal psychology.

Stability–Change Are the characteristics we develop in childhood more or less permanent and fixed, or do we change significantly over the course of our lives? Developmental psychologists are especially interested in these and other questions, as are psychologists who specialize in personality, adjustment, abnormal psychology, and therapy.

Diversity–Universality Because we are all human, each person is like every other person. But in some respects, each person is only like certain other people. And in other respects, each of us is like no other person. Thus, anywhere humans exist there will be both similarity and diversity. Throughout this book, we will encounter these questions: Does our understanding of human behavior apply equally well to every human being? Does it apply only to men or just to women, or only to particular racial or ethnic groups or particular societies (especially our own)? Do we perhaps need "different psychologies" to account for the wide diversity of human behaviors (Arnett, 2008)?

Mind–Body Finally, how are mind and body connected? Many psychologists are fascinated by the relationship between what we experience (such as thoughts and feelings) and what our biological processes are (such as activity in the nervous system). This mind–body

"I told my parents that if grades were so important they should have paid for a smarter egg donor."

To understand human behavior, we must appreciate the rich diversity of culture throughout the world.

issue will arise most clearly in our discussions of the biological basis of behavior, sensation and perception, altered states of consciousness, emotion and motivation, adjustment and health psychology, and disorders and therapy.

These five issues represent enduring themes in the history of psychology. Depending on the events and intellectual climate of a given time period, one or another of these issues has assumed special prominence in the history of psychology. For example, at the beginning of the 21st century the role of genetics (heredity) is receiving much greater attention than in the past. Diversity is also an issue of much greater concern, as is the role of biological processes.

Throughout this book, we will highlight the importance of these matters. Several times in each chapter we will call your attention to the way in which the topic under consideration reflects one of these issues. In this way, we will show the surprising unity and coherence within the diverse science of psychology.

Psychology as Science
What does psychology have in common with other sciences?

Earlier we defined psychology as the science of behavior and mental processes. The key word in this definition is *science*. Psychologists rely on the **scientific method** when seeking to answer questions. They collect data through careful, systematic observation; attempt to explain what they have observed by developing theories; make new predictions based on those theories; and then systematically test those predictions through additional observations and experiments to determine whether they are correct. Thus, like all scientists, psychologists use the scientific method to describe, understand, predict, and, eventually, achieve some measure of control over what they study.

For example, consider the question of whether males are more aggressive than females. How would psychologists approach the issue? First, they would want to find out whether in fact men and women actually differ in aggressive behavior. Hundreds of research studies have addressed this question, and the evidence seems conclusive: Although males and females do not differ significantly in feelings of anger, males are more physically and verbally aggressive than females (Archer, 2009). Males are usually more physically aggressive than females in non-human species as well. Once psychologists have established that there are indeed sex differences in aggression, the next step is to attempt to explain those differences. A number of explanations are possible. For example, if you are a physiological psychologist, you will probably ascribe these differences to genetics or body chemistry. If you are a social psychologist, you might explain the differences in terms of cultural norms, which require males to "stand up for themselves" and hold that physical aggression isn't "feminine." If you are an evolutionary psychologist, you might point out that females of many species (especially mammals) have traditionally born greater responsibility than males for caring for their offspring and ensuring their survival. Perhaps females have evolved to avoid hostile confrontations that could harm or kill them.

Each of these explanations stands as a **theory** about the causes of sex differences in aggression. And each theory allows you to make new **hypotheses,** or predictions, about the phenomenon in question. For example, if gender differences in aggression arise because males have higher levels of testosterone than females do, you would predict that extremely violent men should have higher levels of testosterone than do men who are generally nonviolent. If sex differences in aggression reflect cultural norms, you would predict that within societies that encourage nonviolence and peaceful coexistence the difference in aggression across the sexes should be small. If sex differences are due to an evolutionary advantage for females to avoid direct, aggressive confrontations in order to reproduce and care for their offspring, you would expect sex differences to be greatest for physical aggression and somewhat less for verbal aggression. You would also expect such inborn sex differences to appear very early in life.

Each of these predictions or hypotheses can be tested through research, and the results should indicate whether one theory is better than another at accounting for known facts

scientific method An approach to knowledge that relies on collecting data, generating a theory to explain the data, producing testable hypotheses based on the theory, and testing those hypotheses empirically.

theory Systematic explanation of a phenomenon; it organizes known facts, allows us to predict new facts, and permits us to exercise a degree of control over the phenomenon.

hypotheses Specific, testable predictions derived from a theory.

and predicting new facts. You will learn in Chapters 2 and 8 that there is no simple relationship between testosterone and aggressiveness. In Chapter 8 ("Motivation and Emotion") you will also learn that indeed cultural norms do affect sex difference in aggressiveness among humans, but that doesn't explain sex differences in non-human species. In Chapter 2 ("The Biological Basis of Behavior") you will also learn that research data do provide some support for the evolutionary theory of sex differences in aggression.

Critical Thinking: Thinking Like a Scientist

What does it mean to "think critically?"

Consider the statement "Opposites attract." Do you agree with this statement? Many people answer yes without hesitation on the grounds that "Everybody knows that." Critical thinkers, however, question common knowledge. Learning to think critically is one of the "fringe benefits" of studying psychology. (See "Applying Psychology: The Benefits of Studying Psychology.")

When we think critically, we define problems, examine evidence, analyze assumptions, consider alternatives and, ultimately, find reasons to support or reject an argument. To think critically, you must adopt a state of mind that is characterized by objectivity, caution, a willingness to challenge other people's opinions, and—perhaps most difficult of all—a willingness to subject your deepest beliefs to scrutiny. In other words, you must think like a scientist. 👁

Psychologists use a number of strategies in questioning assumptions and examining data. Here, we use the rules of psychological investigation to judge whether the previously mentioned assertion that "opposites attract" is correct:

- ***Define the problem or the question you are investigating.*** Do opposites attract each other?
- ***Suggest a theory or a reasonable explanation for the problem.*** People who are dissimilar balance each other in a relationship.
- ***Collect and examine all the available evidence.*** Be skeptical of people's self-reports, as they may be subjectively biased. If data conflict, try to find more evidence.

👁 **Watch** the **Video** Thinking Like a Psychologist: Debunking Myths on **MyPsychLab**

Males are more physically aggressive than females. Different areas within psychology have different explanations for why this is the case.

Research on attraction yields no support for the idea that opposites attract, whereas many studies confirm that people of similar looks, interests, age, family background, religion, values, and attitudes seek each other.

- *Analyze assumptions.* Because balancing different people's strengths and weaknesses is a good way to form a group, you might assume it is a good basis for personal relationships as well, which would explain why people of opposite temperaments would be attracted to each other. Yet research evidence shows that such an assumption is false. Why should people of similar temperaments attract each other? One important reason is that they often belong to the same social circles. Research suggests proximity is a big factor in attraction.

APPLYING PSYCHOLOGY

The Benefits of Studying Psychology

Although psychology is the fourth most popular undergraduate major (after Business, Social Sciences & History, and Education) (American Psychological Association, 2008b), we know that many students take psychology classes in order to fulfill a general requirement for their degree, rather than out of a compelling interest in the subject. Those students, and even some who are keenly interested in psychology, may wonder, "What am I going to gain from taking this course?" There are several benefits that you can gain from studying psychology:

- **Self-understanding.** Almost all of us want to understand ourselves and others better. In our daily lives, we often look for answers by relying on our own experience, knowledge, and assumptions. But, as you will see, that barely scratches the surface. As a psychology student, you will be challenged to go beyond the superficial in your life and confront what really lies behind your most basic actions. You will learn to look deeply into human behavior and ask complex and precise questions. In the process, you will not only achieve a better understanding of yourself and your fellow human beings, but also come to realize that much of what we consider "just plain common sense about people" doesn't hold up under scrutiny.
- **Critical thinking skills.** In addition to greater understanding of yourself and others, by studying psychology you will

also have an opportunity to acquire some specific skills. One of those skills is the ability to think critically about psychological issues: to clearly define issues, to examine the evidence bearing on them, to become more aware of hidden assumptions, to resist the temptation to oversimplify, to draw conclusions carefully, and above all to realize the relevance of empirical research to understanding psychological issues. As a result of practicing critical thinking, you will become a more sophisticated consumer of the information available to you in the mass media (Bensley, Crowe, Bernhardt, Buckner, & Allman, 2010; Gray, 2008). You will also become more cautious about too quickly accepting what looks like "common sense."

- **Skill in the application of the scientific method.** Because psychology uses the scientific method to understand behavior, studying psychology helps students understand and become proficient in the principles and application of the scientific method. Perhaps this is why increasing numbers of educators use psychology to teach the fundamentals of the scientific method to undergraduates who show little interest in more traditional scientific disciplines like chemistry or physics (Dingfelder, 2007).
- **Study skills.** You will also have the opportunity to acquire better study skills that will serve you well in all your courses. You will find an entire chapter on human memory (Chapter 6) containing excellent

information about making the most of your study time. But you will also find information about the relation between sleep and learning and the effects of drugs on memory (Chapter 4), about the nature of intelligence and its relation to success in school and in later life (Chapter 7), about the effects of motivation and arousal on the ability to learn and to perform (Chapter 8), and about age differences in the ability to learn and remember (Chapter 9).

- **Job skills.** Finally, you may acquire some skills that will help you find a job. This chapter lists many career possibilities for students who earn degrees in psychology. In addition, many careers outside psychology draw on a person's knowledge of psychology. For example, personnel administrators deal with employee relations, vocational rehabilitation counselors help people with disabilities find employment, and day-care center supervisors oversee the care of preschool children. Indeed, employers in areas such as business and finance seek out psychology majors because of their knowledge of the principles of human behavior and their skills in experimental design and data collection and analysis.

Of course, all of these benefits are much more likely to accrue to students who regularly attend class, study, and try to apply what they learn to their own lives. As with many other opportunities, the benefits you receive are, in large part, up to you.

- *Avoid oversimplifying.* Don't overlook the evidence that people of similar temperaments find living together rather difficult in some ways. For example, living with someone who is as tense as you are may be harder than living with someone of calm temperament—your opposite.
- *Draw conclusions carefully.* It seems safe to conclude that, in general, opposites don't attract, but there are specific exceptions to this general rule.
- *Consider every alternative interpretation.* People may cite cases that conflict with your conclusion. Remember, however, that their arguments are likely to be based on subjective observations and a far narrower database than researchers have used when studying this question.
- *Recognize the relevance of research to events and situations.* Let's say you have been thinking of dating someone whose temperament seems quite different from yours. You may decide, based on what you now know, not to rush into things but to go more slowly, testing your own observations against your knowledge of research findings. But since there are cases where opposites do attract, you may indeed find that person attractive.

CHECK YOUR UNDERSTANDING

1. Indicate whether each of the following statements is true (T) or false (F):
   a. _____ Psychologists collect data through careful, systematic observation.
   b. _____ Psychologists try to explain their observations by developing theories.
   c. _____ Psychologists form hypotheses or predictions on the basis of theories.
   d. _____ Psychologists appeal to common sense in their arguments.
   e. _____ Psychologists systematically test hypotheses.
   f. _____ Psychologists base their conclusions on widely shared values.

Answers: a. (T). b. (T). c. (T). d. (F). e. (T). f. (F).

APPLY YOUR UNDERSTANDING

1. Caroline is interested in the extent to which personality characteristics are determined for life by genetics or the extent to which they can be changed as a result of the experiences of our lives. Which of the enduring issues discussed in this chapter best describes Caroline's interests?
   a. mind–body
   b. diversity–universality
   c. nature–nurture
   d. tastes great–less filling

2. Dakota spends most of his work time in his office helping clients with adjustment problems, such as troubled marriages, and coping with career changes, such as retirement. Dakota is most likely a(n) _____ psychologist.
   a. industrial
   b. organizational
   c. clinical
   d. counseling

Answers: 1. c. 2. d.

THE GROWTH OF PSYCHOLOGY

"Psychology has a long past, but a short history." What does that mean?

Prior to about the 5th century B.C.E., nobody thought much about trying to understand human thoughts and behavior. People regarded their mental processes with awe, assuming that thoughts and emotions were the work of spirits and gods. That all changed when Greek philosophers began to speculate about how the mind works, about where thoughts and feelings come from if not from the gods, and about how the mind might

LEARNING OBJECTIVES

- Describe the emergence of scientific psychology in the late 19th and early 20th centuries.
- Explain the differences between psychodynamic, behavioral, humanistic, cognitive, evolutionary, and positive psychology.
- Describe the role of women in the history of psychology.

Dualism View that thoughts and feelings (the mind) are distinct from the world of real objects and our bodies.

affect behavior. Socrates (470–399 B.C.E.) believed that we are born with knowledge and, by reasoning correctly, we gain access to it. He also believed that our minds (souls) do not cease to exist when we die. In other words, thoughts and ideas are distinct from the world of real objects and our bodies, a concept that is known as **dualism.** Plato (427–347 B.C.E.) was a student of Socrates. Not surprisingly, he believed in innate knowledge that we access through careful reasoning. He also divided the world into two realms, with mind being pure and abstract, and all else physical and mundane. He also suggested that reason is responsible for balancing our desires (appetites) on the one hand with our (spirit) on the other in pursuit of reason's goals. As we will see, this notion is remarkably similar to ideas put forth by Sigmund Freud thousands of years later. Aristotle (384–322 B.C.E.) was a student of Plato but he came to very different conclusions about the sources of knowledge. In particular, he believed that we acquire knowledge by observing the physical world and using logic and reasoning to make sense of our observations. We perceive the world, remember at least some of what we have perceived, and by thinking we arrive at understanding. In other words, there is no innate knowledge. His emphasis on careful observation and reasoning about facts are precursors to the modern, scientific study of behavior.

For the next 2,000 years hardly anyone spent time pondering the nature of human thought and its relationship to behavior. With the end of the Dark Ages and the beginnings of the scientific revolution, René Descartes (1596–1650) took the position that the human mind, unlike the physical world, is not subject to laws. Moreover, though the mind is not observable, it controls the body; and in turn, the body provides information for the mind. You will recognize this as another example of dualism. And indeed understanding the relation between mind and body continues to challenge psychologists today, as we will see. John Locke (1632–1704) took a very different view. Like Aristotle, he concluded that we gain knowledge through experience. In sharp contrast to Socrates and Plato, he said the human mind at the moment of birth is a *tabula rasa,* a "blank slate" that contains no innate knowledge. And unlike Descartes, he believed that even the human mind operates according to laws. Thomas Hobbes (1588–1679) went even further. He claimed that such things as "soul" and "spirit" and "mind" are meaningless. According to Hobbes, thoughts and experiences are simply by-products of the workings of our brain. In this respect, Hobbes anticipated the position of psychological behaviorists as we shall soon see. Charles Darwin (1809–1882) followed in Hobbes' path by asserting that while the mind is unobservable (and thus not a proper subject for scientific study), behavior is observable and thus open to scientific examination. Moreover, Darwin took the position that behavior evolves—behavior that contributes to the survival of a species tends to persist while behavior that is detrimental to survival tends to disappear over time. Evolutionary psychologists today follow in that same tradition.

It was not until the late 1800s that the scientific method began to be applied to questions that had puzzled philosophers for centuries. Only then did psychology come into being as a formal, scientific discipline separate from philosophy. The history of psychology can be divided into three main stages: the emergence of a science of the mind, the behaviorist decades, and the "cognitive revolution."

The "New Psychology": A Science of the Mind

**How did Wundt help to define psychology as a science of the mind?
Why did James think that sensation and perception alone couldn't explain behavior?
Why was Freud's theory of the unconscious shocking at the turn of the 20th century?**

At the beginning of the 20th century, most university psychology programs were located in philosophy departments. But the foundations of the "new psychology"—the science of psychology—had been laid.

Wilhelm Wundt and Edward Bradford Titchener: Voluntarism and Structuralism Most psychologists agree that psychology was born in 1879, the year that Wilhelm Wundt founded the first psychological laboratory at the University of Leipzig in Germany. In the public eye, a laboratory identified a field of inquiry as "science" (Benjamin, 2000). At the outset, Wundt did not attract much attention; only four students attended his first lecture. By the mid-1890s, however, his classes were filled to capacity.

Wundt attempted to explain immediate experience and to develop ways to study it scientifically, though he also believed that some mental processes could not be studied through scientific experiments. Wundt was primarily interested in memory and *selective attention*—the process by which we determine what we are going to attend to at any given moment. Wundt used the term *voluntarism* to describe his view of psychology. He believed that attention is actively controlled by intentions and motives, and that this sets human attention apart from attention in other organisms. In turn, attention controls such other psychological processes as perceptions, thoughts, and memories. We will examine the role of attention more closely in Chapter 4 ("States of Consciousness") and Chapter 6 ("Memory"), but for the moment it is sufficient to note that, in establishing a laboratory and insisting on measurement and experimentation, Wundt moved psychology out of the realm of philosophy and into the world of science.

One important product of the Leipzig lab was its students who carried the new science of psychology to universities in other countries, including the United States: G. Stanley Hall (who established the first American psychology laboratory at Johns Hopkins University in 1883), J. M. Cattell (a professor at the University of Pennsylvania in 1888, who was the first American to be called a "professor of psychology"), and British-born Edward Bradford Titchener, who went to Cornell University. Titchener's ideas differed sharply in many respects from those of his mentor (Sundqvist, 2007). Titchener was impressed by recent advances in chemistry and physics, achieved by analyzing complex compounds (molecules) in terms of their basic elements (atoms). Similarly, Titchener reasoned, psychologists should analyze complex experiences in terms of their simplest components. For example, when people look at a banana they immediately think, "Here is a fruit, something to peel and eat." But this perception is based on associations with past experience; what are the most fundamental elements, or "atoms," of thought?

Titchener broke down consciousness into three basic elements: physical sensations (what we see), feelings (such as liking or disliking bananas), and images (memories of other bananas). Even the most complex thoughts and feelings, he argued, can be reduced to these simple elements. Titchener saw psychology's role as identifying these elements and showing how they can be combined and integrated—an approach known as **structuralism**. Although the structuralist school of psychology was relatively short-lived and has had little long-term effect, the study of perception and sensation continues to be very much a part of contemporary psychology, as you will see in Chapter 3, "Sensation and Perception."

William James: Functionalism One of the first academics to challenge structuralism was an American, William James (son of the transcendentalist philosopher Henry James, Sr., and brother of novelist Henry James). As a young man, James earned a degree in physiology and also studied philosophy on his own, unable to decide which interested him more. In psychology, he found the link between the two. In 1875, James offered a class in psychology at Harvard. He later commented that the first lecture he ever heard on the subject was his own.

James argued that Titchener's "atoms of experience"—pure sensations without associations—simply do not exist in real-life experience. Our minds are constantly weaving associations, revising experience, starting, stopping, and jumping back and forth in time. Perceptions, emotions, and images cannot be separated, James argued; consciousness flows in a continuous stream. If we could not recognize a banana, we would have to figure out what it was each time we saw one. Mental associations allow us to benefit from previous experience. When we get up in the morning, get dressed, open the door, and walk down the street, we don't have to think about what we are doing: We act out of habit. James suggested that when we repeat something, our nervous systems are changed so that each repetition is easier than the last.

James developed a **functionalist theory** that focused on how individuals use their perceptual abilities to adapt and function in their environment. This theory raised questions about learning, the complexities of mental life, the impact of experience on the brain, and humankind's place in the natural world that still seem current today. Although

structuralism School of psychology that stresses the basic units of experience and the combinations in which they occur.

functionalist theory Theory of mental life and behavior that is concerned with how an organism uses its perceptual abilities to function in its environment.

Wilhelm Wundt

William James

Sigmund Freud

impatient with experiments, James shared Wundt and Titchener's belief that the goal of psychology was to analyze experience.

Sigmund Freud: Psychodynamic Psychology Of all psychology's pioneers, Sigmund Freud is by far the best known—and the most controversial. A medical doctor, unlike the other figures we have introduced, Freud was fascinated by the central nervous system. He spent many years conducting research in the physiology laboratory of the University of Vienna and only reluctantly became a practicing physician. After a trip to Paris, where he studied with a neurologist who was using hypnosis to treat nervous disorders, Freud established a private practice in Vienna in 1886. His work with patients convinced him that many nervous ailments are psychological, rather than physiological, in origin. Freud's clinical observations led him to develop a comprehensive theory of mental life that differed radically from the views of his predecessors.

Freud held that human beings are not as rational as they imagine and that "free will," which was so important to Wundt, is largely an illusion. Rather, we are motivated by unconscious instincts and urges that are not available to the rational, conscious part of our mind. Other psychologists had referred to the unconscious, in passing, as a dusty warehouse of old experiences and information we could retrieve as needed. In contrast, Freud saw the unconscious as a dynamic cauldron of primitive sexual and aggressive drives, forbidden desires, nameless fears and wishes, and traumatic childhood memories. Although hidden from awareness, unconscious impulses press on the conscious mind and find expression in disguised or altered form, including dreams, mannerisms, slips of the tongue, and symptoms of mental illness, as well as in socially acceptable pursuits such as art and literature. To uncover the unconscious, Freud developed the technique of *free association*, in which the patient lies on a couch, recounts dreams, and says whatever comes to mind.

Freud's psychodynamic theory was controversial at the turn of the century. Many of Freud's Victorian contemporaries were shocked, not only by his emphasis on sexuality, but also by his suggestion that we are often unaware of our true motives and thus are not entirely in control of our thoughts and behavior. Conversely, members of the medical community in Vienna at that time generally held Freud's new theory in high regard, nominating him for the position of Professor Extraordinarious at the University of Vienna (Esterson, 2002). Freud's lectures and writings attracted considerable attention in the United States as well as in Europe; he had a profound impact on the arts and philosophy, as well as on psychology. However, Freud's theories and methods continue to inspire heated debate.

Psychodynamic theory, as expanded and revised by Freud's colleagues and successors, laid the foundation for the study of personality and psychological disorders, which we will discuss in Chapters 10, 12 and 13. His revolutionary notion of the unconscious and his portrayal of human beings as constantly at war with themselves are taken for granted today, at least in literary and artistic circles. Freud's theories were never totally accepted by mainstream psychology, however; and in recent decades his influence on clinical psychology and psychotherapy has declined.

Redefining Psychology: The Study of Behavior

How was Watson's approach to human behavior different from that of Freud?

How did Skinner expand behaviorism?

Until the beginning of the 20th century, psychology was defined as the study of mental processes. The primary method of collecting data was introspection or self-observation, which occurred in a laboratory or on an analyst's couch. At the beginning of the 20th century, however, a new generation of psychologists rebelled against this "soft" approach. The leader of the challenge was the American psychologist John B. Watson.

John B. Watson: Behaviorism While Freud explored unconscious forces in Vienna, across the ocean, John B. Watson argued that the whole idea of mental life was superstition, a relic left over from the Middle Ages. In "Psychology as a Behaviorist Views It" (1913),

psychodynamic theories Personality theories contending that behavior results from psychological factors that interact within the individual, often outside conscious awareness.

Watson contended that you cannot see or even define consciousness any more than you can observe a soul. And if you cannot locate or measure something, it cannot be the object of scientific study. For Watson, psychology was the scientific study of observable, measurable behavior—and nothing more.

Watson's view of psychology, known as **behaviorism,** was based on the work of the Russian physiologist Ivan Pavlov, who had won a Nobel Prize for his research on digestion. In the course of his experiments, Pavlov noticed that the dogs in his laboratory began to salivate as soon as they heard their feeder coming, even before they could see their dinner. He decided to find out whether salivation, an automatic reflex, could be shaped by learning. He began by repeatedly pairing the sound of a buzzer with the presence of food. The next step was to observe what happened when the buzzer was sounded without introducing food. This experiment clearly demonstrated what Pavlov had noticed incidentally: After repeated pairings, the dogs salivated in response to the buzzer alone. Pavlov called this simple form of training *conditioning*. Thus, a new school of psychology was inspired by a casual observation—followed by rigorous experiments. We will learn more about the findings of this approach in Chapter 5, "Learning."

Watson came to believe that all mental experiences—thinking, feeling, awareness of self—are nothing more than physiological changes in response to accumulated experiences of conditioning. Experience may write virtually anything. He held the position that if he were able to completely control the environment, he could train any healthy infant to become any kind of adult he chose, physician, lawyer, artist, or even thief or beggar (J. B. Watson, 1924).

John B. Watson

Watson attempted to demonstrate that all psychological phenomena—even Freud's unconscious motivations—are the result of conditioning. In one of the most infamous experiments in psychology's history, Watson attempted to create a conditioned fear response in an 11-month-old boy. "Little Albert" was a secure, happy baby who enjoyed new places and experiences. On his first visit to Watson's laboratory, Albert was delighted by a tame, furry white rat, but he became visibly frightened when Watson banged a steel bar with a hammer just behind the infant's head. On his second visit, Watson placed the rat near Albert, and the moment the baby reached out and touched the rat, Watson banged the hammer. After half a dozen pairings, little Albert began crying the instant the rat was introduced, without any banging. Further experiments found that Albert was frightened by anything white and furry—a rabbit, a dog, a sealskin coat, cotton wool, and Watson wearing a Santa Claus mask (J. B. Watson & Rayner, 1920; also see Beck, Levinson, & Irons, 2009). Freud had labeled the transfer of emotions from one person or object to another "displacement," a neurotic response that he traced to the unconscious. Drawing on Pavlov, Watson called the same phenomenon "generalization," a simple matter of conditioning. As far as Watson was concerned, psychodynamic theory and psychoanalysis were "voodooism."

Watson was also interested in showing that fears could be eliminated by conditioning. Mary Cover Jones, one of his graduate students, successfully reconditioned a boy who showed a fear of rabbits (not caused by laboratory conditioning) to overcome this fear. Her technique, which involved presenting the rabbit at a great distance and then gradually bringing it closer while the child was eating, is similar to conditioning techniques used by psychologists today.

B. F. Skinner: Behaviorism Revisited Following in the footsteps of Pavlov and Watson, B. F. Skinner became one of the leaders of the behaviorist school of psychology in the mid-20th century. Like Watson, Skinner fervently believed that psychologists should study only observable and measurable behavior. He, too, was primarily interested in changing behavior through conditioning—and in discovering natural laws of behavior in the process. But Skinner added a new element to the behaviorist repertoire: reinforcement. He rewarded his subjects for behaving the way he wanted them to behave. For example, an animal was put into a special cage and allowed to explore it. Eventually, the animal reached up and pressed a lever or pecked at a disk on the wall, whereupon a food pellet dropped into the box. Gradually, the animal learned that pressing the bar or pecking

Mary Cover Jones

behaviorism School of psychology that studies only observable and measurable behavior.

B. F. Skinner

at the disk always brought food. Why did the animal learn this? It learned because it was *reinforced,* or rewarded, for doing so. Skinner thus made the animal an active agent in its own conditioning.

Behaviorism dominated academic psychology in the United States well into the 1960s. One unintended and, at the time, largely unnoticed consequence was that psychology developed an *environmental bias:* Virtually every aspect of human behavior was attributed to learning and experience. Investigating evolutionary influences on behavior or studying hereditary, genetic influences on individual and group differences was considered taboo (R. B. Evans, 1999).

The Cognitive Revolution

How did Gestalt psychologists influence the way we think about perception?
What aspects of life do humanistic psychologists stress?

In the late 1960s, behaviorism began to loosen its grip on the field. On one hand, research on perception, personality, child development, interpersonal relations, and other topics that behaviorists had ignored raised questions they couldn't readily explain. On the other hand, research in other fields (especially anthropology, linguistics, neurobiology, and computer science) was shedding new light on the workings of the mind. Psychologists came to view behaviorism not as an all-encompassing theory, but as only one piece of the puzzle that played an important role in the development of psychology as a science (Moore, 2010). They began to look into the "black box" of the human mind and put more emphasis on humans (and other animals) as conscious, perceptive, and alert beings; that is, as active learners, rather than passive recipients of life's lessons.

The Precursors: Gestalt and Humanistic Psychology Even during the period that behaviorism dominated American psychology, not all psychologists had accepted behaviorist doctrines. Two schools that paved the way for the cognitive revolution were Gestalt psychology and humanistic psychology.

In Germany, psychologists Max Wertheimer, Wolfgang Köhler, and Kurt Koffka were all interested in perception, particularly in certain tricks that the mind plays on itself. For example, when we see a series of still pictures flashed at a constant rate (for example, movies or "moving" neon signs), why do the pictures seem to move? Phenomena like these launched a new school of thought, **Gestalt psychology.** Roughly translated from German, *Gestalt* means "whole" or "form." When applied to perception, it refers to our tendency to see patterns, to distinguish an object from its background, to complete a picture from a few cues. Like William James, the Gestalt psychologists rejected the structuralists' attempt to break down perception and thought into their elements. When we look at a tree, we see just that, a tree, rather than a series of isolated leaves and branches. We'll see in Chapter 3 that Gestalt psychology paved the way for the modern study of perception.

During the same period, the American psychologist Abraham Maslow, who studied under Gestalt psychologist Max Wertheimer and anthropologist Ruth Benedict, developed a more holistic approach to psychology, in which feelings and yearnings play a key role. Maslow referred to **humanistic psychology** as the "third force"—beyond Freudian theory and behaviorism. Humanistic psychologists emphasize human potential and the importance of love, belonging, self-esteem and self-expression, peak experiences (when one becomes so involved in an activity that self-consciousness fades), and self-actualization (the spontaneity and creativity that result from focusing on problems outside oneself and looking beyond the boundaries of social conventions). These psychologists focus on mental health and well-being, on self-understanding and self-improvement, rather than on mental illness.

Humanistic psychology has made important contributions to the study of motivation and emotions (see Chapter 8), as well as to the subfields of personality and psychotherapy (Chapters 10 and 13). But this doctrine has never been totally accepted by mainstream psychology. Because humanistic psychology is interested in questions of meaning, values, and ethics, many people—including its own members—see this school of psychology more

Gestalt psychology School of psychology that studies how people perceive and experience objects as whole patterns.

humanistic psychology School of psychology that emphasizes nonverbal experience and altered states of consciousness as a means of realizing one's full human potential.

as a cultural and spiritual movement than as a branch of science. In recent years, however, positive psychologists (whom we discuss further later in this chapter) have begun to reinvestigate some of the questions that humanistic psychologists raised a half century ago.

The Rise of Cognitive Psychology As behaviorism fell out of favor in the late 1960s, psychology began to come full circle in what can be described as a *cognitive revolution*—a shift away from a limited focus on behavior toward a broad interest in such mental processes as memory, decision making, and information processing. The field evolved from a period in which consciousness was considered inaccessible to scientific inquiry to one in which researchers resumed investigating and theorizing about the mind—but now with new research methods and behaviorism's commitment to objective, empirical research. As a result of this shift in focus, even the definition of psychology changed. Psychology is still the study of human behavior, but psychologists' concept of "behavior" has been expanded to include thoughts, feelings, and states of consciousness.

This new focus applies to existing fields of psychology as well as to new subfields. In developmental psychology, for example, the idea that a child is a blank slate was replaced by a new view of babies and children as aware, competent, social beings. In this new view, children actively seek to learn about and make sense of their world. Moreover, all healthy children are "equipped" with such distinctively human characteristics as the ability to acquire language through exposure, without formal education. Developmental psychology is one of several subfields contributing to and benefiting from the emergence of cognitive psychology.

Cognitive psychology is the study of our mental processes in the broadest sense: thinking, feeling, learning, and remembering, for example. If the behaviorist model of learning resembled an old-fashioned telephone switchboard (a call or a stimulus comes in, is relayed along various circuits in the brain, and an answer or a response goes out), the cognitive model resembles a high-powered, modern computer. Cognitive psychologists are interested in the ways in which people acquire information, process that information using their cognitive "hardware" and "software," and use the results to make sense out of the world, to solve problems, and so on.

In contrast to behaviorists, cognitive psychologists believe that mental processes can and should be studied scientifically. Although we cannot observe memories or thoughts directly, we can observe behavior and make inferences about the kinds of cognitive processes that underlie that behavior. For example, we can read a lengthy story to people and then observe what they remember from that story, the ways in which their recollections change over time, and the sorts of errors in recall that they make. On the basis of systematic research of this kind, we can gain insight into the cognitive processes underlying human memory (which we discuss in Chapter 6, "Memory"). Moreover, with the advent of new brain-imaging techniques (described in Chapter 2, "The Biological Basis of Behavior"), cognitive psychologists have begun to address questions about the neurological mechanisms that underlie such cognitive processes as learning, memory, intelligence, and emotion, giving rise to the rapidly expanding field of *cognitive neuroscience* (Yarkoni, Poldrack, Van Essen, & Wager, 2010).

cognitive psychology School of psychology devoted to the study of mental processes in the broadest sense.

New Directions

Where do evolutionary psychologists look for the roots of human behavior?
What new focus is positive psychology bringing to the study of human behavior?
Is there a single perspective dominating psychology today?

During much of the 20th century, psychology was divided into competing theoretical schools. Crossing theoretical lines was considered intellectual heresy. In the 21st century, by contrast, psychologists are more flexible in considering the merits of new approaches, combining elements of different perspectives as their interests or research findings dictate. As a result, new theories and initiatives are emerging.

evolutionary psychology An approach to, and subfield of, psychology that is concerned with the evolutionary origins of behaviors and mental processes, their adaptive value, and the purposes they continue to serve.

positive psychology An emerging field of psychology that focuses on positive experiences, including subjective well-being, self-determination, the relationship between positive emotions and physical health, and the factors that allow individuals, communities, and societies to flourish.

Evolutionary Psychology As the name indicates, **evolutionary psychology** focuses on the origins of behavior patterns and mental processes, the adaptive value they have or had, and the functions they serve or served in our emergence as a distinct species (Buss, 2005). Evolutionary psychologists ask, how did human beings get to be the way we are? In what ways might the roots of behavior serve to promote the survival of the species?

Evolutionary psychologists study such diverse topics as perception, language, helping others (altruism), parenting, happiness, sexual attraction, mate selection, jealousy, morality and violence (Brosnan, 2011; Confer et al., 2010). By studying such phenomena in different species, different habitats, different cultures, and in males and females, evolutionary psychologists seek to understand the basic programs that guide thinking and behavior.

We have said that cognitive psychologists tend to see the human mind as a "general purpose" computer that requires software (experience) to process information. In contrast, many evolutionary psychologists see the mind as having "evolved psychological circuits" that predispose human beings to think and act in certain ways (Confer et al., 2010; Ermer, Cosmides, & Tooby, 2007). Further, they contend that these fixed programs evolved thousands of years ago when our ancestors lived as hunter–gatherers, although the problem-solving strategies that benefited early humans may or may not be adaptive in the modern era. Though the application of evolutionary theory to the understanding of human behavior was initially advanced by Charles Darwin himself more than a century ago (Burghardt, 2009), few psychologists adopted this perspective until recently. Today, the application of evolutionary theory to understanding human behavior has experienced a renaissance, particularly as psychologists pay increased attention to the biological foundations of behaviors, behavioral genetics and human diversity (Buss, 2011). As stated by David Buss, one of the foremost evolutionary psychologists, "Evolutionary psychology synthesizes modern evolutionary biology and psychology to penetrate some of life's deep mysteries: Why do many struggles center around sex? Why is social conflict pervasive? And what are the mechanisms of mind that define human nature?" (Buss, 2009, p. 140).

Positive Psychology Another emerging perspective is **positive psychology,** which traces its roots back to humanistic psychology. According to this view, psychology should devote more attention to "the good life": the study of subjective feelings of happiness and well-being; the development of such individual traits as intimacy, integrity, leadership, altruism, and wisdom; and the kinds of families, cooperative lifestyles, work settings, and communities that encourage individuals to flourish (Snyder, Lopez, & Pedrotti, 2011).

Positive psychologists argue that psychologists have learned a great deal about the origins, diagnosis, and treatment of mental illness but relatively little about the origins and nurturance of mental wellness. There have been many studies of prejudice and intergroup hostility, for example, but very few about tolerance and intergroup harmony.

Today's positivists do not argue that psychologists should abandon their role in the science of healing. To the contrary, they support efforts to promote better, more

Positive psychology seeks to understand more about ordinary human strengths and virtues such as altruism, tolerance, happiness, philanthropy and wisdom. For instance, what factors led to the volunteerism displayed here by a member of the Japanese Red Cross, feeding a baby in the aftermath of the 8.9 earthquake and tsunami that devastated the coastline of Japan in 2011?

widespread use of what psychologists have learned. But they argue that psychology has reached a point where building positive qualities should receive as much emphasis as repairing damage (Duckworth, Steen, & Seligman, 2005; Guðmundsdóttir, 2011).

Multiple Perspectives of Psychology Today   Contemporary psychologists tend to see different perspectives as complementary, with each perspective contributing to our understanding of human behavior. Sometimes these theoretical perspectives mesh and enhance each other beautifully; at other times, adherents of one approach challenge their peers, arguing for one viewpoint over others. But psychologists agree that the field advances only when new evidence is added to support or challenge existing theories. ✳

✳ Explore the Concept A History of Psychology on MyPsychLab

Where Are the Women?

What obstacles did women face in the early years of psychology?

As you read the brief history of modern psychology, you may have concluded that the founders of the new discipline were all men. But did psychology really have only fathers and no mothers? If there were women pioneers in the field, why are their names and accomplishments missing from historical accounts?

In fact, women have contributed to psychology from its beginnings. In the United States, women presented papers and joined the national professional association as soon as it was formed in 1892. Often, however, they faced discrimination. Some colleges and universities did not grant degrees to women; professional journals were reluctant to publish their work; and teaching positions were often closed to them. Despite these barriers, a number of early women psychologists made important contributions and were acknowledged by some of the men in the growing discipline.

In 1906, James McKeen Cattell published *American Men of Science*, which, despite its title, included a number of women, among them 22 female psychologists. Cattell rated 3 of these women as among the 1,000 most distinguished scientists in the country: Mary Whiton Calkins (1863–1930), for her analysis of how we learn verbal material and her contributions to self-psychology; Christine Ladd-Franklin (1847–1930), for her work in color vision; and Margaret Floy Washburn (1871–1939) for her pioneering research examining the role of imagery in thought processes and the experimental study of animal cognition. In addition, Mary Whiton Calkins was elected and served as the first female president of the American Psychological Association (APA) in 1905, a position also held by Margaret Floy Washburn in 1921. However, because the doors to an academic career remained closed, other early female psychologists found positions in therapeutic and other nonacademic settings; pursued careers in allied professions, such as child development and education, which were considered acceptable fields for women; or gained recognition by collaborating on research projects and books with their spouses.

In recent decades, the situation has changed dramatically. The number of women who receive PhDs in psychology has grown by leaps and bounds. (See **Figure 1–1.**) For example, by 2008, the number of PhDs in psychology awarded to men had fallen to less than 30 percent (Willyard, 2011). Indeed, among members of the American Psychological Association, women now outnumber men almost 2 to 1 (64% to 36%) (American Psychological Association, 2011). No doubt some of this progress has resulted from the efforts of teachers of psychology to raise their students' awareness of the important accomplishments of female psychologists. Because female psychologists perform key research in all of the psychology subfields, you will find their work referred to throughout this text. For example, Terry Amabile has studied creativity, in particular the positive effects that exposure to creative role models can have on people. Elizabeth Loftus's research on memory has uncovered how unreliable eyewitness accounts of a crime can be. Eleanor Maccoby, Alice Eagly, and Jacqueline Eccles are prominent among the growing number of women and men who are studying sex differences in a variety of areas, such as emotionality, math and verbal ability, and helping behavior.

The relative absence of women from the history of psychology is only one aspect of a much bigger and more troubling concern: the relative inattention to human diversity that characterized psychology through most of the 20th century. Only recently have

Margaret Floy Washburn

Elizabeth Loftus's research on the memory of eyewitnesses is helping us understand more about cognitive processes.

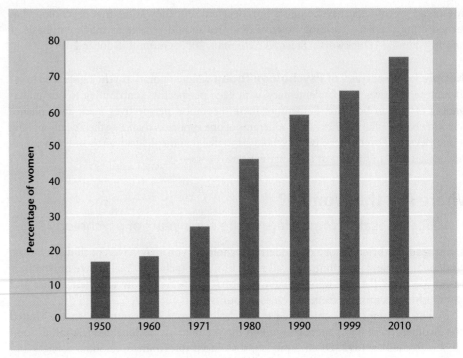

FIGURE 1–1
Percentage of women recipients of PhDs in psychology, 1950–2010.

Source: *Summary Report: Doctorate Recipients from United States Universities (Selected Years)*. National Research Council. Figure compiled by the American Psychological Association Research Office. Copyright © 2000. 1999 data from the National Research Foundation, 2002. 2010 data from Willyard, 2011.

psychologists looked closely at the ways in which culture, gender, race, and ethnicity can affect virtually all aspects of human behavior. In the next section, we begin our examination of this important topic.

✓●⌐ **Study** and **Review** on **MyPsychLab**

CHECK YOUR UNDERSTANDING

1. It was not until the late _____ that psychology came into its own as a separate discipline.

Answers: 1800s or 19th century.

APPLY YOUR UNDERSTANDING

1. Gregory believes that most of human behavior can be explained by examining our unconscious impulses. Gregory takes a _____ view of psychology.
   a. psychodynamic
   b. behavioral
   c. Gestalt
   d. structuralist

2. As a contestant on the television show *Jeopardy!*, you are delighted that you took a psychology course when you read the clue, "Founder of the first psychological laboratory," and you know that the correct answer (phrased in the form of a question, as required by the show) is, "Who was _____?"
   a. B. F. Skinner
   b. John B. Watson
   c. William James
   d. Wilhelm Wundt

Answers: 1. a. 2. d.

HUMAN DIVERSITY

Why should you learn about human diversity?

In the early 20ᵗʰ century, the great majority of research studies were conducted by White male professors at American universities, using White male American college students as participants. This arrangement was not a conscious or deliberate decision to study just one particular group. As in the medical community and in other sciences and prestigious professions in Europe and North America, psychology took for granted that what was true of White Western males would be true for other people as well. One critical history of psychology during this period was entitled *Even the Rat Was White!* (Guthrie, 1976).

For students like you, however, understanding human diversity is essential. Our major cities are home to people from diverse backgrounds, with diverse values and goals, living side by side. But proximity does not always produce harmony; sometimes it leads to aggression, prejudice, and conflict. Understanding cultural, racial, ethnic, and gender differences in thinking and behavior gives us the tools to reduce some of these interpersonal tensions. Looking at human diversity from a scientific perspective will allow you to separate fact from fiction in your daily interactions. Moreover, once you understand how and why groups differ in their values, behaviors, approaches to the world, thought processes, and responses to situations, you will be better able to savor the diversity around you. Finally, the more you comprehend human diversity, and realize that the vast majority of the world's population lives in conditions very different than those experienced by Americans, the more you will appreciate the many universal features of humanity (Arnett, 2008).

The process of examining and overcoming past assumptions and biases has been slow and uneven, but a new appreciation of human diversity is taking shape (Crisp, 2010). Psychologists have begun to question assumptions that are explicitly based on gender, race, and culture. Are women more likely than men to help a person in distress? Are African Americans more vulnerable to certain types of mental illness than are European Americans, or vice versa? Do the Japanese view children's ability to learn in the same way Americans do? Do homosexuals have different motives and emotions than heterosexuals? Research indicates that the answer to such questions often is "no."

gender The psychological and social meanings attached to being biologically male or female.

Gender

How are psychologists helping us to understand the differences between men and women?

Gender has many layers. The words *male* and *female* refer to one's biological makeup, the physical and genetic facts of being one sex or the other. Some scientists use the term *sex* to refer exclusively to biological differences in anatomy, genetics, or physical functioning, and **gender** to refer to the psychological and social meanings attached to being biologically male or female. Because distinguishing what is biologically produced from what is socially influenced is almost impossible, in our discussion of these issues, we will use the terms *sex* and *gender* interchangeably.

Gender Stereotypes In the past, men and women led very different lives. Today, women in many societies are as likely as men to obtain higher education; to work full-time, pursue careers, start businesses; and to be active in politics. And men are more likely to be more active parents and homemakers than their fathers were. Yet, stereotypes about how the "typical male" or "typical female" looks and acts still lead to confusion and misunderstandings between the sexes. In general, our culture promotes the idea that men are dominant, strong, and aggressive, whereas women are accommodating, emotional, and affectionate. As a result, many boys learn to hide their emotions, to deny feelings of weakness even to themselves, and to fight. Many girls, by contrast, learn to hide their ambitions, to deny their talents and strengths even to themselves, and perhaps to give in. Stereotypes are rarely benign. As we will see in Chapter 9, "Life-Span Development," the negative effects of these particular stereotypes on both boys and girls are significant and lasting.

Despite stereotypes of fathers as distant from their children, many fathers today take a very active role in parenting.

Carol Gilligan

As psychologists study the origins of homosexuality, gay couples seek social acceptance as parents.

feminist theory Feminist theories offer a wide variety of views on the social roles of women and men, the problems and rewards of those roles, and prescriptions for changing those roles.

sexual orientation Refers to the direction of one's sexual interest toward members of the same sex, the other sex, or both sexes.

race A subpopulation of a species, defined according to an identifiable characteristic (that is, geographic location, skin color, hair texture, genes, facial features, and so forth).

Beyond our stereotypes about what males and females "typically" are like, we have general beliefs about gender roles—that is, cultural expectations regarding acceptable behavior and activities for males and females, respectively. As a rule, cultural norms change more slowly than behavior patterns. Although most modern American families depend on two salaries, the assumption that the husband should be the chief breadwinner and the wife should put her home and children first remains powerful. Working wives and mothers work a "second shift" (keeping house and caring for children) at home—as much because they feel that doing so is their responsibility and area of expertise, as because their husbands still expect them to do so (Dillaway & Paré, 2008; Konishi, 2010).

The study of gender similarities and differences has become part of mainstream psychology. Psychologists in virtually every subfield conduct research to determine whether their findings apply equally to males and females, and if not, why not. As we will see, **feminist theory** is not for women only.

Feminist Psychology As the number of female psychologists has grown in recent decades (see **Figure 1–1**), so have their concerns about traditional psychological theories, research, and clinical practices (Basow, 2010; Robb, 2006). Feminist psychologists such as Carol Gilligan make three main points. As we have noted, much of the research supporting key psychological theories, such as moral development, was based on all-male samples. Second, reports of gender differences tend to focus on the extremes, exaggerating small differences and ignoring much greater similarities. Third, the questions that psychologists ask and the topics that they study reflect what they consider to be important; male and female psychologists differ to some extent in that regard.

Beyond research and theory, contemporary feminist psychology has begun to influence every facet of psychological practice by seeking mechanisms to empower women in the community, by advocating action to establish policies that advance equality and social justice, and by increasing women's representation in global leadership. Feminists also took the lead in urging other psychologists to recognize sexual orientation as simply another aspect of human diversity.

Sexual Orientation The term **sexual orientation** refers to whether a person is sexually attracted to members of the opposite sex (heterosexuality), the same sex (homosexuality), or both sexes (bisexuality). Division 44 of the American Psychological Association, "Society for the Psychological Study of Lesbian, Gay, and Bisexual Issues," was founded in 1985 to promote research and education regarding sexual orientation, for psychologists as well as the general public. Psychologists have only just begun to investigate the many sensitive issues associated with this dimension of human diversity—including such topics as the origins of sexual orientation, brain differences between heterosexual and homosexual men, discrimination and aggression toward people with different sexual orientations (Nadal, 2011), and the ethical issues that may arise if genes that influence sexual orientation are identified.

Race and Ethnicity

Why are psychologists interested in racial and ethnic differences?

Race is a biological term used to refer to a subpopulation whose members have reproduced exclusively among themselves and therefore are genetically similar and distinct from other members of the same species. Most people simply take for granted the idea that the human species can be divided into a number of distinct races (Asians, Africans, Caucasians, Native Americans, and so on). However, human beings have migrated, intermarried, and commingled so frequently over time that it is impossible to identify biologically separate races. Moreover, the criteria people use to differentiate among different races are arbitrary. In the United States, we assign people to different races primarily on the basis of skin color and facial features. In central Africa, members of the Tutsi and Hutu tribes see themselves as different races, although they are similar in skin color and facial features. In spite of these different definitions, most people continue to believe that racial categories are meaningful; and as a result, race shapes people's social identities, their sense of self, their experiences in their own and other societies, and even their health.

Whereas racial categories are based on physical differences, **ethnicity** is based on cultural characteristics. An *ethnic group* is a category of people who have migrated to another country, but still identify themselves—and are perceived by others—as distinctive because of a common homeland and history, language, religion, or traditional cultural beliefs and social practices. For example, Hispanic Americans may be Black, White, or any shade in between. What unites them is their language and culture. By the mid-1980s, there was sufficient interest among psychologists in ethnicity for the APA to create a new division (Division 45), devoted to the psychological study of ethnic minority issues. Increasing numbers of psychologists are now studying why ethnicity is so important both in our country and in others and how individuals select or create an ethnic identity and respond to ethnic stereotypes.

Racial and Ethnic Minorities in Psychology Most ethnic minorities are still underrepresented among the ranks of American psychologists (Chandler, 2011). Why? One possibility is that when Black, Hispanic American, Native American, and other students look at the history of psychology or the psychology faculties of modern universities, they find few role models; likewise, when they look at psychological research, they find little about themselves and their realities (Strickland, 2000). One survey of psychology journals found that less than 2% of the articles focused on U.S. racial and ethnic minorities (Iwamasa & Smith, 1996). Nonetheless, their small numbers have not prevented them from achieving prominence and making significant contributions to the field. For example, the late Kenneth Clark (1914–2005), a former president of the American Psychological Association, received national recognition for the important work he and his wife, the late Mamie Clark (1917–1983), did on the effects of segregation on Black children. This research was cited by the Supreme Court in the *Brown v. Board of Education* decision of 1954 that outlawed segregated schools in the United States.

In an effort to remedy the underrepresentation of ethnic minorities, the APA's Office of Ethnic Minority Affairs is sponsoring programs to attract ethnic-minority students to psychology (Clay, 2009; Munsey, 2009). This initiative includes summer programs for high school students, recruitment at the high school and college levels, mentor and other guidance programs, and a clearinghouse for college students who meet the requirements for graduate programs.

Psychologists are also working to uncover and overcome biases in psychological research that are related to gender, race, and ethnicity. The field of psychology is broadening its scope to probe the full range and richness of human diversity, and this text mirrors that expansive and inclusive approach. We will consider the problem of bias in psychological research more fully later in the chapter.

Kenneth Clark's research on the effects of segregation influenced the Supreme Court to outlaw segregated schools in *Brown v. Board of Education.*

ethnicity A common cultural heritage—including religion, language, or ancestry—that is shared by a group of individuals.

THINKING CRITICALLY ABOUT...

Psychology and Minority Students

In the text, we cited Strickland's conclusion that members of minority groups are underrepresented among psychology majors and in psychology postgraduate programs because a majority of their instructors and professors are White, and because so many of the research studies they read about in introductory psychology are based on White-only participants (Strickland, 2000).

- Do you agree with Strickland? Why or why not?
- What other reasons might explain why Whites are more likely than people of color to choose psychology as their main area of study and future career?
- How might you go about determining whether those various explanations are valid? What kind of research evidence would lead you to favor one explanation over another?

Culture

How does culture contribute to human diversity?

"Humans are a cultural species" (Heine & Norenzayan, 2006, p. 251). A **culture** provides modes of thinking, acting, and communicating; ideas about how the world works and why people behave as they do; beliefs and ideals that shape our individual dreams and desires;

culture The tangible goods and the values, attitudes, behaviors, and beliefs that are passed from one generation to another.

cross-cultural research Research involving the exploration of the extent to which people differ from one culture to another.

information about how to use and improve technology; and, perhaps most important, criteria for evaluating what natural events, human actions, and life itself mean. All large, complex modern societies also include subcultures—groups whose values, attitudes, behavior, and vocabulary or accent distinguish them from the cultural mainstream. Most Americans participate in a number of subcultures as well as in mainstream culture.

Many of the traits we think of as defining us as human—especially language, morals, and technology—are elements of culture. Even one's sense of self is dependent on culture and subculture. In **cross-cultural research,** psychologists examine the way cultures and subcultures affect behavior. For example, cross-cultural research on motivation and emotions, personality, and self-esteem has called attention to a broad distinction between *individualistic cultures* (which value independence and personal achievement) and *collectivist cultures* (which value interdependence, fitting in, and harmonious relationships). Moreover, cross-cultural studies have had a significant impact on the study of gender. Anthropologist Margaret Mead's classic work, *Sex and Temperament in Three Primitive Societies* (1935), is still cited by feminists and others as showing that definitions of masculinity and femininity are not biological givens, but are instead created by cultures and learned by their members along with other cultural norms, which makes them subject to change. Finally, in our increasingly multicultural society, psychologists are now dealing with diverse clients, research participants, and students. To meet this challenge, psychologists and other mental health professionals have begun working to educate and train "culturally competent" professionals (Fung, Andermann, Zaretsky, & Lo, 2008; Whealin & Ruzek, 2008).

Throughout this book, we will explore similarities and differences among individuals and groups of people. For example, we will examine differences in personality characteristics and intelligence; also, we will look at similarities in biological functioning and developmental stages. In most chapters we will examine research on males and females, members of different racial and ethnic groups, and cross-cultural studies.

CHECK YOUR UNDERSTANDING

1. A _____ is a group within a larger society that shares a certain set of values, beliefs, outlooks, and norms of behavior.

2. People who have ancestors from the same region of the world and who share a common language, religion, and set of social traditions are said to be part of the same _____ group.

3. "Minority groups are seriously underrepresented among psychologists." Is this statement true (T) or false (F)?

Answers: 1. subculture. 2. ethnic. 3. (T).

APPLY YOUR UNDERSTANDING

1. Which of the following is NOT a reason you should study human diversity?
   a. _____ because our society is made up of so many different kinds of people
   b. _____ as a way of helping to solve interpersonal tensions based on misunderstandings of other people
   c. _____ to help define what humans have in common
   d. _____ because diversity psychology is one of the major subdivisions of psychology

2. Which of the following subcultures has been historically overrepresented in psychological research?
   a. _____ African Americans
   b. _____ homosexual men and women
   c. _____ White males
   d. _____ the homeless

Answers: 1. d. 2. c.

RESEARCH METHODS IN PSYCHOLOGY

What are some of the research methods that psychologists use in their work?

To collect data systematically and objectively, psychologists use a variety of research methods, including naturalistic observation, case studies, surveys, correlational research, and experimental research.

Naturalistic Observation

Why is a natural setting sometimes better than a laboratory for observing behavior?

Psychologists use **naturalistic observation** to study human or animal behavior in its natural context. One psychologist with this real-life orientation might observe behavior in a school or a factory; another might observe monkeys in the wild rather than viewing them in captivity. The primary advantage of naturalistic observation is that the behavior observed in everyday life is likely to be more natural, spontaneous, and varied than that observed in a laboratory.

Naturalistic observation is not without its drawbacks. Psychologists using naturalistic observation have to take behavior as it comes. They cannot suddenly yell, "Freeze!" when they want to study in more detail what is going on. Nor can psychologists tell people to stop what they are doing because it is not what the psychologists are interested in researching. Moreover, simply describing one's impressions of "a day in the life" of a particular group or the way that different people behave in the same setting is not science. Observers must measure behavior in a systematic way, for example, by devising a form that enables them to check what people are doing at planned timed intervals.

The main drawback in naturalistic observation is **observer bias.** Even psychologists who are trained observers may subtly distort what they see to make it conform to what they were hoping to see. For this reason, contemporary researchers often use video that can be analyzed and scored by other researchers who do not know what the study is designed to find out. Another potential problem is that psychologists may not observe or record behavior that seems to be irrelevant. Therefore, many observational studies employ a team of trained observers who pool their notes. This strategy often generates a more complete picture than one observer could draw alone.

Despite these disadvantages, naturalistic observation is a valuable tool. After all, real-life behavior is what psychology is all about. Naturalistic observation often provides new ideas and suggests new theories, which can then be studied more systematically and in more detail in the laboratory. This method also helps researchers maintain their perspective by reminding them of the larger world outside the lab.

naturalistic observation Research method involving the systematic study of animal or human behavior in natural settings rather than in the laboratory.

observer bias Expectations or biases of the observer that might distort or influence his or her interpretation of what was actually observed.

The world-famous primatologist Jane Goodall has spent most of her adult life observing chimpanzees in their natural environment in Africa.

case study Intensive description and analysis of a single individual or just a few individuals.

survey research Research technique in which questionnaires or interviews are administered to a selected group of people.

Case Studies
When can a case study be most useful?

A second research method is the **case study:** a detailed description of one person or a few individuals. A case study usually includes real-life observation, interviews, scores on various psychological tests, and whatever other measures the researcher considers revealing. For example, the Swiss psychologist Jean Piaget developed a comprehensive theory of cognitive development by carefully studying each of his three children as they grew and changed during childhood. Other researchers have tested Piaget's theory with experiments involving larger numbers of children, both in our own culture and in others. (See Chapter 9, "Life-Span Development.")

Like naturalistic observation, case studies can provide valuable insights but they also can have significant drawbacks. Observer bias is as much a problem here as it is with naturalistic observation. Moreover, because each person is unique, we cannot confidently draw general conclusions from a single case. Nevertheless, case studies figure prominently in psychological research. For example, the famous case of Phineas Gage, who suffered severe and unusual brain damage, led researchers to identify the front portion of the brain as important for the control of emotions and the ability to plan and carry out complex tasks. (See Chapter 2, "The Biological Basis of Behavior.")

Surveys
What are some of the benefits of survey research?

In some respects, surveys address the shortcomings of naturalistic observation and case studies. In **survey research,** a carefully selected group of people is asked a set of predetermined questions in face-to-face interviews or in questionnaires. Surveys, even those with a low-response rate, can generate a great deal of interesting and useful information at relatively low cost, but for results to be accurate, researchers must pay close attention to the survey questions (Saris & Gallhofer, 2007). In addition, the people surveyed must be selected with great care and be motivated to respond to the

Jean Piaget based his theory of cognitive development on case studies of children.

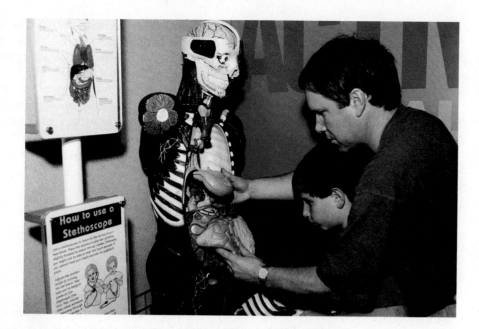

Can the experiences we have as children actually increase intelligence? Researchers might want to study the relationship between stimulating activities, such as frequent visits to science museums, and children's IQ scores. The relationship between the two may show a correlation, but researchers would not conclude from a correlational study that such experiences alone would cause a change in a child's IQ.

survey thoughtfully and carefully. For example, asking parents, "Do you ever use physical punishment to discipline your children?" may elicit the socially correct answer, "No." Asking "When was the last time you spanked your child?" is more likely to elicit honest responses, because the question is specific and implies that most parents use physical punishment—the researcher is merely asking when. At the same time, survey researchers must be careful not to ask leading questions, such as "Most Americans approve of physical punishment; do you?" Guaranteeing anonymity to participants in a survey can also be important.

Naturalistic observations, case studies, and surveys can provide a rich set of raw data that describes behaviors, beliefs, opinions, and attitudes. But these research methods are not ideal for making predictions, explaining, or determining the causes of behavior. For these purposes, psychologists use more powerful research methods, as we will see in the next two sections.

Correlational Research

What is the difference between correlation and cause and effect?

A psychologist, under contract to the U.S. Air Force, is asked to predict which applicants for a pilot-training program will make good pilots. An excellent approach to this problem would be **correlational research.** The psychologist might select several hundred trainees, give them a variety of aptitude and personality tests, and then compare the results with their performance in training school. This approach would tell him whether some characteristic or set of characteristics is closely related to, or correlated with, eventual success as a pilot.

Suppose that the psychologist finds that the most successful trainees score higher than the unsuccessful trainees on mechanical aptitude tests and that they are also cautious people who do not like to take unnecessary risks. The psychologist has discovered that there is a *correlation,* or relationship, between these traits and success as a pilot trainee. If these correlations are confirmed in new groups of trainees, then the psychologist could recommend with some confidence that the Air Force consider using these tests to select future trainees.

Correlational data are useful for many purposes, but they do not permit the researcher to explain cause and effect. This important distinction is often overlooked. Correlation means that two phenomena seem to be related: When one goes up, the other goes up (or down). In our pilot trainee example, high scores on tests of mechanical aptitude and caution predict success as a pilot trainee. But correlation does not identify the direction of influence. Does the tendency to shy away from taking risks make a trainee a good pilot? Or is the reverse

correlational research Research technique based on the naturally occurring relationship between two or more variables.

true: Learning to be a skillful pilot makes people cautious? Or is there some unknown factor that causes people to be both cautious and capable of acquiring the different skills needed in the cockpit? Although the psychologist has *described a relation* between skill as a pilot and two other characteristics, he has no basis for drawing conclusions about cause and effect.

Despite limitations, correlational research often sheds light on important psychological phenomena. In this book, you will come across many examples of correlational research. As you will learn, these interesting findings allow us to make some predictions, but psychologists want to move beyond simply making predictions. To explain the causes of psychological phenomena, psychologists most often use experimental research. ✳

✳ **Explore** the **Concept** Correlations Do Not Show Causation on **MyPsychLab**

Experimental Research

What kinds of research questions are best studied by experimental research?

A psychology instructor notices that on Monday mornings, most students in her class do not remember materials as well as they do later in the week. She has discovered a relationship between the day of the week and memory for course-related material. On the basis of this correlation, she could predict that every Monday thereafter, the students in her class will not absorb material as well as on other days. But she wants to go beyond simply predicting her students' behavior. She wants to understand or explain why their memories are poorer on Mondays than on other days of the week.

As a result of her own experiences and some informal interviews with students, she suspects that students stay up late on weekends and that their difficulty remembering information presented on Mondays is due to lack of sleep. This theory appears to make sense, but the psychologist wants to prove that it is correct. To determine whether lack of sleep actually causes memory deficits, she turns to the **experimental method.**

Her first step is to select **participants,** people whom she can observe to find out whether her hypothesis is correct. She decides to use student volunteers. To keep her results from being influenced by sex differences or intelligence levels, she chooses a group made up of equal numbers of men and women, all of whom scored between 520 and 550 on the verbal section of their college board exams.

The psychologist then needs to know which participants are sleep deprived. Simply asking people whether they have slept well is not ideal: Some may say "no," so that they will have an excuse for doing poorly on the test, and others may say "yes," because they do not want a psychologist to think that they are so unstable that they cannot sleep. And two people who both say they "slept well" may not mean the same thing by that phrase. So the psychologist decides to intervene—that is, to *control* the situation more closely—to determine which participants have sleep deficits. Everyone in the experiment, she decides, will spend the night in the same dormitory. They will be kept awake until 4:00 A.M. and then awakened at 7:00 A.M. She and her colleagues will patrol the halls to make sure no one falls asleep ahead of schedule. By manipulating the amount of time the participants sleep, the psychologist is introducing and controlling an essential element of the experimental method: an **independent variable.**

Next, she needs to know how well the students remember new information after they are deprived of sleep. For this, she designs a memory task. She needs something that none of her participants will know in advance. If she chooses a chapter in a history book, for example, she runs the risk that some of her participants are history buffs. Given the various possibilities, the psychologist decides to print a page of geometric shapes, each labeled with a nonsense word. Circles are "glucks," triangles are "rogs," and so on. She gives students half an hour to learn the names from this page, then takes it away and asks them to assign those same labels to geometric shapes on a new page. The psychologist believes that the students' ability to learn and remember the labels will depend on their having had a good night's sleep. Performance on the memory task (the number of correct answers) thus becomes the **dependent variable.** According to the psychologist's hypothesis, changing the independent variable (the amount of sleep) should also change the dependent variable (performance on

experimental method Research technique in which an investigator deliberately manipulates selected events or circumstances and then measures the effects of those manipulations on subsequent behavior.

participants Individuals whose reactions or responses are observed in an experiment.

independent variable In an experiment, the variable that is manipulated to test its effects on the other, dependent variables.

dependent variable In an experiment, the variable that is measured to see how it is changed by manipulations in the independent variable.

the memory task). Her prediction is that this group of participants, who get no more than 3 hours of sleep, should do quite poorly on the memory test.

At this point, the experimenter begins looking for loopholes in her experimental design. How can she be sure that poor test results mean that the participants did less well than they would have done if they had more sleep? For example, their poor performance could simply be the result of knowing that they were being closely observed. To be sure that her experiment measures only the effects of inadequate sleep, the experimenter creates another group, containing equal numbers of males and females of the same ages and with the same college board scores. The first group, the **experimental group,** will be kept awake, as described, until 4:00 A.M. That is, they will be subjected to the experimenter's manipulation of the independent variable—amount of sleep. Members of the second group, the **control group,** will be allowed to go to sleep whenever they please. If the only consistent difference between the two groups is the amount of sleep they get, the experimenter can be much more confident that if the groups differ in their test performance, the difference is due to the length of time they slept the night before.

Finally, the psychologist questions her own objectivity. Because she believes that lack of sleep inhibits students' learning and memory, she does not want to prejudice the results of her experiment; that is, she wants to avoid **experimenter bias.** So she decides to ask a neutral person, someone who does not know which participants did or did not sleep all night, to score the tests.

The experimental method is a powerful tool, but it, too, has limitations. First, many intriguing psychological variables, such as love, hatred, or grief, do not readily lend themselves to experimental manipulation. And even if it were possible to induce such strong emotions as part of a psychological experiment, this treatment would raise serious ethical questions. In some cases, psychologists may use animals rather than humans for experiments. But some subjects, such as the ability to remember historical facts or group problem solving, cannot be studied with other species. Second, because experiments are conducted in an artificial setting, participants—whether human or non-human animals—may behave differently than they would in real life.

The accompanying **Summary Table** groups the main advantages and disadvantages of each of the research methods we have discussed. Because each method has drawbacks, psychologists often use more than one method to study a single problem.

Multimethod Research

What does multimethod research allow psychologists to do?

Suppose that a psychologist were interested in studying creativity. She would probably combine several of the methods we have described. She might begin her research by giving a group of college students a creativity test that she had invented to measure their capacity to discover or produce something new, and look for *correlations* among the students' scores on her test, their grades, and their scores on commonly used intelligence tests. Then, she might spend several weeks *observing* a college class and *interviewing* teachers, students, and parents to correlate classroom behavior and the interview data with the students' scores on the creativity test. She might then go on to test some of her ideas with an *experiment* by using a group of students as participants. Her findings at any point in this research program might prompt her to revise her creativity test or her understanding of creativity. Eventually, her research might provide new insights into the nature of creativity and its relationship to other mental abilities.

The Importance of Sampling

How can sampling affect the results of a research study?

One obvious drawback to every form of research is that it is usually impossible to include everyone as participants. No one could expect to study the responses of all individuals who suffer from the irrational fears known as phobias or to record the maternal behavior of

experimental group In a controlled experiment, the group subjected to a change in the independent variable.

control group In a controlled experiment, the group not subjected to a change in the independent variable; used for comparison with the experimental group.

experimenter bias Expectations by the experimenter that might influence the results of an experiment or its interpretation.

SUMMARY TABLE   BASIC METHODS OF RESEARCH

Research Method		Advantages	Limitations
Naturalistic Observation	Behavior is observed in the environment in which it occurs naturally.	Provides a great deal of firsthand behavioral information that is more likely to be accurate than reports after the fact. The participant's behavior is more natural, spontaneous, and varied than behaviors taking place in the laboratory. A rich source of hypotheses as well.	The presence of an observer may alter the participants' behavior; the observer's recording of the behavior may reflect a preexisting bias; and it is often unclear whether the observations can be generalized to other settings and other people.
Case Studies	Behavior of one person or a few people is studied in depth.	Yields a great deal of detailed descriptive information. Useful for forming hypotheses.	The case(s) studied may not be a representative sample. This method can be time consuming and expensive. Observer bias is a potential problem.
Surveys	A large number of participants are asked a standard set of questions.	Enables an immense amount of data to be gathered quickly and inexpensively.	Sampling biases can skew results. Poorly constructed questions can result in answers that are ambiguous, so data are not clear. Accuracy depends on ability and willingness of participants to answer questions honestly.
Correlational Research	This approach employs statistical methods to examine the relationship between two or more variables.	May clarify relationships between variables that cannot be examined by other research methods. Allows prediction of behavior.	This method does not permit researchers to draw conclusions regarding cause-and-effect relationships.
Experimental Research	One or more variables are systematically manipulated, and the effect of that manipulation on other variables is studied.	Because of strict control of variables, offers researchers the opportunity to draw conclusions about cause-and-effect relationships.	The artificiality of the lab setting may influence subjects' behavior; unexpected and uncontrolled variables may confound results; many variables cannot be controlled and manipulated.

sample A subgroup of a population.

random sample Sample in which each potential participant has an equal chance of being selected.

representative sample Sample carefully chosen so that the characteristics of the participants correspond closely to the characteristics of the larger population.

all female monkeys. No matter what research method is used, researchers almost always have to study a small **sample,** or subset of the population, and then use the results of that limited study to generalize about larger populations. For example, the psychology instructor who studied the effect of lack of sleep on memory assumed that her results would apply to other students in her classes (past and future), as well as to students in other classes and at other colleges.

How realistic are these assumptions? How confident can researchers be that the results of research conducted on a relatively small sample apply to the much larger population from which the sample was drawn? (See "Applying Psychology: Internet Users: A Flawed Study?") By reducing *sampling errors* social scientists have developed several techniques to improve the generalizability of their results. One is to select participants at random from the larger population. For example, the researcher studying pilot trainees might begin with an alphabetical list of all trainees and then select every third name on the list to be in his study. These participants would constitute a **random sample** from the larger group of trainees, because every trainee had an equal chance of being chosen for the study.

Another way to make sure that conclusions apply to the larger population is to pick a **representative sample** of the population being studied. For example, researchers looking for a representative cross section of Americans would want to ensure that the proportion of males and females in the study matched the national proportion, that the number of participants from each state matched the national population distribution, and so on. The importance of sampling has received a great deal of attention recently as psychologists have become increasingly sensitive to the great diversity among humans. In the next section of the chapter, we will explore the implications of human diversity for psychological research.

Human Diversity and Research

Can we generalize about research findings from one group to another?

As we noted earlier, psychologists have recently begun to question early assumptions that the results of research conducted with White male participants would also apply to women, to people of other racial and ethnic groups, and to people of different cultures. Similarly, do feminist theories, developed by and tested primarily with White, college-educated women, apply to women of color (B. Roth, 2004)? As you will see throughout this book, research indicates that people's gender, race, ethnic background, and culture often have profound effects on their behavior. That is why, earlier in this chapter, we raised the possibility that perhaps we need "different psychologies" to account for the wide diversity of human behaviors.

Diversity also presents a challenge to the way that research is conducted. The gender, race, or ethnicity of the experimenter may also introduce subtle, unintended biases. For example, some early research concluded that women were more likely than men to conform to social pressure in the laboratory. Later research revealed no gender differences, however, when the experimenter is female (Eagly & Carli, 1981). More recent studies continue to demonstrate that the gender of the experimenter may produce different results when testing male versus female participants (Lundström & Olsson, 2005).

Similarly, evidence suggests that the results of research with African American participants may be significantly affected by the race of the experimenter (Graham, 1992; Weisse, Foster, & Fisher, 2005). For example, African Americans score higher on IQ and other tests when the person administering the test is also an African American (Graham, 1992).

√•—Study and **Review** on **MyPsychLab**

CHECK YOUR UNDERSTANDING

1. A method of research known as _____ allows psychologists to study behavior as it occurs in real-life settings.
2. Psychologists use _____ research to examine relationships between two or more variables without manipulating any variable.
3. The method of research best suited to explaining behavior is _____ research.
4. The _____ variable in an experiment is manipulated to see how it affects a second variable; the _____ variable is the one observed for any possible effects.
5. To ensure that the results of a particular study apply to a larger population, researchers use _____ or _____ samples.

Answers: 1. naturalistic observation. 2. correlational. 3. experimental. 4. independent, dependent. 5. random, representative.

APPLY YOUR UNDERSTANDING

1. Proper use of the experimental method is associated with all of the following, EXCEPT
   a. hypotheses.
   b. variables.
   c. experimenter bias.
   d. subjects or participants.

2. Margaret would like to be able to apply her research results to college sophomores as a whole. Which of the following would be the LEAST appropriate method for her to use?
   a. experiments that use college sophomores
   b. a case study of a college sophomore
   c. surveys of college sophomores
   d. interviews with college sophomores

Answers: 1. c. 2. b.

APPLYING PSYCHOLOGY

Internet Users: A Flawed Study?

"Sad, Lonely World Discovered in Cyberspace"

"Isolation Increases with Internet Use"

"Online and Bummed Out"

What's behind these headlines that appeared in various publications during the fall of 1998 while the Internet was still relatively new in our culture? Researchers had found that—as these publications phrased it—"using the Internet can cause isolation, loneliness, and depression"; "the Internet is actually bad for some people's psychological well-being"; and "greater use of the Internet leads to shrinking social support and happiness" (Kraut et al., 1998).

As a critical thinker, you should ask a number of questions about these headlines. Who was studied? How did the researchers determine Internet use? How did they measure such things as isolation, loneliness, depression, social support, and happiness? Did the researchers actually conduct a genuine experiment, manipulating the independent variable of Internet use and observing its effect on the dependent variables, or did they use some other, less powerful research design? If the latter, how do they know that Internet use caused any changes they might have observed?

The answers should motivate you to be far more cautious than the headline writers about what the research actually showed. To begin with, the researchers studied 256 people from only 93 families in Pittsburgh, and 20 of the families and 87 of the people dropped out before the study was completed. Also, households with preexisting Internet connections were excluded. Are you confident that the results from this sample can be generalized as broadly as the mass media did?

Because this was not a true experiment with an experimental group and a control group, is it possible that the Internet users were already unusually lonely or isolated or depressed? If so, how might Internet use affect these individuals?

Going further, the researchers actually tracked Internet use through software on the computer. To measure social involvement and psychological well-being, however, they relied entirely on *self-report measures*. Does this reliance on self-reports cause you to be cautious about the results of the research? How do we know whether these reports were accurate? (You might read ahead to Chapter 10 where we discuss concerns about research that relies heavily on self-reports.)

If you relied solely on the headlines, you might conclude that the study found dramatic differences between Internet users and nonusers. In fact, the most that could be said is that heavier users of the Internet showed very slight declines in some aspects of self-reported social involvement and only slight increases in self-reported feelings of loneliness and depression. Moreover, even those slight negative effects disappeared over time (Kraut et al., 2002). And as you might expect, more recent research indicates that greater Internet use is associated with various positive outcomes (M. Ito et al., 2009; Kraut & Kiesler, 2003). For example, Mizuko Ito and her colleagues recently completed a 3-year study of computer use among young people. They concluded "Today's youth may be coming of age and struggling for autonomy and identity as did their predecessors, but they are doing so amid new worlds for communication, friendship, play, and self-expression…. Online spaces enable youth to connect with peers in new ways…. A smaller number of youth also use the online world to explore interests and find information that goes beyond what they have access to at school or in their local community…. In both friendship-driven and interest-driven online activity, youth create and navigate new forms of expression and rules for social behavior…. Others "geek out" and dive into a topic or talent. Contrary to popular images, geeking out is highly social and engaged…. New media allow for a degree of freedom and autonomy for youth that is less apparent

in a classroom setting… while hanging out online, youth are picking up basic social and technological skills they need to fully participate in contemporary society…." (M. Ito et al., 2009, pp. 1–3). Though you may find the results of the recent research more closely match your own experiences, don't fail to be a critical thinker! What questions would you ask about the sample and the methods by which Ito and her colleagues collected their data?

You should always ask yourself questions about sampling and research methods when you read accounts of psychological research in the mass media. And in fairness, they are questions these researchers themselves have raised although they rarely appear in reports in the popular media.

About Internet Users

1. What other questions about this research would you add to the ones already mentioned?

2. If you read sensationalistic headlines about another research topic, such as obesity and social activity, or parenting and juvenile crime, how would you go about learning the details of the research, so you could answer your own critical thinking questions?

Ethics and Psychology: Research on Humans and Animals

Are there ethical guidelines for conducting psychological research? What objections have been raised regarding research on animal subjects?

LEARNING OBJECTIVE

- Identify key ethical issues in psychological research with humans and nonhumans.

If the college or university you attend has a research facility, you may have a chance to participate in a psychology experiment. You will probably be offered a small sum of money or class credit to participate. But you may not learn the true purpose of the experiment until after it's over. Is this deception necessary to the success of psychology experiments? And what if the experiment causes you discomfort? Before answering, consider the ethical debate that flared up in 1963 when Stanley Milgram published the results of several experiments he had conducted.

Milgram hired people to participate in what he said was a learning experiment. In a typical session, a young man would arrive at the laboratory to participate. He was met by a stern-faced researcher in a lab coat; another man in street clothes was sitting in the waiting room. The researcher explained that he was studying the effects of punishment on learning. When the two men drew slips out of the hat, the participant's slip said "teacher." The teacher watched as the "learner" was strapped into a chair and an electrode attached to his wrist. Then the teacher was taken into an adjacent room and seated at an impressive-looking "shock generator" with switches from 15 to 450 volts (V), labeled "Slight Shock," "Very Strong Shock," up to "Danger: Severe Shock," and, finally, "XXX." The teacher's job was to read a list of paired words, which the learner would attempt to memorize and repeat. The teacher was instructed to deliver a shock whenever the learner gave a wrong answer and to increase the intensity of the shock each time the learner made a mistake. At 90 V, the learner began to grunt; at 120 V, he shouted, "Hey, this really hurts!" At 150 V, he demanded to be released, and at 270 V, his protests became screams of agony. Beyond 330 V, the learner appeared to pass out. If the teacher became concerned and asked whether he could stop, the experimenter politely but firmly replied that he was expected to continue, that this experiment was being conducted in the interests of science.

In reality, Milgram was studying obedience, not learning. He wanted to find out whether ordinary people would obey orders to cause another person pain. As part of his research, Milgram (1974) described the experiment to 110 psychiatrists, college students, and middle-class adults, and he asked them at what point they thought participants would stop. Members of all three groups guessed that most people would refuse to continue beyond 130 V and that no one would go beyond 300 V. The psychiatrists estimated that only one in a thousand people would continue to the XXX shock panel. Astonishingly, 65% of Milgram's participants administered the highest level of shock, even though many worried aloud that the shocks might be causing serious damage to the learners.

To find out what he wanted to know, Milgram had to deceive his participants. The stated purpose of the experiment—to test learning—was a lie. The "learners" were Milgram's accomplices, who had been trained to act as though they were being hurt; the machines were fake; and the learners received no shocks at all (Milgram, 1963). But, critics argued, the "teachers"—the real subjects of the study—were hurt. Not only did most voice concern, but also they showed clear signs of stress: They sweated, bit their lips, trembled, stuttered, or in a few cases, broke into uncontrollable nervous laughter. Critics also worried about the effect of the experiment on the participants' self-esteem. How would you like to be compared with the people who ran the death camps in Nazi Germany? (In Chapter 14, "Social Psychology," we will describe a 2009 study that attempted to replicate the Milgram study without raising the same ethical concerns.)

Although the design of this experiment was not typical of the vast majority of psychological experiments, it sparked such a public uproar that the APA reassessed its ethical guidelines, which were first published in 1953. A new code of ethics on psychological experimentation was approved. The code is assessed each year and periodically revised to ensure that it adequately protects participants in research studies. In addition to outlining the ethical principles

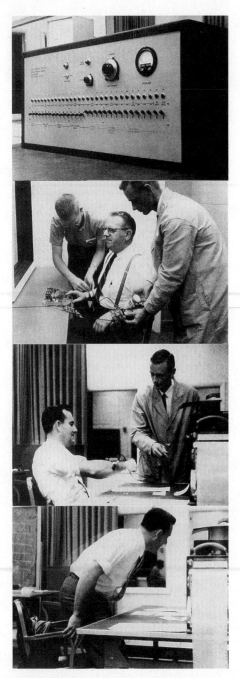

Stanley Milgram's Obedience Experiment. (A) The shock generator used in the experiment. (B) With electrodes attached to his wrists, the learner provides answers by pressing switches that light up on an answer box. (C) The subject administers a shock to the learner. (D) The subject breaks off the experiment. Milgram's study yielded interesting results, but it also raised serious questions about the ethics of such experimentation.

guiding research and teaching, the code spells out a set of ethical standards for psychologists who offer therapy and other professional services, such as psychological testing.

The APA code of ethics requires that researchers obtain informed consent from participants and stipulates the following:

- Participants must be informed of the nature of research in clearly understandable language.
- Informed consent must be documented.
- Risks, possible adverse effects, and limitations on confidentiality must be spelled out in advance.
- If participation is a condition of course credit, equitable alternative activities must be offered.
- Participants cannot be deceived about aspects of the research that would affect their willingness to participate, such as risks or unpleasant emotional experiences.
- Deception about the goals of the research can be used only when absolutely necessary to the integrity of the research.

In addition, psychological researchers are required to follow the U.S. government's Code of Federal Regulations, which includes an extensive set of regulations concerning the protection of human participants in all kinds of research. Failure to abide by these federal regulations may result in the termination of federal funding for the researcher and penalties for the research institution.

Despite these formal ethical and legal guidelines, controversy still rages about the ethics of psychological research on humans. Some people contend that research procedures should never be emotionally or physically distressing. Others assert that ethical guidelines that are too strict may undermine the scientific value of research or cripple future research. Still others maintain that psychology, as a science, should base its ethical code on documented evidence about the effects of research procedures on participants, not on conjecture about what is "probably" a good way to conduct research. Yet another view is that developing the explanations necessary to produce informed consent may help researchers themselves get a better understanding of the goals and methods of research.

Animal Research

In recent years, serious questions have also been raised about the ethics of using animals in psychological research (Herzog, 2005). Psychologists study animal behavior to shed light on human behavior. Crowding mice into small cages, for example, has yielded valuable insights into the effects of overcrowding on humans. Animals are used in experiments in which it would be clearly unethical to use human participants—such as studies involving brain lesions (requiring cutting into the brain). In fact, much of what we know about sensation, perception, drugs, emotional attachment, and the neural basis of behavior is derived from animal research (Ringach & Jentsch, 2009). Yet, animal protectionists and others question whether it is ethical to use nonhuman animals, which cannot give their consent to serve as subjects, in psychological research (Greek & Greek, 2010).

In its "Ethical Principles of Psychologists and Code of Conduct," the American Psychological Association (2010) has defined the standards that apply to the use of animals in research:

a. Psychologists acquire, care for, use, and dispose of animals in compliance with current federal, state, and local laws and regulations, and with professional standards.

b. Psychologists trained in research methods and experienced in the care of laboratory animals supervise all procedures involving animals and are responsible for ensuring appropriate consideration of their comfort, health, and humane treatment.

c. Psychologists ensure that all individuals under their supervision who are using animals have received instruction in research methods and in the care, maintenance, and handling of the species being used, to the extent appropriate to their role. (See also Standard 2.05, Delegation of Work to Others.)

d. Psychologists make reasonable efforts to minimize the discomfort, infection, illness, and pain of animal subjects.

e. Psychologists use a procedure subjecting animals to pain, stress, or privation only when an alternative procedure is unavailable and the goal is justified by its prospective scientific, educational, or applied value.

f. Psychologists perform surgical procedures under appropriate anesthesia and follow techniques to avoid infection and minimize pain during and after surgery.

g. When it is appropriate that an animal's life be terminated, psychologists proceed rapidly, with an effort to minimize pain and in accordance with accepted procedures.

Those principles have been expanded by the APA's Committee on Animal Research and Ethics (CARE) into a full set of guidelines for psychologists who use animals in research (American Psychological Association, 2011).

✔●⎯Study and Review on MyPsychLab

CHECK YOUR UNDERSTANDING

Are the following statements true (T) or false (F)?

1. _____ Controversy over ethical standards in psychology has almost disappeared.
2. _____ The APA code of ethics used today is unchanged since 1953.
3. _____ Researchers who fail to follow the Federal Code of Regulations are subject to penalties.

Answers: 1. (F), 2. (F), 3. (T).

APPLY YOUR UNDERSTANDING

1. Your classmate Jared says he does not need to be concerned about ethical standards for his naturalistic observation study. On the basis of what you have learned from this chapter, your reply should be

   a. "You're right, because there are only ethical guidelines for the protection of animals."

   b. "You're right. Only laboratory experiments must conform to ethics standards."

   c. "That's incorrect. All psychological research is subject to ethical guidelines."

   d. "That's incorrect. Actually, naturalistic observation is the only kind of research subject to ethics rules."

2. Before they agree to be in her experiment, Yolanda gives the participants a short description of what they will be asked to do in the study, the reasons she is conducting the study, and any risks or discomfort that they might face. Yolanda is

   a. getting informed consent from her participants.

   b. mollycoddling her participants.

   c. deceiving her participants.

   d. not adhering to ethical guidelines for the treatment of human research participants.

Answers: 1. c. 2. a.

CAREERS IN PSYCHOLOGY

What can you do with a background in psychology or with an advanced degree?

Some readers may be studying psychology out of general interest; others may be considering careers in psychology. What kinds of careers are open to psychology graduates? Community college graduates with associate's degrees in psychology are well qualified for paraprofessional positions in state hospitals, mental health centers, and other human service settings. Job responsibilities may include screening and evaluating new patients, record-keeping, and assisting in consultation sessions.

Graduates with bachelor's degrees in psychology may find jobs assisting psychologists in mental health centers, vocational rehabilitation facilities, and correctional centers. They

LEARNING OBJECTIVE

- Describe some of the career paths that are available to people who have studied psychology. Distinguish among psychiatrists, psychoanalysts, clinical psychologists, counseling psychologists, and social workers.

❋ Explore the Concept Psychologists at Work on MyPsychLab

may also take positions as research assistants, teach psychology in high school, or find jobs in government or business. ❋

For those who pursue advanced degrees in psychology—a master's degree or a doctorate—career opportunities span a wide range. Many doctoral psychologists join the faculties of colleges and universities. Others work in applied fields such as school, health, industrial, commercial, and educational psychology. Nearly half of doctoral psychologists are clinicians or counselors who treat people experiencing mental, emotional, or adaptational problems. Master's degree graduates in psychology often work as researchers at universities; in government; or for private companies. Students with a master's degree in industrial/organizational psychology are particularly sought by large corporations to work in personnel and human resource departments, while doctoral graduates in industrial/organizational psychology are hired into management or consulting positions in industry. Other graduates work in health and education.

Many students who major in psychology want to become therapists. For these students, there are five main career paths:

- A *psychiatrist* is a medical doctor who, in addition to 4 years of medical training, has completed 3 years of residency training in psychiatry, most of which is spent in supervised clinical practice. Psychiatrists specialize in the diagnosis and treatment of behavior disorders. In addition to providing psychotherapy, in many states, psychiatrists are the only mental health professionals who are licensed to prescribe medications.
- A *psychoanalyst* is a psychiatrist or psychologist who has received additional specialized training in psychoanalytic theory and practice, usually at a psychoanalytic institute that requires him or her to undergo psychoanalysis before practicing.
- *Clinical psychologists* assess and treat mental, emotional, and behavioral disorders, ranging from short-term crises to chronic disorders such as schizophrenia. They hold advanced degrees in psychology (a PhD or PsyD)—the result of a 4- to 6-year graduate program, plus a 1-year internship in psychological assessment and psychotherapy and at least 1 more year of supervised practice. With additional training, some states also permit clinical psychologists to prescribe medications for the treatment of mental disorders (see Chapter 13, "Therapies").
- *Counseling psychologists* help people cope with situational problems, such as adjusting to college, choosing a vocation, resolving marital problems, or dealing with the death of a loved one.
- *Social workers* may also treat psychological problems. They typically have a master's degree (MSW) or a doctorate (DSW). Social workers often work under the supervision of psychiatrists or clinical psychologists, although in some states they may be licensed to practice independently.

A free booklet, *Psychology: Scientific Problem Solvers, Careers for the Twenty-First Century*, is available online at www.apa.org/careers/resources/guides/careers.pdf Point your browser to www.apa.org/careers/resources/index.aspx for more information about careers in psychology.

Two additional resources are well worth reading:

Eric Landrum and Stephen Davis have written an excellent book on *The Psychology Major: Career Options and Strategies for Success (4th edition)*

If you are interested in careers with a bachelor's degree in psychology, in addition to *The Psychology Major* you will find the book *Finding Jobs With a Psychology Bachelor's Degree: Expert Advice for Launching Your Career* by Eric Landrum very informative.

✔● Study and Review on MyPsychLab

CHECK YOUR UNDERSTANDING

Is each of the following statements true (T) or false (F)?

1. _____ Careers in psychology are largely limited to people with PhDs.
2. _____ Almost all the careers related to a knowledge of psychology are in the mental health field.

Answers: 1. (F). 2. (F).

1. KeShawn is a medical doctor who specializes in diagnosing and treating people suffering from psychological disorders. He is a
   a. psychiatrist.
   b. counseling psychologist.
   c. clinical psychologist.
   d. social worker.

2. Psychologists can be found working in which of the following settings?
   a. research laboratories
   b. schools
   c. government and corporations
   d. all of the above

Answers: 1.a. 2.d.

KEY TERMS

What Is Psychology?
psychology, p. 3
scientific method, p. 8
theory, p. 8
hypotheses, p. 8

The Growth of Psychology
dualism, p. 12
structuralism, p. 13
functionalist theory, p. 13
psychodynamic theories, p. 14

behaviorism, p. 15
Gestalt psychology, p. 16
humanistic psychology, p. 16
cognitive psychology, p. 17
evolutionary psychology, p. 18
positive psychology, p. 18

Human Diversity
gender, p. 21
feminist theory, p. 22
sexual orientation, p. 22

race, p. 22
ethnicity, p. 23
culture, p. 23
cross-cultural research, p. 24

Research Methods in Psychology
naturalistic observation, p. 25
observer bias, p. 25
case study, p. 26
survey research, p. 26

correlational research, p. 27
experimental method, p. 28
participants, p. 28
independent variable, p. 28
dependent variable, p. 28
experimental group, p. 29
control group, p. 29
experimenter bias, p. 29
sample, p. 30
random sample, p. 30
representative sample, p. 30

CHAPTER REVIEW ((•⌐Listen to the **Chapter Audio** on **MyPsychLab**

WHAT IS PSYCHOLOGY?

"Most psychologists study mental and emotional problems and work as psychotherapists." Is this statement true or false? **Psychology** is the scientific study of behavior and mental processes. Through its many subdivisions its proponents seek to describe and explain human thoughts, feelings, perceptions, and actions.

Developmental psychologists are concerned with processes of growth and change over the life course, from the prenatal period through old age and death. *Physiological psychologists* focus on the biological basis of body's neural and chemical systems, studying how these affect thoughts, emotions, and behavior. *Experimental psychologists* investigate basic psychological processes, such as learning, memory, sensation, perception, cognition, motivation, and emotion. *Personality psychologists* look at the differences among people in such traits as sociability, anxiety, aggressiveness, and self-esteem. *Clinical* and *counseling psychologists* specialize in the diagnoses and treatment of psychological disorders, whereas *social psychologists* focus on how other people and social situations influence thoughts and actions. *Industrial* and *organizational psychologists* apply the principles of psychology to the workplace.

Given the broad range of careers and interests, what holds the subfields of psychology together as a distinct scientific discipline? Five enduring issues or fundamental themes unify the various subfields of psychology:

- Person–Situation: To what extent is behavior caused by processes inside the person as opposed to factors outside the individual?
- Nature–Nurture: How do genes and experiences interact to influence behavior?
- Stability–Change: To what extent do we stay the same as we develop and how much do we change?
- Diversity–Universality: In what ways do people differ in how they think and act?
- Mind–Body: What is the relationship between experiences such as thoughts and feelings and biological processes?

What does psychology have in common with other sciences? Like the other sciences, psychology relies on the **scientific method** to find answers to questions. This method involves careful observation and collection of data, the development of **theories** about relationships and causes, and the systematic testing of **hypotheses** (or predictions) to disprove invalid theories.

CRITICAL THINKING

What does it mean to "think critically?" Thinking critically means that you think like a scientist. You base your beliefs on solid evidence, analyze assumptions, avoid oversimplifying and draw conclusions carefully.

THE GROWTH OF PSYCHOLOGY

"Psychology has a long past, but a short history." What does that mean? The roots of psychology can be found among the Greek philosophers (particularly Socrates, Plato, and Aristotle) who first began to speculate about how the mind works, about where thoughts and feelings come from, and about the relationship between the mind and behavior. From their thinking emerged the concept of **dualism** which holds that thoughts and feelings (the mind) are distinct from the world of real objects and our bodies.

The 17th century witnessed renewed interest in human thought and its relationship to behavior. Rene Descartes, John Locke, Thomas Hobbes, and Charles Darwin took very different positions on the nature of the mind, the source of knowledge, and the relationship between the mind and the brain. It was not until the late 18th century that the tools of science were applied to answering such questions.

How did Wundt help to define psychology as a science of the mind? Why did James think that sensation and perception alone couldn't explain behavior? Why was Freud's theory of the unconscious shocking at the turn of the 20th century? Wilhelm Wundt established the first psychology laboratory in 1879 at the University of Leipzig in Germany. His use of experiment and measurement marked the beginnings of psychology as a science. One of his students, Edward Titchener, established a perspective called **structuralism,** which was based on the belief that psychology's role was to identify the basic elements of experience and how they combine.

In his perspective known as **functionalism,** American psychologist William James criticized structuralism, arguing that sensations cannot be separated from the mental associations that allow us to benefit from past experiences. James believed that our rich storehouse of ideas and memories is what enables us to function in our environment.

The **psychodynamic theories** of Sigmund Freud, his colleagues, and successors added another new dimension to psychology: the idea that much of our behavior is governed by unconscious conflicts, motives, and desires.

How was Watson's approach to human behavior different from that of Freud? How did Skinner expand behaviorism? John B. Watson, a spokesman for **behaviorism**, argued that psychology should concern itself only with observable, measurable behavior. Watson based much of his work on the conditioning experiments of Ivan Pavlov.

B. F. Skinner's beliefs were similar to those of Watson, but he added the concept of reinforcement or reward. In this way, he made the learner an active agent in the learning process.

How did Gestalt psychologists influence the way we think about perception? What aspects of life do humanistic psychologists stress? According to **Gestalt psychology,** perception depends on the human tendency to see patterns, to distinguish objects from their backgrounds, and to complete pictures from a few clues. In this emphasis on wholeness, the Gestalt school differed radically from structuralism.

Humanistic psychology, with its focus on meaning, values, and ethics, emphasizes the goal of reaching one's fullest potential. **Cognitive psychology** is the study of mental processes in the broadest sense, focusing on how people perceive, interpret, store, and retrieve information. Unlike behaviorists, cognitive psychologists believe that mental processes can and should be studied scientifically. This view has dramatically changed American psychology from its previous behaviorist focus.

Where do evolutionary psychologists look for the roots of human behavior? What new focus is positive psychology bringing to the study of human behavior? Is there a single perspective dominating psychology today? Evolutionary psychology focuses on the functions and adaptive value of various human behaviors and the study of how those behaviors have evolved. **Positive psychology** studies subjective feelings of happiness and well-being; the development of individual traits such as integrity and leadership; and the settings that encourage individuals to flourish. Most contemporary psychologists do not adhere to a single school of thought. They believe that different theories can often complement one another and together enrich our understanding of human behavior.

What obstacles did women face in the early years of psychology? Although psychology has profited from the contributions of women from its beginnings, women often faced discrimination: Some colleges and universities did not grant degrees to women, professional journals were often reluctant to publish their work, and teaching positions were often closed to them. In recent decades, the situation has changed dramatically.

HUMAN DIVERSITY

Why should you learn about human diversity? A rich diversity of behavior and thought exists in the human species, among individuals and groups. Being attuned to this diversity can help reduce the tensions that arise when people misunderstand one another. It can also help us to define what humans have in common.

How are psychologists helping us to understand the differences between men and women? **Feminist theory** explores the differences and similarities in thought and behavior between the two sexes or **genders.** Culturally generated beliefs regarding these differences are called *gender stereotypes.* Psychologists are trying to determine the hereditary and cultural causes of gender differences as well as the origins of sexual orientation.

Why are psychologists interested in racial and ethnic differences? Race, a biological term, refers to subpopulations that are genetically similar. **Ethnicity** involves a shared cultural heritage based on common ancestry, which can affect norms of behavior.

How does culture contribute to human diversity? The intangible aspects of **culture**—the beliefs, values, traditions, and norms of behavior that a particular people share—make an important contribution to human diversity. Because many subcultural groups exist, psychology must take both inter- and cross-cultural influences into account.

RESEARCH METHODS IN PSYCHOLOGY

What are some of the research methods that psychologists use in their work? Psychologists use naturalistic observation, case studies, surveys, correlational research, and experiments to study behavior and mental processes.

Why is a natural setting sometimes better than a laboratory for observing behavior? Psychologists use **naturalistic observation** to study behavior in natural settings. Because there is minimal interference from the researcher, the behavior observed is likely to be more accurate, spontaneous, and varied than behavior studied in a laboratory. Researchers using this method must be careful to avoid **observer bias.**

When can a case study be most useful? Researchers conduct a **case study** to investigate in depth the behavior of one person or a few persons. This method can yield a great deal of detailed, descriptive information that is useful for forming hypotheses, but is vulnerable to observer bias and overgeneralization of results.

What are some of the benefits of survey research? Survey research generates a large amount of data quickly and inexpensively by asking a standard set of questions of a large number of people. Great care must be taken, however, in the wording of questions and in the selection of respondents.

What is the difference between correlation and cause and effect? Correlational research investigates the relation, or correlation, between two or more variables. Although two variables may be *related* to each other, that does not imply that one *causes* the other.

What kinds of research questions are best studied by experimental research? An **experiment** is called for when a researcher wants to draw conclusions about cause and effect. In an experiment, the impact of one factor can be studied while all other factors are held constant. The factor whose effects are being studied is called the **independent variable,** since the researcher is free to manipulate it at will. The factor on which there is apt to be an impact is called the **dependent variable.** Usually an experiment includes both an **experimental group** of **participants** and a **control group** for comparison purposes. Often a neutral person records data and scores results, so **experimenter bias** doesn't creep in.

What does multimethod research allow psychologists to do? Many psychologists overcome the limitations of using a single research method by using multiple methods to study a single problem.

How can sampling affect the results of a research study? Regardless of the research method used, psychologists usually study a small **sample** of subjects and then generalize their results to larger populations. Proper sampling is critical to ensure that results have broader application. **Random samples,** in which each potential participant has an equal chance of being chosen, and **representative samples,** in which subjects are chosen to reflect the general characteristics of the population as a whole, are two ways of doing this.

Can we generalize about research findings from one group to another? Because of differences among people based on age, sex, ethnic background, culture, and so forth, findings from studies that use White, male, American college students as participants cannot always be generalized to other groups. In addition, the gender, race, and ethnic background of a psychologist can have a biasing impact on the outcome of research.

ETHICS AND PSYCHOLOGY: RESEARCH ON HUMANS AND ANIMALS

Are there ethical guidelines for conducting psychological research? What objections have been raised regarding research on animal subjects? The APA has a code of ethics for conducting research involving human participants or animal subjects. Researchers must obtain informed consent from study participants. Participants must be told in advance about the nature and possible risks of the research. People should not be pressured to participate.

Although much of what we know about certain areas of psychology has come from animal research, the practice of experimenting on animals has strong opponents because of the pain and suffering that are sometimes involved. Although APA and the federal government have issued guidelines for the humane treatment of laboratory animals, many animal rights advocates argue that the only ethical research on animals is naturalistic observation.

CAREERS IN PSYCHOLOGY

What can you do with a background in psychology or with an advanced degree? A background in psychology is useful in a wide array of fields because so many jobs involve a basic understanding of people. Careers for those with advanced degrees in psychology include teaching, research, jobs in government and private business, and occupations in the mental health field. Opportunities in the mental health field depend on one's degree of training. Practice in psychiatry requires medical training; practice in clinical psychology requires a doctoral degree. Positions in counseling psychology and social work are additional career options.

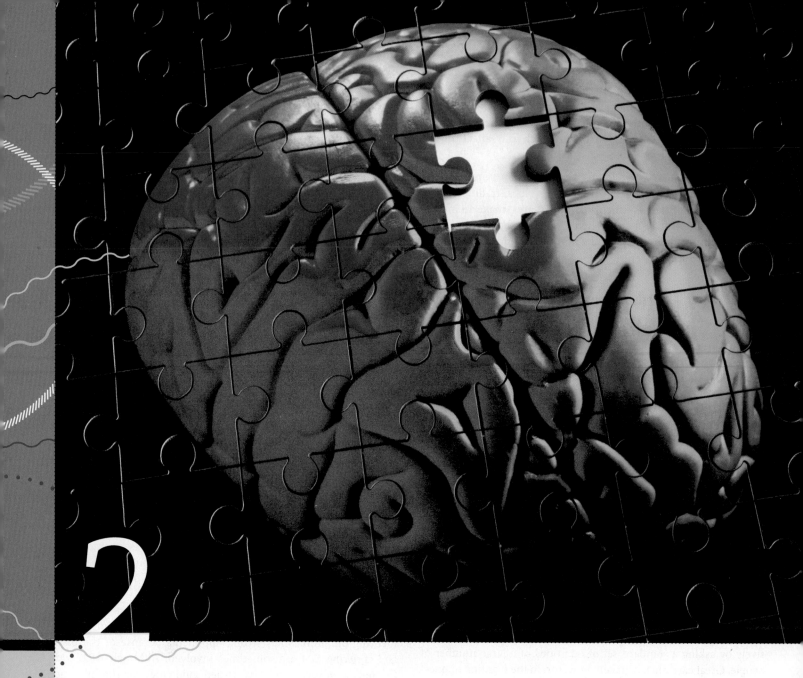

2

The Biological Basis of Behavior

OVERVIEW

If you observed 5-year-old Nico, you would never guess how different he is from other children. People are enchanted by his infectious smile and friendly conversation. He shows an aptitude for creating computer graphics and his ability to use language is well above average. Nico also interacts well with other children. In fact, the only thing unusual about him is a slight limp and some difficulty in using his left arm. This is amazing because inside Nico is not at all like other children. Nico, you see, has only half a brain (Battro, 2006).

He was not born with this condition. What Nico was born with is a left *hemiplegia,* or partial paralysis on the left side of his body. Despite this, he learned to walk at 1½. But as he approached his second birthday, he began to suffer epileptic seizures. Over time the seizures became much worse and Nico would frequently lose consciousness during them. Tests revealed an area on the right side of his brain where the seizures started and spread. Medications were useless in calming this area's erratic electrical activity; so when Nico was aged 3½, his parents authorized surgical removal of the afflicted region. After this treatment failed, his desperate parents reluctantly agreed to a much more radical procedure—removal of the entire right half of Nico's brain.

Wouldn't the impact of this surgery be devastating, adversely affecting all of Nico's thinking and behavior? Remarkably, it was not. Nico's epileptic seizures immediately stopped and he fully retained his ability to speak. Within a few days he was up and walking, displaying his typical good humor. How could this be when removing half a brain entails removing about 50 billion brain cells? The answer lies in some extraordinary traits possessed by the human brain: its complexity and plasticity.

The human brain is enormously complex. Its 100 billion cells, on average, interconnect to form a multitude of pathways and networks. In addition, although the two sides of the brain constantly work together, they are not symmetrical in terms of their specialized tasks. For example, in most people the left side of the brain houses language abilities while the right side excels at certain nonverbal skills, especially spatial ones like those needed to assemble a puzzle. This is why removal of Nico's right brain had virtually no effect on his use of language.

But most important of all to Nico's recovery is the fact that the brain of a very young child is remarkably adaptable, or *plastic.* The left side of Nico's brain readily took over most of the functions that the right side was designed to perform. This shift probably began even before his operation and intensified after the right half of his brain was removed, demonstrating that although the brain is the command center of the body, it also responds to sensory and environmental feedback. As a result, for Nico, half a brain is enough.

The journey through the brain that you will take in this chapter is part of the branch of psychology known as **psychobiology,** which deals with the biological bases of behavior and mental processes. Psychobiology overlaps with a much larger interdisciplinary field of study called **neuroscience,** which specifically focuses on the study of the brain and the nervous system. Many psychobiologists who study the brain's influence on behavior call themselves *neuropsychologists.*

We begin by looking at the basic building blocks of the brain and *nervous system:* the cells known as neurons. The electrical and chemical messages that neurons transmit are what allow you to react with such speed and complexity to events around you. Next, we consider the *endocrine system* of glands that secrete chemical messages called hormones into the blood. Finally, we examine the influence of heredity and evolution on human behavior.

ENDURING ISSUES **in The Biological Basis of Behavior**

As you read this chapter, you will encounter all five "Enduring Issues" introduced in Chapter 1. To what extent is behavior caused by internal processes, as opposed to environmental factors (*Person–Situation*)? The core of this chapter—the notion that biological processes affect thoughts, emotions, and behavior—directly addresses this question. The chapter also sheds light on the connection between what we experience and our biological processes (*Mind–Body*) and on the extent to which heredity affects behavior (*Nature–Nurture*). In addition, you may be surprised to learn that the nervous system changes permanently as a result of experience (*Stability–Change*). Finally, you will learn that there are significant differences between men and women in the way that the brain works (*Diversity–Universality*).

ENDURING ISSUES

Mind–Body   Window on the Mind

In the mind–body debate, neuropsychologists stand at the crossroad, where our sense of self intersects with advances in scientific knowledge. How does the organ we call the brain create the experience of what we call the mind? Until recently this question

psychobiology The area of psychology that focuses on the biological foundations of behavior and mental processes.

neuroscience The study of the brain and the nervous system.

seemed unanswerable. After all, the body and brain are observable, physical entities. In contrast, the mind is a subjective entity, private and unique, and observable only to its owner.

Since the early 1990s (called the Decade of the Brain), neuropsychologists have learned more about the brain than during the entire previous history of psychology. New technology has enabled researchers to identify—in a normal, living person—which areas of the brain are active during such different activities as naming an object or studying a face. A number of neuropsychologists believe that in the near future we will be able to describe and explain the mind, and even complex social behaviors such as empathy and intuition, in biological terms (Cacioppo & Berntson, 2005; A. R. Damasio, 2010). ■

neurons Individual cells that are the smallest unit of the nervous system.

dendrites Short fibers that branch out from the cell body and pick up incoming messages.

axon Single long fiber extending from the cell body; it carries outgoing messages.

nerve (or tract) Group of axons bundled together.

myelin sheath White fatty covering found on some axons.

sensory (or afferent) neurons Neurons that carry messages from sense organs to the spinal cord or brain.

motor (or efferent) neurons Neurons that carry messages from the spinal cord or brain to the muscles and glands.

interneurons (or association neurons) Neurons that carry messages from one neuron to another.

mirror neurons Specialized neurons that respond when we observe others perform a behavior or express an emotion.

NEURONS: THE MESSENGERS

What types of cells are found in the nervous system?

The brain of an average human being contains as many as 100 billion nerve cells, or **neurons.** Billions more neurons are found in other parts of the nervous system. Neurons vary widely in size and shape, but they are all specialized to receive and transmit information. A typical neuron is shown in **Figure 2–1.** Like other cells, the neuron's cell body is made up of a nucleus, which contains a complete set of chromosomes and genes; cytoplasm, which keeps the cell alive; and a cell membrane, which encloses the whole cell. What makes a neuron different from other cells is the tiny fibers that extend out from the cell body, called **dendrites.** Their role is to pick up incoming messages from other neurons and transmit them to the cell body. The single long fiber extending from the cell body is an **axon.** The axon's job is to carry outgoing messages to neighboring neurons or to a muscle or gland. Axons vary in length from 1 or 2 millimeters to 3 feet. Although a neuron has only one axon, near its end the axon splits into many terminal branches. When we talk about a **nerve** (or **tract**), we are referring to a group of axons bundled together like wires in an electrical cable. *Terminal buttons* at the end of each axon release chemical substances called *neurotransmitters*. We will examine this process in the next section.

The axon in **Figure 2–1** is surrounded by a white, fatty covering called a **myelin sheath.** The myelin sheath is "pinched" at intervals, making the axon resemble a string of microscopic sausages. Not all axons have this covering, but myelinated axons are found in all parts of the body. (Because of this white covering, tissues made up primarily of myelinated axons are known as "white matter," whereas tissues made up primarily of unmyelinated axons are called "gray matter.") The myelin sheath has two functions: First, it provides insulation, so that signals from adjacent neurons do not interfere with each other; second, it increases the speed at which signals are transmitted.

Neurons that collect messages from sense organs and carry those messages to the spinal cord or the brain are called **sensory** (or **afferent**) **neurons.** Neurons that carry messages from the spinal cord or the brain to the muscles and glands are called **motor** (or **efferent**) **neurons.** And neurons that carry messages from one neuron to another are called **interneurons** (or **association neurons**).

A recently identified group of specialized cells called **mirror neurons** are involved in mimicking the behavior of others. First discovered in monkeys just over a decade ago, mirror neurons fire not only when an action is performed, but also when a similar action is witnessed (Fadiga, Fogassi, Pavesi, & Rizzolatti, 1995). Found in the brains of humans and other primates, mirror neurons appear to play a key role in how a primate's brain is wired to mimic the sensations and feelings experienced by other related animals and, thus, to identify and empathize with them (Ehrenfeld, 2011; Rizzolatti, Fogassi, & Gallese, 2008). Mirror neurons may also play a key role in how humans represent events cognitively, in processes we refer to as thinking and understanding (Fogassi, 2011).

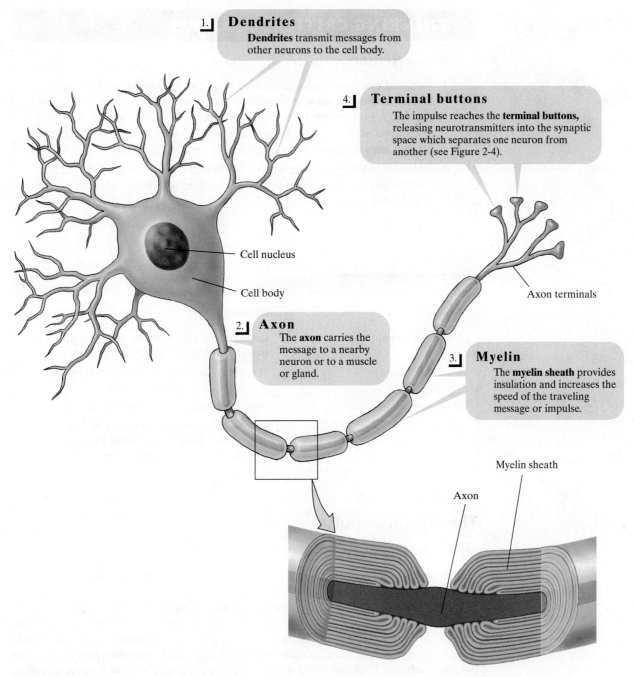

1. **Dendrites**
Dendrites transmit messages from other neurons to the cell body.

4. **Terminal buttons**
The impulse reaches the **terminal buttons,** releasing neurotransmitters into the synaptic space which separates one neuron from another (see Figure 2-4).

Cell nucleus

Cell body

Axon terminals

2. **Axon**
The **axon** carries the message to a nearby neuron or to a muscle or gland.

3. **Myelin**
The **myelin sheath** provides insulation and increases the speed of the traveling message or impulse.

Myelin sheath

Axon

FIGURE 2–1
This typical myelinated neuron shows the cell body, dendrites, axon, myelin sheath, and terminal buttons.

Source: Adapted from *Fundamentals of Human Neuropsychology* (4th ed.), by Brian Kolb and Ian Q. Whishaw. Copyright © 1980, 1985, 1990, 1996 by W. H. Freeman and Company. Reprinted with permission.

The nervous system also contains a vast number of **glial cells** (or **glia;** the word *glia* means "glue"). Glial cells hold the neurons in place, provide nourishment, remove waste products, prevent harmful substances from passing from the bloodstream into the brain, and form the myelin sheath that insulates and protects neurons. Recent evidence suggests that glial cells and *astrocytes* (a type of star-shaped glial cell) also may play an important role in neuron regeneration, learning and memory, and enhancing communication between neurons (Emamian, Naghdi, Sepehri, Jahanshahi, Sadeghi, & Choopani, 2010; Moore, Abdullah, Brown, Arulpragasam, & Crocker, 2011).

glial cells (or glia) Cells that insulate and support neurons by holding them together, provide nourishment and remove waste products, prevent harmful substances from passing into the brain, and form the myelin sheath.

SUMMARY TABLE	TYPES OF NEURONS
Type of Neuron	**Description**
Sensory or afferent	Collect information from the sensory organs and transmit it to the central nervous system
Motor or efferent	Transmit information from the central nervous system to the muscles and glands
Interneurons or association	Transmit information between neurons
Mirror	Specialized neurons in the central nervous system that become active when a behavior or emotion is witnessed in another organism

The Neural Impulse

What "language" do neurons speak?

Explore the Concept Action Potential on MyPsychLab

Neurons speak in a language that all cells in the body understand: simple "yes–no," "on–off" electrochemical impulses. ✹

When a neuron is at rest, the membrane surrounding the cell forms a partial barrier between the fluids that are inside and outside the neuron. Both solutions contain electrically charged particles, or **ions.** (See **Figure 2–2A.**) Because there are more negative ions inside the neuron than outside, there is a small electrical charge (called the **resting potential**) across the cell membrane. Thus, the resting neuron is said to be in a state of **polarization.** A resting, or polarized, neuron is like a spring that has been compressed but not released. All that is needed to generate a neuron's signal is the release of this tension.

When a small area on the cell membrane is adequately stimulated by an incoming message, pores (or channels) in the membrane at the stimulated area open, allowing a sudden inflow of positively charged sodium ions. (See **Figure 2–2B.**) This process is called *depolarization;* now the inside of the neuron is positively charged relative to the outside. Depolarization sets off a chain reaction. When the membrane allows sodium to enter the neuron at one point, the next point on the membrane opens. More sodium ions flow into the neuron at the second spot and depolarize this part of the neuron, and so on, along the entire length of the neuron. As a result, an electrical charge, called a **neural impulse** (or **action potential**), travels down the axon, much like a fuse burning from one end to the other. (See **Figure 2–2C.**) When this happens, we say that the neuron has "fired." The speed at which neurons carry impulses varies widely, from as fast as nearly 400 feet per second on largely myelinated axons to as slow as about 3 feet per second on those with no myelin.

ions Electrically charged particles found both inside and outside the neuron.

resting potential Electrical charge across a neuron membrane resulting from more positive ions concentrated on the outside and more negative ions on the inside.

polarization The condition of a neuron when the inside is negatively charged relative to the outside; for example, when the neuron is at rest.

neural impulse (or action potential) The firing of a nerve cell.

FIGURE 2-2
The neural impulse—communication within the neuron.

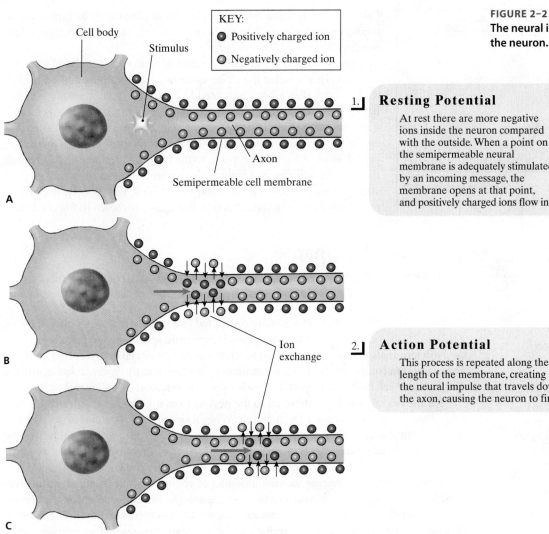

KEY:
- Positively charged ion
- Negatively charged ion

Cell body
Stimulus
Axon
Semipermeable cell membrane
Ion exchange

A
B
C

1. **Resting Potential**

At rest there are more negative ions inside the neuron compared with the outside. When a point on the semipermeable neural membrane is adequately stimulated by an incoming message, the membrane opens at that point, and positively charged ions flow in.

2. **Action Potential**

This process is repeated along the length of the membrane, creating the neural impulse that travels down the axon, causing the neuron to fire.

A single neuron may have many hundreds of dendrites and its axon may branch out in numerous directions, so that it is in touch with hundreds or thousands of other cells at both its input end (dendrites) and its output end (axon). At any given moment, a neuron may be receiving messages from other neurons, some of which are primarily excitatory (telling it to "fire"), and from others, primarily inhibitory (telling it to "rest"). The constant interplay of excitation and inhibition determines whether the neuron is likely to fire or not.

As a rule, single impulses received from neighboring neurons do not make a neuron fire. The incoming message causes a small, temporary shift in the electrical charge, called a **graded potential,** which is transmitted along the cell membrane and may simply fade away, leaving the neuron in its normal polarized state. For a neuron to fire, graded potentials caused by impulses from many neighboring neurons—or from one neuron firing repeatedly—must exceed a certain minimum **threshold of excitation.** Just as a

graded potential A shift in the electrical charge in a tiny area of a neuron.

threshold of excitation The level an impulse must exceed to cause a neuron to fire.

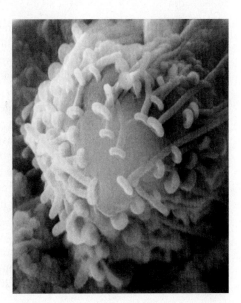

A photograph taken with a scanning electron microscope, showing the synaptic knobs at the ends of axons. Inside the knobs are the vesicles that contain neurotransmitters.

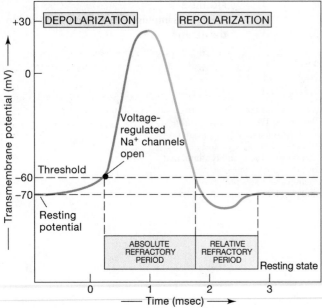

FIGURE 2–3

Electrical changes during the action potential.

The incoming message must be above a certain threshold to cause a neuron to fire. After it fires, the neuron is returned to its resting state. This process happens very quickly; and within a few thousandths of a second (msec), the neuron is ready to fire again.

all-or-none law Principle that the action potential in a neuron does not vary in strength; either the neuron fires at full strength, or it does not fire at all.

synaptic space (or synaptic cleft) Tiny gap between the axon terminal of one neuron and the dendrites or cell body of the next neuron.

synapse Area composed of the axon terminal of one neuron, the synaptic space, and the dendrite or cell body of the next neuron.

terminal button (or synaptic knob) Structure at the end of an axon terminal branch.

synaptic vesicles Tiny sacs in a terminal button that release chemicals into the synapse.

neurotransmitters Chemicals released by the synaptic vesicles that travel across the synaptic space and affect adjacent neurons.

receptor sites Locations on a receptor neuron into which a specific neurotransmitter fits like a key into a lock.

light switch requires a minimum amount of pressure to be turned on, an incoming message must be above the minimum threshold to make a neuron fire.

Every firing of a particular neuron produces an impulse of the same strength. This is called the **all-or-none law.** However, the neuron is likely to fire *more often* when stimulated by a strong signal. Immediately after firing, the neuron goes through an *absolute refractory period:* For about a thousandth of a second, the neuron will not fire again, no matter how strong the incoming messages may be. Following that is a *relative refractory period,* when the cell is returning to the resting state. During this period, the neuron will fire, but only if the incoming message is considerably stronger than is normally necessary to make it fire. Finally, the neuron returns to its resting state, ready to fire again, as shown in **Figure 2–3.**

The Synapse

What happens as information moves from one neuron to the next?

Neurons are not directly connected like links in a chain. Rather, they are separated by a tiny gap, called a **synaptic space,** or **synaptic cleft,** where the axon terminals of one neuron *almost* touch the dendrites or cell body of other neurons. The entire area composed of the axon terminals of one neuron, the synaptic space, and the dendrites and cell body of the next neuron is called the **synapse.** (See **Figure 2–4.**)

For the neural impulse to move on to the next neuron, it must somehow cross the synaptic space. The transfer is made by chemicals: When a neuron fires, an impulse travels down the axon, out through the axon terminals, into a tiny swelling called a **terminal button,** or **synaptic knob.** Most terminal buttons contain a number of tiny oval sacs called **synaptic vesicles.** (See **Figure 2–4.**) When the neural impulse reaches the end of the terminals, it causes these vesicles to release varying amounts of chemicals called **neurotransmitters** into the synaptic space. Each neurotransmitter has specific matching **receptor sites** on the other side of the synaptic space. Neurotransmitters fit into their corresponding receptor sites just as a key fits into a lock. This lock-and-key system ensures that neurotransmitters do not randomly stimulate other neurons, but follow orderly pathways.

Once their job is complete, neurotransmitters detach from the receptor site. In most cases, they are either reabsorbed into the axon terminals to be used again, broken down and recycled to make new neurotransmitters, or disposed of by the body as waste. The synapse is cleared and returned to its normal state.

Neurotransmitters In recent decades, neuroscientists have identified hundreds of neurotransmitters; their exact functions are still being studied. (See "**Summary Table:** Major Neurotransmitters and Their Effects.") However, a few brain chemicals are well known.

Acetylcholine (ACh) acts where neurons meet skeletal muscles. It also appears to play a critical role in arousal, attention, memory, and motivation. Alzheimer's disease, which involves loss of memory and severe language problems, has been linked to degeneration of the brain cells that produce and respond to ACh (Kihara & Shimohama, 2004).

Dopamine generally affects neurons associated with voluntary movement, learning, memory, and emotions. As with most neurotransmitters, the precise location in the brain where dopamine is released determines the effect it will have on behavior. For instance, in studies with rats, increasing the amount of dopamine in one brain center resulted in binge eating, while in a nearby center an increase in dopamine resulted in a fear response (Faure, Reynolds, Richard, & Berridge, 2008).

Serotonin is popularly known as "the mood molecule" because it is often involved in emotional experiences. Serotonin is an example of a neurotransmitter that has widespread effects. Serotonin is like a master key that opens many locks—that is, it attaches to as many as a dozen receptor sites (N. Thierry et al., 2004).

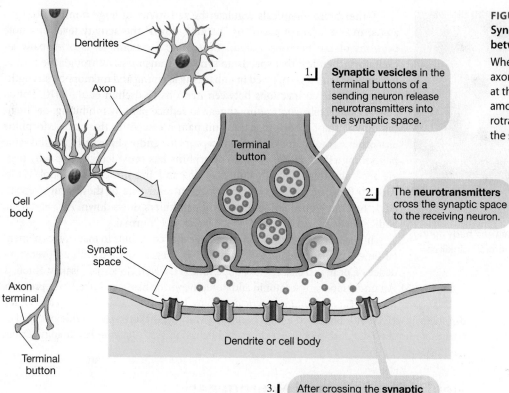

1. **Synaptic vesicles** in the terminal buttons of a sending neuron release neurotransmitters into the synaptic space.

Terminal button

2. The **neurotransmitters** cross the synaptic space to the receiving neuron.

Synaptic space

Dendrite or cell body

3. After crossing the **synaptic space** the neurotransmitters fit into **receptor sites** located on the dendrites or cell body of the receiving neuron.

Dendrites

Axon

Cell body

Axon terminal

Terminal button

FIGURE 2–4
Synaptic transmission—communication between neurons.

When a neural impulse reaches the end of an axon, tiny oval sacs, called synaptic vesicles, at the end of most axons release varying amounts of chemical substances called neurotransmitters. These substances travel across the synaptic space and affect the next neuron.

SUMMARY TABLE	MAJOR NEUROTRANSMITTERS AND THEIR EFFECTS
Acetylcholine (ACh)	Distributed widely throughout the central nervous system, where it is involved in arousal, attention, memory, motivation, and movement. Involved in muscle action through presence at neuromuscular junctions (specialized type of synapse where neurons connect to muscle cells). Degeneration of neurons that produce ACh has been linked to Alzheimer's disease. Too much ACh can lead to spasms and tremors; too little, to paralysis or torpor.
Dopamine	Involved in a wide variety of behaviors and emotions, including pleasure and pain. Implicated in schizophrenia and Parkinson's disease.
Serotonin	Involved in the regulation of sleep, dreaming, mood, eating, pain, and aggressive behavior. Implicated in depression.
Norepinephrine	Affects arousal, wakefulness, learning, memory, and mood.
Endorphins	Involved in the inhibition of pain. Released during strenuous exercise. May be responsible for "runner's high."
GABA (Gamma aminobutyric acid)	A largely inhibitory neurotransmitter distributed widely throughout the central nervous system. Implicated in sleep and eating disorders, GABA has also been linked to extreme anxiety.
Glutamate	Involved in learning and memory and the perception of pain.
Glycene	Principally responsible for inhibition in the spinal cord and lower brain centers.

Endorphins, which are released into the brain and body during exercise, are neurotransmitters that act as natural painkillers.

Other brain chemicals regulate the sensitivity of large numbers of synapses, in effect "turning up" or "turning down" the activity level of whole portions of the nervous system. *Glutamate* for example, is principally an excitatory chemical that speeds up synaptic transmission through the central nervous system. It is involved in enhancing learning and memory by strengthening synaptic connections between neurons (Balschun et al., 2010; Potter, 2009). Conversely, *endorphins* appear to reduce pain by inhibiting, or "turning down," the neurons that transmit pain messages in the brain. Morphine and other narcotics lock into the receptors for endorphins and have the same painkilling effects. Research on endorphins has provided clues to why people become addicted to morphine, heroin, and, in some cases, alcohol (Haile, Kosten, & Kosten, 2008). When a person takes one of these drugs repeatedly, the body's production of *natural* painkillers slows down. As a result, an addict needs more of the artificial drug to feel "normal."

Imbalances in neurotransmitters appear to contribute to many types of mental illness. Schizophrenia, for example, has been associated with an overabundance of, or hypersensitivity to, dopamine (H. Silver, Goodman, Isakov, Knoll, & Modai, 2005). An undersupply of serotonin and norepinephrine has been linked to depression. Imbalances in *GABA (Gamma aminobutyric acid)* have been associated with sleep and eating disorders as well as with increased levels of anxiety (Murphy, Ihekoronze, & Wideman, 2011). (For more on the relationship between drugs and behavior, see "Applying Psychology: Drugs and Behavior.")

Neural Plasticity and Neurogenesis

How does experience change the brain? Can the brain and the nervous system repair themselves?

ENDURING ISSUES

Stability–Change　Neural Plasticity

From the beginning, your brain has been encoding experience, developing the patterns of emotion and thought that make you who you are. At the same time, your brain is continually changing as you learn new information and skills and adjust to changing conditions. How do neurons perform this intricate balancing act, maintaining stability while adapting to change? Even more remarkably, how does the brain recover from injury or reorganize itself after surgery (as in the example at the beginning of the chapter)? The answer lies in *neural plasticity*, the ability of the brain to be changed structurally and chemically by experience. ■

In a classic series of experiments, M. R. Rosenzweig (1984) demonstrated the importance of experience to neural development and the establishment of *neural networks*. In the laboratory, Rosenzweig assigned baby rats into two groups. Members of one group were raised in an impoverished environment, isolated in barren cages. Members of the second group were raised in an enriched environment; they lived in cages with other rats and a variety of toys that offered opportunities for exploration, manipulation, and social interaction. Rosenzweig found that the rats raised in enriched environments had larger neurons with more synaptic connections than those raised in impoverished environments. (See **Figure 2–5.**) More recent experiments, by Rosenzweig (1996) and others (Ruifang & Danling, 2005), have shown that similar changes occur in rats of any age. Other researchers have found that rats raised in stimulating environments perform better on a variety of problem-solving tests and develop more synapses when required to perform complex tasks (Kleim, Vij, Ballard, & Greenough, 1997). These combined results suggest that the brain changes in response to the organism's experiences, a principle called **neural plasticity.** Furthermore, they demonstrate that neural plasticity is a feedback loop: Experience leads to changes in the brain, which, in turn, facilitate new learning, which leads to further neural change, and so on (Singer et al., 2011).

neural plasticity　The ability of the brain to change in response to experience.

APPLYING PSYCHOLOGY

Drugs and Behavior

Understanding how neurotransmitters work can also help you understand how chemical substances, including some common ones that you may use, affect your brain. You have already learned that opiates such as morphine work because they fit into the same receptors as naturally occurring endorphins. Other psychoactive drugs as well as many toxins also work by either blocking or enhancing the transmission of chemicals across synapses. Consider the following examples:

- *Botulism* (produced by the bacteria in improperly canned or frozen food) prevents the release of acetylcholine (Ach), which carries signals to the muscles. The result is paralysis and, sometimes, rapid death.
- The poison of the *black widow spider* produces the opposite effect. It causes ACh to spew into the synapses of the nervous system. As a result, neurons fire repeatedly, causing spasms and tremors.
- Antipsychotic medications *chlorpromazine* (trade name Thorazine) and *clozapine* prevent dopamine from binding to receptor sites; this reduction in stimulation apparently reduces schizophrenic hallucinations.
- *Caffeine* works in a slightly more complex way. It blocks the action of adenosine, a transmitter that inhibits the release of other neurotransmitters such as epinephrine. Without the restraining effects of adenosine, more of these other excitatory, arousing neurotransmitters are released. Two or three cups of coffee contain enough caffeine to block half the adenosine receptors for several hours, producing a high state of arousal and, in some cases, anxiety and insomnia.

- *Cocaine* works in yet another way. It prevents dopamine from being reabsorbed from the synapse after it has done its job of stimulating the next neuron. As a result, excess amounts of dopamine accumulate in the synapses, producing heightened arousal of the entire nervous system.
- Some *antidepressant medications* also work by preventing or slowing the removal of neurotransmitters from the synapse. We will say more about these "miracle drugs" that help reduce the hopelessness of severe depression in Chapter 12, "Psychological Disorders," and Chapter 13, "Therapies."

We will have much more to say about drugs and their effects in Chapter 4, "States of Consciousness."

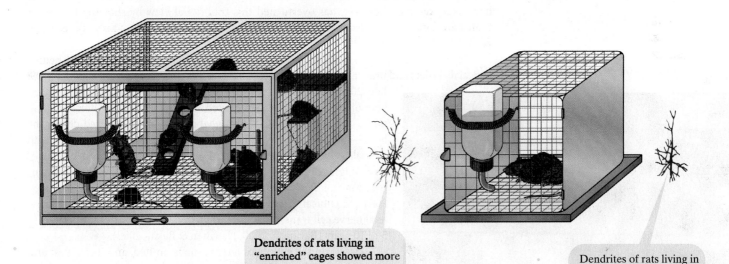

Dendrites of rats living in "enriched" cages showed more synaptic connections

Dendrites of rats living in bare cages

FIGURE 2–5

Brain growth and experience.

In Rosenzweig's experiment, young rats lived in two kinds of cages: "impoverished," with nothing to manipulate or explore, or "enriched," with a variety of objects. When Rosenzweig examined the rats' brains, he found that the enriched group had larger neurons with more synaptic connections (shown as dendrites in the drawing) than the rats that lived in the bare cages. Experience, then, can actually affect the structure of the brain.

Source: Illustration from Bunji Tagawa from "Brain changes in response to experience" by M. R. Rosenzweig, E. L. Bennett, and M. C. Diamond, *Scientific American*, 1972. Copyright © 1972 by *Scientific American*, Inc. Adapted with permission from the Estate of Bunji Tagawa.

neural network A group of neurons that are functionally connected.

neurogenesis The growth of new neurons.

As we saw in the story of Nico at the beginning of the chapter, reorganization of the brain as a result of experience is not limited to rats (Kolb, Gibb, & Robinson, 2003). For example, violinists, cellists, and other string musicians spend years developing precise left-hand sensitivity and dexterity. Researchers have found that the area of the musicians' brains associated with left-hand sensation is larger than the area that represents the right hand, and larger than the left-hand area in nonmusicians (Stewart, 2008). Plasticity in the brain is not just limited to changes that affect motor behaviors. The brains of female mammals apparently change in response to hormonal changes that occur during pregnancy (Kinsley & Lambert, 2006). Plasticity also permits changes in the way our nervous system responds to sensation. For example, in blind people, the portion of the brain normally responsible for vision reorganizes to respond to touch and hearing (Amedi, Merabet, Bermpohl, & Pascual-Leone, 2005).

Experience also causes changes in the *strength* of communication across synapses. For example, when neurons in the hippocampus (a brain structure involved in forming memories in humans and other animals) are stimulated by an electrical pulse, the initial response in nearby neurons is very weak. But repeated stimulation of the same pathway causes the nearby neurons to respond vigorously, an effect that lasts weeks after the stimulation was stopped (Taufiq et al., 2005). *Long-term potentiation* (LTP), as this is called, appears to help the brain learn and store new information (Bliss, Collingridge, & Morris, 2004).

The effects of neural plasticity are made more profound because neurons are functionally connected to one another forming circuits or **neural networks** that mature and develop in response to experience. These complex neural networks, made up of thousands of individual cells, serve as the foundation for all psychological processes, including thoughts, behaviors, emotions, and consciousness. These uniquely different neural networks are what underlie individual differences in thinking and behaving, and also appear to play an important role in producing cultural differences. For example, because people from the same culture share similar experiences, their neural networks would tend to be more similar to one another than they would be to people from a different culture. Conversely, people from different cultures often have very different experiences, leading to the development of very different neural networks, thus causing them to think, perceive, and behave very differently from one another (Park and Huang, 2010).

Finally, there is evidence that experience can also produce new neurons. For many years, psychologists believed that organisms are born with all the brain cells they will ever have. New research however, has overturned this traditional view by showing that adult brains are capable of **neurogenesis,** the production of new brain cells (Yang, Bi, & Feng, 2011; Yirmiya & Goshen, 2011).

✳️ Explore the Concept Brain Damage and Neuralplasticity on MyPsychLab

The discovery of adult neurogenesis raises new possibilities in the treatment of neurological disorders and brain and spinal cord injuries (Hayashi, Ohta, Kawakami, & Toda, 2009; Luo, 2011). Scientists have long known that embryos contain large numbers of stem cells: undifferentiated, precursor cells or "precells" that, under the right conditions, can give rise to any specialized cell in the body—liver, kidney, blood, heart, or neurons. Remarkably, in tests with animals, stem cells transplanted into a brain or spinal cord spontaneously migrated to damaged areas and began to generate specialized neurons for replacement (Kokaia & Lindvall, 2003; Nowakowski & Hayes, 2004). In clinical trials with patients suffering from Parkinson's disease, fetal nerve cell transplants have improved motor control for periods of 5 to 10 years (Barinaga, 2000; Newman & Bakay, 2008). ✳️

However, the supply of fetal tissue is limited, and its harvest and use raise ethical questions (Kuflik, 2008). Fortunately, scientists have recently found ways to coax mature cells to behave like stem cells, eliminating the need to use fetal cells to stimulate neurogenesis. One study for example, demonstrated that the skin cells of mice could be transformed into neurons by using viruses to alter their genetic code (Vierbuchen, Ostermeier, Pang, Kokubu, Südhof, & Wernig, 2010). Research like this has enormous promise in helping researchers overcome the ethical issues associated with using stem cells to promote neurogenesis.

Severing the spinal cord at the neck typically causes paralysis of everything below the head because nerves connecting to the body's muscles no longer have a cable to the brain. People with spinal cord injuries may someday benefit from research on neurogenesis.

Another potential use of new research findings is to stimulate the brain's own stem cells to provide "self-repair." For instance, research aimed at identifying specific chemicals that stimulate neurogenesis in the brain and spinal cord has shown promising results (Telerman, Lapter, Sharabi, Zinger, & Mozes, 2011). Other research has demonstrated that exercise may stimulate neurogenesis, resulting in improved learning and memory (Kerr & Swain, 2011). To translate these discoveries into treatments, scientists need to learn more, but people suffering from such neurological disorders as Parkinson's and Alzheimer's diseases, as well as victims of spinal cord injuries and stroke, now have hope (Gage, 2000; Newman & Bakay, 2008).

CHECK YOUR UNDERSTANDING

✓● Study and Review on MyPsychLab

Match each term with the appropriate definition.

1. ___ neuron
2. ___ neural plasticity
3. ___ dendrites
4. ___ axons
5. ___ neural impulse
6. ___ resting potential
7. ___ absolute refractory period
8. ___ neurogenesis
9. ___ synapse
10. ___ neurotransmitters
11. ___ dopamine
12. ___ serotonin
13. ___ all-or-none law
14. ___ mirror neurons

a. growth of new neurons
b. long, cellular fibers carrying outgoing messages
c. when a nerve cell cannot fire again
d. neurotransmitter that affects emotions, arousal, and sleep
e. cell that transmits information
f. when experience changes the brain
g. chemicals that carry messages across synapses
h. short, cellular fibers that pick up incoming messages
i. neurotransmitter with a role in schizophrenia and Parkinson's disease
j. action potential
k. a neuron either fires at full strength or not at all
l. terminal button, synaptic space, and dendrite of neighboring neuron
m. electrical imbalance across a neural membrane at rest
n. special neurons that fire in response to the actions of others

Answers: 1. e. 2. f. 3. h. 4. b. 5. j. 6. m. 7. c. 8. a. 9. l. 10. g. 11. i. 12. d. 13. k. 14. n.

APPLY YOUR UNDERSTANDING

1. You return from a day at the beach to find you have developed a severe sunburn. Which neurons are sending messages from your burned skin to your brain informing you of the pain from the burn?
   a. afferent neurons
   b. efferent neurons
   c. interaction neurons
   d. motor neurons

2. John is a 75-year-old male who is in the early stages of Alzheimer's disease. The cause of his disorder is most likely a deficiency of
   a. acetylcholine.
   b. dopamine.
   c. serotonin.
   d. norepinephrine.

Answers: 1. a. 2. a.

- Identify the parts of the brain and their function. Explain what is meant by "hemispheric specialization" and the functional differences between the two cerebral hemispheres.
- Discuss how microelectrode techniques, macroelectrode techniques, structural imaging, and functional imaging provide information about the brain.
- Explain how the spinal cord works.

THE CENTRAL NERVOUS SYSTEM

The Organization of the Nervous System

How is the nervous system organized?

Every part of the nervous system is connected to every other part. To understand its anatomy and functions, however, it is useful to analyze the nervous system in terms of the divisions and subdivisions shown in **Figure 2–6**. The **central nervous system** includes the brain and spinal cord, which together contain more than 90% of the body's neurons. The **peripheral nervous system** consists of nerves that connect the brain and spinal cord to every other part of the body, carrying messages back and forth between the central nervous system and the sense organs, muscles, and glands. The peripheral nervous system is subdivided into the *somatic nervous system,* which transmits information about body movements and the external environment, and the *autonomic nervous system,* which transmits information to and from the internal organs and glands. (We will discuss the endocrine system, which works hand in hand with the nervous system, later in the chapter.)

The Brain

What are the major structures and areas of the brain, and what functions do they serve?

The human brain is the product of millions of years of evolution through which our brains have increased in size and synaptic complexity. As new, more complex structures were added, older structures were retained. One way to understand the brain is to look at three layers that evolved in different stages of evolution: (1) the primitive *central core;* (2) the *limbic system,* which evolved later; and (3) the *cerebral hemispheres,* which are in charge of higher mental processes such as problem solving and language. (See **Figure 2–7.**) We will use these three basic divisions to describe the parts of the brain, what they do, and how they interact to influence our behavior. (See "**Summary Table:** Parts of the Brain and Their Functions.")

The Central Core At the point where the spinal cord enters the skull, it becomes the hindbrain. Because the **hindbrain** is found in even the most primitive vertebrates, it is believed to have been the earliest part of the brain to evolve. The part of the hindbrain

central nervous system (CNS) Division of the nervous system that consists of the brain and spinal cord.

peripheral nervous system (PNS) Division of the nervous system that connects the central nervous system to the rest of the body.

hindbrain Area containing the medulla, pons, and cerebellum.

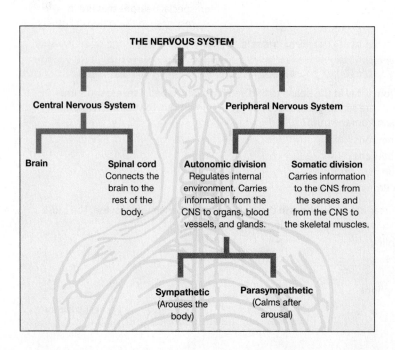

FIGURE 2–6
A schematic diagram of the divisions of the nervous system and their various subparts.

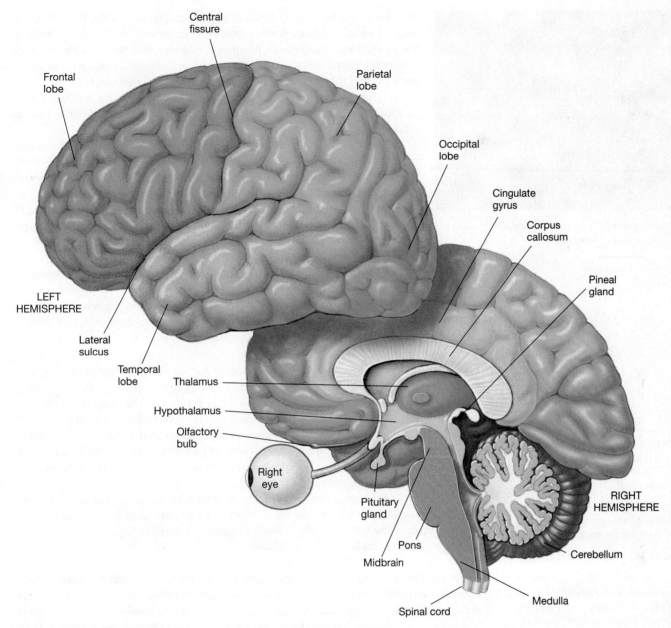

FIGURE 2–7
The divisions of the brain.

Source: Figure 2–6, p. 36, from *Psychology: The Core*, 1st edition, by Charles G. Morris and Albert A. Maisto. Copyright © 2008. Reproduced by permission of Pearson Education, Inc., Upper Saddle River, NJ.

nearest to the spinal cord is the **medulla,** a narrow structure about 1.5 inches long. The medulla controls such bodily functions as breathing, heart rate, and blood pressure. The medulla is also the point at which many of the nerves from the body cross over on their way to and from the higher brain centers; nerves from the left part of the body cross to the right side of the brain and vice versa (a topic to which we will return). Near the medulla lies the **pons,** which produces chemicals that help maintain our sleep–wake cycle. (See Chapter 4, "States of Consciousness.") Both the medulla and the pons transmit messages to the upper areas of the brain.

The part of the hindbrain at the top and back of the brain stem is the **cerebellum,** sometimes called the "little brain." Though the cerebellum takes up only a small space, its surface area is almost two-thirds that of the much larger cerebrum. It also contains more neurons than the rest of the brain. Traditionally, it has been thought that the cerebellum is responsible for our sense of balance and for coordinating the body's actions to ensure that

medulla Structure in the hindbrain that controls essential life support functions including breathing, heart rate, and blood pressure.

pons Structure in the midbrain that regulates sleep and wake cycles.

cerebellum Structure in the hindbrain that controls certain reflexes and coordinates the body's movements.

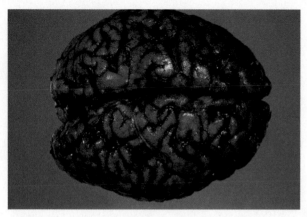

The human brain, viewed from the top. Its relatively small size belies its enormous complexity.

movements go together in efficient sequences. Damage to the cerebellum in adults does indeed cause severe problems in movement, such as jerky motions and stumbling. Recent research suggests, however, that the cerebellum is also involved in psychological processes, including emotional control, attention, memory, and coordinating sensory information (Della Sala, 2011).

Above the cerebellum, the brain stem widens to form the **midbrain.** The midbrain is especially important for hearing and sight. It is also one of several places in the brain where pain is registered.

Almost directly over the brain stem are the two egg-shaped structures that make up the **thalamus.** The thalamus is often described as a relay station: Almost all sensory information passes through the thalamus on the way to higher levels of the brain, where it is translated and routed to the appropriate brain location. Directly below the thalamus is the smaller **hypothalamus,** which exerts an enormous influence on many kinds of motivation. Portions of the hypothalamus govern hunger, thirst, sexual drive, and body temperature and are directly involved in emotional behavior such as experiencing rage, terror, or pleasure.

The **reticular formation (RF)** is a netlike system of neurons that weaves through all of these structures. Its main job is to send "Alert!" signals to the higher parts of the brain in response to incoming messages. The RF can be subdued, however; during sleep, the RF is turned down. Anesthetics work largely by temporarily shutting this system off, and permanent damage to the RF can even induce a coma.

The Cerebrum Ballooning out over and around the central core, virtually hiding it, is the **cerebrum.** The cerebrum is divided into two hemispheres. This is what most people think of first when they talk about "the brain"; it is the part of the brain that processes thought, vision, language, memory, and emotions. The cerebrum is the most recently evolved part of the nervous system and is more highly developed in humans than in any other animal. The human cerebrum takes up most of the room inside the skull, accounting for about 80% of the weight of the human brain. It contains about 70% of the neurons in the entire central nervous system.

The surface of the cerebrum is a thin layer of gray matter (unmyelinated cells) called the **cerebral cortex.** Spread out, the human cortex would cover 2 to 3 square feet and be about as thick as the letter "T." To fit inside the skull, in humans the cerebral cortex has developed intricate folds called *convolutions*. In each person, these convolutions form a pattern that is as unique as a fingerprint.

A number of landmarks on the cerebral cortex allow us to identify distinct areas, each with different functions. The first is a deep cleft, running from front to back, that divides the brain into *right* and *left* hemispheres. As seen in **Figure 2–7,** each of these hemispheres can be divided into four *lobes* (described later), which are separated from one another by crevices, or fissures, such as the *central fissure*. In addition, there are large areas on the cortex of all four lobes called **association areas** that integrate information from diverse parts of the cortex and are involved in mental processes such as learning, thinking, and remembering.

The different lobes of the cerebral hemispheres are specialized for different functions. (See **Figure 2–8.**) The **frontal lobe,** located just behind the forehead, accounts for about half the volume of the human cerebrum. It receives and coordinates messages from the other three lobes of the cerebrum and seems to keep track of previous and future movements of the body. This ability to monitor and integrate the complex tasks that are going on in the rest of the brain has led some investigators to hypothesize that the frontal lobe serves as an "executive control center" for the brain (E. Goldberg, 2009). The area on the surface of the frontal lobe known as the **primary motor cortex** plays a key role in voluntary action. The frontal lobe also seems to play a key role in the behaviors we associate with personality, including motivation, persistence, emotional responses, character, and even moral decision making (J. Greene & Haidt, 2002; Jackson et al., 2003).

Until recently, our knowledge of the frontal lobes was based on research with nonhuman animals, whose frontal lobes are relatively undeveloped, and on studies of rare cases of people with frontal lobe damage. One famous case, involving a bizarre accident,

midbrain Region between the hindbrain and the forebrain; it is important for hearing and sight, and it is one of several places in the brain where pain is registered.

thalamus Forebrain region that relays and translates incoming messages from the sense receptors, except those for smell.

hypothalamus Forebrain region that governs motivation and emotional responses.

reticular formation (RF) Network of neurons in the hindbrain, the midbrain, and part of the forebrain, whose primary function is to alert and arouse the higher parts of the brain.

cerebrum The main portion of the brain, occupying the upper part of the cranial cavity.

cerebral cortex The outer surface of the two cerebral hemispheres that regulates most complex behavior.

association areas Areas of the cerebral cortex where incoming messages from the separate senses are combined into meaningful impressions and outgoing messages from the motor areas are integrated.

frontal lobe Part of the cerebrum that is responsible for voluntary movement; it is also important for attention, goal-directed behavior, and appropriate emotional experiences.

primary motor cortex The section of the frontal lobe responsible for voluntary movement.

Central fissure
Separates the primary somatosensory cortex from the primary motor cortex

Primary somatosensory cortex
Registers sensory messages from the entire body

Primary motor cortex
Part of the frontal lobe; sends messages to muscles and glands; key role in voluntary movement

Parietal lobe
Receives sensory information from sense receptors all over the body (in the skin, muscles, joints, organs, taste buds); also involved in spatial abilities

Frontal lobe
Coordinates messages from the other cerebral lobes; involved in complex problem-solving tasks

Temporal lobe
Involved in complex visual tasks; balance; regulates emotions; strong role in understanding language

Prefrontal cortex
Involved in goal-directed behavior, impulse control, judgment, and awareness

Occipital lobe
Receives and processes visual information

FIGURE 2–8
The four lobes of the cerebrum.
Deep fissures in the cerebral cortex separate the cerebrum into four lobes. Also shown are the prefrontal cortex and the primary motor cortex (both part of the frontal lobe) and the somatosensory cortex (part of the parietal lobe).

was reported in 1848. Phineas Gage, the foreman of a railroad construction gang, made a mistake while using some blasting powder. The explosion blew a nearly 4-foot-long tamping iron more than an inch thick into his cheek and all the way through the top of his head, severely damaging his frontal lobes. To the amazement of those who witnessed the accident, Gage remained conscious, walked part of the way to a doctor, and suffered few physical aftereffects. He did, however, suffer lasting psychological changes, including difficulty reasoning and making decisions, as well as difficulty controlling his emotions. These changes were so radical that, in the view of his friends, he was no longer the same man. A century later, most neuroscientists agree that personality change—especially loss of motivation and ability to concentrate—is the major outcome of frontal lobe damage.

The forward-most surface of the frontal lobe, known as the **prefrontal cortex** (see **Figure 2–8**), plays a crucial role in goal-directed behavior, the ability to control impulses, judgment, and *metacognition*—which involves awareness and control of our thoughts (Modirrousta & Fellows, 2008).

Much more research needs to be done before psychologists can understand how this part of the brain contributes to such a wide and subtle range of mental activities. (See "**Summary Table:** Parts of the Brain and Their Functions.")

prefrontal cortex The forward-most region of the frontal lobe involved in impulse control, judgment, and conscious awareness.

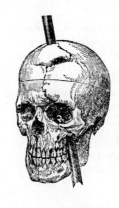

The skull of Phineas Gage, showing where the tamping iron passed through it, severely damaging his frontal lobes.

SUMMARY TABLE		PARTS OF THE BRAIN AND THEIR FUNCTIONS
Central Core	Medulla	Regulates respiration, heart rate, blood pressure.
	Pons	Regulates sleep–wake cycles.
	Cerebellum	Regulates reflexes and balance; coordinates movement.
	Reticular formation	Regulates attention and alertness.
	Thalamus	Major sensory relay center; regulates higher brain centers and peripheral nervous system.
	Hypothalamus	Influences emotion and motivation; governs stress reactions.
Limbic System	Hippocampus	Regulates formation of new memories.
	Amygdala	Governs emotions related to self-preservation.
Cerebrum	Frontal lobe	Goal-directed behavior; concentration; emotional control and temperament; voluntary movements; coordinates messages from other lobes; complex problem solving; involved in many aspects of personality.
	Parietal lobe	Receives sensory information; visual/spatial abilities.
	Occipital lobe	Receives and processes visual information.
	Temporal lobe	Smell and hearing; balance and equilibrium; emotion and motivation; some language comprehension; complex visual processing and face recognition.

The **occipital lobe,** located at the very back of the cerebral hemispheres, receives and processes visual information. Damage to the occipital lobe can produce blindness or visual hallucinations. (See **Figure 2–8.**)

The **parietal lobe** occupies the top back half of each hemisphere. This lobe receives sensory information from all over the body—from sense receptors in the skin, muscles, joints, internal organs, and taste buds. Messages from these sense receptors are registered in the **primary somatosensory cortex.** The parietal lobe also seems to oversee spatial abilities, such as the ability to follow a map (Silver & Kastner, 2009). This lobe is also typically involved in eye-hand coordination. In one study of young men in their twenties who were asked to perform complex visual-motor tasks, those who rarely played video games relied primarily on the parietal lobe of the brain. Interestingly, those men who played video games at least four hours a week relied primarily on an entirely different portion of the cerebrum: the prefrontal cortex (Granek, Gorbet, & Sergio, 2010). You might recognize this as yet another example of neural plasticity.

The **temporal lobe,** located roughly behind the temples, plays an important role in complex visual tasks such as recognizing faces and interpreting the facial emotions of others (Martens, Leuthold, & Schweinberger, 2010). The temporal lobe also receives and processes information from the ears, contributes to balance and equilibrium, and regulates emotions and motivations such as anxiety, pleasure, and anger. The ability to understand and comprehend language is concentrated primarily in the rear portion of the temporal lobes, though some language comprehension may also occur in the parietal and frontal lobes (Crinion, Lambon-Ralph, & Warburton, 2003; Hutsler, 2003).

Beneath the temporal lobe, hidden deep within the lateral fissure, which separates the parietal and temporal lobes, is an area known as the **insula.** Involved in the conscious expression of emotion and desire, the insula has recently been shown to play an

occipital lobe Part of the cerebrum that receives and interprets visual information.

parietal lobe Part of the cerebrum that receives sensory information from throughout the body.

primary somatosensory cortex Area of the parietal lobe where messages from the sense receptors are registered.

temporal lobe Part of the cerebral hemisphere that helps regulate hearing, balance and equilibrium, and certain emotions and motivations.

insula An area of the brain between the parietal and temporal lobes involved in addiction and the conscious expression of emotion and desire.

important role in addiction by controlling the conscious urge to seek drugs and assess risk (Naqvi & Bechara, 2009). For example, cigarette smokers who have sustained damage to this area stop smoking quickly and resist the urge to take up the habit again (Naqvi, Rudrauf, Damasio, & Bechara, 2007). Other studies have demonstrated a link between the insula and addiction to amphetamines, cocaine, and alcohol (Contreras, Ceric, & Torrealba, 2007).

The Limbic System The **limbic system** is a ring of loosely connected structures located between the central core and the cerebral hemispheres. (See **Figure 2–9.**) In evolutionary terms, the limbic system is more recent than the central core and is fully developed only in mammals.

The limbic system plays a central role in times of stress, coordinating and integrating the activity of the nervous system. One part of the limbic system, the **hippocampus,** plays an essential role in the formation of new memories. People with severe damage to this area can still remember names, faces, and events that they recorded in memory before they were injured, but they cannot remember anything new. Another structure, the **amygdala** (working together with the hippocampus) is involved in governing and regulating emotions and in establishing emotional memories (R. J. Davidson, Jackson, & Kalin, 2000; LaBar & Cabeza, 2006), particularly those related to fear and self-preservation (Donley, Schulkin, & Rosen, 2005). In one case, a woman whose amygdala was destroyed by disease in her childhood reported that she never felt fear, even when threatened by a knife or a gun (Feinstein, Adolphs, Damasio, & Tranel, 2010). The amygdala also plays a role in the experience of pleasure (Salzman & Fusi, 2010), as do other limbic structures (Burgdorf & Panksepp, 2006). Even our ability to read the facial expressions of emotion in other people (such as smiling or frowning) is registered in the limbic system (L. Carr, Lacoboni, Dubeau, Mazziotta, & Lenzi, 2005; Guyer et al., 2008). For example, people with a rare genetic disorder known as *Williams syndrome,* which involves amygdala damage, are often characterized by an inability to properly interpret the facial expressions of anger or worry in other people. As a result, individuals with Williams syndrome are socially awkward and lack social fear (Järvinen-Pasley et al., 2008; Sarpal et al., 2008). (We will return to the limbic system in Chapter 8, "Motivation and Emotion.")

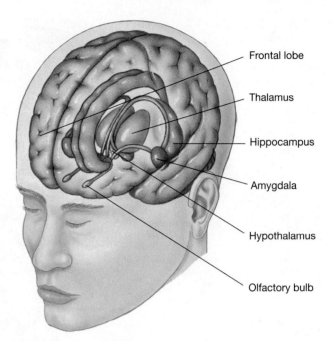

FIGURE 2–9
The limbic system.
A system of brain structures, including the thalamus, hippocampus, amygdala, hypothalamus, and olfactory bulb. This system is primarily involved in regulating behaviors having to do with motivation and emotion.

Hemispheric Specialization

How are the left and right hemispheres specialized for different functions?

The cerebrum, as noted earlier, consists of two separate cerebral hemispheres. Quite literally, humans have a "right half-brain" and a "left half-brain." The primary connection between the left and the right hemispheres is a thick, ribbonlike band of nerve fibers under the cortex called the **corpus callosum.** (See **Figure 2–10.**)

Under normal conditions, the left and right cerebral hemispheres are in close communication through the corpus callosum and work together as a coordinated unit (Funnell, 2010). But research suggests that the cerebral hemispheres are not really equivalent. (See **Figure 2–10.**)

The most dramatic evidence comes from "split-brain" patients. In some cases of severe epilepsy, surgeons cut the corpus callosum to stop the spread of epileptic seizures from one hemisphere to the other. In general, this procedure is successful: The patients' seizures are reduced and sometimes eliminated. But their two hemispheres are functionally isolated; in effect, their right brain doesn't know what their left brain is doing (and vice versa). Since sensory information typically is sent to both hemispheres, in everyday life, split-brain patients function quite normally. However, a series of ingenious experiments revealed what happens when the two hemispheres cannot communicate (Gazzaniga, 2005; Sperry, 1964). ⊙➔

limbic system Ring of structures that plays a role in learning and emotional behavior.

hippocampus A limbic system structure which plays an important role in the formation of new memories.

amygdala A limbic system structure involved in governing emotions and establishing emotional memories.

corpus callosum A thick band of nerve fibers connecting the left and right cerebral hemispheres.

Simulate the **Experiment** Split Brain on **MyPsychLab**

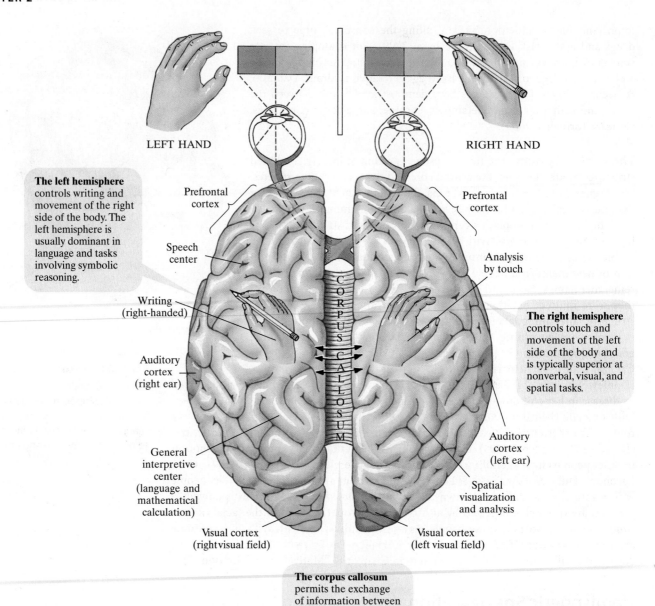

LEFT HAND

RIGHT HAND

The left hemisphere controls writing and movement of the right side of the body. The left hemisphere is usually dominant in language and tasks involving symbolic reasoning.

Prefrontal cortex

Prefrontal cortex

Speech center

Analysis by touch

Writing (right-handed)

CORPUS CALLOSUM

The right hemisphere controls touch and movement of the left side of the body and is typically superior at nonverbal, visual, and spatial tasks.

Auditory cortex (right ear)

General interpretive center (language and mathematical calculation)

Auditory cortex (left ear)

Spatial visualization and analysis

Visual cortex (right visual field)

Visual cortex (left visual field)

The corpus callosum permits the exchange of information between the two hemispheres.

FIGURE 2–10
The two cerebral hemispheres.
Each hemisphere specializes in processing specific types of information, as shown on the diagram.

In one such experiment, split-brain patients were asked to stare at a spot on a projection screen. When pictures of various objects were projected to the left of that spot, they could pick them out of a group of hidden objects by feeling them with their left hands but they couldn't say what the objects were! In fact, when asked what objects they saw on the left side of the screen, split-brain patients usually said "nothing." (See **Figure 2–11A.**) When asked to pick out the objects with their right hands, they couldn't do so even though they were able to name the objects. (See **Figure 2–11B.**)

The explanation for these unusual results is found in the way each hemisphere of the brain operates. When the corpus callosum is cut, the right hemisphere receives information only from the left side of the visual field and the left side of the body. As a result, it can match an object shown in the left visual field with information received by touch from the left hand, but it cannot verbally identify those objects. Conversely, the left hemisphere receives information only from the right side of the body and the right half of the visual field. Consequently, it cannot match an object shown in the left

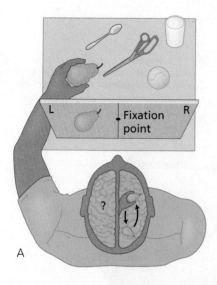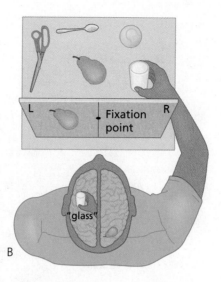

FIGURE 2–11
The split-brain experiment.
(A) When split-brain patients stare straight ahead at the "fixation point" and an object is briefly displayed on the left side of the screen, the visual information goes to the right hemisphere which does not control language. They can successfully pick out the object by touch using the left hand, but they cannot name the object. (B) When they are asked to pick out the object with their right hand, they cannot do so since the visual information is in their right hemisphere but their right hand is controlled by the left hemisphere. However, they can name whatever object they touch.

Source: Figure 2-19, p. 81, from Psychology: Core Concepts, 6th edition, by P. G. Zimbardo, R. L. Johnson, & V. McCann. Copyright © 2009. Reprinted with permission.

visual field using only the right hand, but it can verbally identify any objects touched with the right hand.

But why can't the right hemisphere verbally identify an object that is shown in the left visual field? The answer is that for the great majority of people (even for most left-handers), in the process of learning to read, language ability becomes concentrated primarily in the left hemisphere. As a result, when an object is in the left visual field, the nonverbal right hemisphere can see the object, but can't name it. The verbal left hemisphere, in contrast, can't see an object in this location, so when asked what it sees, it answers that nothing is on the screen.

Does the left hemisphere specialize in any other tasks besides language? Some researchers think that it may also operate more analytically, logically, rationally, and sequentially than the right hemisphere does (Kingstone, Enns, Mangun, & Gazzaniga, 1995; Martins, Caeiro, & Ferro, 2007). In contrast, the right hemisphere excels at visual and spatial tasks—nonverbal imagery, including music, face recognition, and the perception of emotions and color (K. J. Barnett, 2008; Buklina, 2005; Steinke, 2003). Put another way, the left hemisphere specializes in analyzing sequences and details, whereas the right hemisphere specializes in holistic processing and in solving problems that require *insight* or creative solutions (Shamay-Tsoory, Adler, Aharon-Peretz, Perry, & Mayseless, 2011).

Although such research is fascinating and fun to speculate about, be cautious in interpreting it. First, not everyone shows the same pattern of differences between the left and right hemispheres. In particular, the differences between the hemispheres may be greater in men than in women (Mucci et al., 2005). Second, it is easy to oversimplify and exaggerate differences between the two sides of the brain. Split-brain research has given rise to several popular but misguided books that classify people as "right-brain" or "left-brain" thinkers. It is important to remember that under normal conditions, the right and left hemispheres are in close communication through the corpus callosum and so work together in a coordinated, integrated way (Gazzaniga, 2005, 2008). Furthermore, as we saw in the story of Nico at the beginning of the chapter, the plasticity of the brain means that both hemispheres have the potential to perform a range of tasks.

Language The notion that human language is controlled primarily by the left cerebral hemisphere was first set forth in the 1860s by a French physician named Paul Broca. Broca's ideas were modified a decade later by the scientist Karl Wernicke. Thus, it should come as no surprise that the two major language areas in the brain have traditionally been called *Broca's area* and *Wernicke's area*. (See **Figure 2–12**.)

Wernicke's area lies toward the back of the temporal lobe. This area is crucial in processing and understanding what others are saying. In contrast, Broca's area, found in the frontal lobe, is considered to be essential to our ability to talk. Support for these distinctions comes from patients who have suffered left-hemisphere strokes and resulting brain damage. Such strokes often produce predictable language problems, called

FIGURE 2–12
Processing of speech and language.
Broca's and Wernicke's areas, generally found only on the left side of the brain, work together, enabling us to produce and understand speech and language.

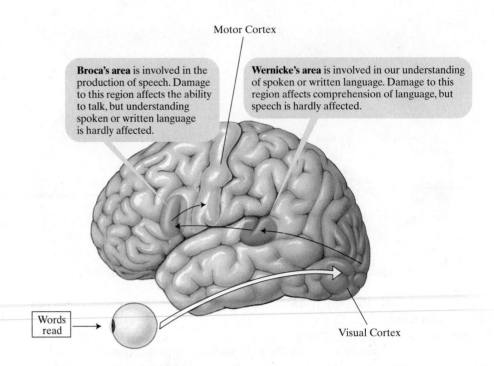

Motor Cortex

Broca's area is involved in the production of speech. Damage to this region affects the ability to talk, but understanding spoken or written language is hardly affected.

Wernicke's area is involved in our understanding of spoken or written language. Damage to this region affects comprehension of language, but speech is hardly affected.

Words read

Visual Cortex

aphasias Impairments of the ability to use (expressive aphasia) or understand (receptive aphasia) language that usually results from brain damage.

aphasias. If the brain damage primarily affects Broca's area, the aphasia tends to be "expressive." That is, the patients' language difficulties lie predominantly in sequencing and producing language (talking). If the damage primarily affects Wernicke's area, the aphasia tends to be "receptive," and patients generally have profound difficulties understanding language (listening).

Interestingly, the areas of the brain involved in processing speech and language may not be as uniquely human as once thought (Belin, 2008). Investigators have identified a similar region in the brain of macaque monkeys, which is also involved in voice recognition for members of their own species (Petkov et al., 2008).

Handedness A common misconception is that hemispheric specialization is related to handedness. The fact is that speech is most often localized in the left hemisphere for both right- and left-handed people. However, in a small percentage of left-handed individuals, language functions are concentrated in the right hemisphere (Knecht et al., 2000).

Nevertheless, psychologists have uncovered a number of interesting facts about handedness. Approximately 90% of humans are right-handed, with slightly more males than females showing a tendency toward left-handedness. Though research has not fully explained why some people are left-handed and others are right-handed, the tendency toward right-handedness appears to be a trait humans have possessed for quite some time, as anthropological studies of prehistoric cave drawing, tools, and human skeletons have shown (James Steele, 2000). Most chimpanzees, bonobos, and gorillas also favor their right hands, but most orangutans favor their left hands (Hopkins et al., 2011).

Tools for Studying the Brain

What methods have been developed to study the brain?

For centuries, our understanding of the brain depended entirely on observing patients who had suffered brain injury or from examining the brains of cadavers. Another approach—that is still in use—is to remove or damage the brains of nonhuman animals and study the effects. But the human brain is far more complicated than that of any other animal. How can scientists study the living, fully functioning human brain? Contemporary neuroscientists have four basic techniques—microelectrodes, macroelectrodes, structural imaging, and functional imaging. (The "**Summary Table**: Tools for Studying the Nervous System" reviews these techniques and their uses.) ◉

◉ **Watch** the **Video** Brain Building on **MyPsychLab**

SUMMARY TABLE	TOOLS FOR STUDYING THE NERVOUS SYSTEM
Microelectrode Techniques	Used to study the functions of individual neurons.
Macroelectrode Techniques	Used to obtain a picture of the activity in a particular region of the brain. The EEG is one such technique.
Structural Imaging	Family of techniques used to map structures in a living brain.
Computerized axial tomography (CAT or CT)	Permits three-dimensional imaging of a living human brain.
Magnetic resonance imaging (MRI)	Produces pictures of inner brain structures.
Functional Imaging Techniques	Family of techniques that can image activity in the brain as it responds to various stimuli.
EEG imaging	Measures brain activity on a millisecond-by-millisecond basis.
Magnetoencephalography (MEG) Magnetic source imaging (MSI)	Two procedures that are similar to EEG imaging but have greater accuracy.
Positron emission tomography (PET) scanning Radioactive PET Single photon emission computed tomography (SPECT)	Three techniques that use radioactive energy to map exact regions of brain activity.
Functional magnetic resonance imaging (fMRI)	Measures the movement of blood molecules in the brain, pinpointing specific sites and details of neuronal activity.

Microelectrode Techniques   *Microelectrode* recording techniques are used to study the functions of single neurons. A microelectrode is a tiny glass or quartz pipette or tube (smaller in diameter than a human hair) that is filled with a conducting liquid. When technicians place the tip of this electrode inside a neuron, they can study changes in the electrical conditions of that neuron. Microelectrode techniques have been used to understand action potentials, the effects of drugs or toxins on neurons, and even processes that occur in the neural membrane.

Macroelectrode Techniques   *Macroelectrode* recording techniques are used to obtain an overall picture of the activity in particular regions of the brain, which may contain millions of neurons. The first such device—the *electroencephalograph* (EEG)—is still in use today. Flat electrodes, taped to the scalp, are linked by wires to a device that translates electrical activity into lines on a moving roll of paper (or, more recently, images on a computer screen). This graph of so-called brain waves provides an index of both the strength and the rhythm of neural activity. As we will see in Chapter 4, "States of Consciousness," this technique has given researchers valuable insights into changes in brain waves during sleep and dreaming.

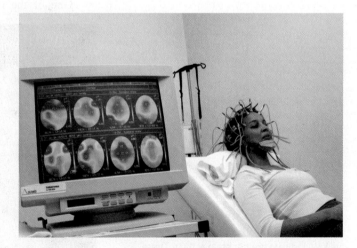

In an EEG, electrodes attached to the scalp are used to create a picture of neural activity in the brain.

Structural Imaging   When researchers want to map the structures in a living human brain, they turn to two newer techniques. *Computerized axial tomography* (CAT or CT) *scanning* allows scientists to create three-dimensional images of a human brain without performing surgery. To produce a CAT scan, an X-ray photography unit rotates around the person, moving from the top of the head to the bottom; a computer then combines the resulting images. *Magnetic resonance imaging* (MRI) is even more successful at producing pictures of the

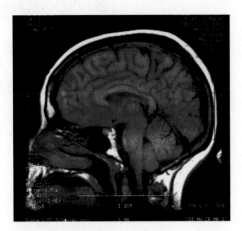

MRI image of the human head.

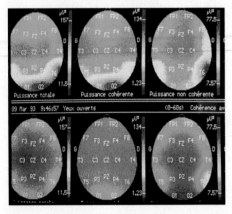

EEG imaging of one person's alpha brain waves (looking down on the brain, front of the head toward the top of the page). Red and yellow colors indicate greater alpha-wave activity.

inner regions of the brain, with its ridges, folds, and fissures. With MRI, the person's head is surrounded by a magnetic field and the brain is exposed to radio waves, which causes hydrogen atoms in the brain to release energy. The energy released by different structures in the brain generates an image that appears on a computer screen.

Recent advances in MRI technology now enable scientists to compare precise three-dimensional images obtained over extended periods. This permits tracking of progressive structural changes in the brain that accompany slow neurodegenerative disorders like Alzheimer's disease (Bruen, McGeown, Shanks, & Venneri, 2008).

Functional Imaging In many cases, researchers are interested in more than structure; they want to look at the brain's *activity* as it actually reacts to sensory stimuli such as pain, tones, and words. Such is the goal of several *functional imaging* methods. EEG imaging measures brain activity millisecond-by-millisecond. In this technique, more than two dozen electrodes are placed at important locations on the scalp. These electrodes record brain activities, which are then converted by a computer into colored images on a television screen. The technique has been extremely useful in detecting abnormal cortical activity such as that observed during epileptic seizures, like those suffered by Nico, the boy described at the beginning of the chapter.

Two related techniques, called *magnetoencephalography* (MEG) and *magnetic source imaging* (MSI), take the procedure a step further. In standard EEG, electrical signals are distorted as they pass through the skull; and their exact source is difficult to determine. However, those same electrical signals create magnetic fields that are unaffected by bone. Both MEG and MSI measure the strength of the magnetic field and identify its source with considerable accuracy. By using these procedures, neuroscientists have begun to determine exactly which parts of the brain do most of the work in such psychological processes as memory (Campo et al., 2005), language processing (Ressel, Wilke, Lidzba, Lutzenberger, & Krägeloh-Mann, 2008), and reading, and shed light on mental disorders such as schizophrenia (Haenschel & Linden, 2011).

Another family of functional imaging techniques—including *positron emission tomography* (PET) *scanning*—uses radioactive energy to map brain activity. In these techniques, a person first receives an injection of a radioactive substance. Brain structures that are especially active immediately after the injection absorb most of the substance. When the substance starts to decay, it releases subatomic particles. By studying where most of the particles come from, researchers can determine exactly which portions of the brain are most active. PET has been used to investigate how our memory for words and images is stored in the brain (Cabeza & Nyberg, 2000; Craik et al., 1999), and locate damage resulting from Alzheimer's disease (Zetterberg, 2008).

One of the newest and most powerful techniques for recording activity in the brain is called *functional magnetic resonance imaging* (fMRI). Functional MRI measures the movement of blood molecules (which is related to neuron activity) in the brain, permitting neuroscientists to pinpoint specific sites and details of neuronal activity. By comparing brain activity in normal learners with brain activity in children

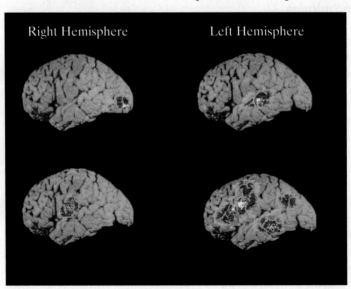

PET scans of a person at rest (top) and using language (bottom). The "hot" colors (red and yellow) indicate greater brain activity. These scans show that language activity is located primarily, but not exclusively, in the brain's left hemisphere.

with learning problems, researchers have begun to identify the neurological mechanisms associated with attention deficit hyperactivity disorder (ADHD) (Schneider et al., 2010); dyslexia (T. L. Richards & Berninger, 2008); Huntington's disease (Bohanna, Georgiou-Karistianis, Hannan, & Egan, 2008); and disorders that involve difficulties in controlling emotions (Heinzel et al., 2005). With fMRI it is even possible to determine with some accuracy what a person is thinking about, may decide to do, and whether he or she is lying (Ganis, Rosenfeld, Meixner, Kievit, & Schendan, 2011). FMRI studies have even debunked the myth that we use only 10% of our brain since studies using fMRI have not shown any area of the brain that is perpetually inactive (Lilienfeld & Arkowitz, 2008). Because fMRI enables us to collect extremely precise images rapidly and is noninvasive in that it does not require the injection of radioactive chemicals, it is especially promising as a research tool.

THINKING CRITICALLY ABOUT . . .

Tools for Studying the Brain

Stop for a minute and think about what you have just read. These remarkable tools for studying the brain allow researchers to identify specific areas in the brain that become more active when people engage in various activities such as identifying objects, learning new information, and so on. The temptation is to conclude that those areas of the brain *cause* people to be able to identify the objects or to learn the new information. But in fact, all that has been shown is that there is an *association* or *correlation* between the mental activity and those brain regions. Recall that in Chapter 1 ("The Science of Psychology") you were warned about drawing causal inferences from correlational data. There may be a causal relationship or there may not. We simply don't yet know. Moreover, "Psychological states such as thoughts and feelings are real. Brain states are real. The problem is that the two are not real in the same way" (Barrett, 2009). You might recognize this as yet another example of the enduring issue *Mind–Body*. For more on these complex issues, see the series of articles that appeared in the journal *Perspectives on Psychological Science*, 2010, Vol. 5, pp. 714–775.

---

spinal cord Complex cable of neurons that runs down the spine, connecting the brain to most of the rest of the body.

The Spinal Cord

What does the spinal cord do? How does it work with the brain to sense events and act on them?

We talk of the brain and the spinal cord as two distinct structures, but in fact, there is no clear boundary between them; at its upper end, the spinal cord enlarges into the brain stem. (See **Figure 2–13.**)

The **spinal cord** is our communications superhighway, connecting the brain to most of the rest of the body. When the spinal cord is severed, parts of the body are literally disconnected from the brain. Thus, people who suffer damage to the spinal cord lose all sensations from the parts of the body that can no longer send information to higher brain areas, as well as control over the movements of those body parts.

The spinal cord is made up of soft, jellylike bundles of long axons, wrapped in insulating myelin (white matter) and surrounded and protected by the bones in the spine. There are two major neural pathways in the spinal cord. One consists of motor neurons, descending from the brain, that control internal organs and muscles and help to regulate the autonomic nervous system (described later). The other consists of ascending, sensory neurons that carry information from the extremities and internal organs to the brain. In addition, the spinal cord contains neural circuits that produce reflex movements (and control some aspects of walking). These circuits do not require input from the brain.

To understand how the spinal cord works, consider the simple act of burning your finger on a hot pan. (See **Figure 2–14.**) You pull your hand away without thinking, but that quick response was the last event in a series of reactions in your nervous system. First, special sensory cells pick up the message that your finger is burned. They pass this information along to *interneurons* located in the spinal cord. The interneurons, in turn, connect to motor neurons, triggering a quick withdrawal of your hand. At the same time, the message is being sent to other parts of your nervous system. Your body goes on "emergency alert": You breathe faster, your heart pounds, your entire body (including the endocrine system) mobilizes itself against the wound. Meanwhile, your brain is interpreting the messages it receives: You feel pain, you look at the burn, and you run cold water over your hand. A simple, small burn, then, triggers a complex, coordinated sequence of activities.

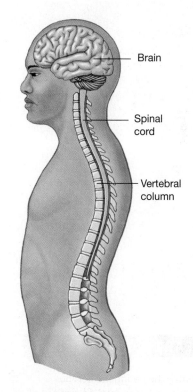

FIGURE 2–13
Brain and spinal cord.

Source: Reprinted from *Human Physiology: An Integrated Approach* by A. C. Silverthorn. Copyright © 1989. Reprinted by permission of Pearson Education, Inc., Upper Saddle River, NJ.

FIGURE 2–14
The spinal cord and reflex action.

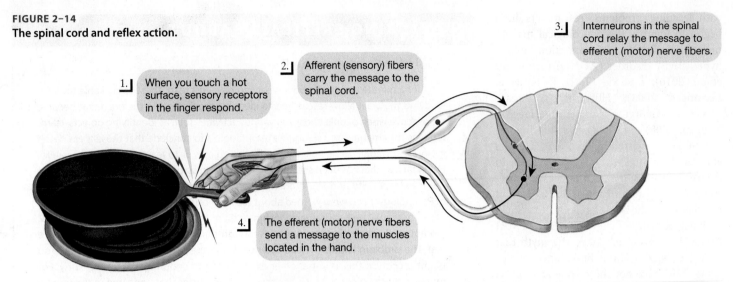

1. When you touch a hot surface, sensory receptors in the finger respond.

2. Afferent (sensory) fibers carry the message to the spinal cord.

3. Interneurons in the spinal cord relay the message to efferent (motor) nerve fibers.

4. The efferent (motor) nerve fibers send a message to the muscles located in the hand.

CHECK YOUR UNDERSTANDING

Match the lobes of the cerebral cortex with their functions.

1. ____ frontal lobes
2. ____ occipital lobes
3. ____ temporal lobes
4. ____ parietal lobes

a. process language and information from the ears
b. process body sensations and spatial information
c. plan goal-directed behavior
d. process visual information

Answers: 1. c. 2. d. 3. a. 4. b.

APPLY YOUR UNDERSTANDING

1. Susan has a degenerative disease that causes her to lose her balance easily and to move in a jerky and uncoordinated way. She cannot drink from a glass without spilling or touch her toes without falling over. This disease is probably affecting her _____.

   a. hypothalamus
   b. midbrain
   c. cerebellum
   d. reticular formation

2. After a head injury a person reports that she is unable to see, although her eyes are uninjured. A doctor would suspect an injury in the _____ lobe.

   a. frontal
   b. occipital
   c. parietal
   d. temporal

Answers: 1. c. 2. b.

LEARNING OBJECTIVES

- Identify the peripheral nervous system and contrast the functions of the somatic and autonomic nervous systems.
- Explain the differences between the sympathetic and the parasympathetic nervous systems.

THE PERIPHERAL NERVOUS SYSTEM

How does the brain communicate with the rest of the body? How is the autonomic branch of the peripheral nervous system involved in controlling emotions?

The origins of the quick response your body makes to touching a hot pan are in your peripheral nervous system. The peripheral nervous system (PNS) links the brain and spinal cord to the rest of the body, including the sensory receptors, glands, internal organs, and skeletal muscles. (See **Figure 2–6.**) It consists of both *afferent neurons*, which carry messages *to* the central nervous system (CNS), and *efferent neurons*, which carry messages *from* the CNS. All the things that register through your senses—sights, sounds, smells, temperature, pressure, and so on—travel to your brain via afferent neurons. The efferent neurons carry signals from the brain to the body's muscles and glands.

Some neurons belong to a part of the PNS called the **somatic nervous system.** Neurons in this system are involved in making voluntary movements of the skeletal muscles. Other neurons belong to a part of the PNS called the autonomic nervous system. Neurons in the **autonomic nervous system** govern involuntary activities of your internal organs, from the beating of your heart to the hormone secretions of your glands.

The autonomic nervous system is of special interest to psychologists because it is involved not only in vital body functions, such as breathing and blood flow, but also in important emotions as well. To understand the workings of the autonomic nervous system, you must know about the system's two parts: the *sympathetic* and the *parasympathetic* divisions. (See **Figure 2–15.**)

The nerve fibers of the **sympathetic division** are busiest when you are intensely aroused, such as being enraged or very frightened. For example, if you were hiking through the woods and suddenly encountered a large, growling bear, your sympathetic division would be instantaneously triggered. In response to messages from it, your heart would begin to pound, your breathing would quicken, your pupils would enlarge, and your digestion would stop. All these changes would help direct your energy and attention to the emergency you faced, giving you the keen senses, stamina, and strength needed to flee from the danger or to stand and fight it. Your sympathetic division would also tell your glands to start pumping hormones into your blood to further strengthen your body's reactions. Sympathetic nerve fibers connect to every internal organ—a fact that explains why the body's response to sudden danger is so widespread.

somatic nervous system The part of the peripheral nervous system that carries messages from the senses to the central nervous system and between the central nervous system and the skeletal muscles.

autonomic nervous system The part of the peripheral nervous system that carries messages between the central nervous system and the internal organs.

sympathetic division Branch of the autonomic nervous system; it prepares the body for quick action in an emergency.

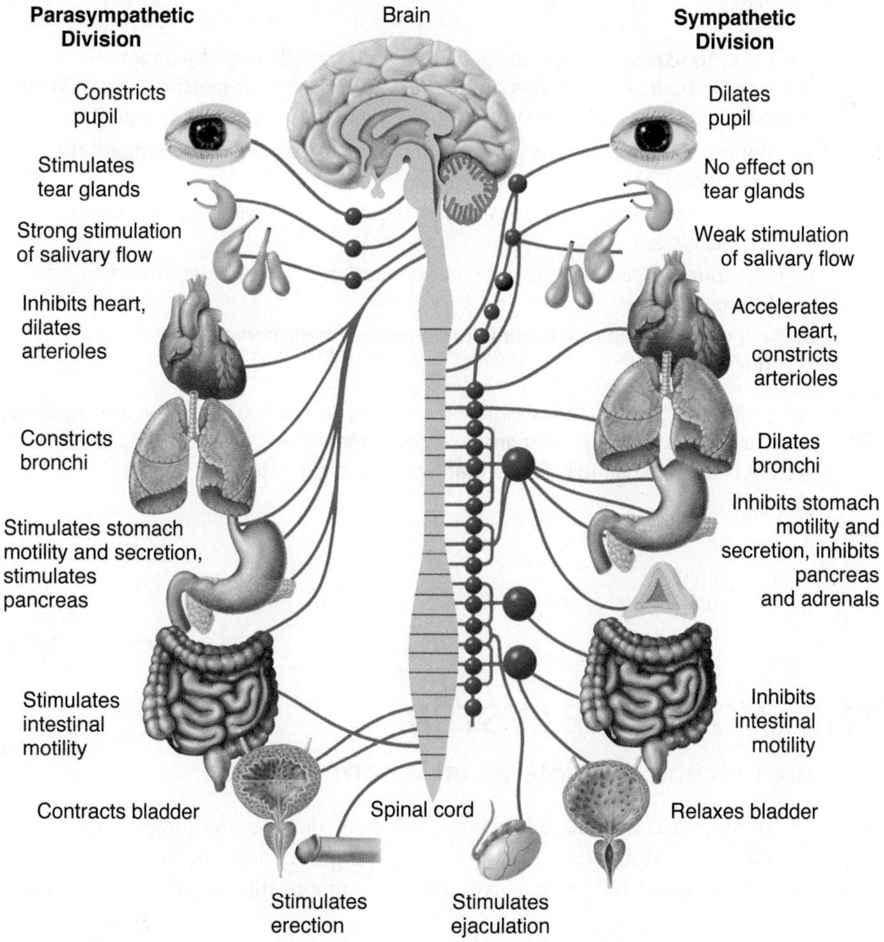

Parasympathetic Division

Brain

Sympathetic Division

Constricts pupil — Dilates pupil

Stimulates tear glands — No effect on tear glands

Strong stimulation of salivary flow — Weak stimulation of salivary flow

Inhibits heart, dilates arterioles — Accelerates heart, constricts arterioles

Constricts bronchi — Dilates bronchi

Stimulates stomach motility and secretion, stimulates pancreas — Inhibits stomach motility and secretion, inhibits pancreas and adrenals

Stimulates intestinal motility — Inhibits intestinal motility

Contracts bladder — Relaxes bladder

Spinal cord

Stimulates erection — Stimulates ejaculation

FIGURE 2–15

The sympathetic and parasympathetic divisions of the autonomic nervous system.

The sympathetic division generally acts to arouse the body, preparing it for "fight or flight." The parasympathetic follows with messages to relax.

Source: Figure 15.14, p. 262, from *General Biology,* Revised Edition by Willis Johnson. Copyright © 1961 by Brooks/Cole, a part of Cengage Learning, Inc. Reproduced by permission. *www.cengage.com/permissions.*

When you are in a frightening situation, such as being confronted with an angry bear, the sympathetic division of the autonomic nervous system triggers a number of responses within your body. These responses give you the strength and stamina to either fight the danger or flee from it.

parasympathetic division Branch of the autonomic nervous system; it calms and relaxes the body.

✔•—☐**Study** and **Review** on **MyPsychLab**

Although sympathetic reactions are often sustained even after danger is passed, eventually even the most intense sympathetic division reaction fades and the body calms down, returning to normal. The heart then goes back to beating at its regular rate, the stomach muscles relax, digestion resumes, breathing slows down, and the pupils contract. This calming effect is promoted by the **parasympathetic division** of the autonomic nervous system. Parasympathetic nerve fibers connect to the same organs as sympathetic nerve fibers do, but they cause the opposite reaction.

Traditionally, the autonomic nervous system was regarded as the "automatic" part of the body's response mechanism (hence its name). You could not, it was believed, tell your own autonomic nervous system when to speed up or slow down your heartbeat or when to stop or start your digestive processes. However, more recent studies have shown that humans (and animals) have some control over the autonomic nervous system. For example, people can learn to moderate the severity of high blood pressure (Reineke, 2008) or migraine headaches (Nestoriuc, Martin, Rief, & Andrasik, 2008), and even treat hyperactive attention deficit disorder (Monastra, 2008) through *biofeedback,* a subject we will look at more closely in Chapter 5, "Learning."

CHECK YOUR UNDERSTANDING

Indicate whether each function is associated with the sympathetic (S) or the parasympathetic (P) division of the autonomic nervous system.

1. ____ heartbeat increases
2. ____ stomach starts digesting food
3. ____ breathing speeds up
4. ____ body recovers from an emergency situation

Answers: 1. (S). 2. (P). 3. (S). 4. (P).

APPLY YOUR UNDERSTANDING

1. The heavy footsteps on the stairs get closer and closer. Slowly, the door to the bedroom creaks open. As a stranger lunges in, you let out an ear-piercing scream. Which of the following most accurately describes your nervous system at this point?
   a. Your sympathetic nervous system is more active than your parasympathetic nervous system.
   b. Your parasympathetic nervous system is more active than your sympathetic nervous system.
   c. Both your sympathetic and your parasympathetic nervous systems are extremely active.
   d. Neither your sympathetic nor your parasympathetic nervous systems are unusually active.

2. John started jogging to lose weight. The first day he ran two miles. The next morning, as he lay in bed relaxing and trying to recover, the nerves of his _____ nervous system made him painfully aware that he had overexercised.
   a. parasympathetic
   b. somatic
   c. autonomic
   d. sympathetic

Answers: 1. a. 2. b.

- Describe the endocrine glands and the way their hormones affect behavior.

▷ THE ENDOCRINE SYSTEM

Why are psychologists interested in hormones?

The nervous system is not the only mechanism that regulates the functioning of our bodies. The endocrine system plays a key role in helping to coordinate and integrate complex psychological reactions. In fact, as we've noted throughout this chapter, the nervous system and the endocrine system work together in a constant chemical conversation. The **endocrine glands** release chemical substances called **hormones** that are carried throughout your body by the bloodstream. Hormones serve a similar function to neurotransmitters: They carry messages. Indeed, the same substance—for example, norepinephrine—may serve both as a neurotransmitter and as a hormone. A main difference between the nervous and the endocrine systems is speed. A nerve impulse may travel through the body in a few hundredths of a second, but hormones may take seconds, even minutes, to reach their target.

Hormones interest psychologists for two reasons. First, at certain stages of development, hormones *organize* the nervous system and body tissues. At puberty, for example, hormone surges trigger the development of secondary sex characteristics, including breasts in females and a deeper voice in males. Second, hormones *activate* behaviors. They affect such things as alertness or sleepiness, excitability, sexual behavior, ability to concentrate, aggressiveness, reactions to stress, even desire for companionship. Hormones can also have dramatic effects on mood, emotional reactivity, ability to learn, and ability to resist disease. Radical changes in some hormones may also contribute to serious psychological disorders, such as depression. The locations of the endocrine glands are shown in **Figure 2–16.**

The **pituitary gland,** which is located on the underside of the brain, is connected to the hypothalamus. The pituitary produces the largest number of different hormones

endocrine glands Glands of the endocrine system that release hormones into the bloodstream.

hormones Chemical substances released by the endocrine glands; they help regulate bodily activities.

pituitary gland Gland located on the underside of the brain; it produces the largest number of the body's hormones.

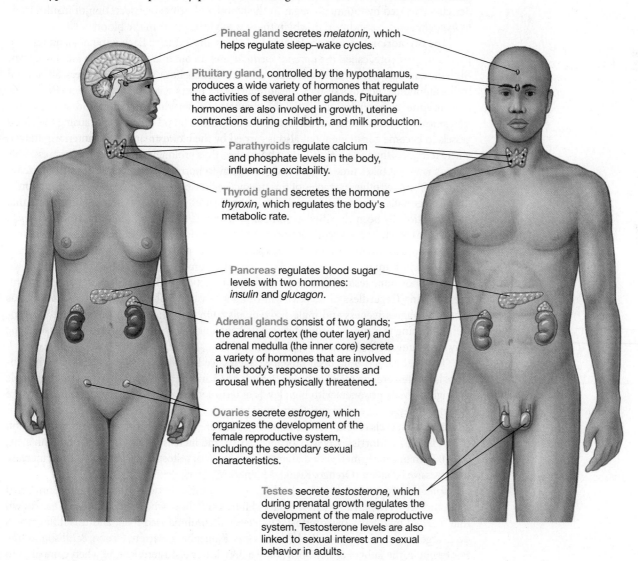

Pineal gland secretes *melatonin,* which helps regulate sleep–wake cycles.

Pituitary gland, controlled by the hypothalamus, produces a wide variety of hormones that regulate the activities of several other glands. Pituitary hormones are also involved in growth, uterine contractions during childbirth, and milk production.

Parathyroids regulate calcium and phosphate levels in the body, influencing excitability.

Thyroid gland secretes the hormone *thyroxin,* which regulates the body's metabolic rate.

Pancreas regulates blood sugar levels with two hormones: *insulin* and *glucagon.*

Adrenal glands consist of two glands; the adrenal cortex (the outer layer) and adrenal medulla (the inner core) secrete a variety of hormones that are involved in the body's response to stress and arousal when physically threatened.

Ovaries secrete *estrogen,* which organizes the development of the female reproductive system, including the secondary sexual characteristics.

Testes secrete *testosterone,* which during prenatal growth regulates the development of the male reproductive system. Testosterone levels are also linked to sexual interest and sexual behavior in adults.

FIGURE 2–16
The glands of the endocrine system.
Endocrine glands secrete hormones that produce widespread effects on the body.

pineal gland A gland located roughly in the center of the brain that appears to regulate activity levels over the course of a day.

thyroid gland Endocrine gland located below the voice box; it produces the hormone thyroxin.

parathyroids Four tiny glands embedded in the thyroid.

pancreas Organ lying between the stomach and small intestine; it secretes insulin and glucagon to regulate blood-sugar levels.

adrenal glands Two endocrine glands located just above the kidneys.

gonads The reproductive glands—testes in males and ovaries in females.

and thus has the widest range of effects on the body's functions. In fact, it is often called the "master gland" because of its influential role in regulating other endocrine glands. The pituitary influences blood pressure, thirst, sexual behavior, body growth, as well as other functions.

The pea-sized **pineal gland** is located in the middle of the brain. It secretes the hormone *melatonin*, which helps to regulate sleep–wake cycles. We will discuss the biological clock in greater detail in Chapter 4, "States of Consciousness."

The **thyroid gland** is located just below the larynx, or voice box. It produces one primary hormone, *thyroxin*, which regulates the body's rate of metabolism and, thus, how alert and energetic people are and how fat or thin they tend to be. An overactive thyroid can produce a variety of symptoms, including: overexcitability, insomnia, and reduced attention span. Too little thyroxin leads to the other extreme: constantly feeling tired and wanting to sleep.

Embedded in the thyroid gland are the **parathyroids**—four tiny organs that control and balance the levels of calcium and phosphate in the body, which in turn influence levels of excitability.

The **pancreas** lies in a curve between the stomach and the small intestine. The pancreas controls the level of sugar in the blood by secreting two regulating hormones: *insulin* and *glucagon.* These two hormones work against each other to keep the blood-sugar level properly balanced. Underproduction of insulin leads to *diabetes mellitus,* a chronic disorder characterized by too much sugar in the blood and urine; oversecretion of insulin leads to *hypoglycemia,* a condition in which there is too little sugar in the blood.

The two **adrenal glands** are located just above the kidneys. Each adrenal gland has two parts: an inner core, called the *adrenal medulla,* and an outer layer, called the *adrenal cortex.* Both the adrenal cortex and the adrenal medulla affect the body's reaction to stress. Stimulated by the autonomic nervous system, the adrenal cortex pours several hormones into the bloodstream. One, *epinephrine,* activates the sympathetic nervous system. Another hormone, *norepinephrine* (also a neurotransmitter), not only raises blood pressure by causing the blood vessels to become constricted, but also is carried by the bloodstream to the anterior pituitary, where it triggers the release of still more hormones, thus prolonging the response to stress. This process is why it takes time for the body to return to normal after extreme emotional excitement. (We will see other examples of this interaction in Chapter 8, "Motivation and Emotion.")

The **gonads**—the *testes* in males and the *ovaries* in females—secrete hormones that have traditionally been classified as masculine (the *androgens*) and feminine (the *estrogens*). (Both sexes produce both types of hormone, but androgens predominate in males, whereas estrogens predominate in females.) These hormones play a number of important organizing roles in human development. For example, human and animal studies have shown that if the hormone testosterone is present during critical periods of prenatal development, the offspring (regardless of its sex) will develop a variety of male characteristics such as increased aggressiveness and male sex-type play. On the other hand, the absence of testosterone during this period promotes female behaviors such as nesting and female sex-type play (Auyeung, 2009; Kalat, 2001; Knickmeyer et al., 2005).

Testosterone has long been linked to aggressive behavior, perhaps explaining why violence is greatest among males between the ages of 15 and 25, the years when testosterone levels are highest. Male prisoners with high levels of testosterone are likely to have committed more violent crimes, at an earlier age, than other prisoners (Dabbs, Carr, Frady, & Riad, 1995). In addition, high levels of testosterone in normal men are associated with competitive aggression (Carré Gilchrist, Morrissey, & McCormick, 2010), and increased risk taking (Goudriaan et al., 2010). Even in elderly men with dementia, high levels of testosterone are related to an increase in aggressive behavior (Orengo, Kunik, Molinari, Wristers, & Yudofsky, 2002).

Interestingly, testosterone levels also appear to differ between married and unmarried men, and between married men who have children and those who do not. Research has shown that married men have lower testosterone levels than unmarried men, and this difference is even larger for married men with children (Gray, Kahlenberg, Barrett, Lipson, & Ellison, 2002). For example, the fathers of newborns have a 33% lower testosterone level when compared to fathers-to-be (Berg & Wynne-Edwards, 2001). Evolutionary psychologists suggest these variations in testosterone level may be associated with a physiological response of the male body that increases the nurturing capacity of men who become fathers and husbands.

CHECK YOUR UNDERSTANDING

1. Communication in the endocrine system depends on _____, which are chemicals secreted directly into the bloodstream.

2. Match each gland with its major function.

____ thyroid gland

____ parathyroid glands

____ pineal gland

____ pancreas

____ pituitary gland

____ gonads

____ adrenal glands

a. balance calcium and phosphate in the body
b. controls sugar level in the blood
c. involved in stress response
d. produce androgens and estrogens
e. regulates rate of metabolism
f. controls other endocrine glands
g. controls daily cycle of activity levels

Answers: 1. hormones. **2.** thyroid gland (e); parathyroid glands (a); pineal gland (g); pancreas (b); pituitary gland (f); gonads (d); adrenal glands (c).

APPLY YOUR UNDERSTANDING

1. A clinical psychologist refers a new client to a medical doctor because the client's psychological symptoms could indicate an overactive thyroid gland. What symptoms might the psychologist be responding to?

a. The client is having trouble getting to sleep and staying asleep.
b. The client, who in the past was usually careful and thoughtful, is now making careless "snap decisions."
c. The client finds it increasingly difficult to concentrate and to focus on tasks.
d. All of the above could be symptoms of an overactive thyroid gland.

2. Mary has been under a great deal of stress lately. Her blood pressure has increased, she has lost her appetite, and her heart is beating faster than usual. These changes are most likely the result of

a. increased activity in the pineal gland.
b. reduced activity in the pancreas.
c. increased activity in the adrenal glands.
d. reduced activity in the thyroid gland.

Answers: 1. d. **2.** c.

GENES, EVOLUTION, AND BEHAVIOR

Our brain, nervous system, and endocrine system keep us aware of what is happening outside (and inside) our bodies; enable us to use language, think, and solve problems; affect our emotions; and thus guide our behavior. To understand why they function as they do, we need to look at our genetic heritage, as individuals and as members of the human species.

ENDURING ISSUES

Heredity–Environment   The Pendulum Swings

For many years, scientists were divided by the so-called "nature versus nurture" debate. Psychologists in one camp emphasized genes and heredity (or nature). Psychologists in the other camp emphasized the environment and experience (or nurture). Most contemporary psychologists view this debate as artificial: Both genes and environment shape human behavior. As described in our section on neural plasticity, researchers have made great

LEARNING OBJECTIVES

- Distinguish among genetics, behavior genetics, and evolutionary psychology.
- Differentiate among genes, chromosomes, DNA, and the human genome. Describe what is meant by dominant and recessive genes, polygenic inheritance, and genotype vs. phenotype.
- Compare and contrast strain studies, selection studies, family studies, twin studies, and adoption studies as sources of information about the effects of heredity.
- Identify the key ethical issues that arise as society gains more control over genetics.
- Describe how evolutionary psychologists view the influence of natural selection on human social behavior.

behavior genetics Study of the relationship between heredity and behavior.

evolutionary psychology Study of the evolutionary roots of behaviors and mental processes.

genetics Study of how traits are transmitted from one generation to the next.

genes Elements that control the transmission of traits; they are found on the chromosomes.

chromosomes Pairs of threadlike bodies within the cell nucleus that contain the genes.

deoxyribonucleic acid (DNA) Complex molecule in a double-helix configuration that is the main ingredient of chromosomes and genes and that forms the code for all genetic information.

strides in understanding how these two forces interact. Nonetheless, strong disagreement still exists regarding the relative influence of heredity and environment on our thoughts, abilities, personalities, and behaviors.

Two different but related fields address the influence of heredity on human behavior. **Behavior genetics** focuses on the extent to which heredity accounts for individual differences in behavior and thinking. **Evolutionary psychology** studies the evolutionary roots of behaviors and mental processes that all human beings share. To understand the contributions of these fields, we must first understand the process of inheritance. ■

Genetics

How are traits passed from one generation to the next?

Genetics is the study of how living things pass on traits from one generation to the next. Offspring are not carbon copies or "clones" of their parents, yet some traits reappear from generation to generation in predictable patterns. Around the beginning of the 20th century, scientists named the basic units of inheritance **genes**. To understand more about these blueprints for development, let's take a look at some cellular components.

As shown in **Figure 2–17,** the nucleus of each cell contains **chromosomes,** tiny threadlike bodies that carry genes—the basic units of heredity. Each chromosome contains hundreds or thousands of genes in fixed locations. Chromosomes vary in size and shape, and usually come in pairs. Each species has a constant number: mice have 20 pairs, monkeys have 27, and peas have 7. Human beings have 23 pairs of chromosomes in every normal cell, except the sex cells (eggs and sperm), which have only half a set of chromosomes.

At fertilization, the chromosomes from the father's sperm link to the chromosomes from the mother's egg, creating a new cell called a *zygote.* That single cell and all of the billions of body cells that develop from it (except sperm and eggs) contain 46 chromosomes, arranged as 23 pairs.

Genes are composed primarily of **deoxyribonucleic acid (DNA),** a complex organic molecule that looks like two chains twisted around each other in a double-helix pattern. Amazingly, a six-foot strand of DNA is crammed into the nucleus of every cell of your body. DNA is the only known molecule that can replicate or reproduce itself, which happens each time a cell divides.

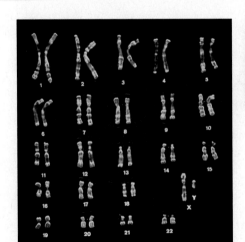

(Left) The 23 pairs of chromosomes found in every normal human cell. The two members of 22 of these pairs look exactly alike. The two members of the 23rd pair, the sex chromosomes, may or may not look alike. Females have equivalent X chromosomes, while males have one X and one Y chromosome, which look very different. (Right) The chromosome pattern that causes Down syndrome: the presence of three chromosomes in pair 21.

FIGURE 2–17
The relation among chromosomes, genes, and DNA.

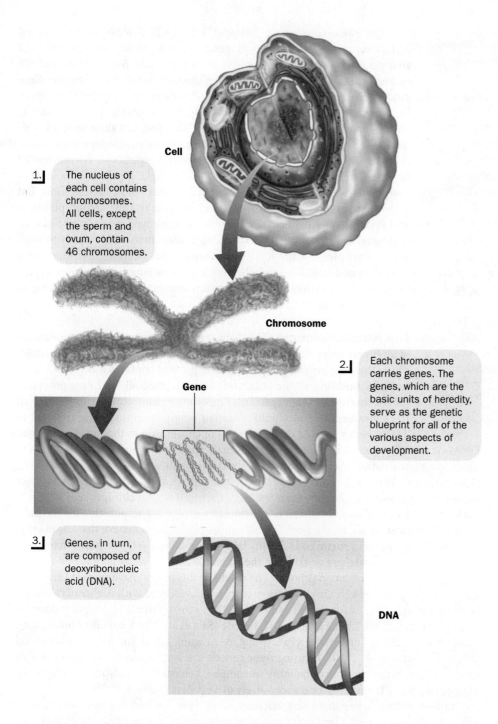

Cell

1. The nucleus of each cell contains chromosomes. All cells, except the sperm and ovum, contain 46 chromosomes.

Chromosome

2. Each chromosome carries genes. The genes, which are the basic units of heredity, serve as the genetic blueprint for all of the various aspects of development.

Gene

3. Genes, in turn, are composed of deoxyribonucleic acid (DNA).

DNA

Genes, like chromosomes, occur in pairs. In some cases, such as eye color, one may be a **dominant gene** (B for brown eyes) and the other a **recessive gene** (b for blue eyes). A child who inherits the gene for blue eyes from both parents (bb) will have blue eyes. (See **Figure 2–18.**) A sibling who inherits the gene for brown eyes from both parents (BB) will have brown eyes. And, because the brown-eye gene dominates, so will a sibling who inherits the gene for brown eyes from one parent and the gene for blue eyes from the other (Bb or bB).

Polygenic Inheritance

Thus far, we have been talking about single-gene inheritance: We have said that a gene is a small segment of DNA that carries directions for a particular trait or group of traits. Examples of a single gene that controls a single trait are rare, however. In **polygenic inheritance,** multiple genes contribute to a particular trait. Weight, height, skin pigmentation, intelligence, and countless other characteristics are polygenic.

dominant gene Member of a gene pair that controls the appearance of a certain trait.

recessive gene Member of a gene pair that can control the appearance of a certain trait only if it is paired with another recessive gene.

polygenic inheritance Process by which several genes interact to produce a certain trait; responsible for our most important traits.

Two brown-eyed parents each have a recessive gene for blue eyes.

Brown-eyed mother   Brown-eyed father

Offspring

Brown eyes   Brown eyes   Brown eyes   Blue eyes

Chances are 1 in 4 that a child will inherit both recessive genes and have blue eyes.

FIGURE 2–18

Transmission of eye color by dominant (B) and recessive (b) genes.

This figure represents the four possible combinations of eye-color genes in these parents' offspring. Because three out of the four combinations result in brown-eyed children, the chance that any child will have brown eyes is 75%.

The twisted chain of the long DNA molecule contains the genetic code.

Your own unique genetic "blueprint" is internally coded on your 46 matched chromosomes and is called your **genotype.** Except for reproductive cells, your genotype is contained in every cell in your body. But heredity need not be immediately or fully apparent. Even identical twins, who have the same genotype, differ in small ways that allow family members to tell them apart. In some cases, expression of a trait is delayed until later in life. For example, many men inherit "male-pattern baldness" that does not show up until middle age. Moreover, genes may predispose a person to developing a particular trait, but full expression of the characteristic depends on environmental factors. Given the same environment, for example, a person who inherits "tall" genes will be tall, and a person who inherits "short" genes, short. But if the first person is malnourished in childhood and the second person is well nourished as a child, they may be the same height as adults. Since an individual's genotype does not always obviously correspond directly to what is expressed, we use the term **phenotype** when referring to the *outward expression* of a trait. For example, people with an inherited tendency to gain weight (genotype) may or may not become obese (phenotype), depending on their diet, exercise program, and overall health.

The Human Genome   The term *genome* refers to the full complement of an organism's genetic material (all the genes and all the chromosomes). Thus, the genome for any particular organism contains a complete blueprint for building all the structures and directing all the living processes for the lifetime of that organism. The **human genome,** the sum total of all the genes necessary to build a human being, is approximately 20,000 to 25,000 genes, located on the 23 pairs of chromosomes that make up human DNA. At first that seems like a surprisingly small number for our species since these genes, contained within every cell of our body, distinguish us from other forms of life. However, only very small variations in the genetic code distinguish humans from other organisms. For instance, humans share 98.7% of their genes with chimpanzees (Olson & Varki, 2003). Even smaller variations in the human genome are responsible for the individual differences we see in the world's 6 billion people. Experts believe that the average variation in the human genetic code for any two different people is much less than 1%.

In June 2000, researchers working on the *Human Genome Project* announced the first rough map of the entire human genome. The results of this project have since led researchers to identify genes on specific chromosomes that are associated with Alzheimer's disease (Eriksson et al., 2011), alcoholism (Cao et al., 2011), schizophrenia and bipolar disorder (Georgieva et al., 2008; Lipina et al., 2011), suicide (Saiz et al., 2008), cognitive functioning (Szekely et al., 2011), intelligence (Pan, Wang, & Aragam, 2011) and even mathematical ability (Docherty et al., 2010). By using these genetic markers, researchers expect not only to understand better the role of heredity in complex behaviors, but also to develop individualized genetic treatments for a wide variety of disorders (Collins, 2010).

In this section, we've discussed mechanisms of heredity and dramatic advances in genetics that may someday lead to functional improvements in a variety of medical arenas. For the most part, we have used physical characteristics as examples. Behavior geneticists apply the same principles to *psychological* characteristics.

Behavior Genetics

What methods do psychologists use to study the effects of genes on behavior?

Behavior geneticists study the topics that interest all psychologists—perception, learning and memory, motivation and emotions, personality, and psychological disorders—but from a genetic perspective. Their goal is to identify what genes contribute to intelligence, temperament, talents, and other characteristics, as well as genetic predispositions to psychological and neurological disorders (Willner, Bergman, & Sanger, 2008). Of course, genes do not directly cause behavior. Rather, they affect both the development and operation of the nervous system and the endocrine system, which, in turn, influence the likelihood that a certain behavior will occur under certain circumstances (Vinkhuyzen, van der Sluis, & Posthuma, 2010).

In the remainder of this chapter, we will look at some of the methods used by behavior geneticists as well as some of their more interesting discoveries.

Animal Behavior Genetics Much of what we know about behavior genetics comes from studies of nonhuman animals. Mice are favorite subjects because they breed quickly and have relatively complex behavior patterns. In **strain studies,** close relatives, such as siblings, are intensively inbred over many generations to create strains of animals that are genetically similar to one another, but different from other strains. When animals from different strains are raised together in the same environment, differences between them largely reflect genetic differences in the strains. This method has shown that performance on learning tasks, as well as sense of smell and susceptibility to seizures, are affected by heredity.

Selection studies are another way to assess *heritability,* the degree to which a trait is inherited. If a trait is closely regulated by genes, when animals with the trait are interbred, more of their offspring should have the trait than one would find in the general population. Humans have practiced selective breeding for thousands of years to create breeds of dogs and other domesticated animals that have desirable traits—both physical and psychological.

Human Behavior Genetics For obvious reasons, scientists cannot conduct strain or selection studies with human beings. But there are a number of ways to study behavioral techniques indirectly.

Family studies are based on the assumption that if genes influence a trait, close relatives should share that trait more often than distant relatives, because close relatives have more genes in common. For example, overall, schizophrenia occurs in only 1% to 2% of the general population (N. L. Nixon & Doody, 2005; L. N. Robins & Regier, 1991). Siblings of people with schizophrenia, however, are about 8 times more likely (and children of schizophrenic parents about 10 times more likely) to develop the disorder than someone chosen randomly from the general population. Unfortunately, because family members share not only some genes but also similar environments, family studies alone cannot clearly distinguish the effects of heredity and environment.

To obtain a clearer picture of the influences of heredity and environment, psychologists often use **twin studies. Identical twins** develop from a single fertilized ovum and are therefore identical in genetic makeup at conception. Any differences between them must be due to their experiences. **Fraternal twins,** however, develop from two separate fertilized egg cells and are no more similar genetically than are other brothers and sisters. If twin pairs grow up in similar environments and if identical twins are no more alike in a particular characteristic than fraternal twins, then heredity cannot be very important for that trait.

Twin studies suggest that heredity plays a crucial role in schizophrenia. When one identical twin develops schizophrenia, the chances that the other twin will develop the disorder are about 50%. For fraternal twins, the chances are about 15% (Gottesman, 1991). Such studies have also provided evidence for the heritability of a wide variety of other behaviors, including verbal skills (Viding et al., 2004), mild intellectual impairment (Spinath, Harlaar, Ronald, & Plomin, 2004), aggressiveness (Eley, Lichenstein, & Stevenson, 1999), compulsive gambling (Shah, Eisen, Xian, & Potenza, 2005), depression, anxiety, and eating disorders (Eley & Stevenson, 1999; O'Connor, McGuire, Reiss, Hetherington, & Plomin, 1998; Silberg & Bulik, 2005).

Similarities between twins, even identical twins, cannot automatically be attributed to genes, however; twins nearly always grow up together. Parents and others may treat them alike—or try to emphasize their differences, so that they grow up as separate individuals. In either case, the data for heritability may be biased. To avoid this problem, researchers attempt to locate identical twins who were separated at birth or in

genotype An organism's entire unique genetic makeup.

phenotype The characteristics of an organism; determined by both genetics and experience.

human genome The full complement of genes within a human cell.

strain studies Studies of the heritability of behavioral traits using animals that have been inbred to produce strains that are genetically similar to one another.

selection studies Studies that estimate the heritability of a trait by breeding animals with other animals that have the same trait.

family studies Studies of heritability in humans based on the assumption that if genes influence a certain trait, close relatives should be more similar on that trait than distant relatives.

twin studies Studies of identical and fraternal twins to determine the relative influence of heredity and environment on human behavior.

identical twins Twins developed from a single fertilized ovum and therefore identical in genetic makeup at the time of conception.

fraternal twins Twins developed from two separate fertilized ova and therefore different in genetic makeup.

People clearly do inherit physical traits from their parents. Whether—and to what extent—they also inherit behavioral traits remains uncertain.

adoption studies Research carried out on children, adopted at birth by parents not related to them, to determine the relative influence of heredity and environment on human behavior.

very early childhood and then raised in different homes. A University of Minnesota team led by Thomas Bouchard followed separated twins for more than 10 years (Bouchard, 1984, 1996; Bouchard et al., 1990; W. Johnson, Bouchard, Segal, & Samuel, 2005). They confirmed that genetics plays a major role in mental retardation, schizophrenia, depression, reading skill, and intelligence. Bouchard and his colleagues have also found that complex personality traits, interests, and talents, and even the structure of brain waves, are guided by genetics.

Studies of twins separated shortly after birth have also drawn criticism. For example, the environment in the uterus may be more traumatic for one twin than the other (Foley, Neale, & Kendler, 2000; J. A. Phelps, Davis, & Schartz, 1997). Also, since adoption agencies usually try to place twins in similar families, their environments may not be much different (Joseph, 2001). Finally, the number of twin pairs separated at birth is fairly small. For these reasons, scientists sometimes rely on other types of studies to investigate the influence of heredity.

Adoption studies focus on children who were adopted at birth and brought up by parents not genetically related to them. Adoption studies provide additional evidence for the heritability of intelligence and some forms of mental illness (Insel & Wang, 2010; Jacobs, van Os, Derom, & Thiery, 2008) and the role of genetics in behavior previously thought to be solely determined by environmental influences like smoking (Boardman, Blalock, & Pampel, 2010).

By combining the results of *twin, adoption, and family* studies, psychologists have obtained a clearer picture of the role of heredity in many human characteristics, including schizophrenia. As shown in **Figure 2–19,** the average risk of schizophrenia steadily increases in direct relation to the closeness of one's biological relationship to an individual with the disorder.

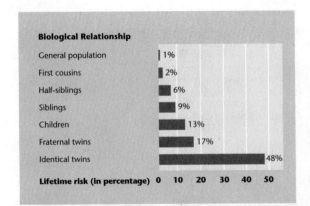

Identical twins develop from a single ovum and consequently start out with the same genetic material.

Social Implications

What are some of the ethical issues that arise as society gains more control over genetics?

Science is not simply a process that takes place in a laboratory; it can also have widespread effects on society at large. To the extent that we can trace individual differences in human behavior to chromosomes and genes, we have a potential, biologically, to control people's lives. This potential raises new ethical issues.

Contemporary techniques of prenatal screening now make it possible to detect many genetic defects even before a baby is born. *Chorionic villus sampling* and *amniocentesis* are two procedures for obtaining samples of cells from fetuses in order to analyze their genes. In the first, the cells are taken from membranes surrounding the fetus; in the second, the cells are harvested from the fluid in which the fetus grows. Using these procedures, genetic problems are detected in about 2% of pregnancies. Do the parents have a right to abort the fetus? Should society protect all life, no matter how imperfect it is in the eyes of some? If not, which defects are so unacceptable that abortion is justified? Most of these questions have a long history, but recent progress in behavior genetics and medicine has given them a new urgency. We are reaching the point at which we will be able to intervene in a fetus's development by replacing some of its genes with others. For which traits might this procedure be considered justified, and who has the right to make those decisions? Such questions pose major ethical dilemmas, and it is important that we all think critically about them (Leuzinger-Bohleber, Engels, & Tsiantis, 2008).

So far, we have been talking about the environment as if it were something *out there,* something that happens *to* people, over which they have little control. But individuals also shape their environments. The genes and predispositions individuals inherit alter the environment in several ways (Plomin, DeFries, Craig, & McGuffin, 2003). For example, people tend to seek environments in which they feel comfortable. A

Biological Relationship

General population	1%
First cousins	2%
Half-siblings	6%
Siblings	9%
Children	13%
Fraternal twins	17%
Identical twins	48%

Lifetime risk (in percentage)   0   10   20   30   40   50

FIGURE 2–19

Average risk of schizophrenia among biological relatives of people with schizophrenia.

Source: Graph, p. 96, from *Schizophrenia Genesis: The Origins of Madness* by I. I. Gottesman. Copyright © 1991 by Henry Holt & Company, LLC. Reprinted by permission of the publisher.

shy child might prefer a quieter play group than would a child who is more outgoing. In addition, our own behavior causes others to respond in particular ways. For example, one study showed that children with a genetic predisposition toward fearfulness were treated differently by their caregivers, which in turn reshaped their neurocircuitry through plasticity thus exacerbating their fearfulness (Fox, Hane, & Pine, 2007). Because genes and environments interact in so many intricate ways, trying to separate and isolate the effects of heredity and environment—nature and nurture—is artificial (Kline, 2008).

The study of behavior genetics and that of evolutionary psychology, which we will consider next, makes many people uneasy. Some fear that it may lead to the conclusion that who we are is written in some kind of permanent ink before we are born. Some people also fear that research in these fields could be used to undermine movements toward social equality. But far from finding human behavior to be genetically predetermined, recent work in behavior genetics shows just how important the environment is in determining which genetic predispositions come to be expressed and which do not. In other words, we may inherit predispositions, but we do not inherit destinies. The emerging picture confirms that both heredity and environment (nature and nurture) work together as allies to shape most significant behaviors and traits (Kline, 2008).

THINKING CRITICALLY ABOUT . . .

Media Accounts of Research

What is wrong with this headline?

"Scientists Find Gene for Intelligence"

Robert Plomin (1998) compared genetic data on 50 children whose SAT scores were equivalent to IQ scores of 160 or higher to a control group. He found that a variant of a particular gene was twice as common in children with ultra-high IQs as in children with average IQs (scores of 100). Scientists estimate that about 50% of the variation in IQ scores is due to heredity. The gene had a small effect, accounting for about 2% of the variance among individuals, or 4 IQ points, but the researchers made an important first step in uniting biological technology with behavioral genetics.

What rules of critical thinking did this headline ignore? How would you rewrite this headline?

Hints: Consider the size of the sample, the danger of focusing on extremes, and what "heritability" means.

Evolutionary Psychology

How might the process of natural selection influence human social behaviors?

Much as behavior geneticists try to explain the individual differences in human behavior, evolutionary psychologists try to explain the behavioral traits that people have in common. The key to these shared characteristics, they feel, is the process of evolution by **natural selection,** first described by Charles Darwin in *On the Origin of Species* (1859).

According to the principle of natural selection, those organisms that are best adapted to their environments are most likely to survive and reproduce. If the traits that give them a survival advantage are genetically based, those same genetic characteristics are passed on to their offspring. Organisms that do not possess the adaptive traits tend to die off before they reproduce, and hence, the less-adaptive traits do not get passed along to future generations. Natural selection, therefore, promotes the survival and reproduction of individuals who are genetically well adapted to their particular environment.

As described in Chapter 1, evolutionary psychologists study the origins of behaviors and mental processes, emphasizing the adaptive or survival value of such traits. Evolutionary psychologists look at the role that natural selection might have played in selecting for adaptive *behaviors,* especially during the long period that our ancestors lived as hunter–gatherers. They argue that, just as our hands and upright posture are products of natural selection, so are our brains. As a result, our brains are "prewired" to learn some things more easily than others, to analyze problems in certain ways, and to communicate in distinctively human ways.

Evolutionary psychologists cite language as a prime example (Pinker, 2007). As we will see in Chapter 9, "Life-Span Development," all normal children acquire language without specific instruction; children in different cultures acquire language at about the

natural selection The mechanism proposed by Darwin in his theory of evolution, which states that organisms best adapted to their environment tend to survive, transmitting their genetic characteristics to succeeding generations, whereas organisms with less adaptive characteristics tend to vanish from the earth.

same ages and in predictable stages; and the underlying structure of all human languages (nouns and verbs, subjects and objects, questions and conditional phrases, and so on) is basically the same. Taken as a whole, evolutionary psychologists argue, the evidence strongly suggests that our human brains have a built-in "program" for language. In support of this notion, scientists have begun to identify specific genes (collectively known as the "human lexinome") which were pivotal to the development of human language (Gibson & Gruen, 2008). Evolutionary psychologists cite mate selection as another example. In choosing a partner, males and females tend to pursue different strategies. Why? Evolutionary psychologists answer this way: Human females usually have only one child at a time. Women also invest more in each child than men do—going through pregnancy, caretaking, and providing nourishment. It would seem to be most adaptive for females to look for males who will provide the best genes, resources, and long-term parental care. Males, on the other hand, are limited only by the number of prospective mates they can attract, because sperm are plentiful and quickly replaced. It may be most adaptive for males to seek to mate with as many females as they can and to compete with other males for access to females.

Evolutionary psychology is not without its critics (Siegert & Ward, 2002). Some opponents argue that science is being used to justify perpetuating unjust social policies. These critics claim that simply by saying a trait is adaptive implies that it is both genetically determined and good. In the past, racists and fascists have misused biological theories to promote social injustices. In Nazi Germany, for example, Jews were considered genetically inferior, a view that was used to justify their extermination. Similarly, the evolutionary theory of male–female differences in mate selection could be seen as endorsing male promiscuity, since it is biologically adaptive. In response, evolutionary psychologists are quick to point out that their aim is not to shape social policy, but to understand the origins of human behavior.

Other critics chide evolutionary psychologists for too hastily explaining behaviors from an evolutionary perspective, rather than investigating other plausible origins of them. Evolutionary psychologists answer that their goal is not to propose evolutionary theories that exclude all other possible explanations; instead, their aim is to offer an evolutionary perspective that may complement other points of view.

✔●─**Study** and **Review** on **MyPsychLab**

CHECK YOUR UNDERSTANDING

Are the following statements true (T) or false (F)?

1. ___ "Individual differences in intelligence, emotional reactivity, and susceptibility to schizophrenia and depression may all be influenced by genes."

2. ___ *Neuropsychology* is the study of how traits are passed from one generation to another.

Answers: 1. (T). 2. (F).

APPLY YOUR UNDERSTANDING

1. A woman exhibits a recessive characteristic such as blue eyes. Her children _____ exhibit the same trait.
   a. definitely will
   b. may or may not
   c. will definitely *not*

2. Imagine that psychologists document a long history of criminal behavior in a family: Children, their parents, their grandparents, and even their great-grandparents have long lists of convictions for crimes. Knowing only this, the most reasonable conclusion you can draw is that criminal behavior is most likely due to
   a. genetic factors.
   b. environmental factors.
   c. a combination of genetic and environmental factors.

Answers: 1. b. 2. c.

KEY TERMS

psychobiology, p. 41
neuroscience, p. 41

Neurons: The Messengers
neurons, p. 42
dendrites, p. 42
axon, p. 42
nerve (or tract), p. 42
myelin sheath, p. 42
sensory (or afferent)
  neurons, p. 42
motor (or efferent)
  neurons, p. 42
interneurons (or association
  neurons), p. 42
mirror neurons, p. 42
glial cells (or glia), p. 43
ions, p. 44
resting potential, p. 44
polarization, p. 44
neural impulse (or action
  potential), p. 44
graded potential, p. 45
threshold of excitation, p. 45
all-or-none law, p. 46
synaptic space (or synaptic
  cleft, p. 46
synapse, p. 46

terminal button (or synaptic
  knob), p. 46
synaptic vesicles, p. 46
neurotransmitters, p. 46
receptor sites, p. 46
neural plasticity, p. 48
neural network, p. 50
neurogenesis, p. 50

The Central Nervous System
central nervous system
  (CNS), p. 52
peripheral nervous system
  (PNS), p. 52
hindbrain, p. 52
medulla, p. 53
pons, p. 53
cerebellum, p. 53
midbrain, p. 53
thalamus, p. 54
hypothalamus, p. 54
reticular formation
  (RF), p. 54
cerebrum, p. 54
cerebral cortex, p. 54
association areas, p. 54
frontal lobe, p. 54
primary motor cortex, p. 54

prefrontal cortex, p. 55
occipital lobe, p. 56
parietal lobe, p. 56
primary somatosensory
  cortex, p. 56
temporal lobe, p. 56
insula, p. 56
limbic system, p. 57
hippocampus, p. 57
amygdala, p. 57
corpus callosum, p. 57
aphasias, p. 60
spinal cord, p. 63

The Peripheral Nervous System
somatic nervous system, p. 65
autonomic nervous
  system, p. 65
sympathetic division, p. 65
parasympathetic division, p. 65

The Endocrine System
endocrine glands, p. 67
hormones, p. 67
pituitary gland, p. 67
pineal gland, p. 67
thyroid gland, p. 67

parathyroids, p. 67
pancreas, p. 67
adrenal glands, p. 67
gonads, p. 67

Genes, Evolution, and Behavior
behavior genetics, p. 70
evolutionary psychology, p. 70
genetics, p. 70
genes, p. 70
chromosomes, p. 70
deoxyribonucleic acid
  (DNA), p. 70
dominant gene, p. 71
recessive gene, p. 71
polygenic inheritance, p. 71
genotype, p. 72
phenotype, p. 72
human genome, p. 72
strain studies, p. 73
selection studies, p. 73
family studies, p. 73
twin studies, p. 73
identical twins, p. 73
fraternal twins, p. 73
adoption studies, p. 74
natural selection, p. 75

CHAPTER REVIEW ((•─Listen to the **Chapter Audio** on **MyPsychLab**

Biological processes are the basis of our thoughts, feelings, and actions. All of our behaviors are kept in tune with our surroundings and coordinated with one another through the work of two interacting systems: the nervous system and the endocrine system.

NEURONS: THE MESSENGERS

What types of cells are found in the nervous system? The basic building block of the nervous system is the **neuron,** or nerve cell. Neurons have several characteristics that distinguish them from other cells. Neurons receive messages from other neurons through short fibers called **dendrites.** A longer fiber, called an **axon,** carries outgoing messages from the cell. A group of axons bundled together forms a nerve or tract. Some axons are covered with a fatty **myelin sheath** made up of **glial cells;** this increases neuron efficiency and provides insulation. There are many different types of neurons including: **sensory** or **afferent neurons, motor** or **efferent neurons, interneurons** or **association neurons,** and **mirror neurons,** which are involved in imitation.

What "language" do neurons speak? When a neuron is at rest (a state called the **resting potential**), there is a slightly higher concentration of negatively charged ions inside its membrane than

there is outside. The membrane is said to be **polarized**—that is, the electrical charge inside it is negative relative to its outside. When an incoming message is strong enough, this electrical imbalance abruptly changes (the membrane is depolarized), and an **action potential** (**neural impulse**) is generated. Incoming messages cause **graded potentials,** which, when combined, may exceed the minimum **threshold of excitation** and make the neuron "fire." After firing, the neuron briefly goes through the **absolute refractory period,** when it will not fire again, and then through the relative refractory period, when firing will occur only if the incoming message is much stronger than usual. According to the **all-or-none law,** every firing of a particular neuron produces an impulse of equal strength. More rapid firing of neurons is what communicates the strength of a message.

What happens as information moves from one neuron to the next? **Neurotransmitter** molecules, released by **synaptic vesicles,** cross the tiny **synaptic space** (or **cleft**) between an **axon terminal** (or **terminal button**) of a sending neuron and a dendrite of a receiving neuron. Here they latch on to **receptor sites,** much as keys fit into locks, and pass on their excitatory or inhibitory messages. Psychologists need to understand how **synapses** function because neurotransmitters affect an enormous range of physical and emotional responses.

How does experience change the brain? Can the brain and the nervous system repair themselves? Research demonstrates that experiences in our environments can produce changes in the brain, a principle called **neural plasticity.** Neural plasticity leads to the development of **neural networks**—neurons that are functionally connected to one another. Human brains also are capable of **neurogenesis**—the production of new brain cells. The study of neurogenesis may help treat neurological disorders, but also raises ethical questions.

THE CENTRAL NERVOUS SYSTEM

How is the nervous system organized? The nervous system is organized into two parts: the **central nervous system (CNS),** which consists of the brain and spinal cord, and the **peripheral nervous system (PNS),** made up of nerves that radiate throughout the body, linking all of the body's parts to the CNS.

What are the major structures and areas of the brain, and what functions do they serve? Physically, the brain has three more-or-less distinct areas: the central core, the limbic system, and the cerebral hemispheres.

The central core consists of the hindbrain, cerebellum, midbrain, thalamus and hypothalamus, and reticular formation. The **hindbrain** is made up of the **medulla,** a narrow structure nearest the spinal cord that controls breathing, heart rate, and blood pressure, and the **pons,** which produces chemicals that maintain our sleep–wake cycle. The medulla is the point at which many of the nerves from the left part of the body cross to the right side of the brain and vice versa. The **cerebellum** controls the sense of balance and coordinates the body's actions. The **midbrain,** which is above the cerebellum, is important for hearing and sight and is one of the places in which pain is registered. The **thalamus** is a relay station that integrates and shapes incoming sensory signals before transmitting them to the higher levels of the brain. The **hypothalamus** is important to motivation, drives, and emotional behavior. The **reticular formation,** which is woven through all of these structures, alerts the higher parts of the brain to incoming messages.

The **cerebrum** takes up most of the room inside the skull. The outer covering of the cerebral hemispheres is known as the cerebral cortex. They are the most recently evolved portion of the brain, and they regulate the most complex behavior. Each cerebral hemisphere is divided into four lobes, delineated by deep fissures on the surface of the brain. The **occipital lobe,** located at the back of the head, receives and processes visual information. The **temporal lobe,** located roughly behind the temples, helps us perform complex visual tasks, such as recognizing faces. The **parietal lobe,** which sits on top of the temporal and occipital lobes, receives sensory information from all over the body and oversees spatial abilities. Messages from sensory receptors are registered in the **primary somatosensory cortex.** The frontal lobe receives and coordinates messages from the other lobes and keeps track of past and future body movement. The **prefrontal cortex** is primarily responsible for goal-directed behavior, the ability to control impulses, judgment, and metacognition. The **primary motor cortex** is responsible for voluntary movement. The **insula,** which lies between the temporal and parietal lobes, is involved in the conscious expression of emotion, desire, and addiction. The **association areas**—areas that are free to process all kinds of information—make up most of the cerebral cortex and enable the brain to produce behaviors requiring the coordination of many brain areas.

The **limbic system,** a ring of structures located between the central core and the cerebral hemispheres, is a more recent evolutionary development than the central core. It includes the **hippocampus,** which is essential to the formation of new memories, and the **amygdala,** which, together with the hippocampus, governs emotions related to self-preservation. Other portions of the limbic system heighten the experience of pleasure. In times of stress, the limbic system coordinates and integrates the nervous system's response.

How are the left and right hemispheres specialized for different functions? The two cerebral hemispheres are linked by the **corpus callosum,** through which they communicate and coordinate their activities. Nevertheless, each hemisphere appears to specialize in certain tasks (although they also have overlapping functions). The right hemisphere excels at visual and spatial tasks, nonverbal imagery, and the perception of emotion, whereas the left hemisphere excels at language and perhaps analytical thinking, too. The right hemisphere controls the left side of the body, and the left hemisphere controls the right side.

What methods have been developed to study the brain? An increasingly sophisticated technology exists for investigating the brain. Among the most important tools are microelectrode techniques, macroelectrode techniques (EEG), structural imaging (CT scanning and MRI), and functional imaging (EEG imaging, MEG, and MSI). Two new functional imaging techniques, PET scanning and fMRI, allow us to observe not only the structure, but also the functioning of parts of the brain. Scientists often combine these techniques to study brain activity in unprecedented detail—information that can help in the treatment of medical and psychological disorders.

What does the spinal cord do? How does it work with the brain to sense events and act on them? The **spinal cord** is a complex cable of nerves that connects the brain to most of the rest of the body. It is made up of bundles of long nerve fibers and has two basic functions: to permit some reflex movements and to carry messages to and from the brain. When a break in the cord disrupts the flow of impulses from the brain below that point, paralysis occurs.

THE PERIPHERAL NERVOUS SYSTEM

How does the brain communicate with the rest of the body? How is the autonomic branch of the peripheral nervous system involved in controlling emotions? The peripheral nervous system (PNS) contains two types of neurons: *afferent neurons,* which carry sensory messages to the central nervous system, and *efferent neurons,* which carry messages *from* the CNS. Neurons involved in making voluntary movements of the skeletal muscles belong to a part of the PNS called the **somatic nervous system,** whereas neurons involved in governing the actions of internal organs belong to a part of the PNS called the autonomic nervous system. The **autonomic nervous system** is itself divided into two parts: the **sympathetic division,** which acts primarily to arouse the body when it is faced with threat, and the **parasympathetic division,** which acts to calm the body down, restoring it to normal levels of arousal.

THE ENDOCRINE SYSTEM

Why are psychologists interested in hormones? The endocrine system is the other communication system in the body. It is made up of **endocrine glands** that produce **hormones,** chemical substances released into the bloodstream to either *trigger* developmental changes in the body or to activate certain behavioral responses. The **thyroid gland** secretes thyroxin, a hormone involved in regulating the body's rate of metabolism. Symptoms of an overactive thyroid are agitation and tension, whereas an underactive thyroid produces lethargy. The **parathyroids** control and balance the levels of calcium and phosphate in the blood and tissue fluids. This process in turn affects the excitability of the nervous system. The **pineal gland** regulates activity levels over the course of the day and also regulates the sleep–wake cycle. The **pancreas** controls the level of sugar in the blood by secreting insulin and glucagon. When the pancreas secretes too much insulin, the person can suffer *hypoglycemia.* Too little insulin can result in *diabetes mellitus.* Of all the endocrine glands, the **pituitary gland** regulates the largest number of different activities in the body. It affects blood pressure, thirst, uterine contractions in childbirth, milk production, sexual behavior and interest, and the amount and timing of body growth, among other functions. Because of its influences on other glands, it is often called the "master gland." The **gonads**—the testes in males and the ovaries in females—secrete hormones called androgens (including testosterone) and estrogens. Testosterone plays an important role during critical periods of prenatal development to organize sex typed behaviors, and has long been linked to aggressive behavior. Each of the two **adrenal glands** has two parts: an outer covering, the *adrenal cortex,* and an inner core, the *adrenal medulla.* Both affect our response to stress, although the adrenal cortex affects other body functions, too. One stress-related hormone of the adrenal medulla is epinephrine, which amplifies the effects of the sympathetic nervous system.

GENES, EVOLUTION, AND BEHAVIOR

How are traits passed from one generation to the next? The related fields of **behavior genetics** and **evolutionary psychology** explore the influences of heredity on human behavior. Both are helping to settle the nature-versus-nurture debate over the relative contributions of genes and the environment to human similarities and differences. **Genetics** is the study of how traits are passed on from one generation to the next via genes. This process is called heredity. Each **gene,** or basic unit of inheritance, is lined up on tiny threadlike bodies called **chromosomes,** which in turn are made up predominantly of a complex molecule called **deoxyribonucleic acid (DNA).** The human genome is the full complement of genes necessary to build a human body—approximately 20,000 to 25,000 genes. The *Human Genome Project* has produced a rough map of the genes on the 23 pairs of human chromosomes. Each member of a gene pair can be either **dominant** or **recessive.** In **polygenic inheritance** a number of genes interact to produce a trait.

What methods do psychologists use to study the effects of genes on behavior? Psychologists use a variety of methods to study *heritability*—that is, the contribution of genes in determining variations in certain traits. **Strain studies** approach the problem by observing strains of highly inbred, genetically similar animals, whereas **selection studies** try to determine the extent to which an animal's traits can be passed on from one generation to another. In the study of humans, **family studies** tackle heritability by looking for similarities in traits as a function of biological closeness. Also useful in studying human heritability are **twin studies** and **adoption studies.**

What are some of the ethical issues that arise as society gains more control over genetics? Manipulating human genes in an effort to change how people develop is a new technology that makes many people uneasy, but their concerns may be exaggerated because genes are not all-powerful. Both heredity and environment play a part in shaping most significant human behaviors and traits.

How might the process of natural selection influence human social behaviors? The theory of evolution by **natural selection** states that organisms best adapted to their environment tend to survive, transmitting their genetic ch*aracteristics to succeeding generations, whereas organisms with fewer adaptive characteristics tend to die off. Evolutionary psychology analyzes human behavioral tendencies by examining their adaptive value from an evolutionary perspective. While not without its critics, it has proved useful in helping to explain some of the commonalities in human behavior that occur across cultures.

3

Sensation and Perception

OVERVIEW

Smell is sometimes considered the "dispensable" sense—the one we could easily live without if necessary. We are not like dogs, who depend on a keen sense of smell to navigate through the world. Since we use the senses of sight and sound so extensively, how bad could an absence of a sense of smell really be?

Robin Henig lost her sense of smell after a bad fall. When her head hit the ground, her brain rebounded forward, smashed into the front of her skull, and severely damaged the delicate nerves of the olfactory system. For Robin the world had become strangely sterile, as though encased in an impenetrable film of plastic wrap. Odors simply didn't get through to her brain. She said "... I felt vulnerable. Smelling is what told me not to eat spoiled egg salad and to stay clear of skunks ... Without scent, I felt as if I were walking around without my contact lenses, dealing with people while wearing earplugs, moving through something sticky and thick. The sharpness of things, their specificity, diminished" (Henig, 2004, p. 110). For someone who loses the sense of smell, walking into a bakery is the same as entering a restroom, which is no different than walking through a hyacinth garden in spring.

At 85 years of age, Doris Stowens was losing her sight as a result of macular degeneration. "One day a few years ago, [she] saw the monsters from Maurice Sendak's 'Where the Wild Things Are' stomping into her bedroom. Then the creatures morphed into traditional Thai dancers with long brass fingernails, whose furious dance took them from the floor to the walls to the ceiling" (Kruglinski, 2004, p. D7). Though she was terrified, she realized that the hallucinations were somehow related to her loss of vision.

Smell and vision are just two of the senses giving us a window on the world. Evolution has provided us with many others—hearing, taste, touch, pain, pressure, warmth, cold, and the kinesthetic senses—that combine into a rich mosaic of awareness forming the basis of consciousness. It is sensation that gives us connections both to our own selves and to our surroundings.

We begin this chapter by looking at the basic principles of sensation—how we acquire information from the external (and internal) world. We examine the body's various sense organs to see how each converts physical stimuli, such as light waves, into nerve impulses. But sensation is only half the story. To be meaningful, this kaleidoscope of sensory input must be organized and interpreted. Our eyes register only light, dark, and color; but our brains "perceive" distinctive visual objects—a tree, a branch, a leaf—in three-dimensional space. Our ears are designed to detect the movement of vibrating air molecules, yet we distinguish between a baby's cry and a Bach concerto. We explore these phenomena in the last section of this chapter, which deals with *perception*.

ENDURING ISSUES in Sensation and Perception

Two key questions we address in this chapter concern the extent to which our perceptual experiences accurately reflect what is in the outside world (*Person–Situation*) and the ways in which our experiences depend on biological processes (*Mind–Body*). We will also examine the extent to which people around the world perceive events in the same way (*Diversity–Universality*) and the ways that our experience of the outside world changes as a result of experience over the course of our lives (*Stability–Change* and *Nature–Nurture*).

THE NATURE OF SENSATION

What causes sensory experiences? How is energy, such as light or sound, converted into a message to the brain?

Sensation begins when energy stimulates a receptor cell in one of the sense *organs*, such as the eye or the ear. Each **receptor cell** responds to one particular form of energy—light waves (in the case of vision) or vibration of air molecules (in the case of hearing). When there is sufficient energy, the receptor cell "fires" and sends to the brain a coded signal that varies according to the characteristics of the stimulus. The process of converting physical energy, such as light or sound, into electrochemical codes is called **transduction.** For instance, a very bright light might be coded by the rapid firing of a set of nerve cells, but a dim light would set off a much slower firing sequence. The neural signal is coded still further as it passes along the sensory nerves to the central nervous system, so the message that reaches the brain is precise and detailed.

The impulses on the optic nerve reliably produce an experience we call vision, just as impulses moving along an auditory nerve produce the experience we call hearing, or audition. The one-to-one relationship between stimulation of a specific nerve and the resulting sensory experience is known as the *doctrine of specific nerve energies*. Even if the impulses on the optic nerve are caused by something other than light, the result is still a

LEARNING OBJECTIVE

- Explain the difference between absolute and difference thresholds and the effect of adaptation on sensory thresholds. Summarize the evidence for subliminal perception.

sensation The experience of sensory stimulation.

receptor cell A specialized cell that responds to a particular type of energy.

transduction The conversion of physical energy into coded neural signals.

absolute threshold The least amount of energy that can be detected as a stimulation 50% of the time.

adaptation An adjustment of the senses to the level of stimulation they are receiving.

difference threshold or **just-noticeable difference (jnd)** The smallest change in stimulation that can be detected 50% of the time.

Weber's law The principle that the jnd for any given sense is a constant fraction or proportion of the stimulation being judged.

visual experience. Gentle pressure on an eye, for instance, results in signals from the optic nerve that the brain interprets as visual patterns—the visual pattern of "seeing stars" when we're hit in the eye is so familiar that even cartoons depict it.

Sensory Thresholds

What are the limits on our ability to sense stimuli in our environment?

To produce any sensation at all, the physical energy reaching a receptor cell must achieve a minimum intensity, or **absolute threshold.** Any stimulation below the absolute threshold will not be experienced. But how much sensory stimulation is enough?

To answer such a question, psychologists present a stimulus at different intensities and ask people whether they sense anything. You might expect that there would come a point at which people would suddenly say, "Now I see the flash" or "Now I hear a sound." But actually, there is a range of intensities over which a person sometimes—but not always—can sense a stimulus. The absolute threshold is defined as the point at which a person can detect the stimulus 50% of the time that it is presented. (See **Figure 3–1.**)

Although there are differences among people, the absolute threshold for each of our senses is remarkably low. The approximate absolute thresholds under ideal circumstances are as follows (McBurney & Collings, 1984):

- Hearing: The tick of a watch from 6 m (20 feet) in very quiet conditions
- Vision: A candle flame seen from 50 km (30 miles) on a clear, dark night
- Taste: 1 g (0.0356 ounces) of table salt in 500 L (529 quarts) of water
- Smell: One drop of perfume diffused throughout a three-room apartment
- Touch: The wing of a bee falling on the cheek from a height of 1 cm (0.39 inches)

Under normal conditions, absolute thresholds vary according to the level and nature of ongoing sensory stimulation. For example, your threshold for the taste of salt would be considerably higher after you ate salted peanuts. In this case, the absolute threshold would rise because of sensory **adaptation,** in which our senses automatically adjust to the overall average level of stimulation in a particular setting. When confronted by a great deal of stimulation, they become much less sensitive than when the overall level of stimulation is low. Similarly, when the level of stimulation drops, our sensory apparatus becomes much more sensitive than under conditions of high stimulation. This process of adaptation allows all of our senses to be keenly attuned to a multitude of environmental cues without getting overloaded. ⊙→

Simulate the **Experiment** Methods of Constant Stimuli on **MyPsychLab**

Imagine now that you can hear a particular sound. How much stronger must the sound become before you notice that it has grown louder? The smallest change in stimulation that you can detect 50% of the time is called the **difference threshold,** or the **just-noticeable difference (jnd).** Like the absolute threshold, the difference threshold varies from person to person and from moment to moment. And, like absolute thresholds, difference thresholds tell us something about the flexibility of sensory systems. For example, adding 1 pound to a 5-pound load will certainly be noticed, so we might assume that the difference threshold must be considerably less than 1 pound. Yet adding 1 pound to a 100-pound load probably would not make much of a difference, so we might conclude that the difference threshold must be considerably more than 1 pound. But how can the jnd be both less than and greater than 1 pound? It turns out that the difference threshold varies according to the strength or intensity of the original stimulus. The greater the stimulus, the greater the change necessary to produce a jnd.

In the 1830s, Ernst Weber concluded that the difference threshold is a constant *fraction or proportion* of the original stimulus; this is a theory known as **Weber's law.** It is important to note that the values of these fractions vary significantly for the different senses. Hearing, for example, is very sensitive: We can detect a change in loudness of 10%. By contrast, producing a jnd in taste requires a 20% change. To return to our earlier example of weight, a change in weight of 2% is necessary to produce a jnd. So adding 1 pound to a 50-pound load would produce a noticeable difference half of the time; adding 1 pound to a 100-pound load would not.

Adding one ounce to this load would not produce a noticeable difference because one ounce would fall below the difference threshold for this amount of weight.

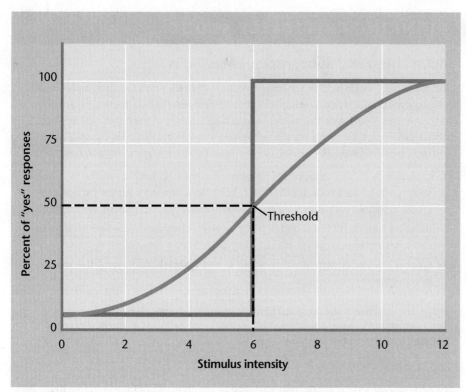

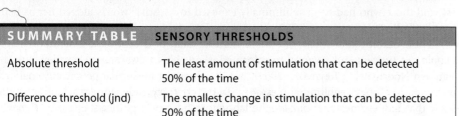

FIGURE 3–1
Determining a sensory threshold.
The red line represents an ideal case: At all intensities below the threshold, the person reports no sensation or no change in intensity; at all intensities above the threshold, the person reports a sensation or a change in intensity. In reality, however, we never come close to the ideal of the red line. The blue line shows the actual responses of a typical person. The threshold is taken as the point where a person reports a sensation or a change in intensity 50% of the time.

SUMMARY TABLE	SENSORY THRESHOLDS
Absolute threshold	The least amount of stimulation that can be detected 50% of the time
Difference threshold (jnd)	The smallest change in stimulation that can be detected 50% of the time

Subliminal Perception

Under what circumstances might messages outside our awareness affect our behavior?

The idea of an absolute threshold implies that some events occur *subliminally*—below our level of awareness. Can subliminal messages used in advertisements and self-help tapes change people's behavior? For decades, the story has circulated that refreshment sales increased dramatically when a movie theater in New Jersey flashed subliminal messages telling people to "Drink Coca-Cola" and "Eat Popcorn." In fact, sales of Coke and popcorn did not change (Dijksterhuis, Aarts, & Smith, 2005).

Similarly, audiotapes with subliminal self-help messages often promise more than they deliver (Dijksterhuis, Aarts, & Smith, 2005). In one series of studies, volunteers used such tapes for several weeks. About half said they had improved as a result of listening to the tapes, but objective tests detected no measurable change. Moreover, the perceived improvement had more to do with the label on the tape than its subliminal content: About half the people who received a tape labeled "Improve Memory" said that their memory had improved even though many of them had actually received a tape intended to boost self-esteem (Greenwald, Spangenberg, Pratkanis, & Eskenazi, 1991).

Nevertheless, there is clear evidence that under carefully controlled conditions, people can be influenced by information outside their awareness. In one study, a group of people was subliminally exposed to words conveying honesty (a positive trait), while another group was subliminally exposed to words conveying hostility (a negative trait). Subsequently, all the participants read a description of a woman whose behavior could be looked at as either honest or hostile. When asked to assess various personality characteristics of the woman,

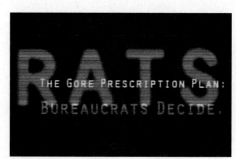

Subliminal advertising.

Advertisers have tried to use subliminal messages, which occur below our level of awareness, to encourage people to buy products such as refreshments at the movie theater. The use of subliminal messages reached a new low in their suspected application in the 2000 U.S. presidential campaign. A storm of controversy brewed over the word "RATS" allegedly superimposed over the image of a presidential contender.

THINKING CRITICALLY ABOUT . . .

Advertising and Subconscious Messages

TV ads do not contain hidden, subliminal messages, but they do attempt to make viewers associate products with idealized images and lifestyles. They do this by trying to play on our senses. Visual cues (the models) and auditory cues (the voice-over) are the most obvious examples. But tactile cues (a car's leather interior) and kinesthetic cues (the feeling of a test drive created by placing the camera inside a moving car) are also common.

1. Analyze a television series of ads for sensory content. Choose a specific category, such as ads for vacations or pain medications. What sensory cues are the advertisers using to hold your attention? to create conscious or subconscious associations?

   (Hint: Try turning off the sound to focus on visual cues; close your eyes to analyze auditory cues.)

2. What is the underlying message—that is, the associations beyond the specific information the ad conveys?

NOTE: This exercise is not designed to make you more skeptical of advertising (although this may be one outcome), but rather to make you as aware of sensory communication as advertisers are!

the people who had been subliminally exposed to "honest" words rated her as more honest, and those who had been subliminally exposed to "hostile" words judged her as being hostile (Erdley & D'Agostino, 1988).

These studies and others like them indicate that, *in a controlled laboratory setting,* people can process and respond to information outside of awareness (Van den Bussche, Van den Noortgate, & Reynvoet, 2009). But this does *not* mean that people automatically or mindlessly "obey" subliminal messages. To the contrary, independent scientific studies show that hidden messages *outside* the laboratory have no significant effect on behavior (Dijksterhuis, Aarts, & Smith, 2005).

So far, we have talked about the general characteristics of sensation; however, each of the body's sensory systems works a little differently. We now turn to the unique features of each of the major sensory systems.

✔•─ **Study** and **Review** on **MyPsychLab**

CHECK YOUR UNDERSTANDING

1. A _____ converts energy into a neural signal.
2. Perception of sensory information that is below the threshold of awareness is called _____ perception.

Answers: 1. receptor cell. 2. subliminal.

APPLY YOUR UNDERSTANDING

1. A psychologist who asked you to make a series of judgments to determine whether or not a light was present in an unlighted room would be trying to assess your _____ for perceiving light.
   - **a.** psychometric function
   - **b.** just-noticeable difference (jnd)
   - **c.** response bias
   - **d.** absolute threshold

2. According to Weber's law, in order for a person to detect a change in the weight of an object, the weight must change by at least 10%. If you are lifting a 50-pound weight, how much must the weight change before you will notice at least half the time that it is lighter or heavier?
   - **a.** 1 ounce
   - **b.** 8 ounces
   - **c.** 1 pound
   - **d.** 5 pounds

Answers: 1.d. 2.d.

VISION

Why have psychologists studied vision more than any other sense?

Different animal species depend more on some senses than on others. Bats rely heavily on hearing and some fish rely on taste. But for humans, vision is the most important sense; hence, it has received the most attention from psychologists. To understand vision, we need to look at the parts of the visual system.

LEARNING OBJECTIVES

- Describe the role of rods, cones, bipolar cells, ganglion cells, the optic nerve, the optic chiasm, and feature detectors in the brain in causing a visual experience.
- Explain how dark and light adaptation affect our vision and how they cause afterimages.
- Distinguish among hue, saturation, brightness, and additive and subtractive color mixing. Explain the two major theories of color perception.

The Visual System

How does light create a neural impulse?

The structure of the human eye, including the cellular path to the brain, is shown in **Figure 3–2.** Light enters the eye through the **cornea,** the transparent protective coating over the front part of the eye. It then passes through the **pupil,** the opening in the center of the **iris** (the colored part of the eye). In very bright light, the muscles in the iris contract to make the pupil smaller and thus protect the eye from damage. This contraction also helps us to see better in bright light. In dim light, the muscles relax to open the pupil wider and let in as much light as possible.

Explore the Concept Light and the Optic Nerve on MyPsychLab

Inside the pupil, light moves through the **lens,** which focuses it onto the **retina,** the light-sensitive inner lining of the back of the eyeball. Directly behind the lens is a depressed spot in the retina called the **fovea.** (See **Figure 3–3.**) The fovea occupies the center of the visual field, and images that pass through the lens are in sharpest focus here. Thus, the words you are now reading are hitting the fovea, while the rest of what you see—a desk, walls, or whatever—is striking other areas of the retina.

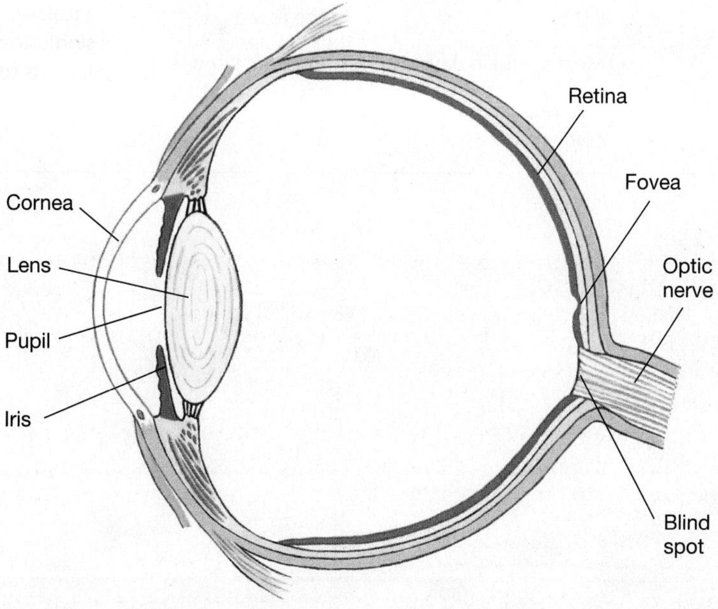

FIGURE 3–2
A cross section of the human eye.
Light enters the eye through the cornea, passes through the pupil, and is focused by the lens onto the retina.
Source: Adapted from Hubel, 1963.

cornea The transparent protective coating over the front part of the eye.

pupil A small opening in the iris through which light enters the eye.

iris The colored part of the eye that regulates the size of the pupil.

lens The transparent part of the eye behind the pupil that focuses light onto the retina.

retina The lining of the eye containing receptor cells that are sensitive to light.

fovea The area of the retina that is the center of the visual field.

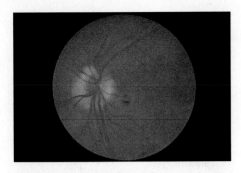

FIGURE 3–3
The retina.
View of the retina through an ophthalmo-scope, an instrument used to inspect blood vessels in the eye. The small dark spot near the center is the fovea. The yellow circle marks the blind spot, where the optic nerve leaves the eye.

The Receptor Cells The retina contains the receptor cells responsible for vision. These cells are sensitive to only one small part of the spectrum of electromagnetic energy known as *visible light*. (See **Figure 3–4**.) Energies in the electromagnetic spectrum are referred to by their **wavelength**. Although we receive light waves from the full spectrum, only a portion of it is *visible light* to us. There are two kinds of receptor cells in the retina—**rods** and **cones**—named for their characteristic shapes. (See **Figure 3–5**.) About 120 million rods and 8 million cones are present in the retina of each eye. Rods and cones differ from each other in a number of ways, as listed in "**Summary Table**: Rods and Cones." Rods, chiefly responsible for *night vision*, respond only to varying degrees or intensities of light and dark. Cones, in contrast, allow us to see colors. Operating chiefly in daylight, cones are also less sensitive to light than rods are.

Rods and cones differ in other ways as well. Cones are found mainly in the fovea, which contains no rods. Rods predominate just outside the fovea. The greater the distance from the fovea, the sparser both rods and cones become. Rods and cones also differ in the ways that they connect to nerve cells leading to the brain. Both rods and cones connect to specialized neurons called **bipolar cells**, which have only one axon and one dendrite. (See **Figure 3–6**.) In the fovea, cones generally connect with only one bipolar cell, while several rods share a single bipolar cell.

wavelengths The different energies represented in the electromagnetic spectrum.

rods Receptor cells in the retina responsible for night vision and perception of brightness.

cones Receptor cells in the retina responsible for color vision.

bipolar cells Neurons that have only one axon and one dendrite; in the eye, these neurons connect the receptors on the retina to the ganglion cells.

SUMMARY TABLE	RODS AND CONES		
Type of Receptor Cell	**Features and Functions**	**Location**	**Connections**
Rods	• Highly sensitive to light • Responsible for night vision • Responsible for perception of brightness	• Missing from the fovea • Concentrated just outside the fovea	Typically, many rods connect to a single bipolar cell.
Cones	• Moderately sensitive to light • Most useful in daylight • Responsible for color vision	• Located mainly in the fovea • Concentrated in the center of the fovea	In the fovea, typically, only a single cone connects to a single bipolar cell.

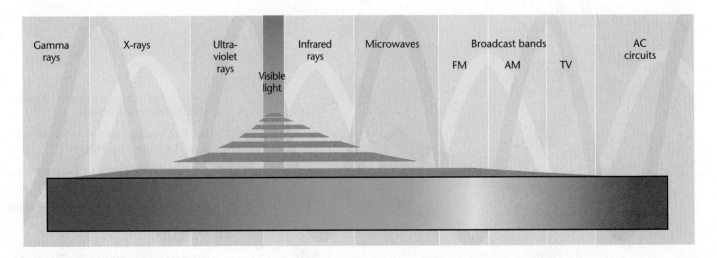

Gamma rays　X-rays　Ultra-violet rays　Visible light　Infrared rays　Microwaves　Broadcast bands　FM　AM　TV　AC circuits

FIGURE 3–4
The electromagnetic spectrum.
The eye is sensitive to only a very small segment of the spectrum, known as visible light.

The one-to-one connection between cones and bipolar cells in the fovea allows for maximum **visual acuity.** To see it for yourself, hold this book about 18 inches from your eyes and look at the "X" in the center of the following line:

This is a test to show how visual **X** acuity varies across the retina.

Your fovea picks up the "X" and about four letters to each side. This is the area of greatest visual acuity. Notice how your vision drops off for words and letters toward the left or right end of the line. Because rods normally pool their signals to the bipolar cells, they send a less-detailed message to the brain. As a consequence, outside the fovea visual acuity drops by as much as 50%.

In the dark, the fovea is almost useless because it contains no light-sensitive rods. To see a dim object, we have to look slightly to one side so that the image falls just outside the fovea where there are lots of highly sensitive rods. Conversely, if you want to examine something closely and in detail, move it into the sunlight or under a bright lamp. Up to a point, the more light, the better: Stronger light stimulates more cones in the fovea, increasing the likelihood that bipolar cells will start a precise, detailed message on its way to the brain.

Adaptation Earlier in the chapter, we introduced the term *adaptation,* the process by which our senses adjust to different levels of stimulation. In the case of vision, adaptation occurs as the sensitivity of rods and cones changes according to how much light is available. In bright light, the rods and cones become less sensitive to light. So when you go from bright sunlight into a dimly lit theater, you can see very little as you look for a seat. First the cones and then the rods slowly adapt until they reach their maximum sensitivity, a process that takes about 30 minutes. Since there is usually not enough energy in very dim light to stimulate many cones, you see the inside of the theater and the people around you primarily in black, white, and gray. The process by which rods and cones become more sensitive to light in response to lowered levels of illumination is called **dark adaptation.**

visual acuity The ability to distinguish fine details visually.

dark adaptation Increased sensitivity of rods and cones in darkness.

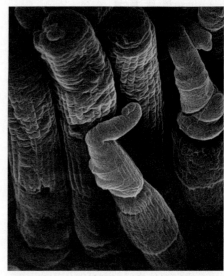

FIGURE 3–5
Rods and cones.

As you can see from this photomicrograph, the rods and cones are named for their shape.

Source: E. R. Lewis, Y. Y. Zeevi, & F. S. Werblin (1969). Scanning electron microscopy of vertebrate receptors. *Brain Research*, 15, 559–562.

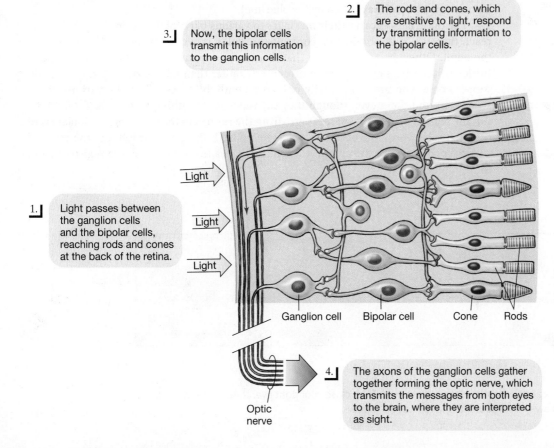

3. Now, the bipolar cells transmit this information to the ganglion cells.

2. The rods and cones, which are sensitive to light, respond by transmitting information to the bipolar cells.

1. Light passes between the ganglion cells and the bipolar cells, reaching rods and cones at the back of the retina.

Light

Light

Light

Ganglion cell   Bipolar cell   Cone   Rods

Optic nerve

4. The axons of the ganglion cells gather together forming the optic nerve, which transmits the messages from both eyes to the brain, where they are interpreted as sight.

FIGURE 3–6

A close-up of the layers of the retina.

Light must pass between the ganglion cells and the bipolar cells to reach the rods and cones. The sensory messages then travel back out from the receptor cells, via the bipolar cells, to the ganglion cells. The axons of the ganglion cells gather together to form the optic nerve, which carries the messages from both eyes to the brain. (See Figure 3–2.)

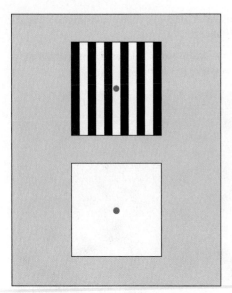

FIGURE 3–7

An afterimage.

First, stare continuously at the center of the upper square for about 20 seconds, then look at the dot in the lower square. Within a moment, a gray-and-white afterimage should appear inside the lower square.

light adaptation Decreased sensitivity of rods and cones in bright light.

afterimage Sense experience that occurs after a visual stimulus has been removed.

ganglion cells Neurons that connect the bipolar cells in the eyes to the brain.

optic nerve The bundle of axons of ganglion cells that carries neural messages from each eye to the brain.

blind spot The place on the retina where the axons of all the ganglion cells leave the eye and where there are no receptors.

optic chiasm The point near the base of the brain where some fibers in the optic nerve from each eye cross to the other side of the brain.

By the time you leave the theater, your rods and cones have grown very sensitive. As a result, all the neurons fire at once when you go into bright outdoor light. You shield your eyes and your irises contract in order to reduce the amount of light entering your pupils and striking your retinas. As this process of **light adaptation** proceeds, the rods and cones become less sensitive to stimulation. Within about a minute, both rods and cones are fully adapted and you no longer need to shield your eyes.

Dark and light adaptation can cause an **afterimage,** as shown in **Figure 3–7.** The gray-and-white afterimage appears because the part of the retina that is exposed to the dark stripes of the upper square becomes more sensitive (dark adapted). The area exposed to the white part of the upper square becomes less sensitive (light adapted). When you shift your eyes to the lower square, the less sensitive parts of the retina produce the sensation of gray rather than white. This afterimage fades within a minute as the retina adapts again, this time to the solid white square.

From Eye to Brain We have so far directed our attention to the eye, but messages from the eye must travel to the brain in order for a visual experience to occur. (See **Figure 3–6.**) The first step in this process is for rods and cones to connect to bipolar cells. The bipolar cells then hook up with the **ganglion cells** which lead out of the eye. The axons of the ganglion cells then join to form the **optic nerve,** which carries messages from each eye to the brain. The place on the retina where the axons of the ganglion cells join to form the optic nerve is called the **blind spot.** This area contains no receptor cells, so when light from a small object is focused directly on the blind spot, the object will not be seen. (See **Figure 3–8.**)

After the nerve fibers that make up the optic nerves leave the eyes, they separate, and some of them cross to the other side of the head at the **optic chiasm.** (See **Figure 3–9.**) The nerve fibers from the right side of each eye travel to the right hemisphere of the brain; those from the left side of each eye travel to the left hemisphere. Therefore, visual information about any object in the left visual field, the area to the left of the viewer, will go to the right hemisphere (the pathway traced by the red line in Figure 3–9). Similarly, information about any object in the right visual field, the area to the right of the viewer, will go to the left hemisphere (the pathway traced by the blue line).

The optic nerves carry their messages to various parts of the brain. Some messages reach the area of the brain that controls the reflex movements that adjust the size of the pupil. Others go to the region that directs the eye muscles to change the shape of the lens. Still others go to lower brain centers, rather than the visual cortex. As a result, some people who are temporarily or permanently blind can describe various visual stimuli around them even though they say they "saw" nothing (ffytche & Zeki, 2011). But the main destinations for messages from the retina are the visual projection areas of the cerebral cortex—the occipital lobe (see Figure 2–8, "The four lobes of the cerebral cortex," p. 55), where the complex coded messages from the retina are registered and interpreted.

FIGURE 3–8

Finding your blind spot.

To locate your blind spot, hold the book about a foot away from your eyes. Then close your right eye, stare at the "X," and slowly move the book toward you and away from you until the red dot disappears.

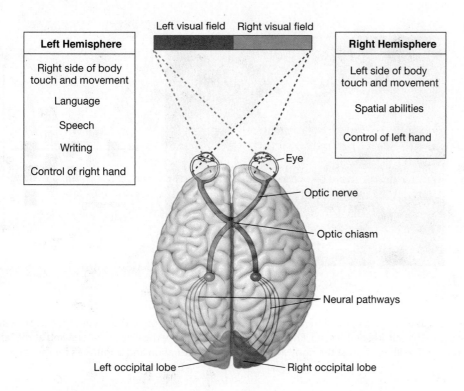

FIGURE 3-9

The neural connections of the visual system.

Messages about the red-colored area in the left visual field of each eye travel to the right occipital lobe; information about the blue area in the right visual field of each eye goes to the left occipital lobe. The crossover point is the optic chiasm.

Source: Adapted from "The Split Brain of Man," by Michael S. Gazzaniga, illustrations by Eric Mose. Copyright © 1967. Reprinted by permission of the Estate of Eric Mose.

How does the brain register and interpret these signals, "translating" light into visual images? First, the ganglion cells in the retina do some preliminary coding of the information entering the eye. Some ganglion cells send messages about the edges of objects. Others convey information about motion. Still others convey information about shadows or highlights. In the brain itself, certain brain cells—called **feature detectors**—are highly specialized to detect particular elements of the visual field, such as horizontal or vertical lines. Other feature-detector cells register more complex information, with some being sensitive to movement, depth, or color. These different types of feature detectors send messages to specific, but nearby, regions of the cortex. Visual experience, then, depends on the brain's ability to combine these pieces of information into a meaningful image.

Color Vision

How do we see color?

Humans, like many other animals, see in color, at least during the day. Color vision is highly adaptive for an animal that needs to know when fruit is ripe or how to avoid poisonous plants and berries (which tend to be brightly hued). There are different ideas, however, about how it is that we are able to see colors.

Properties of Color Look at the color solid in **Figure 3-10.** What do you see? Most people report that they see some oranges, some yellows, some reds—a number of different colors. We call these different colors **hues,** and to a great extent, the hues you see depend on the wavelength of the light reaching your eyes. (See Figure 3-4.)

Now look at the triangle of green colors on the right side of Figure 3-10. Although each color patch on the triangle is the same hue, the green color is deepest or richest toward the left side of the triangle. The vividness or richness of a hue is its **saturation.**

Finally, notice that the colors near the top of the color patches are almost white, whereas those close to the bottom are almost black. This is the dimension of **brightness,** which depends largely on the strength of the light entering your eyes. If you squint and look at the color solid, you will reduce the apparent brightness of all the colors in the solid, and many of them will appear to become black.

feature detectors Specialized brain cells that only respond to particular elements in the visual field such as movement or lines of specific orientation.

hues The aspects of color that correspond to names such as red, green, and blue.

saturation The vividness or richness of a hue.

brightness The nearness of a color to white as opposed to black.

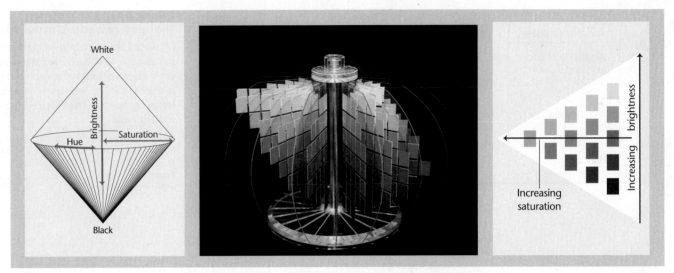

FIGURE 3–10
The color solid.

In the center portion of the figure, known as a color solid, the dimension of hue is represented around the circumference. *Saturation* ranges along the radius from the inside to the outside of the solid. *Brightness* varies along the vertical axis. The drawing at the left illustrates this arrangement schematically. The illustration at the right shows changes in saturation and brightness for the same hue.

Hue, saturation, and brightness are three separate aspects of our experience of color. Although people can distinguish only about 150 hues, gradations of saturation and brightness within those 150 hues allow us to see more than 2 million different colors (Travis, 2003). Some of this variety is captured in Figure 3–10.

Theories of Color Vision If you look closely at a color television screen, you will see that the picture is actually made up of tiny red, green, and blue dots. The same principle is at work in our own ability to see thousands of colors. Specifically, red, green, and blue lights—the primary colors for light mixtures—can be combined to create any hue. (See **Figure 3–11.**) This process is called **additive color mixing,** because each light adds additional wavelengths to the overall mix.

additive color mixing The process of mixing lights of different wavelengths to create new hues.

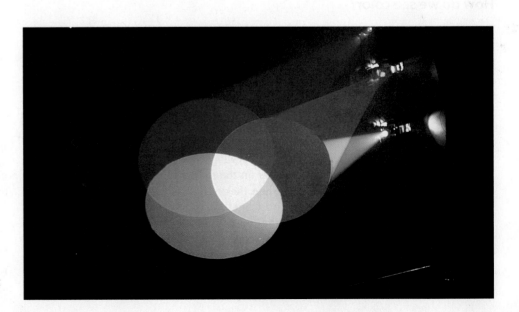

FIGURE 3–11
Additive color mixing.

Mixing light waves is an additive process. When red and green lights are combined, the resulting hue is yellow. Adding blue light to the other two yields white light.

Color mixing with paint follows different rules than does color mixing with light. The color of paint depends not on which wavelengths are *present,* but rather on which are *absorbed* and which are *reflected.* For example, red paint absorbs light from the blue end of the spectrum and reflects light from the red end. Since paint mixing depends on what colors are absorbed, or subtracted, the process is called **subtractive color mixing.** (See **Figure 3–12.**)

In the early 1800s, the German physiologist Hermann von Helmholtz proposed a theory of color vision based on additive color mixing. Helmholtz reasoned that the eye must contain three types of cones that are sensitive to red, green, or blue–violet light. According to this view, color experiences come from mixing the signals from the three receptors. Helmholtz's explanation of color vision is known as **trichromatic (or three-color) theory.**

Trichromatic theory explains how three primary colors can be combined to produce any other hue. Trichromatic theory does not, however, explain some aspects of normal color vision. Why, for example, don't people with normal color vision ever see a light or a pigment that can be described as "reddish green" or "yellowish blue"? And what accounts for *color afterimages?* (See **Figure 3–13.**)

In the later 19th century, another German scientist, Ewald Hering, proposed an alternative theory of color vision that can explain these phenomena. Hering proposed the existence of three *pairs* of color receptors: a yellow–blue pair and a red–green pair that determine the hue you see; and a black–white pair that determines the brightness of the colors you see. Hering's theory is now known as the **opponent-process theory.**

Opponent-process theory does a good job of explaining color afterimages. While you were looking at the green stripes in Figure 3–13, the red–green receptors were sending "green" messages to your brain, but they were also adapting to the stimulation by becoming less sensitive to green light. When you later looked at the white page, the red–green receptors responded vigorously to wavelengths in the red portion of the spectrum, so you saw red stripes instead of green.

Trichromatic and opponent-process theories are summarized in the "**Summary Table:** Theories of Color Vision." Today, psychologists believe that both the trichromatic and opponent-process theories are valid, but at different stages of the visual process. As trichromatic theory asserts, there are three kinds of cones for color. Thus, trichromatic theory corresponds fairly closely to the types of color receptors that actually exist in the retina. The opponent-process theory closely reflects what happens along the neural pathways that connect the eye and the brain. Together these two theories account for most color phenomena.

subtractive color mixing The process of mixing pigments, each of which absorbs some wavelengths of light and reflects others.

trichromatic (or three-color) theory
The theory of color vision that holds that all color perception derives from three different color receptors in the retina (usually red, green, and blue receptors).

opponent-process theory Theory of color vision that holds that three sets of color receptors (yellow–blue, red–green, black–white) respond to determine the color you experience.

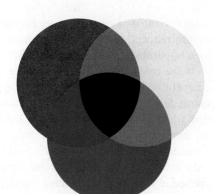

FIGURE 3–12
Subtractive color mixing.
The process of mixing paint pigments rather than lights is a subtractive process, because the pigments absorb some wavelengths and reflect others. A mixture of the three primary pigments (red, yellow, and blue) absorbs all wavelengths, producing black.

FIGURE 3–13

Afterimage.

Stare at the white spot in the center of the flag for about 30 seconds. Then look at a blank piece of white paper, and you will see an afterimage in complementary colors. Although the flag is printed in green, yellow, and black, its afterimage will appear in red, blue, and white.

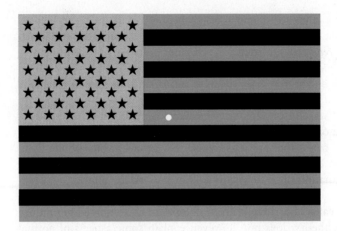

Color Vision in Other Species Most of us assume that color is in the environment. But studies of other species show that, to a great extent, color is in the eye of the beholder. Humans and most other primates perceive a wide range of colors. Most other mammals experience the world only in reds and greens or blues and yellows (Travis, 2003). Hamsters, rats, squirrels, and other rodents are completely color blind. However, some animals can see colors that we can't. Bees can see ultraviolet light. To a bee's eyes, flowers with white petals flash like neon signs pointing the way to nectar.

SUMMARY TABLE	THEORIES OF COLOR VISION	
Theory	**Developed By**	**Main Ideas**
Trichromatic theory	Helmholtz	Three kinds of receptors in the retina (red, green, blue)
Opponent-process theory	Hering	Three pairs of receptors in the retina (yellow–blue, red–green, black–white)

APPLYING PSYCHOLOGY

A Rose by Any Other Name

Folklore tells us that colors can affect our emotional state and our behavior. Marketers spend huge sums deciding what colors should go on a box of cereal as opposed to a box of detergent and interior decorators ponder the correct color to put on walls. Although there has been very little research on the influence of different colors, several recent studies suggest that is about to change. Andrew Elliot and his colleagues have begun to explore the effect of the color red on achievement. Their thinking is that "… red carries the meaning of failure in achievement contexts, warning that a dangerous possibility is at hand. This warning signal is posited to produce avoidance-based motivation that primarily has negative implications for achievement outcomes" (Elliot, Maier, Moller, Friedman, & Meinhart, 2007, p. 251). A series of experiments showed that although participants were unaware of the effect of colors on their performance, they did significantly worse on tests with red covers compared to tests with green or gray covers (Elliot et al., 2007). Researchers studying Web-based testing of knowledge have also discovered that showing a red (vs. green) progress bar or a red (vs. blue) forward button reduced test performance among men (Gnambs, Appel, & Batinic, 2010).

Is the color red always a bad thing in competitive situations? Not always. Hagemann, Strauss, and Leissing (2008) found that when the performance of tae kwon do competitors was identical, referees assigned more points to those dressed in red trunks and head protectors than those dressed in blue. And in relational contexts, "…specifically those involving sexual attraction, red carries the meaning of love, passion, and sexual readiness" (Elliot et al., 2007, p. 253).

CHECK YOUR UNDERSTANDING

✓•—[Study and Review on MyPsychLab

Match the terms with the appropriate definitions.

1. ____ cornea
2. ____ pupil
3. ____ iris
4. ____ lens
5. ____ fovea
6. ____ retina

   a. colored part of the eye
   b. center of the visual field
   c. opening in the iris through which light enters
   d. protective layer over front part of the eye
   e. part that contains the receptor cells that respond to light
   f. part that focuses light onto the retina

Answers: 1. d. 2. c. 3. a. 4. f. 5. b. 6. e.

APPLY YOUR UNDERSTANDING

1. Imagine that you are wearing a multicolored shirt when you go out for a walk on a dark night. During the walk you look down and notice that the colors all look like patches of gray. The reason that you no longer see the colors as different hues is that

   a. you are seeing primarily with the cones.
   b. you are seeing primarily with the rods.
   c. the image of your shirt is falling on your blind spot.
   d. the colors have become saturated.

2. Your six-year-old nephew asks you to use crayons to draw a green car and a red fire truck, but you have no green crayon. He says "My teacher says yellow and blue make green." You realize your nephew understands the basics of

   a. additive color mixing.
   b. subtractive color mixing.
   c. the trichromatic theory of color vision.
   d. the opponent-process theory of color vision.

Answers: 1. b. 2. b.

HEARING

If a tree falls in the forest and no one is there, does the tree make a sound?

If you had to make a choice, would you give up your sight or your hearing? Presented with this hypothetical choice, most people say they would give up hearing first. But the great teacher and activist Helen Keller, who was both blind and deaf from infancy, regretted her inability to hear more than anything else.

> I am just as deaf as I am blind. The problems of deafness are deeper and more complex, if not more important than those of blindness. Deafness is a much worse misfortune. For it means the loss of the most vital stimulus—the sound of the voice that brings language, sets thoughts astir and keeps us in the intellectual company of man. (Keller, 1948; quoted in D. Ackerman, 1995, pp. 191–192)

LEARNING OBJECTIVES

- Explain the characteristics of sound waves and their effect on the sensation we call sound.
- Describe the path that information about sound travels from the ears to the brain. Explain place theory, frequency theory, and the volley principle.
- Explain the two major kinds of hearing disorders (deafness and tinnitus).

Sound

How do the characteristics of sound waves cause us to hear different sounds?

The sensation we call **sound** is our brain's interpretation of the ebb and flow of air molecules pounding on our eardrums. When something in the environment moves, pressure is caused as molecules of air or fluid collide with one another and then move apart again. This pressure transmits energy at every collision, creating **sound waves**. The simplest sound wave—what we hear as a pure tone—can be pictured as the sine wave shown in **Figure 3–14.** The tuning fork vibrates, causing the molecules of air first to contract and then to expand. The **frequency** of the waves is measured in cycles per second, expressed in a unit called **hertz (Hz).**

sound A psychological experience created by the brain in response to changes in air pressure that are received by the auditory system.

sound waves Changes in pressure caused when molecules of air or fluid collide with one another and then move apart again.

frequency The number of cycles per second in a wave; in sound, the primary determinant of pitch.

hertz (Hz) Cycles per second; unit of measurement for the frequency of sound waves.

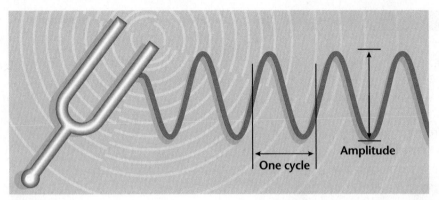

FIGURE 3–14

Sound waves.

As the tuning fork vibrates, it alternately compresses and expands the molecules of air, creating a sound wave.

Frequency primarily determines the **pitch** of the sound—how high or how low it is. The human ear responds to frequencies from approximately 20 Hz to 20,000 Hz. Cats can hear noises as high as 64,000 Hz and mice can hear sounds up to 100,000 Hz.

The height of the sound wave represents its **amplitude** (Figure 3–14), which, together with frequency, determines the perceived loudness of a sound. Sound intensity is measured by a unit called **decibel.** (See **Figure 3–15.**) As we grow older, we lose some of our ability to hear soft sounds; however, we can hear loud sounds as well as ever.

The sounds that we hear seldom result from pure tones. Unlike a tuning fork, musical instruments produce **overtones**—accompanying sound waves that are different multiples of the frequency of the basic tone. This complex pattern of overtones determines the **timbre,** or texture, of the sound. A note played on the piano sounds different from the same note played on a violin because of the differing overtones of the two instruments. Music synthesizers can mimic different

FIGURE 3–15

A decibel scale for several common sounds.

Prolonged exposure to sounds above 85 decibels can cause permanent damage to the ears, as can even brief exposure to sounds near the pain threshold.

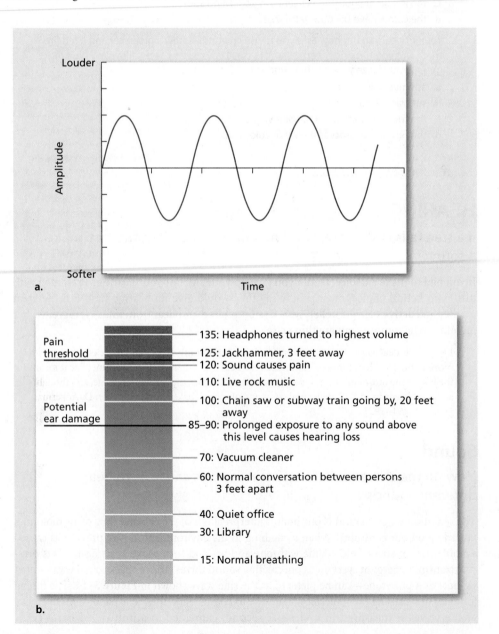

pitch Auditory experience corresponding primarily to frequency of sound vibrations, resulting in a higher or lower tone.

amplitude The magnitude of a wave; in sound, the primary determinant of loudness.

decibel Unit of measurement for the loudness of sounds.

instruments electronically because they are able to produce the timbre of different musical instruments.

Like our other senses, hearing undergoes adaptation and can function optimally under a wide variety of conditions. City residents enjoying a weekend in the country may be struck at how quiet everything seems. However, after they have adapted to the quieter environment, they may find that the country starts to sound very noisy.

The Ear

What path does sound follow from the ear to the brain?

Hearing begins when sound waves are gathered by the outer ear and passed along to the eardrum (see **Figure 3–16**) causing it to vibrate. The quivering of the eardrum prompts three tiny bones in the middle ear—the *hammer,* the *anvil,* and the *stirrup*—to hit each other in sequence and thus carry the vibrations to the inner ear. The stirrup is attached to a

overtones Tones that result from sound waves that are multiples of the basic tone; primary determinant of timbre.

timbre The quality or texture of sound; caused by overtones.

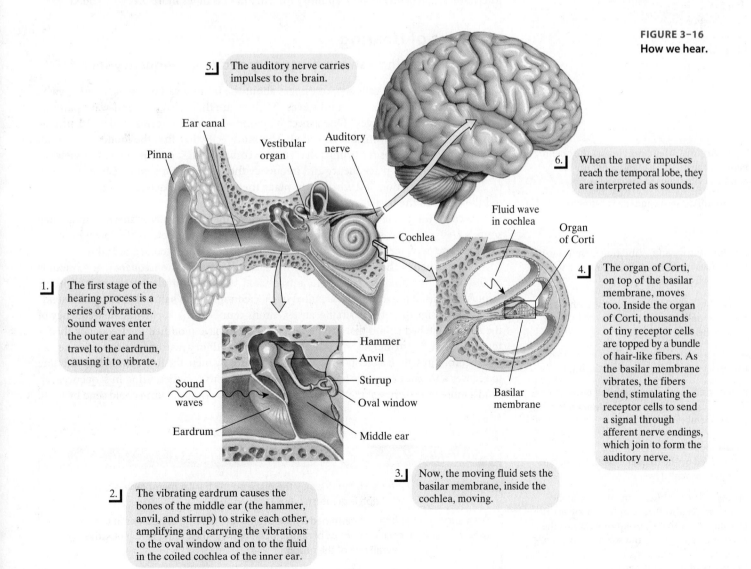

FIGURE 3–16
How we hear.

5. The auditory nerve carries impulses to the brain.

6. When the nerve impulses reach the temporal lobe, they are interpreted as sounds.

4. The organ of Corti, on top of the basilar membrane, moves too. Inside the organ of Corti, thousands of tiny receptor cells are topped by a bundle of hair-like fibers. As the basilar membrane vibrates, the fibers bend, stimulating the receptor cells to send a signal through afferent nerve endings, which join to form the auditory nerve.

1. The first stage of the hearing process is a series of vibrations. Sound waves enter the outer ear and travel to the eardrum, causing it to vibrate.

2. The vibrating eardrum causes the bones of the middle ear (the hammer, anvil, and stirrup) to strike each other, amplifying and carrying the vibrations to the oval window and on to the fluid in the coiled cochlea of the inner ear.

3. Now, the moving fluid sets the basilar membrane, inside the cochlea, moving.

Pinna
Ear canal
Vestibular organ
Auditory nerve
Cochlea
Fluid wave in cochlea
Organ of Corti
Basilar membrane
Hammer
Anvil
Stirrup
Oval window
Middle ear
Sound waves
Eardrum

Watch the Video Noise and the Brain on MyPsychLab

Hair cells on the basilar membrane.

Explore and Concept Major Structures of the Ear on MyPsychLab

oval window Membrane across the opening between the middle ear and inner ear that conducts vibrations to the cochlea.

cochlea Part of the inner ear containing fluid that vibrates, which in turn causes the basilar membrane to vibrate.

basilar membrane Vibrating membrane in the cochlea of the inner ear; it contains sense receptors for sound.

organ of Corti Structure on the surface of the basilar membrane that contains the receptor cells for hearing.

auditory nerve The bundle of axons that carries signals from each ear to the brain

place theory Theory that pitch is determined by the location of greatest vibration on the basilar membrane.

frequency theory Theory that pitch is determined by the frequency with which hair cells in the cochlea fire.

volley principle Refinement of frequency theory; it suggests that receptors in the ear fire in sequence, with one group responding, then a second, then a third, and so on, so that the complete pattern of firing corresponds to the frequency of the sound wave.

membrane called the **oval window;** vibrations of the oval window, in turn, are transmitted to the fluid inside a snail-shaped structure called the **cochlea.** The cochlea is divided lengthwise by the **basilar membrane,** which is stiff near the oval window but gradually becomes more flexible toward its other end. When the fluid in the cochlea begins to move, the basilar membrane ripples in response.

Lying on top of the basilar membrane and moving in sync with it is the **organ of Corti.** Here the messages from the sound waves finally reach the receptor cells for the sense of hearing: thousands of tiny hair cells that are embedded in the organ of Corti. As you can see in **Figure 3–17,** each hair cell is topped by a bundle of fibers. These fibers are pushed and pulled by the vibrations of the basilar membrane. When these fibers move, the receptor cells send a signal through afferent nerve endings that join to form the **auditory nerve** to the brain. The brain pools the information from thousands of hair cells to create sounds.

Neural Connections The sense of hearing is truly bilateral: Each ear sends messages to both cerebral hemispheres. The switching station where the nerve fibers from the ears cross over is in the medulla, part of the brain stem. (See Figure 2–7.) From the medulla, other nerve fibers carry the messages from the ears to the higher parts of the brain. Some messages go to the brain centers that coordinate the movements of the eyes, head, and ears. Others travel through the reticular formation. But the primary destinations for these auditory messages are the auditory areas in the temporal lobes of the two cerebral hemispheres. (See Figure 2–8.) En route to the temporal lobes, auditory messages pass through at least four lower brain centers where auditory information becomes more precisely coded.

Theories of Hearing

How do we distinguish low-frequency and high-frequency sounds?

Thousands of tiny hair cells send messages about the infinite variations in the frequency, amplitude, and overtones of sound waves. But how are the different sound-wave patterns coded into neural messages? One aspect of sound—loudness—seems to depend primarily on how many neurons are activated: The more cells that fire, the louder the sound. The coding of messages regarding pitch is more complicated. There are two basic views of pitch discrimination: place theory and frequency theory. (See "**Summary Table:** Theories of Pitch Discrimination.") According to **place theory,** the brain determines pitch by noting the place on the basilar membrane at which the message is strongest. High-frequency sounds cause the greatest vibration at the stiff base of the basilar membrane; low-frequency sounds resonate most strongly at the opposite end. The brain detects the location of the most intense nerve-cell activity and uses this to determine the pitch of a sound.

The **frequency theory** of pitch discrimination holds that the frequency of vibrations of the basilar membrane as a whole is translated into an equivalent frequency of nerve impulses. Thus, if a hair bundle is pulled or pushed rapidly, its hair cell fires rapidly, sending a rush of signals to the brain. Because neurons cannot fire as rapidly as the frequency of the highest pitched sound that can be heard, theorists have modified the frequency theory to include a **volley principle.** According to this view, auditory neurons can fire in sequence: One neuron fires, then a second one, and then a third. By then, the first neuron has had time to recover and can fire again. In this way, a set of neurons together, firing in sequence, can send a more rapid series of impulses to the brain than any single neuron could send by itself.

SUMMARY TABLE	THEORIES OF PITCH DISCRIMINATION
Place theory	Pitch is determined by the place on the basilar membrane where vibration is greatest.
Frequency theory	Pitch is determined by the overall rate of firing of neurons in the cochlea. Groups of neurons can "volley" their firing to increase the overall rate of the group.

Loud music can cause damage to the sensitive structures of the ears, leading to hearing loss.

Because neither place theory nor frequency theory alone fully explains pitch discrimination, some combination of the two is necessary. Frequency theory appears to account for the ear's responses to frequencies up to about 4000 Hz; above that, place theory provides a better explanation of what is happening.

Hearing Disorders Since the mechanisms that allow us to hear are so complicated, the potential is great for a large number of possible problems that may interfere with hearing. Of the 28 million Americans with hearing loss, about 10 million are victims of exposure to noise. About 6.5 million teenagers have some hearing loss (an increase of nearly one-third from the levels in 1988–1994 (Shargorodsky, Curhan, Curhan, & Eavey, 2010)). The chief culprits are leaf blowers, chain saws, and snowmobiles (Biassoni et al., 2005). (See Figure 3–16.)

For people with irreversible hearing loss, a number of remedies are available. New digital technology has made hearing aids, which amplify sound, more precise by enhancing speech perception and reducing background noise. Surgery can help people with conductive hearing loss due to a stiffening of the connections between the bones of the middle ear.

Implants offer hope to people who suffer from deafness due to cochlear damage. One or more platinum electrodes are inserted into the cochlea of one ear. The electrodes bypass the damaged hair cells and convey electrical signals from a miniature sound synthesizer directly to the auditory nerve, which conveys an auditory message to the brain. There is also evidence that a new kind of implant may be able to stimulate the auditory nerve directly without going through the cochlea (Middlebrooks & Snyder, 2008).

ENDURING ISSUES

Diversity–Universality Deaf Culture

Should doctors do everything possible to restore hearing in children who are born deaf or become deaf at an early age? The National Association of the Deaf argues no. Many of these procedures only partially restore hearing. As a result, the association argues, children are left in limbo. On the one hand, they are denied access to sign language and to the deaf subculture; on the other, they are pushed into a hearing culture that labels them "disabled," reducing self-esteem. The association holds that sign language is a legitimate language and should be recognized as such. Children who learn sign language as their native language function quite well, often better than children who struggle to understand spoken language they can barely hear.

Underlying this position is the view that deafness is not a disability. Rather, it is just another form of human diversity. ■

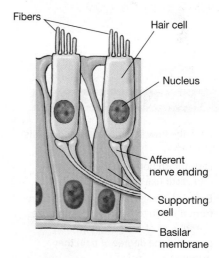

FIGURE 3–17

A detailed drawing of a hair cell.

At the top of each hair cell is a bundle of fibers. If the fibers bend as much as 100 trillionths of a meter, the receptor cells transmit a sensory message to the brain.

Source: Drawing adapted from "The Hair Cells of the Inner Ear" by A. J. Hudspeth, illustrated by Bunji Tagawa. Copyright © 1983. Adapted with permission from the Estate of Bunji Tagawa.

Far from not hearing enough sound, millions of people hear too much of the wrong kind of sound and suffer greatly because of it. Almost everybody has at some time heard a steady, high-pitched hum that persists even in the quietest room. This sound, which seems to come from inside the head, is called *tinnitus,* and it is estimated to afflict approximately one out of every eight persons. In some people, it becomes unbearably loud—like the screeching of subway brakes—and does not go away. In most cases, tinnitus results from irritation or damage to the hair cells. Prolonged exposure to loud sound or toxins, certain medical conditions, and even some antibiotics can cause permanent damage to the hair cells. In many cases, drug therapies, implants that create "white noise" (or sound blockage), and biofeedback can provide relief.

✓●─[Study and Review on MyPsychLab

CHECK YOUR UNDERSTANDING

In which order would a sound wave reach the following structures when traveling from the outer ear to the inner ear? Number the following terms in the correct order.

1. ___ oval window
2. ___ anvil
3. ___ cochlea
4. ___ auditory nerve
5. ___ eardrum

Answers: 1. 3rd, 2. 2nd, 3. 4th, 4. 5th, 5. 1st.

APPLY YOUR UNDERSTANDING

1. As you sit in front of a sound generator, the frequency of the sound is gradually increased. You are most likely to notice an increase in
   a. pitch.
   b. loudness.
   c. saturation.
   d. overtones.

2. A friend says, "I hear this loud ringing in my ears. Sometimes it's so loud I have trouble sleeping. It's driving me crazy!" Your friend is most likely describing
   a. cochlear degeneration.
   b. timbre.
   c. rippling of the basilar membrane.
   d. tinnitus.

Answers: 1. a. 2. d.

LEARNING OBJECTIVES

- Describe how stimuli give rise to smells and tastes.
- Distinguish between the kinesthetic and vestibular senses.
- Explain how sensory messages are sent from the skin to the brain. Summarize the sources of differences among people in the degree of pain they experience.

THE OTHER SENSES

What are the chemical senses?

Researchers have focused most of their attention on vision and hearing because humans rely primarily on these two senses to gather information about their environment. Our other senses—including smell, taste, balance, motion, pressure, temperature, and pain—are also at play, even when we are less conscious of them. We turn first to the chemical senses: smell and taste.

Smell

What activates the sense of smell?

Although the sense of smell in humans is much weaker than in most animals, it is still about 10,000 times more acute than taste. Like our other senses, smell undergoes adaptation.

Research has unlocked many of the mysteries of our other senses, but exactly how we smell is still an open question. Scientists do know that when we breathe in, air flows over the roughly 12 million odor-detecting cells high up in the nasal cavity. Each cell is specialized to respond to only some odorant molecules. (See **Figure 3–18.**) The axons from millions of these receptors go directly to the **olfactory bulb,** where some recoding takes place. Then messages are routed

olfactory bulb The smell center in the brain.

to the olfactory cortex in the temporal lobes of the brain, resulting in our ability to recognize and remember about 10,000 different smells. There our understanding comes to a halt: Exactly how the coded messages from the nose result in the sensation of smell is still a mystery.

Odor sensitivity is related to gender. Numerous studies confirm that women generally have a better sense of smell than men (Chrisler & McCreary, 2010). Age also makes a difference since adults aged 20–40 have the sharpest sense of smell (Doty, 1989; Schiffman, 1997). Of the people tested by Doty and his colleagues, half of those 65–80 years old and three-quarters of those over the age of 80 had meaningful loss of smell (Doty, 2006). *Anosmia*, the complete loss of smell, can be devastating, but some experimental treatments hold out promise that smell, once lost, can be restored (Raloff, 2007).

Most mammals, including humans, have a second sensory system devoted to the sense of smell—which some animals use in daily living for such important things as marking their territory, identifying sexually receptive mates, and recognizing members of their group. Receptors located in the roof of the nasal cavity detect chemicals called **pheromones**, which can have quite specific and powerful effects on behavior. Humans also have receptors for pheromones and, like other mammals, there is evidence that pheromones can significantly affect behavior. For example, studies have demonstrated that pheromones can affect the menstrual cycles in women (McClintock, 1999; K. Stern & McClintock, 1998). Researchers also have shown that when males and lesbians are exposed to a natural female pheromone, their general mood is elevated and their ratings of the *sexual attractiveness* of females described in a story are enhanced. Findings are similar when females and gay men are exposed to a natural male pheromone (Berglund, Lindström, & Savic, 2006; Savic, Berglund, & Lindström, 2005; Scholey, Bosworth, & Dimitrakaki, 1999; Thorne, Neave, Scholey, Moss, & Fink, 2002; Thorne, Scholey, & Neave, 2000). One study of three dozen heterosexual female university students showed that women who used a perfume laced with a synthetic pheromone engaged in significantly more sexual behavior, although they were not approached more often by men nor did they have more informal dates compared with women who used the same perfume, but without the pheromone (McCoy & Pitino, 2002). Similar findings were reported in an earlier study of 17 heterosexual men (W. B. Cutler, Friedmann, & McCoy, 1998). 👁

Certain animal species rely more on their sense of smell than humans do. This dog has been trained to use its keen sense of smell to help security forces at the airport.

pheromones Chemicals that communicate information to other organisms through smell.

👁 **Watch** the **Video** Alzheimer's Smell Test on **MyPsychLab**

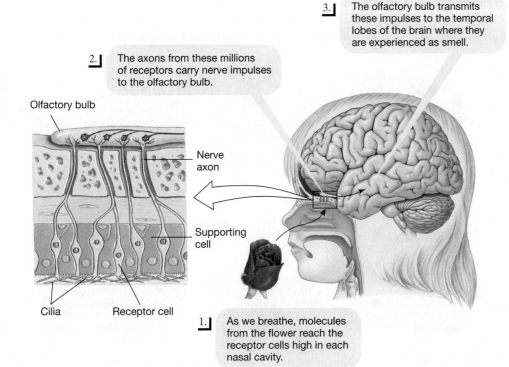

2. The axons from these millions of receptors carry nerve impulses to the olfactory bulb.

3. The olfactory bulb transmits these impulses to the temporal lobes of the brain where they are experienced as smell.

Olfactory bulb

Nerve axon

Supporting cell

Cilia

Receptor cell

1. As we breathe, molecules from the flower reach the receptor cells high in each nasal cavity.

FIGURE 3–18

The human olfactory system.

The sense of smell is triggered when odor molecules in the air reach the olfactory receptors located inside the top of the nose. Inhaling and exhaling odor molecules from food does much to give food its flavorful "taste."

Source: Adapted from *Human Anatomy and Physiology* by Anthony J. Gaudin and Kenneth C. Jones. Copyright © 1989. Reprinted by permission of Harcourt Publishing Co.

taste buds Structures on the tongue that contain the receptor cells for taste.

kinesthetic senses Senses of muscle movement, posture, and strain on muscles and joints.

Taste

How do we detect the basic tastes?

To understand taste, we must distinguish it from flavor—a complex interaction of taste and smell (Bartoshuk, 2009). Try holding your nose when you eat. You will notice that most of the food's flavor will disappear, and you will experience only the basic taste qualities: *sweet, sour, salty, bitter,* and *umami* (umami accounts for our sensitivity to monosodium glutamate—MSG—and related proteins).

The receptor cells for the sense of taste are housed in roughly 10,000 **taste buds**, most of which are found on the tip, sides, and back of the tongue (see **Figure 3–19**). Each area of the tongue can distinguish all taste qualities, though some areas may be more sensitive to certain tastes than others.

The taste buds are embedded in the tongue's *papillae,* bumps that you can see if you look at your tongue in the mirror. When we eat something, the chemical substances in the food dissolve in saliva and go into the crevices between the papillae, where they come into contact with the taste buds. In turn, the taste buds release a neurotransmitter that causes adjacent neurons to fire, sending a nerve impulse to the parietal lobe of the brain and to the limbic system.

Taste, like the other senses, experiences adaptation. When you first start eating salted peanuts or potato chips, the saltiness is quite strong, but after a while it becomes less noticeable. Furthermore, exposure to one quality of taste can modify other taste sensations—after brushing your teeth in the morning, you may notice that your orange juice has lost its sweetness. Because the number of taste buds decreases with age, older people often lose interest in food because they cannot taste it as well as they used to.

Kinesthetic and Vestibular Senses

How do we know which way is up and whether we are moving or standing still?

The **kinesthetic senses** provide information about the speed and direction of our movement in space. More specifically, they relay information about muscle movement, changes in posture, and strain on muscles and joints. Specialized receptors provide constant

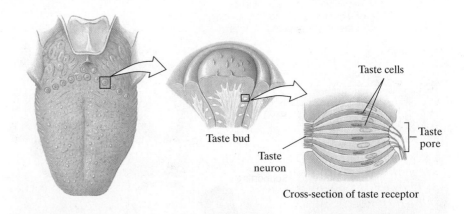

FIGURE 3–19

The structure of a taste bud.

The sensory receptors for taste are found primarily on the tongue. Taste cells can detect only sweet, sour, salty, bitter, and umami qualities. All other tastes result from different combinations of these taste sensations.

1. The taste buds are embedded in small lumps on the tongue called papillae.

2. When we eat, chemicals in the food dissolve in saliva and come into contact with the taste cells (receptors) within the taste buds.

3. Now, adjacent neurons fire, sending nerve impulses to the brain's parietal lobe, where the messages are perceived as taste.

Taste cells

Taste bud

Taste neuron

Taste pore

Cross-section of taste receptor

feedback from the stretching and contraction of individual muscles. The information from these receptors travels via the spinal cord to the cortex of the parietal lobes, the same brain area that perceives the sense of touch.

The **vestibular senses** provide information about our orientation or position in space that helps determine which way is up and which way is down. Like hearing, the vestibular senses originate in the inner ear, where hair cells serve as the sense organs. The impulses from these hair cells travel to the brain along the auditory nerve, but their ultimate destinations in the brain are still something of a mystery. Certain messages from the vestibular system go to the cerebellum, which controls many of the reflexes involved in coordinated movement. Others reach the areas that regulate the internal body organs, and some find their way to the parietal lobe of the cerebral cortex for analysis and response.

Perhaps we are most acutely aware of our vestibular senses when we experience *motion sickness*. Certain kinds of motion, such as riding in ships, trigger strong reactions in some people. According to one theory, motion sickness stems from discrepancies between visual information and vestibular sensations (Bubka & Bonato, 2003; R. M. Stern & Koch, 1996). In other words, our eyes and our body are sending our brain contradictory information. Our eyes tell our brain that we are moving, but the organs in our inner ear insist that we are sitting still. Susceptibility to motion sickness appears to be related to both race and genetics: People of Asian ancestry are particularly susceptible to motion sickness (Muth, Stern, Uijtdehaage, & Koch, 1994).

The Skin Senses

What types of sensory messages are sent from the skin to the brain?

Our skin is our largest sense organ—a person 6 feet tall has about 21 square feet of skin. Skin contains receptors for our sense of touch, which plays an important role in human interaction and emotion. In most societies, hellos and good-byes are accompanied by gestures involving touch, like shaking hands. Touching and being touched by others bridges, at least momentarily, our isolation. In fact, research shows that touching someone for just a few seconds can successfully convey emotions such as anger, fear, disgust, love, gratitude, sympathy, happiness and sadness (Hertenstein, Holmes, McCullough, & Keltner, 2009).

The skin's numerous nerve receptors, distributed in varying concentrations throughout its surface, send nerve fibers to the brain by two routes. Some information goes through the medulla and the thalamus and from there to the sensory cortex in the parietal lobe of the brain—which is presumably where our experiences of touch, pressure, and so on arise. (See Figure 2–8.) Other information goes through the thalamus and then on to the reticular formation, which is responsible for arousing the nervous system or quieting it down.

Skin receptors give rise to sensations of pressure, temperature, and pain, but the relationship between the receptors and our sensory experiences is subtle. Researchers believe that our brains draw on complex information about the patterns of activity received from many different receptors to detect and discriminate among skin sensations. For example, our skin has "cold fibers" that increase their firing rate as the skin cools down and that slow their firing when the skin heats up. Conversely, we also have "warm fibers" that accelerate their firing rate when the skin gets warm and that slow down when the skin cools. The brain apparently uses the combined information from these two sets of fibers as the basis for determining skin temperature. If both sets are activated at once, the brain may read their combined pattern of firings as "hot." Thus, you might think that you are touching something hot when you are really touching something warm and something cool at the same time, a phenomenon known as *paradoxical heat*. (See **Figure 3–20.**)

The skin senses are remarkably sensitive. For example, skin displacement of as little as 0.0000025 of an inch can result in a sensation of pressure. Moreover, various parts of the

vestibular senses The senses of equilibrium and body position in space.

This dancer is utilizing information provided by both her kinesthetic and her vestibular senses. Her kinesthetic senses are relaying messages pertaining to muscle strain and movements; her vestibular senses are supplying feedback about her body position in space.

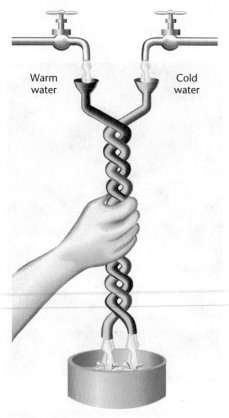

FIGURE 3-20
Paradoxical heat.
Touching a warm pipe and a cold pipe at the same time causes two sets of skin receptors to signal at once to the brain. The brain reads their combined pattern of firings as "hot," a phenomenon known as paradoxical heat.

Glowing coals smolder under the feet of these participants in an annual ritual at Mt. Takao, Japan. How do they do it? Is it mind over matter—the human ability to sometimes "turn off" pain sensations? The secret in this case may actually lie more in the coals than in the men. Because wood is a poor conductor of heat, walking over wood coals quickly may not be that painful after all.

body differ greatly in their sensitivity to pressure: Your face and fingertips are extremely sensitive, whereas your legs, feet, and back are much less so.

Like other senses, the skin senses undergo various kinds of sensory adaptation. When we first get into a bath, it may be uncomfortably hot; but in a few minutes we adapt to the heat. Skin senses are also influenced by our expectations. When someone tickles us, our skin senses respond with excitement, but tickling ourselves produces no effect. Clearly, the brain draws on many sources of information in interpreting the sense of touch.

Pain

What differences among people have an effect on the degree of pain they experience?

Although pain plays an important role in everyday life—alerting us to both minor and major injuries—more people visit doctors for relief of pain than for any other reason. The economic impact of pain is more than $100 billion a year in the United States alone (Mackey, 2005). Yet, to a great extent, pain remains a puzzle. What is the purpose of pain? An old adage holds that pain is nature's way of telling you that something is wrong; and it does seem reasonable to assume that damage to the body causes pain. But in many cases, actual physical injury is not accompanied by pain. Conversely, some people feel pain without having been injured or long after an injury has healed. One of the most perplexing examples of this is the *phantom limb phenomenon,* which occurs in at least 90% of amputees and perhaps half of the people who experience a stroke (Antoniello, Kluger, Sahlein, & Heilman, 2010). After amputation of an arm or a leg, a patient often continues to feel the missing limb; in fact some patients report that they can actually move their phantom limb (Ramachandran & Rogers-Ramachandran, 2007). Surprisingly, children who are born without arms or legs also often report having phantom limbs (Melzack, Israel, Lacroix, & Schultz, 1997). And therein lies an important clue to how the sensation of a phantom limb arises: not in the damaged nerves at the site of the amputation (which the children don't have), but higher up in the brain itself where there apparently is some kind of neural "picture" of what the intact human body should be like. As the brain slowly reorganizes itself to reflect the missing limb, the pain and other sensations often subside with time, demonstrating yet again the force of neural plasticity (Flor, Nikolajsen, & Jensen, 2006) (see Chapter 2).

Gate-Control Theory The sensation of pain in many ways remains mysterious, but some progress has been made in understanding why and how pain occurs. Sensory information about pain begins when *free nerve endings* are stimulated.

Information from these receptors travels to the spinal cord where, according to the **gate-control theory** of pain, a "neurological gate" in the spinal cord controls the transmission of pain impulses to the brain (Melzack, & Katz, 2004). If the gate is open, we experience more pain than when it is closed.

When pain messages reach the brain, a complex series of reactions begins. As we saw in Chapter 2, the sympathetic nervous system springs into action. The nervous system and endocrine system go on alert to help deal with the crisis. Meanwhile, chemicals to reduce or stop the pain messages may be released both in the brain and in the spinal cord. Certain areas of the brain stem may also reduce the flow of incoming pain information by sending signals to fibers in the spinal cord to partially or completely close the "gate." These processes account for the fact that, despite an injury, little or no pain may be experienced.

Biopsychosocial Theory Some psychologists believe that the gate-control theory oversimplifies the complex experience we call pain. According to **biopsychosocial theory,** pain sensations involve three interrelated phenomena: biological mechanisms, psychological mechanisms, and social mechanisms (Edwards, Campbell, Jamison, & Wiech, 2009).

Biological mechanisms involve the degree to which tissue is injured and our pain pathways have adapted. For example, chronic pain can alter pathways in the nervous system. As a result, the nerves in the spinal cord can become hypersensitive. Let's say you break a bone in your foot and don't get medical attention until pain prevents you from walking. Even after the break heals, a mild blow to your foot may be painful.

Genetics also appears to play a role. Scientists have identified a small genetic variation that accounts partially for individual differences in the experience of pain (Cox et al., 2006). Mutations of this gene can cause individuals to experience no pain, while other mutations can lead to hypersensitivity to pain.

Psychological mechanisms—our thoughts, beliefs, and emotions—also can affect our experience of pain (Wickelgren, 2009). In one study, heat pulses were administered to the lower right leg. Participants who expected only moderate pain reported much less pain when the stimulus was actually severe. Moreover, there was much lower activity in pain-related brain areas; and participants' expectations of lower pain were almost as effective as morphine in relieving physical pain (Koyama, McHaffie, Laurienti, & Coghill, 2005).

Some people make an active effort to cope with pain: Confident that they can overcome pain, they avoid negative feelings, engage in diverting activities, and refuse to let pain interfere with their daily lives. By contrast, others with the same injuries or disorders can be overwhelmed: They feel "victimized," that their pain is ruling their life, and that no one understands. Studies indicate that believing in one's ability to cope may actually cause higher brain centers to reduce or block pain signals (Padhi, 2005; Wall & Melzack, 1996). Even temporary psychological states can have an impact; researchers have found that distracting people with sounds or pleasant aromas can reduce not only the sensation of pain, but also activity in portions of the brain that respond to pain (Moont, Pud, Sprecher, Sharvit, & Yarnitsky, 2010).

Social mechanisms, such as the degree of family support, also play a role (Master et al., 2009). In one large study of chronic pain patients, those who described their families as being supportive reported significantly less pain intensity, less reliance on medication, and greater activity levels than patients who reported family disharmony and limited support (Jamison & Virts, 1990). Cultural expectations can also affect the experience of pain as well as ways of coping with pain (Bonham, 2001; D. Gordon & Bidar-Sielaff, 2006; Sullivan, 2004).

Alternative Treatments There is a vast array of treatments for reducing pain though none of them is fully effective against all kinds of pain. Some of them work by affecting the gate-control mechanisms in the spinal cord. Others, such as pain relievers, work directly in the brain. But the ways in which other treatments work remain a mystery. For example, many studies have shown that if you give pain sufferers a chemically inert pill, or *placebo,* but tell them that it is an effective pain reducer, they often report some relief (National Institutes of Health, 2007). There is no doubt many home remedies rely on the **placebo effect.** Research indicates that both placebos and acupuncture, which involves the insertion of thin needles into parts of the body, work in part through the release of endorphins, pain-blocking neurotransmitters (Hollins, 2010). But recent research shows that even for placebos and acupuncture, endorphin release alone does not account for pain reduction (Kong et al., 2006; Matre, Casey, & Knardahl, 2006). Moreover, some other pain-reduction techniques—such as hypnosis or concentration exercises (as in the Lamaze birth technique)—appear to have nothing at all to do with endorphins, but rely on some other means of reducing the pain sensation (deCharms et al., 2005). Clearly, much more research is needed before we will fully understand the sensation of pain. ◉

gate-control theory The theory that a "neurological gate" in the spinal cord controls the transmission of pain messages to the brain.

biopsychosocial theory The theory that the interaction of biological, psychological, and cultural factors influences the intensity and duration of pain.

placebo effect Pain relief that occurs when a person believes a pill or procedure will reduce pain. The actual cause of the relief seems to come from endorphins.

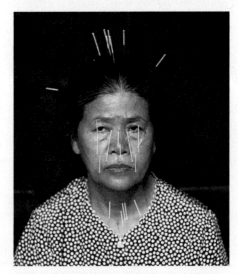

Traditional Asian medicine has used acupuncture to reduce or eliminate pain. Studies indicate that acupuncture works by releasing endorphins into the body.

Watch the **Video** Brain Pain on **MyPsychLab**

✓•─[Study and Review on MyPsychLab]

CHECK YOUR UNDERSTANDING

1. The basic tastes are _____, _____, _____, _____, and _____.

2. Skin senses include sensations of _____, _____, and _____.

3. Our _____ sense provides awareness of our body's position.

Answers: 1. sweet, sour, salty, bitter, and umami. 2. pressure, temperature, pain. 3. kinesthetic.

APPLY YOUR UNDERSTANDING

1. A seven-year-old is asked to eat something that he would rather not eat. He holds his nose, eats it, and says, "Ha! I couldn't taste it!" You remember what you have learned in this course, and you decide to correct him: "Actually, you have only gotten rid of
   a. the flavor, not the taste."
   b. the taste, not the flavor."
   c. the smell, not the taste or flavor."
   d. the papillae, not the taste."

2. George suffers from chronic back pain. His doctor suggests that he try a form of therapy in which electrical stimulation is applied to his back. He explains that stimulating large sensory nerves in the spinal cord can prevent the transmission of pain impulses to the brain, and that it is an application of the _____ theory of pain.
   a. gate-control
   b. contra-stimulation
   c. free nerve ending
   d. patterned-firing

Answers: 1. a. 2. a.

LEARNING OBJECTIVES ····▷

- Distinguish between sensation and perception. Explain the Gestalt principles of perceptual organization. Describe the several perceptual constancies.

- Identify the major cues to distance and depth, distinguishing between monocular and binocular cues.

- Explain how we can localize sound and perceive movement, distinguishing between real movement and apparent movement.

- Explain how visual illusions arise.

- Describe how observer characteristics and culture can influence perception.

PERCEPTION

How is perception different from sensation?

Our senses provide us with raw data about the external world. But unless we interpret this raw information, it is nothing more than what William James (1890) called a "booming, buzzing confusion." The eye records patterns of lightness and darkness, but it does not "see" a bird flittering from branch to branch. Deciphering *meaningful* patterns in the jumble of sensory information is what we mean by perception. But how does perception differ from sensation?

Perception is the brain's process of organizing and making sense of sensory information. Using sensory information as raw material, the brain creates perceptual experiences that go beyond what is sensed directly. The close up of the painting in **Figure 3–21** corresponds to sensation: discrete "blips" of color. Viewed as a whole, however, these units of color become a picture. Another graphic illustration of the way perception transforms mere sensations into a meaningful whole can be seen in **Figure 3–22**. Although we tend to perceive a white triangle in the center of the pattern, the sensory input consists only of three circles from which "pie slices" have been cut and three 60-degree angles. Or consider **Figure 3–23**. At first glance most people see only an assortment of black blotches. However, when you are told that the blotches represent a person riding a horse, suddenly your perceptual experience changes. What was meaningless sensory information now takes shape as a horse and rider.

How do we see objects and shapes? Psychologists assume that perception begins with some real-world object with real-world properties "out there." Psychologists call that object, along with its important perceptual properties, the *distal stimulus*. We never experience the distal stimulus directly. Energy from it (or in the case of our chemical senses, molecules from it) must activate our sensory system. We call the information that reaches our sensory receptors the *proximal* stimulus. Remarkably, although the distal stimulus and

perception The brain's interpretation of sensory information so as to give it meaning.

the proximal stimulus are never the same thing, our perception of the distal stimulus is usually very accurate.

However, sometimes you perceive things that could not possibly exist. The trident shown in **Figure 3–24** exemplifies such an "impossible" figure. On closer inspection, you discover that the object that you "recognized" is not really there. In all these cases, the brain actively creates and organizes perceptual experiences out of raw sensory data—sometimes even from data we are not aware of receiving. We now explore how perceptual processes organize sensory experience.

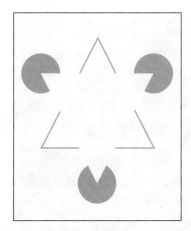

FIGURE 3–22

An illusory triangle.

When sensory information is incomplete, we tend to create a complete perception by supplying the missing details. In this figure we fill in the lines that let us perceive a white triangle in the center of the pattern.

FIGURE 3–23

Perceiving a pattern.

Knowing beforehand that the black blotches in this figure represent a person riding a horse changes our perception of it.

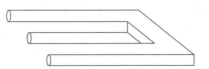

FIGURE 3–24

An optical illusion.

In the case of the trident, we go beyond what is sensed (blue lines on flat white paper) to perceive a three-dimensional object that isn't really there.

It's not what it looks like.

Source: © *The New Yorker Collection,* 2000, John O'Brien from *cartoonbank.com.* All Rights Reserved.

Simulate the **Experiment**
Distinguishing Figure-Ground Relationships on **MyPsychLab**

Perceptual Organization

How do we organize our perceptual experiences?

As we saw in Chapter 1 "The Science of Psychology," early in the 20th century a group of German psychologists, calling themselves *Gestalt psychologists,* set out to discover the principles through which we interpret sensory information. They demonstrated many of the ways in which the brain creates a coherent perceptual experience that is more than simply the sum of the available sensory information and that it does so in predictable ways.

In one important facet of the perceptual process, we distinguish *figures* from the *ground* against which they appear. A colorfully upholstered chair stands out from the bare walls of a room. We can distinguish a violin solo against the ground of a symphony orchestra or a single voice amid cocktail-party chatter. Sometimes, however, there are not enough cues in a pattern to permit us to easily distinguish a figure from its ground. **Figure 3–25** illustrates this problem. This is the principle behind camouflage: to make a figure blend into its background.

Sometimes a figure with clear contours can be perceived in two very different ways because it is unclear which part of the stimulus is the figure and which is the ground. (See **Figures 3–26** and **3–27.**) At first glance, you perceive figures against a specific background, but as you stare at the illustrations, you will discover that the figures and the ground reverse, making for two very different perceptions of the same illustration. The artwork or stimulus hasn't changed, but your perception has changed.

Figure 3–28 demonstrates some other important principles of perceptual organization. As all these figures demonstrate, in its search for meaning, our brain tries to fill in missing information, to see whole objects and to hear meaningful sounds, rather than just random bits and pieces of raw, sensory data.

FIGURE 3–25

Random dots or something more?

This photo does not give us enough cues to allow us to easily distinguish the figure of the Dalmatian dog from the ground behind it.

FIGURE 3-27
Figure–ground relationship …
How do you perceive this figure?

Do you see a goblet or the silhouettes of a man and a woman? Both interpretations are possible, but not at the same time. Reversible figures like this work because it is unclear which part of the stimulus is the figure and which is the neutral ground against which the figure is perceived.

FIGURE 3-26
The reversible figure and ground in this M. C. Escher woodcut cause us first to see black devils and then to see white angels in each of the rings.

Source: M. C. Escher's "Circle Limit IV" © 2003, Cordon Art B. V. Baarn, Holland. All rights reserved.

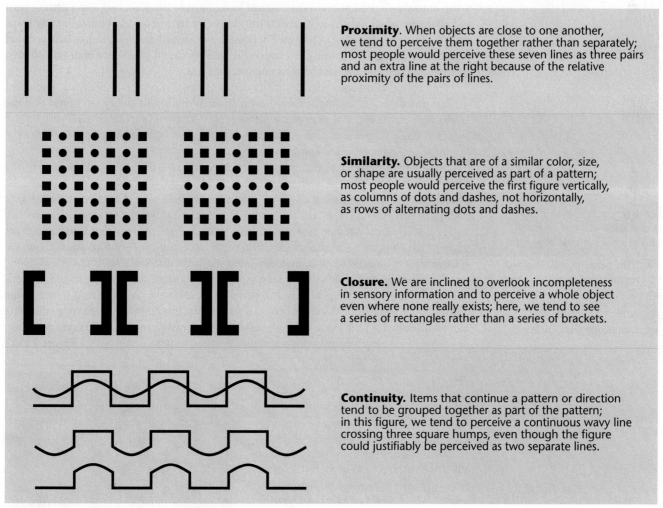

Proximity. When objects are close to one another, we tend to perceive them together rather than separately; most people would perceive these seven lines as three pairs and an extra line at the right because of the relative proximity of the pairs of lines.

Similarity. Objects that are of a similar color, size, or shape are usually perceived as part of a pattern; most people would perceive the first figure vertically, as columns of dots and dashes, not horizontally, as rows of alternating dots and dashes.

Closure. We are inclined to overlook incompleteness in sensory information and to perceive a whole object even where none really exists; here, we tend to see a series of rectangles rather than a series of brackets.

Continuity. Items that continue a pattern or direction tend to be grouped together as part of the pattern; in this figure, we tend to perceive a continuous wavy line crossing three square humps, even though the figure could justifiably be perceived as two separate lines.

FIGURE 3-28
Gestalt principles of perceptual organization.

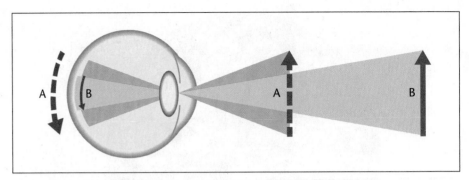

FIGURE 3–29

The relationship between distance and the size of the retinal image.

Object A and object B are the same size, but A, being much closer to the eye, casts a much larger image on the retina.

Perceptual Constancies

How do we perceive things as unchanging despite changing sensory information?

When anthropologist Colin Turnbull (1961) studied the Mbuti pygmies of Zaire, most of them had never left the dense Ituri rain forest and had rarely encountered objects that were more than a few feet away. On one occasion, Turnbull took a pygmy guide named Kenge on a trip onto the African plains. When Kenge looked across the plain and saw a distant herd of buffalo, he asked what kind of insects they were. He refused to believe that the tiny black spots he saw were buffalo. As he and Turnbull drove toward the herd, Kenge believed that magic was making the animals grow larger. Because he had no experience of distant objects, he could not perceive the buffalo as having constant size.

Perceptual constancy refers to the tendency to perceive objects as relatively stable and unchanging despite changing sensory information. Without this ability, we would find the world very confusing. For example, a house looks like the same house day or night and from any angle. The sensory information changes as illumination and perspective change, but the object is perceived as constant.

We tend to perceive familiar objects at their true size regardless of the size of the image that they cast on the retina. As **Figure 3–29** shows, the farther away an object is, the smaller the retinal image it casts. We might guess that a woman some distance away is 5 feet 4 inches tall when she is really 5 feet 8 inches, but hardly anyone would perceive her as being 3 feet tall, no matter how far away she is. We know from experience that adults are seldom that short. **Size constancy** depends partly on experience—information about the relative sizes of objects stored in memory—and partly on distance cues.

Familiar objects also tend to be seen as having a constant shape, even though the retinal images they cast change as they are viewed from different angles. This is called **shape constancy.** A rectangular door will project a rectangular image on the retina only when it is viewed directly from the front. From any other angle, it casts a trapezoidal image on the retina, but it is not perceived as having suddenly become a trapezoidal door. (See **Figure 3–30**.)

perceptual constancy A tendency to perceive objects as stable and unchanging despite changes in sensory stimulation.

size constancy The perception of an object as the same size regardless of the distance from which it is viewed.

shape constancy A tendency to see an object as the same shape no matter what angle it is viewed from.

FIGURE 3–30

Examples of shape constancy.

Even though the image of the door on the retina changes greatly as the door opens, we still perceive the door as being rectangular.

Similarly, we tend to perceive familiar objects as keeping their colors, regardless of information that reaches the eye. If you own a red automobile, you will see it as red whether it is on a brightly lit street or in a dark garage. But **color constancy** does not always hold true. When objects are unfamiliar or there are no customary color cues to guide us, color constancy may be distorted—as when you buy a sweater in a brightly lit store, only to discover that in ordinary daylight, it is not the shade you thought it was.

Brightness constancy means that even though the amount of light available to our eyes varies greatly over the course of a day, the perceived brightness of familiar objects hardly varies at all. We perceive a sheet of white paper as brighter than a piece of coal whether we see these objects in candlelight or under bright sunlight. Brightness constancy occurs because an object reflects the same percentage of the light falling on it whether that light is from a candle or the sun. Rather than basing our judgment of brightness on the absolute amount of light that the object reflects, we assess how the relative reflection compares with the surrounding objects.

Memory and experience play important roles in perceptual constancies. Look at **Figure 3–31.** If you see former President Clinton and Vice President Gore, look again! Clinton's face has been superimposed over Gore's. Because we focus on the perceptual cues of head shape, hair style, and context (the microphones and the president are standing in front of the vice president, as protocol requires), we perceive the more likely image of the president and vice president standing together.

FIGURE 3–31
Look again!
Context, hair style, and head shape lead us to believe that this is a picture of former President Clinton and former Vice President Gore when, in reality, Clinton's face is superimposed over the face of Gore.

color constancy An inclination to perceive familiar objects as retaining their color despite changes in sensory information.

brightness constancy The perception of brightness as the same, even though the amount of light reaching the retina changes.

monocular cues Visual cues requiring the use of one eye.

binocular cues Visual cues requiring the use of both eyes.

interposition Monocular distance cue in which one object, by partly blocking a second object, is perceived as being closer.

linear perspective Monocular cue to distance and depth based on the fact that two parallel lines seem to come together at the horizon.

aerial perspective Monocular cue to distance and depth based on the fact that more distant objects are likely to appear hazy and blurred.

elevation Monocular cue to distance and depth based on the fact that the higher on the horizontal plane an object is, the farther away it appears.

Perception of Distance and Depth

How do we know how far away something is?

We are constantly judging the distance between ourselves and other objects. When we walk through a classroom, our perception of distance helps us to avoid bumping into desks or tripping over the wastebasket. We also assess the depth of objects—how much total space they occupy. We use many cues to determine the distance and the depth of objects. Some of these cues depend on visual messages that one eye alone can transmit; these are called **monocular cues.** Others, known as **binocular cues,** require the use of both eyes. Having two eyes allows us to make more accurate judgments about distance and depth, particularly when objects are relatively close. But monocular cues alone are often sufficient to allow us to judge distance and depth quite accurately, as we'll see in the next section.

Monocular Cues One important monocular distance cue that provides us with information about relative position is called interposition. **Interposition** occurs when one object partly blocks a second object. The first object is perceived as being closer, the second as more distant. (See **Figure 3–32.**)

As art students learn, there are several ways in which perspective can help in estimating distance and depth. In **linear perspective,** two parallel lines that extend into the distance seem to come together at some point on the horizon. In **aerial perspective,** distant objects have a hazy appearance and a somewhat blurred outline. On a clear day, mountains often seem to be much closer than on a hazy day, when their outlines become blurred. The **elevation** of an object also serves as a perspective cue to depth: An object that is on a higher horizontal plane seems to be farther away than one on a lower plane. (See **Figure 3–33.**)

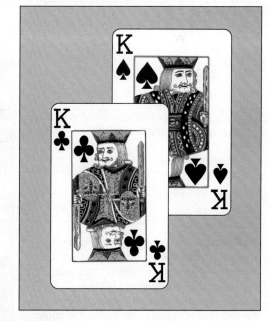

FIGURE 3–32
Interposition.
Because the King of Clubs appears to have been superimposed on the King of Spades, we perceive it to be closer to us.

FIGURE 3-33
Elevation as a visual cue.
Because of the higher elevation and the suggestion of depth provided by the road, the tree on the right is perceived as being more distant and about the same size as the tree at lower left. Actually, it is appreciably smaller, as you can see if you measure the heights of the two drawings.

texture gradient Monocular cue to distance and depth based on the fact that objects seen at greater distances appear to be smoother and less textured.

shadowing Monocular cue to distance and depth based on the fact that shadows often appear on the parts of objects that are more distant.

Another useful monocular cue to distance and depth is **texture gradient**. An object that is close seems to have a rough or detailed texture. As distance increases, the texture becomes finer, until finally the original texture cannot be distinguished clearly, if at all. For example, when standing on a pebbly beach, you can distinguish among the gray stones and the gravel in front of your feet. However, as you look down the beach, you cannot make out individual stones at all. (See **Figure 3–35.**) **Shadowing**, another important cue to the distance, depth, and solidity of an object, is illustrated in **Figure 3–34.**

Bus or train passengers often notice that nearby trees or telephone poles seem to flash past the windows, whereas buildings and other objects farther away seem to move slowly. These differences in the speeds of movement of images across the retina as you move give an important cue to distance and depth. You can observe the same effect if you stand still and move your head from side to side as you focus your gaze on something in the middle distance: Objects close to you seem to move in the direction opposite to the direction in which your head is moving, whereas objects far away seem to move in the same direction as your head. This distance cue is known as **motion parallax.**

Binocular Cues All the visual cues examined so far depend on the action of only one eye. Many animals—such as horses, deer, and fish—rely entirely on monocular cues. Although they have two eyes, the two visual fields do not overlap, because their eyes are located on the sides of the head rather than in front. Humans, apes, and many predatory animals—such as lions and wolves—have a distinct physical advantage. Since both eyes are set in the front of the

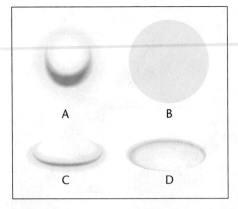

FIGURE 3-34
Shadowing.
Shadowing on the outer edges of a spherical object, such as a ball or globe, gives it a three-dimensional quality (A). Without shadowing (B), it might be perceived as a flat disk. Shadowing can also affect our perception of the direction of depth. In the absence of other cues, we tend to assume overhead lighting, so image C appears to be a bump because its top edge is lit, whereas image D appears to be a dent. If you turn the book upside down, the direction of depth is reversed.

FIGURE 3-35
Texture gradient.
Note how the nearby stones on this beach appear larger and clearer than the distant ones.

head, the visual fields overlap. The **stereoscopic vision** derived from combining the two retinal images—one from each eye—makes the perception of depth and distance more accurate.

Because our eyes are set approximately 2½ inches apart, each one has a slightly different view of things. The difference between the two images is known as **retinal disparity.** The left eye receives more information about the left side of an object, and the right eye receives more information about the right side. Here's how to test this: Close one eye and line up a finger with some vertical line, like the edge of a door. Then open that eye and close the other one. Your finger will appear to have moved. When you look at the finger with both eyes, however, the two different images become one.

An important binocular cue to distance comes from the muscles that control the **convergence** of the eyes. When we look at objects that are fairly close to us, our eyes tend to converge—to turn slightly inward toward each other. The sensations from the muscles that control the movement of the eyes thus provide a cue to distance. If the object is very close, such as at the end of the nose, the eyes cannot converge, and two separate images are perceived. If the object is more than a few yards (meters) away, the sight lines of the eyes are more or less parallel, and there is no convergence.

Location of Sounds Just as we use monocular and binocular cues to establish visual depth and distance, we draw on **monaural** (single-ear) and **binaural** (two-ear) **cues** to locate the source of sounds. (See **Figure 3–36.**) In one monaural cue, loud sounds are perceived as closer than faint sounds, with changes in loudness translating into changes in distance. Binaural cues work on the principle that because sounds off to one side of the head reach one ear slightly ahead of the other, the time difference between sound waves reaching the two ears helps us make accurate judgments about location.

In a second binaural cue, sound signals arriving from a source off to one side of you are slightly louder in the nearer ear than in the ear farther from the source. The slight difference occurs because your head, in effect, blocks the sound, reducing the intensity of sound in the opposite ear. This relative loudness difference between signals heard separately by the two ears is enough for the brain to locate the sound source and to judge its distance.

Most of us rely so heavily on visual cues that we seldom pay much attention to the rich array of auditory information available around us. But people who have been blind since birth often compensate for their lack of vision by sharpening their awareness of sounds. As a result tvhey can figure out where obstacles lie in their paths by listening to the echoes from a cane and their own voices. In fact, many blind people can judge the size and distance of one object in relation to another by using nothing more than sound cues. This increased sensitivity to sound is less among people who became blind when they were small children and it is often lacking in people who became blind after the age of 10 (Gougoux et al., 2004; Gougoux, Zatorre, Lassonde, Voss, & Lepore, 2005).

Perception of Movement

How do we perceive movement?

The perception of movement is a complicated process involving both visual information from the retina and messages from the muscles around the eyes as they follow an object. On occasion, our perceptual processes play tricks on us, and we think we perceive movement when the objects that we are looking at are in fact stationary. We must distinguish, therefore, between real and apparent movement.

Real movement refers to the physical displacement of an object from one position to another. The perception of real movement depends only in part on movement of images across the retina of the eye. If you stand still and move your head to look around you, the images of all the objects in the room will pass across your retina. But messages from the eye muscles counteract the changing information from the retina, so the objects in the room will be perceived as motionless.

The perception of real movement is determined by how the position of objects changes in relation to a background that is perceived as stationary. When we perceive a car moving along a street, for example, we see the street, the buildings, and the sidewalk as a stationary background and the car as a moving object.

motion parallax Monocular distance cue in which objects closer than the point of visual focus seem to move in the direction opposite to the viewer's moving head, and objects beyond the focus point appear to move in the same direction as the viewer's head.

stereoscopic vision Combination of two retinal images to give a three-dimensional perceptual experience.

retinal disparity Binocular distance cue based on the difference between the images cast on the two retinas when both eyes are focused on the same object.

convergence A visual depth cue that comes from muscles controlling eye movement as the eyes turn inward to view a nearby stimulus.

monaural cues Cues to sound location that require just one ear.

binaural cues Cues to sound location that involve both ears working together.

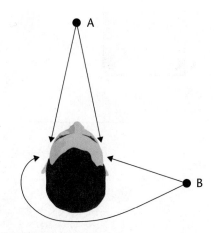

FIGURE 3–36
Cues used in sound localization.
Sound waves coming from source A will reach both ears simultaneously. Sound waves from source B reach the right ear first, where they are also louder. The head casts a "shadow" over the other ear, thus reducing the intensity of the delayed sound in that ear.

When we look at an electronic marquee such as this one, we see motion, even though the sign consists of stationary lights that are flashed on and off.

autokinetic illusion The perception that a stationary object is actually moving.

stroboscopic motion Apparent movement that results from flashing a series of still pictures in rapid succession, as in a motion picture.

phi phenomenon Apparent movement caused by flashing lights in sequence, as on theater marquees.

Apparent movement occurs when we perceive movement in objects that are actually standing still. One form of apparent movement is referred to as the **autokinetic illusion**—the perceived motion created by the absence of visual cues surrounding a single stationary object. If you stand in a room that is absolutely dark except for one tiny spot of light and stare at the light for a few seconds, you will begin to see the light drift. In the darkened room, your eyes have no visible framework; there are no cues telling you that the light is really stationary. The slight movements of the eye muscles, which go unnoticed most of the time, make the light appear to move.

Another form of apparent movement is **stroboscopic motion**—the apparent motion created by a rapid series of still images. This form of apparent movement is illustrated best by a motion picture, which is not in motion at all. The film consists of a series of still pictures showing people and objects in slightly different positions. When the separate images are projected sequentially onto a screen at a specific rate of speed, the people and objects seem to be moving because of the rapid change from one still picture to the next.

Another common perceptual illusion, known as the **phi phenomenon,** occurs as a result of stroboscopic motion. When a light is flashed on at a certain point in a darkened room, then flashed off, and a second light is flashed on a split second later at a point a short distance away, most people will perceive these two separate lights as a single spot of light moving from one point to another. This perceptual process causes us to see motion in neon signs, where words appear to move across the sign, from one side to the other, as the different combinations of stationary lights are flashed on and off.

Visual Illusions

What causes visual illusions?

Visual illusions graphically demonstrate the ways in which we use sensory cues to create perceptual experiences that may (or may not) correspond to what is out there in the real world. By understanding how we are fooled into "seeing" something that isn't there, psychologists can figure out how perceptual processes work in the everyday world and under normal circumstances.

Psychologists generally distinguish between physical and perceptual illusions. One example of a *physical illusion* is the bent appearance of a stick when it is placed in water—an illusion easily understood because the water acts like a prism, bending the light waves before they reach our eyes. *Perceptual illusions* occur because the stimulus contains misleading cues that give rise to inaccurate or impossible perceptions.

The illusions in **Figure 3–37** and **Figure 3–38** result from false and misleading depth cues. For example, in **Figure 3–38**C, both monsters cast the same size image on the retina in our eyes. But the depth cues in the tunnel suggest that we are looking at a three-dimensional scene and that therefore the top monster is much farther away. In the real world, this perception would mean that the top monster is actually much larger than the bottom monster. Therefore we "correct" for the distance and actually perceive the top monster as larger, despite other cues to the contrary. We know that the image is actually two dimensional, but we still respond to it as if it were three dimensional.

Artists rely on many of these perceptual phenomena both to represent reality accurately and to distort it deliberately. In paintings and sketches drawn on a two-dimensional surface, it is almost always necessary to distort objects for them to be perceived correctly by viewers. For example, in representational art, the railroad tracks, sidewalks, and tunnels are always drawn closer together in the distance. Thus, our understanding of perceptual illusion enables us to manipulate images for deliberate effect—and to delight in the results.

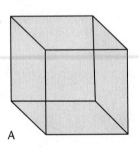

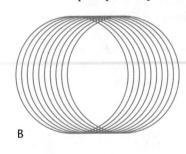

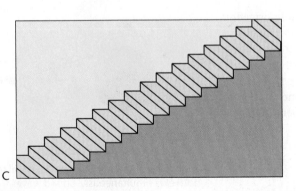

FIGURE 3–37
Reversible figures.

Images A, B, and C are examples of reversible figures—drawings that we can perceive two different ways, but not at the same time.

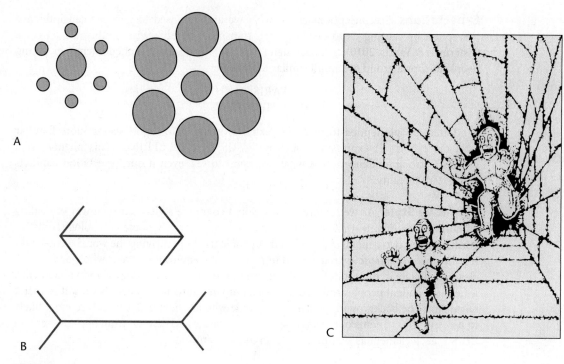

FIGURE 3–38
Misleading depth cues.
Images A, B, and C show how, through the use of misleading depth cues, we misjudge the size of objects. The middle circles in image A are exactly the same size, as are the lines in Image B and the monsters in Image C.

Observer Characteristics

What personal factors influence our perceptions?

ENDURING ISSUES

Diversity–Universality   How Does Ethnicity Influence Perception?

All normal human beings have the same sense organs and perceptual capacity. Yet our individuality—our motivations, values, expectations, cognitive style, and cultural preconceptions—influences what we perceive. We focus on individual differences in this section. But as you read, think about the degree to which people's sensory and perceptual experiences differ depending on their race, culture, or gender. ■

Motivation and Emotion Our desires and needs shape our perceptions. People in need are likely to perceive something that they think will satisfy that need (Balcetis & Dunning, 2007). The best known example of this, at least in fiction, is a *mirage:* People lost in the desert have visual fantasies of an oasis over the next dune. In real life most people have a fear of snakes. When shown an array of pictures, even very young children locate pictures of snakes more quickly than nonthreatening pictures (LoBue & DeLoache, 2008). Thus, people with strong emotions toward certain objects are likely to detect those objects more rapidly than other people do.

Values Values also affect perception. In one classical experiment, nursery school children were shown a poker chip. Each child was asked to compare the size of the chip with the size of an adjustable circle of light until the child said that the chip and the circle of light were the same size. The children were then brought to a machine that produced a poker chip that could be exchanged for candy. Thus, the children were taught to value the poker chips more highly than they had before. After the children had been rewarded with candy for the poker chips, they were again asked to compare the size of the chips with a circle of light. This time the chips seemed larger to the children (W. W. Lambert, Solomon, & Watson, 1949).

Expectations Preconceptions about what we are supposed to perceive can influence perception by causing us to delete, insert, transpose, or otherwise modify what we see (Esterman & Yantis, 2010). S. J. Lachman (1984) demonstrated this phenomenon by asking people to copy a group of stimuli similar to this one:

PARIS IN THE
THE SPRING

Often, people tended to omit the "extra" words and to report seeing more familiar (and more normal) expressions, such as PARIS IN THE SPRING. This phenomenon reflects a strong tendency to see what we *expect* to see, even if our expectation conflicts with external reality.

Cognitive Style As we mature, we develop a cognitive style—our own way of dealing with the environment—that also affects how we see the world. Some psychologists distinguish between two general approaches that people use in perceiving the world. People taking the *field-dependent approach* tend to perceive the environment as a whole and do not clearly delineate in their minds the shape, color, size, or other qualities of individual items. If field-dependent people are asked to draw a human figure, they generally draw it so that it blends into the background. By contrast, people who are *field independent* are more likely to perceive the elements of the environment as separate and distinct from one another and to draw each element as standing out from the background.

Experience and Culture Cultural background also influences people's perceptions. For example, Westerners' perceptions tend to focus on salient foreground objects, whereas Asians are more inclined to focus on contexts (Kitayama, Duffy, Kawamura, & Larsen, 2003; Miyamoto, Nisbett, & Masuda, 2006). Shown a scene of an elephant in the jungle: "An Asian would see a jungle that happened to have an elephant in it . . . . a Westerner would see the elephant and might notice the jungle." (Denise Park quoted in Binns, 2007, p. 9). There is increasing evidence that cultural differences in people's experiences can actually rewire the nervous system (Goh et al., 2007; Park & Huang, 2010).

Personality A number of researchers have shown that our individual personalities influence perception. For example, one study compared clinically depressed college students to students with eating disorders in terms of their ability to identify words related to depression and food (von Hippel, Hawkins, & Narayan, 1994). The students saw a series of words very quickly (for less than one-tenth of a second each). In general, students with an eating disorder were faster at identifying words that referred to foods that they commonly thought about than they were at identifying foods that they rarely thought about. Similarly, depressed students were faster at identifying adjectives describing personality traits that they commonly thought about (such as "timid") than adjectives that described traits that they rarely thought about (such as "extroverted").

ENDURING ISSUES

Person–Situation   Do Perceptual Experiences Reflect the Outside World?

After reading this chapter, have your ideas changed about the relative importance of processes that occur inside the individual (thoughts, emotions, motives, attitudes, values, personalities) as opposed to objects and events in the real world? If someone were to ask you whether perceptual experiences match more closely the image on the retina or the outside world, what would you say? What examples would you select from the chapter to make your point most effectively? ◾

CHECK YOUR UNDERSTANDING

Match the following principles of perception with the appropriate definitions.

1. ____ similarity
2. ____ continuity
3. ____ proximity
4. ____ closure

a. tendency to perceive a whole object even where none exists
b. elements that continue a pattern are likely to be seen as part of the pattern
c. objects that are like one another tending to be grouped together
d. elements found close together tending to be perceived as a unit

Answers: 1. c. 2. b. 3. d. 4. a.

APPLY YOUR UNDERSTANDING

1. You are seated at a small table talking to a friend opposite you who is drinking coffee. As she lifts the cup off the saucer and raises it to her mouth, the image made on your retina by the cup actually changes shape, but you still "see" it as being a cup. This is due to

   a. good continuation.
   b. motion parallax.
   c. perceptual constancy.
   d. the phi phenomenon.

2. As you study a painting, you notice that a pathway in the painting is made up of stones that become smaller and smaller as you look "down the lane." The artist has used which one of the following distance cues to create the impression of depth?

   a. interposition
   b. texture gradient
   c. elevation
   d. shadowing

Answers: 1. c. 2. b.

KEY TERMS

The Nature of Sensation
sensation, p. 81
receptor cell, p. 81
transduction, p. 81
absolute threshold, p. 82
adaptation, p. 82
difference threshold or just-noticeable difference (jnd), p. 82
Weber's law, p. 82

Vision
cornea, p. 85
pupil, p. 85
iris, p. 85
lens, p. 85
retina, p. 85
fovea, p. 85
wavelengths, p. 86
rods, p. 86
cones, p. 86
bipolar cells, p. 86
visual acuity, p. 87
dark adaptation, p. 87

light adaptation, p. 88
afterimage, p. 88
ganglion cells, p. 88
optic nerve, p. 88
blind spot, p. 88
optic chiasm, p. 88
feature detectors, p. 89
hues, p. 89
saturation, p. 89
brightness, p. 89
additive color mixing, p. 90
subtractive color mixing, p. 91
trichromatic theory (or three-color) theory, p. 91
opponent-process theory, p. 91

Hearing
sound, p. 93
sound waves, p. 93
frequency, p. 93
hertz (Hz), p. 93
pitch, p. 94
amplitude, p. 94
decibel, p. 94

overtones, p. 95
timbre, p. 95
oval window, p. 96
cochlea, p. 96
basilar membrane, p. 96
organ of Corti, p. 96
auditory nerve, p. 96
place theory, p. 96
frequency theory, p. 96
volley principle, p. 96

The Other Senses
olfactory bulb, p. 98
pheromones, p. 99
taste buds, p. 100
kinesthetic senses, p. 100
vestibular senses, p. 101
gate-control theory, p. 102
biopsychosocial theory, p. 103
placebo effect, p. 103

Perception
perception, p. 104
perceptual constancy, p. 108

size constancy, p. 108
shape constancy, p. 108
color constancy, p. 108
brightness constancy, p. 108
monocular cues, p. 109
binocular cues, p. 109
interposition, p. 109
linear perspective, p. 109
aerial perspective, p. 109
elevation, p. 109
texture gradient, p. 109
shadowing, p. 109
motion parallax, p. 110
stereoscopic vision, p. 111
retinal disparity, p. 111
convergence, p. 111
monaural cues, p. 111
binaural cues, p. 111
autokinetic illusion, p. 112
stroboscopic motion, p. 112
phi phenomenon, p. 112

CHAPTER REVIEW   ((•[Listen to the **Chapter Audio** on **MyPsychLab**

THE NATURE OF SENSATION

What causes sensory experiences? Humans have sensory experiences of sight, hearing, smell, taste, touch, pain, and balance, which are known as **sensations.** These experiences begin when the body's sensory receptors are stimulated. In each case, some form of physical energy is converted into neural impulses that are carried to the brain.

How is energy, such as light or sound, converted into a message to the brain? The process of sending a sensory message to the brain begins when energy stimulates **receptor cells** in one of the sense organs. Through the process of **transduction,** receptor cells convert the stimulation into coded signals that vary according to the characteristics of the stimulus. Further coding occurs as the signal passes along sensory nerve fibers, so that the message finally reaching the brain is very detailed and precise.

What are the limits on our ability to sense stimuli in our environment? The amount of physical energy that reaches sensory receptors must be of a minimal intensity to produce a detectable sensation. The least amount of energy needed to produce a sensation 50% of the time is called the **absolute threshold.** For hearing, the absolute threshold is roughly the tick of a watch from 6 m (20 feet) away in a very quiet room, and for vision, it is a candle flame seen from 50 km (30 miles) on a clear, dark night. Absolute thresholds vary according to the intensity of the stimulus present at any given time—a process called **adaptation.** Also, we are very sensitive to *changes* in the stimulus intensity. The **difference threshold** or the **just-noticeable difference (jnd)** is the smallest change in stimulation that can be detected 50% of the time.

Under what circumstances might messages outside our awareness affect our behavior? When people respond to sensory messages that are below their threshold level of awareness, they are said to be responding subliminally. Such subliminal processing can occur in controlled laboratory settings, but there is no scientific evidence that subliminal messages have any effect in everyday life.

VISION

Why have psychologists studied vision more than any other sense? Different animal species depend more on some senses than others. In bats and dogs, hearing and sense of smell, respectively, are particularly important. In humans, vision is paramount, which is why it has received the most research attention.

How does light create a neural impulse? Light enters an eye through the **cornea** (a transparent protective coating) and passes through the **pupil** (the opening in the **iris**) as well as through the **lens,** which focuses it onto the eye's light-sensitive inner lining called the **retina.** Neural impulses are generated in the retina by receptor cells known as **rods** and **cones.** The rods and cones connect to nerve cells called **bipolar cells,** which in turn connect to **ganglion cells.** The axons of ganglion cells converge to form the **optic nerve,** which carries to the brain the neural impulses triggered in the retina. **Light** and **dark adaptation** occur as the sensitivity of rods and cones changes with the availability of light.

How do we see color? The **trichromatic theory** of color vision is based on the principles of **additive color mixing.** It holds that the eyes contain three different kinds of color receptors, one of which is most responsive to red, another to green, and another to blue. By combining signals from these three types of receptors, the brain can detect a wide range of shades. In contrast, the **opponent-process theory** of color vision maintains that receptors in the eyes are specialized to respond to one member of three basic color pairs: red–green, yellow–blue, and black–white (or light–dark). Research gives some support for both these theories. There are indeed three kinds of color receptors in the retinas, but the messages they initiate are coded by other neurons into opponent-process form. **Hue, saturation,** and **brightness** are properties of color vision.

HEARING

If a tree falls in the forest and no one is there, does the tree make a sound? Our ability to hear **sound** is important as it permits us to understand language and communicate with other people.

How do the characteristics of sound waves cause us to hear different sounds? The physical stimuli for the sense of hearing are **sound waves,** which produce vibration in the eardrums. **Frequency,** the number of cycles per second in a sound wave, is the primary determinant of **pitch** (how high or low the tones seems to be). The complex patterns of **overtones** which accompany real world sounds determine the **timbre** or texture of a sound. **Amplitude,** or loudness, refers to the magnitude of a sound wave, and is measured using a **decibel** scale.

What path does sound follow from the ear to the brain? When sound waves strike an eardrum and cause it to vibrate, three bones in the middle ear—the hammer, the anvil, and the stirrup—are stimulated to vibrate in sequence. These vibrations are magnified in their passage through the middle ear and into the inner ear beyond it. In the inner ear, movement of the **basilar membrane** stimulates sensory receptors in the **organ of Corti.** This stimulation of the hair cells produces auditory signals that travel to the brain through the **auditory nerve.**

How do we distinguish low-frequency and high-frequency sounds? The **place theory** holds that the brain distinguishes low-frequency sounds from high-frequency sounds by noting the place on the basilar membrane at which the greatest stimulation is occurring. For high-frequency sounds, this is the base of the basilar membrane; for low-frequency sounds, it is the membrane's opposite end. According to the **frequency theory** of pitch discrimination, the frequency of vibrations on the basilar membrane as a whole is translated into an equivalent frequency of nerve impulses that travel to the brain. This theory, with its associated **volley principle,** can account for pitch detection up to frequencies of about 4000 Hz. Above that, the place theory seems to provide a better explanation.

THE OTHER SENSES

What are the chemical senses? Two senses—smell and taste—are designed to detect the presence of various chemical substances in the air and in food.

What activates the sense of smell? Substances carried by airborne molecules into the nasal cavities activate highly specialized receptors for smell. From here, messages are carried directly to the **olfactory bulb** in the brain, where they are sent to the brain's temporal lobe, resulting in our awareness of smell. **Pheromones** are chemicals produced by organisms to communicate using their sense of smell.

How do we detect the basic tastes? Flavor is a complex blend of taste and smell. There are five basic ones—sweet, sour, salty, bitter, and umami—and other tastes derive from combinations of these. The five receptors for taste are housed in the **taste buds** on the tongue. When these receptors are activated by the chemical substances in food, their adjacent neurons fire, sending nerve impulses to the brain.

How do we know which way is up and whether we are moving or standing still? The **vestibular senses** provide information about our orientation or position in space, such as whether we are right side up or upside down. The receptors for these senses are in two vestibular organs in the inner ear—the semicircular canals and the vestibular sacs. The vestibular organs are responsible for motion sickness. This queasy feeling may be triggered by discrepancies between visual information and vestibular sensations. The kinesthetic senses provide information about the speed and direction of our movements. They rely on feedback from specialized receptors, which are attached to muscle fibers and the tendons that connect muscle to bone.

What types of sensory messages are sent from the skin to the brain? The skin is the largest sense organ, and sensations that arise from the receptors embedded in it produce our sensation of touch, which includes pressure, temperature, and pain. Research has not yet established a simple, direct connection between these three sensations and the various types of skin receptors whose nerve fibers lead to the brain.

What differences among people have an effect on the degree of pain they experience? People have varying degrees of sensitivity to pain based on their physiological makeup, their current mental and emotional state, their expectations, and their cultural beliefs and values. One commonly accepted explanation of pain is the **gate-control theory,** which holds that a "neurological gate" in the spinal cord controls the transmission of pain messages to the brain. **Biopsychosocial theory** proposes that pain results from the interaction of biological, psychological, and social mechanisms. As pain reducers, placebos and acupuncture work in part through the release of pain-blocking neurotransmitters called endorphins.

PERCEPTION

How is perception different from sensation? Sensation refers to the raw sensory data that the brain receives from the senses of sight, hearing, smell, taste, balance, touch, and pain. **Perception,** which takes place in the brain, is the process of organizing, interpreting, and giving meaning to those data.

How do we organize our perceptual experiences? Twentieth-century Gestalt psychologists believed that the brain creates a coherent perceptual experience that is more than simply the sum of the available sensory data. The brain imposes order on the data it receives partly by distinguishing patterns such as figure and ground, proximity, similarity, closure, and continuity.

How do we perceive things as unchanging despite changing sensory information? **Perceptual constancy** is our tendency to perceive objects as unchanging even given many changes in sensory stimulation. Once we have formed a stable perception of something, we see it as essentially the same regardless of differences in viewing angle, distance, lighting, and so forth. These **size, shape, brightness,** and **color constancies** help us better to understand and relate to the world.

How do we know how far away something is? We perceive distance and depth through both **monocular cues** (received even by one eye alone) and **binocular cues** (requiring the interaction of both eyes). Examples of monocular cues are **interposition** (in which one object partly covers another), **linear perspective, elevation** (or closeness of something to the horizon), **texture gradient** (from coarser to finer depending on distance), **shadowing,** and **motion parallax** (differences in the relative movement of close and distant objects as we change position). An important binocular cue is **stereoscopic vision,** which is derived from combining our two retinal images to produce a 3-D effect. Two other binocular cues are **retinal disparity** (the difference between the two separate images received by the eyes) and **convergence** of the eyes as viewing distance decreases. Just as we use monocular and binocular cues to sense depth and distance, we use **monaural** (one-ear) and **binaural** (two-ear) cues to locate the source of sounds.

How do we perceive movement? Perception of movement is a complicated process involving both visual messages from the retina and messages from the muscles around the eyes as they shift to follow a moving object. At times our perceptual processes trick us into believing that an object is moving when in fact it is not. There is a difference, then, between real movement and apparent movement. Examples of apparent movement are the **autokinetic illusion** (caused by the absence of visual cues surrounding a stationary object), **stroboscopic motion** (produced by rapidly flashing a series of pictures), and the **phi phenomenon** (produced by a pattern of flashing lights).

What causes visual illusions? Visual illusions occur when we use a variety of sensory cues to create perceptual experiences that do not actually exist. Some are *physical illusions,* such as the bent appearance of a stick in water. Others are *perceptual illusions,* which occur because a stimulus contains misleading cues that lead to inaccurate perceptions.

What personal factors influence our perceptions? In addition to past experience and learning, our perceptions are also influenced by our motivation, values, expectations, cognitive style, experience and culture, and personality. So far, we have talked about the general characteristics of sensation; however, each of the body's sensory systems works a little differently. We now turn to the unique features of each of the major sensory systems.

4

States of Consciousness

OVERVIEW

As a student, you probably know what extreme fatigue is like. When studying for final exams far into the night, a dusty cloud seems to gradually envelop your brain. Awareness dulls as you struggle to keep your focus, gluing your eyes to words on the page that begin to blur together. Now transfer this same state of fatigue to the wards of a large hospital, where resident doctors in training are sometimes expected to work shifts lasting as long as 36 nonstop hours. One physician, looking back on his days as a resident, recalls how he once assisted a team of neurosurgeons in a complicated operation after working 30 consecutive hours. His mind was bleary and unfocused as he stood behind the performing surgeon, dutifully holding the retractors as the minutes ticked monotonously by. A mental fuzziness slowly descended; and then his state of utter exhaustion slipped quietly into slumber. The next moment he was asleep on the surgeon's shoulder, snoring softly in his ear.

Extreme fatigue is just one of many states of consciousness. Psychologists define **consciousness** as a person's awareness of and responsiveness to mental processes and the environment. Normal **waking consciousness** includes such things as concentrating, making decisions, planning, solving problems, and remembering—all the different thoughts, feelings, and perceptions that occupy the mind when we are awake and reasonably alert. The hallmark of normal waking consciousness is the highly selective nature of attention. Even when we are fully awake and alert, we are usually conscious of only a small portion of what is going on around us. To make sense of our environment, we must select only the most important information to attend to and then filter out everything else. At times we pay such close attention to what we are doing that we are oblivious to what is going on around us. How the process of attention works is examined at some length in Chapter 6, "Memory."

Other forms of consciousness, to varying degrees, are more detached from the external world. These are known as **altered states of consciousness.** Some—such as sleep—occur spontaneously during the course of a day. Others are intentionally induced. When you drink a cup of coffee, take a Ritalin, or calm your mind through yoga, you are purposely undertaking to change your state of consciousness.

Normal waking consciousness is the subject of other chapters in this book (especially Chapters 3, 6, 7, and 8). In this chapter we focus on altered states of consciousness, beginning with sleep and dreaming. We then turn to drug-altered consciousness, meditation, and hypnosis.

ENDURING ISSUES in States of Consciousness

In this chapter, you will quickly recognize several of the "Enduring Issues" that were introduced in Chapter 1. The mind–body relation is central to this entire chapter since we will be exploring the ways in which psychological states can affect biological processes and, conversely, the ways in which biological changes can profoundly affect psychological experiences. In addition, we will discover that there are significant differences among people in their susceptibility to various altered states of consciousness (*Diversity–Universality*) and that the settings in which consciousness-altering substances are taken can greatly alter their effects (*Person–Situation*).

SLEEP

Why do we need to sleep?

Human beings spend about one-third of their lives in the altered state of consciousness known as sleep: a natural state of rest characterized by a reduction in voluntary body movement and decreased awareness of the surroundings. No one who has tried to stay awake longer than 20 hours at a time could doubt the necessity of sleep. When people are deprived of sleep, they crave sleep just as strongly as they would food or water after a period of deprivation. Merely resting doesn't satisfy us.

All birds and mammals sleep; frogs, fish, and even insects go into "rest states" similar to sleep. Indeed, Drosophila fruit flies, a favorite subject for genetic studies because they reproduce rapidly, are remarkably like us: They are active during the day and somnolent at night; when deprived of sleep, they need long naps to recover. Caffeine keeps them awake, whereas antihistamines make them drowsy (Hendricks & Sehgal, 2004; Wu, Ho, Crocker, Yue, Koh, & Sehgal, 2009). How long organisms sleep, where, in what positions and the consequences of sleep deprivation vary from species to species (J. M. Siegel, 2008).

Nobody knows exactly why we need to sleep, although evidence has begun to accumulate that sleep plays an important restorative function, both physically and mentally.

consciousness Our awareness of various cognitive processes, such as sleeping, dreaming, concentrating, and making decisions.

waking consciousness Mental state that encompasses the thoughts, feelings, and perceptions that occur when we are awake and reasonably alert.

altered states of consciousness Mental states that differ noticeably from normal waking consciousness.

Sleep researchers monitor volunteers' brain waves, muscle tension, and other physiological changes during sleep.

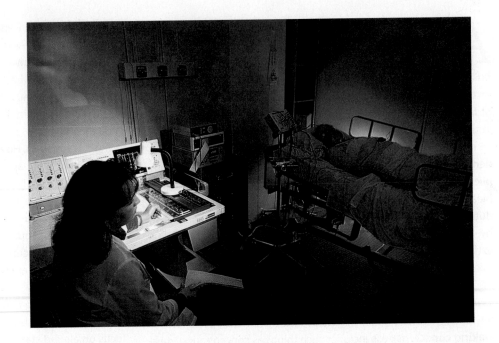

For instance, recent research has shown that getting adequate sleep boosts our immune response, making us less susceptible to disease (Faraut et al., 2010). Sleep also cleanses the body of chemicals released when cells use energy to do their jobs (Tobin, 2007). One of those chemicals is adenosine, which builds up during the day and eventually signals the brain that is time to sleep (Thakkar, Winston, & McCarley, 2003). Caffeine works by temporarily blocking adenosine receptors in the brain. Sleep also contributes to cognitive functioning. For example, when people are presented with complex problems and are permitted to sleep prior to solving them, they are more likely to generate insightful solutions than if they are kept from sleeping (Wagner, Gais, Haider, Verleger, & Born, 2004). This latter finding supports the idea that creativity, decision-making and problem-solving skills may be enhanced by getting adequate sleep (Leitzell, 2008). Sleep is also crucial to the formation of long-term memories (Rasch & Born, 2008; Tamminen, Payne, Stickgold, Wamsley, & Gaskell, 2010), perhaps by enhancing neural plasticity and increasing the formation of new neural networks (see Chapter 2, "The Biological Basis of Behavior") (Cohen, Freitas, Tormos, Oberman, Eldaief, & Pascual-Leone, 2010).

Circadian Cycles: The Biological Clock

What is the biological clock?

Like many other biological functions, sleep and waking follow a daily, or circadian, cycle (from the Latin expression *circa diem,* meaning "about a day"). **Circadian rhythms** are a fundamental adaptation to the 24-hour solar cycle of light and dark, found not only in humans and other animals, but also in plants and even one-celled organisms. The human *biological clock* is largely governed by a tiny cluster of neurons just above the optic chiasm in the lower region of the hypothalamus (see Figures 2–7 and 3–9) known as the **suprachiasmatic nucleus (SCN)** (R. Y. Moore, 2007). The SCN receives information about the daily light and dark cycles via a direct pathway from the retina of the eye (Pobojewski, 2007). In response to the light and dark cycles detected by the eye, the SCN releases specific neurotransmitters that control our body's temperature, metabolism, blood pressure, hormone levels, and hunger, which vary predictably through the course of the day. For example, the level of the hormone epinephrine (which causes the body to go on alert) reaches a peak in the late morning hours and then steadily declines until around midnight, when it suddenly drops to a very low level and remains there until morning. By contrast, levels of melatonin (which promotes sleep) surge at night and drop off during the day.

circadian rhythm A regular biological rhythm with a period of approximately 24 hours.

suprachiasmatic nucleus (SCN) A cluster of neurons in the hypothalamus that receives input from the retina regarding light and dark cycles and is involved in regulating the biological clock.

Working late at night runs counter to the body's natural circadian rhythm. The result is that tens of millions of night workers around the world find themselves trying to work while feeling sleepy and having difficulty paying attention (Price, 2011). This is an especially critical problem among workers whose jobs require that they remain alert and able to make split-second decisions. For example, in the spring of 2011 a number of air traffic controllers were found late at night to be asleep on the job. In one case, several large jets had to land at Reagan National Airport in Washington without any assistance from the control tower whose operator was fast asleep.

Travel, especially across many time zones, can disrupt people's circadian rhythms, leaving them groggy and tired—a feeling known as jet lag.

The Rhythms of Sleep

What physical changes mark the rhythms of sleep?

"Going to sleep" means losing awareness and failing to respond to a stimulus that would produce a response in the waking state. As measured by an EEG, brain waves during this "twilight" state are characterized by irregular, low-voltage alpha waves. This brain-wave pattern mirrors the sense of relaxed wakefulness that we experience while lying on a beach or resting after a big meal.

After this initial twilight phase, the sleeper enters *Stage 1* of sleep. Stage-1 brain waves are tight and of very low amplitude (height), resembling those recorded when a person is alert or excited (see **Figure 4–1**). But, in contrast to normal waking consciousness, Stage 1 of the sleep cycle is marked by a slowing of the pulse, muscle relaxation, and side-to-side rolling movements of the eyes—the last being the most reliable indication of this first stage of sleep. Stage 1 usually lasts only a few moments. The sleeper is easily aroused at this stage and, once awake, may be unaware of having slept at all.

Stages 2 and *3* are characterized by progressively deeper sleep. During Stage 2, short rhythmic bursts of brain-wave activity called *sleep spindles* periodically appear. In Stage 3, *delta waves*—slow waves with very high peaks—begin to emerge. During these stages, the sleeper is hard to awaken and does not respond to stimuli such as noises or lights. Heart rate, blood pressure, and temperature continue to drop.

In *Stage 4* sleep, the brain emits very slow delta waves. Heart rate, breathing rate, blood pressure, and body temperature are as low as they will get during the night. In young adults, delta sleep occurs in 15- to 20-minute segments—interspersed with lighter sleep—mostly during the first half of the night. Delta sleep time lessens with age, but continues to be the first sleep to be made up after sleep has been lost.

About an hour after falling asleep, the sleeper begins to ascend from Stage 4 sleep to Stage 3, Stage 2, and back to Stage 1—a process that takes about 40 minutes. The brain waves return to the low-amplitude, saw-toothed shape characteristic of Stage 1 sleep and waking alertness. Heart rate and blood pressure also increase, yet the muscles are more relaxed than at any other point in the sleep cycle, and the person is very difficult to awaken. The eyes move rapidly under closed eyelids. This **rapid-eye movement (REM)** sleep stage is distinguished from all other stages of sleep (called **non-REM or NREM**) that precede and follow it.

rapid-eye movement (REM) or paradoxical sleep Sleep stage characterized by rapid-eye movements and increased dreaming.

non-REM (NREM) sleep Non-rapid-eye-movement stages of sleep that alternate with REM stages during the sleep cycle.

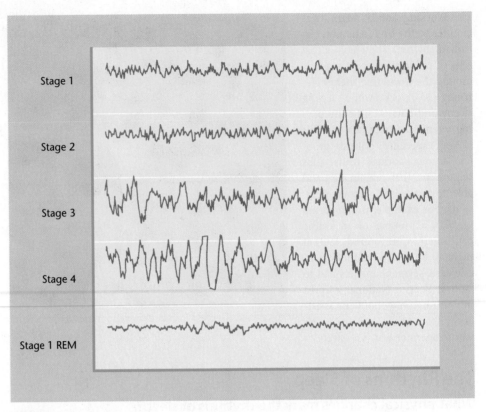

FIGURE 4–1

The brain-wave patterns typical of the five stages of sleep.

The four NREM stages and the first REM stage. The brain waves in REM sleep closely resemble Stage 1 of NREM sleep, but the person in REM is very deeply asleep.

REM sleep is also called **paradoxical sleep,** because although measures of brain activity, heart rate, blood pressure, and other physiological functions closely resemble those recorded during waking consciousness, the person in this stage appears to be deeply asleep and is incapable of moving; the body's voluntary muscles are essentially paralyzed. REM sleep is also the stage when most dreaming occurs, though dreams also take place during NREM sleep. The first Stage 1–REM period lasts about 10 minutes and is followed by Stages 2, 3, and 4 of NREM sleep. This sequence of sleep stages repeats itself all night, averaging 90 minutes from Stage 1–REM to Stage 4 and back again. Normally, a night's sleep consists of 4 to 5 sleep cycles of this sort. But the pattern of sleep changes as the night progresses. At first, Stages 3 and 4 dominate; but as time passes, the Stage 1–REM periods gradually become longer, and Stages 3 and 4 become shorter, eventually disappearing altogether. Over the course of a night, then, about 45 to 50% of the sleeper's time is spent in Stage 2, whereas REM sleep takes up another 20 to 25% of the total. (See "**Summary Table:** Stages of Sleep.")

ENDURING ISSUES

Diversity–Universality   Individual Differences in Sleep

Sleep requirements and patterns vary considerably from person to person. Some adults need hardly any sleep. Researchers have documented the case of a Stanford University professor who slept for only 3 to 4 hours a night over the course of 50 years and that of a woman who lived a healthy life on only 1 hour of sleep per night (Rosenzweig & Leiman, 1982). Sleep patterns also change with age (Philip et al., 2004; Sadeh, Raviv, & Gruber, 2000). Infants sleep much longer than adults—13 to 16 hours during the first year—and much more of their sleep is REM sleep. (See **Figure 4–2**.) Moreover, young children in Asian countries sleep less than children in the United States and Canada (Mindell, Sadeh, Wiegand, & How, 2008). Finally, many people in non-Western societies drift in and out of sleep during the course of the night, a sleep pattern that lends itself well to protecting oneself from predators (Worthman & Melby, 2002). ■

SUMMARY TABLE	**STAGES OF SLEEP**	
	Brain Waves	**Characteristics**
Twilight state	Low-voltage alpha waves	Relaxed wakefulness
Stage 1	Low-voltage alpha waves	Slower pulse; relaxed muscles; side-to-side rolling of eyes; easily aroused
Stage 2	Sleep spindles	Still lower pulse, blood pressure, body temperature; hard to awaken; unresponsive to stimuli
Stage 3	Some delta waves	
Stage 4	Delta waves	Very low pulse rate, blood pressure, body temperature; slow breathing
REM (paradoxical)	Low-voltage alpha waves	Increased heart rate, blood pressure; muscles very relaxed; rapid eye movements (REM); very difficult to awaken

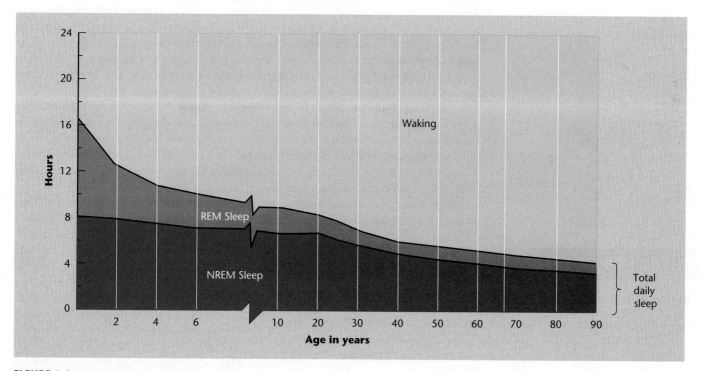

FIGURE 4–2
Changes in REM and NREM sleep.
The amount of REM sleep people need declines sharply during the first few years of life. Newborns spend about 8 hours, or almost half of their total sleep time in REM sleep, whereas older children and adults spend just 1 to 2 hours or about 20%–25% of their total sleep time in REM sleep (Roffwarg et al., *Science, 152* [1966]).

Sleep Deprivation

What happens when people don't get enough sleep?

Between one-third and one-half of all adults regularly fail to get enough sleep. According to the National Sleep Foundation, adolescents need at least 9 hours of sleep a night but 80% of them get less sleep than that (National Sleep Foundation, 2006). As a result, at least once a week 28% of high school students fall asleep in class. Another 22% fall asleep while doing homework and 14% arrive late or miss school entirely because they oversleep. Thus, it is not surprising that chronic sleep deprivation among adolescents results in diminished attention, reduced arousal, and lower test scores (Beebe, Rose, & Amin, 2010).

Despite common beliefs, people do not adapt to chronic sleep loss. Extensive research shows that losing an hour or two of sleep every night, week after week, month after month, makes it more difficult for people to pay attention (especially to monotonous tasks) and to remember things (Van Dongen, Belenky, & Krueger, 2011). Reaction time slows down, behavior becomes unpredictable, logical reasoning is impaired, and accidents and errors in judgment increase, while productivity and the ability to make decisions decline (Durmer & Dinges, 2005; Oken & Salinsky, 2007; Scott, McNaughton, & Polman, 2006). These findings have important implications. For example, experts estimate that sleep loss is a contributing factor in more than 200,000 automobile accidents each year in the United States, resulting in more than a thousand deaths and tens of thousands of injuries. Research suggests that driving while sleepy is just as dangerous as driving while drunk (Orzeł-Gryglewska, 2010). Combining sleep deprivation with drinking, even moderate drinking, is especially dangerous (Oken & Salinsky, 2007).

Sleep deprivation may also affect the performance of people in high-risk positions such as nuclear power plant operators, who often have to make critical decisions on short notice. In 1979, there was an accident at the nuclear power plant at Three Mile Island, Pennsylvania, in which human error transformed a minor mishap into a major nuclear disaster. Hospital residents who work long hours without rest experience twice as many failures of attention while working at night compared to residents who work shorter shifts. They make over one-third of serious medical errors regarding patients, including five times as many serious diagnostic mistakes that could be life-threatening (Landrigan et al., 2004; Landrigan, 2005). To put the state of exhaustion into further perspective, residents working heavy schedules perform similarly on cognitive tasks to people with blood alcohol levels between 0.04% and 0.05%—the level reached when an average-sized man consumes three beers in a single hour (Arnedt, Owens, Crouch, Stahl, & Carskadon, 2005).

Awareness of the relationship between sleep deprivation and accidents has led to changes in the working patterns of people whose jobs can have life-and-death consequences. For example, the Accreditation Council for Graduate Medical Education (2003) has developed common duty hour standards that set a cap of 80 hours per week and that limit continuous duty time to 24 hours for physicians in training. Evidence indicates that the standards are having a positive effect, though additional safeguards are needed (Ulmer, Wolman, & Johns, 2008).

Lack of sleep has been shown to contribute to such diseases as heart attacks, asthma, strokes, high blood pressure, and diabetes (Sabanayagam & Shankar, 2010). In children, insufficient sleep is associated with increased risk of being overweight (Lumeng et al., 2007). Sleep deprivation is also clearly related to depression in high school and college students. According to Mary Alice Carskadon, a leading researcher in the area of sleep among college students, "Every study we have ever done over the past decade on high school and college students shows the less sleep they get the more depressed mood they report" (Markel, 2003, p. D6). Even for college students who are not depressed, a lack of sleep results in lower academic performance (Gilbert & Weaver, 2010).

THINKING CRITICALLY ABOUT . . .

Sleep Deprivation

1. The Accreditation Council for Graduate Medical Education (2003) (ACGME) duty standards are intended to reduce serious errors and improve patient care. How might you go about determining whether indeed they have the desired effect?

2. One study cited below concluded that even a brief nap can "increase alertness, reduce irritability, and improve efficiency." But many people report that they feel more tired after taking a brief nap than they did before! How might you explain the apparent contradiction between these two facts?

APPLYING PSYCHOLOGY

Are You Getting Enough Sleep?

Sleep is sometimes elusive. The ancient Greeks believed that sleep was a gift of the god Morpheus, who granted or refused it to mortals. Like most people, you probably have had at least a few nights when you found it difficult to fall asleep. Episodes of even temporary or occasional insomnia can impair your ability to function during the day. So what can you do if you suddenly find yourself going through a period when you are unable to get a good night's sleep? Here are some tips that may help:

- Maintain regular bedtime hours; don't sleep late on weekends.
- Establish a regular, relaxing bedtime routine that you follow each night before retiring, such as a warm bath, followed by a little reading or making an entry into a journal.
- Abstain from drugs, including alcohol, caffeine, and nicotine, as well as the routine use of sleeping pills. Tryptophan, a substance that promotes sleep, may be taken as a sleep aid in the form of warm milk, confirming a folk remedy for sleeplessness.
- Adjust the temperature of the room if it is too cold or too warm.
- Avoid foods that may cause sleeplessness, such as chocolate. And don't overeat.
- Establish a regular exercise program during the day, but never exercise within several hours of bedtime.

- Avoid anxious thoughts while in bed. Set aside regular times during the day—well before bedtime—to mull over your worries. This technique may be supplemented by relaxation training, using such methods as biofeedback, self-hypnosis, or meditation (Gathchel & Oordt, 2003).
- Don't fight insomnia when it occurs. The old saying "If I can't sleep, I mop the kitchen floor" makes sense to sleep researchers, who counsel their clients to get out of bed and engage in a relaxing activity for a while until they feel sleepy again.

Sleep quiz: Are you getting enough sleep? Test yourself.

Take the following sleep quiz and see if you need more sleep.
Answer yes or no to the following questions.

____ Do you often fall asleep while watching TV?
____ Is it common for you to fall asleep after large meals or while relaxing after dinner?
____ Do you often fall asleep or fear nodding off during boring lectures, tedious activities, or in warm rooms?
____ Do you need an alarm clock to wake up in the morning?
____ Do you often press the snooze button on your alarm clock to get more sleep?

____ Do you struggle to get out of bed in the morning?
____ Do you often feel tired, irritable, or stressed out during the day?
____ Do you have trouble concentrating or remembering?
____ Are you easily distracted or feel slow while performing tasks that require thinking, problem solving, or creativity?
____ Do you sometimes feel drowsy or fear nodding off while driving?
____ Do you need a nap to help you get through the day?

According to sleep researcher James Maas, if you answered yes to three or more of these questions you may need more sleep than you are getting. In addition to the techniques recommended above, there are a number of excellent books that describe techniques for getting a good night's sleep including the following:

Epstein, L., & Mardon, S. (2007). *The Harvard Medical School guide to a good night's sleep.* New York: McGraw-Hill.

Krugman, M. (2005). *The insomnia solution.* New York: Grand Central Publishing.

Jacobs, G. D., & Benson, H. (1999). *Say good night to insomnia: The six-week, drug-free program developed at Harvard Medical School.* New York: Holt Paperbacks.

Source: Adapted from: Maas, J. B. (1999). *Power sleep: The revolutionary program that prepares your mind for peak performance.* New York: Harper Collins.

Unfortunately, people do not always know when they are not getting enough sleep (see "Applying Psychology: Are You Getting Enough Sleep?"). In a laboratory study, one group of healthy college students who were getting 7–8 hours of sleep a night showed no apparent signs of sleep deprivation. Yet 20% of them fell asleep immediately when they were put into a dark room, a symptom of chronic sleep loss. Another group for a period of time went to bed 60–90 minutes earlier than their normal bedtime. These students reported that they felt much more vigorous and alert—indeed, they performed significantly better on tests of psychological and mental acuity (Carskadon, Acebo, & Jenni, 2004; Carskadon & Dement, 1982).

nightmares Frightening dreams that occur during REM sleep and are remembered.

night terrors Frightening, often terrifying dreams that occur during NREM sleep from which a person is difficult to awaken and doesn't remember the content.

According to a well-known sleep researcher, Dr. William Dement, one way to reduce your sleep debt is to take short naps. Even a 20-minute nap can increase alertness, reduce irritability, and improve efficiency, while 1-hour naps lead to more marked increases in performance (Leitzell, 2008; S. C. Mednick et al., 2002).

Sleep Disorders

What is the difference between a nightmare and night terror?

At any given time, at least 50 million Americans suffer from chronic, long-term sleep disorders; and 20 million other Americans experience occasional sleep problems. A study of 72,000 female nurses found that women who sleep either too much (more than 9 hours) or too little (less than 5 hours) have an increased risk for heart disease. Although researchers could not determine exactly why this relationship was present, they suggested the tendency to sleep too much or too little might be indicative of underlying medical conditions (Ayas et al., 2003). The scientific study of typical sleep patterns has yielded further insights into several sleep disorders, including the ones we discuss next: sleeptalking and sleepwalking, nightmares and night terrors, insomnia, apnea, and narcolepsy.

Sleeptalking, Sleepwalking, and Night Terrors *Sleeptalking* and *sleepwalking* usually occur during Stage 4. Both are more common among children than adults: About 20% of children have at least one episode of either sleepwalking or sleeptalking. Boys are more likely to walk in their sleep than girls. Contrary to popular belief, waking a sleepwalker is not dangerous (in fact, it may be more dangerous *not* to wake the person), but because sleepwalking commonly takes place during a very deep stage of sleep, waking a sleepwalker is not easy (National Sleep Foundation, 2005).

Sometimes sleep can be frightening, when people experience nightmares or night terrors, also known as sleep terrors. Although both these phenomena are bad dreams, they are very different (Mindell & Owens, 2003; Zadra, Pilon, & Donderi, 2006). **Nightmares** occur during REM sleep and we can remember them in the morning. These frightening dreams are also very common; virtually everyone has them occasionally. **Night terrors,** a form of nocturnal fright that makes the dreamer suddenly sit up in bed—often screaming out in fear—occur during NREM sleep. People generally cannot be awakened from night terrors and will push away anyone trying to comfort them. Unlike nightmares, night terrors cannot be recalled the next morning.

The frequency of nightmares and night terrors increases for both children and adults during times of stress (Schredl, Biemelt, Roos, Dünkel, & Harris, 2008), though neither nightmares nor night terrors alone indicate psychological problems. Anxious people have no more

Children who are awakened by night terrors wake up suddenly, are difficult to comfort, and rarely remember the experience the next day.

nightmares than other people do. However, people whose nightmares stem from a traumatic experience, such as posttraumatic stress disorder, may be plagued by terrifying nighttime episodes for years (Gehrman & Harb, 2010; Van Liempt, Vermetten, Geuze, & Westenberg, 2006).

Insomnia, Apnea, and Narcolepsy **Insomnia,** the inability to fall or remain asleep, afflicts approximately 30% of adults around the world, especially women and older adults (T. Roth, 2007). Most episodes of insomnia grow out of stressful events and are temporary (Cano, Mochizuki, & Saper, 2008). But for as much as 20% of the population, insomnia is a persistent disruption that results in decreased quality of life, increased likelihood of accidents, decreased job performance, and health problems (T. Roth, 2007; Tobin, 2007).

The causes of insomnia vary for different individuals. For some people, insomnia is a consequence of a larger psychological problem, so its cure requires treating the underlying disorder. For others, interpersonal difficulties, such as loneliness, can contribute to difficulty sleeping (Cacioppo et al., 2002). Some people worry so much about not sleeping that even simple "good sleep hygiene" bedtime rituals may unwittingly usher in anxiety, rather than set the stage for relaxation. Finally, bad sleep habits—such as varying bedtimes or talking on a cell phone just before going to sleep—and distracting sleep settings may aggravate or even cause insomnia (Hamblin, Croft, Wood, Stough, & Spong, 2008).

Sleeping pills are occasionally prescribed to help people recover from short bouts with insomnia. However, when used over a long period of time, patients may become dependent upon them to sleep, requiring an increased dosage to be effective. Even the short-term use of many sedatives can interfere with the normal sleep cycle, decreasing both REM and deep stage sleep. The result is often a reduction in sleep quality, accompanied by fatigue and irritability during the day (Watson, Baghdoyan, & Lydic, 2010).

Another sleep disorder, obstructive sleep **apnea,** affects 10 to 12 million Americans, many of whom have inherited the condition (Khalyfa, Serpero, Kheirandish-Gozal, Capdevila, & Gozal, 2011). Apnea is associated with breathing difficulties at night: In severe cases, the victim actually stops breathing after falling asleep. When the level of carbon dioxide in the blood rises to a certain point, apnea sufferers are spurred to a state of arousal just short of waking consciousness. Because this process may happen hundreds of times a night, apnea patients typically feel exhausted and fall asleep repeatedly the next day. They may also complain of depression, sexual dysfunction, difficulty concentrating, and headaches (El-Ad & Lavie, 2005; Strollo & Davé, 2005). Moreover, sleep-related breathing disorders have been shown to be related to hyperactivity, conduct disorders, and aggressiveness among children and adolescents (Chervin, Killion, Archbold, & Ruzicka, 2003). Depending on its severity, sleep apnea can also double or triple the risk of having a stroke or dying (Yaggi et al., 2005).

insomnia Sleep disorder characterized by difficulty in falling asleep or remaining asleep throughout the night.

apnea Sleep disorder characterized by breathing difficulty during the night and feelings of exhaustion during the day.

Nearly 1 in 3 adults suffers from insomnia and the resulting decreased quality of life, increased likelihood of accidents, decreased job performance, and health problems.

narcolepsy Hereditary sleep disorder characterized by sudden nodding off during the day and sudden loss of muscle tone following moments of emotional excitement.

dreams Vivid visual and auditory experiences that occur primarily during REM periods of sleep.

THINKING CRITICALLY ABOUT . . .

Sleep Loss and Illness

"Too little sleep—or too much—may raise the risk of developing heart disease."
That headline referred to a study of more than 70,000 nurses conducted over more than a decade in which it was shown that those who slept less than 5 hours a night were almost 40% more likely to develop heart disease than those who averaged the normal 8 hours of sleep (Ayas et al., 2003).

1. The headline implies that the findings from this study apply universally—to women who are not nurses, to men, and to people around the world. Do you agree or disagree? Why or why not?

2. Note that the headline says that too little sleep "may" raise the risk of developing heart disease. Can you think of other factors that might cause both sleep loss and increase the risk of heart disease, and thus account for the relationship between the two?

3. The research depended on self-report of sleep: In other words, those who *said* they slept little were also those who were at greater risk of developing heart disease. Does that fact change your interpretation of the research results and your answers to the first two questions?

4. Interestingly, the study also showed that *too much* sleep is also associated with a higher risk of heart disease. Nurses who said they slept more than 9 hours a night on average were 37% more likely to develop heart disease than those who said they slept the normal 8 hours. Does this additional piece of information change your thinking about this issue? How might you explain the relationship between self-reports of too much sleep and risk of developing heart disease?

Too much sleep has serious repercussions as well. **Narcolepsy** is a hereditary disorder whose victims nod off without warning in the middle of a conversation or other alert activity. People with narcolepsy often experience a sudden loss of muscle tone upon expression of any sort of emotion. A joke, anger, sexual stimulation—all bring on the muscle paralysis associated with deep sleep. Suddenly, without warning, they collapse. Another symptom of the disorder is immediate entry into REM sleep, which produces frightening hallucinations that are, in fact, dreams that the person is experiencing while still partly awake. New medications show promise in treating some patients with narcolepsy (Majid & Hirshkowitz, 2010).

LEARNING OBJECTIVE

• Explain what dreams are. Summarize the explanations of dream activity and content as set forth in Freudian theory, information processing theory, and neural activation theory.

DREAMS

What are dreams?

Every culture, including our own, attributes meaning to dreams. In some cultures, people believe that dreams contain messages from their gods or that dreams predict the future. Psychologists define **dreams** as visual and auditory experiences that our minds create during sleep. The average person has four or five dreams a night, accounting for about one to two hours of the total time spent sleeping. People awakened during REM sleep report graphic dreams about 80 to 85% of the time (Domhoff, 2003). Less striking dreamlike experiences that resemble normal wakeful consciousness are reported about 50% of the time during NREM sleep.

Most dreams last about as long as the events would in real life; they do not flash on your mental screen just before waking, as was once believed. Generally, dreams consist of a sequential story or a series of stories. Stimuli, both external (such as a train whistle or a low-flying airplane) and internal (such as hunger pangs), may modify an ongoing dream, but they do not initiate dreams. Often, dreams are so vivid that it is difficult to distinguish them from reality (Domhoff, 2005).

Why Do We Dream?

Psychologists have long been fascinated by dream activity and the contents of dreams, and a number of explanations have been proposed.

Dreams as Unconscious Wishes   Sigmund Freud (1900), the first modern theorist to investigate this topic, called dreams the "royal road to the unconscious." Believing that dreams represent unfulfilled wishes, he asserted that people's dreams reflect the motives guiding their behavior—motives of which they may not be consciously aware. Freud distinguished between the *manifest,* or surface, *content* of dreams and their *latent content*—the hidden, unconscious thoughts or desires that he believed were expressed indirectly through dreams.

In dreams, according to Freud, people permit themselves to express primitive desires that are relatively free of moral controls. For example, someone who is not consciously aware of hostile feelings toward a sister may dream about murdering her. However, even in a dream, such hostile feelings may be censored and transformed into a symbolic form. For example, the desire to do away with one's sister (the dream's latent content) may be recast into the dream image of seeing her off at a train "terminal" (the dream's manifest content). According to Freud, this process of censorship and symbolic transformation accounts for the highly illogical nature of many dreams. Deciphering the disguised meanings of dreams remains one of the principal tasks of many psychoanalysts (Hill, Liu, Spangler, Sim, & Schottenbauer, 2008). Freud's pioneering work, focused on exploring the meaning of dreams, paved the way for contemporary investigations of dream content (Schneider, 2010).

Dreams and Information Processing   A completely different explanation for dreaming emerged in the later part of the 20th century with the advent of *information processing theory* (see Chapter 6, "Memory"). This view holds that in our dreams, we reprocess information gathered during the day as a way of strengthening memories of information that is crucial to survival (Ji & Wilson, 2007; Wagner & Born, 2008). During our waking hours, our brains are bombarded with sensory data. We need a "time out" to decide what information is valuable, whether it should be filed in long-term memory, where it should be filed, and what information should be erased so that it doesn't clutter neural pathways (Payne & Nadel, 2004). According to this view, dreams seem illogical because the brain is rapidly scanning old files and comparing them with new, unsorted "clippings." 👁

In support of this view, research has demonstrated that both humans and nonhumans spend more time in REM sleep after learning difficult material; furthermore, interfering with REM sleep immediately after learning severely disrupts the memory for the newly learned material (C. T. Smith, Nixon, & Nader, 2004; Wetzel, Wagner, & Balschun, 2003). Brain-imaging studies have also demonstrated that the specific area of the brain most active while learning new material is also active during subsequent REM sleep (Maquet et al., 2000).

👁 **Watch** the **Video** In the Real World: REM Sleep and Memory on **MyPsychLab**

Dreams and Waking Life   Still another theory maintains that dreams are an extension of the conscious concerns of daily life in altered (but not disguised) form (Domhoff, 2003). Research has shown that what people dream about is generally similar to what they think about and do while awake (Domhoff, 2010). For example, a parent who's having problems with a child may dream about childhood confrontations with his or her own parents. Dream content is also related to where you are in your sleep cycle, what you've been doing before you sleep, your gender, your age, and even your socioeconomic status. For example, although the dreams of men and women have become more similar over the last several decades, men more often dream about weapons, unfamiliar characters, male characters, aggressive interactions, and failure outcomes, whereas women are more likely to dream about being the victims of aggression (Bursik, 1998). Dream content also appears to be relatively consistent for most individuals, displaying similar themes across years and even decades (Domhoff & Schneider, 2008).

Dreams and Neural Activity Research using advanced brain-imaging techniques has indicated that the limbic system, which is involved with emotions, motivations, and memories, is very active during dreams; so, to a lesser extent, are the visual and auditory areas of the forebrain that process sensory information. However, areas of the forebrain, including the prefrontal cortex, involved in working memory, attention, logic, and self-monitoring are relatively inactive during dreams (Dang-Vu, Schabus, Desseilles, Schwartz, & Maquet, 2007). This fact might explain the highly emotional texture of dreams, as well as the bizarre imagery and the loss of critical insight, logic, and self-reflection. This uncensored mixture of desires, fears, and memories comes very close to the psychoanalytic concept of unconscious wishes, suggesting that Freud may have come closer to the meaning of dreams than many contemporary psychologists have acknowledged.

Dreams are the most common alteration of normal consciousness; and as we have seen, they occur naturally under normal conditions. Altered states of consciousness can also be induced by drugs, a topic to which we next turn our attention.

✔️—Study and Review on MyPsychLab

CHECK YOUR UNDERSTANDING

1. Our awareness of the mental processes of our everyday life is called _____.
2. Technological innovations such as _____ (_____) enable scientists to study brain activity during various states of consciousness.
3. The major characteristic of waking consciousness is _____.
4. In humans, sleeping and waking follow a _____ cycle.
5. Most vivid dreaming takes place during the _____ stage of sleep.
6. We normally spend about _____ hours each night dreaming.
7. Freud distinguished between the _____ and _____ content of dreams.

Answers: 1. consciousness. 2. electroencephalography (EEG). 3. selective attention. 4. circadian. 5. REM. 6. two. 7. manifest, latent.

APPLY YOUR UNDERSTANDING

1. You are a psychologist studying an elderly person's sleep cycle. Compared with a younger person, you would expect to find that this person spends _____ time in Stage 3 and Stage 4 sleep.
   a. less
   b. more
   c. about the same

2. Recently, your sister has found it difficult to stay awake during the day. In the middle of a conversation, she will suddenly nod off. At night when she goes to bed, she often describes frightening hallucinations. Your sister is probably suffering from
   a. sleep apnea.
   b. REM deprivation.
   c. narcolepsy.
   d. insomnia.

Answers: 1. a. 2. c.

LEARNING OBJECTIVES

- Define psychoactive drugs and summarize how their use has changed over the centuries.
- Differentiate substance abuse and substance dependence.
- Explain how double-blind procedures and placebos are used in drug research.
- Describe the major depressants, their effects, the effects of an overdose, and the extent to which they are susceptible to dependence.
- Describe the major stimulants, their effects, the effects of an overdose, and the extent to which they are susceptible to dependence.
- Describe the effects of LSD and marijuana.
- Describe the biological, psychological, social, and cultural factors that make it more likely someone will abuse drugs.

⤳ DRUG-ALTERED CONSCIOUSNESS

How is today's drug problem different from the drug use in other societies and times?

In Chapter 2, "The Biological Basis of Behavior," we examined how various drugs affect the function of the nervous system by fitting into the same receptor sites as naturally occurring chemicals or by blocking or enhancing transmission across the synapse. Here we will address the impact drugs have on behavior and consciousness.

The use of **psychoactive drugs**—substances that change people's moods, perceptions, mental functioning, or behavior—is almost universal. In nearly every known culture throughout history, people have sought ways to alter waking consciousness. Many legal and illegal drugs currently available have been used for thousands of years. Of all psychoactive substances, alcohol has the longest history of widespread use. Archaeological evidence suggests that Late-Stone-Age groups began producing mead (fermented honey flavored with sap or fruit) about 10,000 years ago. The Egyptians, Babylonians, Greeks, and Romans viewed wine as a "gift from the gods." Wine is frequently praised in the Bible, and drinking water is hardly mentioned. As recently as the 19th century, most people in Western civilizations drank alcohol with every meal (including breakfast) and between meals, as a "pick-me-up," as well as on social and religious occasions.

Is the use of drugs today different from the drug use in other societies and times? In many ways, the answer is yes. First, motives for using psychoactive drugs have changed. In most cultures, psychoactive substances have been used as part of religious rituals, as medicines and tonics, as nutrient beverages, or as culturally approved stimulants (much as we drink coffee). By contrast, the use of alcohol and other drugs in contemporary society is primarily recreational. The French often drink wine with dinner, the British have their pubs, and Greeks have their festivals. Americans most often imbibe in settings specifically designed for recreation and inebriation: bars, clubs, and cocktail parties. In addition, people use and abuse drugs privately and secretly in their homes, sometimes without the knowledge of their family and friends—leading to hidden addiction.

Second, the drugs themselves have changed. Modern psychoactive substances often are stronger than those used in other cultures and times. For most of Western history, wine (12% alcohol) was often diluted with water. Hard liquor (40%–75% alcohol) appeared only in the 10th century C.E., and the heroin available on the streets today is stronger and more addictive than that which was available in the 1930s and 1940s.

In addition, new, synthetic drugs appear regularly, with unpredictable consequences. In the 1990s, the National Institute for Drug Abuse created a new category, "Club Drugs," for increasingly popular psychoactive substances manufactured in small laboratories or even home kitchens. Because the source, the psychoactive ingredients, and any possible contaminants are unknown, the symptoms, toxicity, and short- or long-term consequences are also unknown—making these drugs especially dangerous. The fact that they are often consumed with alcohol multiplies the risks. Examples include "Meth" or "Crystal Meth" (methamphetamine); "Grievous Bodily Harm" (gammahydroxybutyrate [GHB]), a combination of sedatives and growth hormone stimulant; "Special K" (ketamine), an anesthetic approved for veterinary use that induces dreamlike states and hallucinations in humans; and "Roofies" (flunitrazepam), a tasteless, odorless sedative/anesthetic that can cause temporary amnesia, which is why it is also known as the "Forget-Me Pill" and is associated with sexual assault.

Finally, scientists and the public know more about the effects of psychoactive drugs than in the past. Nicotine is an obvious example. The Surgeon General's Report issued in 1964 confirmed a direct link between smoking and heart disease, as well as lung cancer. Subsequent research establishing that cigarettes are harmful not only to smokers, but also to people around them (as a result of secondhand smoke), as well as to their unborn babies (Schick & Glantz, 2005), transformed a personal health decision into a moral issue. Nonetheless, tens of millions of Americans still smoke, and millions of others use drugs they know to be harmful. ☑•

psychoactive drugs Chemical substances that change moods and perceptions.

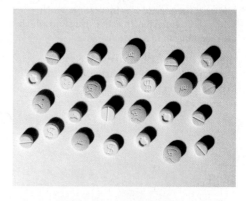

So-called "designer drugs" like Ecstasy are produced illegally by chemists who sometimes put cartoon characters or dollar signs on the tablets.

Complete the **Survey** What Drugs Have You Used? on **MyPsychLab**

Substance Use, Abuse, and Dependence

How can we tell whether someone is dependent on a psychoactive substance?

If we define drugs broadly to include caffeine, tobacco, and alcohol, then most people throughout the world use some type of drug on an occasional or a regular basis. Most of these people use such drugs in moderation and do not suffer ill effects. But for some,

substance abuse A pattern of drug use that diminishes the ability to fulfill responsibilities at home, work, or school that results in repeated use of a drug in dangerous situations or that leads to legal difficulties related to drug use.

substance dependence A pattern of compulsive drug taking that results in tolerance, withdrawal symptoms, or other specific symptoms for at least a year.

double-blind procedure Experimental design useful in studies of the effects of drugs, in which neither the subject nor the researcher knows at the time of administration which subjects are receiving an active drug and which are receiving an inactive substance.

placebo Chemically inactive substance used for comparison with active drugs in experiments on the effects of drugs.

substance use escalates into **substance abuse**—a pattern of drug use that diminishes a person's ability to fulfill responsibilities, that results in repeated use of the drug in dangerous situations, or that leads to legal difficulties related to drug use. For example, people whose drinking causes ill health and problems within their families or on their jobs are abusing alcohol. Substance abuse is America's leading health problem (S. Martin, 2001).

The ongoing abuse of drugs, including alcohol, may lead to compulsive use of the substance, or **substance dependence,** which is also known as *addiction.* (See **Table 4–1.**) Although not everyone who abuses a substance develops dependence, dependence usually follows a period of abuse. Dependence often includes *tolerance,* the phenomenon whereby higher doses of the drug are required to produce its original effects or to prevent *withdrawal symptoms,* the unpleasant physical or psychological effects following discontinuance of the substance. Many organizations publicize self-tests based on these and other elements in the definition of substance abuse. For example, a self-test from the National Council on alcoholism includes the questions, "Can you handle more alcohol now than when you first started to drink?" and "When drinking with other people, do you try to have a few extra drinks the others won't know about?"

The causes of substance abuse and dependence are a complex combination of biological, psychological, and social factors that varies for each individual and for each substance. Also, the development of substance dependence does not follow an established timetable. One person might drink socially for years before abusing alcohol, whereas someone else might become addicted to cocaine in a matter of days. Before we examine specific drugs and their effects, we first look at how psychologists study drug-related behaviors.

How Drug Effects are Studied The effects of particular drugs are studied under carefully controlled scientific conditions. In most cases, researchers compare people's behavior before the administration of the drug with their behavior afterward, taking special precautions to ensure that any observed changes in behavior are due to the drug alone.

To eliminate research errors based on subject or researcher expectations, most drug experiments use the **double-blind procedure,** in which some participants receive the active drug while others take a neutral, inactive substance called a **placebo.** Neither the researchers nor the participants know who is taking the active drug and who is taking the placebo. If the behavior of the participants who actually received the drug differs from the behavior of those who got the placebo, the cause is likely to be the active ingredient in the drug.

TABLE 4–1   **Signs of Substance Dependence**

The most recent clinical definition of dependence (American Psychiatric Association, 2000; Newton, 2006) describes a broad pattern of drug-related behaviors characterized by at least three of the following seven symptoms over a 12-month period:

1. Developing tolerance, that is, needing increasing amounts of the substance to gain the desired effect or experiencing a diminished effect when using the same amount of the substance. For example, the person might have to drink an entire six-pack to get the same effect formerly experienced after drinking just one or two beers.

2. Experiencing withdrawal symptoms, which are physical and psychological problems that occur if the person tries to stop using the substance. Withdrawal symptoms range from anxiety and nausea to convulsions and hallucinations.

3. Using the substance for a longer period or in greater quantities than intended.

4. Having a persistent desire or making repeated efforts to cut back on the use of the substance.

5. Devoting a great deal of time to obtaining or using the substance.

6. Giving up or reducing social, occupational, or recreational activities as a result of drug use.

7. Continuing to use the substance even in the face of ongoing or recurring physical or psychological problems likely to be caused or made worse by the use of the substance.

Studying drug-altered consciousness is complicated by the fact that most drugs not only affect different people in different ways, but also produce different effects in the same person at different times or in different settings (S. Siegel, 2005). For example, some people are powerfully affected by even small amounts of alcohol, whereas others are not. And drinking alcohol in a convivial family setting usually produces somewhat different effects than does consuming alcohol under the watchful eyes of a scientist.

Recently, sophisticated neuroimaging procedures have proved useful for studying drug effects. Techniques such as PET imaging have enabled researchers to isolate specific differences between the brains of addicted and nonaddicted people. For example, the "addicted brain" has been found to differ qualitatively from the nonaddicted brain in a variety of ways, including metabolically and in responsiveness to environmental cues. Investigators have also focused on the role played by neurotransmitters in the addictive process (see Chapter 2, "The Biological Basis of Behavior")—noting that every addictive drug causes dopamine levels in the brain to increase (Addolorato, Leggio, Abenavoli, & Gasbarrini, 2005). Results like these may lead not only to better understanding of the biological basis of addiction, but also to more effective treatments.

In analyzing drugs and drug use, it is convenient to group psychoactive substances into three categories: depressants, stimulants, and hallucinogens. (See "**Summary Table:** Drugs: Characteristics and Effects.") (We will look at a fourth category of psychoactive drugs, medications used in the treatment of mental illness, in Chapter 13, "Therapies.") These categories are not rigid, as the same drug may have multiple effects or different effects on different users, but this division helps organize our knowledge about drugs.

depressants Chemicals that slow down behavior or cognitive processes.

alcohol Depressant that is the intoxicating ingredient in whiskey, beer, wine, and other fermented or distilled liquors.

Depressants: Alcohol, Barbiturates, and the Opiates

Why does alcohol, a depressant, lead to higher rates of violence?

Depressants are chemicals that retard behavior and thinking by either speeding up or slowing down nerve impulses. Generally speaking, alcohol, barbiturates, and the opiates have depressant effects. People take depressants to reduce tension, to forget their troubles, or to relieve feelings of inadequacy, loneliness, or boredom.

Alcohol The most frequently used psychoactive drug in Western societies is **alcohol.** In spite of, or perhaps because of, the fact that it is legal and socially approved, alcohol is America's number-one drug problem. A large-scale survey of adults in the United States found that nearly 9% of those surveyed reported alcohol dependence or abuse in the previous 12 months. More than 30% reported alcohol dependence or abuse sometime in the course of their lives (Hasin, Stinson, Ogburn, & Grant, 2007). More than 25% of high school seniors say that they got drunk sometime in the past 30 days; and alcohol is also a significant problem among middle-school students. (See **Figure 4–3.**) At least 14 million Americans (more than 7% of the population aged 18 and older) have problems with drinking, including more than 8 million alcoholics, who are addicted to alcohol. Three times as many men as women are problem drinkers. For both sexes, alcohol abuse and addiction is highest in the 18- to 29-year-old age group (Hingson, Heeren, Winter, & Wechsler, 2005; National Institute on Alcohol Abuse and Alcoholism, 2003).

Excessive chronic alcohol use can harm virtually every organ in the body, beginning with the brain, and is associated with impairments in perceptual–motor skills, visual–spatial processing, problem solving, and abstract reasoning (Samokhvalov, Popova, Room, Ramonas, & Rehm, 2010). Alcohol is the leading cause of liver disease and kidney damage, is a major factor in cardiovascular disease, increases the risk of certain cancers, and can lead to sexual dysfunction and infertility. Alcohol is particularly damaging to the nervous system during the teenage years (K. Butler, 2006). The total economic cost of alcohol abuse and dependence in America is estimated at nearly $200 billion annually (National Institutes of Health, n.d.). In addition, alcohol abuse is directly involved in more than 20,000 deaths annually and the number is rising (Kung, Hoyert, Xu, & Murphy, 2008).

The social costs of abusing alcohol are high as well. Alcohol is involved in a substantial proportion of violent and accidental deaths, including suicides, which makes it the leading

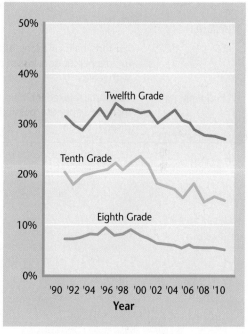

FIGURE 4–3

Teenage use of alcohol (% drunk in past 30 days).

A national survey found that the percent of teenagers who said they got drunk at least one time during the past 30 days remained relatively steady through the 1990s, with a modest but steady decline from 2000 through 2010. More than 25% of 12th graders reported getting drunk during the past 30 days in 2010.

Source: Monitoring the future: A continuing study of American Youth. http://www.monitoringthefuture.org/data/10data/pr10t3.pdf

SUMMARY TABLE   DRUGS: CHARACTERISTICS AND EFFECTS

	Typical Effects	Effects of Overdose	Tolerance/Dependence
Depressants			
Alcohol	Biphasic; tension-reduction "high," followed by depressed physical and psychological functioning	Disorientation, loss of consciousness, death at extremely high blood-alcohol levels	Tolerance; physical and psychological dependence, withdrawal symptoms
Barbiturates, Tranquilizers	Depressed reflexes and impaired motor functioning, tension reductions	Shallow respiration, clammy skin, dilated pupils, weak and rapid pulse, coma, possible death	Tolerance; high psychological and physical dependence on barbiturates, low to moderate physical dependence on such tranquilizers as Valium, although high psychological dependence; withdrawal symptoms
Opiates	Euphoria, drowsiness, "rush" of pleasure, little impairment of psychological functions	Slow, shallow breathing, clammy skin, nausea, vomiting, pinpoint pupils, convulsions, coma, possible death	High tolerance; physical and psychological dependence; severe withdrawal symptoms
Stimulants			
Amphetamines, Cocaine, Caffeine, Nicotine	Increased alertness, excitation, euphoria, increased pulse rate and blood pressure, sleeplessness	For amphetamines and cocaine: agitation and, with chronic high doses, hallucinations (e.g., "cocaine bugs") For caffeine and nicotine: restlessness, insomnia, rambling thoughts, heart arrhythmia, possible circulatory failure For nicotine: increased blood pressure	For amphetamines, cocaine, and nicotine: tolerance; psychological and physical dependence For caffeine: physical and psychological dependence; withdrawal symptoms
Hallucinogens			
LSD	Illusions, hallucinations, distortions in time perception, loss of contact with reality	Psychotic reactions	No physical dependence for LSD; degree of psychological dependence unknown for LSD
Marijuana	Euphoria, relaxed inhibitions, increased appetite, possible disorientation	Fatigue, disoriented behavior, possible psychosis	Psychological dependence

contributor (after AIDS) to death among young people. Alcohol is implicated in more than two-thirds of all fatal automobile accidents, two-thirds of all murders, two-thirds of all spouse beatings, and more than half of all cases of violent child abuse. Moreover, the use of alcohol during pregnancy has been linked to a variety of birth defects, the most notable being fetal alcohol syndrome. (See Chapter 9, "Life-Span Development.") More than 40% of all heavy drinkers die before the age of 65 (compared with less than 20% of nondrinkers). In addition, there is the untold cost in psychological trauma suffered by the nearly 30 million children of alcohol abusers.

What makes alcohol so powerful? Alcohol first affects the frontal lobes of the brain, which figure prominently in inhibitions, impulse control, reasoning, and judgment (Zahr, Pitel, Chanraud, & Sullivan, 2010). As consumption continues, alcohol impairs functions of the cerebellum, the center of motor control and balance (Manto & Jacquy, 2002). Eventually, alcohol consumption affects the spinal cord and medulla, which regulate such involuntary functions as breathing, body temperature, and heart rate. A blood-alcohol level of 0.25% or more may cause this part of the nervous system to shut down and may severely impair functioning; slightly higher levels can cause death from alcohol poisoning. (See **Table 4–2.**)

Even in moderate quantities, alcohol affects perception, motor processes, memory, and judgment. It diminishes the ability to see clearly, to perceive depth, and to distinguish the differences between bright lights and colors, and it generally affects spatial–cognitive functioning—all clearly necessary for driving a car safely. Alcohol interferes with memory storage: Heavy drinkers may also experience *blackouts*, which make them unable to

TABLE 4-2   The Behavioral Effects of Blood-Alcohol Levels

Levels of Alcohol in the Blood (%)	Behavioral Effects
0.05	Feels good; less alert; reduced inhibitions
0.10	Is slower to react; less cautious; slurred speech
0.15	Reaction time is much slower
0.20	Sensory-motor abilities are suppressed
0.25	Is staggering (motor abilities severely impaired); perception is limited as well
0.30	Is in semistupor; confused
0.35	Is at level for anesthesia; death is possible
0.40	Stupor
0.50	Coma
0.60	Respiratory paralysis and death

Source: Data from *Drugs, Society, and Human Behavior*, 10th ed., by Oakley Ray, 2003, New York: McGraw-Hill; U.S. National Library of Medicine. (2006). *Alcohol use.* Retrieved December 19, 2008, from http://www.nlm.nih.gov/medlineplus/ency/article/001944.htm.

Excessive drinking and public drunkenness have been widely frowned on in many cultures.

remember anything that occurred while they were drinking; but even long-term alcoholics show improvements in memory, attention, balance, and neurological functioning after three months of sobriety (R. S. Moser, Frantz, & Brick, 2008).

Heavy drinkers have difficulty focusing on relevant information and ignoring inaccurate, irrelevant information, thus leading to poor judgments, a condition called **alcoholic myopia** (Schreiber Compo et al., 2011). Dozens of studies demonstrate that alcohol use is correlated with increases in aggression, hostility, violence, and abusive behavior (Giancola, Josephs, Parrott, & Duke, 2010). Thus, intoxication makes people less aware of and less concerned about the negative consequences of their actions, increasing their likelihood to engage in risky behavior (S. George, Rogers, & Duka, 2005). The same principle applies to potential victims. For instance, when women are intoxicated, their ability to accurately evaluate a dangerous situation with a potential male aggressor is diminished, so that their risk of being sexually assaulted increases. Not surprisingly, people who are intoxicated are more likely to engage in unprotected sex than if they were sober (Griffin, Umstattd, & Usdan, 2010). The dangers of alcohol notwithstanding, alcohol continues to be popular because of its short-term effects. As a depressant, it calms the nervous system, much like a general anesthetic (McKim, 2007). Thus, people consume alcohol to relax or to enhance their mood. ✳

It is often experienced as a stimulant because it inhibits centers in the brain that govern critical judgment and impulsive behavior. Alcohol makes people feel more courageous, less inhibited, more spontaneous, and more entertaining. To drinkers, the long-term negative consequences of alcoholism pale beside these short-term positive consequences.

✳ **Explore** the **Concept** Behavioral Effects Associated with Various Blood Alcohol Levels on **MyPsychLab**

ENDURING ISSUES

Diversity–Universality   Women and Alcohol

Women are especially vulnerable to the effects of alcohol (National Institute on Alcohol Abuse and Alcoholism [NIAAA], 2003). Because women generally weigh less than men, the same dose of alcohol has a stronger effect on the average woman than on the average man. Most women also have lower levels of the stomach enzyme that regulates alcohol metabolism. The less of this enzyme in the stomach, the greater the amount of alcohol that passes into the bloodstream and spreads through the body. (This is the reason why drinking on an empty stomach has more pronounced effects than drinking with meals.) In addition, neuroimaging studies reveal that women's brains may also be more

alcoholic myopia A condition resulting from alcohol consumption involving poor judgments arising from misdirected attention and failure to consider negative consequences.

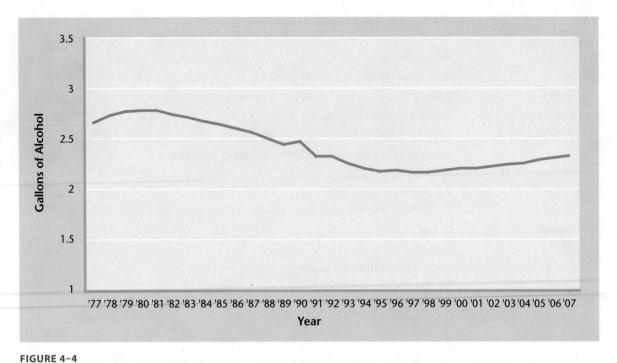

FIGURE 4–4
Per capita annual alcohol consumption in the United States, 1977–2007

Source: http://www.niaaa.nih.gov/Resources/DatabaseResources/QuickFacts/AlcoholSales/Pages/consum01.aspx

vulnerable to damage from alcohol consumption than male brains (K. Mann et al., 2005). As a rough measure, one drink is likely to have the same effects on a woman as two drinks have on a man. ■

The good news is that since 1977, the overall consumption of alcohol is generally down with only a slight increase in the recent decade due largely to increased consumption of wine (see **Figure 4–4**) (Nekisha, Gerald, Hsiao-ye, & Michael, 2005). Alcohol-related traffic deaths, while still too common, are also declining (Yi, Williams, & Dufour, 2002). (See **Figure 4–5**).

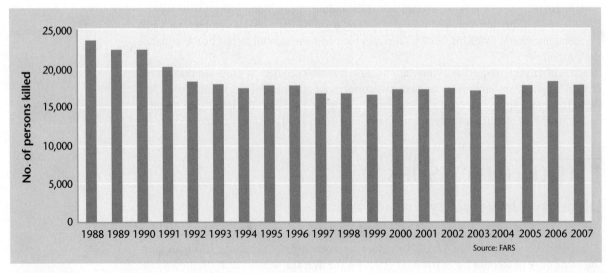

FIGURE 4–5
Persons killed in alcohol-related traffic crashes.

Deaths in alcohol-related traffic accidents have generally declined since the 1980s, although the total number for the most recent year is still tragically high.

Source: http://www.alcoholalert.com/drunk-driving-statistics-2007.html

Binge Drinking on College Campuses One of the few places today where drunkenness is tolerated, and often expected, is the American college campus. According to the National Center on Addiction and Drug Abuse (NCADA), "In 2005, 67.9 percent of students (approximately 5.3 million students) reported drinking in the past month and 40.1 percent (approximately 3.1 million students) reported binge drinking.... The proportion of students reporting frequent binge drinking increased 15.7 percent (from 19.7 percent to 22.8 percent)" (NCADA, 2007, p. 3). "Binge drinking" is defined as five or more drinks in a row for men, four or more drinks for women. "Frequent binge drinking" is defined as binge drinking three or more times in the past two weeks. Nearly half of the college students who drink report that they do so in order to get drunk.

It is not surprising that frequent binge drinkers had more problems, and more serious problems, than other students. Many had missed classes, fallen behind in schoolwork, engaged in unplanned—and unprotected—sex, gotten in trouble with campus police, engaged in vandalism or violence, or been hurt or injured (National Center on Addiction and Drug Abuse, 2007). Bingers were more likely than other students to have used other drugs, especially cigarettes and marijuana (R. D. Brewer & Swahn, 2005; National Center on Addiction and Substance Abuse, 2007; Pirkle & Richter, 2006). They were 10 times more likely to have driven a car after drinking and more than 15 times more likely to have ridden with a driver who was drunk or high.

The effects of binge drinking are not limited to students who participate. At schools with high binge rates, a majority of students report that they have been unable to study or sleep because of binge drinking. Many sober students have cared for drunken friends, endured drunken insults, and fended off unwanted sexual advances. Yet most are reluctant to report these problems to campus or other authorities. Strict campus alcohol policies have been shown to be effective in reducing binge drinking rates over time (Harris, Sherritt, Van Hook, Wechsler, & Knight, 2010).

Barbiturates Barbiturates, commonly known as "downers," include such medications as Amytal, Nembutal, Seconal, and phenobarbital. Discovered about a century ago, this class of depressants was first prescribed for its sedative and anticonvulsant qualities. But after researchers recognized in the 1950s that barbiturates had potentially deadly effects—particularly in combination with alcohol—their use declined. Though barbiturates are sometimes prescribed to help people sleep, they actually disrupt the body's natural sleep patterns and cause dependence when used for long periods.

The general effects of barbiturates are strikingly similar to those of alcohol: Taken on an empty stomach, a small dose causes light-headedness, silliness, and poor motor coordination (McKim, 2007), whereas larger doses may bring on slurred speech, loss of inhibition, and increases in aggression. When taken during pregnancy, barbiturates, like alcohol, produce such birth defects as a cleft palate and malformations of the heart, skeleton, and central nervous system (Olney, Wozniak, Farber, Jevtovic-Todorovic, & Bittigau, 2002).

Opiates Psychoactive substances derived from, or resembling, sap taken from the seedpod of the opium poppy, **opiates** have a long history of use—though not always abuse. Originating in Turkey, opium spread west around the Mediterranean and east through India into China, where it was used in pill or liquid form in folk medicines for thousands of years. But changes in the way opium and its derivative, morphine, were used opened the door to abuse. In the mid-17th century, when the emperor of China banned tobacco and the Chinese began to smoke opium, addiction quickly followed. During the American Civil War, physicians used a new invention, the hypodermic needle, to administer morphine, a much-needed painkiller for soldiers. In this form, morphine was far more addictive than smoking opium. Heroin—introduced in 1898 as a cure for morphine addiction—created an even stronger dependency.

Morphine compounds are still used in painkillers and other medications, such as codeine cough syrups. The nonmedicinal distribution of opiates was banned early in the 20th century. After that, a black market for heroin developed.

Heroin and other opiates resemble endorphins, the natural painkillers produced by the body, and occupy many of the same nerve-receptor sites. (See Chapter 2, "The Biological

barbiturates Potentially deadly depressants, first used for their sedative and anticonvulsant properties, now used only to treat such conditions as epilepsy and arthritis.

opiates Drugs, such as opium and heroin, derived from the opium poppy, that dull the senses and induce feelings of euphoria, well-being, and relaxation. Synthetic drugs resembling opium derivatives are also classified as opiates.

stimulants Drugs, including amphetamines and cocaine, that stimulate the sympathetic nervous system and produce feelings of optimism and boundless energy.

Basis of Behavior.") Heroin users report a surge of euphoria soon after taking the drug, followed by a period of "nodding off" and clouded mental functioning. Regular use leads to tolerance; tolerance may lead to physical dependence. In advanced stages of addiction, heroin becomes primarily a painkiller to stave off withdrawal symptoms. These symptoms, which may begin within hours of the last dose, include profuse sweating; alternating hot flashes and chills with goose bumps resembling the texture of a plucked turkey (hence, the term *cold turkey*); severe cramps, vomiting, and diarrhea; and convulsive shaking and kicking (as in "kicking the habit").

Heroin abuse is associated with serious health conditions, including fatal overdose, spontaneous abortion, collapsed veins, pulmonary problems, and infectious diseases, especially HIV/AIDS and hepatitis, as a result of sharing needles (Bourgeois, 1999; McCurdy, Williams, Kilonzo, Ross, & Leshabari, 2005; Meade, McDonald, & Weiss, 2009). Perhaps not surprisingly, the highest cause of death among heroin users is overdosing (Degenhardt et al., 2011).

Stimulants: Caffeine, Nicotine, Amphetamines, and Cocaine

How do people tend to feel after a stimulant wears off?

The drugs classified as **stimulants**—caffeine, nicotine, amphetamines, and cocaine—have legitimate uses, but because they produce feelings of optimism and boundless energy, the potential for abuse is high.

Caffeine Caffeine, which occurs naturally in coffee, tea, and cocoa, belongs to a class of drugs known as *xanthine stimulants*. The primary ingredient in over-the-counter stimulants, caffeine is popularly believed to maintain wakefulness and alertness, but many of its stimulant effects are illusory. In one study, research participants performing motor and perceptual tasks thought they were doing better when they were on caffeine, but their actual performance was no better than without it. In terms of wakefulness, caffeine reduces the total number of sleep minutes and increases the time it takes to fall asleep. It is the only stimulant that does not appear to alter sleep stages or cause REM rebound, making it much safer than amphetamines.

Caffeine is found in many beverages and nonprescription medications, including pain relievers, cold and allergy remedies, and a wide variety of energy drinks. (See **Figure 4–6.**)

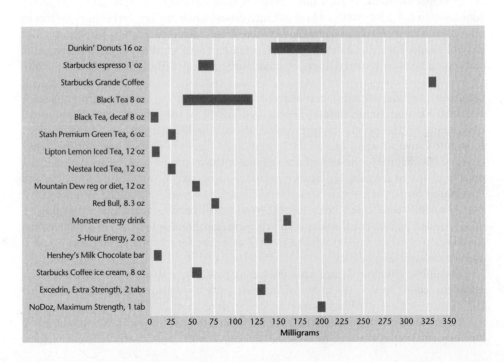

FIGURE 4–6

The amount of caffeine in some common preparations.

Caffeine occurs in varying amounts in coffee, tea, soft drinks, and many nonprescription medications.

Source: Based on Get Pharmacy Advice http://www.getpharmacyadvice.com/caffeine-content-in-various-beverages-and-foods/

It is generally considered a benign drug, although large doses—more than five or six cups of strong coffee per day, for example—may cause anxiety, headaches, heart palpitations, insomnia, and diarrhea. Caffeine interferes with prescribed medications, such as tranquilizers and sedatives, and appears to aggravate the symptoms of many psychiatric disorders. It is not clear what percentage of coffee drinkers are dependent on caffeine. Those who are dependent experience tolerance, difficulty in giving it up, and physical and psychological distress, such as headaches, lethargy, and depression, whether the caffeine is in soda, coffee, or tea (Juliano & Griffiths, 2004).

In recent years, beverages combining caffeine and alcohol have become popular, especially among college students. Early evidence suggested these "caffeinated alcoholic beverages" may pose a greater health risk than alcohol or caffeine consumed separately (Howland, Rohsenow, Calise, MacKillop, & Metrik, 2011), prompting the FDA to quickly remove many of these beverages from the market (U.S. Food and Drug Administration, 2010). Among the concerns raised by the consumption of caffeinated alcoholic beverages are an increase in the tendency to engage in risky behaviors, and a strong association with developing alcohol dependence among regular users (Arria, Caldeira, Kasperski, Vincent, Griffiths, & O'Grady, 2011).

Nicotine Nicotine, the psychoactive ingredient in tobacco, is probably the most dangerous and addictive stimulant in use today. Recent studies have found that the neurochemical properties of nicotine are similar to those of cocaine, amphetamines, and morphine (Fredrickson, Boules, Lin, & Richelson, 2005). When smoked, nicotine tends to arrive at the brain all at once following each puff—a rush similar to the "high" experienced by heroin users. The smoker's heart rate increases and blood vessels constrict, causing dull skin and cold hands and accelerating the process of wrinkling and aging. Nicotine affects levels of several neurotransmitters, including norepinephrine, dopamine, and serotonin. Depending on the time, the amount smoked, and other factors, it may have sedating or stimulating effects. Symptoms of withdrawal from nicotine include nervousness, difficulty concentrating, both insomnia and drowsiness, headaches, irritability, and intense craving, which continue for weeks and may recur months or even years after a smoker has quit (Haro & Drucker-Colín, 2004).

Despite well-known health risks and strong social pressures, millions of Americans continue to smoke, either for the pleasure of the combined stimulant-sedative effects or to prevent cravings and withdrawal symptoms. Particularly worrisome is that the number of teenagers who start smoking each year has hardly changed and nicotine addiction in young people happens very quickly (DiFranza et al., 2007). Youths aged 12–17 who smoke are about 12 times more likely to use illicit drugs, and 16 times more likely to drink heavily, than their nonsmoking peers (National Household Survey on Drug Abuse, 1998; D. Smith, 2001). The suggestion that nicotine may serve as a "gateway" drug receives some support from research showing that, taken during the adolescent years, nicotine may alter the way specific brain cells respond to serotonin increasing the likelihood of becoming addicted to other drugs (McQuown, 2010) (see Chapter 2, The Biological Basis of Behavior).

Amphetamines **Amphetamines** are powerful synthetic stimulants, first marketed in the 1930s as a nasal spray to relieve symptoms of asthma. At the chemical level, amphetamines resemble epinephrine, a hormone that stimulates the sympathetic nervous system. (See Chapter 2, "The Biological Basis of Behavior.") During World War II, the military routinely gave soldiers amphetamines in pill form to relieve fatigue. After the war, the demand for "pep pills" grew among night workers, truck drivers, students, and athletes. Because amphetamines tend to suppress the appetite, they were widely prescribed as "diet pills." Today, the only legitimate medical uses for amphetamines are to treat narcolepsy and attention deficit disorder. (Paradoxically, amphetamines have a calming effect on hyperactive children.) They are, however, widely used for nonmedical, "recreational" reasons.

Amphetamines not only increase alertness, but also produce feelings of competence and well-being. People who inject them intravenously report a "rush" of euphoria. After the drug's

Antismoking ads target teenagers who often start smoking while they are still young and then find it difficult to quit as adults.

amphetamines Stimulant drugs that initially produce "rushes" of euphoria often followed by sudden "crashes" and, sometimes, severe depression.

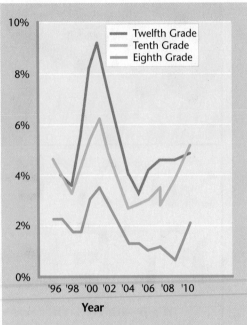

FIGURE 4–7

Teenage use of Ecstacy.

Teenage use of Ecstacy showed a dramatic increase between 1998 and 2001, and then it dropped sharply after 2001. In recent years, Ecstasy use has shown a disturbing increase, particularly among young adolescents.

Source: Monitoring the future: A continuing study of American Youth. http://www.monitoringthefuture.org/data/10data/pr10t2.pdf

cocaine Drug derived from the coca plant that, although producing a sense of euphoria by stimulating the sympathetic nervous system, also leads to anxiety, depression, and addictive cravings.

effects wear off, however, users may "crash" into a state of exhaustion and depression. Amphetamines are habit forming: Users may come to believe that they cannot function without them. High doses can cause sweating, tremors, heart palpitations, anxiety, and insomnia—which may lead people to take barbiturates or other drugs to counteract these effects. Excessive use of amphetamines may cause personality changes, including paranoia, homicidal and suicidal thoughts, and aggressive, violent behavior (Baker & Dawe, 2005). Chronic users may develop *amphetamine psychosis,* which resembles paranoid schizophrenia and is characterized by delusions, hallucinations, and paranoia.

Methamphetamine—known on the street as "speed" and "fire," or in a crystal, smokable form as "ice," "crystal," "crystal meth," and "crank"—is easily produced in clandestine laboratories from ingredients available over the counter. A variation that was briefly popular around the turn of the 21st century, Ecstasy (methylenedioxymethamphetamine, or MDMA), acts as both a stimulant and a hallucinogen. The name "Ecstasy" reflects the users' belief that the drug makes people love and trust one another, puts them in touch with their own emotions, and heightens sexual pleasure.

Short-term physical effects include involuntary teeth clenching (which is why users often wear baby pacifiers around their neck or suck lollipops), faintness, and chills or sweating. Although early research on Ecstasy with primates suggested that even short-term recreational use could have long-term harmful consequences, more recent studies have not verified evidence of permanent damage from short-term use (Navarro & Maldonado, 2004; Ricaurte, Yuan, Hatzidimitriou, Cord, & McCann, 2003; Sumnall, Jerome, Doblin, & Mithoefer, 2004). There is still some reason to be concerned, however, especially by heavy use. Animal research going back more than 20 years shows that high doses of methamphetamine damage the axon terminals of dopamine- and serotonin-containing neurons (National Institute on Drug Abuse, 2005b). Increased aggression in rats has been observed following a single low dose administration of methamphetamine (Kirilly et al., 2006). One study also found that the recreational use of Ecstasy may lead to a decrease in intelligence test scores (Gouzoulis-Mayfrank et al., 2000), and heavy use of MDMA has been associated with a decline in visual memory (Back-Madruga et al., 2003). Moreover, the use of Ecstasy during pregnancy has been associated with birth defects (McElhatton, Bateman, Evans, Pughe, & Thomas, 1999). Increased public awareness of the potential dangers associated with Ecstasy explains in part the sharp decline in its usage after 2000. Unfortunately, usage among young teenagers in particular, has shown a slight upturn in recent years (See **Figure 4–7.**)

Cocaine First isolated from cocoa leaves in 1885, **cocaine** came to be used widely as a topical anesthetic for minor surgery (and still is, for example, in the dental anesthetic Novocain). Around the turn of the century, many physicians believed that cocaine was beneficial as a general stimulant, as well as a cure for excessive use of alcohol and morphine addiction. Among the more famous cocaine users was Sigmund Freud. When he discovered how addictive cocaine was, Freud campaigned against it, as did many of his contemporaries, and ingesting the drug fell into disrepute.

Cocaine made a comeback in the 1970s in such unlikely places as Wall Street, among investment bankers who found that the drug not only made them high, but also allowed them to wheel and deal around the clock with little sleep (Califano, 1999). In the white-powdered form that is snorted (street names include "coke" and "snow"), it became a status drug; the amphetamine of the wealthy. In the 1980s, a cheaper, smokable, crystallized form known as "crack" (made from the by-products of cocaine extraction) appeared in inner-city neighborhoods. Crack reaches the brain in less than 10 seconds, producing a high that lasts from 5 to 20 minutes, followed by a swift and equally intense depression. Users report that crack leads to almost instantaneous addiction. Addiction to powdered cocaine, which has longer effects, is not inevitable, but is likely. Babies born to women addicted to crack and cocaine often are premature or have low-birth weight, may have withdrawal symptoms, and enter school with subtle deficits in intelligence and language skills (Bandstra, Morrow, Mansoor, & Accornero, 2010).

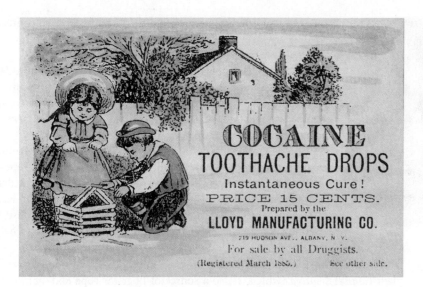

On the biochemical level, cocaine blocks the reabsorption of the neurotransmitter dopamine, which is associated with awareness, motivation, and, most significantly, pleasure (Bressan & Crippa, 2005). Excess dopamine intensifies and prolongs feelings of pleasure—hence the cocaine user's feelings of euphoria. Normally, dopamine is reabsorbed, leading to feelings of satiety or satisfaction; dopamine reabsorption tells the body, "That's enough." But cocaine short-circuits this feeling of satisfaction, in effect telling the body, "More!" The addictive potential of cocaine may be related to the fact that cocaine alters the way brain cells produce and respond to dopamine, so that an increasing amount of cocaine is needed to get the same high in the future (Perez, Ford, Goussakov, Stutzmann, & Hu, 2011).

Hallucinogens and Marijuana

How does marijuana affect memory?

Certain natural or synthetic drugs can cause striking shifts in perception of the outside world or, in some cases, can cause their users to experience imaginary landscapes, settings, and beings that may seem more real than the outside world. Because such experiences resemble hallucinations, the drugs causing them are known as **hallucinogens.** The hallucinogens include lysergic acid diethylamide (LSD, also known as "acid"), mescaline, peyote, psilocybin, and salvia. Marijuana is sometimes included in this group, although its effects are normally less powerful. How many cultural groups have used hallucinogens is not known. Historians believe that Native Americans have used mescaline, a psychedelic substance found in the mushroom-shaped tops or "buttons" of peyote cactus, for at least 8,000 years.

By contrast, the story of **lysergic acid diethylamide (LSD),** the drug that triggered the current interest in the hallucinogens, began in the 20th century. In 1943, an American pharmacologist synthesized LSD, and after ingesting it, he reported experiencing "an uninterrupted stream of fantastic pictures and extraordinary shapes with an intense, kaleidoscopic play of colors." His report led others to experiment with LSD as an artificial form of psychosis, a painkiller for terminal cancer patients, and a cure for alcoholism in the 1950s (Ashley, 1975). LSD came to public attention in the 1960s, when Harvard psychologist Timothy Leary, after trying the related hallucinogen psilocybin, began spreading the "Turn On, Tune In, Drop Out" gospel of the hippie movement. Use of LSD and marijuana declined steadily in the 1970s, but became popular once again in the 1990s, especially with high school and college students (Janofsky, 1994).

About an hour after ingesting LSD, people begin to experience an intensification of sensory perception, loss of control over their thoughts and emotions, and feelings of depersonalization and detachment. Some LSD users say that things never looked or sounded or smelled so beautiful; others have terrifying, nightmarish visions. Some users experience a

hallucinogens Any of a number of drugs, such as LSD and mescaline, that distort visual and auditory perception.

lysergic acid diethylamide (LSD) Hallucinogenic or "psychedelic" drug that produces hallucinations and delusions similar to those occurring in a psychotic state.

This Native American women is grinding dry peyote that will be mixed with water and drunk during an upcoming festival. Many Native American peoples have traditionally included peyote in their religious ceremonies.

marijuana A mild hallucinogen that produces a "high" often characterized by feelings of euphoria, a sense of well-being, and swings in mood from gaiety to relaxation; may also cause feelings of anxiety and paranoia.

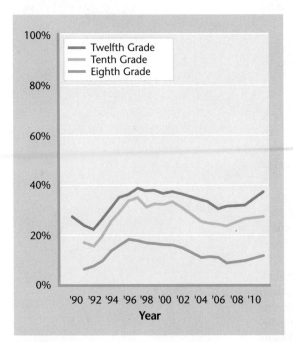

FIGURE 4–8

Teenage use of marijuana in past years.

A national survey found that use of marijuana by American teenagers reached a peak in the mid-1990s and then began a steady decline through 2007. Since 2007 the use of marijuana has shown a steady increase almost reaching levels not seen for more than a decade.

Source: Monitoring the future: A continuing study of American Youth. http://www.monitoringthefuture.org/data/10data/pr10t2.pdf

sense of extraordinary mental lucidity; others become so confused that they fear they are losing their minds. The effects of LSD are highly variable, even for the same person on different occasions.

"Bad trips," or unpleasant experiences, may be set off by a change in dosage or an alteration in setting or mood. Flashbacks, or recurrences of hallucinations, may occur weeks after ingesting LSD. Other consequences of frequent use may include memory loss, paranoia, panic attacks, nightmares, and aggression (Pechnick & Ungerleider, 2004).

Unlike depressants and stimulants, LSD and the other hallucinogens do not appear to produce withdrawal effects. If LSD is taken repeatedly, tolerance builds up rapidly: After a few days, no amount of the drug will produce its usual effects, until its use is suspended for about a week (McKim, 2007). This effect acts as a built-in deterrent to continuous use, which helps explain why LSD is generally taken episodically, rather than habitually.

Marijuana Marijuana is a mixture of dried, shredded flowers and leaves of the hemp plant *Cannabis sativa* (which is also a source of fiber for rope and fabrics). Unlike LSD, marijuana usage has a long history. In China, cannabis has been cultivated for at least 5,000 years. The ancient Greeks knew about its psychoactive effects; and it has been used as an intoxicant in India for centuries. But only in the 20th century did marijuana become popular in the United States. **Figure 4–8** shows the trend in marijuana use by American teenagers in recent years.

Although the active ingredient in marijuana, *tetrahydrocannabinol* (THC), shares some chemical properties with hallucinogens like LSD, it is far less potent. Marijuana smokers report feelings of relaxation; heightened enjoyment of food, music, and sex; a loss of awareness of time; and on occasion, dreamlike experiences. As with LSD, experiences are varied. Many users experience a sense of well-being, and some feel euphoric, but others become suspicious, anxious, and depressed.

Marijuana has direct physiological effects, including dilation of the blood vessels in the eyes, making the eyes appear bloodshot; a dry mouth and coughing (because it is generally smoked); increased thirst and hunger; and mild muscular weakness, often in the form of drooping eyelids (Donatelle, 2004). The use of marijuana during pregnancy has been associated with depression, attention disorders, and delinquency in children born to mothers who smoked marijuana while pregnant (Day, Leech, & Goldschmidt, 2011). Among the drug's psychological effects is a distortion of time, which appears to be related to the impact marijuana has on specific regions of the brain (D. S. O'Leary et al., 2003). Feelings that minutes occur in slow motion or that hours flash by in seconds are common. Marijuana use also produces alterations in short-term memory and attention (S. D. Lane, Cherek, Lieving, & Tcheremissine, 2005). In addition, neuroimaging studies have shown that chronic marijuana use may lead to poor decision making by altering the way specific brain centers respond to negative consequences (Wesley, Hanlon, & Porrino, 2011).

While under the influence of marijuana, people often lose the ability to remember and coordinate information, a phenomenon known as *temporal disintegration*. For instance, someone who is "high" on marijuana may forget what he or she was talking about in midsentence. While high, marijuana users have shortened attention spans and delayed reactions, which contribute to concerns about their ability to drive a car or to study or work effectively (National Institute on Drug Abuse, 2004b).

Is marijuana a "dangerous" drug? This question is the subject of much debate in scientific circles as well as public forums. On the one hand are those who contend that marijuana can be psychologically if not physiologically addictive (Haney et al., 2004; Levin et al., 2004); that frequent, long-term use has a negative impact on learning and motivation; and that legal prohibitions against marijuana should be continued. The evidence for cognitive or psychological damage is mixed. One study of college students showed that critical skills related to attention, memory, and learning are impaired among people who use marijuana heavily, even after discontinuing its use for at least 24 hours

THINKING CRITICALLY ABOUT . . .

Teenage Use of Marijuana

According to the National Institute on Drug Abuse (2005): Longitudinal research on marijuana use among young people below college age indicates those who used marijuana have lower achievement than the nonusers, more acceptance of deviant behavior, more delinquent behavior and aggression, greater rebelliousness, poorer relationships with parents, and more associations with delinquent and drug-using friends.

1. Write down as many possible explanations for the relationship between using marijuana and other behaviors mentioned as you can think of—the more, the better.

2. Now decide which of these explanations you consider most likely and why. How might you go about determining whether those explanations are, in fact, correct?

3. Examine the assumptions underlying your decisions, or exchange your list with classmates and evaluate each other's assumptions.

(National Institute on Drug Abuse, 2004a). Another found that marijuana use is associated with microscopic reductions in the white matter of the frontal lobes, leading to an increase in impulsive behavior (Gruber, Silveri, Dahlgren, & Yurgelun-Todd, 2011). On the other hand are those who maintain that marijuana is less harmful than the legal drugs, alcohol and nicotine. They argue that the criminalization of marijuana forces people to buy unregulated cannabis from illegal sources, which means that they might smoke "pot" contaminated with more harmful substances. Moreover, some evidence indicates that marijuana can relieve some of the unpleasant side effects of chemotherapy and can reduce suffering among terminal cancer patients. In short, the jury is still out, and the debate over marijuana is likely to continue (Cohen, 2009).

Explaining Abuse and Addiction

What combination of factors makes it more likely that someone will abuse drugs?

Some people drink socially and never develop a problem with alcohol, whereas others become dependent or addicted. Some experiment with crack or use "club drugs," whereas others "just say no." Each year, millions of Americans stop smoking cigarettes. Given the known hazards of smoking, why do a significant number of them relapse after months, even years, of not smoking?

The causes of substance abuse and dependence are complex; the result of a combination of biological, psychological, social, and cultural factors that varies from person to person, and depend on what psychoactive drug or drugs are used. But psychologists have identified a number of factors that, especially in combination, make it more likely that a person will abuse drugs.

Biological Factors There is mounting evidence that "At least half of a person's susceptibility to drug addiction can be linked to genetic factors" (Price, 2008, p. 16; see also Nurnberger & Bierut, 2007). The evidence for a genetic predisposition for alcohol abuse is strong, though there is not just one gene that is involved (Nurnberger & Bierut, 2007). People whose biological parents have alcohol-abuse problems are more likely to abuse alcohol—even if they are adopted and are raised by people who do not abuse alcohol. Identical twins are far more likely to have similar patterns relating to alcohol, tobacco, and marijuana use than are fraternal twins (Gordis, 1996; C. Lerman et al., 1999; I-C. Liu et al., 2004; National Institute on Drug Abuse, 2004a). Even the *subjective effects* alcohol, tobacco, and marijuana produce on users, such as the degree of euphoria, pleasantness, or unpleasantness, appear to have a strong genetic component (Haberstick, 2011).

Psychologists have not reached consensus on the exact role that heredity plays in a predisposition for alcoholism (or abuse of other substances). Some psychologists point to hereditary differences in enzymes that break down alcohol in the body (Nurnberger & Bierut, 2007). People also appear to differ genetically in their tolerance for alcohol in the blood and in the ways they react to alcohol (Ball, 2004). Heredity can also profoundly affect the quantity of key neurotransmitters in the brain, (Nurnberger & Bierut, 2007; Vadasz et al., 2007) as well as the number of receptors that respond to those neurotransmitters (Dalley et al., 2007; Sherva et al., 2008). In turn, those changes in the brain appear to affect the likelihood that a person will become addicted to drugs.

Is addiction a disease, like diabetes or high blood pressure? Alcoholics Anonymous (AA), the oldest and probably the most successful self-help organization in this country, has long endorsed this view. According to the disease model, alcoholism is not a moral issue, but a medical one; and rather than being a sign of character flaws, alcohol abuse is a symptom of a physiological condition. An important aspect of the disease model is that, regardless of the initial source of the addiction, addictive substances dramatically change the brain. Those changes can take months or years to reverse and, during that time, cravings to use the drug can be intense.

The disease model has been applied to many addictions. For example, a relatively new organization called Nicotine Anonymous, dedicated to helping smokers quit, now operates over 450 active groups in the United States and additional groups in 35 other countries (Nicotine Anonymous, 2008). To some degree, the disease model has become part of conventional wisdom: Many Americans view substance abuse as a biological problem, often the result of "bad" genes, which requires medical treatment. Not all psychologists agree, however. Problems with alcohol are better described as a continuum, ranging from mild to severe dependence with many stages in between. The either/or view tends to discourage people from seeking help until their problems have become severe and are more difficult to overcome, and to stigmatize those who go through cycles of sobriety and relapse as weak and contemptible, emphasizing their setbacks rather than their success. It is more appropriate to consider addiction to have a physical basis but important psychological, social, and cultural implications as well.

Psychological, Social, and Cultural Factors   Whether a person uses a psychoactive drug and what effects that drug has depends in part on the person's expectations, the social setting, and cultural beliefs and values. For instance, one survey found that the principal reason American college students drink alcohol, smoke cigarettes, or use other drugs is to reduce stress, forget about their problems, and to fit in socially (National Center on Addiction and Substance Abuse, 2007).

The environment in which a child grows up also shapes attitudes and beliefs about drugs. It also appears to play a larger role than does heredity in determining whether an individual starts to drink, smoke, or use other drugs, though "genetic factors are more influential in determining who progresses to problem use or abuse" (National Center on Addiction and Substance Abuse, 2007, p. 42). For example, children whose parents do not use alcohol tend to abstain or to drink only moderately; children whose parents abuse alcohol tend to drink heavily (Chassin, Pitts, Delucia, & Todd, 1999; Chassin, Flora, & King, 2004). Parents are not the only family influence; some research indicates that siblings' and peers' attitudes and behavior have as much or more impact on young people than parents do (Ary, Duncan, Duncan, & Hops, 1999; J. R. Harris, 1998).

Culture, too, may steer people toward or away from alcohol. Parents and spouses may introduce people by example to a pattern of heavy drinking. Alcohol is also more acceptable in some ethnic cultures than in others—for example, many religions frown on the excessive use of alcohol, and Muslims, Mormons, conservative Baptists, and Seventh-Day Adventists prohibit it.

In sum, many researchers believe that a full understanding of the causes of alcoholism and other drug addictions will not be achieved unless we take account of a wide variety of factors: heredity, personality, social setting, and culture.

As we have seen, a wide variety of psychoactive drugs may alter consciousness, often with negative consequences such as abuse and addiction. In the next section we will look at meditation and hypnosis, two procedures that have been used for centuries to promote positive outcomes through altered states of consciousness.

ENDURING ISSUES

Person–Situation   Factors Affecting Drug Effects

The setting in which drugs are taken is another powerful determinant of their effects (S. Siegel, 2005). Every year thousands of hospital patients are given opiate-based pain-killers before and after surgery. They may have experiences that a heroin or cocaine user would label as a "high," but they are more likely to consider them confusing than pleasant. In this setting, psychoactive substances are defined as medicine, dosage is supervised by physicians, and patients take them to get well, not to get high. In contrast, at teenage raves, college beer parties, and all-night clubs, people drink specifically to get drunk and take other drugs to get high. But even in these settings, some individuals participate without using or abusing drugs, and motives for using drugs vary. People who drink or smoke marijuana because they think that they need a drug to overcome social inhibitions and to be accepted are more likely to slip into abuse than people who use the same substances in the same amounts because they want to have more fun. ■

✓●─Study and Review on MyPsychLab

CHECK YOUR UNDERSTANDING

Indicate whether the following statements are true (T) or false (F):

1. ____ Alcohol is implicated in more than two-thirds of all automobile accidents.
2. ____ Caffeine is not addictive.
3. ____ Many users become dependent on crack cocaine almost immediately after beginning to use it.
4. ____ Recurring hallucinations are common among users of hallucinogens.
5. ____ Marijuana interferes with short-term memory.

Answers: 1. (T). 2. (F). 3. (T). 4. (T). 5. (T).

APPLY YOUR UNDERSTANDING

1. Although you know that alcohol is a central nervous system depressant, your friend says it is actually a stimulant because he does things that he wouldn't otherwise do after having a couple of drinks. He also feels less inhibited, more spontaneous, and more entertaining. The reason your friend experiences alcohol as a stimulant is that
   a. alcohol has the same effect on the nervous system as amphetamines.
   b. alcohol has a strong placebo effect.
   c. the effects of alcohol depend almost entirely on the expectations of the user.
   d. alcohol depresses areas in the brain responsible for critical judgment and impulsiveness.

2. John drinks five or six cups of strong coffee each day. Which of the following symptoms is he most likely to report?
   a. nausea, loss of appetite, cold hands, and chills
   b. feelings of euphoria and well-being
   c. anxiety, headaches, insomnia, and diarrhea
   d. time distortion and reduced emotional sensitivity

Answers: 1. d. 2. c.

LEARNING OBJECTIVES

- Describe the biological and psychological effects of meditation.
- Explain why it is difficult to define hypnosis, the process of inducing hypnosis, and the role of hypnotic suggestions.

meditation Any of the various methods of concentration, reflection, or focusing of thoughts undertaken to suppress the activity of the sympathetic nervous system.

MEDITATION AND HYPNOSIS

Can hypnosis help you overcome a problem, such as smoking or overeating?

At one time, Western scientists viewed meditation and hypnosis with great skepticism. However, research has shown that both techniques can produce alterations in consciousness that can be measured through such sophisticated methods as brain imaging.

Meditation

What are the effects of meditation?

For centuries, people have used various forms of **meditation** to experience an alteration in consciousness. Each form of meditation focuses the meditator's attention in a slightly different way. *Zen meditation* concentrates on respiration, for example, whereas *Sufism* relies on frenzied dancing and prayer. In *transcendental meditation* (TM), practitioners intone a mantra, which is a sound, specially selected for each person, to keep all other images and problems at bay and to allow the meditator to relax more deeply. The fact that mediation may take many different forms presents one of the challenges facing psychologists who study meditation (Caspi & Burleson, 2005). Some forms of meditation result in a restful, yet fully alert state that enables the self-regulation of one's emotions. Other forms lead to a state of *mindfulness,* which is "a full-spectrum awareness of the present moment just as it is, accepting whatever is happening simply because it is already happening" (Kabat-Zinn, 2006, p. 61).

In all its forms, meditation suppresses the activity of the sympathetic nervous system which, as we noted in Chapter 2, is the part of the nervous system that prepares the body for strenuous activity during an emergency. Meditation also lowers the rate of metabolism, reduces heart and respiratory rates, and decreases blood lactate, a chemical linked to stress. Alpha brain waves (which accompany relaxed wakefulness) increase noticeably during meditation. Not surprisingly, brain-imagining studies indicate that practicing meditation activates brain centers involved in attention and regulation of the autonomic nervous system activity (Cahn & Polich, 2006; Lazar et al., 2000).

Meditation has been used to treat certain medical problems, especially so-called functional complaints (those for which no physical cause can be found). For example, stress often leads to muscle tension and, sometimes, to pressure on nerves—and pain. Relaxation techniques such as meditation may bring relief of such physical symptoms (Blanchard et al., 1990; Moriconi, 2004). Other evidence suggests that meditation may even be useful in treating children diagnosed with attention-deficit hyperactive disorder, and in

Meditation can help relieve anxiety and promote peace of mind and a sense of well-being.

helping their parents manage the additional stress often placed on their families (Harrison, Manocha, & Rubia, 2004). Studies have also shown that mindfulness-meditation is effective in helping people stop using drugs, and in the prevention of relapses among past drug users (Witkiewitz, Marlatt, & Walker, 2005). Finally, some evidence indicates that meditation may increase the effectiveness of the immune system (R. J. Davidson et al., 2003; Pace et al., 2009).

Besides physiological benefits, research has shown that even brief periods of meditation can reduced fatigue, anxiety, and blood pressure, and improve mood, visual-spatial processing, and memory (Zeidan, 2010).

Hypnosis

What clinical uses have been found for hypnosis?

In mid-18th-century Europe, Anton Mesmer, a Viennese physician, fascinated audiences by putting patients into trances to cure their illnesses. Mesmerism—now known as **hypnosis**—was initially discredited by a French commission chaired by Benjamin Franklin (Forrest, 2002). But some respectable 19th-century physicians revived interest in hypnosis when they discovered that it could be used to treat certain forms of mental illness. Nevertheless, even today considerable disagreement persists about how to define hypnosis.

One reason for the controversy is that from a behavioral standpoint, there is no simple definition of exactly what it means to be hypnotized. Different people who are believed to have undergone hypnosis describe their experiences in very different ways. Similarly, some researchers who study hypnosis still debate whether or not it should be characterized as a state of altered consciousness (Lynn & Kirsch, 2006c). Other researchers stress that studying the phenomena that characterize a hypnotic state, such as the social interactions and the neurophysiological changes (Gruzelier, 2005), is of more importance than reaching a consensus on whether hypnosis is an altered state (Kihlström, 2005; Lynn, Fassler, & Knox, 2005).

The Process of Hypnosis The Society of Psychological Hypnosis (Division 30 of the APA) states that

> Hypnosis typically involves an introduction to the procedure during which the subject is told that suggestions for imaginative experiences will be presented.... When using hypnosis, one person (the subject) is guided by another (the hypnotist) to respond to suggestions for changes in subjective experience, alterations in perception, sensation, emotion, thought or behavior. (American Psychological Association, 2005)

Although the specifics of the procedure may vary depending on the hypnotist and the purpose for the hypnosis, most hypnotic induction procedures involve a suggestion to relax. Some people learn to administer hypnotic procedures to themselves, in which case it is referred to as *self-hypnosis*.

Hypnotic Suggestions Individuals also vary in their susceptibility to hypnosis. Several studies have shown that although susceptibility to hypnosis is not related to personal characteristics such as trust, gullibility, submissiveness, and social compliance, it is related to the ability of an individual to *dissociate,* or become absorbed in reading, music, and daydreaming (Terhune, Cardena, & Lindgren, 2011).

One measure of susceptibility is whether people respond to hypnotic suggestion. Some people who are told that they cannot move their arms or that their pain has vanished do, in fact, experience paralysis or anesthesia; if told that they are hearing a certain piece of music or are unable to hear anything, they may hallucinate or become deaf temporarily (Montgomery, DuHamel, & Redd, 2000). But, contrary to rumors, hypnotic suggestion cannot force people to do something foolish and embarrassing—or dangerous—against their will.

Another measure of the success of hypnosis is whether people respond to *posthypnotic commands.* For example, under hypnosis, a person suffering from back pain may be instructed that when he feels a twinge, he will imagine that he is floating on a cloud, his body is weightless, and the pain will stop—a technique also called "imaging." A runner

hypnosis Trancelike state in which a person responds readily to suggestions.

Susceptibility to hypnosis varies from person to person, but many people have found it useful in a variety of medical and counseling situations.

may be told that when she pulls on her ear, she will block out the noise of the crowd and the runners on either side of her to heighten her concentration—a form of self-hypnosis. As the last example suggests, hypnosis has become increasingly popular among professional athletes and their weekend counterparts (Edgette & Rowan, 2003; Liggett, 2000).

ENDURING ISSUES

Mind–Body   Clinical Applications of Hypnosis

Because hypnotic susceptibility varies significantly from one person to another, its value in clinical and therapeutic settings is difficult to assess (Smith, 2011). Nevertheless, hypnosis is used in a variety of medical and counseling situations (Lynn, Kirsch, & Rhue, 2010). Some research indicates that it can enhance the effectiveness of traditional forms of psychotherapy (Chapman, 2006; Kirsch, Montgomery, & Sapirstein, 1995), especially when it is used to treat anxiety disorders (Lynn & Kirsch, 2006a) and posttraumatic stress disorder (Lynn & Kirsch, 2006b). Hypnosis has been shown to be effective in controlling various types of physical pain (D. R. Patterson, 2010). Dentists have used it as an anesthetic for years. Hypnosis has also been used to alleviate pain in children with leukemia who have to undergo repeated bone-marrow biopsies (Hilgard, Hilgard, & Kaufmann, 1983). Moreover, it also has a role in treating some medical conditions, such as irritable bowel syndrome (Gonsalkorale, Miller, Afzal, & Whorwell, 2003).

Can hypnosis make someone change or eliminate bad habits? In some cases, posthypnotic commands temporarily diminish a person's desire to smoke, abuse alcohol, or overeat (Tramontana, 2009). But even certified hypnotists agree that this treatment is effective only if people are motivated to change their behavior. Hypnosis may shore up their will, but so might joining a support group, such as Nicotine Anonymous or Weight Watchers. ■ ◉

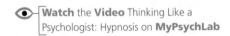

Watch the **Video** Thinking Like a Psychologist: Hypnosis on **MyPsychLab**

Study and **Review** on **MyPsychLab**

CHECK YOUR UNDERSTANDING

Match the following terms with the appropriate description:

1. ____ meditation
2. ____ hypnosis
3. ____ hypnotic susceptibility

a. varies tremendously over time
b. is a controversial altered state of consciousness
c. suppresses sympathetic nervous system

Answers: 1.c. 2.b. 3.a.

1. Marie is a professional athlete involved in competitive sports. She regularly practices transcendental meditation as part of her training. The most likely reason she finds this practice beneficial is that meditation

    a. increases the rate of metabolism.
    b. increases the activity of the sympathetic nervous system.
    c. produces deep relaxation.
    d. increases the respiratory rate.

2. You overhear some people discussing the effects of hypnosis. On the basis of what you have learned in this chapter, you agree with everything they say EXCEPT

    a. "Some people can easily be hypnotized and some people can't."
    b. "If you tell someone under hypnosis to forget everything that happens, some people will actually do that."
    c. "Under hypnosis, people can be forced to do foolish or embarrassing things against their will."
    d. "Hypnosis can actually be used to control some kinds of pain."

Answers: 1. c. 2. c.

KEY TERMS

consciousness, p. 119
waking consciousness, p. 119
altered states of consciousness, p. 119

Sleep
circadian rhythm, p. 120
suprachiasmatic nucleus (SCN), p. 120
rapid-eye movement (REM) or paradoxical sleep, p. 122
non-REM (NREM) sleep, p. 122

nightmares, p. 126
night terrors, p. 126
insomnia, p. 127
apnea, p. 127
narcolepsy, p. 128

Dreams
dreams, p. 128

Drug-Altered Consciousness
psychoactive drugs, p. 131
substance abuse, p. 132

substance dependence, p. 132
double-blind procedure, p. 132
placebo, p. 132
depressants, p. 133
alcohol, p. 133
alcoholic myopia, p. 135
barbiturates, p. 137
opiates, p. 137
stimulants, p. 138
amphetamines, p. 139
cocaine, p. 140
hallucinogens, p. 141

lysergic acid diethylamide (LSD), p. 141
marijuana, p. 142

Meditation and Hypnosis
meditation, p. 146
hypnosis, p. 147

CHAPTER REVIEW ((•─[Listen to the **Chapter Audio** on **MyPsychLab**

Consciousness is our awareness of various cognitive processes that operate in our daily lives such as sleeping, dreaming, concentrating, and making decisions. To make sense of our complex environment, we selectively choose which stimuli to absorb and we filter out the rest. Psychologists divide consciousness into two broad areas: **waking consciousness,** which includes thoughts, feelings, and perceptions that arise when we are awake and reasonably alert; and **altered states of consciousness,** during which our mental state differs noticeably from normal waking consciousness.

SLEEP

Why do we need to sleep? Nobody knows exactly why we need to sleep, although sleep appears to play an important restorative function, both physically and mentally. Getting adequate sleep boosts our immune response and cleanses the body of chemicals like adenosine, which is released when cells use energy. Sleep also appears to play a crucial role in long-term memory formation.

What is the biological clock? Like many other biological functions, sleep and waking follow a daily biological cycle known as a **circadian rhythm.** The human *biological clock* is governed by a tiny cluster of neurons in the brain known as the **suprachiasmatic nucleus (SCN)** that regulates proteins related to metabolism and alertness. Normally, the rhythms and chemistry of the body's cycles interact smoothly; but when we cross several time zones in one day, hormonal, temperature, and digestive cycles become desynchronized.

What physical changes mark the rhythms of sleep? Normal sleep consists of several stages. During *Stage 1,* the pulse slows, muscles relax, and the eyes move from side to side. The sleeper is easily awakened from Stage 1 sleep. In *Stages 2* and *3,* the sleeper is hard to awaken and does not respond to noise or light. Heart rate, blood pressure, and temperature continue to drop. During *Stage 4* sleep, heart and breathing rates, blood pressure, and body temperature are at their lowest points of the night. About an hour after first falling asleep, the sleeper begins to ascend through the stages back to Stage 1—a process that takes about 40 minutes. At this stage in the sleep cycle, heart rate and blood pressure increase, the muscles become more relaxed than at any other time in the cycle, and the eyes move rapidly under closed eyelids. This stage of sleep is known as **rapid-eye movement (REM) or paradoxical sleep.**

What happens when people don't get enough sleep? Between one-third and one-half of adults fail to get enough sleep. Among adolescents, not getting enough sleep may result in falling asleep at school. Sleep deprivation negatively affects reaction time, memory, judgment, and the ability to pay attention. Driving while sleepy is just as dangerous as driving drunk. Sleep deprivation has been associated with errors and poor performance at work leading to serious mishaps in high-risk professions such as medicine or working at a nuclear power plant. The lack of sleep also contributes to such diseases as heart attacks, asthma, strokes, high blood pressure, and diabetes and is associated with depression and being overweight. Unfortunately, people do not always know when they are not getting enough sleep.

What is the difference between a nightmare and night terror? Sleep disorders include sleeptalking, sleepwalking, night terrors, insomnia, apnea, and narcolepsy. Most episodes of sleeptalking and sleepwalking occur during a deep stage of sleep. Unlike **nightmares,** frightening dreams that most often occur during REM sleep and are remembered, **night terrors** are more common among children than adults, prove difficult to be awakened from, and are rarely remembered the next morning. **Insomnia** is characterized by difficulty in falling asleep or remaining asleep throughout the night. **Apnea** is marked by breathing difficulties during the night and feelings of exhaustion during the day. **Narcolepsy** is a hereditary sleep disorder characterized by sudden nodding off during the day and sudden loss of muscle tone following moments of emotional excitement.

DREAMS

What are dreams? Dreams are visual or auditory experiences that occur primarily during REM periods of sleep. Less vivid experiences that resemble conscious thinking tend to occur during **NREM** sleep.

Why do we dream? Several theories have been developed to explain the nature and content of dreams. According to Freud, dreams have two kinds of content: manifest (the surface content of the dream itself) and latent (the disguised, unconscious meaning of the dream). According to a more recent hypothesis, dreams arise out of the mind's reprocessing of daytime information that is important to the survival of the organism. With this hypothesis, dreaming thus strengthens our memories of important information.

DRUG-ALTERED CONSCIOUSNESS

How is today's drug problem different from drug use in other societies and times? Chemical substances that change moods and perceptions are known as **psychoactive drugs.** Although many of the psychoactive drugs available today have been used for thousands of years, the motivation for using drugs is different today. Traditionally, these drugs were used in religious rituals, as nutrient beverages, or as culturally approved stimulants. Today, most psychoactive drug use is recreational, divorced from religious or family traditions.

How can we tell whether someone is dependent on a psychoactive substance? Substance abuse is a pattern of drug use that diminishes the person's ability to fulfill responsibilities at home, work, or school and that results in repeated use of a drug in dangerous situations or that leads to legal difficulties related to drug use. Continued abuse over time can lead to **substance dependence,** a pattern of compulsive drug taking that is much more serious than substance abuse. It is often marked by tolerance, the need to take higher doses of a drug to produce its original effects or to prevent withdrawal symptoms. Withdrawal symptoms are the unpleasant physical or psychological effects that follow discontinuance of the psychoactive substance. When studying drug effects, most researchers use the **double-blind procedure** in which some participants receive the active drug while others take a neutral, inactive substance called a **placebo.**

Why does alcohol, a depressant, lead to higher rates of violence? Depressants are chemicals that slow down behavior or cognitive processes. **Alcohol** calms down the nervous system, working like a general anesthetic. It is often experienced subjectively as a stimulant because it inhibits centers in the brain that govern critical judgment (**alcoholic myopia**) and impulsive behavior. This accounts for its involvement in a substantial proportion of violent and accidental deaths. **Barbiturates** are potentially deadly depressants, first used for their sedative and anticonvulsant properties, but today their use is limited to the treatment of such conditions as epilepsy and arthritis. The **opiates** are highly addictive drugs such as opium, morphine, and heroin that dull the senses and induce feelings of euphoria, well-being, and relaxation. Morphine and heroin are derivatives of opium.

How do people tend to feel after a stimulant wears off? Stimulants are drugs that stimulate the sympathetic nervous system and produce feelings of optimism and boundless energy, making the potential for their abuse significant. Caffeine occurs naturally in coffee, tea, and cocoa. Considered a benign drug, in large doses caffeine can cause anxiety, insomnia, and other unpleasant conditions. Nicotine occurs naturally only in tobacco. Although it is a stimulant, it acts like a depressant when taken in large doses. **Amphetamines** are stimulants that initially produce "rushes" of euphoria often followed by sudden "crashes" and, sometimes, depression. **Cocaine** brings on a sense of euphoria by stimulating the sympathetic nervous system, but it can also cause anxiety, depression, and addictive cravings. Its crystalline form—crack—is highly addictive.

How does marijuana affect memory? Hallucinogens include drugs such as **LSD,** psilocybin, and mescaline that distort visual and auditory perception. **Marijuana** is a mild hallucinogen capable of producing feelings of euphoria, a sense of well-being, and swings in mood from gaiety to relaxation to paranoia. Though similar to hallucinogens in certain respects, marijuana is far less potent, and its effects on consciousness are far less profound. Marijuana can disrupt memory, causing people to forget what they are talking about in midsentence.

What combination of factors makes it more likely that someone will abuse drugs? A possible genetic predisposition, the person's expectations, the social setting, and cultural beliefs and values make drug abuse more likely.

MEDITATION AND HYPNOSIS

What are the effects of meditation? Meditation refers to any of several methods of concentration, reflection, or focusing of thoughts intended to suppress the activity of the sympathetic nervous system. Meditation not only lowers the metabolic rate but also reduces heart and respiratory rates. Brain activity during meditation resembles that experienced during relaxed wakefulness; and the accompanying decrease in blood lactate reduces stress.

What clinical uses have been found for hypnosis? Hypnosis is a trancelike state in which the hypnotized person responds readily to suggestions. Susceptibility to hypnosis depends on how easily people can become absorbed in concentration. Hypnosis can ease the pain of certain medical conditions and can help people stop smoking and break other habits.

5

Learning

What do the following anecdotes have in common?

- In Mozambique, a giant pouched rat the size of a cat scurries across a field, pauses, sniffs the air, turns, sniffs again, and then begins to scratch at the ground with her forepaws. She has discovered yet another land mine buried a few, inches underground. After a brief break for a bit of banana and a pat or two from her handler, she scurries off again to find more land mines.

- In the middle of a winter night, Adrian Cole—4 years old and three feet tall—put on his jacket and boots and drove his mother's car to a nearby video store. When he found the store closed, he drove back home. Since he was driving very slowly with the lights off and was also weaving a bit, he understandably attracted the attention of police officers who followed him. When he got home, he collided with two parked cars and then backed into the police cruiser! When the police asked him how he learned to drive, he explained that his mother would put him on her lap while she drove and he just watched what she did.

- "I just can't stand to eat shrimp. I don't like the smell of it, or the sight of it. Once when I young, I had some for dinner while vacationing at the beach and it made me sick for the rest of the week. Now just the thought of it disgusts me."

The common element in all these stories—and the topic of this chapter—is learning. Although most people associate learning with classrooms and studying for tests, psychologists define it more broadly. To them, **learning** occurs whenever experience or practice results in a relatively permanent change in behavior or in potential behavior. This definition includes all the examples previously mentioned, plus a great many more. When you remember how to park a car or where the library water fountain is, you are showing a tiny part of your enormous capacity for learning.

Human life would be impossible without learning; it is involved in virtually everything we do. You could not communicate with other people or recognize yourself as human if you were unable to learn. In this chapter, we explore several kinds of learning. One type is learning to associate one event with another. When pouched rats associate the smell of TNT and receiving food or when a person associates the sight or smell of a food with illness they are engaging in two forms of learning called *operant* and *classical conditioning*. Because psychologists have studied these forms of learning so extensively, much of this chapter is devoted to them. But making associations isn't all there is to human learning. Our learning also involves the formation of concepts, theories, ideas, and other mental abstractions. Psychologists call it *cognitive learning,* and we discuss it at the end of this chapter.

Our tour of learning begins in the laboratory of a Nobel Prize–winning Russian scientist at the turn of the 20th century. His name is Ivan Pavlov, and his work is helping to revolutionize the study of learning. He has discovered classical conditioning.

ENDURING ISSUES in Learning

This chapter addresses how humans and other animals acquire new behaviors as a result of their experiences. Thus, it bears directly on the enduring issue of Stability versus Change (the extent to which organisms change over the course of their lives). The events that shape learning not only vary among different individuals (diversity–universality) but also are influenced by an organism's inborn characteristics (nature–nurture). Finally, some types of learning can affect our physical health by influencing how our body responds to disease (mind–body).

CLASSICAL CONDITIONING

How did Pavlov discover classical conditioning?

The Russian physiologist Ivan Pavlov (1849–1936) discovered **classical (or Pavlovian) conditioning,** a form of learning in which a response elicited by a stimulus becomes elicited by a previously neutral stimulus, almost by accident. While measuring how much saliva dogs produce when given food, he noticed that the mere sight of food or the sound of his footsteps made them drool. This aroused Pavlov's curiosity. How had the dogs learned to salivate to sights and sounds?

To answer this question, Pavlov sounded a bell just before presenting his dogs with food. A ringing bell does not usually make a dog's mouth water, but after hearing the bell many times right before getting fed, Pavlov's dogs began to salivate as soon as the bell rang. It was as if they had learned that the bell signaled the appearance of food; and

- Define learning.
- Describe the elements of classical conditioning, distinguishing among unconditioned stimulus, unconditioned response, conditioned stimulus and conditioned response.
- Describe the process of establishing a classically conditioned response, including the effect of intermittent pairing.
- Provide examples of classical conditioning in humans, including desensitization therapy. Explain the statement that "classical conditioning is selective" and illustrate with examples of conditioned taste aversions.

learning The process by which experience or practice results in a relatively permanent change in behavior or potential behavior.

classical (or Pavlovian) conditioning The type of learning in which a response naturally elicited by one stimulus comes to be elicited by a different, formerly neutral, stimulus.

unconditioned stimulus (US) A stimulus that invariably causes an organism to respond in a specific way.

unconditioned response (UR) A response that takes place in an organism whenever an unconditioned stimulus occurs.

conditioned stimulus (CS) An originally neutral stimulus that is paired with an unconditioned stimulus and eventually produces the desired response in an organism when presented alone.

conditioned response (CR) After conditioning, the response an organism produces when a conditioned stimulus is presented.

their mouths watered on cue even if no food followed. The dogs had been *conditioned* to salivate in response to a new stimulus (Pavlov, 1927). **Figure 5–1** shows one of Pavlov's procedures in which the bell has been replaced by a touch to the dog's leg just before food is given.

Elements of Classical Conditioning

How might you classically condition a pet?

Figure 5–2 diagrams the four basic elements in classical conditioning: the unconditioned stimulus, the unconditioned response, the conditioned stimulus, and the conditioned response. The **unconditioned stimulus (US)** is an event that automatically elicits a certain reflex reaction, which is the **unconditioned response (UR)**. In Pavlov's studies, food in the mouth was the unconditioned stimulus, and salivation to it was the unconditioned response. The third element in classical conditioning, the **conditioned stimulus (CS)**, is an event that is repeatedly paired with the unconditioned stimulus. For a conditioned stimulus, Pavlov often used a bell. At first, the conditioned stimulus does not elicit the desired response. But eventually, after repeatedly being paired with the unconditioned stimulus, the conditioned stimulus alone comes to trigger a reaction similar to the unconditioned response. This learned reaction is the **conditioned response (CR).**

Classical conditioning has been demonstrated in virtually every animal species, even cockroaches, bees, and sheep. You yourself may have inadvertently classically conditioned one of your pets. For instance, you may have noticed that your cat begins to purr when it hears the sound of the electric can opener running. For a cat, the taste and smell of food

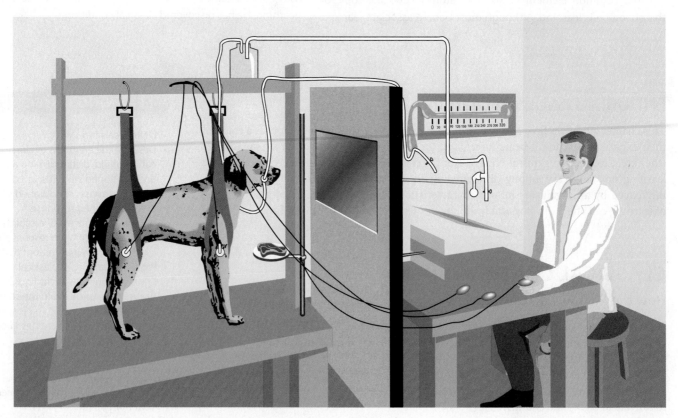

FIGURE 5–1

Pavlov's apparatus for classically conditioning a dog to salivate.

The experimenter sits behind a one-way mirror and controls the presentation of the conditioned stimulus (touch applied to the leg) and the unconditioned stimulus (food). A tube runs from the dog's salivary glands to a vial, where the drops of saliva are collected as a way of measuring the strength of the dog's response.

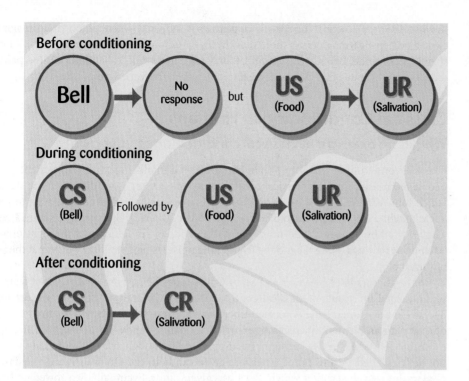

FIGURE 5–2
A model of the classical conditioning process.

are unconditioned stimuli for a purring response. By repeatedly pairing the can opener whirring with the delivery of food, you have turned this sound into a conditioned stimulus that triggers a conditioned response.

Establishing a Classically Conditioned Response

If you once burned your finger on a match while listening to a certain song, why doesn't that song now make you reflexively jerk your hand away?

As shown in **Figure 5–3**, it generally takes repeated pairings of an unconditioned stimulus and a cue before the unconditioned response eventually becomes a conditioned response. The likelihood or strength of the conditioned response increases each time these two stimuli are paired. This learning, however, eventually reaches a point of diminishing returns. The amount of each increase gradually becomes smaller, until finally no further learning occurs. The conditioned response is now fully established.

The spacing of pairings is also important in establishing a classically conditioned response. If pairings of the CS and US follow each other very rapidly, or if they are very far apart, learning

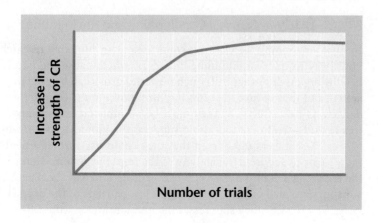

FIGURE 5–3
Response acquisition.

At first, each pairing of the US and CS increases the strength of the response. After a number of trials, learning begins to level off; and eventually it reaches a point of diminishing returns.

Desensitization therapy is based on the belief that we can overcome fears by learning to remain calm in the face of increasingly fear-arousing situations. Here people being desensitized to a fear of heights are able to swing high above the ground without panicking.

the association is slower. If the spacing of pairings is moderate—neither too far apart nor too close together—learning occurs more quickly. It is also important that the CS and US rarely, if ever, occur alone. Pairing the CS and US only once in a while, called **intermittent pairing**, reduces both the rate of learning and the final strength of the learned response.

Classical Conditioning in Humans

What is an example of classical conditioning in your own life?

Classical conditioning is as common in humans as it is in other animals. For example, some people learn fears through classical conditioning. In Chapter 1, we discussed the study in which John Watson and his assistant, Rosalie Rayner, used classical conditioning to instill a fear of white rats in a 1-year-old baby named Little Albert (J. B. Watson & Rayner, 1920). They started by pairing a loud noise (an unconditioned stimulus) with the sight of a rat. After a few pairings of the rat and the frightening noise, Albert would cry in fear at the sight of the rat alone.

Several years later, psychologist Mary Cover Jones demonstrated a way that fears can be unlearned by means of classical conditioning (M. C. Jones, 1924). Her subject was a 3-year-old boy named Peter who, like Albert, had a fear of white rats. Jones paired the sight of a rat with an intrinsically pleasant experience—eating candy. While Peter sat alone in a room, a caged white rat was brought in and placed far enough away so that the boy would not be frightened. At this point, Peter was given candy to eat. On each successive day, the cage was moved closer, after which, Peter was given candy. Eventually, he showed no fear of the rat, even without any candy.

In more recent times, psychiatrist Joseph Wolpe (1915–1997) adapted Jones's method to the treatment of certain kinds of anxiety (Wolpe, 1973, 1990). Wolpe reasoned that because irrational fears are learned (conditioned), they could also be unlearned through conditioning. He noted that it is not possible to be both fearful and relaxed at the same time. Therefore, if people could be taught to relax in fearful or anxious situations, their anxiety should disappear. Wolpe's **desensitization therapy** begins by teaching a system of deep-muscle relaxation. Then the person constructs a list of situations that prompt various degrees of fear or anxiety, from intensely frightening to only mildly so. A person with a fear of heights, for example, might construct a list that begins with standing on the edge of the Grand Canyon and ends with climbing two rungs on a ladder. While deeply relaxed, the person imagines the least distressing situation on the list first. If he or she succeeds in remaining relaxed, the person proceeds to the next item on the list, and so on until no anxiety is felt. In this way, classical conditioning is used to change an undesired reaction. In Chapter 13 ("Therapies") we will return to examine desensitization therapy in greater depth.

ENDURING ISSUES

Mind–Body   Classical Conditioning and the Immune System

In another example of classical conditioning in humans, researchers have devised a novel way to treat autoimmune disorders, which cause the immune system to attack healthy organs or tissues. Although powerful drugs can be used to suppress the immune system and thus reduce the impact of the autoimmune disorder, these drugs often have dangerous side effects, so they must be administered sparingly. The challenge, then, was to find a treatment that could suppress the immune system without damaging vital organs. Researchers discovered that they could use formerly neutral stimuli either to increase or to suppress the activity of the immune system. Here's how it works: As US, the researchers use immune-suppressing drugs and pair them with a specific CS, such as a distinctive smell or taste. After only a few pairings of the drug (US) with the smell or taste (CS), the CS alone suppresses the immune system (the CR) without any dangerous

intermittent pairing Pairing the conditioned stimulus and the unconditioned stimulus on only a portion of the learning trials.

desensitization therapy A conditioning technique designed to gradually reduce anxiety about a particular object or situation.

side effects! In this case, classical conditioning works on the mind but ultimately affects the body. While the use of classical conditioning to treat autoimmune disorders shows promise, additional research is still necessary to validate its effectiveness and evaluate its potential application as a therapy to treat these disorders (Schedlowski & Pacheco-López, 2010). ■

Classical Conditioning Is Selective

Why are people more likely to develop a phobia of snakes than of flowers?

A bird's nervous system is adapted to remember sight–illness combinations, such as the distinctive color of a certain berry and subsequent food poisoning. In mammals, by contrast, taste–illness combinations are quickly and powerfully learned.

If people can develop phobias, or intense fears through classical conditioning, why don't we acquire phobias of virtually everything that is paired with harm? For example, many people get shocks from electric sockets, but almost no one develops a socket phobia. Why should this be the case?

Psychologist Martin Seligman (1971) has offered an answer: The key, he says, lies in the concept of **preparedness.** Some things readily become conditioned stimuli for fear responses because we are biologically prepared to learn those associations. Among the common objects of phobias are heights, snakes, and the dark. In our evolutionary past, fear of these potential dangers probably offered a survival advantage, and so a readiness to perceive such threats and to respond quickly with fear may have become "wired into" our species(LoBue, Rakison & DeLoache, 2010).

Preparedness also underlies **conditioned taste aversion,** a learned association between the taste of a certain food and a feeling of nausea and revulsion. Conditioned taste aversions are acquired very quickly. It usually takes only one pairing of a distinctive flavor and subsequent illness to develop a learned aversion to the taste of that food. Readily learning connections between distinctive flavors and illness has clear benefits. If we can quickly learn which foods are poisonous and avoid those foods in the future, we greatly increase our chances of survival. Other animals with a well-developed sense of taste, such as rats and mice, also readily develop conditioned taste aversions, just as humans do (Anderson, Varlinskaya, & Spear, 2010; Guitton, Klin, & Dudai, 2008).

preparedness A biological readiness to learn certain associations because of their survival advantages.

conditioned taste aversion Conditioned avoidance of certain foods even if there is only one pairing of conditioned and unconditioned stimuli.

ENDURING ISSUES

Nature–Nurture   The Evolutionary Basis of Fear

To what extent does our evolutionary heritage condition our fears; and to what extent are fears the result of our experiences? Recent studies suggest that the two work in tandem. For example, some stimuli unrelated to human survival through evolution, but which we have learned to associate with danger, can serve as CSs for fear responses. Pictures of handguns and butcher knives, for example, are as effective as pictures of snakes and spiders in conditioning fear in some people (Lovibond, Siddle, & Bond, 1993). These studies suggest that preparedness may be the result of learning rather than evolution. Other studies have shown that people who do not suffer from phobias can rather quickly unlearn fear responses to spiders and snakes if those stimuli appear repeatedly without painful or threatening USs. Thus, even if humans are prepared to fear these things, that fear can be overcome through conditioning. In other words, our evolutionary history and our personal learning histories interact to increase or decrease the likelihood that certain kinds of conditioning will occur. ■

Seligman's theory of preparedness argues that we are biologically prepared to associate certain stimuli, such as heights, the dark, and snakes, with fear responses. In our evolutionary past, fear of these potential dangers probably offered a survival advantage.

✓• ⌐Study and Review on MyPsychLab

1. The simplest type of learning is called _____ _____. It refers to the establishment of fairly predictable behavior in the presence of well-defined stimuli.

2. Match the following in Pavlov's experiment with dogs:

   ____ unconditioned stimulus   a. bell
   ____ unconditioned response   b. food
   ____ conditioned stimulus   c. salivating to bell
   ____ conditioned response   d. salivating to food

3. The intense, irrational fears that we call phobias can be learned through classical conditioning. Is this statement true (T) or false (F)?

4. A learned association between the taste of a certain food and a feeling of nausea is called _____ _____ _____.

5. Teaching someone to relax even when he or she encounters a distressing situation is called _____ _____.

6. In the experiment with Little Albert, the unconditioned stimulus was _____.

Answers: 1. classical conditioning. 2. unconditioned stimulus—b; unconditioned response—d; conditioned stimulus—a; conditioned response—c. 3. T. 4. conditioned taste aversion. 5. desensitization therapy. 6. loud noises.

1. Which of the following are examples of classical conditioning?
   a. eating when not hungry just because we know it is lunchtime
   b. a specific smell triggering a bad memory
   c. a cat running into the kitchen to the sound of a can opener
   d. All of the above are examples of classical conditioning.

2. You feel nauseated when you read about sea scallops on a restaurant menu, because you once had a bad episode with some scallops that made you sick. For you in this situation, the menu description of the scallops is the
   a. US.
   b. CS.
   c. CR.

Answers: 1. d. 2. b.

- Explain how operant conditioning differs from classical conditioning.
- Explain the law of effect (the principle of reinforcement) and the role of reinforcers, punishers, and shaping in establishing an operantly conditioned response. Differentiate between positive reinforcers, negative reinforcers, and punishment. Explain the circumstances under which punishment can be effective and the drawbacks to using punishment.
- Explain what is meant by learned helplessness.
- Describe how biofeedback and neurofeedback can be used to change behavior.

operant (or instrumental) conditioning
The type of learning in which behaviors are emitted (in the presence of specific stimuli) to earn rewards or avoid punishments.

OPERANT CONDITIONING

How are operant behaviors different from the responses involved in classical conditioning?

Around the turn of the 20th century, while Pavlov was busy with his dogs, the American psychologist Edward Lee Thorndike (1874–1949) was using a "puzzle box," or simple wooden cage, to study how cats learn. As illustrated in **Figure 5–4,** Thorndike confined a hungry cat in the puzzle box, with food just outside where the cat could see and smell it. To get to the food, the cat had to figure out how to open the latch on the box door, a process that Thorndike timed. In the beginning, it took the cat quite a while to discover how to open the door. But on each trial, it took the cat less time, until eventually it could escape from the box in almost no time at all. Thorndike was a pioneer in studying the kind of learning that involves making a certain response due to the consequences it brings. This form of learning has come to be called **operant** or **instrumental conditioning.** The pouched rat described at the opening of this chapter learned to find land mines through operant conditioning.

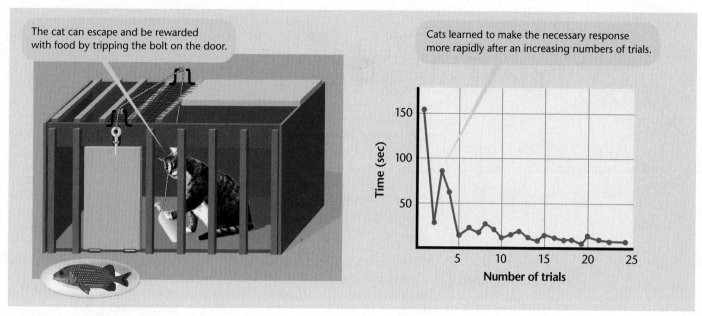

The cat can escape and be rewarded with food by tripping the bolt on the door.

Cats learned to make the necessary response more rapidly after an increasing numbers of trials.

FIGURE 5–4

A cat in a Thorndike "puzzle box."

The cat can escape and be rewarded with food by tripping the bolt on the door. As the graph shows, Thorndike's cats learned to make the necessary response more rapidly after an increasing number of trials.

Elements of Operant Conditioning

What two essential elements are involved in operant conditioning?

One essential element in operant conditioning is *emitted behavior.* This is one way in which operant conditioning differs from classical conditioning. In classical conditioning, a response is automatically triggered by some stimulus, such as a loud noise automatically triggering fear. In this sense, classical conditioning is passive in that the behaviors are *elicited* by stimuli. In contrast, Thorndike's cats *spontaneously* tried to undo the latch on the door of the box. You *spontaneously* wave your hand to signal a taxi to stop. You *voluntarily* put money into machines to obtain food. These and similar actions are called **operant behaviors** because they involve "operating" on the environment.

A second essential element in operant conditioning is a *consequence* following a behavior. Thorndike's cats gained freedom and a piece of fish for escaping from the puzzle boxes. Consequences like this one, which increase the likelihood that a behavior will be repeated, are called **reinforcers.** In contrast, consequences that **decrease** the chances that a behavior will be repeated are called **punishers.** Imagine how Thorndike's cats might have acted had they been greeted by a large, snarling dog when they escaped from the puzzle boxes. Thorndike summarized the influence of consequences in his **law of effect:** Behavior that brings about a satisfying effect (reinforcement) is likely to be performed again, whereas behavior that brings about a negative effect (punishment) is likely to be suppressed. Contemporary psychologists often refer to the **principle of reinforcement,** rather than the law of effect, but the two terms mean the same thing.

Establishing an Operantly Conditioned Response

How might an animal trainer teach a tiger to jump through a flaming hoop?

Because the behaviors involved in operant conditioning are voluntary, it is not always easy to establish an operantly conditioned response. The desired behavior must first be performed spontaneously in order for it to be rewarded and strengthened. Sometimes you can

operant behaviors Behaviors designed to operate on the environment in a way that will gain something desired or avoid something unpleasant.

reinforcers Stimuli that follow a behavior and increase the likelihood that the behavior will be repeated.

punishers Stimuli that follow a behavior and decrease the likelihood that the behavior will be repeated.

law of effect (principle of reinforcement) Thorndike's theory that behavior consistently rewarded will be "stamped in" as learned behavior, and behavior that brings about discomfort will be "stamped out."

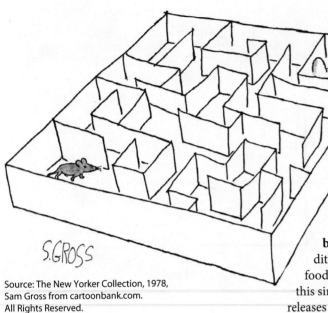

Watch the **Video** B. F. Skinner Biography
on **MyPsychLab**

Skinner box A box often used in operant
conditioning of animals; it limits the available
responses and thus increases the likelihood that
the desired response will occur.

shaping Reinforcing successive approximations
to a desired behavior.

simply wait for this action to happen. Thorndike, for example, waited for his cats to trip the latch that opened the door to his puzzle boxes. Then he rewarded them with fish.

But when there are many opportunities for making irrelevant responses, waiting can be slow and tedious. If you were an animal trainer for a circus, imagine how long you would have to wait for a tiger to jump through a flaming hoop spontaneously so you could reward it. One way to speed up the process is to increase motivation. Even without food in sight, a hungry animal is more active than a well-fed one and so is more likely, just by chance, to make the response you're looking for. Another strategy is to reduce opportunities for irrelevant responses, as Thorndike did by making his puzzle boxes small and bare. Many researchers do the same thing by using Skinner boxes to train small animals in. A **Skinner box** (named after B. F. Skinner, another pioneer in the study of operant conditioning), is a small cage with solid walls that is relatively empty, except for a food cup and an activating device, such as a bar or a button. (See **Figure 5–5.**) In this simple environment, it doesn't take long for an animal to press the button that releases food into the cup, thereby reinforcing the behavior. ⦿

Usually, however, the environment cannot be controlled so easily; hence a different approach is called for. Another way to speed up operant conditioning is to reinforce successive approximations of the desired behavior. This approach is called **shaping.** To teach a tiger to jump through a flaming hoop, the trainer might first reinforce the animal simply for jumping up on a pedestal. After that behavior has been learned, the tiger might be reinforced only for leaping from that pedestal to another. Next, the tiger might be required to jump through a hoop between the pedestals to gain a reward. And finally, the hoop is set on fire, and the tiger must leap through it to be rewarded.

As in classical conditioning, the learning of an operantly conditioned response eventually reaches a point of diminishing returns. If you look back at **Figure 5–4,** you'll see that the first few reinforcements produced quite large improvements in performance, as indicated by the rapid drop in time required to escape from the puzzle box. But each successive reinforcement produced less of an effect until, eventually, continued reinforcement brought no evidence of further learning. After 25 trials, for instance, Thorndike's cats were escaping from the box no more quickly than they had been after 15 trials. The operantly conditioned response had then been fully established. Can operant conditioning influence human behavior? See "Applying Psychology: Modifying Your Own Behavior," to learn about how you can use operant conditioning to modify your own behavior.

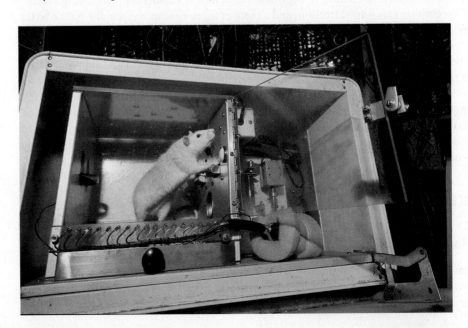

FIGURE 5–5

A rat in a Skinner box.

By pressing the bar, the rat releases food pellets into the box; this procedure reinforces its bar-pressing behavior.

APPLYING PSYCHOLOGY

Modifying Your Own Behavior

Can you modify your own undesirable behaviors by using operant conditioning techniques? Yes, but first you must observe your own actions, think about their implications, and plan a strategy of intervention.

1. Begin by identifying the behavior you want to acquire: This is called the "target" behavior. You will be more successful if you focus on acquiring a new behavior rather than on eliminating an existing one. For example, instead of setting a target of being less shy, you might define the target behavior as becoming more outgoing or more sociable.

2. The next step is defining the target behavior precisely: What exactly do you mean by "sociable"? Imagine situations in which the target behavior could be performed. Then describe in writing the way in which you now respond to these situations. For example, you might write, "When I am sitting in a lecture hall, waiting for class to begin, I don't talk to the people around me." Next, write down how you would rather act in that situation: "In a lecture hall before class, I want to talk to at least one other person. I might ask the person sitting next to me how he or she likes the class or the professor or simply comment on some aspect of the course."

3. The third step is monitoring your present behavior: You may do so by keeping a daily log of activities related to the target behavior. This will establish your current "base rate" and give you something concrete against which to gauge improvements. At the same time, try to figure out whether your present, undesirable behavior is being reinforced in some way. For example, if you find yourself unable to study, record what you do instead (Get a snack? Watch television?) and determine whether you are inadvertently rewarding your failure to study.

4. The next step—the basic principle of self-modification—is providing yourself with a positive reinforcer that is contingent on specific improvements in the target behavior: You may be able to use the same reinforcer that now maintains your undesirable behavior, or you may want to pick a new reinforcer. For example, if you want to increase the amount of time you spend studying, you might reward yourself with a token for each 30 minutes of study. Then, if your favorite pastime is watching movies, you might charge yourself three tokens for an hour of television, whereas the privilege of going to a movie might cost six.

A Closer Look at Reinforcement

What is the difference between positive and negative reinforcement? What are some of the unintentional effects that reinforcement can have?

We have been talking about reinforcement as if all reinforcers are alike, but in fact this is not the case. Think about the kinds of consequences that would encourage you to perform some behavior. Certainly these include consequences that give you something positive, like praise, recognition, or money. But the removal of some negative stimulus is also a good reinforcer of behavior. When new parents discover that rocking a baby will stop the infant's persistent crying, they sit down and rock the baby deep into the night; the removal of the infant's crying is a powerful reinforcer.

These examples show that there are two kinds of reinforcers. **Positive reinforcers,** such as praise, add something rewarding to a situation, whereas **negative reinforcers,** such as stopping an aversive noise, subtract something unpleasant. Animals will learn to press bars and open doors not only to obtain food and water (positive reinforcement), but also to turn off a loud buzzer or an electric shock (negative reinforcement).

Both positive and negative reinforcement results in the learning of new behaviors or the strengthening of existing ones. Remember, in everyday conversation when we say that we have "reinforced" something, we mean that we have strengthened it. Similarly, in operant conditioning, reinforcement—whether positive or negative—always strengthens or encourages a behavior. A child might practice the piano because she or he receives praise for practicing (positive reinforcement) or because it gives her or him a break from doing tedious homework (negative reinforcement), but in either case the end result is a higher incidence of piano playing.

positive reinforcers Events whose presence increases the likelihood that ongoing behavior will recur.

negative reinforcers Events whose reduction or termination increases the likelihood that ongoing behavior will recur.

But what if a particular behavior is just *accidentally* reinforced because it happens by chance to be followed by some rewarding incident? Will the behavior still be more likely to occur again? B. F. Skinner (1948) showed that the answer is yes. He put a pigeon in a Skinner box and at fixed intervals dropped a few grains of food into the food cup. The pigeon began repeating whatever it had been doing just before the food was given, such as standing on one foot. This action had nothing to do with getting the food, of course. But still the bird repeated it over and over again. Skinner called the bird's behavior *superstitious,* because it was learned in a way that is similar to how some human superstitions are learned. If you happen to be wearing an Albert Einstein T-shirt when you get your first A on an exam, you may come to believe that wearing this shirt was a factor. Even though the connection at first was pure coincidence, you may keep on wearing your "lucky" shirt to every test thereafter. Interestingly, there is evidence that such a superstition may actually improve your performance in the future by increasing your expectation that your efforts will be successful (Damisch, Stoberock & Mussweiler, 2010). In turn, the improved performance provides some positive reinforcement for continuing to engage in the superstitious behavior.

In the case of forming superstitions, reinforcement has an illogical effect on behavior, but that effect is generally harmless. Some psychologists believe that reinforcement can also lead inadvertently to negative results. They believe that offering certain kinds of reinforcers (candy, money, play time) for a task that could be intrinsically rewarding (that is, reinforcing in and of itself) can undermine the intrinsic motivation to perform it. People may begin to think that they are working only for the reward and lose enthusiasm for what they are doing. They may no longer see their work as an intrinsically interesting challenge in which to invest creative effort and strive for excellence. Instead, they may see work as a chore that must be done to earn some tangible payoff. This warning can be applied to many situations, such as offering tangible rewards to students for their work in the classroom, or giving employees a "pay for performance" incentive to meet company goals (Kohn, 1993; Rynes, Gerhart, & Parks, 2005).

Other psychologists, however, suggest that this concern about tangible reinforcers may be exaggerated. Although the use of rewards may sometimes produce negative outcomes, this is not always the case (Cameron, Banko, & Pierce, 2001). For example, children who were rewarded with stickers or praise for eating healthful vegetables that they initially disliked reported liking those vegetables more three months later. They also ate more of those vegetables when given a chance to eat as much or as little as they wished (Cooke et al., 2011). In fact, one extensive review of more than 100 studies showed that when used appropriately, rewards do not compromise intrinsic motivation, and under some circumstances, they may even help to encourage creativity (Eisenberger & Cameron, 1996; Selarta, Nordström, Kuvaas, & Takemura, 2008). For example, research has shown that rewarding highly creative behavior on one task often enhances subsequent creativity on other tasks (Eisenberger & Rhoades, 2001).

punishment Any event whose presence decreases the likelihood that ongoing behavior will recur.

Punishment

What problems can punishment create?

Although we all hate to be subjected to it, **punishment** is a powerful controller of behavior. After receiving a heavy fine for failing to report extra income to the IRS, we are less likely to make that mistake again. In this case, an unpleasant consequence reduces the likelihood that we will repeat a behavior. This is the definition of punishment.

Punishment is different from negative reinforcement. Reinforcement of whatever kind *strengthens* (reinforces) behavior. Negative reinforcement strengthens behavior by removing something unpleasant from the environment. In contrast, punishment adds something unpleasant to the

The use of punishment has potential drawbacks. It cannot "unteach" unwanted behavior, only suppress it. Punishment may also stir up negative feelings in the person who is punished or inadvertently provide a model of aggressive behavior.

environment; and as a result, it tends to *weaken* the behavior that caused it. If going skiing during the weekend rather than studying for a test results in getting an F, the F is an unpleasant consequence (a punisher) that makes you less likely to skip homework for ski time again.

Is punishment effective? We can all think of instances when it doesn't seem to work. Children often continue to misbehave even after they have been punished repeatedly for that particular misbehavior. Some drivers persist in driving recklessly despite repeated fines. Why are there these seeming exceptions to the law of effect? Why, in these cases, isn't punishment having the result it is supposed to?

THINKING CRITICALLY ABOUT . . .

Corporal Punishment

Some school systems still use some form of corporal punishment, such as paddling, for students who misbehave. The justification is that it is an effective method of changing undesirable behavior, it develops a sense of personal responsibility, it teaches self-discipline, and it helps develop moral character.

Based on what you now know about operant conditioning,

1. under what circumstances (if any) should corporal punishment be used in schools?

2. what factors, besides the student's immediate actions, should adults consider before using corporal punishment?

3. what unintended consequences might arise from the use of corporal punishment?

For punishment to be effective, it must be imposed properly. First, punishment should be *swift*. If it is delayed, it doesn't work as well. Sending a misbehaving child immediately to a time-out seat (even when it is not convenient to do so) is much more effective than waiting for a "better" time to punish. Punishment should also be *sufficient* without being cruel. If a parent briefly scolds a child for hitting other children, the effect will probably be less pronounced than if the child is sent to his or her room for the day. At the same time, punishment should be *consistent*. It should be imposed for all infractions of a rule, not just for some.

Punishment is particularly useful in situations in which a behavior is dangerous and must be changed quickly. A child who likes to poke things into electric outlets, or runs out into a busy street must be stopped immediately, so punishment may be the best course of action. But even in situations like these, punishment has drawbacks.

Punishment Cannot Unteach Unwanted Behaviors First, it only *suppresses* the undesired behavior; it doesn't prompt someone to "unlearn" the behavior, and it doesn't teach a more desirable one. If the threat of punishment is removed, the negative behavior is likely to recur. This result is apparent on the highway. Speeders slow down when they see a police car (the threat of punishment), but speed up again as soon as the threat is passed. Punishment, then, rarely works when long-term changes in behavior are wanted (Pogarsky & Piquero, 2003).

Punishment Can Backfire Second, punishment often stirs up negative feelings (frustration, resentment, self-doubt), which can impede the learning of new, more desirable behaviors. For example, when a child who is learning to read is scolded for every mispronounced word, the child may become very frustrated and hesitant. This frustration and doubt about ability can prompt more mispronunciations, which lead to more scolding. In time, the negative feelings that punishment has caused can become so unpleasant that the child may avoid reading altogether. In addition, some studies have shown that children who frequently experience corporal punishment have a higher incidence of depression, antisocial behavior, decreased self-control, and increased difficulty relating to their peers (C. E. Leary, Kelley, Morrow, & Mikulka, 2008; Slessareva & Muraven, 2004).

Punishment Can Teach Aggression. A third drawback of punishment, when it is harsh, is the unintended lesson that it teaches: Harsh punishment may encourage the learner to copy that same harsh and aggressive behavior toward other people. In laboratory studies, monkeys that are harshly punished tend to attack other monkeys (Barry Schwartz, 1989). In addition, punishment often makes people angry, aggressive, and hostile.

Because of these drawbacks, punishment should be used carefully, and always together with reinforcement of desirable behavior. Once a more desirable response is established, punishment should be removed to reinforce negatively that new behavior. Positive reinforcement (praise, rewards) should also be used to strengthen the desired behavior because it teaches an alternative behavior to replace the punished one. Positive reinforcement also makes the learning environment less threatening.

Sometimes, after punishment has been administered a few times, it needn't be continued, because the mere threat of punishment is enough to induce the desired behavior. Psychologists call it **avoidance training,** because the person is learning to avoid the possibility of a punishing consequence. Avoidance training is responsible for many everyday behaviors. It has taught you to keep your hand away from a hot iron to avoid the punishment of a burn. Avoidance training, however, doesn't always work in our favor. For instance, a child who has been repeatedly criticized for poor performance in math may learn to shun difficult math problems in order to avoid further punishment. Unfortunately, the child fails to develop math skills and therefore fails to improve any innate capabilities, and so a vicious cycle has set in. The avoidance must be unlearned through some positive experiences with math in order for this cycle to be broken.

ENDURING ISSUES

Diversity–Universality   What Is Punishment?

We do not know whether something is reinforcing or punishing until we see whether it increases or decreases the occurrence of a response. We might also assume that having to work alone, rather than in a group of peers, would be punishing, but some children prefer to work alone. Teachers must understand the children in their classes as individuals before they decide how to reward or punish them. Similarly, what is reinforcing for people in one culture might not have the same effect for people in other cultures.

In addition, an event or object might not be consistently rewarding or punishing over time. So even if candy is initially reinforcing for some children, if they eat large amounts of it, it can become neutral or even punishing. We must therefore be very careful in labeling items or events as "reinforcers" or "punishers." ■

Learned Helplessness

In what ways do some college students exhibit learned helplessness?

Have you ever met someone who has decided he will never be good at science? We have said that through avoidance training, people learn to prevent themselves from being punished, but what happens when such avoidance of punishment isn't possible? The answer is often a "giving-up" response that can generalize to other situations. This response is known as **learned helplessness.** ✳

Martin Seligman and his colleagues first studied learned helplessness in experiments with dogs (Seligman & Maier, 1967).They placed two groups of dogs in chambers that delivered a series of electric shocks to the dogs' feet at random intervals. The dogs in the control group could turn off (escape) the shock by pushing a panel with their nose. The dogs in the experimental group could not turn off the shock—they were, in effect, helpless. Next, both the experimental and the control animals were placed in a different situation, one in which they could escape shock by jumping over a hurdle. A warning light always came on 10 seconds before each 50-second shock was given. The dogs in the control group quickly learned to jump the hurdle as soon as the warning light flashed, but the dogs in the experimental group didn't. These dogs, which had previously experienced unavoidable shocks, didn't even jump the hurdle *after* the shock started. They just lay there and accepted the shocks. Also, many of these dogs were generally listless, suffered loss of appetite, and displayed other symptoms associated with depression.

✳—⌐Explore the Concept, Learned Helplessness, on MyPsychLab

avoidance training Learning a desirable behavior to prevent the occurrence of something unpleasant, such as punishment.

learned helplessness Failure to take steps to avoid or escape from an unpleasant or aversive stimulus that occurs as a result of previous exposure to unavoidable painful stimuli.

Many subsequent studies have shown that learned helplessness can occur both in animals and in humans. Once established, the condition generalizes to new situations and can be very persistent, even given evidence that an unpleasant circumstance can now be avoided. For example, when faced with a series of unsolvable problems, a college student may eventually give up trying and make only halfhearted efforts to solve new problems, even when the new problems are solvable. Moreover, success in solving new problems has little effect on the person's behavior. He or she continues to make only halfhearted tries, as if never expecting *any* success at all. Similarly, children raised in an abusive family, where punishment is unrelated to behavior, often develop a feeling of helplessness (C. Peterson & Bossio, 1989). Even in relatively normal settings outside their home, they often appear listless, passive, and indifferent. They make little attempt either to seek rewards or to avoid discomfort.

biofeedback A technique that uses monitoring devices to provide precise information about internal physiological processes, such as heart rate or blood pressure, to teach people to gain voluntary control over these functions.

neurofeedback A biofeedback technique that monitors brain waves with the use of an EEG to teach people to gain voluntary control over their brain wave activity.

Shaping Behavioral Change Through Biofeedback

How can operant conditioning be used to control biological functions?

Patrick, an 8-year-old third grader, was diagnosed with *attention-deficit disorder (ADD)*. He was unable to attend to what was going on around him, was restless, and was unable to concentrate. An EEG showed increased numbers of slow brain waves. After a course of 40 training sessions using special computer equipment that allowed Patrick to *monitor* his brain-wave activities, he learned how to produce more of the fast waves that are associated with being calm and alert. As a result, Patrick became much more "clued in" to what was going on around him and much less likely to become frustrated when things didn't go his way (Fitzgerald, 1999; Fuchs, Birbaumer, Lutzenberger, Gruzelier, & Kaiser, 2003; Monastra, 2008).

When operant conditioning is used to control certain biological functions, such as blood pressure, skin temperature or heart rate, it is referred to as **biofeedback.** Instruments are used to measure particular biological responses—muscle contractions, blood pressure, and heart rate. Variations in the strength of the response are reflected in signals, such as light or tones. By using these signals, the person can learn to control the response through shaping. For example, Patrick learned to control his brain waves by controlling the movement of a Superman icon on a computer screen. When biofeedback is used to monitor and control brain waves, as in Patrick's case, it is referred to as **neurofeedback.**

Biofeedback and neurofeedback have become well-established treatments for a number of medical problems, including migraine headaches (Kropp, Siniatchkin, & Gerber, 2005), hypertension (Reineke, 2008), and panic attacks (Meuret, Wilhelm, & Roth, 2004). Biofeedback has also been used by athletes, musicians, and other performers to control the anxiety that can interfere with their performance.

Biofeedback treatment does have some drawbacks. Learning the technique takes considerable time, effort, patience, and discipline. And it does not work for everyone. But it gives many patients control of their treatment, a major advantage over other treatment options, and it has achieved impressive results in alleviating certain medical problems.

THINKING CRITICALLY ABOUT . . .

Biofeedback and Neurofeedback

Assume for the moment that you are skeptical about the benefits of biofeedback and neurofeedback. What questions would you ask about research studies that claim to show they are beneficial? To get started, refer back to Chapter 1 and the section on "Critical Thinking."

1. What kind of evidence would you look for to support your skeptical position? What kind of evidence would cause you to rethink your position? Are you swayed by reports of single cases (such as Patrick) or would you be more influenced by studies of large numbers of people? Would you be interested in short-term effects, or would you want to see results over a much longer period of time?

2. What assumptions would you need to watch out for? How would you know whether biofeedback or neurofeedback really worked? (Remember that you should be skeptical of self-reports.)

3. Might there be alternative explanations for the results of the research you find? In other words, is it possible that something quite apart from biofeedback or neurofeedback could explain the results?

4. Once you have formulated your position on the benefits of biofeedback or neurofeedback, how would you avoid oversimplifying your conclusions?

✓•─[**Study** and **Review** on **MyPsychLab**]

CHECK YOUR UNDERSTANDING

1. An event whose reduction or termination increases the likelihood that ongoing behavior will recur is called _____ reinforcement, whereas any event whose presence increases the likelihood that ongoing behavior will recur is called _____ reinforcement.

2. A type of learning that involves reinforcing the desired response is known as _____ _____.

3. When a threat of punishment induces a change to more desirable behavior, it is called _____ _____.

4. Superstitious behavior can result when a behavior is rewarded by pure _____.

5. Any stimulus that follows a behavior and decreases the likelihood that the behavior will be repeated is called a _____.

6. Which of the following problems may result from avoidance training?

    a. A person may continue to avoid something that no longer needs to be avoided.

    b. The effects of avoidance training tend to last for only a short time.

    c. Avoidance training may produce latent learning.

    d. Avoidance training tends to take effect when it is too late to make a difference in avoiding the problem situation.

Answers: 1. negative; positive. 2. operant conditioning. 3. avoidance training. 4. coincidence. 5. punishment. 6. a.

APPLY YOUR UNDERSTANDING

1. Imagine that you want to teach a child to make his or her bed. What kind of reinforcement could you use to do that?

    a. punishment

    b. positive reinforcement

    c. negative reinforcement

    d. both (b) and (c) would work

2. You are hired to make a commercial for a company that manufactures dog food. They want you to get a dog to run from a hallway closet, under a coffee table, around a sofa, leap over a wagon, rush to the kitchen, and devour a bowl of dog food. The most effective way to accomplish this task would be to

    a. wait for this chain of events to happen and then use a reinforcer to increase the likelihood that the behavior will occur again on demand.

    b. use shaping.

    c. teach the dog to discriminate between the various landmarks on its way to the food.

    d. hire a smart dog.

Answers: 1. d. 2. b.

LEARNING OBJECTIVES

- Describe the importance of contingencies in both operant and classical conditioning.
- Differentiate between the four schedules of reinforcement in operant conditioning and their effect on learned behavior.
- Describe the processes of extinction, spontaneous recovery, generalization, and discrimination in classical and operant conditioning.
- Explain what is meant by higher order conditioning and differentiate between primary and secondary reinforcers.

FACTORS SHARED BY CLASSICAL AND OPERANT CONDITIONING

Can you think of any similarities between classical and operant conditioning?

Despite the differences between classical and operant conditioning, these two forms of learning have many things in common. First, they both involve the learning of associations. In classical conditioning, it is a learned association between one stimulus and another, whereas in operant conditioning, it is a learned association between some action and a consequence. Second, the responses in both classical and operant conditioning are under the control of stimuli in the environment. A classically conditioned fear might be triggered by the sight of a white rat; an operantly conditioned jump might be cued by the flash of a red light. In both cases, moreover, the learned responses to a cue can generalize to similar stimuli. Third, neither classically nor operantly conditioned responses will last forever if they aren't periodically renewed. This doesn't necessarily mean that they are totally forgotten, however. Even after you think that these responses have long vanished, either one can suddenly reappear in the right situation. And fourth, in both kinds of learning—classical *and* operant conditioning—new behaviors can build on previously established ones.

The Importance of Contingencies

How can changes in the timing of a conditioned stimulus lead to unexpected learning? Why does intermittent reinforcement result in such persistent behavior?

Because classical and operant conditioning are both forms of associative learning, they both involve perceived contingencies. A **contingency** is a relationship in which one event *depends* on another. Graduating from college is *contingent* on passing a certain number of courses. In both classical and operant conditioning, perceived contingencies are very important.

Contingencies in Classical Conditioning In classical conditioning, a contingency is perceived between the CS and the US. The CS comes to be viewed as a signal that the US is about to happen. This is why, in classical conditioning, the CS not only must occur in close proximity to the US, but also should precede the US and provide predictive information about it (Rescorla, 1966, 1967, 1988).

Scientists once believed that no conditioning would occur if the CS *followed* the US; this belief, however, turns out not to be entirely true. The explanation again lies in contingency learning. Imagine a situation in which a tone (the CS) always follows a shock (the US). This process is called *backward conditioning*. After a while, when the tone is sounded alone, the learner will not show a conditioned fear response to it. After all, the tone has never predicted that a shock is about to be given. But what the learner *does* show is a conditioned *relaxation* response to the sound of the tone, because the tone has served as a signal that the shock is over and will not occur again for some time. Again, we see the importance of contingency learning: The learner responds to the tone on the basis of the information that it gives about what will happen next.

Other studies similarly show that predictive information is crucial in establishing a classically conditioned response. In one experiment with rats, for instance, a noise was repeatedly paired with a brief electric shock until the noise soon became a conditioned stimulus for a conditioned fear response (Kamin, 1969). Then a second stimulus—a light—was added right before the noise. You might expect that the rat came to show a fear of the light as well, because it, too, preceded the shock. But this is not what happened. Apparently, the noise–shock contingency that the rat had already learned had a **blocking** effect on learning that the light also predicted shock. Once the rat had learned that the noise signaled the onset of shock, adding yet another cue (a light) provided no new predictive information about the shock's arrival, and so the rat learned to ignore the light. Classical conditioning, then, occurs only when a stimulus tells the learner something *new* or *additional* about the likelihood that a US will occur.

Contingencies in Operant Conditioning Contingencies also figure prominently in operant conditioning. The learner must come to perceive a connection between performing a certain voluntary action and receiving a certain reward or punishment. If no contingency is perceived, there is no reason to increase or decrease the behavior.

But once a contingency is perceived, does it matter how often a consequence is actually delivered? When it comes to rewards, the answer is yes. Fewer rewards are often better than more. In the language of operant conditioning, *partial* or *intermittent*

contingency A reliable "if–then" relationship between two events, such as a CS and a US.

blocking A process whereby prior conditioning prevents conditioning to a second stimulus even when the two stimuli are presented simultaneously.

schedule of reinforcement In operant conditioning, the rule for determining when and how often reinforcers will be delivered.

fixed-interval schedule A reinforcement schedule in which the correct response is reinforced after a fixed length of time since the last reinforcement.

variable-interval schedule A reinforcement schedule in which the correct response is reinforced after varying lengths of time following the last reinforcement.

fixed-ratio schedule A reinforcement schedule in which the correct response is reinforced after a fixed number of correct responses.

variable-ratio schedule A reinforcement schedule in which a varying number of correct responses must occur before reinforcement is presented.

extinction A decrease in the strength or frequency, or stopping, of a learned response because of failure to continue pairing the US and CS (classical conditioning) or withholding of reinforcement (operant conditioning).

reinforcement results in behavior that will persist longer than behavior learned by *continuous reinforcement*. Why would this be the case? The answer has to do with expectations. When people receive only occasional reinforcement, they learn not to expect reinforcement with every response, so they continue responding in the hopes that eventually they will gain the desired reward. Vending machines and slot machines illustrate these different effects of continuous versus partial reinforcement. A vending machine offers continuous reinforcement. Each time you put in the right amount of money, you get something desired in return (reinforcement). If a vending machine is broken and you receive nothing for your coins, you are unlikely to put more money in it. In contrast, a casino slot machine pays off intermittently; only occasionally do you get something back for your investment. This intermittent payoff has a compelling effect on behavior. You might continue putting coins into a slot machine for a very long time even though you are getting nothing in return.

Psychologists refer to a pattern of reward payoffs as a **schedule of reinforcement.** Partial or intermittent reinforcement schedules are either fixed or variable, and they may be based on either the number of correct responses or the time elapsed between correct responses. **Table 5–1** gives some everyday examples of different reinforcement schedules.

On a **fixed-interval schedule,** learners are reinforced for the first response after a certain amount of time has passed since that response was previously rewarded. That is, they have to wait for a set period before they will be reinforced again. With a fixed-interval schedule, performance tends to fall off immediately after each reinforcement and then tends to pick up again as the time for the next reinforcement draws near. For example, when exams are given at fixed intervals—like a weekly quiz—students tend to decrease their studying right after one test is over and then increase studying as the next test approaches. (See **Figure 5–6.**)

TABLE 5–1   Examples of Reinforcement in Everyday Life

Continuous reinforcement (reinforcement every time the response is made)	Putting money in a parking meter to avoid getting a ticket Putting coins in a vending machine to get candy or soda
Fixed-ratio schedule (reinforcement after a fixed number of responses)	Being paid on a piecework basis. In the garment industry, for example, workers may be paid a fee per 100 dresses sewn.
Variable-ratio schedule (reinforcement after a varying number of responses)	Playing a slot machine. The machine is programmed to pay off after a certain number of responses have been made, but that number keeps changing. This type of schedule creates a steady rate of responding, because players know that if they play long enough, they will win. Sales commissions. You have to talk to many customers before you make a sale, and you never know whether the next one will buy. The number of sales calls you make, not how much time passes, will determine when you are reinforced by a sale, and the number of sales calls will vary.
Fixed-interval schedule (reinforcement of first response after a fixed amount of time has passed)	You have an exam coming up, and as time goes by and you haven't studied, you have to make up for it all by a certain time, and that means cramming. Picking up a salary check, which you receive every week or every 2 weeks
Variable-interval response (reinforcement of first response after varying amounts of time)	Surprise quizzes in a course cause a steady rate of studying because you never know when they'll occur; you have to be prepared all the time. Watching a football game; waiting for a touchdown. It could happen anytime. If you leave the room, you may miss it, so you have to keep watching continuously.

Source: From Landy, 1987, p. 212. Adapted by permission.

A **variable-interval schedule** reinforces correct responses after varying lengths of time following the last reinforcement. One reinforcement might be given after 6 minutes and the next after 4 minutes. The learner typically gives a slow, steady pattern of responses, being careful not to be so slow as to miss all the rewards. For example, if quizzes are given during a semester at unpredictable intervals, students have to keep studying at a steady rate, because on any given day there might be a test.

On a **fixed-ratio schedule,** a certain number of correct responses must occur before reinforcement is provided, resulting in a high response rate, since making many responses in a short time yields more rewards. Being paid on a piecework basis is an example of a fixed-ratio schedule. Under a fixed-ratio schedule, a brief pause after reinforcement is followed by a rapid and steady response rate until the next reinforcement. (See **Figure 5–6.**)

On a **variable-ratio schedule,** the number of correct responses needed to gain reinforcement is not constant. The casino slot machine is a good example of a variable-ratio schedule. It will eventually pay off, but you have no idea when. Because there is always a chance of hitting the jackpot, the temptation to keep playing is great. Learners on a variable-ratio schedule tend not to pause after reinforcement and have a high rate of response over a long period of time. Because they never know when reinforcement may come, they keep on testing for a reward.

Extinction and Spontaneous Recovery

Can you ever get rid of a conditioned response? Under what circumstances might old learned associations suddenly reappear?

Another factor shared by classical and operant conditioning is that learned responses sometimes weaken and may even disappear. If a CS and a US are never paired again or if a consequence never follows a learned behavior, the learned association will begin to fade until eventually the effects of prior learning are no longer seen. This outcome is called **extinction** of a conditioned response.

Fixed Ratio

Cumulative responses

Time →

Fixed Interval

Cumulative responses

Time →

Variable Ratio

Cumulative responses

Time →

Variable Interval

Cumulative responses

Time →

FIGURE 5–6

Response patterns to schedules of reinforcement.

On a fixed-interval schedule, as the time for reinforcement approaches, the number of responses increases, and the slope becomes steeper. On a variable-interval schedule, the response rate is moderate and relatively constant. Notice that each tick mark on the graph represents one reinforcement. The fixed-ratio schedule is characterized by a high rate of response and a pause after each reinforcement. A variable-ratio schedule produces a high rate of response with little or no pause after each reinforcement.

The slot machine is a classic example of a variable-ratio schedule of reinforcement. The machine eventually pays off, but always after a variable number of plays. Because people keep hoping that the next play will be rewarded, they maintain a high rate of response over a long period of time.

THINKING CRITICALLY ABOUT . . .

Reinforcement Schedules

Think about how you could apply the principles of behavioral learning to

1. design the ideal slot machine–one that would keep people playing over and over again, even though they won very little money.

2. design a reward system for a fifth-grade class that would result in both effort at schoolwork and in good behavior.

3. design an ideal lottery or mail-in contest.

4. design an ideal payment system for salespeople (you may include both salary and commission).

For each type of reward system, think about what the reinforcers should be, what contingencies are operating, and what behaviors you want to elicit. Also think about how you would demonstrate to a skeptic that your procedures have actually resulted in a change in the desired direction.

Extinction and Spontaneous Recovery in Classical Conditioning For an example of extinction in classical conditioning, let's go back to Pavlov's dogs. What would you predict happened over time when the dogs heard the bell (the CS), but food (the US) was no longer given? The conditioned response to the bell—salivation—gradually decreased until eventually it stopped altogether. The dogs no longer salivated when they heard the bell. Extinction had taken place.

Once such a response has been extinguished, is the learning gone forever? Pavlov trained his dogs to salivate when they heard a bell, then extinguished this conditioned response. A few days later, the dogs were exposed to the bell again in the laboratory setting. As soon as they heard it, their mouths began to water. The response that had been learned and then extinguished reappeared on its own with no retraining. This phenomenon is known as **spontaneous recovery.** The dogs' response was now only about half as strong as it had been before extinction, and it was very easy to extinguish a second time. Nevertheless, the fact that the response occurred at all indicated that the original learning was not completely forgotten (see **Figure 5–7**).

How can extinguished behavior disappear and then reappear later? The explanation is that extinction does not erase learning. Rather, extinction occurs because new learning interferes with a previously learned response. New stimuli in other settings come to be paired with the conditioned stimulus; and these new stimuli may elicit responses different from (and sometimes incompatible with) the original conditioned response. For example, if you take a break from watching the latest horror movies in theaters and instead watch reruns of classic horror films on television, these classic films may seem so amateurish that they make you laugh rather than scare you. Here you are learning to associate the scary music in such films with laughter, which in effect opposes your original fear response. The result is interference and extinction. Spontaneous recovery consists of overcoming this interference. For instance, if you return to the theater to see the latest Stephen King movie, the conditioned response of fear to the scary music may suddenly reappear. It is as if the unconditioned stimulus of watching "up-to-date"

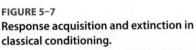

spontaneous recovery The reappearance of an extinguished response after the passage of time, without training.

FIGURE 5–7

Response acquisition and extinction in classical conditioning.

From point A to point B, the conditioned stimulus and the unconditioned stimulus were paired; and learning increased steadily. From B to C, however, the conditioned stimulus was presented alone. By point C, the response had been extinguished. After a rest period from C to D, spontaneous recovery occurred—the learned response reappeared at about half the strength that it had at point B. When the conditioned stimulus was again presented alone, the response extinguished rapidly (point E).

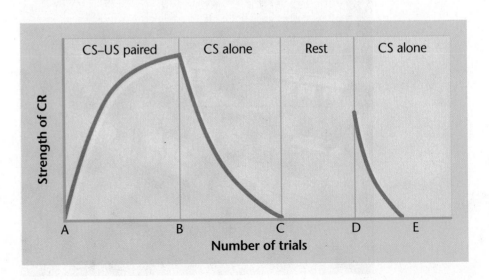

horror acts as a reminder of your earlier learning and renews your previous classically conditioned response. Such "reminder" stimuli work particularly well when presented in the original conditioning setting.

Extinction and Spontaneous Recovery in Operant Conditioning Extinction and spontaneous recovery also occur in operant conditioning. In operant conditioning, extinction happens as a result of withholding reinforcement. The effect usually isn't immediate. In fact, when reinforcement is first discontinued, there is often a brief *increase* in the strength or frequency of responding before a decline sets in. For instance, if you put coins in a vending machine and it fails to deliver the goods, you may push the button more forcefully and in rapid succession before you finally give up.

Just as in classical conditioning, extinction in operant conditioning doesn't completely erase what has been learned. Even though much time has passed since a behavior was last rewarded and the behavior seems extinguished, it may suddenly reappear. This spontaneous recovery may again be understood in terms of interference from new behaviors. If a rat is no longer reinforced for pressing a lever, it will start to engage in other behaviors—turning away from the lever, attempting to escape, and so on. These new behaviors will interfere with the operant response of lever pressing, causing it to extinguish. Spontaneous recovery is a brief victory of the original learning over interfering responses. The rat decides to give the previous "reward" lever one more try, as if testing again for a reward.

The difficulty of extinguishing an operantly conditioned response depends on a number of factors:

When reinforcement has been frequent, a learned behavior tends to be retained even after reinforcement is reduced. A dog "shaking hands" is an excellent example. Many previous rewards for this response tend to keep the dog offering people its paw even when no reward follows.

- *Strength of the original learning.* The stronger the original learning, the longer it takes the response to extinguish. If you spend many hours training a puppy to sit on command, you will not need to reinforce this behavior very often once the dog grows up.
- *Pattern of reinforcement.* As you learned earlier, responses that were reinforced only occasionally when acquired are usually more resistant to extinction than responses that were reinforced every time they occurred.
- *Variety of settings in which the original learning took place.* The greater the variety of settings, the harder it is to extinguish the response. Rats trained to run several different types of alleys in order to reach a food reward will keep running longer after food is withdrawn than will rats trained in a single alley.
- *Complexity of the behavior.* Complex behavior is much more difficult to extinguish than simple behavior is. Complex behavior consists of many actions put together, and each of those actions must be extinguished in order for the whole to be extinguished.
- *Learning through punishment versus reinforcement.* Behaviors learned through punishment rather than reinforcement are especially hard to extinguish. If you avoid jogging down a particular street because a vicious dog there attacked you, you may never venture down that street again, so your avoidance of the street may never extinguish.

One way to speed up the extinction of an operantly conditioned response is to put the learner in a situation that is different from the one in which the response was originally learned. The response is likely to be weaker in the new situation, and therefore it will extinguish more quickly. Of course, when the learner is returned to the original learning setting after extinction has occurred elsewhere, the response may undergo spontaneous recovery, just as in classical conditioning. But now the response is likely to be weaker than it was initially, and it should be relatively easy to extinguish once and for all. You may have experienced this phenomenon yourself when you returned home for the holidays after your first semester in college. A habit that you thought you had outgrown at school may have suddenly reappeared. The home setting worked as a "reminder" stimulus, encouraging the response, just as we mentioned when discussing classical conditioning. Because you have already extinguished the habit in another setting, however, extinguishing it at home shouldn't be difficult.

The skills a person learns in playing tennis may also be utilized in such sports as Ping-Pong, squash, and badminton. This is an example of stimulus generalization in operant conditioning.

Stimulus Control, Generalization, and Discrimination

How can anxiety about math in grade school affect a college student? Why do people often slap the wrong card when playing a game of slapjack?

The home setting acting as a "reminder" stimulus is just one example of how conditioned responses are influenced by surrounding cues in the environment. This outcome is called **stimulus control,** and it occurs in both classical and operant conditioning. In classical conditioning, the conditioned response (CR) is under the control of the conditioned stimulus (CS) that triggers it. Salivation, for example, might be controlled by the sound of a bell. In operant conditioning, the learned response is under the control of whatever stimuli come to be associated with delivery of reward or punishment. A leap to avoid electric shock might come under the control of a flashing light, for instance. In both classical and operant conditioning, moreover, the learner may respond to cues that are merely similar (but not identical) to the ones that prevailed during the original learning. This tendency to respond to similar cues is known as **stimulus generalization.**

Generalization and Discrimination in Classical Conditioning There are many examples of stimulus generalization in classical conditioning. One example is the case of Little Albert, who was conditioned to fear white rats. When the experimenters later showed him a white rabbit, he cried and tried to crawl away, even though he had not been taught to fear rabbits. He also showed fear of other white, furry objects like cotton balls, a fur coat, even a bearded Santa Claus mask. Little Albert had generalized his learned reactions from rats to similar stimuli. In much the same way, a person who learned to feel anxious over math tests in grade school might come to feel anxious about any task involving numbers, even balancing a checkbook.

Stimulus generalization is not inevitable, however. Through a process called **stimulus discrimination,** learners can be trained not to generalize, but rather to make a conditioned response only to a single specific stimulus. This process involves presenting several similar stimuli, only one of which is followed by the unconditioned stimulus. For instance, Albert might have been shown a rat and other white, furry objects, but only the rat would be followed by a loud noise (the US). Given this procedure, Albert would have learned to discriminate the white rat from the other objects, and the fear response would not have generalized as it did.

Learning to discriminate is essential in everyday life. We prefer for children to learn not to fear *every* loud noise and *every* insect, but only those that are potentially harmful. Through stimulus discrimination, behavior becomes more finely tuned to the demands of our environment.

Generalization and Discrimination in Operant Conditioning Stimulus generalization also occurs in operant conditioning. A baby who is hugged and kissed for saying "Mama" when he sees his mother may begin to call everyone "Mama." Although the person whom the baby sees—the stimulus—changes, he responds with the same word.

In operant conditioning, responses, too, can be generalized, not just stimuli. For example, the baby who calls everyone "Mama" may also call people "Nana." His learning has generalized to other sounds that are similar to the correct response, "Mama." This is called **response generalization.** Response generalization doesn't occur in classical conditioning. If a dog is taught to salivate when it hears a high-pitched tone, it will salivate less when it hears a low-pitched tone, but the response is still salivation.

Just as discrimination is useful in classical conditioning, it is also useful in operant conditioning. Learning *what* to do has little value if you do not know *when* to do it. Learning that a response is triggered is pointless if you do not know which response is right. Discrimination training in operant conditioning consists of reinforcing *only* a specific, desired response and *only* in the presence of a specific stimulus. With this procedure, pigeons have been trained to peck at a red disk, but not at a green one. First they are taught to peck at a disk. Then they are presented with two disks, one red and one green. They get food when they peck at the red one, but not when they peck at the green. Eventually they learn to discriminate between the two colors, pecking only at the red.

stimulus control Control of conditioned responses by cues or stimuli in the environment.

stimulus generalization The transfer of a learned response to different but similar stimuli.

stimulus discrimination Learning to respond to only one stimulus and to inhibit the response to all other stimuli.

response generalization Giving a response that is somewhat different from the response originally learned to that stimulus.

New Learning Based on Original Learning

How might you build on a conditioned response to make an even more complex form of learning? Why is money such a good reinforcer for most people?

There are other ways, besides stimulus generalization and discrimination, that original learning can serve as the basis for new learning. In classical conditioning, an existing conditioned stimulus can be paired with a new stimulus to produce a new conditioned response. This is called **higher order conditioning.** In operant conditioning, objects that have no intrinsic value can nevertheless become reinforcers because of their association with other, more basic reinforcers. These learned reinforcers are called *secondary reinforcers.*

Higher Order Conditioning Pavlov demonstrated higher order conditioning with his dogs. After the dogs had learned to salivate when they heard a bell, Pavlov used the bell (*without* food) to teach the dogs to salivate at the sight of a black square. Instead of showing them the square and following it with food, he showed them the square and followed it with the bell until the dogs learned to salivate when they saw the square alone. In effect, the bell served as a substitute unconditioned stimulus, and the black square became a new conditioned stimulus. This procedure is known as *higher order conditioning* not because it is more complex than other types of conditioning or because it incorporates any new principles, but simply because it is conditioning based on previous learning.

Higher order conditioning is difficult to achieve because it is battling against extinction of the original conditioned response. The unconditioned stimulus no longer follows the original conditioned stimulus and that is precisely the way to extinguish a classically conditioned response. During higher order conditioning, Pavlov's dogs were exposed to the square followed by the bell, but no food was given. Thus, the square became a signal that the bell would not precede food, and soon all salivation stopped. For higher order conditioning to succeed, the unconditioned stimulus must be occasionally reintroduced. Food must be given once in a while after the bell sounds so that the dogs will continue to salivate when they hear the bell. ✳

Secondary Reinforcers Some reinforcers, such as food, water, and sex, are intrinsically rewarding in and of themselves. These are called **primary reinforcers.** No prior learning is required to make them reinforcing. Other reinforcers have no intrinsic value. They have acquired value only through association with primary reinforcers. These are the **secondary reinforcers** we mentioned earlier. They are called secondary not because they are less important, but because prior learning is needed before they will function as reinforcers.

For humans, money is one of the best examples of a secondary reinforcer. Although money is just paper or metal, through its exchange value for primary reinforcers, it becomes a powerful reinforcer. Children come to value money only after they learn that it will buy such things as candy (a primary reinforcer). Then the money becomes a secondary reinforcer. And through the principles of higher order conditioning, stimuli paired with a secondary reinforcer can acquire reinforcing properties. Checks and credit cards, for example, are one step removed from money, but they can also be highly reinforcing.

Summing Up

Does operant conditioning ever look like classical conditioning?

Classical and operant conditioning both entail forming associations between stimuli and responses, and perceiving contingencies between one event and another. Both are subject to extinction and spontaneous recovery, as well as to stimulus control, generalization, and discrimination. The main difference between the two is that in classical conditioning, the learner is passive and the behavior involved is usually involuntary, whereas in operant conditioning, the learner is active and the behavior involved is usually voluntary.

✳ **Explore** the **Concept**, Higher Order Conditioning, on **MyPsychLab**

higher order conditioning Conditioning based on previous learning; the conditioned stimulus serves as an unconditioned stimulus for further training.

primary reinforcers Reinforcers that are rewarding in themselves, such as food, water, or sex.

secondary reinforcers Reinforcers whose value is acquired through association with other primary or secondary reinforcers.

✓•─[**Study** and **Review** on **MyPsychLab**]

1. After extinction and a period of rest, a conditioned response may suddenly reappear. This phenomenon is called _____ _____.

2. The process by which a learned response to a specific stimulus comes to be associated with different, but similar stimuli is known as _____ _____.

3. Classify the following as primary (P) or secondary (S) reinforcers.

   a. food _____
   b. money _____
   c. college diploma _____
   d. sex _____

Answers: 1. spontaneous recovery. 2. stimulus generalization. 3. a. (P); b. (S); c. (S); d. (P).

1. On the first day of class, your instructor tells you that there will be unscheduled quizzes *on average* about every 2 weeks throughout the term, but not exactly every 2 weeks. This is an example of a _____ reinforcement schedule.

   a. continuous
   b. fixed-interval
   c. fixed-ratio
   d. variable-interval

2. In the situation in question 1, what study pattern is the instructor most likely trying to encourage?

   a. slow, steady rates of studying
   b. cramming the night before quizzes
   c. studying a lot right before quizzes, then stopping for a while right after them

Answers: 1. d. 2. a.

- Define cognitive learning and how it can be inferred from evidence of latent learning and cognitive maps.
- Explain what is meant by insight and its relation to learning sets.
- Explain the process of observational (vicarious) learning and the conditions under which it is most likely to be reflected in behavior.
- Give examples of cognitive learning in nonhumans.

COGNITIVE LEARNING

How would you study the kind of learning that occurs when you memorize the layout of a building?

Some psychologists insist that because classical and operant conditioning can be *observed* and *measured,* they are the only legitimate kinds of learning to study scientifically. But others contend that mental activities are crucial to learning and so can't be ignored. How do you grasp the layout of a building from someone else's description of it? How do you enter into memory abstract concepts like *conditioning* and *reinforcement?* You do all these things and many others through **cognitive learning**—the mental processes that go on inside us when we learn. Cognitive learning is impossible to observe and measure directly, but it can be *inferred* from behavior, and so it is also a legitimate topic for scientific study.

Latent Learning and Cognitive Maps

Did you learn your way around campus solely through operant conditioning (rewards for correct turns, punishments for wrong ones), or was something more involved?

Interest in cognitive learning began shortly after the earliest work in classical and operant conditioning. In the 1930s, Edward Chace Tolman, one of the pioneers in the study of cognitive learning, argued that we do not need to show our learning in order for learning to have occurred. Tolman called learning that isn't apparent because it is not yet demonstrated **latent learning.** ◉→

cognitive learning Learning that depends on mental processes that are not directly observable.

latent learning Learning that is not immediately reflected in a behavior change.

◉→[**Simulate** the **Experiment**, Learning, on **MyPsychLab**]

Tolman studied latent learning in a famous experiment (Tolman & Honzik, 1930). Two groups of hungry rats were placed in a maze and allowed to find their way from a start box to an end box. The first group found food pellets (a reward) in the end box; the second group found nothing there. According to the principles of operant conditioning, the first group would learn the maze better than the second group—which is, indeed, what happened. But when Tolman took some of the rats from the second, unreinforced group and started to give them food at the goal box, almost immediately they ran the maze as well as the rats in the first group. (See **Figure 5–8.**) Tolman argued that the unrewarded rats had actually learned a great deal about the maze as they wandered around inside it. In fact, they may have even learned *more* about it than the rats that had been trained with food rewards, but their learning was *latent*—stored internally, but not yet reflected in their behavior. It was not until they were given a motivation to run the maze that they put their latent learning to use.

Since Tolman's time, much work has been done on the nature of latent learning regarding spatial layouts and relationships. From studies of how animals or humans find their way around a maze, a building, or a neighborhood with many available routes, psychologists have proposed that this kind of learning is stored in the form of a mental image, or **cognitive map.** When the proper time comes, the learner can call up the stored image and put it to use.

In response to Tolman's theory of latent learning, Thorndike proposed an experiment to test whether a rat could learn to run a maze and store a cognitive image of the maze without experiencing the maze firsthand. He envisioned researchers carrying each rat through the maze in a small wire-mesh container and then rewarding the rat at the end of each trial as if it had run the maze itself. He predicted that the rat would show little or no evidence of learning as compared with rats that had learned the same maze on their own through trial and error. Neither he nor Tolman ever conducted the experiment.

Two decades later, however, researchers at the University of Kansas did carry out Thorndike's idea (McNamara, Long, & Wike, 1956). But instead of taking the passive rats through the "correct" path, they carried them over the same path that a free-running rat had taken in that maze. Contrary to Thorndike's prediction, the passenger rats learned the maze just as well as the free-running rats. They did, however, need visual cues to learn the maze's layout. If carried through the maze only in the dark, they later showed little latent learning.

More recent research confirms this picture of cognitive spatial learning. Animals show a great deal more flexibility in solving problems than can be explained by simple conditioning (Collett & Graham, 2004). In experiments using rats in a radial maze, rats are able to recall which arms of the maze contain food, even when scent cues are removed (Grandchamp & Schenk, 2006). Moreover, when the configuration of the maze is repeatedly changed, the rats not only quickly adapt but also remember previous maze configurations (J. Tremblay & Cohen, 2005). Studies such as these suggest that the rats develop a cognitive map of the maze's layout (Save & Poucet, 2005). Even in rats, learning involves more than just a new behavior "stamped in" through reinforcement. It also involves the formation of new mental images and constructs that may be reflected in future behavior.

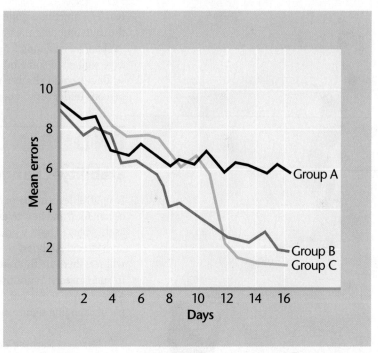

FIGURE 5–8
Graph showing the results of the Tolman and Honzik study.

The results of the classic Tolman and Honzik study are revealed in the graph. Group A never received a food reward. Group B was rewarded each day. Group C was not rewarded until the 11th day, but note the significant change in the rats' behavior on Day 12. The results suggest that Group C had been learning all along, although this learning was not reflected in their performance until they were rewarded with food for demonstrating the desired behaviors.

Source: Tolman & Honzik, 1930.

Insight and Learning Sets

Do you have a learning set for writing a term paper?

During World War I, the German Gestalt psychologist Wolfgang Köhler conducted a classic series of studies into another aspect of cognitive learning: sudden **insight** into a problem's solution. Outside a chimpanzee's cage, Köhler placed a banana on the ground, not quite within the animal's reach. When the chimp realized that it couldn't reach the banana, it reacted with frustration. But then it started looking at what was in the cage, including a stick left there by

cognitive map A learned mental image of a spatial environment that may be called on to solve problems when stimuli in the environment change.

insight Learning that occurs rapidly as a result of understanding all the elements of a problem.

Köhler's experiments with chimpanzees illustrate learning through insight. In this photo, one of the chimps has arranged a stack of boxes to reach bananas hanging from the ceiling. Insights gained in this problem-solving situation may transfer to similar ones.

Köhler. Sometimes quite suddenly the chimp would grab the stick, poke it through the bars of the cage, and drag the banana within reach. The same kind of sudden insight occurred when the banana was hung from the roof of the cage, too high for the chimp to grasp. This time the cage contained some boxes, which the chimp quickly learned to stack up under the banana so that it could climb up to pull the fruit down. Subsequent studies have shown that even pigeons under certain conditions can display insight (Aust & Huber, 2006).

ENDURING ISSUES

Stability–Change   Human Insight

Insightful learning is particularly important in humans, who must learn not only where to obtain food and how to escape from predators but also such complex ethical and cultural ideas as the value of hard work, helping others, or overcoming addictions. In Chapter 7, "Cognition and Mental Abilities," we will explore the role of insight in creative problem solving. As we will see, there are times when all other problem-solving techniques fail to produce a solution; in such cases, it is not unusual for the solution to suddenly "pop up" in a moment of insight. Moreover, to the extent that people gain insight into their own behavior, they should be capable of changing significantly over the course of their lives (see Chapter 13, "Therapies"). ■

Previous learning can often be used to help solve problems through insight. This was demonstrated by Harry Harlow in a series of studies with rhesus monkeys (Harlow, 1949). Harlow presented each monkey with two boxes—say, a round green box on the left side of a tray and a square red box on the right side. A morsel of food was put under one of the boxes. The monkey was permitted to lift just one box; if it chose the correct box, it got the food. On the next trial, the food was put under the same box (which had been moved to a new position), and the monkey again got to choose just one box. Each monkey had six trials to figure out that the same box covered the food no matter where that box was located. Then the monkeys were given a new set of choices—say, between a blue triangular box and an orange oval one—and another six trials, and so on with other shapes and colors of boxes. The solution was always the same: The food was invariably under only one of the boxes. Initially the monkeys chose boxes randomly, sometimes finding the food, sometimes not. After a while, however, their behavior changed: In just one or two trials, they would find the correct box, which they chose consistently thereafter until the experimenter changed the boxes. They seemed to have learned the underlying principle—that the food would always be under the same box—and they used that learning to solve almost instantly each new set of choices given.

Harlow concluded that the monkeys "learned how to learn," that is, they had established a **learning set** regarding this problem: Within the limited range of choices available to them, they had discovered how to tell which box would give the reward. Similarly, Köhler's chimps could be said to have established a learning set regarding how to get food that was just out of reach. When presented with a new version of the problem, they simply called upon past learning in a slightly different situation (reaching a banana on the ground versus reaching one hanging from the ceiling). In both Harlow's and Köhler's studies, the animals seemed to have learned more than just specific behaviors: They had apparently learned *how* to learn. More recent studies confirm learning sets can be formed by other species of primates such as capuchin and rhesus monkeys (Beran, 2008), and even by rats (Bailey, 2006).

Learning by Observing

Why would it be harder to learn to drive a car if you had never been in one before? Why is it hard for deaf children to learn spoken language when they can easily be reinforced for correct speech sounds?

The first time you drove a car, you successfully turned the key in the ignition, put the car in gear, and pressed the gas pedal without having ever done any of those things before. How were you able to do that without step-by-step shaping of the correct behaviors? The answer

learning set The ability to become increasingly more effective in solving problems as more problems are solved.

is that like Adrian Cole, the 4-year-old driver described at the start of the chapter, you had often watched other people driving, a practice that made all the difference. There are countless things we learn by watching other people and listening to what they say. This process is called **observational or vicarious learning,** because although we are learning, we don't have to do the learned behaviors firsthand; we merely view or hear the modeled behavior. Observational learning is a form of "social learning," in that it involves interaction with other people. Psychologists who study it are known as **social learning theorists.**

Observational learning is very common. In fact, recent evidence shows that young children often "over imitate"—slavishly following what they are shown to do, even when that is not the most effective way to behave (Horner & Whiten, 2005; Zimmer, 2005). By watching other people who model new behavior we can learn such things as how to start a lawn mower and how to saw wood. Research has shown that we can even learn bad habits, such as smoking, by watching actors smoke in a movie (Dal Cin, Gibson, Zanna, Shumate, & Fong, 2007; Heatherton & Sargent, 2009). When the Federal Communications Commission (FCC) banned cigarette commercials on television, it was acting on the belief that providing models of smokers would prompt people to imitate smoking. It is hard for deaf children to learn spoken language because they have no auditory model of correct speech.

Of course, we do not imitate *everything* that other people do. Why are we selective in our imitation? There are several reasons (Bandura, 1977, 1986). First, we can't pay attention to everything going on around us. The behaviors we are most likely to imitate are those that are modeled by someone who commands our attention (as does a famous or attractive person, or an expert). Second, we must remember what a model does in order to imitate it. If a behavior isn't memorable, it won't be learned. Third, we must make an effort to convert what we see into action. If we have no motivation to perform an observed behavior, we probably won't show what we've learned. This is a distinction between *learning* and *performance,* which is crucial to social learning theorists: We can learn without any change in overt behavior that demonstrates our learning. Whether or not we act depends on our motivation.

One important motivation for acting is the kind of consequences associated with an observed behavior—that is, the rewards or punishments it appears to bring. These consequences do not necessarily have to happen to the observer. They may happen simply to the other people whom the observer is watching. This is called **vicarious reinforcement** or **vicarious punishment,** because the consequences aren't experienced firsthand by the learner: They are experienced *through* other people. If a young teenager sees adults drinking and they seem to be having a great deal of fun, the teenager is experiencing vicarious reinforcement of drinking and is much more likely to imitate it.

The foremost proponent of social learning theory is Albert Bandura, who refers to his perspective as a *social cognitive theory* (Bandura, 1986, 2004). In a classic experiment, Bandura (1965) showed that people can learn a behavior without being reinforced directly for it and that learning a behavior and performing it are not the same thing. Three groups of nursery schoolchildren watched a film in which an adult model walked up to an adult-size plastic inflated doll and ordered it to move out of the way. When the doll failed to obey, the model became aggressive, pushing the doll on its side, punching it in the nose, hitting it with a rubber mallet, kicking it around the room, and throwing rubber balls at it. However, each group of children saw a film with a different ending. Those in the *model-rewarded condition* saw the model showered with candies, soft drinks, and praise by a second adult (vicarious reinforcement). Those in the *model-punished condition* saw the second adult shaking a finger at the model, scolding, and spanking him (vicarious punishment). And those in the *no-consequences condition* saw nothing happen to the model as a result of his aggressive behavior.

Immediately after seeing the film, the children were individually escorted into another room where they found the same large inflated doll, rubber balls, and mallet, as well as many other toys. Each child played alone for 10 minutes, while observers behind a one-way mirror recorded the number of imitated aggressive behaviors that the child spontaneously performed in the absence of any direct reinforcement for those actions. After 10 minutes, an experimenter entered the room and offered the child treats in return for imitating things

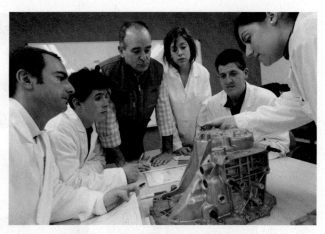

In observational or vicarious learning, we learn by watching a model perform a particular action and then trying to imitate that action correctly. Some actions would be very difficult to master without observational learning.

observational (or vicarious) learning Learning by observing other people's behavior.

social learning theorists Psychologists whose view of learning emphasizes the ability to learn by observing a model or receiving instructions, without firsthand experience by the learner.

vicarious reinforcement (or punishment) Reinforcement or punishment experienced by models that affects the willingness of others to perform the behaviors they learned by observing those models.

After watching an adult behave aggressively toward an inflated doll, the children in Bandura's study imitated many of the aggressive acts of the adult model.

the model had done. This was a measure of how much the child had previously learned from watching the model, but perhaps hadn't yet displayed.

The green bars in **Figure 5–9** show that *all* the children had learned aggressive actions from watching the model, even though they were not overtly reinforced for that learning. When later offered treats to copy the model's actions, they all did so quite accurately. In addition, the yellow bars in the figure show that the children tended to suppress their inclination spontaneously to imitate an aggressive model when they had seen that model punished for aggression. This result was especially true of girls. Apparently, vicarious punishment provided the children with information about what might happen to them if they copied the "bad" behavior. Vicarious reinforcement similarly provides information about likely consequences, but in this study, its effects were not large. For children of this age (at least those not worried about punishment), imitating aggressive behavior toward a doll seems to have been considered "fun" in its own right, even without being associated with praise and candy. This outcome was especially true for boys.

This study has important implications regarding how not to teach aggression unintentionally to children. Suppose that you want to get a child to stop hitting other children. You might think that slapping the child as punishment would change the behavior, and it probably would suppress it to some extent. But slapping the child also demonstrates that hitting is an effective means of getting one's way. So slapping not only provides a model of aggression; it also provides a model associated with vicarious reinforcement. Perhaps this is why children who experience corporal punishment are more likely to imitate the violent behavior of their parents when they become adults (Barry, 2007). You and the child would both be better off if the punishment given for hitting was not a similar form of aggression and if the child could also be rewarded for showing appropriate interactions with others (Gershoff & Bitensky, 2007).

Social learning theory's emphasis on expectations, insights, and information broadens our understanding of how people learn. According to social learning theory, humans use their powers of observation and thought to interpret their own experiences and those of others when deciding how to act. Moreover, human beings are capable of setting performance

Complete the **Survey**, Media Violence and Societal Aggression on **MyPsychLab**

standards for themselves and then rewarding (or punishing) themselves for achieving or failing to achieve those standards as a way to regulate their own behavior. This important perspective can be applied to the learning of many different things, from skills and behavioral tendencies to attitudes, values, and ideas.

Cognitive Learning in Nonhumans

Are non-human animals capable of cognitive learning?

We have seen that classical and operant conditioning are no longer viewed as purely mechanical processes that can proceed without at least some cognitive activity. Moreover, animals are capable of latent learning, learning cognitive maps, and insight, all of which involve cognitive processes. Do non-human animals also exhibit other evidence of cognitive learning? The answer seems to be a qualified yes.

For example, in the wild, chimpanzees learn to use long sticks to fish for termites by watching their mothers (Lonsdorf, 2005). Capuchin monkeys have shown they can benefit from watching the *mistakes* of other monkeys that made unsuccessful attempts at opening a container (Kuroshima, Kuwahata, & Fujita, 2008). Some female dolphins in Australia cover their sensitive beaks with sponges when foraging for food on the sea floor, a skill they apparently learn by imitating their mothers (Krützen et al., 2005). Meerkats have been observed teaching their young how to hunt and handle difficult prey (A. Thornton, 2008). And even rats that watch other rats try a novel or unfamiliar food without negative consequences show an increased tendency to eat the new food (Galef & Whiskin, 2004; Galef, Dudley, & Whiskin, 2008). These results, along with reports that animals as diverse as chickens and octopi, whales and bumblebees learn by watching others, further support the notion that nonhuman animals do indeed learn in ways that support the cognitive theory of learning.

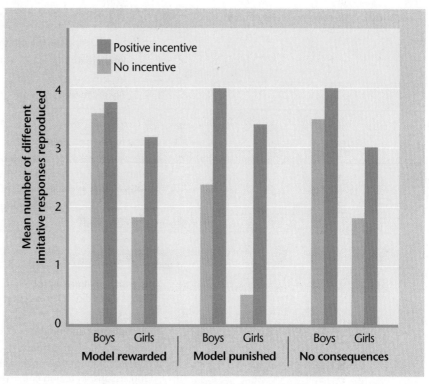

FIGURE 5–9
Results of Bandura's study.

As the graph shows, even though all the children in Bandura's study of imitative aggression learned the model's behavior, they performed differently depending on whether the model whom they saw was rewarded or punished.

Source: Results of Bandura's study. From "Influence of models' reinforcement contingencies on the acquisition of imitative responses" by A. Bandura, *Journal of Personality and Social Psychology*, 1, 592, 1965. Reprinted by permission of the American Psychological Association and the author.

Use of sponges as tools among some dolphins.

Dolphins have been observed using sponges to protect their snouts as they probe the sea floor searching for fish. Researchers believe mother dolphins teach this sponge-tool technique to their young. See http://animal.discovery.com/news/briefs/20050606/dolphin.html

✓● Study and Review on MyPsychLab

CHECK YOUR UNDERSTANDING

Match the following terms with the appropriate definition.

1. _____ latent learning
2. _____ insight
3. _____ observational learning

a. new, suddenly occurring idea to solve a problem
b. learning by watching a model
c. learning that has not yet been demonstrated in behavior

Are the following statements true (T) or false (F)?

4. _____ "Social learning theory broadens our understanding of how people learn skills and gain abilities by emphasizing expectations, insight, information, self-satisfaction, and self-criticism."

5. _____ "Social learning theory supports spanking as an effective way to teach children not to hit."

Answers: 1. (c). 2. (a). 3. (b). 4. (T). 5. (F).

APPLY YOUR UNDERSTANDING

1. An ape examines a problem and the tools available for solving it. Suddenly the animal leaps up and quickly executes a successful solution. This is an example of
   a. insight.
   b. operant conditioning.
   c. trial-and-error learning.

2. Before Junior got his driver's license, he rode along whenever his older sister had driving lessons, watching and listening carefully, especially when she had trouble learning to parallel park and another driver yelled at her for denting his fender. When Junior's turn to drive came, he was especially careful never to bump other cars when parallel parking. Junior learned to avoid parallel parking collisions as a result of
   a. insight.
   b. vicarious punishment.
   c. trial-and-error learning.
   d. higher order conditioning.

Answers: 1. a. 2. b.

KEY TERMS

learning, p. 153

Classical Conditioning
classical (or Pavlovian) conditioning, p. 153
unconditioned stimulus (US), p. 154
unconditioned response (UR), p. 154
conditioned stimulus (CS), p. 154
conditioned response (CR), p. 154
intermittent pairing, p. 156
desensitization therapy, p. 156
preparedness, p. 157
conditioned taste aversion, p. 157

Operant Conditioning
operant (or instrumental) conditioning, p. 158
operant behaviors, p. 159
reinforcers, p. 159
punishers, p. 159
law of effect (principle of reinforcement), p. 159
Skinner box, p. 160
shaping, p. 160
positive reinforcers, p. 161
negative reinforcers, p. 161
punishment, p. 162
avoidance training, p. 164
learned helplessness, p. 164
biofeedback, p. 165
neurofeedback, p. 165

Factors Shared by Classical and Operant Conditioning
contingency, p. 167
blocking, p. 167
schedule of reinforcement, p. 168
fixed-interval schedule, p. 168
variable-interval schedule, p. 169
fixed-ratio schedule, p. 169
variable-ratio schedule, p. 169
extinction, p. 169
spontaneous recovery, p. 170
stimulus control, p. 172
stimulus generalization, p. 172
stimulus discrimination, p. 172
response generalization, p. 172

higher order conditioning, p. 173
primary reinforcers, p. 173
secondary reinforcers, p. 173

Cognitive Learning
cognitive learning, p. 174
latent learning, p. 174
cognitive map, p. 175
insight, p. 175
learning set, p. 176
observational (or vicarious) learning, p. 177
social learning theorists, p. 177
vicarious reinforcement (or punishment), p. 177

CHAPTER REVIEW ((•-[Listen to the Chapter Audio on MyPsychLab

CLASSICAL CONDITIONING

How did Pavlov discover classical conditioning? Learning is the process by which experience or practice produces a relatively permanent change in behavior or potential behavior. One basic form of learning involves learning to associate one event with another. **Classical conditioning** is a type of associative learning that Pavlov discovered while studying digestion. Pavlov trained a dog to salivate at the sound of a bell when he rang the bell just before food was given. The dog learned to associate the bell with food and began to salivate at the sound of the bell alone.

How might you classically condition a pet? Suppose you wanted to classically condition salivation in your own dog. You know that food is an **unconditioned stimulus** (US) that automatically evokes the **unconditioned response** (UR) of salivation. By repeatedly pairing food with a second, initially neutral stimulus (such as a bell), the second stimulus would eventually become a **conditioned stimulus (CS)** eliciting a **conditioned response (CR)** of salivation.

If you once burned your finger on a match while listening to a certain song, why doesn't that song now make you reflexively jerk your hand away? Establishing a classically conditioned response usually is easier if the US and CS are paired with each other repeatedly, rather than a single time or even once in a while (**intermittent pairing**). That is why a single burn to your finger is not usually enough to produce a classically conditioned response. It is also important that the spacing of pairings be neither too far apart nor too close together.

What is an example of classical conditioning in your own life? In the case of Little Albert, Watson conditioned a child to fear white rats by always pairing a loud, frightening noise with a rat. Perhaps you have acquired a classically conditioned fear or anxiety (to the sound of a dentist's drill, for instance) in much the same way; or perhaps you have also unlearned a conditioned fear by repeatedly pairing the feared object with something pleasant. Mary Cover Jones paired the sight of a feared rat (at gradually decreasing distances) with a child's pleasant experience of eating candy. This procedure was the precursor to **desensitization therapy.**

Why are people more likely to develop a phobia of snakes than of flowers? The concept of **preparedness** accounts for the fact that certain conditioned responses are acquired very easily. The ease with which we develop **conditioned taste aversions** illustrates preparedness. Because animals are biologically prepared to learn them, conditioned taste aversions can occur with only one pairing of the taste of a tainted food and later illness, even when there is a lengthy interval between eating the food and becoming ill. A fear of snakes may also be something that humans are prepared to learn.

OPERANT CONDITIONING

How are operant behaviors different from the responses involved in classical conditioning? Operant or **instrumental conditioning** is learning to make or withhold a certain response because of its consequences. **Operant behaviors** are different from the responses involved in classical conditioning because they are voluntarily emitted, whereas those involved in classical conditioning are elicited by stimuli.

What two essential elements are involved in operant conditioning? One essential element in operant conditioning is an operant behavior, or a behavior performed by one's own volition while "operating" on the environment. The second essential element is a consequence associated with that operant behavior. When a consequence increases the likelihood of an operant behavior's being emitted, it is called a **reinforcer.** When a consequence decreases the likelihood of an operant behavior, it is called a **punisher.** These relationships are the basis of the **law of effect,** or **principle of reinforcement:** Consistently rewarded behaviors are likely to be repeated, whereas consistently punished behaviors are likely to be suppressed.

How might an animal trainer teach a tiger to jump through a flaming hoop? To speed up establishing an operantly conditioned response in the laboratory, the number of potential responses may be reduced by restricting the environment, as in a **Skinner box.** For behaviors outside the laboratory, which cannot be controlled so conveniently, the process of **shaping** is often useful. In shaping, reinforcement is given for successive approximations to the desired response. An animal trainer might use shaping to teach a tiger to jump through a flaming hoop.

What is the difference between positive and negative reinforcement? What are some of the unintentional effects that reinforcement can have? Several kinds of reinforcers strengthen or increase the likelihood of behavior. **Positive reinforcers** (such as food) add something rewarding to a situation. **Negative reinforcers** (for example, stopping an electric shock) subtracts something unpleasant. When an action is followed closely by a reinforcer, we tend to repeat the action, even if it did not actually produce the reinforcement. Such behaviors are called *superstitious.*

What problems can punishment create? Punishment is any unpleasant consequence that decreases the likelihood that the preceding behavior will recur. Whereas negative reinforcement strengthens behavior, punishment weakens it. Although punishment can be effective, it also can stir up negative feelings and serve to model aggressive behavior. Also, rather than teaching a more desirable response, it only suppresses an undesirable one. After punishment has occurred a few times, further repetitions sometimes are unnecessary because the threat of punishment is enough. With this process, called **avoidance training,** people learn to avoid the possibility of a punishing consequence.

In what ways do some college students exhibit learned helplessness? When people or other animals are unable to escape from a punishing situation, they may acquire a "giving-up" response, called learned helplessness. **Learned helplessness** can generalize to new situations, causing resignation in the face of unpleasant outcomes, even when the outcomes can be avoided. A college student who gives up trying to do well in school after a few poor grades on tests is exhibiting learned helplessness.

How can operant conditioning be used to control biological functioning? When operant conditioning is used to control biological functions, such as blood pressure or heart rate, it is referred to as **biofeedback.** When it is used to control brain waves it is called **neurofeedback.** Biofeedback and neurofeedback have been successfully applied to a variety of medical problems, including migraine headaches, hypertension, and asthma. Biofeedback has also been used by athletes and musicians to improve performance and control anxiety.

FACTORS SHARED BY CLASSICAL AND OPERANT CONDITIONING

Can you think of any similarities between classical and operant conditioning? Despite the differences between classical and operant conditioning, these two forms of learning have many things in common. (1) Both cases involve learned associations; (2) in both cases, responses come under control of stimuli in the environment; (3) in both cases, the responses will gradually disappear if they are not periodically renewed; and (4) in both cases, new behaviors can build upon previously established ones.

How can changes in the timing of a conditioned stimulus lead to unexpected learning? Why does intermittent reinforcement result in such persistent behavior? In both classical and operant conditioning, an "if–then" relationship, or contingency, exists either between two stimuli or between a stimulus and a response. In both these kinds of learning, perceived contingencies are very important.

In classical conditioning, the contingency is between the CS and the US. The CS comes to be viewed as a signal that the US is about to happen. For that reason, the CS must not only occur in close proximity to the US, but must also precede the US and provide predictive information about it. If the CS occurs *after* the US, it will come to serve as a signal that the US is over, not that the US is imminent.

In operant conditioning, contingencies exist between responses and consequences. Contingencies between responses and rewards are called **schedules of reinforcement.** *Partial reinforcement,* in which rewards are given only for some correct responses, generates behavior that persists longer than that learned by *continuous reinforcement.* A **fixed-interval schedule,** by which reinforcement is given for the first correct response after a fixed time period, tends to result in a flurry of responding right before a reward is due. A **variable-interval schedule,** which reinforces the first correct response after an unpredictable period of time, tends to result in a slow, but steady pattern of responding. In a *fixed-ratio schedule,* behavior is rewarded after a fixed number of correct responses, so the result is usually a high rate of responding. Finally, a **variable-ratio schedule** provides reinforcement after a varying number of correct responses. It encourages a high rate of response that is especially persistent.

Can you ever get rid of a conditioned response? Under what circumstances might old learned associations suddenly reappear? Learned responses sometimes weaken and may even disappear, a phenomenon called **extinction.** The learning is not necessarily completely forgotten, however. Sometimes a **spontaneous recovery** occurs, in which the learned response suddenly reappears on its own, with no retraining.

Extinction is produced in classical conditioning by failure to continue pairing the CS and the US. The CS no longer serves as a signal that the US is about to happen, and so the conditioned response dies out. An important contributing factor is often new, learned associations that interfere with the old one. In situations in which you are reminded of the old association, spontaneous recovery may occur.

Extinction occurs in operant conditioning when reinforcement is withheld until the learned response is no longer emitted. The ease with which an operantly conditioned behavior is extinguished varies according to several factors: the strength of the original learning, the variety of settings in which learning took place, and the schedule of reinforcement used during conditioning.

How can anxiety about math in grade school affect a college student? Why do people often slap the wrong card when playing a game of slapjack? When conditioned responses are influenced by surrounding cues in the environment, **stimulus control** occurs. The tendency to respond to cues that are similar, but not identical, to those that prevailed during the original learning is known as **stimulus generalization.** An example of stimulus generalization in classical conditioning is a student's feeling anxious about studying math in college because he or she had a bad experience learning math in grade school. **Stimulus discrimination** enables learners to perceive differences among cues so as not to respond to all of them.

In operant conditioning, the learned response is under the control of whatever cues come to be associated with delivery of reward or punishment. Learners often generalize about these cues, responding to others that are broadly similar to the ones that prevailed during the original learning. An example is slapping any face card in a game of slapjack. Learners may also generalize their responses by performing behaviors that are similar to the ones that were originally reinforced. This result is called **response generalization.** Discrimination in operant conditioning is taught by reinforcing only a certain response and only in the presence of a certain stimulus.

How might you build on a conditioned response to make an even more complex form of learning? Why is money such a good reinforcer for most people? In both classical and operant conditioning, original learning serves as a building block for new learning. In classical conditioning, an earlier CS can be used as an US for further training. For example, Pavlov used the bell to condition his dogs to salivate at the sight of a black square. This effect, which is called **higher order conditioning,** is difficult to achieve because of extinction. Unless the original unconditioned stimulus is presented occasionally, the initial conditioned response will die out.

In operant conditioning, initially neutral stimuli can become reinforcers by being associated with other reinforcers. A **primary reinforcer** is one that, like food and water, is rewarding in and of itself. A **secondary reinforcer** is one whose value is learned through its association with primary reinforcers or with other secondary reinforcers. Money is such a good secondary reinforcer because it can be exchanged for so many different primary and secondary rewards.

Does operant conditioning ever look like classical conditioning? Despite their differences, classical and operant conditioning share many similarities: Both involve associations between stimuli and responses; both are subject to extinction and spontaneous recovery as well as generalization and discrimination; in both, new learning can be based on original learning. Operant conditioning can even be used, in **biofeedback** and **neurofeedback** training, to learn to control physiological responses that are usually learned through classical conditioning. Many psychologists now wonder whether classical and operant conditioning aren't just two ways of bringing about the same kind of learning.

COGNITIVE LEARNING

How would you study the kind of learning that occurs when you memorize the layout of a chessboard? **Cognitive learning** refers to the mental processes that go on inside us when we learn. Some kinds of learning, such as memorizing the layout of a chessboard, seem to be purely cognitive, because the learner does not appear to be "behaving" while the learning takes place. Cognitive learning, however, can always affect future behavior, such as reproducing the layout of a memorized chessboard after it is cleared away. It is from such observable behavior that cognitive learning is inferred.

Did you learn your way around campus solely through operant conditioning (rewards for correct turns, punishments for wrong ones) or was something more involved? **Latent learning** is any learning that has not yet been demonstrated in behavior. Your knowledge of psychology is latent if you have not yet displayed it in what you say, write, and do. One kind of latent learning is knowledge of spatial layouts and relationships, which is usually stored in the form of a **cognitive map.** Rewards or punishments aren't essential for latent learning to take place. You did not need rewards and punishments to learn the layout of your campus,

for example. You acquired this cognitive map simply by storing your visual perceptions.

Do you have a learning set for writing a term paper? A **learning set** is a concept or procedure that provides a key to solving a problem even when its demands are slightly different from those of problems you have solved in the past. As a student, you probably have a learning set for writing a term paper that allows you successfully to develop papers on many different topics. A learning set can sometimes encourage insight or the sudden perception of a solution even to a problem that at first seems totally new. In this case, you are perceiving similarities between old and new problems that weren't initially apparent.

Why would it be harder to learn to drive a car if you had never been in one before? Why is it hard for deaf children to learn spoken language when they can easily be reinforced for correct speech sounds? **Social learning theorists** argue that we learn much by observing other people who model a behavior or by simply hearing about something. This process is called **observational** (or **vicarious**) **learning.** It would be harder to learn to drive a car without ever having been in one because you would lack a model of "driving behavior." It is hard for deaf children to learn spoken language because they have no auditory model of correct speech.

The extent to which we imitate behaviors learned through observation depends on our motivation to do so. One important motivation is any reward or punishment that we have seen the behavior bring. When a consequence isn't experienced firsthand, but only occurs to other people, it is called **vicarious reinforcement or vicarious punishment.**

Are nonhuman animals capable of cognitive learning? Research has shown that many animals, including chimpanzees, dolphins, whales, rats, octopi, and even bumblebees are capable of various forms of cognitive learning.

6

Memory

Most of us remember certain days or moments more distinctly than others. Your first day of school, your first kiss, a special holiday, the loss of a loved one—these experiences may be etched so indelibly on your memory that it seems that they happened just yesterday, rather than many years in the past. But imagine if you had a distinct memory of not only your first day of school, but of the second one, too; as well as the third, fourth, fifth, and so on. Imagine if you recalled not just the most important events of your life, but, in addition, all of the tiny, insignificant details of each and every day: what the weather was like, what you ate for dinner, what you watched on television. Imagine these visions of the past—some ordinary and mundane, some comforting and pleasant, others, terribly painful and sad—ran through your head in a constant loop, a random compilation of all of the moments of your life assaulting your consciousness with ceaseless persistence. Jill Price, a 42-year-old woman who lives in California, need not imagine such a scenario; for her, this is life.

In her 2008 memoir, *The Woman Who Can't Forget,* Jill Price recounts a life lived with what psychologist James L. McGaugh has diagnosed as hyperthymestic syndrome, or "overdeveloped memory." If given a date over the course of the past thirty years, Price can typically recount what day of the week it was in addition to details about something that happened to her that day. Moreover, according to Price, autobiographical memories, unpredictably summoned by various stimuli—a familiar smell, for example, or a song on the radio—constantly dominate her thoughts in a mechanism beyond her conscious control. As Price contends, her unusual powers of memory are more a burden than a blessing, forcing her to relive every argument, every disappointment, every moment of despair she has ever known at arbitrary intervals. Indeed, as Price's case illustrates, while the ability to remember has its merits, so too, it seems, does the ability to forget.

Accounts of people with extraordinary memories raise many questions about the nature of **memory** itself: Why are some people so much better at remembering things than others? Why is it that remembering may sometimes be so simple (think how effortlessly baseball fans remember the batting averages of their favorite players) and other times so difficult (as when we grope for answers on an exam)? Just how does memory work, and what makes it fail?

Among the first to seek scientific answers to these questions was the 19th-century German psychologist Hermann Ebbinghaus. Using himself as a subject, Ebbinghaus composed lists of "nonsense syllables," meaningless combinations of letters, such as PIB, WOL, or TEB. He memorized lists of 13 nonsense syllables each. Then, after varying amounts of time, he relearned each list of syllables. He found that the longer he waited after first learning a list, the longer it took to learn the list again. Most of the information was lost in the first few hours. Ebbinghaus's contributions dominated memory research for many years.

Many contemporary psychologists, by contrast, perceive memory as a series of steps in which we process information, much as a computer stores and retrieves data. Together, these steps form the **information-processing model** of memory. In this chapter you will find terms like *encoding, storage,* and *retrieval,* which are convenient ways of comparing human memory with computers. But we will also consider the social, emotional, and biological factors that make us human and that also distinguish our memories from those of computers.

Far more information bombards our senses than we can possibly process, so the first stage of information processing involves selecting some of this material to think about and remember. Therefore, we turn first to the sensory registers and to attention, the process that allows us to select incoming information for further processing.

ENDURING ISSUES **in Memory**

In this chapter, we will again encounter the "Enduring Issues" in psychology that were introduced in Chapter 1. We will explore the biological bases of memory (*Mind–Body*), the ways that memory differs among people and across cultures (*Diversity–Universality*), and the ways that memory changes in the first few years of life (*Stability–Change*). Finally, we will consider the extent to which memories can be changed by events outside the person as well as the importance of environmental cues in triggering memories (*Person–Situation*).

THE SENSORY REGISTERS

What is the role of sensory registers?

Look slowly around the room. Each glance takes in an enormous amount of visual information, including colors, shapes, textures, relative brightness, and shadows. At the same time, you pick up sounds, smells, and other kinds of sensory data. All of this raw information flows from your senses into the **sensory registers,** which are like waiting rooms in which information enters and stays for only a short time. Whether we remember

memory The ability to remember the things that we have experienced, imagined, and learned.

information-processing model A computer-like model used to describe the way humans encode, store, and retrieve information.

sensory registers Entry points for raw information from the senses.

LEARNING OBJECTIVES

- Describe the role of the sensory registers and the length of time information remains there. Distinguish between the *icon* and the *echo*.
- Compare Broadbent and Treisman's theories of attention. Explain what is meant by the "cocktail-party phenomenon" and "inattentional blindness."

If you were to walk into this room, your eyes and your other sense organs would pick up many impressions of what is to be found here. How much of this information would you remember later?

any of the information depends on which operations we perform on it, as you will see throughout this chapter. Although there are registers for each of our senses, the visual and auditory registers have been studied most extensively.

Visual and Auditory Registers

What would happen if auditory information faded as quickly as visual information fades?

Although the sensory registers have virtually unlimited capacity, information disappears from them quite rapidly (Cowan et al., 2005). A simple experiment can demonstrate how much visual information we take in—and how quickly it is lost. Bring a digital camera into a darkened room, and then take a photograph with a flash. During the split second that the room is lit up by the flash, your visual register will absorb a surprising amount of information about the room and its contents. Try to hold on to that visual image, or *icon*, as long as you can. You will find that in a few seconds, it is gone. Then compare your remembered image of the room with what you actually saw, as captured in the photograph. You will discover that your visual register took in far more information than you were able to retain for even a few seconds.

Classic experiments by George Sperling (1960) clearly demonstrate how quickly information disappears from the visual register. Sperling flashed groups of letters, organized into three rows, on a screen for just a fraction of a second. When the letters were gone, he sounded a tone to tell his participants which row of letters to recall: A high-pitched tone indicated that they should try to remember the top row of letters, a low-pitched tone meant that they should recall the bottom row, and a medium-pitched tone signaled them to recall the middle row. Using this *partial-report technique,* Sperling found that if he sounded the tone immediately after the letters were flashed, people could usually recall 3 or 4 of the letters in *any* of the three rows; that is, they seemed to have at least 9 of the original 12 letters in their visual registers. But if he waited for even 1 second before sounding the tone, his participants were able to recall only 1 or 2 letters from any single row—in just 1 second, then, all but 4 or 5 of the original set of 12 letters had vanished from their visual registers. In everyday life, new visual information keeps coming into the register; and the new information replaces the old information almost immediately (in about a quarter of a second), a process often called *masking.*

Auditory information fades more slowly than visual information. The auditory equivalent of the icon, the *echo,* tends to last for several seconds, which, given the nature of speech, is certainly lucky for us. Otherwise, "*You* did it!" would be indistinguishable from "You *did* it!" because we would be unable to remember the emphasis on the first words by the time the last words were registered.

Attention

Why does some information capture our attention, whereas other information goes unnoticed?

If information disappears from the sensory registers so rapidly, how do we remember *anything* for more than a second or two? One way is that we select some of the incoming information for further processing by means of attention. (See **Figure 6–1.**) **Attention** is the process of *selectively* looking, listening, smelling, tasting, and feeling. At the same time, we give meaning to the information that is coming in. Look at the page in front of you. You will see a series of black lines on a white page. For you to make sense of this jumble of data, you process the information in the sensory registers for meaning.

How do we select what we are going to pay attention to at any given moment, and how do we give that information meaning? Donald Broadbent (1958) suggested that a filtering

attention The selection of some incoming information for further processing.

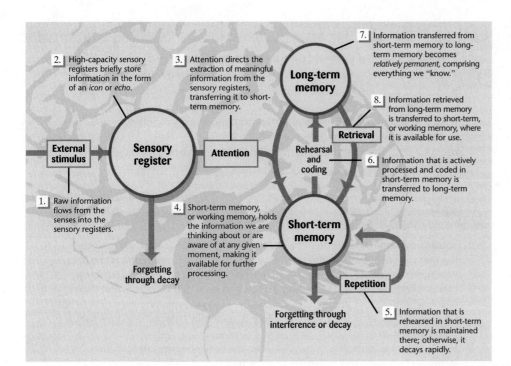

FIGURE 6–1
The sequence of information processing.

process at the entrance to the nervous system allows only those stimuli that meet certain requirements to pass through. Those stimuli that do get through the filter are compared with what we already know, so that we can recognize them and figure out what they mean. If you and a friend are sitting in a restaurant talking, you filter out all other conversations taking place around you, a process known as the *cocktail-party phenomenon* (Cherry, 1966; Haykin & Chen, 2006). Although you later might be able to describe certain characteristics of those other conversations, such as whether the people speaking were men or women, according to Broadbent, you normally cannot recall what was being discussed, even at neighboring tables. Since you filtered out those other conversations, the processing of that information did not proceed far enough for you to understand what you heard.

Broadbent's filtering theory helps explain some aspects of attention, but sometimes unattended stimuli do capture our attention. To return to the restaurant example, if someone nearby were to mention your name, your attention probably would shift to that conversation. Anne Treisman (1960, 1964, 2004) modified the filter theory to account for phenomena like this. She contended that the filter is not a simple on-and-off switch, but rather a variable control—like the volume control on a radio, which can "turn down" unwanted signals without rejecting them entirely. According to this view, although we may be paying attention to only some incoming information, we monitor the other signals at a low volume. Thus, we can shift our attention if we pick up something particularly meaningful. This automatic processing can work even when we are asleep: Parents often wake up immediately when they hear their baby crying, but sleep through other, louder noises.

At times, however, our automatic processing monitor fails, and we can overlook even meaningful information. In research studies, for example, some people watching a video of a ball-passing game failed to notice a person dressed as a gorilla who was plainly visible for nearly 10 seconds (Mack, 2003). In other words, just because we are *looking* or *listening* to something, doesn't mean we are *attending* to it. Psychologists refer to our failure to attend to something we are looking at as **inattentional blindness.** Research has shown, for example, that attending to auditory information can reduce one's ability to accurately process visual information, which makes driving while talking on a cell phone a distinctly bad idea (Pizzighello & Bressan, 2008)!

This student is working attentively in spite of other activity around her. If someone calls her name, though, the student's attention will be quickly diverted.

inattentional blindness Failure to notice or be aware of something that is in plain sight.

✓•─[Study and Review on MyPsychLab]

CHECK YOUR UNDERSTANDING

1. Indicate whether the following statements are true (T) or false (F):
   a. _____ The sensory registers have virtually unlimited capacity.
   b. _____ Some kinds of information are stored permanently in the sensory registers.
   c. _____ Auditory information fades from the sensory registers more quickly than visual information does.
   d. _____ The filter theory as modified by Treisman holds that attention is like an on-and-off switch.

   Answers: 1. a. (T). b. (F). c. (F). d. (F).

APPLY YOUR UNDERSTANDING

1. You are in a large, noisy group in which everyone seems to be talking at once. In order to concentrate on the conversation you are having with one of the people, you "tune out" all the other conversations that are going on around you. A few minutes later, someone nearby turns to you and says, "Did you hear what I was saying to John?" You have to admit that even though you were standing right next to her, you don't know what she said. Your failure to remember that other conversation is an example of
   a. selective attention.
   b. the partial-report technique.
   c. the cocktail-party phenomenon.
   d. masking.

2. A few minutes later in that same group, while talking to someone else, you suddenly hear someone nearby mention your name. This time your attention is immediately drawn to that other conversation. This is an example of
   a. Broadbent's filtering theory.
   b. the partial-report technique.
   c. the cocktail-party phenomenon.
   d. masking.

3. Failure to notice something that is in plain sight is called
   a. automatic blindness.
   b. inattentional blindness.
   c. partial blindness.
   d. masking.

   Answers: 1. a. 2. c. 3. b.

LEARNING OBJECTIVES

• Define short-term memory (STM), explain why it is called "working memory" and describe the way information is encoded in STM.
• Describe the capacity of STM including the role of chunking and interference, maintenance of information in STM, and the effect of stress on STM.

SHORT-TERM MEMORY

What are the two primary tasks of short-term memory?

Short-term memory (STM) holds the information that we are thinking about or are aware of at any given moment. When you listen to a conversation, when you watch a television show, when you become aware of a headache—in all these cases, you are using STM both to hold onto and to think about new information coming in from the sensory registers. Short-term memory has two primary tasks: to store new information briefly and to work on that (and other) information. Short-term memory is sometimes called *working memory,* to emphasize the active or working component of this memory system (Nairne, 2003).

Capacity of STM

How much information can be held in short-term memory?

Chess masters at tournaments demand complete silence while they ponder their next move. You shut yourself in a quiet room to study for final exams. As these examples illustrate, STM can handle only so much information at any given moment. Research

short-term memory (STM) Working memory; briefly stores and processes selected information from the sensory registers.

suggests that STM can hold about as much information as can be repeated or rehearsed in 1.5 to 2 seconds (Baddeley, 1986, 2002).

To get a better idea of the limits of STM, read the first row of letters in the list that follows just once. Then close your eyes, and try to remember the letters in the correct sequence. Repeat the procedure for each subsequent row.

1. C X W
2. M N K T Y
3. R P J H B Z S
4. G B M P V Q F J D
5. E G Q W J P B R H K

Like most other people, you probably found rows 1 and 2 fairly easy, row 3 a bit harder, row 4 extremely difficult, and row 5 impossible to remember after just one reading.

Now try reading through the following set of 12 letters just once, and see whether you can repeat them:

TJYFAVMCFKIB

How many letters were you able to recall? In all likelihood, not all 12. But what if you had been asked to remember the following 12 letters instead?

TV FBI JFK YMCA

Could you remember them? Almost certainly the answer is yes. These are the same 12 letters as before, but here they are grouped into four separate "words." This way of grouping and organizing information so that it fits into meaningful units is called **chunking** (Cowan & Chen, 2009).

By chunking words into sentences or sentence fragments, we can process an even greater amount of information in STM. For example, suppose that you want to remember the following list of words: *tree, song, hat, sparrow, box, lilac, cat.* One strategy would be to cluster as many of them as possible into phrases or sentences: "The sparrow in the tree sings a song"; "a lilac hat in the box"; "the cat in the hat." But isn't there a limit to this strategy? Would five sentences be as easy to remember for a short time as five single words? No. As the size of any individual chunk increases, the number of chunks that can be held in STM declines (Fendrich & Arengo, 2004). STM can easily handle five unrelated letters or words at once, but five unrelated sentences are much harder to remember.

Keep in mind that STM usually has to perform more than one task at a time. During the brief moments you spent memorizing the preceding rows of letters, you probably gave them your full attention. But normally you have to attend to new incoming information while you work on whatever is already present in short-term memory. Competition between these two tasks for the limited work space in STM means that neither task will be done as well

Chess players demand complete silence as they consider their next move. This is because there is a definite limit to the amount of information STM can handle at any given moment.

chunking The grouping of information into meaningful units for easier handling by short-term memory.

"Hold on a second, Bob. I'm putting you on a stickie."

rote rehearsal Retaining information in memory simply by repeating it over and over.

as it could be. Try counting backward from 100 while trying to learn the rows of letters in our earlier example. What happens?

Now turn on some music and try to learn the rows of letters. You'll find that the music doesn't interfere much, if at all, with learning the letters. Interestingly, when two memory tasks are presented in different sensory modalities (for instance, visual and auditory), they are less likely to interfere with each other than if they are in the same modality (Lehnert & Zimmer, 2008). This suggests the existence of *domain-specific* working memory systems that can operate at the same time with very little interference.

Not surprisingly, stress and worry have also been shown to be detrimental to the operation of short-term memory (Matthews & Campbell, 2010). This is particularly true when the task at hand involves mathematics, because the worry created by stress competes for working memory space, which would otherwise be allocated to solving the math problem (Beilock, 2008).

Encoding in STM

Do we store material in short-term memory as it sounds or as it looks?

We encode verbal information for storage in STM *phonologically*—that is, according to how it sounds. This is the case even if we see the word, letter, or number on a page, rather than hear it spoken (Vallar, 2006). We know this because numerous experiments have shown that when people try to retrieve material from STM, they generally mix up items that sound alike. A list of words such as *mad, man, mat, cap* is harder for most people to recall accurately than is a list such as *pit, day, cow, bar* (Baddeley, 1986).

But not all material in short-term memory is stored phonologically. At least some material is stored in visual form, and other information is retained on the basis of its meaning (R. G. Morrison, 2005). For example, we don't have to convert visual data such as maps, diagrams, and paintings into sound before we can code them into STM and think about them. Moreover, research has shown that memory for images is generally better than memory for words because we often store images both phonologically and as images, while words are usually stored only phonologically. The *dual coding* of images accounts for the reason it is sometimes helpful to form a mental picture of something you are trying to learn (Paivio, 2007). ✳

✳ Explore the Concept Encoding, Storage and Retrieval in Memory on **MyPsychLab**

Maintaining STM

How can we hold information in STM?

As we have said, short-term memories are fleeting, generally lasting a matter of seconds. However, we can hold information in STM for longer periods through rote rehearsal, also called *maintenance rehearsal*. **Rote rehearsal** consists of repeating information over and over, silently or out loud. Although it may not be the most efficient way to remember something permanently, it can be quite effective for a short time.

✓● Study and Review on **MyPsychLab**

CHECK YOUR UNDERSTANDING

1. _____ memory is what we are thinking about at any given moment. Its function is to briefly store new information and to work on that and other information.
2. _____ enables us to group items into meaningful units.
3. Strings of letters and numbers are encoded _____ in short-term memory.
4. _____ rehearsal, or simply repeating information over and over, is an effective way of retaining information for just a minute or two.

Answers: 1. short-term. 2. chunking. 3. phonologically. 4. rote.

1. You try to remember the letters CNOXNPEHFOBSN, but despite your best efforts you can't seem to remember more than half of them. Then you are told that the letters can be rearranged as CNN FOX HBO ESPN (four TV channels). After that, you are able to remember all the letters even weeks later. Rearranging the letters into groups that are easier to retain in memory is known as

   a. shadowing.
   b. chunking.
   c. rote rehearsal.
   d. cueing.

2. Your sister looks up a phone number in the phone book, but then can't find the phone. By the time she finds the phone, she has forgotten the number. While she was looking for the phone, she apparently failed to engage in

   a. rote rehearsal.
   b. parallel processing.
   c. phonological coding.
   d. categorizing.

Answers: 1.b. 2.a.

LONG-TERM MEMORY

What types of information are retained in long-term memory?

Our ability to store vast quantities of information for indefinite periods of time is essential if we are to master complex skills, acquire an education, or remember the personal experiences that contribute to our identity. Everything that we learn is stored in **long-term memory (LTM):** the words to a popular song; the meaning of *justice;* how to roller skate or draw a face; your enjoyment of opera or your disgust at the sight of raw oysters; and what you are supposed to be doing tomorrow at 4:00 P.M.

Capacity of LTM

What is the limit of LTM?

We have seen that short-term memory can hold only a few items, normally only for a matter of seconds. By contrast, long-term memory can store a vast amount of information for many years. In one study, for example, adults who had graduated from high school more than 40 years earlier were still able to recognize the names of 75% of their classmates (Lindsay & Read, 2006).

Encoding in LTM

How are most memories encoded in LTM?

Can you picture the shape of Florida? Do you know what a trumpet sounds like? Can you imagine the smell of a rose or the taste of coffee? Your ability to do most of these things means that at least some long-term memories are coded in terms of nonverbal images: shapes, sounds, smells, tastes, and so on.

Yet, most of the information in LTM seems to be encoded in terms of *meaning.* If material is especially familiar (the words of the national anthem, for example), you may have stored it verbatim in LTM, and you can often retrieve it word for word when you need it. Generally speaking, however, we do not use verbatim storage in LTM. If someone tells you a long, rambling story, you may listen to every word, but you certainly will not try to remember the story verbatim. Instead, you will extract the main points of the

- Define long-term memory (LTM) including the capacity of LTM and the way information is encoded in LTM. Explain the serial position effect.
- Differentiate rote rehearsal from elaborative rehearsal and explain the role of mnemonics and schemata as forms of elaborative rehearsal.
- Distinguish among episodic memories, semantic memories, procedural memories, emotional memories, explicit memories, and implicit memories. Explain how priming and the tip-of-the-tongue phenomenon shed light on memory.

long-term memory (LTM) The portion of memory that is more or less permanent, corresponding to everything we "know."

serial position effect The finding that when asked to recall a list of unrelated items, performance is better for the items at the beginning and end of the list.

story and try to remember those. Even simple sentences are usually encoded in terms of their meaning. Thus, when people are asked to remember that "Tom called John," they often find it impossible to remember later whether they were told "Tom called John" or "John was called by Tom." They usually remember the *meaning* of the message, rather than the exact words (R. R. Hunt & Ellis, 2003).

Serial Position Effect

Which items in a list are hardest to remember?

When given a list of items to remember (such as a list of grocery items), people tend to do better at recalling the first items (*primacy effect*) and the last items (*recency effect*) in the list. They also tend to do poorest of all on the items in the middle of the list. (See **Figure 6–2**.)

The explanation for this **serial position effect** resides in understanding how short- and long-term memory work together. The recency effect occurs because the last items that were presented are still contained in STM and thus are available for recall. The primacy effect, on the other hand, reflects the opportunity to rehearse the first few items in the list—increasing their likelihood of being transferred to LTM.

Poor performance occurs on the items in the middle of the list because they were presented too long ago to still be in STM, and because so many items requiring attention were presented before and after them that there was little opportunity for rehearsal. The serial position effect has been shown to occur under a wide variety of conditions and situations (Neath, 1993; Suhr, 2002; W. S. Terry, 2005).

Maintaining LTM

What three processes are used to hold information in LTM?

Rote Rehearsal Rote rehearsal, the principal tool for holding information in STM, is also useful for holding information in LTM. Rote rehearsal is probably the standard method of storing conceptually meaningless material, such as phone numbers, Social Security numbers, security codes, computer passwords, birth dates, and people's names.

Indeed, although everyone hates rote drill, there seems to be no escaping its use in mastering a wide variety of skills, from memorizing the alphabet to playing a work of Mozart on the piano or doing a back flip on the balance beam. Mastering a skill means achieving *automaticity,* or fluid, immediate performance. Expertise in typing, for example, involves the ability to depress the keys quickly and accurately without thinking about it. Automaticity is achieved only through tedious practice.

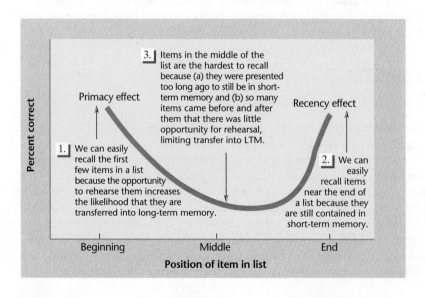

FIGURE 6–2
The serial position effect.
The serial position effect demonstrates how short- and long-term memory work together.

Research suggests, however, that repetition without any intention to learn generally has little effect on subsequent recall (Van-Hooff & Golden, 2002). You can probably prove this phenomenon to yourself: Stop here and try to imagine from memory the front side of a U.S. penny. Now look at **Figure 6–3,** and pick the illustration that matches your memory. For most people, this task is surprisingly difficult: Despite the repetition of seeing thousands of pennies, most people cannot accurately draw one, or even pick one out from among other, similar objects (Nickerson & Adams, 1979).

Elaborative Rehearsal As we have seen, rote rehearsal with the intent to learn is sometimes useful in storing information in LTM. But often, an even more effective procedure is **elaborative rehearsal** (Craik, 2002; Craik & Lockhart, 1972), the act of relating new information to something that we already know. Through elaborative rehearsal, you extract the meaning of the new information and then link it to as much of the material already in LTM as possible. We tend to remember meaningful material better than arbitrary facts; and the more links or associations of meaning you can make, the more likely you are to remember the new information later.

Clearly, elaborative rehearsal calls for a deeper and more meaningful processing of new data than does simple rote rehearsal. Unless we rehearse material in this way, we often soon forget it. For example, have you ever been in a group in which people were taking turns speaking up—perhaps on the first day of class when all present are asked to introduce themselves briefly, or at the beginning of a panel discussion when the speakers are asked to do the same in front of a large audience? Did you notice that you forgot virtually everything that was said by the person who spoke just before you did? According to research, you failed to remember because you did not elaboratively rehearse what that person was saying (C. F. Bond, Pitre, & Van Leeuwen, 1991). That person's comments simply "went in one ear and out the other" while you were preoccupied with thinking about your own remarks.

In some situations, special techniques called **mnemonics** (pronounced ni-MON-iks) may help you to tie new material to information already in LTM. Some of the simplest mnemonic techniques are the rhymes and jingles that we often use to remember dates and other facts. *Thirty days hath September, April, June, and November …* enables us to recall how many days are in a month. With other simple mnemonic devices, words or sentences can be made out of the material to be recalled. We can remember the colors of the visible spectrum—red, orange, yellow, green, blue, indigo, and violet—by using their first letters to form the acronym ROY G. BIV.

Schemata A variation on the idea of elaborative rehearsal is the concept of **schema** (plural: *schemata*). A schema is a mental representation of an event, an object, a situation, a person, a process, or a relationship that is stored in memory and that leads you

Information in LTM is highly organized and cross-referenced, like a cataloging system in a library. The more carefully we organize information, the more likely we will be able to retrieve it later.

elaborative rehearsal The linking of new information in short-term memory to familiar material stored in long-term memory.

mnemonics Techniques that make material easier to remember.

schema (skee-mah; plural: schemata) A set of beliefs or expectations about something that is based on past experience.

FIGURE 6–3
A penny for your thoughts.
Which of these accurately illustrates a real U.S. penny? The answer is on page 194.

THINKING CRITICALLY ABOUT . . .

Elaborative Rehearsal

Elaborative rehearsal requires that you relate new material to information already stored in LTM. Sometimes, this requires thinking abstractly, visually, or conceptually about the things you want to remember. How would you use elaborative rehearsal to store the following information?

1. In Japanese, the word for difficult is *muzukashii*.

2. The *p* in pterodactyl is silent.

3. The square root of *pi* is approximately 1.772.

Now try to develop an elaborative rehearsal strategy for something you are trying to learn, say in this or another class you are taking.

Did using an elaborative rehearsal strategy increase your ability to recall the material? What types of elaborative rehearsal strategies did you devise? Which ones seem to work best for you? Why do you think that was the case?

to expect your experience to be organized in certain ways. For example, you may have a schema for eating in a restaurant, for driving a car, or for attending a class lecture. A class lecture schema might include sitting down in a large room with seats arranged in rows, opening your notebook, and expecting the professor or lecturer to come in and address the class from the front of the room.

Schemata such as these provide a framework into which incoming information is fitted. Schemata also may color what you recall by prompting you to form a *stereotype*; that is, to ascribe certain characteristics to all members of a particular group. (We will explore the process of stereotyping in Chapter 14, "Social Psychology.") Thus, becoming aware of your particular schemata is one way to improve your ability to remember. (See "Applying Psychology: Improving Your Memory" for more on improving your memory.)

To summarize, we have seen that the capacity of LTM is immense and material stored there may endure, more or less intact, for decades. By comparison, STM has a sharply limited capacity and information may disappear quickly from it. The sensory registers can take in an enormous volume of information, but they have no ability to process memories. Together, these three stages of memory—the sensory registers, STM, and LTM—comprise the information-processing view of memory, as reviewed in the "**Summary Table:** Memory as an Information-Processing System." (Answer to question on page 193: The accurate illustration of a penny in Figure 6–3 is the third from the left.)

Types of LTM

How do types of LTM differ?

The information stored in LTM can take many forms. However, most long-term memories can be classified into one of several types: episodic, semantic, procedural, and emotional memories.

Episodic memories are memories for events experienced in a specific time and place. These are *personal* memories, rather than historical facts. If you can recall what you ate for dinner last night or how you learned to ride a bike when you were little, then you are calling up episodic memories. Episodic memory is like a diary that lets you go back in time and space to relive a personal experience (Knierim, 2007). For Jill Price, profiled at the beginning of this chapter, every waking moment is characterized by a barrage of episodic memories.

In addition to permitting us to relive past experiences, episodic memories also play a crucial role in our ability to anticipate and envision the future (Schacter & Addis, 2009). That is, by recombining elements of past experiences (episodic memories), we can imagine or simulate future events. For example, in preparation for an important job interview, you would be well-served to remember how previous job interviews took place. Then by restructuring the key elements of those past experiences you will be better able to anticipate potential questions and hopefully devise better answers than you may have otherwise. Indeed, some researchers have suggested that even personal goals may emerge as a result of recombining elements of episodic memories to simulate future possibilities and aspirations (D'Argembeau & Mathy, 2011).

episodic memories The portion of long-term memory that stores personally experienced events.

SUMMARY TABLE   MEMORY AS AN INFORMATION-PROCESSING SYSTEM

System	Means by Which Information Is Stored	Form in Which Information Is Stored	Storage Organization	Storage Duration	Means by Which Information Is Retrieved	Factors in Forgetting
Sensory Register	Visual and auditory registers	Raw sensory data	None	From less than 1 second to only a few seconds	Reconsideration of registered information	Decay or masking
Short-Term Memory	Rote or maintenance rehearsal	Visual and phonological representation	None	Usually 15 to 20 seconds	Rote or maintenance rehearsal	Interference or decay
Long-Term Memory	Rote rehearsal, elaborative rehearsal, schemata	Some nonverbal representations, mostly stored by meaning	Logical frameworks, such as hierarchies or categories	Perhaps for an entire lifetime	Retrieval cues linked to organized information	Retrieval failure or interference

APPLYING PSYCHOLOGY

Improving Your Memory

What can you do to improve your memory? It's the active decision to get better and the number of hours you push yourself to improve that makes the difference. Regardless of your innate ability, anyone can improve their memory by doing the following.

1. **Develop motivation.** Without a strong desire to learn or remember something, you probably won't. But if you find a way to keep yourself alert and stimulated, you will have an easier time learning and remembering things.

2. **Practice memory skills.** To stay sharp, memory skills, like all skills, must be practiced and used. Memory experts recommend exercises such as crossword puzzles, acrostics, anagrams, Scrabble, Monopoly, Trivial Pursuit, and bridge. Practice testing on the material you want to learn is also helpful. After you have read something, write down what you remember, compare it to the original, and once again write down what you remember. Research shows that this kind of self-testing increases retention of material more than simply studying (Karpicke & Blunt, 2011).

3. **Be confident in your ability to remember.** Self-doubt often leads to anxiety, which, in turn, interferes with the ability to retrieve information from memory. Relaxation exercises, experts agree, may substantially boost your ability to retrieve information from memory.

4. **Minimize distractions.** Although some people can study for an exam and listen to the radio simultaneously, most people find that outside distractions interfere with both learning and remembering. Look for a quiet, even secluded setting before attempting to commit something to memory.

5. **Stay focused.** Paying close attention to details, and focusing on your surroundings, emotions, and other elements associated with an event will help you remember it clearly.

6. **Make connections between new material and other information already stored in your long-term memory.** The more links you forge between new information and old information already in LTM, the more likely you are to remember the new material. Discuss things you want to remember with other people. Think about or write down ways in which the new information is related to things you already know.

7. **Use mental imagery.** Imagery works wonders as an aid to recalling information from memory. Whenever possible, form mental pictures of the items, people, words, or activities you want to remember. If you have

a sequence of stops to make, picture yourself leaving each place and heading for the next. To remember that someone's last name is Glass, you might imagine her holding a glass or looking through a glass.

8. **Use retrieval cues.** The more retrieval cues you have, the more likely it is that you will remember something. One way to establish automatic retrieval cues is to create routines and structure. For example, when you come in the door, put your house and car keys in the same place every time. Then when you ask yourself, "Where did I put my keys?" the fact that you have a special place for the keys serves as a retrieval cue.

9. **Rely on more than memory alone.** Write down the things you need to remember, and then post a note or list of those things somewhere obvious, such as on your bulletin board or refrigerator door. Put all the dates you want to remember on a calendar, and then put the calendar in a conspicuous place.

10. **Be aware that your own personal schemata may distort your recall of events.** People sometimes unknowingly "rewrite" past events to fit their current image or their desired image of themselves and their past decisions. Being on guard against such distortions may help you avoid them.

THINKING CRITICALLY ABOUT . . .

Types of Memory

Experts disagree about how many different kinds of memory there are. Recently, some psychologists have suggested that the classification of memories into different types is artificial and merely confuses matters. They suggest that we should consider memory a unitary thing.

What arguments can you come up with to support the practice of making distinctions among different kinds of memory?

Once skills such as playing tennis have been stored in our procedural memory, they are seldom lost.

semantic memories The portion of long-term memory that stores general facts and information.

procedural memories The portion of long-term memory that stores information relating to skills, habits, and other perceptual-motor tasks.

emotional memories Learned emotional responses to various stimuli.

explicit memory Memory for information that we can readily express in words and are aware of having; these memories can be intentionally retrieved from memory.

implicit memory Memory for information that we cannot readily express in words and may not be aware of having; these memories cannot be intentionally retrieved from memory.

Semantic memories are facts and concepts not linked to a particular time. Semantic memory is like a dictionary or an encyclopedia, filled with facts and concepts, such as the meaning of the word *semantic*, the location of the Empire State Building, the value of 2 times 7, and the identity of George Washington.

Procedural memories are motor skills and habits (A. Johnson, 2003). They are not memories about skills and habits; they *are* the skills and habits. Procedural memories have to do with knowing how: how to ride a bicycle, play a violin, make coffee, write your name, walk across a room, or slam on a car's brakes. The information involved usually consists of a precise sequence of coordinated movements that are often difficult to describe in words. Repetition, and in many cases deliberate practice, are often required to master skills and habits, but once learned, they are rarely completely lost.

Emotional memories are learned emotional responses to various stimuli: all of our loves and hates, our rational and irrational fears, our feelings of disgust and anxiety. If you are afraid of flying insects, become enraged at the sight of a Nazi flag, or are ashamed of something you did, you have emotional memories.

Explicit and Implicit Memory

What are the differences between implicit and explicit memories?

Because of the differences among types of memories, psychologists distinguish between **explicit memory,** which includes episodic and semantic memories, and **implicit memory,** which includes procedural and emotional memories. These terms reflect the fact that sometimes we are aware that we know something (explicit memory) and that sometimes we are not aware (implicit memory).

Serious interest in the distinction between explicit and implicit memory began as a result of experiments with amnesic patients. For example, Brenda Milner (Milner, Corkin, & Teuber, 1968) studied the now-famous case of patient "H. M." (Henry Molaison, 1926–2008), a young man who had severe, uncontrollable epileptic seizures. The seizures became life threatening, so that as a last resort, surgeons removed most of the afflicted area of his brain. The surgery greatly reduced the frequency and severity of seizures, but it left behind a new problem: H. M. could no longer form new memories. He could meet someone again and again, but each time it was as if he were meeting the person for the first time. Old memories were intact: He could remember things that he had learned long before the operation, but he could not learn anything new. Or so it seemed!

Then one day Milner asked H. M. to trace the outline of a star while looking in a mirror. This simple task is surprisingly difficult, but with practice most people show steady progress. Surprisingly, so did H. M. Each day he got better and better at tracing the star, just as a person with an undamaged brain would do—yet each day he had no recollection of ever having attempted the task. H. M.'s performance demonstrated not only that he could learn, but also that there are different kinds of memories. Some are explicit: We know things, and we know that we know them. And some are implicit: We know things, but that knowledge is unconscious. (See **Table 6–1** for a summary of implicit and explicit memory.)

Additional support for the distinction between explicit and implicit memory is derived from clinical observations of the ways in which strong emotional experiences can affect

TABLE 6–1   Types of Memories

Explicit		Implicit	
Semantic	Episodic	Procedural	Emotional
Memories of facts and concepts	Memories of personally experienced events	Motor skills and habits	Learned emotional reactions
Example: recalling that Albany is the capital of New York	*Example:* recalling a trip to Albany	*Example:* ice skating	*Example:* recoiling at the sight of a rat

behavior years later even without any conscious recollection of the experiences (Öhman, 2010; Westen, 1998). In cases of war, abuse, or terrorism, emotional memories are sometimes so overwhelming and painful they can lead to a psychiatric disorder called posttraumatic stress disorder or PTSD (Kekelidze & Portnova, 2011). (We will consider PTSD in more detail in Chapter 11, "Stress and Health Psychology.")

The fact that strong emotional memories can affect behavior without conscious awareness seem at first to give credence to Freud's notion of the unconscious mind—that repressed memories for traumatic incidents can still affect our behavior. But implicit memory research suggests instead that people store emotional experiences separately from the memories of the experience itself. Thus, we may feel anxiety about flying because of a traumatic plane ride in early childhood, yet we may not remember the experience that gives rise to that anxiety. Memory of the event is out of reach, not because (as Freud thought) it has been repressed, but because the episodic and emotional components of the experience were stored separately.

Priming   Research on a phenomenon called *priming* also demonstrates the distinction between explicit and implicit memory. In priming, a person is exposed to a stimulus, usually a word or picture. Later, the person is shown a fragment of the stimulus (a few letters of a word or a piece of a picture) and is asked to complete it. The typical result is that people are more likely to complete fragments with items seen earlier than they are with other, equally plausible items. For example, you might be shown a list of words, including the word *tour*. Later on, you might be shown a list of word fragments, including __ *ou* __, and be asked to fill in the blanks to make a word. In comparison to others who had not been primed by seeing the word *tour*, you are far more likely to write *tour* than you are *four*, *pour*, or *sour*, all of which are just as acceptable as *tour*. The earlier exposure to *tour* primes you to write that word.

The Tip-of-the-Tongue Phenomenon   Everyone has had the experience of knowing a word but not quite being able to recall it. This is called the **tip-of-the-tongue phenomenon** (or **TOT**) (R. Brown & McNeil, 1966; Hamberger & Seidel, 2003; B. L. Schwartz, 2002; Widner, Otani, & Winkelman, 2005). Although everyone experiences TOTs, these experiences become more frequent during stressful situations (Schwartz, 2010) and as people get older, especially when attempting to recall personal names (Juncos-Rabadán, Facal, Rodríguez, & Pereiro, 2010; Schwartz, 2010; B. L. Schwartz & Frazier, 2005; K. K. White & Abrams, 2002). Moreover, other words—usually with a sound or meaning similar to the word you are seeking—occur to you while you are in the TOT state and these words interfere with and sabotage your attempt to recall the desired word. The harder you try, the worse the TOT state gets. The best way to recall a blocked word, then, is to stop trying to recall it! Most of the time, the word you were searching for will pop into your head, minutes or even hours after you stopped consciously searching for it (B. L. Schwartz, 2002). (If you want to experience TOT yourself, try naming Snow White's seven dwarfs.)

The distinction between explicit and implicit memories means that some knowledge is literally unconscious. Moreover, as we shall soon see, explicit and implicit memories also seem to involve different neural structures and pathways (Voss & Paller, 2008). However, memories typically work together. When we remember going to a Chinese restaurant, we recall not only when and where we ate and whom we were with (episodic memory), but

Looking into a bakery window, perhaps smelling the aromas of the cakes inside, may prime the memory, triggering distinct memories associated with those sights and smells, formed many years ago.

tip-of-the-tongue phenomenon (or TOT) Knowing a word, but not being able to immediately recall it.

also the nature of the food we ate (semantic memory), the skills we learned such as eating with chopsticks (procedural memory), and the embarrassment we felt when we spilled the tea (emotional memory). When we recall events, we typically do not experience these kinds of memories as distinct and separate; rather, they are integrally connected, just as the original experiences were. Whether we will continue to remember the experiences accurately in the future depends to a large extent on what happens in our brain, as we will see in the next section.

✔●─[**Study** and **Review** on **MyPsychLab**

CHECK YOUR UNDERSTANDING

1. The primacy effect accounts for why we remember items at the _____ of a list, while the recency effect accounts for why we remember items at the _____ of the list.

2. If information is learned through repetition, this process is _____ rehearsal; if it is learned by linking it to other memories, this process is _____ rehearsal.

3. A schema is a framework in memory into which new information is fit. Is this statement true (T) or false (F)?

4. Implicit memories consist of _____ and _____ memories, whereas explicit memories consist of _____ and _____ memories.

Answers: 1. beginning; end. **2.** rote; elaborative. **3.** (T). **4.** procedural and emotional; episodic and semantic.

APPLY YOUR UNDERSTANDING

1. You run into an old friend who gives you his phone number and asks you to call. You want to be sure to remember the phone number, so you relate the number to things that you already know. "555" is the same as the combination to your bicycle lock. "12" is your brother's age. And "34" is the size of your belt. This technique for getting information into long-term memory is called
   a. rote rehearsal.
   b. relational rehearsal.
   c. elaborative rehearsal.
   d. episodic rehearsal.

2. *He:* "We've been to this restaurant before."

   She: "I don't think so."

   He: "Didn't we eat here last summer with your brother?"

   She: "That was a different restaurant, and I think it was last fall, not last summer."

   This couple is trying to remember an event they shared and, obviously, their memories differ. The information they are seeking is most likely stored in
   a. procedural memory.
   b. emotional memory.
   c. semantic memory.
   d. episodic memory.

Answers: 1. c. **2.** d.

- Define long-term potentiation. Identify the areas of the brain that play a role in the formation and storage of long-term memories. Describe the role of sleep in the formation of new memories.

THE BIOLOGY OF MEMORY

What role do neurons play in memory?

Research on the biology of memory focuses mainly on the question, *How and where are memories stored?* Simple as the question is, it has proved enormously difficult to answer and our answers are still not entirely complete.

Current research indicates that memories consist of changes in the synaptic connections among neurons (Asrican, 2007; Kandel, 2001). When we learn new things, new connections are formed in the brain; when we review or practice previously learned things, old connections are strengthened. These chemical and structural changes build *neural networks* which grow over a period of months or years (Abraham & Williams, 2008; Bekinschtein et al., 2008; Lu, Christian, & Lu, 2008), during which time the number of connections among neurons increases as does the likelihood that cells will excite one another through electrical discharges, a process known as **long-term potentiation (LTP).**

Although learning takes place in the brain, it is also influenced by events occurring elsewhere in the body. Two hormones in particular, epinephrine and cortisol, have been shown to affect long-term retention, especially for unpleasant experiences (Korol & Gold, 2007). Another hormone found to influence memory is *ghrelin.* Secreted from the lining of stomach when it is empty, ghrelin travels to the brain where it primarily stimulates receptors in the hypothalamus to signal hunger. However, some ghrelin also finds its way to the hippocampus, where studies with mice have shown it can enhance learning and memory (Diano et al., 2006; Olszewski, Schiöth, & Levine, 2008). As a result, hungry mice are more likely to remember where they have found food in the past.

long-term potentiation (LTP) A long-lasting change in the structure or function of a synapse that increases the efficiency of neural transmission and is thought to be related to how information is stored by neurons.

ENDURING ISSUES

Mind–Body   Effects of Stress on Body and Brain

Epinephrine secretion is part of the "fight or flight" syndrome (see Chapter 11, "Stress and Health Psychology"), and has the effect of arousing the organism to action. However, the effect on memory of epinephrine and other stress-related hormones is not merely the result of general arousal. Apparently these hormones indirectly act on specific brain centers, such as the hippocampus and the amygdala, that are critical for memory formation (Vermetten & Bremner, 2002). Increased blood levels of epinephrine probably also explain improved performance in humans under conditions of mild stress (L. Cahill & Alkire, 2003). Extreme stress, however, often interferes with both the learning and later recall of specific information. For example, research has demonstrated that when people are exposed to highly stressful events, their memory for the emotional aspect of the event may be enhanced (LaBar, 2007) but their ability to recall the nonemotional aspects of the event is disrupted (Payne et al., 2006). If you are studying for an exam, then, a little anxiety will probably improve your performance, but a high level of anxiety will work against you. ∎

Where Are Memories Stored?

Are STM and LTM found in the same parts of the brain?

Memories are not all stored in one place. Instead, our brains appear to depend on a large number of neural networks distributed throughout the brain working in concert to form and store memories (Tsien, 2007). As a general rule however, studies have shown that the areas of the brain involved in encoding a particular event are reactivated when the event is remembered. This suggests that "…the process of remembering an episode involves literally returning to the brain state that was present during that episode" (Danker & Anderson, 2010, p. 87). This may help explain why, when we have difficulty remembering something, it is often helpful to think about related events or details, thus returning our brain to the initial state we were in when we stored the memory.

Different regions of the brain are specialized for the storage of different kinds of memories (See **Figure 6–4**). Short-term and working memory, for example, seem to be located primarily in the prefrontal cortex and temporal lobe (Izaki, Takita, & Akema,

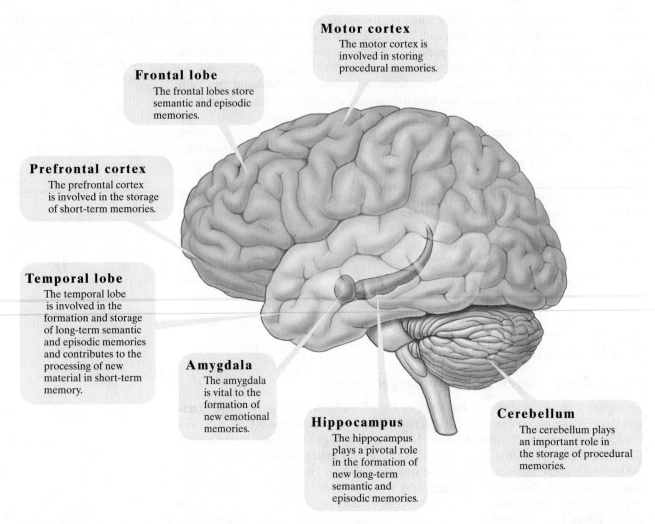

Frontal lobe
The frontal lobes store semantic and episodic memories.

Motor cortex
The motor cortex is involved in storing procedural memories.

Prefrontal cortex
The prefrontal cortex is involved in the storage of short-term memories.

Temporal lobe
The temporal lobe is involved in the formation and storage of long-term semantic and episodic memories and contributes to the processing of new material in short-term memory.

Amygdala
The amygdala is vital to the formation of new emotional memories.

Hippocampus
The hippocampus plays a pivotal role in the formation of new long-term semantic and episodic memories.

Cerebellum
The cerebellum plays an important role in the storage of procedural memories.

FIGURE 6–4
The biological basis of memory.
Many different parts of the brain are specialized for the storage of memories.

2008; Rainer & Miller, 2002; Scheibel & Levin, 2004). Long-term semantic memories seem to be located primarily in the frontal and temporal lobes of the cortex, which interestingly also play a prominent role in consciousness and awareness. Research shows increased activity in a particular area of the left temporal lobe—for example, when people are asked to recall the names of people. A nearby area shows increased activity when they are asked to recall the names of animals, and another neighboring area becomes active when they are asked to recall the names of tools (H. Damasio, Grabowski, Tranel, Hichwa, & Damasio, 1996). (See **Figure 6–5.**) Destruction of these areas of the

FIGURE 6–5
PET scanning shows increased activity (yellow and orange areas) in different areas of the brain when people ar e asked to recall the names of people, animals, and tools.

Source: From H. Damasio, T. Grabowski, R. Frank, A.M. Galaburda & A.R. Damasio (1994) The return of Phineas Gage: clues about the brain from a famous patient, Science, 264, 1102-1105. Dornsife Neuroscience Imaging Center and Brain and Creativity Institute, University of Southern California

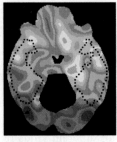
Persons

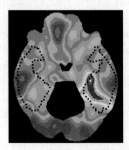
Animals

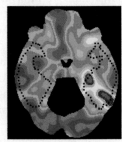
Tools

cortex (through head injury, surgery, stroke, or disease) results in selective memory loss H. Damasio et al., 1996).

Episodic memories also find their home in the frontal and temporal lobes (Jackson, 2004; Nyberg et al., 2003; Stevens & Grady, 2007). But some evidence shows that episodic and semantic memories involve different portions of these brain structures (Prince, Tsukiura, & Cabeza, 2007). In addition, because episodic memories depend on integrating different sensations (vision, audition, and so on) to create a personal memory experience, they also draw upon several distinct sensory areas of the brain (MacKenzie & Donaldson, 2009). Thus, episodic memory is probably best thought of as the integration of memories that are located throughout the brain into a coherent personal experience (D. C. Rubin, 2006).

Procedural memories appear to be located primarily in the cerebellum (an area required for balance and motor coordination) and in the motor cortex (Gabrieli, 1998; Hermann et al., 2004). As you might expect, damage to the cerebellum generally has a negative impact on one's ability to perform specific tasks (Hermann et al., 2004).

Subcortical structures also play a role in long-term memory. For example, the hippocampus has been implicated in the functioning of both semantic and episodic memory (Eichenbaum & Fortin, 2003; Manns, Hopkins, & Squire, 2003), as well as being involved in the ability to remember spatial relationships (Astur, Taylor, Marnelak, Philpott, & Sutherland, 2002; Bilkey & Clearwater, 2005). If the hippocampus is damaged, people can remember events that have just occurred (and are in STM), but their long-term recall of those same events is impaired. The amygdala, a structure that lies near the hippocampus, seems to play a role in emotional memory that is similar to the role the hippocampus plays in episodic, semantic, and procedural memory (LaBar, 2007; Payne et al., 2006; Vermetten & Bremner, 2002). For example, damage to the amygdala reduces the ability to recall new emotional experiences, but it does not prevent the recall of emotional events that occurred prior to the damage, though they are often remembered as neutral facts, devoid of emotional content. This may explain why people with amygdala damage are sometimes unable to "read" facial expressions, even though they recognize the person's face (Pegna, Caldara-Schnetzer, & Khateb, 2008; Pegna, Khateb, & Lazeyras, 2005).

The Role of Sleep

What role does sleep play in memory?

In Chapter 4 ("States of Consciousness"), we noted that sleep appears to play an important role in the formation of new memories. For example, a study with adolescents showed that sleeping less than 8 hours a night had a negative impact on working memory (Gradisar, Terrill, Johnston, & Douglas, 2008). Similarly, a study of procedural memory with musicans showed that adequate sleep following practice resulted in improved memory and performance (Allen, 2008). Even remembering to execute a goal or task, such as remembering an appointment or to take medication, is improved following a period of sleep compared to a period of wakefulness (Scullin & McDaniel, 2010).

Studies like this have prompted neuroscientists to explore precisely how sleep is involved in the formation and storage of new memories (Rasch & Born, 2008). Brain imaging with animals and humans shows that the same hippocampal neurons and patterns of neuron activity that accompany initial learning are reactivated during subsequent deep sleep. Thus, it is not surprising that deep sleep after learning serves to strengthen new memories (M. P. Walker & Stickgold, 2006). In particular, sleep appears to selectively enhance our ability to remember emotionally important experiences (Payne & Kensinger, 2010). Not surprisingly, research has also shown that sleep deprivation interferes with the process of long-term potentiation precisely in the regions of the brain involved in memory consolidation (Süer, Dolu, Artis, Sahin, Yilmaz, & Cetin, 2011). Clearly, psychologists have a long way to go before they will fully understand the biology of memory, but progress is being made in this fascinating area.

✓•─ **Study** and **Review** on **MyPsychLab**

Match the following types of memory to the location in the brain where they appear to be stored:

1. ___ short-term memories
2. ___ long-term semantic and episodic memories
3. ___ procedural memories
4. ___ emotional memories

   a. frontal and temporal lobes
   b. cerebellum and motor cortex
   c. amygdala
   d. prefrontal cortex and temporal lobe

Answers: 1.d. 2.a. 3.b. 4.c.

APPLY YOUR UNDERSTANDING

1. Oliver Sacks, the author of *The Man Who Mistook His Wife for a Hat,* describes Jimmie G., who was an otherwise healthy 49-year-old man whose long-term memory stopped changing when he was 19. New information in his short-term memory simply never got stored in long-term memory. Which part of his brain was most likely not working correctly?

   a. the prefrontal cortex
   b. the hippocampus
   c. Broca's area
   d. the occipital lobe

2. Imagine now that you encounter someone like Jimmie G., but in this case, the person cannot form new emotional memories. He has emotional reactions to things he encountered early in his life, but he has no such reactions to things he encountered more recently—no new loves or hates, no new fears, no new sources of anger or happiness. Which part of his brain is most likely not working correctly?

   a. the amygdala
   b. the temporal lobe
   c. the prefrontal cortex
   d. the cerebellum

Answers: 1.b. 2.a.

LEARNING OBJECTIVES

- Describe the biological factors that influence forgetting, including the phenomenon of retrograde amnesia.
- Differentiate between retroactive and proactive interference.
- Explain what is meant by "state-dependent memory" and the "reconstructive" nature of remembering.

decay theory A theory that argues that the passage of time causes forgetting.

FORGETTING

What factors explain why we sometimes forget?

Why do memories, once formed, not remain forever in the brain? Part of the answer has to do with the biology of memory, and another part has to do with the experiences that we have before and after learning.

The Biology of Forgetting

How does the deterioration of the brain help to explain forgetting?

According to the **decay theory,** memories deteriorate because of the passage of time. Most of the evidence supporting decay theory comes from experiments known as *distractor studies.* For example, in one experiment, participants learned a sequence of letters, such as PSQ. Then they were given a three-digit number, such as 167, and asked to count backwards by threes: 167, 164, 161, and so on, for up to 18 seconds (L. R. Peterson & Peterson, 1959). At the end of that period, they were asked to recall the three letters. The results of this test astonished the experimenters. The participants showed a rapid decline in their ability to remember the letters. Because the researchers assumed that counting backwards would not *interfere* with remembering, they could only account for the forgotten letters by noting that they had simply faded from short-term memory in a matter of seconds. Decay, then, seems to be at least partly responsible for forgetting in short-term memory.

Information in LTM also can be lost if the storage process is disrupted. Head injuries often result in **retrograde amnesia,** a condition in which people cannot remember what happened to them shortly before their injury. In such cases, forgetting may occur because memories are not fully consolidated in the brain.

Severe memory loss is invariably traced to brain damage caused by accidents, surgery, poor diet, or disease (Roncadin, Guger, Archibald, Barnes, & Dennis, 2004). For example, chronic alcoholism can lead to a form of amnesia called *Korsakoff's syndrome* caused by a vitamin deficiency in the nutritionally poor diet that is typical of people who abuse alcohol (Brand, 2007). Other studies show the importance of the hippocampus to long-term memory formation. Studies of elderly people who have trouble remembering names, for instance, show alterations in hippocampal functioning and connectivity to other areas of the brain (Tsukiura et al., 2011). Brain scans (see **Figure 6–6**) also reveal hippocampus damage in people suffering from *Alzheimer's disease,* a neurological disorder that causes severe memory loss (Sankari, Adeli, & Adeli, 2011). (See Chapter 9, "Life-Span Development," for more information about Alzheimer's disease.)

Alzheimer's may also involve below-normal levels of the neurotransmitter acetylcholine in the brain. Indeed, some research suggests that drugs and surgical procedures that increase acetylcholine levels may serve as effective treatments for age-related memory problems (Penner, Rupsingh, Smith, Wells, Borrie, & Bartha, 2010). ◉

retrograde amnesia The inability to recall events preceding an accident or injury, but without loss of earlier memory.

◉ **Watch** the **Video** What Happens with Alzheimers on **MyPsychLab**

Experience and Forgetting

What environmental factors contribute to our inability to remember?

Although sometimes caused by biological factors, forgetting can also result from inadequate learning. A lack of attention to critical cues, for example, is a cause of the forgetting commonly referred to as absentmindedness. For example, if you can't remember where you parked your car, most likely you can't remember because you didn't pay attention to where you parked it.

Forgetting also occurs because, although we attended to the matter to be recalled, we did not rehearse the material enough. Merely "going through the motions" of rehearsal does little good. Prolonged, intense practice results in less forgetting than a few, halfhearted repetitions. Elaborative rehearsal can also help make new memories more durable. When you park your car in space G-47, you will be more likely to remember its location if you think, "G-47. My uncle George is about *47* years old." In short, we cannot expect to remember information for long if we have not learned it well in the first place.

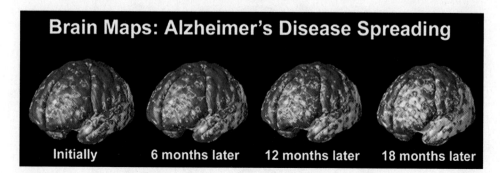

FIGURE 6–6

The progression of Alzheimer's disease.

A computerized brain scan taken of a single patient over time shows the spread of Alzheimer's disease throughout the brain. Diseased tissue is shown as red and white. Notice how the damaged tissue replaces normal brain tissue shown here as blue.

Source: Dr. Paul Thompson

retroactive interference The process by which new information interferes with information already in memory.

proactive interference The process by which information already in memory interferes with new information.

Interference Inadequate learning accounts for many memory failures, but learning itself can cause forgetting. This is the case because learning one thing can interfere with learning another. Information gets mixed up with, or pushed aside by, other information and thus becomes harder to remember. Such forgetting is said to be due to *interference*. As portrayed in **Figure 6–7,** there are two kinds of interference. In **retroactive interference,** new material interferes with information already in long-term memory. Retroactive interference occurs every day. For example, once you learn a new telephone number, you may find it difficult to recall your old number, even though you used that old number for years.

In the second kind of interference, **proactive interference,** old material interferes with new material being learned. Like retroactive interference, proactive interference is an everyday phenomenon. Suppose you always park your car in the lot behind the building where you work, but one day all those spaces are full, so you have to park across the street. When you leave for the day, you are likely to head for the lot behind the building—and may even be surprised at first that your car is not there. Learning to look for your car behind the building has interfered with your memory that today you parked the car across the street.

The most important factor in determining the degree of interference is the similarity of the competing items. Learning to swing a golf club may interfere with your ability to hit a baseball, but probably won't affect your ability to make a free throw on the basketball courts. The more dissimilar something is from other things that you have already learned, the less likely it will be to mingle and interfere with other material in memory (G. H. Bower & Mann, 1992).

Situational Factors Whenever we try to memorize something, we are also unintentionally picking up information about the context in which the learning is taking place. That information becomes useful when we later try to retrieve the corresponding information from LTM. If those environmental cues are absent when we try to recall what we learned, the effort to remember is often unsuccessful. Context-dependent memory effects tend to be small, so studying in the same classroom where you are scheduled to take an exam will probably not do too much to improve your grade. Nevertheless, contextual cues are occasionally used by police who sometimes take witnesses back to the scene of a crime in the hope that they will recall crucial details that can be used to solve the crime.

FIGURE 6–7

Diagram of experiments measuring retroactive and proactive interference.

In retroactive interference, the experimental group usually does not perform as well on tests of recall as those in the control group, who experience no retroactive interference from a list of words in Step 2. In proactive interference, people in the experimental group suffer the effects of proactive interference from the list in Step 1. When asked to recall the list from Step 2, they perform less well than those in the control group.

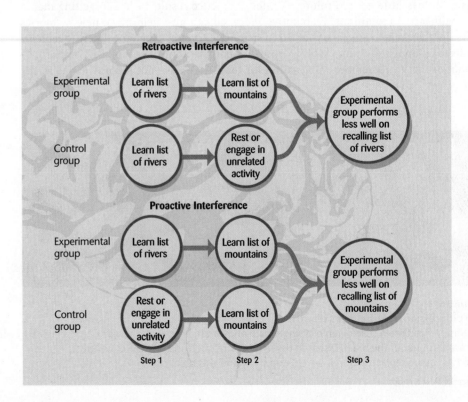

SUMMARY TABLE	FACTORS THAT AFFECT FORGETTING
Factor	**Effect**
Decay	Information in memory deteriorates with the passage of time.
Retrograde amnesia	Storage of new information is disrupted; most often due to injury.
Hippocampal damage	Damage to the hippocampus interferes with the formation of new memories; often caused by brain injury, advanced aging or Alzheimer's disease.
Retroactive interference	Learning new material interferes with information already stored in memory.
Proactive interference	Information already stored in memory interferes with learning new material.
Situational factors	Attempting to remember something in a different situation or internal state may negatively impact memory.
Reconstruction	Memories are reconstructed or replaced with incorrect information which is often more consistent with a current image or perception.

Our ability to accurately recall information is also affected by internal cues, a phenomenon known as *state-dependent memory*. Researchers have found that people who learn material in a particular physiological state tend to recall that material better if they return to the same state they were in during learning (de-l'Etoile, 2002; Kelemen & Creeley, 2003; Riccio, Millin, & Gisquet-Verrier, 2003). For example, if people learn material while under the influence of caffeine, recall of the material is slightly improved when they are again under the influence of caffeine (Kelemen & Creeley, 2003).

The Reconstructive Process Forgetting also occurs because of what is called the "reconstructive" nature of remembering. Earlier, we talked about how schemata are used in storing information in long-term memory. Bartlett proposed that people also use schemata to "reconstruct" memories (Bartlett, 1932). This reconstructive process can lead to huge errors. Indeed, we are sometimes more likely to recall events that never happened than events that actually took place (Brainerd & Reyna, 1998)! The original memory is not destroyed; instead, people are sometimes unable to tell the difference between what actually happened and what they merely heard about or imagined (Neuschatz, Lampinen, Toglia, Payne, & Cisneros, 2007).

We may also reconstruct memories for social reasons or personal self-defense (Feeney & Cassidy, 2003). Each time you tell someone the story of an incident, you may unconsciously make subtle changes in the details of the story. Consequently, these changes become part of your memory of the event. When an experience doesn't fit our view of the world or ourselves, we tend, unconsciously, to adjust it or to blot it out of memory altogether (Bremner & Marmar, 1998).

CHECK YOUR UNDERSTANDING   ✔●—[**Study** and **Review** on **MyPsychLab**

Match the following terms with their appropriate definitions:

1. ____ retrograde amnesia
2. ____ retroactive interference
3. ____ proactive interference

  a. forgetting because new information makes it harder to remember information already in memory
  b. forgetting because old information in memory makes it harder to learn new information
  c. can result from head injury or electroconvulsive therapy

Answers: 1.c. 2.a. 3.b.

(continued)

1. You are trying to explain to someone that "forgetting" sometimes occurs because of the reconstructive nature of long-term memory. Which of the following would be an example that you might use to support your position?

   a. People can distinguish between real and fictional accounts in narratives.

   b. People who learn material in a particular setting tend to recall that material better if they return to that same setting.

   c. Rote rehearsal with no intention to remember has little effect on long-term memory.

   d. People often rewrite their memories of past events to fit their current view or desired view of themselves.

2. You are given a chance to earn $10 if you can correctly learn a list of 20 words. You have 5 minutes to learn the entire list. At the end of that time, you can recite the list perfectly. But before you are given a chance to show what you have learned, you are required to learn a second list of similar words. When it comes time to show how well you learned the first list, to your dismay, you discover that you have forgotten half the words that you once knew perfectly! What is the most likely cause of your forgetting the words on the first list?

   a. negative transfer

   b. retroactive interference

   c. retroactive facilitation

   d. proactive interference

Answers: 1. d. 2. b.

- Describe the influence of culture on memory.
- Define autobiographical memory and describe the several theories that attempt to explain childhood amnesia.
- Describe examples of extraordinary memory (including eidetic imagery and flashbulb memories).
- Discuss the accuracy of eyewitness testimony and recovered memories.

SPECIAL TOPICS IN MEMORY

What factors can influence how well you remember a specific incident?

Now that we have reviewed the various types of memory and how our memory for different events is stored in the brain, we will turn our attention to some special factors that affect memory.

Cultural Influences

Are the memory tasks in Western schools different from those in cultures that pass on traditions orally?

Remembering has practical consequences for our daily life and takes place within a particular context. It's not surprising, then, that many researchers believe that the physical environments, values, self-views, and customs of a given culture have a profound effect on what and how easily people remember (Ross & Wang, 2010). In many Western cultures, for example, being able to recite a long list of words or numbers, to repeat the details of a scene, and to provide facts and figures about historical events are all signs of a "good memory." In fact, tasks such as these are often used to test people's memory abilities. However, these kinds of memory tasks do not necessarily reflect the type of learning, memorization, and categorization skills taught in non-Western schools. Members of other cultures often perform poorly on such memory tests because the exercises seem so odd to them.

In contrast, consider the memory skills of a person living in a society in which cultural information is passed on from one generation to the next through a rich oral tradition. Such an individual may be able to recite the deeds of the culture's heroes in verse or rattle off the lines of descent of families, larger lineage groups, and elders. Or perhaps the individual has a storehouse of information about the migration of animals or the life cycles of plants that help people to obtain food and to know when to harvest crops.

Studies have also shown that culture affects not just our musical preferences, but also our ability to remember and detect small changes in music. Young Japanese children, for example, are better at detecting small variations in pitch of familiar television theme

Look carefully at these cows and try to notice significant distinguishing characteristics of each animal. Is this task difficult for you? It probably is, unless you have been working closely with cattle all your life.

shows than are Canadian children of the same age. Researchers speculate the superior performance of the Japanese children on this task is due to the role that pitch plays in distinguishing different accents in the Japanese language (Trehub, Schellenberg, & Nakata, 2008). In addition, cross-cultural brain imaging research has shown that different regions of the brain are activated when recognizing and remembering music from one's own culture compared to the music of an unfamiliar culture (Demorest et al., 2010).

ENDURING ISSUES

Diversity–Universality   Memory and Culture

Frederic Bartlett, whose work on memory was discussed earlier in this chapter, anticipated the intertwining of memory and culture long ago. Bartlett (1932) related a tale of a Swazi cowherd who had a prodigious memory for facts and figures about cattle. The cowherd could recite, with virtually no error, the selling price, type of cattle bought, and circumstances of the sale for purchases dating back several years. These skills are not surprising when you know that in Swazi culture the care and keeping of cattle are very important in daily life, and many cultural practices focus on the economic and social importance of cattle. In contrast, Bartlett reported, Swazi children did no better than his young European participants in recalling a 25-word message. Stripped of its cultural significance, their memory performance was not exceptional. More recent research showed that college students in Ghana, a culture with a strong oral tradition, were much better than college students in New York at remembering a short story they had heard (Matsumoto, 2000). ▪

Autobiographical Memory

What kinds of events are most likely to be remembered?
Why do we have so few memories from the first 2 years of life?

Autobiographical memory refers to our recollection of events that happened in our life and when those events took place; as such, it is a form of episodic memory. As Martin Conway (1996, p. 295) contends, "autobiographical memory is central to self, to identity, to emotional experience, and to all those attributes that define an individual."

In general, recent life events are, of course, easier to recall than earlier ones. In a classic study of autobiographical memory, researchers asked young adults to report the earliest personal memory that came to mind when they saw each of 20 words and then to estimate how long ago each event had occurred. The words were all common nouns, such as *hall* and *oven,* for which people can easily create images. In general, most personal memories concerned relatively recent events: The longer ago an event occurred, the less likely people were to report it (Crovitz & Schiffman, 1974). Other research, however, shows that people over age 50 are more likely than younger people to recall events from relatively early in life, probably because many of the most critical choices we make in our lives occur in late adolescence and early adulthood (Janssen, Chessa, & Murre, 2005; Mackavey, Malley, & Stewart, 1991).

Exactly how the vast amount of autobiographical information stored in memory is organized is not fully understood, but research in this area has supported two interesting theories. It may be that we store autobiographical information according to important events in our lives, such as beginning college, getting married, or experiencing the death of a loved one. This view explains why we can usually remember when events occurred relative to these major landmarks in our lives (Shum, 1998). We may also store autobiographical memories in *event clusters,* which are groups of memories on a related theme or that take place close together in time (N. R. Brown, 2005). However, it is important to remember that like all memory, autobiographical memory is not always accurate, though its accuracy does increase when distinctive cues are present to help elicit the recall of information (McDonough & Gallo, 2008). ☑•

Complete the **Survey** What Do You Remember? on **MyPsychLab**

ENDURING ISSUES

Stability–Change   Childhood Amnesia

Despite the richness of our autobiographical memories, research shows that people rarely if ever recall events that occurred before they were 2 years old (Howe, 2003). This phenomenon is sometimes called **childhood amnesia,** or *infantile amnesia.*

Exactly why people have difficulty remembering events from their first years of life is not well understood, although several explanations have been advanced. One hypothesis holds that childhood amnesia is a result of the child's brain not being fully developed at birth. Consistent with this line of reasoning, Patricia Bauer and her colleagues (Bauer, 2008; Bauer, Burch, Scholin, & Güler, 2007) found that memories formed early in life may not consolidate properly because the specific regions of the brain devoted to memory consolidation are not yet fully developed, and as such remain vulnerable to interference. Childhood amnesia may also be linked to language skills: Young children do not have the language skills necessary to strengthen and consolidate early experiences (Hudson & Sheffield, 1998; Simcock & Hayne, 2002). Other research suggests that age-related changes in encoding, retention, and retrieval processes that accompany the transition from infancy to early childhood account for childhood amnesia (Hayne, 2004). Still other researchers contend appropriate cues and repetition are the primary influences on efficient recall, not age (Bauer, 1996). Further research is needed before we can evaluate each of these alternative explanations. ■

Extraordinary Memory

What is photographic memory?

Some people are able to perform truly amazing feats of memory. From time to time, the newspaper will carry a report of a person with a "photographic memory." This phenomenon, called **eidetic imagery,** enables people to see the features of an image in minute detail, sometimes even to recite an entire page of a book they read only once.

One study screened 500 elementary schoolchildren before finding 20 with eidetic imagery (Haber, 1969). The children were told to scan a picture for 30 seconds, moving their eyes to see all its various parts. The picture was then removed, and the children were told to look at a blank easel and report what they saw in an eidetic image. They needed at least 3 to

childhood amnesia The difficulty adults have remembering experiences from their first 2 years of life.

eidetic imagery The ability to reproduce unusually sharp and detailed images of something one has seen.

5 seconds of scanning to produce an image, even when the picture was familiar. In addition, the quality of eidetic imagery seemed to vary from child to child. One girl in this study could move and reverse images and recall them several weeks later. Three children could produce eidetic images of three-dimensional objects; and some could superimpose an eidetic image of one picture onto another and form a new picture. However, the children with eidetic imagery performed no better than their noneidetic classmates on other tests of memory.

One of the most famous documented cases of extraordinary memory comes from the work of the distinguished psychologist Alexander Luria (Luria & Solotaroff, 1987). For over 20 years, Luria studied a Russian newspaper reporter named Shereshevskii ("S"). In *The Mind of a Mnemonist* (1968), Luria described how "S" could recall masses of senseless trivia as well as detailed mathematical formulas and complex arrays of numbers. He could easily repeat lists of up to 70 words or numbers after having heard or seen them only once.

"S" and other people with exceptional memories were not born with a special gift for remembering things. Rather, they have carefully developed memory techniques using certain principles. For example, Luria discovered that when "S" studied long lists of words, he would form a graphic image for every item. When reading a long and random list of words, for example, "S" might visualize a well-known street, specifically associating each word with some object along the way. When asked to recite the lists of words, he would take an imaginary walk down that street, recalling each object and the word associated with it. By organizing his data in a way that was meaningful to him, he could more easily link them to existing material in his long-term memory.

Developing an exceptional memory takes time and effort (Takahashi, Shimizu, Saito, & Tomoyori, 2006). **Mnemonists** (pronounced nee-MON-ists), people who are highly skilled at using memory techniques, frequently have compelling reasons for developing their memories. "S" used his memory skills to his advantage as a newspaper reporter. As we will see in the next chapter, chess masters also sometimes display astonishing recall of meaningful chessboard configurations (Campitelli, Gobet, & Parker, 2005).

Millions of people will forever have a vivid flashbulb memory of planes flying into the twin towers of the World Trade Center in New York City on September 11, 2001.

Flashbulb Memories

Are flashbulb memories always accurate?

A **flashbulb memory** is the experience of remembering vividly a certain event and the incidents surrounding it even after a long time has passed. We often remember events that are shocking or otherwise highly significant in this way (Cubelli & Della Sala, 2008; Wooffitt, 2005). The death of a close relative, a birth, a graduation, or a wedding day may all elicit flashbulb memories. So can dramatic events in which we were not personally involved, such as the attacks on the World Trade Center and the Pentagon on September 11, 2001 (Edery & Nachson, 2004; Talarico & Rubin, 2003): 97% of Americans surveyed 1 year after the September 11 attacks claimed they could remember exactly where they were and what they were doing when they first heard about the attacks (Pew Research Center for the People and the Press, 2002).

The assumptions that flashbulb memories are accurate, that they form at the time of an event, and that we remember them better because of their highly emotional content have all been questioned (Lanciano, Curci, & Semin, 2010). First, flashbulb memories are certainly not always accurate. Although this is a difficult contention to test, let's consider just one case. Psychologist Ulric Neisser vividly recalled what he was doing on the day in 1941 when the Japanese bombed Pearl Harbor. He clearly remembered that he was listening to a professional baseball game on the radio, which was interrupted by the shocking announcement. But professional baseball is not played in December, when the attack took place, so this sharp flashbulb memory was simply incorrect (Neisser, 1982).

Even if an event is registered accurately, it may undergo periodic revision, just like other long-term memories (Cubelli & Della Sala, 2008). We are bound to discuss and rethink a major event many times, and we probably also hear a great deal of additional information about that event in the weeks and months after it occurs. As a result, the flashbulb memory may undergo reconstruction and become less accurate over the years until it sometimes bears little or no resemblance to what actually happened.

mnemonists People with highly developed memory skills.

flashbulb memory A vivid memory of a certain event and the incidents surrounding it even after a long time has passed.

Eyewitness Testimony

How much can we trust eyewitness testimony?

I know what I saw! When an eyewitness to a crime gives evidence in court, that testimony often overwhelms evidence to the contrary. Faced with conflicting or ambiguous testimony, jurors tend to put their faith in people who saw an event with their own eyes. However, there is now compelling evidence that this faith in eyewitnesses is often misplaced.

For more than 20 years, Elizabeth Loftus (1993; Loftus & Pickrell, 1995; D. B. Wright & Loftus, 2008) has been the most influential researcher into eyewitness memory. In a classic study, Loftus and Palmer (1974) showed experimental participants a film depicting a traffic accident. Some of the participants were asked, "About how fast were the cars going when they hit each other?" Other participants were asked the same question, but with the words *smashed into, collided with, bumped into,* or *contacted* in place of *hit.* The researchers discovered that people's reports of the cars' speeds depended on which word was inserted in the question. Those asked about cars that "smashed into" each other reported that the cars were going faster than those who were asked about cars that "contacted" each other. In another experiment, the participants were also shown a film of a collision and then were asked either "How fast were the cars going when they hit each other?" or "How fast were the cars going when they smashed into each other?" One week later, they were asked some additional questions about the accident that they had seen on film the week before. One of the questions was "Did you see any broken glass?" More of the participants who had been asked about cars that had "smashed into" each other reported that they had seen broken glass than did participants who had been asked the speed of cars that "hit" each other. These findings illustrate how police, lawyers, and other investigators may, often unconsciously, sway witnesses and influence subsequent eyewitness accounts. On the basis of experiments like these, Loftus and Palmer concluded that eyewitness testimony is unreliable.

Why do eyewitnesses make mistakes? Some research suggests that the problem may be *source error:* People are sometimes unable to tell the difference between what they witnessed and what they merely heard about or imagined (Garry & Polaschek, 2000; Reyna & Titcomb, 1997). This is especially true for young children (Shapiro, 2002; K. L. Thierry & Spence, 2002). Studies have shown that simply imagining an event sometimes makes people believe it actually happened (Garry & Polaschek, 2000; Henkel, Franklin, & Johnson, 2000; Mazzoni & Memon, 2003). Similarly, if you hear information about an event you witnessed, you might later confuse your memory of that information with your memory of the original event. For instance, studies have shown that if an eyewitness receives confirming feedback after picking a suspect out of a police lineup, or has the opportunity to meet with a co-witness who shares their memory for the event, their confidence in the accuracy of their memory increases (Mori & Mori, 2008; Neuschatz et al., 2005; Wright, Memon, Skagerberg, & Gabbert, 2009). The impact of subsequent information seems to be particularly strong when it is repeated several times

THINKING CRITICALLY ABOUT . . .

Eyewitness Testimony

T. R. Benton, Ross, Bradshaw, Thomas, and Bradshaw (2006) studied 111 jurors drawn from a jury pool in Hamilton County, Tennessee. Using a questionnaire with 30 statements about eyewitness testimony (Kassin et al., 2001), they found that jurors significantly disagreed with eyewitness experts on more than 85% of the items. For example, while almost all of the experts agreed that instructions by police can affect the willingness of an eyewitness to make an identification, less than half of the jurors agreed. Over three-quarters of the experts agreed that an eyewitness may mistakenly identify someone they saw in another situation as a culprit, less than a third of the jurors agreed. And while more than nine out of ten of the experts agreed that Hypnosis may influence a witnesses' suggestibility toward leading and misleading questions, less than a quarter of the jurors believed that hypnosis could have such an impact. In sum, the authors concluded that jurors have limited knowledge concerning the veracity of eyewitness testimony and their beliefs concerning the accuracy of eyewitness testimony differ significantly from the opinions of experts.

1. What questions might you raise about the authors' conclusion? For example, do you think that their sample of jurors is representative of jurors throughout the United States? If so, why do you think so? If not, in what ways do you think it differed significantly and how do you think that might have affected their results?

2. The authors note that some courts exclude the need for eyewitness expert testimony on the grounds that it only requires common sense to understand how eyewitness testimony should be interpreted. Do you agree that testimony from eyewitness experts should be excluded on the grounds that it is not necessary? Why or why not? Are there some circumstances when such testimony might be more valuable than others? How might you go about determining whether, in fact, expert testimony is valuable at least sometimes?

(Zaragoza & Mitchell, 1996), as is often the case with extensive media coverage, or when it comes from an authority figure such as a police officer (Roper & Shewan, 2002). Other studies have shown that simply describing the perpetrator shortly after the incident occurs actually interferes with memories of what the person actually looked like, thus making it more difficult for the eyewitness to pick the correct person out of a lineup at a later date (B. Bower, 2003a; Fiore & Schooler, 2002).

Whatever the reason for eyewitness errors, there is good evidence that such mistakes can send thousands of innocent people to jail each year in the United States (Pezdek, 2007). For example, based almost entirely on the eyewitness identification testimony of a single individual, Steven Avery was convicted of brutally attacking, raping, and nearly killing a woman in 1985 and was sentenced to 32 years in prison. Although Avery offered alibis from 14 witnesses and documentation showing he wasn't at the scene of the crime, it took repeated legal challenges and new advances in DNA testing for him to overcome the conviction. Finally, on September 11, 2003, Mr. Avery was exonerated of all charges and released from prison. Increasingly, courts are recognizing the limits of eyewitness testimony and are taking steps to teach jurors how to properly evaluate it (Martire & Kemp, 2011).

Recovered Memories

Can people be persuaded to "create" new memories about events that never occurred?

In recent years, a controversy has raged, both within the academic community and in society at large, about the validity of *recovered memories* (Geraerts, Raymaekers, & Merckelbach, 2010; Gleaves, Smith, Butler, Spiegel, & Kihlstrom, 2010; Loftus, Garry, & Hayne, 2008). The idea is that people experience an event, then lose all memory of it, and then later recall it, often in the course of psychotherapy or under hypnosis. Frequently, the recovered memories concern physical or sexual abuse during childhood. The issue is important not only for theoretical reasons, but also because of the fact that people have been imprisoned for abuse solely on the basis of the recovered memories of their "victims" (Geraerts, Raymaekers, & Merckelbach, 2008). Adding to this confusion is research that shows children's memories are particularly influenced by negative emotions. Thus, when recalling events associated with an uncomfortable experience, such as abuse, children are more likely to make factual errors than when recalling neutral or positive events (Brainerd, Stein, Silveira, Rohenkold, & Reyna, 2008). No one denies the reality of childhood abuse or the damage that such experiences cause. But are the recovered memories real? Did the remembered abuse really occur? ⦿➤

Simulate the Experiment Creating False Memories on **MyPsychLab**

The answer is by no means obvious. There is ample evidence that people can be induced to "remember" events that never happened (Saletan, 2010; S. M. Smith et al, 2003). Research confirms that it is relatively easy to implant memories of an experience merely by asking about it. Sometimes these memories become quite real to the participant. In one experiment, 25% of adults "remembered" fictitious events by the third time they were interviewed about them. One of the fictitious events involved knocking over a punch bowl onto the parents of the bride at a wedding reception. At the first interview, one participant said that she had no recollection whatsoever of the event; by the second interview, she "remembered" that the reception was outdoors and that she had knocked over the bowl while running around. Some people even "remembered" details about the event, such as what people looked like and what they wore. Yet, the researchers documented that these events never happened (Hyman, Husband, & Billings, 1995).

The implication of this and similar research is that it is quite possible for people to "remember" abusive experiences that never happened. And some people who have "recovered" abuse memories have later realized that the events never occurred. Some of these people have brought suit against the therapists who, they came to believe, implanted the memories. In one case, a woman won such a suit and was awarded $850,000 (Imrie, 1999; also see Geraerts, Raymaekers, & Merckelbach, 2008).

However, there is reason to believe that not all recovered memories are merely the products of suggestion. There are numerous case studies of people who have lived through traumatic experiences, including natural disasters, accidents, combat, assault, and rape, who then apparently forgot these events for many years, but who later remembered them. For example, Wilbur J. Scott, a sociologist, claimed to remember nothing of his tour of duty in Vietnam during 1968–1969, but during a divorce in 1983, he discovered his medals and souvenirs from Vietnam, and the memories then came back to him (Arrigo & Pezdek, 1997).

What is needed is a reliable way of separating real memories from false ones, but so far no such test is available (Bernstein & Loftus, 2009). The sincerity and conviction of the person who "remembers" long-forgotten childhood abuse is no indication of the reality of that abuse. However, evidence does suggest that people who recover memories during suggestive therapy are at an increased risk of fabricating false memories compared to individuals who spontaneously recover memories of abuse (Geraerts et al., 2009). Nevertheless, we are left with the conclusion that recovered memories are not, in themselves, sufficiently trustworthy to justify criminal convictions. There must also be corroborative evidence, since without corroboration, there is no way that even the most experienced examiner can separate real memories from false ones (Loftus, Garry, & Hayne, 2008; Loftus, 1997).

Study and **Review** on **MyPsychLab**

CHECK YOUR UNDERSTANDING

Is each of the following statements true (T) or false (F)?

1. Retrograde amnesia is the phenomenon that we seldom remember events that occurred before our second birthday.

2. A long-lasting and vivid memory for a certain event and the incidents surrounding it is called a flashbulb memory.

3. Research demonstrates that it is nearly impossible to change a person's memory once that memory has been stored.

Answers: 1. (F). 2. (T). 3. (F).

APPLY YOUR UNDERSTANDING

1. You are talking with someone from a different culture who is not very good at remembering long lists of random words or numbers, but who can recite from memory all of his ancestors going back hundreds of years. What is the most likely explanation for this difference in memory skills?

   a. The values and customs of a given culture have a profound effect on what people remember.

   b. The person's autobiographical memory is stronger than his semantic memory.

   c. The list of his ancestors has been stored in flashbulb memory.

   d. The list of his ancestors is an example of a "recovered memory."

2. Your mother is reminiscing about your first birthday party and asks you, "Do you remember when Aunt Mary dropped her piece of cake in your lap?" Try as you might, you can't recall that incident. This is most likely an example of

   a. memory decay.

   b. retrograde amnesia.

   c. infantile amnesia.

   d. proactive interference.

Answers: 1. a. 2. c.

KEY TERMS

CHAPTER REVIEW   ((•-[Listen to the **Chapter Audio** on **MyPsychLab**

THE SENSORY REGISTERS

What is the role of sensory registers? Many psychologists view **memory** as a series of steps in which we encode, store, and retrieve information, much as a computer does. This is called the **information-processing** model of memory. The first step in the model is inputting data through our senses into temporary holding bins, called **sensory registers.** These registers give us a brief moment to decide whether something deserves our attention.

What would happen if auditory information faded as quickly as visual information fades? Information entering a sensory register disappears very quickly if it isn't processed further. Information in the visual register lasts for only about a quarter of a second before it is replaced by new information. If sounds faded from our auditory register as rapidly as this, spoken language would be more difficult to understand. Luckily, information in the auditory register can linger for several seconds.

Why does some information capture our attention, while other information goes unnoticed? The next step in the memory process is **attention**—selectively looking at, listening to, smelling, tasting, or feeling what we deem to be important. The nervous system filters out peripheral information, allowing us to zero in on what is essential at a particular time. Unattended information receives at least some processing, however, so that we can quickly shift attention to it if it suddenly strikes us as significant.

SHORT-TERM MEMORY

What are the two primary tasks of short-term memory? How much information can be held in short-term memory? **Short-term memory (STM),** also called working memory, holds whatever information we are actively attending to at any given time. Its two primary tasks are to store new information briefly and to "work" on information that we currently have in mind. We

can process more information in STM by grouping it into larger meaningful units, a process called **chunking.**

Do we store material in short-term memory as it sounds or as it looks? Information can be stored in STM according to the way it sounds, the way it looks, or its meaning. Verbal information is encoded by sound, even if it is written rather than heard. The capacity for visual encoding in STM is greater than for encoding by sound.

How can we hold information in STM? Through rote rehearsal, or maintenance rehearsal, we retain information in STM for a minute or two by repeating it over and over again. However, rote memorization does not promote long-term memory.

LONG-TERM MEMORY

What types of information are retained in long-term memory? **Long-term memory (LTM)** stores everything we learn.

What is the limit of LTM? Long-term memory can store a vast amount of information for many years.

How are most memories encoded in LTM? Most of the information in LTM seems to be encoded according to its meaning.

Which items in a list are hardest to remember? Short- and long-term memory work together to explain the **serial position effect,** in which people tend to recall the first and last items in a list better than items in the middle. The *recency effect* explains that items at the end are still held in STM, whereas the *primacy effect* describes the extra LTM rehearsal given to items early in the list.

What three processes are used to hold information in LTM? The way in which we encode material for storage in LTM affects the ease with which we can retrieve it later on. Rote rehearsal is particularly useful for holding conceptually meaningless material, such as phone numbers, in LTM. Through the deeper and more meaningful mechanism of **elaborative rehearsal,** we extract the meaning of information and link it to as much material as possible that is already in LTM. Memory techniques such as **mnemonics** rely on elaborative processing.

A **schema** is a mental representation of an object or event that is stored in memory. Schemata provide a framework into which incoming information is fitted. They may prompt the formation of stereotypes and the drawing of inferences.

How do types of LTM differ? Episodic memories are personal memories for events experienced in a specific time and place. **Semantic memories** are facts and concepts not linked to a particular time. **Procedural memories** are motor skills and habits. **Emotional memories** are learned emotional responses to various stimuli.

What are the differences between implicit and explicit memories? Explicit memory refers to memories we are aware of, including episodic and semantic memories. **Implicit memory** refers to memories for information that either was not intentionally committed to LTM or is retrieved unintentionally from LTM, including procedural and emotional memories. This distinction is illustrated by research on *priming,* in which people are more likely to complete fragments of stimuli with items seen earlier than with other, equally plausible items.

THE BIOLOGY OF MEMORY

What role do neurons play in memory? Memories consist of changes in the chemistry and structure of neurons. The process by which these changes occur is called **long-term potentiation (LTP).**

Are STM and LTM found in the same parts of the brain? Different parts of the brain are specialized for the storage of memories. Short-term memories seem to be located primarily in the prefrontal cortex and temporal lobe. Long-term memories seem to involve both subcortical and cortical structures. Semantic and episodic memories seem to be located primarily in the frontal and temporal lobes of the cortex, and procedural memories appear to be located primarily in the cerebellum and motor cortex. The hippocampus seems especially important in the formation of semantic, episodic, and procedural memories. Emotional memories are dependent on the amygdala.

What role does sleep play in memory? During deep sleep, the same hippocampal neurons and patterns of neuron activity that accompany initial learning are reactivated. As a result, new memories are further strengthened.

FORGETTING

What factors explain why we sometimes forget? Both biological and experiential factors can contribute to our inability to recall information.

How does the deterioration of the brain help to explain forgetting? According to the **decay theory,** memories deteriorate because of the passage of time. Severe memory loss can be traced to brain damage caused by accidents, surgery, poor diet, or disease. Head injuries can cause **retrograde amnesia**, the inability of people to remember what happened shortly before their accident. The hippocampus may have a role in long-term memory formation. Below-normal levels of the neurotransmitter acetylcholine may be implicated in memory loss seen in Alzheimer's disease.

What environmental factors contribute to our inability to remember? To the extent that information is apparently lost from LTM, researchers attribute the cause to inadequate learning or to interference from competing information. Interference may come from two directions: In **retroactive interference,** new information interferes with old information already in LTM; **proactive interference** refers to the process by which old information already in LTM interferes with new information.

When environmental cues present during learning are absent during recall, context-dependent forgetting may occur. The ability to recall information is also affected by one's physiological state when the material was learned; this process is known *as state-dependent memory.*

Sometimes we "reconstruct" memories for social or personal self-defense. Research on long-term memory and on forgetting offers ideas for a number of steps that can be taken to improve recall.

SPECIAL TOPICS IN MEMORY

What factors can influence how well you remember a specific incident? Cultural values and customs profoundly affect what people remember and how easily they recall it. So do the emotions we attach to a memory, with some emotion-laden events being remembered for life. Also affecting how well we remember are the strategies we use to store and retrieve information.

Are the memory tasks in Western schools different from those in cultures that pass on traditions orally? Many Western schools stress being able to recall long lists of words, facts, and figures that are divorced from everyday life. In contrast, societies in which cultural information is passed on through a rich oral tradition may instead emphasize memory for events that directly affect people's lives.

What kinds of events are most likely to be remembered? *Autobiographical memory* refers to recollection of events from one's life. Not all of these events are recalled with equal clarity, of course, and some are not recalled at all. Autobiographical memories are typically strongest for events that had a major impact on our lives or that aroused strong emotion.

Why do we have so few memories from the first 2 years of life? People generally cannot remember events that occurred before age 2, a phenomenon called childhood amnesia. Childhood amnesia may result from the incomplete development of brain structures before age 2, from the infants' lack of a clear sense of self, or from the lack of language skills used to consolidate early experience. Research also suggests it may be related to an adult's inability to recall memories that were, in fact, stored during the first 2 years.

What is a photographic memory? People with exceptional memories have carefully developed memory techniques. **Mnemonists** are individuals who are highly skilled at using those techniques. A phenomenon called **eidetic imagery** enables some people to see features of an image in minute detail.

Are flashbulb memories always accurate? Years after a dramatic or significant event occurs, people often report having vivid memories of that event as well as the incidents surrounding it. These memories are known as **flashbulb memories.** Recent research has challenged the assumptions that flashbulb memories are accurate and stable.

How much can we trust eyewitness testimony? Jurors tend to put their faith in witnesses who saw an event with their own eyes. However, some evidence suggests that eyewitnesses sometimes are unable to tell the difference between what they witnessed and what they merely heard about or imagined.

Can people be persuaded to "create" new memories about events that never occurred? There are many cases of people who experience a traumatic event, lose all memory of it, but then later recall it. Such recovered memories are highly controversial, since research shows that people can be induced to "remember" events that never happened. So far there is no clear way to distinguish real recovered memories from false ones.

Cognition and Mental Abilities

OVERVIEW

"At the Braefield School for the Deaf, I met Joseph, a boy of 11 who had just entered school for the first time—an 11-year-old with no language whatever. ... Joseph longed to communicate, but could not... It was not only language that was missing: there was not, it was evident, a clear sense of the past, of 'a day ago' as distinct from 'a year ago.' There was a strange lack of historical sense, the feeling of a life that lacked autobiographical and historical dimension ... a life that only existed in the moment, in the present. ...

Joseph saw, distinguished, categorized, used; he had no problems with perceptual categorization or generalization, but he could not, it seemed, go much beyond this, hold abstract ideas in mind, reflect, play, plan. He seemed completely literal—unable to juggle images or hypotheses or possibilities, unable to enter an imaginative or figurative realm. And yet, one still felt, he was of normal intelligence, despite the manifest limitations of intellectual functioning. It was not that he lacked a mind, but that he was not using his mind fully. ..." (Sacks, 2000, pp. 32–34)

As Sacks suggests, language and thought are intertwined. We find it difficult to imagine one without the other, and we consider both part of what it means to be human. Psychologists use the term **cognition** to refer to all the processes that we use to acquire and apply information. We have already considered the cognitive processes of perception, learning, and memory. In this chapter, we focus on three cognitive processes that we think of as characteristically human: thinking, problem solving, and decision making. We also discuss two mental abilities that psychologists have tried to measure: intelligence and creativity.

ENDURING ISSUES in Cognition and Mental Abilities

The "Enduring Issues" in this chapter are highlighted in four prominent places. We will encounter the diversity–universality theme when we explore the differences and similarities in the way people process information and again when we discuss exceptional abilities. We make two additional references to the enduring issues as we discuss the stability–change of intelligence test scores over time, and again when we explore how measures of intelligence and performance sometimes vary as a function of expectations and situations (*Person–Situation*).

BUILDING BLOCKS OF THOUGHT

What are the three most important building blocks of thought?

When you think about a close friend, you may have in mind complex statements about her, such as "I'd like to talk to her soon" or "I wish I could be more like her." You may also have an image of her—probably her face, but perhaps the sound of her voice as well. Or you may think of your friend by using various concepts or categories such as *woman, kind, strong, dynamic,* and *gentle.* When we think, we make use of all these things—language, images, and concepts—often simultaneously. These are the three most important building blocks of thought.

LEARNING OBJECTIVE

• Describe the three basic building blocks of thought and give an example of each. Explain how phonemes, morphemes, and grammar (syntax and semantics) work together to form a language.

Language

What steps do we go through to turn a thought into a statement?

Human **language** is a flexible system of symbols that enables us to communicate our ideas, thoughts, and feelings. Joseph, the deaf boy described at the beginning of this chapter, had great difficulty communicating because he knew no languages. Although all animals communicate with each other, language is unique to humans (MacWhinney, 2005).

One way to understand language is to consider its basic structure. Spoken language is based on units of sound called **phonemes.** The sounds of *t, th,* and *k,* for instance, are all phonemes in English. By themselves, phonemes are meaningless and seldom play an important role in helping us to think. But phonemes can be grouped together to form words, prefixes (such as *un-* and *pre-*), and suffixes (such as *-ed* and *-ing*). These meaningful combinations of phonemes are known as **morphemes**—the smallest meaningful units in a language. Unlike phonemes, morphemes play a key role in human thought. They can

cognition The processes whereby we acquire and use knowledge.

language A flexible system of communication that uses sounds, rules, gestures, or symbols to convey information.

phonemes The basic sounds that make up any language.

morphemes The smallest meaningful units of speech, such as simple words, prefixes, and suffixes.

grammar The language rules that determine how sounds and words can be combined and used to communicate meaning within a language.

represent important ideas such as "red" or "calm" or "hot." The suffix -*ed* captures the idea of "in the past" (as in *visited* or *liked*). The prefix *pre-* conveys the idea of "before" or "prior to" (as in *preview* or *predetermined*).

We can combine morphemes to create words that represent quite complex ideas, such as *pre-exist-ing, un-excell-ed, psycho-logy.* In turn, words can be arranged to form sentences according to the rules of **grammar.** The two major components of grammar are *syntax* and *semantics. Syntax* is the system of rules that governs how we combine words to form meaningful phrases and sentences. For example, in English and many other languages, the meaning of a sentence is often determined by word order. "Sally hit the car" means one thing; "The car hit Sally" means something quite different; and "Hit Sally car the" is meaningless.

Semantics describes how we assign meaning to morphemes, words, phrases, and sentences—in other words, the content of language. When we are thinking about something—say, the ocean—our ideas often consist of phrases and sentences, such as "The ocean is unusually calm tonight." Sentences have both a *surface structure*—the particular words and phrases—and a *deep structure*—the underlying meaning. The same deep structure can be conveyed by different surface structures:

The ocean is unusually calm tonight.

Tonight the ocean is particularly calm.

Compared with most other nights, tonight the ocean is calm.

Alternatively, the same surface structure can convey different meanings or deep structures, but a knowledge of language permits one to know what is meant within a given context:

Surface Structure	Might mean... Or...
Flying planes can be dangerous.	An airborne plane...
	The profession of pilot...
Visiting relatives can be a nuisance.	Relatives who are visiting...
	The obligation to visit relatives...
The chicken is ready to eat.	Food has been cooked sufficiently...
	The bird is hungry...

Syntax and semantics enable speakers and listeners to perform what linguist Noam Chomsky calls *transformations* between surface structure and deep structure. According to Chomsky (1957; Chomsky, Place, & Schoneberger, 2000), when you want to communicate an idea, you start with a thought, then choose words and phrases that will express the idea, and finally, produce the speech sounds that make up those words and phrases, as shown by the left arrow in **Figure 7–1.** When you want to understand a sentence, your task is reversed. You must start with speech sounds and work your way up to the meaning of those sounds, as represented by the right arrow in Figure 7–1.

Our remarkable ability to perform these transformations becomes clear when you attempt to comprehend the following sentence: when lettres wihtin wrods are jubmled or trnasposed (as they are in this sentence), raeding speed is redcued, though not as much as you might expect (approximately 11%–26%). However, it is much more difficult to extract the meaning of a sentence when letter substitutions are made (such as "qroblem" or "problnc" for "problem") (Rayner, White, Johnson, & Liversedge, 2006).

Images

What role do images play in thinking?

Using language is not the only way to think about things. Think for a moment about Abraham Lincoln. Your thoughts of Lincoln may have included such phrases as "wrote the Gettysburg Address" and "president during the Civil War." But you probably also

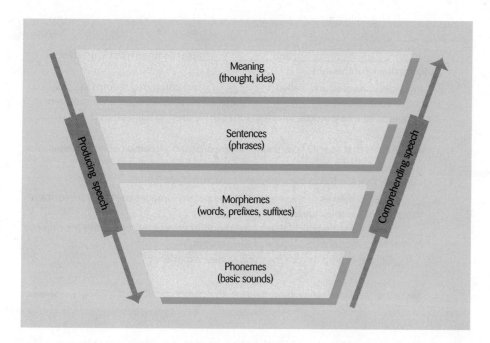

had some mental images about him: bearded face, lanky body, or log cabin. An **image** is a mental representation of some sensory experience, and it can be used to think about things. Images also allow us to use concrete forms to represent complex and abstract ideas, as when newspapers use pie charts and graphs to illustrate how people voted in an election.

Concepts

How do concepts help us to think more efficiently?

Concepts are mental categories for classifying specific people, things, or events. *Dogs, books, fast, beautiful,* and *interesting* are all concepts. When you think about a specific thing—say, Mt. Everest—you may think of facts. You may also have an image of it. But you are also likely to think of the concepts that apply to it, such as *mountain, highest, dangerous,* and *snow-covered.* Concepts help us to think efficiently about things and how they relate to one another. They also give meaning to new experiences and allow us to organize our experiences. For example, most children soon develop a concept of fish that allows them to recognize, think about, and understand new kinds of fish when they see them for the first time.

Although it is tempting to think of concepts as simple and clear-cut, most of the concepts that we use are rather "fuzzy": They overlap one another and are often poorly defined. For example, most people can tell a mouse from a rat, but listing the critical differences between the two is difficult (Rosch, 2002). If we cannot explain the difference between mouse and rat, how can we use these *fuzzy concepts* in our thinking? It turns out that we often construct a **prototype (or model)** of a representative mouse and one of a representative rat, and then use those prototypes in our thinking (Rosch, 2002; Voorspoels, Vanpaemel, & Storms, 2008). For example, when thinking about birds, most of us have a prototype in mind—such as a robin or a sparrow—that captures for us the essence of *bird.* When we encounter new objects, we compare them with this prototype to determine whether they are, in fact, birds. And when we think about birds, we usually think about our prototypical bird.

Concepts, then, like words and images, help us to think. But human cognition involves more than just passively thinking about things. It also involves actively using words, images, and concepts to fashion an understanding of the world, to solve problems, and to make decisions. In the next three sections, we see how this is done.

"Well, you don't look like an experimental psychologist to *me.*"

image A mental representation of a sensory experience.

concepts Mental categories for classifying objects, people, or experiences.

prototype (or model) According to Rosch, a mental model containing the most typical features of a concept.

✓•[**Study** and **Review** on **MyPsychLab**

Pablo Picasso, the great 20th-century artist, developed a style of painting known as Cubism. In paintings such as *Nude with Bunch of Irises and Mirror,* 1934, shown here, he reformed objects into basic geometric shapes. We recognize the figure in this painting as a woman because its shapes represent the "concept" of a female.

CHECK YOUR UNDERSTANDING

1. _____, _____, and _____ are the three most important building blocks of thought.

2. In language, units of sound, called _____, are combined to form the smallest units of meaning, called _____. These smallest meaningful units can then be combined to create words, which in turn can be used to build phrases and whole _____.

3. Language rules that specify how sounds and words can be combined into meaningful sentences are called rules of _____.

4. Indicate whether the following statements are true (T) or false (F).
   a. _____ Images help us to think about things because images use concrete forms to represent complex ideas.
   b. _____ People decide which objects belong to a concept by comparing the object's features to a model or prototype of the concept.
   c. _____ Concepts help us give meaning to new experiences.

Answers: 1. language, images, concepts. **2.** phonemes, morphemes, sentences. **3.** grammar. **4. a.** (T); **b.** (T); **c.** (T).

APPLY YOUR UNDERSTANDING

1. "I will spend tonight studying." "Tonight I will be studying." These two sentences exhibit the same
   a. surface structure.
   b. syntax.
   c. phonology.
   d. deep structure.

2. Harry cannot list the essential differences between dogs and cats, but he has no trouble thinking about dogs and cats. This is most likely due to the fact that he
   a. has a prototype of a representative dog and another of a representative cat.
   b. has developed a morpheme for a dog and another morpheme for a cat.
   c. is exhibiting functional fixedness.
   d. is using heuristics.

Answers: 1. d. **2.** a.

> LANGUAGE, THOUGHT, AND CULTURE

How do language, thought, and culture influence each other?

ENDURING ISSUES

Diversity–Universality   Do We All Think Alike?

For at least 100 years, psychologists and philosophers assumed the basic processes of human cognition are universal. They accepted that cultural differences affect thought—thus, Masai elders in the Serengeti count their wealth in heads of cattle, whereas Wall Street bankers measure theirs in stocks and bonds. But habits of thought—the ways people process information—were assumed to be the same everywhere. The tendency to categorize objects and experiences, the ability to reason logically, and the desire to understand situations in terms of cause and effect were thought to be part of human nature, regardless of cultural setting. In this section, we will examine the validity of these viewpoints. ■

Do people from different cultures perceive and think about the world in different ways? A series of controlled experiments suggests they do. In one experiment (Nisbett, Peng, Choi, & Norenzayan, 2001), American and Japanese students were shown an underwater scene and asked to describe what they saw. Most Japanese participants described the scene as a whole, beginning with the background; by contrast, most American participants described the biggest, brightest, fastest fish. Similar differences exist between Eastern Europeans and Americans and between Russians and Germans (Varnum, Grossmann, Kitayama, & Nisbett (2010). These studies demonstrate fundamental, qualitative differences in how people in different cultures perceive and think about the world that are not due to genetic differences or differences in language.

As we have seen, language is one of the building blocks of thought. Can language influence how we think and what we can think about? Benjamin Whorf (1956) strongly believed that it does. According to Whorf's **linguistic relativity hypothesis,** the language we speak determines the pattern of our thinking and our view of the world—a position known more generally as **linguistic determinism.** For Whorf, if a language lacks a particular expression, the corresponding thought will probably not occur to speakers of that language. For example, the Hopi of the southwestern United States have only two nouns for things that fly. One noun refers to birds; the other is used for everything else. A plane and a dragonfly, for instance, are both referred to with the same noun. According to Whorf, Hopi speakers would not see as great a difference between planes and dragonflies as we do, because their language labels the two similarly.

The linguistic relativity hypothesis has intuitive appeal—it makes sense to think that limits of language will produce limits in thinking. However, research indicates that language doesn't restrict thinking to the extent that some linguistic determinists believed. For example, English has only three words for lightness: white (or light), black (or dark), and gray. Yet English speakers can discriminate hundreds of levels of visual intensity (Baddeley & Attewell, 2009). Moreover, experience and thought actually influence language. For example, the growth of personal computers and the Internet has inspired a vocabulary of its own, such as *gigabyte, CPU, smartphone,* and *blogs.* In short, people create new words when they need them.

Psychologists have not dismissed the Whorf hypothesis altogether, but rather have softened it, recognizing that language, thought, and culture are intertwined (Chiu, Leung, & Kwan, 2007). Experience shapes language; and language, in turn, affects subsequent experience (K. Fiedler, 2008). This realization has caused us to examine our use of language more carefully, as we will see in the next section.

linguistic relativity hypothesis Whorf's idea that patterns of thinking are determined by the specific language one speaks.

linguistic determinism The belief that thought and experience are determined by language.

The Dani of New Guinea can perceive and remember the many colors of their world just as readily as you can, even though their language has only two color terms—*light* and *dark*. Human thought is not limited to the words in a person's language. Language may indeed influence thought, but it doesn't seem to restrict thought to the extent that Whorf believed.

✓•◦〔**Study** and **Review** on **MyPsychLab**〕

CHECK YOUR UNDERSTANDING

1. According to Whorf's _____ _____ hypothesis, the language we speak shapes our thinking.

2. Indicate whether the following statements are true (T) or false (F).
   a. _____ Many words in our language correspond to concepts.
   b. _____ Experience shapes language.
   c. _____ Thoughts are limited to the words in the language that a person speaks.

Answers: 1. linguistic relativity. **2. a.** (T); **b.** (T); **c.** (F).

APPLY YOUR UNDERSTANDING

1. Cross-cultural studies indicate that people from different cultures with very different languages nonetheless perceive and are able to think about such things as colors in very similar ways even if their language contains no words for these things. These data _____ Whorf's theory.
   a. support
   b. contradict
   c. neither support nor contradict

Answer: 1. b.

Is Language Male Dominated?

Does language contribute to gender stereotyping?

The English language has traditionally used masculine terms such as *man* and *he* to refer to all people—female as well as male. Several studies suggest that this affects the way English speakers think. Hyde (1984) discovered that the use of "he" or "she" to describe a factory worker affected how children assessed the performance of male and female workers. Children who heard workers described by the masculine pronoun "he" rated female workers poorly; those who heard workers identified by the pronoun "she" judged female workers most positively; and the ratings of children who heard gender-neutral descriptions of workers fell in between those of the two other groups.

More recent research has focused on the unconscious, automatic nature of gender stereotyping and language (Palomares, 2004; Parks & Roberton, 2004). In an experiment requiring men and women to respond rapidly to gender-neutral and gender-specific pronouns, both sexes responded more quickly to stimuli containing traditional gender stereotypes (e.g., nurse/she) than to stimuli containing nontraditional ones (e.g., nurse/he). This occurred even among participants who were explicitly opposed to gender stereotyping (Banaji & Hardin, 1996).

As we have seen, language, cognition, and culture are interrelated in a complex fashion, each contributing to how people communicate, think, and behave. However, as we noted at the beginning of this chapter, non-humans do communicate with one another. The nature of communication and cognition in non-human animals is a topic to which we will now turn.

LEARNING OBJECTIVE

- Summarize research evidence that supports the statement that "non-human animals have some humanlike cognitive capacities." Explain the following statement: "All animals communicate, but only humans use language to communicate."

NON-HUMAN LANGUAGE AND THOUGHT

Can scientists learn what is on an animal's mind?

The Question of Language

What kind of communication and language do other animals use?

The forms of animal communication vary widely. Honeybees enact an intricate waggle dance that tells their hive mates not only exactly where to find pollen, but also the quality of that pollen (Biesmeijer & Seeley, 2005). Humpback whales perform long, haunting

Professor Sue Savage-Rumbaugh and Kanzi. Savage-Rumbaugh continued Kanzi's naturalistic education through social interaction during walks outside. Kanzi now understands spoken English and more than 200 keyboard symbols. He responds to completely new vocal and keyboard requests and uses the keyboard to make requests, comment on his surroundings, state his intentions, and—sometimes—indicate what he is thinking about.

solos ranging from deep bass rumblings to high soprano squeaks. The technical term for such messages is **signs,** general or global statements about the animal's *current* state. But fixed, stereotyped signs don't constitute a language. The distinguishing features of language are *meaningfulness* (or semantics), *displacement* (talking or thinking about the past or the future), and *productivity* (the ability to produce and understand new and unique words and expressions). Using these criteria, as far as we know, no other species has its own language.

For more than two decades, however, Francine Patterson (Bonvillian & Patterson, 1997; F. G. Patterson, 1981) used American Sign Language with a lowland gorilla named Koko. By age 5, Koko had a working vocabulary of 500 signs—similar to a 5-year-old deaf child using sign language, though far lower than a hearing, speaking child's vocabulary of 1,000–5,000 words. In her mid-20s, Koko signed about her own and her companions' happy, sad, or angry emotions. Most interesting, Koko referred to the past and the future (displacement). Using signs *before* and *later, yesterday* and *tomorrow* appropriately, she mourned the death of her pet kitten and expressed a desire to become a mother.

Critics suggest that researchers such as Patterson may be reading meaning and intentions into simple gestures. To reduce the ambiguity of hand signs, other researchers have used computer keyboards to teach and record communications with apes (Rumbaugh, 1977; Rumbaugh & Savage-Rumbaugh, 1978); to document behavior with and without humans on camera; and also to study another ape species, bonobos. Most impressive—and surprising—was a bonobo named Kanzi (Savage-Rumbaugh & Lewin, 1994). Initially in the lab, Kanzi was adopted by an older female who lacked keyboard skills. Some months later, Kanzi, who had been accompanying his "mother" to lessons but who was not receiving formal training, was learning keyboard symbols and spoken English on his own—much as children do.

That non-human great apes can learn signs without intensive training or rewards from human trainers is clear. Whether they can grasp the deep structure of language is less clear. Moreover, at best, apes have reached the linguistic level of a 2- to 2-1/2-year-old child. Critics see this as evidence of severe limitations, whereas others view it as an extraordinary accomplishment.

Animal Cognition

Do some animals think like humans?

As we have seen, language is only one of the building blocks of thought. Without language, can non-humans nonetheless think? The question is particularly difficult to answer because psychologists have only recently developed techniques for learning how other

signs Stereotyped communications about an animal's current state.

👁—|**Watch** the **Video** Birds and Language
at **MyPsychLab**

animals use their brains and for identifying the similarities and differences between human and non-human thought. 👁

Numerous studies indicate that other animals have some humanlike cognitive capacities (Herrmann, Hernández-Lloreda, Call, Haer, & Tomasello, 2010; Kluger, 2010; Patton, 2008-2009; Tomasello & Herrmann, 2010).

Parrots, for example, are exceptionally good vocal mimics. But do parrots know what they are saying? According to Irene Pepperberg (2000, 2007), Alex, an African gray parrot, did. Alex could count to 6; identify more than 50 different objects; and classify objects according to color, shape, material, and relative size. Pepperberg contends that rather than demonstrating simple mimicry, the parrot's actions reflected reasoning, choice, and, to some extent, thinking.

Other researchers have taught dolphins to select which of two objects is identical to a sample object—the basis of the concepts *same* and *different* (Herman, Uyeyama, & Pack, 2008)—and to respond accurately to numerical concepts such as *more* and *less* (Jaakkola, Fellner, Erb, Rodriguez, & Guarino, 2005). What's more, rhesus and capuchin monkeys can learn the concept of *numeration,* or the capacity to use numbers, and *serialization,* or the ability to place objects in a specific order based on a concept (Terrace, Son, & Brannon, 2003; A. A. Wright & Katz, 2007). In short, humans are not unique in their ability to form concepts, one of the building blocks of thought.

But do chimps, dolphins and parrots know what they know? Do non-human animals have a *sense of self?* George Gallup (1985, 1998) noticed that after a few days' exposure, captive chimpanzees began making faces in front of a mirror and used it to examine and groom parts of their bodies they had never seen before. To test whether the animals understood that they were seeing themselves, Gallup anesthetized them and painted a bright red mark above the eyebrow ridge and on the top of one ear. The first time the chimps looked at the mirror after awakening, they reached up and touched the red marks, presumably recognizing themselves.

Since Gallup's initial study, hundreds of researchers have used the mirror test and more recently live video displays with many other animals. So far, only seven non-human species—chimpanzees, bonobos (formerly called "pygmy chimpanzees"), orangutans, dolphins, elephants, magpies, and less frequently, gorillas—have been shown to have self-awareness (Bard, Todd, Bernier, Love, & Leavens, 2006; Boysen & Himes, 1999; Gallup, 1985; Heschl & Burkart, 2006; Prior, Schwarz, & Güntürkün, 2008; Vauclair, 1996). For that matter, even human infants do not demonstrate mirror-recognition until 18 to 24 months of age.

If chimpanzees possess self-awareness, do they understand that others have information, thoughts, and emotions that may differ from their own? Observational studies suggest they do have at least a limited sense of other-awareness. One measure of other-awareness is *deception.* For example, if a chimpanzee discovers a hidden store of food and another chimpanzee happens along, the first may begin idly grooming himself. Presumably, the first chimpanzee recognizes that the second (a) is equally interested in food, and (b) will interpret the grooming behavior as meaning there is nothing interesting nearby. Both in the wild and in captive colonies, chimpanzees frequently practice deception in matters of food, receptive females, and power or dominance.

So far, we have been talking about *what* humans and non-humans think about. As we will see in the next section, cognitive psychologists are equally interested in *how* people use thinking to solve problems and make decisions.

CHECK YOUR UNDERSTANDING

1. Chimpanzees, orangutans, and bonobos are the only three non-human species to consistently show
   a. self-awareness.
   b. problem-solving ability.
   c. numeration comprehension.
2. Humans use language to communicate. What is the non-human animal equivalent of language?
   a. grunts   b. squeaks   c. signs

Answers: 1. a. 2. c.

APPLY YOUR UNDERSTANDING

1. When you visit the zoo, you notice a chimpanzee using a mirror to groom itself. This is a sign of:
   a. self-awareness
   b. numeration
   c. displacement

Answer: 1. a.

PROBLEM SOLVING

What are three general aspects of the problem-solving process?

Solve the following problems:

Problem 1 You have three measuring spoons. (See **Figure 7–2.**) One is filled with 8 teaspoons of salt; the other two are empty, but have a capacity of 2 teaspoons each. Divide the salt among the spoons so that only 4 teaspoons of salt remain in the largest spoon.

   Most people find this problem easy. Now try solving a more complex problem (the answers to all of the problems are at the end of this chapter).

Problem 2 You have three measuring spoons. (See **Figure 7–3.**) One (spoon A) is filled with 8 teaspoons of salt. The second and third spoons are both empty. The second spoon (spoon B) can hold 5 teaspoons, and the third (spoon C) can hold 3 teaspoons. Divide the salt among the spoons so that spoon A and spoon B each have exactly 4 teaspoons of salt and spoon C is empty.

   Most people find this problem much more difficult than the first one. Why? The answer lies in interpretation, strategy, and evaluation. Problem 1 is considered trivial because

LEARNING OBJECTIVES

- Explain why problem representation is an important first step in solving problems. In your explanation include divergent and convergent thinking, verbal, mathematical and visual representation, and problem categorization.
- Distinguish between trial and error, information retrieval, algorithms, and heuristics as ways of solving problems. Give an example of hill climbing, sub-goals, means-end analysis, and working backward. Explain how "mental sets" can help or hinder problem solving.

FIGURE 7–2
Figure for Problem 1

FIGURE 7–3
Figure for Problem 2

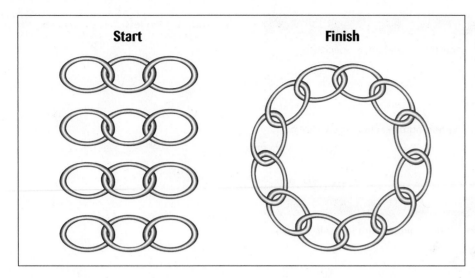

Start **Finish**

FIGURE 7–4
Figure for Problem 3

interpreting what is needed is easy, the strategies for solving it are simple, and the steps required to move closer to a solution can be verified effortlessly. Problem 2, by contrast, requires some thought to interpret what is needed; the strategies for solving it are not immediately apparent; and the steps required to see actual progress toward the goal are harder to evaluate. These three aspects of problem solving—interpretation, strategy, and evaluation—provide a useful framework for investigating this topic.

Interpreting Problems

Why is representing the problem so important to finding an effective solution?

The first step in solving a problem is called **problem representation,** which means interpreting or defining the problem. It is tempting to leap ahead and try to solve a problem just as it is presented, but this impulse often leads to poor solutions. For example, if your business is losing money, you might define the problem as deciphering how to cut costs. But by defining the problem so narrowly, you have ruled out other options. A better representation of this problem would be to figure out ways to boost profits—by cutting costs, by increasing income, or both. Problems that have no single correct solution and that require a flexible, inventive approach call for **divergent thinking**—or thinking that involves generating many different possible answers. In contrast, **convergent thinking** is thinking that narrows its focus in a particular direction, assuming that there is only one solution (or at most a limited number of right solutions).

To see the importance of problem representation, consider the next two problems.

Problem 3 You have four pieces of chain, each of which is made up of three links. (See **Figure 7–4**.) All links are closed at the beginning of the problem. It costs 2 cents to open a link and 3 cents to close a link. How can you join all 12 links together into a single, continuous circle without paying more than 15 cents?

Problem 3 is difficult because people assume that the best way to proceed is to open and close the end links on the pieces of chain. As long as they persist with this "conceptual block," they will be unable to solve the problem. If the problem is represented differently, the solution is obvious almost immediately (see Answer Key at the end of this chapter for solutions).

If you have successfully interpreted Problem 3, give Problem 4 a try.

Problem 4 A monk wishes to get to a retreat at the top of a mountain. He starts climbing the mountain at sunrise and arrives at the top at sunset of the same day. During the course of his ascent, he travels at various speeds and stops often to rest. He spends the night engaged in meditation. The next day, he starts his descent at sunrise, following the same narrow path that he used to climb the mountain. As before, he travels at various speeds and stops often to rest. Because he takes great care not to trip and fall on the way down, the descent takes as long as the ascent, and he does not arrive at the bottom until sunset. Prove that there is one place on the path that the monk passes at exactly the same time of day on the ascent and on the descent.

This problem is extremely difficult to solve if it is represented verbally or mathematically. It is considerably easier to solve if it is represented visually, as you can see from the explanation that appears at the end of this chapter. Interestingly, Albert Einstein relied heavily on his powers of visualization to understand phenomena that he would later describe by using complex mathematical formulas. This great thinker believed his extraordinary genius resulted in part from his skill in representing problems visually.

problem representation The first step in solving a problem; it involves interpreting or defining the problem.

divergent thinking Thinking that meets the criteria of originality, inventiveness, and flexibility.

convergent thinking Thinking that is directed toward one correct solution to a problem.

Another aspect of successfully representing a problem is deciding to which category the problem belongs. In fact, gaining expertise in any field consists primarily of increasing your ability to represent and categorize problems so that they can be solved quickly and effectively. Star chess players, for example, can readily categorize a game situation by comparing it with various standard situations stored in their long-term memories (Huffman, Matthews, & Gagne, 2001; A. J. Waters, Gobet, & Leyden, 2002). This strategy helps them interpret the current pattern of chess pieces with greater speed and precision than a novice chess player can. ✳

✳ **Explore** the **Concept** Intuition and Discovery in Problem Solving on **MyPsychLab**

Implementing Strategies and Evaluating Progress

Why are heuristics usually better for solving problems than is trial and error?

Once you have properly interpreted a problem, the next steps are to select a solution strategy and evaluate progress toward your goal. A solution strategy can be anything from simple trial and error, to information retrieval based on similar problems, to a set of step-by-step procedures guaranteed to work (called an algorithm), to rule-of-thumb approaches known as heuristics.

Trial and Error Trial and error is a strategy that works best when choices are limited. For example, if you have only three or four keys to choose from, trial and error is the best way to find out which one unlocks your friend's front door. In most cases, however, trial and error wastes time because there are many different options to test.

Information Retrieval One approach is to retrieve information from long-term memory about how such a problem was solved in the past. Information retrieval is an especially important option when a solution is needed quickly. For example, pilots simply memorize the slowest speed at which a particular airplane can fly before it stalls.

Algorithms Complex problems require complex strategies. An **algorithm** is a problem-solving method that guarantees a solution if it is appropriate for the problem and is properly carried out. For example, to calculate the product of 323 and 546, we multiply the numbers according to the rules of multiplication (the algorithm). If we do it accurately, we are guaranteed to get the right answer.

Heuristics Because we don't have algorithms for every kind of problem, we often turn to **heuristics,** or rules of thumb. Heuristics do not guarantee a solution, but they may bring it within reach.

A very simple heuristic is **hill climbing:** We try to move continually closer to our goal without going backward. At each step, we evaluate how far "up the hill" we have come, how far we still have to go, and precisely what the next step should be. On a multiple-choice test, for example, one useful hill-climbing strategy is first to eliminate the alternatives that are obviously incorrect.

Another problem-solving heuristic is to create **subgoals,** which involves breaking a problem into smaller, more manageable pieces that are easier to solve individually than the problem as a whole. Consider the problem of the Hobbits and the Orcs.

Problem 5 Three Hobbits and three Orcs are on the bank of a river. They all want to get to the other side, but their boat will carry only two creatures at a time. Moreover, if at any time the Orcs outnumber the Hobbits, the Orcs will attack the Hobbits. How can all the creatures get across the river without danger to the Hobbits?

You can find the solution to this problem by thinking of it in terms of a series of subgoals. What has to be done to get just one or two creatures across the river safely, temporarily leaving aside the main goal of getting everyone across? We could first send two

algorithm A step-by-step method of problem solving that guarantees a correct solution.

heuristics Rules of thumb that help in simplifying and solving problems, although they do not guarantee a correct solution.

hill climbing A heuristic, problem-solving strategy in which each step moves you progressively closer to the final goal.

subgoals Intermediate, more manageable goals used in one heuristic strategy to make it easier to reach the final goal.

of the Orcs across and have one of them return. That gets one Orc across the river. Now we can think about the next trip. It's clear that we can't then send a single Hobbit across with an Orc, because the Hobbit would be outnumbered as soon as the boat landed. Therefore, we have to send either two Hobbits or two Orcs. By working on the problem in this fashion—concentrating on subgoals—we can eventually get everyone across.

Once you have solved Problem 5, try Problem 6, which is considerably more difficult (the answers to both problems are at the end of the chapter).

Problem 6 This problem is identical to Problem 5, except that there are five Hobbits and five Orcs, and the boat can carry only three creatures at a time.

Subgoals are often helpful in solving a variety of everyday problems. For example, a student whose goal is to write a term paper might set subgoals by breaking the project into a series of separate tasks: choosing a topic, doing research, writing the first draft, editing, and so on. Even the subgoals can sometimes be broken down into separate tasks: Writing the first draft might break down into the subgoals of writing the introduction, describing the position to be taken, supporting the position with evidence, drawing conclusions, writing a summary, and writing a bibliography. Subgoals make problem solving more manageable because they free us from the burden of having to "get to the other side of the river" all at once.

One of the most frequently used heuristics, called **means-end analysis,** combines hill climbing and subgoals. Like hill climbing, means-end analysis involves analyzing the difference between the current situation and the desired end, and then doing something to reduce that difference. But in contrast to hill climbing—which does not permit detours away from the final goal in order to solve the problem—means-end analysis takes into account the entire problem situation. It formulates subgoals in such a way as to allow us temporarily to take a step that appears to be backward in order to reach our goal in the end. One example is the pitcher's strategy in a baseball game when confronted with the best batter in the league. The pitcher might opt to walk this batter intentionally even though doing so moves away from the major subgoal of keeping runners off base. Intentional walking might enable the pitcher to keep a run from scoring and so contribute to the ultimate goal of winning the game. This flexibility in thinking is a major benefit of means-end analysis.

But means-end analysis also poses the danger of straying so far from the end goal that the goal disappears altogether. One way of avoiding this situation is to use the heuristic of **working backward.** With this strategy, the search for a solution begins at the goal and works backward toward the "givens." Working backward is often used when the goal has more information than the givens and when the operations involved can work in two directions. For example, if you wanted to spend exactly $100 on clothing, it would be difficult to reach that goal simply by buying some items and hoping that they totaled exactly $100. A better strategy would be to buy one item, subtract its cost from $100 to determine how much money you have left, then purchase another item, subtract its cost, and so on, until you have spent $100.

Obstacles to Solving Problems

How can a "mental set" both help and hinder problem solving?

Many factors can either help or hinder problem solving. One factor is a person's level of motivation, or emotional arousal. Generally, we must generate a certain surge of excitement to motivate ourselves to solve a problem, yet too much arousal can hamper our ability to find a solution. (See Chapter 8, "Motivation and Emotion.")

Another factor that can either help or hinder problem solving is **mental set**—our tendency to perceive and to approach problems in certain ways. A mental set can be helpful if we have learned operations that can legitimately be applied to the present situation. In fact, much of our formal education involves learning useful mental sets. But sets can also create obstacles, especially when a novel approach is needed. The most successful problem solvers can choose from many different mental sets and can also judge when to change sets or when to abandon them entirely.

means-end analysis A heuristic strategy that aims to reduce the discrepancy between the current situation and the desired goal at a number of intermediate points.

working backward A heuristic strategy in which one works backward from the desired goal to the given conditions.

mental set The tendency to perceive and to approach problems in certain ways.

APPLYING   PSYCHOLOGY

Becoming a More Skillful Problem Solver

Even the best problem solvers occasionally get stumped, but you can do some things that will help you find a solution. These tactics encourage you to discard unproductive approaches and find strategies that are more effective.

1. **Eliminate poor choices.** When we are surer of what won't work than what will, the *tactic of elimination* can be very helpful. After listing all the possible solutions you can think of, discard all the solutions that seem to lead in the wrong direction. Now, examine the list more closely. Some solutions that seem to be ineffective may turn out to be good on closer examination.

2. **Visualize a solution.** If you are stumped by a problem, try using visual images. For example, in the Hobbit and Orc problems draw a picture of the river, and show the Hobbits and Orcs at each stage of the solution as they are ferried across. Drawing a diagram might help you grasp what a problem calls for, but you also can visualize mentally.

3. **Develop expertise.** We get stumped on problems because we lack the knowledge to find a quick solution. Experts not only know more about a particular subject but also organize their information in larger "chunks" that are extensively interconnected, much like a cross-referencing system in a library.

4. **Think flexibly.** Striving to be more flexible and creative is an excellent tactic for becoming a better problem solver. This will help you avoid *functional fixedness* or prevent a *mental set* from standing in the way of solving a problem.

One type of mental set that can seriously hinder problem solving is called **functional fixedness.** Consider **Figure 7–5.** Do you see a way to mount the candle on the wall? If not, you are probably stymied by functional fixedness. (The solution to this problem appears at the end of the chapter.) The more you use an object in only one way, the harder it is to see new uses for it and to realize that an object can be used for an entirely different purpose. See "Applying Psychology: Becoming a More Skillful Problem

functional fixedness The tendency to perceive only a limited number of uses for an object, thus interfering with the process of problem solving.

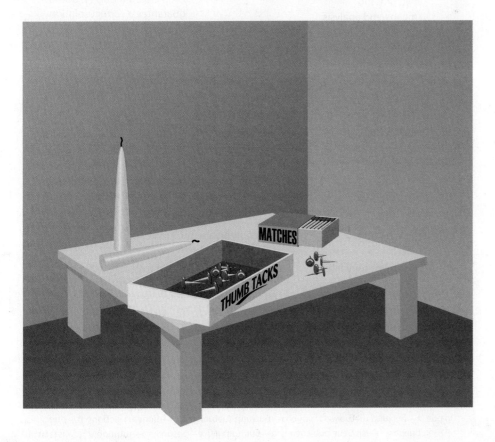

FIGURE 7–5
To test the effects of functional fixedness, participants might be given the items shown on the table and asked to mount a candle on the wall. See **Figure 7–12** for a solution.

THINKING CRITICALLY ABOUT . . .

Solving Problems

Think for a moment of the last time you were confronted with a difficult problem.

1. What types of thinking or reasoning did you use to deal with that problem?

2. Having read this portion of the chapter, would you respond differently if you were faced with a similar problem? If so, what would you do differently?

3. You are headed for Mount Rushmore, and you can see it from a distance. You have no map. What is the best problem-solving strategy you can use to get there, and why?

brainstorming A problem-solving strategy in which an individual or a group produces numerous ideas and evaluates them only after all ideas have been collected.

Solver," for techniques that will improve your problem-solving skills.

Because creative problem solving requires generating original ideas, deliberate strategies don't always help. Solutions to many problems rely on insight, often a seemingly arbitrary flash "out of the blue." (See Chapter 5, "Learning.") Psychologists have only recently begun to investigate such spontaneous problem-solving processes as insight and intuition, but research indicates that such "mental breakthroughs" are likely to occur only when we widen our scope of attention from a few obvious but incorrect alternatives to more diverse possible solutions (B. Bower, 2008). This conclusion is supported by neuroimaging, which reveals that insight is generally preceded by periods of increased electrical activity in the frontal regions of the brain involved in *suppressing* unwanted thoughts (Kounios et al., 2008; Qiu, Li, Jou, Wu, & Zhang, 2008).

The value of looking for new ways to represent a difficult problem cannot be over-stressed. Be open to potential solutions that at first seem unproductive. The solution may turn out to be more effective, or it may suggest related solutions that will work. This is the rationale behind the technique called **brainstorming:** When solving a problem, generate a lot of ideas before you review and evaluate them.

✔●─Study and Review on MyPsychLab

CHECK YOUR UNDERSTANDING

1. Match each problem-solving strategy with the appropriate definition.

___ algorithm
___ heuristic
___ hill climbing
___ means-end analysis
___ working backward
___ subgoal creation

   a. rule-of-thumb approach that helps in simplifying and solving problems, although it doesn't guarantee a correct solution

   b. strategy in which each step moves you closer to a solution

   c. step-by-step method that guarantees a solution

   d. strategy in which one moves from the goal to the starting point

   e. strategy that aims to reduce the discrepancy between the current situation and the desired goal at a number of intermediate points

   f. breaking down the solution to a larger problem into a set of smaller, more manageable steps

2. Match each form of thinking with its definition and the kind of problems to which it is suited.

   ___ divergent thinking
   ___ convergent thinking

   a. suited to problems for which there is one correct solution or a limited number of solutions

   b. thinking that involves generating many different ideas

   c. suited to problems that have no one right solution and require an inventive approach

   d. thinking that limits its focus to a particular direction

Answers: 1. Algorithm—c, heuristic—a, hill climbing—b, means-end analysis—e, working backward—d, subgoal creation—f. **2.** divergent thinking—b, and c. convergent thinking—a, and d.

1. Your car is not operating correctly. The mechanic opens the hood and says, "We've been seeing lots of cars recently with fouled plugs or dirty fuel filters. Let's start there and see if that's your problem, too." The mechanic is using a(n)

   a. heuristic.
   b. algorithm.
   c. compensatory decision model.
   d. noncompensatory decision model.

2. You are at a football game when it begins to rain heavily. As you get soaked, you see the people next to you pull folded plastic trash bags out of their pockets to use as a temporary "raincoat." Your failure to realize that the trash bag might also be used as rain protection is an example of

   a. an algorithm.
   b. a heuristic.
   c. means-end analysis.
   d. functional fixedness.

Answers: 1. a. 2. d.

DECISION MAKING

How does decision making differ from problem solving?

Decision making is a special kind of problem solving in which we already know all the possible solutions or choices. The task is not to come up with new solutions, but rather to identify the best available one. This process might sound fairly simple, but sometimes we have to juggle a large and complex set of criteria as well as many possible options. For example, suppose that you are looking for an apartment among hundreds available. A reasonable rent is important to you, but so are good neighbors, a good location, a low noise level, and cleanliness. If you find an inexpensive, noisy apartment with undesirable neighbors, should you take it? Is it a better choice than a more expensive, less noisy apartment in a better location? How can you make the best choice?

- Explain how decision making differs from problem solving. Describe the process of compensatory decision making and the use of decision-making heuristics. Explain how framing can affect decisions, and how hindsight bias and counterfactual thinking affect the way we view our decisions after the fact.

Compensatory Decision Making

How would you go about making a truly logical decision?

The logical way to make a decision is to rate each of the available choices on all the criteria you are using, arriving at some overall measure of the extent to which each choice matches your criteria. For each choice, the attractive features can offset or compensate for the unattractive features. This approach to decision making is therefore called a **compensatory model.**

Table 7–1 illustrates one of the most useful compensatory models applied to a car-buying decision. The buyer's three criteria are weighted in terms of importance: price (not weighted heavily), gas mileage, and service record (both weighted more heavily). Next, each car is rated from 1 (poor) to 5 (excellent) on each of the criteria. Car 1 has an excellent price (5) but relatively poor gas mileage (2) and service record (1); and Car 2 has a less desirable price but fairly good mileage and service record. Each rating is then multiplied by the weight for that criterion (e.g., for Car 1, the price rating of 5 is multiplied by the

TABLE 7–1   Compensatory Decision Table for Purchase of a New Car

	Price (weight = 4)	Gas mileage (weight = 8)	Service record (weight = 10)	Weighted Total
Car 1	5 (20)	2 (16)	1 (10)	(46)
Car 2	1 (4)	4 (32)	4 (40)	(76)

Ratings: 5 = excellent; 1 = poor

compensatory model A rational decision-making model in which choices are systematically evaluated on various criteria.

weight of 4, and the result is put in parentheses next to the rating). Finally, the ratings in parentheses are totaled for each car. Clearly, Car 2 is the better choice: It is more expensive, but that disadvantage is offset by its better mileage and service record and these two criteria are more important than price to this particular buyer.

Although most people would agree that using such a table is a good way to decide which car to buy, at times people will abandon the compensatory decision-making process in the face of more vivid anecdotal information. For example, if a friend had previously bought Car 2 and found it to be a lemon, many people will choose Car 1 despite Car 2's well-thought out advantages. Moreover, as we will see in the next section, it is often not possible or desirable to rate every choice on all criteria. In such situations people typically use heuristics that have worked well in the past to simplify decision making, even though they may lead to less-than-optimal decision making.

Decision-Making Heuristics

How can heuristic approaches lead us to make bad decisions?

Research has identified a number of common heuristics that people use to make decisions. We use the **representativeness** heuristic whenever we make a decision on the basis of certain information that matches our model of the typical member of a category. For example, if every time you went shopping you bought the least expensive items and if all of these items turned out to be poorly made, you might eventually decide not to buy anything that seems typical of the category "very cheap."

Another common heuristic is **availability.** In the absence of full and accurate information, we often base decisions on whatever information is most readily available, even though this information may not be accurate or complete. A familiar example of the availability heuristic is the so-called *subway effect*. It seems to be a law of nature that if you are waiting at a subway station, one train after another will come along headed in the opposite direction from the direction that you want to go. The problem here is that by the time a subway train does come along, we have already left the scene, so we never get to see the opposite situation: several subway trains going in our direction before one comes the other way. As a result, we tend to assume that those situations seldom or never occur, and so we make our decisions accordingly.

Yet another heuristic, closely related to availability, is **confirmation bias**—the tendency to notice and remember evidence that supports our beliefs and to ignore evidence that contradicts them. For example, individuals who believe that AIDS is something that happens to "other people" (homosexual men and intravenous drug users, not middle-class heterosexuals) are more likely to remember articles about rates of HIV infection in these groups or in third-world countries than articles about AIDS cases among people like themselves (Fischhoff & Downs, 1997). Convinced that HIV is not something that they personally need to worry about, they ignore evidence to the contrary.

A related phenomenon is our tendency to see *connections or patterns of cause and effect* where none exist. For example, many parents strongly believe that sugar can cause hyperactivity in children and that arthritis pain is related to weather—despite research evidence to the contrary. The list of commonsense beliefs that persist in the face of contrary evidence is long (Redelmeier & Tversky, 2004).

Framing

Does the way information is presented affect decisions?

Numerous studies have shown that subtle changes in the way information is presented can dramatically affect the final decision. A classic study (McNeil, Pauker, Sox, & Tversky, 1982) illustrates how **framing** can influence a medical decision. In this study, experimental participants were asked to choose between surgery and radiation therapy to treat lung cancer. However, the framing of the information they were provided was manipulated. In the *survival frame*, participants were given the statistical outcomes of both procedures in the form of survival statistics, thus emphasizing the 1- and 5-year survival rates after

representativeness A heuristic by which a new situation is judged on the basis of its resemblance to a stereotypical model.

availability A heuristic by which a judgment or decision is based on information that is most easily retrieved from memory.

confirmation bias The tendency to look for evidence in support of a belief and to ignore evidence that would disprove a belief.

framing The perspective from which we interpret information before making a decision.

treatment. In the *mortality frame,* the participants were given the same information, presented (or framed) according to death rates after 1 year and after 5 years. Although the actual number of deaths and survivors associated with each procedure was identical in both the survival and mortality frames, the percentage of participants who chose one procedure over another varied dramatically *depending on how the information was framed.* Probably most surprising was that this framing effect was found even when 424 experienced radiologists served as the research participants!

Explaining Our Decisions

How do we explain to ourselves the decisions we make?

Hindsight Whether a choice is exceptionally good, extraordinarily foolish, or somewhere in between, most people think about their decisions after the fact. The term **hindsight bias** refers to the tendency to view outcomes as inevitable and predictable after we know the outcome, and to believe that we could have predicted what happened, or perhaps that we did. For example, physicians remember being more confident about their diagnoses when they learn that they were correct than they were at the time of the actual diagnoses.

"If Only" At times, everyone imagines alternatives to reality and mentally plays out the consequences. Psychologists refer to such thoughts about things that never happened as **counterfactual thinking**—in which thoughts are counter to the facts. Counterfactual thinking often takes the form of "If only" constructions, in which we mentally revise the events or actions that led to a particular outcome: "If only I had studied harder"; "If only I had said no"; "If only I had driven straight home." It is tempting to think that such imaginary, after-the-fact thinking, is of no value. However, research shows that under some circumstances counterfactual thinking can play a constructive role helping one to regulate behavior, learn from mistakes, and improve future performance (Epstude & Roese, 2008).

MULTITASKING

With the advent of the digital age, multitasking has become a way of life. We listen to iPods while jogging, program our TiVo while watching a movie, e-mail and surf the Web simultaneously, and follow the directions of a GPS while driving and talking to a passenger in a car. Fortunately, our brains appear reasonably well equipped for at least some multitasking. The prefrontal cortex (Figure 2–8), which as we saw in Chapter 2 ("The Biological Basis of Behavior") governs goal-directed behavior and suppresses impulses, also enables us to mentally toggle between separate tasks with relative ease (Jäncke, Brunner, & Esslen, 2008; Modirrousta & Fellows, 2008).

Is multitasking really efficient? Research indicates that if the tasks are dissimilar and the person is an experienced multitasker and is intelligent, multitasking can be effective up to a point. But in general, research has shown that multitasking often slows down thinking, decreases accuracy, and in some cases increases stress (Bühner, König, Pick, & Krumm, 2006; Clay, 2009; Kinney, 2008; Mark, Gudith & Klocke, 2008; J. S. Rubinstein, Meyer, & Evans, 2001). Moreover, despite a commonly held belief that young people are more adept at multitasking than older adults, research that compared 18- to 21-year-olds to 35- to 39-year-olds found the negative effects of multitasking were generally more pronounced in the younger group (Westwell, 2007).

Perhaps nowhere is the impact of multitasking more important than when driving a car (Strayer & Drews, 2007). For example, while talking on a "hands-free" cell phone, braking time is slowed and attention to events in the peripheral visual field is reduced. Even when the participants in one study were specifically instructed to give more attention to driving than the extraneous task, or were well practiced at multitasking, driving performance was adversely affected by multitasking (J. Levy & Pashler, 2008; J. Levy, Pashler, & Boer, 2006).

Texting while driving is even worse. One British study using 17- to 24-year-old participants found that texting while driving reduced braking time by 35%, which was much worse than the effect of alcohol or marijuana. Steering control while texting was reduced

hindsight bias The tendency to see outcomes as inevitable and predictable after we know the outcome.

counterfactual thinking Thinking about alternative realities and things that never happened.

91%, compared to a 35% reduction under the influence of marijuana (RAC Foundation, 2008). Research such as this has prompted Professor David Meyer, a noted researcher in the area of multitasking, to conclude that "If you're driving while cell-phoning, then your performance is going to be as poor as if you were legally drunk" (Hamilton, 2008).

✓• Study and Review on MyPsychLab

CHECK YOUR UNDERSTANDING

1. Match each decision-making heuristic with the appropriate definition.

____ representativeness heuristic
____ availability heuristic
____ confirmation bias

a. making judgments on the basis of whatever information can be most readily retrieved from memory

b. attending to evidence that supports your existing beliefs and ignoring other evidence

c. making decisions on the basis of information that matches your model of what is "typical" of a certain category

2. The way a question is framed usually will not affect its answer. Is this statement true (T) or false (F)?

3. Julio's girlfriend gets a speeding ticket, and he blames himself, saying, "If only I hadn't let her borrow my car." His thinking is an example of _____.

4. "Young people are better than older people at multitasking." Is this statement true (T) or false (F)?

Answers: 1. representativeness heuristic—c. availability heuristic—a. confirmation bias—b. 2. (F) 3. hindsight bias. 4. (F)

APPLY YOUR UNDERSTANDING

1. In deciding where to go on vacation, you decide you want a place where you can relax, a place that is warm, and a place that you can reach inexpensively. But you will not consider any place that is more than 1,000 miles away. What kind of decision-making model are you using?

a. visualization
b. brainstorming
c. noncompensatory
d. compensatory

2. You are driving down the highway at the posted speed limit. After a while you mention to your passenger, "It sure looks like everyone is either going slower or faster than the speed limit. Hardly anyone seems to be going the same speed as I am." In fact, most of the cars on the highway are also traveling at the speed limit. Your erroneous conclusion is most likely due to

a. framing.
b. hindsight bias.
c. mental set.
d. the availability heuristic.

Answers: 1. c. 2. d.

LEARNING OBJECTIVES

- Compare and contrast the theories of intelligence put forth by Spearman, Thurstone, Sternberg, Gardner, and Goleman.
- Describe the similarities and differences between the Stanford-Binet Intelligence Scale and the Wechsler Intelligence Scales, and explain how they differ from group tests, performance tests, and culture-fair tests of intelligence. Explain what is meant by test "reliability" and "validity" and how psychologists determine whether an intelligence test is reliable or valid.
- Summarize the criticisms of intelligence tests and the relationship between IQ test scores and job success.

⟩ INTELLIGENCE AND MENTAL ABILITIES

What types of questions are used to measure intelligence?

In many societies, one of the nicest things you can say is "You're smart"; and one of the most insulting is "You're stupid." Intelligence is so basic to our view of human nature that any characterization of a person that neglects to mention that person's intelligence is likely to be considered incomplete. Although psychologists have studied intelligence almost since psychology emerged as a science, they still struggle to understand this complex and elusive concept. In the next few sections, you may come to appreciate the difficulty of their task. Toward that end, we begin by asking you some questions intended to measure intelligence:

1. Describe the difference between *laziness* and *idleness*.
2. Which direction would you have to face so that your right ear would be facing north?
3. What does *obliterate* mean?
4. In what way are an hour and a week alike?
5. Choose the lettered block that best completes the pattern in the following figure.

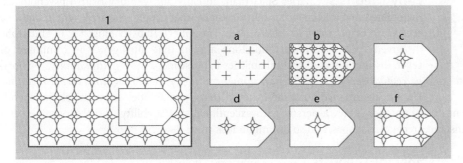

6. If three pencils cost 25 cents, how many pencils can you buy for 75 cents?
7. Select the lettered pair that best expresses a relationship similar to that expressed in the original pair:
   Crutch: Locomotion::

   a. paddle: canoe
   b. hero: worship
   c. horse: carriage
   d. spectacles: vision
   e. statement: contention

8. Decide how the first two items in the following figure are related to each other. Then find the one item at the right that goes with the third item in the same way that the second item goes with the first.

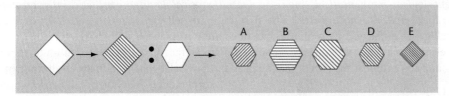

9. For each item in the following figure, decide whether it can be completely covered by using some or all of the given pieces without overlapping any.

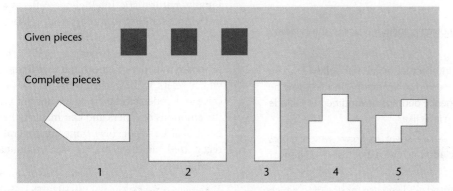

These questions were taken from various tests of **intelligence,** or general mental ability. (The answers appear at the end of the chapter.) We will discuss intelligence tests later in this chapter. But first, let's consider some historical and contemporary theories of intelligence.

intelligence A general term referring to the ability or abilities involved in learning and adaptive behavior.

This dancer possesses an abundance of what Howard Gardner calls bodily-kinesthetic intelligence.

Theories of Intelligence

What are some of the major theories of intelligence?

For more than a century, one of the most basic questions addressed by psychologists has been whether intelligence is a single, general mental ability or whether it is composed of many separate abilities.

Early Theorists Charles Spearman, an early 20th-century British psychologist, maintained that intelligence is quite general—that people who are bright in one area are usually bright in other areas as well. The American psychologist L. L. Thurstone disagreed with Spearman. Thurstone argued that intelligence is composed of seven distinct kinds of mental abilities (Thurstone, 1938): *spatial ability, memory, perceptual speed, word fluency, numerical ability, reasoning, and verbal meaning.* Unlike Spearman, Thurstone believed that these abilities are relatively independent of one another. Thus, a person with exceptional spatial ability (the ability to perceive distance, recognize shapes, and so on) might lack word fluency.

triarchic theory of intelligence Sternberg's theory that intelligence involves mental skills (analytical intelligence), insight and creative adaptability (creative intelligence), and environmental responsiveness (practical intelligence).

theory of multiple intelligences Howard Gardner's theory that there is not one intelligence, but rather many intelligences, each of which is relatively independent of the others.

emotional intelligence According to Goleman, a form of intelligence that refers to how effectively people perceive and understand their own emotions and the emotions of others, and can regulate and manage their emotional behavior.

Contemporary Theorists Contemporary psychologists have considerably broadened the concept of intelligence and how it can best be measured. For example, Robert Sternberg (2009) has proposed a **triarchic theory of intelligence.** Sternberg argues that human intelligence encompasses a much broader array of abilities than the limited skills assessed by traditional intelligence tests. *Analytical intelligence,* the aspect of intelligence assessed by most intelligence tests, refers to the ability to learn how to do things, acquire new knowledge, solve problems, and carry out tasks effectively. *Creative intelligence* is the ability to adjust to new tasks, use new concepts, respond effectively in new situations, gain insight, and adapt creatively. *Practical intelligence* is the ability to find solutions to practical and personal problems.

Another contemporary theory of intelligence is the **theory of multiple intelligences** advanced by Howard Gardner and his associates at Harvard (J.-Q. Chen, Moran, & Gardner, 2009). Gardner, like Thurstone, believes that intelligence is made up of several distinct abilities, each of which is relatively independent of the others. Precisely how many separate abilities might exist is difficult to determine, but Gardner lists eight: *logical–mathematical, linguistic, spatial, musical, bodily-kinesthetic, interpersonal, intrapersonal, and naturalistic.* The first four are self-explanatory. Bodily-kinesthetic intelligence is the ability to manipulate one's body in space; a skilled athlete shows high levels of this kind of intelligence. People who are extraordinarily talented at understanding and communicating with others, such as exceptional teachers and parents, have strong interpersonal intelligence. People who understand themselves and who use this knowledge effectively to attain their goals rank high in intrapersonal intelligence. Finally, naturalistic intelligence reflects an individual's ability to understand, relate to, and interact with the world of nature.

Finally, Daniel Goleman (1997) has proposed a theory of **emotional intelligence,** which refers to how effectively people perceive and understand their own emotions and the emotions of others and can manage their emotional behavior. Five traits are generally recognized as contributing to emotional intelligence.

- *Knowing one's own emotions.* The ability to monitor and recognize our own feelings. This is of central importance to self-awareness and all other dimensions of emotional intelligence.

THINKING CRITICALLY ABOUT . . .

Multiple Intelligences

Gardner's theory clearly includes abilities not normally included under the heading of intelligence.

1. We earlier defined intelligence as general intellectual or mental ability. Do you agree that all of Gardner's facets of intelligence fit that definition? Should some be excluded? Or should the definition of intelligence perhaps be modified to include them? What might such a modified definition look like?

2. Some people have excellent "color sense"—they seem to know which colors go well together. Should this ability be included as one aspect of intelligence? What about rhyming ability?

3. In answering the first two questions, what criteria did you use for deciding which abilities to include as aspects of intelligence and which to exclude? Do other people share your viewpoint, or do their criteria differ? How might you go about deciding which viewpoints have most merit?

SUMMARY TABLE	COMPARING GARDNER'S, STERNBERG'S, AND GOLEMAN'S THEORIES OF INTELLIGENCE	
Gardner's multiple intelligences	Sternberg's triarchic intelligence	Goleman's emotional intelligence
Logical–mathematical	Analytical	
Linguistic		
Spatial	Creative	
Musical		
Bodily-kinesthetic		
Interpersonal	Practical	Recognizing emotions in others and managing relationships
Intrapersonal		Knowing yourself and motivating yourself with emotions
Naturalistic		

- *Managing one's emotions.* The ability to control impulses, to cope effectively with sadness, depression, and minor setbacks, as well as to control how long emotions last.
- *Using emotions to motivate oneself.* The capacity to marshal emotions toward achieving personal goals.
- *Recognizing the emotions of other people.* The ability to read subtle, nonverbal cues that reveal what other people really want and need.
- *Managing relationships.* The ability to accurately acknowledge and display one's own emotions, as well as being sensitive to the emotions of others.

The "**Summary Table**" reviews the contemporary theories described here. These theories shape the content of intelligence tests and other measures that evaluate the abilities of millions of people. We consider these next.

Intelligence Tests

What kinds of intelligence tests are in use today?

The Stanford–Binet Intelligence Scale   The first test developed to measure intelligence was designed by two Frenchmen, Alfred Binet and Théodore Simon. The test, first used in Paris in 1905, was designed to identify children who might have difficulty in school. ◉

The first *Binet–Simon Scale* consisted of 30 tests arranged in order of increasing difficulty. With each child, the examiner started with the easiest tests and worked down the list until the child could no longer answer questions. A well-known adaptation of the Binet–Simon Scale, the *Stanford–Binet Intelligence Scale,* was prepared at Stanford University by L. M. Terman, first published in 1916 and updated repeatedly since then. The current Stanford–Binet Intelligence Scale is designed to measure four virtually universal abilities related to traditional views of intelligence: *verbal reasoning, abstract/visual reasoning, quantitative reasoning,* and *short-term memory.* The Stanford–Binet is best suited for children, adolescents, and very young adults. Questions 1 and 2 on page 235 were drawn from an early version of the Stanford–Binet.

Terman also introduced the now famous term **intelligence quotient (IQ)** to establish a numerical value of intelligence, setting the score of 100 for a person of average intelligence. **Figure 7–6** shows an approximate distribution of IQ scores in the population.

The Wechsler Intelligence Scales   The most commonly used individual test of intelligence for adults is the **Wechsler Adult Intelligence Scale—Fourth Edition (WAIS-IV)**, originally developed in the late 1930s by psychologist David Wechsler. The Stanford–Binet emphasizes verbal skills, but Wechsler believed adult intelligence consists more of the ability to handle life situations than to solve verbal and abstract problems.

Watch the **Video** Intelligence Testing, Then and Now on **MyPsychLab**

intelligence quotient (IQ) A numerical value given to intelligence that is determined from the scores on an intelligence test on the basis of a score of 100 for average intelligence.

Wechsler Adult Intelligence Scale—Fourth Edition (WAIS-IV) An individual intelligence test developed especially for adults.

FIGURE 7-6
The approximate distribution of IQ scores in the population.
Note that the greatest percentage of scores fall around 100. Very low percentages of people score at the two extremes of the curve.

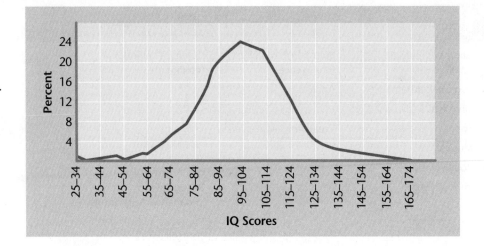

Wechsler Intelligence Scale for Children—Fourth Edition (WISC-IV) An individual intelligence test developed especially for school-age children.

group tests Written intelligence tests administered by one examiner to many people at one time.

performance tests Intelligence tests that minimize the use of language.

culture-fair tests Intelligence tests designed to eliminate cultural bias by minimizing skills and values that vary from one culture to another.

The Wechsler Intelligence Scales, developed by David Wechsler, are individual intelligence tests administered to one person at a time. There are versions of the Wechsler Scales for both adults and children. Here, a child is being asked to copy a pattern using blocks.

The WAIS-IV assesses verbal comprehension, perceptual reasoning, working memory, and processing speed. Scores on all four of those indices can be combined to give a *Full-Scale IQ*. Scores on just the first two indices can be combined to give a *General Ability Index*. Questions 3, 4, and 9 on page 235 resemble questions on the WAIS-IV. Wechsler also developed a similar intelligence test for use with school-age children. Like the WAIS-IV, the **Wechsler Intelligence Scale for Children–Fourth Edition (WISC-IV)** yields a Full-Scale IQ score as well as scores for verbal comprehension, perceptual reasoning, working memory and processing speed.

Group Tests With the Stanford–Binet, the WAIS-IV, and the WISC-IV, an examiner takes a single person to an isolated room, spreads the materials on a table, and spends from 60 to 90 minutes administering the test. The examiner may then take another hour or so to score the test according to detailed instructions in a manual. This is a time-consuming, costly operation. Moreover, under some circumstances the examiner's behavior can influence the score. For these reasons, test makers have devised **group tests,** which a single examiner can administer to many people at once. Instead of sitting across the table from a person who asks you questions, you receive a test booklet that contains questions for you to answer in writing within a certain amount of time.

Group tests have some distinct advantages over individualized tests. They eliminate bias on the part of the examiner, answer sheets can be scored quickly and objectively, and it is possible to collect data from large numbers of test takers. But group tests also have some distinct disadvantages. The examiner is less likely to notice whether a person is tired, ill, or confused by the directions. People who are not used to being tested tend to do less well on group tests than on individual tests. Questions 5 through 9 on page 235 are drawn from group tests.

Performance and Culture-Fair Tests To perform well on the intelligence tests that we have discussed, people must be proficient in the language in which the test is given. How, then, can we test non-native English speakers in English-speaking countries? Psychologists have designed two general forms of tests for such situations: performance tests and culture-fair tests.

Performance tests consist of problems that minimize or eliminate the use of words. One of the earliest performance tests, the *Seguin Form Board,* is essentially a puzzle. The examiner removes specifically designed cutouts, stacks them in a predetermined order, and asks the person to replace them as quickly as possible. A more recent performance test, the *Porteus Maze,* consists of a series of increasingly difficult printed mazes. People trace their way through the maze without lifting the pencil from the paper. Such tests require the test taker to pay close attention to a task for an extended period and continuously to plan ahead in order to make the correct choices.

Culture-fair tests, like performance tests, minimize or eliminate the use of language. But they also try to downplay skills and values—such as the need for speed—that vary from culture to culture. In the *Goodenough–Harris Drawing Test,* for example, people are asked to draw the best picture of a person that they can. Drawings are scored for proportions, correct and complete representation of the parts of the body, detail in clothing, and so on. An example of a culture-fair item from the *Progressive Matrices* is Question 5 on page 235 This test consists of 60 designs, each with a missing part. The person is given six to eight possible choices to replace the part.

Biological Measures of Intelligence Thus far we have considered psychological measures of intelligence. However, numerous efforts have been made to assess intelligence using biological measures (Deary, Penke, & Johnson, 2010; Tang et al., 2010). Beginning early in the 20th century, psychologists attempted to correlate brain size with intelligence. The correlations were very weak but always positive, suggesting a slight relation between the two. More recently, investigators have compared the sizes and metabolic functioning of such brain structures as the cerebellum and hippocampus, revealing small but significant differences among the brains of people with different forms of mental retardation (Lawrence, Lott, & Haier, 2005). Other researchers have found modest relationships between intelligence and the electrical response of brain cells to stimulation (Stelmack, Knott, & Beauchamp, 2003).

To date, no known biological measure of intelligence approaches the accuracy of psychological tests, but findings such as these suggest that measures of intelligence may someday involve a biological component.

What Makes a Good Test?

What are some important characteristics of a good test?

How can we tell whether intelligence tests will produce consistent results no matter when they are given? And how can we tell whether they really measure what they claim to measure? Psychologists address these questions by referring to a test's *reliability* and *validity*. Issues of reliability and validity apply equally to all psychological tests, not just to tests of mental abilities. In Chapter 10, for example, we reexamine these issues as they apply to personality assessment.

Reliability By **reliability,** psychologists mean the dependability and consistency of the scores that a test yields. How do we know whether a test is reliable? The simplest way to find out is to give the test to a group and then, after a while, give the same people the same test again. If they obtain similar scores each time, the test is said to have high *test-retest reliability*. For example, **Table 7–2** shows the IQ scores of eight people tested 1 year apart using the same test. Although the scores did change slightly, none changed by more than six points.

But there's a problem. How do we know that people have not simply remembered the answers from the first testing and repeated them the second time around? To avoid this possibility, psychologists prefer to give two equivalent tests, both designed to measure the same thing. If people score the same on both forms, the tests are considered reliable. One way to create alternate forms is to split a single test into two parts—for example, to assign odd-numbered items to one part and even-numbered items to the other. If scores on the two halves agree, the test has **split-half reliability.**

TABLE 7–2   IQ Scores on the Same Test Given 1 Year Apart

Person	First Testing	Second Testing
A	130	127
B	123	127
C	121	119
D	116	122
E	109	108
F	107	112
G	95	93
H	89	94

reliability Ability of a test to produce consistent and stable scores.

split-half reliability A method of determining test reliability by dividing the test into two parts and checking the agreement of scores on both parts.

ENDURING ISSUES

Stability–Change   Test Reliability and Changes in Intelligence

If a person takes an intelligence test on Monday and obtains an IQ score of 90, and then retakes the test on Tuesday and scores 130, clearly something is amiss. But what? People vary from moment to moment and day to day. Changes in health and motivation can affect test results even with the most reliable tests. And although IQ scores tend to be remarkably stable after the age of 5 or 6, intellectual ability does sometimes change dramatically—for better or worse. One person's mental ability may decline substantially after a mild head injury; another person's scores on intelligence tests may rise after years of diligent study.

Since scores on even the best tests vary somewhat from one day to the next, many testing services now report a person's score along with a range of scores that allows for variations. For example, a score of 110 might be reported with a range of 104–116. This implies that the true score is most likely within a few points of 110, but almost certainly does not fall lower than 104 or higher than 116. ∎

These methods of testing reliability can be very effective. But psychological science demands more precise descriptions than "very reliable" or "fairly reliable." Psychologists express reliability in terms of **correlation coefficients,** which measure the relation between two sets of scores (see Appendix A for a discussion of correlation coefficients). If test scores on one occasion are absolutely consistent with those on another occasion, the correlation coefficient is 1.0. If there is no relationship between the scores, the correlation coefficient is zero. In Table 7–2, where there is a very close, but not perfect, relationship between the two sets of scores, the correlation coefficient is .96.

How reliable are intelligence tests? In general, people's IQ scores on most intelligence tests are quite stable (Meyer et al., 2001). Performance and culture-fair tests are somewhat less reliable. However, as we've discussed, scores on even the best tests vary somewhat from one day to another.

Validity   Do intelligence tests really measure "intelligence"? When psychologists ask this question, they are concerned with test validity. **Validity** refers to a test's ability to measure what it has been designed to measure. How do we know whether a given test actually measures what it claims to measure?

One measure of validity is known as **content validity**—whether the test contains an adequate sample of the skills or knowledge that it is supposed to measure. Most widely used intelligence tests seem to measure at least some of the mental abilities that we think of as part of intelligence. These include planning, memory, understanding, reasoning, concentration, and the use of language. Although they may not adequately sample all aspects of intelligence equally well, they at least seem to have some content validity.

Another way to measure a test's validity is to see whether a person's score on that test closely matches his or her score on another test designed to measure the same thing. The two different scores should be very similar if they are both measures of the same ability. Most intelligence tests do this well: Despite differences in test content, people who score high on one test tend to score high on others. However, this outcome doesn't necessarily mean that the two tests actually measure intelligence. Conceivably, they could both be measuring the same thing, but that thing might not be intelligence. To demonstrate that the tests are valid measures of intelligence, we need an independent measure of intelligence against which to compare test scores. Determining test validity in this way is called **criterion-related validity.** Ever since Binet invented the intelligence test, the main criterion against which intelligence test scores have been compared has been school achievement. Even the strongest critics agree that IQ tests predict school achievement very well (Groth-Marnat, 2009).

Criticisms of IQ Tests   What is it about IQ tests, then, that makes them controversial? As you might guess from our earlier discussion of theories of intelligence, one source of disagreement and criticism concerns their content. Since psychologists disagree on the very nature of intelligence, it follows that they will disagree on the merits of particular tests of intelligence.

correlation coefficients Statistical measures of the degree of association between two variables.

validity Ability of a test to measure what it has been designed to measure.

content validity Refers to a test's having an adequate sample of questions measuring the skills or knowledge it is supposed to measure.

criterion-related validity Validity of a test as measured by a comparison of the test score and independent measures of what the test is designed to measure.

That said, there is general agreement among psychologists that at the least, intelligence tests measure the ability to take tests. This fact could explain why people who do well on one IQ test also tend to do well on other tests. And it could also explain why intelligence test scores correlate so closely with school performance since academic grades also depend heavily on test-taking ability.

Apart from predicting academic grades, how useful are intelligence tests? IQ tests also tend to predict success after people finish their schooling. People with high IQ scores tend to enter high-status occupations: Physicians and lawyers tend to have higher IQs than truck drivers and janitors. Critics point out, however, that this pattern can be explained in various ways. For one thing, because people with higher IQs tend to do better in school, they stay in school longer and earn advanced degrees, thereby opening the door to high-status jobs. Moreover, children from wealthy families generally grow up in environments that encourage academic success and reward good performance on tests (Blum, 1979; Ceci & Williams, 1997). In addition, they are more likely to have financial resources for post-graduate education or advanced occupational training, as well as family connections that pave the way to occupational success. Still, higher grades and intelligence test scores do predict occupational success and performance on the job (Kuncel, Hezlett, & Ones, 2004; Mcquillan, 2007; Ree & Earles, 1992).

Goleman's concept of emotional intelligence is specifically intended to predict success in the real world. Since this is a relatively new concept, researchers have only begun to evaluate it. However, some studies have shown promising results. For example, one study found that students with higher emotional intelligence scores adapted better socially and academically at school (Mestre, Guil, Lopes, Salovey, & Gil-Olarte, 2006). As you might expect, the ability to manage and regulate one's emotions is also important to success in the workplace (Cherniss & Goleman, 2001; Druskat, Sala, & Mount, 2006).

Though some investigators argue that emotional intelligence is no different from abilities that are already assessed by more traditional measures of intelligence and personality (M. Davies, Stankov, & Roberts, 1998; Waterhouse, 2006), the theory of emotional intelligence continues to gain support from psychological research (Mayer, Salovey, & Caruso, 2008). It has captured the attention of managers and others responsible for hiring, promoting, and predicting the performance of people in the workplace (Salovey, 2006; Yu & Yuan, 2008). In addition, recent research on emotional intelligence is advancing our understanding of the factors that contribute to the development of some forms of mental illness (Malterer, Glass, & Newman, 2008). (See Chapter 12, "Psychological Disorders.")

Another major criticism of intelligence tests is that their content and administration do not take into account cultural variations and, in fact, discriminate against minorities. High scores on most IQ tests require considerable mastery of standard English, thus biasing the tests in favor of middle- and upper-class White people. Moreover, White middle-class examiners may not be familiar with the speech patterns of lower income African American children or children from homes in which English is not the primary language, a complication that may hamper good test performance (Sattler, 2005). In addition, certain questions may have very different meanings for children of different social classes. 👁

Watch the **Video** In the Real World: Intelligence Tests and Stereotypes on **MyPsychLab**

ENDURING ISSUES

Person–Situation   Tracking the Future

Tracking, the practice of assigning students who "test low" to special classes for slow learners, can work to the student's disadvantage if the test results do not reflect the student's true abilities. However, the opposite mistake may sometimes work to the student's advantage: A student of mediocre ability who is identified early on as above average may receive special attention, encouragement, and tutoring that would otherwise have been considered "wasted effort" on the part of teachers. Thus, intelligence test scores can set up a self-fulfilling prophecy, so that students defined as slow become slow, and those defined as quick become quick. In this way, intelligence tests may not only predict achievement but also help determine it (R. Rosenthal, 2002). ■

Although some investigators argue that the most widely used and thoroughly studied intelligence tests are not unfairly biased against minorities (Gottfredson, 2009), others contend that a proper study of cultural bias has yet to be made (E. Hunt & Carlson, 2007). Clearly, the issue of whether tests are unfair to minorities will be with us for some time.

✓● Study and Review on MyPsychLab

CHECK YOUR UNDERSTANDING

1. Indicate whether the following statements are true (T) or false (F).
   a. _____ Intelligence is synonymous with problem-solving ability.
   b. _____ The early American psychologist L. L. Thurstone maintained that intelligence was quite general and should not be thought of as several distinct abilities.
   c. _____ Intrapersonal intelligence reflects the adage, "Know thyself."
   d. _____ Sternberg's and Gardner's theories of intelligence both include practical abilities.
2. In 1916, the Stanford psychologist L. M. Terman introduced the term _____ _____, or _____, and set the score of _____ for a person of average intelligence.
3. _____ tests eliminate or minimize the use of words in assessing mental abilities. Like these tests, _____-_____ tests minimize the use of language, but they also include questions that minimize skills and values that vary across cultures.

Answers: **1. a.** (F). **b.** (F). **c.** (T). **d.** (T). **2.** Intelligence quotient, I.Q., 100. **3.** Performance, culture-fair.

APPLY YOUR UNDERSTANDING

1. Margaret is trying to create a 10-item intelligence test. She compares scores from her test to scores on the Stanford–Binet test in an attempt to determine her test's
   a. reliability.
   b. validity.
   c. standard scores.
   d. standard deviation.

2. A friend of yours says, "Everyone has different talents and abilities. Some people are really good at math but just kind of average at everything else. Other people are really good at music or athletics or dancing but can't add two numbers to save their lives. Just because you have an ability in one area doesn't mean you're talented at other things." Your friend's view of abilities most closely matches which of the following theorists discussed in this section of the chapter?
   a. Spearman
   b. Gardner
   c. Thurstone
   d. Binet

Answers: **1.** b. **2.** b.

LEARNING OBJECTIVES

- Summarize the evidence that both heredity and environment (including intervention programs) affect intelligence.
- What is the "Flynn Effect"? What are some of the explanations that have been offered for it?
- Summarize the evidence regarding gender differences and cultural differences in mental abilities.
- Explain what is required for a diagnosis of mental retardation and summarize what is known about its causes. Describe what is meant by "inclusion" and whether it has been shown to be beneficial.
- Explain what is meant by saying a person is "gifted." Explain the pros and cons of special programs for gifted children.

⟫ HEREDITY, ENVIRONMENT, AND INTELLIGENCE

What determines individual differences in intelligence?

To what extent is intelligence inherited and to what extent is it the product of the environment? Sorting out the importance of each factor as it contributes to intelligence is a complex task.

Heredity

Why are twin studies useful in studying intelligence?

As we saw in Chapter 2, "The Biological Basis of Behavior," scientists can use studies of identical twins to measure the effects of heredity in humans. Twin studies of intelligence begin by comparing the IQ scores of identical twins who have been raised together. As **Figure 7–7**

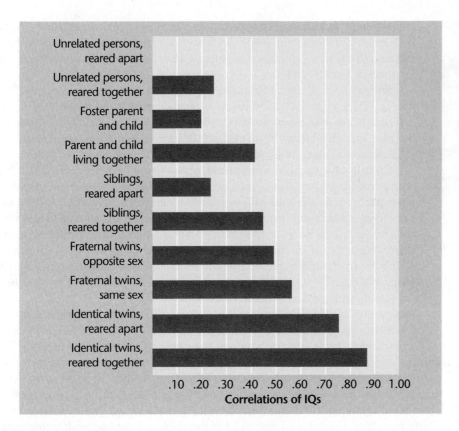

FIGURE 7–7
Correlations of IQ scores and family relationships.
Identical twins who grow up in the same household have IQ scores that are almost identical to each other. Even when they are reared apart, their scores are highly correlated. (Erienmeyer-Kimling & Jarvik, (1963)

shows, the correlation between their IQ scores is very high. In addition to identical genes, however, these twins grew up in very similar environments: They shared parents, home, teachers, vacations, and probably friends, too. These common experiences could explain their similar IQ scores. To check this possibility, researchers have tested identical twins who were separated early in life—generally before they were 6 months old—and raised in different families. As Figure 7–7 shows, even when identical twins are raised in different families, they tend to have very similar intelligence test scores; in fact, the similarity is much greater than that between non-twin siblings who grow up in the *same* environment.

These findings make a strong case for the heritability of intelligence, though as we pointed out in Chapter 2 twin studies do not constitute "final proof." However, other evidence also demonstrates the role of heredity (Deary, Johnson, & Houlihan, 2009). For example, adopted children have been found to have IQ scores that are more similar to those of their *biological* mothers than to those of the mothers who are raising them. Do psychologists, then, conclude that intelligence is an inherited trait and that environment plays little, if any, role?

Environment

What have we learned from early intervention programs about the influence of the environment on intellectual development?

Probably no psychologist denies that genes play a role in determining intelligence, but most believe that genes provide only a base or starting point. Each of us inherits a certain body build from our parents, but our actual weight is greatly determined by what we eat and how much we exercise. Similarly, although we inherit certain mental capacities, their development depends on what we see around us as infants, how our parents respond to our first attempts to talk, what schools we attend, which books we read, which television programs we watch—even what we eat (Sternberg & Grigorenko, 2001; Nisbett, 2009). Moreover, recent evidence indicates that the role of heredity varies with social economic status: In impoverished families, it appears to have little or no bearing on intelligence; in

Individual differences in intelligence can be partly explained by differences in environmental stimulation and encouragement. The specific forms of stimulation given vary from culture to culture. Because our culture assigns importance to developing academic skills, the stimulation of reading and exploring information in books can give children an edge over those who are not so encouraged.

affluent families, its influence appears to be stronger (Turkheimer, Haley, Waldron, D'Onofrio, & Gottesman, 2003). Evidence also shows that the effect of heredity increases from early childhood to middle childhood and into adulthood (Davis, Haworth, & Plomin, 2009).

Environment affects children even before birth, such as through prenatal nutrition (M. D. Sigman, 2000). During infancy, malnutrition can lower IQ scores by an average of 20 points (Stock & Smythe, 1963). Conversely, vitamin supplements can increase young children's IQ scores, possibly even among well-nourished children (D. Benton & Roberts, 1988; Schoenthaler, Amos, Eysenck, Peritz, & Yudkin, 1991).

Quite by chance, psychologist H. M. Skeels found evidence in the 1930s that IQ scores among children also depend on environmental stimulation. While investigating orphanages for the state of Iowa, Skeels observed that the children lived in very overcrowded wards and that the few adults there had almost no time to play with the children, to talk to them, or to read them stories. Many of these children were classified as "subnormal" in intelligence. Skeels followed the cases of two girls who, after 18 months in an orphanage, were sent to a ward for women with severe retardation. Originally, the girls' IQs were in the range of retardation, but after a year on the adult ward, as if by magic, their IQs had risen to normal (Skeels, 1938). Skeels regarded this fact as quite remarkable—after all, the women with whom the girls had lived were themselves severely retarded. When he placed 13 other "slow" children as houseguests in such adult wards, within 18 months their mean IQ rose from 64 to 92 (within the normal range)—all apparently because they had had someone (even someone of below-normal intelligence) to play with them, to read to them, to cheer them on when they took their first steps, and to encourage them to talk (Skeels, 1942). During the same period, the mean IQ of a group of children who had been left in orphanages dropped from 86 to 61. Thirty years later, Skeels found that all 13 of the children raised on adult wards were self-supporting, their occupations ranging from waiting on tables to real-estate sales. Of the contrasting group, half were unemployed, four were still in institutions, and all of those who had jobs were dishwashers (Skeels, 1966). Later studies have reinforced Skeels's findings on the importance of intellectually stimulating surroundings as well as the importance of good nutrition (Capron & Duyme, 1989).

Intervention Programs: How Much Can We Boost IQ? In 1961, the Milwaukee Project set out to learn whether intervening in a child's family life could offset the negative effects of cultural and socioeconomic deprivation on IQ scores (Garber & Heber, 1982; Heber, Garber, Harrington, & Hoffman, 1972). The average score of the 40 pregnant women in the study was less than 75 on the Wechsler scale. Women in the control group received no special education or training; those in the experimental group were sent to school, given job training, and instructed in child care, household management, and personal relationships.

After the babies were born, the research team shifted their focus to them. For 6 years, the children whose mothers received special training spent most of each day in an infant-education center, where they were fed, taught, and cared for by paraprofessionals. The children whose mothers received no special training did not attend the center. Ultimately the children in the experimental group achieved an average IQ score of 126, 51 points higher than their mothers' average scores. In contrast, the average score of the children in the control group was 94. Thus, this landmark study supported the notion that intervention may indeed counter the negative effects of cultural and socioeconomic deprivation on IQ scores.

Head Start, the nation's largest intervention program, began in 1965. Since its inception, Head Start has provided comprehensive services to more than 25 million children and their families through child care, education, health, nutrition, and family support (National Head Start Association, 2008). Focusing on preschoolers between the ages of 3 and 5 from low-income families, the program has two key goals: to provide children with educational and social skills before they go to school, and to provide information about nutrition and health to both the children and their families. Head Start involves parents in all its aspects, from daily activities to administration of the program itself.

Some studies evaluating the long-term effects of Head Start have found that it boosts cognitive and language abilities (W. S. Barnett, 1998; Wasik, Bond, & Hindman, 2006; Zhai, 2008; Zigler & Styfco, 2008). However, the congressionally mandated *Head Start Impact Study* found much more modest benefits (Puma, Bell, Cook, & Hyde, 2010). Specifically, that study concluded that access to Head Start does have a positive impact on children's preschool experiences in some areas but almost all of those advantages faded by the end of the first grade. Thus, it is questionable whether Head Start provides any appreciable, long-term, practical benefits.

Overall, the effectiveness of early intervention appears to depend on the quality of the particular program (S. L. Ramey, 1999; C. T. Ramey & Ramey, 2007; Zigler & Styfco, 1993). Intervention programs that have clearly defined goals; that explicitly teach such basic skills as counting, naming colors, and writing the alphabet; and that take into account the broad context of human development, including health care and other social services, achieve the biggest and most durable gains.

The IQ Debate: A Useful Model

How can the study of plants help us to understand the relationship between heredity and environment?

Both heredity and environment have important effects on individual differences in intelligence, but is one of these factors more important than the other? A useful analogy comes from studies of plants. Suppose that you grow one group of randomly assigned plants in enriched soil, and another group in poor soil. The enriched group will grow to be taller and stronger than the nonenriched group; the difference between the two groups in this case is due entirely to differences in their environment. *Within* each group of plants, however, differences among individual plants are likely to be primarily due to genetics, because all plants in the same group share essentially the same environment. Thus, the height and strength of any single plant reflects both heredity *and* environment.

Similarly, group differences in IQ scores might be due to environmental factors, but differences among people *within* groups could be due primarily to genetics. At the same time, the IQ scores of particular people would reflect the effects of both heredity *and* environment. Robert Plomin, an influential researcher in the field of human intelligence, concludes that "the world's literature suggests that about half of the total variance in IQ scores can be accounted for by genetic variance" (Plomin, 1997, p. 89). This finding means that environment accounts for the other half.

The Flynn Effect   An interesting side note to this discussion is the fact that IQ scores have *gone up* in the population as a whole. Because James Flynn (1984, 1987) of the University of Otago in New Zealand was the first to report this finding, it is often called the *Flynn Effect*. In his original research, Professor Flynn gathered evidence showing that, between 1932 and 1978, intelligence test scores rose about three points per decade. More recently, by pulling together data from five nations (Britain, Netherlands, Israel, Norway, and Belgium) Flynn (1999) has shown that the average increase in IQ may be as high as six points per decade. Consistent with this result is a finding by Flieller (1999) that children today between the ages of 10 and 15 years display significant cognitive advancement compared with children of the same age tested 20 and 30 years ago. And, as Neisser (1998) points out, accompanying this general increase in IQ scores is a decrease in the difference in intelligence scores between Blacks and Whites.

Although the Flynn Effect has many possible explanations, none of them seem to account entirely for the magnitude of the effect (Sundet, Borren, & Tambs, 2008). Rather than getting smarter, maybe people are simply getting better at taking tests. Environmental factors, such as improved nutrition and health care, may also contribute to this trend (Teasdale & Owen, 2005). Some psychologists have suggested that the sheer complexity of the modern world is responsible (Schooler, 1998). For example, the proliferation of televisions, computers, and video games could be contributing to the rise in IQ scores (Greenfield, 1998; Neisser, 1998).

Head Start is a program designed to do just what its name implies: to give children from disadvantaged environments a head start in acquiring the skills and attitudes needed for success in school. Although researchers debate whether Head Start produces significant and lasting boosts in IQ, it does have many school-related benefits for those who participate in it.

Mental Abilities and Human Diversity: Gender and Culture

Do culture and gender influence mental abilities?

Gender In 1974, psychologists Eleanor Maccoby and Carol Jacklin published a review of psychological research on gender differences. They found no differences between males and females in most of the studies they examined. However, a few differences did appear in cognitive abilities: Girls tended to display greater verbal ability, and boys tended to exhibit stronger spatial and mathematical abilities. Largely as a result of this research, gender differences in verbal, spatial, and mathematical abilities became so widely accepted that they were often cited as one of the established facts of psychological research.

A closer examination of the research literature, including more recent work, indicates that while gender differences in some math and verbal skills exist, they are relatively small and often concentrated in very specific skills. For example, an analysis of 242 studies involving more than a million people showed no difference between men and women in mathematical ability (Lindberg, Hyde, Petersen, & Linn, 2010). While girls do appear to display stronger verbal skills than boys, female superiority is generally only found when the assessment of verbal skill includes writing. Conversely, boys tend to outperform girls primarily on measures of visual-spatial skill (Halpern et al., 2007). Interestingly, the advantage males have over females in visual-spatial ability has been detected in infants as young as 3–5 months (D. S. Moore & Johnson, 2008; Quinn & Liben, 2008). Men also differ from women in another way: They are more likely than women to fall at the extremes of the mathematical intelligence range (Ceci & Williams, 2010; Halpern et al., 2007; Wai, Cacchio, Putallaz, & Makel, 2010). Conversely, women outnumber men at the very high end of the scale when it comes to verbal reasoning and writing ability (Wai et al., 2010).

What should we conclude from these findings? First, cognitive differences between males and females appear to be restricted to specific cognitive skills. Scores on tests such as the Stanford–Binet or the WAIS reveal no overall gender differences in general intelligence (Halpern, 1992). Second, gender differences typically are small (Skaalvik & Rankin, 1994). Third, we do not know whether the differences that do exist are a result of biological or cultural factors (Hyde & Mezulis, 2002). Finally, one extensive review of the literature concluded that "There is no single factor by itself that has been shown to determine sex differences in science and math. Early experience, biological constraints, educational policy, and cultural context each have effects, and these effects add and interact in complex and sometimes unpredictable ways" (Halpern et al., 2007, p. 41).

Culture For years, U.S. media have been reporting an achievement gap, especially in math, between American and Asian students. Recent media reports suggest even broader differences. ◉

Psychological research tells us something about the causes of these achievement gaps. Two decades ago, a team of researchers led by the late Harold Stevenson (1924–2005) began to study the performance of first- and fifth-grade children in American, Chinese, and Japanese elementary schools (Stevenson, Lee, & Stigler, 1986). At that time, the American students at both grade levels lagged far behind the other two countries in math and came in second in reading. A decade later, when

◉ **Watch** the **Video** Cultural Influences: Robert Sternberg on **MyPsychLab**

Research shows there are only negligible differences between men and women in mathematical ability.

the study was repeated with a new group of fifth-graders, the researchers discovered that the American students performed even worse than they had earlier. In 1990, the research team also studied the original first-graders from all three cultures, now in the eleventh grade. The result? The American students retained their low standing in mathematics compared with the Asian students (Stevenson, 1992, 1993; Stevenson, Chen, & Lee, 1993).

The next question was, Why? Stevenson's team wondered whether cultural attitudes toward ability and effort might, in part, explain the differences. To test this hypothesis, the researchers asked students, their parents, and their teachers in all three countries whether they thought effort or ability had a greater impact on academic performance. From first through eleventh grade, American students on the whole disagreed with the statement that "everyone in my class has about the same natural ability in math." In other words, the Americans thought that "studying hard" has little to do with performance. Their responses appear to reflect a belief that mathematical skill is primarily a function of innate ability. American mothers expressed a similar view. Moreover, 41% of the American eleventh-grade teachers thought "innate intelligence" is the most important factor in mathematics performance. By contrast, Asian students, parents, and teachers believed that effort and "studying hard" determine success in math.

Such culturally influenced views of the relative importance of effort and innate ability may have profound consequences for the way that children, their parents, and their teachers approach the task of learning. Students who believe that learning is based on natural ability see little value in working hard to learn a difficult subject. By contrast, students who believe that academic success comes from studying are more likely to work hard. Indeed, even the brightest students will not get far without making an effort. Although many Americans no doubt believe in the value of effort and hard work, our widespread perception that innate ability is the key to academic success may be affecting the performance of U.S. students.

In short, while Stevenson's research confirms the existence of significant differences in student performance across various cultures, the evidence suggests that these differences reflect cultural attitudes toward the importance of ability and effort, rather than an underlying difference in intelligence across the cultures.

THINKING CRITICALLY ABOUT . . .

International Comparisons of School Achievement

1. Do you agree or disagree with the conclusions of Stevenson and his colleagues that cultural attitudes may account for some of the academic performance differences between American students and students from other countries? What additional evidence might provide support for your position?

2. If you were to research this topic today, would you do things differently than Stevenson's team did? Are there any other factors that might account for the differences in achievement that you would investigate? What specific questions would you ask of the parents, students, and teachers? What additional information about the school systems would you collect?

3. Given the results of this research, what specific steps would you take to improve the academic performance of American children?

Extremes of Intelligence

What do psychologists know about the two extremes of human intelligence: very high and very low?

The average IQ score on intelligence tests is 100. Nearly 70% of all people have IQs between 85 and 115, and all but 5% of the population have IQs between 70 and 130. In this section, we focus on people who score at the two extremes of intelligence—those with mental retardation and those who are intellectually gifted.

Mental Retardation **Mental retardation** encompasses a vast array of mental deficits with a wide variety of causes, treatments, and outcomes. The American Psychiatric Association (1994) defines mental retardation as "significantly subaverage general intellectual functioning ... that is accompanied by significant limitations in adaptive functioning" and that appears before the age of 21 (p. 39). There are also various degrees of mental retardation. Mild retardation corresponds to Stanford–Binet IQ scores ranging from a high

mental retardation Condition of significantly subaverage intelligence combined with deficiencies in adaptive behavior.

of about 70 to a low near 50. Moderate retardation corresponds to IQ scores from the low 50s to the middle 30s. People with IQ scores between the middle 30s and 20 are considered severely retarded, and the profoundly retarded are those whose scores are below 20. (See **Table 7–3.**)

But a low IQ is not in itself sufficient for diagnosing mental retardation. The person must also be unable to perform the daily tasks needed to function independently (Rust & Wallace, 2004). A person who is able to live independently, for example, is not considered to have mental retardation even if his or her IQ may be extremely low. To fully assess individuals and to place them in appropriate treatment and educational programs, mental health professionals need information on physical health and on emotional and social adjustment (Borthwick-Duffy, 2007).

Some people with mental handicaps exhibit remarkable abilities in highly specialized areas, such as numerical computation, memory, art, or music (Pring, Woolf, & Tadic, 2008; Treffert & Wallace, 2002). Probably the most dramatic and intriguing examples involve *savant performance* (Boelte, Uhlig, & Poustka, 2002; L. K. Miller, 2005). Savant performances include mentally calculating large numbers almost instantly, determining the day of the week for any date over many centuries, and playing back a long musical composition after hearing it played only once.

What causes mental retardation? In most cases, the causes are unknown—especially in cases of mild retardation, which account for nearly 90% of all retardation. When causes can be identified, most often they stem from a wide variety of genetic, environmental, social, nutritional, and other risk factors (A. A. Baumeister & Baumeister, 2000; Moser, 2004).

About 25% of cases—especially the more severe forms of retardation—appear to involve genetic or biological disorders. Scientists have identified more than 100 forms of mental retardation caused by single defective genes (Plomin, 1997). One is the genetically based disease *phenylketonuria,* or *PKU,* which occurs in about one person out of 25,000. In people suffering from PKU, the liver fails to produce an enzyme necessary for early brain development. Fortunately, placing a PKU baby on a special diet can prevent mental retardation from developing (Merrick, Aspler, & Schwarz, 2005; Widaman, 2009). In the disorder known as *Down syndrome,* which affects 1 in 600 newborns, an extra 21st chromosome is the cause. Down syndrome, named for the physician who first described its symptoms, is marked by moderate to severe mental retardation.

Biologically caused mental retardation can be moderated through education and training (C. T. Ramey, Ramey, & Lanzi, 2001). The prognosis for those with no underlying physical causes is even better. People whose retardation is due to a history of social and educational deprivation can respond dramatically to appropriate interventions. Today,

TABLE 7–3   Levels of Mental Retardation

Type of Retardation	IQ Range	Attainable Skill Level
Mild retardation	Low 50s to low 70s	People may be able to function adequately in society and learn skills comparable to a sixth-grader, but they need special help at times of unusual stress.
Moderate retardation	Mid-30s to low 50s	People profit from vocational training and may be able to travel alone. They learn on a second-grade level and perform skilled work in a sheltered workshop under supervision.
Severe retardation	Low 20s to mid-30s	People do not learn to talk or to practice basic hygiene until after age 6. They cannot learn vocational skills but can perform simple tasks under supervision.
Profound retardation	Below 20 or 25	Constant care is needed. Usually, people have a diagnosed neurological disorder.

Source: Based on APA, *DSM-IV*, 1994.

Down syndrome is a common biological cause of mental retardation, affecting one in 600 newborns. The prognosis for Down syndrome children today is much better than it was in the past. With adequate support, many children with the affliction can participate in regular classrooms and other childhood activities.

the majority of children with physical or mental disabilities are educated in local school systems (Doré, Wagner, Doré, & Brunet, 2002), in *inclusion* arrangements (Kavale, 2002) (previously known as *mainstreaming*), which help these students to socialize with their nondisabled peers. The principle of mainstreaming has also been applied successfully to adults with mental retardation, by taking them out of large, impersonal institutions and placing them in smaller community homes that provide more normal life experiences (I. Brown, Buell, Birkan, & Percy, 2007).

Giftedness   At the other extreme of the intelligence scale are "the gifted"—those with exceptional mental abilities, as measured by scores on standard intelligence tests. As with mental retardation, the causes of **giftedness** are largely unknown.

The first and now-classic study of giftedness was begun by Lewis Terman and his colleagues in the early 1920s. They defined giftedness in terms of academic talent and measured it by an IQ score in the top 2 percentile (Terman, 1925). More recently, some experts have sought to broaden the definition of giftedness beyond that of simply high IQ (L. J. Coleman & Cross, 2001; Csikszentmihalyi, Rathunde, & Whalen, 1993; Subotnik & Arnold, 1994). One view is that giftedness is often an interaction of above-average general intelligence, exceptional creativity, and high levels of commitment. Various criteria can identify gifted students, including scores on intelligence tests, teacher recommendations, and achievement test results. School systems generally use diagnostic testing, interviews, and evaluation of academic and creative work (Sattler, 1992). These selection methods can identify students with a broad range of talent, but they can miss students with specific abilities, such as a talent for mathematics or music (Cramond & Kim, 2008). This is important because research suggests that most gifted individuals display special abilities in only a few areas. "Globally" gifted people are rare (Achter, Lubinski, & Benbow, 1996; Lubinski & Benbow, 2000; Olzewski-Kubilius, 2003; Winner, 1998, 2000).

A common view of gifted people is that they have poor social skills and are emotionally maladjusted. However, research does not support this stereotype (J. Richards, Encel, & Shute, 2003; Robinson & Clinkenbeard, 1998). Indeed, one review (Janos & Robinson, 1985) concluded that "being intellectually gifted, at least at moderate levels of ability, is clearly an asset in terms of psychosocial adjustment in most situations" (p. 181). Nevertheless, children who are exceptionally gifted sometimes do experience difficulty "fitting in" with their peers.

giftedness   Refers to superior IQ combined with demonstrated or potential ability in such areas as academic aptitude, creativity, and leadership.

ENDURING ISSUES

Diversity–Universality   Not Everyone Wants to Be Special

Because gifted children sometimes become bored and socially isolated in regular class-rooms, some experts recommend that they be offered special programs (Olzewski-Kubilius, 2003). Special classes for the gifted would seem to be something the gifted themselves would want, but this is not always the case. Special classes and special schools can sepa-rate gifted students from their friends and neighbors. And stereotypes about the gifted can mean that, once identified as gifted, the student is less likely to be invited to participate in certain school activities, such as dances, plays, and sports. Gifted students also sometimes object to being set apart, labeled "brains," and pressured to perform beyond the ordinary. Many but not all gifted students welcome the opportunities offered by special programs. ■

Any discussion of giftedness inevitably leads to the topic of creativity. The two topics are, indeed, closely related, as we shall see in the next section.

✔ **Study** and **Review** on **MyPsychLab**

CHECK YOUR UNDERSTANDING

1. Indicate whether the following statements are true (T) or false (F):
   a. ____ When identical twins are raised apart, their IQ scores are not highly correlated.
   b. ____ Environmental stimulation has little, if any, effect on IQ.
   c. ____ The Head Start program appears to have a positive impact on children's preschool experiences in some areas.
2. As psychologists learn more about giftedness, the definition of it has become (broader/narrower) _____.

Answers: 1. a. (F). b. (F). c. (T). 2. broader.

APPLY YOUR UNDERSTANDING

1. Imagine that an adoption agency separates identical twins at birth and places them randomly in very different kinds of homes. Thirty years later, a researcher discovers that the pairs of twins have almost identical scores on IQ tests. Which of the following conclusions is most consistent with that finding?
   a. Heredity has a significant effect on intelligence.
   b. Environment has a significant effect on intelligence.
   c. Heredity provides a starting point, but environment determines our ultimate intelligence.
   d. Because the twins were placed in very different environments, it's not possible to draw any conclusions.
2. Ten-year-old John has an IQ score of 60 on the Wechsler Intelligence Scale for Children. Which of the following would you need to know before you could determine whether John is mildly retarded?
   a. whether his score on the Stanford–Binet Intelligence Scale is also below 70
   b. whether he can perform the daily tasks needed to function independently
   c. whether he has a genetic defect in the X chromosome
   d. whether he suffered from malnutrition before birth

Answers: 1. a. 2. b.

LEARNING OBJECTIVE

- Describe the relationship between creativity and intelligence, and the ways in which creativity has been measured.

creativity The ability to produce novel and socially valued ideas or objects.

CREATIVITY

What is creativity?

Creativity is the ability to produce novel and socially valued ideas or objects ranging from philosophy to painting, from music to mousetraps. As we saw earlier in this chapter, Sternberg included creativity and insight as important elements in human intelligence. Most IQ tests, however, do not measure creativity, and many researchers would argue that intelligence and creativity are not the same thing.

Intelligence and Creativity

How is creativity related to intelligence?

Early studies typically found little or no relationship between creativity and intelligence (for example, Getzels & Jackson, 1962; Wing, 1969), but these studies were concerned only with bright students. Perhaps creativity and intelligence are indeed linked, but only until IQ reaches a certain threshold level, after which higher intelligence isn't associated with higher creativity. There is some evidence for this *threshold theory* (Barron, 1963; Yamamoto & Chimbidis, 1966). However, other studies have failed to provide support (Preckel, Holling, & Wiese, 2006) finding instead that the relationship between intelligence and creativity is best understood only when the individual facets of intelligence and creativity (such as musical or artistic) are considered (K. H. Kim, 2008; Sligh, Conners, & Roskos-Ewoldsen, 2005).

Creative people are often *perceived* as being more intelligent than less creative people who have equivalent IQ scores. But this may be the result of other characteristics that creative people share. For instance, research has shown that creative people also tend to score high on measures of *extraversion*—a personality trait reflecting gregariousness, assertiveness, and excitement seeking (Furnham & Bachtiar, 2008; Furnham, Batey, Anand, & Manfield, 2008). (See Chapter 10, "Personality.")

In general, creative people are *problem finders* as well as problem solvers. The more creative people are, the more they like to work on problems that they have set for themselves. Creative scientists (such as Charles Darwin and Albert Einstein) often work for years on a problem that has sprung from their own curiosity (Gruber & Wallace, 2001). Also, "greatness" rests not just on "talent" or "genius"; such people also have intense dedication, ambition, and perseverance (Stokes, 2006). ⊙➔

⊙➔ **Simulate** the **Experiment** Problem Solving and Creativity on **MyPsychLab**

Creativity Tests

Can creativity be measured?

Measuring creativity poses special problems (Cramond & Kim, 2008; Naglieri & Kaufman, 2001; Runco, 2008). Because creativity involves original responses to situations, questions that can be answered *true* or *false* or *a* or *b* are not good measures. More open-ended tests are better. Instead of asking for one predetermined answer to a problem, the examiner asks the test takers to let their imaginations run free. Scores are based on the originality of a person's answers and often on the number of responses as well.

In one such test, the *Torrance Test of Creative Thinking,* people must explain what is happening in a picture, how the scene came about, and what its consequences are likely to be. In the *Christensen–Guilford Test,* they are to list as many words containing a given letter as possible, to name things belonging to a certain category (such as "liquids that will burn"), and to write four-word sentences beginning with the letters RDLS—"Rainy days look sad, Red dogs like soup, Renaissance dramas lack symmetry." One of the most widely used creativity tests, S. A. Mednick's (1962) *Remote Associates Test (RAT),* asks people to relate three apparently unrelated words. For example, a test taker might relate the stimulus words *poke, go,* and *molasses* using the word *slow:* "Slowpoke, go slow, slow as molasses." In the newer *Wallach and Kogan Creative Battery,* people form associative groupings. For instance, children are asked to "name all the round things you can think of" and to find similarities between objects, such as between a potato and a carrot.

Although people who do not have high IQs can score well on the Wallach and Kogan test, the Torrance test seems to require a reasonably high IQ for adequate performance. This finding raises the question of which of these tests is a valid measure of creativity. In general, current tests of creativity do not show a high degree of validity (Baer, 2008; Clapham, 2004), so measurements derived from them must be interpreted with caution.

As with intelligence, there is considerable interest in identifying the neural mechanisms that underlie creative thinking, but to date the results have been discouraging. One recent, comprehensive review of the literature concludes that creativity as a whole is not clearly associated with any particular brain area. The authors point out that "It is hard to believe that creative behavior, in all its manifestations, from carrying out exquisitely choreographed dance moves, to scientific discovery, constructing poems, and coming up with ingenious ideas of what to do with a brick, engages a common set of brain areas or depends on a limited set of mental processes" (Dietrich & Kanso, 2010, p. 845). Whether there are brain areas associated with *specific kinds* of creativity remains to be seen.

✔•─[**Study** and **Review** on **MyPsychLab**

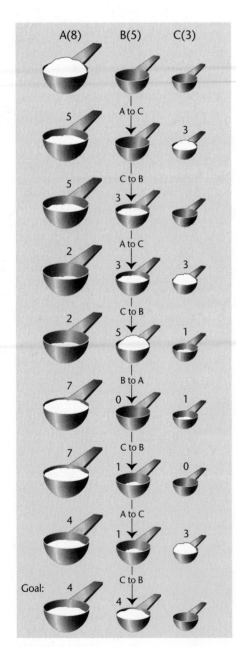

FIGURE 7–8
Answer to Problem 2.

CHECK YOUR UNDERSTANDING

1. The ability to produce novel and unique ideas or objects, ranging from philosophy to painting, from music to mousetraps, is termed _____.
2. Two important features of creative people are that they
   a. take risks and like to work on problems that they invent themselves.
   b. are perceived as less intelligent and more irresponsible than other people.
   c. excel at art but are poor at science.
3. _____ tests are the best type for measuring creativity.

Answers: 1. creativity. **2.** a. **3.** Open-ended.

APPLY YOUR UNDERSTANDING

1. You are discussing creativity and intelligence with a friend who says, "Those are two different things. There's no relationship between being intelligent and being creative." Based on what you have learned in this chapter, which of the following would be the most accurate reply?
   a. "You're right. There is no evidence of a relationship between creativity and intelligence."
   b. "You're wrong. There is a relationship between intelligence and creativity but it is complex and is understood only when the individual facets of intelligence and creativity are taken into account."
   c. "That's apparently true only among very bright people. For most people, creativity and intelligence tend to go together."
   d. "That's true for people with IQ scores below about 100, but above that point, intelligence and creativity tend to go together."

Answer: 1. c.

ANSWERS TO PROBLEMS IN THE CHAPTER

Problem 1 Fill each of the smaller spoons with salt from the larger spoon. That step will require 4 teaspoons of salt, leaving exactly 4 teaspoons of salt in the larger spoon.

Problem 2 As shown in **Figure 7–8,** fill spoon C with the salt from spoon A (now A has 5 teaspoons of salt and C has 3). Pour the salt from spoon C into spoon B (now A has 5 teaspoons of salt, and B has 3). Again fill spoon C with the salt from spoon A. (This leaves A with only 2 teaspoons of salt, while B and C each have 3.) Fill spoon B with the salt from spoon C. (This step leaves 1 teaspoon of salt in spoon C, while B has 5 teaspoons, and A has only 2.) Pour all of the salt from spoon B into spoon A. (Now A has 7 teaspoons of salt, and C has 1.) Pour all of the salt from spoon C into spoon B, and then fill spoon C from spoon A. (This step leaves 4 teaspoons of salt in A, 1 teaspoon in B, and 3 teaspoons in C.) Finally, pour all of the salt from spoon C into spoon B. (This step leaves 4 teaspoons of salt in spoons A and B, which is the solution.)

Problem 3 Take one of the short pieces of chain shown in **Figure 7–9,** and open all three links. (This step costs 6 cents.) Use those three links to connect the remaining three pieces of chain. (Hence, closing the three links costs 9 cents.)

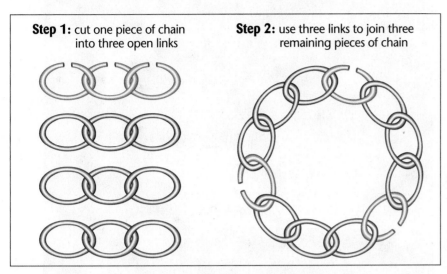

Step 1: cut one piece of chain into three open links

Step 2: use three links to join three remaining pieces of chain

FIGURE 7–9
Answer to Problem 3.

Problem 4 One way to solve this problem is to draw a diagram of the ascent and the descent, as in **Figure 7–10.** From this drawing, you can see that indeed there is a point that the monk passes at exactly the same time on both days. Another way to approach this problem is to imagine that there are two monks on the mountain; one starts ascending at 7 A.M., while the other starts descending at 7 A.M. on the same day. Clearly, sometime during the day the monks must meet somewhere along the route.

Problem 5 This problem has four possible solutions, one of which is shown in **Figure 7–11.**

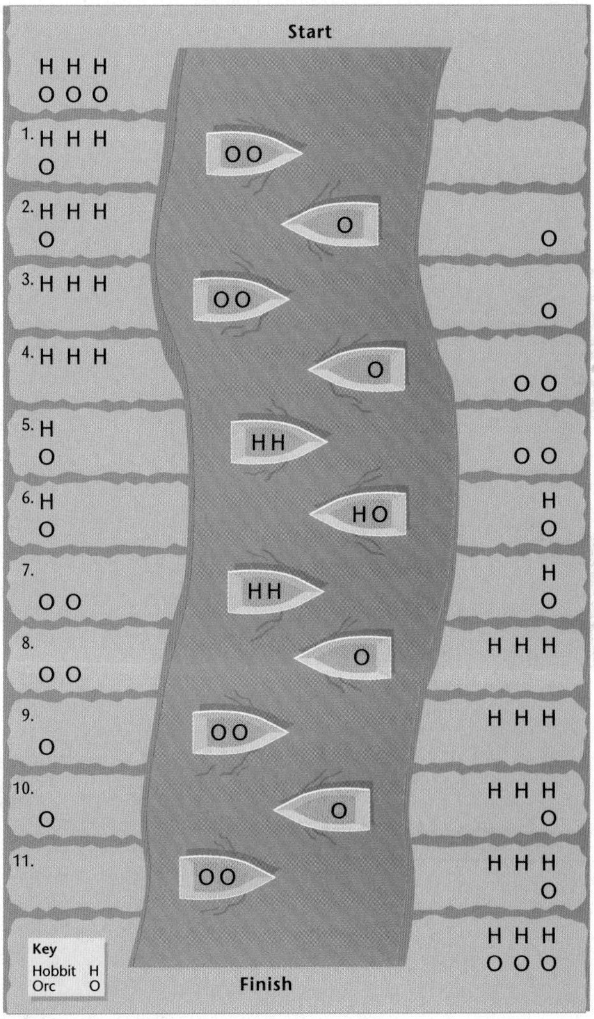

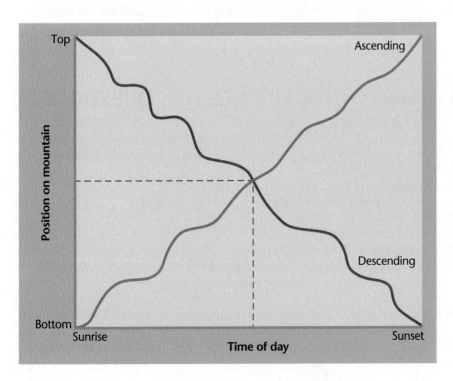

FIGURE 7–11
Answer to Problem 5.

FIGURE 7–10
Answer to Problem 4.

FIGURE 7–12
Solution to Figure 7–5.

In solving the problem given in Figure 7–5, many people have trouble realizing that the box of tacks can also be used as a candle-holder, as shown here.

Problem 6 There are 15 possible solutions to this problem, of which this is one: First, one Hobbit and one Orc cross the river in the boat; the Orc remains on the opposite side while the Hobbit rows back. Next, three Orcs cross the river; two of those Orcs remain on the other side (making a total of three Orcs on the opposite bank) while one Orc rows back. Now three Hobbits and one Orc row the boat back. Again, three Hobbits row across the river, at which point all five Hobbits are on the opposite bank with only two Orcs. Then, one of the Orcs rows back and forth across the river twice to transport the remaining Orcs to the opposite side.

ANSWERS TO INTELLIGENCE TEST QUESTIONS

1. *Idleness* refers to the state of being inactive, not busy, unoccupied; *laziness* means an unwillingness or a reluctance to work. Laziness is one possible cause of idleness, but not the only cause.
2. If you face west, your right ear will face north.
3. *Obliterate* means to erase or destroy something completely.
4. Both an hour and a week are measures of time.
5. Alternative (f) is the correct pattern.
6. Seventy-five cents will buy nine pencils.
7. Alternative (d) is correct. A crutch is used to help someone who has difficulty with locomotion; spectacles are used to help someone who has difficulty with vision.
8. Alternative D is correct. The second figure is the same shape and size but with diagonal cross-hatching from upper left to lower right.
9. Figures 3, 4, and 5 can all be completely covered by using some or all of the given pieces.

KEY TERMS

CHAPTER REVIEW   ((•⏽ Listen to the **Chapter Audio** on **MyPsychLab**

BUILDING BLOCKS OF THOUGHT

What are the three most important building blocks of thought? The three most important building blocks of thought are language, images, and concepts. As we think, we use words, sensory "snapshots," and categories that classify things.

What steps do we go through to turn a thought into a statement? **Language** is a flexible system of symbols that allows us to communicate ideas to others. When we express thoughts as statements, we must conform to our language's rules. Every language has rules indicating which sounds (or **phonemes**) are part of that particular language, how those sounds can be combined into meaningful units (or **morphemes**), and how those meaningful units can be ordered into phrases and sentences (rules of **grammar**). To communicate an idea, we start with a thought and then choose sounds, words, and phrases that will express the idea clearly. To understand the speech of others, the task is reversed.

What role do images play in thinking? **Images** are mental representations of sensory experiences. Visual images in particular can be powerful aids in thinking about the relationships between things. Picturing things in our mind's eye can sometimes help us solve problems.

How do concepts help us to think more efficiently? **Concepts** are categories for classifying objects, people, and experiences based on their common elements. Without the ability to form concepts, we would need a different name for every new thing we encounter. We draw on concepts to anticipate what new experiences will

be like. Many concepts are "fuzzy," lacking clear-cut boundaries. Therefore we often use **prototypes,** mental models of the most typical examples of a concept, to classify new objects.

LANGUAGE, THOUGHT, AND CULTURE

How do language, thought, and culture influence each other? According to Benjamin Whorf's **linguistic relativity hypothesis,** thought is greatly influenced by language. But critics contend that thought and experience can shape and change a language as much as a language can shape and change thought.

Does language contribute to gender stereotyping? Some evidence indicates that the use of "man" and "he" to refer to all people affects the way that English speakers think. Referring to doctors, college professors, bankers, and executives by the generic "he" may contribute to the gender stereotyping of these respected occupations as appropriate for men but not for women. In contrast, referring to secretaries and housekeepers as "she" may reinforce the stereotype that those occupations are appropriate for women, not men.

NON-HUMAN LANGUAGE AND THOUGHT

Can scientists learn what is on an animal's mind? What kind of communication and language do other animals use? Non-human animals communicate primarily through **signs:** general or global statements about the animal's current state. Using the distinguishing features of language, which include semantics, displacement, and productivity as criteria, no other species has its own language, although chimpanzees have been taught to use American Sign Language.

Do some animals think like humans? Research indicates that some animals have humanlike cognitive capacities, such as the ability to form concepts and to reason. Apes have demonstrated sophisticated problem-solving skills. However, only chimpanzees, bonobos, and orangutans consistently show signs of self-awareness.

PROBLEM SOLVING

What are three general aspects of the problem-solving process? Interpreting a problem, formulating a strategy, and evaluating progress toward a solution are three general aspects of the problem-solving process. Each in its own way is critical to success at the task.

Does the way information is presented affect decisions? Why is representing the problem so important to finding an effective solution? Problem representation—defining or interpreting the problem—is the first step in problem solving. We must decide whether to view the problem verbally, mathematically, or visually; and to get clues about how to solve it we must categorize it. Some problems require **convergent thinking,** or searching for a single correct solution, while others call for **divergent thinking,** or generating many possible solutions. Representing a problem in an unproductive way can block progress completely.

Why are heuristics usually better for solving problems than is trial and error? Selecting a solution strategy and evaluating progress toward the goal are also important steps in the problem-solving process. A solution strategy can range from trial and error, to information retrieval based on similar problems, to a set of step-by-step procedures guaranteed to work (an **algorithm**), to rule-of-thumb approaches known as **heuristics.** An algorithm is often preferable over trial and error because it guarantees a solution and does not waste time. But because we lack algorithms for so many things, heuristics are vital to human problem solving. Some useful heuristics are **hill climbing,** creating **subgoals, means-end analysis,** and **working backward.**

How can a "mental set" both help and hinder problem solving? A **mental set** is a tendency to perceive and approach a problem in a certain way. Although sets can enable us to draw on past experience to help solve problems, a strong set can also prevent us from using essential new approaches. One set that can seriously hamper problem solving is **functional fixedness**—the tendency to perceive only traditional uses for an object. One way to minimize mental sets is the technique of **brainstorming** in which an individual or group collects numerous ideas and evaluates them only after all possible ideas have been collected.

DECISION MAKING

How does decision making differ from problem solving? Decision making is a special kind of problem solving in which all possible solutions or choices are known. The task is not to come up with new solutions, but rather to identify the best one available based on whatever criteria are being used.

How would you go about making a truly logical decision? The logical way to make a decision is to rate each available choice in terms of weighted criteria and then to total the ratings for each choice. This approach is called a **compensatory model** because heavily weighted attractive features can compensate for lightly weighted unattractive ones.

How can heuristic approaches lead us to make bad decisions? Heuristics can save a great deal of time and effort, but they do not always result in the best choices. Errors in judgment may occur based on the **representativeness** heuristic, which involves making decisions based on information that matches our model of the "typical" member of a category. Other examples are overreliance on the **availability** heuristic (making choices based on whatever information we can most easily retrieve from memory, even though it may not be accurate) and the **confirmation bias** (the tendency to seek evidence in support of our existing beliefs and to ignore evidence that contradicts them).

Does the way information is presented affect decisions? How do we explain to ourselves the decisions we make? **Framing,** or perspective in which a problem is presented, can also affect the outcome of a decision. And regardless of whether a decision proves to be good or bad, we often use **hindsight bias,** which refers to our tendency to view outcomes as inevitable or predictable after we know the outcome to "correct" our memories so that the decision seems to be a good one. **Counterfactual thinking** involves revisiting our decisions by considering "what if" alternatives.

MULTITASKING

Contrary to what many people believe, multitasking often results in reduced speed, decreased accuracy, and increased stress. Numerous studies have shown that driving is particularly affected by multitasking. Talking on a cell phone or texting while driving may be as bad as driving legally drunk.

INTELLIGENCE AND MENTAL ABILITIES

What types of questions are used to measure intelligence? Psychologists who study **intelligence** ask what intelligence entails and how it can be measured. To accomplish this, they use a variety of questions to assess general knowledge, vocabulary, arithmetic reasoning, and spatial manipulation.

What are some of the major theories of intelligence? Intelligence theories fall into two categories: those that argue in favor of a "general intelligence" that affects all aspects of cognitive functioning, and those that say intelligence is composed of many separate abilities, in which a person will not necessarily score high in all. Spearman's theory of intelligence is an example of the first category. Thurstone's theory is an example of the second category, as are Sternberg's **triarchic theory of intelligence** and Gardner's **theory of multiple intelligences.** Goleman's theory of **emotional intelligence** emphasizes skill in social relationships and awareness of others' and one's own emotions.

What kinds of intelligence tests are in use today? The *Binet–Simon Scale,* developed in France by Alfred Binet and Theodore Simon, was adapted by Stanford University's L. M. Terman to create a test that yields an **intelligence quotient (IQ),** the *Stanford–Binet Intelligence Scale.* The **Wechsler Adult Intelligence Scale** and the **Wechsler Intelligence Scale for Children** provide scores for several different kinds of mental abilities as well as an overall IQ score. In contrast to these individual intelligence tests, **group tests** of intelligence are administered by one examiner to many people at a time. Alternatives to traditional IQ tests include **performance tests** of mental abilities that exclude the use of language and **culture-fair tests** that reduce cultural bias in a variety of ways.

What are some important characteristics of a good test? **Reliability** refers to the ability of a test to produce consistent and stable scores. Psychologists express reliability in terms of **correlation coefficients,** which measure the relationship between two sets of scores. **Validity** is the ability of a test to measure what it has been designed to measure. **Content validity** exists if a test contains an adequate sample of questions relating to the skills or knowledge it is supposed to measure. **Criterion-related** validity refers to the relationship between test scores and whatever the test is designed to measure. In the case of intelligence, the most common independent measure is academic achievement. Although the reliability of IQ tests is seldom questioned, their validity is questioned. Critics charge that these tests assess a very limited set of mental skills and that some tests may be unfairly biased against minority groups. Also, poor school performance may be the result of, rather than caused by, low test scores. Finally, although IQ tests tend to predict occupational success and performance on the job after college, they are not ideally suited to that important task. New tests are being developed to address these concerns.

HEREDITY, ENVIRONMENT, AND INTELLIGENCE

What determines individual differences in intelligence? Why are twin studies useful in studying intelligence? Although there has been extended debate about the extent to which heredity and environment contribute to IQ, studies comparing the IQ scores of identical and fraternal twins raised in the same and different families indicate that approximately 50% of differences in intelligence are due to genetics and the other half due to differences in environment, including education.

What have we learned from early intervention programs about the influence of the environment on intellectual development? With such a sizable percentage of the differences in IQ scores being attributable to the environment and education, many psychologists are strongly in favor of compensatory education programs for young children from disadvantaged homes. Two such programs are the Milwaukee Project and Head Start. Although they may not boost IQ scores greatly in the long run, such programs do seem to have significant educational benefits.

How can the study of plants help us to understand the relationship between heredity and environment? Plants grown in rich soil under ideal environmental conditions generally do better than plants grown in poor soil under less than ideal conditions, thus showing the importance of environment. But differences between plants grown under the same environmental conditions demonstrate the importance of heredity. Similarly, individual differences in human intelligence reflect both the genetic and environmental factors. However, psychologists cannot yet account for the fact that IQ scores on the whole are increasing (the Flynn Effect).

Do culture and gender influence mental abilities? While males and females do not differ in general intelligence, females do tend to have slightly stronger verbal skills while males tend to have slightly stronger visual-spatial skills. Research indicates that these differences emerge in early infancy. As for cultural differences, research does not support the notion that people from certain cultures have a natural tendency to excel at academic skills.

What do psychologists know about the two extremes of human intelligence: very high and very low? The IQs of nearly 70% of the population fall between 85 and 115; and all but 5% have IQs between 70 and 130. **Mental retardation** and **giftedness** are the two extremes of intelligence. About 25% of cases of mental retardation can be traced to biological causes, including Down syndrome, but causes of the remaining 75% are not fully understood; nor are the causes of giftedness. Gifted people do not necessarily excel in all mental abilities.

CREATIVITY

What is creativity? **Creativity** is the ability to produce novel and socially valued ideas or objects.

How is creativity related to intelligence? The threshold theory holds that a minimum level of intelligence is needed for creativity, but above that threshold level, higher intelligence doesn't necessarily make for greater creativity. Apparently factors other than intelligence contribute to creativity.

Can creativity be measured? Creativity tests are scored on the originality of answers and, frequently, on the number of responses (demonstrating divergent thinking). Some psychologists question how valid these tests are, however.

8

Motivation and Emotion

Classic detective stories are usually studies of motivation and emotion. At the beginning, all we know is that a murder has been committed: After eating dinner with her family, sweet old Amanda Jones collapses and dies of strychnine poisoning. "Now, why would anyone do a thing like that?" everybody wonders. The police ask the same question, in different terms: "Who had a motive for killing Miss Jones?" In a good mystery, the answer is "Practically everybody."

There is, for example, the younger sister—although she is 75 years old, she still bristles when she thinks of that tragic day 50 years ago when Amanda stole her sweetheart. And there is the next-door neighbor, who was heard saying that if Miss Jones's poodle trampled his peonies one more time, there would be consequences. Then there is the spendthrift nephew who stands to inherit a fortune from the deceased. Finally, the parlor maid has a guilty secret that Miss Jones knew and had threatened to reveal. All four suspects were in the house on the night of the murder, had access to the poison (which was used to kill rats in the basement), and had strong feelings about Amanda Jones. All of them had a motive for killing her.

In this story, motivation and emotion are so closely intertwined that drawing distinctions between them is difficult. However, psychologists do try to separate them. A **motive** is a specific need or desire that arouses the organism and directs its behavior toward a goal. All motives are triggered by some kind of stimulus: a bodily condition, a cue in the environment, or a feeling.

Emotion refers to the experience of feelings such as fear, joy, surprise, and anger. Like motives, emotions also activate and affect behavior, but it is more difficult to predict the kind of behavior that a particular emotion will prompt. If a man is hungry, we can be reasonably sure that he will seek food. If, however, this same man experiences a feeling of joy or surprise, we cannot know with certainty how he will act.

The important thing to remember about both motives and emotions is that they push us to take some kind of action whether or not we are aware of it. We do not need to think about feeling hungry to make a beeline for the refrigerator. Similarly, we do not have to realize that we are afraid before stepping back from a growling dog. Moreover, the same motivation or emotion may produce different behaviors in different people. Ambition might motivate one person to go to law school and another to join a crime ring. Feeling sad might lead one person to cry alone and another to seek out a friend. On the other hand, the same behavior might arise from different motives or emotions: You may go to a movie because you are happy, bored, or lonely. In short, the workings of motives and emotions are very complex.

In this chapter, we will first look at some specific motives that play important roles in human behavior. Then we will turn our attention to emotions and the various ways they are expressed. We begin our discussion of motivation with a few general concepts.

ENDURING ISSUES in Motivation and Emotion

The heart of this chapter concerns the ways in which motives and emotions affect behavior and are affected by the external environment (*Person–Situation*). While discussing those key issues, we will explore the question of whether motives and emotions are inborn or acquired (*Nature–Nurture*) and whether they change significantly over the life span (*Stability–Change*). We will also consider the extent to which individuals differ in their motives and emotions (*Diversity–Universality*) and the ways in which motives and emotions arise from and, in turn, affect biological processes (*Mind–Body*). ■

PERSPECTIVES ON MOTIVATION

How can you use intrinsic and extrinsic motivation to help you succeed in college?

Instincts

Early in the 20th century, psychologists often attributed behavior to **instincts**—specific, inborn behavior patterns characteristic of an entire species. In 1890, William James compiled a list of human instincts that included hunting, rivalry, fear, curiosity, shyness, love, shame, and resentment. But by the 1920s, instinct theory began to fall out of favor as an explanation of human behavior for three reasons: (1) Most important human behavior is learned; (2) human behavior is rarely rigid, inflexible, unchanging, and found throughout the species, as is the case with instincts; and (3) ascribing every conceivable human behavior to a corresponding instinct explains nothing (calling a person's propensity to be alone an "antisocial instinct," for example, merely names the behavior without pinpointing its origins).

LEARNING OBJECTIVE

- Compare and contrast instincts, drive-reduction theory, and arousal theory (including the Yerkes–Dodson law) as explanations of human behavior. Distinguish between primary and secondary drives, intrinsic and extrinsic motivation, and summarize Maslow's hierarchy of motives.

motive Specific need or desire, such as hunger, thirst, or achievement, that prompts goal-directed behavior.

emotion Feeling, such as fear, joy, or surprise, that underlies behavior.

instincts Inborn, inflexible, goal-directed behaviors that are characteristic of an entire species.

THINKING CRITICALLY ABOUT . . .

Primary Drives

Primary drives are, by definition, unlearned. But learning clearly affects how these drives are expressed: We learn how and what to eat and drink.

1. Given that information, how might you design a research study to determine what aspects of a given drive, say hunger, are learned and which are not?

2. What steps would you take to increase the likelihood that your results apply to people in general and not just to a small sample of people?

3. Would you have to rely on self-reports or could you directly observe behavior?

 Watch the **Video** The Big Picture: What Drives Us? on **MyPsychLab**

Drive-Reduction Theory

An alternative view of motivation holds that bodily needs (such as the need for food or the need for water) create a state of tension or arousal called a **drive** (such as hunger or thirst). According to **drive-reduction theory,** motivated behavior is an attempt to reduce this unpleasant state of tension in the body and to return the body to a state of **homeostasis,** or balance. When we are hungry, we look for food to reduce the hunger drive. When we are tired, we find a place to rest.

According to drive-reduction theory, drives can generally be divided into two categories. **Primary drives** are unlearned, are found in all animals (including humans), and motivate behavior that is vital to the survival of the individual or species. Primary drives include hunger, thirst, and sex. **Secondary drives** are acquired through learning. For instance, no one is born with a drive to acquire great wealth, yet many people are motivated by money. 👁

Arousal Theory

Drive-reduction theory is appealing, but it cannot explain all kinds of behavior. It implies, for example, that once drives are reduced, people will do little. They would literally have no motivation. Yet this is obviously not the case. People work, play, do Sudoku puzzles, and do many other things for which there is no known drive that needs to be reduced.

Arousal theory suggests that each of us has an optimum level of arousal that varies over the course of the day and from one situation to another. According to this view, behavior is motivated by the desire to maintain the optimum level of arousal for a given moment. Sometimes, as envisioned in drive-reduction theory, that may call for reducing the level of arousal. But other times, behavior appears to be motivated by a desire to increase the state of arousal. For example, when you are bored, you may turn on the television, take a walk, or check for text messages.

Interestingly, overall level of arousal affects performance in different situations but psychologists agree that there is no "best" level of arousal necessary to perform all tasks (Gray, Braver, & Raichle, 2002). Rather, it is largely a question of degree. The **Yerkes–Dodson law** puts it this way: The more complex the task, the lower the level of arousal that can be tolerated without interfering with performance (Yerkes & Dodson, 1908/2007). Thus, to perform optimally on a simple task, you may need to increase your level of arousal. Conversely, you may need to reduce your level of arousal to perform well on a complex task. (See **Figure 8–1.**)

Arousal theory has some advantages over drive-reduction theory, but neither one can readily account for some kinds of behavior. For example, many people today participate in activities that are stimulating in the extreme: rock climbing, skydiving, bungee jumping, kitesurfing, and hang gliding. Such thrill-seeking activities do not seem to be drive-reducing and do not seem to be done in pursuit of an optimal level of arousal. Zuckerman (2007a) accounts for such activities by suggesting that *sensation seeking* is itself a basic motivation, at least some aspects of which are inherited and neurologically based (Joseph, Liu, Jiang, Lynam, & Kelly, 2009; Zuckerman, 2009). In general, high sensation seekers, compared to low sensation seekers, are more likely to

- prefer dangerous sports (Diehm & Armatas, 2004; Eachus, 2004; Zuckerman, 2007b);
- choose vocations that involve an element of risk and excitement (Zuckerman, 2006);
- smoke, drink heavily, gamble, and use illicit drugs (D'Silva, Grant-Harrington, Palmgreen, Donohew, & Pugzles-Lorch, 2001; Gurpegui et al., 2007; Nower, Derevensky, & Gupta, 2004);

drive State of tension or arousal that motivates behavior.

drive-reduction theory States that motivated behavior is aimed at reducing a state of bodily tension or arousal and returning the organism to homeostasis.

homeostasis State of balance and stability in which the organism functions effectively.

primary drives Unlearned drive, such as hunger, that are based on a physiological state.

secondary drives Learned drives, such as ambition, that are not based on a physiological state.

arousal theory Theory of motivation that proposes that organisms seek an optimal level of arousal.

Yerkes–Dodson law States that there is an optimal level of arousal for the best performance of any task; the more complex the task, the lower the level of arousal that can be tolerated before performance deteriorates.

- engage in unsafe driving (S. L. Pedersen & McCarthy, 2008);
- have more sexual partners and engage in more varied and dangerous sexual activities (Berg, 2008; Cohen, 2008); and
- be classified in school as delinquent or hyperactive (though not more aggressive) (Ang & Woo, 2003; Modecki, 2008).

intrinsic motivation A desire to perform a behavior that stems from the enjoyment derived from the behavior itself.

extrinsic motivation A desire to perform a behavior to obtain an external reward or avoid punishment.

ENDURING ISSUES

Nature–Nurture   The Evolutionary Basis of Arousal Seeking

Some evolutionary theorists argue that sensation seeking may have an evolutionary basis. For example, Cosmides and Tooby (2000) propose that risk-taking behavior may have played an important adaptive role for our ancestors by providing them with opportunities to develop successful strategies to deal with potentially dangerous situations. Those who took risks, and who were thereby better equipped to cope with danger and turmoil in their environment, improved their social status and sexual competitiveness more than those who did not (Ermer, Cosmides, & Tooby, 2008). ■

Intrinsic and Extrinsic Motivation

Some psychologists further distinguish between intrinsic and extrinsic motivation. **Intrinsic motivation** refers to motivation provided by an activity itself. Children climb trees, finger paint, and play games for no other reason than the fun they get from the activity itself. In the same way, adults may solve crossword puzzles, play a musical instrument, or tinker in a workshop largely for the enjoyment they get from the activity. **Extrinsic motivation** refers to motivation that derives from the consequences of an activity. For example, a child may do chores not because he enjoys them but because doing so earns an allowance, and an adult who plays a musical instrument may do so to earn some extra money.

Whether behavior is intrinsically or extrinsically motivated can have important consequences (Deci & Ryan, 2008). For example, if parents offer a reward to their young daughter for writing to her grandparents, the likelihood of her writing to them when rewards are no longer available may actually decrease. One analysis of some 128 studies that examined the effect of extrinsic rewards on the behavior of children, adolescents, and adults found that when extrinsic rewards are offered for a behavior, intrinsic motivation and sense of personal responsibility for that behavior are likely to decrease, at least for a short time (Deci, Koestner, & Ryan, 1999, 2001). However, unexpected (as opposed to contractual) rewards

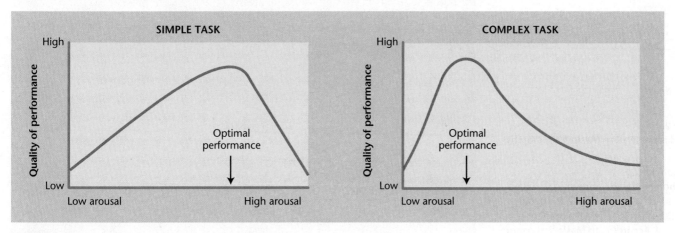

FIGURE 8–1

The Yerkes–Dodson law.

A certain amount of arousal is needed to perform most tasks, but a very high level of arousal interferes with the performance of complicated activities. That is, the level of arousal that can be tolerated is higher for a simple task than for a complex one.

Source: After Hebb, 1955.

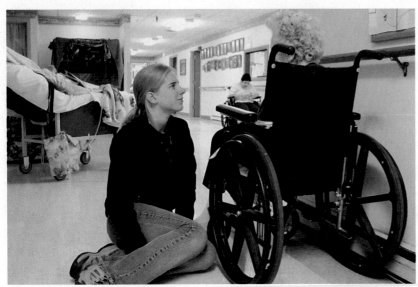

The same activity might be motivated intrinsically, just for the pleasure of doing it, or extrinsically, by rewards unrelated to the activity itself.

hierarchy of needs A theory of motivation advanced by Maslow holding that higher order motives involving social and personal growth only emerge after lower level motives related to survival have been satisfied.

do not necessarily reduce intrinsic motivation, and positive feedback (including praise) may actually increase intrinsic motivation (Reiss, 2005). For example, one study showed that rewarding small children for eating vegetables they initially disliked resulted in the children consuming more of those vegetables and reporting that the they liked them more (Cooke, 2011).

A Hierarchy of Motives

Humanistic psychologist Abraham Maslow (1954) arranged motives in a hierarchy, from lower to higher. The lower motives spring from physiological needs that must be satisfied. As we move higher in Maslow's **hierarchy of needs,** the motives have more subtle origins: the desire to live as safely as possible, to connect meaningfully with other human beings, and to make the best possible impression on others. Maslow believed that the highest motive in the hierarchy is self-actualization—the drive to realize one's full potential. Maslow's hierarchy of motives is illustrated in **Figure 8–2.**

According to Maslow's theory, higher motives emerge only after the more basic ones have been largely satisfied: A person who is starving doesn't care what people think of her table manners.

Maslow's model offers an appealing way to organize a wide range of motives into a coherent structure. But recent research challenges the universality of his views. In many societies, people live on the very edge of survival, yet they form strong and meaningful social ties and possess a firm sense of self-esteem (E. Hoffman, 2008; Wubbolding, 2005). As a result of such research findings, many psychologists now view Maslow's model with

FIGURE 8–2

A pyramid representing Maslow's hierarchy of needs.

From bottom to top, the stages correspond to how fundamental the motive is for survival and how early it appears in both the evolution of the species and the development of the individual. According to Maslow, the more basic needs must largely be satisfied before higher motives can emerge.

Source: From *Motivation and Personality* by Abraham H. Maslow. Copyright © 1970. Reprinted by permission of Pearson Education, Upper Saddle River, NJ.

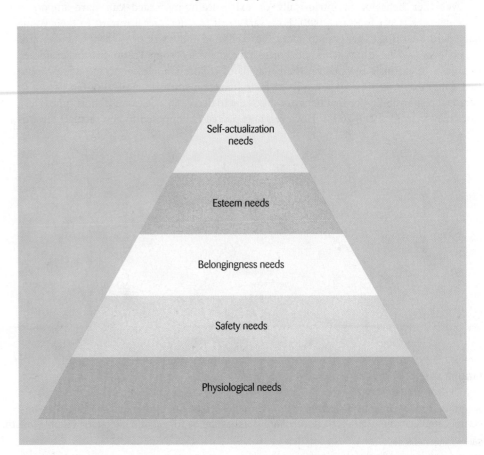

Self-actualization needs

Esteem needs

Belongingness needs

Safety needs

Physiological needs

a measure of skepticism although it continues to be a convenient way to think of the wide range of human motives.

We have reviewed some basic concepts about motivation. With these concepts in mind, we now turn our attention to specific motives.

✓● Study and Review on MyPsychLab

CHECK YOUR UNDERSTANDING

Match the following terms with the appropriate definition.

1. ___ drive
2. ___ drive reduction
3. ___ homeostasis
4. ___ self-actualization
5. ___ intrinsic motivation
6. ___ extrinsic motivation

a. the drive to realize one's full potential
b. state of balance in which the organism functions effectively
c. theory that motivated behavior is focused on reducing bodily tension
d. tending to perform behavior to receive some external reward or avoid punishment
e. state of tension brought on by biological needs
f. motivation arising from behavior itself

Answers: 1. e. 2. c. 3. b. 4. a. 5. f. 6. d.

APPLY YOUR UNDERSTANDING

1. You are home alone and have nothing to do. You find yourself walking around. You look for something to read, but nothing seems quite right. Then you check to see if anything interesting is on TV, but again nothing seems worth watching. Finally, you decide to go jogging. This kind of motivated behavior that increases the state of arousal is a problem for
   a. the instinct theory of motivation.
   b. any theory of motivation.
   c. the drive-reduction theory of motivation.
   d. the Yerkes–Dodson law.

2. While you are working on a complex task, your boss stops by your desk and says, "You've only got 10 more minutes to finish that up. It's really important that it be done right. I know you can do it and I'm depending on you." When you complain that he's making you nervous and your performance will suffer, he replies, "I'm just trying to motivate you." Which of the following does your boss apparently not understand?
   a. drive-reduction theory
   b. homeostasis
   c. extrinsic motivation
   d. the Yerkes–Dodson law

Answers: 1. c. 2. d.

HUNGER AND THIRST

Why do people usually get hungry at mealtime?

When you are hungry, you eat. If you don't eat, your need for food will increase but your hunger will come and go. Moreover, shortly after lunch when you have no need for further food, if you pass a bakery and smell the baked goods, you may crave a donut or a scone. In other words, the psychological state of hunger is not the same as the biological need for food, although that need often sets the psychological state in motion.

Thirst also is stimulated by both internal and external cues. Internally, thirst is controlled by two regulators that monitor the level of fluids inside and outside the cells. But we may also become thirsty just seeing a TV commercial featuring people savoring tall, cool drinks in a lush, tropical setting. Even what we thirst for can be influenced by what we see.

LEARNING OBJECTIVES

- Identify the areas of the brain that are involved in hunger and describe the role of glucose, leptin, and ghrelin in determining a biological need for food. Distinguish between the biological need for food and the experience of hunger (including the role of incentives).
- List the symptoms that are used to diagnose anorexia nervosa, bulimia nervosa, muscle dysmorphia, and obesity. Describe the people who are most likely to develop these disorders and the most likely causes of them.

glucose A simple sugar used by the body for energy.

leptin A hormone released by fat cells that reduces appetite.

ghrelin A hormone produced in the stomach and small intestines that increases appetite.

✳ ⌐Explore the Concept Virtual Brain: Hunger and Eating on MyPsychLab

One study showed, for example, that women watching a movie with commercials advertising sweetened soda were more likely to consume soda during movie breaks than where women who viewed commercials advertising water (Koordeman, Anschutz, van Baaren, & Engels, 2010).

Biological and Emotional Factors

How can external cues influence our desire to eat?

Early research identified two regions in the hypothalamus that served as a kind of "switch" that turned eating on or off. When one of these centers was stimulated, animals began to eat; and when it was destroyed the animals stopped eating to the point of starvation. When the second region was stimulated, animals stopped eating; when it was destroyed, animals ate to the point of extreme obesity. However, recent studies have challenged this simple "on–off" explanation for the control of eating by showing that a number of other areas of the brain are also involved in regulating food intake including regions of the cerebrum, amygdala, the insula and the spinal cord (Garavan, 2010; Olszewski, Cedernaes, Olsson, Levine, & Schiöth, 2008; Siep et al., 2009). ✳

How do these various areas of the brain know when to stimulate hunger? It turns out that the brain monitors the blood levels of **glucose** (a simple sugar used by the body for energy), fats, carbohydrates, and the hormone *insulin*. (See **Figure 8–3**.) Changes in the levels of these substances signal the need for food. In addition, fat cells within our body produce the hormone **leptin** which travels in the bloodstream and is sensed by the hypothalamus. High levels of leptin signal the brain to reduce appetite, or to increase the rate at which fat is burned.

The brain also monitors the amount of food that you have eaten. Specialized cells in the stomach and the upper part of the small intestine sense the volume of food in the digestive system. When only a small quantity of food is present, these cells release a hormone called **ghrelin** into the bloodstream. Ghrelin travels to the brain where it stimulates appetite and focuses our thoughts and imagination on food (Näslund & Hellström, 2007; Faulconbridge, 2008).

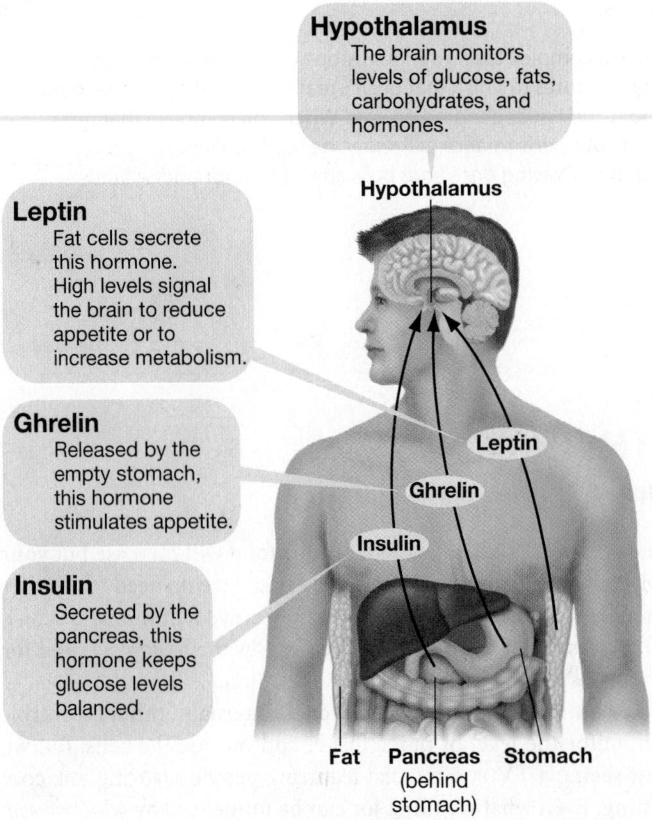

FIGURE 8–3
Physiological factors regulating appetite and body weight.

A variety of chemical messengers interact to stimulate and suppress appetite. Among these are insulin, leptin, and ghrelin.

Hypothalamus
The brain monitors levels of glucose, fats, carbohydrates, and hormones.

Hypothalamus

Leptin
Fat cells secrete this hormone. High levels signal the brain to reduce appetite or to increase metabolism.

Ghrelin
Released by the empty stomach, this hormone stimulates appetite.

Insulin
Secreted by the pancreas, this hormone keeps glucose levels balanced.

Leptin
Ghrelin
Insulin

Fat   Pancreas   Stomach
(behind stomach)

But, as we noted earlier, the biological need for food is not the only thing that can trigger the experience of hunger. For example, a single night of sleep deprivation can leave one feeling hungry by increasing ghrelin levels and decreasing leptin levels (Schmid, Hallschmid, Jauch-Chara, Born, & Schultes, 2008). Moreover, the mere sight, smell, or thought of food causes an increase in insulin production, which, in turn, lowers glucose levels in the body's cells, mirroring the body's response to a physical need for food (Logue, 2000; van der Laan, de Ridder, Viergever, & Smeets, 2011). Thus, the aroma from a nearby restaurant may serve as more than an **incentive** to eat; it may actually cause the body to react as though there is a real biological need for food. Most Americans eat three meals a day at fairly regular intervals. Numerous studies with both humans and animals have shown that regularly eating at particular times during the day leads to the release at those times of the hormones and neurotransmitters that cause hunger (Woods, Schwartz, Baskin, & Seeley, 2000). In other words, we get hungry around noon partly because the body "learns" that if it's noon, it's time to eat.

incentive External stimulus that prompts goal-directed behavior.

ENDURING ISSUES

Diversity–Universality   Hunger and Eating

The hunger drive is tied to emotions in complex ways. Some people head for the refrigerator whenever they are depressed, bored, anxious, or angry. Others lose all interest in food at these times and complain that they are "too upset to eat." One student studying for an important exam spends as much time eating as reading; another student studying for the same exam lives on coffee until the exam is over. Under emotionally arousing conditions, what one person craves may turn another person's stomach.

What people eat when they are hungry also varies greatly as a result of learning and social conditioning. Although most Americans will not eat horsemeat, it is very popular in several European countries. Yet many Americans consume pork, which violates both Islamic and Jewish dietary laws. In some parts of South Asia, Africa, and China, people consider monkey brains a delicacy. And in Cambodia, fried tarantulas are popular and cheap! ■

How and when you satisfy hunger and thirst depends on social, psychological, environmental, and cultural influences as well as on physiological needs. For example, the Japanese tea ceremony *(right)* is concerned more with restoring inner harmony than with satisfying thirst. Do you think the office worker *(left)* is drinking coffee because she is thirsty?

anorexia nervosa A serious eating disorder that is associated with an intense fear of weight gain and a distorted body image.

bulimia nervosa An eating disorder characterized by binges of eating followed by self-induced vomiting.

muscle dysmorphia A disorder generally seen in young men involving an obsessive concern with muscle size.

Eating Disorders and Obesity

How can you tell if someone is suffering from anorexia nervosa or bulimia?

Anorexia Nervosa and Bulimia Nervosa "When people told me I looked like someone from Auschwitz [the Nazi concentration camp], I thought that was the highest compliment anyone could give me." This confession comes from a young woman who as a teenager suffered from a serious eating disorder known as **anorexia nervosa.** She was 18 years old, 5 feet 3 inches tall, and weighed 68 pounds. This young woman was lucky. She managed to overcome the disorder and has since maintained normal body weight. Many others are less fortunate. In fact, researchers have found that over 10% of the young women with anorexia nervosa die as a result of the disorder, one of the highest fatality rates for psychiatric disorders affecting young females (Birmingham, Su, Hlynsky, Goldner, & Gao, 2005; Huas, 2011).

The following four symptoms are used in the diagnosis of anorexia nervosa (American Psychiatric Association, 2000):

1. Intense fear of becoming obese, which does not diminish as weight loss progresses.
2. Disturbance of body image (for example, claiming to "feel fat" even when emaciated).
3. Refusal to maintain body weight at or above a minimal normal weight for age and height.
4. In females, the absence of at least three consecutive menstrual cycles.

Approximately 1% of all adolescents suffer from anorexia nervosa; about 90% of these are White upper- or middle-class females (Bulik et al., 2006).

Anorexia is frequently compounded by another eating disorder known as **bulimia nervosa** (Herpertz-Dahlmann, 2009). The following criteria are used for its diagnosis (American Psychiatric Association, 2000):

1. Recurrent episodes of binge eating (rapid consumption of a large amount of food, usually in less than 2 hours).
2. Recurrent inappropriate behaviors to try to prevent weight gain, such as self-induced vomiting.
3. Binge eating and compensatory behaviors occurring at least twice a week for three months.
4. Body shape and weight excessively influencing the person's self-image.
5. Occurrence of the just-mentioned behaviors at least sometimes in the absence of anorexia.

Approximately 1 to 2% of all adolescent females suffer from bulimia nervosa, though some evidence suggests this number may be decreasing (Keel, Heatherton, Dorer, Joiner, & Zalta, 2006). Once again, the socioeconomic group at highest risk for bulimia is upper-middle- and upper-class women.

Although anorexia and bulimia are much more prevalent among females than males (Gleaves, Miller, Williams, & Summers, 2000; S. Turnbull, Ward, Treasure, Jick, & Derby, 1996), many more men are affected by these disorders than was once suspected (Gila, Castro, & Cesena, 2005). Both men and women with eating disorders are preoccupied with body image, but men are not necessarily obsessed with losing weight (Ey, 2010; Ousley, Cordero, & White, 2008). For example, a related phenomenon called **muscle dysmorphia** appears to be on the increase among young men (Olivardia, 2007). Muscle dysmorphia is an obsessive concern with one's muscle size. Men with muscle dysmorphia, many of whom are well muscled, are nonetheless distressed at their perceived puniness, and spend an inordinate amount of time fretting over their diet and exercising to increase their muscle mass (C. G. Pope, Pope, & Menard, 2005).

Little is known about the factors that contribute to eating disorders among men (Crosscope-Happel, 2005), though research has shown that muscle dysmorphia is associated with low self-esteem and having been bullied as a child (Wolke & Sapouna, 2008). We know considerably more about the factors that contribute to eating disorders in women

Does the American obsession with super slimness lead adolescents to become anorexic?

(Garner & Magana, 2006). On one hand, mass media promote the idea that a woman must be thin to be attractive. In addition, women with bulimia commonly have low self-esteem, are hypersensitive to social interactions, and are more likely to come from families where negative comments are often made about weight (Crowther, Kichler, Sherwood, & Kuhnert, 2002; Zonnevylle-Bender et al., 2004). Many also display clinical depression or obsessive–compulsive disorder (see Chapter 12, "Psychological Disorders") and have engaged in self-injurious behaviors such as cutting themselves (Herpertz-Dahlmann, 2009). Finally, there is growing evidence that genetics plays a significant role in both anorexia nervosa and bulimia nervosa (Helder & Collier, 2011).

Anorexia and bulimia are notoriously hard to treat, and there is considerable disagreement on the most effective approach to therapy (G. T. Wilson, Grilo, & Vitousek, 2007; Yager, 2008), though some research suggests a multimodal treatment approach involving nutritional counseling, individual therapy, and family therapy may be most effective (Herpertz-Dahlmann & Salbach-Andrae, 2009). Unfortunately, some psychologists doubt that we can ever eliminate eating disorders in a culture bombarded with the message that "thin is in" (Fairburn, Cooper, Shafran, & Wilson, 2008). Regrettably, in many developing countries such as Taiwan, Singapore, and China, where dieting is becoming a fad, eating disorders, once little known, are now becoming a serious problem (H. Chen & Jackson, 2008).

Obesity and Weight Control According to the U.S. Surgeon General, obesity is the most pressing health problem in America (Office of the Surgeon General, 2007). *Obesity* refers to an excess of body fat in relation to lean body mass, while *overweight* refers to weighing more than a desirable standard, whether from high amounts of fat or being very muscular. Obesity has increased by more than 50% during the past decade, with more than two-thirds of Americans being either overweight or obese. In contrast to anorexia nervosa and bulimia nervosa, obesity is more prevalent among Black women than among White women (Y. C. Wang, Colditz, & Kuntz, 2007).

Even more disturbing, the rate of obesity among young people has more than tripled since 1980, with over 9 million overweight adolescents in America today. (See **Figure 8–4**).

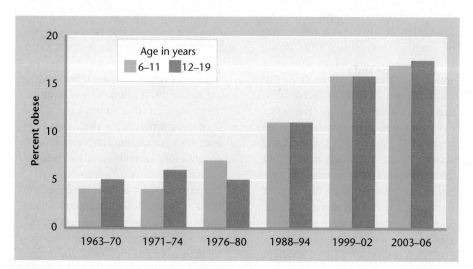

FIGURE 8–4

Rising obesity among American youth.

The number of overweight children and adolescents has increased sharply in recent years. From 1980 to 2002, the percentage of overweight adolescents tripled. This trend is particularly disturbing since overweight children and adolescents are likely to become overweight adults, placing them at increased risk for cardiovascular disease, hypertension, and diabetes.

Source: CDC/NCHS, NHES, and NHANES.

Notes: Excludes pregnant women starting with 1971–74. Pregnancy status not available for 1963–65 and 1966–70. Data for 1963–65 are for children 6–11 years of age; data for 1966–70 are for adolescents 12–17 years of age, not 12–19 years.

set point theory A theory that our bodies are genetically predisposed to maintaining a certain weight by changing our metabolic rate and activity level in response to caloric intake.

This problem is particularly serious since overweight children and adolescents are more likely to become overweight adults who are at an increased risk for serious diseases like hypertension, cardiovascular disease, diabetes, and sleep apnea (American Heart Association, 2009).

Many factors contribute to overeating and obesity (Hebebrand & Hinney, 2009). As stated above, many people inherit a tendency to be overweight (Frayling et al., 2007; Ramadori et al., 2008). Neuroimaging studies suggest part of this problem may stem from an inherited tendency in some people to become addicted to compulsive eating (similar to the genetic predisposition toward drug and alcohol addiction). As a result of this predisposition, these individuals are more vulnerable to cravings triggered by food cues in their environment, and less responsive to their body's internal signaling of satiety (Leutwyler-Ozelli, 2007).

Eating habits established during childhood are also important because they determine the number of fat cells that develop in the body and that number remains fairly constant throughout life. Dieting during adulthood only decreases the amount of fat each cell stores; it doesn't reduce the total number of fat cells (Spalding et al., 2008).

APPLYING PSYCHOLOGY

The Slow (but Lasting) Fix for Weight Gain

The study of hunger and eating has led to some compelling insights into the problem of weight control. It appears that our bodies are genetically "set" to maintain a certain weight by means of neural networks that monitor and control energy homeostasis (Levin, 2010). According to this **set point theory,** if you consume more calories than you need for that weight, your metabolic rate will increase. As a result, you will feel an increase in energy that will prompt you to be more active, thereby burning more calories. If, however, you eat fewer calories than are needed to maintain your weight, your metabolic rate will decrease; you will feel tired and become less active, thereby burning fewer calories. This mechanism was no doubt helpful during the thousands of years that our species lived literally hand to mouth, but it is less helpful where food is abundant, as in modern industrialized nations.

An implication of our current understanding of hunger and weight regulation is that a successful weight-control program must be long term and must work with, rather than against, the body's normal tendency to maintain weight. On the basis of studies of the hunger drive and the relationship between eating and body weight, here are our recommendations for weight control:

1. First, check with your doctor before you start. People want quick fixes, so they often go overboard on dieting or exercise, sometimes with disastrous consequences. Make sure your weight loss program will be safe.
2. Increase your body's metabolism through regular exercise. The most effective metabolism booster is 20–30 minutes of moderate activity several times a week. Although only about 200–300 calories are burned off during each exercise session, the exercise increases the resting metabolic rate. This means that you burn more calories when not exercising. Thus, exercise is an important part of a weight reduction program.
3. Modify your diet. A moderate reduction in calories is beneficial. Also, reduce your consumption of fats (particularly saturated fats) and sugars. Sugars trigger an increase in the body's level of insulin; and high levels of fat and insulin in the blood stimulate hunger.
4. Reduce external cues that encourage you to eat undesirable foods. The mere sight or smell of food can increase the amount of insulin in the body, thus triggering hunger. Many people find that if they do their grocery shopping on a full stomach, it is easier to resist the temptation to buy junk foods.
5. Set realistic goals. Focus at least as much on preventing weight gain as on losing weight. If you must lose weight, try to shed just one pound a week for 2 or 3 months. After that, concentrate on maintaining that new, lower weight for several months before moving on to further weight loss.
6. Reward yourself—in ways unrelated to food—for small improvements. Use some of the behavior-modification techniques described in Chapter 5: Reward yourself not only for each pound of weight lost but also for each day or week that you maintain that weight loss. And remember, numerous studies have shown that losing weight is much easier than keeping weight off (T. Mann et al., 2007). The only way you can keep the weight off is by continuing to adhere to a reasonable diet and exercise plan.

A sedentary lifestyle also contributes to obesity. Children in the United States today are more likely to watch television and play video games than to play soccer or hockey; and many adults lack adequate physical activity, too. Abundant opportunities and encouragement to overeat in American culture also play a role. Several studies have shown that many obese people eat more than half their calories at night (Mieda, Williams, Richardson, Tanaka, & Yanagisawa, 2006). Portion size has also increased in recent years, as has the constant availability of food from vending machines and fast-food restaurants.

Adding to the medical difficulties accompanying obesity, overweight people often face ridicule and discrimination resulting in significant economic, social, and educational loss. For example, overweight women have reported lowered self-confidence owing to victimization in school and at work because of their weight (C. Johnson, 2002; Rothblum, Brand, Miller, & Oetjen, 1990). Obese male lawyers earn less than male lawyers of normal weight (Saporta & Halpern, 2002). Even children who are overweight display increased rates of behavior problems, including aggression, lack of discipline, immaturity, anxiety, low self-esteem, and depression when compared with their normal-weight peers (Ward-Begnoche et al., 2009; Q. Yang & Chen, 2001).

With all of the problems associated with being overweight, many people are constantly trying to lose weight. There are no quick fixes to weight loss, but the suggestions in "Applying Psychology: The Slow (but Lasting) Fix for Weight Gain" can help people lose weight and keep it off.

✔●—Study and Review on MyPsychLab

CHECK YOUR UNDERSTANDING

1. The level of _____ in the blood signals hunger.
2. Hunger can be stimulated by both _____ and _____ cues.

Match the following terms with the appropriate definition.

3. ____ hypothalamus
4. ____ anorexia nervosa
5. ____ bulimia nervosa

a. recurrent episodes of binge eating, followed by vomiting, taking laxatives, or excessively exercising

b. contains both a hunger center and a satiety center

c. intense fear of obesity, disturbance of body image, and very little intake of food, with resulting weight well below normal minimums

Answers: 1. glucose. 2. internal, external. 3. b. 4. c. 5. a.

APPLY YOUR UNDERSTANDING

1. You are on your way out to a play, and you notice that you are hungry. While you are watching the play, you no longer feel hungry. But when the play is over, you notice that you are hungry again. This demonstrates that
   a. the biological need for food causes hunger.
   b. if you are distracted, primary drives but not secondary drives will decrease.
   c. hunger does not necessarily correspond to a biological need for food.
   d. primary drives are unlearned and are essential to survival of the individual or species.

2. You've noticed that when you are hungry, eating a carrot doesn't satisfy you, but eating a chocolate bar does. This is probably because the chocolate bar, to a greater extent than the carrot
   a. increases the amount of glucose in your bloodstream, which in turn reduces hunger.
   b. reduces your biological need for food.
   c. is an extrinsic motivator.
   d. serves as an incentive.

Answers: 1. c. 2. a.

LEARNING OBJECTIVES

- Describe how sexual motivation is both similar to and different from other primary drives. Identify the factors (biological and nonbiological) that affect sexual motivation.
- Describe the sexual response cycle and how it differs for men and women. Briefly explain what is meant by the statement that "research indicates that the sex lives of most Americans differ significantly from media portrayals."
- Summarize the research evidence for and against a biological basis for sexual orientation.

SEX

How is the sex drive different from other primary drives?

Sex is the primary drive that motivates reproductive behavior. Like the other primary drives, it can be turned on and off by biological conditions in the body as well as by environmental cues. The human sexual response is also affected by social experience, sexual experience, nutrition, emotions, and age. In fact, just thinking about, viewing, or having fantasies about sex can lead to sexual arousal in humans (Bogaert & Fawcett, 2006). Sex differs from other primary drives in one important way: Hunger and thirst are vital to the survival of the individual, but sex is vital only to the survival of the species.

Biological Factors

How well do we understand the biology of the sex drive?

Biology clearly plays a major role in sexual motivation. At one time, the level of hormones such as **testosterone**—the male sex hormone—was believed to *determine* the male sex drive. Today, scientists recognize that hormonal influences on human sexual arousal are considerably more complex (Gades et al., 2008). While moment-to-moment fluctuations in testosterone levels are not directly linked to sex drive, *baseline* levels of testosterone are associated with the frequency of sexual behavior and satisfaction (Persky, 1978). In addition, research has shown that just thinking about sex can increase testosterone levels in women (Goldey & van Anders, 2010) and that testosterone supplements can increase the sex drive in women (Bolour & Braunstein, 2005). However, unlike lower animals, whose sexual activity is tied to the female's reproductive cycle, humans are capable of sexual arousal at any time.

Explore the **Concept** Virtual Brain: Hormones and Sex on **MyPsychLab**

Many animals secrete substances called *pheromones* that promote sexual readiness in potential partners (see Chapter 3, "Sensation and Perception"). Some evidence suggests that humans, too, secrete pheromones, in the sweat glands of the armpits and in the genitals, and that they may influence human sexual attraction (Boulkroune, Wang, March, Walker, & Jacob, 2007; Hummer & McClintock, 2009). The brain exerts a powerful influence on the sex drive, too. In particular, the limbic system and the insula, located deep within the brain, are involved in sexual excitement (Balfour, 2004; Bianchi-Demicheli & Ortigue, 2007) (see Chapter 2, "Biological Basis of Behavior").

testosterone The primary male sex hormone.

sexual response cycle The typical sequence of events, including excitement, plateau, orgasm, and resolution, characterizing sexual response in males and females.

Explore the **Concept** Sexual Response Cycle on **MyPsychLab**

The biology of sexual behavior is better understood than that of the sex drive itself. Sex researchers William Masters and Virginia Johnson long ago identified a **sexual response cycle** that consists of four phases: *excitement, plateau, orgasm,* and *resolution* (W. H. Masters & Johnson, 1966). In the *excitement phase,* the genitals become engorged with blood. In the male, this causes erection of the penis; in the female, it causes erection of the clitoris and nipples. This engorgement of the sexual organs continues into the *plateau phase,* in which sexual tension levels off. During this phase, breathing becomes more rapid and genital secretions and muscle tension increase. During *orgasm,* the male ejaculates and the woman's uterus contracts rhythmically; and both men and women experience some loss of muscle control. Following orgasm males experience a *refractory period,* which can last from a few minutes to several hours, during which time they cannot have another orgasm. Women do not have a refractory period, and may, if stimulation is reinitiated, experience another orgasm almost immediately. The *resolution phase* is one of relaxation in which muscle tension decreases and the engorged genitals return to normal. Heart rate, breathing, and blood pressure also return to normal. **Figure 8–5** displays the pattern of sexual responses for men and women.

THINKING CRITICALLY ABOUT . . .

The Sex Drive

The sex drive is said to have no survival value for the individual; its only value is the survival of the species. Suppose that humans were capable of reproducing, but no longer had a sex drive. How would life be different? In answering that question, would it help to collect data on people alive today who, for one reason or another, have lost their sex drive? Are there ways in which information from such people might not be useful to you?

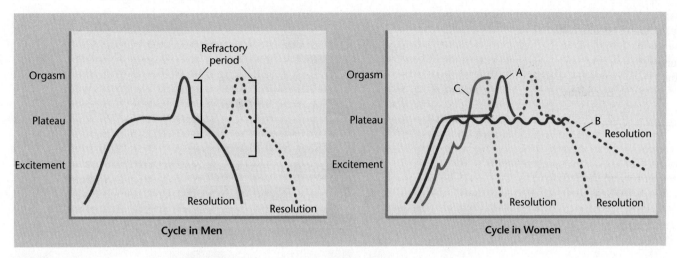

FIGURE 8–5

The sexual response cycle in males and females.

As the illustration shows, males typically go through one complete response cycle and are then capable of becoming excited again after a refractory period. Females have three characteristic patterns: one similar to the male cycle, with the added possibility of multiple orgasms (A); one that includes a lengthy plateau phase with no orgasm (B); and a rapid cycle including several increases and decreases of excitement before reaching orgasm (C).

Source: Adapted from Masters & Johnson, 1966. Reprinted by permission of The Masters and Johnson Institute.

Cultural and Environmental Factors

How does culture influence sexual behavior?

Although hormones and the nervous system do figure in the sex drive, human sexual motivation, especially in the early stages of excitement and arousal, is much more dependent on experience and learning than on biology.

What kinds of stimuli activate the sex drive? It need not be anything as immediate as a sexual partner. The sight of one's lover, as well as the smell of perfume or aftershave lotion, can stimulate sexual excitement. Soft lights and music often have an aphrodisiac effect. One person may be unmoved by an explicit pornographic movie but aroused by a romantic love story, whereas another may respond in just the opposite way. Ideas about what is moral, appropriate, and pleasurable also influence our sexual behavior. Finally, as shown in **Figure 8–6,** one global survey of reported sexual activity indicated the rate at which couples have sex varies dramatically around the world (Durex Global Sex Survey, 2005). This survey also revealed that the frequency of sexual activity varies by age, with 35- to 44-year-olds reporting to have sex an average of 112 times a year, 25- to 34-year-olds having sex an average of 108 times per year, and 16- to 20-year-olds having sex 90 times annually.

Gender equality is also an important cultural factor in how much people report enjoying their sex lives (Petersen & Hyde, 2010). For example, heterosexual couples living in countries where women and men hold equal status are the most likely to report that their sex lives are emotionally and physically satisfying. Conversely, both men and women in countries where men traditionally are more dominant report the least satisfying sex lives (Harms, 2006).

Patterns of Sexual Behavior Among Americans

Contrary to media portrayals of sexual behavior in publications like *Playboy* or TV shows like *Sex in the City,* which depict Americans as oversexed and unwilling to commit to long-term relationships, research indicates that most people are far more conservative in

FIGURE 8-6
Frequency (annual) of sexual behavior around the world.

A global survey of reported sexual activity indicates the frequency that couples have sex varies dramatically by country.

Source: http://www.durex.com/cm/ gss2005result. pdf. Used with permission of Durex.com.

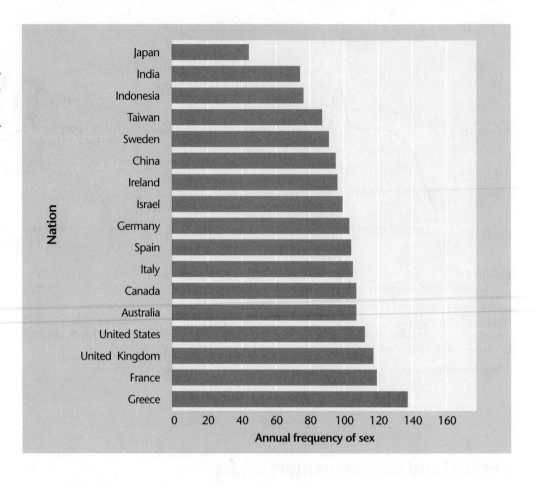

their sex lives. One carefully designed study (Michael, Gagnon, Laumann, & Kolata, 1994) of 3,432 randomly selected people between the ages of 18 and 59 revealed the following patterns in the sexual activity of American men and women:

- About one-third of those sampled had sex twice a week or more, one-third a few times a month, and the remaining third a few times a year or not at all.

- The overwhelming majority of respondents did not engage in kinky sex. Instead, vaginal intercourse was the preferred form of sex for over 90% of those sampled. Watching their partner undress was ranked second, and oral sex, third.

- Married couples reported having sex more often—and being more satisfied with their sex lives—than did unmarried persons (see also Waite & Joyner, 2001).

- The average duration of sexual intercourse reported by most people was approximately 15 minutes.

- The median number of partners over the lifetime for males was 6 and for females 2 (17% of the men and 3% of the women reported having sex with over 20 partners).

- About 25% of the men and 15% of the women had committed adultery.

Extensive research has also documented at least four significant differences in sexuality between American men and women: Men are more interested in sex than are women; women are more likely than men to link sex to a close, committed relationship; aggression, power, dominance, and assertiveness are more closely linked to sex among men than among women; and women's sexuality is more open to change over time (Lykins, Meana, & Strauss, 2008; Peplau, 2003). However, it is important to point out that gender differences in sexuality are smallest in nations that have gender equality, suggesting many of the observed differences in sexuality between men and women are based in culture (Petersen & Hyde, 2011).

Sexual Orientation

What are the arguments for and against a biological explanation of homosexuality?

Sexual orientation refers to the direction of an individual's sexual interest. People with a *heterosexual orientation* are sexually attracted to members of the opposite sex; those with a *homosexual orientation* are sexually attracted to members of their own sex; and *bisexuals* are attracted to members of both sexes. Recent studies indicate that in the United States about 3% of young adult males and 4% of young adult females identify themselves as homosexual, though estimates vary considerably depending on the age of the respondents and how sexual orientation is defined. Sexual orientation also varies by culture. For example, about 21% of adolescent females in Norway report being attracted to members of their own sex, while less than 2% of Turkish females identify themselves as being homosexual (L. Ellis, Robb, & Burke, 2005; John Hughes, 2006; Savin-Williams, 2006).

Homosexual activity is common among animals. For example, male giraffes often engage in extreme necking, entwining, and rubbing, becoming sexually aroused as they do.

What determines sexual orientation? This issue has been argued for decades in the form of the classic nature-versus-nurture debate. Those on the nature side hold that sexual orientation is rooted in biology and is primarily influenced by genetics (LeVay, 2011). They point out that homosexual men and women generally know before puberty that they are "different" and often remain "in the closet" regarding their sexual orientation for fear of recrimination (Lippa, 2005). Evidence from family and twin studies shows a higher incidence of male homosexuality in families with other gay men (Camperio-Ciani, Corna, & Capiluppi, 2004), and a higher rate of homosexuality among men with a homosexual twin even when the twins were raised separately (LeVay & Hamer, 1994). The nature position also derives support from studies revealing anatomical and physiological differences between the brains of homosexual and heterosexual men (Fitzgerald, 2008; M. Hines, 2004, 2010; LeVay, 1991). In addition, research has shown that the brains of gay and lesbian people respond to sexual pheromones like the brains of heterosexual people of the opposite gender (Berglund, Lindström, & Savic, 2006; Savic, Berglund, & Lindström, 2007). Finally, if homosexuality is primarily the result of early learning and socialization, children raised by gay or lesbian parents should be more likely to become homosexual. Research, however, has clearly demonstrated that this is not the case (C. J. Patterson, 2000).

Among other animals, homosexual activity occurs with some degree of regularity. For instance, among pygmy chimpanzees, about 50% of all observed sexual activity is between members of the same sex. In zoos, sexual activity between members of the same sex has been observed in several species including penguins and koalas bears. Even male giraffes commonly entwine their necks until both become sexually stimulated. And among some birds, such as greylag geese, homosexual unions have been found to last up to 15 years (Bagemihl, 2000; Driscoll, 2008).

Those on the nurture side argue that sexual orientation is primarily a learned behavior, influenced by early experience and largely under voluntary control. They find support for their position from cross-cultural studies that show sexual orientations occurring at different frequencies in various cultures.

Regardless of the origin of homosexuality, the general consensus among medical and mental health professionals is that heterosexuality and homosexuality both represent normal expressions of human sexuality, and that there is no convincing evidence that sexual orientation can be changed by so-called "*reparative*" or "*conversion therapy*" (American Psychological Association, 2011).

sexual orientation Refers to the direction of one's sexual interest toward members of the same sex, the other sex, or both sexes.

✔●─ **Study** and **Review** on **MyPsychLab**

CHECK YOUR UNDERSTANDING

1. The sex drive is necessary for the survival of the (individual/species) _____.
2. The four stages of the sexual response cycle are _____, _____, _____, and _____.

Match the following terms with the appropriate definitions.

3. ____ pheromones
4. ____ testosterone
5. ____ the limbic system

a. brain center involved in sexual excitement
b. hormone that influences some aspects of sexual development
c. scents that may cause sexual attraction

Answers: 1. species. 2. excitement, plateau, orgasm, and resolution. 3. c. 4. b. 5. a.

APPLY YOUR UNDERSTANDING

1. Rebecca has just "come out" to her friend Charles, telling him that she is a lesbian. She says she has known since she was a child that she was different from other girls because she was never attracted to boys, and she has concluded that this is just the way she is meant to be. Charles's reaction, however, is negative. He suggests that Rebecca just isn't trying hard enough and that counseling could help her learn new patterns of attraction. Rebecca is expressing the _____ view of homosexual orientation, while Charles's response demonstrates the _____ view.
   a. interventionist; interactionist
   b. interactionist; interventionist
   c. nurture; nature
   d. nature; nurture

2. You are reading an article in the newspaper when you come across the following statement: "The extent to which a male is interested in sex is determined by the level of the hormone testosterone at that moment." Which of the following would be an accurate response, based on what you have learned in this chapter?
   a. "That would be true only for adolescent and young adult males, not older adults."
   b. "Actually, there is very little relationship between moment-to-moment levels of testosterone and sex drive in males."
   c. "That's true, but testosterone is a pheromone, not a hormone."
   d. "That's true, but only during the excitement phase of the sexual response cycle."

Answers: 1. d. 2. b.

·⟩ OTHER IMPORTANT MOTIVES

How are stimulus motives different from primary drives?

So far, we have moved from motives that depend on biological needs (hunger and thirst) to a motive that is far more sensitive to external cues—sex. Next, we consider motives that are even more responsive to environmental stimuli. These motives, called **stimulus motives,** include *exploration, curiosity, manipulation,* and *contact.* They push us to investigate and often to change our environment. Finally, we will turn our attention to the motives of *aggression, achievement,* and *affiliation.*

Exploration and Curiosity

What motives cause people to explore and change their environment?

Where does that road go? What is in that dark little shop? Answering these questions has no obvious benefit: You do not expect the road to take you anywhere you need to go or the shop to contain anything you really want. You just want to know. Exploration and

stimulus motives Unlearned motives, such as curiosity or contact, that prompts us to explore or change the world around us.

curiosity are motives sparked by the new and unknown and are directed toward no more specific goal other than "finding out." They are not unique to humans. The family dog will run around a new house, sniffing and checking things out, before it settles down to eat its dinner. Even rats, when given a choice, will opt to explore an unknown maze rather than run through a familiar one.

Psychologists disagree about the nature of curiosity, its causes, and even how to measure it (Kashdan & Silvia, 2009). William James viewed it as an emotion; Freud considered it a socially acceptable expression of the sex drive. Others have seen it as a response to the unexpected and as evidence of a human need to find meaning in life. We might assume that curiosity is a key component of intelligence, but research has failed to confirm that hypothesis. Curiosity has been linked to creativity (Kashdan & Fincham, 2002). Interestingly, people who score high on novelty-seeking tests have a reduced number of dopamine receptors, suggesting curiosity and exploration may arise from a need for increased dopamine stimulation (Golimbet, Alfimova, Gritsenko, & Ebstein, 2007; Zald et al., 2008).

This toddler is exhibiting curiosity, a stimulus motive.

Manipulation and Contact

Is the human need for contact universal?

Why do museums have "Do Not Touch" signs everywhere? It is because the staff knows from experience that the urge to touch is almost irresistible. Unlike curiosity and exploration, manipulation focuses on a specific object that must be touched, handled, played with, and felt before we are satisfied. Manipulation is a motive limited to primates, who have agile fingers and toes. In contrast, the need for *contact* is more universal than the need for manipulation. Furthermore, it is not limited to touching with the fingers—it may involve the whole body. Manipulation is an active process, but contact may be passive.

In a classic series of experiments, Harry Harlow demonstrated the importance of the need for contact (Harlow, 1958; Harlow & Zimmerman, 1959). Newborn baby monkeys were separated from their mothers and given two "surrogate mothers." Both surrogate mothers were the same shape, but one was made of wire mesh and had no soft surfaces. The other was cuddly—layered with foam rubber and covered with terry cloth. Both surrogate mothers were warmed by means of an electric light placed inside them, but only the wire-mesh mother was equipped with a nursing bottle. Thus, the wire-mesh mother fulfilled two physiological needs for the infant monkeys: the need for food and the need for warmth. But baby monkeys most often gravitated to the terry-cloth mother, which did not provide food. When they were frightened, they would run and cling to it as they would to a real mother. Because both surrogate mothers were warm, the researchers concluded that the need for closeness goes deeper than a need for mere warmth. The importance of contact has also been demonstrated with premature infants. Low-birth-weight babies who are held and massaged gain weight faster, are calmer, and display more activity than those who are seldom touched (Hernandez-Reif, Diego, & Field, 2007; Weiss, Wilson, & Morrison, 2004).

An infant monkey with Harlow's surrogate "mothers"—one made of bare wire, the other covered with soft terry cloth. The baby monkey clings to the terry-cloth mother, even though the wire mother is heated and dispenses food. Apparently, there is contact comfort in the cuddly terry cloth that the bare wire mother can't provide.

Aggression

Is aggression a biological response or a learned one?

Human **aggression** encompasses all behavior that is intended to inflict physical or psychological harm on others. Intent is a key element of aggression. Accidentally hitting a pedestrian with your car is not an act of aggression—whereas deliberately running down a person would be.

Judging from the statistics (which often reflect underreporting of certain types of crimes), aggression is disturbingly common in this country. According to the *FBI's Uniform Crime Reports,* more than 1.3 million violent crimes were reported in the United States in 2009. These crimes included more than 13,600 murders, more than 88,000 forcible rapes, 408,000 robberies, and more than 807,000 aggravated assaults (Federal Bureau of Investigation, 2009).

aggression Behavior aimed at doing harm to others; also, the motive to behave aggressively.

The need for contact, closeness, and affection goes beyond simply the need to touch.

Why are people aggressive? Freud considered aggression an innate drive, similar to hunger and thirst, that builds up until it is released. In his view, one important function of society is to channel the aggressive drive into constructive and socially acceptable avenues, such as sports, debate, and other forms of competition. If Freud's analysis is correct, then expressing aggression should reduce the aggressive drive. Research shows, however, that under some circumstances, venting one's anger is more likely to increase than to reduce future aggression (Bushman, 2002; Schaefer & Mattei, 2005).

Another view holds that aggression is a vestige of our evolutionary past that can be traced to defensive behaviors characteristic of our ancestors (G. S. McCall & Shields, 2008). According to this view, the potential for aggression became hard-wired in the human brain, since it served an important adaptive function which enabled our ancestors to effectively compete for food and mates (Wallner & Machatschke, 2009).

Frustration also plays an important role in aggression. However, frustration does not always produce aggression. For example, if frustration doesn't generate anger, aggression is unlikely (Berkowitz & Harmon-Jones, 2004). Moreover, people react to frustration in different ways: some seek help and support, others withdraw from the source of frustration, some become aggressive, and some choose to escape into drugs or alcohol. Finally, there is some evidence that frustration is most likely to cause aggression in people who have learned to be aggressive as a means of coping with unpleasant situations (R. E. Tremblay, Hartup, & Archer, 2005).

One way we learn aggression is by observing aggressive models, especially those who get what they want (and avoid punishment) when they behave aggressively. For example, in contact sports, we often applaud acts of aggression. In professional hockey, fistfights between players may elicit as much fan fervor as does goal scoring.

But what if the aggressive model does not come out ahead or is even punished for aggressive actions? Observers usually will avoid imitating a model's behavior if it has negative consequences. However, as we saw in Chapter 5, "Learning," children who viewed aggressive behavior learned aggressive behavior, regardless of whether the aggressive model was rewarded or punished. The same results were obtained in a study in which children were shown films of aggressive behavior. Children who saw the aggressive model being punished were less aggressive than those who saw the aggressive model rewarded, but both groups of children were more aggressive than those who saw no aggressive model at all. These data are consistent with research showing that exposure to cinematic violence of any sort causes a small to moderate increase in aggressive behavior among children and adolescents (J. P. Murray, 2008). Indeed, one large-scale meta-analysis of 136 studies that were conducted in several different countries found clear evidence that playing violent video games was associated with increased aggressive behavior and decreased empathy and prosocial behavior (Anderson et al., 2010).

Aggression and Culture Further evidence that aggression is learned can be seen in the cultural variations that exist for handling of aggression (Lansford & Dodge, 2008; Triandis, 1994). For example, cultures as diverse as the Semai of the Malaysian rain forest, the Tahitian Islanders of the Pacific, the Zuni and Blackfoot nations in North America, the Pygmies of Africa, and the residents of Japan and the Scandinavian nations place a premium on resolving conflicts peacefully. Most of these are *collectivist* societies that emphasize the good of the group over the desires of the individual. Members of collectivist societies are more likely to seek compromise or to withdraw from a threatening interaction because of their concern for maintaining group harmony. In contrast, cultures such as the Yanomanö of South America, the Truk Islanders of Micronesia, and the Simbu of New Guinea encourage aggressive behavior, particularly among males. Members of these *individualist* societies are more likely to follow the adage "Stand up for yourself." Actually, we need not travel to exotic, faraway lands to find such diversity. Within the United States, such subcultures as Quakers, the Amish, the Mennonites, and the Hutterites have traditionally valued nonviolence and peaceful coexistence. This outlook contrasts markedly with individualist attitudes and practices in mainstream American culture.

Gender and Aggression Across cultures and at every age, males are more likely than females to behave aggressively. Three studies that reviewed more than 100 studies of aggression concluded that males are more aggressive than females both verbally (i.e., with taunts, insults, and threats) and, in particular, physically (i.e., with hitting, kicking, and fighting) (Bettencourt & Miller, 1996; Eagly & Steffen, 1986; Hyde, 1986). These gender differences tend to be greater in natural settings than in controlled laboratory settings (Hyde, 2005a) and appear to be remarkably stable (Arsenio, 2004; Knight, Fabes, & Higgins, 1996). Indeed, even historical data that go back to 16th-century Europe show that males committed more than three times as many violent crimes as females (L. Ellis & Coontz, 1990).

Is the origin of gender difference in aggression biological or social? The answer is not simple. On the one hand, certain biological factors appear to contribute to aggressive behavior. As we saw in Chapter 2, "The Biological Basis of Behavior," high levels of testosterone are associated with aggressiveness. At the same time, our society clearly tolerates and even encourages greater aggressiveness in boys than in girls (Sommers-Flanagan, Sommers-Flanagan, & Davis, 1993). For example, we are more likely to give boys toy guns and to reward them for behaving aggressively; girls are more likely than boys to be taught to feel guilty for behaving aggressively or to expect parental disapproval for their aggressive behavior. The most accurate conclusion seems to be that, like most of the complex behaviors that we have reviewed, gender differences in aggression undoubtedly depend on the interaction of nature and nurture (Geen, 1998; Verona, Joiner, Johnson, & Bender, 2006).

Some psychologists believe that aggression is largely a learned behavior. Professional athletes in contact sports often serve as models of aggressive behavior.

Achievement

Is being highly competitive important to high achievement?

Climbing Mount Everest, sending rockets into space, making the dean's list, rising to the top of a giant corporation—all these actions may have mixed underlying motives. But in all of them there is a desire to excel. It is this desire for achievement for its own sake that leads psychologists to suggest that there is a separate **achievement motive.** Perhaps not surprisingly, achievement motivation is correlated with measures of life satisfaction, success in life, and quality of life. Research also confirms that parental support for achievement is directly correlated with achievement motivation in children (Acharya & Joshi, 2011).

From psychological tests and personal histories, psychologists have developed a profile of people with high achievement motivation. These people are fast learners. They relish the opportunity to develop new strategies for unique and challenging tasks. Driven less by the desire for fame or fortune than by the need to live up to a high, self-imposed standard of performance (M. Carr, Borkowski, & Maxwell, 1991), they are self-confident, willingly take on responsibility, and do not readily bow to outside social pressures. They are energetic and allow few things to stand in the way of their goals.

achievement motive The need to excel, to overcome obstacles.

THINKING CRITICALLY ABOUT . . .

Culture and Aggression

The United States has one of the world's highest living standards and sends more young people to college than most other industrialized nations. Yet we have a very high incidence of violent crime.

1. Why do you think violence is so prevalent in U.S. culture? Can you design a research study to test your ideas?

2. How might the problem of widespread violence be reduced? What kind of evidence would be required to show that your ideas in fact work?

3. This critical-thinking exercise begins with several assertions about living standards, college attendance, and violent crime. However, no sources were cited to support those claims. Did you ask yourself whether there is any evidence to support them and, if so, whether the evidence is clear? What kinds of data would you want to see in order to determine if those assertions are correct?

Are males naturally more aggressive than females? Research suggests that both biology and culture encourage aggression in boys more than in girls. Adults often look the other way when two boys are fighting, sending the message that violence is an acceptable way to settle disputes.

Affiliation

How do psychologists explain the human need to be with other people?

Generally, people have a need for affiliation—to be with other people. The **affiliation motive** is likely to be especially strong when people feel threatened (Rofe, 1984). *Esprit de corps*—the feeling of being part of a sympathetic group—is critical among troops going into a battle, just as a football coach's pregame pep talk fuels team spirit. Both are designed to make people feel they are working for a common cause or against a common foe. Moreover, being in the presence of someone who is less threatened or fearful can reduce fear and anxiety. For example, patients with critical illnesses tend to prefer being with healthy people, rather than with other seriously ill patients or by themselves (Rofe, Hoffman, & Lewin, 1985). In the same way, if you are nervous on a plane during a bumpy flight, you may strike up a conversation with the calm-looking woman sitting next to you.

Some have argued that our need for affiliation has an evolutionary basis (Buss, 2006). In this view, forming and maintaining social bonds provided our ancestors with both survival and reproductive benefits. Social groups can share resources such as food and shelter, provide opportunities for reproduction, and assist in the care of offspring. Children who chose to stay with adults were probably more likely to survive (and ultimately reproduce) than those who wandered away from their groups. Thus, it is understandable that people in general tend to seek out other people.

Recently, neuroscientists have shown how various hormones, including oxytocin and dopamine, are released during times of stress prompting us to build social bonds (Carter, 2005). Not surprisingly, these same hormones also play an important role in romantic attachments and the formation of parental bonds to children (Leckman, Hrdy, Keverne, & Carter, 2006).

affiliation motive The need to be with others.

CHECK YOUR UNDERSTANDING

1. A person who is willing to contend with the high risks of a career in sales is probably motivated by a high _____ motive.

2. Indicate whether the following statements are true (T) or false (F).
   a. ____ Curiosity has been linked to creativity.
   b. ____ Research shows that low-birth-weight babies gain weight faster with frequent physical contact.
   c. ____ Aggression may be a learned response to numerous stimuli.

Answers: 1. achievement. 2. a. (T). b. (T). c. (T).

APPLY YOUR UNDERSTANDING

1. Susan scores high on tests of achievement motivation. Which of the following would you LEAST expect to be true of her?
   a. She is a fast learner who willingly takes on responsibility.
   b. She seldom deviates from methods that have worked for her in the past.
   c. She has a strong desire to live up to high, self-imposed standards of excellence.
   d. She is self-confident and resists outside social pressures.

2. You are watching a children's TV show in which the "bad guys" eventually are punished for their aggressive behavior. Your friend says, "It's a good thing the bad guys always lose. Otherwise, kids would learn to be aggressive from watching TV shows like this." You think about that for a minute and then, on the basis of what you have learned in this chapter, you reply,
   a. "Actually, seeing an aggressor punished for his or her actions leads to more aggression than seeing no aggression at all."
   b. "You're right. Seeing aggressors punished for their actions is a good way to reduce the amount of aggressiveness in children."
   c. "Aggression is an instinctual response to frustration, so it really doesn't matter what children see on TV. If they are frustrated, they will respond with aggression."

Answers: 1. b. 2. a.

EMOTIONS

How many basic emotions are there?

Ancient Greek rationalists thought that emotions, if not held in check, would wreak havoc on higher mental abilities such as rational thought and decision making. In his classic book, *The Expression of Emotions in Man and Animals* (1872/1965), Charles Darwin argued that emotional expression in man evolved by natural selection to serve an adaptive and communicative function (Hess & Thibault, 2009). Many early psychologists, too, often viewed emotions as a "base instinct"—a vestige of our evolutionary heritage that needed to be repressed.

More recently however, psychologists have begun to see emotions in a more positive light. Today, they are considered essential to survival and a major source of personal enrichment and resilience (Tugade & Fredrickson, 2004). Emotions are linked to variations in immune function and, thereby, to disease (see Chapter 11, "Stress and Health Psychology"). And as we saw in Chapter 7, "Cognition and Mental Abilities," emotions may also influence how successful we are (Goleman, 1997; Goleman, Boyatzis, & McKee, 2002). It is clear, then, that if we are going to understand human behavior, we must understand emotions. Unfortunately, that task is easier said than done. As you will soon see, even identifying how many emotions there are is difficult.

LEARNING OBJECTIVES

- Discuss the evidence for a set of basic emotions that are experienced by all humans.
- Compare and contrast the James–Lange theory, Cannon–Bard theory, and cognitive theories of emotion.

Basic Emotions

Are there basic emotions that all people experience regardless of their culture?

Many people have attempted to identify and describe the basic emotions experienced by humans (Cornelius, 1996; Schimmack & Crites, 2005). Some years ago, Robert Plutchik (1927–2006), for example, proposed that there are eight basic emotions: *fear, surprise, sadness, disgust, anger, anticipation, joy,* and *acceptance* (Plutchik, 1980). Each of these emotions helps us adjust to the demands of our environment, although in different ways. Fear, for example, underlies flight, which helps protect animals from their enemies; anger propels animals to attack or destroy.

Emotions adjacent to each other on Plutchik's emotion "circle" (see **Figure 8–7**) are more alike than those situated farther away. Surprise is more closely related to fear than to anger; joy and acceptance are more similar to each other than either is to disgust. Moreover, according to Plutchik's model, different emotions may combine to produce an even wider and richer spectrum of experience. Occurring together, anticipation and joy, for example, yield optimism; joy and acceptance fuse into love; and surprise and sadness make for disappointment. Within any of Plutchik's eight categories, emotions also vary in intensity.

ENDURING ISSUES

Diversity–Universality   Are Emotions Universal?

Some scientists challenge Plutchik's model, noting that it may apply only to the emotional experience of English-speaking people. Anthropologists report enormous differences in the ways that other cultures view and categorize emotions. Some languages, in fact, do not even have a word for "emotion." Languages also differ in the number of words that they have to name emotions. English includes over 2,000 words to describe emotional experiences, but Taiwanese Chinese has only 750 such descriptive words. One tribal language has only seven words that can be translated into categories of emotion. Some cultures lack words for "anxiety" or "depression" or "guilt." Samoans have just one word encompassing love, sympathy, pity, and liking—all distinct emotions in our own culture (Frijda, Markam, & Sato, 1995; Russell, 1991). ■

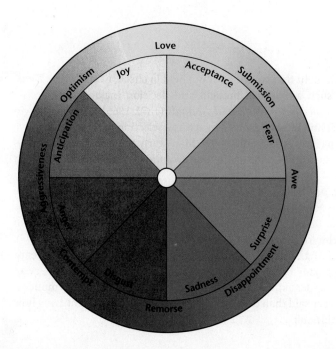

FIGURE 8–7
Plutchik's eight basic categories of emotion.

Source: From Plutchik, 1980.

FIGURE 8–8
Display of emotion in animal and human.
Compare the facial expressions of this girl and her dog. Notice not only their mouths but also their eyes.

Because of the differences in emotions from one culture to another, the tendency now is to distinguish between primary and secondary emotions. Primary emotions are those that are evident in all cultures, contribute to survival, associated with a distinct facial expression, and evident in non-human primates. Secondary emotions are those that are not found in all cultures. They may be thought of as subtle combinations of the primary emotions. (See **Figure 8–8.**)

Attempts to identify primary emotions have generally used cross-cultural studies (Matsumoto, Olide, Schug, Willingham, & Callan, 2009). For example, one group of researchers asked participants from 10 countries to interpret photographs depicting various facial expressions of emotions (Ekman et al., 1987). The percentage of participants from each country who correctly identified the emotions ranged from 60% to 98%. (See **Figure 8–9.**) The researchers used this and other evidence to argue for the existence of 6 primary emotions—*happiness, surprise, sadness, fear, disgust,* and *anger.* Notice that love is not included in this list. Although Ekman did not find a universally recognized facial expression for love, many psychologists nevertheless hold that love is a primary emotion (Hendrick & Hendrick, 2003; Sabini & Silver, 2005). Its outward expression, however, may owe much to the stereotypes promoted by a culture's media (Fehr, 1994). In one study in which American college students were asked to display a facial expression for love, the participants mimicked the conventional "Hollywood" prototypes such as sighing deeply, gazing skyward, and holding their hand over their heart (Cornelius, 1996).

Theories of Emotion

What is the relationship among emotions, biological reactions, and thoughts?

In the 1880s, the American psychologist William James formulated the first modern theory of emotion. The Danish psychologist Carl Lange reached the same conclusions. According to the **James–Lange theory,** stimuli in the environment (say, seeing a large growling dog running toward us) cause physiological changes in our bodies (accelerated heart rate, enlarged pupils, deeper or shallower breathing, increased perspiration, and goose bumps), and emotions arise from those physiological changes. The emotion of *fear,* then, would simply be the almost instantaneous and automatic awareness of physiological changes.

There is some supporting evidence for this theory (R. J. Davidson, 1992; Prinz, 2008), but if you think back to the biology of the nervous system (Chapter 2: "The Biological Basis

James–Lange theory States that stimuli cause physiological changes in our bodies, and emotions result from those physiological changes.

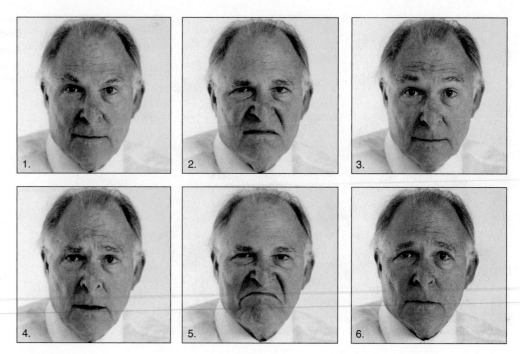

FIGURE 8-9
Name That Face.

Dr. Paul Ekman believes that facial expressions are distinct, predictable, and easy to read for someone who has studied them. His research involved breaking the expressions down into their specific muscular components and developing programs to help train people to become more accurate observers of the feelings that flit briefly across others' faces. Here, he demonstrates six emotional states. How many of them can you match to the pictures? The answers are below.

a. fear
b. neutral (no emotion)
c. sadness
d. anger
e. surprise
f. disgust

Source: Photos by Peter DaSilva for The New York Times

Answers: 1. b (neutral) 2. f (disgust) 3. e (surprise) 4. a (fear) 5. d (anger) 6. c (sadness).

of Behavior"), you should be able to identify a major flaw in the James–Lange theory. Recall that sensory information about bodily changes flows to the brain through the spinal cord. If bodily changes are the source of emotions, then people with severe spinal cord injuries should experience fewer and less intense emotions, but this is not the case (Cobos, Sánchez, Pérez, & Vila, 2004). Moreover, most emotions are accompanied by very similar physiological changes. Bodily changes, then, do not cause specific emotions and may not even be necessary for emotional experience.

Recognizing these facts, the **Cannon–Bard theory** holds that we mentally process emotions and physically respond simultaneously, not one after another. When you see the dog, you feel afraid *and* your heart races at the same time.

Cognitive Theories of Emotion Cognitive psychologists have taken Cannon–Bard's theory a step further. They argue that our emotional experience depends on our perception of a situation (Lazarus, 1991; C. Phelps, Bennett, & Brain, 2008; Scherer, Schorr, & Johnstone, 2001). According to the **cognitive theory** of emotion, the situation gives us clues as to how we should interpret our state of arousal. One of the first theories of emotion that took into account cognitive processes was advanced by Stanley Schachter and Jerome

Cannon–Bard theory States that the experience of emotion occurs simultaneously with biological changes.

cognitive theory States that emotional experience depends on one's perception or judgment of a situation.

Singer (1962; 2001). According to Schachter and Singer's *Two-Factor Theory of Emotion,* when we see a bear, there are indeed bodily changes; but we then use information about the situation to tell us how to respond to those changes. Only when we *cognitively* recognize that we are in danger do we experience those bodily changes as fear. (See **Figure 8–10** for a comparison of these three theories of emotion.)

Challenges to Cognitive Theory   Although a cognitive theory of emotion makes a lot of sense, some critics reject the idea that feelings always stem from cognitions. Quoting the poet e. e. cummings, Robert Zajonc (1923–2008) argued that "feelings is first." Human infants can imitate emotional expressions at 12 days of age, well before they acquire language. We have the ability to respond instantaneously to situations without taking time to interpret and evaluate them. But some emotional responses are not clear-cut. When we feel jittery, a cross between nervous and excited, we ask ourselves, "What's going on?" Zajonc (1984) believed that we invent explanations to label feelings: In his view, cognition follows emotion.

Another direct challenge to the cognitive theory claims that emotions can be experienced without the intervention of cognition (C. E. Izard, 1971, 1994). According to this view, a situation such as separation or pain provokes a unique pattern of unlearned facial movements and body postures that may be completely independent of conscious thought. When information about our facial expressions and posture reaches the brain, we automatically experience the corresponding emotion. According to Carroll Izard, then, the James–Lange theory was essentially correct in suggesting that emotional experience arises from bodily reactions. But Izard's theory stresses facial expression and body posture as crucial to the experience of emotion, whereas the James–Lange theory emphasized muscles, skin, and internal organs.

While considerable evidence supports the view that facial expressions influence emotions (Ekman, 2003; Soussignan, 2002), a growing body of research also indicates that the most accurate recognition of emotional expression occurs when the expresser and receiver are from the same cultural group (Jack, Caldara, & Schyns, 2011; Young & Hugenberg, 2010). Exactly how the unlearned and learned components of emotional expression are communicated and recognized is the topic we turn to now.

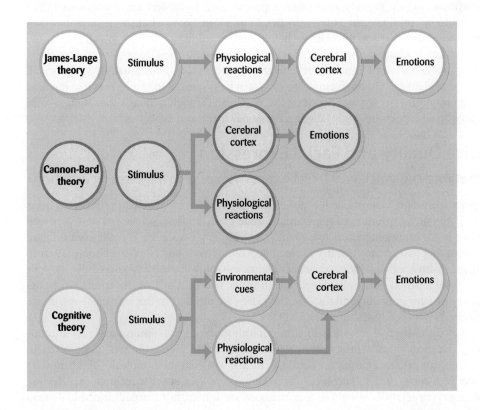

FIGURE 8–10

The three major theories of emotion.

According to the James–Lange theory, the body first responds physiologically to a stimulus, and then the cerebral cortex determines which emotion is being experienced. The Cannon–Bard theory holds that impulses are sent simultaneously to the cerebral cortex and the peripheral nervous system; thus, the response to the stimulus and the processing of the emotion are experienced at the same time, but independently. Cognitive theorists assert that the cerebral cortex interprets physiological changes in the light of information about the situation to determine which emotions we feel.

✓•⊢**Study** and **Review** on **MyPsychLab**

1. Robert Plutchik asserts that emotions vary in _____, a fact that accounts in part for the great range of emotions we experience.

Answer: 1. intensity.

APPLY YOUR UNDERSTANDING

1. Ralph believes that if you're feeling depressed, you should smile a lot and your depression will fade away. His view is most consistent with
   a. Izard's theory.
   b. the Schachter–Singer theory.
   c. the James–Lange theory.
   d. the Cannon–Bard theory.
2. You are on a camping trip when you encounter a bear. You get butterflies in your stomach, your heart starts racing, your mouth gets dry, and you start to perspire. A psychologist who takes the cognitive perspective on emotion would say,
   a. "Seeing the bear caused the physical changes, which in turn caused you to experience fear."
   b. "Seeing the bear caused you to experience fear, which in turn caused all those physical changes."
   c. "Seeing the bear caused the physical changes. When you realized they were caused by the bear, you experienced fear."
   d. "Seeing the bear caused the physical changes and the emotion of fear at the same time."

Answers: 1.a. 2.c.

LEARNING OBJECTIVES

- Explain the importance of facial expressions in communicating emotion and identify the areas of the brain that are responsible for interpreting facial expressions. Describe the role of body language, gestures, and personal space in communicating emotions.
- Summarize the research evidence regarding gender and cultural differences in emotion, the role of "display rules," and whether it is advantageous to express anger as opposed to "holding it in."

COMMUNICATING EMOTION

What is the most obvious signal of emotion?

Sometimes you are vaguely aware that a person makes you feel uncomfortable. When pressed to be more precise, you might say, "You never know what she is thinking." But you do not mean that you never know her opinion of a film or what she thought about the last election. It would probably be more accurate to say that you do not know what she is feeling. Almost all of us conceal our emotions to some extent, but usually people can tell what we are feeling. Although emotions can often be expressed in words, much of the time we communicate our feelings nonverbally. We do so through, among other things, voice quality, facial expression, body language, personal space, and explicit acts.

Voice Quality and Facial Expression

What role can voice and facial expression play in expressing emotion?

If your roommate is washing the dishes and says acidly, "I *hope* you're enjoying your novel," the literal meaning of his words is quite clear, but you probably know very well that he is not expressing a concern about your reading pleasure. He is really saying, "I am annoyed that you are not helping to clean up." Similarly, if you receive a phone call from someone who has had very good or very bad news, you will probably know how she feels before she has told you what happened. In other words, much of the emotional information we convey is not contained in the words we use, but in the way those words are expressed (Gobl & Chasaide, 2003).

Among nonverbal channels of communication, facial expressions seem to communicate the most specific information (Horstmann, 2003). Hand gestures or posture can communicate general emotional states (e.g., feeling bad), but the complexity of the muscles in the face allows facial expressions to communicate very specific feelings (e.g., feeling sad, angry, or fearful). Many facial expressions are innate, not learned. Individuals who are born blind use the same facial expressions of emotion as do sighted persons to express the same emotions (Matsumoto & Willingham, 2009). Moreover, most animals share a common pattern of muscular facial movements. For example, dogs, tigers, and humans all bare their teeth in rage, and research has shown that the same pattern of facial muscles is used to display emotions among most primates, including monkeys, chimpanzees, and humans (Waller, Parr, Gothard, Burrows, & Fuglevand, 2008). Psychologists who take an evolutionary approach believe that facial expressions served an adaptive function, enabling our ancestors to compete successfully for status, to win mates, and to defend themselves (Tooby & Cosmides, 2008). ↱

THINKING CRITICALLY ABOUT . . .

Nonverbal Communication of Emotion

Some people are clearly better than others at reading and sending emotional messages. The question is, why? How might you determine

1. if differences in these skills are learned or inherited?
2. the kinds of learning experiences that produce high skills?
3. whether it is possible to teach the skills?

Simulate the **Experiment** Recognizing Facial Expressions of Emotions on **MyPsychLab**

How the Brain Reads the Face

What parts of the brain are responsible for interpreting facial expressions?

Scientists have known for quite some time that activity in brain circuits centering on the amygdala (Figure 6–4) and insula are critical for the release of emotions (Schafe & LeDoux, 2002; Philip Shaw et al., 2005). The amygdala and insula also appear to play an important role in our ability to correctly interpret facial expressions (Adolphs, 2008; Jehna et al., 2011). Interestingly, some of the underlying brain processes that are used to interpret facial expression take place so quickly (less than 1/10 of a second), it is unlikely that they are consciously driven (Adolphs, 2006).

Adolphs and his colleagues (Adolphs, Tranel, Damasio, & Damasio, 1994) reported the remarkable case of a 30-year-old woman (S. M.) with a rare disease that caused nearly complete destruction of the amygdala. Although S. M. could correctly identify photographs of familiar faces with 100% accuracy, and easily learned to recognize new faces, she had great difficulty recognizing fear and discriminating between different emotions, such as happiness and surprise. More recent research has also shown that people with amygdala damage have trouble "reading faces" (Adolphs, Baron-Cohen, & Tranel, 2002; Adolphs & Tranel, 2003). For example, some patients with severe depressive disorder have an impaired ability to accurately judge another person's facial expression of emotion, and this impairment contributes to their difficulty in interpersonal functioning (Surguladze et al., 2004). In addition, some researchers have suggested that abnormalities in the brain circuits associated with the amygdala can, in some cases, make it difficult for people to perceive threat accurately and that, in turn, can lead to unprovoked violence and aggression (R. J. Davidson, Putnam, & Larson, 2000; Marsh & Blair, 2008).

Body Language, Personal Space, and Gestures

How can posture, personal space, and mimicry affect the communication of emotion?

Body language is another way that we communicate messages nonverbally. How we hold our back, for example, communicates a great deal. When we are relaxed, we tend to stretch back into a chair; when we are tense, we sit more stiffly with our feet together.

The distance we maintain between ourselves and others is called *personal space*. This distance varies depending on the nature of the activity and the emotions felt. If someone stands closer to you than is customary, that proximity may indicate either anger or affection; if farther away than usual, it may indicate fear or dislike. The normal conversing distance between people varies from culture to culture. Two Swedes conversing would ordinarily stand much farther apart than would two Arabs or Greeks.

When having a conversation, most people of middle-Eastern descent stand closer to one another than most Americans do. In our society, two men would not usually stand as close together as these two Arabs unless they were very aggressively arguing with each other (a baseball player heatedly arguing with an umpire, for example).

Explicit acts, of course, can also serve as nonverbal clues to emotions. A slammed door may tell us that the person who just left the room is angry. If friends drop in for a visit and you invite them into your living room, that is a sign that you are probably less at ease with them than with friends whom you invite to sit down with you at the kitchen table. Gestures, such as a slap on the back, an embrace, whether people shake your hand briefly or for a long time, firmly or limply, also tell you something about how they feel about you.

You can see from this discussion that nonverbal communication of emotions is important. However, a word of caution is needed here. Although nonverbal behavior may offer a clue to a person's feelings, it is not an *infallible* clue. Laughing and crying can sound alike, yet crying may signal sorrow, joy, anger, or nostalgia—or that you are slicing an onion. Moreover, as with verbal reports, people sometimes "say" things nonverbally that they do not mean. We all have done things thoughtlessly—turned our backs, frowned when thinking about something else, or laughed at the wrong time—that have given offense because our actions were interpreted as an expression of an emotion that we were not, in fact, feeling.

Many of us overestimate our ability to interpret nonverbal cues. For example, in one study of several hundred "professional lie catchers," including members of the Secret Service, government lie detector experts, judges, police officers, and psychiatrists, every group except for the psychiatrists rated themselves above average in their ability to tell whether another person was lying. Only the Secret Service agents managed to identify the liars at a better-than-chance rate (Ekman & O'Sullivan, 1991). Similar results have been obtained with other groups of people (Frank, 2006). In part, the reason seems to be that many behaviors that might seem to be associated with lying (such as avoiding eye contact, rapid blinking, or shrugs) are not in fact associated with lying; and other behaviors that are associated with lying (such as tenseness and fidgeting) also occur frequently when people are not lying (DePaulo et al., 2003). Thus, even the best nonverbal cues only indicate that a person *may* be lying. Despite our apparent inability to accurately detect lies in other adults, research does show that adults are reasonably accurate at detecting when a *child* is lying (Edelstein, Luten, Ekman, & Goodman, 2006). However, even with young children experts are not necessarily any better at detecting lies than novice adults (Nysse-Carris, Bottoms, & Salerno, 2011).

Sometimes we use *mimicry* to help us understand what others are feeling. Research confirms that during the course of conversation, people often mimic each other's accents, gestures, postures, and facial expressions (McIntosh, 2006). Not surprisingly, research has shown that spontaneous mimicry makes conversations flow more smoothly, helps people feel closer to one another, and fosters friendship (Kobayashi, 2007). In addition, as described previously, because specific emotions are tied to behaviors, and in particular specific facial expressions, mimicking the facial expressions of other helps us to emphasize, or literally feel what another person is feeling (Stel, Van Baaren, & Vonk, 2008). However, even the use of mimicry doesn't overcome our tendency to being deceived. For example, research has also shown that mimicry may actually reduce our accuracy to judge another person's emotions if the person expressing the emotion is purposely trying to be deceptive. In other words, when we mimic a person who is attempting to mislead us, mimicry diminishes our ability to detect that they are trying to deceiving us (Stel, van Dijk, & Olivier, 2009).

Gender and Emotion

Are men less emotional than women?

Men are often said to be less emotional than women. But do men feel less emotion, or are they simply less likely to express the emotions they feel? And are there some emotions that men are more likely than women to express?

Research sheds some light on these issues. In one study, when men and women saw depictions of people in distress, the men showed little emotion, but the women expressed feelings of concern (Eisenberg & Lennon, 1983). However, physiological measures of emotional arousal (such as heart rate and blood pressure) showed that the men in the study were actually just as affected as the women were. The men simply inhibited the expression of their emotions, whereas the women were more open about their feelings. Emotions such as sympathy, sadness, empathy, and distress are often considered "unmanly," and tradition-ally, in Western culture, boys are trained from an early age to suppress those emotions in public (L. Brody & Hall, 2000). The fact that men are less likely than women to seek help in dealing with emotional issues (Komiya, Good, & Sherrod, 2000) is probably a result of this early training. (See **Figure 8–11**.)

Men and women are also likely to react with very different emotions to the same situa-tion. For example, being betrayed or criticized by another person will elicit anger in males, whereas females are more likely to feel hurt, sad, or disappointed (L. Brody & Hall, 2000; Fischer, Rodriguez-Mosquera, van-Vianen, & Manstead, 2004). And, when men get angry, they generally turn their anger outward, against other people and against the situation in which they find themselves. Women are more likely to see themselves as the source of the problem and to turn their anger inward, against themselves. These gender-specific reactions are consistent with the fact that men are four times more likely than women to become violent in the face of life crises; women, by contrast, are much more likely to become depressed.

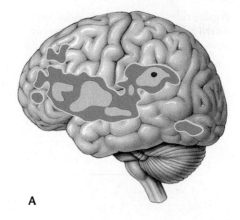

A

B

FIGURE 8–11

Emotion and brain activity in men and women.

When asked to think of something sad, women (A) generate more activity in their brains than men (B) (Carter, 1998).

ENDURING ISSUES

Mind–Body   Holding Anger In

People who frequently feel anger and hostility may be at a serious health risk if they don't allow themselves to express and learn to regulate their anger (Carrère, Mittmann, Woodin, Tabares, & Yoshimoto, 2005). In a study that tracked a group of women over 18 years, researchers found that those scoring high on hostility were three times more likely to die during the course of the study than those who scored low (Julius, Harburg, Cottington, & Johnson, 1986). However, this higher level of risk applied only to participants who said they got angry in many situations but did not vent their anger. Other participants who reported frequent bouts of anger, which they expressed, were in the same low-risk group as those who said they rarely or never felt angry. ■

Men and women also differ in their ability to interpret nonverbal cues of emotion. In particular, women and young girls are more skilled than men or young boys at decod-ing the facial expressions of emotion (Bosacki & Moore, 2004; Hall & Matsumoto, 2004). Perhaps not surprisingly, research has also shown that men are more likely than women to misperceive friendliness as sexual interest; interestingly, they are also more likely to per-ceive sexual interest as friendliness (Farris, Treat, Vikden, & McFall, 2008).

How can we explain these gender differences? One possibility is that because women tend to be the primary caregivers for preverbal infants, they need to become more attuned than men to the subtleties of emotional expressions. Some psychologists have even sug-gested that this skill may be genetically programmed into females. Consistent with this evolutionary perspective, research has shown that male and female infants express and self-regulate emotions differently (McClure, 2000; Weinberg, Tronick, Cohn, & Olson, 1999).

Another explanation of gender differences in emotional sensitivity is based on the rela-tive power of women and men. Because women historically have occupied less powerful positions, they may have felt the need to become acutely attuned to the emotional displays of others, particularly those in more powerful positions (namely, men). This idea is sup-ported by evidence that, regardless of gender, followers are more sensitive to the emotions of leaders than vice versa (Aries, 2006; Judith Hall, Bernieri, & Carney, 2006). ✳

✳ **Complete** the **Survey** How to Deal with Your Emotions on **MyPsychLab**

Culture and Emotion

How can culture influence the way we express emotion?

Does where we live affect what we feel? And if so, why? For psychologists, the key issue is how cultures help shape emotional experiences.

Some researchers have argued that across cultures, peoples, and societies, the face looks the same whenever certain emotions are expressed; this phenomenon is known as the

display rules Culture-specific rules that govern how, when, and why expressions of emotion are appropriate.

universalist position. In contrast, other researchers support the *culture-learning* position, which holds that members of a culture learn the appropriate facial expressions for emotions. These expressions, then, can differ greatly from one culture to the next. Which view is more accurate?

As we saw earlier, Ekman and his colleagues have concluded from cross-cultural studies that at least six emotions are accompanied by universal facial expressions: happiness, sadness, anger, surprise, fear, and disgust. Carroll Izard (1980) conducted similar studies in England, Germany, Switzerland, France, Sweden, Greece, and Japan with similar results. These studies seem to support the universalist position: Regardless of culture, people tended to agree on which emotions others were expressing facially. However, this research does not completely rule out the culture-learning view. Because the participants were all members of developed countries that likely had been exposed to one another through movies, magazines, and tourism, they might simply have become familiar with the facial expressions seen in other cultures. A stronger test was needed that reduced or eliminated this possibility.

Such a test was made possible by the discovery of several contemporary cultures that had been totally isolated from Western culture for most of their existence. Members of the Fore and the Dani cultures of New Guinea, for example, had their first contact with anthropologists only a few years before Ekman's research took place. They provided a nearly perfect opportunity to test the universalist/culture-learning debate. If members of these cultures gave the same interpretation of facial expressions and produced the same expressions on their own faces as did people in Western cultures, there would be much stronger evidence for the universality of facial expressions of emotion. Ekman and

his colleagues presented members of the Fore culture with three photographs of people from outside their culture and asked them to point to the picture that represented how they would feel in a certain situation. For example, if a participant was told "Your child has died, and you feel very sad," he or she would have the opportunity to choose which of the three pictures most closely corresponded to sadness. The results indicated very high rates of agreement on facial expressions of emotions (Ekman & Friesen, 1971; Ekman, Sorenson, & Friesen, 1969). Moreover, when photographs of the Fore and Dani posing the primary emotions were shown to college students in the United States, the same high agreement was found (Ekman & Friesen, 1975). This finding suggests that at least some emotional expressions are inborn and universal.

If this is true, why are people so often confused about the emotions being expressed by people in other cultures? It turns out that the answer is not simple. Part of the explanation involves **display rules.** Display rules concern the circumstances under which it is appropriate for people to show emotion. Display rules differ substantially from culture to culture (Matsumoto, Yoo, & Chung, 2010; Safdar et al., 2009). In a study of Japanese and American college students, the participants watched graphic films of surgical procedures, either by themselves or in the presence of an experimenter. The students' facial expressions were secretly videotaped as they viewed the films. The results showed that when the students were by

Can you identify the emotions being expressed by this man from New Guinea? The finding that U.S. college students could recognize the emotional expressions of people who had been largely isolated from Western cultures—and vice versa—lent support to the *universalist* position of facial expression.

themselves, both the Japanese and the Americans showed facial expressions of disgust, as expected. But when the participants watched the films in the presence of an experimenter, the two groups displayed different responses. American students continued to show disgust on their faces, but the Japanese students showed facial expressions that were more neutral, even somewhat pleasant (Ekman, Friesen, & Ellsworth, 1972). Why the sudden switch? The answer in this case appears to lie in the different display rules of the two cultures. The Japanese norm says, "Don't display strong negative emotion in the presence of a respected elder" (in this case, the experimenter). Americans typically don't honor this display rule; hence, they expressed their true emotions whether they were alone or with someone else.

However, display rules don't tell the whole story. In a comprehensive review of the literature, Elfenbein and Ambady (2002, 2003) have demonstrated that differences in language, familiarity, majority or minority status within a culture, cultural learning, expressive style, and a number of other factors may also account for the fact that "we understand emotions more accurately when they are expressed by members of our own cultural or subcultural group" (p. 228). Since research indicates that learning to correctly identify emotions of people from a different culture contributes to intercultural adjustment (Yoo, Matsumoto, & LeRoux, 2006), further research in this area is important as the nations of the world become increasingly interdependent and multicultural.

✓• ⎡**Study** and **Review** on **MyPsychLab**

CHECK YOUR UNDERSTANDING

1. Cultural differences, particularly _____, influence how we experience emotion.

2. Two important nonverbal cues to emotions are _____ _____ and _____ _____.

3. Men tend to interpret the source of their anger to be in their _____.

4. Research shows that some _____ _____ are recognized universally.

5. _____ _____ are the cultural circumstances under which it is appropriate to show emotions on the face.

6. _____ Overt behavior is an infallible clue to emotions. Is this statement true (T) or false (F)?

Answers: 1. language. **2.** facial expression, body language. **3.** environment. **4.** facial expressions. **5.** Display rules. **6.** (F).

APPLY YOUR UNDERSTANDING

1. Which of the following would probably be best at "reading" nonverbal emotional cues?
   a. a young man
   b. an older woman
   c. an older man
   d. They would all be equally accurate since gender is not related to the ability to understand nonverbal cues to emotion.

2. You are studying gender differences in emotion. You show men and women various films of people in distress. On the basis of what you have read in this chapter, you would predict that the men will show _____ amount of physiological arousal, and _____ emotional expression as the women.
   a. the same; the same
   b. the same; less
   c. a greater; less
   d. a smaller; less

Answers: 1. b. **2.** b.

KEY TERMS

CHAPTER REVIEW
((•─|Listen to the **Chapter Audio** on **MyPsychLab**

PERSPECTIVES ON MOTIVATION

How can you use intrinsic and extrinsic motivation to help you succeed in college? The idea that motivation is based on **instincts** was popular in the early 20th century but since has fallen out of favor. Human motivation has also been viewed as an effort toward **drive reduction** and **homeostasis,** or balance in the body. Another perspective, reflected in **arousal theory,** suggests behavior stems from a desire to maintain an optimum level of arousal. Motivational inducements or incentives can originate from within (**intrinsic motivation**) or from outside (**extrinsic motivation**) the person. The effects of intrinsic motivation are greater and longer-lasting.

Abraham Maslow suggested human motives can be arranged in a **hierarchy of needs,** with primitive ones based on physical needs positioned at the bottom and higher ones such as self-esteem positioned toward the top. Maslow believed that the higher motives don't emerge until the more basic ones have been met, but recent research challenges his view.

HUNGER AND THIRST

Why do people usually get hungry at mealtime? How can external cues influence our desire to eat? Hunger is regulated by several centers within the brain. These centers are stimulated by receptors that monitor blood levels of **glucose,** fats, and carbohydrates as well as the hormones **leptin** and **ghrelin.** Hunger is also stimulated by **incentives** such as cooking aromas and by emotional, cultural, and social factors.

How can you tell if someone is suffering from anorexia nervosa or bulimia? Eating disorders, particularly **anorexia nervosa** and **bulimia nervosa,** are more prevalent among females than among males. They are characterized by extreme preoccupation with body image and weight. **Muscle dysmorphia** is a disorder generally seen among young men involving an obsession with muscle size leading to inordinate worry about diet and exercise. Another food-related problem, obesity, affects millions of Americans. Obesity has complex causes and negative consequences particularly for obese children, who are likely to have health problems as adults.

SEX

How is the sex drive different from other primary drives? Sex is a primary drive that gives rise to reproductive behavior essential for the survival of the species.

How well do we understand the biology of the sex drive? Although hormones such as **testosterone** are involved in human sexual responses, they don't play as dominant a role as they do in some other species. In humans, the brain exerts a powerful influence on the sex drive as well. The human **sexual response cycle,** which differs somewhat for males and females, has four stages—excitement, plateau, orgasm, and resolution.

How does culture influence sexual behavior? Experience and learning affect preferences for sexually arousing stimuli. What is sexually attractive is also influenced by culture. Research suggests a more conservative pattern of sexual behavior in the United States than is portrayed in popular media.

What are the arguments for and against a biological explanation of homosexuality? People with a heterosexual orientation are sexually attracted to members of the opposite sex; those with a homosexual orientation are sexually attracted to members of their own sex. It is likely that both biological and environmental factors play a role in explaining homosexuality.

OTHER IMPORTANT MOTIVES

How are stimulus motives different from primary drives? Stimulus motives are less obviously associated with the survival of the organism or the species, although they often help humans adapt to their environments. **Stimulus motives,** such as the urge to explore and manipulate things, are associated with obtaining information about the world.

What motives cause people to explore and change their environment? A gap in understanding may stimulate curiosity, motivating us to explore and, often, to change our environment.

Is the human need for contact universal? Another important stimulus motive in humans and other primates is to seek various forms of tactile stimulation. The importance of contact has been demonstrated in non-human animal studies as well as in premature human infants.

Is aggression a biological response or a learned one? Any behavior intended to inflict physical or psychological harm on others is an act of **aggression.** Some psychologists see aggression as an innate drive in humans that must be channeled to constructive ends, but others see it more as a learned response that is greatly influenced by modeling, norms, and values. Aggression differs markedly across cultures, supporting the latter view. Males generally are more inclined than females to strike out at others and commit acts of violence. This gender difference probably stems from an interaction of nature and nurture.

Is being highly competitive important to high achievement? People who display a desire to excel, to overcome obstacles, and to accomplish difficult things well and quickly score high in **achievement motive.** Although hard work and a strong desire to master challenges both contribute to achievement, excessive competitiveness toward others can actually interfere with achievement.

How do psychologists explain the human need to be with other people? The **affiliation motive,** or need to be with other people, is especially pronounced when we feel threatened or anxious. Affiliation with others in this situation can counteract fear and bolster spirits.

EMOTIONS

How many basic emotions are there? Are there basic emotions that all people experience regardless of their culture? Robert Plutchik's circular classification system for **emotions** encompasses eight basic emotions. But not all cultures categorize emotions this way. Some lack a word for emotion; others describe feelings as physical sensations. Cross-cultural research by Paul Ekman argues for the universality of at least six emotions—happiness, surprise, sadness, fear, disgust, and anger. Many psychologists add *love* to this list.

What is the relationship among emotions, biological reactions, and thoughts? According to the **James–Lange theory,** environmental stimuli can cause physiological changes; and emotions then arise from our awareness of those changes. In contrast, the **Cannon–Bard theory** holds that emotions and bodily responses occur simultaneously. A third perspective, the **cognitive theory** of emotion, contends that our perceptions and judgments of situations are essential to our emotional experiences. Without these cognitions we would have no idea how to label our feelings. Not everyone agrees with this view, however, because emotions sometimes seem to arise too quickly to depend on mental evaluations. Counter to the cognitive view, C. E. Izard argues that certain inborn facial expressions and body postures are automatically triggered in emotion-arousing situations and are then "read" by the brain as particular feelings.

COMMUNICATING EMOTION

What is the most obvious signal of emotion? What role can voice and facial expression play in expressing emotion? People express emotions verbally through words, tone of voice, exclamations, and other sounds. Facial expressions are the most obvious nonverbal indicators of emotion.

What parts of the brain are responsible for interpreting facial expressions? The amygdala and insula play an important role in our ability to correctly interpret facial expressions. Abnormalities in these brain circuits may be a factor in depression and unprovoked aggression.

How can posture and personal space communicate emotion? Other indicators involve body language—our posture, the way we move, our preferred personal distance from others when talking to them, our degree of eye contact. Explicit acts, such as slamming a door, express emotions, too. People vary in their skill at reading these nonverbal cues.

Are men less emotional than women? Research confirms some gender differences in expressing and perceiving emotions. For instance, when confronted with a person in distress, women are more likely than men to express emotion, even though the levels of physiological arousal are the same for the two sexes. Also, being betrayed or criticized elicits more anger in men, versus more disappointment and hurt in women. Women are generally better than men at reading other people's emotions: decoding facial expressions, body cues, and tones of voice. This skill may be sharpened by their role as caretakers of infants and their traditional subordinate status to men.

How can culture influence the way we express emotion? Regardless of a person's cultural background, the facial expressions associated with certain basic emotions appear to be universal. This finding contradicts the culture-learning view, which suggests facial expressions of emotion are learned within a particular culture. This is not to say that there are no cultural differences in emotional expression, however. Overlaying the universal expression of certain emotions are culturally varying **display rules** that govern when it is appropriate to show emotion—to whom, by whom, and under what circumstances. Other forms of nonverbal communication of emotion vary more from culture to culture than facial expressions do.

9

Life-Span Development

OVERVIEW

Opinionated and always ready and able to defend her views on politics and world affairs, Ann Dunham was not a typical teenager in 1960. When her father, a World War II veteran and furniture salesman, moved his family to Hawaii in 1960, she did not want to go. But in her first year at the University of Hawaii, she met and fell in love with a graduate student from Kenya who shared her ideals. This student was named Barack Obama.

He was well respected among their circle of friends from the university, who described him as self-assured, opinionated, and energetic. Within a year, he and Ann were married, and in 1961, they had a son. They named their son Barack Obama, after his father.

When their son was 2 years old, his father left Hawaii to attend Harvard University, and his parents divorced soon afterward. He and his mother lived with his grandparents, Stanley and Madelyn Dunham, for the next several years while his mother continued her studies at the University of Hawaii. She fell in love with and married an Indonesian student, and they moved to Jakarta when Obama was in first grade. Obama's teachers at the Catholic school he attended in Jakarta have noted the leadership qualities they saw in him at a young age, always willing to help his friends and look out for the little ones.

By fifth grade, however, Obama's mother had moved back to Hawaii so he could attend the elite Punahou school. When she returned to Indonesia several years later, Barack once again moved in with his maternal grandparents. After years of upheaval, Obama's grandparents provided a stable, loving environment. Growing up with issues of abandonment—first from his father's early departure and later his mother's—Obama has said that his grandfather's love and kindness made it clear to him that he was not alone. He has often spoken warmly of his grandmother, crediting her with his sense of practicality and toughness.

In high school, Obama was one of only a handful of Black students at the prep school he attended in Honolulu. Although he struggled with his racial identity, identifying with other Black students but also with his White grandparents, he was charismatic and had many friends from diverse racial backgrounds.

Obama went on to attend Columbia University and Harvard Law School, where he became the first Black president of the *Harvard Law Review*. Despite adversity and family instability, Obama rose up to achieve unparalleled success, becoming the 44th president of the United States.

Barack Obama's life is a fascinating example of both continuity and change. The study of how and why people change over the course of the life span is called **developmental psychology**. Developmental psychologists want to learn about the changes in thought, emotion, and behavior that everyone experiences as they age. In addition, researchers want to understand individual differences in development. To what extent and for what reasons has your own development differed from that of your friends or your siblings? And why does the course of a person's development sometimes suddenly change direction? These are some of the topics we explore in this chapter.

ENDURING ISSUES **in Life-Span Development**

In trying to understand human development, psychologists primarily focus on three enduring issues that were introduced in Chapter 1, "The Science of Psychology."

1. **Individual characteristics versus shared human traits (Diversity–Universality).** We all take essentially the same developmental journey, but each of us travels a different road and experiences events in different ways. Barack Obama's life illustrates this well. Like other people, he progressed through the stages of childhood, adolescence, and adulthood; he embarked on a career, developed a number of close friendships, and dealt with the normal challenges of growing up to become a mature adult. These are all common developmental milestones. Yet in other ways, Obama's development was not like everyone else's. Not everyone grows up in such an unstable, multicultural family, a child of divorce who is ultimately left in the care of his grandparents, goes to elite schools and colleges, or achieves such professional heights. This combination of shared and distinctive elements is common to human development.

2. **Stability versus change (Stability–Change).** The extent to which our thoughts, behaviors, and personalities remain stable or change throughout life's journey is also of central concern to developmental psychologists. Again, Obama's life is an excellent example. The move back to Hawaii to live with his supportive grandparents was certainly a major turning point in his development. Attending Columbia University and Harvard Law School also had a profound effect upon him. And yet with all the changes that these transitions brought, we still see many of the qualities he displayed as a young child in Indonesia.

developmental psychology The study of the changes that occur in people from birth through old age.

How does Barack Obama's life illustrate several key issues in developmental psychology?

cross-sectional study A method of studying developmental changes by comparing people of different ages at about the same time.

cohort A group of people born during the same period in historical time.

3. **Heredity versus environment (Nature–Nurture).** There is probably no issue of more importance to developmental psychologists than the nature–nurture question. How do biological and environmental forces interact to shape human behavior and growth throughout the life span? Obama's parents were both intelligent. Even in the first grade he showed unusual signs of leadership. But his gifts might have gone undeveloped if his mother hadn't enrolled him in the Punahou school and his grandparents had not supported and encouraged him. How different might he have been had he been born into a different family or chosen a different life's work?

METHODS IN DEVELOPMENTAL PSYCHOLOGY

What are some of the limitations of the methods used to study development?

As developmental psychologists study growth and change across the life span, they use the same research methods used by psychologists in other specialized areas: naturalistic observations, correlational studies, and experiments. (See Chapter 1.) But because developmental psychologists are interested in processes of change over time, they use these methods in three special types of studies: cross-sectional, longitudinal, and biographical.

These three types are listed in the "**Summary Table:** Advantages and Disadvantages of Different Types of Developmental Research Methods."

In a **cross-sectional study,** researchers examine developmental change by observing or testing people of different ages at the same time. For example, they might study the development of logical thought by testing a group of 6-year-olds, a group of 9-year-olds, and a group of 12-year-olds, looking for differences among the age groups. However, one problem with cross-sectional studies is that they don't distinguish age differences from **cohort** differences, which are due to the fact that individuals were born and grew up during different historical times. All Americans born in 1960, for example, form a cohort. If we find that 40-year-olds are able to solve harder math problems than 80-year-olds, we wouldn't know whether this difference is due to better cognitive ability in younger people (an age difference) or to better math education 40 years ago (a cohort difference).

SUMMARY TABLE   ADVANTAGES AND DISADVANTAGES OF DIFFERENT TYPES OF DEVELOPMENTAL RESEARCH METHODS

Method	Procedure	Advantages	Disadvantages
Cross-sectional	Studies development by observing people of different ages at the same point in time	• Inexpensive • Takes relatively little time to complete • Avoids high attrition rate (dropout of participants from study)	• Different age groups are not necessarily very much alike • Differences across age groups may be due to cohort differences rather than age
Longitudinal	Studies development by observing the same people at two or more times as they grow older	• Generates detailed information about individuals • Allows for the study of developmental change in great detail • Eliminates cohort differences	• Expensive and time consuming • Potential for high attrition rate—participants may drop out over a long period of time • Differences over time may be due to differences in assessment tools rather than age
Biographical or retrospective	Studies development by interviewing people about past experiences	• Generates rich detail about one individual's life • Allows for in-depth study of one individual	• Individual's recall often untrustworthy • Can be very time consuming and expensive

Longitudinal studies address this problem by testing the same people two or more times as they grow older. For instance, researchers who are interested in the development of logical thought might begin their study by testing a group of 6-year-olds, then test the same children again at age 9, then test them again at age 12. One potential problem with longitudinal studies is that they may not distinguish age differences from differences caused by using different assessment or measurement tools. For example, researchers retesting a cohort at age 12 would probably use a different measure of logical thought than they did when they tested that cohort at age 6. So if they found significant improvement in logical thought over this 6-year period, they wouldn't know to what extent it reflected the advance in age and to what extent it reflected the different measuring tools.

Another drawback to a longitudinal study is that it takes considerable time. When studying the entire life span, a longitudinal study would take decades to complete. To avoid the huge expense of such a long study, researchers have devised a third way of studying adulthood: the **biographical (or retrospective) study**. With this approach, the researcher might start with some 70-year-olds and pursue their lives backward by interviewing them and consulting other sources. However, biographical data are less trustworthy than either longitudinal or cross-sectional data, because people's recollections of the past may be inaccurate.

PRENATAL DEVELOPMENT

Why can an organism or another substance cause devastating effects at one point in prenatal development but not at others?

During the earliest period of **prenatal development**—the stage of development from conception to birth—the fertilized egg divides, beginning the 9-month process that will transform it from a one-celled organism into a complex human being. Two weeks after conception, the cells begin to specialize: Some will form the baby's internal organs, others will form muscles and bones, and still others will form the skin and nervous system. No longer an undifferentiated mass of cells, the developing organism is now called an **embryo.**

The embryo stage ends 3 months after conception, when the *fetal stage* begins. At this point, although it is only 1 inch long, the **fetus** roughly resembles a human being, with arms and legs, a large head, and a heart that has begun to beat. The mother's blood vessels transmit nutritive substances to the embryo or fetus, and carry waste products away from it through the *placenta*. Although the mother's blood never actually mingles with that of her unborn child, toxic agents that she eats, drinks, or inhales (known as **teratogens**) are capable of crossing the placenta and compromising the baby's development. Diseases can also cross the placenta and harm the fetus.

There is a **critical period** during prenatal development when many substances are most likely to have a major effect on the fetus. At other times, the same substance may have no effect at all. For example, if a woman contracts rubella (German measles) during the first 3 months of pregnancy, the effects can range from death of the fetus to a child who is born deaf. If she gets rubella during the final 3 months of pregnancy, however, severe damage to the fetus is unlikely, because the critical period for the formation of major body parts has passed.

Pregnancy is most likely to have a favorable outcome when the mother gets good nutrition and good medical care, and when she avoids exposure to substances that could be harmful to her baby, including alcohol and nicotine. Alcohol is the drug most often abused by pregnant women, often with devastating consequences such as **fetal alcohol spectrum disorder (FASD)**, a condition characterized by multiple problems including cognitive impairments and brain damage (McBee, 2005; E. S. Moore et al., 2007; Paley & O'Connor, 2007). Even small amounts of alcohol can cause neurological problems (Irene Choi, Allan, & Cunningham, 2005). Nicotine is also harmful because it restricts the oxygen supply to the fetus, slows its breathing, and disrupts the

---

longitudinal studies A method of studying developmental changes by evaluating the same people at different points in their lives.

biographical (or retrospective) study A method of studying developmental changes by reconstructing a person's past through interviews and inferring the effects of past events on current behaviors.

◄‥‥

LEARNING OBJECTIVE

- Explain how toxic agents, diseases, and maternal stress can affect an unborn child. Include the concept of *critical period* in your explanation.

prenatal development Development from conception to birth.

embryo A developing human between 2 weeks and 3 months after conception.

fetus A developing human between 3 months after conception and birth.

teratogens Toxic substances such as alcohol or nicotine that cross the placenta and may result in birth defects.

critical period A time when certain internal and external influences have a major effect on development; at other periods, the same influences will have little or no effect.

fetal alcohol spectrum disorder (FASD) A disorder that occurs in children of women who drink alcohol during pregnancy; this disorder is characterized by facial deformities, heart defects, stunted growth, brain damage and cognitive impairments.

Children born with fetal alcohol spectrum disorder (FASD) often exhibit facial deformities, heart defects, stunted growth, and cognitive impairments that can last throughout life. The syndrome is entirely preventable, but not curable.

regular rhythm of the fetal heartbeat (Zeskind & Gingras, 2006). These changes are associated with a significantly increased risk of miscarriage and low birth weight (Ness et al., 1999).

The mother's level of psychological stress during pregnancy and the way she copes with it also can affect the health of a newborn. Research with several species of animals, including non-human primates, has shown that maternal distress increases the concentration of certain hormones in the mother raising the risk for learning, attention, and emotional impairments in the offspring (Emack, Kostaki, Walker, & Matthews, 2008; Kaiseer & Sachser, 2009; Weinstock, 2008). Studies with humans have also shown that the risks of prematurity and low birth weight were higher in mothers with low self-esteem who felt pessimistic, stressed, and anxious during pregnancy (Schetter, 2009; Schetter & Glynn, 2011).

✔•⌐ **Study** and **Review** on **MyPsychLab**

CHECK YOUR UNDERSTANDING

Match each of the following terms with the appropriate definition:

1. ＿＿ prenatal development
2. ＿＿ teratogens
3. ＿＿ critical periods
4. ＿＿ placenta

a. substances that cross the placenta, causing birth defects
b. times at which harmful agents can do major damage to the fetus
c. the period from conception to birth
d. the organ that nourishes the fetus

Answers: 1. c. 2. a. 3. b. 4. d.

APPLY YOUR UNDERSTANDING

1. Sue recently discovered she is pregnant. She asks you whether you think it would be all right if she drinks a beer or two at the end of the week. Based on what you have read in this chapter, which of the following would be the most appropriate reply?
   a. "Not during the first 3 months of pregnancy, and no more than one drink a week thereafter."
   b. "Not during the last 6 months of pregnancy, but it would be okay prior to that."
   c. "Avoid alcohol at all times during pregnancy."
   d. "Only one drink a week, and then only if you get good nutrition and good medical care."

2. Mary Jane is pregnant and a heavy smoker. If her baby has a health problem, it is most likely to
   a. have mental retardation.
   b. have a low birth weight.
   c. be blind.
   d. be prone to disease.

Answers: 1. c. 2. b.

neonates Newborn babies.

LEARNING OBJECTIVE

• Summarize the reflexes and perceptual abilities of newborns. Describe the four basic temperaments that are visible at birth, the extent to which those inborn temperaments remain stable over time, and the reasons for both stability and change.

THE NEWBORN

How competent are newborns?

Research has disproved the old idea that **neonates,** or newborn babies, are oblivious to the world. Although newborns can sleep up to 20 hours a day, when awake they are much more aware and competent than they may seem at first glance.

Reflexes

What early reflexes enable newborns to respond to their environment?

Newborns come equipped with a number of essential reflexes. For example, the baby's tendency to turn his or her head toward anything that touches the cheek, called the *rooting reflex,* helps the baby find the mother's nipple. The *sucking reflex* is the tendency to suck on anything that enters the mouth; and the *swallowing reflex* enables the baby to swallow liquids without choking. Infants are also capable of reflexively imitating the facial expressions of adults (B. Bower, 2003b). For example, if an adult sticks out his or her tongue, newborn babies often respond by sticking out their tongues. And from the very beginning, infants can communicate their needs: They can cry. After only about 6 weeks they have an even better method of communication: They can smile.

If they are raised in a compatible environment, easy, uninhibited babies will most likely grow to be outgoing children and adults.

Temperament

Is your temperament the same as when you were a newborn?

Babies display individual differences in **temperament** from the time they are born. Some cry much more than others; some are much more placid. Some babies love to be cuddled; others seem to wriggle uncomfortably when held.

To some extent these differences in temperament appear to be hereditary. But there is also some evidence that prenatal factors play a significant role (Huizink et al., 2002; Susman, Schmeelk, Ponirakis, & Gariepy, 2001). In particular, maternal stress produces reliable changes in heartbeat and movement in the fetus; these, in turn, have been correlated with temperament (Gutteling et al., 2005).

Regardless of what initially causes a baby's temperament, it often remains stable even into adulthood (McAdams & Olson, 2010). A combination of biological and environmental factors contributes to this stability in behavior. For instance, if a newborn has an innate predisposition to cry often and react negatively to things, the parents may find themselves tired, frustrated, and often angry. These reactions in the parents may serve to reinforce the baby's difficult behaviors, and so they tend to endure. In other cases, environmental factors can cause basic changes in temperament. Thus, a child born with a particular temperament will not necessarily have that temperament for life. Each child's predispositions interact with his or her experiences, and how the child turns out is the result of that interaction (Booth-LaForce & Oxford, 2008; Hane, Cheah, Rubin, & Fox, 2008).

ENDURING ISSUES

Diversity–Universality   Different from Birth

In a classic study of infant temperament, Alexander Thomas and Stella Chess (1977) identified three types of babies:

- "Easy" babies are good natured and adaptable, easy to care for and to please.
- "Difficult" babies are moody and intense, with strong, negative reactions to new people and situations.
- "Slow to warm up" babies are relatively inactive and slow to respond to new things; when they do react, their reactions are mild.

To these three types, Jerome Kagan and his associates (Kagan & Snidman, 2004) have added a fourth: the "shy child." Shy children are timid and inhibited, fearful of anything new or strange. Evidence from neuroimaging studies indicates that there is a biological basis for this temperament: the amygdala (see **Figure 2–9**) of shy infants overreacts when they are presented with a novel stimulus or situation, a response that continues into adolescence (C. E. Schwartz, Wright, et al., 2003). ■

temperament Characteristic patterns of emotional reactions and emotional self-regulation.

When placed on a visual cliff, babies of crawling age (about 6 to 14 months) will not cross the deep side, even to reach their mothers. This classic experiment tells us that by the time they can crawl, babies can also perceive depth.

Watch the **Video** Visual Cliff on **MyPsychLab**

Perceptual Abilities

Which senses are the most developed at birth, and which are the least developed?

Neonates begin to absorb and process information from the outside world as soon as they enter it—in some cases, even before.

Vision Unlike puppies and kittens, human babies are born with their eyes open and functioning, even though the world looks a bit fuzzy to them at first. They see most clearly when faces or objects are only 8 to 10 inches away from them. Visual acuity (the clarity of vision) improves rapidly, however, and so does the ability to focus on objects at different distances. By 6 or 8 months of age, babies can see almost as well as the average college student, though their visual system takes another 3 or 4 years to develop fully.

Even very young babies have visual preferences. They would rather look at a new picture or pattern than one they have seen many times before. If given a choice between two pictures or patterns, both of which are new to them, they generally prefer the one with the clearer contrasts and simpler patterns. As babies get older and their vision improves, they prefer more complex patterns (Acredolo & Hake, 1982; Fantz, Fagan, & Miranda, 1975; Slater, 2000).

In general, infants find human faces and voices particularly interesting (Flavell, 1999; Turati, 2004). Just a few days after birth babies can discriminate different facial expressions in adults. For example, they look longer at a happy adult face than a fearful one (Farroni, Menon, Rigato, & Johnson, 2007). They also will follow the other person's gaze. For example, when presented with a human face depicted as looking to the left or right, infants as young as 2 days old notice the direction of the adult's gaze and shift their gaze accordingly (Farroni, Massaccesi, Pividori, & Johnson, 2004). Newborns also prefer to look at their own mother rather than at a stranger (Bushnell, 2003).

Depth Perception Although researchers have been unable to find evidence of depth perception in babies younger than 4 months, the ability to see the world in three dimensions is well developed by the time a baby learns to crawl, between 6 and 12 months of age.

This was demonstrated in a classic experiment using a device called a *visual cliff* (Walk & Gibson, 1961). Researchers divided a table into three parts, with a solid runway in the center. On one side of this runway was a solid surface decorated in a checkerboard pattern and covered with a sheet of clear glass. The other side was also covered with a thick sheet of clear glass, but on this side—the visual cliff—the checkerboard surface was not directly under the glass, but 40 inches below it. An infant of crawling age was placed on the center runway, and the mother stood on one side or the other, encouraging the baby to crawl toward her across the glass. All of the 6- to 14-month-old infants tested refused to crawl across the visual cliff, even though they were perfectly willing to cross the "shallow" side of the table.

Other Senses Even before babies are born, their ears are in working order. They can hear sounds and will startle at a sudden, loud noise in the uterine environment. After birth, babies show signs that they remember sounds they heard in the womb. For example, immediately after birth, newborns prefer the sound of their mother's voice to that of an unfamiliar female voice (Kisilevsky et al., 2003).

Infants are particularly tuned in to the sounds of human speech (T. M. Hernandez, Aldridge, & Bower, 2000). In some ways, young infants are even better at distinguishing speech sounds than are older children and adults. As children grow older, they often lose their ability to hear the difference between two very similar speech sounds that are not distinguished in their native language. For example, young Japanese infants have no trouble hearing the difference between "ra" and "la," sounds that are not distinguished in the Japanese language. By the time they are 1 year old, however, Japanese infants can no longer tell these two sounds apart (Werker, 1989).

With regard to taste and smell, newborns have clear-cut likes and dislikes. They like sweet flavors, a preference that persists through childhood. Babies only a few hours old will show pleasure at the taste of sweetened water but will screw up their faces in disgust at the taste of lemon juice (Rosenstein & Oster, 2005).

As infants grow older, their perceptions of the world become keener and more meaningful. Two factors are important in this development. One is physical maturation of the sense organs and the nervous system; the other is gaining experience in the world.

Study and Review on MyPsychLab

---

CHECK YOUR UNDERSTANDING

1. What are the four types of temperament?
2. Indicate whether each of the following statements is true (T) or false (F):

   a. _____ A newborn baby's ability to imitate facial expressions is best thought of as a reflex.

   b. _____ Newborns prefer to look at their mothers more than at strangers.

   c. _____ A young infant may be better at distinguishing speech sounds than an older child.

   d. _____ The visual cliff is used to determine which visual stimuli babies prefer.

Answers: 1. easy, difficult, slow to warm up, shy. 2. a. (T) b. (T) c. (T) d. (F).

APPLY YOUR UNDERSTANDING

1. You show a 6-month-old baby a checkerboard pattern with big, bright, red and white squares. The baby seems fascinated and stares at the pattern for a long time but eventually turns her attention to other things. You then show her two patterns: the familiar checkerboard and a new pattern. Which pattern is she likely to look at more?

   a. the familiar checkerboard

   b. the new pattern

   c. There should be no difference since 6-month-olds do not have visual preferences.

   d. There should be no difference since 6-month-olds cannot yet see patterns.

2. Baby John is moody and intense; he reacts to new people and new situations both negatively and strongly. In contrast, Baby Michael is relatively inactive and quiet; he reacts only mildly to new situations. John's temperament is _____ and Michael's is _____.

   a. slow to warm up; easy

   b. shy; slow to warm up

   c. difficult; shy

   d. difficult; slow to warm up

Answers: 1. b. 2. d.

INFANCY AND CHILDHOOD

What kinds of developmental changes occur during infancy and childhood?

During the first dozen or so years of life, a helpless baby becomes a competent member of society. Many important kinds of developments occur during these early years. Here we will focus on neurological, cognitive, and social changes.

Neurological Development

How does the human brain change during infancy and early childhood?

The human brain changes dramatically during infancy and early childhood. During the first 2 years after birth, children have heads that are large relative to their bodies as the brain undergoes rapid growth. A child's brain reaches three-quarters of its adult size by about the age of 2, at which point head growth slows down, and the body does most of the growing. Head growth is virtually complete by age 10, but the body continues to grow for

---

LEARNING OBJECTIVES

- Describe how the human brain changes during infancy and early childhood. Summarize the course of physical and motor development in childhood.

- Describe Piaget's stages of cognitive development and Kohlberg's stages of moral development and summarize the criticisms of each. Describe the course of language development in childhood. Compare and contrast the views of Skinner, Chomsky, and Pinker regarding language development.

- Distinguish *imprinting* from *attachment.* Describe the nature of parent–child relationships in the first 12 years of life with specific reference to Erikson's stages of development. Describe how peer relationships develop during childhood and the importance of *non-shared environments.*

- Distinguish *gender identity, gender constancy, gender-role awareness,* and *gender stereotypes.* Describe *sex-typed behavior* including the extent to which biology and experience shape sex-typed behavior.

- Summarize the research on the effects of television and video games on children.

several more years. As noted in Chapter 2, "The Biological Basis of Behavior," infants are born with approximately 100 billion neurons, though the number of connections between neurons immediately after birth is relatively small. During the first 2 years of life, however, dendrites begin to bloom and branch out; and the number of interconnections between neurons increases dramatically. The developing nervous system also sees the rapid growth of myelin sheaths, the fatty covering that encases many neurons to provide insulation and increase the speed of conduction (see Figure 2–1). With this rapid growth in the number of connections and speed, the developing brain has an enhanced potential to respond to new and varied experiences, which, in turn, further increases the number of connections between neurons.

As the number of interconnections between neurons increases during early childhood, the density of synaptic connections in the brain also swells dramatically. Recall from Chapter 2, synapses are the areas where neurons communicate with one another. During infancy, synaptic growth is particularly prominent in the prefrontal cortex, which is involved in reasoning and self-regulation, and in the visual and auditory areas of the cortex. (See **Figure 9–1**.) Surprisingly, in the third year of life there is actually a decrease in both the number and density of synaptic connections. This decrease appears to result from a natural process in which neurons that are stimulated and used grow stronger and more complex, while those that are unused are replaced or "pruned" away (Huttenlocher, 2002; M. S. C. Thomas & Johnson, 2008).

These patterns of neurological growth, complexity, and reorganization provide a striking example of how nature and nurture work together, underscoring the importance of early and varied stimulation during development. Indeed, as noted in Chapter 2 (see Figure 2–5), a lack of stimulation during this early period of development can negatively impact the growth of neurons and the number of connections between them, adversely affecting development.

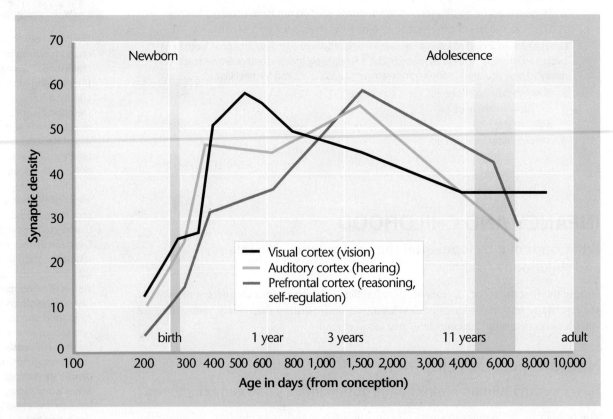

FIGURE 9–1

Synaptic density in the human brain from infancy to adulthood.

Note the dramatic increase and pruning in synaptic density over time in the vision, hearing, and reasoning centers of the brain.

Source: From "Regional Differences in the Synaptogenesis in the Human Cerebral Cortex" by Huttenlocher and Debholkar, *Journal of Comparative Neurology, 387* (October 20, 1997) 2, pp. 167–178. Copyright © 1997. Reprinted by permission of John Wiley & Sons, Inc.

Physical and Motor Development

Do children grow at a steady pace?

During the first year of life, the average baby grows 10 inches and gains 15 pounds. By 4 months, birth weight has doubled and by the first birthday, birth weight has tripled. During the second year, physical growth slows considerably. Rapid increases in height and weight will not occur again until early adolescence.

An infant's growth does not occur in the smooth, continuous fashion depicted in growth charts. Rather, growth takes place in fits and starts. When babies are measured daily over their first 21 months, most show no growth 90% of the time, but when they do grow, they do so rapidly. Incredible though it may sound, some children gain as much as 1 inch in height overnight!

Marked changes in body proportions accompany changes in a baby's size. During the first 2 years after birth, children have heads that are large relative to their bodies as the brain undergoes rapid growth. A child's brain reaches three-quarters of its adult size by about the age of 2, at which point head growth slows down, and the body does most of the growing. Head growth is virtually complete by age 10, but the body continues to grow for several more years. (See **Figure 9–2**.)

Motor development refers to the acquisition of skills involving movement, such as grasping, crawling, and walking. Much early motor development consists of substituting voluntary actions for reflexes. The newborn stepping reflex, for instance, gives way to voluntary walking in the older baby (Gallahue & Ozmun, 2006).

The *average ages* at which such skills are achieved are called *developmental norms*. By about 9 months, for example, the average infant can stand up while holding onto something. Crawling occurs, on average, at 10 months, and walking occurs at about 1 year. These ages are not exact; a baby who is 3 or 4 months behind schedule may be perfectly normal, and one who is 3 or 4 months ahead is not necessarily destined to become a star athlete. To some extent, parents can accelerate the acquisition of motor skills in children by providing them with ample training, encouragement, and practice. As coordination improves, children learn to run, skip, and climb. At 3 and 4, they begin to use their hands for increasingly complex tasks, such as learning how to put on shoes, then grappling with shoelaces. Gradually, through a combination of practice and the physical maturation of the body and the brain, they acquire increasingly complex motor abilities, such as bike riding and swimming. By the age of about 11, some children begin to be highly skilled at such tasks (Gallahue & Ozmun, 2006).

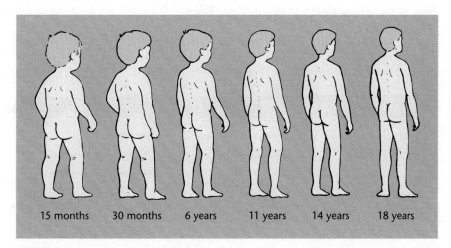

| 15 months | 30 months | 6 years | 11 years | 14 years | 18 years |

FIGURE 9–2

Body proportions at various ages.

Young children are top heavy: They have large heads and small bodies. As they get older, the body and legs become longer, and the head is proportionately smaller.

Source: Figures from "Individual Patterns of Development" by N. Bayley, *Child Development* (1956) Vol. 70, Issue 1. Copyright © 1956 by the Society for Research in Child Development. Reprinted by permission of Wiley-Blackwell.

Cognitive Development

How does a child's ability to think change over time?

The most influential theorist in the area of cognitive development was the Swiss psychologist Jean Piaget (1896–1980). Piaget observed and studied children, including his own three. As a result of his observations, Piaget believed that cognitive development is a way of adapting to the environment. In Piaget's view, children are intrinsically motivated to explore and understand things. As they do so, according to Piaget, they progress through four basic stages of cognitive development. These are outlined in the following "**Summary Table.**"

Sensory-Motor Stage (Birth to 2 Years)   According to Piaget, babies spend the first 2 years of life in the **sensory-motor stage** of development. They start out by simply applying the skills with which they were born—primarily sucking and grasping—to a broad range of activities. Young babies delight in taking things into their mouths—their mother's breast, their own thumb, or anything else within reach. Similarly, young babies will grasp a rattle reflexively. When they eventually realize that the noise comes from the rattle, they begin to shake everything they can grasp in an effort to reproduce the sound. Eventually, they distinguish between things that make noise and things that do not. In this way, infants begin to organize their experiences, fitting them into rudimentary categories such as "suckable" and "not suckable," "noise making," and "not noise making."

Another important outcome of the sensory-motor stage, according to Piaget, is the development of **object permanence,** an awareness that objects continue to exist even when out of sight. For a newborn child, objects that disappear simply cease to exist—"out of sight, out of mind." But as children gain experience with the world, they develop a sense of object permanence. By the time they are 18 to 24 months old, they can even imagine the movement of an object that they cannot actually see move. This last skill depends on the ability to form **mental representations** of objects and to manipulate those representations in their heads. This is a major achievement of the late sensory-motor stage.

By the end of the sensory-motor stage, toddlers have also developed a capacity for self-recognition—that is, they are able to recognize the child in the mirror as "myself." In one famous study, mothers put a dab of red paint on their child's nose while pretending to wipe the child's face. Then each child was placed in front of a mirror. Babies under 1 year of age stared in fascination at the red-nosed baby in the mirror; some of them even reached out to touch the nose's reflection. But babies between 21 and 24 months reached up and touched their own reddened noses, thereby showing that they knew the red-nosed baby in the mirror was "me" (Bard, Todd, Bernier, Love, & Leavens, 2006; Brooks-Gunn & Lewis, 1984).

sensory-motor stage In Piaget's theory, the stage of cognitive development between birth and 2 years of age in which the individual develops object permanence and acquires the ability to form mental representations.

object permanence The concept that things continue to exist even when they are out of sight.

mental representations Mental images or symbols (such as words) used to think about or remember an object, a person, or an event.

SUMMARY TABLE	PIAGET'S STAGES OF COGNITIVE DEVELOPMENT	
Stage	**Approximate age**	**Key features**
Sensory-motor	0–2 years	Object permanence
		Mental representations
Preoperational	2–7 years	Representational thought
		Fantasy play
		Symbolic gestures
		Egocentrism
Concrete-operational	7–11 years	Conservation
		Complex classification
Formal-operational	Adolescence-adulthood	Abstract and hypothetical thought

Preoperational Stage (2 to 7 Years) When children enter the **preoperational stage** of cognitive development, their thought is still tightly bound to their physical and perceptual experiences. But their increasing ability to use mental representations lays the groundwork for the development of language—using words as symbols to represent events and to describe, remember, and reason about experiences. (We will say more about language development shortly.) Representational thought also lays the groundwork for two other hallmarks of this stage—engaging in *fantasy play* (a cardboard box becomes a castle) and using *symbolic gestures* (slashing the air with an imaginary sword to slay an imaginary dragon).

Although children of this age have made advances over sensory-motor thought, in many ways they don't yet think like older children and adults. For example, preschool children are **egocentric**; they have difficulty seeing things from another person's point of view. An illustration of egocentric behavior can sometimes be seen during the game of hide-and-seek, when young children cover their own eyes to prevent others from seeing them.

Children of this age are also easily misled by appearances. In a famous experiment, Piaget showed preoperational children two identical glasses, filled to the same level with juice. The children were asked which glass held more juice, and they replied (correctly) that both had the same amount. Then Piaget poured the juice from one glass into a taller, narrower glass. Again the children were asked which glass held more juice. They looked at the two glasses, saw that the level of the juice in the tall, narrow one was much higher, and then replied that the narrow glass had more.

In Piaget's famous experiment, the child has to judge which glass holds more liquid: the tall, thin one or the short, wide one. Although both glasses hold the same amount, children in the preoperational stage say that the taller glass holds more, since they focus their attention on only one thing—the height of the column of liquid.

Concrete-Operational Stage (7 to 11 Years) During the **concrete-operational stage**, children become more flexible in their thinking. They learn to consider more than one dimension of a problem at a time and to look at a situation from someone else's viewpoint. This is the age at which they become able to grasp **principles of conservation,** such as the idea that the volume of a liquid stays the same regardless of the size and shape of the container into which it is poured. All related conservation concepts, such as those dealing with number or mass, involve an understanding that basic amounts remain constant despite superficial changes in appearance that can be reversed.

Another accomplishment of this stage is the ability to grasp complex classification schemes such as those involving superordinate and subordinate classes. For instance, if you show a preschooler four toy dogs and two toy cats and ask whether there are more dogs or more animals, the child will probably answer "more dogs." It is not until age 7 or 8 that children are able to think about objects as being simultaneously members of two classes, one more inclusive than the other. Yet even well into the elementary school years, children's thinking is still very much stuck in the "here and now." Often, they are unable to solve problems without concrete reference points that they can handle or imagine handling.

Formal-Operational Stage (Adolescence Through Adulthood) This limitation is overcome in the **formal-operational stage** of cognitive development, often reached during adolescence. Most, but not all, youngsters at this stage can think in abstract terms (Kuhn, 2009). They can formulate hypotheses, test them mentally, and accept or reject them according to the outcome of these mental experiments. Therefore, they are capable of going beyond the here and now to understand things in terms of cause and effect, to consider possibilities as well as realities, and to develop and use general rules, principles, and theories. Does this mean that adolescents should be held to the same legal standard as adults? The American Psychological Association has successfully argued before the Supreme Court that when deliberative, reasoned decision making is called for (such as medical and legal decisions), adolescents are as capable of mature decision making as adults. However, where high levels of emotional arousal or social coercion are involved and decisions must be made impulsively, adolescents are less mature than adults and thus less blameworthy (Steinberg, Cauffman, Woolard, Graham & Banich, 2009). Thus in the eyes of the law, a 16-year-old

preoperational stage In Piaget's theory, the stage of cognitive development between 2 and 7 years of age in which the individual becomes able to use mental representations and language to describe, remember, and reason about the world, though only in an egocentric fashion.

egocentric Unable to see things from another's point of view.

concrete-operational stage In Piaget's theory, the stage of cognitive development between 7 and 11 years of age in which the individual can attend to more than one thing at a time and understand someone else's point of view, though thinking is limited to concrete matters.

principles of conservation The concept that the quantity of a substance is not altered by reversible changes in its appearance.

formal-operational stage In Piaget's theory, the stage of cognitive development beginning about 11 years of age in which the individual becomes capable of abstract thought.

adolescent is capable of deciding to have an abortion without consulting her parents, but a 16-year-old adolescent who commits a capital crime will not face capital punishment as an adult would for the same crime.

Criticisms of Piaget's Theory Piaget's work has produced a great deal of controversy (Shayer, 2003). Many question his assumption that there are distinct stages in cognitive development that always progress in an orderly, sequential way, and that a child must pass through one stage before entering the next (Kagan, 2008). Some see cognitive development as a more gradual process, resulting from the slow acquisition of experience and practice rather than the abrupt emergence of distinctly higher levels of ability (Boom, 2004; Courage & Howe, 2002).

Piaget's theory has also sparked criticism for assuming that young infants understand very little about the world, such as the permanence of objects in it (Kiss, 2001; A. Woodward & Needham, 2009). When young babies are allowed to reveal their understanding of object permanence without being required to conduct a search for a missing object, they often seem to know perfectly well that objects continue to exist when hidden by other objects (Baillargeon, 1994). They also show other quite sophisticated knowledge of the world that Piaget thought they lacked, such as a rudimentary grasp of numbers, the ability to take the perspective of another person, and sophisticated reasoning (Gopnik, 2009; V. Izard, Dehaene-Lambertz, & Dehaene, 2008).

Other critics have argued that Piaget underplayed the importance of social interaction in cognitive development. For instance, the influential Russian psychologist Lev Vygotsky contended that people who are more advanced in their thinking provide opportunities for cognitive growth for children with whom they interact (Harreé, 2000; Vygotsky, 1978). These learning experiences greatly depend on a society's culture, another factor that Piaget ignored (Siegal, 2003).

Despite these criticisms, Piaget's theory provides a useful schematic road map of cognitive development (Morra, Gobbo, Marini, & Sheese, 2008). Moreover, Piaget profoundly impacted our understanding with his observation that children play an active role in the learning process, his description of qualitative changes in the way children think at various ages, and his emphasis on "readiness to learn."

Moral Development

How do gender and ethnic background affect moral development?

One of the important changes in thinking that occurs during childhood and adolescence is the development of moral reasoning. Lawrence Kohlberg (1979, 1981) studied this kind of development by telling his participants stories that illustrate complex moral issues. For example, in one of the best known of these stories, the "Heinz dilemma," a woman is described as near death from cancer. Her only hope for treatment requires that she be given a drug developed by a local pharmacist. However, the price of the drug is $2,000, despite that it only cost $200 for the pharmacist to make. Heinz, the woman's husband, can only raise half the money to purchase the drug, so he asks the pharmacist to sell him the drug for half the price or permit him to pay the remainder in installments. But the pharmacist says "No". Driven by desperation, the husband breaks into the pharmacy and steals the drug to save his wife (Kohlberg, 1969). The children and adolescents who heard this story were asked if the husband should have done what he did, and to explain the reason for their answer. On the basis of his participants' replies to these questions, Kohlberg theorized that moral reasoning develops in stages, much like Piaget's account of cognitive development:

- *Preconventional level* Preadolescent children are at what Kohlberg called the preconventional level of moral reasoning: They tend to interpret behavior in terms of its concrete consequences. Younger children at this level base their judgments of "right" and "wrong" behavior on whether it is rewarded or punished. Somewhat older children, still at this level, guide their moral choices on the basis of what satisfies needs, particularly their own. ◉

◉ **Watch** the **Video** Moral Development: Preconventional at **MyPsychLab**

- *Conventional level*   With the arrival of adolescence and the shift to formal-operational thought, the stage is set for progression to the conventional level of moral reasoning. At this level, the adolescent at first defines right behavior as that which pleases or helps others and is approved by them. Around mid-adolescence, there is a further shift toward considering various abstract social virtues, such as being a "good citizen" and respecting authority. Both forms of conventional moral reasoning require an ability to think about such abstract values as "duty" and "social order," to consider the intentions that lie behind behavior, and to put oneself in the "other person's shoes."
- *Postconventional level*   The postconventional level of moral reasoning requires a still more abstract form of thought. This level is marked by an emphasis on abstract principles such as justice, liberty, and equality. Personal and strongly felt moral standards become the guideposts for deciding what is right and wrong. Whether these decisions correspond to the rules and laws of a particular society at a particular time is irrelevant. For the first time, people may become aware of discrepancies between what they judge to be moral and what society has determined to be legal.

Kohlberg's views have been criticized on several counts. First, research indicates that many people in our society, adults as well as adolescents, never progress beyond the conventional level of moral reasoning. Does this finding mean that these people are morally "underdeveloped," as Kohlberg's theory implies?

Second, Kohlberg's theory does not consider cultural differences in moral values. Kohlberg put considerations of "justice" at the highest level of moral reasoning. In Nepal, however, Buddhist monks place the highest moral value on alleviating suffering and showing compassion, concepts that have no place in Kohlberg's scheme of moral development (Huebner, Garrod, & Snarey, 1990). Nevertheless, research supporting Kohlberg has shown that there are some common moral values and basic moral judgment stages that are consistent across cultures (Boom, Wouters, & Keller, 2007; Gibbs, Basinger, Grime, & Snarey, 2007).

Third, Kohlberg's theory has been criticized as sexist. Kohlberg found that boys usually scored higher than girls on his test of moral development. According to Carol Gilligan (1982, 1992), this was the case because boys are more inclined to base their moral judgments on the abstract concept of justice, whereas girls tend to base theirs more on the criteria of caring about other people and the importance of maintaining personal relationships. In Gilligan's view, there is no valid reason to assume that one of these perspectives is morally superior to the other.

More recent research on moral development has moved in the direction of broadening Kohlberg's focus on changes in moral reasoning. Researchers are increasingly interested in the factors that influence moral choices in everyday life, and the extent to which those choices are actually put into action. In other words, they want to understand moral behavior as much as moral thinking (D. C. Reed, 2008; Tappan, 2006).

Language Development

How does a child develop language skills?

The development of language follows a predictable pattern. At about 2 months of age, an infant begins to *coo* (a word for nondescript sounds). In another month or two, the infant enters the **babbling** stage and starts to repeat sounds such as *da* or even meaningless sounds that developmental psychologists refer to as "grunts"; these sounds are the building blocks for later language development. A few months later, the infant may string together the same sound, as in *dadadada*. Finally, the baby will form combinations of different sounds, as in *dabamaga*.

Even deaf babies who communicate with sign language engage in a form of babbling. Like hearing infants, these babies begin to babble before they are 10 months old—but they babble with their hands! Just as hearing infants utter sounds over and over, deaf babies make repetitive movements of their hands, like those of sign language (Goldin-Meadow, 2003).

Gradually, an infant's babbling takes on certain features of adult language. At about age 4 to 6 months, the infant's vocalizations begin to show signs of *intonation,* the rising and lowering of pitch that allows adults to distinguish, for example, between questions ("You're tired?")

babbling A baby's vocalizations, consisting of repetition of consonant–vowel combinations.

From 12 to 24 months, babies typically point at and name, although not always correctly, whatever object interests them.

and statements ("You're tired."). Also around this time, babies learn the basic sounds of their native language and can distinguish them from the sounds of other languages. By 6 months, they may recognize commonly used words, such as their own names and the words *mommy* and *daddy*.

By around their first birthday, babies begin to use intonation to indicate commands and questions. At about the same age, they show signs of understanding what is said to them, and they begin not only to imitate what others say but also to use sounds to get attention. Vocalization also becomes increasingly communicative and socially directed. Caregivers facilitate this process by speaking to babies in what is called *infant-directed speech*. They speak slowly and use simple sentences, a higher pitched voice, repetition, and exaggerated intonations—all of which engage babies' attention and help them distinguish the sounds of their language.

All this preparation leads up to the first word at about 12 months. During the next 6 to 8 months, children build a vocabulary of one-word sentences called **holophrases**: "Up!"; "Out!"; "More!" Children may also use compound words such as *awgone* [all gone]. To these holophrases, they add words used to address people—*Bye-bye* is a favorite—and a few exclamations, such as *Ouch!* These first words play an important role in the formation of the child's vocabulary and pave the way for their understanding of grammar.

In the second year of life, children begin to distinguish between themselves and others. Possessive words become a big part of the vocabulary: [The shoes are] "Daddy's." But the overwhelming passion of children from 12 to 24 months old is naming. With little or no prompting, they will name virtually everything they see, though not always correctly! If they don't know the name of an object, they will simply invent one or use another word that is almost correct. Feedback from parents ("No, that's not a dog, it's a cow") enhances vocabulary and helps children understand what names can and cannot be assigned to classes of things ("dog" is not used for big four-legged animals that live on farms and moo rather than bark).

During the third year of life, children begin to form two- and three-word sentences such as "Baby cry" and "My ball." Recordings of mother–child conversations show that children from 24 to 36 months old noticeably omit auxiliary verbs and verb endings ("I [am] eat[ing] it up"), as well as prepositions and articles ("It [is] time [for] Sarah [to] take [a] nap"). Children this age seize on the most important parts of speech—those that contain the most meaning.

After 3 years of age, children begin to fill in their sentences ("Nick school" becomes "Nick goes to school"), and language production increases dramatically. Children start to use the past tense as well as the present. Sometimes they *overregularize* the past tense, by applying the regular form when an irregular one is called for (saying "Alex goed" instead of "Alex went," for example). Such mistakes are signs that the child has implicitly grasped the basic rules of language. Preschoolers also ask more questions and learn to employ "Why?" effectively and endlessly! By the age of 5 or 6, most children have a vocabulary of over 2,500 words and can construct sentences of 6 to 8 words.

Theories of Language Development Several very different theories explain how language develops. B. F. Skinner (1957) believed that parents and other people listen to the infant's cooing and babbling and reinforce those sounds that most resemble adult speech. If the infant says something that sounds like *mama*, mommy reinforces this behavior with smiles and attention. As children get older, the things they say must sound more like adult speech to be reinforced. Skinner believed that an understanding of grammar, word construction, and so on are acquired in much the same way.

Most psychologists and linguists now believe that learning alone cannot explain the speed, accuracy, and originality with which children learn to use language (Christiansen

holophrases One-word sentences commonly used by children under 2 years of age.

& Chater, 2008a, 2008b; Pinker, 1994, 1999). Noam Chomsky (1965, 1986) has proposed that children are born with a **language acquisition device,** an internal mechanism that is "wired into" the human brain that enables young children to detect general patterns of grammar in adult speech, thus permitting them to quickly learn the words and rules of any language to which they are exposed.

A more recent theory of language acquisition, advanced by Steven Pinker (1994, 2007; Pinker and Jackendoff, 2005), holds that, to a large extent, evolutionary forces may have shaped language, providing humans with what he calls a *language instinct.* Drawing extensively from the fields of linguistics, evolutionary psychology, and neurolinguistics, Pinker constructs a convincing case that language should not be viewed as a "cultural artifact." Instead, Pinker (1994) argues that language is "a distinct piece of the biological makeup of our brains" (p. 18). He contends, "people know how to talk in more or less the sense that spiders know how to spin webs" (p. 18).

According to Pinker, the language instinct, like other instincts, evolved through natural selection, taking the form of an innate circuitry in the brain that uses complex computational rules to perceive, organize, and transmit information (Pinker, 2007). It is because of this adapted circuitry, for instance, that humans are predisposed to attach meaning to words, a process that cognitive neuroscientists recognize as exceedingly complex. According to Pinker, this circuitry also guides the language acquisition process, which enables children to attend to minor but important differences in the pronunciation of words, such as *talk* and *talks,* when they listen to adult speech (Pinker, 1999; 2004). This is important because only by focusing on the relevant aspects of speech could a child ever master the grammatical rules of a language.

Not everyone agrees with Pinker's position (Fitch, Hauser, & Chomsky, 2005; Karmiloff-Smith, 2002; Sampson, 1999). Critics are quick to point out that research has not yet identified any of the specific neural circuits that Pinker describes. They also contend that other theories, based more on learning than on instinct, can just as easily explain many aspects of human language.

language acquisition device A hypothetical neural mechanism for acquiring language that is presumed to be "wired into" all humans.

Bilingualism In the past two decades, psychologists have come to fully realize that the ability to speak more than one language is not unusual. For the great majority of people in the world, it is quite normal. As a result, research on the acquisition and use of multiple languages has not only expanded rapidly but it also sheds new light on the nature of language, the mind and the brain. It is now clear that, contrary to some earlier beliefs, exposure to multiple languages very early in life is not harmful but is, in fact, beneficial to children (Bialystok & Craik, 2010). It is also clear that bilingualism provides long-term benefits, specifically providing some protection from cognitive declines in old age (Bialystok, Craik, Green, & Gollan, 2009; Kroll, 2009).

In a comprehensive review of the research literature, Bialystok, Craik, Green & Gollan (2009) draw the following conclusions:

- Bilingual children learn their languages in the same way as monolinguals, though as children and adults they have a smaller vocabulary in each language than do monolinguals.

- Bilinguals of all ages have better "executive control" which means the ability to control attention, ignore distractions, to switch between tasks, and to hold information in mind while performing a task.

- Bilinguals use the same brain networks for executive control as do monolinguals.

The fact that young children can learn a second language as easily and effortlessly as they acquire one language demonstrates the critical importance of the environment in which they are raised. The fact that children can learn a second language more quickly and speak it more fluently than adults supports the idea of a critical period during which languages are most readily acquired. Moreover, the languages to which a child is exposed during that critical period determine the languages in which the child will

Approximately 10 million students in U.S. schools have a first language other than English. Researchers and educators debate the best way to help these students achieve in school.

Konrad Lorenz discovered that goslings will follow the first moving object they see, regardless of whether it is their mother, a mechanical toy, or a human. Here, Lorenz is trailed by goslings who have imprinted on him.

be truly proficient. This critical period starts to close with the onset of puberty (Sakai, 2005; Sakai & Muto, 2007), which is why it is difficult for even a young adolescent to learn to speak a second language without an accent (Flege, Munro, & MacKay, 1995).

Social Development

How can parents help their children become both securely attached and independent?

Learning to interact with others is an important aspect of childhood development. Early in life, children's most important relationships are with their parents and other caregivers. But by the time they are 3 years old, their important relationships have usually expanded to include siblings, playmates, and other adults outside the family. Their social world expands further when they start school.

Parent–Child Relationships in Infancy: Development of Attachment Young animals of many species follow their mothers because of **imprinting.** Shortly after they are born or hatched, they form a strong bond to the first moving object they see. In nature, this object is most often the mother, the first source of nurturance and protection. But in laboratory experiments, certain species of animals, such as geese, have been hatched in incubators and have imprinted on decoys, mechanical toys, and even human beings (H. S. Hoffman & DePaulo, 1977; Lorenz, 1935). These goslings faithfully follow their human "mother," showing no interest whatever in adult females of their own species.

Human newborns do not imprint on first-seen moving objects, but they do gradually form an **attachment,** or emotional bond, to the people who take care of them. As we saw in Chapter 8, "Motivation and Emotion," classic studies of baby monkeys suggest that the sense of security engendered by physical contact and closeness is one important root of attachment (Harlow, 1958; Harlow & Zimmerman, 1959).

In humans, this attachment is built on many hours of interaction during which baby and parent come to form a close relationship. Signs of attachment are evident by the age of 6 months or even earlier. The baby will react with smiles and coos at the caregiver's appearance and with whimpers and doleful looks when the caregiver goes away. At around 7 months, attachment behavior becomes more intense. The infant will reach out to be picked up by the caregiver, and will cling to the caregiver, especially when tired, frightened, or hurt. The baby will also begin to display **stranger anxiety,** often reacting with loud wails at even the friendliest approach by an unfamiliar person. If separated from the caregiver even for a few minutes in an unfamiliar place, the baby will usually become quite upset. Stranger anxiety usually begins around 7 months, reaching its peak at 12 months, and then declines during the second year of life.

Parents are often puzzled by this new behavior in their previously nonchalant infants, but it is perfectly normal. In fact, anxiety over separation from the parent indicates that the infant has developed a sense of "person permanence" along with a sense of object permanence. For 5-month-olds, it's still "out of sight, out of mind" when Mom or Dad leaves the room, but for 9-month-olds, the memory of their parent lingers, and they announce at the top of their lungs that they want Mommy or Daddy to come back!

Ideally, infants learn in their first year of life that their primary caregivers can be counted on to be there when needed. Psychologist Erik Erikson (1902–1994) called this result the development of *basic trust.* (See the "**Summary Table:** Erikson's Eight Psychosocial Stages, with Corresponding Freudian Stage Indicated.") If babies' needs are generally met, they come to develop faith in other people and also in themselves. They see the world as a secure, dependable place and have optimism about the future. In contrast, babies whose needs are not usually met, perhaps because of an unresponsive or often-absent caregiver, develop what Erikson referred to as *mistrust.* They grow to be fearful and overly anxious about their own security.

imprinting The tendency in certain species to follow the first moving thing (usually its mother) it sees after it is born or hatched.

attachment Emotional bond that develops in the first year of life that makes human babies cling to their caregivers for safety and comfort.

stranger anxiety Fear of unfamiliar people which usually emerges around 7 months, reaching its peak at 12 months and declining during the second year.

SUMMARY TABLE	ERIKSON'S EIGHT PSYCHOSOCIAL STAGES, WITH CORRESPONDING FREUDIAN STAGE INDICATED		
Stage	**Age**	**Challenge**	**Freudian Psychosexual Stage**
Trust vs. mistrust	Birth to 1 year	Developing a sense that the world is safe and good	Oral
Autonomy vs. shame and doubt	1 to 3 years	Realizing that one is an independent person with the ability to make decisions	Anal
Initiative vs. guilt	3 to 6 years	Developing a willingness to try new things and to handle failure	Phallic
Industry vs. inferiority	6 years to adolescence	Learning competence in basic skills and to cooperate with others	Latency
Identity vs. role confusion	Adolescence	Developing a coherent, integrated sense of inner self	Genital
Intimacy vs. isolation	Young adulthood	Establishing ties to another in a trusting, loving relationship	
Generativity vs. stagnation	Middle adulthood	Finding meaning in career, family, and community via productive work	
Ego integrity vs. despair	Late life	Viewing one's life as satisfactory and worth living	

As infants develop basic trust, they venture away from the caregiver to investigate objects and other people around them. This exploration is a first indication of children's developing **autonomy,** or a sense of independence. Autonomy and attachment may seem to be opposites, but they are actually closely related. The child who has formed a secure attachment to a caregiver can explore the environment without fear. Such a child knows that the caregiver will be there when really needed, and so the caregiver serves as a "secure base" from which to venture forth (Ainsworth, 1977; Dwyer, 2006).

At about 2 years of age, children begin to assert their growing independence. They refuse everything: getting dressed ("No!"), going to sleep ("No!"), using the potty ("No!"). The usual outcome of these first declarations of independence is that the parents begin to discipline the child. The conflict between the parents' need for peace and order and the child's desire for autonomy often creates difficulties. But it is an essential first step in **socialization,** the process by which children learn the behaviors and attitudes appropriate to their family and their culture.

Erikson saw two possible outcomes of this early conflict: *autonomy versus shame and doubt.* If a toddler fails to acquire a sense of independence and separateness from others, self-doubt may take root. The child may begin to question his or her own ability to act effectively in the world. If parents and other adults belittle a toddler's efforts, the child may also begin to feel ashamed. The need for both autonomy and socialization can be met if parents allow the child a reasonable amount of independence, while insisting that the child follow certain rules. ☞

autonomy Sense of independence; a desire not to be controlled by others.

socialization Process by which children learn the behaviors and attitudes appropriate to their family and culture.

Simulate the **Experiment** Attachment Classifications in the Strange Situation on **MyPsychLab**

Parent–Child Relationships in Childhood As children grow older, their social worlds expand. Erikson saw the stage between ages 3 and 6 as one of growing initiative, surrounded by a potential for guilt (*initiative versus guilt*). Children of this age become increasingly involved in independent efforts to accomplish goals—making plans, undertaking projects, mastering new skills—from bike riding to drawing to writing simple words. Parental encouragement of these initiatives leads to a sense of joy in taking on new tasks. But if children are repeatedly criticized and scolded for things they do wrong, they may develop strong feelings of unworthiness, resentment, and guilt. In Erikson's view, avoiding these negative feelings is the major challenge of this stage.

According to Erik Erikson, children around age 2 are struggling to establish autonomy from their parents.

The effect of parenting style on a child's outlook and behavior has been the subject of extensive research. For example, Diana Baumrind (1972, 1991, 1996) identified four basic parenting styles:

- *Authoritarian* parents control their children's behavior rigidly and insist on unquestioning obedience. Authoritarian parents are likely to produce children who generally have poor communication skills and are moody, withdrawn, and distrustful.
- *Permissive-indifferent* parents exert too little control, failing to set limits on their children's behavior. They are also neglectful and inattentive, providing little emotional support to their children, who tend to be overly dependent and lacking in social skills and self-control.
- *Permissive-indulgent* parents are very supportive of their children, but fail to set appropriate limits on their behavior. The children of permissive-indulgent parents tend to be immature, disrespectful, impulsive, and out of control.
- *Authoritative* parents, according to Baumrind, represent the most successful parenting style. Authoritative parents provide firm structure and guidance without being overly controlling. They listen to their children's opinions and give explanations for their decisions, but it is clear that they are the ones who make and enforce the rules. Children of authoritative parents are most likely to be self-reliant and socially responsible.

Although many studies show a relationship between parental behavior and child development, be cautious when drawing conclusions about cause and effect. Understand that parents do not determine the parent–child relationship on their own. Children also affect it (Collins, Maccoby, Steinberg, Hetherington, & Bornstein, 2000). Parents do not act the same way toward every child in the family (even though they may try) because each child is a different individual. A thoughtful, responsible child is more likely to elicit authoritative parenting, whereas an impulsive child who is difficult to reason with is more likely to elicit an authoritarian style. Thus, children influence the behavior of their caregivers at the same time that the caregivers are influencing them.

So far we have seen that parents can have a profound effect on the development of their children. In the next section, we will examine the extent to which peers also influence development.

peer group A network of same-aged friends and acquaintances who give one another emotional and social support.

Relationships with Other Children
At a very early age, infants begin to show an interest in other children, but the social skills required to play with them develop only gradually. Among the first peers that most children encounter are their siblings. The quality of sibling relationships can have a major impact, especially on how children learn to relate to other peers. Once children enter school, peer influences outside the family increase greatly. Now they are under a great deal of pressure to be part of a **peer group** of friends. In peer groups, children learn many valuable things, such as how to engage in cooperative activities and how to negotiate the social roles of leader and follower (Barber, Stone, Hunt, & Eccles, 2005).

When young children engage in *parallel play*, each plays alone, but near the other.

As children get older, they develop a deeper understanding of the meaning of friendship. For preschoolers, a friend is simply "someone I play with," but around age 7, children begin to realize that friends "do things" for one another. At this still egocentric age, however, friends are defined largely as people who "do things for *me*." Later, at about age 9, children come to understand that friendship is a two-way street and that, although friends do things for us, we are also expected to do things for them. During these early years, friendships often come and go at dizzying speed; they endure only as long as needs are being met. It is not until late childhood or early adolescence that friendship is viewed as a stable and continuing social relationship requiring mutual support, trust, and confidence.

Successfully making friends is one of the tasks that Erikson saw as centrally important to children between the ages of 7 and 11, the stage of *industry versus inferiority*. At this age, children must master many increasingly difficult skills, social interaction with peers being only one of them. Others have to do with mastering academic skills at school, meeting growing responsibilities placed on them at home, and learning to do various tasks they will need as independent adults. In Erikson's view, if children become stifled in their efforts to prepare themselves for the adult world, they may conclude that they are inadequate and lose faith in their power to become self-sufficient. Those whose industry is rewarded develop a sense of competence and self-assurance.

Non-shared Environments Most developmental psychologists believe that peer influence is just one example of a much broader class of environmental factors called the **non-shared environment** (R. J. Rose et al., 2003). Even children who grow up in the same home with the same parents are likely to have very different day-to-day human relationships, and this non-shared environment can have a significant effect on their development (Suitor, Sechrist, Plikuhn, Pardo, & Pillemer, 2008). One review of the research concludes that although family experiences are important, the crucial environmental influences that shape personality development are "specific to each child, rather than general to an entire family" (Plomin & Rende, 1991, p. 180).

In the United States, over half of the children between birth and third grade spend some time being regularly cared for by persons other than their parents. Some people have expressed concern that being entrusted to caregivers outside the immediate family may interfere with the development of secure attachments and put children at greater risk for emotional maladjustment. But according to the findings of one large-scale longitudinal study (NICHD Early Child Care Research Network, 1997), placing a baby in full-time day care even in the first few months of life doesn't in itself undermine attachment. Working parents and their babies still have ample opportunity to engage in the daily give-and-take of positive feelings on which secure attachments are built. Day care, however, can be a negative factor if working parents generally provide insensitive and unresponsive care. Such behavior is, in itself, associated with insecure attachment, but these babies are even *more* likely to form an insecure attachment if they also experience extensive day care, especially poor-quality care or changing day-care arrangements.

One conclusion, then, is that quality of care counts (Brobert, Wessels, Lamb, & Hwang, 1997; H. Steele, 2008; Votruba-Drzl, Coley, & Chase-Lansdale, 2004). A secure, affectionate, stimulating environment is likely to produce children who are healthy, outgoing, and ready to learn, just as an environment that encourages fears and doubts is likely to stunt development. Research shows, for example, that children of working mothers who are placed in a quality day care generally develop strong cognitive and linguistic skills and are no more likely to display behavior problems than children who stay at home (Belsky, 2006).

Sex-Role Development

When do children learn about their gender?

By about age 3, both boys and girls have developed a **gender identity**—that is, a little girl knows that she is a girl, and a little boy knows that he is a boy. At this point, however, children have little understanding of what that means. A 3-year-old boy might think that if you put a dress on him, he will turn into a girl. By the age of 4 or 5, most children know that gender depends on what kind of genitals a person has. They have also acquired **gender constancy**, the realization that gender cannot be changed.

At quite a young age, children also start to acquire **gender-role awareness**, a knowledge of what behaviors are expected of males and females in their society (Bronstein, 2006). As a result, they develop **gender stereotypes**, or oversimplified beliefs about what the "typical" male and female are like (Sinnott, 1994; Jennifer Steele, 2003). For example, girls are supposed to be clean, neat, and careful, whereas boys are supposed to like rough, noisy, physical play. At the same time that children acquire gender-role awareness and gender stereotypes, they also develop their own **sex-typed behavior**: Girls play with dolls, and boys run around and wrestle with each other.

Although the behavioral differences between boys and girls are minimal in infancy, major differences tend to develop as children grow older. Boys tend to become more active and physically aggressive, and tend to play in larger groups. Girls tend to talk more, shove less, and interact in pairs.

non-shared environment The unique aspects of the environment that are experienced differently by siblings, even though they are reared in the same family.

gender identity A little girl's knowledge that she is a girl, and a little boy's knowledge that he is a boy.

gender constancy The realization that gender does not change with age.

gender-role awareness Knowledge of what behavior is appropriate for each gender.

gender stereotypes General beliefs about characteristics that men and women are presumed to have.

sex-typed behavior Socially prescribed ways of behaving that differ for boys and girls.

By school age, boys and girls tend to play by the rules of sex-typed behavior. Typically, girls play nonaggressive games, in pairs or small groups, whereas boys prefer more active group games.

ENDURING ISSUES

Nature–Nurture   Sex-Typed Behavior

The source of sex-typed behavior is a matter of considerable debate. Because gender-related differences in styles of interaction appear very early in development (even before the age of 3), Eleanor Maccoby, a specialist in this area, believes that they are at least partly biological in origin. In addition to the influence of genes, some evidence suggests that prenatal exposure to hormones plays a part (Collaer & Hines, 1995). But Maccoby thinks that biologically based differences are small at first and later become exaggerated because of the different kinds of socialization experienced by boys and girls. She suggests that a lot of gender-typical behavior is the product of children playing with others of their sex (Maccoby, 1998). Undoubtedly, popular culture—especially as portrayed on television—also influences the norms of gender-appropriate behavior that develop in children's peer groups. And parents, too, can sometimes add input, especially during critical transitions in the child's life when parents feel it is important to behave in more sex-stereotyped ways (Fagot, 1994). The end result is substantial sex-typed behavior by middle childhood. Research on this topic continues, but the growing consensus is that both biology and experience contribute to gender differences in behavior (Collaer & Hines, 1995; Collins et al., 2000). ∎

Television, Video Games, and Children

Is watching TV or playing video games a good or bad influence on the development of children?

On average, American children spend 30 hours a week watching television and 1–2 hours a week playing video games (McDonough, 2009). Not surprisingly, psychologists, educators, and parents are very concerned about the influence TV and video games may have on children. Indeed, the American Academy of Pediatrics (1999, 2007) recommends that children under the age of 2 should not watch television at all and that parents limit their children's time watching TV and playing video games to no more than 1 or 2 hours a day.

One concern is the violence that pervades many TV programs and video games. Children who watch 2 hours of TV daily will see about 8,000 murders and 100,000 other acts of violence by the time they leave elementary school (Kunkel et al., 1996). Even Saturday-morning cartoons average more than 20 acts of violence per hour (Seppa, 1997). The great majority of video games also contain violence—often extreme violence directed toward other game characters (Dill, Gentile, Richter, & Dill, 2005). Does witnessing and, in the case of video games, participating in fictional violence make children more aggressive? And if so, does this exposure to violence account, at least in part, for the rapid rise in violent crime among adolescents?

According to two comprehensive reviews of the research, the answer appears to be "yes" (C. A. Anderson et al., 2003; Huesmann, 2007). In fact, the authors of both of these reviews found that the effects of media violence can extend well into adulthood even for people who are not highly aggressive. Short-term exposure was found to increase the incidence of physically and verbally aggressive thoughts, emotions, and behaviors, whereas longitudinal studies linked exposure to media violence in childhood with aggression later in life, including physical assaults and spouse abuse. Finally, although media violence affects some people more than others, these authors concluded no one is exempt from its deleterious effects.

In addition to the issue of violence, every moment spent watching TV or playing video games takes time away from such activities as chatting with friends or playing sports, which may be more beneficial. Obesity in children has also been correlated with the amount of time spent watching TV (Vandewater, Shim, & Caplovitz, 2004). Watching too much television can also lead to a variety of sleep disturbances in children, including night wakings, daytime sleepiness, increased anxiety at bedtime, shortened sleep duration, and difficulty falling asleep (Van den Bulck, 2004).

Studies confirm that watching television is associated with aggressive behavior in children, but only if the content of the shows is violent.

CHECK YOUR UNDERSTANDING

✓•—Study and **Review** on **MyPsychLab**

1. List, in order, Piaget's four stages of cognitive development.

2. Match each phase of childhood with its major challenge, according to Erik Erikson's theory.

___ infancy

___ toddlerhood

___ preschool years

___ elementary school years

a. industry versus inferiority

b. trust versus mistrust

c. autonomy versus shame and doubt

d. initiative versus guilt

Answers: 1. sensory-motor, preoperational, concrete-operational, formal-operational. 2. infancy: b; toddlerhood: c; preschool years: d; elementary school years: a.

APPLY YOUR UNDERSTANDING

1. At age 10 months, a child watches a red ball roll under a chair, but fails to search for it. At 2 years, the same child watches the same event, but now searches systematically for the ball. What change most likely accounts for the different reactions?

    a. The 10-month-old lacks depth perception.

    b. The 10-month-old does not yet understand the principle of conservation.

    c. The 2-year-old has acquired a sense of object permanence.

    d. All of the above are equally likely explanations.

2. Three preschoolers of different ages are sitting in a room watching a playful puppy. Child 1 exclaims, "I play puppy tail." Child 2 reaches for the dog and cries out, "Gimme!" Child 3 asks, "Who left the puppy here?" On the basis of your knowledge of language development, which child is most likely to be the youngest and which is most likely to be the oldest?

    a. Child 3 is youngest, child 1 is oldest.

    b. Child 3 is youngest, child 2 is oldest.

    c. Child 2 is youngest, child 3 is oldest.

    d. Child 1 is youngest, child 3 is oldest.

Answers: 1. c. 2. c.

Nonetheless, children can learn worthwhile things from watching television and playing *educational video games* (D. R. Anderson, 1998; J. C. Wright et al., 1999). For example, one study compared the performance of kindergarten children who played the *Playstation* educational video game *Lightspan* for 40 minutes a day in school for 11 weeks to a group that did not play the game. Students who played the game performed better on a test of reading and spelling (but not arithmetic) than the control group who did not play the game (Din & Calao, 2001). In another longitudinal study, the TV viewing habits of 5-year-olds were monitored by parents and recorded by electronic devices. Years later, high school records showed the more time these children had spent viewing such educational programs as *Sesame Street* and *Mr. Rogers,* the higher their high school grades were. In contrast, same-age children who watched a lot of noneducational and violent programming had comparatively lower high school grades than their peers (D. R. Anderson, Huston, Wright, & Collins, 1998).

THINKING CRITICALLY ABOUT . . .

Television's Effects

Unless you are a rare exception, you watched a great deal of television when you were growing up. Consider the effects this may have had on you:

1. Do you think you would be very different now if there had been no television in your home when you were growing up? If so, how do you think you would be different?

2. What kinds of things did you miss out on as a result of TV viewing? How would you have spent your time differently?

3. Will your own (or future) children be better off without TV in the house? How would you determine whether in fact this is so?

ADOLESCENCE

Is adolescence characterized only by physical change?

Adolescence is the period of life roughly between ages 10 and 20, when a person is transformed from a child into an adult. This period involves not just the physical changes of a maturing body, but also many cognitive and social-emotional changes.

Physical Changes

What are the consequences of going through puberty early or late?

A series of dramatic physical milestones ushers in adolescence.

Teenagers are acutely aware of the changes taking place in their bodies. Many become anxious about whether they are the "right" shape or size and obsessively compare themselves with the models and actors they see on television and in magazines. When asked what they most dislike about themselves, physical appearance is mentioned most often (Altabe & Thompson, 1994; Rathus, 2006). These concerns can lead to serious eating disorders, as we saw in Chapter 8, "Motivation and Emotion."

Sexual Development The visible signs of **puberty**—the onset of sexual maturation—occurs in a different sequence for boys and girls. In boys, the initial sign is growth of the testes at around age 11½. Roughly a year later comes enlargement of the penis. Development of pubic hair takes a little longer, followed by development of facial hair. Deepening of the voice is one of the last noticeable changes of male maturation.

In females, around age 11 the breasts begin to develop and pubic hair appears. **Menarche,** the first menstrual period, occurs about a year or so later—at age 12½ for the average American girl (Sarah Anderson, Dallal, & Must, 2003). The onset of menstruation does not necessarily mean that a girl is biologically capable of becoming a mother. Female fertility increases gradually during the first year after menarche. The same is true of male fertility. Boys achieve their first ejaculation at an average age of 13½, often during sleep. First ejaculations contain relatively few sperm (Tanner, 1978). Nevertheless, adolescents are capable of producing babies long before they are mature enough to take care of them.

Psychologists used to believe that the beginnings of sexual attraction and desire in young people coincided with puberty, but recent research has changed this view. Hundreds of case histories put the first stirrings of sexual interest in the fourth and fifth grades. Thus, the onset of the obvious physical changes in puberty may actually be more of an ending to a process than a start.

Early and Late Developers Individuals differ greatly in the age at which they go through the changes of puberty. Among boys, early maturing has psychological advantages. Boys who mature earlier do better in sports and in social activities and receive greater respect from their peers. In contrast, although an early maturing girl may be admired by other girls, she may feel self-conscious and often dissatisfied with her developing body (Ohring, Graber, & Brooks-Gunn 2002). Early maturing girls are also more likely to be exposed to drugs and alcohol in high school than later maturing girls (Lanza & Collins, 2002).

Adolescent Sexual Activity Achieving the capacity to reproduce is probably the single most important development in adolescence. But sexuality is a confusing issue for adolescents in the United States. Fifty years ago, young people were expected to postpone sex until they were responsible, married adults. Since then, major changes have occurred in sexual customs. As shown in **Figure 9–3**, in 2007, 48% of adolescents reported having had sex, and 15% reported having had sex with four or more partners.

Boys and girls tend to view their early sexual behavior in significantly different ways (T. Lewin, 1994). Fewer high school girls (46%) than boys (65%) report feeling good about their sexual experiences. Similarly, more girls (65%) than boys (48%) say that they should have waited until they were older before having sex.

Teenage Pregnancy and Childbearing Despite a one-third decline since the early 1990s, the United States still has the highest teen birth rate in the industrialized world: more than five times the rate in France and eight times the rate in Japan (United Nations Statistics Division, 2006).

puberty The onset of sexual maturation, with accompanying physical development.

menarche First menstrual period.

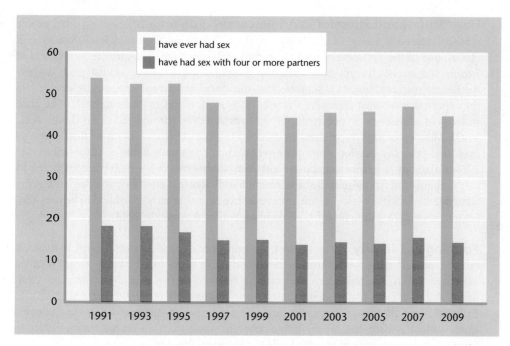

FIGURE 9–3
Sex among high school students.
The percentage of high school students who have had sex has decreased since the early nineties.

Source: Centers for Disease Control, http://www.cdc. gov/healthyyouth/sexualbehaviors/

Whatever the causes, the consequences of teenage pregnancy can be devastating. The entire future of a young unmarried mother is in jeopardy, particularly if she has no parental support or is living in poverty. She is less likely to graduate from high school, less likely to improve her economic status, and less likely to get married and stay married than a girl who postpones childbearing (Coley & Chase-Lansdale, 1998). The babies of teen mothers are more likely to be of low birth weight, which is associated with learning disabilities and later academic problems, childhood illnesses, and neurological problems (Furstenberg, Brooks-Gunn, & Chase-Lansdale, 1989; K. A. Moore, Morrison, & Greene, 1997). In addition, children of teenage mothers are more likely to be neglected and abused than are children of older mothers (Coley & Chase-Lansdale, 1998; George & Lee, 1997).

Cognitive Changes

What change characterizes adolescent thinking?

Just as bodies mature during adolescence, so do patterns of thought. As we saw earlier in the chapter, Piaget (1969) viewed the cognitive advances of adolescence as an increased ability to reason abstractly, called *formal-operational thought* (see "**Summary Table:** Piaget's Stages of Cognitive Development" on page 302). This ability allows them to debate complex issues. Not all adolescents reach the stage of formal operations; and many of those who do, fail to apply formal-operational thinking to the everyday problems they face (Flavell, Miller, & Miller, 2002). Moreover, achieving formal-operational thinking can lead to overconfidence in new mental abilities and a tendency to place too much importance on one's own thoughts. Some adolescents also fail to realize that not everyone thinks the way they do and that other people may hold different views. Piaget called these tendencies the "egocentrism of formal operations" (Piaget, 1967).

Personality and Social Development

What important tasks do adolescents face in their personal and social lives?

Adolescents are eager to establish independence from their parents, but simultaneously fear the responsibilities of adulthood. As a result, this period of development is bound to involve some stress.

identity formation Erickson's term for the development of a stable sense of self necessary to make the transition from dependence on others to dependence on oneself.

identity crisis A period of intense self-examination and decision making; part of the process of identity formation.

cliques Groups of adolescents with similar interests and strong mutual attachment.

How "Stormy and Stressful" Is Adolescence? Early in the 20th century, many people saw adolescence as a time of instability and strong emotions. For example, G. Stanley Hall (1904), one of the first developmental psychologists, portrayed adolescence as a period of "storm and stress," fraught with suffering, passion, and rebellion against adult authority. Recent research, however, suggests that the storm-and-stress view greatly exaggerates the experiences of most teenagers (Arnett, 1999; A. R. Hines & Paulson, 2007). The great majority of adolescents do not describe their lives as rent by turmoil and chaos (Eccles et al., 1993). Most manage to keep stress in check, experience little disruption in their everyday lives, and generally develop more positively than is commonly believed (Bronfenbrenner, 1986; Galambos & Leadbeater, 2002). Although adolescence is inevitably accompanied by some school- and family-related stress, research indicates that effective parenting and secure attachments during adolescence are just as effective as during early childhood in helping adolescents cope during difficult times (Galambos, Barker, & Almeida, 2003).

Forming an Identity To make the transition from dependence on parents to dependence on oneself, the adolescent must develop a stable sense of self. This process is called **identity formation,** a term derived from Erik Erikson's theory, which sees the major challenge of this stage of life as *identity versus role confusion* (Côté, 2006; Erikson, 1968). In Erikson's view, the adolescent must integrate a number of different roles—say, talented math student, athlete, and artist—into a coherent whole that "fits" comfortably. Failure to form this coherent sense of identity leads to confusion about roles.

James Marcia (1980; 2002) believes that finding an identity requires a period of intense self-exploration called an **identity crisis.** He recognizes four possible outcomes of this process. One is *identity achievement.* Adolescents who have reached this status have passed through the identity crisis and succeeded in making personal choices about their beliefs and goals. In contrast are adolescents who have taken the path of *identity foreclosure.* In prematurely settling on an identity chosen for them by others, they have become what others want them to be without ever going through an identity crisis. Other adolescents are in *moratorium* regarding the choice of an identity. They are in the process of actively exploring various role options, but they have not yet committed to any of them. Finally, some teens experience *identity diffusion:* They avoid considering role options in any conscious way. Some who are dissatisfied with this condition but are unable to start a search to "find themselves" resort to escapist activities such as drug or alcohol abuse. Of course, an adolescent's identity status can change over time as the person matures. Moreover, some evidence suggests that the process of identity development varies by social class or ethnic background. For instance, teens from poor families are less likely to experience a period of identity moratorium, in large part because financial constraints make it harder for them to explore many different role options (Forthun, Montgomery, & Bell, 2006; C. Levine, 2003).

Relationships with Peers For most adolescents, peers provide a network of social and emotional support that enables greater independence from adults and facilitates the search for personal identity. But peer relationships change during the adolescent years. Friendship groups in early adolescence tend to be small unisex groups, called **cliques,** of three to nine members. Especially among girls, these unisex friendships deepen and become more mutually self-disclosing as the teens develop the cognitive abilities to better understand themselves and one another (Holmbeck, 1994). Then, in mid-adolescence, unisex cliques usually give way to mixed-sex groups. These, in turn, are normally replaced by groups consisting of couples. At first, adolescents tend to have short-term heterosexual relationships within the group that fulfill short-term needs without exacting the commitment of "going steady" (Sorensen, 1973). Such relationships do not demand love and can dissolve overnight. But between the ages of 16 and 19, most adolescents settle into more stable dating patterns.

In the recent past, new communication technologies have had a profound effect on adolescent peer relationships. Cell phone texting, in particular, has become a true social networking tool that allows teenagers to connect with their friends instantly. Research shows that this connectivity provides a greater sense of connectedness and well-being in part because teenagers can talk about very personal issues that are otherwise difficult to discuss. In turn this heightened self-disclosure leads to closer and higher quality friendships than would otherwise be the case (Valkenberg & Peter, 2009).

Relationships with Parents While they are still searching for their own identity and learning to think through the long-term consequences of their actions, adolescents require guidance and structure from their parents. In their struggle for independence, adolescents question everything and test every rule. Unlike young children who believe that their parents know everything and are all-powerful and good, adolescents are very aware of their parents' shortcomings. It takes years for adolescents to see their mothers and fathers as real people with their own needs and strengths as well as weaknesses (Woodhouse, Dykas, & Cassidy, 2009).

The low point of parent–child relationships generally occurs in early adolescence, when the physical changes of puberty are occurring. Moreover, some significant neurobiological changes are also taking place. Early in adolescence the limbic regions of the brain are well developed and highly active. You may recall from Chapter 2 that the limbic system is central to the experience of emotions. As adolescence progresses, the prefrontal cortex (primarily involved in reasoning and self-control) continues to mature. In turn, this ushers in "a shift from behavior that is driven by affective impulses to more regulated behavior that is guided by consideration of future personal and social consequences" (Whittle et al., 2008, p. 3652). Warm and caring relationships with adults outside the home, such as those at school or at a supervised community center, are especially valuable to adolescents during this transition period.

"Is everything all right, Jeffrey? You never call me 'dude' anymore."

Some Problems of Adolescence

What are some major problems faced by adolescents in our society?

Declines in Self-Esteem We saw earlier that adolescents are especially likely to be dissatisfied with their appearance. Adolescents who are least satisfied with their physical appearance tend also to have low self-esteem (Kuseske, 2008). Since adolescent girls are especially likely to be dissatisfied with their appearance, and because perceived attractiveness and self-esteem are more closely related for females than for males, it is no surprise that adolescent girls have significantly lower self-esteem than do adolescent boys. For boys, there is little or no decline in self-esteem during adolescence (Kling, Hyde, Showers, & Buswell, 1999).

Depression and Suicide The rate of suicide among adolescents has increased more than 600% since 1950, though there are signs that since the mid-1990s it has begun to decrease, at least among males. Suicide is the third leading cause of death among adolescents, after accidents and homicides (Goldston et al., 2008; National Mental Health Association, 2006). Although successful suicide is more common in males than in females, twice as many females *attempt* suicide (National Adolescent Health Information Center, 2004).

Youth Violence In April 1999, two teenaged boys opened fire on their classmates at Columbine High School in Littleton, Colorado. Armed with sawed-off shotguns, a semiautomatic rifle, and a semiautomatic pistol, they killed 13 people and wounded 23 others before killing themselves.

Why did this happen? What causes children as young as 11 to kill other people and, equally often, to kill themselves? Although it is tempting to look for simple answers to these questions, the causes of youth violence are complex (Heckel & Shumaker, 2001).

THINKING CRITICALLY ABOUT . . .

Kids Who Kill

1. After reading the review of the preceding research on youth violence, have your opinions about what causes school-aged children to kill their classmates been changed? In what way?

2. What steps would you recommend to reduce the incidence of tragedies like the one that occurred at Columbine High School? Be specific.

3. In almost all instances, the schoolchildren who commit these violent crimes are middle-class White children living in rural or suburban communities. Why do you think this is the case? What evidence would you accept as supporting your hypotheses?

Biology definitely plays a role, although its influence is certainly much more complex than simply identifying a "murderer gene." For example, researchers have identified a specific gene found in people who display a lack of compassion and an inability to control emotional impulses early in life. As adolescents and adults, their behavior is marked by higher rates of delinquency, violence, and aggression. Research has also shown that the effects of this gene on behavior may either be amplified or reduced depending on the environment in which the child is raised (Buckholtz & Meyer-Lindenberg, 2008). Other research has found that early trauma may cause a brain structure to become hyperactive, causing obsession with a single thought (such as violence) at the same time the prefrontal cortex becomes less able to control impulsive behavior (Amen, Stubblefield, Carmichael, & Thisted, 1996; Schmahl, Vermetten, Elzinga, & Bremmer, 2004).

Environment also plays a role. Most psychologists believe that the "gun culture" in which most of the youthful murderers were raised is an important factor, along with the relatively easy availability of guns (Cooke, 2004; Duke, Resnick, & Borowsky, 2005).

Severe neglect or rejection contributes as well. All of the young killers have indicated that they felt outcast and abandoned by those who should have loved them. In turn, this condition led to feelings of powerlessness and injustice (M. R. Leary, Kowalski, Smith, & Phillips, 2003). In other cases, the youths lacked adult supervision and support, often having no real attachment to even one loving and reliable adult (Garbarino, 1999).

What are the warning signs that might alert family and friends to potential violence? Lack of social connection, masking emotions, withdrawal (being habitually secretive and antisocial), silence, rage, increased lying, trouble with friends, hypervigilance, and cruelty toward other children and animals—these factors should all be a cause for concern. This is especially true if they are exhibited by a boy who comes from a family with a history of criminal violence, who has been abused or bullied, who belongs to a gang, who abuses drugs or alcohol, who has previously been arrested, or who has experienced problems at school (Leschied & Cummings, 2002; Newsome & Kelly, 2006).

✓●─[**Study** and **Review** on **MyPsychLab**

CHECK YOUR UNDERSTANDING

1. In early adolescence, a series of physical changes leads to sexual maturation, the onset of which is called _____.

2. Erikson's view of the major challenge in adolescence is one of _____ versus _____.

3. List the four identity statuses described by James Marcia.

4. True (T) or false (F): The most difficult time in the relationship between a teenager and parents is usually in late adolescence, when the young person is anxious to leave the family "nest."

Answers: 1. puberty. 2. identity; role confusion. 3. identity achievement, identity foreclosure, identity moratorium, identity diffusion. 4. (F).

APPLY YOUR UNDERSTANDING

1. Beth is 14 years old. In the last year or two, she has begun to enjoy debating complex issues such as human rights, poverty, and justice. Which of the following is most likely to be true?

   a. Beth has become capable of formal-operational thought.

   b. Beth is experiencing identity foreclosure.

   c. Beth is experiencing identity diffusion.

   d. Beth's thinking demonstrates adolescent egocentrism.

2. Andrew is 18. He has accepted an identity that was provided to him by his parents and peers. In other words, he has chosen to become what others want him to be. He best fits the description of a(n)

   a. identity achiever.

   b. forecloser.

   c. person in moratorium.

   d. identity diffuser.

Answers: 1.a. 2.b.

ADULTHOOD

Does personality change during adulthood?

The course of adult development varies because it is a result of personal decisions, circumstances, and even luck. Although developmental milestones do not occur at particular ages, certain experiences and changes eventually occur in nearly every adult's life.

Love, Partnerships, and Parenting

What factors are important in forming satisfying relationships in adulthood?

Nearly all adults form a long-term, loving partnership with another adult at some point in their lives. Forming such a partnership is especially common in young adulthood. According to Erik Erikson, the major challenge of young adulthood is *intimacy versus isolation*. Failure to form an intimate partnership with someone else can cause a young adult to feel painfully lonely and incomplete.

Forming Partnerships   Almost 90% of Americans eventually get married (U.S. Bureau of the Census, 2002a), but that percentage is dropping as fewer people choose to marry. In 1960, 72% of those Americans over 18 were married; in 2008 that number had dropped to 52% (Pew Research Center, 2010). Moreover, those who do marry are waiting longer to do so. For example, in 1970, the median age of an American woman marrying for the first time was 20.8 years; this increased to 25.3 years by 2005. Similarly, for American men, the median age for first marriages was 23.2 years in 1970, increasing to 27.1 years by 2005 (U.S. Bureau of the Census, 2006).

Although heterosexual marriage is still the statistical norm in the United States, other types of partnerships exist. Cohabiting relationships are one example. In 2008, more than 5% of Americans over 18 were cohabiting compared to 3% in 1990. In 2008, more than half of Americans 30 to 49 years old say they have lived with an unmarried partner (Pew Research Center, 2010). Some of those in cohabiting relationships are gays and lesbians who seek the same loving, committed, and meaningful partnerships as their heterosexual counterparts (Kurdek, 2005). Moreover, successful homosexual relationships share the same characteristics as successful heterosexual ones: high levels of mutual trust, respect, and appreciation; sexual compatibility; shared decision making; good communication; and good conflict-resolution skills (Holmberg & Blair, 2009; Kurdek, 2005; Laird, 2003). (See "Applying Psychology: Resolving Conflicts in Intimate Relationships.")

Parenthood   For most parents, loving and being loved by their children is an unparalleled source of fulfillment. However, the birth of the first child is also a major turning point in a couple's relationship, one that requires many adjustments. Since young children demand a lot of time and energy, parents may be left with little time or energy for each other.

Parenthood may also heighten conflicts between pursuit of careers and responsibilities at home. This outcome is especially likely among women with an active career outside the home. They may be torn between feelings of loss and resentment at the prospect of leaving their job, and anxiety or guilt over the idea of continuing to work. It is no wonder that women feel the need for their partner's cooperation more strongly during this period of life than men do (Kendall-Tackett, 2001). Contemporary fathers spend more time with their children than their fathers did, but mothers still bear the greater responsibility for both child rearing and housework.

Although homosexual couples as a group believe more strongly in equally dividing household duties than heterosexual couples do, homosexuals tend to make an exception when it comes to child rearing. Child-care responsibilities tend to fall more heavily on one member of a homosexual couple, whereas the other spends more time in paid employment (C. J. Patterson, 1995; Peplau & Beals, 2004). Notably, more than a decade of research has shown that children reared by

< LEARNING OBJECTIVES **>**

- Explain Erikson's concept of *intimacy versus isolation* in young adulthood, the kinds of partnerships that adults form, parenthood, and the difficulties of ending intimate relationships.
- Describe gender differences in the world of work and the demands of dual-career families.
- Describe the changes and challenges of midlife including Erikson's notion of *generativity versus stagnation* and the concept of *midlife crisis* as opposed to *midlife transition*.

Like heterosexuals in successful relationships, gays in loving partnerships share decision making, trust, respect, and appreciation.

FIGURE 9–4
Marital satisfaction.

This graph shows when married people are most and least content with their marriage, on a scale of 1 (very unhappy) to 7 (very happy).

Source: Data from American Sociological Association

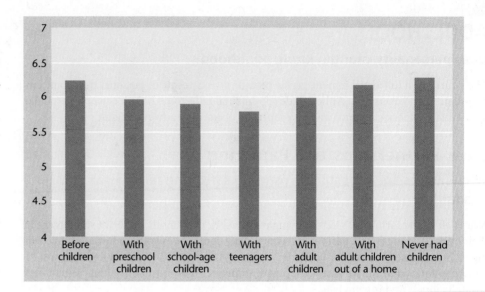

homosexual couples do not show any significant differences in adjustment or development compared to children reared by traditional heterosexual couples (C. J. Patterson, 2009).

Given the demands of parenthood, it isn't surprising that marital satisfaction tends to decline after the arrival of the first child (Ruble, Fleming, Hackel, & Stangor, 1988). (See **Figure 9–4**.) But once children leave home, many parents experience renewed satisfaction in their relationship as a couple. Rather than lamenting over their "empty nests," many couples experience an increase in positive mood and well-being (Gorchoff, John, & Helson, 2008; Stone, Schwartz, Broderick, & Deaton, 2010). For the first time in years, the couple can be alone together and enjoy one another's company.

Ending a Relationship   Intimate relationships frequently end. Although this is the case for all types of couples—married and unmarried, heterosexual and homosexual—most of the research on ending relationships has focused on married, heterosexual couples. The U.S. divorce rate has risen substantially since the 1960s, as it has in many other developed nations (T. Lewin, 1995). Although the divorce rate appears to have stabilized, it has settled at a very high level. Almost half of American marriages eventually end in divorce (U.S. Bureau of the Census, 2007).

Rarely is the decision to separate a mutual one. Most often, one partner takes the initiative in ending the relationship after a long period of slowly increasing unhappiness. Making the decision does not necessarily bring relief. In the short term, it often brings turmoil, animosity, and apprehension. Most children whose parents divorce do not have long-term problems. However, in some cases divorce can have more serious effects on children. In general, younger children are at greater risk, but adolescents whose parents divorce are at greater risk academically and in their social relationships. Children whose parents continue to be in conflict are also at greater risk (Lansford, 2009). Children adapt more successfully to divorce when they have good support systems, when the divorcing parents maintain a good relationship, and when sufficient financial resources are made available to them (Eldar-Avidan, Haj-Yahia, & Greenbaum, 2008; Sandler, Miles, Cookston, & Braver, 2008). The effects of divorce also vary with the children themselves: Those who have easygoing temperaments and who were generally well behaved before the divorce usually have an easier time adjusting (Lansford, 2009; Storksen, Roysamb, & Holmen, 2006). ◉

◉—**Watch** the **Video** Pam: Divorced Mother of 9-year-old, Part 1 on **MyPsychLab**

The World of Work

What are the satisfactions and stresses of adult work?

For many young people, the period from the late teens through the early twenties is crucial because it sets the stage for much of adult life. The educational achievements and training obtained during these transitional years often establish the foundation that will shape the income and occupational status for the remainder of adult life.

APPLYING PSYCHOLOGY

Resolving Conflicts in Intimate Relationships

People have different desires, approaches, priorities, and viewpoints. For those reasons, conflict is inevitable in every intimate relationship. But conflict can be resolved constructively. Psychologists suggest a number of steps that lead to constructive conflict resolution:

1. *Carefully choose the time and place for an argument.* Try not to begin a major disagreement while your partner is in the middle of an important task or is ready to fall asleep after a long, tiring day.

2. *Be a good listener.* Listen calmly and carefully without interrupting. Avoid going on the defensive and try to understand your partner's point of view. Don't let your body give nonverbal cues (shrugging your shoulders, rolling your eyes) that contradict good listening.

3. *Give feedback regarding your understanding of the other person's grievance.* Avoid misunderstandings by restating what your partner has told you in your own words. Clarify by asking questions.

4. *Be candid. Level with your partner about your feelings.* If you are angry, don't make your partner guess your feelings by being silent or showing anger indirectly. But remember that being candid does not mean being hurtful. Avoid using counterproductive tactics such as sarcasm or insults.

5. *Use "I" rather than "you" statements.* For instance, if you're angry with your partner for being late, say, "I've been really worried for the last hour," rather than "You're a whole hour late!" "You" statements sound like accusations and tend to put people on the defensive. "I" statements sound more like efforts to communicate feelings in nonjudgmental ways.

6. *Focus on behavior, not on the person.* For example, focus on your partner's lateness as a problem. Don't accuse your partner of being thoughtless and self-centered.

7. *Don't overstate the frequency of a problem or overgeneralize about it.* Don't tell your partner that he or she is "always late."

8. *Focus on a limited number of specific issues.* Don't overwhelm your partner with a long list of past and present grievances. Stick to current concerns of high priority.

9. *Don't find scapegoats for every grievance against you.* Take responsibility for your actions and encourage your partner to do the same.

10. *Suggest specific, relevant changes to solve a problem.* Both participants in the conflict should propose at least one reasonable solution. Consider the other person's viewpoint as well as your own.

11. *Be open to compromise.* To settle a dispute successfully, both people must be willing to give in a little. Don't back your partner into a corner by making an ultimatum. Partners need to be willing to change themselves to some extent in response to each other's feelings.

12. *Don't think in terms of winner and loser.* A competitive approach to conflict resolution doesn't work in intimate relationships. Strive for solutions that are satisfactory to both parties. Think of each other as allies attacking a mutual problem. In this way, your relationship will become stronger.

Three or four generations ago, choosing a career was not an issue for most young adults. Men followed in their fathers' footsteps or took whatever apprenticeships were available in their communities. Most women were occupied in child care and housework or they pursued such "female" careers as secretarial work, nursing, and teaching. Modern career choices are far more numerous for both men and women. At the end of 2010, for example, women made up almost 47% of the labor force in the United States (U.S. Department of Labor, 2010a). Of employed women, 73% worked full-time; the rest worked part-time (U.S. Department of Labor, 2010b). The largest percentage of employed women (nearly 41%) worked in management, professional, and related occupations, while 32% worked in sales and office occupations (U.S. Department of Labor, 2010c).

Dual-Career Families The percentage of women in the paid labor force has increased dramatically from 42% in 1973 to 54% in 2010 (U.S. Department of Labor, 2010a). The change is even greater for married women (Engemann & Owyang, 2006). This increasing role of women as economic providers is a worldwide trend (Elloy & Mackie, 2002).

As we noted earlier, balancing the demands of career and family is a problem in many families, especially for women. Even when the wife has a full-time job outside the home, she is likely to end up doing the majority of the housework and child care. She is also likely to be aware of this imbalance and to resent it. The "double shift"—one at paid work

Erik Erikson suggested that a major goal in middle adulthood is to achieve a sense of generativity, or doing something to help future generations.

outside the home and another at unpaid household labor—is the common experience of millions of women throughout the world. True equality—the hopeful goal of the dual-career movement—has yet to be achieved (Sabattini & Crosby, 2009). However, despite the pressures associated with the double shift, most women report increases in self-esteem and well-being when they have a paid job (Perrig-Chiello, Hutchison, & Hoepflinger, 2008).

Cognitive Changes

In what ways do adults think differently than adolescents?

Only recently have researchers begun to explore the ways in which adult and adolescent thinking differ. Nonetheless, a few conclusions have begun to emerge. Although adolescents are able to test alternatives and to arrive at what they see as the "correct" solution to a problem, adults gradually come to realize that there isn't a single correct solution to every problem—there may, in fact, be no correct solution, or there may be several. Adults are also more practical: They know that a solution to a problem must be realistic as well as reasonable. No doubt these changes in adult thinking derive from greater experience of the world. Dealing with the kinds of complex problems that arise in adult life requires moving away from the literal, formal, and somewhat rigid thinking of adolescence and young adulthood (G. Goldstein, 2004).

Most measurable cognitive changes during adulthood do not simply involve a rise or fall in general ability. Instead, for most people, such cognitive skills as vocabulary and verbal memory increase steadily through the sixth decade of life. In contrast, perceptual speed (the ability to make quick and accurate visual discriminations) and the ability to perform mathematical computations show the largest decrease with age, with the former beginning to decline as early as age 25, and the latter starting to decline around age 40 (Schaie & Willis, 2001; Schaie & Zanjani, 2006).

For optimal cognitive development, mental exercise is a necessity. Although some decline in cognitive skills is inevitable as people age, the decline can be minimized if people stay mentally active (Stine-Morrow, Parisi, Morrow, & Park, 2008; R. S. Wilson et al., 2003).

Midlife

What are the changes and challenges of midlife?

Psychological health generally improves in adulthood. And adolescents with better psychological health tend to improve even further in adulthood (C. J. Jones & Meredith, 2000; Shiner, Masten, & Roberts, 2003). Both men and women tend to show increased emotional stability, warmth, self-confidence, and self-control with age (B. W. Roberts & Mroezek, 2008). One meta-analysis of several studies found that on average, conscientiousness, emotional stability, agreeableness, and openness to new experience all increased in middle adulthood (B. W. Roberts, Walton, & Viechtbauer, 2006). Such findings suggest that the majority of people are successfully meeting what Erik Erikson saw as the major challenge of middle adulthood: *generativity versus stagnation.* Generativity refers to the ability to continue being productive and creative, especially in ways that guide and encourage future generations. For those who fail to achieve this state, life becomes a meaningless routine, and the person feels stagnant and bored.

Feelings of boredom and stagnation in middle adulthood may be part of what is called a **midlife crisis.** The person in midlife crisis feels painfully unfulfilled and ready for a radical, abrupt shift in career, personal relationships, or lifestyle. Research shows, however, that the midlife crisis is not typical; most people do not make sudden dramatic changes in their lives in mid-adulthood (M. E. Lachman, 2004; Strenger, 2009). In fact, one large-scale study found that the majority of middle-aged adults reported lower levels of anxiety and worry than young adults, and generally felt positively about their lives. Daniel Levinson, who studied personality development in men and women throughout adulthood (Levinson, 1978, 1986, 1987), preferred the term **midlife transition** for the period when people tend to take stock of their lives. Many of the men and women in his studies, confronted with the first signs of aging, began to think about the finite nature of life. They realized that they may never accomplish all they had hoped to do, and they questioned the value of some of the things they had accomplished so far. As a result, some gradually reset their life priorities, establishing new goals based on their new insights.

midlife crisis A time when adults discover they no longer feel fulfilled in their jobs or personal lives and attempt to make a decisive shift in career or lifestyle.

midlife transition According to Levinson, a process whereby adults assess the past and formulate new goals for the future.

ENDURING ISSUES

Stability–Change   The "Change of Life"

A decline in reproductive function occurs during middle age in both men and women. In women, the amount of estrogen produced by the ovaries drops sharply at around age 45, although the exact age varies considerably. Breasts, genital tissues, and the uterus begin to shrink; and menstrual periods become irregular and then cease altogether at around age 50. The cessation of menstruation is called **menopause.** The hormonal changes that accompany menopause often cause certain physical symptoms; the most noticeable are "hot flashes." Some women also may experience serious thinning of the bones, making them more vulnerable to fractures.

Experts disagree about whether a "male menopause" exists. Men never experience as severe a drop in testosterone as women do with estrogen. Instead, studies have found a more gradual decline—perhaps 30% to 40%—in testosterone in men between the ages of 48 and 70 (J. E. Brody, 2004; Crooks & Bauer, 2002). Recent evidence also confirms that with increasing age, male fertility slowly decreases as well (Gooren, 2008). ■

menopause The time in a woman's life when menstruation ceases.

✓●—Study and Review on MyPsychLab

CHECK YOUR UNDERSTANDING

1. According to Erik Erikson, the major challenge of young adulthood is _____ versus _____, whereas the major challenge of middle adulthood is _____ versus _____.

2. The cessation of menstruation in middle-age women is called _____.

Answers: 1. intimacy, isolation; generativity, stagnation. 2. menopause.

APPLY YOUR UNDERSTANDING

1. If you were to poll a group of older couples, you would expect to find that most of them say that their marital satisfaction
   a. has steadily decreased over the years.
   b. has not changed over the years.
   c. declined during the child-rearing years, but has increased since then.
   d. has steadily increased over the years.

2. Imagine that you survey a large group of women who have full-time jobs outside the home as well as families (the so-called "double shift"). Compared with women who do not have paying jobs outside the home, what would you expect to find about this group of dual-career women?
   a. They are more likely to be anxious and depressed.
   b. They are more likely to have higher self-esteem.
   c. They are more likely to say they wouldn't work if they didn't need the money.
   d. Both (a) and (c) are correct.

Answers: 1. c. 2. b.

LATE ADULTHOOD

What factors are related to life expectancy?

During the 20th century, the percentage of Americans over 65 more than tripled; and those over 85 now represent the fastest-growing segment of the population (National Institute on Aging, 2006). In the 2010 census, more than 40 million Americans were over age 65; by the year 2050, there may be nearly 90 million in this age group (U.S. Bureau of the Census, 2010). (See **Figure 9–5**.) This dramatic rise stems from the aging of the large baby-boom generation, coupled with increases in life expectancy due primarily to better health care and nutrition.

However, a sizable gender gap exists in life expectancy. The average American woman today enjoys a life span that is 5.2 years longer than that of the average American man,

LEARNING OBJECTIVES

- Describe the factors that affect life expectancy, the physical changes that occur in late adulthood, and the possible reasons for those physical changes. Include in your description an answer to the question "What kind of lifestyle and sex life can be expected after age 65?"
- Describe Kübler-Ross's stages of dying and the criticisms of her model. Discuss the burden of widowhood and whether it falls more heavily on men or women.

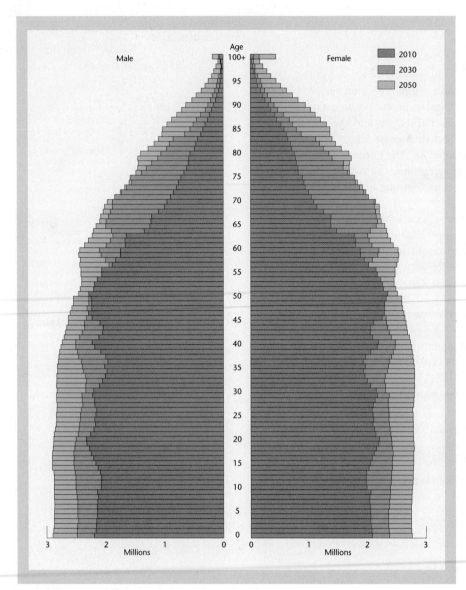

FIGURE 9–5

Population age structure, 2010–2050.

The U.S. population will continue to age over the next several decades, as the huge baby-boom generation matures.

Source: U. S. Census Bureau (2010).

Although physical changes are inevitable during late adulthood, how people respond to these changes has a major effect on their quality of life.

but that difference has been shrinking since 1980 as the life expectancy of males increases more rapidly than that of females (Miniño, Heron, & Smith, 2006). The reasons for this gender gap are still unclear, but likely factors include differences in hormones, exposure to stress, health-related behaviors (Möller-Leimkühler, 2003), and genetic makeup.

There is also a gap in life expectancy between Whites and African Americans in the United States, although that gap also is closing. The average White American child born today is likely to live 5 years longer than the average African American child (Miniño, Heron, & Smith, 2006). This difference seems to stem largely from socio-economic disparities.

Because older adults are becoming an increasingly visible part of American society, it is important to understand their development. Unfortunately, our views of older adults are often heavily colored by myths. For example, many people believe that most older adults are lonely, poor, and troubled by ill health. The false belief that "senility" is inevitable in old age is another damaging myth, as is the belief that most older adults are helpless and dependent on their families for care and financial support. Research contradicts these stereotypes. Increasingly, people age 65 and over are healthy, productive, and able (D. M. Cutler, 2001; Manton & Gu, 2001).

Physical Changes

How does the body change with age?

Most people in midlife have few serious illnesses. However, in middle adulthood and continuing through late adulthood, physical appearance changes, as does the functioning of every organ in the body. The hair thins and turns white or gray. Bones become more fragile. Circulation slows, blood pressure rises, and because the lungs hold less oxygen, the older adult has less energy. Vision, hearing, and the sense of smell all become less acute (Cavanaugh & Blanchard-Fields, 2005).

We do not yet know why physical aging happens (Pankow & Solotoroff, 2007). Whatever the ultimate explanation for physical decline, many factors affect adults' physical well-being. Among these are things they can control, such as diet, exercise, and health care. Attitudes and interests also matter. People who have a continuing sense of usefulness, who maintain old ties, develop new interests, and feel in control of their lives have the lowest rates of disease and the highest survival rates (R. N. Butler, Lewis, & Sunderland, 1998.) Self-perceptions also matter: Adults who enter late adulthood with negative beliefs about aging have more health problems and die much sooner than those who begin late adulthood with positive expectations (Levy, 2009; Levy, Zonderman, Slade, & Ferrucci, 2009).

In fact, despite the normal physical decline that occurs in late adulthood, a survey of 355,334 Americans age 18 to 85 showed that psychological well-being increased

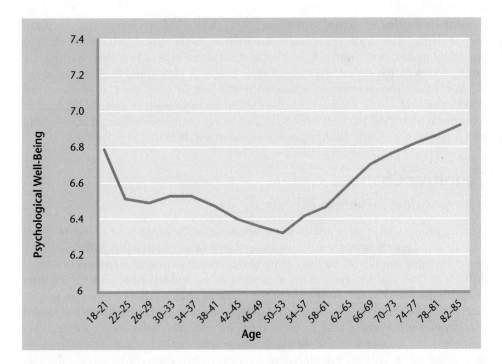

FIGURE 9–6
Psychological well-being across the life-span.
Psychological well-being declines until the early 50s, at which point it sharply increases.

Source: Adapted from Stone, A. A., Schwartz, J. E., Broderick, J. E., & Deaton, A. (2010). A snapshot of the age distribution of psychological well-being in the United States. *PNAS Proceedings of the National Academy of Sciences of the United States of America, 107,* 9985–9990.

dramatically beginning in the early 50s (Stone, Schwartz, Broderick, & Deaton, 2010). (See **Figure 9–6.**) Personal relationships also improve with age (Fingerman & Charles, 2010).

Simulate the **Experiment** Aging and Changes in Physical Appearance on **MyPsychLab**

Social Development

What kind of lifestyle and sex life can be expected after age 65?

Far from being weak and dependent, most men and women over age 65 live apart from their children and outside nursing homes. The ability to live independently and take enjoyment from everyday situations is an important predictor of satisfaction among the elderly (Rioux, 2005). Moreover, those who remain physically and mentally active, travel, exercise, and attend meetings are more likely to report being happier and more satisfied with their lives than those who stay at home (L. K. George, 2001).

Still, gradual social changes do take place in late adulthood. In general, older people interact with fewer people and perform fewer social roles. Behavior becomes less influenced by social rules and expectations. Most older people step back and assess life, realize there is a limit to their capacity for social involvement, and learn to live comfortably with those restrictions. This process does not necessarily entail a psychological "disengagement" from the social world, as some researchers have contended. Instead, older people may simply make sensible choices that suit their more limited time frames and physical capabilities (Carstensen, 1995).

Retirement In late adulthood, most people retire from paid employment. Individual reactions to this major change vary widely, partly because society has no clear idea of what retirees are supposed to do (Schlossberg, 2004). Men generally see retirement as a time to slow down and do less, whereas women often view it as a time to learn new things and explore new possibilities (Helgesen, 1998). This difference can cause obvious problems for retired couples.

Of course, the nature and quality of retired life depend in part on financial status. If retirement means a major decline in a person's standard of living, that person will be less eager to retire and will lead a more limited life after retirement. Another factor in people's attitudes toward retirement is their feelings about work. People who are fulfilled by their jobs are usually less interested in retiring than people whose jobs are unrewarding (Atchley, 1982). Similarly, people who have very ambitious, hard-driving personalities tend to want to stay at work longer than those who are more relaxed.

Sexual Behavior A common misconception is that elderly people have outlived their sexuality. This myth reflects our stereotypes. To the extent that we see them as physically unattractive and frail, we find it difficult to believe that they are sexually active. Although the sexual response of older people is slower and they are less sexually active than younger people, the majority can and do enjoy sex and have orgasms (Herbenick et al., 2010; Lindau et al., 2007). Similar to younger people, a high level of self-esteem and good physical health are important predictors of sexual activity and satisfaction in the elderly (Kontula & Haavio-Mannila, 2009).

Cognitive Changes

Is memory loss inevitable in old age?

Healthy people who remain intellectually active maintain a high level of mental functioning in old age (Schaie, 1984; Shimamura, Berry, Mangels, Rusting, & Jurica, 1995). Since the aging mind works a little more slowly, certain types of memories are more difficult to store and retrieve and the ability to process and attend to information does gradually decline. For the most part, however, these changes do not interfere significantly with the ability to enjoy an active, independent life. In fact, research has shown that because older adults tend to focus more on positive than negative events, they are better able to cope with the inevitable ups and downs of life than are adolescents or younger adults (Kisley, Wood, & Burrows, 2007). Moreover, older adults who stay both mentally and physically active generally experience significantly less cognitive decline than those who are inactive (Erickson et al., 2011; Forstmeier & Maercker, 2008; Hertzog, Kramer, Wilson, & Lindenberger, 2009; Novotney, 2010). Training and practice on cognitive tasks can also help reduce the decline in cognitive performance in later adulthood (Guenther, Schaefer, Holzner, & Kemmler, 2003; S.-C. Li et al., 2008), though the benefits of training are often limited only to the skills that are practiced (Kramer & Willis, 2002; Schooler, 2007).

Alzheimer's disease A neurological disorder, most commonly found in late adulthood, characterized by progressive losses in memory and cognition and by changes in personality.

Alzheimer's Disease For people suffering from **Alzheimer's disease,** the picture is quite different. The disease causes brain changes resulting in the progressive loss of the ability to communicate and reason.

According to current estimates, about 10% of adults over age 65 and nearly half of adults over age 85 suffer from Alzheimer's disease (Alzheimer's Association, 2006). Alzheimer's usually begins with minor memory losses, such as difficulty in recalling words and names or in remembering where something was placed (Storandt, 2008). As it progresses—a process that may take anywhere from 2 to 20 years—personality changes are also likely (Duchek, Balota, Storandt, & Larsen, 2007). First, people may become emotionally withdrawn or flat. Later, they may suffer from delusions, such as thinking that relatives are stealing from them. These people become confused and may not know where they are or what time of day it is. Eventually, they lose the ability to speak, to care for themselves, and to recognize family members. Eventually, Alzheimer's is fatal (Wolfson et al., 2001). There is no known cure, but breakthroughs in research are occurring so fast that a drug to slow the progress of the disorder or even a vaccine to prevent it may be developed in the near future (Mayo Foundation for Medical Education and Research, 2005a).

Facing the End of Life

How well do most elderly people cope with the end of life?

Fear of death is seldom a central concern for people in later adulthood (DeWall & Baumeister, 2007). In fact, such fear seems to be a greater problem in young adulthood or in middle age, when the first awareness of mortality coincides with a greater interest in living (Tomer, 2000).

Because people with Alzheimer's disease suffer memory loss, signs can remind them to perform ordinary activities.

But elderly people do have some major fears associated with dying. They fear the pain, indignity, and depersonalization that they might experience during a terminal illness, as well as the possibility of dying alone. They also worry about burdening their relatives with the expenses of their hospitalization or nursing care. Sometimes, too, relatives are not able to provide much support for the elderly as they decline, either because they live too far away or because they may be unable to cope either with the pain of watching a loved one die or with their own fears of mortality (Tacker, 2007). 👁

Watch the **Video** Aging and Culture on **MyPsychLab**

Stages of Dying In her classic work, the late psychiatrist Elisabeth Kübler-Ross (1926–2004) interviewed more than 200 dying people of all ages to try to understand death's psychological aspects. She described a sequence of five stages people pass through as they react to their own impending death (Kübler-Ross, 1969):

1. *Denial*–The person denies the diagnosis, refuses to believe that death is approaching, insists that an error has been made, and seeks other, more acceptable opinions or alternatives.
2. *Anger*–The person now accepts the reality of the situation but expresses envy and resentment toward those who will live to fulfill a plan or dream, asking "Why me?" Anger may be directed at the doctor or directed randomly. The patience and understanding of other people are particularly important at this stage.
3. *Bargaining*–The person desperately tries to buy time, negotiating with doctors, family members, clergy, and God in a healthy attempt to cope with the realization of death.
4. *Depression*–As bargaining fails and time is running out, the person may succumb to depression, lamenting failures and mistakes that can no longer be corrected.
5. *Acceptance*–Tired and weak, the person at last enters a state of "quiet expectation," submitting to fate.

According to Kübler-Ross, Americans have a greater problem coping with death than people in some other cultures. She observed that some cultures are *death affirming*. For example, the Trukese of Micronesia start preparing for death at age 40. One of the most important national holidays in Mexico is El Día de los Muertos (Day of the Dead) which is a celebration of remembrance that often involves parties, dancing, and even picnics. The living can pay tribute to relatives who have died, and the deceased relatives can once again spend time with the living (Gutiérrez, 2009, 2010). In contrast, American culture is *death denying*. We dye our hair and spend fortunes on plastic surgery to hide our wrinkles. We also shelter children from knowledge of death and dying. By trying to protect them from these unpleasant realities, however, we may actually make them more fearful of death.

Some observers have found fault with Kübler-Ross's model of dying (K. Wright, 2003). Most of the criticisms have focused on her methodology. She studied only a relatively small sample of people and provided little information about how they were selected and how often they were interviewed. Also, all her patients were suffering from cancer. Does her model apply as well to people dying from other causes? Finally, some critics question the universality of her model. Death itself is universal, but reactions to dying may differ greatly from one culture to another.

Despite these questions, there is nearly universal agreement that Kübler-Ross deserves credit for pioneering the study of the transitions that people undergo during the dying process. She was the first to investigate an area long considered taboo; and her research has made dying a more "understandable" experience.

Widowhood The death of one's spouse may be the most severe challenge of late adulthood. People often respond to such a loss with initial disbelief, followed by numbness. Only later is the full impact of the loss felt, which can be severe. The incidence of depression rises significantly following the death of a spouse (Bonanno, Wortman, & Nesse, 2004; Nakao, Kashiwagi, & Yano, 2005). One long-term study revealed that older widows and widowers had a higher incidence of dying within 6 months after the death of their spouse than other married persons of their age. Moreover, this death rate was much higher for widowers than for widows and for people between the age of 55 and 70 than for those over age 70. After this initial 6-month period however, the mortality rate of both the men and the women fell gradually to a more normal level (Impens, 2005).

For somewhat different reasons, then, the burden of widowhood is heavy for both men and women (Feinson, 1986; Wilcox et al., 2003). But because women have a longer life expectancy, there are many more widows than widowers. Thus, men have a better chance of remarrying. More than half the women over 65 are widowed, of whom half will live another 15 years without remarrying.

✓●─**Study** and **Review** on **MyPsychLab**

CHECK YOUR UNDERSTANDING

1. Indicate whether the following statements are true (T) or false (F):
   a. ___ The average man lives as long as the average woman.
   b. ___ The physical changes of aging inevitably become incapacitating.
   c. ___ Most elderly people are dependent on their adult children.
   d. ___ Healthy people who remain intellectually involved maintain a high level of mental functioning in old age.
2. List the five stages of dying described by Elisabeth Kübler-Ross.

Answers: 1. a. (F); b. (F); c. (F); d. (T). 2. Denial, anger, bargaining, depression, acceptance.

APPLY YOUR UNDERSTANDING

1. Elisabeth Kübler-Ross notes that Americans "are reluctant to reveal our age; we spend fortunes to hide our wrinkles; we prefer to send our old people to nursing homes." She suggests that this is because American culture is
   a. death affirming.
   b. death denying.
   c. moratorial.
   d. foreclosed.

2. You are having a discussion about cognitive changes in late adulthood, during which people make the claims that follow. Based on what you have learned in this chapter, you agree with all of them EXCEPT
   a. "If you are healthy and remain intellectually active, you are likely to maintain a high level of mental functioning in old age."
   b. "As you get older, it will become more difficult to process and attend to information."
   c. "If you practice mental tasks, you can help to minimize the decline in those skills."
   d. "As you get older, you will become increasingly confused, gradually lose the ability to speak, and eventually be unable to recognize friends and family."

Answers: 1. b. 2. d.

KEY TERMS

developmental psychology, p. 293

Methods in Developmental Psychology
cross-sectional study, p. 294
cohort, p. 294
longitudinal study, p. 295
biographical (or retrospective study), p. 295

Prenatal Development
embryo, p.295
fetus, p. 295
prenatal development, p. 295
teratogens, p. 295
critical period, p. 295

fetal alcohol spectrum disorder (FASD), p. 295

The Newborn
neonates, p. 296
temperament, p. 297

Infancy and Childhood
sensory-motor stage, p. 302
object permanence, p. 302
mental representations, p. 302
preoperational stage, p. 303
egocentric, p. 303
concrete-operational stage, p. 303
principles of conservation, p. 303

formal-operational stage, p. 303
babbling, p. 305
holophrases, p. 306
language acquisition device, p. 307
imprinting, p. 308
attachment, p. 308
stranger anxiety, p. 308
autonomy, p. 309
socialization, p. 309
peer group, p. 310
non-shared environment, p. 311
gender identity, p. 311
gender constancy, p. 311
gender-role awareness, p. 311

gender stereotypes, p. 311
sex-typed behavior, p. 311

Adolescence
puberty, p. 314
menarche, p. 314
identity formation, p. 316
identity crisis, p. 316
cliques, p. 316

Adulthood
midlife crisis, p. 322
midlife transition, p. 322
menopause, p. 323

Late Adulthood
Alzheimer's disease, p. 326

CHAPTER REVIEW ((•─[Listen to the **Chapter Audio** on **MyPsychLab**

METHODS IN DEVELOPMENTAL PSYCHOLOGY

What are some of the limitations of the methods used to study development? **Cross-sectional** studies involve studying different age groups of people at the same time, whereas longitudinal studies involve the same group of individuals at different times in their lives. **Longitudinal studies** are more time consuming, but do account for **cohort** differences in the typical experiences of members of different generations. **Biographical, or retrospective, studies** involve reconstructing a person's past through interviews.

PRENATAL DEVELOPMENT

Why can an organism or another substance cause devastating effects at one point in prenatal development but not at others? The period of development from conception to birth is called **prenatal development.** During this time, **teratogens**—disease-producing organisms or potentially harmful substances, such as drugs—can pass through the placenta and cause irreparable harm to the **embryo** and **fetus.** This harm is greatest if the drug or other substance is introduced at the same time that some major developmental process is occurring. If the same substance is introduced outside this **critical period,** little or even no harm may result. Pregnant women who consume alcohol may give birth to a child with **fetal alcohol spectrum disorder (FASD).** The mother's level of psychological stress can also affect the health of an unborn baby.

THE NEWBORN

How competent are newborns? Although **neonates** (newborn babies) appear helpless, they are much more competent and aware than they seem. Newborns see and hear, are capable of reflexive behavior, and are distinctly unique in their underlying temperaments.

What early reflexes enable newborns to respond to their environment? Certain reflexes are critical to survival. For instance, the rooting reflex causes newborns, when touched on the cheek, to turn their head in that direction and locate a nipple with their mouths. Nursing is further facilitated by the sucking reflex, which causes newborns to suck on anything placed in their mouth, and the swallowing reflex, which enables them to swallow liquids without choking.

Is your temperament the same as it was when you were a newborn? Babies are born with individual differences in personality, or **temperament** differences. Often a baby's temperament remains quite stable over time due to a combination of genetic and environmental influences, but stability in temperament is not inevitable. Your own temperament may be both similar to and different from the temperament you displayed as a newborn.

Which senses are the most developed at birth, and which are the least developed? All of a baby's senses are functioning at birth: sight, hearing, taste, smell, and touch. Newborns seem particularly adept at discriminating speech sounds, suggesting their hearing is quite keen. Their least developed sense is probably vision, which takes 6 to 8 months to become as good as the average college student's.

INFANCY AND CHILDHOOD

What kinds of developmental changes occur during infancy and childhood? During the first dozen years of life, a helpless infant becomes a competent older child. This transformation encompasses many important kinds of changes, including physical, motor, cognitive, and social developments.

How does the human brain change during infancy and early childhood? During the first 3 years of life, there are rapid increases in the number of connections between neurons in the brain, the speed of conduction between neurons, and the density of synaptic connections. Beginning in the third year of life, both the number and density of synaptic connections decreases markedly as unused neurons are removed.

Do children grow at a steady pace? Growth of the body is most rapid during the first year, with the average baby growing approximately 10 inches and gaining about 15 pounds. It then slows down considerably until early adolescence. When growth does occur, it happens suddenly—almost overnight—rather than through small, steady changes.

Babies tend to reach the major milestones in early motor development at similar ages. The average ages are called *developmental norms.* Those who are somewhat ahead of their peers are not necessarily destined for athletic greatness. Motor development that is slower or faster than the norm tells us little or nothing about a child's future characteristics.

How does a child's ability to think change over time? According to Jean Piaget, children undergo qualitative cognitive changes as they grow older. During the **sensory-motor stage** (birth to age 2), children acquire **object permanence,** the understanding that things continue to exist even when they are out of sight. In the **preoperational stage** (ages 2 to 7), they become increasingly adept at using **mental representations;** and language assumes an important role in describing, remembering, and reasoning about the world. They are **egocentric** in that they have difficulty appreciating others' viewpoints. Children in the concrete-operational stage (ages 7 to 11) are able to pay attention to more than one factor at a time, grasp **principles of conservation,** and can understand someone else's point of view. Finally, in the **formal-operational stage** (adolescence through adulthood), teenagers acquire the ability to think abstractly and test ideas mentally using logic. Not all psychologists agree with Piaget's theory, however.

How do gender and ethnic background affect moral development? Lawrence Kohlberg's stage theory of cognition focused exclusively on moral thinking. He proposed that children at different levels of moral reasoning base their moral choices on different factors: first, a concern about physical consequences, next, a concern about what other people think, and finally, a concern about abstract principles. One problem with this view is that it doesn't consider how cultural values (associated with being female, African American, Japanese, and so on) may affect moral development.

How does a child develop language skills? Language begins with cooing and progresses to **babbling,** the repetition of speech-like sounds. The first word is usually uttered at 12 months. During the next 6 to 8 months, children build a vocabulary of one-word sentences called **holophrases.** Chomsky proposed that children are born with a **language acquisition device,** an innate mechanism that enables them to build a vocabulary, master the rules of grammar, and form intelligible sentences. According to Steven Pinker, human beings have a language instinct. Shaped by natural selection, this language instinct is hardwired into our brains, predisposing infants and young children to focus on the relevant aspects of speech and attach meaning to words. Contrary to earlier beliefs, the ability to speak more than one language is beneficial for children. The fact that young children learn a second language more quickly and speak it more fluently than adults demonstrates the importance of the environment in which they were raised.

How can parents help their children become both securely attached and independent? Developing a sense of independence is just one of the tasks that children face in their social development. During the toddler period, a growing awareness of being a separate person makes developing some **autonomy** from parents a very important issue. Parents can encourage independence in their children by allowing them to make choices and do things on their own within a framework of reasonable and consistently enforced limits. Another major task during this period is forming a secure **attachment,** or emotional bond, with other people. Young animals of many species form a strong bond to the first moving object they see, a process known as **imprinting.** In contrast, human newborns only gradually form emotional bonds with their caregivers. Some of the other important tasks during infancy and early childhood include overcoming **stranger anxiety,** trusting other people (infancy), learning to take initiative in tackling new tasks (the preschool years), and mastering some of the many skills that will be needed in adulthood (middle and later childhood). Parenting style affects children's behavior and self-image. The most successful parenting style is authoritative, in which parents provide firm guidance but are willing to listen to the child's opinions. However, parents do not act the same way toward every child in the family because children are different from each other and elicit different parental responses. The **non-shared environment** refers to the unique aspects of the environment that are experienced differently by siblings even though they are reared in the same family.

Socialization, the process by which children learn their cultures' behaviors and attitudes, is an important task of childhood. As children get older, they develop a deeper understanding of the meaning of friendship and come under the influence of a **peer group.**

When do children learn about their gender? By age 3, a child has developed a **gender identity,** a girl's knowledge that she is a girl and a boy's knowledge the he is a boy. But children of this age have little idea of what it means to be a particular gender. By 4 or 5, most children develop **gender constancy,** the realization that gender depends on what kind of genitals one has and cannot be changed.

Children develop **sex-typed behavior,** or behavior appropriate to their gender, through a process of **gender-role awareness** and the formation of **gender stereotypes** reflected in their culture.

Is watching TV and playing video games a good or bad influence on the development of children? Watching television and playing video games can be worthwhile when the programs or games have an educational context and provide positive role models. However, TV and video games also reduce the time children could spend on other positive activities. When TV and video games contain aggressive content and negative role models, they can encourage aggressive behavior.

ADOLESCENCE

Is adolescence characterized only by physical change? Adolescence involves significant physical changes as well as cognitive and social-emotional changes.

What are the consequences of going through puberty early or late? Puberty—the onset of sexual maturation—occurs in a different sequence for boys and girls. Moreover, individuals differ greatly in the age at which they go through puberty. Signs of puberty begin around 11½ in boys. In girls, **menarche,** the first menstrual period, occurs at 12½ for the average American girl. But individuals vary widely in when they go through puberty. Boys who mature early do better in sports and in social activities and receive greater respect from their peers. Very early maturing girls like the admiration they get from other girls, but dislike the embarrassing sexual attention given to them by boys. And teenage pregnancy can have devastating consequences for the young mother.

These physical changes of adolescence are just part of the transformation that occurs during this period. The child turns into an adult, not only physically, but also cognitively, socially, and emotionally.

What change characterizes adolescent thinking? In terms of cognitive development, teenagers often reach the level of *formal-operational thought,* in which they can reason abstractly and speculate about alternatives. These newfound abilities may make them overconfident that their own ideas are right, turning adolescence into a time of cognitive egocentrism.

What important tasks do adolescents face in their personal and social lives? Contrary to earlier thinking, psychologists now realize that the great majority of adolescents do not experience great "storm and stress." However, adolescents must develop a stable sense of self, a process known as **identity formation.** Identity formation usually follows a period of self-exploration called an **identity crisis.** In Erik Erikson's theory, *identity versus role confusion* is the major challenge of this period. Most adolescents rely on a peer group for social and emotional support, often rigidly conforming to the values of their friends. From small unisex **cliques** in early adolescence, friendship groups change to mixed-sex groups in which short-lived romantic interests are common. Later, stable dating patterns emerge. New communication technologies such as texting can provide a greater sense of connectedness and well-being. Parent–child relationships may become temporarily rocky during adolescence as teenagers, struggling for independence, become aware of their parents' faults and question parental rules.

What are some major problems among adolescents in our society? Developmental problems often emerge for the first time during adolescence. A sizable number of adolescents think about committing suicide; a much smaller number attempt it; however, suicide is the third leading cause of death among adolescents. Statistics reflect a common decline in self-esteem during adolescence, especially among girls.

ADULTHOOD

Does personality change during adulthood? Reaching developmental milestones in adulthood is much less predictable than in earlier years; it is much more a function of the individual's decisions, circumstances, and even luck. Still, certain experiences and changes eventually take place and nearly every adult tries to fulfill certain needs.

What factors are important in forming satisfying relationships in adulthood? Almost every adult forms a long-term loving partnership with at least one other adult at some point in life. According to Erik Erikson, the task of finding intimacy versus being isolated and lonely is especially important during young adulthood.

What are the satisfactions and stresses of adult work? Most adults are moderately or highly satisfied with their jobs and would continue to work even if they didn't need to do so for financial reasons. Balancing the demands of job and family is often difficult, however, especially for women, because they tend to have most of the responsibility for housework and child care. Yet despite this stress of a "double shift," a job outside the home is a positive, self-esteem-boosting factor in most women's lives.

In what ways do adults think differently than adolescents? An adult's thinking is more flexible and practical than that of an adolescent. Whereas adolescents search for the one "correct" solution to a problem, adults realize that there may be several "right" solutions—or none at all. Adults also place less faith in authority than adolescents do.

What are the changes and challenges of midlife? Certain broad patterns of personality change occur in adulthood. As people grow older, they tend to become less self-centered and more comfortable in interpersonal relationships. They also develop better coping skills and new ways of adapting. By middle age, many adults feel an increasing commitment to, and responsibility for, others. This suggests that many adults are successfully meeting what Erik Erikson saw as the major challenge of middle adulthood: *generativity* (the ability to continue being productive and creative, especially in ways that guide and encourage future generations) *versus stagnation* (a sense of boredom or lack of fulfillment, sometimes called a **midlife crisis**). Most adults, however, do not experience dramatic upheaval in their middle years, so this period may be better thought of as one of **midlife transition.**

Middle adulthood brings a decline in the functioning of the reproductive organs. In women, this is marked by **menopause,** the cessation of menstruation, accompanied by a sharp drop in estrogen levels, which may be associated with "hot flashes" and thinning bones. Men experience a slower decline in testosterone levels.

LATE ADULTHOOD

What factors are related to life expectancy? Over the past century, life expectancy in America has increased mainly because of improved health care and nutrition. There is, however, a sizable gender gap, with women living an average of 5.2 years longer than men. There is also a sizable racial gap, with White Americans living an average of 5 years longer than Blacks.

How does the body change with age? The physical changes of late adulthood affect outward appearance and the functioning of every organ. We don't yet know why these changes happen. Whatever the reason, physical aging is inevitable, although it can be slowed by a healthy lifestyle. Moreover, despite the physical changes, psychological well-being increases dramatically from the early 50s to at least age 85.

What kind of lifestyle and sex life can be expected after 65? Most older adults have an independent lifestyle and engage in activities that interest them. Although their sexual responses may be slowed, most continue to enjoy sex beyond the 70s. Still, gradual social changes occur in late adulthood. Older adults start to interact with fewer people and perform fewer social roles. They may also become less influenced by social rules and expectations. Realizing that there is a limit to the capacity for social involvement, they learn to live with some restrictions.

Is memory loss inevitable in old age? The aging mind works a little more slowly and certain kinds of memories are more difficult to store and retrieve, but these changes are generally not extensive enough to interfere with most everyday tasks. Healthy older adults who engage in intellectually stimulating activities usually maintain a high level of mental functioning, unless they develop a condition such as **Alzheimer's disease,** a progressive neurological condition characterized by losses of memory and cognition and changes in personality.

How well do most elderly people cope with the end of life? Most elderly people fear death less than younger people fear it. They do fear the pain, indignity, depersonalization, and loneliness associated with a terminal illness. They also worry about becoming a financial burden to their families. The death of a spouse may be the most severe challenge that the elderly face. Kübler-Ross described a sequence of five stages that people go through when they are dying: *denial, anger, bargaining, depression,* and *acceptance.*

10

Personality

Thirty-year-old Jaylene Smith is a talented physician who meets with a psychologist because she is troubled by certain aspects of her social life. Acquaintances describe Jay in glowing terms, saying she is highly motivated, intelligent, attractive, and charming. But Jay feels terribly insecure and anxious. When the psychologist asked her to pick out some self-descriptive adjectives, she selected "introverted," "shy," "inadequate," and "unhappy."

Jay was the firstborn in a family of two boys and one girl. Her father is a quiet, gentle medical researcher. His work often allowed him to study at home, so he had extensive contact with his children when they were young. He loved all his children, but clearly favored Jay. His ambitions and goals for her were extremely high; and as she matured, he responded to her every need and demand almost immediately and with full conviction. Their relationship remains as close today as it was during Jay's childhood.

Jay's mother worked long hours away from home as a store manager and consequently saw her children primarily at night and on an occasional free weekend. When she came home, Mrs. Smith was tired and had little energy for "nonessential" interactions with her children. She had always been career oriented, but she experienced considerable conflict and frustration trying to reconcile her roles as mother, housekeeper, and financial provider. Mrs. Smith was usually amiable toward all her children but tended to argue more with Jay, until the bickering subsided when Jay was about 6 or 7 years of age. Today, their relationship is cordial but lacks the closeness apparent between Jay and Dr. Smith. Interactions between Dr. and Mrs. Smith were sometimes marred by stormy outbursts over seemingly trivial matters. These episodes were always followed by periods of mutual silence lasting for days.

Jay was very jealous of her first brother, born when she was 2 years old. Her parents recall that Jay sometimes staged temper tantrums when the new infant demanded and received a lot of attention (especially from Mrs. Smith). The temper tantrums intensified when Jay's second brother was born, just 1 year later. As time passed, the brothers formed an alliance to try to undermine Jay's supreme position with their father. Jay only became closer to her father, and her relationships with her brothers were marked by greater-than-average jealousy and rivalry from early childhood to the present.

Throughout elementary, junior high, and high school, Jay was popular and did well academically. Early on, she decided on a career in medicine. Yet, off and on between the ages of 8 and 17, she had strong feelings of loneliness, depression, insecurity, and confusion—feelings common enough during this age period, but stronger than in most youngsters and very distressing to Jay.

Jay's college days were a period of great personal growth, but several unsuccessful romantic involvements caused her much pain. The failure to achieve a stable and long-lasting relationship persisted after college and troubled Jay greatly. Although even-tempered in most circumstances, Jay often had an explosive fit of anger that ended each important romantic relationship that she had. "What is wrong with me?" she would ask herself. "Why do I find it impossible to maintain a serious relationship for any length of time?"

In medical school, her conflicts crept into her consciousness periodically: "I don't deserve to be a doctor"; "I won't pass my exams"; "Who am I, and what do I want from life?"

How can we describe and understand Jaylene Smith's personality? How did she become who she is? Why does she feel insecure and uncertain despite her obvious success? Why do her friends see her as charming and attractive, though she describes herself as introverted and inadequate? These are the kinds of questions that personality psychologists are likely to ask about Jay—and the kinds of questions we will try to answer in this chapter.

ENDURING ISSUES in Personality

As we explore the topic of personality in this chapter, the enduring issues that interest psychologists emerge at several points. The very concept of personality implies that our behavior differs in significant ways from that of other people (*Diversity–Universality*) and that our behavior in part reflects our personality as opposed to the situations in which we find ourselves (*Person–Situation*). We will also assess the extent to which personality is a result of inheritance, rather than a reflection of life experiences (*Nature–Nurture*). Finally, we will consider the extent to which personality changes as we grow older (*Stability–Change*).

STUDYING PERSONALITY

What do psychologists mean when they talk about personality?

Many psychologists define **personality** as an individual's unique pattern of thoughts, feelings, and behaviors that persists over time and across situations. There are two important parts to this definition. On the one hand, personality refers to *unique differences*—those

LEARNING OBJECTIVE

• Define personality. Explain the difference between describing personality (in particular trait theory) and understanding the causes of personality (psychodynamic, humanistic, and cognitive–social learning theories).

personality An individual's unique pattern of thoughts, feelings, and behaviors that persists over time and across situations.

aspects that distinguish a person from everyone else. On the other hand, the definition asserts that personality is relatively *stable and enduring*—that these unique differences persist through time and across situations.

Psychologists vary in their approach to the study of personality. Some set out to identify the most important characteristics of personality, whereas others seek to understand why there are differences in personality. Among the latter group, some consider the family to be the most important factor in personality development, whereas others emphasize the importance of influences outside the family. Still others see personality as the product of how we think about ourselves and our experiences. In this chapter, we explore representative theories of these various approaches. We see how each theoretical paradigm sheds light on the personality of Jaylene Smith. Finally, we will evaluate the strengths and weaknesses of each approach and will see how psychologists go about assessing personality.

LEARNING OBJECTIVES

- Describe the five propositions that are central to all psychodynamic personality theories.
- Describe Freud's theory of personality, including the concepts of *sexual instinct, libido, id, ego, superego,* and *pleasure principle versus reality principle.* Summarize Freud's stages of development and the consequences of *fixation* at a particular stage.
- Compare and contrast Freud's theory, Carl Jung's theory, Adler's theory, Horney's theory, and Erikson's theory of personality.
- Explain how contemporary psychologists view the contributions and limitations of the psychodynamic perspective.

PSYCHODYNAMIC THEORIES
What ideas do all psychodynamic theories have in common?

Psychodynamic theories see behavior as the product of internal psychological forces that often operate outside our conscious awareness. Freud drew on the physics of his day to coin the term *psychodynamics:* As thermodynamics is the study of heat and mechanical energy and the way that one may be transformed into the other, psychodynamics is the study of psychic energy and the way that it is transformed and expressed in behavior. Although psychodynamic theorists disagree about the exact nature of this psychic energy, the following five propositions are central to all psychodynamic theories and have withstood the tests of time (Huprich & Keaschuk, 2006; Westen, 1998):

1. Much of mental life is unconscious; as a result, people may behave in ways that they themselves do not understand.
2. Mental processes (such as emotions, motivations, and thoughts) operate in parallel and thus may lead to conflicting feelings.
3. Not only do stable personality patterns begin to form in childhood, but early experiences also strongly affect personality development.
4. Our mental representations of ourselves, of others, and of our relationships tend to guide our interactions with other people.
5. Personality development involves learning to regulate sexual and aggressive feelings as well as becoming socially interdependent rather than dependent.

Sigmund Freud

When Freud proposed that sexual instinct is the basis of behavior, how was he defining "sexual instinct"?

To this day, Sigmund Freud (1856–1939) is the best known and most influential of the psychodynamic theorists. As we saw in Chapter 1, "The Science of Psychology," Freud created an entirely new perspective on the study of human behavior. Up to his time, the field of psychology had focused on thoughts and feelings of which we are aware. In a radical departure, Freud stressed the **unconscious**—the ideas, thoughts, and feelings of which we are *not* normally aware (Zwettler-Otte, 2008). Freud's ideas form the basis of **psychoanalysis,** a term that refers both to his particular psychodynamic theory of personality and to the form of therapy that he invented.

According to Freud, human behavior is based on unconscious instincts, or drives. Some instincts are aggressive and destructive; others, such as hunger, thirst, self-preservation, and sex, are necessary to the survival of the individual and the species. Freud used the term *sexual instinct* to refer not just to erotic sexuality, but to the craving for pleasure of all kinds. He used the term **libido** for the energy generated by the sexual instinct. As we will see, Freud regarded the sexual instinct as the most critical factor in the development of personality.

unconscious In Freud's theory, all the ideas, thoughts, and feelings of which we are not and normally cannot become aware.

psychoanalysis The theory of personality Freud developed, as well as the form of therapy he invented.

libido According to Freud, the energy generated by the sexual instinct.

How Personality is Structured Freud theorized that personality is formed around three structures: the *id,* the *ego,* and the *superego.* The **id** is the only structure present at birth and is completely unconscious. (See **Figure 10–1.**) Consisting of all the unconscious urges and desires that continually seek expression, it operates according to the **pleasure principle**—that is, it tries to obtain immediate pleasure and to avoid pain. As soon as an instinct arises, the id seeks to gratify it. Because the id is not in contact with the real world, however, it has only two ways of obtaining gratification. One way is by reflex actions, such as coughing, which immediately relieve unpleasant sensations. The other is through fantasy, or *wish fulfillment:* A person forms a mental image of an object or a situation that partially satisfies the instinct and relieves the uncomfortable feeling. This kind of thought occurs most often in dreams and daydreams, but it may take other forms. For instance, if someone insults you and you spend the next half hour imagining clever retorts, you are engaging in wish fulfillment.

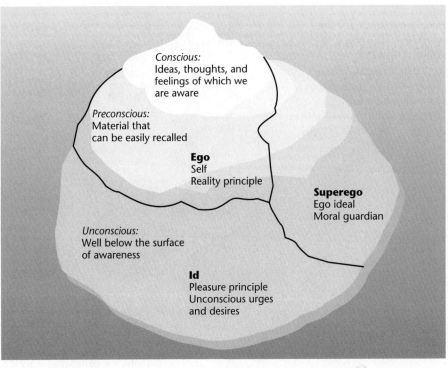

FIGURE 10–1

The structural relationship formed by the id, ego, and superego.

Freud's conception of personality is often depicted as an iceberg to illustrate how the vast workings of the mind occur beneath its surface. Notice that the ego is partly conscious, partly unconscious, and partly preconscious; it derives knowledge of the external world through the senses. The superego also works at all three levels. But the id is an entirely unconscious structure.

Source: Data from *New Introductory Lectures on Psychoanalysis* by Sigmund Freud, 1933. New York: Carlton House.

Mental images of this kind provide fleeting relief, but they cannot fully satisfy most needs. For example, just thinking about being with someone you love is a poor substitute for actually being with that person. Therefore, the id by itself is not very effective at gratifying instincts. It must link to reality if it is to relieve its discomfort. The id's link to reality is the ego.

Freud conceived of the **ego** as the psychic mechanism that controls all thinking and reasoning activities. The ego operates partly consciously, partly *preconsciously,* and partly unconsciously. ("Preconscious" refers to material that is not currently in awareness but can easily be recalled.) The ego seeks to satisfy the id's drives in the external world. But instead of acting according to the pleasure principle, the ego operates by the **reality principle:** By means of intelligent reasoning, the ego tries to delay satisfying the id's desires until it can do so safely and successfully. For example, if you are thirsty, your ego will attempt to determine how effectively and safely to quench your thirst. (See **Figure 10–2.**)

"Some people, Remson, are born to push the envelope, and some are born to lick it."

id In Freud's theory of personality, the collection of unconscious urges and desires that continually seek expression.

pleasure principle According to Freud, the way in which the id seeks immediate gratification of an instinct.

ego Freud's term for the part of the personality that mediates between environmental demands (reality), conscience (superego), and instinctual needs (id); now often used as a synonym for "self."

reality principle According to Freud, the way in which the ego seeks to satisfy instinctual demands safely and effectively in the real world.

FIGURE 10-2
How Freud conceived the workings of the pleasure and reality principles.

Note that according to the reality principle, the ego uses rational thought to postpone the gratification of the id until its desires can be satisfied safely.

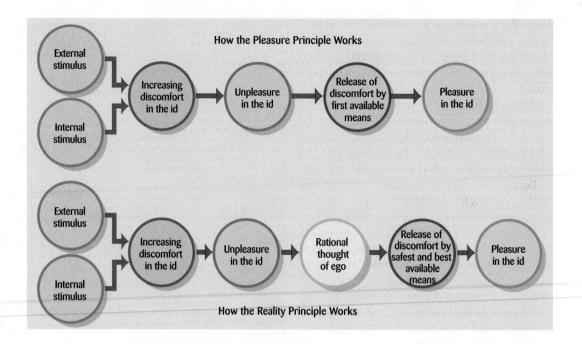

A personality consisting only of ego and id would be completely selfish. It would behave effectively, but unsociably. Fully adult behavior is governed not only by reality, but also by the individual's conscience or by the moral standards developed through interaction with parents and society. Freud called this moral watchdog the **superego.**

The superego is not present at birth. In fact, in Freud's view young children are amoral and do whatever is pleasurable. As we mature, however, we adopt as our own the judgments of our parents about what is "good" and "bad." In time, the external restraint applied by our parents gives way to our own internal self-restraint. The superego, eventually acting as our conscience, takes over the task of observing and guiding the ego, just as the parents once observed and guided the child. In addition, the superego compares the ego's actions with an **ego ideal** of perfection and then rewards or punishes the ego accordingly. Like the ego, the superego works at the conscious, preconscious, and unconscious levels.

Ideally, our id, ego, and superego work in harmony, with the ego satisfying the demands of the id in a reasonable manner that is approved by the superego. We are then free to love and hate and to express our emotions sensibly and without guilt. When our id is dominant, our instincts are unbridled and we are likely to endanger both ourselves and society. When our superego dominates, our behavior is checked too tightly and we are inclined to judge ourselves too harshly or too quickly, impairing our ability to act on our own behalf and enjoy ourselves.

How Personality Develops Freud's theory of personality development focuses on the way in which we satisfy the sexual instinct during the course of life. As infants mature, their libido becomes focused on various sensitive parts of the body during sequential stages of development. If a child is deprived of pleasure (or allowed too much gratification) from the part of the body that dominates a certain stage, some sexual energy may remain permanently tied to that part of the body, instead of moving on in normal sequence to give the individual a fully integrated personality. This is called **fixation** and, as we shall see, Freud believed that it leads to immature forms of sexuality and to certain characteristic personality traits. Let's look more closely at the psychosexual stages that Freud identified and their presumed relationship to personality development.

In the **oral stage** (birth to 18 months), infants, who depend completely on other people to satisfy their needs, relieve sexual tension by sucking and swallowing; when their baby teeth come in, they obtain oral pleasure from chewing and biting. According to Freud, infants who receive too much oral gratification at this stage grow into overly optimistic and dependent adults; they are likely to lack confidence and to be gullible. Those who receive

superego According to Freud, the social and parental standards the individual has internalized; the conscience and the ego ideal.

ego ideal The part of the superego that consists of standards of what one would like to be.

fixation According to Freud, a partial or complete halt at some point in the individual's psychosexual development.

oral stage First stage in Freud's theory of personality development, in which the infant's erotic feelings center on the mouth, lips, and tongue.

too little gratification may turn into pessimistic and hostile people later in life who are sarcastic and argumentative.

During the **anal stage** (roughly 18 months to $3^1/_2$ years), the primary source of sexual pleasure shifts from the mouth to the anus. Just about the time children begin to derive pleasure from holding in and excreting feces, toilet training takes place, and they must learn to regulate this new pleasure in ways that are acceptable to their superego. In Freud's view, if parents are too strict in toilet training, some children throw temper tantrums and may live in self-destructive ways as adults. Others are likely to become obstinate, stingy, and excessively orderly. If parents are too lenient, their children may become messy, unorganized, and sloppy.

When children reach the **phallic stage** (after age 3), they discover their genitals and develop a marked attachment to the parent of the opposite sex while becoming jealous of the same-sex parent. In boys, Freud called this the **Oedipus complex,** after the character in Greek mythology who killed his father and married his mother. Girls go through a corresponding **Electra complex,** involving possessive love for their father and jealousy toward their mother. Most children eventually resolve these conflicts by identifying with the parent of the same sex. However, Freud contended that fixation at this stage leads to vanity and egotism in adult life, with men boasting of their sexual prowess and treating women with contempt, and with women becoming flirtatious and promiscuous. Phallic fixation may also prompt feelings of low self-esteem, shyness, and worthlessness.

At the end of the phallic period, Freud believed, children lose interest in sexual behavior and enter a **latency period.** During this period, which begins around the age of 5 or 6 and lasts until age 12 or 13, boys play with boys, girls play with girls, and neither sex takes much interest in the other.

At puberty, the individual enters the last psychosexual stage, the **genital stage**. Sexual impulses reawaken and, ideally, the quest for immediate gratification of these desires yields to mature sexuality in which postponed gratification, a sense of responsibility, and caring for others all play a part.

Freud's theories continue to have a significant influence on the field of psychology, though they are not without critics. As we will see, even members of Freud's own psychoanalytic school did not completely endorse his emphasis on sexuality. Contemporary psychodynamic theorists tend to put greater emphasis on the ego and its attempts to gain mastery over the world. Finally, some critics have suggested that male and female personality development occur in very different ways, and that Freud's male-centered theory sheds relatively little light on female personality development (Zeedyk & Greemwood, 2008).

Carl Jung

How did Carl Jung's view of the unconscious differ from that of Freud?

Carl Jung (1875–1961) agreed with many of Freud's tenets, including his emphasis on the role of the unconscious in human behavior, but he expanded the role of the unconscious. Jung contended that libido represents *all* life forces, not just pleasure-seeking. And where Freud viewed the id as a "cauldron of seething excitations" that the ego has to control, Jung saw the unconscious as the ego's source of strength and vitality. He also believed that the unconscious consists of the personal unconscious and the collective unconscious. The **personal unconscious** includes our repressed thoughts, forgotten experiences, and undeveloped ideas, which may enter consciousness if an incident or a sensation triggers their recall.

ENDURING ISSUES

Diversity–Universality   Universal Human Archetypes

The **collective unconscious,** Jung's most original concept, comprises memories and behavior patterns that are inherited from past generations and therefore are shared by all humans. Just as the human body is the product of millions of years of evolution, so too,

anal stage Second stage in Freud's theory of personality development, in which a child's erotic feelings center on the anus and on elimination.

phallic stage Third stage in Freud's theory of personality development, in which erotic feelings center on the genitals.

Oedipus complex and Electra complex According to Freud, a child's sexual attachment to the parent of the opposite sex and jealousy toward the parent of the same sex; generally occurs in the phallic stage.

latency period In Freud's theory of personality, a period in which the child appears to have no interest in the other sex; occurs after the phallic stage.

genital stage In Freud's theory of personality development, the final stage of normal adult sexual development, which is usually marked by mature sexuality.

personal unconscious In Jung's theory of personality, one of the two levels of the unconscious; it contains the individual's repressed thoughts, forgotten experiences, and undeveloped ideas.

collective unconscious In Jung's theory of personality, the level of the unconscious that is inherited and common to all members of a species.

According to Carl Jung, we all inherit from our ancestors collective memories or "thought forms" that people have had in common since the dawn of human evolution. The image of a motherlike figure with protective, embracing arms is one such primordial thought form that stems from the important, nurturing role of women throughout human history. This thought form is depicted here in this Bulgarian clay figure of a goddess that dates back some six or seven thousand years.

archetypes In Jung's theory of personality, thought forms common to all human beings, stored in the collective unconscious.

persona According to Jung, our public self, the mask we wear to represent ourselves to others.

extraverts According to Jung, people who usually focus on social life and the external world instead of on their internal experience.

introverts According to Jung, people who usually focus on their own thoughts and feelings.

compensation According to Adler, the person's effort to overcome imagined or real personal weaknesses.

inferiority complex In Adler's theory, the fixation on feelings of personal inferiority that results in emotional and social paralysis.

according to Jung, is the human mind. Over millennia, it has developed "thought forms," or collective memories, of experiences that people have had in common since prehistoric times. He called these thought forms **archetypes**. Archetypes appear in our thoughts as mental images. Because all people have mothers, for example, the archetype of "mother" is universally associated with the image of one's own mother, with Mother Earth, and with a protective presence.

Jung felt that specific archetypes play special roles in shaping personality. The **persona** (an archetype whose meaning stems from the Latin word for "mask") is the element of our personality that we project to other people—a shell that grows around our inner self. For some people, the public self so predominates that they lose touch with their inner feelings, leading to personality maladjustments.

Jung also divided people into two general attitude types—introverts and extraverts. **Extraverts** turn their attention to the external world. They are "joiners" who take an active interest in other people and in the events going on around them. **Introverts** are more caught up in their own private worlds. They tend to be unsociable and lack confidence in dealing with other people. Everyone, Jung felt, possesses some aspects of both attitude types, but one is usually dominant.

Jung further divided people into *rational individuals,* who regulate their actions by thinking and feeling, and *irrational individuals,* who base their actions on perceptions, whether through the senses (sensation) or through unconscious processes (intuition). Most people exhibit all four psychological functions: thinking, feeling, sensing, and intuiting. Jung felt, however, that one or more of these functions is usually dominant. Thus, the thinking person is rational and logical, and decides on the basis of facts. The feeling person is sensitive to his or her surroundings, acts tactfully, and has a balanced sense of values. The sensing type relies primarily on surface perceptions and rarely uses imagination or deeper understanding. And the intuitive type sees beyond obvious solutions and facts to consider future possibilities.

While Freud emphasized the primacy of the sexual instincts, Jung stressed people's rational and spiritual qualities. And while Freud considered development to be shaped in childhood, Jung thought that psychic development comes to fruition only during middle age. Jung brought a sense of historical continuity to his theories, tracing the roots of human personality back through our ancestral past; yet he also contended that a person moves constantly toward self-realization—toward blending all parts of the personality into a harmonious whole. ■

Alfred Adler

What did Alfred Adler believe was the major determinant of personality?

Alfred Adler (1870–1937) disagreed sharply with Freud's concept of the conflict between the selfish id and the morality-based superego. To Adler, people possess innate positive motives and they strive for personal and social perfection. One of his earliest theories grew out of personal experience: As a child, Adler was frail and almost died of pneumonia at the age of 5. This early brush with death led him to believe that personality develops through the individual's attempt to overcome physical weaknesses, an effort he called **compensation.**

Adler later modified and broadened his views, contending that people seek to overcome *feelings* of inferiority that may or may not have a basis in reality. He thought that such feelings often spark positive development and personal growth. Still, some people become so fixated on their feelings of inferiority that they become paralyzed and develop what Adler called an **inferiority complex.** Later in his life, Adler again shifted his theoretical emphasis in a more positive direction suggesting that people strive both for personal perfection and for the perfection of the society to which they belong.

The emphasis Adler placed on positive, socially constructive goals and on striving for perfection is in marked contrast to Freud's pessimistic vision of the selfish person locked into eternal conflict with society. Because of this emphasis, Adler has been hailed by many psychologists as the father of humanistic psychology (Cain, 2002), a topic we will explore in greater depth later in this chapter.

A contemporary representation from U.S. culture of the Jungian archetype of the Wise Old Man can be seen in Albus Dumbledore (from the movies based on J. K. Rowling's *Harry Potter* series).

Karen Horney

What major contributions did Karen Horney make to the psychodynamic perspective?

Karen Horney (1885–1952), another psychodynamic personality theorist greatly indebted to Freud, nevertheless took issue with some of his most prominent ideas, especially his analysis of women and his emphasis on sexual instincts. Based on her experience as a practicing therapist in Germany and the United States, Horney concluded that environmental and social factors are the most important influences in shaping personality; and among these, the most pivotal are the human relationships we experience as children (W. B. Smith, 2007).

In Horney's view, Freud overemphasized the sex drive, resulting in a distorted picture of human relationships. Horney believed that sexuality does figure in the development of personality, but nonsexual factors—such as the need for a sense of basic security and the person's response to real or imagined threats—play an even larger role. For example, all people share the need to feel loved and nurtured by their parents, regardless of any sexual feelings they might have about them. Conversely, parents' protective feelings toward their children emerge not only from biological forces but also from the value that society places on the nurturance of children.

For Horney, *anxiety*—an individual's reaction to real or imagined dangers—is a powerful motivating force. Whereas Freud believed that anxiety usually emerges from unconscious sexual conflicts, Horney stressed that feelings of anxiety also originate in a variety of nonsexual contexts. For example, in childhood anxiety arises because children depend on adults for their very survival. Insecure about receiving continued nurturance and protection, children develop inner protections, or defenses, that provide both satisfaction and security. They experience more anxiety when those defenses are threatened.

In adulthood, anxiety and insecurity can lead to neurotic lifestyles that that may help to deal with emotional problems and ensure safety but only at the expense of personal independence (Horney, 1937). Some people develop an overriding need to give in or submit to others and feel safe only when receiving their protection and guidance. Others deal with basic feelings of insecurity and anxiety by adopting a hostile and domineering manner. Still others withdraw from other people, as if saying "If I withdraw, nothing can hurt me." In contrast, well-adjusted people deal with anxiety without becoming trapped in neurotic lifestyles because their childhood environment enabled them to satisfy their basic emotional needs.

"I'm only a _good_ dane."

Twenty-two-time Grammy Award winner Stevie Wonder, who cultivated particularly acute auditory abilities, illustrates what Alfred Adler referred to as *compensation*.

ENDURING ISSUES

Stability–Change   Is Biology Destiny?

Horney's conviction that social and cultural forces are far more important than biological ones had a profound effect on her views of human development. For example, in contrast to Freud's view that personality is largely formed by the end of childhood, Horney believed that adults can continue to develop and change throughout life by coming to understand the source of their basic anxiety and trying to eliminate neurotic anxiety. Horney also opened the way to a more constructive and optimistic understanding of male and female personality. She emphasized that culture, rather than anatomy, determines many of the characteristics that differentiate women from men. For example, if women feel dissatisfied with their gender or men are overly aggressive, the explanation is likely to be found in their social status and social roles, not in their anatomy; and fortunately, social status and social roles can be changed. Indeed, she was a forerunner of contemporary thinkers who believe that we can change culture and society and, in the process, transform human relationships (Gilman, 2001). ∎

Karen Horney, a psychotherapist during the first half of the 20th century, disagreed with Freud's emphasis on sexual instincts. She considered environmental and social factors, especially the relationships we have as children, to be the most important influences on personality.

Erik Erikson, another psychodynamic theorist, also stressed the importance of parent–child relationships for shaping personality. His eight-stage theory of personality development is still influential today.

Erik Erikson

Erikson's theory focused less on unconscious conflict and more on what factors?

Like Horney, Erik Erikson—a psychodynamic theorist who studied with Freud in Vienna—took a socially oriented view of personality development. While Erikson agreed with much of Freud's thinking on sexual development and the influence of libidinal needs on personality, he put much greater emphasis on the quality of parent–child relationships. According to Erikson, only if children feel competent and valuable, in their own eyes and in society's view, will they develop a secure sense of identity. In this way, Erikson shifted the focus of Freud's personality theory to ego development.

Whereas Freud's stages of personality development ended with adolescence, Erikson believed that personality continues to develop and change throughout life. But in contrast to Horney, he believed that the various stages of life present a variety of different challenges. Success in dealing with early challenges lays the groundwork for effective adjustment at later stages. Conversely, failure to resolve early crises makes later adjustment more difficult. In Chapter 9 ("Life-Span Development") we explored each of Erikson's stages in considerable detail. **Figure 10–3** provides a concise comparison of Erikson's and Freud's stages of personality development.

A Psychodynamic View of Jaylene Smith

How would a psychodynamic theorist view the personality of Jaylene Smith?

According to Freud, personality characteristics such as insecurity, introversion, and feelings of inadequacy and worthlessness often arise from fixation at the phallic stage of development. Thus, had Freud been Jaylene's therapist, he would probably have concluded that Jay has not yet effectively resolved her Electra complex. Working from this premise, he would

Erikson's stages of personality development

	Stage	1	2	3	4	5	6	7	8
Freud's stages of personality development	Oral	Basic trust vs. mistrust							
	Anal		Autonomy vs. shame, doubt						
	Phallic			Initiative vs. guilt					
	Latency				Industry vs. inferiority				
	Genital					Identity vs. role confusion			
	Young adulthood						Intimacy vs. isolation		
	Adulthood							Generativity vs. stagnation	
	Maturity								Ego integrity vs. despair

FIGURE 10–3

Erikson's eight stages of personality development.

Each stage involves its own developmental crisis, whose resolution is crucial to adjustment in successive stages. The first five of the eight stages correspond to Freud's stages of personality development.

Source: Data from "Erickson's Stages of Personality Development" from *Childhood and Society* by Erik H. Erikson. Copyright 1950, © 1963 by W. W. Norton & Company, Inc. Renewed 1978, 1991 by Erik H. Erikson.

have hypothesized that Jay's relationship with her father was either very distant and unsatisfying or unusually close and gratifying. We know, of course, that it was the latter.

In all likelihood, Freud would also have asserted that at around age 5 or 6, Jay had become aware that she could not actually marry her father and do away with her mother, as he would say she wished to do. This possibility might account for the fact that fights between Jay and her mother subsided when Jay was about 6 or 7 years of age. Moreover, we know that shortly thereafter, Jay began to experience "strong feelings of loneliness, depression, insecurity, and confusion." Clearly, something important happened in Jay's life when she was 6 or 7.

THINKING CRITICALLY ABOUT . . .

Psychoanalysis

Freud's original theory was based on case studies of his patients; and the literature on psychoanalysis consists mainly of case studies—descriptions of individual cases of psychopathology, probable causes, and their treatment. Today, however, psychological science depends increasingly on experimental evidence and biological explanations for mental phenomena. Review the five basic concepts of psychodynamic theory described by Westen on page 334 and think about what kinds of evidence might convince you that they are indeed correct. What evidence would lead you to conclude that they are not in fact correct?

Finally, the continued coolness of Jay's relationship with her mother and the unusual closeness with her father would probably have confirmed Freud's suspicion that Jay has still not satisfactorily resolved her Electra complex. Freud would have predicted that Jay would have problems making the progression to mature sexual relationships with other men. Jay, of course, is very much aware that she has problems relating to men, at least when these relationships get "serious."

And what does Erikson's theory tell us about Jaylene Smith's personality? Recall that for Erikson, one's success in dealing with later developmental crises depends on how effectively one has resolved earlier crises. Because Jay is having great difficulty in dealing with intimacy (Stage 6), he would have suggested that she is still struggling with problems from earlier developmental stages. Erikson would have looked for the source of these problems in the quality of Jay's relationship with others. We know that her mother subtly communicated her own frustration and dissatisfaction to her children and spent little time on "nonessential" interactions with them.

These feelings and behavior patterns would not have instilled in a child the kind of basic trust and sense of security that Erikson believed are essential to the first stage of development. In addition, her relationship with her mother and brothers continued to be less than fully satisfactory. It is not surprising, then, that Jay had some difficulty working through subsequent developmental crises. Although she developed a close and caring relationship with her father, Jay was surely aware that his affection partly depended on her fulfilling the dreams, ambitions, and goals that he had for her.

Evaluating Psychodynamic Theories

How do modern psychologists view the contributions and limitations of the psychodynamic perspective?

Freud's emphasis on the fact that we are not always—or even often—aware of the real causes of our behavior has fundamentally changed the way people view themselves and others. Freud's ideas have also had a lasting impact on history, literature, and the arts as well as psychology (Katrios, 2009; Krugler, 2004). Yet, Freud was a product of his time and place. Critics who contend his theory reflects a sexist view of women have pointed out that he was apparently unable to imagine a connection between his female patients' sense of inferiority and their subordinate position in society. However, recent psychoanalytic theorists have made significant strides in updating psychoanalytic theory to account for gender differences (Buhle, 1998; Burack, 1998; Solomon, 2004).

Although it is sometimes difficult to translate psychodynamic personality theories into hypotheses that can be tested experimentally (Cloninger, 2003), Freud's theory has received some confirmation from research (Bornstein, 2005; Leichsenring, 2005). For example, people with eating disorders often have oral personalities (J. Perry, Silvera, & Rosenvinge, 2002). Orally fixated people generally eat and drink too much, tend to mention oral images when interpreting inkblot tests, and also seem to depend heavily on others, as Freud predicted (Fisher & Greenberg, 1985). Moreover, research confirms an association between specific personality types in childhood and later development of psychological problems. For example, a child with an inhibited temperament is more likely to develop social anxiety disorder as an adult (Gladstone, Parker, Mitchell, Wilhelm, & Malhi, 2005). The effectiveness of psychoanalysis as a therapy has also been cited as evidence in support of Freud's theories (Leichsenring, 2005). Still, as we shall see in Chapter 13 , "Therapies," psychoanalysis does not seem to be any more or less effective than therapies based on other theories (J. A. Carter, 2006).

Freud's theories have clearly had a profound effect on our understanding of personality, or they would not still be so vigorously debated today, more than 100 years after he proposed them. Psychodynamic theories attempt to explain the root causes of all human behavior. The sheer magnitude of this undertaking helps to account for their lasting attractiveness.

✔•─ **Study** and **Review** on **MyPsychLab**

CHECK YOUR UNDERSTANDING

Match the following Jungian terms with the appropriate definition.

1. persona
2. collective unconscious
3. archetype

   a. typical mental image or mythical representation
   b. memories and behavior patterns inherited from past generations
   c. aspect of the personality by which one is known to other people

4. According to Alfred Adler, a person with a fixation on or belief in a negative characteristic has an _____. They may try to overcome their perceived weakness through _____.

5. Horney believed that _____ is a stronger source of emotional disturbance than sexual urges.

Answers: 1. c. 2. b. 3. a. 4. inferiority complex; compensation. 5. anxiety.

APPLY YOUR UNDERSTANDING

1. An angry parent imagines hitting a child for misbehaving, but decides instead to discuss the misbehavior with the child and to point out why the behavior was wrong. After hearing the child's explanation for the behavior, the parent feels guilty for having been so angry. The parent's anger and fantasy are the result of the _____; the decision to discuss the problem is the result of the _____; and the guilt derives from the _____.

   a. ego; superego; id
   b. id; ego; superego
   c. ego; id; superego
   d. id; superego; ego

2. John is a young adult. According to Erikson, the major challenge he faces is _____, which will be followed in middle adulthood by the crisis of _____.

   a. intimacy vs. isolation; integrity vs. despair
   b. intimacy vs. isolation; generativity vs. stagnation
   c. identity vs. role confusion; intimacy vs. isolation
   d. identity vs. role confusion; integrity vs. despair
   e. identity vs. role confusion; initiative vs. guilt

Answers: 1. b. 2. b.

HUMANISTIC PERSONALITY THEORIES

What are the major ways that humanistic personality theory differs from psychodynamic theories?

Freud believed that personality grows out of the resolution of unconscious conflicts and developmental crises. Many of his followers—including some who modified his theory and others who broke away from his circle—also embraced this basic viewpoint.

But in the theory of Alfred Adler, we glimpsed a very different view of human nature. Adler focused on forces that contribute to positive growth and a move toward personal perfection. For these reasons, Adler is sometimes called the first *humanistic* personality theorist.

Humanistic personality theory emphasizes that we are positively motivated and progress toward higher levels of functioning—in other words, there is more to human existence than dealing with hidden conflicts. Humanistic psychologists believe that life is a process of opening ourselves to the world around us and experiencing joy in living. They stress people's potential for growth and change as well as the ways they experience their lives right now, rather than dwelling on how they felt or acted in the past. Finally, humanists also believe that given reasonable life conditions, people will develop in desirable directions (Criswell, 2003). Adler's concept of striving for perfection laid the groundwork for later humanistic personality theorists such as Abraham Maslow and Carl Rogers. We discussed Maslow's theory of the hierarchy of needs leading to self-actualization in Chapter 8, "Motivation and Emotion." We now turn to Rogers's theory of self-actualization.

Carl Rogers

According to Rogers, how can thinking of yourself as self-assured help you to become so?

One of the most prominent humanistic theorists, Carl Rogers (1902–1987), contended that men and women develop their personalities in the service of positive goals. According to Rogers, every organism is born with certain innate capacities, capabilities, or potentialities—"a sort of genetic blueprint, to which substance is added as life progresses" (Maddi, 1989, p. 102). The goal of life, Rogers believed, is to fulfill this genetic blueprint, to become the best of whatever each of us is inherently capable of becoming. Rogers called this biological push toward fulfillment the **actualizing tendency.** Although Rogers maintained that the actualizing tendency characterizes all organisms—plants, animals, and humans—he noted that human beings also form images of themselves, or *self-concepts.* Just as we try to fulfill our inborn biological potential, so, too, we attempt to fulfill our self-concept, our conscious sense of who we are and what we want to do with our lives. Rogers called this striving the **self-actualizing tendency.** If you think of yourself as "intelligent" and "athletic," for example, you will strive to live up to those images of yourself. **⊙→**

When our self-concept is closely matched with our inborn capacities, we are likely to become what Rogers called a **fully functioning person.** Such people are self-directed: They decide for themselves what it is they wish to do and to become, even though their choices may not always be sound ones. Fully functioning people are also open to experience—to their own feelings as well as to the world and other people around them—and thus find themselves "increasingly willing to be, with greater accuracy and depth, that self which [they] most truly [are]" (Rogers, 1961, pp. 175–176).

According to Rogers, people tend to become more fully functioning if they are brought up with **unconditional positive regard,** or the experience of being treated with warmth, respect, acceptance, and love regardless of their own feelings, attitudes, and behaviors. But often parents and other adults offer children what Rogers called **conditional positive regard:** They value and accept only certain aspects of the child. The acceptance, warmth, and love that the child receives from others then depend on the child's behaving in certain ways and fulfilling certain conditions. In the process, self-concept comes to resemble the inborn capacity less and less, and the child's life deviates from the genetic blueprint.

When people lose sight of their inborn potential, they become constricted, rigid, and defensive. They feel threatened and anxious, and experience considerable discomfort and uneasiness. Because their lives are directed toward what other people want and value, they are unlikely to experience much real satisfaction in life. At some point, they may realize that they don't really know who they are or what they want.

Simulate the **Experiment** Multiple Selves on **MyPsychLab**

humanistic personality theory Any personality theory that asserts the fundamental goodness of people and their striving toward higher levels of functioning.

actualizing tendency According to Rogers, the drive of every organism to fulfill its biological potential and become what it is inherently capable of becoming.

self-actualizing tendency According to Rogers, the drive of human beings to fulfill their self-concepts, or the images they have of themselves.

fully functioning person According to Rogers, an individual whose self-concept closely resembles his or her inborn capacities or potentials.

unconditional positive regard In Rogers's theory, the full acceptance and love of another person regardless of his or her behavior.

conditional positive regard In Rogers's theory, acceptance and love that are dependent on another's behaving in certain ways and on fulfilling certain conditions.

A Humanistic View of Jaylene Smith

How would humanistic theorists view the development of Jaylene Smith's personality?

Humanistic personality theory would focus on the discrepancy between Jay's self-concept and her inborn capacities. For example, Rogers would point out that Jay is intelligent and achievement-oriented but nevertheless feels that she doesn't "deserve to be a doctor," worries about whether she will ever be "truly happy," and remembers that when she was 13, she never was able to be herself and really express her feelings, even with a good friend. Her unhappiness, fearfulness, loneliness, insecurity, and other dissatisfactions similarly stem from Jay's inability to become what she "most truly is." Rogers would suspect that other people in Jay's life made acceptance and love conditional on her living up to their ideas of what she should become. We know that for most of her life, Jay's father was her primary source of positive regard. Very possibly, he conditioned his love for Jay on her living up to his goals for her.

Evaluating Humanistic Theories

What have humanistic theories contributed to our understanding of personality?

The central tenet of most humanistic personality theories—that the overriding purpose of the human condition is to realize one's potential—is difficult if not impossible to verify scientifically. The resulting lack of scientific evidence and rigor is one of the major criticisms of these theories. In addition, some critics claim that humanistic theories present an overly optimistic view of human beings and fail to take into account the evil in human nature. Others contend that the humanistic view fosters self-centeredness and narcissism, and reflects Western values of individual achievement rather than universal human potential.

Nonetheless, Maslow and especially Rogers did attempt to test some aspects of their theories scientifically. For example, Rogers studied the discrepancy between the way people perceived themselves and the way they ideally wanted to be. He discovered that people whose real selves differed considerably from their *ideal* selves were more likely to be unhappy and dissatisfied.

✓● **Study** and **Review** on **MyPsychLab**

CHECK YOUR UNDERSTANDING

Indicate whether the following are true (T) or false (F).

1. _____ Humanistic personality theory emphasizes that we are motivated by conflicts, whereas psychodynamic personality theory emphasizes positive strivings.
2. _____ The goal of life, Rogers believed, is to become the best person that we can inherently become.
3. _____ Our self-concept is our inborn biological potential.
4. _____ When people lose sight of their inborn potential, they are unlikely to experience much satisfaction.

Answers: 1. (F), 2. (T), 3. (F), 4. (T).

APPLY YOUR UNDERSTANDING

1. Barbara was brought up with unconditional positive regard. According to Rogers, she is likely to
   a. be vain and narcissistic.
   b. feel she is valued regardless of her attitudes and behavior.
   c. have self-concepts that do not correspond very closely to her inborn capacities.
   d. Both (b) and (c) are true.
2. Your friend has always known that she wants to be a doctor. When you ask her how she knows that, she says, "That's just who I am. It's what I want to do with my life." Rogers calls the push toward fulfilling this sense of who she is
   a. being fully functioning.
   b. engaging in a compensatory process.
   c. expressing a high need for achievement.
   d. the self-actualizing tendency.

Answers: 1. b. 2. d.

TRAIT THEORIES

What is the key focus of trait theories?

The personality theories that we have examined so far all emphasize early childhood experiences; and all attempt to explain the varieties of human personality. Other personality theorists focus on the present, describing the ways in which already-developed adult personalities differ from one another. These *trait theorists* assert that people differ according to the degree to which they possess certain **personality traits,** such as dependency, anxiety, aggressiveness, and sociability. We infer a trait from how a person behaves. If someone consistently throws parties, goes to great lengths to make friends, and travels in groups, we might safely conclude that this person possesses a high degree of sociability.

Our language has many words that describe personality traits. Gordon Allport, along with his colleague H. S. Odbert (1936), found nearly 18,000 dictionary entries that might refer to personality traits. However, only about 2,800 of the words on Allport and Odbert's list concern the kinds of stable or enduring characteristics that most psychologists would call personality traits; and when synonyms and near-synonyms are removed, the number of possible personality traits drops to around 200—which is still a formidable list. Psychologist Raymond Cattell (1965), using a statistical technique called **factor analysis,** found that those 200 traits tend to cluster in groups. Thus, a person who is described as persevering or determined is also likely to be thought of as responsible, ordered, attentive, and stable and probably would not be described as frivolous, neglectful, and changeable. On the basis of extensive research, Cattell originally concluded that just 16 traits account for the complexity of human personality; later he suggested that it might be necessary to add another seven traits to the list (Cattell & Kline, 1977).

Other theorists thought that Cattell used too many traits to describe personality. Eysenck (1976) argued that personality could be reduced to three basic dimensions: *emotional stability, introversion–extraversion*, and *psychoticism*. According to Eysenck, *emotional stability* refers to how well a person controls emotions. On a continuum, individuals at one end of this trait would be seen as poised, calm, and composed, whereas people at the other end might be described as anxious, nervous, and excitable. *Introversion–extraversion* refers to the degree to which a person is inwardly or outwardly oriented. At one end of this dimension would be the socially outgoing, talkative, and affectionate people, known as *extraverts. Introverts*—generally described as reserved, silent, shy, and socially withdrawn—would be at the other extreme. Eysenck used the term *psychoticism* to describe people characterized by insensitivity and uncooperativeness at one end and warmth, tenderness, and helpfulness at the other end.

ENDURING ISSUES

Nature–Nurture   Is Personality Inherited?

For Allport, traits—or "dispositions," as he called them—are literally encoded in the nervous system as structures that guide consistent behavior across a wide variety of situations. Allport also believed that while traits describe behaviors that are common to many people, each individual personality is composed of a unique constellation of traits. While few psychologists today would deny the influence of the environment in shaping personality, recent evidence substantiating the importance of genetic factors to the development of specific personality traits supports Allport's hunch that at least some personality traits are encoded biologically (Rushton, Bons, & Hur, 2008). ■

The Big Five

What five basic traits describe most differences in personality?

As listed in **Table 10–1,** contemporary trait theorists have boiled down personality traits to five basic dimensions: *extraversion, agreeableness, conscientiousness, emotional stability,* and *culture* (Costa & McCrae, 2006; McCrae et al., 2008). There is a growing consensus

personality traits Dimensions or characteristics on which people differ in distinctive ways.

factor analysis A statistical technique that identifies groups of related objects; it was used by Cattell to identify clusters of traits.

Big Five Five traits or basic dimensions currently considered to be of central importance in describing personality.

TABLE 10–1   The "Big Five" Dimensions of Personality

Traits	Facets of Each Big Five Trait
Extraversion	Warmth, gregariousness, assertiveness, activity, excitement-seeking, positive emotions
Agreeableness	Trust, straightforwardness, altruism, compliance, modesty, tender mindedness
Conscientiousness/Dependability	Competence, order, dutifulness, achievement-striving, self-discipline, deliberation
Emotional Stability (Neuroticism)	Anxiety, hostility, depression, self-consciousness, impulsiveness, vulnerability
Openness to Experience/Culture/ Intellect	Fantasy, aesthetics, feelings, actions, ideas, values

Source: Adapted Table 3, p. 1560 in "Heritability of Facet-Level Traits in a Cross-Cultural Twin Sample: Support for a Hierarchical Model of Personality" by K. L. Jang, W. J. Livesley, R. R. McCrae, A. Angleitner, & R. Reimann, *Journal of Personality & Social Psychology, 74* (1998), 1556–65. Copyright © 1998 by American Psychological Association.

today that these **Big Five** personality dimensions, also known as the *five-factor model,* capture the most salient dimensions of human personality (Costa & McCrae, 2006), although there is some disagreement about whether the fifth dimension should be called "culture" or "openness to experience" or "intellect." In addition, each of the Big Five traits has been shown to have at least six *facets,* or components, as shown in **Table 10–1.**

Research has shown that the Big Five dimensions of personality may have some important real-world applications—particularly as they relate to employment decisions (Guohua & Jiliang, 2005). For example, one study (Conte & Gintoft, 2005) found that the dimensions of extraversion and conscientiousness were reliable predictors of performance in sales. In another study, the measures of agreeableness, conscientiousness, and emotional stability predicted employee burnout (Zeng & Shi, 2007). The Big Five personality traits

Explore the **Concept** Five Factor Model on **MyPsychLab**

have also been shown to be useful in predicting the job performance of police officers (Schneider, 2002). Research has also shown that absenteeism in the workplace is related to the conscientiousness, extraversion, and neuroticism scales (Conte & Jacobs, 2003). In addition to predicting job performance, the emotional stability dimension of the Big Five has been found to correlate with measures of job and career satisfaction across a wide variety of occupations (Cook, 2006). In sum, the Big Five dimensions of personality show promise as reliable predictors of job performance and satisfaction, especially when other criteria (such as technical skills and experience) are also considered (Conte & Gintoft, 2005; R. Hogan, Hogan, & Roberts, 1996).

The Big Five personality traits have also proved useful in describing and predicting behavior across a wide range of age groups and social settings. For instance, longitudinal and cross-sectional studies have demonstrated the validity and consistency of the Big Five personality traits across the life span (Asendorpf & Van-Aken, 2003; Soto, John, Gosling, & Potter, 2010). Other studies have shown the Big Five can reliably predict alcohol consumption, grade point average, and academic motivation among college students (Paunonen, 2003; Komarraju, Karau, & Schmeck, 2009).

Are the Big Five Personality Traits Universal? Most studies of the Big Five have been conducted in the United States. Would the same five personality dimensions be evident in other cultures? The answer appears to be yes. P. T. Costa and McCrae (1992) developed a test to measure the Big Five personality dimensions that has since been translated into numerous languages including German, Portuguese, Hebrew, Chinese, Korean, and Japanese. McCrae and Costa (1997) then compared the results from the various questionnaires in an effort to determine whether the same Big Five personality dimensions would emerge. The results from the six foreign cultures

"My feeling is that while we should have the deepest respect for reality, we should not let it control our lives."

were virtually identical to the data from American samples: The Big Five personality dimensions were clearly evident. As the authors noted, "The structure found in American volunteers was replicated in Japanese undergraduates and Israeli job applicants. A model of personality rooted in English-language trait adjectives could be meaningfully applied not only in a closely related language like German, but also in such utterly distinct languages as Chinese and Korean" (p. 514). Other researchers have reached the same conclusions using quite different techniques (Mlacic & Goldberg, 2007; Salgado, Moscoso & Lado, 2003).

Surprisingly, many of these same personality traits apparently exist in a number of species besides humans. For example, studies have found that the Big Five, with the two added factors of dominance and activity, could be used to rate and describe personality characteristics in species including gorillas, chimpanzees, rhesus and vervet monkeys, hyenas, dogs, cats, and pigs (Gosling & John, 1999; King, Weiss, & Farmer, 2005).

How Might the Big Five be Represented in the Brain?
Structural neuroimaging studies indicate that measures on at least some of the Big Five traits may be related to the size or volume of specific brain regions (DeYoung et al., 2010). For example, *neuroticism* scores correlate with the volume of the brain regions associated with threat, punishment, and negative emotions. Scores on the *agreeableness* trait correlate with the volume of the brain regions known to process information related to the awareness and intentions of others. *Extraversion* scores correlate with the volume of the brain region thought to be involved in processing reward information. And *conscientiousness* is related to the volume of the prefrontal cortex, a brain region discussed in Chapter 2 ("The Biological Basis of Behavior") that plays a central role in planning, judgment, impulse control, and conscious awareness.

Do the Big Five have a Genetic Basis?
Recent evidence shows that not only the Big Five but also many of their individual facets are strongly influenced by heredity (W. Johnson & Krueger, 2004; Livesley, Jang, & Vernon, 2003). Although some early theorists (Eysenck, 1947) suggested that physiological mechanisms underlie basic personality traits, only recently has solid evidence from twin studies begun to support this idea (Jang, Livesley, McCrae, Angleitner, & Riemann, 1998; Luciano, Wainwright, Wright, & Martin, 2006; Rushton, Bons, & Hur, 2008). For example, Jang and colleagues (1998, 2002) tested almost 1,000 sets of twins from Germany and Canada on the 30 facets of the Big Five. They concluded that genetic effects accounted for a substantial portion of the differences between people's scores on 26 of the 30 facet scales. In addition, the genetic and environmental influences were similar for the Canadian and German samples.

Researchers have also confirmed that genetic factors play a significant role in shaping abnormal and dysfunctional personality traits. In one study comparing 128 pairs of identical and fraternal twins on both normal and abnormal personality traits, the influence of genetic factors was found to slightly outweigh the influence of the environment. In addition, the pattern of genetic and environmental influence was similar for both the abnormal traits and the normal ones (Markon, Krueger, Bouchard, & Gottesman, 2002). Other studies have confirmed that genetic factors also contribute to the personality traits that predispose individuals toward substance abuse (Kotov, Gamez, Schmidt, & Watson, 2010), eating disorders (Mazzeo & Bulik, 2009), narcissism and psychopathy (Vernon, Villani, Vickers, & Harris, 2008), depression, marijuana dependence, aggression, and antisocial personality disorder (Alia-Klein et al., 2008; Forsman, Lichtenstein, Andershed, & Larsson, 2008; Fu et al., 2002).

What are the implications of these findings? There are several, although it is important to keep in mind that saying a particular trait such as extraversion has a genetic component does *not* mean that researchers have found a *gene* for extraversion. Nor are they likely to, because genes represent a code for specific proteins, not complex personality traits. It does mean, however, that the Big Five traits and their facets may be hardwired into the human species rather than being cultural artifacts. Many genes—perhaps thousands of them—surely work in combination to account for such complex traits. Though the precise role that genes play in personality is still far from clear, most psychologists would agree that biological factors contribute significantly to the development of most personality traits.

THINKING CRITICALLY ABOUT . . .

Cultural Universals

Is it fair to conclude that the Big Five are in fact universal traits? To answer this question, think about the following questions:

- What types of cultures have so far been studied? What do all of these cultures have in common? What types of cultures have not been studied?

- How would researchers determine whether the Big Five traits are in fact the most important ones in the cultures they have studied? Might other, equally important, traits not be measured? Did the researchers explore what personality traits are important in various cultures or simply confirm that people in a variety of cultures recognize the Big Five traits?

- What do we have to know in order to say that something is universal?

A Trait View of Jaylene Smith

How would trait theorists describe Jaylene Smith's personality?

A psychologist working from the trait perspective would infer certain traits from Jay's behavior. Since Jay chose at an early age to become a doctor, did well academically year after year, and graduated first in her medical-school class, it seems reasonable to infer a trait of determination or persistence to account for her behavior. Taking the Big Five perspective, it seems that Jaylene's personality is high in conscientiousness but perhaps low in emotional stability and extraversion. These relatively few traits provide a thumbnail sketch of what Jay is like. It is likely that there is some biological basis for her unique personality.

Evaluating Trait Theories

What major contributions have trait theories made to our understanding of personality?

Traits are the language that we commonly use to describe other people, such as when we say someone is shy or insecure or arrogant. Thus, the trait view of personality has considerable commonsense appeal. Moreover, it is scientifically easier to study personality traits than to study such things as self-actualization and unconscious motives. But trait theories have several shortcomings (Costa & McCrae, 2006). First, they are primarily descriptive: They seek to describe the basic dimensions of personality, but they generally do not try to explain causes. As you can see from the trait view of Jaylene Smith, trait theory tells us little about why she is the way she is.

In addition, some critics argue that it is dangerous to reduce human complexity to just a few traits (Mischel & Shoda, 1995). Moreover, although the Big Five model is well supported by research, some disagreement remains among psychologists about whether a five-factor model is the best way to describe the basic traits of personality (Boyle, 2008).

The issue of consistency in human behavior has long intrigued personality theorists who are interested in the interaction between personality traits and the social environment. In the view of these theorists, behavior is a product of the person *and* the situation (Mischel, 2004). That interaction is the focus of cognitive–social learning theorists, whom we will consider next.

ENDURING ISSUES

Stability–Change   How Stable Is Personality Over Time?

Some psychologists question whether traits describe and predict behavior very well over time. Are "agreeable" people at age 20 still agreeable at age 60? As we saw in Chapter 9, "Life-Span Development," numerous research studies have shown that temperament remains quite stable over time. Similarly, the Big Five dimensions of personality show considerable stability during early childhood and appear to be "essentially fixed by age 30" (McCrae & Costa, 1994, p. 173; Asendorpf & Van-Aken, 2003). Though to some extent adults can vary their behavior to fit the situations in which they find themselves, in general it seems that when it comes to personality traits, "You can't teach old dogs new tricks." ■

CHECK YOUR UNDERSTANDING

1. Eysenck stated that personality could be reduced to three basic dimensions: _____, _____, and _____.

2. There is evidence that suggests that personality is almost entirely due to environmental factors. Is this statement true (T) or false (F)?

Answers: 1. emotional stability, introversion–extraversion, psychoticism. 2. (F)

APPLY YOUR UNDERSTANDING

1. Peter is competent, self-disciplined, responsible, and well organized. In terms of the Big Five model of personality, he is high in

   a. agreeableness.

   b. conscientiousness.

   c. emotional stability.

   d. intellect.

2. Sherry is warm, assertive, energetic, and enthusiastic. According to the Big Five model of personality, she is high in

   a. extraversion.

   b. agreeableness.

   c. emotional stability.

   d. openness to experience.

Answers: 1. b. 2. a.

COGNITIVE–SOCIAL LEARNING THEORIES

How do personal and situational factors combine to shape behavior?

In contrast to personality trait theories, **cognitive–social learning theories** hold that expectancies and values guide behavior. This set of personal standards is unique to each one of us, growing out of our own life history. Our behavior is the product of our cognitions (how we think about a situation and how we view our behavior in that situation), our learning and past experiences (including reinforcement, punishment, and modeling), and the immediate environment.

Expectancies, Self-Efficacy, and Locus of Control

How does locus of control affect self-efficacy?

Albert Bandura (1977, 1997) asserts that people evaluate a situation according to certain internal **expectancies,** such as personal preferences, and this evaluation affects their behavior. Environmental feedback that follows the actual behavior, in turn, influences future expectancies. These experience-based expectancies lead people to conduct themselves according to unique **performance standards,** individually determined measures of excellence by which they judge their own behavior. Those who succeed in meeting their own internal performance standards develop an attitude that Bandura calls **self-efficacy** (Bandura & Locke, 2003). For example, two young women trying a video game for the first time may experience the situation quite differently, even if their scores are similarly low. One with a high sense of self-efficacy may find the experience fun and be eager to gain the skills necessary to go on to the next level, whereas the one with a lower sense of self-efficacy may be disheartened by getting a low score, assume she will never be any good at video games, and never play again.

In our example, the two young women approach the experience with different expectancies. To Rotter (1954), **locus of control** is an especially prevalent expectancy by which people evaluate situations. People with an *internal locus* of control are

LEARNING OBJECTIVES

- Explain how cognitive–social learning theories of personality differ from other theories. Be sure to include *expectancies, performance standards, self-efficacy,* and *locus of control* in your explanation.
- Summarize the contributions and limitations of the cognitive–social learning perspective.

cognitive–social learning theories Personality theories that view behavior as the product of the interaction of cognitions, learning and past experiences, and the immediate environment.

expectancies In Bandura's view, what a person anticipates in a situation or as a result of behaving in certain ways.

performance standards In Bandura's theory, standards that people develop to rate the adequacy of their own behavior in a variety of situations.

self-efficacy According to Bandura, the expectancy that one's efforts will be successful.

locus of control According to Rotter, an expectancy about whether reinforcement is under internal or external control.

According to cognitive–social learning theorists, people who meet their own internal standards of performance develop a sense of self-efficacy, a confidence that they can meet their goals.

convinced they can control their own fate. They believe that through hard work, skill, and training, they can find reinforcements and avoid punishments. People with an *external locus* of control do not believe they control their fate. Instead, they are convinced that chance, luck, and the behavior of others determine their destiny and that they are helpless to change the course of their lives.

Both Bandura and Rotter have tried to combine personal variables (such as expectancies) with situational variables in an effort to understand the complexities of human behavior. Both theorists believe that expectancies become part of a person's *explanatory style*, which, in turn, greatly influences behavior. Explanatory style, for example, separates optimists from pessimists. It is what causes two beginners who get the same score on a video game to respond so differently. Moreover, studies have shown that a pessimistic explanatory style negatively impacts physical health, academic and career achievement, and many aspects of mental health including depression and anxiety disorders. Conversely, having a positive explanatory style appears to serve as a "protective factor" enhancing an individual's experience of well-being (K. K. Bennett & Elliott, 2005; Wise & Rosqvist, 2006).

In a now-famous study, researchers tracked 99 students from the Harvard graduation classes of 1939 to 1944. The men were interviewed about their experiences and underwent physical checkups every 5 years. When researchers analyzed the men's interviews for signs of pessimism or optimism, they found that the explanatory style demonstrated in those interviews predicted the state of an individual's health decades later. Those men who were optimists at age 25 tended to be healthier at age 65, whereas the health of the pessimists had begun to deteriorate at about age 45 (C. Peterson, Vaillant, & Seligman, 1988). Another study looked at insurance agents in their first 2 years on the job (Seligman & Schulman, 1986). Explanatory style predicted which agents would become excellent agents and which would quit the company (three-fourths of all agents quit within 3 years). Optimists sold 37% more insurance than pessimists in the first 2 years and persisted through the difficulties of the job.

How Consistent are we? We have seen that trait theorists tend to believe that behavior is relatively consistent across situations. "Agreeable" people tend to be agreeable in most situations most of the time. In contrast, cognitive–social learning theorists believe that our actions are influenced by the people around us, and by the way we think we are supposed to behave in a given situation. According to this latter view, although underlying personality is relatively stable, behavior is likely to be more inconsistent than consistent from one situation to another. 👁

If behavior is relatively inconsistent across situations, why does it *appear* to be more consistent than it actually is? Why is the trait view of personality so compelling? One explanation is that, since we see a person only in those situations that tend to elicit the same behavior, we tend to assume that their behavior is similar across a wide range of situations. Moreover, there is considerable evidence that people need to find consistency and stability even in the face of inconsistency and unpredictability. We therefore see consistency in the behavior of others even when there is none (Mischel, 2003; Mischel & Shoda, 1995).

👁—|Watch the **Video** Locus on MyPsychLab|

A Cognitive–Social Learning View of Jaylene Smith

How would cognitive–social learning theorists describe the factors that shaped Jaylene Smith's personality?

Jaylene developed extraordinarily high performance standards, no doubt because her father's goals for her were so high. Although she has succeeded academically and professionally, in the face of such high performance standards it is understandable that she might harbor some feelings of low self-efficacy, pessimism, insecurity, and uncertainty. She might have been genetically predisposed toward shyness and introversion, but it is also likely that she was rewarded for spending much time by herself studying. Moreover, long hours of studying helped her to avoid the discomfort that she felt being around other people for long periods. Reinforcement may also have shaped Jay's self-discipline and her need to achieve academically.

In addition, at least some aspects of Jaylene's personality were formed by watching her parents and brothers and by learning subtle lessons from these family interactions. As a young child, she observed that some people deal with conflict by means of outbursts. That might help to explain her aggressive behavior with boyfriends. Moreover, as Bandura's concept of self-efficacy would predict, Jay surely noticed that her father, a successful medical researcher, enjoyed and prospered in both his career and his family life, whereas her mother's two jobs as homemaker and store manager left her frustrated and tired. This contrast may have contributed to Jay's interest in medicine and to mixed feelings about establishing a close relationship that might lead to marriage.

Evaluating Cognitive–Social Learning Theories

What contributions have cognitive–social learning theories made to our understanding of personality, and what are their limitations?

Cognitive–social learning theories of personality seem to have great potential. They put mental processes back at the center of personality, and they focus on conscious behavior and experience. We can define and scientifically study the key concepts of these theories, such as self-efficacy and locus of control; that is not true of the key concepts of psychodynamic and humanistic theories. Moreover, cognitive–social learning theories help explain why people behave inconsistently, an area in which trait approaches fall short. Cognitive–social learning theories of personality have also spawned useful therapies that help people recognize and change a negative sense of self-efficacy or explanatory style. In particular, as we will see in Chapter 13, "Therapies," these therapies have helped people overcome depression. Self-efficacy theory has also been embraced by management theorists because of its practical implications for work performance. Many studies, conducted over more than 20 years, have shown a positive correlation between self-efficacy and performance in workplaces, schools, and clinical settings.

✓• Study and Review on MyPsychLab

CHECK YOUR UNDERSTANDING

1. In Bandura's view, the belief that people can control their own fate is known as
   _____ _____.

2. According to cognitive–social learning theorists, _____ _____ is what separates
   optimists from pessimists.

Answers: 1. self-efficacy. 2. explanatory style.

APPLY YOUR UNDERSTANDING

1. Rey Ramos grew up in the South Bronx, an urban ghetto where young males are more
   likely to go to jail than they are to graduate from high school. He said, "My father always
   said you can't change anything; destiny has everything written for you. But, I rebelled
   against that, and I told him I was going to make my own destiny." According to cognitive–
   social learning theories of personality, which of the following is most descriptive of Rey?
   a. He has an internal locus of control.
   b. He has a low sense of self-efficacy.
   c. He is compensating for feelings of inferiority.
   d. He has an external locus of control.

2. You introduce a friend to a new video game. On her first try, she doesn't do well but
   she says, "This is fun. I have to climb that ladder more quickly to escape the bombs.
   Let me try again!" According to Bandura, her optimism reflects
   a. positive internal expectancies.
   b. environmental feedback.
   c. external locus of control.
   d. a low sense of self-efficacy.

Answers: 1.a. 2.a.

PERSONALITY ASSESSMENT

How do psychologists measure personality?

In some ways, testing personality is much like testing intelligence. In both cases, we are trying to measure something intangible and invisible. And in both cases, a "good test" is one that is both *reliable and valid:* It gives dependable and consistent results, and it measures what it claims to measure. (See Chapter 7 , "Cognition and Mental Abilities.") But there are special difficulties in measuring personality.

Because personality reflects *characteristic* behavior, we are not interested in someone's *best* behavior. We are interested in *typical* behavior. Further complicating the measurement process, such factors as fatigue, a desire to impress the examiner, and fear of being tested can profoundly affect a person's behavior in a personality assessment situation. For the intricate task of measuring personality, psychologists use four basic tools: the personal interview, direct observation of behavior, objective tests, and projective tests. The tools most closely associated with each of the major theories of personality are shown in the "**Summary Table:** Theories of Personality" and are discussed next.

The Personal Interview

What are the purposes of structured and unstructured interviews?

An interview is a conversation with a purpose: to obtain information from the person being interviewed. Interviews are often used in clinical settings to learn, for example, why someone is seeking treatment and to help diagnose the person's problem. Such interviews are generally *unstructured*—that is, the interviewer asks the client questions about any issues that arise and asks follow-up questions whenever appropriate. The interviewer may also pay attention to the person's manner of speaking, poise, or tenseness when certain topics are raised.

When conducting systematic research on personality, investigators more often rely on *structured* interviews. In these interviews, the order and content of the questions are fixed, and the interviewer adheres to the set format. Although less personal, this kind of interview allows the interviewer to obtain comparable information from everyone interviewed. Generally speaking, structured interviews elicit information about sensitive topics that might not come up in an unstructured interview.

Explore the **Concept** Psychodynamic, Behavioral, and other Approaches to Personality on **MyPsychLab**

SUMMARY TABLE	THEORIES OF PERSONALITY	
Theory	**Roots of Personality**	**Methods of Assessing**
Psychodynamic	Unconscious thoughts, feelings, motives, and conflicts; repressed problems from early childhood	Projective tests, personal interviews
Humanistic	A drive toward personal growth and higher levels of functioning	Objective tests, personal interviews
Trait	Relatively permanent dispositions within the individual that cause the person to think, feel, and act in characteristic ways	Objective tests
Social Learning	Determined by past reinforcement and punishment as well as by observing what happens to other people	Interviews, objective tests, observations

Direct Observation

What are the advantages and limits of the observational method?

Another way to find out how a person usually behaves is to observe that person's actions in everyday situations over a long period. Behaviorists and social learning theorists prefer this method of assessing personality because it allows them to see how situation and environment influence behavior and to note a range of behaviors.

In *direct observation*, observers watch people's behavior firsthand. Systematic observation allows psychologists to look at aspects of personality (e.g., traits, moods, or motives) as they are expressed in real life (Back & Egloff, 2009). Ideally, the observers' unbiased accounts of behavior paint an accurate picture of that behavior, but an observer runs the risk of misinterpreting the true meaning of an act. For example, the observer may think that children are being hostile when they are merely protecting themselves from the class bully. Direct observation is expensive and time-consuming, and there is always the possibility that the presence of the observer will affect people's behavior.

Objective Tests

Why are objective tests preferred by trait theorists?

To avoid depending on the skills of an interviewer or the interpretive abilities of an observer in assessing personality, psychologists devised **objective tests,** or personality inventories. Generally, these are written tests that are administered and scored according to a standard procedure. The tests are usually constructed so that the person merely chooses a "yes" or "no" response, or selects one answer among many choices. Objective tests are the most widely used tools for assessing personality, but they have two serious drawbacks. First, they rely entirely on self-report. If people do not know themselves well, cannot be entirely objective about themselves, or want to paint a particular picture of themselves, self-report questionnaire results have limited usefulness (Bagby & Marshall, 2005; Marshall, De Fruyt, Rolland, & Bagby, 2005). In fact, some research indicates that peers who know you well often do a better job characterizing you than you do yourself (Funder, 1995). Second, if people have previously taken personality questionnaires, their familiarity with the test format may affect their responses to it. (See "Applying Psychology: Evaluating Your Personality.")

objective tests Personality tests that are administered and scored in a standard way.

APPLYING PSYCHOLOGY

Evaluating Your Personality

The following scales provide a way for you to assess your own personality on the Big Five personality traits. It will examine the extent to which others agree with your assessment, the extent to which your behavior is consistent across a range of situations, and the extent to which your personality has been stable over time. The adjectives correspond to the six facets for each of the Big Five traits. (See **Table 10–1.**)

For each of the adjectives, indicate the extent to which you think it applies to you. If you write your answers on a separate sheet of paper, you can then ask others to do the same and compare their answers to your own. Friends, close relatives, and others who know you well are likely to provide the most useful information. You also might try to get ratings from people who see you in different situations—perhaps some people who see you only in class, some who see you only in informal social situations, and others who have known you for a very long time in a wide variety of situations. That will give you an opportunity to see the extent to which different situations cause you to behave in different ways; in turn, this could lead others, who see you only in those situations, to conclude that your *personality* is different than perhaps it really is.

You might also fill out the form, or have others fill it out, as you were in the past, and compare that with how you are today. It would be interesting to speculate on the reasons for any significant changes over time.

Use the following scales to rate yourself on each adjective:

1. Very true of me
2. Often true of me
3. Sometimes true of me
4. Seldom true of me
5. Almost never true of me

Extraversion					
Outgoing	1	2	3	4	5
Sociable	1	2	3	4	5
Forceful	1	2	3	4	5
Energetic	1	2	3	4	5
Adventurous	1	2	3	4	5
Enthusiastic	1	2	3	4	5

Agreeableness					
Forgiving	1	2	3	4	5
Not demanding	1	2	3	4	5
Warm	1	2	3	4	5
Not stubborn	1	2	3	4	5
Modest	1	2	3	4	5
Sympathetic	1	2	3	4	5

Conscientiousness					
Efficient	1	2	3	4	5
Organized	1	2	3	4	5
Responsible	1	2	3	4	5
Thorough	1	2	3	4	5
Self-disciplined	1	2	3	4	5
Deliberate	1	2	3	4	5

Emotional Stability					
Tense	1	2	3	4	5
Irritable	1	2	3	4	5
Depressed	1	2	3	4	5
Self-conscious	1	2	3	4	5
Moody	1	2	3	4	5
Not self-confident	1	2	3	4	5

Openness					
Curious	1	2	3	4	5
Imaginative	1	2	3	4	5
Artistic	1	2	3	4	5
Wide interests	1	2	3	4	5
Excitable	1	2	3	4	5
Unconventional	1	2	3	4	5

Because of their interest in accurately measuring personality traits, trait theorists favor objective tests. Cattell, for example, developed a 374-question personality test called the **Sixteen Personality Factor Questionnaire.** The 16PF (as it is usually called) provides scores on each of the 16 traits originally identified by Cattell. More recently, objective tests such as the **NEO-PI-R** have been developed to assess the Big Five major personality traits (Costa & McCrae, 2006). The NEO-PI-R yields scores for each trait and its six facets. For each of over 200 questions, the test taker indicates to what degree he or she disagrees with the statement made. The primary use of the test is to assess the personality of a normal adult, although recent studies suggest it may also prove useful in some clinical settings (Bagby, Sellbom, Costa, & Widiger, 2008).

The most widely used and thoroughly researched objective personality test is the **Minnesota Multiphasic Personality Inventory (MMPI-2)** (Hoelzle & Meyer, 2008). Originally developed as an aid in diagnosing psychiatric disorders, the MMPI-2 remains in use as an effective diagnostic tool (Egger, Delsing, & DeMey, 2003), for detecting *malingering,* or faking a psychiatric disorder (Kucharski, Johnsen, & Procell, 2004; Walters et al., 2008) and for the forensic (legal) evaluation of personality (Nelson, Hoelzle, Sweet, Arbisi, & Demakis, 2010). Respondents are asked to answer "true," "false," or "cannot say" to such questions as "Once in a while I put off until tomorrow what I ought to do today," "At times I feel like swearing," and "There are people who are trying to steal my thoughts and ideas." Some of the items repeat very similar thoughts in different words: For example, "I tire easily" and "I feel weak all over much of the time." This redundancy provides a check on the possibility of false or inconsistent answers. **Table 10–2** shows the 10 clinical scales that are assessed by the MMPI-2.

Projective Tests

What do projective tests try to measure?

Owing to their belief that people are often unaware of the determinants of their behavior, psychodynamic theorists tend to discount self-report-based objective personality tests. Instead, they prefer **projective tests** of personality. Most projective tests consist of simple ambiguous stimuli. After looking at an essentially meaningless graphic image or at a vague picture, the test taker explains what the material means. Alternatively, the person may be asked to complete a sentence fragment, such as "When I see myself in the mirror, I …" The tests offer no clues regarding the "best way" to interpret the material or to complete the sentence.

Sixteen Personality Factor Questionnaire Objective personality test created by Cattell that provides scores on the 16 traits he identified.

NEO-PI-R An objective personality test designed to assess the Big Five personality traits.

Minnesota Multiphasic Personality Inventory (MMPI-2) The most widely used objective personality test, originally intended for psychiatric diagnosis.

projective tests Personality tests, such as the Rorschach inkblot test, consisting of ambiguous or unstructured material.

Rorschach test A projective test composed of ambiguous inkblots; the way people interpret the blots is thought to reveal aspects of their personality.

TABLE 10-2   The 10 Clinical Scales of the MMPI-2

Clinical Scale	Symbol	Description
Hypochondriasis	Hs	Excessive concern with physical health and bodily function, somatic complaints, chronic weakness
Depression	D	Unhappiness, loss of energy, pessimism, lack of self-confidence, hopelessness, feeling of futility
Hysteria	Hy	Reacts to stress with physical symptoms such as blindness or paralysis; lacks insights about motives and feelings
Psychopathic Deviation	Pd	Disregard for rules, laws, ethics, and moral conduct; impulsiveness, rebellious toward authority figures, may engage in lying, stealing and cheating
Masculinity–Femininity	Mf	Adherence to nontraditional gender traits, or rejection of the typical gender role
Paranoia	Pa	Suspiciousness, particularly in the area of interpersonal relations, guarded, moralistic, and rigid; overly responsive to criticism
Psychasthenia	Pt	Obsessiveness and compulsiveness, unreasonable fears, anxious, tense, and high-strung
Schizophrenia	Sc	Detachment from reality, often accompanied by hallucinations, delusions, and bizarre thought processes; often confused, disorganized
Hypomania	Ma	Elevated mood, accelerated speech, flight of ideas, overactivity, energetic, and talkative
Social Introversion	Sl	Shy, insecure, and uncomfortable in social situations; timid, reserved, often described by others as cold and distant

THINKING CRITICALLY ABOUT . . .

Projective Tests

Critics of projective tests say that it is the clinician whose personality is actually revealed by the tests, because the clinician's report is itself an interpretation of an ambiguous stimulus (the client's verbal response).

1. Do you agree or disagree? Why?

2. How might this potential source of error be reduced?

3. What are the real or potential advantages to using projective tests?

The **Rorschach test** is the best known and one of the most frequently used projective personality tests (I. B. Weiner, 2006). It is named for Hermann Rorschach, a Swiss psychiatrist who in 1921 published the results of his research on interpreting inkblots as a key to personality. (See **Figure 10–4.**) Each inkblot design is printed on a separate card and is unique in form, color, shading, and white space. People are asked to specify what they see in each blot. Test instructions are minimal, so people's responses will be completely their own. After interpreting all the blots, the person goes over the cards again with the examiner and explains which part of each blot prompted each response. There are different methods of interpreting a person's responses to the blots on the Rorschach test, some of which produce more valid results than others (Masling, 2002; Viglione & Taylor, 2003).

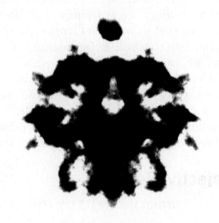

FIGURE 10–4

Inkblots used in the Rorschach projective test.

Projective tests have several advantages. Because they are flexible and can even be treated as games or puzzles, people can take them in a relaxed atmosphere, without the tension and self-consciousness that sometimes accompany objective tests. Often, the person doesn't even know the true purpose of the test, so responses are less likely to be faked. Some psychologists believe that the projective test can uncover unconscious thoughts and fantasies, such as latent sexual or family problems. In any event, the accuracy and usefulness of projective tests depend largely on the skill of the examiner in eliciting and interpreting responses.

Somewhat more demanding is the **Thematic Apperception Test (TAT).** It consists of 20 cards picturing one or more human figures in deliberately ambiguous situations. (See **Figure 10–5.**) A person is shown the cards one by one and asked to write a complete story about each picture, including what led up to the scene depicted, what the characters are doing at that moment, what their thoughts and feelings are, and what the outcome will be.

Although various scoring systems have been devised for the TAT (Aranow, Weiss, & Rezikoff, 2001), examiners usually interpret the stories in the light of their personal knowledge of the storyteller. One key in evaluating the TAT is determining who the test taker identifies with—the story's hero or heroine, or one of the minor characters. The examiner then determines what the attitudes and feelings of the character reveal about the storyteller. The examiner also assesses each story for content, language, originality, organization, consistency, and recurring themes such as the need for affection, repeated failure, or parental domination.

Both the Rorschach and the TAT may open up a conversation between a clinician and a patient who is reluctant or unable to talk about personal problems. Both tests may also provide insight into motives, events, or feelings of which the person is unaware. However, because projective tests are often not administered in a standard fashion, their validity and reliability, especially in cross-cultural settings, have been called into question (Hofer & Chasiotis, 2004; Wood et al., 2010). As a result, their use has declined since the 1970s. Still, when interpreted by a skilled examiner, these tests can offer insight into a person's attitudes and feelings. ◉➤

Thematic Apperception Test (TAT)
A projective test composed of ambiguous pictures about which a person is asked to write a complete story.

Simulate the **Experiment** Personality on **MyPsychLab**

FIGURE 10–5
A sample item from the Thematic Apperception Test (TAT).

In the photo, the person is making up a story to explain the scene in the painting. The examiner then interprets and evaluates the person's story for what it reveals about her personality.

Source: Reprinted by permission of the publishers from Henry A. Murray, *Thematic Apperception Test,* Cambridge, Mass.: Harvard University Press, Copyright © 1943 by the President and Fellows of Harvard College, © 1971 by Henry A. Murray.

✔•⌐ **Study** and **Review** on **MyPsychLab**

1. _____ tests require people to fill out questionnaires, which are then scored according to a standardized procedure.

2. In _____ tests of personality, people are shown ambiguous stimuli and asked to describe them or to make up a story about them.

Answers: 1. Objective. 2. projective.

1. You are consulting a psychologist who asks you to take a personality test. She shows you pictures of people and asks you to write a complete story about each picture. The test is most likely the
   a. Minnesota Multiphasic Personality Inventory.
   b. Rorschach Test.
   c. Thematic Apperception Test.
   d. NEO-PI-R.

2. "They are often not administered in a standard fashion, they are seldom scored objectively, but when interpreted by a skilled examiner, they can provide insight into a person." To what does this quotation most likely refer?
   a. structured interviews
   b. objective personality tests
   c. projective personality tests
   d. the NEO-PI-R and the MMPI-2

Answers: 1. c. 2. c.

KEY TERMS

Studying Personality
personality, p. 333

Psychodynamic Theories
unconscious, p. 334
psychoanalysis, p. 334
libido, p. 334
id, p. 335
pleasure principle, p. 335
ego, p. 335
reality principle, p. 335
superego, p. 336
ego ideal, p. 336
fixation, p. 336
oral stage, p. 336
anal stage, p. 337
phallic stage, p. 337

Oedipus complex and Electra
  complex, p. 337
latency period, p. 337
genital stage, p. 337
personal unconscious, p. 337
collective unconscious, p. 337
archetypes, p. 338
persona, p. 338
extraverts, p. 338
introverts, p. 338
compensation, p. 338
inferiority complex, p. 338

Humanistic Personality Theories
humanistic personality theory,
  p. 343
actualizing tendency, p. 343

self-actualizing tendency, p. 343
fully functioning person, p. 343
unconditional positive regard,
  p. 343
conditional positive regard, p. 343

Trait Theories
personality traits, p. 345
factor analysis, p. 345
Big Five, p. 346

Cognitive–Social Learning Theories
cognitive–social learning
  theories, p. 349
expectancies, p. 349

performance standards, p. 349
self-efficacy, p. 349
locus of control, p. 349

Personality Assessment
objective tests, p. 353
Sixteen Personality Factor
  Questionnaire, p. 355
NEO-PI-R, p. 355
Minnesota Multiphasic
  Personality Inventory
  (MMPI-2), p. 355
projective tests, p. 355
Rorschach test, p. 356
Thematic Apperception Test
  (TAT), p. 357

CHAPTER REVIEW ((•─Listen to the **Chapter Audio** on **MyPsychLab**

STUDYING PERSONALITY

What do psychologists mean when they talk about personality? **Personality** refers to an individual's unique pattern of thoughts, feelings, and behaviors that persists over time and across situations. Key to this definition is the concept of distinctive differences among individuals and the concept of personality's stability and endurance.

PSYCHODYNAMIC THEORIES

What ideas do all psychodynamic theories have in common? *Psychodynamic theories* of personality consider behavior to be the transformation and expression of psychic energy within the individual. Often these psychological dynamics are **unconscious** processes.

When Freud proposed that the sexual instinct is the basis of behavior, how was he defining "sexual instinct"? According to Freud, personality is made of three structures. The **id,** the only personality structure present at birth, operates in the unconsciousness according to the **pleasure principle.** The ego, operating at the conscious level according to the **reality principle,** controls all conscious thinking and reasoning. The **superego** acts as the moral guardian or conscience helping the person function in society by comparing the ego's actions with the **ego ideal** of perfection. Freud used the term *sexual instinct* to refer to the desire for virtually any form of pleasure. As infants mature, their **libido,** or energy generated by the sexual instinct, becomes focused on sensitive parts of the body. A **fixation** occurs if a child is deprived of or receives too much pleasure from the part of the body that dominates one of the five developmental stages—**oral, anal, phallic, latency,** and **genital.** During the phallic stage, strong attachment to the parent of the opposite sex and jealousy of the parent of the same sex is termed the **Oedipus complex** in boys and the **Electra complex** in girls. Next, the child enters the latency period, characterized by a lack of interest in sexual behavior. Finally, at puberty, the individual enters the genital stage of mature sexuality.

How did Carl Jung's view of the unconscious differ from that of Freud? Freud saw the id as a "cauldron of seething excitations," whereas Jung viewed the unconscious as the ego's source of strength. Jung believed that the unconscious consisted of the **personal unconscious,** encompassing an individual's repressed thoughts, forgotten experiences, and undeveloped ideas; and the **collective unconscious,** a subterranean river of memories and behavior patterns flowing to us from previous generations. Certain universal thought forms, called **archetypes,** give rise to mental images or mythological representations and play a special role in shaping personality. Jung used the term **persona** to describe that part of personality by which we are known to other people, like a mask we put on to go out in public.

What did Alfred Adler believe was the major determinant of personality? Adler believed that people possess innate positive motives and strive toward personal and social perfection. He originally proposed that the principal determinant of personality was the individual's attempt to **compensate** for actual physical weakness, but he later modified his theory to stress the importance of *feelings* of inferiority, whether or not those feelings are justified. Adler concluded that strivings for superiority and perfection, both in one's own life and in the society in which one lives, are crucial to personality development.

What major contributions did Karen Horney make to the psychodynamic perspective? For Horney, anxiety—a person's reaction to real or imagined dangers or threats—is a stronger motivating force than the sexual drive, or libido. Overly anxious adults may adopt one of three maladaptive coping strategies—moving toward people (submission), moving against people (aggression), and moving away from people (detachment). By emphasizing that culture and not anatomy determines many of the personality traits that differentiate women from men and that culture can be changed, Horney became a forerunner of feminist psychology.

Erikson's theory focused less on unconscious conflict and more on what factors? Erikson argued that the quality of the parent–child relationship affects the development of personality because, out of this interaction, the child either feels competent and valuable and is able to form a secure sense of identity or feels incompetent and worthless and fails to build a secure identity. Erikson proposed that each person moves through eight stages of development, each involving a more successful versus a less successful adjustment.

How would a psychodynamic theorist view the personality of Jaylene Smith? Freud would probably conclude that Jay had not successfully resolved her Electra complex. Erikson might suggest that Jay has problems achieving intimacy (Stage 6) because she had failed to develop satisfactory relations with other people earlier in her life.

How do modern psychologists view the contributions and limitations of the psychodynamic perspective? Psychodynamic theories have had a profound impact on the way we view ourselves and others, but some of Freud's theories have been criticized as unscientific and culture bound, based on the anecdotal accounts of troubled individuals. As a therapy, **psychoanalysis** has been shown to be beneficial in some cases but no more so than are other therapies.

HUMANISTIC PERSONALITY THEORIES

What are the major ways that humanistic personality theory differs from psychodynamic theories? Freud and many of his followers believed that personality grows out of the resolution of unconscious conflicts and developmental crises from the past. **Humanistic personality theory** emphasizes that we are positively motivated and progress toward higher levels of functioning; and it stresses people's potential for growth and change in the present.

According to Rogers, how can thinking of yourself as self-assured help you to become so? Rogers contended that every person is born with certain innate potentials and the **actualizing tendency** to realize our biological potential as well as our conscious sense of who we are. A **fully functioning person** is one whose self-concept closely matches the person's inborn capabilities, and is encouraged when a child is raised in an atmosphere characterized by **unconditional positive regard.**

How would humanistic theorists view the development of Jaylene Smith's personality? Humanistic theorists would focus on the difference between Jay's self-concept and her actual capacities. Her inability to become what she "most truly is" would account for her anxiety, loneliness, and general dissatisfaction. Rogers would suspect that throughout Jay's life, acceptance and love came from satisfying other people's ideas of what she should become.

What have humanistic theories contributed to our understanding of personality? There is a lack of scientifically derived evidence for humanistic theories of personality. In addition, these theories are criticized for taking too rosy a view of human nature, for fostering self-centeredness, and for reflecting Western values of individual achievement.

TRAIT THEORIES

What is the key focus of trait theories? Trait theorists reject the notion that there are just a few distinct personality types. Instead, they insist that each person possesses a unique constellation of fundamental **personality traits,** which can be inferred from how the person behaves.

What five basic traits describe most differences in personality? Recent research suggests that there may be just five overarching and universal personality traits: extraversion, agreeableness, conscientiousness, emotional stability, and openness to experience (also called culture or intellect). Research shows these traits have some real world applications and are strongly influenced by heredity.

How would trait theorists describe Jaylene Smith's personality? Trait theorists would probably ascribe Jaylene's high achievements to the traits of determination or persistence. Sincerity, motivation, intelligence, anxiety, and introversion would also describe Jay. In terms of Big Five factors, she would be considered high in conscientiousness, but low in emotional stability and extraversion.

What major contributions have trait theorists made to our understanding of personality? Trait theories are primarily descriptive and provide a way of classifying personalities, but they do not explain why someone's personality developed as it did. Unlike psychodynamic and humanistic theories, however, trait theories are relatively easy to test experimentally, and research confirms the value of the five-factor model, referred to as the **"Big Five,"** in pinpointing personality. Also, although most personality theories assume that behavior is consistent across situations and over a lifetime, a number of psychologists believe that situational variables have a significant effect on behavior.

COGNITIVE–SOCIAL LEARNING THEORIES

How do personal and situational factors combine to shape behavior? **Cognitive–social learning theories** of personality view behavior as the product of the interaction of cognitions, learning and past experiences, and the immediate environment.

How does one's locus of control affect self-efficacy? Albert Bandura maintains that certain internal **expectancies** determine how a person evaluates a situation and that this evaluation has an effect on the person's behavior. These expectancies prompt people to conduct themselves according to unique **performance standards,** individually determined measures of excellence by which they judge their behavior. According to Rotter, people with an internal **locus of control**—one type of expectancy—believe that they can control their own fate through their actions. Those who succeed in meeting their own internal performance standards develop an attitude that Bandura calls **self-efficacy.**

How would cognitive–social learning theorists describe the factors that shaped Jaylene Smith's personality? These theorists would assert that Jaylene acquired extraordinarily high performance standards that almost inevitably left her with feelings of low self-efficacy, insecurity, and uncertainty. She probably learned to be shy because she was rewarded for the many hours she spent alone studying. Reinforcement would also have shaped her self-discipline and high need to achieve. By watching her parents, Jay could have learned to respond to conflicts with aggressive outbursts.

What contributions have cognitive–social learning theories made to our understanding of personality, and what are their limitations? Cognitive–social learning theories avoid the narrowness of trait theories, as well as the reliance on case studies and anecdotal evidence that weakens psychodynamic and humanistic theories. They also explain why people behave inconsistently, an area where the trait theories fall short. Cognitive–social learning theories have also spawned therapies that have been effectively used to treat depression.

PERSONALITY ASSESSMENT

How do psychologists measure personality? Psychologists use four different methods to assess personality: the personal interview, direct observation of behavior, objective tests, and **projective tests.** Factors such as a desire to impress the examiner, fatigue, and fear of being tested can profoundly affect the reliability and validity of such tests.

What are the purposes of structured and unstructured interviews? During an unstructured interview, the interviewer asks questions about any issues that arise and poses follow-up questions where appropriate. In a structured interview, the order and the content of the questions are fixed, and the interviewer does not deviate from the format. Structured interviews are more likely to be used for systematic research on personality because they elicit comparable information from all interviewees.

What are the advantages and limits of the observational method? Direct observation of a person over a period of time, which enables researchers to assess how situation and environment influence behavior, has the advantage of not relying on people's self-reported behavior. However, the observer runs the risk of misinterpreting the meaning of a given behavior.

Why are objective tests preferred by trait theorists? Objective tests ask respondents to answer "yes–no" questions about their own behavior and thoughts. Cattell's **Sixteen Personality Factor Questionnaire (16PF)** provides scores on 16 basic personality traits, whereas the NEO-PI-R reports scores for each of the Big Five traits and their associated facets. The **Minnesota Multiphasic Personality Inventory (MMPI-2),** originally developed as an aid to diagnose mental disorders, includes questions that measure the truthfulness of a person's response.

What do projective tests try to measure? Psychodynamic theorists, who believe that much behavior is determined by unconscious processes, tend to discount tests that rely on self-reports. They are more likely to use projective tests consisting of ambiguous stimuli that can elicit an unlimited number of interpretations based on these unconscious processes. Two such tests are the **Rorschach Test** and the **Thematic Apperception Test (TAT).**

11

Stress and Health Psychology

OVERVIEW

For many people, imagining a life-altering experience—such as a car accident—that results in paralysis or the sudden amputation of a limb is nearly unfathomable. Scenarios like these seem devastating and horrific; how do you continue any semblance of a normal life when suddenly, you cannot participate in the same activities or move around as freely as you once did? For Austin Whitney, this seemingly unimaginable set of circumstances became a reality when he lost the use of both legs as a result of a car accident on the very day he learned he had been accepted to the University of California.

In the book *You're Stronger Than You Think: Tapping Into the Secrets of Emotionally Resilient People,* author Peter Ubel, M.D., explains that people typically have time to consider and come to terms with the reality of going from a mobile person with two working legs to a paraplegic who must rely on other methods of mobility. But in Whitney's case, he was a healthy guy up until the moment of the accident. He had no opportunity to think about a life without the use of his legs.

Despite this unfortunate set of circumstances, Austin was determined not only to graduate from college on time but also to walk across the stage and receive his diploma just like all the other graduates in his class. On May 14, 2011, that is exactly what happened. Each of his legs was strapped to a bionic leg brace. A computer in a small backpack sent instructions to the motors and gears that caused his legs to move while Austin concentrated on maintaining his balance. He rose slowly out of his wheelchair in front of 15,000 people who stood up with him and roared their support. He walked slowly across the stage where he was met by the Chancellor of the University of California, Berkeley (see the photo on p. 350). And he received his diploma along with his classmates. Austin has also been recertified to scuba dive, is working on his scuba diving instructor certification, and is considering going to law school. He is a prime example of the way that some people can take extraordinary tragedy and trauma and "get it back."

We begin this chapter by looking at common sources of stress and why some people, such as Austin Whitney, are less vulnerable to stress than others. We then examine strategies for coping with stress. Next we turn to how acute or chronic stress can sometimes make people more susceptible to physical illness by weakening their immune system. The challenge, which we take up in the sections that follow, is to find ways to reduce stress and promote good health and a sense of well-being.

ENDURING ISSUES in Stress and Health Psychology

In this chapter, we again encounter several of the enduring issues that interest all psychologists regardless of their area of specialization. To what extent do the methods that people use in coping with stress depend on the environment in which they find themselves (*Person–Situation*)? Can psychological stress cause physical illness (*Mind–Body*)? To what extent do people respond differently to severe stress (*Diversity–Universality*)?

SOURCES OF STRESS

What are stressors?

The term **stressor** refers to any environmental demand that creates a state of tension or threat (**stress**) and requires change or adaptation (**adjustment**). Many situations prompt us to change our behavior in some way, but only some cause stress. Consider, for example, stopping at a traffic signal that turns red. Normally, this involves no stress. But now imagine that you are rushing to an important appointment or to catch a train and the red light will surely make you late. Here, stress is triggered because the situation not only requires adaptation, but it produces tension and distress as well.

Some events, such as wars and natural disasters, are inherently stressful for virtually everyone. Other less dramatic, day-to-day events are nonetheless sources of significant stress for large numbers of people. An August 2010 survey found that most Americans were experiencing moderate to high stress due to concerns about such things as money, work, the economy, family responsibilities and relationships (see Figure 11–1). Stress is not limited, however, to dangerous or unpleasant situations. Even everyday events or good things can also cause stress, because they necessitate a change or adaptation. For example, a wedding is often both stressful and exciting (Ma, 2004).

> ### LEARNING OBJECTIVES
> - Distinguish between *stressors* and *stress*. Identify the major sources of stress. Describe the three types of conflict. Explain what is meant by "self-imposed stress."
> - Describe the role of optimism and pessimism, locus of control, hardiness, and resilience in affecting people's response to stress.

stressor Any environmental demand that creates a state of tension or threat and requires change or adaptation.

stress A state of psychological tension or strain.

adjustment Any effort to cope with stress.

Change

Why is change so stressful for most people?

All stressful events involve change. But most people have a strong preference for order, continuity, and predictability in their lives. Therefore, anything—good or bad—that requires change has the potential to be experienced as stressful. The more change required, the more stressful the situation.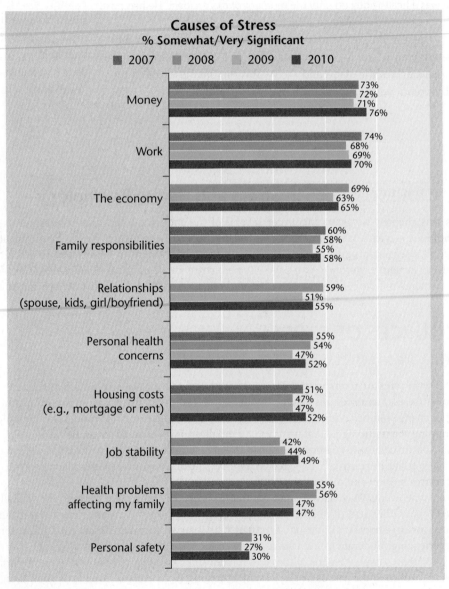

Questionnaires like the College Life Stress Inventory (CLSI) measure the amount of change and, hence, the amount of stress in an individual's life (Renner & Mackin, 1998, 2002). As you can see in **Table 11–1**, both positive and negative life events can cause stress; and the more of these life events that are experienced, the higher the person's overall "stress rating."

Watch the **Videos** Stress About the Future: Amanda, 22 Years Old & Stress About the Future: Gary, 25 Years Old on **MyPsychLab**

Causes of Stress
% Somewhat/Very Significant

■ 2007   ■ 2008   ■ 2009   ■ 2010

Money
73%
72%
71%
76%

Work
74%
68%
69%
70%

The economy
69%
63%
65%

Family responsibilities
60%
58%
55%
58%

Relationships
(spouse, kids, girl/boyfriend)
59%
51%
55%

Personal health concerns
55%
54%
47%
52%

Housing costs
(e.g., mortgage or rent)
51%
47%
47%
52%

Job stability
42%
44%
49%

Health problems affecting my family
55%
56%
47%
47%

Personal safety
31%
27%
30%

FIGURE 11–1

Sources of Stress in America.

In a 2010 survey, most Americans reported experiencing moderate to severe stress from a variety of every-day stressors.

Source: Clay (2011).

TABLE 11-1 College Life Stress Inventory

Copy the "stress rating" number into the column titled "Your Items" for any item that has happened to you in the last year, and then add these numbers for your total.

Event	Stress Ratings	Your Items	Event	Stress Ratings	Your Items
Being raped	100		Lack of sleep	69	
Finding out that you are HIV positive	100		Change in housing situation (hassles, moves)	69	
Being accused of rape	98		Competing or performing in public	69	
Death of a close friend	97		Getting in a physical fight	66	
Death of a close family member	96		Difficulties with a roommate	66	
Contracting a sexually transmitted disease (other than AIDS)	94		Job changes (applying, new job, work hassles)	65	
Concerns about being pregnant	91		Declaring a major or having concerns about future plans	65	
Finals week	90		A class you hate	62	
Concerns about your partner being pregnant	90		Drinking or use of drugs	61	
Oversleeping for an exam	89		Confrontations with professors	60	
Flunking a class	89		Starting a new semester	58	
Having a boyfriend or girlfriend cheat on you	85		Going on a first date	57	
Ending a steady dating relationship	85		Registration	55	
Serious illness in a close friend or family member	85		Maintaining a steady dating relationship	55	
Financial difficulties	84		Commuting to campus or work, or both	54	
Writing a major term paper	83		Peer pressures	53	
Being caught cheating on a test	83		Being away from home for the first time	53	
Drunk driving	82		Getting sick	52	
Sense of overload in school or work	82		Concerns about your appearance	52	
Two exams in one day	80		Getting straight A's	51	
Cheating on your boyfriend or girlfriend	77		A difficult class that you love	48	
Getting married	76		Making new friends; getting along with friends	47	
Negative consequences of drinking or drug use	75		Attending a fraternity or sorority "rush"	47	
Depression or crisis in your best friend	73		Falling asleep in class	40	
Difficulties with parents	73		Attending an athletic event (e.g., football game)	20	
Talking in front of a class	72		Total	_____	

Source: From "A Life-Stress Instrument for Classroom Use" by M. J. Renner & R. S. Mackin, *Teaching of Psychology,* 25 (1), p. 47. Copyright © 1998 by Lawrence Erlbaum Associates. Reprinted by permission of Copyright Clearance Center on behalf of the publisher.

All major life changes involve a certain amount of stress. This is partly because major life changes typically bring strong emotions, and even joy and elation can arouse the body and begin to take a toll on its resources. Major life events can also be stressful because any new experience requires some adjustment.

pressure A feeling that one must speed up, intensify, or change the direction of one's behavior or live up to a higher standard of performance.

frustration The feeling that occurs when a person is prevented from reaching a goal.

conflict Simultaneous existence of incompatible demands, opportunities, needs, or goals.

In Renner and Mackin's work, college students' scores on the CLSI ranged from a low of 182 to a high of 2,571, but two-thirds had scores between 800 and 1,700. Take a few moments to compute your score and see how you compare. Although there is considerable individual variation in how well people adapt to life changes such as those represented in the CLSI, in general, very high scores correspond to an enhanced risk of developing a stress-induced illness.

Everyday Hassles

How can everyday hassles contribute to stress?

Many of the items on the College Life Stress Inventory concern stress that arises from fairly dramatic, relatively infrequent events. However, many psychologists have pointed out that much stress is generated by "hassles," life's petty annoyances, irritations, and frustrations (M. D. Bennett & Miller, 2006; Safdar & Lay, 2003). Such seemingly minor matters as a having a zipper break, waiting in long lines, or dealing with the normal, daily stressors at work or at school can have a long term impact because they affect family life (Repetti, Wang, & Saxbe, 2009). Richard Lazarus believed that big events matter so much, because they trigger numerous little hassles that eventually overwhelm us with stress. "It is not the large dramatic events that make the difference," Lazarus noted, "but what happens day in and day out, whether provoked by major events or not" (Lazarus, 1981, p. 62). Research confirms that people who have recently suffered a major traumatic event are more likely to experience a sustained stress reaction when exposed to minor stressors or hassles they might usually be able to tolerate (Cross, 2003). In the end, both major and minor events are stressful, since they lead to feelings of pressure, frustration, and conflict.

Pressure occurs when we feel forced to speed up, intensify, or shift direction in our behavior, or when we feel compelled to meet a higher standard of performance. Pressure on the job or in school is a familiar example. In our private lives, trying to live up to social and cultural norms about what we *should* be doing, as well as our family's and friends' expectations, also adds pressure.

Frustration Frustration occurs when a person is prevented from reaching a goal because something or someone stands in the way. *Delays* are annoying because our culture puts great stock in the value of time. *Lack of resources* is frustrating to those who cannot afford the new cars or lavish vacations they desire. *Losses,* such as the end of a love affair or a cherished friendship, cause frustration because they often make us feel helpless, unimportant, or worthless. *Failure* generates intense frustration—and accompanying guilt—in our competitive society. We imagine that if we had done things differently, we might have succeeded; thus, we may feel personally responsible for our setbacks and tend to assume that others blame us for not trying harder or being smarter. *Discrimination* also contributes to frustration: Being denied opportunities or recognition simply because of one's sex, age, religion, sexual orientation, or skin color is extremely frustrating.

Conflict Of all life's troubles, conflict is probably the most common. A boy does not want to go to his aunt's for dinner, but neither does he want to listen to his parents complain if he stays home. A student finds that both the required courses she wanted to take this semester are given at the same hours on the same days. **Conflict** arises when we face two or more incompatible demands, opportunities, needs, or goals. We can never completely resolve conflict. We must either give up some of our goals, modify some of them, delay our pursuit of some of them, or resign ourselves to not attaining all of our goals. Whatever we do, we are bound to experience some frustration, thereby adding to the stressfulness of conflicts.

In the 1930s, Kurt Lewin described two opposite tendencies of conflict: approach and avoidance. When something attracts us, we want to approach it; when something frightens us, we try to avoid it. Lewin (1935) showed how different combinations of these tendencies create three basic types of conflict: approach/approach conflict, avoidance/avoidance conflict, and approach/avoidance conflict. (See the **Summary Table:** "Types of Conflict.")

Much of the stress we experience in our lives arises not from major traumas but from small everyday hassles such as traffic jams, petty arguments, and equipment that fails when we need it most.

Approach/approach conflict occurs when a person is simultaneously attracted to two appealing goals. Being accepted for admission at two equally desirable colleges or universities is an example. The stress that occurs in approach/approach conflict is that in choosing one desirable option, we must give up the other.

The reverse is **avoidance/avoidance conflict,** in which we confront two undesirable or threatening possibilities, neither of which has any positive attributes. When faced with an avoidance/avoidance conflict, people usually try to escape the situation altogether. If escape is impossible, some people vacillate between choosing one threat or the other, like a baseball player's being caught in a rundown between first and second base, while other people simply wait for events to resolve their conflict for them.

An **approach/avoidance conflict,** in which a person is both attracted to and repelled by the same goal, is the most common form of conflict. The closer we come to a goal with good and bad features, the stronger grow our desires both to approach and to avoid, but according to Lewin the tendency to avoid increases more rapidly than the tendency to approach. In an approach/avoidance conflict, therefore, we approach the goal until we reach the point at which the tendency to approach equals the tendency to avoid the goal. Afraid to go any closer, we stop and vacillate, making no choice at all, until the situation changes. A familiar example is a couple whose only quarrel is that one wants to get married, but the other is unsure. The second person wants to continue the relationship (approach), but is wary of making a life-long commitment (avoidance).

THINKING CRITICALLY ABOUT . . .

Road Rage and You

As our highways have become more congested, incidents of aggressive driving—popularly known as "road rage"—have become more common and more dangerous (R. E. Mann et al., 2007). One survey found that 9 in 10 drivers had been threatened by speeding, tailgating, failure to yield right of way, lane changes without signaling, weaving, cutting in, and rude, provocative gestures and comments during the previous year. Psychologist Leon James (James & Nahl, 2000) has studied driving patterns for more than a decade. One of the techniques Professor James uses in his research is to ask people to record their experiences and feelings (a technique called "self-witnessing") when they are driving in traffic. At first he was shocked by how often ordinarily polite, considerate people became intolerant and antisocial when they got behind the wheel—what he calls a "Jekyll and Hyde effect." Try recording your thoughts as you drive (and be honest); ask several friends to do the same. Do you find James' "Jekyll and Hyde effect"?

There are three main theories of road rage:

- The **crowding** *hypothesis:* More cars→more traffic→more frustration→more stress→more anger→more hostility→more violence.

- The **cultural** *hypothesis:* Americans learn aggressive and dangerous driving patterns as children, by watching their parents and other adults behind the wheel, and by viewing risky driving in movies and television commercials.

- The **displacement** *hypothesis:* People are more likely to lose their tempers while driving if they have suffered recent blows to their self-esteem, and seek to recoup their sense of worth by winning battles on the road.

Which theory do you find most convincing? Why? How might you go about determining which has the most merit?

Self-Imposed Stress

How do we create stress?

So far, we have considered external sources of stress. Sometimes, however, people create problems for themselves quite apart from stressful events in their environment (Henig, 2009). Some psychologists argue that many people carry around a set of irrational, self-defeating beliefs that add unnecessarily to the normal stresses of living (A. Ellis & Harper, 1975;

SUMMARY TABLE	TYPES OF CONFLICT
Type of Conflict	**Nature of Conflict**
Approach/approach	You are attracted to two incompatible goals at the same time.
Avoidance/avoidance	Repelled by two undesirable alternatives at the same time, you are inclined to escape, although other factors often prevent such an escape.
Approach/avoidance	You are both repelled by, and attracted to, the same goal.

approach/approach conflict According to Lewin, the result of simultaneous attraction to two appealing possibilities, neither of which has any negative qualities.

avoidance/avoidance conflict According to Lewin, the result of facing a choice between two undesirable possibilities, neither of which has any positive qualities.

approach/avoidance conflict According to Lewin, the result of being simultaneously attracted to and repelled by the same goal.

T. Lucas, Alexander, Firestone, & Lebreton, 2008). For example, some people believe that "I must be competent, adequate, and successful at everything I do." Still other people believe that "it is disastrous if everything doesn't go the way I would like." These people feel upset, miserable, and unhappy when things don't go perfectly. As described in Chapter 12, "Psychological Disorders," self-defeating thoughts like these can contribute to depression (Beck, 1984; Young, Rygh, Weinberger, & Beck, 2008). ⊙→

⊙→ **Simulate** the **Experiment** How Stressed Are You? on **MyPsychLab**

Stress and Individual Differences

Do people who are resistant to stress share certain traits?

Just as some people create more stress for themselves than others do, some people—such as Austin Whitney whose story opened this chapter—cope well with major life stresses, whereas others are thrown by even minor problems. What accounts for these differences? In part, the answer is to be found in the way we interpret our situation (Suzuki, 2006). Seeing a challenging situation as an opportunity for success rather than for failure is typically associated with positive emotions such as eagerness, excitement, and confidence (Bouckenooghe, Buelens, Fontaine, & Vanderheyden, 2005). People's overall view of the world also affects how well they cope with stress. *Optimists,* who tend to appraise events as challenges rather than threats, are generally better able to cope with stressful events than are *pessimists,* who are more likely to dwell on failure (Ben-Zur, 2008; C. Peterson, 2000). Similarly, people with an *internal locus of control* see themselves as being able to affect their situations while those with an *external locus of control* are more likely to appraise events negatively (Ryan & Deci, 2000) (see Chapter 10, "Personality," for a discussion of locus of control).

Hardiness and Resilience Even after experiencing a major disaster, only a minority of people experience serious psychological harm (Bonanno, Brewin, Kaniasty, & La Greca, 2010). People with a trait we call *hardiness* tolerate stress exceptionally well or seem to thrive on it (Kobasa, 1979; Leyro, Zvolensky, & Bernstein, 2010; Maddi 2008; Zvolensky, Vulanovic, Bernstein, & Leyro, 2010). They also feel that they control their own destinies and are confident about being able to cope with change (Kessler, Price, & Wortman, 1985; S. E. Taylor, 2003). Conversely, individuals who have little confidence that they can master new situations and can exercise control over events feel powerless and apathetic (C. Peterson, Maier, & Seligman, 1993b). (Recall our discussion of learned helplessness in Chapter 5, "Learning.") Even when change offers new opportunities for taking charge of their situation, they remain passive.

Psychologists are also interested in *resilience:* the ability to "bounce back," recovering one's self-confidence, good spirits, and hopeful attitude after extreme or prolonged stress (Beasley, Thompson, & Davidson, 2003; Bonanno, Galea, Bucciarelli, & Vlahov, 2006). In one study, half of the people in a sample of those were actually inside the World Trade Center at the time of the terrorist attacks showed only mild, short-lived symptoms of stress (Bonannon et al., 2010). Resilience may partially explain why some children who grow up in adverse circumstances (such as extreme poverty, dangerous neighborhoods, abusive parents, or exposure to drugs and alcohol) become well-adjusted adults, whereas others remain troubled—and frequently get into trouble—throughout their lives (Bonanno, 2004; Feinauer, Hilton, & Callahan, 2003; Leifer, Kilbane, & Kalick, 2004). In 2010, the U. S. Army initiated a Comprehensive Soldier Fitness (CSF) program designed to enhance resilience among soldiers, family members and civilians in the Department of

Why do some children living in adverse conditions remain troubled throughout their lives, while more resilient children in the same circumstances become well-adjusted adults? Here, the children of migrant workers in Beijing, China, play in front of their ramshackle housing.

the Army. It works by assessing resiliency strengths, providing online self-help modules based on the results of the assessment, training master resilience trainers, and requiring resilience training at every Army leader development school (Casey, 2011). This is a ground-breaking program based on the belief that resilience can be learned. Researchers are monitoring the program closely to determine whether, in fact, it is effective (Lester, McBride, Bliese, & Adler, 2011). The entire January, 2001, issue of *American Psychologist* was devoted to describing this program in depth.

✔•⎯ **Study** and **Review** on **MyPsychLab**

CHECK YOUR UNDERSTANDING

Indicate whether the following statements are true (T) or false (F):

1. ____ Change that results from "good" events, like marriage or job promotion, does not produce stress.
2. ____ Stressful events almost always involve changes in our lives.
3. ____ Big events in life are always much more stressful than everyday hassles.
4. ____ Optimists are generally better able to cope with stress than are pessimists.

Answers 1. (F); 2. (T); 3. (F); 4. (T).

APPLY YOUR UNDERSTANDING

1. Bob wants to go to graduate school in pharmacology, but he is very concerned about the intense studying that will be required to complete the curriculum. Bob is faced with a(n)
   a. offensive/defensive coping dilemma.
   b. direct/defensive coping dilemma.
   c. avoidance/avoidance conflict.
   d. approach/avoidance conflict.
2. LaShondra is a caterer. She has just finished the prep work for a 15-person dinner that is scheduled for 7:30 P.M. that night. At 4:00 P.M., the client calls to tell her that there will actually be 30 people, and they need to start dinner at 7:00 P.M. instead of 7:30 P.M. LaShondra feels stressed because this call creates
   a. frustration.
   b. pressure.
   c. self-imposed stress.
   d. conflict.

Answers: 1. d. 2. b.

COPING WITH STRESS

What is the difference between direct coping and defensive coping?

Whatever its source, stress requires that we cope—that is, it requires us to make cognitive and behavioral efforts to manage psychological stress. There are many different ways of coping with stress, but two general types of adjustment stand out: direct coping and defensive coping.

Direct Coping

What are three strategies that deal directly with stress?

Direct coping refers to intentional efforts to change an uncomfortable situation. Direct coping tends to be problem oriented and to focus on the immediate issue. (See "Applying Psychology: Coping with Stress at College.") When we are threatened, frustrated, or in conflict, we have three basic choices for coping directly: *confrontation, compromise, or withdrawal.*

LEARNING OBJECTIVES

- Compare and contrast direct coping and defensive coping. Describe and give an example of the three strategies for coping directly with stress. Describe and give an example of the major ways of coping defensively.

- Explain how socioeconomic status, culture, and gender affect levels of stress and ways of coping with stress.

confrontation Acknowledging a stressful situation directly and attempting to find a solution to the problem or to attain the difficult goal.

compromise Deciding on a more realistic solution or goal when an ideal solution or goal is not practical.

Consider the case of a woman who has worked hard at her job for years, but has not been promoted. She learns that she has not advanced due to her stated unwillingness to temporarily move to a branch office in another part of the country to acquire more experience. Her unwillingness to move stands between her and her goal of advancing in her career. She has several choices, which we will explore.

Confrontation Acknowledging that there is a problem for which a solution must be found, attacking the problem head-on, and pushing resolutely toward the goal is called **confrontation.** This might involve learning new skills, enlisting other people's help, finding other things, or just trying harder. Or it might require steps to change either oneself or the situation. The woman who wants to advance her career might try to persuade her boss that even though she has never worked in a branch office, she nevertheless has acquired enough experience to handle a better job in the main office.

Confrontation may also include expressions of anger. Anger may be effective, especially if we really have been treated unfairly and if we express our anger with restraint instead of exploding in rage.

Compromise **Compromise** is one of the most common and effective ways of coping directly with conflict or frustration. We often recognize that we cannot have everything we want and that we cannot expect others to do just what we would like them to do. In such cases, we may decide to settle for less than we originally sought. For example, the woman might agree to take a less desirable position that doesn't require relocation.

APPLYING PSYCHOLOGY

Coping with Stress at College

It is 2 weeks before finals, and you must write two papers and study for four exams. You are very worried. You are not alone. There are many techniques you can teach yourself to help cope with the pressures of college life.

1. Plan ahead, do not procrastinate, and get things done well before deadlines. Start work on large projects well in advance.
2. Exercise; do whatever activity you enjoy.
3. Listen to your favorite music, watch a television show, or go to a movie as a study break.
4. Talk to other people.
5. Meditate or use other relaxation techniques.
6. Seek out a stress-reduction workshop. Many colleges and universities offer these.

One very effective technique is to make a list of *everything* you have to do, right down to doing the laundry, getting birthday cards for family and friends, and so on. Then star the highest-priority tasks—the ones that *really* have to be done first or those that will take a long time. Use your available time to work on *only* those tasks. Cross off high-priority tasks as they are done, add new tasks as they arrive, and continually adjust the priorities so that the most critical tasks are always starred.

This technique serves various purposes. It removes the fear that you'll forget something important, because everything is on a single sheet of paper. It helps you realize that things are not as overwhelming as they might otherwise seem. (The list is finite, and there are probably only a few things that truly are high-priority tasks.) It lets you focus your energy on the most important tasks and makes it easy to avoid spending time on less important things that might drift into your attention. Finally, it assures you that you are doing everything possible to do the most important things in your life, and if you don't manage to do them all, you can truly say, "There's no way I could have done any better; it simply wasn't possible in the time available." Actually, that will seldom be the case. Usually the highest priority tasks get done and the lower priority tasks simply wait, often for weeks or months, after which you wonder how important they really are if they always come out on the bottom of the totem pole.

Withdrawal In some circumstances, the most effective way of coping with stress is to withdraw from the situation. The woman whose promotion depends on temporarily relocating might quit her job and join another company. When we realize that our adversary is more powerful than we are, that there is no way we can effectively modify ourselves or the situation, that there is no possible compromise, and that any form of confrontation would be self-defeating, **withdrawal** is a positive and realistic response. However, withdrawal may be a mixed blessing. Perhaps the greatest danger of coping by withdrawal is that the person will come to avoid all similar situations. The woman who did not want to take a job at her company's branch office might not only quit her present job, but might withdraw entirely from the work world leaving her in a poor position to take advantage of an effective alternative if one should come along.

Defensive Coping

What are the major ways of coping defensively?

Thus far, we have discussed coping with stress that arises from recognizable sources. But there are times when we either cannot identify or cannot deal directly with the source of our stress. For example, you return to a parking lot to discover that your car has been damaged. In other cases, a problem is so emotionally threatening that it cannot be faced directly: Perhaps someone close to you is terminally ill, or after 4 years of hard work, you have failed to gain admission to medical school and may have to abandon your plan to become a doctor.

In such situations, people may turn to **defense mechanisms** as a way of coping. Defense mechanisms are techniques for *deceiving* oneself about the causes of a stressful situation to reduce pressure, frustration, conflict, and anxiety. The self-deceptive nature of such adjustments led Freud to conclude that they are entirely unconscious, but not all psychologists agree. Often we realize that we are pushing something out of our memory or are otherwise deceiving ourselves. For example, all of us have blown up at someone when we *knew* we were really angry at someone else. Whether defense mechanisms operate consciously or unconsciously, they provide a means of coping with stress that might otherwise be unbearable.

Denial **Denial** is the refusal to acknowledge a painful or threatening reality. Although denial can be a positive response in some situations, it clearly is not in other situations. Frequent drug users who insist that they are merely "experimenting" with drugs are using denial.

Repression The most common mechanism for blocking out painful feelings and memories is **repression,** a form of forgetting to exclude painful thoughts from consciousness. Soldiers who break down in the field often block out the memory of the experiences that led to their collapse (P. Brown, van der Hart, & Graafland, 1999).

Denial and repression are the most basic defense mechanisms. In denial, we block out situations that we can't handle; in repression, we block out unacceptable impulses or stressful thoughts. These psychic strategies form the basis for several other defensive ways of coping.

Projection If a problem cannot be denied or completely repressed, we may be able to distort its nature so that we can handle it more easily through **projection:** the attribution of one's repressed motives, ideas, or feelings onto others. A corporate executive who feels guilty about the way he rose to power may project his own ruthless ambition onto his colleagues. He simply is doing his job, he believes, whereas his associates are all crassly ambitious and consumed with power.

Identification The reverse of projection is **identification:** taking on the characteristics of someone else, so that we can vicariously share in that person's triumphs and overcome feeling inadequate. The admired person's actions, that is, become a substitute for our own.

withdrawal Avoiding a situation when other forms of coping are not practical.

defense mechanisms Self-deceptive techniques for reducing stress, including denial, repression, projection, identification, regression, intellectualization, reaction formation, displacement, and sublimation.

denial Refusal to acknowledge a painful or threatening reality.

repression Excluding uncomfortable thoughts, feelings, and desires from consciousness.

projection Attributing one's repressed motives, feelings, or wishes to others.

identification Taking on the characteristics of someone else to avoid feeling incompetent.

regression Reverting to childlike behavior and defenses.

intellectualization Thinking abstractly about stressful problems as a way of detaching oneself from them.

reaction formation Expression of exaggerated ideas and emotions that are the opposite of one's repressed beliefs or feelings.

displacement Shifting repressed motives and emotions from an original object to a substitute object.

sublimation Redirecting repressed motives and feelings into more socially acceptable channels.

A parent with unfulfilled career ambitions may share emotionally in a son's or daughter's professional success. Identification is often used as a form of self-defense in situations in which a person feels utterly helpless, for example, in a hostage situation. To survive, victims sometimes seek to please their captors and may identify with them as a way of defensively coping with unbearable and inescapable stress. This is called the "Stockholm Syndrome" (Cassidy, 2002), after four Swedes who were held captive in a bank vault for nearly a week, but defended their captors upon release.

Regression People under stress may revert to childlike behavior through a process called **regression**. Some psychologists say people regress because an adult cannot stand feeling helpless. Conversely, children feel helpless and dependent every day, so becoming more childlike can make total dependency or helplessness more bearable. Regression is sometimes used as a manipulative strategy, too, albeit an immature and inappropriate one. Adults who cry or throw temper tantrums when their arguments fail may expect those around them to react sympathetically, as their parents did when they were children.

Intellectualization **Intellectualization** is a subtle form of denial in which we detach ourselves from our feelings about our problems by analyzing them intellectually and thinking of them almost as if they concerned other people. Parents who start out intending to discuss their child's difficulties in a new school and then find themselves engaged in a sophisticated discussion of educational philosophy may be intellectualizing a very upsetting situation. They appear to be dealing with their problems, but in fact they are not, because they have cut themselves off from their disturbing emotions.

Reaction Formation The term **reaction formation** refers to a behavioral form of denial in which people express, with exaggerated intensity, ideas and emotions that are the opposite of their own. *Exaggeration* is the clue to this behavior. The man who extravagantly praises a rival may be covering up jealousy over his opponent's success.

Displacement **Displacement** involves the redirection of repressed motives and emotions from their original objects to substitute objects. A classic example is the person who has an extremely frustrating and stressful day at work and then yells at his wife and children when he gets home.

Sublimation **Sublimation** refers to transforming repressed motives or feelings into more socially acceptable forms. Anger and aggressiveness, for instance, might be channeled into competitiveness in business or sports. A strong and persistent desire for attention might be transformed into an interest in acting or politics.

Does defensive coping mean that a person is immature, unstable, or on the edge of a "breakdown"? Is direct coping adaptive, and is defensive coping maladaptive? Not necessarily (Cramer, 2000; Rhodewalt & Vohs, 2005). In some cases of prolonged and severe stress, lower level defenses such as denial may not only contribute to our overall ability to adjust but also may be essential to survival. Over the long run, however, defense mechanisms are maladaptive if they interfere with a person's ability to deal directly with a problem or they create more problems than they solve.

ENDURING ISSUES

Person–Situation   Coping Strategies

Individuals use various coping strategies in different combinations and in different ways to deal with stressful events. It is tempting to conclude that styles of coping, like personality, reside within the individual. Yet, a good deal of research indicates that how much stress people encounter and how they cope depend to a significant degree on the environment in which they live (Almeida, 2005; Prokopcává, 2004). ■

Socioeconomic, Cultural, and Gender Differences in Coping with Stress

Who experiences the most stress?

Consider the impact of socioeconomic status on stress and coping. In poor neighborhoods, addressing even the basic tasks of living is stressful. Thus, poor people have to deal with more stress than people who are financially secure (M. A. Barnett, 2008; Gallo, de los Monteros, & Shivpuri, 2009). Moreover, people in lower socioeconomic classes often have fewer means for coping with hardship and stress—fewer people to turn to and fewer community resources to draw on for support during stressful times (Gallo et al., 2009; Hammack, Robinson, Crawford, & Li, 2004). The cumulative effect of these factors over a lifetime helps to explain why stress often takes a greater toll on people in lower socioeconomic classes (Kasper et al., 2008).

Studies have also found that the way individuals cope with stress varies for people from different cultural backgrounds. For example, when stressed, most European Americans seek *explicit* social support from their friends, such as discussing the source of their stress and seeking advice and emotional solace. In contrast Asian Americans are generally more reluctant than European Americans to seek explicit social support because they are concerned about the potential negative relationship consequences that may occur if they disclose the source of their stress. Instead, they are more likely to seek *implicit* social support which involves simply being in close contact with others, without disclosing the source of their stress (H. S. Kim, Sherman, & Taylor, 2008; S. E. Taylor, Welch, Kim, & Sherman, 2007).

Research also indicates that when faced with equally stressful situations, men and women often use different coping strategies (Bellman, Forster, Still, & Cooper, 2003; Kort-Butler, 2009; Narayanan, Shanker, & Spector, 1999; Patton & Goddard, 2006). Women are more likely than men to evaluate the stressful situation positively, to gather information in order to reduce uncertainty, to engage in distracting activities, and turn to prayer. Men are more likely to keep their feelings to themselves, avoid thinking about the situation, and engage in problem-solving to reduce the stress (Spence, Nelson, & Lachlan, 2010). Women under stress are also more likely than men to tend to their young and to seek contact and support from others (particularly other women) rather than to behave aggressively. This "tend-and-befriend" response may be linked to the hormone *oxytocin*, which is linked to maternal behavior and social affiliation. Under stress, both males and females secrete oxytocin, but the male hormone testosterone seems to reduce its effect, whereas the female hormone estrogen amplifies it (S. E. Taylor, 2006). A new line of research suggests that the tend-and-befriend response may also be the result of evolutionary adaptations. In simple terms, when our hunter/gatherer ancestors were threatened with danger, it may have been most adaptive for the species if the men responded with aggression and women responded by guarding the children and seeking social support from others (S. E. Taylor et al., 2000; S. E. Taylor, 2006; Turton & Campbell, 2005; Volpe, 2004).

✔●—[**Study** and **Review** on **MyPsychLab**

CHECK YOUR UNDERSTANDING

1. There are two general types of coping: _____ and _____.
2. Confronting problems, compromising, or withdrawing from the situation entirely are all forms of _____ coping.
3. _____ coping is a means of dealing with situations that people feel unable to resolve.

Answers: 1. direct, defensive. 2. direct. 3. Defensive.

1. You're approaching a deadline by which a project must be finished. Your stress level rises when you realize that it will be nearly impossible to meet the deadline. Which of the following is NOT one of your choices for coping directly with the stressful situation?

   a. trying harder and enlisting the help of others

   b. denying that you will be unable to finish the project on time

   c. admitting defeat and withdrawing from the situation

   d. working out an arrangement through which you submit part of the project on time and get additional time for submitting the rest of it

2. Bill is very frustrated because he did quite poorly on several midterm exams. After returning from an especially difficult exam, he yells at his roommate for leaving clothes strewn around the floor. Bill's reaction is most likely the result of which defense mechanism?

   a. projection

   b. reaction formation

   c. sublimation

   d. displacement

Answers: 1. b. 2. d.

- Explain why "experiencing too much stress over too long a period can contribute to physical problems." In your explanation, include Cannon's theory of the fight-or-flight response and the several stages of Selye's general adaptation syndrome.
- Summarize the evidence that shows chronic stress can contribute to heart disease. Include Type A and Type D personalities in your summary.
- Summarize the research evidence that "stress also affects the functioning of the immune system."

Watch the **Video** The Big Picture: Health Psychology on **MyPsychLab**

health psychology A subfield of psychology concerned with the relationship between psychological factors and physical health and illness.

HOW STRESS AFFECTS HEALTH

What long-lasting effects of stress do we need to be concerned with?

Experiencing too much stress over a long period can contribute to physical problems as well as psychological ones (Kendall-Tackett, 2010). For example, being discriminated against because of one's sex, religion, sexual orientation, or skin color is often a life-long source of stress (Jackson, Knight, & Rafferty, 2010). Research shows that perceived discrimination is linked to mental health problems (depression, distress, anxiety) as well as physical health problems (high blood pressure, poor health, obesity, substance abuse) (Hatzenbuehler, 2009; Okazaki, 2009; Pascoe & Richman, 2009). **Health psychology** focuses on how the mind and body interact. Specifically, health psychologists seek to understand how psychological factors influence wellness and illness. Numerous studies have found that people suffering from acute or chronic stress are likely to be more vulnerable to everything from the common cold to an increased risk for heart disease (S. Cohen et al., 1998; R. O. Stanley & Burrows, 2008; L. M. Thornton, 2005). As you will learn, new research is uncovering the biological mechanisms that link stress to lowered immunity and poor health. The challenge for health psychologists is to find ways to prevent stress from becoming physically and emotionally debilitating, and to *promote* healthy behavior and well-being.

Physicians and psychologists agree that stress management is an essential part of programs to prevent disease and promote health. To understand how our body responds to stress, recall that in Chapter 2 ("The Biological Basis of Behavior"), we discussed how the sympathetic nervous system reacts when you are intensely aroused (see p. 65). Your heart begins to pound, your respiration increases, you develop a queasy feeling in your stomach and your glands start pumping stress hormones such as *adrenaline* and *norepinephrine* into your blood. Other organs also respond; for example, the liver increases the available sugar in the blood for extra energy, and the bone marrow increases the white blood cell count to combat infection.

The noted physiologist Walter Cannon (1929) first described the basic elements of this sequence of events as a *fight-or-flight response,* because it appeared that its primary purpose was to prepare an animal to respond to external threats by either attacking or fleeing from them. The adaptive significance of the fight-or-flight response in people was obvious to Cannon, because it assured the survival of early humans when faced with genuine danger. However, Cannon also observed that this same physiological mobilization occurred regardless of the nature of the threat. In our everyday lives, stressors may be present over long periods of time. As a result, your body may remain on alert for a long time as well. Since the human body is not designed to be exposed for long periods to the powerful biological changes that accompany alarm and mobilization, when stress is prolonged, we are likely to experience some kind of physical disorder.

Extending Cannon's theory of the fight-or-flight response, the Canadian physiologist Hans Selye (pronounced SAY-lee) (1907–1982) contended that we react to physical and psychological stress in three stages that he collectively called the **general adaptation syndrome (GAS)** (Selye, 1956, 1976). These three stages are alarm reaction, resistance, and exhaustion.

Stage 1, *alarm reaction,* is the first response to stress. It begins when the body recognizes that it must fend off some physical or psychological danger. Activity of the sympathetic nervous system is increased and the body is ready to meet the danger. At the alarm stage, we might use either direct or defensive coping strategies. If neither of those approaches reduces the stress, we eventually enter the second stage of adaptation.

general adaptation syndrome (GAS) According to Selye, the three stages the body passes through as it adapts to stress: alarm reaction, resistance, and exhaustion.

ENDURING ISSUES

Mind–Body   Psychological Stress and Physical Illness

How exactly does psychological stress lead to or influence physical illness? First, when we experience stress, our heart, lungs, nervous system, and other physiological systems are forced to work harder. Second, stress has a powerful negative effect on the body's immune system, and prolonged stress can destroy the body's ability to defend itself from disease. Indirectly, stress may also lead to unhealthy behaviors such as smoking, drinking, overeating or skipping meals, not getting enough exercise, and avoiding regular medical checkups, that can, in turn, lead to illness and poor overall health. ■

During Stage 2, *resistance,* physical symptoms and other signs of strain appear. We intensify our use of both direct and defensive coping techniques. If we succeed in reducing the stress, we return to a more normal state. But if the stress is extreme or prolonged, we may turn in desperation to inappropriate coping techniques and cling to them rigidly, despite evidence that they are not working. When that happens, physical and emotional resources are further depleted, and signs of psychological and physical wear and tear become even more apparent.

In the third stage, *exhaustion,* we draw on increasingly ineffective defense mechanisms in a desperate attempt to bring the stress under control. Some people lose touch with reality and show signs of emotional disorder or mental illness at this stage. Others show signs of "burnout," including the inability to concentrate, irritability, procrastination, and a cynical belief that nothing is worthwhile (Y. Li & Hou, 2005; Maslach & Leiter, 1997). Physical symptoms such as skin or stomach problems may erupt, and some victims of burnout turn to alcohol, drugs, or overeating to cope with the stress-induced exhaustion. While these unhealthy behaviors may help to reduce stress and preserve mental health in the short-term, they have long-term health consequences (Jackson et al., 2010). If the stress continues, the person may suffer irreparable physical or psychological damage or even death.

Stress and Heart Disease

How is Type A behavior related to heart disease?

Stress is a major contributing factor in the development of coronary heart disease (CHD), the leading cause of death and disability in the United States (Deary, Weiss, & Batty, 2010; Esler, Schwarz, & Alvarenga, 2008; Rosengren et al., 2004). A great deal of research has been done, for example, on people who exhibit the *Type A behavior pattern*—that is, who respond to life events with impatience, hostility, competitiveness, urgency, and constant striving (M. Friedman & Rosenman, 1959). Type A people are distinguished from more easygoing *Type B* people. The two cardiologists who first identified the characteristics of Type A personalities were convinced that this behavior pattern was most likely to surface

Evidence appears to show that the chronic anger and hostility associated with Type A behavior can predict heart disease.

Watch the Video Thinking Like a Psychologist: Personality and Health on MyPsychLab

in stressful situations. A number of studies have shown that Type A behavior does indeed predict CHD (Carmona, Sanz, & Marin, 2002; T. Q. Miller, Turner, Tindale, Posavac, & Dugoni, 1991). For example, when Type A personalities were subjected to harassment or criticism, their heart rate and blood pressure were much higher than those of Type B personalities under the same circumstances (Griffiths & Dancaster, 1995; Lyness, 1993). Both high heart rate and high blood pressure are known to contribute to CHD.

There is also considerable evidence that *chronic anger* and *hostility* predict heart disease (Mohan, 2006; R. B. Williams, 2001). For example, people who scored high on an anger scale were 2.5 times more likely to have heart attacks or sudden cardiac deaths than their calmer peers (Janice Williams et al., 2000).

Depression, too, appears to increase the risk of heart disease and premature death (Mitka, 2008; Rugulies, 2002). In fact, recent studies have identified a personality type that incorporates the precise elements of depression that are most predictive of heart disease. Called *Type D,* or *Distressed Personality,* it is characterized by depression, negative emotions, and social inhibition. The Type D personality is linked to heart disease because when stressed, people with a Type D personality produce excessive amounts of cortisol, which damages the heart and blood vessels over time (Deary et al., 2010; Denollet, 2005; Huang, Yao, Huang, Guo, & Yang, 2008; Sher, 2004).

Because long-term stress increases the likelihood of developing CHD, reducing stress has become part of the treatment used to slow the progress of hardening of the arteries, which can lead to a heart attack. A very low-fat diet and stress-management techniques, such as yoga and deep relaxation, have been effective in treating this disease (Langosch, Budde, & Linden, 2007; Ornish et al., 1998). Counseling designed to diminish the intensity of time urgency and hostility in patients with Type A behavior has also been moderately successful in reducing the incidence of CHD (M. Friedman et al., 1996; Kop, 2005).

Stress and the Immune System

Why do so many students get sick during finals?

Scientists have long suspected that stress also affects the functioning of the immune system. Recall that the immune system is strongly affected by hormones and signals from the brain. The field of **psychoneuroimmunology (PNI)** studies the interaction between stress on the one hand and immune, endocrine, and nervous system activity on the other (Byrne-Davis & Vedhara, 2008; Dougall & Baum, 2004; Irwin, 2008). Chronic stress—from caring for a sick spouse or elderly parent (Norton, 2010), living in poverty, depression (Kiecolt-Glaser & Glaser, 2002; Oltmanns & Emery, 1998), or even living with a spouse with cancer (Mortimer, Sephton, Kimerling, Butler, Bernstein, & Spiegel, 2005)—has been linked to suppressed functioning of the immune system (Irwin, 2002). To the extent that stress disrupts the functioning of the immune system, it can impair health (S. Cohen & Herbert, 1996; Walls, 2008).

Increased stress has been shown to increase susceptibility to influenza in both mice and humans (E. A. Murphy et al., 2008; Tseng, Padgett, Dhabhar, Engler, & Sheridan, 2005) and upper respiratory infections, such as the common cold (S. Cohen, 1996; S. Cohen et al., 2002). For example, volunteers who reported being under severe stress and who had experienced two or more major stressful events during the previous year were more likely to develop a cold when they were exposed to a cold virus (S. Cohen, Tyrrell, & Smith, 1991). A control group of volunteers who reported lower levels of stress were less likely to develop cold symptoms even though they were equally exposed to the virus. People who report experiencing a lot of positive emotions (for example, happiness, pleasure, or relaxation) are also less likely to develop colds when exposed to the virus than those who report a lot of negative emotions (for example, anxiety, hostility, or depression) (S. Cohen, Doyle, Turner, Alper, & Skoner, 2003a).

Psychoneuroimmunologists have also established a possible relationship between stress and cancer (Herberman, 2002). Stress does not cause cancer, but to the extent that stress impairs the immune system, cancerous cells may be better able to establish

psychoneuroimmunology (PNI) A new field that studies the interaction between stress on the one hand and immune, endocrine, and nervous system activity on the other.

themselves and spread throughout the body. Establishing a direct link between stress and cancer in humans is difficult. For obvious reasons, researchers cannot conduct controlled experiments with human participants. Some early research showed a *correlation* between stress and incidence of cancer (McKenna, Zevon, Corn, & Rounds, 1999; A. O'Leary, 1990), but more recent research has not confirmed these findings (Maunsell, Brisson, Mondor, Verreault, & Deschenes, 2001). In addition, although several new cancer drugs work by boosting the immune system, even this does not necessarily mean that damage to the immune system makes people more vulnerable to cancer (Azar, 1999). Thus, the jury is still out on whether stress contributes to cancer in humans (Reiche, Morimoto, & Nunes, 2005).

Regardless, many medical practitioners agree that psychologists can play a vital role in improving the quality of life for cancer patients (Joanna Smith, Richardson, & Hoffman, 2005). For example, women faced with the diagnosis of late-stage breast cancer understandably experience high levels of depression and mental stress. Many physicians now routinely recommend that their breast-cancer patients attend group therapy sessions, which are effective in increasing the quality of life, reducing depression, mental stress, hostility, insomnia, and the perception of pain (Giese-Davis et al., 2002; Goodwin et al., 2001; Quesnel, Savard, Simard, Ivers, & Morin, 2003; Witek-Janusek et al., 2008). Some initial reports also showed that breast-cancer patients who attended group therapy sessions actually had an increased survival rate (Spiegel & Moore, 1997), although more recent investigations have not supported this claim (DeAngelis, 2002; Edelman, Lemon, Bell, & Kidman, 1999; Goodwin et al., 2001).

STAYING HEALTHY

What two key areas can people control to help themselves stay healthy?

Stress may be part of life, but there are proven ways to reduce the negative impact of stress on your body and your health. The best method, not surprisingly, is to reduce stress. A healthy lifestyle can also prepare you to cope with the unavoidable stress in your life.

Reduce Stress

What steps can people take to reduce stress?

Scientists do not have a simple explanation for the common cold, much less cancer. But they do have advice on how to reduce stress and stay healthy.

Calm Down *Exercise* is a good beginning. Running, walking, biking, swimming, or other aerobic exercise lowers your resting heart rate and blood pressure, so that your body does not react as strongly to stress and recovers more quickly. As we discuss later, exercise is also part of a healthy lifestyle. Moreover, numerous studies show that people who exercise regularly and are physically fit have higher self-esteem than those who do not; are less likely to feel anxious, depressed, or irritable; and have fewer aches and pains, as well as fewer colds (Annesi, 2005; Biddle, 2000; Nguyen-Michel, Unger, Hamilton, & Spruijt-Metz, 2006; Sonstroem, 1997).

LEARNING OBJECTIVES

- Describe the four proven ways to reduce stress.
- Explain the role of proactive coping, positive reappraisal, and humor in reducing stress.
- Describe the four elements of a healthy lifestyle.

THINKING CRITICALLY ABOUT . . .

Genetics and Cancer

According to a report in the *New England Journal of Medicine*, the chances of developing cancer are largely determined by lifestyle, not inheritance (K. L. Lichtenstein et al., 2000). In one of the largest studies of its kind, researchers analyzed longitudinal data on 44,788 pairs of Scandinavian twins born between 1870 and 1958. The data revealed that 10,803 of these individuals developed cancers. Even when one identical twin developed cancer, the chances that the other twin got the same cancer were very low. The authors concluded "that the overwhelming contributor to the causation of cancer in the populations of twins that we studied was the environment" (p. 80).

- How much confidence do you have in this report? Why?
- If this report is correct, what can you do to reduce the risk that you will develop cancer?
- Would you recommend that someone with a family history of cancer nonetheless undergo genetic tests, if and when these are available, to determine whether they are also likely to develop cancer?

Doing yoga exercises regularly is a direct way of coping with stress that can enhance feelings of well-being while improving balance and flexibility.

Research has also shown that expressive writing can alleviate stress and help one cope with a difficult situation. While it is unclear if writing about our feelings provides a safe outlet for our emotions, or helps us focus our thoughts on finding solutions, dozens of research studies have shown that expressing one's feelings in writing can be an effective way to reduce stress (Pennebaker & Chung, 2007; Smyth, Hockemeyer, & Tulloch, 2008). Expressive writing has even been shown to be of value when used as a therapeutic technique, reducing the symptoms of depression and stress in women suffering from intimate partner violence (Koopman, Ismailji, Holmes, Classen, Palesh, & Wales, 2005).

Relaxation training is another stress buster. A number of studies indicate that relaxation techniques lower stress (Pothier, 2002) and improve immune functioning (Andersen, Kiecolt-Glaser, & Glaser, 1994; Antoni, 2003). Relaxation is more than flopping on the couch with the TV remote, however. Healthful physical relaxation requires lying quietly and alternately tensing and relaxing every voluntary muscle in your body—from your head to your toes—to learn how to recognize muscle tension, as well as to learn how to relax your body. Breathing exercises can have the same effect: If you are tense, deep, rhythmic breathing is difficult, but learning to do so relieves bodily tension. (See also Chapter 4, "States of Consciousness," for a discussion of meditation, and Chapter 5, "Learning," for a discussion of biofeedback, both of which can be useful in relaxing and reducing stress.)

Reach Out A strong network of friends and family who provide *social support* can help to maintain good health (S. Cohen, Doyle, Turner, Alper, & Skoner, 2003b; Haslam, Jetten, Postmes, & Haslam, 2009; Jetten, Haslam, & Haslam, 2011; Uchino, 2009). Exactly why the presence of a strong social support system is related to health is not fully understood. Some researchers contend that social support may directly affect our response to stress and health by producing physiological changes in endocrine, cardiac, and immune functioning (Uchino, Uno, & Holt-Lunstad, 1999). Whatever the underlying mechanism, most people can remember times when other people made a difference in their lives by giving them good advice (informational support), helping them to feel better about themselves (emotional support), providing assistance with chores and responsibilities or financial help (tangible support), or simply by "hanging out" with them (belonging support) (Uchino et al., 1999).

Religion and Altruism Health psychologists are also investigating the role religion may play in reducing stress and bolstering health (Freedland, 2004; Joseph, Linley, & Maltby, 2006; W. R. Miller & Thoresen, 2003; Rabin & Koenig, 2002). For example, research has found that elderly people who pray or attend religious services regularly enjoy better health and markedly lower rates of depression than those who do not (Koenig, McCullough, & Larson, 2000). Other studies have shown that having a religious commitment may also help to moderate high blood pressure and hypertension (Levin & Vanderpool, 1989; Wilkins, 2005).

It is unclear why there is an association between health and religion (Contrada et al., 2004; K. S. Masters, 2008). One explanation holds that religion provides a system of social support that includes caring friends and opportunities for close personal interactions. As previously described, a strong network of social support can reduce stress in a variety of ways, and in turn, reduced stress is associated with better health. Other possible explanations are that regular attendance at religious services encourages people to help others, which in turn increases feelings of personal control and reduces feelings of depression; that frequent attendance at religious services increases positive emotions; and that most religions encourage healthy lifestyles.

Altruism—reaching out and giving to others because this brings *you* pleasure—is one of the more effective ways to reduce stress (Vaillant, 2000). Caring for others tends to take our minds off our own problems, to make us realize that there are others who are worse off than we are, and to foster the feeling that we're involved in something larger than our own small slice of life (Allen, Haley, & Roff, 2006). Altruism is a component of most religions, suggesting that altruism and religious commitment may have something in common that helps to reduce stress. Altruism may also channel loss, grief, or anger into constructive action.

Learn to Cope Effectively How you appraise events in your environment—and how you appraise your ability to cope with potentially unsettling, unpredictable events—can minimize or maximize stress and its impact on health.

Proactive coping is the psychological term for anticipating stressful events and taking advance steps to avoid them or to minimize their impact (Aspinwall & Taylor, 1997; Greenglass, 2002). Proactive coping does not mean "expect the worst;" constant vigilance actually increases stress and may damage health. Rather, proactive coping means (as in the Boy Scout motto) "Be prepared." This may include accumulating resources (time, money, social support, and information), recognizing potential stress in advance, and making realistic plans. ✻

In many cases, you cannot change or escape stressful circumstances, but you can change the way you think about things. *Positive reappraisal* helps people to make the best of a tense or painful situation (Lequerica, Forchheimer, Tate, Roller, & Toussaint, 2008). A low grade can be seen as a warning sign, not a catastrophe; similarly, a job you hate may provide information on what you really want in your career. Positive reappraisal does not require you to become a "Pollyanna" (the heroine of a novel who was optimistic to the point of being ridiculous). Rather, it requires finding new meaning in a situation, or finding a perspective or insight that you had overlooked. Positive reappraisal has also been shown to be an effective technique to help people cope with HIV, by improving the quality of their life and increasing their psychological well-being (Moskowitz, Hult, Bussolari, & Acree, 2009).

✻ Explore the Effect of Cognitive Appraisal on Responses to Stressors on **MyPsychLab**

One of the most effective, stress-relieving forms of reappraisal is *humor* (Ayan, 2009). As Shakespeare so aptly put it in *The Winter's Tale*: "A merry heart goes all the day/Your sad tires in a mile" (*Act IV, Scene 3*). Journalist Norman Cousins (1981) attributed his recovery from a life-threatening disease to regular "doses" of laughter. Watching classic comic films, he believed, reduced both his pain and the inflammation in his tissues. He wrote:

> What was significant about the laughter . . . was not just the fact that it provides internal exercise for a person flat on his or her back—a form of jogging for the innards—but that it creates a mood in which the other positive emotions can be put to work, too. In short, it helps make it possible for good things to happen. (pp. 145–146)

Some health psychologists agree that a healthy body and a sense of humor go hand in hand (Myers & Sweeney, 2006; Salovey, Rothman, Detweiler, & Steward, 2000; Vaillant, 2000), while others believe that more research is needed before any firm conclusions can be drawn (R. A. Martin, 2002). Most are in agreement, however, that doing what we can to maintain a healthy body helps us both reduce and cope with stress. ◉

◉ Watch the **Video** In the Real World: Reducing Stress, Improving Health on **MyPsychLab**

Adopt a Healthy Lifestyle

What are the elements of a healthy lifestyle?

While learning how to avoid and cope with stress is important, the *positive psychology* movement (see Chapter 1, "The Science of Psychology") has prompted many health psychologists to explore other ways to promote good health by adopting a healthier lifestyle. Developing healthy habits—like eating a well-balanced diet, getting regular exercise, not smoking, and avoiding high-risk behaviors—are all important to maintaining health (H. S. Friedman, 2002).

Diet A good diet of nutritious foods is important because it provides the energy necessary to sustain a vigorous lifestyle while promoting healthy growth and development. Although there is some disagreement about what *exactly* constitutes a well-balanced diet, most experts advise eating a wide variety of fruits, vegetables, nuts, whole-grain breads and cereals, accompanied by small portions of fish and lean meats. Several studies have documented that eating a healthy diet can improve the quality of life, increase longevity, and reduce the risk of heart disease, cancer, and stroke (Trichopoulou, Costacou, Bamia, & Trichopoulos, 2003). Conversely, eating excessive amounts of fatty meats, deep-fried foods, dairy products that are high in cholesterol (such as whole milk and butter), and foods high in sugars (such as soda and candy) are generally considered unhealthy (H. S. Friedman, 2002). ◉

Exercise The importance of regular aerobic exercise (such as jogging, brisk walking, or swimming) for maintaining a healthy body has been well established. In addition, health psychologists have shown that regular aerobic exercise can also help people cope better with stress, as well as help them feel less depressed, more vigorous, and more energetic. One study, for example, randomly divided mildly depressed college women into three groups. One group participated in regular aerobic exercise, one group received relaxation therapy, and the last group (a control group) received no treatment at all. After 10 weeks, the mildly depressed women in the aerobic activity group reported a marked decrease in their depression when compared to the no treatment group. The relaxation group also showed benefits from relaxation therapy, but they were not as significant as the group that had engaged in the regular aerobic exercise program (McCann & Holmes, 1984). Numerous other studies have also demonstrated a link between regular exercise, reduced stress, increased self-confidence, and improved sleep quality (Gandhi, Depauw, Dolny, & Freson, 2002; Manger & Motta, 2005).

Quit Smoking Fewer Americans smoke today than in the past, and over half of those who did smoke have quit. However, cigarette smoking still poses a serious health threat to the millions of people who continue to smoke (Mody & Smith, 2006). Smoking is linked to chronic lung disease, heart disease, and cancer. In addition, smoking can reduce the quality of life by decreasing lung efficiency. ◉→

Interestingly, the tendency to start smoking occurs almost exclusively during the adolescent years. Almost no one over the age of 21 takes up the habit for first time, but teenagers who seriously experiment with cigarettes or have friends who smoke are more likely to start smoking than those who do not (W. S. Choi, Pierce, Gilpin, Farkas, & Berry, 1997; J. L. Johnson, Kalaw, Lovato, Baillie, & Chambers, 2004). For these reasons, health psychologists realize that initiatives aimed at preventing smoking should primarily focus their efforts on young people (Tilleczek & Hine, 2006).

Most adults who smoke want to quit, but their addiction to nicotine (discussed in Chapter 4, "States of Consciousness") makes quitting very difficult. Fortunately, several alternative methods to help people quit smoking have been developed in recent years. For instance, prescription antidepressant medications such as *Zyban, Wellbutrin,* and *Effexor,* which work at the neurotransmitter level, have proved useful in helping people stop smoking. Nicotine substitutes, usually in the form of chewing gum, patches, or inhalers, have also produced encouraging results (Etter, 2009). Many people who are attempting to quit also find that modifying the environment that they have come to associate with smoking is important. For instance, because people often smoke in bars or during coffee breaks, changing routines that signal lighting up can also help. Finally, some people succeed in quitting "cold turkey." They simply decide to stop smoking without any external support or change in their lifestyle. Regardless of how people quit smoking, studies have shown that quitting will generally add years to your life. Hence, doing whatever it takes to stop is worth it.

Avoid High-Risk Behaviors Every day, we make dozens of small, seemingly insignificant choices that can potentially impact our health and well-being. For instance, choosing to wear a seat belt every time you ride in a car is one of the more significant measures to reduce the risk of injury and early death. Similarly, refusing to have unprotected sex reduces your chances of contracting a sexually transmitted disease. ◉

◉ **Watch** the **Video** You Are What You Eat on **MyPsychLab**

◉→ **Simulate** the **Experiment** Second-Hand Smoke on **MyPsychLab**

◉ **Watch** the **Video** What's In It For Me?: The Challenge Of Quitting Bad Habits on **MyPsychLab**

Health psychologists, working with public agencies, are designing intervention programs to help people make safer choices in their everyday lives. For example, John Jemmott and his colleagues (Jemmott, Jemmott, Fong, & McCaffree, 2002) studied the impact of a *safer sex* program that stressed the importance of condom use and other safer sex practices on a sample of 496 high-risk inner-city African American adolescents. Six months after the program began, a follow-up evaluation of the participants revealed that they reported a lower incidence of high-risk sexual behavior, including unprotected intercourse, than did adolescents who did not participate in the program. Similar results have been obtained in programs designed to prevent drug abuse among adolescents (R. Davies, 2009). Research like this underscores the important role that health psychologists can play in helping people learn to avoid risky behavior and improve their quality of life.

✔•⌐Study and **Review** on **MyPsychLab**

CHECK YOUR UNDERSTANDING

1. _____ is the term given to the set of characteristics, such as hostility and a sense of urgency, that many people believe make a person more susceptible to coronary heart disease.

   Indicate whether the following statements are true (T) or false (F):

2. ____ Research has been unable to find a relationship between stress and the strength of the body's immune system.

3. ____ Increased stress may make us more susceptible to the common cold.

4. ____ Prolonged stress has been shown to increase vulnerability to cancer.

5. ____ People who attend religious services regularly enjoy better health than those who do not attend regularly.

Answers: 1. Type A behavior patterns. 2. (F); 3. (T); 4. (T); 5. (T).

APPLY YOUR UNDERSTANDING

1. During the last year, John has been exposed to extremely loud, harsh noise because a high-rise apartment is going up next to his home. He finds the sound of the jackhammers and other heavy equipment almost deafening. Which of the following is most likely to be true?

   a. The increased stress may make John more vulnerable to illness.

   b. The increased stress may make John less vulnerable to illness as long as he is able to stay in Selye's stage of "resistance."

   c. John is a "Type A" personality.

   d. Both (b) and (c) are true.

2. You are going through a particularly stressful event. According to Selye's *general adaptation syndrome*, your first response to the stress is likely to be

   a. increased activity in the sympathetic nervous system and heightened sensitivity and alertness.

   b. reliance on defense mechanisms in an effort to bring the stress quickly under control.

   c. inability to concentrate, irritability, and procrastination.

   d. increased activity in the immune system to ward off potential diseases.

Answers: 1. a. 2. a.

EXTREME STRESS

How does extreme stress differ from everyday stress?

Extreme stress marks a radical departure from everyday life, such that a person cannot continue life as before and, in some cases, never fully recovers. What are some major causes of extreme stress? What effect do they have on people? How do people cope?

<----- **LEARNING OBJECTIVE**

- Identify the five major sources of extreme stress and describe their impact.

Sources of Extreme Stress

What are some sources of extreme stress, and what impact do they have?

Extreme stress has a variety of sources, ranging from unemployment to wartime combat, from violent natural disaster to rape. More common events, too, can be sources of extreme stress, including bereavement, separation, and divorce.

Unemployment Joblessness is a major source of stress (Lennon & Limonic, 2010). When the jobless rate rises, there is also an increase in first admissions to psychiatric hospitals, infant mortality, deaths from heart disease, alcohol-related diseases, and suicide (Almgren, Guest, Immerwahr, & Spittel, 2002; Goldman-Mellor, Saxton, & Catalano, 2010; Luo, Florence, Quispe-Agnoli, Ouyang, & Crosby, 2011). One survey taken in September 2009 when unemployment was 10% in the United States, showed that compared to those who were still employed, those without jobs were four times as likely to have serious mental health problems (Mental Health America, 2009). Family strain also increases. "Things just fell apart," one worker said after both he and his wife suddenly found themselves unemployed. Not surprisingly, being unemployed also decreases an individual's sense of well-being and happiness (Creed & Klisch, 2005).

Divorce and Separation "The deterioration or ending of an intimate relationship is one of the more potent of stressors and one of the more frequent reasons why people seek psychotherapy" (J. Coleman, Glaros, & Morris, 1987, p. 155). After a breakup, both partners often feel they have failed at one of life's most important endeavors, but strong emotional ties often continue to bind the pair. If only one spouse wants to end the marriage, the initiator may feel sadness and guilt at hurting the other partner; the rejected spouse may feel anger, humiliation, and guilt over his or her role in the failure. Even if the separation was a mutual decision, ambivalent feelings of love and hate can make life turbulent, often for many years (R. E. Lucas, 2005). Of course, adults are not the only ones who are stressed by divorce (Lansford, 2009). Each year more than 1 million American children are also impacted by their parent's divorce, with approximately 40% of all children under the age of 18 being involved in a divorce (S. M. Greene, Anderson, Doyle, & Riedelbach, 2006). A national survey of the impact of divorce on children (Cherlin, 1992) found that a majority suffer intense emotional stress at the time of divorce. Although most recover within a year or two, especially if the custodial parent establishes a stable home and the parents do not fight about child rearing (Bing, Nelson, & Wesolowski, 2009), a minority experience long-term problems (Judith Siegel, 2007; Wallerstein, Blakeslee, & Lewis, 2000).

The death of a loved one is a source of extreme stress for many people. Recently, psychologists have questioned traditional notions about the grieving process.

Bereavement For decades, it was widely held that following the death of a loved one, people go through a necessary period of intense grief during which they work through their loss and, about a year later, pick up and go on with their lives. Psychologists and physicians, as well as the public at large, have endorsed this cultural wisdom. But some have challenged this view of loss (Bonanno, Wortman, & Nesse, 2004; Davis, Wortman, Lehman, & Silver, 2000; Wortman & Silver, 1989).

According to Wortman and her colleagues (Bonanno, Boerner, & Wortman, 2008), the first myth about bereavement is that people should be intensely distressed when a loved one dies; this suggests that people who are not devastated are behaving abnormally, perhaps pathologically. Often, however, people have prepared for the loss, said their goodbyes, and feel little remorse or regret. Indeed, they may be relieved that their loved one is no longer suffering. The second myth—that people need to work through their grief—may lead family, friends, and even physicians to (consciously or unconsciously) encourage the bereaved to feel or act distraught. Moreover, physicians may deny those mourners who are deeply disturbed necessary anti-anxiety or antidepressant medication "for their own good." The third myth holds that people who find meaning in the death, who come to a spiritual or existential understanding of why it happened, cope better than those who do not. In reality, people who do not seek greater understanding are the best adjusted and least depressed. The fourth myth—that people should recover from a loss within a year or so—is perhaps the most damaging. Parents trying to cope with the death of an infant and adults whose spouse or child died suddenly in a vehicle accident often continue to experience painful memories and wrestle with depression years later (S. A. Murphy, 2008). But because they have not recovered "on schedule," members of their social network may become unsympathetic. Unfortunately, the people who need support most may hide their feelings because they do not want to make other people uncomfortable. Often they fail to seek treatment because they, too, believe they should recover on their own.

Not all psychologists agree with this "new" view of bereavement. But most agree that research on loss must consider individual (and group or cultural) differences, as well as variations in the circumstances surrounding a loss (Dobson, 2004; Hayslip & Peveto, 2005; Vanderwerker & Prigerson, 2004).

Catastrophes Catastrophes—natural and otherwise—produce certain psychological reactions common to all stressful events. At first, in the *shock stage,* "the victim is stunned, dazed, and apathetic" and sometimes even "stuporous, disoriented, and amnesic for the traumatic event." Then, in the *suggestible stage,* victims are passive and quite ready to do whatever rescuers tell them to do. In the third phase, the *recovery stage,* emotional balance is regained, but anxiety often persists, and victims may need to recount their experiences over and over again. In later stages, survivors may feel irrationally guilty because they lived while others died (Mallimson, 2006: Straton, 2004).

Combat and Other Threatening Personal Attacks Wartime experiences often cause soldiers intense and disabling combat stress that persists long after they have left the battlefield. Similar reactions—including bursting into rage over harmless remarks, sleep disturbances, cringing at sudden loud noises, psychological confusion, uncontrollable crying, and silently staring into space for long periods—are also frequently seen in survivors of serious accidents, especially children, and of violent crimes such as rapes and muggings (Fairbrother & Rachman, 2006). **Figure 11–2** shows the traumatic effects of war on the civilian population, based on composite statistics obtained after recent civil wars (Mollica, 2000).

Posttraumatic Stress Disorder

What experiences can lead to posttraumatic stress disorder?

Severely stressful events can cause a psychological disorder known as **posttraumatic stress disorder (PTSD).** Dramatic nightmares in which the victim reexperiences the terrifying event exactly as it happened are common. So are daytime flashbacks, in which the victim relives the trauma. Often, victims of PTSD withdraw from social life and from job and family

posttraumatic stress disorder (PTSD) Psychological disorder characterized by episodes of anxiety, sleeplessness, and nightmares resulting from some disturbing past event.

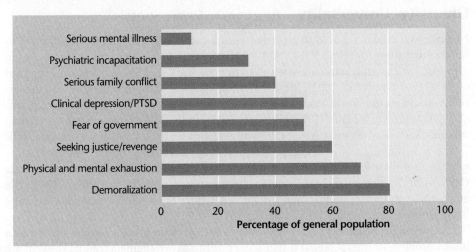

FIGURE 11–2
Mental trauma in societies at war.

In societies that have undergone the stress of war, nearly everyone suffers some psychological reaction, ranging from serious mental illness to feelings of demoralization. Rates of clinical depression are as high as 50%.

Source: Figure from p. 54 by Laurie Gracie in "Invisible Wounds" by R. F. Mollica, *Scientific American,* June 2000. Copyright © 2000. Reprinted by permission.

Soldiers who have been in combat are at risk for developing posttraumatic stress disorder.

responsibilities (Kashdan, Julian, Merritt, & Uswatte, 2006). PTSD can set in immediately after a traumatic event or within a short time afterwards. But sometimes, months or years may go by in which the victim seems to have recovered from the experience, and then, without warning, psychological symptoms reappear, then may disappear only to recur repeatedly (Corales, 2005).

The experiences of soldiers have heightened interest in PTSD. For example, between 18.7% and 30.9% of the soldiers who served in Vietnam experienced PTSD at some point afterward (Dohrenwend et al., 2007; E. J. Ozer, Best, Lipsey, & Weiss, 2003). It is estimated that as many as one-third of Iraq war veterans suffer from PTSD. Many veterans of World War II, who are now old men, still have nightmares from which they awake sweating and shaking. The memories of combat continue to torment them after more than half a century (Port, Engdahl, & Frazier, 2001). Recently, therapists have begun to observe a new phenomenon: Veterans who seemed to be healthy and well adjusted throughout their postwar lives suddenly develop symptoms of PTSD when they retire and enter their "golden years" (Sleek, 1998; van Achterberg, Rohrbaugh, & Southwick, 2001).

Soldiers are not the only victims of war. Indeed, during the 20th century, civilian deaths outnumbered military deaths in most wars. Yet only in the last decade—especially following the tragedy of the September 11 terrorist attacks on the World Trade Center and the Pentagon and the devastation of New Orleans by Hurricane Katrina—have medical researchers begun to investigate the psychological and physiological effects of war, tragedy, and terrorism on civilian survivors. For many, the immediate response following a traumatic event is one of shock and denial. Shock leaves victims feeling stunned, confused, and in some cases, temporarily numb. Denial often causes them to be unwilling to acknowledge the impact and emotional intensity of the event. After the initial shock passes, individual reactions to trauma vary considerably, but commonly include: heightened emotionality, irritability, nervousness, difficulty concentrating, changes in sleep patterns, physical symptoms such as nausea, headaches, chest pain, and even depression. Some civilians also experience long-lasting and severe problems, such as exhaustion, hatred, mistrust, and the symptoms of PTSD (Gurwitch, Sitterle, Young, & Pfefferbaum, 2002; Mollica, 2000). For example, in one survey of adults with no previous history of PTSD, 10% of those who witnessed the collapse of the World Trade Center towers on September 11, 2001, developed symptoms of PTSD that were still present five to six years later. Another 10% first developed symptoms of PTSD after several years had passed since the attacks (Brackbill et al., 2009). Among Holocaust survivors, many continued to show symptoms of PTSD decades after the end of WWII (Barel, Van IJzendoorn, Sagi-Schwartz, & Bakermans-Kranenburg, 2010).

ENDURING ISSUES

Diversity–Universality   Reactions to Severe Stress

Not everyone who is exposed to severely stressful events (such as heavy combat or childhood sexual abuse) develops PTSD. Although more than half of the American population is exposed to a severely traumatic event at some time, less than 10% will develop symptoms of PTSD (E. J. Ozer et al., 2003). More than three-quarters of those who witnessed the terrorist attacks on the World Trade Center towers in 2001 showed no significant symptoms of PTSD several years later (Brackbill et al., 2009). Individual characteristics—including gender, personality, a family history of mental disorders, prior exposure to trauma, substance abuse among relatives, exaggerated reactivity to startling sounds, and preexisting neurological disorders—appear to predispose some people to PTSD more than others (H. Johnson & Thompson, 2008; Najavits, 2004; Parslow, Jorm, & Christensen, 2006; Pole et al., 2009). Both men and women who have a history of emotional problems are more likely to experience severe trauma and to develop PTSD as a consequence of trauma. Not surprisingly, people who may already be under extreme stress (perhaps caused by a health problem or interpersonal difficulties) prior to experiencing a traumatic event are at greatest risk (Elwood, Hahn, Olatunji, & Williams, 2009; Heinrichs et al., 2005; Lipsky, Field, Caetano, & Larkin, 2005). Recent evidence has shown a relationship between PTSD and an increased risk of heart disease (Kubzansky, Koenen, Jones, & Eaton, 2009). In fact, one study found that veterans diagnosed with PTSD were twice as likely to die from early age heart disease compared to veterans not diagnosed with PTSD (Boscarino, 2008).

Some psychologists have found that following a significant trauma, a few particularly stable individuals experience a *positive* form of personal growth called **posttraumatic growth (PTG)** (Bower, Moskowitz, & Epel, 2009; Calhoun & Tedeschi, 2001; Tedeschi & Calhoun, 2008). In the rare instances where posttraumatic growth occurs, it appears to emerge largely from an individual's struggle to reconcile their loss through religious or existential understanding (Ting & Watson, 2007). As with PTSD, personality, psychological well-being, and effective cognitive coping strategies are important factors in determining whether a traumatic event will result in PTG (Garnefski, Kraaij, Schroevers, & Somsen, 2008). When it does occur, posttraumatic growth is more likely to be seen in young adults than in older people (S. Powell, Rosner, Butollo, Tedeschi, & Calhoun, 2003). ■

THINKING CRITICALLY ABOUT . . .

Posttraumatic Stress

1. Obviously, war is not the only cause of extreme stress and trauma. Do you think an individual's response to a personal attack, such as a rape, is similar to or different from that caused by serving in combat?

2. What might you do to help a friend recover from a significant personal trauma? How could you find out about counseling and other resources to provide further help?

Recovery from posttraumatic stress disorder is strongly related to the amount of emotional support survivors receive from family, friends, and community. Treatment consists of helping those who have experienced severe trauma to come to terms with their terrifying memories. Immediate treatment near the site of the trauma coupled with the expectation that the individual will return to everyday life is often effective. Reliving the traumatic event in a safe setting is also crucial to successful treatment (Jaycox, Zoellner, & Foa, 2002). This helps desensitize people to the traumatic memories haunting them (Oltmanns & Emery, 2006).

---

posttraumatic growth (PTG) Positive personal growth that may follow an extremely stressful event.

✔—Study and Review on MyPsychLab

CHECK YOUR UNDERSTANDING

Is each of the following statements true (T) or false (F)?

1. ____ If people who are bereaved following the death of a spouse or child have not recovered by the end of 1 year, this outcome indicates that they are coping abnormally.

2. ____ Catastrophes—including floods, earthquakes, violent storms, fires, and plane crashes—produce different psychological reactions than do other kinds of stressful events.

3. ____ Most children whose parents divorce experience serious and long-term problems.

4. ____ Posttraumatic stress disorder can appear months or even years after a traumatic event.

Answers: 1. (F), 2. (F), 3. (F), 4. (T).

APPLY YOUR UNDERSTANDING

1. Your friend Patrick has just survived a traumatic event. Which of the following would you LEAST expect to observe?
   a. difficulty sleeping, frequent nightmares
   b. physical symptoms, such as nausea and headaches
   c. irritability, rapid mood changes, and nervousness
   d. a healthy appetite and increased interest in food and eating

2. As you try to help Patrick begin to recover from the traumatic event, which of the following would be most beneficial?
   a. Encourage him to get over it as quickly as possible and move on with his life.
   b. Suggest that he change jobs and move to a new location so he can "start over."
   c. Listen supportively without probing.
   d. Encourage him to describe the details of the event so he won't go into denial.

Answers: 1. d. 2. c.

- Describe the several standards for judging whether an individual is well adjusted.

THE WELL-ADJUSTED PERSON

What qualities describe a well-adjusted person?

We noted at the beginning of the chapter that adjustment is any effort to cope with stress. Psychologists disagree, however, about what constitutes *good* adjustment. Some think it is the ability to live according to social norms. Thus, a woman who grows up in a small town, attends college, teaches for a year or two, and then settles down to a peaceful family life might be considered well adjusted because she is living by the predominant values of her community.

Other psychologists disagree strongly with this view. They argue that society is not always right. Thus, if we accept its standards blindly, we renounce the right to make individual judgments. For instance, V. E. O'Leary and Bhaju (2006) argue that well-adjusted people enjoy the difficulties and ambiguities of life, treating them as challenges to be overcome. Such people are aware of their strengths and weaknesses; this awareness empowers them to live in harmony with their inner selves. For example, although aging involves declining health and decreased mobility, successful aging also involves the opportunity for psychological growth and maturation. The idea that adversity may serve as an impetus for psychological growth is also consistent with the positive psychology movement.

We may also evaluate adjustment by using specific criteria, such as the following, to judge an action:

1. Does the action realistically meet the demands of the situation, or does it simply postpone resolving the problem?
2. Does the action meet the individual's needs?
3. Is the action compatible with the well-being of others?

Abraham Maslow, whose hierarchy of needs was discussed in Chapter 8, "Motivation and Emotion," believed that well-adjusted people attempt to "actualize" themselves. That is, they live in a way that enhances their own growth and fulfillment, regardless of what others might think. According to Maslow, well-adjusted people are unconventional and creative thinkers, perceive people and events realistically, and set goals for themselves. They also tend to form deep, close relationships with a few chosen individuals.

As we have seen, there are many standards for judging whether an individual is well adjusted. A person deemed well adjusted by one standard might not be considered well adjusted by other standards. The same principle holds true when we try to specify what behaviors are "abnormal"—the topic of the next chapter.

THINKING CRITICALLY ABOUT . . .

Who Is Well Adjusted?

Write down the names of three individuals whom you consider well adjusted. Take some time before you answer. Include one person whom you know only distantly, perhaps someone you read about.

- What personal qualities set these individuals apart?

- What do these people have in common? What are their individual distinctions?

CHECK YOUR UNDERSTANDING

1. The well-adjusted person has learned to balance
   a. conformity and nonconformity.
   b. self-control and spontaneity.
   c. flexibility and structure.
   d. all of the above.

Answer: 1. d.

APPLY YOUR UNDERSTANDING

1. Your roommate is attempting to deal with a particularly stressful set of events in her life. You wonder whether she is coping well or whether there is cause for concern. Which of the following criteria would be LEAST useful in making that judgment?
   a. Whether her behavior is realistically meeting the demands of the situation.
   b. Whether she is doing what society says people should do in these kinds of situations.
   c. Whether her behavior is interfering with the well-being of others around her.
   d. Whether her actions are effectively meeting her needs.

2. Mary lives in a way that enhances her own growth and fulfillment regardless of what others think. In many ways, she is unconventional, is a creative thinker, and has close relationships with only a few chosen individuals. According to Maslow, Mary is most likely
   a. a well-adjusted, self-actualizing person.
   b. engaging in positive reappraisal.
   c. a Type A personality.
   d. making excessive use of intellectualization.

Answers: 1. b. 2. a.

KEY TERMS

Sources of Stress
stressor, p. 363
stress, p. 363
adjustment, p. 363
pressure, p. 366
frustration, p. 366
conflict, p. 366
approach/approach
   conflict, p. 367

avoidance/avoidance conflict,
   p. 367
approach/avoidance conflict,
   p. 367

Coping with Stress
confrontation, p. 370
compromise, p. 370
withdrawal, p. 371
defense mechanisms, p. 371
denial, p. 371

repression, p. 371
projection, p. 371
identification, p. 371
regression, p. 372
intellectualization, p. 372
reaction formation, p. 372
displacement, p. 372
sublimation, p. 372

How Stress Affects Health
health psychology, p. 374

general adaptation syndrome
   (GAS), p. 375
psychoneuroimmunology
   (PNI), p. 376

Extreme Stress
posttraumatic stress disorder
   (PTSD), p. 383
posttraumatic growth
   (PTG), p. 385

CHAPTER REVIEW   ((•[Listen to the **Chapter Audio** on **MyPsychLab**

SOURCES OF STRESS

What are stressors? We experience **stress** when we are faced with a tense or threatening situation that requires us to change or adapt our behavior (a **stressor**). Life-and-death situations, like war and natural disasters, are inherently stressful. Even events that are usually viewed as positive, like a wedding or a job promotion, can be stressful, because they require change, adaptation, and **adjustment.** How we adjust to the stress affects our health, since prolonged or severe stress can contribute to physical and psychological disorders.

Why is change so stressful for most people? Because most people strongly desire order in their lives, any good or bad event involving change will be experienced as stressful.

How can everyday hassles contribute to stress? Day-to-day petty annoyances and irritations can be as stressful as major life events, because these seemingly minor incidents give rise to feelings of pressure, frustration, conflict, and anxiety.

When we experience **pressure** from either internal or external forces, we feel forced to intensify our efforts or to perform at higher levels. Internal forces include trying to live up to social and cultural norms as well as family and peer expectations.

We feel frustrated when someone or something stands between us and our goal. Five basic sources of **frustration** are delays, lack of resources, losses, failure, and discrimination.

Conflict arises when we are faced with two or more incompatible demands, opportunities, needs, or goals. With **approach/approach conflict,** a person must either choose between two attractive but incompatible goals or opportunities, or modify them so as to take some advantage of both. With **avoidance/avoidance conflict,** a person must choose between two undesirable or threatening possibilities. If escape is impossible, the person may often vacillate between the two possibilities. With **approach/avoidance conflict,** a person is both attracted to and repelled by the same goal or opportunity. Because the desire to approach and the desire to avoid the goal both grow stronger as the person in this dilemma nears the goal, eventually the tendency to approach equals the tendency to avoid. The person then vacillates until finally making a decision or until the situation changes.

How do we create stress? Sometimes we subject ourselves to stress by internalizing a set of irrational, self-defeating beliefs that add unnecessarily to the normal stresses of living.

Do people who are resistant to stress share certain traits? People who cope well with stress tend to be self-confident and optimistic. With their internal locus of control, they also see themselves as being able to affect their situations. Stress-resistant people share a trait called *hardiness*—a tendency to experience difficult demands as challenging rather than threatening. *Resilience,* the ability to bounce back after a stressful event, is also related to positive adjustment.

COPING WITH STRESS

What is the difference between direct coping and defensive coping? People generally adjust to stress in one of two ways: *Direct coping* describes any action people take to change an uncomfortable situation, whereas *defensive coping* denotes the various ways people convince themselves—through a form of self-deception—that they are not really threatened or do not really want something they cannot get.

What are three strategies that deal directly with stress? When we confront a stressful situation and admit to ourselves that there is a problem that needs to be solved, we may learn new skills, enlist other people's aid, or try harder to reach our goal. **Confrontation** may also include expressions of anger. **Compromise** usually requires adjusting expectations or desires;

the conflict is resolved by settling for less than what was originally sought. Sometimes the most effective way of coping with a stressful situation is to distance oneself from it. The danger of **withdrawal,** however, is that it may become a maladaptive habit.

What are the major ways of coping defensively? When a stressful situation arises and there is little that can be done to deal with it directly, people often turn to defense mechanisms as a way of coping. **Defense mechanisms** are ways of deceiving ourselves about the causes of stressful events, thus reducing conflict, frustration, pressure, and anxiety. **Denial** is the refusal to acknowledge a painful or threatening reality. **Repression** is the blocking out of unacceptable thoughts or impulses from consciousness. When we cannot deny or repress a particular problem, we might resort to **projection**—attributing our repressed motives or feelings to others, thereby locating the source of our conflict outside ourselves. **Identification** may occur when people feel completely powerless. People who adopt this technique take on others' characteristics to gain a sense of control or adequacy. People under severe stress sometimes revert to childlike behavior, called **regression.** Because adults can't stand feeling helpless, becoming more childlike can make total dependency or helplessness more tolerable. A subtle form of denial is seen in **intellectualization,** when people emotionally distance themselves from a particularly disturbing situation. **Reaction formation** refers to a behavioral form of denial in which people express with exaggerated intensity ideas and emotions that are the opposite of their own. Through **displacement,** repressed motives and feelings are redirected from their original objects to substitute objects. **Sublimation** involves transforming repressed emotions into more socially accepted forms. Defensive coping can help us adjust to difficult circumstances, but it can also lead to maladaptive behavior if it interferes with our ability to deal constructively with a difficult situation.

Who experiences the most stress? How people handle stress is determined to a significant degree by the environment in which they live. People in low-income groups often experience more stress and have fewer personal and community resources to draw on for support as well as fewer coping strategies. Men and women may cope differently with stress.

HOW STRESS AFFECTS HEALTH

What long-lasting effects of stress do we need to be concerned with? **Health psychologists** try to find ways to prevent stress from becoming debilitating and to promote healthy behaviors. Physiologist Hans Selye contended that people react to physical and psychological stress in three stages. In Stage 1 (*alarm reaction*) of the **general adaptation syndrome (GAS),** the body recognizes that it must fight off some physical or psychological danger, resulting in quickened respiration and heart rate, increased sensitivity and alertness, and a highly charged emotional state—a physical adaptation that augments our coping resources and helps us to regain self-control. If direct or defensive coping mechanisms fail to reduce the stress, we progress to Stage 2 (*resistance stage*), during which physical symptoms of strain appear as we intensify our efforts to cope both directly and defensively. If these attempts to regain psychological equilibrium fail, psychological disorganization rages out of control until we reach Stage 3 (*exhaustion*). During this phase, we use increasingly ineffective defense mechanisms to bring the stress under control. At this point, some people lose touch with reality, whereas others show signs of "burnout," such as shorter attention spans, irritability, procrastination, and general apathy.

How is Type A behavior related to heart disease? Stress is known to be an important factor in chemical changes in the body leading to the development of coronary heart disease (CHD). Research has demonstrated that the type A behavior pattern—characterized by impatience, hostility, urgency, competitiveness, and striving—predicts CHD.

Why do so many students get sick during finals? Stress—such as that experienced by students during examination periods—can suppress the functioning of the immune system, the focus of the relatively new field of **psychoneuroimmunology (PNI)**. Stress can also increase one's susceptibility to the common cold, and it appears to be linked to the development of some forms of cancer.

STAYING HEALTHY

What two key areas can people control to help themselves stay healthy? We can reduce the negative impact of stress on our health by trying to reduce stress and by maintaining a healthy lifestyle, which equips the body to cope with stress that is unavoidable.

What steps can people take to reduce stress? Exercising regularly and learning to relax reduce the body's responses to stress. Having a strong network of social support is also related to healthier adjustment. Religious and altruistic people also typically experience less stress, although the mechanism involved is not clear. Finally, people can take steps to minimize the impact of stressful events (proactive coping), by making the best of difficult situations (positive reappraisal), and by maintaining a sense of humor.

What are the elements of a healthy lifestyle? The *positive psychology* movement has prompted many psychologists to promote good health by adopting a healthier lifestyle. Eating a well-balanced diet, getting regular exercise, not smoking, and avoiding high-risk behaviors are all important to maintaining health.

EXTREME STRESS

How does extreme stress differ from everyday stress? People experiencing extreme stress cannot continue their everyday life as they did before the stress and, in some cases, they never fully recover.

What are some sources of extreme stress, and what impact do they have? Extreme stress derives from a number of sources, including unemployment, divorce and separation, bereavement, combat, and natural catastrophes. One of the impediments to effective coping occurs when a grieving person feels compelled to adjust in socially prescribed ways that do not provide effective relief.

What experiences can lead to posttraumatic stress disorder? Extreme traumas may result in **posttraumatic stress disorder (PTSD),** a disabling emotional disorder whose symptoms include daytime flashbacks, social and occupational withdrawal, sleeplessness, and nightmares. Combat veterans and people with a history of emotional problems are especially vulnerable to PTSD. A few particularly stable individuals experience a *positive* form of personal growth following extreme trauma called **posttraumatic growth (PTG).**

THE WELL-ADJUSTED PERSON

What qualities describe a well-adjusted person? Psychologists disagree on what constitutes good adjustment. Some believe that well-adjusted people live according to social norms. Others disagree, arguing that well-adjusted people enjoy overcoming challenging situations and that this ability leads to growth and self-fulfillment. Finally, some psychologists use specific criteria to evaluate a person's ability to adjust, such as how well the adjustment solves the problem and satisfies both personal needs and the needs of others.

12

Psychological Disorders

Jack was a very successful chemical engineer known for the meticulous accuracy of his work. But Jack also had a "little quirk." He constantly felt compelled to double-, triple-, and even quadruple-check things to assure himself that they were done properly. For instance, when leaving his apartment in the morning, he occasionally got as far as the garage—but invariably he would go back to make certain that the door was securely locked and the stove, lights, and other appliances were all turned off. Going on a vacation was particularly difficult for him because his checking routine was so exhaustive and time-consuming. Yet Jack insisted that he would never want to give up this chronic checking. Doing so, he said, would make him "much too nervous."

For Claudia, every day was more than just a bad-hair day. She was always in utter despair over how "hideous" her hair looked. She perceived some parts of it to be too long, and others to be too short. In her eyes, one area would look much too "poofy," while another area would look far too flat. Claudia got up early each morning just to work on her hair. For about 2 hours she would wash it, dry it, brush it, comb it, curl it, straighten it, and snip away infinitesimal amounts with an expensive pair of hair-cutting scissors. But she was never satisfied with the results. Not even trips to the most expensive salons could make her feel content about her hair. She declared that virtually every day was ruined because her hair looked so bad. Claudia said that she desperately wanted to stop focusing on her hair, but for some reason she just couldn't.

Jonathan was a 22-year-old auto mechanic whom everyone described as a loner. He seldom engaged in conversation and seemed lost in his own private world. At work, the other mechanics took to whistling sharply whenever they wanted to get his attention. Jonathan also had a "strange look" on his face that could make customers feel uncomfortable. But his oddest behavior was his assertion that he sometimes had the distinct feeling his dead mother was standing next to him, watching what he did. Although Jonathan realized that his mother was not really there, he nevertheless felt reassured by the illusion of her presence. He took great care not to look or reach toward the spot where he felt his mother was, because doing so inevitably made the feeling go away.

Cases adapted from J. S. Nevis, S. A. Rathus, & B. Green (2005). *Abnormal Psychology in a Changing World* (5th ed.) Upper Saddle River, NJ: Prentice Hall.

ENDURING ISSUES in Psychological Disorders

As we explore psychological disorders in this chapter, we will again encounter some of the enduring issues that interest psychologists. A recurring topic is the relationship between genetics, neurotransmitters, and behavior disorders (*Mind–Body*). We will also see that many psychological disorders arise because a vulnerable person encounters a particularly stressful environment (*Person–Situation*). As you read the chapter, think about how you would answer the question "What is normal?" and how the answer to that question has changed over time and differs even today across cultures (*Diversity–Universality*). Consider also whether a young person with a psychological disorder is likely to suffer from it later in life and, conversely, whether a well-adjusted young person is immune to psychological disorders later in life (*Stability–Change*).

PERSPECTIVES ON PSYCHOLOGICAL DISORDERS

How does a mental health professional define a psychological disorder?

When is a person's behavior abnormal? This is not always easy to determine. There is no doubt about the abnormality of a man who dresses in flowing robes and accosts pedestrians on the street, claiming to be Jesus Christ, or a woman who dons an aluminum-foil helmet to prevent space aliens from "stealing" her thoughts. But other instances of abnormal behavior aren't always so clear. What about the three people we have just described? All of them exhibit unusual behavior. But does their behavior deserve to be labeled "abnormal"? Do any of them have a genuine psychological disorder?

The answer depends in part on the perspective you take. As **Table 12–1** summarizes, society, the individual, and the mental health professional all adopt different perspectives when distinguishing abnormal behavior from normal behavior. Society's main standard of abnormality is whether the behavior fails to conform to prevailing ideas about what is socially expected of people. In contrast, when individuals assess the abnormality of their own behavior, their main criterion is whether that behavior fosters a sense of unhappiness

LEARNING OBJECTIVES

- Compare the three perspectives on what constitutes abnormal behavior. Explain what is meant by the statement "Identifying behavior as abnormal is also a matter of degree." Distinguish between the *prevalence* and *incidence* of psychological disorders, and between *mental illness* and *insanity*.

- Describe the key features of the biological, psychoanalytic, cognitive–behavioral, diathesis–stress, and systems models of psychological disorders.

- Explain what is meant by and describe the basis on which it categorizes disorders.

TABLE 12-1   Perspectives on Psychological Disorders

	Standards/Values	Measures
Society	Orderly world in which people assume responsibility for their assigned social roles (e.g., breadwinner, parent), conform to prevailing mores, and meet situational requirements	Observations of behavior, extent to which a person fulfills society's expectations and measures up to prevailing standards
Individual	Happiness, gratification of needs	Subjective perceptions of self-esteem, acceptance, and well-being
Mental health professional	Sound personality structure characterized by growth, development, autonomy, environmental mastery, ability to cope with stress, adaptation	Clinical judgment, aided by behavioral observations and psychological tests of such variables as self-concept; sense of identity; balance of psychic forces; unified outlook on life; resistance to stress; self-regulation; the ability to cope with reality; the absence of mental and behavioral symptoms; adequacy in interpersonal relationships

Source: From "A Tripartite Model of Mental Health and Therapeutic Outcomes with Special Reference to Negative Effects on Psychotherapy" by H. H. Strupp and S. W. Hadley, *American Psychologist, 32* (1977), pp. 187–196. Copyright © 1977 by American Psychological Association.

and lack of well-being. Mental health professionals take still another perspective. They assess abnormality chiefly by looking for maladaptive *personality traits, psychological discomfort* regarding a particular behavior, and evidence that the behavior is preventing the person from *functioning well in life.*

These three approaches to identifying abnormal behavior are not always in agreement. For example, of the three people previously described, only Claudia considers her own behavior to be a genuine problem that is undermining her happiness and sense of well-being. In contrast to Claudia, Jack is not really bothered by his compulsive behavior (in fact, he sees it as a way of relieving anxiety); and Jonathan is not only content with being a loner, but he also experiences great comfort from the illusion of his dead mother's presence. But now suppose we shift our focus and adopt society's perspective. In this case, we must include Jonathan on our list of those whose behavior is abnormal. His self-imposed isolation and talk of sensing his mother's ghost violate social expectations of how people should think and act. Society would not consider Jonathan normal. Neither would a mental health professional. In fact, from the perspective of a mental health professional, all three of these cases show evidence of a psychological disorder. The people involved may not always be distressed by their own behavior, but that behavior is impairing their ability to function well in everyday settings or in social relationships. The point is that there is no hard and fast rule as to what constitutes abnormal behavior. Distinguishing between normal and abnormal behavior always depends on the perspective taken.

Identifying behavior as abnormal is also a matter of degree. To understand why, imagine that each of our three cases is slightly less extreme. Jack is still prone to double-checking, but he doesn't check over and over again. Claudia still spends much time on her hair, but she doesn't do so constantly and not with such chronic dissatisfaction. As for Jonathan, he only occasionally withdraws from social contact; and he has had the sense of his dead mother's presence just twice over the last 3 years. In these less severe situations, a mental health professional would not be so ready to diagnose a mental disorder. Clearly, great care must be taken when separating mental health and mental illness into two *qualitatively* different categories. It is often more accurate to think of mental illness as simply being *quantitatively* different from normal behavior—that is, different in degree. The line between one and the other is often somewhat arbitrary. Cases are always much easier to judge when they fall at the extreme end of a dimension than when they fall near the "dividing line."

Historical Views of Psychological Disorders

How has the view of psychological disorders changed over time?

The place and times also contribute to how we define mental disorders. Thousands of years ago, mysterious behaviors were often attributed to supernatural powers and madness was a sign that spirits had possessed a person. As late as the 18th century, the emotionally disturbed person was often thought to be a witch or to be possessed by the devil. Exorcisms, ranging from mild to severe were performed, many people endured horrifying tortures. Some people were even burned at the stake.

Not all people with mental illness were persecuted and tortured. Beginning in the late Middle Ages, some public and private asylums were established to care for people with mental illness. Even though these institutions were founded with good intentions, most were little more than prisons. In the worst cases, inmates were chained down and deprived of food, light, or air in order to "cure" them.

Little was done to ensure humane standards in mental institutions until 1793, when Philippe Pinel (1745–1826) became director of the Bicêtre Hospital in Paris. Under his direction, patients were released from their chains and allowed to move about the hospital grounds, rooms were made more comfortable and sanitary, and questionable and violent medical treatments were abandoned (James Harris, 2003). Pinel's reforms were soon followed by similar efforts in England and, somewhat later, in the United States where Dorothea Dix (1802–1887), a schoolteacher from Boston, led a nationwide campaign for the humane treatment of mentally ill people. Under her influence, the few existing asylums in the United States were gradually turned into hospitals.

In the 17th century, French physicians tried various devices to cure their patients of "fantasy and folly."

The basic reason for the failed—and sometimes abusive—treatment of mentally disturbed people throughout history has been the lack of understanding of the nature and causes of psychological disorders. Although our knowledge is still inadequate, important advances in understanding abnormal behavior can be traced to the late 19th and 20th centuries, when three influential but often conflicting models of abnormal behavior emerged: the biological model, the psychoanalytic model, and the cognitive–behavioral model.

The Biological Model

How can biology influence the development of psychological disorders?

The **biological model** holds that psychological disorders are caused by physiological malfunctions often stemming from hereditary factors. As we shall see, support for the biological model has been growing rapidly as scientists make significant advances in *neuroscience,* which directly links biology and behavior (see Chapter 2, "The Biological Basis of Behavior").

For instance, new neuroimaging techniques have enabled researchers to pinpoint regions of the brain involved in such disorders as schizophrenia (Gur et al., 2011; Kumra, 2008) and antisocial personality (Völlm, 2010). By unraveling the complex chemical interactions that take place at the synapse, *neurochemists* have spawned advances in *neuropharmacology* leading to the development of promising new psychoactive drugs (see Chapter 13, "Therapies"). Many of these advances are also linked to the field of behavior genetics, which is continually increasing our understanding of the role of specific genes in the development of complex disorders such as schizophrenia (Lipina et al., 2011; Ying-Chieh Wang et al., 2008) and autism (Losh, Sullivan, Trembath, & Piven, 2008; Marui et al., 2011).

Although neuroscientific breakthroughs are indeed remarkable, to date no neuroimaging technique can clearly and definitively differentiate among various mental disorders (Pihl, 2010). And despite the availability of an increasing number of medications to alleviate the symptoms of some mental disorders, most drugs can only control—rather than cure—abnormal behavior. There is also some concern that advances in identifying the underlying neurological structures and mechanisms associated with mental illnesses may interfere with the recognition of equally important psychological causes of abnormal behavior (Dudai, 2004; Widiger & Sankis, 2000). Despite this concern, the integration of neuroscientific research and traditional psychological approaches to understanding behavior is taking place at an increasingly rapid pace, and will undoubtedly reshape our view of mental illness in the future (Westen, 2005; Zipursky, 2007).

biological model View that psychological disorders have a biochemical or physiological basis.

The cognitive–behavioral view of mental disorders suggests that people can learn—and unlearn—thinking patterns that affect their lives unfavorably. For example, an athlete who is convinced she will not win may not practice as hard as she should and end up "defeating herself."

The Psychoanalytic Model

What did Freud and his followers believe was the underlying cause of psychological disorders?

Freud and his followers developed the **psychoanalytic model** during the late 19th and early 20th centuries. (See Chapter 10, "Personality.") According to this model, behavior disorders are symbolic expressions of unconscious conflicts, which can usually be traced to childhood. The psychoanalytic model argues that in order to resolve their problems effectively, people must become aware that the source of their problems lies in their childhood and infancy.

The Cognitive–Behavioral Model

According to the cognitive–behavioral model, what causes abnormal behavior?

A third model of abnormal behavior grew out of 20th-century research on learning and cognition. The **cognitive–behavioral model** suggests that psychological disorders, like all behavior, result from learning. For example, a bright student who believes that he is academically inferior to his classmates and can't perform well on a test may not put much effort into studying. Naturally, he performs poorly, and his poor test score confirms his belief that he is academically inferior.

The Diathesis–Stress Model and Systems Theory

Why do some people with a family history of a psychological disorder develop the disorder, whereas other family members do not?

Each of the three major theories is useful in explaining the causes of certain types of disorders. The most exciting recent developments, however, emphasize integration of the various theoretical models to discover specific causes and specific treatments for different mental disorders.

One promising integrative approach is the **diathesis–stress model.** This model suggests that a biological predisposition called a **diathesis** must combine with a stressful circumstance before the predisposition to a mental disorder is manifested (S. R. Jones & Fernyhough, 2007).

The **systems approach,** also known as the *biopsychosocial model,* examines how biological risks, psychological stresses, and social pressures and expectations combine to produce psychological disorders (Fava & Sonino, 2007). According to this model, emotional problems are "lifestyle diseases" that, much like heart disease and many other physical illnesses, result from a combination of risk factors and stresses. Just as heart disease can result from a combination of genetic predisposition, personality styles, poor health habits (such as smoking), and stress, psychological problems result from several risk factors that influence one another. In this chapter, we follow the systems approach in examining the causes and treatments of abnormal behavior.

ENDURING ISSUES

Mind–Body   Causes of Mental Disorders

Throughout this chapter, as we discuss what is known about the causes of psychological disorders, you will see that biological and psychological factors are intimately connected. For example, there is strong evidence for a genetic component in some personality disorders as well as in schizophrenia. However, not everyone who inherits these factors develops a personality disorder or suffers from schizophrenia. Our current state of knowledge allows us to pinpoint certain causative factors for certain conditions, but it does not allow us to completely differentiate biological and psychological factors. ∎

psychoanalytic model View that psychological disorders result from unconscious internal conflicts.

cognitive–behavioral model View that psychological disorders result from learning maladaptive ways of thinking and behaving.

diathesis–stress model View that people biologically predisposed to a mental disorder (those with a certain diathesis) will tend to exhibit that disorder when particularly affected by stress.

diathesis Biological predisposition.

systems approach View that biological, psychological, and social risk factors combine to produce psychological disorders. Also known as the biopsychosocial model of psychological disorders.

The Prevalence of Psychological Disorders

How common are mental disorders?

Psychologists and public-health experts are concerned with both the prevalence and the incidence of mental health problems. *Prevalence* refers to the frequency with which a given disorder occurs at a given time. If there were 100 cases of depression in a population of 1,000, the prevalence of depression would be 10%. The *incidence* of a disorder refers to the number of new cases that arise in a given period. If there were 10 new cases of depression in a population of 1,000 in a single year, the incidence would be 1% per year.

In 2005, the National Institute of Mental Health conducted a survey finding that 26.2% or approximately 57.7 million Americans were suffering from a mental disorder. While only about 6% were regarded as having a serious mental illness, almost half the people (45%) suffering from one mental disorder also met the criteria for two or more other mental disorders (Kessler, Chiu, Demler, & Walters, 2005). Notably, mental disorders are the leading cause of disability in the United States for people between the ages of 15 and 44 (The World Health Organization, 2004). **Figure 12–1** shows the prevalence for some of the more common mental disorders among adult Americans. As shown in Figure 12–1, anxiety disorders are the most common mental disorder followed by mood disorders. (All of these are described in detail later in this chapter.)

Globally, diagnostic interviews with more than 60,000 people in 14 countries around the world showed that over a 1-year period, the prevalence of moderate or serious psychological disorders varied widely from 12% of the population in the Americas to 7% in Europe, 6% in the Middle East and Africa, and just 4% in Asia (World Health Organization [WHO] World Mental Health Survey Consortium, 2004).

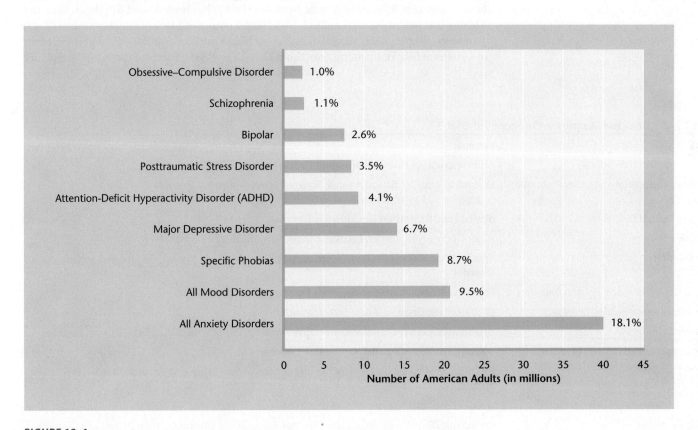

FIGURE 12–1

Prevalence of selected mental disorders in the United States.

A 2005 survey by the National Institute of Mental Health found that approximately 26.2%, or about 57.7 million Americans suffer from a mental disorder. The prevalence among adult Americans for a few of the more common mental disorders is shown here.

Source: National Institute of Mental Health (2005).

insanity Legal term applied to defendants who do not know right from wrong or are unable to control their behavior.

Mental Illness and the Law

Is there a difference between "insanity" and "mental illness"?

Particularly horrifying crimes have often been attributed to mental disturbance, because it seems to many people that anyone who could commit such crimes must be "crazy." But to the legal system, this presents a problem: If a person is truly "crazy," are we justified in holding him or her responsible for criminal acts? The legal answer to this question is a qualified yes. A mentally ill person is responsible for his or her crimes unless he or she is determined to be *insane*. What's the difference between being "mentally ill" and being "insane"? **Insanity** is a legal term, not a psychological one. It is typically applied to defendants who were so mentally disturbed when they committed their offense that they either lacked substantial capacity to appreciate the criminality of their actions (to know right from wrong) or to conform to the requirements of the law (to control their behavior).

When a defendant is suspected of being mentally disturbed or legally insane, another important question must be answered before that person is brought to trial: Is the person able to understand the charges against him or her and to participate in a defense in court? This issue is known as *competency* to stand trial. The person is examined by a court-appointed expert and, if found to be incompetent, is sent to a mental institution, often for an indefinite period. If judged to be competent, the person is required to stand trial.

Classifying Abnormal Behavior

Why is it useful to have a manual of psychological disorders?

For nearly 60 years, the American Psychiatric Association (APA) has issued a manual describing and classifying the various kinds of psychological disorders. This publication, the *Diagnostic and Statistical Manual of Mental Disorders (DSM)*, has been revised five times; the latest revision was published in May, 2013. The *DSM-5* (American Psychiatric Association, 2013) provides a complete list of mental disorders, with each category painstakingly defined in terms of significant behavior patterns (see **Table 12–2**). The *DSM* has gained increasing acceptance

TABLE 12-2   Selected Diagnostic Categories of *DSM-5*

Category	Example
Neurodevelopmental disorders	Autism Spectrum Disorder, Attention-Deficit/Hyperactivity Disorder
Schizophrenia Spectrum and Other Psychotic Disorders	Delusional disorder, Schizophrenia, Schizoaffective Disorder, Catatonia
Bipolar and Related Disorders	Bipolar I and II Disorders, Cyclothymic Disorder
Depressive Disorders	Major Depressive Disorder, Persistent Depressive Disorders
Anxiety Disorders	Specific Phobia, Social Anxiety Disorder, Panic Disorder, Agoraphobia, Generalized Anxiety Disorder
Obsessive-Compulsive and Related Disorders	Obsessive-Compulsive Disorder, Body Dysmorphic Disorder
Trauma- and Stressor-Related Disorders	Posttraumatic Disorder, Acute Stress Disorder
Dissociative Disorders	Dissociative Identity Disorder, Dissociative Amnesia, Depersonalization/Derealization Disorder
Somatic Symptom and Related Disorders	Somatic Symptom Disorder, Conversion Disorder
Sexual Dysfunctions	Erectile Disorder, Female Orgasmic Disorder, Female Sexual Interest-Arousal Disorder, Premature Ejaculation
Gender Dysphoria	Gender Dysphoria
Paraphilic Disorders	Voyeuristic Disorder, Exhibitionistic Disorder, Frotteuristic Disorder, Sexual Masochism Disorder, Sexual Sadism Disorder, Pedophilic Disorder, Fetishistic Disorder, Transvestic Disorder
Personality Disorders	Paranoid Personality Disorder, Schizoid Personality Disorder, Avoidant Personality Disorder, Dependent Personality Disorder, Antisocial Personality Disorder, Borderline Personality Disorder, Narcissistic Personality Disorder

because its detailed criteria for diagnosing mental disorders have made diagnosis much more reliable. Today, it is the most widely used classification of psychological disorders. In the remainder of this chapter, we will explore some of the key categories in greater detail.

✓●—**Study** and **Review** on **MyPsychLab**

CHECK YOUR UNDERSTANDING

1. It is likely that people in early societies believed that _____ forces caused abnormal behavior.

2. There is growing evidence that _____ factors are involved in mental disorders as diverse as schizophrenia, depression, and anxiety.

3. _____ is a legal term that is not the same thing as mental illness.

Indicate whether the following statements are true (T) or false (F):

4. The line separating normal from abnormal behavior is somewhat arbitrary.

5. About two-thirds of Americans are suffering from one or more serious mental disorders at any given time.

6. The cognitive view of mental disorders suggests that they arise from unconscious conflicts, often rooted in childhood.

Answers: 1. supernatural. 2. genetic. 3. Insanity. 4. (T). 5. (F). 6. (F).

APPLY YOUR UNDERSTANDING

1. You are talking to a friend whose behavior has you concerned. She says, "Look, I'm happy, I feel good about myself, and I think things are going well." Which viewpoint on mental health is reflected in her statement?
   a. society's view
   b. the individual's view
   c. the mental health professional's view
   d. Both (b) and (c) are true.

2. A friend asks you, "What causes people to have psychological disorders?" You respond, "Most often, it turns out that some people are biologically prone to developing a particular disorder. When they have some kind of stressful experience, the predisposition shows up in their behavior." What view of psychological disorders are you taking?
   a. psychoanalytic model
   b. cognitive model
   c. behavioral model
   d. diathesis–stress model

Answers: 1.b. 2.d.

MOOD DISORDERS

How do mood disorders differ from ordinary mood changes?

Most people have a wide emotional range; they can be happy or sad, animated or quiet, cheerful or discouraged, or overjoyed or miserable, depending on the circumstances. In some people with **mood disorders,** this range is greatly restricted. They seem stuck at one or the other end of the emotional spectrum—either consistently excited and euphoric or consistently sad—regardless of life circumstances. Others with mood disorders alternate between the extremes of euphoria and sadness.

Depressive Disorders

How does clinical depression differ from ordinary sadness?

The most common mood disorders are **depressive disorders** in which people may feel overwhelmed with sadness, lose interest in the things they normally enjoy, experience intense feelings of worthlessness and guilt, or feel tired and apathetic, sometimes to the

LEARNING OBJECTIVES

- Explain how mood disorders differ from ordinary mood changes. List the key symptoms that are used to diagnose major depression, dysthymia, mania, and bipolar disorder. Describe the causes of mood disorders.

- Describe the factors that are related to a person's likelihood of committing suicide. Contrast the three myths about suicide with the actual facts about suicide.

mood disorders Disturbances in mood or prolonged emotional state.

depressive disorders Mood disorders often characterized by overwhelming feelings of sadness, lack of interest in activities, and perhaps excessive guilt or feelings of worthlessness.

point of being unable to make the simplest decisions. Many depressed people feel as if they have failed utterly in life, and they tend to blame themselves for their problems. Seriously depressed people often have insomnia and lose interest in food and sex. They may have trouble thinking or concentrating—even to the extent of finding it difficult to read a newspaper. In fact, difficulty in concentrating and subtle changes in short-term memory are sometimes the first signs of the onset of depression (Janice Williams et al., 2000). In extreme cases, depressed people may be plagued by suicidal thoughts or may even attempt suicide (Hantouche, Angst, & Azorin, 2010). Sadly, the earlier the age of onset of depressive symptoms, the greater the likelihood that suicide may be attempted (A. H. Thompson, 2008).

Clinical depression is different from the "normal" kind of depression that all people experience from time to time. Only when depression is long lasting and goes well beyond the typical reaction to a stressful life event is it classified as a mood disorder (American Psychiatric Association, 2013). (See "Applying Psychology: Recognizing Depression.")

APPLYING PSYCHOLOGY

Recognizing Depression

From time to time, almost everyone gets "the blues." Failing a major exam, breaking up with a partner, even leaving home and friends to attend college can all produce a temporary state of sadness. More significant life events can have an even greater impact: The loss of one's job or the loss of a loved one can produce a sense of hopelessness about the future that feels very much like a slide into depression. But in all of these instances, either the mood disorder is a normal reaction to a real problem or it passes quickly.

At what point do these normal responses evolve into clinical depression? The *DSM-5* provides the framework for making this distinction. First, clinical depression is characterized by depressed mood or by the loss of interest and pleasure in usual activities, or both. Clinicians also look for significant impairment or distress in social, occupational, or other important areas of functioning. People suffering from depression not only feel sad or empty, but also have significant problems carrying on a normal lifestyle. Clinicians also look for other explanations. Could symptoms be due to substance abuse or medication side effects? Could they be the result of a medical condition such as hypothyroidism (the inability of the thyroid gland to produce an adequate amount of its hormones)? Could the symptoms be better interpreted as an intense but otherwise normal reaction to life events?

If the symptoms do not seem to be explained by the preceding causes, clinicians make a diagnosis of major depressive disorder according to the *DSM-5,* which specifies that at least five of the following symptoms—including at least one of the first two—are present:

1. *Depressed mood:* Does the person feel sad or empty for most of the day, most every day, or do others observe these symptoms?
2. *Loss of interest in pleasure:* Has the person lost interest in performing normal activities, such as working or going to social events? Does the person seem to be "just going through the motions" of daily life without deriving any pleasure from them?
3. *Significant weight loss or gain:* Has the person gained or lost more than 5% of body weight in a month? Has the person lost interest in eating or complained that food has lost its taste?
4. *Sleep disturbances:* Is the person having trouble sleeping? Conversely, is the person sleeping too much?
5. *Disturbances in motor activities:* Do others notice a change in the person's activity level? Does the person just "sit around" or, conversely, behave in an agitated or unusually restless manner?
6. *Fatigue:* Does the person complain of being constantly tired and having no energy?
7. *Feelings of worthlessness or excessive guilt:* Does the person express feelings such as "You'd be better off without me" or "I'm evil and I ruin everything for everybody I love"?
8. *Inability to concentrate:* Does the person complain of memory problems ("I just can't remember anything anymore") or the inability to focus attention on simple tasks, such as reading a newspaper?
9. *Recurrent thoughts of death:* Does the person talk about committing suicide or express the wish that he or she were dead?

If you or someone you know well seems to have these symptoms, that person should consult a doctor or mental health professional. When these symptoms are present and are not due to other medical conditions, a diagnosis of major depression is typically the result, and appropriate treatment can be prescribed. As you will learn in Chapter 13, "Therapies," appropriate diagnosis is the first step in the effective treatment of psychological disorders.

Source: *Diagnostic and Statistical Manual of Mental Disorders,* 5th Edition, Text Revision. Washington, DC, American Psychiatric Association, 2013.

DSM-5 distinguishes between **major depressive disorder**, which can be an episode of intense sadness that may last for several months, and **persistent depressive disorder** which involves less intense sadness (and related symptoms), but persists with little relief for a period of 2 years or more. Depression is two to three times more prevalent in women than in men (Kessler et al., 2003; Nolen-Hoeksema, 2006).

Children and adolescents can also suffer from depression. In very young children, depression is sometimes difficult to diagnose because the symptoms are usually different than those seen in adults. For instance, in infants or toddlers, depression may manifest as a "failure to thrive" or gain weight, or as a delay in speech or motor development. In school-aged children, depression may be manifested as antisocial behavior, excessive worrying, sleep disturbances, or unwarranted fatigue (Kaslow, Clark, & Sirian, 2008).

One of the most severe hazards of depression, as well as some of the other disorders described in this chapter, is that people may become so miserable that they no longer wish to live.

major depressive disorder A depressive disorder characterized by an episode of intense sadness, depressed mood, or marked loss of interest or pleasure in nearly all activities.

persistent depressive disorder A depressive disorder where the symptoms are generally less severe than for major depressive disorder, but are present most days and persist for at least 2 years.

Suicide

What factors are related to a person's likelihood of committing suicide?

Each year in the United States, approximately one suicide occurs every 17 minutes, or over 34,000 annually, making it the 11th leading cause of death (Centers for Disease Control, 2006; Holloway, Brown, & Beck, 2008). In addition, half a million Americans receive hospital treatment each year for attempted suicide. Indeed, suicides outnumber homicides by five to three in the United States. The suicide rate is much higher among Whites than among minorities (Centers for Disease Control, 2006). Compared to other countries, the suicide rate in the United States is below average (the highest rates are found in eastern European countries) (Curtin, 2004). More women than men attempt suicide, but more men succeed, partly because men tend to choose violent and lethal means, such as guns.

Although the largest number of suicides occurs among older White males, since the 1960s suicide attempt rates have been rising among adolescents and young adults (**Figure 12–2**). In fact, adolescents account for 12% of all suicide attempts in the United States, and in many other countries suicide ranks as either the first, second, or third leading cause of death in that age group (Centers for Disease Control and Prevention, 1999; Zalsman & Mann, 2005). We cannot as yet explain the increase, though the stresses of leaving home, meeting the demands of college or a career, and surviving loneliness or broken romantic attachments seem to be particularly great at this stage of life. Although external problems such as unemployment and financial strain may also contribute to personal problems, suicidal behavior is most common among adolescents with psychological problems. Several myths concerning suicide can be quite dangerous:

Myth: Someone who talks about committing suicide will never do it.

Fact: Most people who kill themselves have talked about it. Such comments should always be taken seriously.

Myth: Someone who has tried suicide and failed is not serious about it.

Fact: Any suicide attempt means that the person is deeply troubled and needs help immediately. A suicidal person will try again, picking a more deadly method the second or third time around.

Myth: Only people who are life's losers—those who have failed in their careers and in their personal lives—commit suicide.

Fact: Many people who kill themselves have prestigious jobs, conventional families, and a good income. Physicians, for example, have a suicide rate several times higher than that for the general population; in this case, the tendency to suicide may be related to their work stresses.

People considering suicide are overwhelmed with hopelessness. They feel that things cannot get better and see no way out of their difficulties. This perception is depression in the extreme, and it is not easy to talk someone out of this state of mind. Telling a suicidal

FIGURE 12–2

Gender and race differences in the suicide rate across the life span.

The suicide rate for White males, who commit the largest number of suicides at all ages, shows a sharp rise beyond the age of 65. In contrast, the suicide rate for African American females, which is the lowest for any group, remains relatively stable throughout the life span.

Source: Data from CDC, http://www.cdc.gov/nchs/data/dvs/MortFinal2007_WorkTable210R.pdf

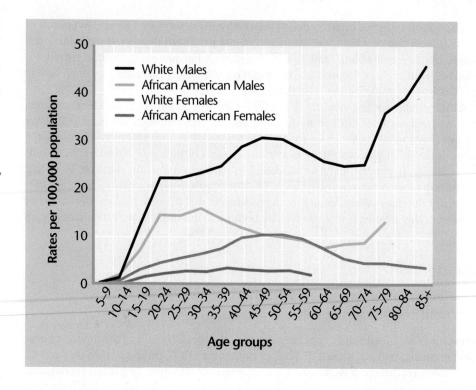

person that things aren't really so bad does no good; in fact, the person may only view this as further evidence that no one understands his or her suffering. But most suicidal people do want help, however much they may despair of obtaining it. If a friend or family member seems at all suicidal, getting professional help is important. A community mental health center is a good starting place, as are the national suicide hotlines.

Bipolar and Related Disorders

What is mania, and how is it involved in bipolar disorder?

Other mood disorders, which are less common than depression, involve **manic episodes,** in which the person becomes euphoric or "high," extremely active, excessively talkative, and easily distracted. People suffering from mania may become grandiose—that is, their self-esteem is greatly inflated. They typically have unlimited hopes and schemes, but little interest in realistically carrying them out. People in a manic state sometimes become aggressive and hostile toward others as their self-confidence grows more and more exaggerated. At the extreme, people going through a manic episode may become wild, incomprehensible, or violent until they collapse from exhaustion.

The mood disorder in which both mania and depression are present is known as bipolar disorder. In people with **bipolar disorder,** periods of mania and depression may alternate (each lasting from a few days to a few months), sometimes with periods of normal vmood in between. Occasionally, bipolar disorder occurs in a mild form, with moods of unrealistically high spirits followed by moderate depression. Research suggests that bipolar disorder is much less common than depression and, unlike depression, occurs equally in men and women. Bipolar disorder, which usually emerges during late adolescence or early adulthood, also seems to have a stronger biological component than depression. In fact, a number of specific genes have been implicated as contributing to the development of bipolar disorder (K. H. Choi et al., 2011). ◉

manic episodes Characterized by euphoric states, extreme physical activity, excessive talkativeness, distractedness, and sometimes grandiosity.

bipolar disorder A mood disorder in which periods of mania and depression may alternate, sometimes with periods of normal mood intervening.

◉ **Watch** and **Video** DSM in Context: Speaking Out: Feliziano: Bipolar Disorder on **MyPsychLab**

Causes of Mood Disorders

What causes some people to experience extreme mood changes?

Mood disorders result from a combination of risk factors although researchers do not yet know exactly how these elements interact to cause a mood disorder (Moffitt, Caspi, & Rutter, 2006).

Biological Factors Genetic factors can play an important role in the development of depression (Haghighi et al., 2008; Karg, Burmeister, Shedden, & Sen, 2011) and bipolar disorder (K. H. Choi et al., 2011; Serretti & Mandelli, 2008). Strong evidence comes from studies of twins. (See Chapter 2, "The Biological Basis of Behavior.") If one identical twin is clinically depressed, the other twin (with identical genes) is likely to become clinically depressed also. Among fraternal twins (who share only about half their genes), if one twin is clinically depressed, the risk for the second twin is much lower (McGuffin, Katz, Watkins, & Rutherford, 1996). In addition, genetic researchers have identified a specific variation on the 22 chromosome that appears to increase an individual's susceptibility to bipolar disorder by influencing the balance of certain neurotransmitters in the brain (Hashimoto et al., 2005; Kuratomi et al., 2008).

A new and particularly intriguing line of research aimed at understanding the cause of mood disorders stems from the diathesis–stress model. Recent research shows that a diathesis (biological predisposition) leaves some people particularly vulnerable to certain stress hormones. Adverse or traumatic experiences early in life can result in high levels of those stress hormones, which in turn increases the likelihood of a mood disorder later in life (Bradley et al., 2008; Gillespie & Nemeroff, 2007).

Psychological Factors Although a number of psychological factors are thought to play a role in causing severe depression, in recent years, researchers have focused on the contribution of maladaptive **cognitive distortions.** According to Aaron Beck (1967, 1976, 1984), during childhood and adolescence, some people undergo wrenching experiences such as the loss of a parent, severe difficulties in gaining parental or social approval, or humiliating criticism from teachers and other adults. One response to such experience is to develop a negative self-concept—a feeling of incompetence or unworthiness that has little to do with reality, but that is maintained by a distorted and illogical interpretation of real events. When a new situation arises that resembles the situation under which the self-concept was learned, these same feelings of worthlessness and incompetence may be activated, resulting in depression. Considerable research supports Beck's view of depression (Clark & Beck, 2010; Kwon & Oei, 2003; Maag, Swearer, & Toland, 2009). Therapy based on Beck's theories has proven quite successful in treating depression. (See Chapter 13, "Therapies.")

Social Factors Many social factors have been linked with mood disorders, particularly difficulties in interpersonal relationships. In fact, some theorists have suggested that the link between depression and troubled relationships explains the fact that depression is two to three times more prevalent in women than in men (National Alliance on Mental Illness, 2003), because women tend to be more relationship oriented than men are in our society (Ali, 2008). Yet, not every person who experiences a troubled relationship becomes depressed. As the systems approach would predict, it appears that a genetic predisposition or cognitive distortion is necessary before a distressing close relationship or other significant life stressor will result in a mood disorder (Wichers et al., 2007).

ENDURING ISSUES

Person–Situation   The Chicken or the Egg?

It is sometimes difficult to tease apart the relative contribution of the person's biological or cognitive tendencies and the social situation. People with certain depression-prone genetic or cognitive tendencies may be more likely than others to encounter stressful life events by

cognitive distortions Illogical and maladaptive responses to early negative life events that lead to feelings of incompetence and unworthiness that are reactivated whenever a new situation arises that resembles the original events.

virtue of their personality and behavior. For example, studies show that depressed people tend to evoke anxiety and even hostility in others, partly because they require more emotional support than people feel comfortable giving. As a result, people tend to avoid those who are depressed, and this shunning can intensify the depression. In short, depression-prone and depressed people may become trapped in a vicious circle that is at least partly of their own creation (Coyne & Whiffen, 1995; Pettit & Joiner, 2006). ■

✓•⌐**Study** and **Review** on **MyPsychLab**

CHECK YOUR UNDERSTANDING

Indicate whether the following statements are true (T) or false (F):

1. _____ People with a mood disorder always alternate between the extremes of euphoria and sadness.
2. _____ More men attempt suicide, but more women actually kill themselves.
3. _____ Most psychologists now believe that mood disorders result from a combination of risk factors.
4. _____ Mania is the most common mood disorder.

Answers: 1. (F). 2. (F). 3. (T). 4. (F).

APPLY YOUR UNDERSTANDING

1. Bob is "down in the dumps" most of the time. He is having a difficult time dealing with any criticism he receives at work or at home. Most days he feels that he is a failure, despite the fact that he is successful in his job and his family is happy. Although he participates in various activities outside the home, he finds no joy in anything. He says he is constantly tired, but he has trouble sleeping. It is most likely that Bob is suffering from

   a. clinical depression.
   b. generalized anxiety disorder.
   c. depersonalization disorder.
   d. somatoform disorder.

2. Mary almost seems to be two different people. At times, she is hyperactive and talks nonstop (sometimes so fast that nobody can understand her). At those times, her friends say she is "bouncing off the walls." But then she changes: She becomes terribly sad, loses interest in eating, spends much of her time in bed, and rarely says a word. It is most likely that Mary is suffering from

   a. dissociative identity disorder.
   b. depression.
   c. bipolar disorder.
   d. schizophrenia.

Answers: 1. a. 2. c.

LEARNING OBJECTIVES

• Explain how anxiety disorders differ from ordinary anxiety. Briefly describe the key features of phobias, panic disorders, generalized anxiety disorder, and obsessive–compulsive disorder.
• Describe the causes of anxiety disorders.

❯ ANXIETY DISORDERS

How does an anxiety disorder differ from ordinary anxiety?

All of us are afraid from time to time, but we usually know why we are fearful, our fear is caused by something appropriate and identifiable, and it passes with time. In the case of **anxiety disorders,** however, either the person does not know why he or she is afraid, or the anxiety is inappropriate to the circumstances. In either case, the person's fear and anxiety just don't seem to make sense.

As shown in Figure 12–1, anxiety disorders are more common than any other form of mental disorder. Anxiety disorders can be subdivided into several diagnostic categories, including specific phobias, panic disorder, and other anxiety disorders, as well as anxiety-related disorders such as obsessive–compulsive disorder and disorders caused by specific traumatic events.

anxiety disorders Disorders in which anxiety is a characteristic feature or the avoidance of anxiety seems to motivate abnormal behavior.

Specific Phobias

Into what three categories are phobias usually grouped?

A **specific phobia** is an intense, paralyzing fear of something that perhaps should be feared, but the fear is excessive and unreasonable. In fact, the fear in a specific phobia is so great that it leads the person to avoid routine or adaptive activities and thus interferes with life functioning. For example, it is appropriate to be a bit fearful as an airplane takes off or lands, but people with a phobia about flying refuse to get on or even go near an airplane. Other common phobias focus on animals, heights, closed places, blood, needles, and injury. Almost 10% of people in the United States suffer from at least one specific phobia.

Most people feel some mild fear or uncertainty in many social situations, but when these fears interfere significantly with life functioning, they are considered to be **social anxiety disorders.** Intense fear of public speaking is a common form of social phobia. In other cases, simply talking with people or eating in public causes such severe anxiety that the phobic person will go to great lengths to avoid these situations.

Agoraphobia is much more debilitating than social phobia. This term comes from Greek and Latin words that literally mean "fear of the marketplace," but the disorder typically involves multiple, intense fears, such as the fear of being alone, of being in public places from which escape might be difficult, of being in crowds, of traveling in an automobile, or of going through tunnels or over bridges. The common element in all of these situations seems to be a great dread of being separated from sources of security. Some sufferers are so fearful that they will venture only a few miles from home; others will not leave their homes at all.

For example, consider the accomplished author, composer, pianist, and educator Allen Shawn, who wrote in his memoir:

> I don't like heights, I don't like being on the water. I am upset by walking across parking lots or open parks or fields where there are no buildings. I tend to avoid bridges, unless they are on a small scale. I respond poorly to stretches of vastness but do equally badly when I am closed in, as I am severely claustrophobic. When I go to a theater, I sit on the aisle. I am petrified of tunnels, making most train travel as well as many drives difficult. I don't take subways. I avoid elevators as much as possible. I experience glassed-in spaces as toxic, and I find it very difficult to adjust to being in buildings in which the windows don't open. I don't like to go to enclosed malls; and if I do, I don't venture very far into them …. In short, I am afraid both of closed and of open spaces, and I am afraid, in a sense, of any form of isolation. (Shawn, 2007, p. xviii)

Panic Disorder

How does a panic attack differ from fear?

Another type of anxiety disorder is **panic disorder,** characterized by recurring episodes of a sudden, unpredictable, and overwhelming fear or terror. Panic attacks occur without any reasonable cause and are accompanied by feelings of impending doom, chest pain, dizziness or fainting, sweating, difficulty breathing, and fear of losing control or dying. Panic attacks usually last only a few minutes, but they may recur for no apparent reason. For example, consider the following description:

> Thirty-year-old Shelly Baker arrived at an anxiety clinic seeking help dealing with "panic attacks." The attacks, which were becoming more frequent, often occurred 2 or 3 times a day. Without any warning, she would suddenly experience a wave of "terrible fear." She was afraid that she would lose control and do something bizarre like running outside and screaming at the top of her lungs.

Panic attacks not only cause tremendous fear while they are happening, but also leave a dread of having another panic attack, which can persist for days or even weeks after the original episode. In some cases, this dread is so overwhelming that it can lead to the development of agoraphobia: To prevent a recurrence, people may avoid any circumstance that might cause anxiety, clinging to people or situations that help keep them calm.

specific phobia Anxiety disorder characterized by an intense, paralyzing fear of something.

social anxiety disorder Anxiety disorders characterized by excessive, inappropriate fears connected with social situations or performances in front of other people.

agoraphobia An anxiety disorder that involves multiple, intense fears of crowds, public places, and other situations that require separation from a source of security such as the home.

panic disorder An anxiety disorder characterized by recurrent panic attacks in which the person suddenly experiences intense fear or terror without any reasonable cause.

generalized anxiety disorder An anxiety disorder characterized by prolonged vague but intense fears that are not attached to any particular object or circumstance.

obsessive–compulsive disorder (OCD) An anxiety-related disorder in which a person feels driven to think disturbing thoughts or to perform senseless rituals.

body dysmorphic disorder A somatoform disorder in which a person becomes so preoccupied with his or her imagined ugliness that normal life is impossible.

Simulate the **Experiment** Obsessive Compulsive Test on **MyPsychLab**

In the various phobias and in panic attacks, there is a specific source of anxiety. In contrast, **generalized anxiety disorder** is defined by prolonged vague but intense fears that are not attached to any particular object or circumstance. Generalized anxiety disorder perhaps comes closest to the everyday meaning attached to the term *neurotic*. Its symptoms include the inability to relax, muscle tension, rapid heartbeat or pounding heart, apprehensiveness about the future, constant alertness to potential threats, and sleeping difficulties (Hazlett-Stevens, Pruitt, & Collins, 2009).

Anxiety-Related Disorders

How does obsessive-compulsive disorder differ from phobias?

As the name suggests, **obsessive–compulsive disorder (OCD)** involves *obsessions*, which are involuntary thoughts or ideas that keep recurring despite the person's attempts to stop them, or *compulsions*, which are repetitive, ritualistic behaviors that a person feels compelled to perform. Obsessive thoughts are often horrible and frightening. One patient, for example, reported that "when she thought of her boyfriend, she wished he were dead"; when her sister spoke of going to the beach with her infant daughter, she "hoped that they would both drown" (Carson & Butcher, 1992, p. 190). Compulsive behaviors may be equally disruptive to the person who feels driven to perform them. Recall Jack, the engineer described at the beginning of the chapter, who couldn't leave his house without double- and triple-checking to be sure the doors were locked and all the lights and appliances were turned off.

People who experience obsessions and compulsions often do not seem particularly anxious, so why is this disorder considered an anxiety-related disorder? The answer is that if such people try to stop their irrational behavior—or if someone else tries to stop them—they experience severe anxiety. In other words, the obsessive–compulsive behavior seems to have developed to keep anxiety under control.

Body dysmorphic disorder, or imagined ugliness, is a poorly understood type of somatoform disorder. Cases of body dysmorphic disorder can be very striking. One man, for example, felt that people stared at his "pointed ears" and "large nostrils" so much that he eventually could not face going to work, so he quit his job. Claudia, the woman described at the beginning of the chapter who displayed such concern about her hair, apparently was suffering from a body dysmorphic disorder. Clearly, people who become that preoccupied with their appearance cannot lead a normal life. Ironically, most people who suffer body dysmorphic disorder are not ugly. They may be average looking or even attractive, but they are unable to evaluate their looks realistically.

Finally, two types of anxiety-related disorders are clearly caused by some specific highly stressful event. Some people who have lived through fires, floods, tornadoes, or disasters such as an airplane crash experience repeated episodes of fear and terror after the event itself is over. If the anxious reaction occurs soon after the event, the diagnosis is *acute stress disorder*. If a period of time elapses before symptoms appear, particularly in cases of military combat or rape, the diagnosis is likely to be *posttraumatic stress disorder*, discussed in Chapter 11, "Stress and Health Psychology."

Causes of Anxiety Disorders

What causes anxiety disorders?

Like all behaviors, phobias can be learned. Consider a young boy who is savagely attacked by a large dog. Because of this experience, he is now terribly afraid of all dogs. In this case, a realistic fear has become transformed into a phobia. However, other phobias are harder to understand. As we saw in Chapter 5, "Learning," many people get shocks from electric sockets, but almost no one develops a socket phobia. Yet snake and spider phobias are common. The reason seems to be that through evolution we have become biologically predisposed to associate certain potentially dangerous objects with intense fears (Hofmann, Moscovitch, & Heinrichs, 2004; Seligman, 1971).

Psychologists working from the biological perspective point to heredity, arguing that we can inherit a predisposition to anxiety disorders (Gelernter & Stein, 2009; Leigh, 2009; Leonardo & Hen, 2006). In fact, anxiety disorders tend to run in families. Researchers have located some specific genetic sites that may generally predispose people toward anxiety disorders (Goddard et al., 2004; Hamilton et al., 2004). In some cases, specific genes have even been linked to specific anxiety disorders, such as obsessive hoarding (Alonso et al., 2008).

Finally, we need to consider the role that internal psychological conflicts may play in producing feelings of anxiety. The very fact that people suffering from anxiety disorders often have no idea why they are anxious suggests that the explanation may be found in unconscious conflicts that trigger anxiety. According to this classical psychoanalytic view, phobias are the result of displacement, in which people redirect their anxiety from the unconscious conflicts toward objects or settings in the real world. (See Chapter 11, "Stress and Health Psychology," for a discussion of displacement.) ◉

◉ **Watch** the **Video** Anxiety and Worry on **MyPsychLab**

✔ **Study** and **Review** on **MyPsychLab**

CHECK YOUR UNDERSTANDING

1. According to the psychoanalytic view, anxiety results from _____.
2. The belief that we inherit the tendency to develop some phobias more easily than others argues that these phobias are _____.

Indicate whether the following statements are true (T) or false (F):

3. _____ The fear in a specific phobia often interferes with life functions.
4. _____ People who experience obsessions and compulsions appear highly anxious.
5. _____ Research indicates that people who feel that they are not in control of stressful events in their lives are more likely to experience anxiety than those who believe that they have control over such events.

Answers: 1. unconscious conflicts. 2. prepared responses. 3. (T). 4. (F). 5. (T).

APPLY YOUR UNDERSTANDING

1. Barbara becomes intensely fearful whenever she finds herself in crowds or in public places from which she might not be able to escape easily. It is most likely that Barbara is suffering from
   a. generalized anxiety disorder.
   b. panic disorder.
   c. agoraphobia.
   d. acute stress disorder.

2. A combat veteran complains of insomnia. If he does fall asleep, he often has horrible nightmares that involve killing and blood. He may be doing something normal—for example, riding a bicycle through a park—when frightening memories of war come upon him as a result of some normal stimulus, like the sound of a low-flying airplane. Given this information, you would suspect that he was suffering from
   a. generalized anxiety disorder.
   b. posttraumatic stress disorder.
   c. panic disorder.
   d. obsessive–compulsive disorder.

Answers: 1. c. 2. b.

SOMATIC SYMPTOM AND RELATED DISORDERS ⟵

What is the difference between psychosomatic illness and somatic symptom and related disorders?

The term *psychosomatic* perfectly captures the interplay of *psyche* (mind) and *soma* (body). A **psychosomatic illness** is a real, physical disorder, but one that has, at least in part, a psychological cause. As we saw in Chapter 11 ("Stress and Health Psychology"), stress,

psychosomatic illness A real physical illness that is largely caused by psychological factors such as stress and anxiety.

somatic symptom and related disorders Disorders in which there is an apparent physical illness for which there is no organic basis.

somatic symptom disorder Disorder characterized by recurrent vague somatic complaints without a physical cause.

conversion disorders Disorders in which a dramatic specific disability has no physical cause but instead seems related to psychological problems.

illness anxiety disorder Disorder in which a person interprets insignificant symptoms as signs of serious illness in the absence of any organic evidence of such illness.

anxiety, and prolonged emotional arousal alter body chemistry, the functioning of bodily organs, and the body's immune system (which is vital in fighting infections). Thus, modern medicine leans toward the idea that all physical ailments are to some extent "psychosomatic."

Psychosomatic disorders involve genuine physical illnesses. In contrast, people suffering from **somatic symptom and related disorders** believe that they are physically ill and describe symptoms that sound like physical illnesses, but medical examinations reveal no organic problems. Nevertheless, the symptoms are real to them and are not under voluntary control. For example, in one kind of somatoform disorder, **somatic symptom disorder,** the person experiences vague, recurring physical symptoms for which medical attention has been sought repeatedly but no organic cause found. Common complaints are back pain, dizziness, abdominal pain, and sometimes anxiety and depression.

Conversion disorders are characterized by complaints of paralysis, blindness, deafness, seizures, loss of feeling, or pregnancy. In these disorders, no physical causes appear, yet the symptoms are very real. In cases of **illness anxiety disorder**, the person interprets some small symptom—perhaps a cough, a bruise, or perspiration—as a sign of a serious disease. Although the symptom may actually exist, there is no evidence that the serious illness does.

Somatic symptom and related disorders (especially conversion disorders) present a challenge for psychological theorists because they seem to involve some kind of unconscious processes. Freud concluded that the physical symptoms were often related to traumatic experiences buried in a patient's past. Cognitive–behavioral theorists look for ways in which the symptomatic behavior is being rewarded. From the biological perspective, research has shown that at least some diagnosed disorders actually were real physical illnesses that were overlooked or misdiagnosed. Nevertheless, most cases of conversion disorder cannot be explained by current medical science. These cases pose as much of a theoretical challenge today as they did when conversion disorders captured Freud's attention more than a century ago.

✓●─ **Study** and **Review** on **MyPsychLab**

CHECK YOUR UNDERSTANDING

Indicate whether the following statements are true (T) or false (F):

1. _____ Modern medicine leans toward the idea that all physical ailments are to some extent "psychosomatic."

2. _____ People who suffer from somatic symptom and related disorders do not consciously seek to mislead others about their physical condition.

3. _____ Research has shown that at least some diagnosed somatic symptom and related disorders actually were real physical illnesses that were overlooked or misdiagnosed.

4. _____ Most cases of conversion disorder can be explained by current medical science.

Answers: 1. (T), 2. (T), 3. (T), 4. (F).

APPLY YOUR UNDERSTANDING

1. Bob is concerned about a few warts that have appeared on his arms. His doctor says that they are just warts and are not a concern, but Bob believes they are cancerous and that he will die from them. He consults another doctor and then another, both of whom tell him they are just normal warts, but he remains convinced they are cancerous and he is going to die. It appears that Bob is suffering from

   a. illness anxiety disorder.

   b. a psychosomatic disorder.

   c. conversion disorder.

   d. a phobia.

2. John is a writer, but work on his latest novel has come to a halt because he has lost all feeling in his arm and his hand. His doctor can find no physical cause for his problem; however, there is no question that he no longer has feeling in his arm and that he can no longer hold a pencil or type on a keyboard. It seems likely that John is suffering from

   a. body dysmorphic disorder.

   b. hypochondriasis.

   c. conversion disorder.

   d. dissociative disorder.

Answers: 1. a. 2. c.

dissociative disorders Disorders in which some aspect of the personality seems separated from the rest.

dissociative amnesia A disorder characterized by loss of memory for past events without organic cause.

dissociative fugue A symptom of dissociative amnesia that involves flight from home and the assumption of a new identity with amnesia for past identity and events.

dissociative identity disorder (Also called multiple personality disorder.) Disorder characterized by the separation of the personality into two or more distinct personalities.

DISSOCIATIVE DISORDERS

What do dissociative disorders have in common?

Dissociative disorders are among the most puzzling forms of mental disorders, both to the observer and to the sufferer. *Dissociation* means that part of an individual's personality appears to be separated from the rest. The disorder sometimes involves memory loss and a complete, though generally temporary, change in identity. Rarely, several distinct personalities appear in one person.

Loss of memory without an organic cause can occur as a reaction to an extremely stressful event or period. During World War II, for example, some hospitalized soldiers could not recall their names, where they lived, where they were born, or how they came to be in battle. But war and its horrors are not the only causes of **dissociative amnesia.** The person who betrays a friend in a business deal or the victim of rape may also forget, selectively, what has happened. Total amnesia, in which people forget everything, is rare, despite its popularity in novels and films. Sometimes an amnesia victim leaves home and assumes an entirely new identity; this phenomenon, known as **dissociative fugue,** is also very unusual.

In **dissociative identity disorder,** commonly known as *multiple personality disorder,* several distinct personalities emerge at different times. In the true multiple personality, the various personalities are distinct people with their own names, identities, memories, mannerisms, speaking voices, and even IQs. Sometimes the personalities are so separate that they don't know they inhabit a body with other "people." At other times, the personalities do know of the existence of other "people" and even make disparaging remarks about them. Typically, the personalities contrast sharply with one another, as if each one represents different aspects of the same person—one being the more socially acceptable, "nice" side of the person and the other being the darker, more uninhibited or "evil" side.

The origins of dissociative identity disorder are still not understood (Dell, 2006). One theory suggests that it develops as a response to childhood abuse (Lev-Wiesel, 2008). The child learns to cope with abuse by a process of dissociation—by having the abuse, in effect, happen to "someone else," that is, to a personality who is not conscious most of the time. The fact that one or more of the multiple personalities in almost every case is a child (even when the person is an adult) seems to support this idea, and clinicians report a history of child abuse in more than three-quarters of their cases of dissociative identity disorder (Kidron, 2008; C. A. Ross, Norton, & Wozney, 1989).

Other clinicians suggest that dissociative identity disorder is not a real disorder at all, but an elaborate kind of role-playing—faked in the beginning and then perhaps genuinely believed by the patient (Lilienfeld & Lynn, 2003; H. G. Pope, Barry, Bodkin, & Hudson, 2006). Some intriguing biological data show that in at least some patients, however, the various personalities have different blood pressure readings, different responses to medication, different allergies, different vision problems (necessitating a different pair of glasses for each personality), and different handedness—all of which would be difficult to feign. Each personality may also exhibit distinctly different brain-wave patterns (Dell'Osso, 2003).

LEARNING OBJECTIVE

• Explain what is meant by *dissociation.* Briefly describe the key features of dissociative amnesia, dissociative fugue, dissociative identity disorder, and depersonalization disorder.

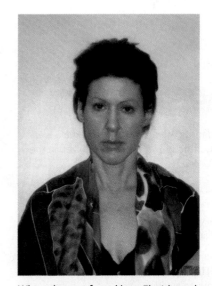

When she was found by a Florida park ranger, Jane Doe was suffering from amnesia. She could not recall her name, her past, or how to read and write. She never regained her memory of the past.

depersonalization/derealization disorder A dissociative disorder whose essential feature is that the person suddenly feels changed or different in a strange way.

A far less dramatic (and much more common) dissociative disorder is **depersonalization/derealization disorder,** in which the person suddenly feels changed or different in a strange way. Some people feel that they have left their bodies, whereas others find that their actions have suddenly become mechanical or dreamlike. This kind of feeling is especially common during adolescence and young adulthood, when our sense of ourselves and our interactions with others change rapidly. Only when the sense of depersonalization becomes a long-term or chronic problem or when the alienation impairs normal social functioning can this be classified as a dissociative disorder (American Psychiatric Association, 2013).

✔●─ **Study** and **Review** on **MyPsychLab**

CHECK YOUR UNDERSTANDING

1. _____ usually involve memory loss and a complete—though generally temporary—change in identity.
2. Clinicians report a history of _____ in over three-quarters of their cases of dissociative identity disorder.
3. Dissociative disorders, like conversion disorders, seem to involve _____ processes.

Answers: 1. Dissociative disorders. 2. child abuse 3. unconscious.

APPLY YOUR UNDERSTANDING

1. A person who was being interrogated by the police confessed on tape to having committed several murders. When the alleged killer was brought to trial, his lawyers agreed that the voice on the tape belonged to their client. But they asserted that the person who confessed was another personality that lived inside the body of their client. In other words, they claimed that their client was suffering from
   a. depersonalization/derealization disorder.
   b. dissociative identity disorder.
   c. conversion disorder.
   d. body dysmorphic disorder.

2. You are reading the newspaper and come across a story of a young man who was found wandering the streets with no recollection of who he was, where he came from, or how he got there. You suspect that he is most likely suffering from
   a. depersonalization/derealization disorder.
   b. dissociative amnesia.
   c. conversion disorder.
   d. body dysmorphic disorder.

Answers: 1. b. 2. b.

LEARNING OBJECTIVE

- Identify the main types of sexual dysfunctions that are recognized in the *DSM-5*.

sexual dysfunction Loss or impairment of the ordinary physical responses of sexual function for at least six months.

erectile disorder (or erectile dysfunction) (ED) The inability of a man to achieve or maintain an erection.

female sexual interest/arousal disorder The inability of a woman to become sexually aroused or to reach orgasm.

─> # SEXUAL DYSFUNCTIONS

What are the main types of sexual dysfunctions?

Sexual dysfunction is the loss or impairment of the ordinary physical responses of sexual function for at least six months (see **Figure 12–3**). In men, this usually takes the form of **erectile disorder** or **erectile dysfunction (ED),** the inability to achieve or maintain an erection. In women, it often takes the form of **female sexual interest/arousal disorder,** loss of interest in sex or the inability to become sexually excited or to reach orgasm. (These conditions were once called "impotence" and "frigidity," respectively, but professionals in the field have rejected these terms as too negative and judgmental.) Occasional problems with achieving or maintaining an erection in men or with lubrication or reaching orgasm in women are common. Only when the condition lasts for at least six months and when enjoyment of sexual relationships becomes impaired should it be considered serious.

ENDURING ISSUES

Diversity–Universality   What's Normal?

Ideas about what is normal and abnormal in sexual behavior vary with the times, the individual, and, sometimes, the culture. Throughout the late 20th century, as psychologists became more aware of the diversity of "normal" sexual behaviors, they increasingly narrowed their definition of abnormal sexual behavior. Today the *DSM-5* recognizes only a limited number of sexual disorders. ■

The incidence of ED is quite high, even among otherwise healthy men. In one survey, 25% of 40- to 70-year-old men had moderate ED. Less than half the men in this age group reported having no ED (Lamberg, 1998). Fortunately, new medications popularly known as *Viagra, Levitra,* and *Cialis* are extremely effective in treating ED (S. B. Levine, 2006; Meston & Frohlich, 2000).

Although medications appear to help most male patients overcome ED, they are of little value unless a man is first sexually aroused. Unfortunately, some men and women find it difficult or impossible to experience any desire for sexual activity to begin with. **Sexual desire disorders** involve a lack of interest in sex or perhaps an active distaste for it. Low sexual desire is more common among women than among men and plays a role in perhaps 40% of all sexual dysfunctions (R. D. Hayes, Dennerstein, Bennett, & Fairley, 2008; Warnock, 2002). The extent and causes of this disorder in men or women is difficult to analyze. Because some people simply have a low motivation for sexual activity, scant interest in sex is normal for them and does not necessarily reflect any sexual disorder (Meston & Rellini, 2008).

Other people are able to experience sexual desire and maintain arousal but are unable to reach orgasm, the peaking of sexual pleasure and the release of sexual tension. These people are said to experience **orgasmic disorders.** Male orgasmic disorder—the inability to ejaculate even when fully aroused—is rare yet seems to be becoming increasingly common as more men find it desirable to practice the delay of orgasm. Masters and Johnson (1970) attributed male orgasmic disorder primarily to such psychological factors as traumatic experiences. The problem may also occur as a side effect of some medications, such as certain antidepressants. This difficulty is considerably more common among women than among men (see Figure 12–3).

Among the other problems that can occur during the sexual response cycle are **premature ejaculation,** a fairly common disorder that the *DSM-5* defines as the male's inability to inhibit orgasm as long as desired, and **vaginismus,** involuntary muscle spasms in the outer part of a woman's vagina during sexual excitement that make intercourse impossible. Again, the occasional experience of such problems is common; the *DSM-5* considers them dysfunctions only if they are persistent and recurrent (Hunter, Goodie, Oordt, & Dobmeyer, 2009).

PARAPHILIC DISORDERS

What key characteristic distinguishes paraphilias from paraphilic disorders?

Paraphilias involve the use of unconventional sex objects or situations to obtain sexual arousal. Most people have unusual sexual fantasies at some time, which can be a healthy stimulant of normal sexual enjoyment. Only when the paraphilia causes distress or impairment to the person or whose satisfaction entails personal harm, or risk of harm, to others is it considered to be a disorder. **Fetishism** refers to the repeated use of a nonhuman object such as a shoe or underwear as the preferred or exclusive method of achieving sexual excitement (Darcangelo, Hollings, & Paladino, 2008). Most people who practice fetishism are male, and the fetish frequently begins during adolescence (Fagan, Lehne, Strand, & Berlin, 2005). Fetishes may derive from unusual learning experiences: As their sexual drive develops during adolescence, some boys learn to associate arousal with inanimate objects, perhaps as a result of early sexual exploration while masturbating or because of difficulties in social relationships (Bertolini, 2001).

sexual desire disorders Disorders in which the person lacks sexual interest or has an active distaste for sex.

orgasmic disorders Inability to reach orgasm in a person able to experience sexual desire and maintain arousal.

premature ejaculation Inability of man to inhibit orgasm as long as desired.

vaginismus Involuntary muscle spasms in the outer part of the vagina that make intercourse impossible.

paraphilias Use of unconventional objects or situations to achieve sexual arousal.

fetishism A nonhuman object is the preferred or exclusive method of achieving sexual excitement.

Using nonhuman objects, such as shoes, underwear, or leather goods, as the preferred or exclusive method of achieving sexual excitement is known as fetishism.

FIGURE 12-3

Sexual dysfunction in the United States.

These graphs show the incidence of the most common types of sexual dysfunction in men and women, by age group.

Source: Data from the American Medical Association, February 1999.

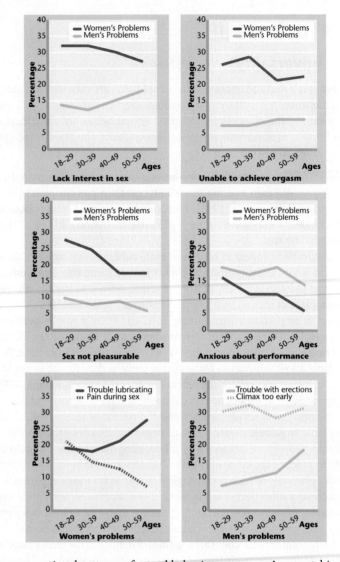

voyeurism Desire to watch others having sexual relations or to spy on nude people.

exhibitionism Exposing one's genitals in public to achieve sexual arousal.

frotteurism Achieving sexual arousal by touching or rubbing against a nonconsenting person in public situations.

transvestic fetishism Wearing the clothes of the opposite sex to achieve sexual gratification.

sexual sadism Obtaining sexual gratification from humiliating or physically harming a sex partner.

sexual masochism Inability to enjoy sex without accompanying emotional or physical pain.

pedophilic disorder Desire to have sexual relations with children as the preferred or exclusive method of achieving sexual excitement.

Other unconventional patterns of sexual behavior are **voyeurism,** watching other people have sex or spying on people who are nude; achieving arousal by **exhibitionism,** the exposure of one's genitals in inappropriate situations, such as to strangers; **frotteurism,** achieving sexual arousal by touching or rubbing against a nonconsenting person in situations like a crowded subway car; and **transvestic fetishism,** wearing clothes of the opposite sex for sexual excitement and gratification. **Sexual sadism** ties sexual pleasure to aggression. To attain sexual gratification, sadists humiliate or physically harm sex partners. **Sexual masochism** is the inability to enjoy sex without accompanying emotional or physical pain. Sexual sadists and masochists sometimes engage in mutually consenting sex, but at times sadistic acts are inflicted on unconsenting partners, sometimes resulting in serious injury or even death (Purcell & Arrigo, 2006).

One of the most serious paraphilic disorders is **pedophilic disorder,** which according to *DSM-5* is defined as engaging in sexual activity with a child, generally under the age of 13. Pedophiles are almost invariably men under age 40 who are close to the victims rather than strangers (Barbaree & Seto, 1997). Although there is no single cause of pedophilic disorder, some of the most common explanations are that pedophiles cannot adjust to the adult sexual role and have been interested exclusively in children as sex objects since adolescence; they turn to children as sexual objects in response to stress in adult relationships in which they feel inadequate; or they have records of unstable social adjustment and generally commit sexual offenses against children in response to a temporary aggressive mood. Studies also indicate that the majority of pedophiles have histories of sexual frustration and failure, low self-esteem, an inability to cope with negative emotions, tend to perceive themselves as immature, and are rather dependent, unassertive, lonely, and insecure (L. J. Cohen & Galynker, 2002; Mandeville-Norden & Beech, 2009).

GENDER DYSPHORIA

What are the key symptoms required for a diagnosis of gender dysphoria?

The word "dysphoria" means an abnormal feeling of discontent or discomfort. **Gender dysphoria** is the strong desire to become—or the insistence that one really is—a member of the other sex. Some little boys, for example, want to be girls instead. They may reject boys' clothing, desire to wear their sisters' clothes, and play only with girls and with toys that are considered "girls' toys." Similarly, some girls wear boys' clothing and play only with boys and "boys' toys." When such children are uncomfortable being a male or a female and are unwilling to accept themselves as such, the diagnosis is gender dysphoria (Zucker, 2005).

The causes of gender dysphoria are not known. Both animal research and the fact that these disorders are often apparent from early childhood suggest that biological factors, such as prenatal hormonal imbalances, are major contributors. Research suggests that children with gender dysphoria have an increased likelihood of becoming homosexual or bisexual as adults (Wallien & Cohen-Kettenis, 2008).

gender dysphoria Disorders that involve the strong desire to become, or the insistence that one really is, a member of the other biological sex.

CHECK YOUR UNDERSTANDING

✔●—Study and Review on MyPsychLab

Match each of the following terms with the appropriate description:

1. ____ pedophilic disorder
2. ____ gender dysphoria
3. ____ female sexual interest/arousal disorder
4. ____ paraphilias

a. The inability for a woman to become sexually excited or to reach orgasm.
b. The use of unconventional sex objects or situations to obtain sexual arousal.
c. Recurrent, intense sexually arousing fantasies, sexual urges, or behaviors involving sexual activity with a prepubescent child.
d. The strong desire to become—or the insistence that one really is—a member of the other biological sex.

Answers: 1. c. 2. d. 3. a. 4. b.

APPLY YOUR UNDERSTANDING

1. Viagra and similar drugs have become best sellers because they provide temporary relief from
   a. erectile disorder.
   b. paraphilias.
   c. generalized anxiety disorder.
   d. body dysmorphic disorder.

2. A man is arrested for stealing women's underwear from clotheslines and adding them to the large collection he has hidden in his home. He says that he finds the clothing sexually exciting. This would appear to be a case of
   a. erectile disorder.
   b. gender dysphoria.
   c. pedophilic disorder.
   d. fetishism.

Answers: 1. a. 2. d.

- Identify the distinguishing characteristic of personality disorders. Briefly describe schizoid, paranoid, dependent, avoidant, narcissistic, borderline, and antisocial personality disorders.

personality disorders Disorders in which inflexible and maladaptive ways of thinking and behaving learned early in life cause distress to the person or conflicts with others.

schizoid personality disorder Personality disorder in which a person is withdrawn and lacks feelings for others.

paranoid personality disorder Personality disorder in which the person is inappropriately suspicious and mistrustful of others.

dependent personality disorder Personality disorder in which the person is unable to make choices and decisions independently and cannot tolerate being alone.

PERSONALITY DISORDERS

Which personality disorder creates the most significant problems for society?

In Chapter 10, "Personality," we saw that despite having certain characteristic views of the world and ways of doing things, people normally can adjust their behavior to fit different situations. But some people, starting at some point early in life, develop inflexible and maladaptive ways of thinking and behaving that are so exaggerated and rigid that they cause serious distress to themselves or problems to others. People with such **personality disorders** range from harmless eccentrics to cold-blooded killers.

One group of personality disorders, **schizoid personality disorder,** is characterized by an inability or desire to form social relationships and have no warm or tender feelings for others. Such loners cannot express their feelings and appear cold, distant, and unfeeling. Moreover, they often seem vague, absentminded, indecisive, or "in a fog." Because their withdrawal is so complete, persons with schizoid personality disorder seldom marry and may have trouble holding jobs that require them to work with or relate to others (American Psychiatric Association, 2013).

People with **paranoid personality disorder** often see themselves as rational and objective, yet they are guarded, secretive, devious, scheming, and argumentative. They are suspicious and mistrustful even when there is no reason to be; they are hypersensitive to any possible threat or trick; and they refuse to accept blame or criticism even when it is deserved.

A cluster of personality disorders characterized by anxious or fearful behavior includes dependent personality disorder and avoidant personality disorder. People with **dependent personality disorder** are unable to make decisions on their own or to do things independently. Rather, they rely on parents, a spouse, friends, or others to make the major choices in their lives and usually are extremely unhappy being alone. In **avoidant personality disorder,** the person is timid, anxious, and fearful of rejection. It is not surprising that this social anxiety leads to isolation, but unlike the schizoid type, the person with avoidant personality disorder *wants* to have close relationships with others.

Another cluster of personality disorders is characterized by dramatic, emotional, or erratic behavior. People with **narcissistic personality disorder,** for example, display a grandiose sense of self-importance and a preoccupation with fantasies of unlimited success. Such people believe that they are extraordinary, need constant attention and admiration, display a sense of entitlement, and tend to exploit others. They are given to envy and arrogance, and they lack the ability to really care for anyone else (American Psychiatric Association, 2013).

Borderline personality disorder is characterized by marked instability in self-image, mood, and interpersonal relationships. People with this personality disorder tend to act impulsively and, often, self-destructively. They feel uncomfortable being alone and often manipulate self-destructive impulses in an effort to control or solidify their personal relationships.

THINKING CRITICALLY ABOUT . . .

Causation

We have offered a number of different theories about the cause of antisocial personality disorder, all supported by research. Think about each of these theories and try to answer the following questions:

- To what extent do the different perspectives conflict? To what extent do they support one another?

- What kind of evidence—what kinds of research studies—is offered in support of each theory?

- Which theory would be most useful from a clinical, or treatment, point of view? Which would be most likely to spawn further research?

- Why do different theoretical perspectives exist?

Family influences may also prevent the normal learning of rules of conduct in the preschool and school years. A child who has been rejected by one or both parents is not likely to develop adequate social skills or appropriate social behavior. Further, the high incidence of antisocial behavior in people with an antisocial parent suggests that antisocial behavior may be partly learned and partly inherited. Once serious misbehavior begins in childhood, there is an almost predictable progression: The child's conduct leads to rejection by peers and failure in school, followed by affiliation with other children who have behavior problems. By late childhood or adolescence, the deviant patterns that will later show up as a full-blown antisocial personality disorder are well established (J. Hill, 2003; T. M. Levy & Orlans, 2004). Cognitive theorists emphasize that in addition to the failure to learn rules and develop self-control, moral development may be arrested in children who are emotionally rejected and inadequately disciplined (K. Davidson, 2008; Soyguet & Tuerkcapar, 2001).

One of the most widely studied personality disorders is **antisocial personality disorder.** People who exhibit this disorder may lie, steal, cheat, and show little or no sense of responsibility, although they often seem intelligent and charming at first. The "con man" exemplifies many of the features of the antisocial personality, as does the person who compulsively cheats business partners, because she or he knows their weak points. Some antisocial personalities show little or no anxiety or guilt about their behavior. Indeed, they are likely to blame society or their victims for the antisocial actions that they themselves commit. As you might suspect, people with antisocial personality disorder are responsible for a good deal of crime and violence.

Approximately 3% of American men and less than 1% of American women suffer from antisocial personality disorder. It is not surprising that prison inmates show high rates of this personality disorder ranging from 35% to 60% (Black, Gunter, Loveless, Allen, & Sieleni, 2010; Moran, 1999). Not all people with antisocial personality disorder are convicted criminals, however. Many manipulate others for their own gain while avoiding the criminal justice system.

Antisocial personality disorder seems to result from a combination of biological predisposition, difficult life experiences, and an unhealthy social environment (Gabbard, 2005; Moffitt, Caspi, & Rutter, 2006). Some findings suggest that heredity is a risk factor for the later development of antisocial behavior (Fu et al., 2002; Lyons et al., 1995). Research suggests that some people with antisocial personalities are less responsive to stress and thus are more likely to engage in thrill-seeking behaviors, such as gambling and substance abuse, which may be harmful to themselves or others (Patrick, 1994; Pietrzak & Petry, 2005). Another intriguing explanation for the cause of antisocial personality disorder is that it arises as a consequence of anatomical irregularities in

avoidant personality disorder Personality disorder in which the person's fears of rejection by others lead to social isolation.

narcissistic personality disorder Personality disorder in which the person has an exaggerated sense of self-importance and needs constant admiration.

borderline personality disorder Personality disorder characterized by marked instability in self-image, mood, and interpersonal relationships.

antisocial personality disorder Personality disorder that involves a pattern of violent, criminal, or unethical and exploitative behavior and an inability to feel affection for others.

✓•─**Study** and **Review** on **MyPsychLab**

CHECK YOUR UNDERSTANDING

Match the following personality disorders with the appropriate description:

1. ___ schizoid personality disorder
2. ___ paranoid personality disorder
3. ___ dependent personality disorder
4. ___ avoidant personality disorder
5. ___ borderline personality disorder

a. shows instability in self-image, mood, and relationships
b. is fearful and timid
c. is mistrustful even when there is no reason
d. lacks the ability to form social relationships
e. is unable to make own decisions

Answers: 1.d. 2.c. 3.e. 4.b. 5.a.

APPLY YOUR UNDERSTANDING

1. John represents himself as a stockbroker who specializes in investing the life savings of elderly people, but he never invests the money. Instead, he puts it into his own bank account and then flees the country. When he is caught and asked how he feels about financially destroying elderly people, he explains, "Hey, if they were stupid enough to give me their money, they deserved what they got." John is most likely suffering from _____ personality disorder.
   a. dependent
   b. avoidant
   c. antisocial
   d. borderline

2. Jennifer is a graduate student who believes that her thesis will completely change the way that scientists view the universe. She believes that she is the only person intelligent enough to have come up with the thesis, that she is not sufficiently appreciated by other students and faculty, and that nobody on her thesis committee is sufficiently knowledgeable to judge its merits. Assuming that her thesis is not, in fact, revolutionary, it would appear that Jennifer is suffering from _____ personality disorder.
   a. paranoid
   b. narcissistic
   c. borderline
   d. antisocial

Answers: 1.c. 2.b.

the prefrontal region of the brain during infancy (Boes, Tranel, Anderson, & Nopoulos, 2008; A. R. Damasio & Anderson, 2003).

Some psychologists believe that emotional deprivation in early childhood predisposes people to antisocial personality disorder. The child for whom no one cares, say some psychologists, cares for no one. Respect for others is the basis of our social code, but when you cannot see things from another person's perspective, behavior "rules" seem like nothing more than an assertion of adult power to be defied.

LEARNING OBJECTIVES

• Describe the common feature in all cases of schizophrenia. Explain the difference between hallucinations and delusions. Briefly describe the key features of disorganized, catatonic, paranoid, and undifferentiated schizophrenia.

• Describe the causes of schizophrenic spectrum disorders.

SCHIZOPHRENIC SPECTRUM DISORDERS

How is schizophrenia different from multiple-personality disorder?

Schizophrenic spectrum disorders are severe conditions marked by disordered thoughts and communications, inappropriate emotions, and bizarre behavior that lasts for months or even years (E. Walker & Tessner, 2008). People with schizophrenia are out of touch with reality, which is to say that they are **psychotic.** Approximately 0.5% to 1.0% of people have schizophrenia. One meta-analysis of data from 46 different countries found the rate of schizophrenia was similar for men and women, and did not vary significantly across countries (Saha, Chant, & McGrath, 2008).

People with schizophrenia often suffer from **hallucinations,** false sensory perceptions that usually take the form of hearing voices that are not really there. (Visual, tactile, or olfactory hallucinations are more likely to indicate substance abuse or organic brain damage.) They also frequently have **delusions**—false beliefs about reality with no factual basis—that distort their relationships with their surroundings and with other people. Typically, these delusions are paranoid: People with schizophrenia often believe that someone is out to harm them. Because their world is utterly different from reality, people with schizophrenia usually cannot live a normal life unless they are successfully treated with medication. (See Chapter 13, "Therapies.") Often, they are unable to communicate with others, since their words are incoherent when they speak. ✳

✳ Explore the **Concept** Types and Symptoms of Schizophrenia on **MyPsychLab**

Traditional Subtypes of Schizophrenic Disorders

What are the traditional categories of schizophrenic disorders?

In the past, the DSM recognized various subtypes of schizophrenic disorders. For example, *disorganized schizophrenia* often was characterized by giggling, grimacing, and frantic gesturing. People suffering from disorganized schizophrenia often showed a childish disregard for social conventions. People suffering from *catatonic schizophrenia* often remained immobile, mute, and impassive. Conversely, they might become excessively excited, talking and shouting continuously. Those suffering from *paranoid schizophrenia* often exhibited extreme suspiciousness and complex delusions. People with paranoid schizophrenia might believe themselves to be Napoleon or the Virgin Mary, or they may insist that Russian spies with laser guns are constantly on their trail because they have learned some great secret. Note that this disorder is far more severe than paranoid personality disorder, which does not involve bizarre delusions or loss of touch with reality. Finally, people suffering from *undifferentiated schizophrenia* had several of the characteristic symptoms of schizophrenia—such as delusions, hallucinations, or incoherence—yet do not show the typical symptoms of any other subtype of the disorder.

DSM-5 no longer distinguishes between these traditional subtypes. Although each subtype was defined by predominant symptoms, the same symptoms sometimes appeared in other subtypes as well. The result was that the distinctions among the subtypes were often blurred, and that rendered them of limited value. Thus, *DSM-5* simply identifies schizophrenic spectrum disorders without breaking them down into distinct subtypes.

schizophrenic spectrum disorders Severe disorders in which there are disturbances of thoughts, communications, and emotions, including delusions and hallucinations.

psychotic Behavior characterized by a loss of touch with reality.

hallucinations Sensory experiences in the absence of external stimulation.

delusions False beliefs about reality that have no basis in fact.

Causes of Schizophrenia

What are the causes of schizophrenia?

Because schizophrenia is a very serious disorder, considerable research has been directed at trying to discover its causes (Keshavan, Tandon, Boutros, & Nasrallah, 2008). Many studies indicate that schizophrenia has a genetic component (Lichtenstein et al., 2009), though no single gene has been identified as a cause for schizophrenia (Pogue-Geile & Yokley, 2010). Instead, more than 20 genes have been implicated as potentially contributing to the development of schizophrenia (Gottesman & Hanson, 2005). People with schizophrenia are more likely than other people to have children with schizophrenia, even when those children have lived with adoptive parents since early in life. If one identical twin suffers from schizophrenia, the chances are almost 50% that the other twin will also develop this disorder. In fraternal twins, if one twin has schizophrenia, the chances are only about 17% that the other twin will develop it as well (Gottesman, 1991).

Considerable research suggests that biological predisposition to schizophrenia may involve the faulty regulation of the neurotransmitters dopamine and glutamate in the central nervous system (Lin, Lane, & Tsai, 2011; Miyake, Thompson, Skinbjerg, & Abi-Dargham, 2011). Some research also indicates that pathology in various structures of the brain may contribute to the onset of schizophrenia (Killgore, Rosso, Gruber, & Yurgelun-Todd, 2009; Lawrie, McIntosh, Hall, Owens, & Johnstone, 2008). Other studies link schizophrenia to some form of early prenatal infection or disturbance (Brown & Derkits, 2010). Despite these findings however, no laboratory tests to date can diagnose schizophrenia on the basis of brain or genetic abnormalities alone. ◉

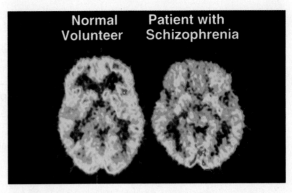

Normal Volunteer   Patient with Schizophrenia

Neuroimaging techniques, such as this PET scan, often reveal important differences between the brains of people with schizophrenia and normal volunteers. Still, neuroimaging does not provide a decisive diagnostic test for schizophrenia.

◉ **Watch** the **Video** Genetics Research in Schizophrenia on **MyPsychLab**

THINKING CRITICALLY ABOUT . . .

Genius and Mental Disorders

Jean-Jacques Rousseau allegedly was paranoid. Mozart composed his *Requiem* while under the delusion that he was being poisoned. Van Gogh cut off his ear and sent it to a prostitute. Schopenhauer, Chopin, and John Stuart Mill were depressed. Robert Burns and Lord Byron apparently were alcoholics. Virginia Woolf suffered from bipolar disorder throughout her entire adult life.

- Do you think that creative people in general are more likely than others to suffer from psychological problems? What leads you to believe as you do?

- What evidence would you need to have in order to answer this question in a scientific way?

  Studies of identical twins have also been used to identify the importance of environment in causing schizophrenia. Because identical twins are genetically identical and because half of the identical twins of people with schizophrenia do not develop schizophrenia themselves, this severe and puzzling disorder cannot be caused by genetic factors alone. Environmental factors—ranging from disturbed family relations to taking drugs to biological damage that may occur at any age, even before birth—must also figure in determining whether a person will develop schizophrenia. Finally, although quite different in emphasis, the various explanations for schizophrenic disorders are not mutually exclusive. Genetic factors are universally acknowledged, but many theorists believe that only a combination of biological, psychological, and social factors produces schizophrenia (van Os, Rutten, & Poulton, 2008). According to systems theory, genetic factors predispose some people to schizophrenia; and family interaction and life stress activate the predisposition.

NEURODEVELOPMENTAL DISORDERS

Why do stimulants appear to slow down hyperactive children and adults?

Children may suffer from conditions already discussed in this chapter—for example, depression and anxiety disorders. But other disorders are either characteristic of children or are first evident in childhood. The *DSM-5* contains a long list of disorders usually first diagnosed in infancy, childhood, or adolescence. Two of these disorders are attention-deficit/hyperactivity disorder and autistic disorder.

Attention-deficit/hyperactivity disorder (ADHD) was once known simply as *hyperactivity*. The new name reflects the fact that children with the disorder typically have trouble focusing their attention in the sustained way that other children do. Instead, they are easily distracted, often fidgety and impulsive, and almost constantly in motion. In the United States about 7% or four and a half million school aged children have ADHD, with boys (11%) being more than twice as likely as girls (4%) to be affected (Bloom & Cohen, 2006). About 4% of adults in the United States also display the symptoms of ADHD (Kessler et al., 2006). Research suggests that ADHD is present at birth, but becomes a serious problem only after a child starts school (Monastra, 2008). The class setting demands that children sit quietly, pay attention as instructed, follow directions, and inhibit urges to yell and run around. The child with ADHD simply cannot conform to these demands.

We do not yet know what causes ADHD, but considerable evidence indicates biological factors play an important role (Monastra, 2008; Nigg, 2005). Neuroimaging studies, for example, reveal individuals with ADHD display altered brain functioning when presented

attention-deficit/hyperactivity disorder (ADHD) A childhood disorder characterized by inattention, impulsiveness, and hyperactivity.

with tasks that require shifting attention. The deficiency appears to involve the frontal lobe (see Chapter 2, "The Biological Basis of Behavior"), which normally recruits appropriate regions of the brain to solve a problem. In people with ADHD, however, the frontal lobe sometimes activates brain centers unrelated to solving a problem (Konrad, Neufang, Hanisch, Fink, & Herpertz-Dahlmann, 2006; Mulas et al., 2006; Murias, Swanson, & Srinivasan, 2007).

Deficits in the prefrontal cortex may also contribute to ADHD. Generally, the prefrontal cortex plays an important role in inhibiting unnecessary motor behaviors and directing attention. This inhibitory role of the prefrontal cortex may not function properly in people with ADHD making it difficult for them to reduce unnecessary motor activity and focus attention (Depue, Burgess, Willcutt, Ruzic, & Banich, 2010).

Family interaction and other social experiences may be more important in preventing the disorder than in causing it (C. Johnston & Ohan, 2005). That is, some exceptionally competent parents and patient, tolerant teachers may be able to teach "difficult" children to conform to the demands of schooling. Although some psychologists train the parents of children with ADHD in these management skills, the most frequent treatment for these children is a type of drug known as a **psychostimulant.** Psychostimulants do not work by "slowing down" hyperactive children; rather, they appear to increase the children's ability to focus their attention so that they can attend to the task at hand, which decreases their hyperactivity and improves their academic performance (Duesenberg, 2006; Gimpel et al., 2005). Unfortunately, psychostimulants often produce only short-term benefits; and their use and possible overuse in treating ADHD children is controversial (Comstock, 2011; Marc Lerner & Wigal, 2008).

A very different and profoundly serious disorder that usually becomes evident in the first few years of life is **autistic disorder.** Autistic children fail to form normal attachments to parents, remaining distant and withdrawn into their own separate worlds. As infants, they may even show distress at being picked up or held. As they grow older, they typically do not speak, or they develop a peculiar speech pattern called *echolalia,* in which they repeat the words said to them. Autistic children typically show strange motor behavior, such as repeating body movements endlessly or walking constantly on tiptoe. They don't play as normal children do; they are not at all social and may use toys in odd ways, constantly spinning the wheels on a toy truck or tearing paper into strips. Autistic children often display the symptoms of retardation (LaMalfa, Lassi, Bertelli, Salvini, & Placidi, 2004), but it is hard to test their mental ability because they generally don't talk (Dawson, Soulières, Gernsbacher, & Mottron, 2007). The disorder lasts into adulthood in the great majority of cases.

In recent years, autistic disorder has come to be viewed as just one dimension of a much broader range of developmental disorders known as **autistic spectrum disorder (ASD)** (Angus, 2011; Ming, Brimacombe, Chaaban, Zimmerman-Bier, & Wagner, 2008). Individuals with disorders in the autistic spectrum display symptoms that are similar to those seen in autistic disorder, but the severity of the symptoms is often quite reduced. For example, some children with ASD may show difficulty interacting with other people, but may have little or no problem with speech or intellectual development.

We don't know exactly what causes autism, although most theorists believe that it results almost entirely from biological conditions (Currenti, 2010; Goode, 2004; Zimmerman, Connors, & Pardo-Villamizar, 2006). Recent evidence suggests that genetics play a strong role in causing the disorder (Campbell, Li, Sutcliffe, Persico, & Levitt, 2008; Rutter, 2005), though no specific gene or chromosome responsible for autistic disorder has yet been identified (Losh, Sullivan, Trembath, & Piven, 2008). Neuroimaging studies have also implicated faulty development of the frontal lobes, the amygdala and cerebellum as contributing to the development of autism, but these results are not conclusive (Amaral, Schumann, & Nordahl, 2008).

Another intriguing line of research has focused on abnormal antibodies found in the blood of some mothers of children with autistic disorder, but not in mothers of healthy children. When pregnant rhesus monkeys were injected with these antibodies, all of their offspring displayed autistic like behaviors, including atypical repetitive movements and hyperactivity (Martin et al., 2008).

Children with autistic disorder often remain distant and withdrawn, rarely engaging in play with other children.

psychostimulant Drugs that increase ability to focus attention in people with ADHD.

autistic disorder A childhood disorder characterized by lack of social instincts and strange motor behavior.

autistic spectrum disorder (ASD) A range of disorders involving varying degrees of impairment in communication skills, social interactions, and restricted, repetitive, and stereotyped patterns of behavior.

✓• Study and Review on MyPsychLab

LEARNING OBJECTIVE

- Describe the differences between men and women in psychological disorders including the prevalence of disorders and the kinds of disorders they are likely to experience. Explain why these differences exist. Explain why "it is increasingly important for mental health professionals to be aware of cultural differences" in psychological disorders.

GENDER AND CULTURAL DIFFERENCES IN PSYCHOLOGICAL DISORDERS

What are the differences between men and women in psychological disorders?

For the most part, men and women are similar with respect to mental disorders, but differences do exist. Many studies have concluded that women have a higher rate of psychological disorders than men do, but this is an oversimplification (Cosgrove & Riddle, 2004). We do know that more women than men are *treated* for mental disorders. But this cannot be taken to mean that more women than men have mental disorders, for in our society, it is much more acceptable for women to discuss their emotional difficulties and to seek professional help openly (H. Lerman, 1996).

Moreover, mental disorders for which there seems to be a strong biological component, such as bipolar disorder and schizophrenia, are distributed fairly equally between the sexes. Differences tend to be found for those disorders *without* a strong biological component— that is, disorders in which learning and experience play a more important role. For example, men are more likely than women to suffer from substance abuse and antisocial personality disorder. Women, on the other hand, are more likely to suffer from depression, agoraphobia, simple phobia, obsessive–compulsive disorder, and somatization disorder (Craske, 2003; Rosenfield & Pottick, 2005). These tendencies, coupled with the fact that gender differences observed in the United States are not always seen in other cultures (Culbertson, 1997), suggest that socialization plays a part in developing a disorder: When men display abnormal behavior, it is more likely to take the forms of drinking too much and acting aggressively;

when women display abnormal behavior, they are more likely to become fearful, passive, hopeless, and "sick" (Rosenfield & Pottick, 2005).

One commonly reported difference between the sexes concerns marital status. Men who are separated, divorced, or who have never married have a higher incidence of mental disorders than do either women of the same marital status or married men. But married women have higher rates than married men. What accounts for the apparent fact that marriage is psychologically less beneficial for women than for men?

Here, too, socialization appears to play a role. For women, marriage, family relationships, and child rearing are likely to be more stressful than they are for men (Erickson, 2005; Stolzenberg & Waite, 2005). For men, marriage and family provide a haven; for women, they are a demanding job. In addition, women are more likely than men to be the victims of incest, rape, and marital battering. As one researcher has commented, "for women, the U.S. family is a violent institution" (Koss, 1990, p. 376). We saw in Chapter 11 that the effects of stress are proportional to the extent that a person feels alienated, powerless, and helpless. Alienation, powerlessness, and helplessness are more prevalent in women than in men. The rate of depression among women is twice that of men, a difference that is usually ascribed to the more negative and stressful aspects of women's lives, including lower incomes and the experiences of bias and physical and sexual abuse (American Psychological Association, 2006; Blehar & Keita, 2003). These factors are especially common among minority women, so it is not surprising that the prevalence of psychological disorders is greater among them than among other women (Laganà & Sosa, 2004).

In summary, women do seem to have higher rates of anxiety disorders and depression than men do; and they are more likely than men to seek professional help for their problems. However, greater stress, due in part to socialization and lower status rather than psychological weakness, apparently accounts for this statistic. Marriage and family life, associated with lower rates of mental disorders among men, introduce additional stress into the lives of women, particularly young women (25 to 45); and in some instances this added stress escalates into a psychological disorder.

More women than men in the United States seek help for mental disorders, but this may not mean mental disorders are more prevalent in women. Women are more likely than men to seek help for a variety of problems, physical and mental.

ENDURING ISSUES

Diversity–Universality   Are We All Alike?

The frequency and nature of some psychological disorders vary significantly among the world's different cultures (Halbreich & Karkun, 2006; López & Guarnaccia, 2000). This suggests that many disorders have a strong cultural component, or that diagnosis is somehow related to culture. On the other hand, disorders that are known to have a strong genetic component generally display a more uniform distribution across different cultures. ■

As the U.S. population becomes more diverse, it is increasingly important for mental health professionals to be aware of cultural differences if they are to understand and diagnose disorders among people of various cultural groups. Many disorders occur only in particular cultural groups. For example, *ataque de nervios*—literally translated as "attack of nerves"—is a culturally specific phenomenon that is seen predominately among Latinos. The symptoms of *ataque de nervios* generally include the feeling of being out of control, which may be accompanied by fainting spells, trembling, uncontrollable screaming, and crying, and, in some cases, verbal or physical aggressiveness. Afterwards, many patients do not recall the attack, and quickly return to normal functioning. Another example, *taijin kyofusho* (roughly translated as "fear of people"), involves a morbid fear that one's body or actions may be offensive to others. *Taijin kyofusho* is rarely seen outside of Japan.

The prevalence of childhood disorders also differs markedly by culture. Of course, it is adults—parents, teachers, counselors—who decide whether a child is suffering from a psychological disorder, and those decisions are likely to be influenced by cultural expectations. For example, in a series of cross-cultural studies, Thai children were more likely to be referred to mental health clinics for internalizing problems, such as anxiety and depression, compared to U.S. children, who were more likely to be referred for externalizing problems, such as aggressive behavior (Weisz et al., 1997).

✔•⌐**Study** and **Review** on **MyPsychLab**

KEY TERMS

Perspectives on Psychological Disorders
biological model, p. 393
psychoanalytic model, p. 394
cognitive–behavioral model, p. 394
diathesis–stress model, p. 394
diathesis, p. 394
systems approach, p. 394
insanity, p. 396

Mood Disorders
mood disorders, p. 397
depressive disorders, p. 397
major depressive disorder, p. 399
persistent depressive disorder, p. 399
manic episodes, p. 400
bipolar disorder, p. 400
cognitive distortions, p. 401

Anxiety Disorders
anxiety disorders, p. 402
specific phobia, p. 403
social anxiety disorder, p. 403
agoraphobia, p. 403
panic disorder, p. 403
generalized anxiety disorder, p. 404

obsessive–compulsive disorder (OCD), p. 404
body dysmorphic disorder, p. 404

Somatic Symptom and Related Disorders
psychosomatic illness, p. 405
somatic symptom and related disorders, p. 406
somatic symptom disorder, p. 406
conversion disorders, p. 406
illness anxiety disorder, p. 406

Dissociative Disorders
dissociative disorders, p. 407
dissociative amnesia, p. 407
dissociative fugue, p. 407
dissociative identity disorder, p. 407
depersonalization/derealization disorder, p. 408

Sexual Dysfunctions
sexual dysfunction, p. 408
erectile disorder (or erectile dysfunction) (ED), p. 408
female sexual interest/arousal disorder, p. 408
sexual desire disorders, p. 409

orgasmic disorders, p. 409
premature ejaculation, p. 409
vaginismus, p. 409

Paraphilic Disorders
paraphilias, p. 409
fetishism, p. 409
voyeurism, p. 410
exhibitionism, p. 410
frotteurism, p. 410
transvestic fetishism, p. 410
sexual sadism, p. 410
sexual masochism, p. 410
pedophilic disorder, p. 410

Gender Dysphoria
gender dysphoria, p. 411

Personality Disorders
personality disorders, p. 412
schizoid personality disorder, p. 412
paranoid personality disorder, p. 412
dependent personality disorder, p. 412
avoidant personality disorder, p. 413
narcissistic personality disorder, p. 413

borderline personality disorder, p. 413
antisocial personality disorder, p. 413

Schizophrenic Spectrum Disorders
Schizophrenic spectrum disorders, p. 414
psychotic, p. 414
hallucinations, p. 414
delusions, p. 414

Neurodevelopmental Disorders
attention-deficit/hyperactivity disorder (ADHD), p. 416
psychostimulant, p. 417
autistic disorder, p. 417
autistic spectrum disorder (ASD), p. 417

CHAPTER REVIEW   ((•⃝— Listen to the **Chapter Audio** on **MyPsychLab**

PERSPECTIVES ON PSYCHOLOGICAL DISORDERS

How does a mental health professional define a psychological disorder? Mental health professionals define a psychological disorder as a condition that either seriously impairs a person's ability to function in life or creates a high level of inner distress, or both. This view does not mean that the category "disordered" is always easy to distinguish from the category "normal." In fact, it may be more accurate to view abnormal behavior as merely quantitatively different from normal behavior.

How has the view of psychological disorders changed over time? In early societies, abnormal behavior was often attributed to supernatural powers. As late as the 18th century, the mentally ill were thought to be witches or possessed by the devil. In modern times, three approaches have helped to advance our understanding of abnormal behavior: the biological, the psychoanalytic, and the cognitive behavioral.

How can biology influence the development of psychological disorders? The **biological model** holds that abnormal behavior is caused by physiological malfunction, especially of the brain. Researchers assume the origin of these malfunctions is often hereditary. Although neuroscientists have demonstrated that genetic/biochemical factors are involved in some psychological disorders, biology alone cannot account for most mental illnesses.

What did Freud and his followers believe was the underlying cause of psychological disorders? The **psychoanalytic model** originating with Freud holds that abnormal behavior is a symbolic expression of unconscious conflicts that generally can be traced to childhood.

According to the cognitive–behavioral model, what causes abnormal behavior? The **cognitive–behavior model** states that psychological disorders arise when people learn maladaptive ways of thinking and acting. What has been learned can be unlearned, however. Cognitive–behavioral therapists strive to modify their patients' dysfunctional behaviors and distorted, self-defeating thought processes.

Why do some people with a family background of a psychological disorder develop the disorder, whereas other family members do not? According to the **diathesis-stress model**, which integrates the biological and environmental perspectives, psychological disorders develop when a biological predisposition is triggered by stressful circumstances. Another attempt at integrating causes is the **systems** (biopsychosocial) **approach**, which contends psychological disorders are "lifestyle diseases" arising from a combination of biological risk factors, psychological stresses, and societal pressures.

How common are mental disorders? According to research, 15% of the population is suffering from one or more mental disorders at any given point in time.

Is there a difference between "insanity" and "mental illness"? **Insanity** is a legal term, not a psychological one. It is typically applied to defendants who were so mentally disturbed when they committed their offense that they either did not know right from wrong or were unable to control their behavior.

Why is it useful to have a manual of psychological disorders? The current fourth edition of the *Diagnostic and Statistical Manual of Mental Disorders (DSM-5)* provides careful descriptions of the symptoms of different disorders so that diagnoses based on them will be reliable and consistent among mental health professionals. The *DSM-5* includes little information on causes and treatments.

MOOD DISORDERS

How do mood disorders differ from ordinary mood changes? Most people have a wide emotional range, but in some people with **mood disorders,** this range is greatly restricted. They seem stuck at one or the other end of the emotional spectrum, or they may alternate back and forth between periods of mania and depression.

How does clinical depression differ from ordinary sadness? The most common mood disorders are **depressive disorders,** in which a person may feel overwhelmed with sadness, lose interest in activities, and display such other symptoms as excessive guilt, feelings of worthlessness, insomnia, and loss of appetite. **Major depressive disorder** is an episode of intense sadness that may last for several months; in contrast, **persistent depressive disorder** involves less intense sadness but persists with little relief for a period of 2 years or more.

What factors are related to a person's likelihood of committing suicide? More women than men attempt suicide, but more men succeed. Suicide attempt rates among American adolescents and young adults have been rising. A common feeling associated with suicide is hopelessness, which is also typical of depression.

What is mania, and how is it involved in bipolar disorder? People suffering from **manic episodes** become euphoric ("high"), extremely active, excessively talkative, and easily distracted. They typically have unlimited hopes and schemes, but little interest in realistically carrying them out. At the extreme, they may collapse from exhaustion. Manic episodes usually alternate with depression. Such a mood disorder, in which both mania and depression are alternately present and are sometimes interrupted by periods of normal mood, is known as **bipolar disorder.**

What causes some people to experience extreme mood changes? Mood disorders can result from a combination of biological, psychological, and social factors. Genetics and chemical imbalances in the brain seem to play an important role in the development of depression and, especially, bipolar disorder. **Cognitive distortions** (unrealistically negative views about the self) occur in many depressed people, although it is uncertain whether these cause the depression or are caused by it. Finally, social factors, such as troubled relationships, have also been linked with mood disorders.

ANXIETY DISORDERS

How does an anxiety disorder differ from ordinary anxiety? Normal fear is caused by something identifiable and the fear subsides with time. With **anxiety disorder,** however, either the person doesn't know the source of the fear or the anxiety is inappropriate to the circumstances.

Into what three categories are phobias usually grouped? A **specific phobia** is an intense, paralyzing fear of something that it is unreasonable to fear so excessively. A **social anxiety disorder** is excessive, inappropriate fear connected with social situations or performances in front of other people. **Agoraphobia,** a less common and much more debilitating type of anxiety disorder, involves multiple, intense fears such as the fear of being alone, of being in public places, or of other situations involving separation from a source of security.

How does a panic attack differ from fear? Panic disorder is characterized by recurring sudden, unpredictable, and overwhelming experiences of intense fear or terror without any reasonable cause.

In contrast, **Generalized anxiety disorder** is defined by prolonged vague, but intense fears that, unlike phobias, are not attached to any particular object or circumstance.

How does obsessive-compulsive disorder differ from phobias? Obsessive–compulsive disorder involves either involuntary thoughts that recur despite the person's attempt to stop them or compulsive rituals that a person feels compelled to perform. A related disorder in this category is called **Body dysmorphic disorder,** which is characterized by imagined ugliness in some part of the body. Two other types of anxiety-related are caused by highly stressful events. If the anxious reaction occurs soon after the event, the diagnosis is *acute stress disorder;* if it occurs long after the event is over, the diagnosis is *posttraumatic stress disorder.*

What causes anxiety disorders? Psychologists with a biological perspective propose that a predisposition to anxiety disorders may be inherited because these types of disorders tend to run in families. Cognitive psychologists suggest that people who believe that they have no control over stressful events in their lives are more likely to suffer from anxiety disorders than other people are. Evolutionary psychologists hold that we are predisposed by evolution to associate certain stimuli with intense fears, serving as the origin of many phobias. Psychoanalytic thinkers focus on inner psychological conflicts and the defense mechanisms they trigger as the sources of anxiety disorders.

SOMATIC SYMPTOM AND RELATED DISORDERS

What is the difference between psychosomatic and somatic symptom and related disorders? Psychosomatic illnesses have a valid physical basis, but are largely caused by psychological factors such as excessive stress and anxiety. In contrast, **somatic symptom and related disorders** are characterized by physical symptoms without any identifiable physical cause. Examples are Somatic symptom disorder, characterized by recurrent vague somatic complaints without a physical cause, **conversion disorder** (a dramatic specific disability without organic cause), and **illness anxiety disorder** (insistence that minor symptoms mean serious illness).

DISSOCIATIVE DISORDERS

What do dissociative disorders have in common? In **dissociative disorders,** some part of a person's personality or memory is separated from the rest. **Dissociative amnesia** involves the loss of at least some significant aspects of memory. When an amnesia victim leaves home and assumes an entirely new identity, the disorder is known as **dissociative fugue.** In **dissociative identity disorder** (*multiple personality disorder*), several distinct personalities emerge at different times. In **depersonalization/derealization disorder,** the person suddenly feels changed or different in a strange way.

SEXUAL DYSFUNCTIONS

What are the main types of sexual dysfunctions? The main types of sexual dysfunctions recognized by *DSM-5* include sexual dysfunction, paraphilias, and gender....

Sexual dysfunction is the loss or impairment of the ability to function effectively during sex. In men, this may take the form of **erectile disorder (ED),** the inability to achieve or keep an erection; in women, it often takes the form of **female sexual interest/ arousal disorder,** loss of interest, the inability to become sexually excited or to reach orgasm. Sexual desire disorders involve a lack of interest in or an active aversion to sex. People with **orgasmic disorders** experience both desire and arousal but are unable to reach orgasm. Other problems that can occur include **premature ejaculation**—the male's inability to inhibit orgasm as long as desired— and **vaginismus**—involuntary muscle spasms in the outer part of a woman's vagina during sexual excitement that make intercourse impossible.

PARAPHILIC DISORDERS

What key characteristic distinguishes paraphilias from paraphilic disorders? Paraphilic disorders involve the use of unconventional sex objects or situations. These disorders include **fetishism, voyeurism, exhibitionism, frotteurism, transvestic fetishism, sexual sadism,** and **sexual masochism.** One of the most serious paraphiliac disorders is **pedophilic disorder,** which involves engaging in sexual relations with children.

GENDER DYSPHORIA

What are the key symptoms required for a diagnosis of gender dysphoria? Gender dysphoria involves the desire to become, or the insistence that one really is, a member of the other sex. In children, gender dysphoria is characterized by rejection of one's biological gender as well as the clothing and behavior society considers appropriate to that gender during childhood.

PERSONALITY DISORDERS

Which personality disorder creates the most significant problems for society? **Personality disorders** are enduring, inflexible, and maladaptive ways of thinking and behaving that are so exaggerated and rigid that they cause serious inner distress or conflicts with others. One group of personality disorders is characterized by odd or eccentric behavior. People who exhibit **schizoid personality disorder** lack the ability or desire to form social relationships and have no warm feelings for other people; those with **paranoid personality disorder** are inappropriately suspicious, hypersensitive, and argumentative. Another cluster of personality disorders is characterized by anxious or fearful behavior. Examples are **dependent personality disorder** (the inability to think or act independently) and **avoidant personality disorder** (social anxiety leading to isolation). A third group of personality disorders is characterized by dramatic, emotional, or erratic behavior. For instance, people with **narcissistic personality disorder** have a highly overblown sense of self-importance, whereas those with **borderline personality disorder** show much instability in self-image, mood, and interpersonal relationships. Finally, people with **antisocial personality disorder** chronically lie, steal, and cheat with little or no remorse. Because this disorder is responsible for a good deal of crime and violence, it creates the greatest problems for society.

SCHIZOPHRENIC SPECTRUM DISORDERS

How is schizophrenia different from multiple-personality disorder? In multiple-personality disorder, consciousness is split into two or more distinctive personalities, each of which is coherent and intact. This condition is different from **schizophrenic disorders,** which involve dramatic disruptions in thought and communication, inappropriate emotions, and bizarre behavior that lasts for years. People with schizophrenia are out of touch with reality and usually cannot live a normal life unless successfully treated with medication. They often suffer from **hallucinations** (false sensory perceptions) and **delusions** (false beliefs about reality).

What are the traditional categories of schizophrenic disorders? Traditional subtypes of schizophrenic disorders include *disorganized schizophrenia* (childish disregard for social conventions), *catatonic schizophrenia* (mute immobility or excessive excitement), *paranoid schizophrenia* (extreme suspiciousness related to complex delusions), and *undifferentiated schizophrenia* (characterized by a diversity of symptoms). *DSM-5* no longer differentiates these various subtypes of schizophrenia.

What are the causes of schizophrenia? Schizophrenia has a genetic component. Pathology in various structures of the brain and prenatal disturbances may also play a role.

NEURODEVELOPMENTAL DISORDERS

Why do stimulants appear to slow down hyperactive children and adults? The *DSM-5* contains a long list of disorders usually first diagnosed in infancy, childhood, or adolescence. Children with **attention-deficit/hyperactivity disorder (ADHD)** are highly distractible, often fidgety and impulsive, and almost constantly in motion. The **psychostimulants** frequently prescribed for ADHD appear to slow such children down because they increase the ability to focus attention on routine tasks. **Autistic disorder** is a profound developmental problem identified in the first few years of life. It is characterized by a failure to form normal social attachments, by severe speech impairment, and by strange motor behaviors. A much broader range of developmental disorders known as **autistic spectrum disorder (ASD)** is used to describe individuals with symptoms that are similar to those seen in autistic disorder, but may be less severe.

GENDER AND CULTURAL DIFFERENCES IN PSYCHOLOGICAL DISORDERS

What complex factors contribute to different rates of abnormal behavior in men and women? Although nearly all psychological disorders affect both men and women, there are some gender differences in the degree to which some disorders are found. Men are more likely to suffer from substance abuse and antisocial personality disorder; women show higher rates of depression, agoraphobia, simple phobia, obsessive–compulsive disorder, and somatization disorder. In general, gender differences are less likely to be seen in disorders that have a strong biological component. This tendency is also seen cross-culturally, where cultural differences are observed in disorders not heavily influenced by genetic and biological factors. These gender and cultural differences support the systems view that biological, psychological, and social forces interact as causes of abnormal behavior.

13

Therapies

OVERVIEW

For most new mothers, giving birth results in an instant bond and feelings of immediate and unconditional love for their new baby. Many describe motherhood as the happiest time in their lives and cannot imagine a life without their children. However, for some, another reaction occurs—one of sadness and apathy, and withdrawal from the world around them. Brooke Shields, the well-known actress and model, was one of these women.

In *Down Came the Rain: My Journey Through Postpartum Depression,* Shields (2006) writes that she had always dreamed of being a mother. Although she and her husband, Chris Henchy, initially had trouble conceiving, Shields eventually became pregnant through in vitro fertilization and gave birth to a daughter in 2003. Just as her attempt at conceiving wasn't without effort, easing into life as a mother wasn't effortless, either.

Almost immediately after returning home from the hospital, Shields began to experience symptoms of postpartum depression. Once referred to as the "baby blues," postpartum depression has recently come to be considered a very legitimate type of depression. Symptoms range from anxiety and tearfulness to feelings of extreme detachment and even being suicidal. Shields notes that her "baby blues" rapidly gave way to full-blown depression, including thoughts of self-harm and frightening visions of harm coming to her baby. In addition to the birth of her child, Shields was also coping with the recent death of her father, as well as the ongoing struggle of coping with the suicide of a close friend two years prior. Doctors note that postpartum depression can be exacerbated by events such as these.

As Shields's mental health began to decline, she felt more anxious and panicky. She felt sadness greater than she'd ever experienced, and began thinking that it would never go away. She felt completely detached from the baby she had gone through so much to have. This detachment depressed her further. It became a vicious cycle, and she suffered tremendously throughout it. It didn't occur to Shields that she might have postpartum depression until she heard someone comment on the shame and depression associated with the disease. It finally hit home and Shields sought help.

As with nearly all forms of depression, there was no quick and easy solution. Treatment requires patience, help from a doctor, a supportive family, and often medication. Shields began treatment and gradually began to feel better. She eventually was able to feel the love that mothers speak of when referring to their children. She bonded with her baby and became tuned in to the child's needs instinctively. With her doctor's guidance, she began to wean herself off the medication. She also sought healing through writing the book that detailed her experience, and in 2006, she and her husband conceived again, adding another child to their family.

Having learned about a wide range of psychological disorders in Chapter 12, "Psychological Disorders," you are probably curious about the kinds of treatments available for them. Brooke Shields's treatment for depression, a combination of medication and **psychotherapy,** exemplifies the help that is available. This chapter describes a variety of treatments that mental health professionals provide.

ENDURING ISSUES in Therapies

The underlying assumption behind therapy for psychological disorders is the belief that people are capable of changing (*Stability–Change*). Throughout this chapter you will have many opportunities to think about whether people suffering from psychological disorders can change significantly and whether they can change without intervention. In the discussion of biological treatments for psychological disorders, we again encounter the issue of mind–body. Finally, the enduring issue of diversity–universality will arise when we discuss the challenges therapists face when treating people from cultures other than their own.

INSIGHT THERAPIES

What do insight therapies have in common?

Although the details of various **insight therapies** differ, their common goal is to give people a better awareness and understanding of their feelings, motivations, and actions in the hope that this will lead to better adjustment. In this section, we consider three major insight therapies: psychoanalysis, client-centered therapy, and Gestalt therapy.

Psychoanalysis

How does "free association" in psychoanalysis help a person to become aware of hidden feelings?

Psychoanalysis is designed to bring hidden feelings and motives to conscious awareness so that the person can deal with them more effectively.

psychotherapy The use of psychological techniques to treat personality and behavior disorders.

insight therapies A variety of individual psychotherapies designed to give people a better awareness and understanding of their feelings, motivations, and actions in the hope that this will help them to adjust.

‹····· **LEARNING OBJECTIVES** ·······

- Describe the common goal of all insight therapies. Compare and contrast psychoanalysis, client-centered therapy, and Gestalt therapy.

- Explain how short-term psychodynamic therapy and virtual therapy differ from the more traditional forms of insight therapy.

The consulting room where Freud met his clients. Note the position of Freud's chair at the head of the couch. In order to encourage free association, the psychoanalyst has to function as a blank screen onto which the client can project his or her feelings. To accomplish this, Freud believed, the psychoanalyst has to stay out of sight of the client.

In Freudian psychoanalysis, the client is instructed to talk about whatever comes to mind. This process is called **free association.** Freud believed that the resulting "stream of consciousness" would provide insight into the person's unconscious mind. During the early stages of psychoanalysis, the analyst remains impassive, mostly silent, and out of the person's sight. The analyst's silence serves as a "blank screen" onto which the person projects unconscious thoughts and feelings.

Eventually, clients may test their analyst by talking about desires and fantasies that they have never revealed to anyone else. When clients discover that their analyst is not shocked or disgusted by their revelations, they are reassured and transfer to their analyst feelings they have toward authority figures from their childhood. This process is known as **transference.** It is said to be *positive transference* when the person feels good about the analyst.

As people continue to expose their innermost feelings, they begin to feel increasingly vulnerable. Threatened by their analyst's silence and by their own thoughts, clients may feel cheated and perhaps accuse their analyst of being a money grabber. Or they may suspect that their analyst is really disgusted by their disclosures or is laughing at them behind their backs. This *negative transference* is thought to be a crucial step in psychoanalysis, for it presumably reveals negative feelings toward authority figures and resistance to uncovering repressed emotions.

As therapy progresses, the analyst takes a more active role and begins to *interpret* or suggest alternative meanings for clients' feelings, memories, and actions. The goal of interpretation is to help people to gain **insight**—to become aware of what was formerly outside their awareness. As what was unconscious becomes conscious, clients may come to see how their childhood experiences have determined how they currently feel and act. By *working through* old conflicts, clients have a chance to review and revise the feelings and beliefs that underlie their problems. In the example of a therapy session that follows, the woman discovers a link between her current behaviors and childhood fears regarding her mother, which she has transferred to the analyst.

Therapist: (*summarizing and restating*) It sounds as if you would like to let loose with me, but you are afraid of what my response would be.

Patient: I get so excited by what is happening here. I feel I'm being held back by needing to be nice. I'd like to blast loose sometimes, but I don't dare.

Therapist: Because you fear my reaction?

Patient: The worst thing would be that you wouldn't like me. You wouldn't speak to me friendly; you wouldn't smile; you'd feel you can't treat me and discharge me from treatment. But I know this isn't so; I know it.

Therapist: Where do you think these attitudes come from?

Patient: When I was 9 years old, I read a lot about great men in history. I'd quote them and be dramatic, I'd want a sword at my side; I'd dress like an Indian. Mother would scold me, "Don't frown; don't talk so much. Sit on your hands," over and over again. I did all kinds of things. I was a naughty child. She told me I'd be hurt. Then, at 14, I fell off a horse and broke my back. I had to be in bed. Mother told me that day not to go riding. I'd get hurt because the ground was frozen. I was a stubborn, self-willed child. Then I went against her will and suffered an accident that changed my life: a fractured back. Her attitude was, "I told you so." I was put in a cast and kept in bed for months.

free association A psychoanalytic technique that encourages the person to talk without inhibition about whatever thoughts or fantasies come to mind.

transference The client's carrying over to the analyst feelings held toward childhood authority figures.

insight Awareness of previously unconscious feelings and memories and how they influence present feelings and behavior.

Therapist: You were punished, so to speak, by this accident.

Patient: But I gained attention and love from Mother for the first time. I felt so good. I'm ashamed to tell you this: Before I healed, I opened the cast and tried to walk, to make myself sick again so I could stay in bed longer.

Therapist: How does that connect with your impulse to be sick now and stay in bed so much?

Patient: Oh. . . . (*pause*)

Therapist: What do you think?

Patient: Oh, my God, how infantile, how ungrownup (*pause*). It must be so. I want people to love me and feel sorry for me. Oh, my God. How completely childish. It is, *is* that. My mother must have ignored me when I was little, and I wanted so to be loved.

Therapist: So that it may have been threatening to go back to being self-willed and unloved after you got out of the cast (*interpretation*).

Patient: It did. My life changed. I became meek and controlled. I couldn't get angry or stubborn afterward.

Therapist: Perhaps if you go back to being stubborn with me, you would be returning to how you were before, that is, active, stubborn, but unloved.

Patient: (*excitedly*) And, therefore, losing your love. I need you, but after all, you aren't going to reject me. But the pattern is so established now that the threat of the loss of love is too overwhelming with everybody, and I've got to keep myself from acting selfish or angry (Wolberg, 1977, pp. 560–561).

A relatively small percentage of people who seek therapy go into traditional psychoanalysis, as this woman did. As Freud recognized, analysis requires great motivation to change and an ability to deal rationally with whatever the analysis uncovers. Moreover, traditional analysis may take 5 years or longer, with three, sometimes five, sessions a week. Few can afford this kind of treatment, and fewer still possess the verbal and analytical skills necessary to discuss thoughts and feelings in this detailed way. And many want more immediate help for their problems. Finally, for those with severe disorders, psychoanalysis is ineffective.

Since Freud's invention around the turn of the 20th century, psychodynamic personality theory has changed significantly. Many of these changes have led to modified psychoanalytic techniques as well as to different therapeutic approaches (McCullough & Magill, 2009; Monti & Sabbadini, 2005). Freud felt that to understand the present we must understand the past, but most neo-Freudians encourage clients to cope directly with current problems in addition to addressing unresolved conflicts from the past. Neo-Freudians also favor face-to-face discussions, and most take an active role in analysis by interpreting their client's statements freely and suggesting discussion topics.

Source: © *The New Yorker Collection*, 1989, Danny Shanahan from *cartoonbank.com*. All Rights Reserved.

Client-Centered Therapy

Why did Carl Rogers call his approach to therapy "client centered"?

Carl Rogers, the founder of **client-centered (or person-centered) therapy,** took pieces of the neo-Freudians' views and revised them into a radically different approach to therapy. According to Rogers, the goal of therapy is to help people to become fully functioning, to open them up to all of their experiences and to all of themselves. Such inner awareness is a form of insight, but for Rogers, insight into current feelings was more important than insight into unconscious wishes with roots in the distant past. Rogers called his approach to therapy *client centered* because he placed the responsibility for change on the person with the problem. Rogers believed that people's defensiveness, anxiety, and other signs of discomfort stem from their experiences of *conditional positive regard.* They have learned that love and acceptance are contingent on conforming to what other people want them to be. By contrast, the cardinal rule in person-centered therapy is for the therapist to express

client-centered (or person-centered) therapy Nondirectional form of therapy developed by Carl Rogers that calls for unconditional positive regard of the client by the therapist with the goal of helping the client become fully functioning.

◉─ **Watch** the **Video** Classic Footage of
Carl Rogers on Role of a Therapist on
MyPsychLab

unconditional positive regard—that is, to show true acceptance of clients no matter what
they may say or do (Bozarth, 2007). Rogers felt that this was a crucial first step toward
clients' self-acceptance. ◉

Rogerian therapists try to understand things from the clients' point of view. They are
emphatically *nondirective*. They do not suggest reasons for a client's feelings or how they
might better handle a difficult situation. Instead, they try to reflect clients' statements,
sometimes asking questions or hinting at feelings that clients have not articulated. Rogers
felt that when therapists provide an atmosphere of openness and genuine respect, clients
can find themselves, as portrayed in the following session.

Client: I guess I do have problems at school . . . . You see, I'm chairman of the Science
Department, so you can imagine what kind of a department it is.

Therapist: You sort of feel that if you're in something that it can't be too good. Is
that . . .

Client: Well, it's not that I . . . It's just that I'm . . . I don't think that I could run it.

Therapist: You don't have any confidence in yourself?

Client: No confidence, no confidence in myself. I never had any confidence in myself.
I—like I told you—like when even when I was a kid I didn't feel I was capable
and I always wanted to get back with the intellectual group.

Therapist: This has been a long-term thing, then. It's gone on a long time.

Client: Yeah, the *feeling* is—even though I know it isn't, it's the feeling that I have
that—that I haven't got it, that—that—that—people will find out that I'm
dumb or—or . . .

Therapist: Masquerade.

Client: Superficial, I'm just superficial. There's nothing below the surface. Just superficial generalities, that . . .

Therapist: There's nothing really deep and meaningful to you (Hersher, 1970, pp. 29–32).

Rogers wanted to discover those processes in client-centered therapy that were associated with positive results. Rogers's interest in the *process* of therapy resulted in important and lasting contributions to the field; research has shown that a therapist's emphasis
on empathy, warmth, and understanding increase success, no matter what therapeutic
approach is used (Bike, Norcross, & Schatz, 2009; Kirschenbaum & Jourdan, 2005).

A number of variations on person-centered therapy have been developed. However,
they all share several common features: the therapist must provide empathy and unconditional positive regard, and the belief that clients are resourceful persons capable of finding
their own directions and solutions to their problems (Cain, 2010).

Carl Rogers (far right) leading a group
therapy session. Rogers was the founder
of client-centered therapy.

Gestalt Therapy

How is Gestalt therapy different from psychoanalysis?

Gestalt therapy is largely an outgrowth of the work of Frederick (Fritz) Perls at the Esalen Institute in California. By emphasizing the present and encouraging face-to-face confrontations, Gestalt therapy attempts to help people become more genuine in their daily interactions (Brownell, 2010). The therapist is active and directive, and the emphasis is on the *whole* person. (The term *Gestalt* means "whole.") The therapist's role is to "fill in the holes in the personality to make the person whole and complete again" (Perls, 1969, p. 2).

Gestalt therapists use various techniques to try to make people aware of their feelings. For example, they tell people to "own their feelings" by talking in an active, rather than a passive way: "I feel angry when he's around" instead of "He makes me feel angry when he's around." They also ask people to speak to a part of themselves that they imagine to be sitting next to them in an empty chair. This *empty-chair technique* and others are illustrated in the following excerpt:

Therapist: Try to describe just what you are aware of at each moment as fully as possible. For instance, what are you aware of now?

Client: I'm aware of wanting to tell you about my problem, and also a sense of shame—yes, I feel very ashamed right now.

Therapist: Okay. I would like you to develop a dialogue with your feeling of shame. Put your shame in the empty chair over here (*indicates chair*), and talk to it.

Client: Are you serious? I haven't even told you about my problem yet.

Therapist: That can wait—I'm perfectly serious, and I want to know what you have to say to your shame.

Client: (*awkward and hesitant at first, but then becoming looser and more involved*) Shame, I hate you. I wish you would leave me—you drive me crazy, always reminding me that I have a problem, that I'm perverse, different, shameful—even ugly. Why don't you leave me alone?

Therapist: Okay, now go to the empty chair, take the role of shame, and answer yourself back.

Client: (*moves to the empty chair*) I am your constant companion—and I don't *want* to leave you. I would feel lonely without you, and I don't hate you. I pity you, and I pity your attempts to shake me loose, because you are doomed to failure.

Therapist: Okay, now go back to your original chair and answer back.

Client: (*once again as himself*) How do you know I'm doomed to failure? (*spontaneously shifts chairs now, no longer needing direction from the therapist; answers himself back, once again in the role of shame*) I know that you're doomed to failure because *I* want you to fail and because I control your life. You can't make a single move without me. For all you know, you were born with me. You can hardly remember a single moment when you were without me, totally unafraid that I would spring up and suddenly remind you of your loathsomeness (Shaffer, 1978, pp. 92–93).

In this way, the client becomes more aware of conflicting inner feelings and, with insight, can become more genuine. Psychoanalysis, client-centered therapy, and Gestalt therapy differ in technique, but all use talk to help people become more aware of their feelings and conflicts, and all involve fairly substantial amounts of time. More recent developments in therapy seek to limit the amount of time people spend in therapy.

Recent Developments

What are some recent developments in insight therapies?

Although Freud, Rogers, and Perls originated the three major forms of insight therapy, others have developed hundreds of variations on this theme. Most involve a therapist who is far more active and emotionally engaged with clients than traditional psychoanalysts

Gestalt therapy An insight therapy that emphasizes the wholeness of the personality and attempts to reawaken people to their emotions and sensations in the present.

short-term psychodynamic therapy
Insight therapy that is time limited and focused on trying to help clients correct the immediate problems in their lives.

thought fit. These therapists give clients direct guidance and feedback, commenting on what they are told rather than just neutral listening.

Another general trend in recent years is toward shorter-term "dynamic therapy." For most people, this usually means meeting once a week for a fixed period. In fact, **short-term psychodynamic therapy** is increasingly popular among both clients and mental health professionals (Abbass, Joffres, & Ogrodniczuk, 2008; McCullough & Magill, 2009). Insight remains the goal, but the course of treatment is usually limited—for example, to 25 sessions. With the trend to a time-limited framework, insight therapies have become more problem- or symptom-oriented, with greater focus on the person's current life situation and relationships. Although contemporary insight therapists do not discount childhood experiences, they view people as being less at the mercy of early childhood events than Freud did.

Perhaps the most dramatic and controversial change in insight therapies is *virtual therapy*. For a hundred years or so, people who wanted to see a therapist have literally gone to *see* a therapist—they have traveled to the therapist's office, sat down, and talked through their problems. In recent years, however, some people have started connecting with their therapists by telephone (S. Williams, 2000). Others pay their visits via cyberspace. The delivery of health care over the Internet or through other electronic means is part of a rapidly expanding field known as *telehealth*.

Although most therapists believe that online therapy is no substitute for face-to-face interactions (Almer, 2000; Rabasca, 2000c), evidence suggests that telehealth may provide cost-effective opportunities for delivery of some mental health services (J. E. Barnett & Scheetz, 2003; T. J. Kim, 2011). Telehealth is a particularly appealing alternative for people who live in remote or rural areas. For example, a university-based telehealth system in Kentucky provides psychological services to rural schools (Thomas Miller et al., 2003), and *video-conferencing therapy* has been used successfully to treat posttraumatic stress disorder in rural Wyoming (Hassija & Gray, 2009). Another study, this time in Canada, demonstrated that psychotherapy delivered by videoconference was as effective as face-to-face therapy in treating posttraumatic stress disorder (Germain, Marchand, Bouchard, Drouin, & Guay, 2009). Though these preliminary results are encouraging, more research is needed to determine under what circumstances virtual therapy is effective, as such services are likely to proliferate in the future (Melnyk, 2008; Zur, 2007).

Even more notable than the trend toward short-term and virtual therapy has been the proliferation of behavior therapies during the past few decades. In this next section, we examine several types.

✓—[**Study** and **Review** on **MyPsychLab**

CHECK YOUR UNDERSTANDING

1. _____ therapies focus on giving people clearer understanding of their feelings, motives, and actions.

2. _____ _____ is a technique in psychoanalysis whereby the client lets thoughts flow without interruption or inhibition.

3. The process called _____ involves having clients project their feelings toward authority figures onto their therapist.

4. Rogerian therapists show that they value and accept their clients by providing them with _____ _____ regard.

5. Indicate whether the following statements are true (T) or false (F):

   a. ____ Psychoanalysis is based on the belief that problems are symptoms of inner conflicts dating back to childhood.

   b. ____ Rogers's interest in the process of therapy was one avenue of exploration that did not prove very fruitful.

   c. ____ In Gestalt therapy, the therapist is active and directive.

   d. ____ Gestalt therapy emphasizes the client's problems in the present.

Answers: 1. Insight. **2.** Free association. **3.** transference. **4.** unconditional positive. **5. a.** (T). **b.** (F). **c.** (T). **d.** (T).

1. Consider the following scenario: The client lies on a couch, and the therapist sits out of sight. The therapist gets to know the client's problems through free association and then encourages the client to "work through" his or her problems. What kind of therapy is this?

   a. psychoanalysis

   b. client-centered therapy

   c. Gestalt therapy

   d. rational–emotive therapy

2. Which of the following choices illustrates client-centered therapy with a depressed person?

   a. The client is encouraged to give up her depression by interacting with a group of people in an encounter group.

   b. The therapist tells the client that his depression is self-defeating and gives the client "assignments" to develop self-esteem and enjoy life.

   c. The therapist encourages the client to say anything that comes into her head, to express her innermost fantasies, and to talk about critical childhood events.

   d. The therapist offers the client her unconditional positive regard and, once this open atmosphere is established, tries to help the client discover why she feels depressed.

Answers: 1. a. 2. d.

BEHAVIOR THERAPIES

What do behaviorists believe should be the focus of psychotherapy?

Behavior therapies sharply contrast with insight-oriented approaches. They are focused on changing *behavior*, rather than on discovering insights into thoughts and feelings. Behavior therapies are based on the belief that all behavior, both normal and abnormal, is learned. People suffering from hypochondriasis *learn* that they get attention when they are sick; people with paranoid personalities *learn* to be suspicious of others. Behavior therapists also assume that maladaptive behaviors *are* the problem, not symptoms of deeper underlying causes. If behavior therapists can teach people to behave in more appropriate ways, they believe that they have cured the problem. The therapist does not need to know exactly how or why a client learned to behave abnormally in the first place. The job of the therapist is simply to teach the person new, more satisfying ways of behaving on the basis of scientifically studied principles of learning, such as classical conditioning, operant conditioning, and modeling (Zinbarg & Griffith, 2008).

Therapies Based on Classical Conditioning

How can classical conditioning be used as the basis of treatment?

As we saw in Chapter 5 ("Learning"), *classical conditioning* involves the repeated pairing of a neutral stimulus with one that evokes a certain reflex response. Eventually, the formerly neutral stimulus alone comes to elicit the same response. The approach is one of learned stimulus-response associations. Several variations on classical conditioning have been used to treat psychological problems.

Desensitization, Extinction, and Flooding **Systematic desensitization,** a method for gradually reducing fear and anxiety, is one of the oldest behavior therapy techniques (Wolpe, 1990). The method works by gradually associating a new response (relaxation) with anxiety-causing stimuli. For example, an aspiring politician might seek

- Explain the statement that "Behavior therapies sharply contrast with insight-oriented approaches."
- Describe the processes of desensitization, extinction, flooding, aversive conditioning, behavior contracting, token economies, and modeling.

behavior therapies Therapeutic approaches that are based on the belief that all behavior, normal and abnormal, is learned, and that the objective of therapy is to teach people new, more satisfying ways of behaving.

systematic desensitization A behavioral technique for reducing a person's fear and anxiety by gradually associating a new response (relaxation) with stimuli that have been causing the fear and anxiety.

The clients in these photographs are overcoming a simple phobia: fear of snakes. After practicing a technique of deep relaxation, clients in desensitization therapy work from the bottom of their hierarchy of fears up to the situation that provokes the greatest fear or anxiety. Here, clients progress from handling rubber snakes (top left) to viewing live snakes through a window (top center) and finally to handling live snakes. This procedure can also be conducted in the therapist's office, where clients combine relaxation techniques with simply imagining anxiety-provoking scenes.

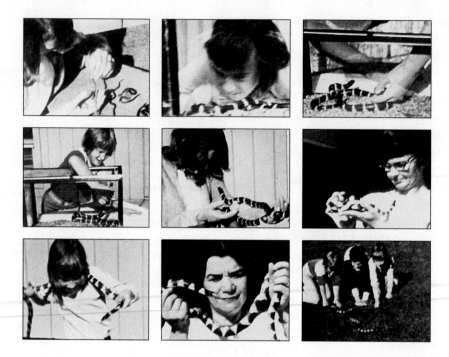

therapy because she is anxious about speaking to crowds. The therapist explores the kinds of crowds that are most threatening: Is an audience of 500 worse than one of 50? Is it harder to speak to men than it is to women? Is there more anxiety facing strangers than a roomful of friends? From this information the therapist develops a *hierarchy of fears*—a list of situations from the least to the most anxiety provoking. The therapist then teaches techniques for relaxation, both mentally and physically. Once the client has mastered deep relaxation, she or he begins work at the bottom of the hierarchy of fears. The person is told to relax while imagining the least threatening situation on the list, then the next most threatening, and so on, until the most fear-arousing one is reached and the client can still remain calm.

Numerous studies show that systematic desensitization helps many people overcome their fears and phobias (Hazel, 2005; D. W. McNeil & Zvolensky, 2000). However, the key to success may not be the learning of a new conditioned relaxation response, but rather the *extinction* of the old fear response through mere exposure. Recall that in classical conditioning, extinction occurs when the learned, conditioned stimulus is repeatedly presented without the unconditioned stimulus following it. Thus, if a person repeatedly imagines a frightening situation without encountering danger, the associated fear should gradually decline. Desensitization is most effective when clients gradually confront their fears in the real world rather than merely in their imaginations.

The technique of *flooding* is a less familiar desensitization method. It involves full-intensity exposure to a feared stimulus for a prolonged period of time (Moulds & Nixon, 2006; Wolpe, 1990). Someone with a fear of snakes might be forced to handle dozens of snakes. Though flooding may seem unnecessarily harsh, remember how debilitating many untreated anxiety disorders can be.

Aversive Conditioning Another classical conditioning technique is **aversive conditioning,** in which pain and discomfort are associated with the behavior that the client wants to unlearn. Aversive conditioning has been used with limited success to treat alcoholism, obesity, smoking, and some psychosexual disorders. For example, the taste and smell of alcohol are sometimes paired with drug-induced nausea and vomiting. Before long, clients feel sick just seeing a bottle of liquor. A follow-up study of nearly 800 people who completed alcohol-aversion treatment found that 63% had maintained continuous abstinence for at least 12 months (Sharon Johnson, 2003; Wiens & Menustik, 1983). The long-term effectiveness of this technique has been questioned; if punishment no longer follows, the undesired behavior may reemerge.

aversive conditioning Behavioral therapy techniques aimed at eliminating undesirable behavior patterns by teaching the person to associate them with pain and discomfort.

Therapies Based on Operant Conditioning

How could "behavior contracting" change an undesirable behavior?

In *operant conditioning,* a person learns to behave a certain way because that behavior is reinforced. One therapy based on the principle of reinforcement is called **behavior contracting.** The therapist and the client agree on behavioral goals and on the reinforcement that the client will receive when he or she reaches those goals. These goals and reinforcements are often written in a contract that "legally" binds both the client and the therapist. A contract to help a person stop smoking might read: "For each day that I smoke fewer than 20 cigarettes, I will earn 30 minutes of time to go bowling. For each day that I exceed the goal, I will lose 30 minutes from the time that I have accumulated."

Another therapy based on operant conditioning is called the **token economy.** Token economies are usually used in schools and hospitals, where controlled conditions are most feasible (Boniecki & Moore, 2003; Comaty, Stasio, & Advokat, 2001). People are rewarded with tokens or points for appropriate behaviors, which can be exchanged for desired items and privileges. In a mental hospital, for example, improved grooming habits might earn points that can be used to purchase special foods or weekend passes. The positive changes in behavior, however, do not always generalize to everyday life outside the hospital or clinic, where adaptive behavior is not always reinforced and maladaptive behavior is not always punished.

behavior contracting Form of operant conditioning therapy in which the client and therapist set behavioral goals and agree on reinforcements that the client will receive on reaching those goals.

token economy An operant conditioning therapy in which people earn tokens (reinforcers) for desired behaviors and exchange them for desired items or privileges.

✔●—**Study** and **Review** on **MyPsychLab**

CHECK YOUR UNDERSTANDING

1. The therapeutic use of rewards to encourage desired behavior is based on a form of learning called _____ _____.

2. When client and therapist agree on a written set of behavioral goals, as well as a specific schedule of reinforcement when each goal is met, they are using a technique called _____ _____.

3. Some therapy involves learning desired behaviors by watching others perform those actions, which is also known as _____.

4. A _____ _____ is an operant conditioning technique whereby people earn some tangible item for desired behavior, which can then be exchanged for more basic rewards and privileges.

5. The technique of _____ involves intense and prolonged exposure to something feared.

Answers: 1. operant conditioning. 2. behavior contracting. 3. modeling. 4. token economy. 5. flooding.

APPLY YOUR UNDERSTANDING

1. Maria is in an alcoholism treatment program in which she must take a pill every morning. If she drinks alcohol during the day, she immediately feels nauseous. This treatment is an example of

   a. transference.
   b. flooding.
   c. aversive conditioning.
   d. desensitization.

2. Robert is about to start a new job in a tall building; and he is deathly afraid of riding in elevators. He sees a therapist who first teaches him how to relax. Once he has mastered that skill, the therapist asks him to relax while imagining that he is entering the office building. Once he can do that without feeling anxious, the therapist asks him to relax while imagining standing in front of the elevator doors, and so on until Robert can completely relax while imagining riding in elevators. This therapeutic technique is known as

   a. transference.
   b. desensitization.
   c. behavior contracting.
   d. flooding.

Answers: 1. c. 2. b.

modeling A behavior therapy in which the person learns desired behaviors by watching others perform those behaviors.

cognitive therapies Psychotherapies that emphasize changing clients' perceptions of their life situation as a way of modifying their behavior.

stress-inoculation therapy A type of cognitive therapy that trains clients to cope with stressful situations by learning a more useful pattern of self-talk.

rational–emotive therapy (RET) A directive cognitive therapy based on the idea that clients' psychological distress is caused by irrational and self-defeating beliefs and that the therapist's job is to challenge such dysfunctional beliefs.

According to cognitive therapists, the confidence this person is showing stems from the positive thoughts she has about herself. Stress-inoculation therapy helps replace negative, anxiety-evoking thoughts with confident self-talk.

Therapies Based on Modeling

What are some therapeutic uses of modeling?

Modeling—learning a behavior by watching someone else perform it—can also be used to treat problem behaviors. In a now classic demonstration of modeling, Albert Bandura and colleagues helped people to overcome a snake phobia by showing films in which models gradually moved closer and closer to snakes (Bandura, Blanchard, & Ritter, 1969). Modeling techniques have also been successfully used as part of job training programs (P. J. Taylor, Russ-Eft, & Chan, 2005) and have been used extensively with people with mental retardation to teach job and independent living skills (Cannella-Malone et al., 2006; Farr, 2008).

COGNITIVE THERAPIES

How can people overcome irrational and self-defeating beliefs?

Cognitive therapies are based on the belief that if people can change their distorted ideas about themselves and the world, they can also change their problem behaviors and make their lives more enjoyable. A cognitive therapist's goal is to identify erroneous ways of thinking and to correct them (Craske, 2009). Three popular forms of cognitive therapy are stress-inoculation therapy, rational–emotive therapy, and Aaron Beck's cognitive approach.

Stress-Inoculation Therapy

How can self-talk help us deal with difficult situations?

As we go about our lives, we talk to ourselves constantly—proposing courses of action, commenting on our performance, expressing wishes, and so on. **Stress-inoculation therapy** makes use of this self-talk to help people cope with stressful situations. The client is taught to suppress any negative, anxiety-evoking thoughts and to replace them with positive, "coping" thoughts. A student facing anxiety with an exam may think, "Another test; I'm so nervous. I'm sure I won't know the answers. If only I'd studied more. If I don't get through this course, I'll never graduate!" This pattern of thought is dysfunctional because it only makes anxiety worse. With the help of a cognitive therapist, the student learns a new pattern of self-talk: "I studied hard, and I know the material well. I looked at the textbook last night and reviewed my notes. I should be able to do well. If some questions are hard, they won't all be, and even if it's tough, my whole grade doesn't depend on just one test." Then the person tries the new strategy in a real situation, ideally one of only moderate stress (like a short quiz). Finally, the person is ready to use the strategy in a more stressful situation, like a final exam (Sheehy & Horan, 2004). Stress-inoculation therapy works by turning the client's thought patterns into a kind of vaccine against stress-induced anxiety.

Rational–Emotive Therapy

What irrational beliefs do many people hold?

Another type of cognitive therapy, **rational–emotive therapy (RET),** developed by Albert Ellis (1973, 2001), is based on the view that most people in need of therapy hold a set of irrational and self-defeating beliefs (Macavei, 2005; Overholser, 2003). They believe that they should be competent at *everything, always* treated fairly, quick to find solutions to *every* problem, and so forth. Such beliefs involve absolutes—"musts" and "shoulds"—and make no room for mistakes. When people with such irrational beliefs come up against real-life struggles, they often experience excessive psychological distress.

Rational–emotive therapists confront such dysfunctional beliefs vigorously, using a variety of techniques, including persuasion, challenge, commands, and theoretical arguments (A. Ellis & MacLaren, 1998). Studies have shown that RET often enables people to reinterpret negative beliefs and experiences more positively, decreasing the likelihood of depression (Blatt, Zuroff, Quinlan, & Pilkonis, 1996; Bruder et al., 1997).

Beck's Cognitive Therapy

How can cognitive therapy be used to combat depression?

One of the most important and promising forms of cognitive therapy for treating depression is known simply as **cognitive therapy** (J. Cahill et al., 2003). Sometimes it is referred to as "Beck's cognitive therapy," after developer Aaron Beck (1967), to distinguish between the broader category of cognitive therapies.

Beck believes that depression results from inappropriately self-critical patterns of thought. Self-critical people have unrealistic expectations, magnify failures, make sweeping negative generalizations based on little evidence, notice only negative feedback from the outside world, and interpret anything less than total success as failure. Although Beck's assumptions about the cause of depression are very similar to those underlying RET, the style of treatment differs considerably. Cognitive therapists are much less challenging and confrontational than rational–emotive therapists (Dozois, Frewen, & Covin, 2006). Instead, they try to help clients examine each dysfunctional thought in a supportive, but objectively scientific manner ("Are you *sure* your whole life will be totally ruined if you break up with Frank? What is your evidence for that? Didn't you once tell me how happy you were *before* you met him?"). Like RET, Beck's cognitive therapy tries to lead the person to more realistic and flexible ways of thinking. ✳

cognitive therapy Therapy that depends on identifying and changing inappropriately negative and self-critical patterns of thought.

✳ **Explore** the **Concept** Psychotherapy Practitioners and Their Activities on **MyPsychLab**

✔ **Study** and **Review** on **MyPsychLab**

CHECK YOUR UNDERSTANDING

1. Developing new ways of thinking that lead to more adaptive behavior lies at the heart of all _____ therapies.

2. An important form of cognitive therapy used to combat depression was developed by Aaron _____.

3. The immediate focus in cognitive therapies is to help clients change their behaviors. Is this statement true (T) or false (F)?

Answers: 1. cognitive. 2. Beck. 3. (F).

APPLY YOUR UNDERSTANDING

1. Larry has difficulty following his boss's directions. Whenever his boss asks him to do something, Larry panics. Larry enters a stress-inoculation program. Which is most likely to be the first step in this program?

   a. Have Larry volunteer to do a task for his boss.
   b. Show Larry a film in which employees are asked to do tasks and they perform well.
   c. Ask Larry what he says to himself when his boss asks him to perform a task.
   d. Ask Larry how he felt when he was a child and his mother asked him to do something.

2. Sarah rushes a sorority but isn't invited to join. She has great difficulty accepting this fact and as a consequence she becomes deeply depressed. She sees a therapist who vigorously challenges and confronts her in an effort to show her that her depression comes from an irrational, self-defeating belief that she must be liked and accepted by everyone. This therapist is most likely engaging in

   a. rational–emotive therapy.
   b. stress-inoculation therapy.
   c. flooding.
   d. desensitization therapy.

Answers: 1. c. 2. a.

LEARNING OBJECTIVES ┈┈┈┈▷

- Describe the potential advantages of group therapy compared to individual therapy.
- Compare and contrast family therapy, couple therapy, and self-help groups.

GROUP THERAPIES

What are some advantages of group therapies?

Some therapists believe that treating several people simultaneously is preferable to individual treatment. **Group therapy** allows both client and therapist to see how the person acts around others. If a person is painfully anxious and tongue-tied, chronically self-critical, or hostile, these tendencies show up quickly in a group.

Group therapies have the other advantage of social support—a feeling that one is not the only person in the world with problems. Group members can help one another learn useful new behaviors, like how to disagree without antagonizing others. Group interactions can lead people toward insights into their own behavior, such as why they are defensive or feel compelled to complain constantly. Because group therapy consists of several clients "sharing" a therapist, it is less expensive than individual therapy.

There are many kinds of group therapy. Some groups follow the general outlines of the therapies we have already mentioned. Others are oriented toward a specific goal, such as stopping smoking or drinking. Others may have a more open-ended goal—for example, a happier family or romantic relationship.

Group therapy can help to identify problems that a person has when interacting with other people. The group also offers social support, helping people to feel less alone with their problems.

group therapy Type of psychotherapy in which clients meet regularly to interact and help one another achieve insight into their feelings and behavior.

family therapy A form of group therapy that sees the family as at least partly responsible for the individual's problems and that seeks to change all family members' behaviors to the benefit of the family unit as well as the troubled individual.

couple therapy A form of group therapy intended to help troubled partners improve their problems of communication and interaction.

Family Therapy

Who is the client in family therapy?

Family therapy is one form of group therapy. Family therapists believe that if one person in the family is having problems, it's a signal that the entire family needs assistance. Therefore, it would be a mistake to treat a client without attempting to meet the person's parents, spouse, or children. Family therapists do not try to reshape the personalities of family members (Gurman & Kniskern, 1991), rather, they attempt to change relational interactions by such things as improving communication, encouraging empathy, sharing responsibilities, and reducing family conflict (Doherty & McDaniel, 2009). To achieve these goals, all family members must believe that they will benefit from behavioral changes.

Although family therapy is appropriate when there are problems between husband and wife or parents and children, it is increasingly used when only one family member has a clear psychological disorder (Keitner, Archambault, Ryan, & Miller, 2003; Mueser, 2006). The goal of treatment in these circumstances is to help mentally healthy members of the family cope more effectively with the impact of the disorder on the family unit, which, in turn, helps the troubled person. Family therapy is also called for when a person's progress in individual therapy is slowed by the family (often because other family members have trouble adjusting to that person's improvement) (Clark, 2009).

Couple Therapy

What are some techniques used in couple therapy?

Another form of group therapy is **couple therapy,** which is designed to assist partners who are having relationship difficulties. Previously termed *marital therapy,* the term "couple therapy" is considered more appropriate today because it captures the broad range of partners who may seek help (Lebow, 2006; Sheras & Koch-Sheras, 2006).

Most couple therapists concentrate on improving patterns of communication and mutual expectations. In *empathy training,* each member of the couple is taught to share inner feelings and to listen to and understand the partner's feelings before responding. This technique requires more time spent listening, grasping what is really being said, and less time in self-defensive rebuttal. Other couple therapists use behavioral techniques, such as helping a couple develop a schedule for exchanging specific caring actions, like helping with chores or making time to share a special meal together. This approach may not sound romantic, but proponents say it can break a cycle of dissatisfaction and hostility in a relationship, and hence, it is an important step in the right direction (N. B. Epstein, 2004). Couple therapy for both partners is generally more effective than therapy for just one (Fraser & Solovey, 2007; Susan Johnson, 2003).

Self-Help Groups

Why are self-help groups so popular?

An estimated 57 million Americans suffer from some kind of psychological problem (Kessler, Chiu, Demler, & Walters, 2005). Since individual treatment can be expensive, more and more people faced with life crises are turning to low-cost self-help groups. Most groups are small, local gatherings of people who share a common problem and who provide mutual support. Alcoholics Anonymous is perhaps the best-known self-help group, but self-help groups are available for virtually every life problem.

Do these self-help groups work? In many cases, they apparently do. Alcoholics Anonymous has developed a reputation for helping people cope with alcoholism. Most group members express strong support for their groups, and studies have demonstrated that they can indeed be effective (Galanter, Hayden, Castañeda, & Franco, 2005; Kurtz, 2004; McKellar, Stewart, & Humphreys, 2003).

Such groups also help to prevent more serious psychological disorders by reaching out to people who are near the limits of their ability to cope with stress. The social support they offer is particularly important in an age when divorce, geographic mobility, and other factors have reduced the ability of the family to comfort people. A list of some self-help organizations is included in "Applying Psychology: How to Find Help."

Watch the *Video* In the Real World: Self-Therapy on **MyPsychLab**

Study and **Review** on **MyPsychLab**

CHECK YOUR UNDERSTANDING

1. Which of the following is an advantage of group therapy?
   a. The client has the experience of interacting with other people in a therapeutic setting.
   b. It often reveals a client's problems more quickly than individual therapy.
   c. It can be cheaper than individual therapy.
   d. All of the above.

Answer: 1.d.

APPLY YOUR UNDERSTANDING

1. You are talking to a clinical psychologist who explains that, in her view, it is a mistake to try to treat a client's problems in a vacuum. Quite often, well-adjusted members of a family can help the client cope more effectively. Other times, the client's progress is slowed due to other people in the family. She is most likely a
   a. self-help therapist.
   b. family therapist.
   c. proximity therapist.
   d. social-attribution therapist.

2. Imagine that you believe most problems between partners arise because they don't share their inner feelings and they don't truly listen to and try to understand each other. You meet with them together and teach them to spend more time listening to the other person and trying to understand what the other person is really saying. Your beliefs are closest to which of the following kinds of therapists?
   a. Gestalt therapists.
   b. rational–emotive therapists.
   c. family therapists.
   d. couple therapists.

Answers: 1.b. 2.d.

APPLYING PSYCHOLOGY

How to Find Help

The attitude that seeking help for psychological problems is a sign of "weakness" is very common in our society. But the fact is that millions of people, including students, are helped by psychological counseling and therapy every year. Therapy is a common, useful aid in coping with daily life.

College is a time of stress and anxiety for many people. The competition for grades, the exposure to many different kinds of people with unfamiliar views, the tension of relating to peers all can take a psychological toll, especially for students away from home for the first time. Most colleges and universities have their own counseling services, and many are as sophisticated as the best clinics in the country. Most communities also have mental health programs. As an aid to a potential search for the right counseling service, we include here a list of some of the available resources for people who seek the advice of a mental health professional. Many of these services have national offices that can provide local branch information and the appropriate people to contact.

For Alcohol and Drug Abuse
National Clearinghouse for Alcohol and Drug Information

Rockville, MD (800) 729-6686
General Service Board

Alcoholics Anonymous, Inc.
New York, NY (212) 870-3400

For Friends or Relatives of Those with an Alcohol Problem
Al-Anon Family Groups
Virginia Beach, VA
(888) 4alanon (meeting information)
(757) 563-1600 (personal assistance)
Web site: www.al-anon.alateen.org

National Association for Children of Alcoholics
Rockville, MD
(301) 468-0985

For Depression and Suicide
Mental Health Counseling Hotline
New York, NY
(212) 734-5876

Heartbeat (for survivors of suicides)
Colorado Springs, CO
(719) 596-2575

For Sexual and Sex-Related Problems
Sex Information and Education Council of the United States (SIECUS)
New York, NY
(212) 819-9770

National Organization for Women
Legislative Office

Washington, DC
(202) 331-0066

For Physical Abuse
Child Abuse Listening and Mediation (CALM)
Santa Barbara, CA
(805) 965-2376

For Help in Selecting a Therapist
National Mental Health Consumer Self-Help Clearinghouse
(215) 751-1810

For General Information on Mental Health and Counseling
The National Alliance for the Mentally Ill
Arlington, VA
(703) 524-7600

The National Mental Health Association
Alexandria, VA
(703) 684-7722

The American Psychiatric Association
Washington, DC
(703) 907-7300

The American Psychological Association
Washington, DC
(202) 336-5500

The National Institute of Mental Health
Rockville, MD
(301) 443-4513

LEARNING OBJECTIVES

- Summarize the research evidence that psychotherapy is, in fact, more effective than no therapy at all. Briefly describe the five major results of the Consumer Reports study.
- Describe the common features shared by all forms of psychotherapy that may account for the fact that there is little or no overall difference in their effectiveness. Explain the statement that "Some kinds of psychotherapy seem to be particularly appropriate for certain people and problems"; include examples.

EFFECTIVENESS OF PSYCHOTHERAPY

How much better off is a person who receives psychotherapy than one who gets no treatment at all?

We have noted that some psychotherapies are generally effective, but how much better are they than no treatment at all? Researchers have found that roughly twice as many people (two-thirds) improve with formal therapy than with no treatment at all (Borkovec & Costello, 1993; M. J. Lambert, 2001). Furthermore, many people who do not receive formal therapy get therapeutic help from friends, clergy, physicians, and teachers. Thus, the recovery rate for people who receive *no* therapeutic help at all is quite possibly even less than one-third. Other studies concur on psychotherapy's effectiveness (Hartmann & Zepf, 2003; M. J. Lambert & Archer, 2006; Leichsenring & Leibing, 2003). However, the effectiveness of psychotherapy appears to be related to a number of other factors. For instance, psychotherapy works best for relatively mild psychological problems (Kopta, Howard, Lowry, & Beutler, 1994) and seems to provide the greatest benefits to people who really *want* to change, such as Brooke Shields (Orlinsky & Howard, 1994).

One very extensive study designed to evaluate the effectiveness of psychotherapy was reported by *Consumer Reports.* Largely under the direction of psychologist Martin E. P. Seligman (1995), this investigation surveyed 180,000 *Consumer Reports* subscribers on everything from automobiles to mental health. Approximately 7,000 people from the total sample responded to the mental health section of the questionnaire that assessed satisfaction and improvement in people who had received psychotherapy, with the following results.

First, the vast majority of respondents reported significant overall improvement after therapy (Seligman, 1995). Second, there was no difference in the overall improvement score among people who had received therapy alone and those who had combined psychotherapy with medication. Third, no differences were found between the various forms of psychotherapy. Fourth, no differences in effectiveness were indicated among psychologists, psychiatrists, and social workers, although marriage counselors were seen as less effective. Fifth, people who received long-term therapy reported more improvement than those who received short-term therapy. This last result, one of the most striking findings of the study, is illustrated in **Figure 13–1.** Though the *Consumer Reports* study lacked the scientific rigor of more traditional investigations designed to assess psychotherapeutic efficacy, it does provide broad support for the idea that psychotherapy works (Jacobson & Christensen, 1996; Seligman, 1995, 1996). 👁

THINKING CRITICALLY ABOUT . . .

Survey Results

The text states that the *Consumer Reports* study lacked the scientific rigor of more traditional investigations. Think about the following questions:

- How were the respondents selected? How does that compare to the way in which scientific surveys select respondents (see Chapter 1, "The Science of Psychology")?
- How did the study determine whether the respondents had improved?
- How would a psychologist conduct a more scientific study of the effectiveness of psychotherapy? What variables would need to be defined? How would the participants be chosen? What ethical issues might need to be considered?

👁 **Watch** the **Video** Thinking Like a Psychologist: Assessing the Effectiveness of Treatments on **MyPsychLab**

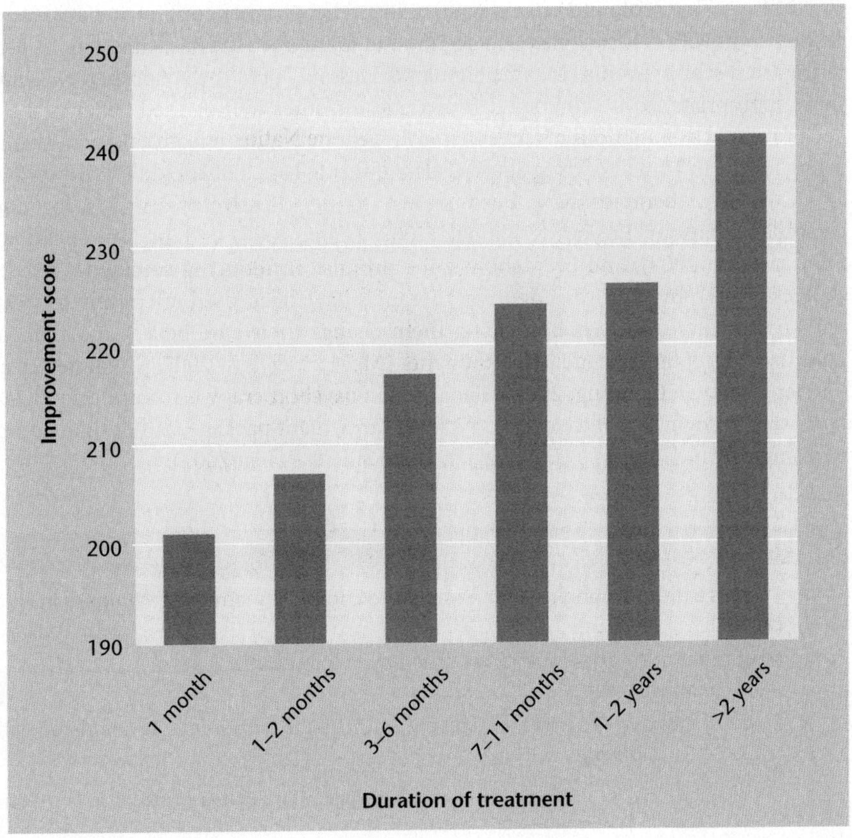

FIGURE 13–1

Duration of therapy and improvement.

One of the most dramatic results of the *Consumer Reports* (1995) study on the effectiveness of psychotherapy was the strong relationship between reported improvement and the duration of therapy.

Source: Data from "The Effectiveness of Psychotherapy: The Consumer Reports Study" by M. E. P. Seligman, *American Psychologist, 50* (1995), pp. 965–974. Copyright © 1995 by American Psychological Association.

Which Type of Therapy Is Best for Which Disorder?

An important question is whether some forms of psychotherapy are more effective than others (Lyddon & Jones, 2001). Is behavior therapy, for example, more effective than insight therapy? In general, the answer seems to be "not much" (J. A. Carter, 2006; Hanna, 2002; Wampold et al., 1997). Most of the benefits of treatment seem to come from being in *some* kind of therapy, regardless of the particular type.

As we have seen, the various forms of psychotherapy are based on very different views about what causes mental disorders and, at least on the surface, approach the treatment of mental disorders in different ways. Why, then, is there no difference in their effectiveness? To answer this question, some psychologists have focused their attention on what the various forms of psychotherapy have in common, rather than emphasizing their differences (J. A. Carter, 2006; A. H. Roberts, Kewman, Mercer, & Hovell, 1993):

1. All forms of psychotherapy provide people with an *explanation for their problems*. Along with this explanation often comes a new perspective, providing people with specific actions to help them cope more effectively.
2. Most forms of psychotherapy offer people *hope*. Because most people who seek therapy have low self-esteem and feel demoralized and depressed, hope and the expectation for improvement increase their feelings of self-worth.
3. All major types of psychotherapy engage the client in a *therapeutic alliance* with a therapist. Although their therapeutic approaches may differ, effective therapists are warm, empathetic, and caring people who understand the importance of establishing a strong emotional bond with their clients that is built on mutual respect and understanding (Norcross, 2002; Wampold, 2001).

Together, these nonspecific factors common to all forms of psychotherapy appear to help explain why most people who receive any form of therapy show some benefits, compared with those who receive none at all.

Some kinds of psychotherapy seem to be particularly appropriate for certain people and problems. Insight therapy, for example, though reasonably effective with a wide range of mental disorders (de Maat, de Jonghe, Schoevers, & Dekker, 2009), seems to be best suited to people seeking profound self-understanding, relief of inner conflict and anxiety, or better relationships with others. It has also been found to improve the basic life skills of people suffering from schizophrenia (Maxine Sigman & Hassan, 2006). Behavior therapy is apparently most appropriate for treating specific anxieties or other well-defined behavioral problems, such as sexual dysfunctions. Couple therapy is generally more effective than individual counseling for the treatment of drug abuse (Fals-Stewart & Lam, 2008; Liddle & Rowe, 2002).

Cognitive therapies have been shown to be effective treatments for depression (Hamdan-Mansour, Puskar, & Bandak, 2009; Leahy, 2004) and anxiety disorders (M. A. Stanley et al., 2009), and even show some promise in reducing suicide (Wenzel, Brown, & Beck, 2009). In addition, cognitive therapies have been used effectively to treat people with personality disorders by helping them change their core beliefs and reducing their automatic acceptance of negative thoughts (McMain & Pos, 2007; S. Palmer et al., 2006; Tarrier, Taylor, & Gooding, 2008). The trend in psychotherapy is toward **eclecticism**—that is, toward recognition of the value of a broad treatment package, rather than commitment to a single form of therapy (J. A. Carter, 2006; Slife & Reber, 2001).

✓•─Study and Review on MyPsychLab

CHECK YOUR UNDERSTANDING

1. There is a trend among psychotherapists to combine treatment techniques in what is called _____.
2. Most researchers agree that psychotherapy helps about _____ _____ of the people treated.
3. Psychotherapy works best for relatively _____ disorders, as compared with _____ ones.

Answers: 1. eclecticism. 2. two-thirds. 3. mild, severe.

eclecticism Psychotherapeutic approach that recognizes the value of a broad treatment package over a rigid commitment to one particular form of therapy.

BIOLOGICAL TREATMENTS

What are biological treatments, and who can provide them?

Biological treatments—a group of approaches including medication, electroconvulsive therapy, and neurosurgery—may be used to treat psychological disorders in addition to, or instead of, psychotherapy. Clients and therapists opt for biological treatments for several reasons. First, some people are too agitated, disoriented, or unresponsive to be helped by psychotherapy. Second, biological treatment is virtually always used for disorders with a strong biological component. Third, biological treatment is often used for people who are dangerous to themselves and to others. Fourth, insurance company reimbursement rates encourage brief encounters between therapists and clients rather than the longer sessions associated with the various talk therapies.

Traditionally, the only mental health professionals licensed to offer biological treatments were psychiatrists, who are physicians. However, an increasing number of states now permit specially trained psychologists to prescribe drugs (Fox et al., 2009). Therapists without such training often work with physicians who prescribe medication for their clients. In many cases where biological treatments are used, psychotherapy is also recommended; medication and psychotherapy used together generally are more effective for treating major depression and for preventing a recurrence than either treatment used alone (M. B. Keller et al., 2000; Manber et al., 2008).

Drug Therapies

What are some of the drugs used to treat psychological disorders?

Medication is frequently and effectively used to treat a number of psychological problems. (See **Table 13–1.**) In fact, Prozac, a drug used to treat depression, today is one of the best selling of all prescribed medications. Two major reasons for the widespread use of drug therapies today are the development of several very effective psychoactive medications and the fact that drug therapies can cost less than psychotherapy. Critics suggest, however, that another reason is our society's "pill mentality," or belief that we can take a medicine to fix any problem. ✳

biological treatments A group of approaches, including medication, electroconvulsive therapy, and neurosurgery, that are sometimes used to treat psychological disorders in conjunction with, or instead of, psychotherapy.

Explore the **Video** Drugs Commonly Used to Treat Psychiatric Disorders on **MyPsychLab**

TABLE 13–1 Major Types of Psychoactive Medications

Therapeutic Use	Chemical Structure	Trade Name[*]
Antipsychotics	Phenothiazines	Thorazine, Therazine, Olanzapine, Risperdal, Clozapine
Antidepressants	Tricyclics	Elavil
	MAO inhibitors	Nardil
	SSRIs	Paxil, Prozac, Zoloft
	SNRI	Effexor
Psychostimulants	Amphetamines	Dexedrine
	Other	Ritalin, Adderall
Antiseizure	Carbamazepine	Tegretol
Antianxiety	Benzodiazepines	Valium, Xanax
Sedatives	Barbiturates	Luminal, Mebaral
Antipanic	Tricyclics	Tofranil
Antiobsessional	Tricyclics	Anafranil

[*]The chemical structures and especially the trade names listed in this table are representative examples, rather than an exhaustive list, of the many kinds of medications available for the specific therapeutic use.

Source: G. L. Klerman, M. M. Weissman, J. C. Markowitz, I. Glick, P. J. Wilner, B. Mason, & M. K. Shear. (1994). Medication and psychotherapy. In A. E. Bergin & S. L. Garfield (Eds.), *Handbook of psychotherapy and behavior change* (4th ed., pp. 734–782). Oxford, England: John Wiley & Sons (adapted and updated).

Antipsychotic Drugs Before the mid-1950s, drugs were not widely used to treat psychological disorders, because the only available sedatives induced sleep as well as calm. Then the major tranquilizers *reserpine* and the *phenothiazines* were introduced. In addition to alleviating anxiety and aggression, both drugs reduce psychotic symptoms, such as hallucinations and delusions; for that reason, they are called **antipsychotic drugs.** Antipsychotic drugs are prescribed primarily for very severe psychological disorders, particularly schizophrenia. They are very effective for treating schizophrenia's "positive symptoms," like hallucinations, but less effective for the "negative symptoms," like social withdrawal. The most widely prescribed antipsychotic drugs are known as *neuroleptics,* which work by blocking the brain's receptors for dopamine, a major neurotransmitter (Leuner & Müller, 2006; Oltmanns & Emery, 2006). The success of antipsychotic drugs in treating schizophrenia supports the notion that schizophrenia is linked in some way to an excess of this neurotransmitter in the brain. (See Chapter 12, "Psychological Disorders.")

Antipsychotic medications sometimes have dramatic effects. People with schizophrenia who take them can go from being perpetually frightened, angry, confused, and plagued by auditory and visual hallucinations to being totally free of such symptoms. It is important to note that these drugs do not cure schizophrenia; they only alleviate the symptoms while the person is taking the drug (Oltmanns & Emery, 2006; P. Thomas et al., 2009). Moreover, antipsychotic drugs can have a number of undesirable side effects (H.-Y. Lane et al., 2006; Roh, Ahn, & Nam, 2006). Blurred vision, weight gain, and constipation are among the common complaints, as are temporary neurological impairments such as muscular rigidity or tremors. A very serious potential side effect is *tardive dyskinesia,* a permanent disturbance of motor control, particularly of the face (uncontrollable smacking of the lips, for instance), which can be only partially alleviated with other drugs (Chong, Tay, Subramaniam, Pek, & Machin, 2009; Eberhard, Lindström, & Levander, 2006). In addition, some of the antipsychotic medications that are effective with adults are not as well tolerated by children who experience an increased risk for many of the side effects described above (Kumra et al., 2008). Another problem is that antipsychotics are of little value in treating the problems of social adjustment that people with schizophrenia face outside an institutional setting. Because many discharged people fail to take their medications, relapse is common. However, the relapse rate can be reduced if drug therapy is effectively combined with psychotherapy.

antipsychotic drugs Drugs used to treat very severe psychological disorders, particularly schizophrenia.

ENDURING ISSUES

Mind–Body   Combining Drugs and Psychotherapy

For some disorders, a combination of drugs and psychotherapy works better than either approach used independently. This underscores the fact that the relationship between mind and body is highly complex. The causes of depression have not yet been fully determined, but they will probably be found to include a mixture of genetic predisposition, chemical changes in the brain, and life situation (see Chapter 12, "Psychological Disorders"). ■

Antidepressant Drugs   A second group of drugs, known as antidepressants, is used to combat depression like that experienced by Brooke Shields. Until the end of the 1980s, there were only two main types of antidepressant drugs: *monoamine oxidase inhibitors (MAO inhibitors)* and *tricyclics*. Both drugs work by increasing the concentration of the neurotransmitters serotonin and norepinephrine in the brain. Both are effective for most people with serious depression, but both produce a number of serious and troublesome side effects.

In 1988, Prozac (fluoxetine) came onto the market. This drug works by reducing the uptake of serotonin in the nervous system, thus increasing the amount of serotonin active in the brain at any given moment. (See **Figure 13–2.**) For this reason, Prozac is part of a group of psychoactive drugs known as *selective serotonin reuptake inhibitors (SSRIs)*. (See Chapter 2, "The Biological Basis of Behavior.") Today, a number of second-generation SSRIs are available to treat depression, including *Paxil* (paroxetine), *Zoloft* (sertraline), and *Effexor* (venlafaxine HCl). For many people, correcting the imbalance in these chemicals in the brain reduces their symptoms of depression and also relieves the associated symptoms of anxiety. Moreover, because these drugs have fewer side effects than do MAO inhibitors or tricyclics (Nemeroff & Schatzberg, 2002), they have been heralded in the popular media as "wonder drugs" for the treatment of depression.

Today, antidepressant drugs are not only used to treat depression, but also have shown promise in treating generalized anxiety disorder, panic disorder, obsessive–compulsive disorder, social phobia, and posttraumatic stress disorder (M. H. Pollack & Simon, 2009; Ralat, 2006). Antidepressant drugs such as the SSRIs do not work for everyone, however. At least a quarter of the patients with major depressive disorder do not respond to antidepressant drugs (Shelton & Hollon, 2000). Moreover, for some patients, these drugs produce unpleasant side effects, including nausea, weight gain, insomnia, headaches, anxiety, and impaired sexual functioning (Demyttenaere & Jaspers, 2008). They can also cause severe withdrawal symptoms in patients who abruptly stop taking them (Kotzalidis et al., 2007).

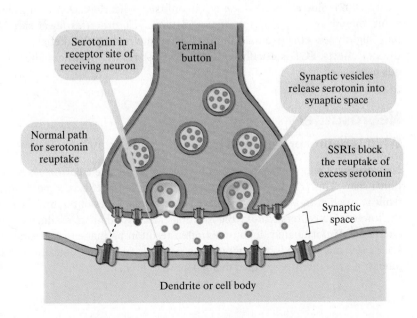

FIGURE 13–2

How do the SSRIs work?

Antidepressants like Prozac, Paxil, and Zoloft belong to a class of drugs called SSRIs (selective serotonin reuptake inhibitors). These drugs reduce the symptoms of depression by blocking the reabsorption (or reuptake) of serotonin in the synaptic space between neurons. The increased availability of serotonin to bind to receptor sites on the receiving neuron is thought to be responsible for the ability of these drugs to relieve the symptoms of depression.

Lithium Bipolar disorder is frequently treated with lithium carbonate. Lithium is not a drug, but a naturally occurring salt that is generally quite effective in treating bipolar disorder (Gnanadesikan, Freeman, & Gelenberg, 2003) and in reducing the incidence of suicide in bipolar patients (Grandjean & Aubry, 2009). We do not know exactly how lithium works, but recent studies with mice indicate that it may act to stabilize the levels of specific neurotransmitters (Dixon & Hokin, 1998) or alter the receptivity of specific synapses (G. Chen & Manji, 2006). Unfortunately, some people with bipolar disorder stop taking lithium when their symptoms improve—against the advice of their physicians; this leads to a relatively high relapse rate (Gershon & Soares, 1997; M. Pope & Scott, 2003).

Other Medications Several other medications can be used to alleviate the symptoms of various psychological problems. (See **Table 13–1.**) *Psychostimulants* heighten alertness and arousal. Some psychostimulants, such as Ritalin, are commonly used to treat children with attention-deficit hyperactivity disorder (Ghuman, Arnold, & Anthony, 2008). In these cases, they have a calming, rather than stimulating effect. *Antianxiety medications*, such as Valium and Xanax, are commonly prescribed as well. Quickly producing a sense of calm and mild euphoria, they are often used to reduce general tension and stress. Because they are potentially addictive, however, they must be used with caution. *Sedatives* produce both calm and drowsiness, and are used to treat agitation or to induce sleep. These drugs, too, can become addictive.

Electroconvulsive Therapy

How is modern electroconvulsive therapy different from that of the past?

Electroconvulsive therapy (ECT) is most often used for cases of prolonged and life-threatening depression that do not respond to other forms of treatment (Birkenhaeger, Pluijms, & Lucius, 2003; Tess & Smetana, 2009). The technique involves briefly passing a mild electric current through the brain or, more recently, through only one of its hemispheres (S. G. Thomas & Kellner, 2003). Treatment normally consists of 10 or fewer sessions of ECT.

No one knows exactly why ECT works, but its effectiveness has been clearly demonstrated. In addition, the fatality rate for ECT is markedly lower than for people taking antidepressant drugs (Henry, Alexander, & Sener, 1995). Still, ECT has many critics and its use remains controversial (Krystal, Holsinger, Weiner, & Coffey, 2000; Shorter & Healy, 2007). Side effects include brief confusion, disorientation, and memory impairment, though research suggests that unilateral ECT produces fewer side effects and is only slightly less effective than the traditional method (Bajbouj et al., 2006). In view of the side effects, ECT is usually considered a "last-resort" treatment after all other methods have failed.

Neurosurgery

What is neurosurgery, and how is it used today?

Neurosurgery refers to brain surgery performed to change a person's behavior and emotional state. This is a drastic step, especially because the effects of neurosurgery are difficult to predict. In a *prefrontal lobotomy,* the frontal lobes of the brain are severed from the lower brain centers (chiefly the thalamus and hypothalamus, which are important to emotions). Unfortunately, lobotomies often result in permanent, undesirable side effects, such as the inability to inhibit impulses or a near-total absence of feeling. Thus, prefrontal lobotomies are rarely performed today (Greely, 2007).

electroconvulsive therapy (ECT) Biological therapy in which a mild electrical current is passed through the brain for a short period, often producing convulsions and temporary coma; used to treat severe, prolonged depression.

neurosurgery Brain surgery performed to change a person's behavior and emotional state; a biological therapy rarely used today.

However, as we learn more about the links between the brain and behavior, it is becoming possible to pinpoint specific neural circuits that control such conditions as severe obsessive–compulsive disorders (OCD) and depression (Shawanda Anderson & Booker, 2006; Weingarten & Cummings, 2001). For example, one area toward the front of the cingulate gyrus (see Figure 2–7) is known to be overactive in people with severe OCD. Thin wires can be threaded into that area to destroy bits of tissue, reducing the overactivity. It is also possible to insert wires permanently, connect them to a kind of pacemaker, and periodically stimulate a particular area of the brain (Cusin et al., 2010; Howland, 2008; Sachdev & Chen, 2009). While these experimental procedures are promising, they do not work in many cases and often there are undesirable side effects (Juckel, Uhl, Padberg, Brüne, & Winter, 2009). Thus researchers are proceeding with great caution (Kringelbach & Aziz, 2009).

The "**Summary Table:** Major Perspectives on Therapy" captures the key characteristics of the wide variety of psychological and biological mental health treatments.

SUMMARY TABLE   MAJOR PERSPECTIVES ON THERAPY

Type of Therapy	Cause of Disorder	Goal	Techniques
Insight therapies			
Psychoanalysis	Unconscious conflicts and motives; repressed problems from childhood	To bring unconscious thoughts and feeling to consciousness; to gain insight	Free association, dream analysis, interpretation, transference
Client-centered therapy	Experiences of conditional positive regard	To help people become fully functioning by opening them up to all of their experiences	Regarding clients with unconditional positive regard
Gestalt therapy	Lack of wholeness in the personality	To get people to "own their feelings" and to awaken to sensory experience in order to become whole	Active rather than passive talk; empty chair techniques, encounter groups
Behavior therapies	Reinforcement for maladaptive behavior	To learn new and more adaptive behavior patterns	Classical conditioning (systematic desensitization, extinction, flooding); aversive conditioning (behavior contracting, token economies); modeling
Cognitive therapies	Misconceptions; negative, self-defeating thinking	To identify erroneous ways of thinking and to correct them	Rational–emotive therapy; stress-inoculation therapy; Beck's cognitive therapy
Group therapies	Personal problems are often interpersonal problems	To develop insight into one's personality and behavior by interacting with others in the group	Group interaction and mutual support; family therapy; couple therapy; self-help therapy
Biological treatments	Physiological imbalance or malfunction	To eliminate symptoms; prevent recurrence	Drugs, electroconvulsive therapy, neurosurgery

✓•〔Study and Review on MyPsychLab

1. Traditionally, the only mental health professionals licensed to provide drug therapy were _____.

2. Bipolar disorder (also called manic–depressive illness) is often treated with _____.

3. Which of the following is true of neurosurgery?
   a. It never produces undesirable side effects.
   b. It is useless in controlling pain.
   c. It is widely used today.
   d. Its effects are hard to predict.

4. Although it is considered effective in treating depression, electroconvulsive therapy (ECT) is considered a treatment of last resort because of its potential negative side effects. Is this statement true (T) or false (F)?

   Match the following antidepressant medications with the neurotransmitter(s) that each is believed to influence. There may be more than one answer for each medication.

5. ____ monoamine oxidase inhibitors   a. norepinephrine
6. ____ tricyclics   b. serotonin
7. ____ SSRIs   c. epinephrine

Answers: 1. psychiatrists. 2. lithium. 3. d. 4. (T). 5. a and b. 6. a and b. 7. b.

1. Blue Haven is a (fictional) state mental hospital where five therapists are responsible for hundreds of patients. These patients are often violent. The therapy most likely to be used here is
   a. psychoanalysis.
   b. biological therapy.
   c. cognitive therapy.
   d. client-centered therapy.

2. Brian is suffering from schizophrenia. Which of the following biological treatments is most likely to be effective in reducing or eliminating his symptoms?
   a. any drug, such as a phenothiazine, that blocks the brain's receptors for dopamine
   b. selective serotonin reuptake inhibitors (SSRIs), such as Paxil and Prozac
   c. lithium carbonate
   d. electroconvulsive therapy

Answers: 1. b. 2. a.

LEARNING OBJECTIVE

- Describe the process of deinstitutionalization and the problems that have resulted from it. Identify alternatives to deinstitutionalization including the three forms of prevention.

INSTITUTIONALIZATION AND ITS ALTERNATIVES

How were people with severe psychological disorders cared for in the past?

For persons with severe mental illness, hospitalization has been the treatment of choice in the United States for the past 150 years. Several different kinds of hospitals offer such care. General hospitals admit many affected people, usually for short-term stays until they can be released to their families or to other institutional care. Private hospitals—some nonprofit and some for profit—offer services to people with adequate insurance. Veterans Administration hospitals admit veterans with psychological disorders.

When most people think of "mental hospitals," however, large, state-run institutions come to mind. These public hospitals, many with beds for thousands of patients, were often built in rural areas in the 19th century. The idea was that a country setting would calm patients and help to restore their mental health. Despite the good intentions behind the establishment of these hospitals, in general they have not provided adequate care or therapy for their residents, as they are perpetually underfunded and understaffed. Except for new arrivals, who were often intensively treated in the hope of quickly discharging them, patients received little therapy besides drugs; and most spent their days watching television or staring into space. Under these conditions, many patients became completely apathetic and accepted a permanent "sick role."

The development of effective drug therapies starting in the 1950s led to a number of changes in state hospitals. First, people who were agitated could now be sedated with drugs, which was considered an improvement over the use of physical restraints. The second major, and more lasting, result of the new drug therapies was the widespread release of people with severe psychological disorders back into the community—a policy called **deinstitutionalization.**

deinstitutionalization Policy of treating people with severe psychological disorders in the larger community or in small residential centers such as halfway houses, rather than in large public hospitals.

Deinstitutionalization

What problems have resulted from deinstitutionalization?

The practice of placing people in smaller, more humane facilities or returning them under medication to care within the community intensified during the 1960s and 1970s. By 1975, 600 regional mental health centers accounted for 1.6 million cases of outpatient care.

In recent years, however, deinstitutionalization has created serious challenges (Lamb & Weinberger, 2001). Discharged people often find poorly funded community mental health centers—or none at all. Many are not prepared to live in the community and they receive little guidance in coping with the mechanics of daily life. Those who return home can become a burden to their families, especially when follow-up care is inadequate. The quality of residential centers such as halfway houses can vary, with many providing poor care and minimal contact with the outside world. Insufficient sheltered housing forces many former patients into nonpsychiatric facilities—often rooming houses located in dirty, unsafe, isolated neighborhoods. The patients are further burdened by the social stigma of mental illness, which may be the largest single obstacle to their rehabilitation. Many released patients have been unable to obtain follow-up care or housing and are incapable of looking after their own needs. Consequently, many have ended up literally on the streets. Without supervision, they have stopped taking the drugs that made their release possible in the first place and their psychotic symptoms have returned. Perhaps one of the most tragic outcomes of the deinstitutionalization movement is the increase in the suicide rate among deinstitutionalized patients (Goldney, 2003). In addition, surveys indicate that nearly 40% of homeless people are mentally ill (Burt et al., 1999). Clearly, providing adequate mental health care to the homeless presents many challenges (Bhui, Shanahan, & Harding, 2006).

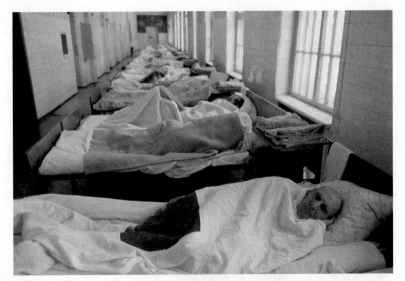

Lacking adequate funding and staff, mental hospitals frequently were crowded and failed to provide adequate treatment to their residents.

Alternative Forms of Treatment

Are there any alternatives to deinstitutionalization other than rehospitalizing patients?

For several decades, Charles Kiesler (1934–2002) argued for a shift from the focus on institutionalization to forms of treatment that avoid hospitalization altogether (Kiesler & Simpkins, 1993). Kiesler (1982b) examined 10 controlled studies in which seriously disturbed people were randomly assigned either to hospitals or to an alternative program. The alternative programs took many forms: training patients living at home to cope with daily activities; assigning patients to a small, homelike facility in which staff and residents share responsibility for residential life; placing patients in a hostel, offering therapy and

Beginning in the 1950s and 1960s, the policy of deinstitutionalization led to the release of many individuals, who, without proper follow-up care, ended up living on the streets. Although not all homeless people are mentally ill, estimates suggest that nearly 40% of homeless persons suffer from some type of mental disorder.

primary prevention Techniques and programs to improve the social environment so that new cases of mental disorders do not develop.

secondary prevention Programs to identify groups that are at high risk for mental disorders and to detect maladaptive behavior in these groups and treat it promptly.

tertiary prevention Programs to help people adjust to community life after release from a mental hospital.

Suicide hotlines and other crisis intervention programs are secondary prevention measures designed to serve individuals and groups at high risk for mental disorders.

crisis intervention; providing family-crisis therapy and day-care treatment; providing visits from public-health nurses combined with medication; and offering intensive outpatient counseling combined with medication. All alternatives involved daily professional contact and skillful preparation of the community to receive the patients. Even though the hospitals to which some people in these studies were assigned provided very good patient care—probably substantially above average for institutions in the United States—9 out of the 10 studies found that the outcome was more positive for alternative treatments than for the more expensive hospitalization.

Prevention

What is the difference between primary, secondary, and tertiary prevention?

Another approach to managing mental illness is attempting prevention. This requires finding and eliminating the conditions that cause or contribute to mental disorders and substituting conditions that foster well-being. Prevention takes three forms: primary, secondary, and tertiary.

Primary prevention refers to efforts to improve the overall environment so that new cases of mental disorders do not develop. Family planning and genetic counseling are two examples of primary prevention programs. Other primary prevention programs aim at increasing personal and social competencies in a wide variety of groups. For example, there are programs designed to help mothers encourage problem-solving skills in their children and programs to enhance competence and adjustment among elderly persons. Current campaigns to educate young people about drugs, alcohol abuse, violence, and date rape are examples of primary prevention (Foxcroft, Ireland, Lister, Lowe, & Breen, 2003; Schinke & Schwinn, 2005).

Secondary prevention involves identifying high risk groups—for example, abused children, people who have recently divorced, those who have been laid off from their jobs, veterans, and victims of terrorist incidents. *Intervention* is the main thrust of secondary prevention—that is, detecting maladaptive behavior early and treating it promptly. One form of intervention is *crisis intervention,* which includes such programs as suicide hotlines or short-term crisis facilities where therapists can provide face-to-face counseling and support.

The main objective of **tertiary prevention** is to help people adjust to community life after release from a mental hospital. For example, hospitals often grant passes to encourage people to leave the institution for short periods of time before their release. Other tertiary prevention measures are halfway houses, where people find support and skills training during the period of transition between hospitalization and full integration into the community, and nighttime and outpatient programs that provide supportive therapy while people live at home and hold down full-time jobs. Tertiary prevention also includes community education.

Prevention has been the ideal of the mental health community since at least 1970, when the final report of the Joint Commission on Mental Health of Children called for a new focus on prevention in mental health work. Ironically, because preventive programs are usually long range and indirect, they are often the first to be

THINKING CRITICALLY ABOUT . . .

Access to Mental Health Care

A friend feels overwhelmed by sadness and is exhibiting depressive symptoms. He comes to you for advice. How likely would you be to suggest that your friend seek psychotherapy or drug treatment? Think about the following questions:

- Would you seek therapy yourself in a similar situation?
- What would you think of a friend who you knew was seeing a therapist?
- Would your friend be able to obtain therapy services? Would he be able to afford these kinds of services?
- Do you think that mental illness and physical illness are equivalent and should be treated the same by insurance companies?

eliminated in times of economic hardship. However, a recent report from the National Research Council and Institute of Medicine concluded that intervention with children and adolescents could improve the well-being of millions of children and save the nation as much as $247 billion dollars a year (O'Connell, Boat, & Warner, 2009).

✓●–Study and **Review** on **MyPsychLab**

CHECK YOUR UNDERSTANDING

1. The practice of treating severely mentally ill people in large, state-run facilities is known as _____.
2. Many people released from mental hospitals have ended up homeless and on the streets. Is this statement true (T) or false (F)?
3. The development of effective antipsychotic drugs and the establishment of a network of community mental health centers starting in the 1950s led to _____, which increased throughout the 1960s and 1970s, and continues today.

Answers: 1. institutionalization. 2. (T) 3. deinstitutionalization.

APPLY YOUR UNDERSTANDING

1. Harold argues that institutionalizing people suffering from serious mental illnesses is not only the most effective way to treat them, but also the least expensive. On the basis of what you have learned in this chapter, which of the following would be the most appropriate reply?
   a. "Mental institutions are indeed the least expensive form of treatment, but they are also the least effective treatment option."
   b. "You're right. Mental institutions are both the least expensive form of treatment and the most effective treatment option."
   c. "Actually, mental institutions are not only the most expensive form of treatment, they are also the least effective treatment option."
   d. "Actually, mental institutions are the most expensive form of treatment, but they are the most effective treatment option."

2. Your community is especially aware of the importance of preventing psychological disorders. So far, financial support has been provided for family planning, genetic counseling, increasing competence among the elderly, and educational programs aimed at reducing the use of drugs and acts of violence. From this description, it is clear that your community is putting its emphasis on
   a. primary prevention efforts.
   b. secondary prevention efforts.
   c. tertiary prevention efforts.

Answers: 1. c. 2. a

CLIENT DIVERSITY AND TREATMENT

Do particular groups of people require special treatment approaches for psychological problems?

A major topic of this book is the wide range of differences that exist in human beings. Do such human differences affect the treatment of psychological problems? The importance of this question is reflected in the fact that there have been seven National Multicultural Conferences and Summits, the most recent held in January 2011, which was attended by more than 900 psychologists and students (Farberman, 2011). Two areas that researchers have explored to answer this question are gender differences and cultural differences.

LEARNING OBJECTIVE

- Explain how gender and cultural differences can affect the treatment of psychological problems and the training of therapists.

Because most traditional therapeutic programs are male oriented, many female clients seek out female therapists who are more sensitive to their situation.

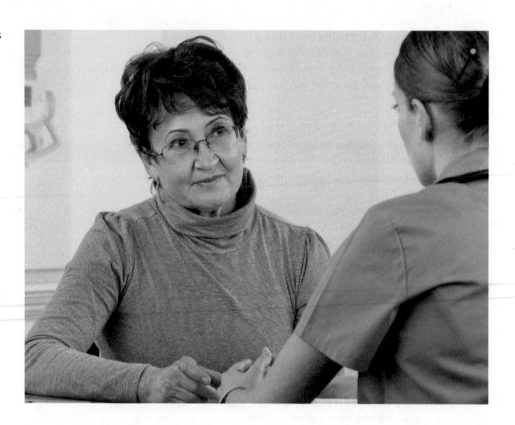

Gender and Treatment

How can gender stereotypes be avoided in treatment?

There are significant gender differences in the prevalence of many psychological disorders. In part, this is because women have traditionally been more willing than men to admit that they have psychological problems and need help to solve them (Addis & Mahalik, 2003; Cochran & Rabinowitz, 2003), and because psychotherapy is more socially accepted for women than for men (Mirkin, Suyemoto, & Okun, 2005). However, the number of males willing to seek psychotherapy and counseling has increased (W. S. Pollack & Levant, 1998). Researchers attribute this growth to the changing roles of men in today's society: Men are increasingly expected to provide emotional as well as financial support for their families.

If gender differences exist in the prevalence of psychological disorders, are there gender differences in their treatment as well? In most respects, the treatment given to women is the same as that given to men, a fact that has become somewhat controversial in recent years (Ogrodniczuk, Piper, & Joyce, 2004; Ogrodniczuk & Staats, 2002). Critics of "equal treatment" have claimed that women in therapy are often encouraged to adopt traditional, male-oriented views of what is "appropriate"; male therapists may urge women to adapt passively to their surroundings. They may also be insufficiently sensitive to the fact that much of the stress that women experience comes from trying to cope with a world in which they are not treated equally (Tone, 2007). In response to this, the number of "feminist therapists" has increased (Brown, 2009). These therapists help their female clients to become aware of the extent to which their problems derive from external controls and inappropriate sex roles, to become more conscious of and attentive to their own needs and goals, and to develop a sense of pride in their womanhood, rather than passively accepting or identifying with the status quo. Consistent with this position, the American Psychological Association has developed a detailed set of guidelines to help psychologists meet the special needs of female patients, which includes exposure to interpersonal victimization and violence, unrealistic media images, and work inequities (American Psychological Association, 2007).

Culture and Treatment

How can a therapist interact appropriately with clients from different cultures?

When a client and a therapist come from different cultural backgrounds or belong to different racial or ethnic groups, misunderstandings can arise in therapy.

ENDURING ISSUES

Diversity—Universality   On Being Culture Bound

Imagine the following scenario: As a Native American client is interviewed by a psychologist, the client stares at the floor. He answers questions politely, but during the entire consultation, he looks away continually, never meeting the therapist's eye. This body language might lead the psychologist to suppose that the man is depressed or has low self-esteem—unless the psychologist knows that in the person's culture, avoiding eye contact is a sign of respect. ▪

This example shows how culture bound our ideas of what constitutes normal behavior are. When psychotherapist and client come from different cultures, misunderstandings of speech, body language, and customs are almost inevitable (Hays, 2008). Even when client and therapist are of the same nationality and speak the same language, there can be striking differences if they belong to different racial and ethnic groups (Casas, 1995). Some Black people, for example, are wary of confiding in a White therapist—so much so that their wariness is sometimes mistaken for paranoia. In addition, Black patients often perceive Black therapists as being more understanding and accepting of their problems than White therapists (V. L. S. Thompson & Alexander, 2006). For this reason, many Black people seek out a Black therapist, a tendency that is becoming more common as larger numbers of Black middle-class people enter therapy (Diala et al., 2000; Snowden & Yamada, 2005).

One of the challenges for U.S. therapists in recent years has been to treat immigrants, many of whom have fled such horrifying circumstances that they arrive in the United States exhibiting posttraumatic stress disorder (Paunovic & Oest, 2001). These refugees must overcome the effects of past trauma, and the new stresses of settling in a strange country— separation from their families, ignorance of the English language, and inability to practice their traditional occupations. Therapists in such circumstances must learn something of their clients' culture. Often they have to conduct interviews through an interpreter—hardly an ideal circumstance for therapy.

Therapists need to recognize that some disorders that afflict people from other cultures may not exist in Western culture at all. For example, as we saw in Chapter 12, "Psychological Disorders," *taijin kyofusho* involves a morbid fear that one's body or actions may be offensive to others. Because this disorder is rarely seen outside Japan, American therapists require specialized training to identify it.

Ultimately, the best solution to the difficulties of serving a multicultural population is to train therapists of many different backgrounds so that members of ethnic, cultural, and racial minorities

Many African American clients are more comfortable dealing with a therapist of the same racial background.

can choose therapists of their own group if they wish to do so (Bernal & Castro, 1994). Research has shown that psychotherapy is more likely to be effective when the client and the therapist share a similar cultural background (Gibson & Mitchell, 2003; Pedersen & Carey, 2003). Similarly, efforts aimed at preventing mental illness in society must also be culturally aware.

✔️ Study and Review on MyPsychLab

CHECK YOUR UNDERSTANDING

Indicate whether the following statements are true (T) or false (F):

1. ___ Men are more likely to be in psychotherapy than women.
2. ___ Our ideas about what constitutes normal behavior are culture bound.
3. ___ Trained mental health professionals rarely misinterpret the body language of a client from another culture.

Answers: 1. (F). 2. (T) 3. (F).

APPLY YOUR UNDERSTANDING

1. An immigrant from the Middle East who speaks very little English seeks assistance from an American psychotherapist who only speaks English. Which of the following problems may interfere with the therapeutic process?
   a. misunderstanding body language
   b. the therapist's lack of familiarity with the cultural norms and values of the immigrant's home country
   c. need for an interpreter
   d. all of the above

2. Preventing and treating psychological disorders is especially challenging in a society such as ours, which has a culturally diverse population. Which of the following is NOT a constructive way of dealing with this challenge?
   a. Therapists need to recognize that some disorders that afflict people from other cultures may not exist in Western culture at all.
   b. Therapists from many different backgrounds need to receive training so that people who wish to do so can be treated by a therapist who shares their cultural background.
   c. Clients should be treated by therapists who represent the dominant culture so that they can best adapt to their new environment.
   d. Intervention programs need to take into account the cultural norms and values of the group being served.

Answers: 1. d. 2. c.

KEY TERMS

psychotherapy, p. 425

Insight Therapies
insight therapies, p. 425
free association, p. 426
transference, p. 426
insight, p. 426
client-centered (or person-centered) therapy, p. 427
Gestalt therapy, p. 429
short-term psychodynamic therapy, p. 430

Behavior Therapies
behavior therapies, p. 431
systematic desensitization, p. 431
aversive conditioning, p. 432
behavior contracting, p. 433
token economy, p. 433
modeling, p. 434

Cognitive Therapies
cognitive therapies, p. 434
stress-inoculation therapy, p. 434

rational–emotive therapy (RET), p. 434
cognitive therapy, p. 435

Group Therapies
group therapy, p. 436
family therapy, p. 436
couple therapy, p. 436

Effectiveness of Psychotherapy
eclecticism, p. 440

Biological Treatments
biological treatments, p. 441
antipsychotic drugs, p. 442
electroconvulsive therapy (ECT), p. 444
neurosurgery, p. 444

Institutionalization and Its Alternatives
deinstitutionalization, p. 447
primary prevention, p. 448
secondary prevention, p. 448
tertiary prevention, p. 448

CHAPTER REVIEW   ((•⊢Listen to the Chapter Audio on MyPsychLab

INSIGHT THERAPIES

What do insight therapies have in common? The various types of **insight therapy** share the common goal of providing people with better awareness and understanding of their feelings, motivations, and actions to foster better adjustment. Among these are psychoanalysis, client-centered therapy, and Gestalt therapy.

How does "free association" in psychoanalysis help a person to become aware of hidden feelings? *Psychoanalysis* is based on the belief that psychological problems stem from feelings and conflicts repressed during childhood. These repressed feelings can be revealed through **free association,** a process in which the client discloses whatever thoughts or fantasies come to mind without inhibition. As therapy progresses, the analyst takes a more active interpretive role.

Why did Carl Rogers call his approach to therapy "client centered"? Carl Rogers believed treatment for psychological problems should be based on the client's view of the world rather than that of the therapist. The therapist's most important task in his approach, called **client-centered** or **person-centered therapy,** is to provide unconditional positive regard for clients so they will learn to accept themselves.

How is Gestalt therapy different from psychoanalysis? **Gestalt therapy** helps people become more aware of their feelings and thus, more genuine. Unlike Freud, who sat quietly out of sight while his clients recalled past memories, the Gestalt therapist confronts the patient, emphasizes the present, and focuses on the *whole* person.

What are some recent developments in insight therapies? Contemporary **insight** therapists are more actively involved than traditional psychoanalysts, offering clients direct guidance and feedback. An especially significant development is the trend toward **short-term psychodynamic therapy,** in which treatment time is limited and oriented toward current life situations and relationships, rather than childhood traumas.

BEHAVIOR THERAPIES

What do behaviorists believe should be the focus of psychotherapy? **Behavior therapies** are based on the belief that all behavior is learned and that people can be taught more satisfying ways of behaving. Maladaptive behaviors are the focus of behavioral psychotherapy, rather than the deeper underlying conflicts that presumably are causing them.

How can classical conditioning be used as the basis of treatment? When new conditioned responses are evoked to old stimuli, classical conditioning principles are being used as a basis for treatment. One therapeutic example is **systematic desensitization,** in which people learn to remain in a deeply relaxed state while confronting feared situations. *Flooding,* which exposes phobic people to feared situations at full intensity for a prolonged period, is a harsh but effective method of desensitization. In **aversive conditioning,** the goal is to eliminate undesirable behavior by associating it with pain and discomfort.

How could "behavior contracting" change an undesirable behavior? Therapies based on operant conditioning encourage or discourage behaviors by reinforcing or punishing them. In **behavior contracting,** client and therapist agree on certain behavioral goals and on the reinforcement that the client will receive on reaching them. In the **token economy** technique, tokens that can be exchanged for rewards are used for positive reinforcement of adaptive behaviors.

What are some therapeutic uses of modeling? In **modeling,** a person learns new behaviors by watching others perform them. Modeling has been used to teach fearless behaviors to phobic people and job skills to mentally retarded people.

COGNITIVE THERAPIES

How can people overcome irrational and self-defeating beliefs about themselves? **Cognitive therapies** focus not so much on maladaptive behaviors as on maladaptive ways of thinking. By changing people's distorted, self-defeating ideas about themselves and the world, cognitive therapies help to encourage better coping skills and adjustment.

How can self-talk help with difficult situations? The things we say to ourselves as we go about our daily lives can encourage success or failure, self-confidence or anxiety. With **stress-inoculation therapy,** clients learn how to use self-talk to "coach" themselves through stressful situations.

What irrational beliefs do many people hold? **Rational–emotive therapy (RET)** is based on the idea that emotional problems derive from a set of irrational and self-defeating beliefs that people hold about themselves and the world. They must be liked by *everyone,* competent at *everything, always* be treated *fairly,* and *never* be stymied by a problem. The therapist vigorously challenges these beliefs, enabling clients to reinterpret their experiences in a more positive light.

How can cognitive therapy be used to combat depression? Aaron Beck believes that depression results from thought patterns that are strongly and inappropriately self-critical. Like RET but in a less confrontational manner, Beck's **cognitive therapy** tries to help such people think more objectively and positively about themselves and their life situations.

GROUP THERAPIES

What are some advantages of group therapies? **Group therapies** are based on the idea that psychological problems are partly interpersonal and therefore, best approached in a group. Group therapies offer a circle of support and shared insight, as well as psychotherapy at a lower cost. Examples include self-help groups, family therapy, and couple therapy.

Who is the client in family therapy? **Family therapy** is based on the belief that a person's psychological problems often signal family problems. Therefore, the therapist treats the entire family, rather than just the troubled individual, with the primary goals of improving communication and empathy and reducing family conflict.

What are some techniques used in couple therapy? **Couple therapy** concentrates on improving patterns of communication and interaction between partners. It attempts to change relationships, rather than individuals. Empathy training and scheduled exchanges of rewards are two techniques used to improve relationships.

Why are self-help groups so popular? Owing to the high cost of private psychotherapy, low-cost self-help groups have become increasingly popular. In groups like Alcoholics Anonymous, people share their concerns and feelings with others who are experiencing similar problems.

EFFECTIVENESS OF PSYCHOTHERAPY

How much better off is a person who receives psychotherapy than one who gets no treatment at all? Formal psychotherapy helps about two-thirds of people treated. Although there is some debate over how many untreated people recover, the consensus is that those who get therapy are generally better off than those who don't.

Which type of therapy is best for which disorder? Although each kind of therapy works better for some problems than for others, most treatment benefits derive from the therapeutic experience, regardless of the therapist's particular perspective. All therapies provide an explanation of problems, hope, and an alliance with a caring, supportive person. The general trend in psychotherapy is toward **eclecticism,** the use of whatever treatment works best for a particular problem.

BIOLOGICAL TREATMENTS

What are biological treatments, and who can provide them? **Biological treatments**—including medication, electroconvulsive therapy, and neurosurgery—are sometimes used when people are too agitated or disoriented to respond to psychotherapy, when there is a strong biological component to the psychological disorder, and when people are dangerous to themselves and others. Medication is often used in conjunction with psychotherapy. Traditionally, psychiatrists were the only mental health professionals licensed to offer biological treatments. However, some states now extend that privilege to specially trained clinical psychologists.

What are some of the drugs used to treat psychological disorders? Drugs are the most common form of biological therapy. **Antipsychotic drugs** are valuable in treating schizophrenia. They do not cure the disorder, but they reduce its symptoms, though side effects can be severe. Many types of medications are used to treat psychological disorders, including antidepressants, antimanic and antianxiety drugs, sedatives, and psychostimulants.

How is modern electroconvulsive therapy different from that of the past? **Electroconvulsive therapy (ECT)** is used for cases of severe depression that do not respond to other treatments. An electric current is briefly passed through a patient's brain. Newer forms of ECT are given to only one side of the brain.

What is neurosurgery, and how is it used today? **Neurosurgery** is brain surgery performed to change a person's behavior and emotional state. Pinpointing and then either destroying or stimulating specific neural circuits reduces symptoms of some psychological disorders in some people. But there are often undesirable side effects. Thus, neurosurgery is still in the experimental stage.

INSTITUTIONALIZATION AND ITS ALTERNATIVES

How were people with severe psychological disorders cared for in the past? For 150 years, institutionalization in large mental hospitals was the most common approach. Patients with serious mental disorders were given shelter and some degree of treatment, but many never recovered enough to be released. With the advent of antipsychotic drugs in the 1950s, a trend began toward **deinstitutionalization.**

What problems have resulted from deinstitutionalization? Poorly funded community mental health centers and other support services have proved inadequate in caring for previously institutionalized patients with mental disorders. Many patients stopped taking their medication, became psychotic, and ended up homeless on the streets. Although the concept of deinstitutionalization may have been good in principle, in practice it has failed for many patients and for society.

Are there any alternatives to deinstitutionalization other than rehospitalizing patients? Alternatives to rehospitalization include living at home with adequate supports provided to all family members; living in small, homelike facilities in which residents and staff share responsibilities; living in hostels with therapy and crisis intervention provided; and receiving intensive outpatient counseling or frequent visits from public health nurses. Most alternative treatments involve daily professional contact and skillful preparation of the family and community. Most studies have found more positive outcomes for alternative treatments than for hospitalization.

What is the difference between primary, secondary, and tertiary prevention? Prevention refers to efforts to reduce the incidence of mental illness before it arises. **Primary prevention** consists of improving the social environment through assistance to parents, education, and family planning. **Secondary prevention** involves identifying high-risk groups and intervention thereof. **Tertiary prevention** involves helping hospitalized patients return to the community and community education.

CLIENT DIVERSITY AND TREATMENT

Do particular groups of people require special treatment approaches for psychological problems? Given that humans differ as much as they do, it isn't surprising that a one-size-fits-all concept isn't always appropriate in the treatment of psychological problems. In recent years, the special needs of women and people from other cultures have particularly occupied the attention of mental health professionals.

How can gender stereotypes be avoided in treatment? Women are more likely than men to be in psychotherapy, and are more likely prescribed psychoactive medication. Because, in traditional therapy, women are often expected to conform to gender stereotypes in order to be pronounced "well," many women have turned to "feminist therapists." The American Psychological Association has issued guidelines to ensure that women receive treatment that is not tied to traditional ideas about appropriate behavior for the sexes.

How can a therapist interact appropriately with clients from different cultures? When a client and therapist come from different cultural backgrounds or belong to different racial or ethnic groups, misunderstandings can arise in therapy. Therapists must recognize that cultural differences exist in the nature of the psychological disorders that affect people. Treatment and prevention must be tailored to the beliefs and cultural practices of the person's ethnic group.

14

Social Psychology

OVERVIEW

O n September 12, 2001, the day after the terrorist attacks on the Pentagon and the World Trade Center, Sher Singh, a telecommunications consultant from Virginia, managed to catch a train home from Boston where he had been on a business trip. "With the horrific images of the terrorist attacks still fresh in my mind," Sher Singh recalls, "I was particularly anxious to get home to my family" (Singh, 2002, p. 1). Singh was very much like any other shocked and sorrowful American on that day—except for one small difference: As a member of the Sikh religion, Singh, unlike most Americans, wore a full beard and a turban.

The train made a scheduled stop in Providence, Rhode Island, about an hour outside of Boston. But oddly, the stop dragged on for a very long time. Singh began to wonder what was wrong. A conductor walking through the coaches announced that the train had mechanical trouble. However, when passengers from neighboring coaches began to disembark and line up on the platform, Singh became suspicious that this was not the true story. He didn't have long to speculate about the genuine cause of the problem, because suddenly law-enforcement officers burst into his coach and pulled him off the train at gunpoint. They were searching for four Arab men who had evaded authorities in a Boston hotel. A Sikh, however, is not an Arab. A Sikh belongs to a Hindu sect that comes from India, not the Middle East.

On the station platform, Singh was abruptly handcuffed and asked about his citizenship. Assurances that he was a U.S. citizen did not satisfy the officers. They asked him if he had a weapon. Singh informed them that, as a devout Sikh, he is required to carry a miniature ceremonial sword. They promptly arrested Singh and pushed him through a crowd of onlookers to a waiting police car. According to news reports, as Singh passed by, some teenagers shouted, "Let's kill him!" while a woman yelled, "Burn in Hell!"

As a terrorist suspect, Singh was photographed, fingerprinted, and strip-searched. He was held in custody at police headquarters until 9:00 PM. While he was jailed, news media nationwide had displayed a photo of him side by side with a photo of Osama bin Laden. Although all charges against Sher Singh were eventually dropped, he never received an apology from the law-enforcement officers involved.

How could this blatant case of mistaken identity have happened? Why were police so convinced that Sher Singh could be a fugitive terrorist? Researchers who specialize in the field of social psychology help provide some answers. **Social psychology** is the scientific study of how people's thoughts, feelings, and behaviors are influenced by the behaviors and characteristics of other people, whether these behaviors and characteristics are real, imagined, or inferred. Sher Singh was clearly a victim of imagined and inferred characteristics formed on the basis of his ethnic appearance. As you read about the findings of social psychologists in this chapter, you will discover that Singh's experience is far from unique (Horry & Wright, 2009). Every day, we all make judgments concerning other people that are often based on very little "real" evidence. The process by which we form such impressions, whether accurate or not, is part of a fascinating area of social psychology known as *social cognition.* We turn to this topic first.

Police never apologized for arresting Sher Singh as a terrorist after the September 11, 2001, attacks in the United States.

ENDURING ISSUES in Social Psychology

A key issue throughout this chapter is the extent to which a particular behavior reflects personal characteristics like attitudes and values, versus situational ones like the behavior of others and social expectations (*Person–Situation*). And especially prominent in this chapter is the extent to which there are differences in social behavior among people in different cultures (*Individuality–Universality*). Finally, you will notice the influence of the neuroscience movement (*Mind–Body*) in this chapter where social psychologists apply the tools of neuroimaging (see Chapter 2: "The Biological Basis of Behavior") to the study of social psychology in the rapidly expanding field of **social neuroscience.**

social psychology The scientific study of the ways in which the thoughts, feelings, and behaviors of one individual are influenced by the real, imagined, or inferred behavior or characteristics of other people.

social neuroscience The application of brain imaging and other neuroscience methods to social psychology.

SOCIAL COGNITION

What do forming impressions, explaining others' behavior, and experiencing interpersonal attraction have in common?

Part of the process of being influenced by other people involves organizing and interpreting information about them to form first impressions, to try to understand their behavior, and to determine to what extent we are attracted to them. This collecting and assessing of information about other people is called **social cognition.** Social cognition is a major area of interest to social psychologists (Shrum, 2007).

Forming Impressions

How do we form first impressions of people?

Research has shown that the impression a student forms about a professor during the first class tends to persist until the end of the semester (Laws, Apperson, Buchert, & Bregman, 2010), supporting the expression "You'll never get a second chance to make a great first impression."

Surprisingly, research indicates it only takes about 100 msec. or 1/10 of a second for an observer to form a durable first impression (Willis & Todorov, 2006). Despite the speed with which we make a first impression, the process is more complex than you may think. You must direct your attention to various aspects of the person's appearance and behavior and then make a rapid assessment of what those characteristics mean. How do you complete this process? What cues do you interpret? How accurate are your impressions? The concept of *schemata,* which we first encountered in Chapter 6, "Memory," helps to answer these questions.

Schemata When we meet someone for the first time, we notice a number of things about that person—clothes, gestures, manner of speaking, body build, and facial features. We then draw on these cues to fit the person into a category. No matter how little information we have or how contradictory it is, no matter how many times our initial impressions have been wrong, we still categorize people after meeting them only briefly. Associated with each category is a *schema*—an organized set of beliefs and expectations based on past experience that is presumed to apply to all members of that category (Aronson, Wilson, & Akert, 2005). *Schemata* (the plural of schema) influence the information we notice and remember. They also help us flesh out our impressions as we peg people into categories. For example, if a woman is wearing a white coat and has a stethoscope around her neck, you could reasonably categorize her as a doctor. Associated with this category is a schema of various beliefs and expectations: highly trained professional, knowledgeable about diseases and their cures, qualified to prescribe medication, and so on.

Over time, as we continue to interact with people, we add new information about them to our mental files. Our later experiences, however, generally do not influence us nearly as much as our earliest impressions. This phenomenon is called the **primacy effect.**

Schemata and the primacy effect reflect a desire to lessen our mental effort. Humans have been called "cognitive misers" (Fiske & Taylor, 1991). Instead of exerting ourselves to interpret every detail that we learn about a person, we are stingy with our mental efforts. Once we have formed an impression about someone, we tend not to exert the mental effort to change it, even if that impression was formed by jumping to conclusions or through prejudice (Fiske, 1995).

Sometimes, schemata can even help us create the behavior we expect from other people. In a classic study, pairs of participants played a competitive game (M. Snyder & Swann, 1978). The researchers told one member of each pair that his or her partner was either hostile or friendly. The players who were led to believe that their partner was hostile behaved differently toward that partner than did the players led to believe that their partner was friendly. In turn, those treated as hostile actually began to display hostility. When we bring about expected behavior in another person in this way, our impression becomes a **self-fulfilling prophecy.**

social cognition Knowledge and understanding concerning the social world and the people in it (including oneself).

primacy effect The fact that early information about someone weighs more heavily than later information in influencing one's impression of that person.

self-fulfilling prophecy The process in which a person's expectation about another elicits behavior from the second person that confirms the expectation.

Considerable scientific research has shown how teacher expectations can take the form of a self-fulfilling prophecy and can influence student performance in the classroom (M. Harris & Rosenthal, 1985; Jussim, Robustelli, & Cain, 2009; Rosenthal, 2002b, 2006). That finding has been named the *Pygmalion effect,* after the mythical sculptor who created the statue of a woman and then brought it to life. Although the research does not suggest that high teacher expectations can turn an "F" student into an "A" student, it does show that both high and low expectations can significantly influence student achievement. One study, for example, compared the performance of "at risk" ninth-grade students who had been assigned to regular classrooms with that of students assigned to experimental classrooms that received a year-long intervention aimed at increasing teachers' expectations. After 1 year, the students in the experimental classrooms had higher grades in English and history than the students who were not in the intervention classrooms. Two years later, the experimental students were also less likely to drop out of high school (Weinstein et al., 1991).

As you have probably noticed, first impressions often contain a significant emotional component. In other words, when we form a first impression, it often includes judgments about an individual's trustworthiness, friendliness, and competence. Thus, one would expect that areas of the brain involved in emotional memory should play an important role in forming first impressions, and this is exactly what one study found. Using neuroimaging techniques, researchers found that the amygdala (see Chapter 2: "The Biological Basis of Behavior"), a region of the brain known to be associated with emotional memory, becomes significantly more active when people form first impressions about individuals they later described as being competent and having the potential to make a good leader (Rule et al., 2010).

Stereotypes   Just as schemata shape our impressions of others, so do stereotypes. As a set of characteristics presumed to be shared by all members of a social category, a **stereotype** is actually a special kind of schema—one that is simplistic, very strongly held, and not necessarily based on firsthand experience. A stereotype can involve almost any distinguishing personal attribute, such as age, sex, race, occupation, place of residence, or membership in a certain group. As Sher Singh learned after the terrorist attacks of September 11, 2001, many Americans developed a stereotype suggesting that all males who "looked" like they were from the Middle East were potential terrorists.

When our first impression of a person is governed by a stereotype, we tend to infer things about that person solely on the basis of some key distinguishing feature and to ignore facts that are inconsistent with the stereotype, no matter how apparent they are. For example, once you have categorized someone as male or female, you may rely more on your stereotype of that gender than on your own observations of how the person acts. Recent studies indicate that sorting people into categories is not automatic or inevitable (Castelli, Macrae, Zogmaister, & Arcuri, 2004). People are more likely to apply stereotyped schemata in a chance encounter than in a structured, task-oriented situation (such as a classroom or the office); more likely to pay attention to individual signals than to stereotypes when they are pursuing a goal; and are more likely to suppress stereotypes that violate social norms.

stereotype A set of characteristics presumed to be shared by all members of a social category.

Suppose you are a new teacher entering this classroom on the first day of school in September. Do you have any expectations about children of any ethnic or racial groups that might lead to a self-fulfilling prophecy?

ENDURING ISSUES

Person–Situation   Interpreting Behavior

The study of attribution, or how people explain their own and other people's behavior, focuses on when and why people interpret behavior as reflecting personal traits or social situations. Suppose you run into a friend at the supermarket. You greet him warmly, but he barely acknowledges you, mumbles "Hi," and walks away. You feel snubbed and try to figure out why he acted like that. Did he behave that way because of something in the situation? Perhaps you did something that offended him; perhaps he was having no luck finding the groceries he wanted; or perhaps someone had just blocked his way by leaving a cart in the middle of an aisle. Or did something within him, some personal trait such as moodiness or arrogance, prompt him to behave that way? ∎

Attribution

How do we decide why people act as they do?

✳ Explore the Concept Internal and External
Attributions on MyPsychLab

Explaining Behavior Social interaction is filled with occasions that invite us to make judgments about the causes of behavior. When something unexpected or unpleasant occurs, we wonder about it and try to understand it. Social psychologists' observations about how we go about attributing causes to behavior form the basis of **attribution theory.** ✳

An early attribution theorist, Fritz Heider (1958), argued that we attribute behavior to either internal or external causes, but not both. Thus, we might conclude that a classmate's lateness was caused by his laziness (a personal factor, or an *internal attribution*) or by traffic congestion (a situational factor, or an *external attribution*).

How do we decide whether to attribute a given behavior to internal or external causes? According to another influential attribution theorist, Harold Kelley (Kelley, 1967, 1973; also see B. Weiner, 2008), we rely on three kinds of information about the behavior: *distinctiveness, consistency,* and *consensus.* For example, if your instructor asks you to stay briefly after class so that she can talk with you, you will probably try to figure out what lies behind her request by asking yourself three questions.

First, how *distinctive* is the instructor's request? Does she often ask students to stay and talk (low distinctiveness) or is such a request unusual (high distinctiveness)? If she often asks students to speak with her, you will probably conclude that she has personal reasons for talking with you. But if her request is highly distinctive, you will probably conclude that something about you, not her, underlies her request.

Second, how *consistent* is the instructor's behavior? Does she regularly ask you to stay and talk (high consistency), or is this a first for you (low consistency)? If she has consistently made this request of you before, you will probably guess that this occasion is like those others. But if her request is inconsistent with past behavior, you will probably wonder whether some particular event—perhaps something you said in class—motivated her to request a private conference.

Finally, what degree of *consensus* among teachers exists regarding this behavior? Do your other instructors ask you to stay and talk with them (high consensus), or is this instructor unique in making such a request (low consensus)? If it is common for your instructors to ask to speak with you, this instructor's request is probably due to some external factor. But if she is the only instructor ever to ask to speak privately with you, it must be something about this particular person—an internal motive or a concern—that accounts for her behavior.

If you conclude that the instructor has her own reasons for wanting to speak with you, you may feel mildly curious for the remainder of class until you can find out what she wants. But if you think external factors—like your own actions—have prompted her request, you may worry about whether you are in trouble and nervously wait for the end of class.

Biases Unfortunately, the causal attributions we make are often vulnerable to *biases.* For instance, imagine that you are at a party and you see an acquaintance, Ted, walk across the room carrying several plates of food and a drink. As he approaches his chair, Ted spills food on himself. You may attribute the spill to Ted's personal characteristics—he is clumsy. Ted, however, is likely to make a very different attribution. He will likely attribute the spill to an external factor—he was carrying too many other things. Your explanation for this behavior reflects the **fundamental attribution error**—the tendency to attribute others' behavior to causes within themselves (Aronson, Wilson, & Akert, 2005; D. L. Watson, 2008).

The fundamental attribution error is part of the *actor-observer bias*—the tendency to explain the behavior of others as caused by internal factors, while attributing one's own behavior to external forces (Hennessy, Jakubowski, & Benedetti, 2005). For example, during World War II, some Europeans risked their own safety to help Jewish refugees. From the perspective of an observer, we tend to attribute this behavior to personal

attribution theory The theory that addresses the question of how people make judgments about the causes of behavior.

fundamental attribution error The tendency of people to overemphasize personal causes for other people's behavior.

qualities. Indeed, Robert Goodkind, chairman of the foundation that honored the rescuers, called for parents to "inculcate in our children the values of altruism and moral courage as exemplified by the rescuers." Clearly, Goodkind was making an internal attribution for the heroic behavior. The rescuers themselves, however, attributed their actions to external factors. One said, "We didn't feel like rescuers at all. We were just ordinary students doing what we had to do." (Lipman, 1991).

A related class of biases is called **defensive attribution.** These types of attributions occur when we are motivated to present ourselves well, either to impress others or to feel good about ourselves. One example of a defensive attribution is the *self-serving bias,* which is a tendency to attribute our successes to our personal attributes while chalking up our failures to external forces beyond our control (Sedikides & Luke, 2008). Students do this all the time. They tend to regard exams on which they do well as good indicators of their abilities and exams on which they do poorly as bad indicators (R. A. Smith, 2005). Similarly, teachers are more likely to assume responsibility for students' successes than for their failures (R. A. Smith, 2005).

A second type of defensive attribution comes from thinking that people get what they deserve: Bad things happen to bad people, and good things happen to good people. This is called the **just-world hypothesis** (Aronson, Wilson, & Akert, 2005; Melvyn Lerner, 1980). When misfortune strikes someone, we often jump to the conclusion that the person deserved it, rather than giving full weight to situational factors that may have been responsible. Why do we behave this way? One reason is that by reassigning the blame for a terrible misfortune from a chance event (something that could happen to us) to the victim's own negligence (a trait that *we,* of course, do not share), we delude ourselves into believing that we could never suffer such a fate (Dalbert, 2001). Interestingly, research has shown that because believing in a just world reduces stress, it may also promote good health, posttraumatic growth, and a sense of well-being following a traumatic event (Fatima & Suhail, 2010; Park, Edmondson, Fenster, & Blank, 2008).

Attribution Across Cultures   Historically, most of the research on attribution theory has been conducted in Western cultures. Do the basic principles of attribution theory apply to people in other cultures as well? The answer appears to be "not always." Some recent research has confirmed the self-serving bias among people from Eastern collectivist cultures like Japan and Taiwan (L. Gaertner, Sedikides, & Chang, 2008; Kudo & Numazaki, 2003; Sedikides, Gaertner, & Toguchi, 2003), while other research has not (Balcetis, Dunning, & Miller, 2008). In one study, Japanese students studying in the United States usually explained failure as a lack of effort (an internal attribution) and attributed their successes to the assistance that they received from others (an external attribution) (Kashima & Triandis, 1986). This process is the reverse of the self-serving bias. Similarly, the fundamental attribution error may not be universal. In some other cultures, people place more emphasis on the role of external, situational factors in explaining both their own behavior and that of others (Incheo Choi, Dalal, Kim-Prieto, & Park, 2003; Morling & Kitayama, 2008). Perhaps research from social neuroscience will someday provide more insight into what role culture plays in shaping the underlying neurological processes that shape the formation of attributions (Mason & Morris, 2010).

Interpersonal Attraction

Do "birds of a feather flock together," or do "opposites attract"?

A third aspect of social cognition involves interpersonal attraction. When people meet, what determines whether they will like each other? This is the subject of much speculation and even mystification, with popular explanations running the gamut from fate to compatible astrological signs. As you might expect, social psychologists take a more

Did this accident happen because of poor driving or because the driver swerved to avoid a child in the street? The fundamental attribution error says that we are more likely to attribute the behavior of others to internal causes, such as poor driving, rather than situational factors, such as a child in the street.

defensive attribution The tendency to attribute our successes to our own efforts or qualities and our failures to external factors.

just-world hypothesis Attribution error based on the assumption that bad things happen to bad people and good things happen to good people.

proximity How close two people live to each other.

data-based approach. Studies have found that attraction and the tendency to like someone else are closely linked to such factors as *proximity, physical attractiveness, similarity, and intimacy.*

Proximity **Proximity** is usually the most important factor in determining attraction (Aronson, Wilson, & Akert, 2005; J. W. Brehm, 2002). The closer two people live to each other, the more likely they are to interact; the more frequent their interaction, the more they will tend to like each other. Conversely, two people separated by considerable geographic distance are not likely to run into each other and thus have little chance to develop a mutual attraction. The proximity effect has less to do with simple convenience than with the security and comfort we feel with people and things that have become familiar. In other words, mere exposure, and especially repeated exposure, enhances familiarity (de Vries, Holland, Chenier, Starr, & Winkielman, 2010) and familiarity leads to liking. Thus, the more people interact with one another, the more likely they are to become attracted to each other (Reis, Maniaci, Caprariello, Eastwick, & Finkel, 2011).

Physical Attractiveness Contrary to the old adage, "beauty is in the eye of the beholder," research has found that people generally agree when rating the attractiveness of others (Gottschall, 2008; Langlois et al., 2000). Even people from different cultures and ethnic groups appear to have a similar standard for who is or is not considered beautiful. This cross-cultural, cross-ethnic agreement suggests the possibility of a universal standard of beauty (Bronstad, Langlois, & Russell, 2008; Rhodes, 2006).

Consistent with the idea of a universal standard of beauty, neuroimaging studies have found specific regions of the brain that are responsive to facial beauty (Chatterjee, Thomas, Smith, & Aguirre, 2009). Perhaps not surprisingly, the areas of the brain that become most active when we view attractive faces are associated with positive emotions, while the areas that respond to less attractive faces are more linked with negative emotions such as disgust (Principe & Langlois, 2011). Even infant brains respond differently to attractive versus less attractive faces, showing more positive emotion toward attractive faces (Partridge, 2010). Finally, social neuroscience has confirmed that there appear to be specific brain regions dedicated to remembering attractive faces which, by the way, are remembered better than less attractive ones (Tsukiura & Cabeza, 2011). ⊙➤

⊙➤ **Simulate** the **Experiment** Perceptions of Attractiveness on **MyPsychLab**

Physical attractiveness can powerfully influence the conclusions that we reach about a person's character. We actually give attractive people credit for more than their beauty (Lorenzo, Biesanz, & Human, 2010). We tend to presume they are more intelligent, interesting, happy, kind, sensitive, moral, and successful than people who are not perceived as attractive. They are also thought to make better spouses and to be more sexually responsive (Griffin & Langlois, 2006; Hosoda, Stone, & Coats, 2003; Katz, 2003; Riniolo, Johnson, Sherman, & Misso, 2006). We also tend to like attractive people more than we do less attractive people. One reason is that physical attractiveness itself is generally considered a positive attribute. We often perceive beauty as a valuable asset that can be exchanged for other things in social interactions. We may also believe that beauty has a "radiating effect"—that the glow of a companion's good looks enhances our own public image (Sedikides, Olsen, & Reis, 1993).

Our preoccupation with physical attractiveness has material consequences. Research has found that mothers of more attractive infants tend to show their children more affection and to play with them more often than mothers of unattractive infants (Langlois, Ritter, Casey, & Sawin, 1995). Even in hospitals, premature infants rated as more attractive by attending nurses thrived better and gained weight faster than those judged as less attractive, presumably because they receive more nurturing (Badr & Abdallah, 2001). Attractive children are also more likely to be better adjusted, to display greater intelligence, and to be treated more leniently by teachers (Langlois et al., 2000; M. McCall, 1997). Similarly, attractive adults enjoy better health, tend to be slightly more intelligent, self-confident, and are generally judged to be more hirable and productive by employers (Desrumaux, De Bosscher, & Léoni, 2009; Hosoda, Stone, & Coats, 2003; L. A. Jackson, Hunter, & Hodge, 1995).

We also tend to give good-looking people the benefit of the doubt: If they don't live up to our expectations during the first encounter, we are likely to give them a second chance, ask for or accept a second date, or seek further opportunities for interaction. These reactions can give attractive people substantial advantages in life and can lead to self-fulfilling prophecies. Physically attractive people may come to think of themselves as good or lovable because they are continually treated as if they are. Conversely, unattractive people may begin to see themselves as bad or unlovable because they have always been regarded that way—even as children.

Similarity Attractiveness isn't everything. In the abstract, people might prefer extremely attractive individuals, but in reality they usually choose friends and partners who are close to their own level of attractiveness (L. Lee, Loewenstein, Ariely, Hong, & Young, 2008). Similarity—of attitudes, interests, values, backgrounds, and beliefs, as well as looks—underlies much interpersonal attraction (AhYun, 2002; Sano, 2002; S. Solomon & Knafo, 2007). When we know that someone shares our attitudes and interests, we tend to have more positive feelings toward that person in part because they are likely to agree with our choices and beliefs. In turn that strengthens our convictions and boosts our self-esteem. Finally, as much as we like people who like us, we are especially drawn to people who like us and who don't generally like others (Eastwick, Finkel, Mochon, & Ariely, 2007).

If similarity is such a critical determinant of attraction, what about the notion that opposites attract? Aren't people sometimes attracted to others who are completely different from them? Extensive research has failed to confirm this notion. In long-term relationships, where attraction plays an especially important role, people overwhelmingly prefer to associate with people who are similar to themselves (Buss, 1985; McPherson, Smith-Lovin, & Cook, 2001). It is true that in some cases, people are attracted to others with complementary characteristics (K. H. Rubin, Fredstrom, & Bowker, 2008). For example, a person who likes to care for and fuss over others could be compatible with a mate who enjoys receiving such attention. But complementarity almost always occurs between people who share similar goals and similar values. True opposites are unlikely even to meet each other, much less interact long enough to achieve such compatibility.

Intimacy When does liking someone become something more? *Intimacy* is the quality of genuine closeness to and trust in another person. People become closer and stay closer through a continuing reciprocal pattern where each person tries to know the other and allows the other to know him or her (Theiss & Solomon, 2008). When you are first getting to know someone, you communicate about "safe," superficial topics like the weather, sports, or shared activities. As you get to know each other better over time, your conversation progresses to more personal subjects: your personal experiences, memories, hopes and fears, goals and failures. Thus, intimate communication is based on a process of gradual *self-disclosure*. Because self-disclosure is possible only when you trust the listener, you will seek—and usually receive—a reciprocal disclosure to keep the conversation balanced and emotionally satisfying (Bauminger, Finzi-Dottan, Chason, & Har-Even, 2008). The pacing of disclosure is important. If you "jump levels" by revealing too much too soon—or to someone who is not ready to make a reciprocal personal response—the other person will probably retreat, and communication will go no further.

THINKING CRITICALLY ABOUT . . .

Intimacy and the Internet

Many of the studies of interpersonal attraction were conducted before the advent of new Internet technologies.

- What impact (if any) has e-mail, instant messaging, online networking communities like Facebook, and dating services like match.com had on close relationships?

- Do these new technology tools make it easier to maintain long-distance relationships? Influence attributions? Encourage self-disclosure with intimates and/or strangers? Subtly shape social cognition in other ways?

- In answering the questions above, what did you use as the source of your opinions? Your personal experiences? Articles in the mass media? Reports of scientific research? Suppose you were conducting a survey to collect data on these questions. What would you ask your participants? How might you determine whether their self-reports are accurate?

Self-disclosure—revealing personal experiences and opinions—is essential to all close relationships.

✓•─|**Study** and **Review** on **MyPsychLab**

1. Associated with the many categories into which we "peg" people are sets of beliefs and expectations called _____ that are assumed to apply to all members of a category. When these are quite simplistic, but deeply held, they are often referred to as _____.

2. When the first information we receive about a person weighs more heavily in forming an impression than later information does, we are experiencing the _____ effect.

3. The tendency to attribute the behavior of others to internal causes and one's own behavior to external causes is called the _____ _____ bias.

4. The belief that people must deserve the bad things that happen to them reflects the _____ _____ _____.

5. The tendency to attribute the behavior of others to personal characteristics is the _____ _____ error.

6. Which of the following is a basis for interpersonal attraction? (There can be more than one correct answer.)
   a. proximity
   b. similarity
   c. attraction of true opposites
   d. all of the above

Answers: 1. schemata, stereotypes. **2.** primacy. **3.** actor–observer. **4.** just-world hypothesis. **5.** fundamental attribution. **6.** a and b.

1. You meet someone at a party who is outgoing and entertaining, and has a great sense of humor. A week later, your paths cross again, but this time the person seems very shy, withdrawn, and humorless. Most likely, your impression of this person after the second meeting is that he or she
   a. is actually shy, withdrawn, and humorless, despite your initial impression.
   b. is actually outgoing and entertaining but was just having a bad day.
   c. is low in self-monitoring.
   d. Both (b) and (c) are correct.

2. Your roommate tells you she did really well on her history midterm exam because she studied hard and "knew the material cold." But she says she did poorly on her psychology midterm because the exam was unfair and full of ambiguous questions. On the basis of what you have learned in this portion of the chapter, this may be an example of
   a. defensive attribution.
   b. the primacy effect.
   c. the ultimate attribution error.
   d. the just-world effect.

Answers: 1. b. **2.** a.

LEARNING OBJECTIVES

- Describe the three major components of attitudes and the variables that determine whether an attitude will be reflected in behavior.
- Distinguish among prejudice, racism, and discrimination. Explain the role of stereotypes and the *ultimate attribution error* in prejudicial attitudes. Compare and contrast the following potential sources of prejudice: frustration–aggression, authoritarian personality, "cognitive misers," and conformity. Describe the three strategies that appear promising as ways to reduce prejudice and discrimination.
- Describe the three steps in the use of persuasion to change attitudes: attention, comprehension, and acceptance. In your description, include the source (credibility and the sleeper effect), the message itself (one-sided vs. two-sided, fear), the medium of communication, and characteristics of the audience.
- Explain what is meant by "cognitive dissonance" and how that can be used to change attitudes.

attitude Relatively stable organization of beliefs, feelings, and behavior tendencies directed toward something or someone—the attitude object.

ATTITUDES

Why are attitudes important?

An **attitude** is a relatively stable organization of beliefs, feelings, and tendencies toward something or someone. Attitudes are important because they often influence our behavior. For example, the phrase "I don't like his attitude" is a telling one. People are often told to "change your attitude" or make an "attitude adjustment." Since attitudes can affect behavior, social psychologists are interested in how attitudes are formed and how they can be changed.

The Nature of Attitudes

What are the three major components of attitudes?

An attitude has three major components: *evaluative beliefs* about an object, *feelings* about that object, and *behavior tendencies* toward that object. Beliefs include facts, opinions, and our general knowledge. Feelings encompass love, hate, like, dislike, and similar sentiments. Behavior tendencies refer to our inclinations to act in certain ways toward the object—to approach it, avoid it, and so on. For example, our attitude toward a political candidate includes our beliefs about the candidate's qualifications and positions on crucial issues and our expectations about how the candidate will vote on those issues. We also have feelings about the candidate—like or dislike, trust or mistrust. And because of these beliefs and feelings, we are inclined to behave in certain ways toward the candidate—to vote for or against the candidate, to contribute time or money to the candidate's campaign, to make a point of attending or staying away from rallies for the candidate, and so forth.

As we will see shortly, these three aspects of an attitude are often consistent with one another. For example, if we have positive feelings toward something, we tend to have positive beliefs about it and to behave positively toward it. This tendency does not mean, however, that our every action will accurately reflect our attitudes. For example, our feelings about going to dentists may be negative, yet most of us make an annual visit anyway. Let's look more closely at the relationship between attitudes and behavior.

Attitudes and Behavior   The relationship between attitudes and behavior is not always straightforward (Ajzen & Cote, 2008). Variables such as the strength of the attitude, how easily it comes to mind, how noticeable a particular attitude is in a given situation, and how relevant the attitude is to the particular behavior in question help to determine whether a person will act in accordance with an attitude.

Moreover, attitudes predict behavior better for some people than for others. People who rate highly on **self-monitoring** are especially likely to override their attitudes to behave in accordance with others' expectations (Jawahar, 2001; O. Klein, Snyder, & Livingston, 2004). For example, before speaking or acting, those who score high in self-monitoring observe the situation for clues about how they should react. Then they try to meet those "demands," rather than behave according to their own beliefs or sentiments. In contrast, those who score low in self-monitoring express and act on their attitudes with great consistency, showing relatively little regard for situational clues or constraints.

Attitude Development   How do we acquire our attitudes? Where do they come from? Many of our most basic attitudes derive from early, direct personal experience. Children are rewarded with smiles and encouragement when they please their parents, and they are punished through disapproval when they displease them. These early experiences give children enduring attitudes (Castelli, Zogmaister, & Tomelleri, 2009). Attitudes are also formed by imitation. Children mimic the behavior of their parents and peers, acquiring attitudes even when no one is deliberately trying to shape them.

But parents are not the only source of attitudes. Teachers, friends, and even famous people are also important in shaping our attitudes. New fraternity or sorority members, for example, may model their behavior and attitudes on upper-class members (McConnell, Rydell, Strain, & Mackie, 2008). A student who idolizes a teacher may adopt many of the teacher's attitudes toward controversial subjects, even if they run counter to attitudes of parents or friends.

The mass media, particularly television, also have a great impact on attitude formation (Lin & Reid, 2009; Nielsen & Bonn, 2008). This is why having his photo televised with the label of terrorist suspect was particularly devastating for Sher Singh. Television and magazines bombard us with messages—not merely through news and entertainment, but also through commercials. Without experience of their own against which to measure the merit of these messages, children are particularly susceptible to the influence of television on their attitudes.

Attitudes are adaptive, because they provide us with a quick way to evaluate a situation or individual. However, to be accurate, attitudes must also be flexible enough to change with self-reflection, and as we acquire new information. Social neuroscience has found that the prefrontal cortex, a brain region principally involved in self-monitoring, plays a pivotal role in reprocessing evaluative information during attitude formation (Cunningham & Zelazo, 2007).

self-monitoring The tendency for an individual to observe the situation for cues about how to react.

Prejudice and Discrimination

How does a person develop a prejudice toward someone else?

Although the terms *prejudice* and *discrimination* are often used interchangeably, they actually refer to different concepts. **Prejudice**—an attitude—is an unfair, intolerant, or unfavorable view of a group of people. **Discrimination**—a behavior—is an unfair act or a series of acts directed against an entire group of people or individual members of that group. To discriminate is to treat an entire class of people in an unfair way.

ENDURING ISSUES

Person–Situation   Does Discrimination Reflect Prejudice?

Prejudice and discrimination do not always occur together. A variety of factors determine whether prejudice will be expressed in discriminative behavior (Monteiro, de França, & Rodrigues, 2009). For example, a prejudiced storeowner may smile at an African American customer to disguise opinions that could hurt his business. Likewise, many institutional practices can be discriminatory even though they are not based on prejudice. For example, regulations establishing a minimum height requirement for police officers may discriminate against women and certain ethnic groups whose average height falls below the standard, even though the regulations do not stem from sexist or racist attitudes. ■

Prejudice Like all other attitudes, prejudice has three components: beliefs, feelings, and behavioral tendencies. Prejudicial beliefs are virtually always negative stereotypes; and, as mentioned earlier, reliance on stereotypes can lead to erroneous thinking about other people. The *ultimate attribution error* refers to the tendency for a person with stereotyped beliefs about a particular group of people to make internal attributions for their shortcomings (they lack ability or motivation) and external attributions for their successes (they were given special advantages) (P. J. Henry, Reyna, & Weiner, 2004). Along with stereotyped beliefs, prejudiced attitudes are usually marked by strong emotions, such as dislike, fear, hatred, or loathing and corresponding negative behavioral tendencies such as avoidance, hostility, and criticism.

Sources of Prejudice Many theories attempt to sort out the causes and sources of prejudice. According to the **frustration–aggression theory,** prejudice is the result of people's frustrations (Allport, 1954; E. R. Smith & Mackie, 2005). As we saw in Chapter 8, "Motivation and Emotion," under some circumstances frustration can spill over into anger and hostility. People who feel exploited and oppressed often cannot vent their anger against an identifiable or proper target, so they displace their hostility onto those even "lower" on the social scale than themselves. The result is prejudice and discrimination. The people who are the victims of this displaced aggression, or *scapegoats,* are blamed for the problems of the times. Recall the experiences of Sher Singh, whom we described at the start of this chapter. After the 2001 terrorist attacks in the United States, many Arabs, Muslims, and even people who looked Middle Eastern, became scapegoats for the frustration of some Americans about the violence.

Another theory locates the source of prejudice in a bigoted or **authoritarian personality** (Adorno, Frenkel-Brunswick, Levinson, & Sanford, 1950; Altemeyer, 2004). Authoritarian people tend to be rigidly conventional. They favor following the rules and abiding by tradition and are hostile to those who defy social norms. They respect and submit to authority and are preoccupied with power and toughness. Looking at the world through a lens of rigid categories, they are cynical about human nature, fearing, suspecting, and rejecting all groups other than those to which they belong. Prejudice is only one expression of their suspicious, mistrusting views (Jost & Sidanius, 2004).

Cognitive sources of prejudice also exist (Cornelis & Van Hiel, 2006). As we saw earlier, people are "cognitive misers" who try to simplify and organize their social thinking as much as possible. Oversimplification can lead to erroneous thinking, stereotypes, prejudice, and

prejudice An unfair, intolerant, or unfavorable attitude toward a group of people.

discrimination An unfair act or series of acts taken toward an entire group of people or individual members of that group.

frustration–aggression theory The theory that, under certain circumstances, people who are frustrated in their goals turn their anger away from the proper, powerful target and toward another, less powerful target that is safer to attack.

authoritarian personality A personality pattern characterized by rigid conventionality, exaggerated respect for authority, and hostility toward those who defy society's norms.

discrimination. For example, belief in a just world—where people get what they deserve and deserve what they get—oversimplifies one's view of the victims of prejudice as somehow "deserving" their plight. This may be why some people watching Sher Singh's arrest jumped to the conclusion that he was a terrorist who "deserved" to be arrested.

In addition, prejudice and discrimination may originate in people's attempts to conform. If we associate with people who express prejudices, we are more likely to go along with their ideas than to resist them. The pressures of social conformity help to explain why children quickly absorb the prejudices of their parents and playmates long before they have formed their own beliefs and opinions on the basis of experience. Peer pressure sometimes makes it "cool" or at least acceptable to harbor biased attitudes toward members of other social groups: Either you are one of "us," or you are one of "them." An *in-group* is any group of people who feels a sense of solidarity and exclusivity in relation to nonmembers. An *out-group,* in contrast, is a group of people who are outside this boundary and are viewed as competitors, enemies, or different and unworthy of respect. These terms can be applied to opposing sports teams, rival gangs, and political parties, or to entire nations, regions, religions, and ethnic or racial groups. According to the *in-group bias,* members see themselves not just as different, but also as superior to members of out-groups (K. Miller, Brewer, & Arbuckle, 2009). In extreme cases, members of an in-group may see members of an out-group as less than human and feel hatred that may lead to violence, civil war, and even genocide.

Racism is the belief that members of certain racial or ethnic groups are *innately* inferior. Racists believe that intelligence, industry, morality, and other valued traits are biologically determined and therefore cannot be changed. The most blatant forms of racism in the United States have declined during the past several decades as evidenced by the election of the first African American President, Barack Obama in 2008. But racism still exists in subtle forms. For example, many Whites say that they approve of interracial marriage, but would be "uncomfortable" if someone in their family married an African American. Blacks and Whites in America also have different views on race-related policies such as school desegregation and affirmative action, with Blacks generally being more supportive of such policies (Julie Hughes, 2009). In one survey of 1,000 Americans shortly after Hurricane Katrina hit the Gulf Coast, 66% of African Americans said that the government's response would have been faster if most victims had been White; only 26% of White Americans agreed. Only 19% of African Americans, compared to 41% of White Americans, felt that the federal government's response was good or excellent. When asked about people who "took things from businesses and homes" during the flooding, 57% of African Americans said they were ordinary people trying to survive; only 38% of White Americans agreed (Pew Research Center for the People and the Press, 2005). 👁

Signs like this were common in the South before the civil rights movement.

👁 **Watch** the **Video** Black Doll White Doll on **MyPsychLab**

Strategies for Reducing Prejudice and Discrimination How can we use our knowledge of prejudice, stereotypes, and discrimination to reduce prejudice and its expression? Three strategies appear promising: recategorization, controlled processing, and improving contact between groups. (See "Applying Psychology: Ethnic Conflict and Violence," page 469, for a discussion of how these strategies can be used to reduce ethnic conflict.)

- *Recategorization.* When we recategorize, we try to expand our schema of a particular group—such as viewing people from different races or genders as sharing similar qualities. These more inclusive schemata become superordinate categories. For instance, both Catholics and Protestants in the United States tend to view themselves as Christians, rather than as separate competing groups (as has occurred in Northern Ireland). If people can create such superordinate categories, they can often reduce stereotypes and prejudice (S. L. Gaertner & Dovidio, 2008).
- *Controlled Processing.* Some researchers believe that we all learn cultural stereotypes, so the primary difference between someone who is prejudiced and someone who is not is the ability to suppress prejudiced beliefs through controlled processing (Cunningham, Johnson, Raye, Gatenby, & Gore, 2004; Dion, 2003). We can train ourselves to be more "mindful" of people who differ from us. For example, to reduce

racism Prejudice and discrimination directed at a particular racial group.

One of the best antidotes to prejudice is contact among people of different racial groups. Working on class projects together, for example, can help children to overcome negative stereotypes about others.

children's prejudice toward people with disabilities, children could be shown slides of handicapped people and be asked to imagine how difficult it might be for such individuals to open a door or drive a car.

- *Improving group contact.* Finally, we can reduce prejudice and tensions between groups by bringing them together (Denson, 2008; McClelland & Linnander, 2006). This was one of the intentions of the famous 1954 U.S. Supreme Court's decision in *Brown v. Board of Education* of Topeka, Kansas, which mandated that public schools become racially integrated. However, intergroup contact alone is generally not enough (D. M. Taylor & Moghaddam, 1994). It only works to undermine prejudicial attitudes if the following conditions are met:

- *The group members must have equal status.*
- *The people involved need to have one-on-one contact with members of the other group.*
- *The members of the two groups must cooperate rather than compete.*
- *The social norms should encourage intergroup contact.*

In all of these suggestions, the primary focus is on changing behavior, not on changing attitudes directly. But changing behavior is often a first step toward changing attitudes. This is not to say that attitude change follows automatically. Attitudes can be difficult to budge because they are often so deeply rooted. Completely eliminating deeply held attitudes, then, can be very difficult. That is why social psychologists have concentrated so much effort on techniques that encourage attitude change. In the next section, we examine some of the major findings in the psychological research on attitude change.

Changing Attitudes

What factors encourage someone to change an attitude?

A man watching television on Sunday afternoon ignores scores of beer commercials, but listens to a friend who recommends a particular brand. A political speech convinces one woman to change her vote in favor of the candidate, but leaves her next-door neighbor determined to vote against him. Why would a personal recommendation have greater persuasive power than an expensively produced television commercial? How can two people with similar initial views derive completely different messages from the same speech? What makes one attempt to change attitudes fail and another succeed? Are some people more resistant to attitude change than others are?

The Process of Persuasion The first step in persuasion is to seize and retain the audience's attention. To be persuaded, you must first pay attention to the message; then you must comprehend it; finally, you must accept it as convincing (Perloff, 2003).

As competition has stiffened, advertisers have become increasingly creative in catching your attention. For example, ads that arouse emotions, especially feelings that make you want to act, can be memorable and thus persuasive (DeSteno & Braverman, 2002; Hansen & Christensen, 2007). Humor, too, is an effective way to keep you watching or reading an ad that you would otherwise ignore (Michael Conway & Dubé, 2002; Strick, van Baaren, Holland, & van Knippenberg, 2009). Other ads "hook" the audience by involving them in a narrative. A commercial might open with a dramatic scene or situation—for example, two people seemingly "meant" for each other but not yet making eye contact—and the viewer stays tuned to find out what happens. Some commercials even feature recurring characters and story lines so that each new commercial in the series is really the latest installment in a

APPLYING PSYCHOLOGY

Ethnic Conflict and Violence

Since the end of the Cold War, interethnic conflict has become the dominant form of war (Mays, Bullock, Rosenzweig, & Wessells, 1998; Rouhana & Bar-Tal, 1998). Bosnia, Croatia, East Timor, Russia, Turkey, Iraq, Ireland, Israel, Sri Lanka … the list of countries torn by ethnic conflict is long; and civilian deaths continue to increase by the thousands. Why does such conflict arise, and why is it so difficult to resolve?

Ethnic conflict has no single cause. In part, it "… is often rooted in histories of colonialism, ethnocentrism, racism, political oppression, human rights abuses, social injustice, poverty, and environmental degradation" (Mays et al., 1998, p. 737; Pederson, 2002; Toft, 2003). But these structural problems are only part of the story, determining primarily who fights whom. The rest of the story is found in psychological processes such as intense group loyalty, personal and social identity, shared memories, polarization and deep-rooted prejudice, and societal beliefs (Phinney, 2008; Tindale, Munier, Wasserman, & Smith, 2002). In other words, structural problems don't have the same effect when people are not prepared to hate and fear others. What are some of the psychological forces at work?

- *Propaganda* causes opponents to be painted in the most negative fashion possible, thus perpetuating racism, prejudice, and stereotypes. In Rwanda, for example, Tutsis (who were almost exterminated by the resulting violence with Hutus) for years were falsely accused in the mass media of having committed horrible crimes and of plotting the mass murder of Hutus (David Smith, 1998).

- When ethnic violence is protracted, *shared collective memories* become filled with instances of violence, hostility, and victimization. Prejudices are thus reinforced, and people increasingly come to view the conflict as inevitable and their differences as irreconcilable (Rouhana & Bar-Tal, 1998).

- *Personal and social identity* can also contribute. Because group memberships contribute to self-image, if your group is maligned or threatened, then by extension you also are personally maligned and threatened. If you are unable to leave the group, you are pressured to defend it to enhance your own feelings of self-esteem (Cairns & Darby, 1998). In this way, what starts out as ethnic conflict quickly becomes a highly personal threat.

- Finally, widespread *societal beliefs* about the conflict and the parties to the conflict also play a role in prolonged ethnic conflicts. Four especially important societal beliefs are "Our goals are just," "The opponent has no legitimacy," "We can do no wrong," and "We are the victims" (Rouhana & Bar-Tal, 1998). These societal beliefs "provide a common social prism through which society members view the conflict."

soap opera. Even annoying ads can still be effective in capturing attention, because people tend to notice them when they appear (Aaker & Bruzzone, 1985).

With so many clever strategies focused on seizing and holding your attention, how can you shield yourself from unwanted influences and resist persuasive appeals? Start by reminding yourself that these are deliberate attempts to influence you and to change your behavior. Research shows that to a great extent, "forewarned is forearmed" (Wood & Quinn, 2003). Another strategy for resisting persuasion is to analyze ads to identify which attention-getting strategies are at work. Make a game of deciphering the advertisers' "code" instead of falling for the ad's appeal. In addition, raise your standards for the kinds of messages that are worthy of your attention and commitment.

Because conflict and violence stem partly from psychological processes, attempts to build peace cannot address only structural problems. Attempts to redistribute resources more equitably, to reduce oppression and victimization, and to increase social justice are essential, but they will succeed only if attention is also given to important psychological processes. Concerted efforts must be made to increase tolerance and improve intergroup relations while also developing new, nonviolent means for resolving conflicts (M. B. Brewer, 2008). The strategies of recategorization, controlled processing, and contact between groups have helped reduce ethnic conflict in some countries (David Smith, 1998). But cognitive changes must also be made: Societal beliefs must be changed, and new beliefs must be developed that are more consistent with conflict resolution and peaceful relationships. In addition, multidisciplinary techniques must be developed if programs are to be fully effective in addressing conflicts in different cultures. As one group of experts put it, "It is both risky and

Conflict among different ethnic groups has led to many years of violence in Africa.

ethnocentric to assume that methods developed in Western contexts can be applied directly in different cultures and contexts. Research on different cultural beliefs and practices and their implications for ethnopolitical conflict analysis and prevention is essential if the field of psychology is going to be successful in its contributions" (Mays et al., 1998, p. 739).

The Communication Model The second and third steps in persuasion—comprehending and then accepting the message—are influenced by both the message itself and the way in which it is presented. The *communication model* of persuasion spotlights four key elements to achieve these goals: the source, the message itself, the medium of communication, and characteristics of the audience.

The effectiveness of a persuasive message first depends on its *source,* the author or communicator who appeals to the audience to accept the message. Credibility makes a big difference, at least initially (Ito, 2002; Jain & Posavac, 2001), especially if we are not inclined to pay attention to the message (Petty & Cacioppo, 1986a). For example, we are more likely to change our attitude about the oil industry's antipollution efforts if we hear the information from an impartial commission appointed to study the situation than if the president of a major refining company tells us about them. However, over a period of time, the credibility of the source becomes less important. Apparently we are inclined to forget the source, while remembering the content. Not surprisingly, this is known as the *sleeper effect* (Kumkale & Albarracín, 2004).

In cases in which we have some interest in the message, the message itself plays the greater role in determining whether we change our attitudes (Petty & Cacioppo, 1986b). Researchers have discovered that we frequently tune out messages that simply contradict our own point of view. Thus, messages are generally more successful when they present both sides of an argument and when they present novel arguments, rather than when they rehash old standbys, heard many times before. Messages that create fear sometimes work well, too (Cochrane & Quester, 2005; Dillard & Anderson, 2004), for example in convincing people to stop smoking (Dahl, Frankenberger, & Manchanda, 2003; K. H. Smith & Stutts, 2003), or to drive safely (Shehryar & Hunt, 2005). However, research has shown that the persuasiveness of fearful ads is relatively short lived compared to the longer term influence of positive ads (Lewis, Watson, & White, 2008).

When it comes to choosing an effective *medium* of persuasion, written documentation is best suited to making people understand complex arguments, whereas videotapes or live presentations are more effective with an audience that already grasps the gist of an argument (Chaiken & Eagly, 1976). Most effective, however, are face-to-face appeals or the lessons of our own experience.

The most critical factors in changing attitudes—and the most difficult to control—have to do with the *audience.* Attitudes are most resistant to change if (1) the audience has

For an ad to affect our behavior, it must first attract our attention. This one also generates fear, which can sometimes be effective.

Source: Patrick Barta/Corbis RF.

a strong commitment to its present attitudes, (2) those attitudes are shared by others, and (3) the attitudes were instilled during early childhood by a pivotal group such as the family. The *discrepancy* between the content of the message and the present attitudes of the audience also affects how well the message will be received. Up to a point, the greater the difference between the two, the greater the likelihood of attitude change, as long as the person delivering the message is considered an expert on the topic. If the discrepancy is too great, however, the *audience* may reject the new information altogether, even though it comes from an expert.

Finally, certain personal characteristics make some people more susceptible to attitude change than others. People with low self-esteem are more easily influenced, especially when the message is complex and hard to understand. Highly intelligent people tend to resist persuasion because they can think of counterarguments more easily.

Cognitive Dissonance Theory One of the more fascinating approaches to understanding the process of attitude change is the theory of **cognitive dissonance,** developed by Leon Festinger (J. Cooper, Mirabile, & Scher, 2005; Festinger, 1957; B. J. Friedman, 2000). Cognitive dissonance exists whenever a person has two contradictory cognitions, or beliefs, at the same time. "I am a considerate and loyal friend" is one cognition; "Yesterday I repeated some juicy gossip I heard about my friend Chris" is another cognition. These two cognitions are dissonant—each one implies the opposite of the other. According to Festinger, cognitive dissonance creates unpleasant psychological tension, which motivates us to try to resolve the dissonance in some way. ◉

Sometimes changing one's attitude is the easiest way to reduce the discomfort of dissonance. I cannot easily change the fact that I have repeated gossip about a friend; therefore, it is easier to change my attitude toward my friend. If I conclude that Chris is not really a friend but simply an acquaintance, then my new attitude now fits my behavior—spreading gossip about someone who is *not* a friend does not contradict the fact that I am loyal and considerate to those who *are* my friends.

Discrepant behavior that contradicts an attitude does not necessarily bring about attitude change, however, because there are other ways a person can reduce cognitive dissonance. One alternative is to *increase the number of consonant elements*—that is, the thoughts that are consistent with one another. For example, I might recall the many times I defended Chris when others were critical of him. Now my repeating a little bit of gossip seems less at odds with my attitude toward Chris as a friend. Another option is to reduce the importance of one or both dissonant cognitions. For instance, I could tell myself, "The person I repeated the gossip to was Terry, who doesn't really know Chris very well. Terry doesn't care and won't repeat it. It was no big deal, and Chris shouldn't be upset about it." By reducing the significance of my disloyal action, I reduce the dissonance that I experience and so make it less necessary to change my attitude toward Chris.

But why would someone engage in behavior that goes against an attitude in the first place? One answer is that cognitive dissonance is a natural part of everyday life. Simply choosing between two or more desirable alternatives leads inevitably to dissonance. Suppose you are in the market for a computer, but can't decide between a PC and a Macintosh. If you choose one, all of its bad features and all the good aspects of the other contribute to dissonance. After you have bought one of the computers, you can reduce the dissonance by changing your attitude: You might decide that the other keyboard wasn't "quite right" and that some of the "bad" features of the computer you bought aren't so bad after all.

You may also engage in behavior at odds with an attitude because you are enticed to do so. Perhaps someone offers you a small bribe or reward: "I will pay you 25 cents just to try my product." Curiously, the larger the reward, the smaller the change in attitude that is likely to result (J. W. Brehm, 2007). When rewards are large, dissonance is at a minimum, and attitude change is small, if it happens at all.

cognitive dissonance Perceived inconsistency between two cognitions.

◉ **Watch** the **Video** Cognitive Dissonance: Need to Justify Our Actions on **MyPsychLab**

THINKING CRITICALLY ABOUT . . .

Attitudes Toward Smoking

Most adolescents and young adults are well aware of the dangers of smoking cigarettes. Nonetheless a significant number of those same people smoke regularly. Based on what you have read concerning attitude change, how would you go about changing people's attitudes toward smoking? For each technique you would use, explain why you think it would be effective. How would you demonstrate whether your program was having the desired effect?

Apparently, when people are convinced that there is a good reason to do something that goes against their beliefs ("I'll try almost anything in exchange for a large cash incentive"), they experience little dissonance, and their attitudes are not likely to shift, even though their behavior may change for a time. If the reward is small, however—just barely enough to induce behavior that conflicts with one's attitude—dissonance will be great, maximizing the chances of attitude change: "I only got 25 cents to try this product, so it couldn't have been the money that attracted me. I must really like this product after all." The trick is to induce the behavior that goes against an attitude, while leaving people feeling personally responsible for the dissonant act. In that way, they are more likely to change their attitudes than if they feel they were blatantly induced to act in a way that contradicted their beliefs.

✔•–Study and Review on MyPsychLab

CHECK YOUR UNDERSTANDING

1. A(n) _____ is a fairly stable organization of beliefs, feelings, and behavioral tendencies directed toward some object, such as a person or group.

2. Are the following statements true (T) or false (F)?
   a. _____ The best way to predict behavior is to measure attitudes.
   b. _____ Prejudice is the act of treating someone unfairly.
   c. _____ Messages are more persuasive when they present both sides of an argument.
   d. _____ A person who has two contradictory beliefs at the same time is likely to experience cognitive dissonance.

3. The message that most likely will result in a change in attitude is one with
   a. high fear from a highly credible source.
   b. high fear from a moderately credible source.
   c. moderate fear from a highly credible source.
   d. moderate fear from a moderately credible source.

Answers: 1. attitude. 2. a. (F), b. (F), c. (T), d. (T), 3. c.

APPLY YOUR UNDERSTANDING

1. You are asked to advise an elementary school on ways to reduce prejudice in an integrated third grade classroom. On the basis of what you have read, which of the following is most likely to be effective?
   a. Seating Black and White children alternately around the drawing table.
   b. Talking to the group regularly about the unfairness of prejudice and discrimination.
   c. Holding frequent competitions to see whether the Black students or the White students perform classroom work better.
   d. Assigning pairs consisting of one Black student and one White student to do interdependent parts of homework assignments.

2. Two people listen to a discussion on why our government should increase defense spending. John has never really thought much about the issue, while Jane has participated in marches and demonstrations against increased defense spending. Which person is LESS likely to change their attitude about defense spending?
   a. Jane
   b. John
   c. Both are equally likely to change their attitudes.

Answers: 1. d. 2. a.

SOCIAL INFLUENCE

What are some areas in which the power of social influence is highly apparent?

In social psychology, **social influence** refers to the process by which others—individually or collectively—affect our perceptions, attitudes, and actions. In the previous section, we examined one form of social influence: attitude change. Next, we'll focus on how the presence or actions of others can control behavior without regard to underlying attitudes.

social influence The process by which others individually or collectively affect one's perceptions, attitudes, and actions.

Cultural Influences

How does your culture influence how you dress or what you eat?

Culture exerts an enormous influence on our attitudes and behavior, and culture is itself a creation of people. As such, culture is a major form of social influence. Consider for a moment the many aspects of day-to-day living that are derived from culture:

1. **Culture dictates how you dress.** A Saudi woman covers her face before venturing outside her home; a North American woman freely displays her face, arms, and legs; and women in some other societies roam completely naked.
2. **Culture specifies what you eat—and what you do not eat.** Americans do not eat dog meat, the Chinese eat no cheese, and the Hindus refuse to eat beef. Culture further guides *how* you eat: with a fork, chopsticks, or your bare hands.
3. **People from different cultures seek different amounts of personal space.** Latin Americans, French people, and Arabs get closer to one another in most face-to-face interactions than do Americans, British, or Swedes.

To some extent, culture influences us through formal instruction. For example, your parents might have reminded you from time to time that certain actions are considered "normal" or the "right way" to behave. But more often, we learn cultural lessons through modeling and imitation. One result of such learning is the unquestioning acceptance of **cultural truisms**—beliefs or values that most members of a society accept as self-evident (Aronson, Wilson, & Akert, 2005; Maio & Olson, 1998). We are rewarded (reinforced) for doing as our companions and fellow citizens do in most situations—for going along with the crowd. This social learning process is one of the chief mechanisms by which a culture transmits its central lessons and values.

In the course of comparing and adapting our own behavior to that of others, we learn the norms of our culture. A **norm** is a culturally shared idea or expectation about how to behave. As in the preceding examples, norms are often steeped in tradition and strengthened by habit. Cultures seem strange to us if their norms are very different from our own. It is tempting to conclude that *different* means "wrong," simply because unfamiliar patterns of behavior can make us feel uncomfortable. To transcend our differences and get along better with people from other cultures, we must find ways to overcome such discomfort.

One technique for understanding other cultures is the *cultural assimilator*, a strategy for perceiving the norms and values of another group (Kempt, 2000). This technique teaches by example, asking students to explain why a member of another culture has behaved in a particular way. For example, why do the members of a Japanese grade school class silently follow their teacher single file through a park on a lovely spring day? Are they afraid of being punished for disorderly conduct if they do otherwise? Are they naturally placid and compliant? Once you understand that Japanese children are raised to value the needs and feelings of others over their own selfish concerns, their orderly, obedient behavior seems much less perplexing. Cultural assimilators encourage us to remain open-minded about others' norms and values by challenging such cultural truisms as "Our way is the right way."

Why do Japanese schoolchildren behave in such an orderly way? How does your answer compare with the discussion of cultural influences?

Conformity

What increases the likelihood that someone will conform?

Accepting cultural norms should not be confused with conformity. For instance, millions of Americans drink coffee in the morning, but not because they are conforming. They drink coffee because they like and desire it. **Conformity,** in contrast, implies a conflict between an individual and a group that is resolved when individual preferences or beliefs yield to the norms or expectations of the larger group.

Since the early 1950s, when Solomon Asch conducted the first systematic study of the subject, conformity has been a major topic of research in social psychology. Asch demonstrated in a series of experiments that under some circumstances, people will

cultural truisms Beliefs that most members of a society accept as self-evidently true.

norm A shared idea or expectation about how to behave.

conformity Voluntarily yielding to social norms, even at the expense of one's preferences.

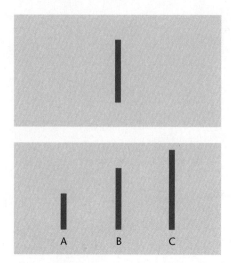

FIGURE 14–1

Asch's experiment on conformity.

In Asch's experiment on conformity, participants were shown a comparison card like the top one and asked to indicate which of the three lines on the bottom card was the most similar. Participants frequently chose the wrong line in order to conform to the group choice.

Watch the **Video** Conformity and Influence in Groups on **MyPsychLab**

conform to group pressures even if this action forces them to deny obvious physical evidence. He asked people to view cards with several lines of differing lengths, then asked them to choose the card with the line most similar to the line on a comparison card. (See **Figure 14–1.**) The lines were deliberately drawn so that the comparison was obvious and the correct choice was clear. All but one of the participants were confederates of the experimenter. On certain trials, these confederates deliberately gave the same wrong answer. This procedure put the lone dissenter on the spot: Should he conform to what he knew to be a wrong decision and agree with the group, thereby denying the evidence of his own eyes, or should he disagree with the group, thereby risking the social consequences of nonconformity?

Overall, participants conformed on about 35% of the trials. There were large individual differences, however; and in subsequent research, experimenters discovered that two sets of factors influence the likelihood that a person will conform: characteristics of the situation and characteristics of the person.

The *size* of the group is one situational factor that has been studied extensively (R. Bond, 2005). Asch (1951) found that the likelihood of conformity increased with group size until four confederates were present. After that point, the number of others made no difference to the frequency of conformity.

Another important situational factor is the degree of *unanimity* in the group. If just one confederate broke the perfect agreement of the majority by giving the correct answer, conformity among participants in the Asch experiments fell from an average of 35% to about 25% (Asch, 1956). Apparently, having just one "ally" eases the pressure to conform. The ally does not even have to share the person's viewpoint—just breaking the unanimity of the majority is enough to reduce conformity (Walther et al., 2002).

Personal characteristics also influence conforming behavior (Griskevicius, Goldstein, Mortensen, Cialdini, & Kenrick, 2006). The more a person is attracted to the group, expects to interact with its members in the future, holds a position of relatively low status, and does not feel completely accepted by the group, the more that person tends to conform. The fear of rejection apparently motivates conformity when a person scores high on one or more of these factors.

Using neuroimaging techniques, not available when Asch did his original work, social neuroscientists have provided some additional insight into the underlying processes involved in making or resisting the decision to conform. Using a mental rotation task in a context of peer pressure to conform to an incorrect judgment, researchers found that for participants that conformed, there were no changes in activity in areas of the brain (such as the prefrontal cortex) known to monitor conflict and plan decisions. However, for *non conformers*, who went against the group pressure to conform, regions of the brain known to be involved in emotional regulation (such as the amygdala) became increasingly active, suggesting nonconformity, or the willingness to stand alone, comes at an emotional cost (Berns et al., 2005).

ENDURING ISSUES

Individuality–Universality   Social Influence Across Cultures

In collectivist cultures, community and harmony are very important. Thus, you might suspect that members of collectivist cultures would conform more frequently to the will of a group than would members of noncollectivist cultures. In fact, psychologists have found that levels of conformity in collectivist cultures are frequently higher than those found by Asch (H. Jung, 2006). In collectivist societies as diverse as Fiji, Zaire, Hong Kong, Lebanon, Zimbabwe, Kuwait, Japan, and Brazil, conformity on tasks similar to those used by Asch ranged from 25% to 51% (P. B. Smith & Bond, 1994).

The fact that conformity in the Asch situation is relatively high across a variety of cultures suggests that there may be some kind of universal "conformity norm" that is strengthened or weakened by a specific cultural context. Further research is needed before we will know the answers to the questions, "What is universal about social influence?" and "What is culturally determined?" ■

Compliance

How could a salesperson increase a customer's compliance in buying a product?

Conformity is a response to pressure exerted by norms that are generally left unstated. In contrast, **compliance** is a change of behavior in response to an explicitly stated request. One technique for inducing compliance is the so-called *foot-in-the-door effect* (Rodafinos, Vucevic, & Sideridis, 2005). Every salesperson knows that the moment a prospect allows the sales pitch to begin, the chances of making a sale improve greatly. The same effect operates in other areas of life: Once people have granted a small request, they are more likely to comply with a larger one.

In the most famous study of this phenomenon, Freedman and Fraser (1966) approached certain residents of Palo Alto, California, posing as members of a committee for safe driving. They asked residents to place a large, ugly sign reading "Drive Carefully" in their front yards. Only 17% agreed to do so. Then other residents were asked to sign a petition calling for more safe-driving laws. When these same people were later asked to place the ugly "Drive Carefully" sign in their yards, an amazing 55% agreed. Compliance with the first small request more than tripled the rate of compliance with the larger request.

Why does the foot-in-the-door technique work so well? One possible explanation is that agreeing to the token act (signing the petition) realigns the person's self-perception with that of someone who more strongly favors the cause. When presented with the larger request, the person then feels obligated to comply (Cialdini & Trost, 1998).

Another strategy commonly used by salespeople is the *lowball procedure* (Cialdini & Trost, 1998; Guéguen, Pascual, & Dagot, 2002). The first step is to induce a person to agree to do something for a comparatively low cost. The second step is to raise the cost of compliance. Among car dealers, lowballing works like this: The dealer persuades the customer to buy a car by reducing the price well below that offered by competitors. Once the customer has agreed to buy the car, the terms of the sale shift so that, in the end, the car is more costly than it would be at other dealerships. Although the original inducement was the low price (the "lowball" that the salesperson originally pitched), once committed, buyers tend to remain committed to the now pricier car.

Under certain circumstances, a person who has refused to comply with one request may be more likely to comply with a second. This phenomenon has been dubbed the *door-in-the-face effect* (Ebster & Neumayr, 2008; Rodafinos, Vucevic, & Sideridis, 2005). In one study, researchers approached students and asked them to make an unreasonably large commitment: Would they counsel delinquent youths at a detention center for 2 years? Nearly everyone declined, thus effectively "slamming the door" in the researcher's face. But when later asked to make a much smaller commitment—supervising children during a trip to the zoo—many of the same students quickly agreed. The door-in-the-face effect appears to work because people interpret the smaller request as a concession and feel pressured to comply.

Obedience

How does the "power of the situation" affect obedience?

Compliance is agreement to change behavior in response to a request. **Obedience** is compliance with a direct order, generally from a person in authority, such as a police officer, principal, or parent. Several of the studies by Stanley Milgram mentioned in Chapter 1, "The Science of Psychology," showed how far some people will go to obey someone in authority (Blass, 2009; Milgram, 1963; Zimbardo, 2007).

What factors influence the degree to which people will do what they are told? Studies in which people were asked to put a dime in a parking meter by people wearing uniforms show that one important factor is the amount of power vested in the person giving the orders. People obeyed a guard whose uniform looked like that of a police officer more often than they obeyed a man dressed either as a milkman or as a civilian. Another factor is surveillance. If we are ordered to do something and then left alone, we are less likely to obey than if we are being watched, especially if the act seems unethical to us. Milgram, for

compliance Change of behavior in response to an explicit request from another person or group.

obedience Change of behavior in response to a command from another person, typically an authority figure.

Nazi concentration camps are a shocking example of the extremes to which people will go to obey orders. How do you explain the behaviors of the people who ran these camps?

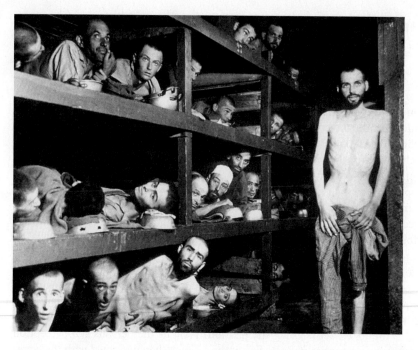

The willingness of prison guards to obey the commands of authority, even when doing so may have violated their own principles, contributed to the abuses that took place at Abu Ghraib Prison during the Iraq War.

✓●─Study and Review on MyPsychLab

instance, found that his "teachers" were less willing to give severe shocks when the experimenter was out of the room.

Milgram's experiments revealed other factors that influence a person's willingness to follow orders. When the victim was in the same room as the "teacher," obedience dropped sharply. When another "teacher" was present, who refused to give shocks, obedience also dropped. But when responsibility for an act was shared, so that the person was only one of many doing it, the degree of obedience was much greater.

Why do people willingly obey an authority figure, even if doing so means violating their own principles? Milgram (1974) suggested that people come to see themselves as the agents of *another* person's wishes and therefore as not responsible for the obedient actions or their consequences. Once this shift in self-perception has occurred, obedience follows, because in their own minds, they have relinquished control of their actions. For example, you may recall that in the aftermath of the Abu Ghraib prison scandal, the enlisted personnel who were photographed abusing prisoners insisted that they did so only on orders from higher authorities.

On a brighter note, some recent studies indicate that the high levels of obedience reported in Milgram's original experiment have declined in recent years. In fact, among males, disobedience has more than doubled since Milgram's original article was published in 1963 (Twenge, 2009). The reasons for this decline, and whether it will continue, remain to be determined.

CHECK YOUR UNDERSTANDING

1. A _____ is a shared idea or expectation about how to behave.
2. Many people are more likely to comply with a smaller request after they have refused a larger one. This is called the _____ effect.
3. Are the following statements true (T) or false (F)?
   a. _____ Research shows that compliance is often higher in collectivist cultures than in noncollectivist ones.
   b. _____ Many people are willing to obey an authority figure, even if doing so means violating their own principles.
   c. _____ Solomon Asch found that people were much more likely to conform in groups of four or more people.
   d. _____ A person is more likely to conform to the group when the group's task is ambiguous or difficult than when it is easy and clear.

Answers: 1. norm. 2. door-in-the-face. 3. a. (T), b. (T), c. (F), d. (T).

1. You answer the telephone and hear the caller say, "Good morning. My name is _____ and I'm calling on behalf of XYZ. How are you today?" Right away you know this caller is using which of the following social influence techniques?

   a. the lowball technique

   b. the assimilator technique

   c. the foot-in-the-door technique

   d. the door-in-the-face technique

2. You would like to say something in class. You raise your hand and wait to be recognized, even though the teacher has not told you to do so. This is an example of

   a. compliance.

   b. conformity.

   c. obedience.

Answers: 1. c. 2. b.

SOCIAL ACTION

Do we behave differently when other people are present?

The various kinds of social influence we have just discussed may take place even when no one else is physically present. We refrain from playing music at full volume when our neighbors are sleeping, comply with jury notices received in the mail, and obey traffic signals even when no one is on the road to enforce them. We now turn to processes that *do* depend on the presence of others. Specifically, we examine processes that occur when people interact one-on-one and in groups. One of these social actions is called *deindividuation*.

Deindividuation

What negative outcomes can result from deindividuation?

We have seen several cases of social influence in which people act differently in the presence of others from the way they would if they were alone. The most striking and frightening instance of this phenomenon is *mob behavior*. Some well-known violent examples of mob behavior are the looting that sometimes accompanies urban rioting and the wanton destruction of property that mars otherwise peaceful protests and demonstrations. One reason for mob behavior is that people can lose their personal sense of responsibility in a group, especially in a group subjected to intense pressures and anxiety. This process

- Explain how deindividuation and the snowball effect can contribute to mob behavior.

- Explain the role of the following factors in influencing helping behavior: altruism, the bystander effect, the ambiguity of the situation, and the personal characteristics of bystanders.

- Describe the process of polarization in group discussion. Identify the factors that affect whether a group is likely to be more or less effective than individuals acting alone.

- Compare and contrast the following theories of leadership: the great-person theory, the right-place-at-the-right-time theory, and contingency theory.

- Briefly summarize cultural and gender differences in leadership.

After natural disasters like the 2010 earthquake in Haiti, strangers often reach out to help each other with physical and financial support.

deindividuation A loss of personal sense of responsibility in a group.

altruistic behavior Helping behavior that is not linked to personal gain.

bystander effect The tendency for an individual's helpfulness in an emergency to decrease as the number of passive bystanders increases.

is called **deindividuation,** because people respond not as individuals, but as anonymous parts of a larger group. In general, the more anonymous that people feel in a group, the less responsible that they feel as individuals (Aronson, Wilson, & Akert, 2005; Zimbardo, 2007). But deindividuation only partly explains mob behavior. Another contributing factor is that, in a group, one dominant and persuasive person can convince people to act through a *snowball effect*: If the persuader convinces just a few people, those few will convince others, who will convince still others, and the group becomes an unthinking mob. Returning to the chapter opening vignette, if Sher Singh had not been in police custody, it is possible that the bystanders who shouted "Let's kill him!" could have had their way.

Helping Behavior

What factors make us more inclined to help a person in need?

Research on deindividuation seems to support the unfortunate—and inaccurate—notion that when people get together, they are likely to become more destructive and irresponsible than they would be individually. But instances of cooperation and mutual assistance are just as abundant as examples of human conflict and hostility. We need only to recall the behavior of people all over the United States in the aftermath of the September 11, 2001, terrorist attacks on the World Trade Center and the Pentagon to find hundreds of examples of people working together and helping each other.

What are some of the social forces that can promote helping behavior? One is perceived self-interest. We may offer our boss a ride home from the office because we know that our next promotion depends on how much she likes us. We may volunteer to feed a neighbor's cat while he is away because we want him to do the same for us. But when helpful actions are not linked to such personal gain, they are considered **altruistic behavior** (Batson, 2011). A person who acts in an altruistic way does not expect any recognition or reward in return, except perhaps the good feeling that comes from helping someone in need. For example, many altruistic acts are directed toward strangers in the form of anonymous charitable donations, as is often demonstrated in the aftermath of a natural disaster. Interestingly, altruism probably played an important role in the early evolution of humans (Marshall, 2011). Moreover, altruism is not unique to humans since it is frequently observed in other primates (de Waal, 2007).

Under what conditions is helping behavior most likely to occur? Like other things that social psychologists study, helping is influenced by two sets of factors: those in the situation and those in the individual.

The most important situational variable is the *presence of other people*. In a phenomenon called the **bystander effect,** the likelihood that a person will help someone else in trouble *decreases* as the number of bystanders present increases (Chekroun & Brauer, 2002; A. M. Rosenthal, 2008). In one experiment, people filling out a questionnaire heard a taped "emergency" in the next room, complete with a crash and screams. Of those who were alone, 70% offered help to the unseen victim, but of those who waited with a companion—a stranger who did nothing to help—only 7% offered help (Latané & Rodin, 1969). However, the bystander effect is attenuated when a situation is *clearly* perceived as dangerous (P. Fischer et al., 2011), which may not have been the case in the experiment described above.

THINKING CRITICALLY ABOUT . . .

Helping Someone in Distress

On August 18, 1999, 24-year-old Kevin Heisinger was on his way home to Illinois from the University of Michigan. In the bathroom of a bus station, he was attacked and beaten to death. Several people were within earshot and heard his cries for help, but none of them helped him or called the police. One person saw him lying on the floor in a pool of blood, but he did nothing. Another person saw him struggling to breathe, but he also walked away. Eventually, a 12-year-old boy called for help. The police arrived in less than 20 seconds, but it was too late to save Kevin's life.

- What factors might have contributed to the unwillingness of people to help Kevin during and after the beating?

- One commentator writing for *The Detroit News* said, "Have our souls been this coarsened, this deadened, by the daily barrage of real and imaginary violence? Or have some of us become like a couple of the contestants on that summer television hit, *Survivor*, so consumed with winning our own pot of gold that we really don't care how we treat others?" (DeRamus, 2000). To what extent do you think the failure of bystanders to help was due to personal characteristics?

- Do your answers to the questions above shed light on the question of why a 12-year-old was the only person to call for help?

In fact, any factors that make it harder for others to recognize a genuine emergency reduce the probability of altruistic actions (Jex, Adams, & Bachrach, 2003). Increasing the amount of personal responsibility that one person feels for another boosts the likelihood that help will be extended (Moriarty, 1975; Ting & Piliavin, 2000). The amount of *empathy* that we feel toward another person also affects our willingness to help (Batson, 2006; Batson, Ahmad, Lishner, & Tsang, 2002). *Mood* also makes a difference: A person in a good mood is more likely to help another in need than is someone who is in a neutral or bad mood (Aronson, Wilson, & Akert, 2005; Salovey, Mayer, & Rosenhan, 1991). In addition, helping behavior is more likely to come from people who are not shy or fear negative evaluation for helping (Karakashian, Walter, Christopher, & Lucas, 2006). Finally, just witnessing another person performing a selfless act or good deed can stimulate altruism in an observer (Schnall, Roper, & Fessler, 2010). 👁

Groups and Decision Making

How is making a decision in a group different from making a decision on your own?

There is a tendency in American society to turn important decisions over to groups. In the business world, key decisions are often made around a conference table rather than behind one person's desk. In politics, major policy decisions are seldom vested in just one person. In the courts, a defendant may request a trial by jury, and for some serious crimes, jury trial is required by law. The nine-member U.S. Supreme Court renders group decisions on legal issues affecting the entire nation.

Many people trust these group decisions more than decisions made by individuals. Yet, the dynamics of social interaction within groups sometimes conspire to make group decisions *less* sound than those made by someone acting alone. Social psychologists are intrigued by how this outcome happens.

Polarization in Group Decision Making People often assume that an individual acting alone is more likely to take risks than a group considering the same issue. This assumption remained unchallenged until the early 1960s. At that time, James Stoner (1961) designed an experiment to test the idea. He asked participants individually to counsel imaginary people who had to choose between a risky, but potentially rewarding course of action and a conservative, but less rewarding alternative. Next, the participants met in small groups to discuss each decision until they reached unanimous agreement. Surprisingly, the groups consistently recommended a riskier course of action than the people working alone did. This phenomenon is known as the **risky shift.**

The risky shift is simply one aspect of a more general group phenomenon called **polarization**—the tendency for people to become more extreme in their attitudes as a result of group discussion. Polarization begins when group members discover during discussion that they share views to a greater degree than they realized. Then, in an effort to be seen in a positive light by the others, at least some group members become strong advocates for what is potentially the dominant sentiment in the group. Arguments leaning toward one extreme or the other not only reassure people that their initial attitudes are correct, but they also intensify those attitudes so that the group as a whole becomes more extreme in its position (J. H. Liu & Latane, 1998). So, if you want a group decision to be made in a cautious, conservative direction, you should be certain that the members of the group hold cautious and conservative views in the first place. Otherwise, the group decision may polarize in the opposite direction (Jerry Palmer & Loveland, 2008).

The Effectiveness of Groups "Two heads are better than one" reflects the common assumption that members of a group will pool their abilities and arrive at a better decision than will individuals working alone. In fact, groups are more effective than individuals only under certain circumstances. For one thing, their success depends on the task they face. If the requirements of the task match the skills of the group members, the group is likely to be more effective than any single individual. However, even if task and personnel

risky shift Greater willingness of a group than an individual to take substantial risks.

polarization Shift in attitudes by members of a group toward more extreme positions than the ones held before group discussion.

👁—Watch the **Video** Prosocial Behavior on **MyPsychLab**

Groups can make decisions and perform tasks very effectively under the right conditions.

groupthink A process that occurs when the members of a group like one another, have similar goals and are isolated, leading them to ignore alternatives and not criticize group consensus.

great-person theory The theory that leadership is a result of personal qualities and traits that qualify one to lead others.

are perfectly matched, the ways in which group members *interact* may reduce the group's efficiency. For example, high-status individuals tend to exert more influence in groups, so if they do not possess the best problem-solving skills, group decisions may suffer (Lovaglia, Mannix, Samuelson, Sell, & Wilson, 2005). Another factor affecting group interaction and effectiveness is group size. The larger the group, the more likely it is to include someone who has the skills needed to solve a difficult problem. On the other hand, it is much harder to coordinate the activities of a large group. In addition, large groups may be more likely to encourage *social loafing,* the tendency of group members to exert less individual effort on the assumption that others in the group will do the work (J. A. Miller, 2002). Finally, the quality of group decision making also depends on the *cohesiveness* of a group. When the people in a group like one another and feel committed to the goals of the group, cohesiveness is high. Under these conditions, members may work hard for the group, spurred by high morale. But cohesiveness can undermine the quality of group decision making. If the group succumbs to **groupthink,** according to Irving Janis (1982, 1989), strong pressure to conform prevents its members from criticizing the emerging group consensus (Henningsen, Henningsen, & Eden, 2006). This is especially likely to happen if a cohesive group is isolated from outside opinion and does not have clear rules defining how to make decisions. The result may be disastrous decisions—such as the Bay of Pigs invasion in Cuba, the ill-fated *Columbia* and *Challenger* space flights, and more recently the decision to invade Iraq in 2004 based on the presumed existence of weapons of mass destruction (Raven, 1998; U.S. Senate, 2004; Vaughn, 1996).

Leadership

What makes a great leader?

Leaders are important to the effectiveness of a group or organization (Kaiser, Hogan, & Craig, 2008). But what makes a good leader? For many years, the predominant answer was the **great-person theory,** which states that leaders are extraordinary people who assume positions of influence and then shape events around them. In this view, people like George Washington, Winston Churchill, and Nelson Mandela were "born leaders"—who would have led any nation at any time in history.

Most historians and psychologists now regard this theory as naive, because it ignores social and economic factors. An alternative theory holds that leadership emerges when the right person is in the right place at the right time. For instance, in the late 1950s and early 1960s, Dr. Martin Luther King, Jr., rose to lead the civil rights movement. Dr. King was clearly a "great person"—intelligent, dynamic, eloquent, and highly motivated. Yet, had the times not been right (for instance, had he lived 30 years earlier), it is doubtful that he would have been as successful as he was.

Many social scientists have argued that there is more to leadership than either the great-person theory or the right-place-at-the-right-time theory implies. Rather, the leader's traits, certain aspects of the situation in which the group finds itself, and the response of the group and the leader to each other are all important considerations (Brodbeck, 2008). Fred Fiedler's *contingency theory* of leader effectiveness is based on such a transactional view of leadership (F. E. Fiedler, 1993, 2002).

According to Fiedler's theory, personal characteristics are important to the success of a leader. One kind of

One theory of leadership holds that the particularly effective leader is the right person in the right place at the right time. For the American civil rights movement, Martin Luther King, Jr., was such a leader.

leader is *task oriented,* concerned with doing the task well—even at the expense of worsening relationships among group members. Other leaders are *relationship oriented,* concerned with maintaining group cohesiveness and harmony. Which style is most effective depends on three sets of situational factors. One is the nature of the task (whether it is clearly structured or ambiguous). The second consideration is the relationship between leader and group (whether the leader has good or bad personal relations with the group members). The third consideration is the leader's ability to exercise great or little power over the group.

The contingency view of leadership, which has received a great deal of support from research conducted in the laboratory as well as in real-life settings, clearly indicates that there is no such thing as an ideal leader for all situations (Ayman, Chemers, & Fiedler, 2007; DeYoung, 2005). "Except perhaps for the unusual case," Fiedler states, "it is simply not meaningful to speak of an effective or of an ineffective leader; we can only speak of a leader who tends to be effective in one situation and ineffective in another" (F. E. Fiedler, 1967, p. 261). We discuss contingency theories of leadership in greater detail in Appendix B, "Psychology Applied to Work."

Recently, Robert J. Sternberg has proposed a systems approach to understanding leadership (Sternberg, 2008; Sternberg, Jarvin, & Grigorenko, 2009). Known as WICS, Sternberg's theory of effective leadership stresses certain essential traits necessary for effective leadership: *wisdom, intelligence,* and *creativity,* synthesized. According to Sternberg, creativity is necessary to devise new ideas, intelligence to evaluate and implement ideas, and wisdom to balance the interests of everyone involved (Sternberg, 2007). Sternberg stresses that efforts to train new leaders should focus on ways to produce individuals who embody these traits and learn effective ways to synthesize them. Though promising, WICS is a relatively new approach to understanding leadership, which has not yet been fully exposed to the scrutiny of empirical research. Only future research will enable psychologists to evaluate the usefulness of this new theory of leadership.

Leadership Across Cultures   An emphasis on the importance of individual leaders seems to apply well to most informal and work groups in the United States. Yet, it is not the only approach to leadership. In a collectivist culture that values cooperation and interdependence among group members, although one member may be named "the manager," it is less likely that individuals will have clearly defined roles as "this type of leader" or "that type of leader." All members see themselves as working together to accomplish the group's goals.

Interestingly, leadership in American businesses has shifted somewhat over the past two decades toward a management style that has proven successful in Japan and other Eastern collectivist cultures (Dean & Evans, 1994; McFarland, Senn, & Childress, 1993; Muczyk & Holt, 2008). This approach emphasizes decision-making input from all group members, small work teams that promote close cooperation, and a leadership style in which managers receive much the same treatment as any other employee. In the West, it is not uncommon for executives to have their own parking spaces, dining facilities, and fitness and social clubs, as well as separate offices and independent schedules. Most Japanese executives consider this privileged style of management very strange. In many Eastern cultures, managers and executives share the same facilities as their workers, hunt for parking spaces like everyone else, and eat and work side by side with their employees. It is interesting that the Japanese model has effectively combined the two leadership approaches—task oriented and relationship oriented—into a single overall style. By being a part of the group, the leader can simultaneously work toward and direct the group's goals, while also contributing to the group's morale and social climate.

Recognition of the diverse styles that effective leadership can take across cultures, ethnicities, gender, and even sexual orientation was the focus of a recent special issue of *The American Psychologist* (Chin, 2010). Perhaps the most important point expressed by the many experts who contributed to this issue is the idea that future leaders must begin to embrace diverse leadership styles and diversity among leaders, if they are to remain competitive in a global workforce that is becoming increasingly diverse.

APPLYING PSYCHOLOGY

Conserving the Environment

This chapter is chock full of information about ways to enlist the support of others in addressing sustainability. Consider the following as examples:

- **Social norms.** We have seen that people look to others to determine what is appropriate behavior. If someone's friends, relatives, and neighbors are engaged in efforts to manage climate change, it is likely that person will also become engaged. In fact, simply informing someone that others around them are taking action can be effective (Biel & Thøgersen, 2007).
- **The process of persuasion.** "For some, ignorance can be a barrier to action in two general ways: not knowing that a problem exists and not knowing what to do once one becomes aware of the problem" (Gifford, 2011, p. 291). In attempting to reduce ignorance, the credibility of the source of information is important, at least initially. However, there is considerable research evidence that people in general distrust scientists and government (Gifford, 2011). Thus, at least initially it is desirable to cite trustworthy experts. Messages that present both sides of the argument or that present novel arguments are likely to be more successful than one-sided messages that simply repeat the "same old, same old." However, there is a relatively low correlation between knowledge about environmental problems and pro-environmental behaviors (Bamberg & Moser, 2007; Kazdin, 2009). It is more effective when it "is linked to a commitment to act, draws on social networks, and focuses on simple, low-cost behaviors" (Kazdin, 2009, p. 346).

- **Social influence.** Once people have granted a small request, they are more likely to comply with a larger one (you should recognize that as the *foot-in-the-door effect*). Asking someone to sign a petition is one way to increase the likelihood that the person will subsequently comply with a larger request. Conversely, asking someone to make an unreasonably large commitment (which they are likely to decline) can increase the likelihood that they will comply with a much smaller commitment (the *door-in-the-face effect*).

There are many other possibilities that grow out of what we know about social psychology. A recent special issue of the *American Psychologist* is also an excellent source of ideas (Swim et al., 2011).

Women in Leadership Positions Just as leadership styles differ across cultures, research has shown that the leadership styles of men and women can also vary considerably. In one 5-year study of 2,482 managers in more than 400 organizations, female and male coworkers said that women make better managers than men (Kass, 1999). The reason seems to be that many female managers have effectively combined such traditionally "masculine" task-oriented traits as decisiveness, planning, and setting standards with such "feminine" relationship-oriented assets as communication, feedback, and empowering other employees; most male managers have not been as successful at combining those two styles (Chin, 2008; Eagly, 2003). For example, one review concluded that, in contrast to the directive and task-oriented leadership style common among men, women tend to have a more democratic, collaborative, and interpersonally oriented style of managing employees (V. E. O'Leary & Flanagan, 2001). Moreover, at least one study found that regardless of gender, leaders are viewed more favorably and considered more competent and efficient when they adopt a traditionally feminine leadership style (Cuadrado, Morales, Recio, & Howard, 2008).

A large-scale review of 45 studies of gender and leadership found women's leadership styles are generally more effective than traditional male leadership styles (Eagly, Johannesen-Schmidt, & van-Engen, 2003). This review also found that female leaders are generally more effective than male leaders at winning acceptance for their ideas and instilling self-confidence in their employees. Results like these have prompted some experts to call for specialized women-only leadership training programs, to assist women in developing their full feminine leadership potential independent of male influence (Vinnicombe & Singh, 2003).

KEY TERMS

CHAPTER REVIEW ((•[Listen to the **Chapter Audio** on **MyPsychLab**

Social psychology is the scientific study of the ways in which the thoughts, feelings, and behaviors of one individual are influenced by the real, imagined, or inferred behavior of other people. **Social neuroscience** involves the application of brain imaging and other neuroscience methods to social psychology.

SOCIAL COGNITION

What do forming impressions, explaining others' behavior, and experiencing interpersonal attraction have in common? Forming impressions, explaining others' behavior, and experiencing interpersonal attraction are all examples of **social cognition,** the process of taking in and assessing information about other people. It is one way in which we are influenced by others' thoughts, feelings, and behaviors.

How do we form first impressions of people? When forming impressions of others, we rely on *schemata,* or sets of expectations and beliefs about categories of people. Impressions are also affected by the order in which information is acquired. First impressions are the strongest (the **primacy effect**), probably because we prefer not to subsequently expend more cognitive effort to analyze or change them. This same preference also encourages us to form impressions by using simplistic, but strongly held schemata called **stereotypes.** First impressions can also bring about the behavior we expect from other people, a process known as **self-fulfilling prophecy.**

How do we decide why people act as they do? Attribution theory holds that people seek to understand human behavior by attributing it either to internal or external causes. Perceptual biases can lead to the **fundamental attribution error,** in which we overemphasize others' personal traits in attributing causes to their behavior. **Defensive attribution** motivates us to explain our own actions in ways that protect our self-esteem. Self-serving bias refers to our tendency to attribute our successes to internal factors and our failures to external ones. The **just-world hypothesis** may lead us to blame the victim when bad things happen to other people.

Do "birds of a feather flock together" or do "opposites attract"? People who are similar in attitudes, interests, backgrounds, and values tend to like one another. **Proximity** also promotes liking. The more we are in contact with certain people, the more we tend to like them. Most people also tend to like physically attractive people, as well as attributing to them, correctly or not, many positive personal characteristics.

ATTITUDES

Why are attitudes important? An **attitude** is a relatively stable organization of beliefs, feelings, and tendencies toward an *attitude object.* Attitudes are important because they often influence behavior.

What are the three major components of attitudes? The three major components of attitudes are (1) evaluative beliefs about the attitude object, (2) feelings about that object, and (3) behavioral tendencies toward it. These three components are very often (but not always) consistent with one another.

How does a person develop a prejudice toward someone else? Prejudice is an unfair negative attitude directed toward a group and its members, whereas **discrimination** is unfair behavior based on prejudice. One explanation of prejudice is the **frustration–aggression theory,** which states that people who feel exploited and oppressed displace their hostility toward the powerful onto *scapegoats*—people who are "lower" on the social scale than they are. Another theory links prejudice to the **authoritarian personality,** a rigidly conventional and bigoted type marked by exaggerated respect for authority and hostility toward those who defy society's norms. A third theory proposes a cognitive source of prejudice—oversimplified or stereotyped thinking about categories of people.

Finally, conformity to the prejudices of one's social group can help to explain prejudice. Three strategies for reducing prejudice appear to be especially promising: recategorization (expanding our schema of a particular group), controlled processing (training ourselves to be mindful of people who differ from us), and improving contact between groups.

What factors encourage someone to change an attitude? Attitudes may be changed when new actions, beliefs, or perceptions contradict preexisting attitudes, called **cognitive dissonance.** Attitudes can also change in response to efforts at persuasion. The first step in persuasion is to get the audience's attention. Then the task is to get the audience to comprehend and accept the message. According to the *communication model,* persuasion is a function of the source, the message itself, the medium of communication, and the characteristics of the audience. The most effective means of changing attitudes—especially important attitudes, behaviors, or lifestyle choices—may be *self-persuasion.*

SOCIAL INFLUENCE

What are some areas in which the power of social influence is highly apparent? **Social influence** is the process by which people's perceptions, attitudes, and actions are affected by others' behavior and characteristics. The power of social influence is especially apparent in the study of cultural influences and of conformity, compliance, and obedience.

How does your culture influence how you dress or what you eat? The culture in which you are immersed has an enormous influence on your thoughts and actions. Culture dictates differences in diet, dress, and personal space. One result of this is the unquestioning acceptance of **cultural truisms**—beliefs or values that most members of a society accept as self-evident. Eating pizza, shunning rattlesnake meat, dressing in jeans instead of a loincloth, and feeling uncomfortable when others stand very close to you when they speak are all results of culture. As we adapt our behavior to that of others, we learn the **norms** of our culture, as well as its beliefs and values.

What increases the likelihood that someone will conform? Voluntarily yielding one's preferences, beliefs, or judgments to those of a larger group is called **conformity.** Research by Solomon Asch and others has shown that characteristics of both the situation and the person influence the likelihood of conforming. Cultural influences on the tendency to conform also exist, with people in collectivist cultures often being more prone to conformity than those in noncollectivist ones.

How could a salesperson increase a customer's compliance in buying a product? **Compliance** is a change in behavior in response to someone's explicit request. One technique to encourage compliance is the *foot-in-the-door approach,* or getting people to go along with a small request to make them more likely to comply with a larger one. Another technique is the *lowball procedure:* initially offering a low price to win commitment, and then gradually escalating the cost. Also effective is the *door-in-the-face tactic,* or initially making an unreasonable request that is bound to be turned down but will perhaps generate enough guilt to foster compliance with another request.

How does the "power of the situation" affect obedience? Classic research by Stanley Milgram showed that many people were willing to obey orders to administer harmful shocks to other people. This **obedience** to an authority figure was more likely when certain situational factors were present. For example, people found it harder to disobey when the authority figure issuing the order was nearby. They were also more likely to obey the command when the person being given the shock was some distance from them. According to Milgram, obedience is brought on by the constraints of the situation.

SOCIAL ACTION

Do we behave differently when other people are present? Conformity, compliance, and obedience may take place even when no one else is physically present, but other processes of social influence depend on the presence of others.

What negative outcomes can result from deindividuation? Immersion in a large, anonymous group may lead to **deindividuation,** the loss of a sense of personal responsibility for one's actions. Deindividuation can sometimes lead to violence or other forms of irresponsible behavior. The greater the sense of anonymity, the more this effect occurs.

What factors make us more inclined to help a person in need? Helping someone in need without expectation of a reward is called **altruistic behavior.** Altruism is influenced by situational factors such as the presence of other people. According to the **bystander effect,** a person is less apt to offer assistance when other potential helpers are present. Conversely, being the only person to spot someone in trouble tends to encourage helping. Also encouraging helping are an unambiguous emergency situation and certain personal characteristics, such as empathy for the victim and being in a good mood.

How is making a decision in a group different from making a decision on your own? Research on the **risky shift** and the broader phenomenon of group **polarization** shows that group decision making actually increases tendencies toward extreme solutions, encouraging members to lean toward either greater risk or greater caution. People deliberating in groups may also display *social loafing,* or a tendency to exert less effort on the assumption that others will do most of the work. And in very cohesive groups and isolated groups, there is a tendency toward **groupthink,** an unwillingness to criticize the emerging group consensus even when it seems misguided.

What makes a great leader? According to the **great-person theory,** leadership is a function of personal traits that qualify one to lead others. An alternative theory attributes leadership to being in the right place at the right time. According to the transactional view, traits of the leader and traits of the group interact with certain aspects of the situation to determine what kind of leader will come to the fore. Fred Fiedler's *contingency theory* focused on two contrasting leadership styles: task oriented and relationship oriented. The effectiveness of each style depends on the nature of the task, the relationship of the leader with group members, and the leader's power over the group.

The task-oriented leadership style typical of American businesses is being transformed through the introduction of a management style that emphasizes small work teams and input from all members of the group. Recent research indicates that women in leadership positions tend to have a more democratic, collaborative, and interpersonally oriented style of managing employees than do men in similar positions.

Appendix A

Measurement and Statistical Methods

Most of the experiments described in this book involve measuring one or more variables and then analyzing the data statistically. The design and scoring of all the tests we have discussed are also based on statistical methods. **Statistics** is a branch of mathematics that provides techniques for sorting out quantitative facts and ways of drawing conclusions from them. Statistics let us organize and describe data quickly, guide the conclusions we draw, and help us make inferences.

Statistical analysis is essential to conducting an experiment or designing a test, but statistics can only handle numbers—groups of them. To use statistics, the psychologist first must measure things—count and express them in quantities.

SCALES OF MEASUREMENT

No matter what we are measuring—height, noise, intelligence, attitudes—we have to use a scale. The data we want to collect determine the scale we will use and, in turn, the scale we use helps determine the conclusions we can draw from our data.

Nominal Scales A **nominal scale** is a set of arbitrarily named or numbered categories. If we decide to classify a group of people by the color of their eyes, we are using a nominal scale. We can count how many people have blue, green, or brown eyes, and so on, but we cannot say that one group has more or less eye color than the other. The colors are simply different. Since a nominal scale is more of a way of classifying than of measuring, it is the least informative kind of scale. If we want to compare our data more precisely, we will have to use a scale that tells us more.

statistics A branch of mathematics that psychologists use to organize and analyze data.

nominal scale A set of categories for classifying objects.

486

Ordinal Scales If we list horses in the order in which they finish a race, we are using an ordinal scale. On an **ordinal scale,** data are ranked from first to last according to some criterion. An ordinal scale tells the order, but nothing about the distances between what is ranked first and second or ninth and tenth. It does not tell us how much faster the winning horse ran than the horses that placed or showed. If a person ranks her preferences for various kinds of soup—pea soup first, then tomato, then onion, and so on—we know which soup she likes most and which soup she likes least, but we have no idea how much better she likes tomato than onion, or if pea soup is far more favored than either one of them.

Since we do not know the distances between the items ranked on an ordinal scale, we cannot add or subtract ordinal data. If mathematical operations are necessary, we need a still more informative scale.

Interval Scales An **interval scale** is often compared to a ruler that has been broken off at the bottom—it only goes from, say, 5½ to 12. The intervals between 6 and 7, 7 and 8, 8 and 9, and so forth are equal, but there is no zero. A Fahrenheit or centigrade thermometer is an interval scale—even though a certain degree registered on such a thermometer specifies a certain state of cold or heat, there is no such thing as the absence of temperature. One day is never twice as hot as another; it is only so many equal degrees hotter.

An interval scale tells us how many equal-size units one thing lies above or below another thing of the same kind, but it does not tell us how many times bigger, smaller, taller, or fatter one thing is than another. An intelligence test cannot tell us that one person is three times as intelligent as another, only that he or she scored so many points above or below someone else.

Ratio Scales We can only say that a measurement is two times as long as another or three times as high when we use a **ratio scale,** one that has a true zero. For instance, if we measure the snowfall in a certain area over several winters, we can say that six times as much snow fell during the winter in which we measured a total of 12 feet as during a winter in which only 2 feet fell. This scale has a zero—there can be no snow.

MEASUREMENTS OF CENTRAL TENDENCY

Usually, when we measure a number of instances of anything—from the popularity of TV shows to the weights of 8-year-old boys to the number of times a person's optic nerve fires in response to electrical stimulation—we get a distribution of measurements that range from smallest to largest or lowest to highest. The measurements will usually cluster around some value near the middle. This value is the **central tendency** of the distribution of the measurements.

Suppose, for example, you want to keep 10 children busy tossing rings around a bottle. You give them three rings to toss each turn, the game has six rounds, and each player scores one point every time he or she gets the ring around the neck of the bottle. The highest possible score is 18. The distribution of scores might end up like this: 11, 8, 13, 6, 12, 10, 16, 9, 12, 3.

What could you quickly say about the ring-tossing talent of the group? First, you could arrange the scores from lowest to highest: 3, 6, 8, 9, 10, 11, 12, 12, 13, and 16. In this order, the central tendency of the distribution of scores becomes clear. Many of the scores cluster around the values between 8 and 12. There are three ways to describe the central tendency of a distribution. We usually refer to all three as the *average.*

ordinal scale Scale indicating order or relative position of items according to some criterion.

interval scale Scale with equal distances between the points or values, but without a true zero.

ratio scale Scale with equal distances between the points or values and with a true zero.

central tendency Tendency of scores to congregate around some middle value.

mean Arithmetical average calculated by dividing a sum of values by the total number of cases.

median Point that divides a set of scores in half.

mode Point at which the largest number of scores occurs.

frequency distribution A count of the number of scores that fall within each of a series of intervals.

The arithmetical average is called the **mean**—the sum of all the scores in the group divided by the number of scores. If you add up all the scores and divide by 10, the total number of scores in this group of ring tossers, you find that the mean for the group is 10.

The **median** is the point that divides a distribution in half—50% of the scores fall above the median, and 50% fall below. In the ring-tossing scores, five scores fall at 10 or below, five at 11 or above. The median is thus halfway between 10 and 11, which is 10.5.

The point at which the largest number of scores occurs is called the **mode.** In our example, the mode is 12. More people scored 12 than any other.

Differences Among the Mean, Median, and Mode

If we take many measurements of anything, we are likely to get a distribution of scores in which the mean, median, and mode are all about the same—the score that occurs most often (the mode) will also be the point that half the scores are below and half above (the median). And the same point will be the arithmetical average (the mean). This is not always true, however, and small samples rarely come out so symmetrically. In these cases, we often have to decide which of the three measures of central tendency—the mean, the median, or mode—will tell us what we want to know.

For example, a shopkeeper wants to know the general incomes of passersby so he can stock the right merchandise. He might conduct a rough survey by standing outside his store for a few days from 12:00 to 2:00 and asking every tenth person who walks by to check a card showing the general range of his or her income. Suppose most of the people checked the ranges between $25,000 and $60,000 a year. However, a couple of the people made a lot of money—one checked $100,000–$150,000 and the other checked the $250,000-or-above box. The mean for the set of income figures would be pushed higher by those two large figures and would not really tell the shopkeeper what he wants to know about his potential customers. In this case, he would be wiser to use the median or the mode.

Suppose instead of meeting two people whose incomes were so great, he noticed that people from two distinct income groups walked by his store—several people checked the box for $25,000–$35,000, and several others checked $50,000–$60,000. The shopkeeper would find that his distribution was bimodal. It has two modes—$30,000 and $55,000. This might be more useful to him than the mean, which could lead him to think his customers were a unit with an average income of about $40,000.

Another way of approaching a set of scores is to arrange them into a **frequency distribution**—that is, to select a set of intervals and count how many scores fall into each interval. A frequency distribution is useful for large groups of numbers; it puts the number of individual scores into more manageable groups.

Suppose a psychologist tests memory. She asks 50 college students to learn 18 nonsense syllables, then records how many syllables each student can recall two hours later. She arranges her raw scores from lowest to highest in a rank distribution:

2	6	8	10	11	14
3	7	9	10	12	14
4	7	9	10	12	15
4	7	9	10	12	16
5	7	9	10	13	17
5	7	9	11	13	
6	8	9	11	13	
6	8	9	11	13	
6	8	10	11	13	

The scores range from 2 to 17, but 50 individual scores are too cumbersome to work with. So she chooses a set of two-point intervals and tallies the number of scores in each interval:

frequency histogram Type of bar graph that shows frequency distributions.

frequency polygon Type of line graph that shows frequency distributions.

Interval	Tally	Frequency
1–2	|	1
3–4	|||	3
5–6	卌 |	6
7–8	卌 ||||	9
9–10	卌 卌 |||	13
11–12	卌 |||	8
13–14	卌 ||	7
15–16	||	2
17–18	|	1

Now she can tell at a glance what the results of her experiment were. Most of the students had scores near the middle of the range, and very few had scores in the high or low intervals. She can see these results even better if she uses the frequency distribution to construct a bar graph—a **frequency histogram.** Marking the intervals along the horizontal axis and the frequencies along the vertical axis would give her the graph shown in **Figure A–1.** Another way is to construct a **frequency polygon,** a line graph. A frequency polygon drawn from the same set of data is shown in **Figure A–2.** Note that the figure is not a smooth curve, since the points are connected by straight lines. With many scores, however, and with small intervals, the angles would smooth out, and the figure would resemble a rounded curve.

THE NORMAL CURVE

Ordinarily, if we take enough measurements of almost anything, we get a *normal distribution.* Tossing coins is a favorite example of statisticians. If you tossed 10 coins into the air 1,000 times and recorded the heads and tails on each toss, your tabulations would reveal a normal distribution. Five heads and five tails would be the most frequent, followed by four heads/six tails and six heads/six tails, and so on down to the rare all heads or all tails.

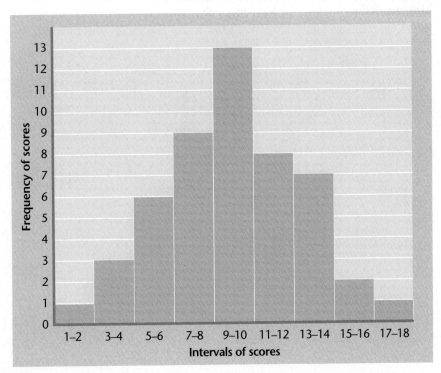

FIGURE A–1

A frequency histogram for a memory experiment.

The bars indicate the frequency of scores within each interval.

FIGURE A–2
A frequency polygon drawn from data used in Figure A–1.

The dots, representing the frequency of scores in each interval, are connected by straight lines.

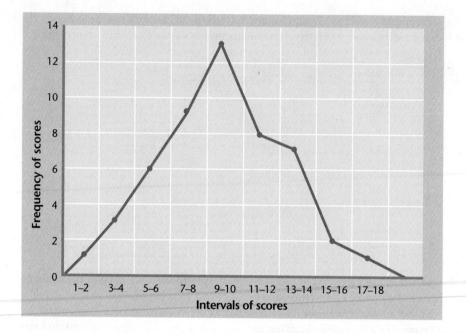

FIGURE A–2
A frequency polygon drawn from data used in Figure A–1.

The dots, representing the frequency of scores in each interval, are connected by straight lines.

normal curve Hypothetical bell-shaped distribution curve that occurs when a normal distribution is plotted as a frequency polygon.

Plotting a normal distribution on a graph yields a particular kind of frequency polygon called a **normal curve. Figure A–3** shows data on the heights of 1,000 men. Superimposed over the bars that reflect the actual data is an "ideal" normal curve for the same data. Note that the curve is absolutely symmetrical—the left slope parallels the right slope exactly. Moreover, the mean, median, and mode all fall on the highest point on the curve.

The normal curve is a hypothetical entity. No set of real measurements shows such a smooth gradation from one interval to the next, or so purely symmetrical a shape. But because so many things do approximate the normal curve so closely, the curve is a useful model for much that we measure.

Skewed Distributions

If a frequency distribution is asymmetrical—if most of the scores are gathered at either the high end or the low end—the frequency polygon will be skewed. The hump will sit to one side or the other, and one of the curve's tails will be disproportionately long.

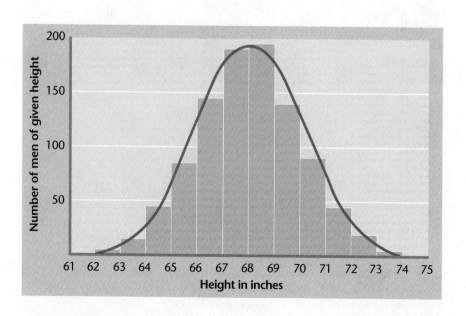

FIGURE A–3
A normal curve.

This curve is based on measurements of the heights of 1,000 adult males.

If a high school mathematics instructor, for example, gives her students a sixth-grade arithmetic test, we would expect nearly all the scores to be quite high. The frequency polygon would probably look like the one in **Figure A–4**. But if a sixth-grade class were asked to do advanced algebra, the scores would probably be quite low. The frequency polygon would be very similar to the one shown in **Figure A–5**.

Note, too, that the mean, median, and mode fall at different points in a skewed distribution, unlike in the normal curve, where they coincide. Usually, if you know that the mean is greater than the median of a distribution, you can predict that the frequency polygon will be skewed to the right. If the median is greater than the mean, the curve will be skewed to the left.

Bimodal Distributions

We have already mentioned a bimodal distribution in our description of the shopkeeper's survey of his customers' incomes. The frequency polygon for a bimodal distribution has two humps—one for each mode. The mean and the median may be the same (**Figure A–6**) or different (**Figure A–7**).

Measures of Variation

Sometimes it is not enough to know the distribution of a set of data and what their mean, median, and mode are. Suppose an automotive safety expert feels that too much damage occurs in tail-end accidents because automobile bumpers are not all the same height. It is not enough to know what the average height of an automobile bumper is. The safety expert also wants to know about the variation in bumper heights: How much higher is the highest bumper than the mean? How do bumpers of all cars vary from the mean? Are the latest bumpers closer to the same height?

Range

The simplest measure of variation is the **range**—the difference between the largest and smallest measurements. Perhaps the safety expert measured the bumpers of 1,000 cars 2 years ago and found that the highest bumper was 18 inches from the ground, the lowest only 12 inches from the ground. The range was thus 6 inches—18 minus 12. This year the highest bumper is still 18 inches high, the lowest still 12 inches from the ground. The range is still 6 inches. Moreover, our safety expert finds that the means of the two distributions are the same—15 inches off the ground. But look at the two frequency polygons in **Figure A–8**—there is still something the expert needs to know, since the measurements cluster around the mean in drastically different ways. To find out how the measurements are distributed around the mean, our safety expert has to turn to a slightly more complicated measure of variation—the standard deviation.

The Standard Deviation

The **standard deviation,** in a single number, tells us much about how the scores in any frequency distribution are dispersed around the mean. Calculating the standard deviation is one of the most useful and widely employed statistical tools.

To find the standard deviation of a set of scores, we first find the mean. Then we take the first score in the distribution, subtract it from the mean, square the difference, and jot it down in a column to be added up later. We do the same for all the scores in the distribution. Then we add up the column of squared differences, divide the total by the number of scores in the distribution, and find the square root of that number. **Figure A–9** shows the calculation of the standard deviation for a small distribution of scores.

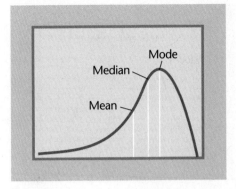

FIGURE A–4
Distribution skewed left.

Most of the scores are gathered at the high end of the distribution, causing the hump to shift to the right. Since the tail on the left is longer, we say that the curve is skewed to the left. Note that the *mean, median,* and *mode* are different.

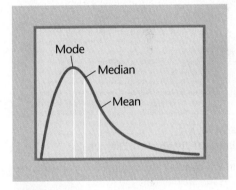

FIGURE A–5
Distribution skewed right.

In this distribution, most of the scores are gathered at the low end, so the curve is skewed to the right. The *mean, median,* and *mode* do not coincide.

range Difference between the largest and smallest measurements in a distribution.

standard deviation Statistical measure of variability in a group of scores or other values.

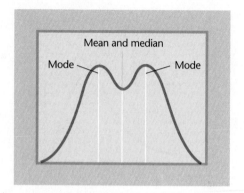

FIGURE A–6
Bimodal distribution: Example 1.

A bimodal distribution in which the *mean* and the *median* are the same.

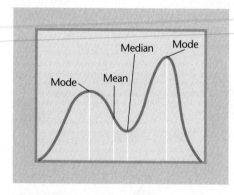

FIGURE A–7
Bimodal distribution: Example 2.

In this bimodal distribution, the *mean* and the *median* are different.

scatter plot Diagram showing the association between scores on two variables.

FIGURE A–8
Frequency polygons for two sets of measurements of automobile bumper heights.

Both are normal curves, and in each distribution the *mean, median,* and *mode* are 15. But the variation from the mean is different, causing one curve to be flattened and the other to be much more sharply peaked.

In a normal distribution, however peaked or flattened the curve, about 68% of the scores fall between one standard deviation above the mean and one standard deviation below the mean (see **Figure A–10**). Another 27% fall between one standard deviation and two standard deviations on either side of the mean, and 4% more between the second and third standard deviations on either side. Overall, then, more than 99% of the scores fall between three standard deviations above and three standard deviations below the mean. This makes the standard deviation useful for comparing two different normal distributions.

Now let us see what the standard deviation can tell our automotive safety expert about the variations from the mean in the two sets of data. The standard deviation for the cars measured 2 years ago is about 1.4. A car with a bumper height of 16.4 is one standard deviation above the mean of 15; one with a bumper height of 13.6 is one standard deviation below the mean. Since the engineer knows that the data fall into a normal distribution, he can figure that about 68% of the 1,000 cars he measured will fall somewhere between these two heights: 680 cars will have bumpers between 13.6 and 16.4 inches high. For the more recent set of data, the standard deviation is just slightly less than 1. A car with a bumper height of about 14 inches is one standard deviation below the mean; a car with a bumper height of about 16 is one standard deviation above the mean. Thus, in this distribution, 680 cars have bumpers between 14 and 16 inches high. This tells the safety expert that car bumpers are becoming more similar, although the range of heights is still the same (6 inches), and the mean height of bumpers is still 15.

MEASURES OF CORRELATION

Measures of central tendency and measures of variation can be used to describe a single set of measurements—like the children's ring-tossing scores—or to compare two or more sets of measurements—like the two sets of bumper heights. Sometimes, however, we need to know if two sets of measurements are in any way associated with each other—if they are correlated. Is parental IQ related to children's IQ? Does the need for achievement relate to the need for power? Is watching violence on TV related to aggressive behavior?

One fast way to determine whether two variables are correlated is to draw a **scatter plot.** We assign one variable (X) to the horizontal axis of a graph and the other variable (Y) to the vertical axis. Then we plot a person's score on one characteristic along the horizontal axis and his or her score on the second characteristic along the vertical axis. Where the two scores intersect, we draw a dot. When several scores have been plotted in this way, the pattern of dots tells whether the two characteristics are in any way correlated with each other.

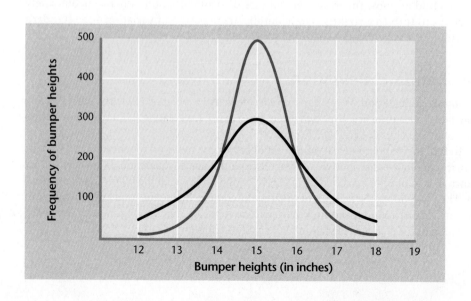

Number of scores = 10		Mean = 7
Scores	Difference from mean	Difference squared
4	$7 - 4 = 3$	$3^2 = 9$
5	$7 - 5 = 2$	$2^2 = 4$
6	$7 - 6 = 1$	$1^2 = 1$
6	$7 - 6 = 1$	$1^2 = 1$
7	$7 - 7 = 0$	$0^2 = 0$
7	$7 - 7 = 0$	$0^2 = 0$
8	$7 - 8 = -1$	$-1^2 = 1$
8	$7 - 8 = -1$	$-1^2 = 1$
9	$7 - 9 = -2$	$-2^2 = 4$
10	$7 - 10 = -3$	$-3^2 = 9$

Sum of squares = 30

Number of scores = 10
Variance = 3
Standard deviation = $\sqrt{3}$ = 1.73

FIGURE A–9
Standard deviation.

Step-by-step calculation of the *standard deviation* for a group of 10 scores with a mean of 7.

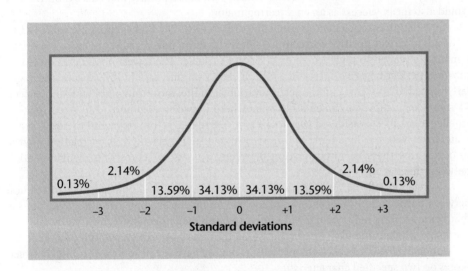

FIGURE A–10
Normal curve.

A normal curve, divided to show the percentage of scores that fall within each *standard deviation* from the *mean*.

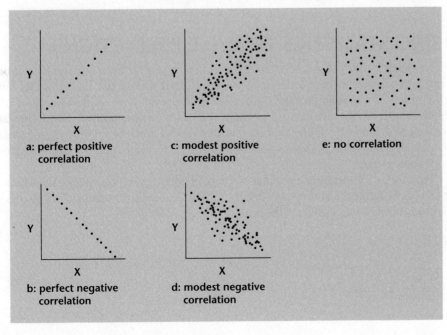

FIGURE A–11
Scatter plots and correlations.

Scatter plots provide a picture of the strength and direction of a correlation.

If the dots on a scatter plot form a straight line running between the lower-left-hand corner and the upper-right-hand corner, as they do in **Figure A–11a,** we have a perfect positive correlation—a high score on one of the characteristics is always associated with a high score on the other one. A straight line running between the upper-left-hand corner and the lower-right-hand corner, as in **Figure A–11b,** is the sign of a perfect negative correlation—a high score on one of the characteristics is always associated with a low score on the other one. If the pattern formed by the dots is cigar shaped in either of these directions, as in **Figures A–11c** and **d,** we have a modest correlation—the two characteristics are related but not highly correlated. If the dots spread out over the whole graph, forming a circle or a random pattern, as they do in **Figure A–11e,** there is no correlation between the two characteristics.

A scatter plot can give us a general idea if a correlation exists and how strong it is. To describe the relation between two variables more precisely, we need a **correlation coefficient**—a statistical measure of the degree to which two variables are associated. The correlation coefficient tells us the degree of association between two sets of matched scores—that is, to what extent high or low scores on one variable tend to be associated with high or low scores on another variable. It also provides an estimate of how well we can predict from a person's score on one characteristic how high he or she will score on another characteristic. If we know, for example, that a test of mechanical ability is highly correlated with success in engineering courses, we could predict that success on the test would also mean success as an engineering major.

Correlation coefficients can run from +1.0 to –1.0. The highest possible value (+1.0) indicates a perfect positive correlation—high scores on one variable are always and systematically related to high scores on a second variable. The lowest possible value (–1.0) means a perfect negative correlation—high scores on one variable are always and regularly related to low scores on the second variable. In life, most things are far from perfect, so most correlation coefficients fall somewhere between +1.0 and –1.0. A correlation smaller than .20 is considered very low, from ±20 to ±40 is low, from ±40 to ±60 is moderate, from ±60 to ±80 is high, and from ±80 to ±1.0 is very high. A correlation of zero indicates that there is no correlation between two sets of scores—no regular relation between them at all.

Correlation tells us nothing about causality. If we found a high positive correlation between participation in elections and income levels, for example, we still could not say that being wealthy made people vote or that voting made people wealthy. We would still not know which came first, or whether some third variable explained both income levels and voting behavior. Correlation only tells us that we have found some association between scores on two specified characteristics.

USING STATISTICS TO MAKE PREDICTIONS

Behind the use of statistics is the hope that we can generalize from our results and use them to predict behavior. We hope, for example, that we can use the record of how well a group of rats runs through a maze today to predict how another group of rats will do tomorrow, that we can use a person's scores on a sales aptitude test to predict how well he or she will sell life insurance, or that we can measure the attitudes of a relatively small group of people about pollution control to indicate what the attitudes of the whole country are.

First, we have to determine whether our measurements are representative and whether we can have confidence in them. In Chapter 1, "The Science of Psychology," we discussed this problem when we considered the problem of proper sampling.

correlation coefficient Statistical measure of the strength of association between two variables.

Probability

Errors based on inadequate sampling procedures are somebody's fault. Other kinds of errors occur randomly. In the simplest kind of experiment, a psychologist will gather a representative sample, split it randomly into two groups, and then apply some experimental manipulation to one of the groups. Afterward, the psychologist will measure both groups and determine whether the experimental group's score is now different from the score of the control group. But even if there is a large difference between the scores of the two groups, it may still be wrong to attribute the difference to the manipulation. Random effects might influence the results and introduce error.

Statistics give the psychologist many ways to determine precisely whether the difference between the two groups is really significant, whether something other than chance produced the results, and whether the same results would be obtained with different subjects. These probabilities are expressed as measures of **significance.** If the psychologist computes the significance level for the results as .05, he or she knows that there are 19 chances out of 20 that the results are not due to chance. But there is still 1 chance in 20—or a .05 likelihood—that the results are due to chance. A .01 significance level would mean that there is only 1 chance in 100 that the results are due to chance.

USING META-ANALYSIS IN PSYCHOLOGICAL RESEARCH

In several places in this text, we have presented findings from reviews of psychological research in which a research team has summarized a wide selection of literature on a topic in order to reach some conclusions on that topic. There are several crucial decisions to be made in such a process: Which research reports should be included? How should the information be summarized? What questions might be answered after all the available information is gathered?

Traditionally, psychologists reviewing the literature in a particular area relied on the *box-score method* to reach conclusions. That is, after collecting all the relevant research reports, the researcher simply counted the number supporting one conclusion or the other, much like keeping track of the scoring in nine innings of a baseball game (hence, the term *box score*). For example, if there were 200 studies of gender differences in aggressive behavior, researchers might find that 120 of them showed that males were more aggressive than females, 40 showed the opposite pattern, and 40 showed no evidence of gender differences. On the basis of these box scores, the reviewer might conclude that males are more likely than females to act aggressively.

Today researchers tend to rely on a more sophisticated strategy known as **meta-analysis.** Meta-analysis provides a way of statistically combining the results of individual research studies to reach an overall conclusion. In a single experiment, each participant contributes data to help the researcher reach a conclusion. In a meta-analysis, each published study contributes data to help the reviewer reach a conclusion, as **Figure A–12** illustrates. Rather than relying on the raw data of individual participants, meta-analysis treats the results of entire studies as its raw data. Meta-analysts begin by collecting all available research reports that are relevant to the question at hand. Next, they statistically transform these results into a common scale for comparison. That way differences in sample size (one study might have used 50 participants, another 500), in the magnitude of an effect (one study might have found a small difference, another a more substantial one), and in experimental procedures (which might vary from study to study) can be examined using the same methods.

significance Probability that results obtained were due to chance.

meta-analysis A statistical procedure for combining the results of several studies so the strength, consistency, and direction of the effect can be estimated.

Meta-Analysis.

Meta-analysis enables researchers to combine the results of individual studies to reach an overall conclusion.

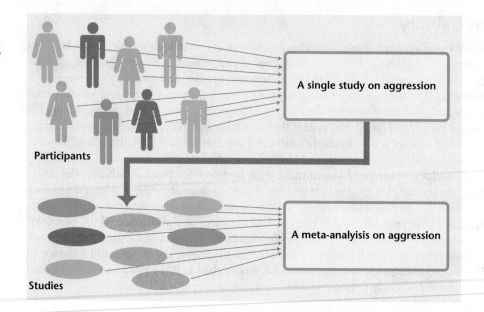

The key element in this process is its statistical basis. Rather than keeping a tally of "yeas" and "nays," meta-analysis allows the reviewer to determine both the strength and the consistency of a research conclusion. For example, instead of simply concluding that there were more studies that found a particular gender difference, the reviewer might determine that the genders differ by 6/10 of a percentage point, or that across all the studies the findings are highly variable.

Meta-analysis has proved to be a valuable tool for psychologists interested in reaching conclusions about a particular research topic. By systematically examining patterns of evidence across individual studies whose conclusions vary, psychologists are able to gain a clearer understanding of the findings and their implications.

Appendix B

Psychology Applied to Work

The field of study that emphasizes the application of psychological principles and theories to work settings is known as **industrial/organizational (I/O) psychology,** in which researchers study how individuals and organizations work and how psychological principles can be applied to improve effectiveness.

The focus of I/O psychology is twofold. Professionals working in the subfield of **industrial psychology** are concerned with effectively managing the *human resources* in organizations. Organizations rely on workers; and the quality and quantity of work that can be done depends heavily on the training, knowledge, and productivity of the workforce. Industrial psychologists identify the knowledge, skills, abilities, and other traits that are required to perform various jobs.

The subfield of **organizational psychology,** by contrast, focuses more broadly on factors pertaining to the organization as a whole. For example, organizational psychologists study the ways in which different organizational systems and structures affect worker productivity and morale.

MATCHING PEOPLE TO JOBS

Organizational productivity increases when jobs fit workers' abilities and interests. To determine which people should be assigned to specific jobs, one must first understand the requirements of each job. This is usually accomplished by performing a **job analysis.**

Job Analysis

Job analysis usually involves collecting data about the behaviors performed by workers while doing the job; the physical, mechanical, social, and informational characteristics of the work environment; and the necessary human attributes for job performance (R. J. Harvey, 1991).

There are several methods for conducting a job analysis. **Functional job analysis** identifies the ways in which workers must manipulate *things,* the ways in which they need to respond to and analyze *data,* and the ways in which they must relate to other *people* (Gatewood & Field, 1998). Functional job analysis, thus, emphasizes the tasks that are required by the job.

An alternative method for analyzing jobs, the **KSAO system of job analysis,** focuses on the human characteristics required to successfully perform the job (R. J. Harvey, 1991).

industrial/organizational (I/O) psychology The study of how individuals and organizations work and how psychological principles can be used to improve organizational effectiveness.

industrial psychology Subfield of industrial/ organizational psychology concerned with effectively managing human resources.

organizational psychology Subfield of industrial/organizational psychology that focuses on the organization as a whole, rather than on the individuals who work within it.

job analysis Identifying the various tasks required by a job and the human qualifications that are required to perform that job.

functional job analysis A method for identifying the procedures and processes that workers must use in the performance of the job.

KSAO system of job analysis A method for identifying the knowledge, skills, abilities, and other human characteristics that are required for the job.

personnel selection The process of selecting from a pool of job applicants those who will be hired to perform a job.

These are most often classified into four categories: knowledge (K), skills (S), abilities (A), and other characteristics (O) such as emotional stability or conscientiousness.

Job analysis lays the foundation for many other business functions: recruiting, hiring, training, and evaluating job performance. Accurate job analysis is so important to the success of organizations that many large companies spend millions of dollars each year simply analyzing jobs (E. L. Levine, Sistrunk, McNutt, & Gael, 1988). Since the purpose of job analysis is to provide both the company and the worker with an understanding of expected duties or responsibilities and required employee qualifications, it serves as the starting point for understanding how to match employees to the job—the organizational function referred to as **personnel selection.**

Predictors of Job Performance

Personnel selection specialists use a number of methods to identify people who are likely to be successful at a particular job. (See **Table B–1.**)

Employment Interviews One of the most frequently used and widely varying selection techniques is the employment interview. Selection interviews vary widely in the content of the specific questions that are asked and in the framework in which the interview is conducted. Interview techniques may have either a structured or unstructured (open-ended) format.

In a *structured job interview,* all job applicants are asked the same questions, usually in a fixed order by the same individual or team of interviewers. The chosen questions, which are usually derived from the job analysis, pertain directly to the applicant's ability to perform the tasks of the job. The applicant's responses usually are scored, often numerically, using a consistent scoring scheme. In contrast, an *unstructured job interview* typically has no fixed format and the questions asked may vary widely from person to person. Furthermore, there usually is no specified method of scoring applicants' responses. Most often an overall rating or ranking is assigned to each applicant based on the interviewer's subjective impression and judgment.

TABLE B–1   Predictive Validity of Commonly Used Selection Methods[a]

Selection Method	Predictive Validity Coefficient (Correlation Between Selection Method Scores and Job Performance)
Structured interview	.51
Unstructured interview	.38
Cognitive (general mental) ability	.51
Conscientiousness	.31
Reference checks	.26
Years of education	.10
Interests	.10
Job knowledge tests	.48
Work-sample tests	.54
Assessment centers	.37
Graphology (handwriting analysis)	.02
Age	−.01

[a]The numbers in this column are correlation coefficients (see Appendix A). The higher the number, the stronger the relationship between predicted job performance and subsequent job performance by those hired.

Source: Adapted from Frank L. Schmidt and John E. Hunter (1998). The validity and utility of selection methods in personnel psychology: Practical and theoretical implications of 85 years of research findings. *Psychological Bulletin, 124,* 262–274.

Compared to scores from unstructured interviews, scores from structured interviews are more highly correlated with measures of subsequent job performance. (See **Table B–1.**) In other words, structured interviews have higher *criterion-related validity*, sometimes called *predictive validity* (see Chapter 7, "Cognition and Mental Abilities," for a discussion of validity).

Whether structured or unstructured, employment interviews also provide an opportunity to talk about the nature of the job. By giving applicants a realistic picture of the demands of a job, employers can help them determine whether the job will be a good match to their expectations.

Employment Tests Interviews are time consuming and relatively expensive. When there are many more applicants than can be hired, organizations often rely on objective, paper-and-pencil tests to screen applicants. This reduces the possibility of bias in favor of applicants whom managers personally like or who are similar to them (T. L. Stanley, 2004).

Industrial psychologists use a wide variety of employment tests. Some measure cognitive abilities, while others measure personality characteristics. Research has shown that both types of tests are excellent predictors of job performance (Barrick & Mount, 1991; Ree, Earles, & Teachout, 1994; F. L. Schmidt & Hunter, 1998). However, tests of cognitive abilities have the highest overall predictive validity and the lowest cost (F. L. Schmidt & Hunter, 2004). Tests of cognitive ability, for the most part, measure general intelligence or general mental ability (see Chapter 7, "Cognition and Mental Abilities"). As one I/O psychologist put it, "If we could know only one attribute of a job candidate upon which to base a prediction, we would want an assessment of intelligence" (Muchinsky, 2006, p. 103).

Unlike tests of general mental ability, which have correct and incorrect answers, objective tests of personality generally include self-descriptive statements about personal preferences ("I would rather go to a baseball game than read a book") and typical behaviors ("I am able to set clear goals and work effectively to achieve them"). In recent years, most I/O researchers have used the *Five Factor Model* of personality to explore the relationship between personality and job performance. (See Chapter 10, "Personality," for a discussion of personality tests and of the Five Factor model.) Of the five major personality traits, conscientiousness is tied most closely to job performance. **Conscientiousness** refers to a person's ability to finish projects that are started, to attend to detail without becoming absorbed by it, and to care enough about the quality of work that it is not compromised by inattention or lack of effort. Although the other four major personality traits (emotional stability, agreeableness, openness to experience, and extraversion) may be related to job performance in some settings (J. Hogan & Holland, 2003), conscientiousness is a valid predictor of job performance in all jobs (Barrick & Mount, 1991; Barrick, Mount, & Judge, 2001; W. S. Dunn, Mount, & Barrick, 1995). Furthermore, conscientiousness is not significantly correlated with general mental ability. Therefore, using both a test of general mental ability and a test of conscientiousness typically results in a better, more accurate prediction of future job performance than is possible from either test alone (F. L. Schmidt & Hunter, 2004).

Other employment tests, known as **integrity tests,** predict negative or counterproductive behavior. These tests include questions that measure three of the five factors linked to counterproductive behavior: *conscientiousness, agreeableness,* and *emotional stability* (F. L. Schmidt & Hunter, 2004). By identifying applicants who score low on these three dimensions, integrity tests can help employers screen out potentially difficult employees before they are hired.

Measures of Previous Performance One of the long-standing dictums in psychology is this: *The best predictor of future performance is past performance.* In other words, high performers in previous positions will most likely perform at a high level in future positions as well. Thus, personnel selection specialists often pay particular attention to job applicants' previous work histories. One method of accomplishing this is by requiring each applicant to provide a prior job history as well as general personal information (such as name, phone number, and so forth). Applications are the most frequently used method of selection (Schultz & Schultz, 1998).

conscientiousness A person's ability to finish projects that are started, to attend to detail without becoming absorbed by it, and to care enough about the quality of work that it is not compromised by inattention or lack of effort.

integrity tests Paper-and-pencil tests that predict the likelihood that a job applicant will engage in counterproductive behavior in the workplace.

Personnel selection specialists also check references to assess an applicant's previous job performance. Job applicants can be required to provide contact data for their former work supervisors. However, many employers are reluctant to comment on the quality of a previous employee's work, since any negative information preventing the employee from securing a new job could result in a costly lawsuit (Fishman, 2005).

Finally, job applicants can be asked to demonstrate content knowledge of the sought-after job or to actually perform relevant skills. The predictive validity of job knowledge and work sample tests is very high, although they are only useful if applicants have had similar roles in the past.

Assessment Centers High-level management positions call for skills that are difficult to evaluate using traditional selection methods (Jansen & Stoop, 2001). In these cases, several applicants may be put into a simulated and highly structured group setting, or **assessment center.** The typical assessment center evaluation lasts two days, involves several group exercises and the administration of a variety of ability and personality tests, and includes a lengthy, detailed, structured interview (Gaugler, Rosenthal, Thornton, & Bentson, 1987). Assessment centers are reasonably good at predicting the long-term performance of individuals in upper management.

Is it possible to use just a few selection methods with good results? Industrial psychologists conclude that the most effective combination generally includes a test of general mental ability along with either a structured interview or a test of conscientiousness (F. L. Schmidt & Hunter, 2004).

MEASURING PERFORMANCE ON THE JOB

Evaluating employee job performance is important for organizations, which depend on high levels of performance to maximize productivity and profitability. But effective performance evaluation also improves the quality of organizational decisions, including pay raises, promotions, and terminations. It helps employees understand how well they are doing their jobs; and can encourage worker loyalty toward the organization (K. R. Murphy & Cleveland, 1995). Finally, formal performance appraisals also can provide a legally defensible rationale for terminating an employee.

Formal methods of evaluating performance, called **performance appraisal systems,** aim to provide an unbiased assessment of the quantity and quality of work contributed by individuals. There are several methods of performance appraisal, each appropriate for different kinds of work.

When productivity can be measured directly, an **objective performance appraisal** is usually used. *Objective* methods are based on *quantitative* measurement, such as counting the number of goods produced, the number of pieces assembled, or the dollars of product sold. However, most jobs do not involve work that can be measured objectively. For example, teachers, managers, nurses, and many other employees do important work that cannot be "counted." For these types of jobs, *subjective* measures of performance must be used. **Subjective performance appraisal** methods rely on *judgments* about the *quality* of an employee's work. Subjective methods are used extensively throughout all types of organizations.

One of the greatest challenges in creating a fair, unbiased performance appraisal system is to identify exactly what is expected of workers. Carefully written job analysis-based descriptions help personnel psychologists identify important tasks. They serve as a good starting point for the development of a performance evaluation system that is clear and relatively free from error.

Generally speaking, evaluations based on *behaviors,* rather than on attitudes or intentions, are less prone to error. Behaviors are observable; therefore, evaluators need to rely less on subjective judgments. One commonly used performance appraisal method is the **behaviorally anchored ratings scale (BARS).** A BARS system first identifies specific behaviors that are associated with high performance, average performance, and substandard

assessment center Method used to select high-level managers that places applicants in a simulated and highly structured group setting where they are given personnel tests and extensive interviews, and they engage in various role-playing activities.

performance appraisal systems Formal methods used to assess the quantity and quality of work contributed by each individual within an organization.

objective performance appraisal Method of performance appraisal based on quantitative measurement of the amount of work done.

subjective performance appraisal Performance appraisal that relies on judgments about the quality of an employee's work.

behaviorally anchored ratings scale (BARS) Performance appraisal that matches employee behavior to specific behaviors associated with high, average, and poor performance.

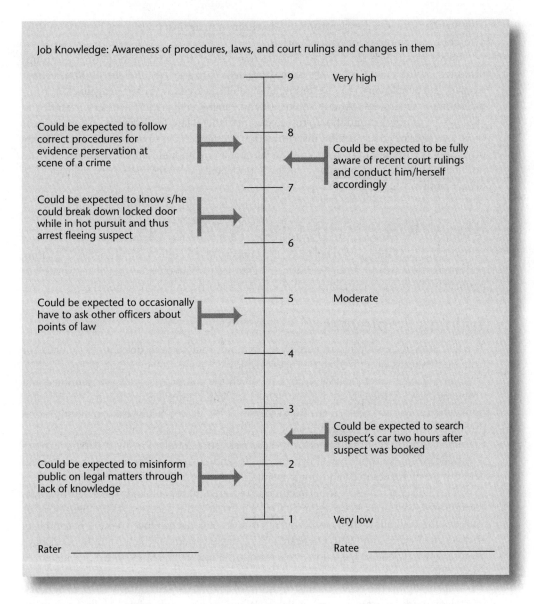

Job Knowledge: Awareness of procedures, laws, and court rulings and changes in them

9 — Very high

Could be expected to follow correct procedures for evidence perservation at scene of a crime — 8

Could be expected to be fully aware of recent court rulings and conduct him/herself accordingly ← 7

Could be expected to know s/he could break down locked door while in hot pursuit and thus arrest fleeing suspect — 6

Could be expected to occasionally have to ask other officers about points of law — 5 — Moderate

4

3

Could be expected to search suspect's car two hours after suspect was booked ← 2

Could be expected to misinform public on legal matters through lack of knowledge —

1 — Very low

Rater _____   Ratee _____

FIGURE B–1
Example of a BARS Performance Evaluation.

Source: Figure, "Example of a BARS Performance Evaluation" from *Psychology of Work Behavior,* rev. ed., by F. J. Landy & D. A. Trumbo. Copyright © 1980 by Wadsworth, a part of Cengage Learning, Inc. Reprinted by permission. *www.cengage.com/ permissions.*

performance for the job being evaluated. These behaviors are then arranged into a rating scale. (See **Figure B–1.**) When evaluators use a BARS scale to rate a particular employee, that employee's typical behavior is compared to the positive and negative incidents identified on the scale. The result is a performance rating that reflects the job-related behaviors that the employee characteristically displays in his or her work.

ISSUES OF FAIRNESS IN EMPLOYMENT

In the past, both in the United States and abroad, some companies have refused to hire employees based on their gender, age, race, or religious beliefs (Brinkley, 1999). Today, most industrialized nations have developed legislation to guard against discriminatory employment practices. In 1964, the United States Congress enacted the **Civil Rights Act of 1964,** a sweeping set of laws and regulations aimed at protecting the rights of individuals and groups who had historically experienced discrimination. The overarching purpose of these laws, and others that have followed, has been to create a society that is fair to all individuals, regardless of their background and beliefs. The Civil Rights Act includes an array of provisions that define and prohibit discriminatory practices in all walks of life.

Civil Rights Act of 1964 A sweeping set of laws and regulations aimed at protecting the rights of people despite their gender, age, race, or religious beliefs.

Title VII of this act expressly prohibits discrimination against employees because of their race, color, religion, sex, or national origin.

In the years since the Civil Rights Act was passed, the scope and number of groups protected by the Civil Rights Act have expanded. Citizens over the age of 40, pregnant women, and people with physical or mental disabilities are now protected against discrimination under federal law. And in some cities and states, civil rights have been extended to members of groups beyond those protected under federal law. For example, in certain areas there are now laws that prohibit discrimination on the basis of sexual orientation, thereby protecting the rights of gay men and lesbian women. Although federal laws currently do not include sexual orientation as a category protected under federal statute, considerable debate on this issue is sure to come.

BEHAVIOR WITHIN ORGANIZATIONS

Industrial/organizational psychologists are concerned not only with employee selection, performance evaluation, and fair treatment. They also are involved in preparing workers to perform to the best of their ability and in creating a motivating organizational environment.

Training Employees

The first step in developing an employee training program is to determine the need for training by means of a three-step process (Landy & Conte, 2004; Ostroff & Ford, 1989). First, an organizational analysis is done in which the company's goals are examined and problems are identified. Next, for problems that lend themselves to training-based solutions, a task analysis is performed. Task analysis identifies which job tasks can be addressed through training. It also determines the knowledge (K), skills (S), abilities (A), and other characteristics (O) required to perform those tasks successfully. Finally, a person analysis is conducted to examine the knowledge, skills, and current performance of workers to determine which ones need additional training.

Where discrepancies exist between tasks required on the job and skill levels of workers, training programs can be designed to teach workers the necessary skills, behaviors, or attitudes that will allow them to perform job tasks effectively. Once training is complete, an assessment of training outcomes can help managers evaluate which training needs have been successfully addressed, and which remain (Alliger & Janak, 1989; I. L. Goldstein & Ford, 2002).

Depending on the type of skills or attitudes that the organization wishes to address, several methods of training are available. When specific, job-related skills need to be learned, on-the-job, vestibule, or simulation training methods are often used.

On-the-Job Training One of the most common methods of teaching new workers the skills they need to perform their job is **on-the-job training,** in which the trainee learns new job tasks while actually performing the job. For example, an assistant chef may have worked in several restaurants before coming to work at a new job, but may be unfamiliar with how the current employer wants food to be plated and sauced. Through on-the-job training, the new assistant chef can be shown by an experienced employee exactly how these tasks are to be performed.

There are many advantages associated with on-the-job training. Employees learn the new skills required for the job on the very equipment they are to use when performing their work. On-the-job training also conserves the organization's resources, since it usually minimizes costs for training equipment and supplies. However, it also has some disadvantages. For example, productivity usually declines during the training period because learning each new task slows performance. Moreover, coworkers functioning as trainers usually cannot instruct trainees and perform their own jobs at the same time, leading to further declines in productivity. Finally, experienced employees do not always make skilled trainers: A highly competent worker may not necessarily have the skills to effectively train a new employee (Riggio, 2003).

on-the-job training Teaching employees a new job by actually performing the job.

One of the oldest on-the-job training programs is *apprenticeship,* which is still used extensively in the crafts and trades. Many jobs associated with apprentice training programs are in heavily unionized occupations; plumbers, carpenters, electricians, and equipment operators in manufacturing industries often learn their skills through apprenticeship training. Today, more than 30,000 apprentice programs exist in the United States involving nearly a half-million trainees, called *apprentices* (U.S. Department of Labor, 2006). Apprentices go through a formal on-the-job training program, which includes both instruction and supervision by a skilled worker.

Another type of on-the-job training is **job rotation,** in which workers are trained to perform all jobs in a particular supervisory unit. For example, in an assembly unit in which five different workers each perform a specific part of the assembly of a machine, each worker would learn each of the five jobs involved. Job rotation programs provide organizations an effective way of staffing jobs that have high turnover, since workers are already trained to take over the job of a person who quits (Riggio, 2003). Job rotation is often part of the training that supervisors receive to help them develop a better understanding of procedures throughout their work division. Research suggests that supervisors who are rotated through several jobs are more likely to remain with a company than those who receive no such training (Grensing-Pophal, 2005; Pooley, 2005).

Vestibule and Simulation Training When new job skills cannot be learned while performing the actual job, an alternative approach is vestibule training. **Vestibule training** allows employees to learn job tasks at work stations similar to those used in production in a training facility, rather than on the actual production floor.

In other cases, *training simulators* are used. For example, flight simulators are used to teach pilots how to fly. Flight simulators operate like real airplanes, with fully equipped cockpits and pitch-and-roll machines that move the simulator to replicate the actual movements of an aircraft. From the pilot's perspective, the only major difference between flying a simulator versus a real airplane is that the simulator doesn't actually leave the ground.

Computer-based simulations also cater to some types of training needs. Today, computer-based simulations are being used to train firefighters, medical personnel, and heavy equipment operators, as well as workers in many other jobs (Construction Equipment, 2006; Foundry Management and Technology, 2006; Scerbo, Bliss, Schmidt, & Thompson, 2006; Jack Smith 2006). Because computer-based training often provides a cost-effective and safe way to provide training, its use is increasing in a wide variety of training applications.

Changing Attitudes in the Workplace Sometimes organizations wish to develop their workforce in terms of attitudes and interpersonal behaviors. Cultural diversity training and sexual harassment training are two examples of such training.

Cultural diversity training is used to help workers adapt their actions and attitudes so they can work effectively in a multicultural work environment. The U.S. workplace broadly reflects the population overall, and that population is becoming much more diverse. For example, of all new additions to the workforce in the 1990s, nearly half (45%) were non-White and nearly two-thirds were women. In response to increasing workplace diversity, a growing trend exists among organizations to offer programs in cultural diversity training. One goal of such training is to create an atmosphere that is fair and nondiscriminatory for all employees; failing to do so puts companies at risk for lawsuits filed under antidiscrimination laws such as the Civil Rights Acts of 1964 and 1991. Cultural diversity training also alerts workers to how their actions may be offensive to others and helps them learn to work cooperatively with coworkers who represent different cultures or gender. Another goal of diversity training is to better capture "the benefits in creativity and problem-solving capabilities that a diverse workforce provides" (Chrobot-Mason & Quinones, 2002). When workers are able to appreciate and embrace the various points of view expressed in a diverse work environment, productivity is enhanced. Finally, the ever-increasing globalization of the workplace means that increasing numbers of employees take assignments abroad, which in turn leads to a need for cultural-diversity training (Speitzer, McCall, & Mahoney, 1997). For these reasons, most industrial/organizational

job rotation Training workers to perform a variety of jobs.

vestibule training Teaching employees new techniques and behaviors in a simulated workplace.

cultural diversity training Teaching employees to adjust their attitudes and actions so they can work effectively as part of a diverse workforce.

psychologists predict that this type of training will become even more important in the future (Bhawuk & Brislin, 2000).

Most organizations also offer employee training that is aimed at reducing sexual harassment in the workplace. **Sexual harassment** can take several forms. *Quid pro quo* (Latin for "this for that") harassment is defined as behavior in which sexual favors are solicited in return for favorable treatment. An example of quid pro quo harassment might involve a manager offering a salary increase or a promotion to a subordinate in exchange for sexual attention. Sexual harassment also exists when managers or coworkers create a *hostile work environment,* perhaps by telling sexist jokes, posting nude "pin-up" photos in lockers, or teasing of a sexual nature. The goals of sexual-harassment-prevention training parallel those of cultural-diversity training: to protect the organization from lawsuits and to create an environment where every worker is able to perform to his or her maximum level of creativity, effort, and productivity.

Motivating Employees

Another means of improving workforce productivity involves motivating workers to give their best effort. Over the years, a variety of theories about worker motivation have been put forward. (See Chapter 8, "Motivation and Emotion.") One way of understanding how these theories approach the topic of motivation is to categorize them into groups (Donovan, 2002).

Cognitive Theories of Motivation Rather than emphasizing inherent individual differences among workers (skills), cognitive-based theories of motivation emphasize how workers think about their jobs and how that in turn affects their attitudes and behaviors on the job. Three cognitive views that have received considerable attention from I/O psychologists are equity theory, expectancy theory, and goal-setting theory.

Equity theory holds that relative to coworkers, employees monitor the amount of effort they expend on the job and the rewards they receive for this effort. In the simplest case, equity theory predicts that when workers believe they are expending equal amounts of effort, they should benefit from equal levels of reward. Motivation, then, depends on the worker's sense of fairness, or *equity.* When employees are either over- or under-rewarded relative to their coworkers, their motivation suffers and they will adjust the quality or quantity of work they produce correspondingly.

Expectancy theory also emphasizes the cognitive processes workers use in evaluating their level of effort and the rewards they receive. However, in expectancy theory the comparison made is not how our own effort and rewards compare to those of others, but rather how we view the connection between our own behavior and the likelihood of attaining desired rewards. According to expectancy theory, employees are aware of the goals or rewards they wish to attain through their work, and they are aware of how their behavior on the job is connected with attaining those rewards. Based on their assessment of the value of the rewards they seek and of the degree to which they expect they can attain those rewards by working harder, they will expend the corresponding amount of effort on the job (Van Eerde & Thierry, 1996; Vroom, 1964). For example, if workers attach high value to a promotion and if they believe that through hard work they will be promoted, this expectancy will motivate them to perform. Conversely, if the rewards offered on the job are not perceived by workers to be valuable, or if workers do not believe that their efforts will result in the attainment of valued rewards, motivation and effort will diminish.

A similar set of assumptions is advanced by **goal-setting theory,** which emphasizes the impact on motivation of clearly articulated goals. According to this theory, when workers believe that their efforts will lead to the attainment of previously set, clearly stated goals, they will be highly motivated toward meeting those goals (Locke & Latham, 2002). Many people apply goal-setting theory in their own lives. For example, a student may work extra hours at a second part-time job to buy a car or pay the rent. The keys in goal-setting theory are to identify appropriate, attainable goals and to clearly communicate to workers what they need to do to reach those goals.

sexual harassment Soliciting sexual favors in exchange for favorable treatment, or creating a hostile work environment.

equity theory Theory that worker motivation depends on the relationship between personal effort expended and rewards received when compared to that of other workers.

expectancy theory Theory that worker motivation depends on the expectation that by working hard they will achieve valued rewards.

goal-setting theory Theory that worker motivation requires clearly stated goals and a belief that good job performance will lead to the attainment of these goals.

Reinforcement Theory Some motivational theories focus less on how workers think about their jobs and more on the outcomes associated with an employee's work. **Reinforcement theory,** which is based on the principles of operant conditioning (see Chapter 5, "Learning"), has been used to explain how workers can be motivated toward high levels of performance.

According to this theory, when work behavior is followed by positive outcomes (reinforcements), that behavior will be maintained and strengthened; when work behavior is punished, that behavior will decrease. An example of reinforcement theory in a production setting is the *piece-rate system.* In a piece-rate system, workers are paid according to the number of "pieces" they assemble. Thus, a worker who builds 25 pieces in a day will be paid more than one who builds only 20 pieces. Sales commission systems, where sales agents are paid a percentage of the price of the products they sell, are another compensation system based on reinforcement theory.

Research indicates that reinforcement can indeed increase workplace productivity. One study that examined the effect of reinforcement-based performance systems over a span of 20 years showed a 17% improvement in productivity (Stajkovic & Luthans, 1997). In a more recent study, more than 90% of organizations experienced sustainable improvements in worker productivity through reinforcement (Komaki, 2003). Moreover, when workers are paid according to their performance, their sense of autonomy and control over their work is also enhanced (Eisenberger, Rhoades, & Cameron, 1999).

However, there are some potential pitfalls associated with the use of reinforcement. For example, when workers are paid according to their own individual successes, they may be reluctant to participate in activities that require cooperation with others. In fact, "pay-for-performance" systems can encourage competitive behavior which, at the extreme, may involve sabotage of coworkers' efforts and an overall decline in workplace productivity. Placing workers in highly stressful, competitive work environments poses yet another issue to consider when evaluating the desirability of reinforcement-based motivational approaches.

Organizational Culture

All of the topics discussed thus far—job analysis, personnel selection and performance evaluation, fair employment practices, and employee training and motivation—occur in the context of a particular organization. Organizations have their own **corporate (organizational) culture,** which refers to the formal and informal rules, procedures, and expectations that define an organization's values, attitudes, beliefs, and customs. In that organizations sometimes differ dramatically from each other, they are characterized by their own unique organizational culture.

As jobs have become more complex, technology has continued to explode, and worker expectations have changed, many organizations have adopted a "team-based" approach to work.

Teams and Teamwork

The basic idea behind work teams is that productivity is enhanced when several people collaborate to solve organizational problems. Teams are particularly effective when problems must be solved by the workers themselves. A good team generally outperforms individual work efforts in tasks that require experience, judgment, and multiple skills (Salas, Stagl, & Burke, 2004). Moreover, research suggests that people who work in teams are more satisfied with their work and are more productive (Glassop, 2002).

Depending on the goals of an organization, there are many different ways that work teams can be organized and several different functions they can perform (Sunstrom, DeMeuse, & Futrell, 1990). Workers on a team may be trained to perform all jobs in their unit (a technique discussed earlier under *job rotation*) and then regularly exchange jobs. Job rotation helps to keeps skills sharp and also helps to relieve the boredom of performing the same job day after day.

Team-based approaches have been gaining popularity (Borman, Ilgen, & Klimoski, 2003). Three factors appear to underlie this trend. First, businesses exist within a complex, information-rich culture in which no employee can know or master everything needed

reinforcement theory Theory that work behavior that is followed by positive outcomes will be maintained and repeated.

corporate (organizational) culture The formal and informal rules, procedures, and expectations that define the values, attitudes, beliefs, and customs of an organization.

to run a successful enterprise. Second, the modern workforce is better educated and thus better prepared to perform complex decision-making functions. Furthermore, workers at every organizational level expect to find challenge in their work; and most are unwilling to work at repetitive, intellectually empty tasks. Finally, the work performed in modern organizations has itself changed. Most jobs no longer consist of performing the same set of simple repetitive tasks; rather, they involve flexible approaches to rapidly changing technologies and business climates (Muchinsky, 2006).

A discussion of team approaches to organizational structure and operation raises the question of leadership. Although workers within a team are interdependent and share responsibilities, team success also depends on effective leadership.

Leadership

As we saw in Chapter 14, "Social Psychology," several theories of leadership have emerged to explain why some individuals become leaders and others do not. Contingency theories are based on the assumption that leadership is the product of both the characteristics of the leader and those of the worker and the workplace.

An important aspect of contingency theories is that there is no specific set of traits, skills, abilities, or attitudes that will guarantee leadership success. On the contrary, to be effective, the leader's characteristics must match the demands of the situation. Consequently, a person who is very effective as a leader in one setting may not be effective in another. This situation is often observed in sales-based organizations that promote managers from within. There is no certainty that someone who is an outstanding leader in one division of a company will be effective if transferred to a different division. Similarly, a person who forms a small start-up company and leads it effectively during its formative years may not be the best person to lead the company when it has hundreds or thousands of employees and multiple offices worldwide.

Certain leadership characteristics do seem to generalize across different types of organizational settings. For example, leaders who are *charismatic,* who exude confidence and have a vision that followers can relate to, are often effective in a wide array of settings (Yukl, 2002). They are also especially effective in motivating the productivity of work teams (R. T. Keller, 2006). Charismatic leaders, sometimes called "transformational leaders," seem to inspire higher levels of job satisfaction in employees as well (Judge & Bono, 2000). Leaders who establish clear expectations are also generally effective in a wide range of situations (R. T. Keller, 2006).

ORGANIZATIONAL ATTITUDES

Effective leadership contributes to organizational productivity in many ways. For example, a leader can have a significant effect on the attitudes that workers develop about their jobs and the organizations for which they work. Among the attitudes that organizational psychologists are most interested in are the degree to which workers derive satisfaction from their jobs and the extent to which they develop a sense of trust in the organization and an appreciation that its processes and procedures are fair.

Job Satisfaction

Organizational psychologists are interested in job satisfaction because it is linked to many important organizational variables. Perhaps the most closely studied relationship is that between job satisfaction and job performance. Intuitively it seems that workers who are satisfied with their jobs will perform at higher levels than those who are unhappy in their work. However, hundreds of research studies have shown that job satisfaction is, at best, only moderately linked to job performance (Judge, Thoresen, Bono, & Patton, 2001). Nevertheless, most employees want satisfying jobs and so most employers seek to create a workplace that contributes to job satisfaction.

The amount of pleasure employees derive from their jobs is determined in large part by the extent to which they feel that their expectations about their jobs are met

(Hulin & Judge, 2003). When expectations are met or exceeded, levels of job satisfaction are generally high. However, there is a limit to what employers can do to increase job satisfaction since it is also affected by employee age, length of employment, overall health, personal motivation, marital status, and leisure activities (Schultz & Schultz, 1998).

Organizational Justice

In recent years, I/O psychologists have become interested in the extent to which employees perceive fairness and justice in the workplace—issues of **organizational justice.** One aspect of organizational justice is employees' perceptions that what they receive in recognition is appropriate for what they contribute to the organization. Most employees expect that when they work hard and contribute positively to the productivity of the organization, they will be rewarded.

Another aspect of organizational justice involves the extent to which the policies and procedures used within the organization are responsive to the feelings of employees. For example, if an organization needs to eliminate a position within a unit, advance notification about the reasons why the position must be terminated, the criteria for deciding which position will be affected, the timeline for making the change, and an appeal process for workers to voice their concerns all contribute to perceived fairness in the workplace.

Finally, organizational justice is high when organizations show concern for workers as individuals. Examples might include a manager sending a get-well card to a subordinate following a surgery or attending the wedding of a worker in the unit he supervises.

Research clearly demonstrates that all three forms of organizational justice contribute to employees' perceptions of fairness in the workplace (Colquitt, Conlon, Wesson, Porter, & Ng, 2001). When workers perceive that rewards are distributed fairly, that rules and procedures are just and are enforced without favoritism, and that they are valued and respected by the organization and its leaders, organizational justice is enhanced. When workers are treated fairly, job satisfaction, commitment, and productivity increase, and negative workplace behaviors, such as absenteeism and sabotage, decline (Simons & Roberson, 2003). Research on the topic of organizational justice is likely to continue as I/O psychologists work to better understand how to enhance workplace productivity while maintaining a positive environment.

organizational justice Degree to which employees perceive fairness in the workplace.

Glossary

Absolute threshold The least amount of energy that can be detected as a stimulation 50% of the time.

Achievement motive The need to excel, to overcome obstacles.

Actualizing tendency According to Rogers, the drive of every organism to fulfill its biological potential and become what it is inherently capable of becoming.

Adaptation An adjustment of the senses to the level of stimulation they are receiving.

Additive color mixing The process of mixing lights of different wavelengths to create new hues.

Adjustment Any effort to cope with stress.

Adoption studies Research carried out on children adopted at birth by parents not related to them, to determine the relative influence of heredity and environment on human behavior.

Adrenal glands Two endocrine glands located just above the kidneys.

Aerial perspective Monocular cue to distance and depth based on the fact that more distant objects are likely to appear hazy and blurred.

Afferent neurons Neurons that carry messages from sense organs to the spinal cord or brain.

Affiliation motive The need to be with others.

Afterimage Sense experience that occurs after a visual stimulus has been removed.

Aggression Behavior aimed at doing harm to others; also, the motive to behave aggressively.

Agoraphobia An anxiety disorder that involves multiple, intense fears of crowds, public places, and other situations that require separation from a source of security such as the home.

Alcohol Depressant that is the intoxicating ingredient in whiskey, beer, wine, and other fermented or distilled liquors.

Alcoholic myopia A condition resulting from alcohol consumption involving poor judgments arising from misdirected attention and failure to consider negative consequences.

Algorithm A step-by-step method of problem solving that guarantees a correct solution.

All-or-none law Principle that the action potential in a neuron does not vary in strength; either the neuron fires at full strength, or it does not fire at all.

Altered states of consciousness Mental states that differ noticeably from normal waking consciousness.

Altruistic behavior Helping behavior that is not linked to personal gain.

Alzheimer's disease A neurological disorder, most commonly found in late adulthood, characterized by progressive losses in memory and cognition and by changes in personality.

Amphetamines Stimulant drugs that initially produce "rushes" of euphoria often followed by sudden "crashes" and, sometimes, severe depression.

Amplitude The magnitude of a wave; in sound, the primary determinant of loudness.

Amygdala A limbic system structure involved in governing emotions and establishing emotional memories.

Anal stage Second stage in Freud's theory of personality development, in which a child's erotic feelings center on the anus and on elimination.

Anorexia nervosa A serious eating disorder that is associated with an intense fear of weight gain and a distorted body image.

Antipsychotic drugs Drugs used to treat very severe psychological disorders, particularly schizophrenia.

Antisocial personality disorder Personality disorder that involves a pattern of violent, criminal, or unethical and exploitative behavior and an inability to feel affection for others.

Anxiety disorders Disorders in which anxiety is a characteristic feature or the avoidance of anxiety seems to motivate abnormal behavior.

Aphasias Impairments of the ability to use (expressive aphasia) or understand (receptive aphasia) language that usually results from brain damage.

Apnea Sleep disorder characterized by breathing difficulty during the night and feelings of exhaustion during the day.

Approach/approach conflict According to Lewin, the result of simultaneous attraction to two appealing possibilities, neither of which has any negative qualities.

Approach/avoidance conflict According to Lewin, the result of being simultaneously attracted to and repelled by the same goal.

Archetypes In Jung's theory of personality, thought forms common to all human beings, stored in the collective unconscious.

Arousal theory Theory of motivation that proposes that organisms seek an optimal level of arousal.

Assessment center Method used to select high-level managers that places applicants in a simulated and highly structured group setting where they are given personnel tests and extensive interviews, and they engage in various role-playing activities.

Association areas Areas of the cerebral cortex where incoming messages from the separate senses are combined into meaningful impressions and outgoing messages from the motor areas are integrated.

Attachment Emotional bond that develops in the first year of life that makes human babies cling to their caregivers for safety and comfort.

Attention The selection of some incoming information for further processing.

Attention-deficit/hyperactivity disorder (ADHD) A childhood disorder characterized by inattention, impulsiveness, and hyperactivity.

Attitude Relatively stable organization of beliefs, feelings, and behavior tendencies directed toward something or someone—the attitude object.

Attribution theory The theory that addresses the question of how people make judgments about the causes of behavior.

Auditory nerve The bundle of axons that carries signals from each ear to the brain.

Authoritarian personality A personality pattern characterized by rigid conventionality, exaggerated respect for authority, and hostility toward those who defy society's norms.

Autistic disorder A childhood disorder characterized by lack of social instincts and strange motor behavior.

Autistic spectrum disorder (ASD) A range of disorders involving varying degrees of impairment in communication skills, social interactions, and restricted, repetitive, and stereotyped patterns of behavior.

Autokinetic illusion The perception that a stationary object is actually moving.

Autonomic nervous system   The part of the peripheral nervous system that carries messages between the central nervous system and the internal organs.

Autonomy   Sense of independence; a desire not to be controlled by others.

Availability   A heuristic by which a judgment or decision is based on information that is most easily retrieved from memory.

Aversive conditioning   Behavioral therapy techniques aimed at eliminating undesirable behavior patterns by teaching the person to associate them with pain and discomfort.

Avoidance training   Learning a desirable behavior to prevent the occurrence of something unpleasant, such as punishment.

Avoidance/avoidance conflict   According to Lewin, the result of facing a choice between two undesirable possibilities, neither of which has any positive qualities.

Avoidant personality disorder   Personality disorder in which the person's fears of rejection by others lead to social isolation.

Axon   Single long fiber extending from the cell body; it carries outgoing messages.

Babbling   A baby's vocalizations, consisting of repetition of consonant–vowel combinations.

Barbiturates   Potentially deadly depressants, first used for their sedative and anticonvulsant properties, now used only to treat such conditions as epilepsy and arthritis.

Basilar membrane   Vibrating membrane in the cochlea of the inner ear; it contains sense receptors for sound.

Behavior contracting   Form of operant conditioning therapy in which the client and therapist set behavioral goals and agree on reinforcements that the client will receive on reaching those goals.

Behavior genetics   Study of the relationship between heredity and behavior.

Behavior therapies   Therapeutic approaches that are based on the belief that all behavior, normal and abnormal, is learned, and that the objective of therapy is to teach people new, more satisfying ways of behaving.

Behaviorally anchored ratings scale (BARS)   Performance appraisal that matches employee behavior to specific behaviors associated with high, average, and poor performance.

Behaviorism   School of psychology that studies only observable and measurable behavior.

Big Five   Five traits or basic dimensions currently considered to be of central importance in describing personality.

Binaural cues   Cues to sound location that involve both ears working together.

Binocular cues   Visual cues requiring the use of both eyes.

Biofeedback   A technique that uses monitoring devices to provide precise information about internal physiological processes, such as heart rate or blood pressure, to teach people to gain voluntary control over these functions.

Biographical (or retrospective) study   A method of studying developmental changes by reconstructing a person's past through interviews and inferring the effects of past events on current behaviors.

Biological model   View that psychological disorders have a biochemical or physiological basis.

Biological treatments   A group of approaches, including medication, electroconvulsive therapy, and psychosurgery, that are sometimes used to treat psychological disorders in conjunction with, or instead of, psychotherapy.

Biopsychosocial theory   The theory that the interaction of biological, psychological, and cultural factors influences the intensity and duration of pain.

Bipolar cells   Neurons that have only one axon and one dendrite; in the eye, these neurons connect the receptors on the retina to the ganglion cells.

Bipolar disorder   A mood disorder in which periods of mania and depression may alternate, sometimes with periods of normal mood intervening.

Blind spot   The place on the retina where the axons of all the ganglion cells leave the eye and where there are no receptors.

Blocking   A process whereby prior conditioning prevents conditioning to a second stimulus even when the two stimuli are presented simultaneously.

Body dysmorphic disorder   A somatoform disorder in which a person becomes so preoccupied with his or her imagined ugliness that normal life is impossible.

Borderline personality disorder   Personality disorder characterized by marked instability in self-image, mood, and interpersonal relationships.

Brainstorming   A problem-solving strategy in which an individual or a group produces numerous ideas and evaluates them only after all ideas have been collected.

Brightness   The nearness of a color to white as opposed to black.

Brightness constancy   The perception of brightness as the same, even though the amount of light reaching the retina changes.

Bulimia nervosa   An eating disorder characterized by binges of eating followed by self-induced vomiting.

Bystander effect   The tendency for an individual's helpfulness in an emergency to decrease as the number of passive bystanders increases.

Cannon–Bard theory   States that the experience of emotion occurs simultaneously with biological changes.

Case study   Intensive description and analysis of a single individual or just a few individuals.

Central nervous system (CNS)   Division of the nervous system that consists of the brain and spinal cord.

Central tendency   Tendency of scores to congregate around some middle value.

Cerebellum   Structure in the hindbrain that controls certain reflexes and coordinates the body's movements.

Cerebrum   The main portion of the brain, occupying the upper part of the cranial cavity.

Cerebral cortex   The outer surface of the two cerebral hemispheres that regulates most complex behavior.

Childhood amnesia   The difficulty adults have remembering experiences from their first two years of life.

Chromosomes   Pairs of threadlike bodies within the cell nucleus that contain the genes.

Chunking   The grouping of information into meaningful units for easier handling by short-term memory.

Circadian rhythm   A regular biological rhythm with a period of approximately 24 hours.

Civil Rights Act of 1964   A sweeping set of laws and regulations aimed at protecting the rights of people despite their gender, age, race, or religious beliefs.

Classical (or Pavlovian) conditioning   The type of learning in which a response naturally elicited by one stimulus comes to be elicited by a different, formerly neutral, stimulus.

Client-centered (or person-centered) therapy   Nondirectional form of therapy developed by Carl Rogers that calls for unconditional positive regard of the client by the therapist with the goal of helping the client become fully functioning.

Cliques   Groups of adolescents with similar interests and strong mutual attachment.

Cocaine Drug derived from the coca plant that, although producing a sense of euphoria by stimulating the sympathetic nervous system, also leads to anxiety, depression, and addictive cravings.

Cochlea Part of the inner ear containing fluid that vibrates, which in turn causes the basilar membrane to vibrate.

Cognition The processes whereby we acquire and use knowledge.

Cognitive dissonance Perceived inconsistency between two cognitions.

Cognitive distortions An illogical and maladaptive response to early negative life events that leads to feelings of incompetence and unworthiness that are reactivated whenever a new situation arises that resembles the original events.

Cognitive learning Learning that depends on mental processes that are not directly observable.

Cognitive map A learned mental image of a spatial environment that may be called on to solve problems when stimuli in the environment change.

Cognitive psychology School of psychology devoted to the study of mental processes in the broadest sense.

Cognitive theory States that emotional experience depends on one's perception or judgment of a situation.

Cognitive therapies Psychotherapies that emphasize changing clients' perceptions of their life situation as a way of modifying their behavior.

Cognitive therapy Therapy that depends on identifying and changing inappropriately negative and self-critical patterns of thought.

Cognitive–behavioral model View that psychological disorders result from learning maladaptive ways of thinking and behaving.

Cognitive–social learning theories Personality theories that view behavior as the product of the interaction of cognitions, learning and past experiences, and the immediate environment.

Cohort A group of people born during the same period in historical time.

Collective unconscious In Jung's theory of personality, the level of the unconscious that is inherited and common to all members of a species.

Color constancy An inclination to perceive familiar objects as retaining their color despite changes in sensory information.

Compensation According to Adler, the person's effort to overcome imagined or real personal weaknesses.

Compensatory model A rational decision-making model in which choices are systematically evaluated on various criteria.

Compliance Change of behavior in response to an explicit request from another person or group.

Compromise Deciding on a more realistic solution or goal when an ideal solution or goal is not practical.

Concepts Mental categories for classifying objects, people, or experiences.

Concrete-operational stage In Piaget's theory, the stage of cognitive development between 7 and 11 years of age in which the individual can attend to more than one thing at a time and understand someone else's point of view, though thinking is limited to concrete matters.

Conditional positive regard In Rogers's theory, acceptance and love that are dependent on another's behaving in certain ways and on fulfilling certain conditions.

Conditioned response (CR) After conditioning, the response an organism produces when a conditioned stimulus is presented.

Conditioned stimulus (CS) An originally neutral stimulus that is paired with an unconditioned stimulus and eventually produces the desired response in an organism when presented alone.

Conditioned taste aversion Conditioned avoidance of certain foods even if there is only one pairing of conditioned and unconditioned stimuli.

Cones Receptor cells in the retina responsible for color vision.

Confirmation bias The tendency to look for evidence in support of a belief and to ignore evidence that would disprove a belief.

Conflict Simultaneous existence of incompatible demands, opportunities, needs, or goals.

Conformity Voluntarily yielding to social norms, even at the expense of one's preferences.

Confrontation Acknowledging a stressful situation directly and attempting to find a solution to the problem or to attain the difficult goal.

Conscientiousness A person's ability to finish projects that are started, to attend to detail without becoming absorbed by it, and to care enough about the quality of work that it is not compromised by inattention or lack of effort.

Consciousness Our awareness of various cognitive processes, such as sleeping, dreaming, concentrating, and making decisions.

Content validity Refers to a test's having an adequate sample of questions measuring the skills or knowledge it is supposed to measure.

Contingency A reliable "if–then" relationship between two events, such as a CS and a US.

Control group In a controlled experiment, the group not subjected to a change in the independent variable; used for comparison with the experimental group.

Convergence A visual depth cue that comes from muscles controlling eye movement as the eyes turn inward to view a nearby stimulus.

Convergent thinking Thinking that is directed toward one correct solution to a problem.

Conversion disorders Disorders in which a dramatic specific disability has no physical cause but instead seems related to psychological problems.

Cornea The transparent protective coating over the front part of the eye.

Corporate (organizational) culture The formal and informal rules, procedures, and expectations that define the values, attitudes, beliefs, and customs of an organization.

Corpus callosum A thick band of nerve fibers connecting the left and right cerebral hemispheres.

Correlation coefficient Statistical measure of the strength of association between two variables.

Correlation coefficients Statistical measures of the degree of association between two variables.

Correlational research Research technique based on the naturally occurring relationship between two or more variables.

Counterfactual thinking Thinking about alternative realities and things that never happened.

Couple therapy A form of group therapy intended to help troubled partners improve their problems of communication and interaction.

Creativity The ability to produce novel and socially valued ideas or objects.

Criterion-related validity Validity of a test as measured by a comparison of the test score and independent measures of what the test is designed to measure.

Critical period A time when certain internal and external influences have a major effect on development; at other periods, the same influences will have little or no effect.

Cross-cultural research Research involving the exploration of the extent to which people differ from one culture to another.

Cross-sectional study A method of studying developmental changes by comparing people of different ages at about the same time.

Cultural diversity training Teaching employees to adjust their attitudes and actions so they can work effectively as part of a diverse workforce.

Cultural truisms   Beliefs that most members of a society accept as self-evidently true.

Culture   The tangible goods and the values, attitudes, behaviors, and beliefs that are passed from one generation to another.

Culture-fair tests   Intelligence tests designed to eliminate cultural bias by minimizing skills and values that vary from one culture to another.

Dark adaptation   Increased sensitivity of rods and cones in darkness.

Decay theory   A theory that argues that the passage of time causes forgetting.

Decibel   Unit of measurement for the loudness of sounds.

Defense mechanisms   Self-deceptive techniques for reducing stress, including denial, repression, projection, identification, regression, intellectualization, reaction formation, displacement, and sublimation.

Defensive attribution   The tendency to attribute our successes to our own efforts or qualities and our failures to external factors.

Deindividuation   A loss of personal sense of responsibility in a group.

Deinstitutionalization   Policy of treating people with severe psychological disorders in the larger community or in small residential centers such as halfway houses, rather than in large public hospitals.

Delusions   False beliefs about reality that have no basis in fact.

Dendrites   Short fibers that branch out from the cell body and pick up incoming messages.

Denial   Refusal to acknowledge a painful or threatening reality.

Deoxyribonucleic acid (DNA)   Complex molecule in a double-helix configuration that is the main ingredient of chromosomes and genes and that forms the code for all genetic information.

Dependent personality disorder   Personality disorder in which the person is unable to make choices and decisions independently and cannot tolerate being alone.

Dependent variable   In an experiment, the variable that is measured to see how it is changed by manipulations in the independent variable.

Depersonalization/derealization disorder   A dissociative disorder whose essential feature is that the person suddenly feels changed or different in a strange way.

Depressants   Chemicals that slow down behavior or cognitive processes.

Depressive disorders   Mood disorders often characterized by overwhelming feelings of sadness, lack of interest in activities, and perhaps excessive guilt or feelings of worthlessness.

Desensitization therapy   A conditioning technique designed to gradually reduce anxiety about a particular object or situation.

Developmental psychology   The study of the changes that occur in people from birth through old age.

Diathesis   Biological predisposition.

Diathesis–stress model   View that people biologically predisposed to a mental disorder (those with a certain diathesis) will tend to exhibit that disorder when particularly affected by stress.

Difference threshold or just-noticeable difference (jnd)   The smallest change in stimulation that can be detected 50% of the time.

Discrimination   An unfair act or series of acts taken toward an entire group of people or individual members of that group.

Displacement   Shifting repressed motives and emotions from an original object to a substitute object.

Display rules   Culture-specific rules that govern how, when, and why expressions of emotion are appropriate.

Dissociative amnesia   A disorder characterized by loss of memory for past events without organic cause.

Dissociative disorders   Disorders in which some aspect of the personality seems separated from the rest.

Dissociative fugue   A symptom of dissociative amnesia that involves flight from home and the assumption of a new identity with amnesia for past identity and events.

Dissociative identity disorder   (Also called multiple personality disorder.) Disorder characterized by the separation of the personality into two or more distinct personalities.

Divergent thinking   Thinking that meets the criteria of originality, inventiveness, and flexibility.

Dominant gene   Member of a gene pair that controls the appearance of a certain trait.

Double-blind procedure   Experimental design useful in studies of the effects of drugs, in which neither the subject nor the researcher knows at the time of administration which subjects are receiving an active drug and which are receiving an inactive substance.

Dreams   Vivid visual and auditory experiences that occur primarily during REM periods of sleep.

Drive   State of tension or arousal that motivates behavior.

Drive-reduction theory   States that motivated behavior is aimed at reducing a state of bodily tension or arousal and returning the organism to homeostasis.

Dualism   View that thoughts and feelings (the mind) are distinct from the world of real objects and our bodies.

Eclecticism   Psychotherapeutic approach that recognizes the value of a broad treatment package over a rigid commitment to one particular form of therapy.

Efferent neurons   Neurons that carry messages from the spinal cord or brain to the muscles and glands.

Ego   Freud's term for the part of the personality that mediates between environmental demands (reality), conscience (superego), and instinctual needs (id); now often used as a synonym for "self."

Ego ideal   The part of the superego that consists of standards of what one would like to be.

Egocentric   Unable to see things from another's point of view.

Eidetic imagery   The ability to reproduce unusually sharp and detailed images of something one has seen.

Elaborative rehearsal   The linking of new information in short-term memory to familiar material stored in long-term memory.

Electroconvulsive therapy (ECT)   Biological therapy in which a mild electrical current is passed through the brain for a short period, often producing convulsions and temporary coma; used to treat severe, prolonged depression.

Elevation   Monocular cue to distance and depth based on the fact that the higher on the horizontal plane an object is, the farther away it appears.

Embryo   A developing human between 2 weeks and 3 months after conception.

Emotion   Feeling, such as fear, joy, or surprise, that underlies behavior.

Emotional intelligence   According to Goleman, a form of intelligence that refers to how effectively people perceive and understand their own emotions and the emotions of others, and can regulate and manage their emotional behavior.

Emotional memories   Learned emotional responses to various stimuli.

Endocrine glands   Glands of the endocrine system that release hormones into the bloodstream.

Episodic memories   The portion of long-term memory that stores personally experienced events.

Erectile disorder (or erectile dysfunction) (ED)   The inability of a man to achieve or maintain an erection.

Ethnicity A common cultural heritage—including religion, language, or ancestry—that is shared by a group of individuals.

Evolutionary psychology An approach to, and subfield of, psychology that is concerned with the evolutionary origins of behaviors and mental processes, their adaptive value, and the purposes they continue to serve.

Exhibitionism Exposing one's genitals in public to achieve sexual arousal.

Expectancies In Bandura's view, what a person anticipates in a situation or as a result of behaving in certain ways.

Expectancy theory Theory that worker motivation depends on the expectation that by working hard they will achieve valued rewards.

Experimental group In a controlled experiment, the group subjected to a change in the independent variable.

Experimental method Research technique in which an investigator deliberately manipulates selected events or circumstances and then measures the effects of those manipulations on subsequent behavior.

Experimenter bias Expectations by the experimenter that might influence the results of an experiment or its interpretation.

Explicit memory Memory for information that we can readily express in words and are aware of having; these memories can be intentionally retrieved from memory.

Extinction A decrease in the strength or frequency, or stopping, of a learned response because of failure to continue pairing the US and CS (classical conditioning) or withholding of reinforcement (operant conditioning).

Extraverts According to Jung, people who usually focus on social life and the external world instead of on their internal experience.

Extrinsic motivation A desire to perform a behavior to obtain an external reward or avoid punishment.

Factor analysis A statistical technique that identifies groups of related objects; it was used by Cattell to identify clusters of traits.

Family studies Studies of heritability in humans based on the assumption that if genes influence a certain trait, close relatives should be more similar on that trait than distant relatives.

Family therapy A form of group therapy that sees the family as at least partly responsible for the individual's problems and that seeks to change all family members' behaviors to the benefit of the family unit as well as the troubled individual.

Feature detectors Specialized brain cells that only respond to particular elements in the visual field such as movement or lines of specific orientation.

Female sexual interest/arousal disorder The inability of a woman to become sexually aroused or to reach orgasm.

Feminist theory Feminist theories offer a wide variety of views on the social roles of women and men, the problems and rewards of those roles, and prescriptions for changing those roles.

Fetal alcohol spectrum disorder (FASD) A disorder that occurs in children of women who drink alcohol during pregnancy; this disorder is characterized by facial deformities, heart defects, stunted growth, brain damage and cognitive impairments.

Fetishism A non-human object is the preferred or exclusive method of achieving sexual excitement.

Fetus A developing human between 3 months after conception and birth.

Fixation According to Freud, a partial or complete halt at some point in the individual's psychosexual development.

Fixed-interval schedule A reinforcement schedule in which the correct response is reinforced after a fixed length of time since the last reinforcement.

Fixed-ratio schedule A reinforcement schedule in which the correct response is reinforced after a fixed number of correct responses.

Flashbulb memory A vivid memory of a certain event and the incidents surrounding it even after a long time has passed.

Formal-operational stage In Piaget's theory, the stage of cognitive development beginning about 11 years of age in which the individual becomes capable of abstract thought.

Fovea The area of the retina that is the center of the visual field.

Framing The perspective from which we interpret information before making a decision.

Fraternal twins Twins developed from two separate fertilized ova and therefore different in genetic makeup.

Free association A psychoanalytic technique that encourages the person to talk without inhibition about whatever thoughts or fantasies come to mind.

Frequency The number of cycles per second in a wave; in sound, the primary determinant of pitch.

Frequency distribution A count of the number of scores that fall within each of a series of intervals.

Frequency histogram Type of bar graph that shows frequency distributions.

Frequency polygon Type of line graph that shows frequency distributions.

Frequency theory Theory that pitch is determined by the frequency with which hair cells in the cochlea fire.

Frontal lobe Part of the cerebrum that is responsible for voluntary movement; it is also important for attention, goal-directed behavior, and appropriate emotional experiences.

Frotteurism Achieving sexual arousal by touching or rubbing against a nonconsenting person in public situations.

Frustration The feeling that occurs when a person is prevented from reaching a goal.

Frustration–aggression theory The theory that, under certain circumstances, people who are frustrated in their goals turn their anger away from the proper, powerful target and toward another, less powerful target that is safer to attack.

Fully functioning person According to Rogers, an individual whose self-concept closely resembles his or her inborn capacities or potentials.

Functional fixedness The tendency to perceive only a limited number of uses for an object, thus interfering with the process of problem solving.

Functional job analysis A method for identifying the procedures and processes that workers must use in the performance of the job.

Functionalist theory Theory of mental life and behavior that is concerned with how an organism uses its perceptual abilities to function in its environment.

Fundamental attribution error The tendency of people to overemphasize personal causes for other people's behavior and to underemphasize personal causes for their own behavior.

Ganglion cells Neurons that connect the bipolar cells in the eyes to the brain.

Gate-control theory The theory that a "neurological gate" in the spinal cord controls the transmission of pain messages to the brain.

Gender The psychological and social meanings attached to being biologically male or female.

Gender constancy The realization that gender does not change with age.

Gender identity A little girl's knowledge that she is a girl, and a little boy's knowledge that he is a boy.

Gender stereotypes   General beliefs about characteristics that men and women are presumed to have.

Gender dysphoria   Disorders that involve the strong desire to become, or the insistence that one really is, a member of the other biological sex.

Gender-role awareness   Knowledge of what behavior is appropriate for each gender.

General adaptation syndrome (GAS)   According to Selye, the three stages the body passes through as it adapts to stress: alarm reaction, resistance, and exhaustion.

Generalized anxiety disorder   An anxiety disorder characterized by prolonged vague but intense fears that are not attached to any particular object or circumstance.

Genes   Elements that control the transmission of traits; they are found on the chromosomes.

Genetics   Study of how traits are transmitted from one generation to the next.

Genital stage   In Freud's theory of personality development, the final stage of normal adult sexual development, which is usually marked by mature sexuality.

Genotype   An organism's entire unique genetic makeup.

Gestalt psychology   School of psychology that studies how people perceive and experience objects as whole patterns.

Gestalt therapy   An insight therapy that emphasizes the wholeness of the personality and attempts to reawaken people to their emotions and sensations in the present.

Ghrelin   A hormone produced in the stomach and small intestines that increases appetite.

Giftedness   Refers to superior IQ combined with demonstrated or potential ability in such areas as academic aptitude, creativity, and leadership.

Glial cells (or glia)   Cells that insulate and support neurons by holding them together, provide nourishment and remove waste products, prevent harmful substances from passing into the brain, and form the myelin sheath.

Glucose   A simple sugar used by the body for energy.

Goal-setting theory   Theory that worker motivation requires clearly stated goals and a belief that good job performance will lead to the attainment of these goals.

Gonads   The reproductive glands—testes in males and ovaries in females.

Graded potential   A shift in the electrical charge in a tiny area of a neuron.

Grammar   The language rules that determine how sounds and words can be combined and used to communicate meaning within a language.

Great-person theory   The theory that leadership is a result of personal qualities and traits that qualify one to lead others.

Group tests   Written intelligence tests administered by one examiner to many people at one time.

Group therapy   Type of psychotherapy in which clients meet regularly to interact and help one another achieve insight into their feelings and behavior.

Groupthink   A process that occurs when the members of a group like one another, have similar goals and are isolated, leading them to ignore alternatives and not criticize group consensus.

Hallucinations   Sensory experiences in the absence of external stimulation.

Hallucinogens   Any of a number of drugs, such as LSD and mescaline, that distort visual and auditory perception.

Health psychology   A subfield of psychology concerned with the relationship between psychological factors and physical health and illness.

Hertz (Hz)   Cycles per second; unit of measurement for the frequency of sound waves.

Heuristics   Rules of thumb that help in simplifying and solving problems, although they do not guarantee a correct solution.

Hierarchy of needs   A theory of motivation advanced by Maslow holding that higher order motives involving social and personal growth only emerge after lower level motives related to survival have been satisfied.

Higher order conditioning   Conditioning based on previous learning; the conditioned stimulus serves as an unconditioned stimulus for further training.

Hill climbing   A heuristic, problem-solving strategy in which each step moves you progressively closer to the final goal.

Hindbrain   Area containing the medulla, pons, and cerebellum.

Hindsight bias   The tendency to see outcomes as inevitable and predictable after we know the outcome.

Hippocampus   A limbic system structure which plays an important role in the formation of new memories.

Holophrases   One-word sentences commonly used by children under 2 years of age.

Homeostasis   State of balance and stability in which the organism functions effectively.

Hormones   Chemical substances released by the endocrine glands; they help regulate bodily activities.

Hues   The aspects of color that correspond to names such as red, green, and blue.

Human genome   The full complement of genes within a human cell.

Humanistic personality theory   Any personality theory that asserts the fundamental goodness of people and their striving toward higher levels of functioning.

Humanistic psychology   School of psychology that emphasizes nonverbal experience and altered states of consciousness as a means of realizing one's full human potential.

Hypnosis   Trancelike state in which a person responds readily to suggestions.

Hypothalamus   Forebrain region that governs motivation and emotional responses.

Hypotheses   Specific, testable predictions derived from a theory.

Id   In Freud's theory of personality, the collection of unconscious urges and desires that continually seek expression.

Identical twins   Twins developed from a single fertilized ovum and therefore identical in genetic makeup at the time of conception.

Identification   Taking on the characteristics of someone else to avoid feeling incompetent.

Identity crisis   A period of intense self-examination and decision making; part of the process of identity formation.

Identity formation   Erickson's term for the development of a stable sense of self necessary to make the transition from dependence on others to dependence on oneself.

Illness anxiety disorder   Disorder in which a person interprets insignificant symptoms as signs of serious illness in the absence of any organic evidence of such illness.

Image   A mental representation of a sensory experience.

Implicit memory   Memory for information that we cannot readily express in words and may not be aware of having; these memories cannot be intentionally retrieved from memory.

Imprinting   The tendency in certain species to follow the first moving thing (usually its mother) it sees after it is born or hatched.

Inattentional blindness   Failure to notice or be aware of something that is in plain sight.

Incentive   External stimulus that prompts goal-directed behavior.

Independent variable   In an experiment, the variable that is manipulated to test its effects on the other, dependent variables.

Industrial psychology   Subfield of industrial/organizational psychology concerned with effectively managing human resources.

Industrial/organizational (I/O) psychology   The study of how individuals and organizations work and how psychological principles can be used to improve organizational effectiveness.

Inferiority complex   In Adler's theory, the fixation on feelings of personal inferiority that results in emotional and social paralysis.

Information-processing model   A computer-like model used to describe the way humans encode, store, and retrieve information.

Insanity   Legal term applied to defendants who do not know right from wrong or are unable to control their behavior.

Insight   (as applied to therapy) Awareness of previously unconscious feelings and memories and how they influence present feelings and behavior.

Insight   (as applied to learning) Learning that occurs rapidly as a result of understanding all the elements of a problem.

Insight therapies   A variety of individual psychotherapies designed to give people a better awareness and understanding of their feelings, motivations, and actions in the hope that this will help them to adjust.

Insomnia   Sleep disorder characterized by difficulty in falling asleep or remaining asleep throughout the night.

Instincts   Inborn, inflexible, goal-directed behaviors that are characteristic of an entire species.

Insula   An area of the brain between the parietal and temporal lobes involved in addiction and the conscious expression of emotion and desire.

Integrity tests   Paper-and-pencil tests that predict the likelihood that a job applicant will engage in counterproductive behavior in the workplace.

Intellectualization   Thinking abstractly about stressful problems as a way of detaching oneself from them.

Intelligence   A general term referring to the ability or abilities involved in learning and adaptive behavior.

Intelligence quotient (IQ)   A numerical value given to intelligence that is determined from the scores on an intelligence test on the basis of a score of 100 for average intelligence.

Intermittent pairing   Pairing the conditioned stimulus and the unconditioned stimulus on only a portion of the learning trials.

Interneurons (or association neurons)   Neurons that carry messages from one neuron to another.

Interposition   Monocular distance cue in which one object, by partly blocking a second object, is perceived as being closer.

Interval scale   Scale with equal distances between the points or values, but without a true zero.

Intrinsic motivation   A desire to perform a behavior that stems from the enjoyment derived from the behavior itself.

Introverts   According to Jung, people who usually focus on their own thoughts and feelings.

Ions   Electrically charged particles found both inside and outside the neuron.

Iris   The colored part of the eye that regulates the size of the pupil.

James–Lange theory   States that stimuli cause physiological changes in our bodies, and emotions result from those physiological changes.

Job analysis   Identifying the various tasks required by a job and the human qualifications that are required to perform that job.

Job rotation   Training workers to perform a variety of jobs.

Just-world hypothesis   Attribution error based on the assumption that bad things happen to bad people and good things happen to good people.

Kinesthetic senses   Senses of muscle movement, posture, and strain on muscles and joints.

KSAO system of job analysis   A method for identifying the knowledge, skills, abilities, and other human characteristics that are required for the job.

Language   A flexible system of communication that uses sounds, rules, gestures, or symbols to convey information.

Language acquisition device   A hypothetical neural mechanism for acquiring language that is presumed to be "wired into" all humans.

Latency period   In Freud's theory of personality, a period in which the child appears to have no interest in the other sex; occurs after the phallic stage.

Latent learning   Learning that is not immediately reflected in a behavior change.

Law of effect (principle of reinforcement)   Thorndike's theory that behavior consistently rewarded will be "stamped in" as learned behavior, and behavior that brings about discomfort will be "stamped out."

Learned helplessness   Failure to take steps to avoid or escape from an unpleasant or aversive stimulus that occurs as a result of previous exposure to unavoidable painful stimuli.

Learning   The process by which experience or practice results in a relatively permanent change in behavior or potential behavior.

Learning set   The ability to become increasingly more effective in solving problems as more problems are solved.

Lens   The transparent part of the eye behind the pupil that focuses light onto the retina.

Leptin   A hormone released by fat cells that reduces appetite.

Libido   According to Freud, the energy generated by the sexual instinct.

Light adaptation   Decreased sensitivity of rods and cones in bright light.

Limbic system   Ring of structures that plays a role in learning and emotional behavior.

Linear perspective   Monocular cue to distance and depth based on the fact that two parallel lines seem to come together at the horizon.

Linguistic determinism   The belief that thought and experience are determined by language.

Linguistic relativity hypothesis   Whorf's idea that patterns of thinking are determined by the specific language one speaks.

Locus of control   According to Rotter, an expectancy about whether reinforcement is under internal or external control.

Long-term memory (LTM)   The portion of memory that is more or less permanent, corresponding to everything we "know."

Long-term potentiation (LTP)   A long-lasting change in the structure or function of a synapse that increases the efficiency of neural transmission and is thought to be related to how information is stored by neurons.

Longitudinal studies   A method of studying developmental changes by evaluating the same people at different points in their lives.

Lysergic acid diethylamide (LSD)   Hallucinogenic or "psychedelic" drug that produces hallucinations and delusions similar to those occurring in a psychotic state.

Major depressive disorder   A depressive disorder characterized by an episode of intense sadness, depressed mood, or marked loss of interest or pleasure in nearly all activities.

Manic episodes   Characterized by euphoric states, extreme physical activity, excessive talkativeness, distractedness, and sometimes grandiosity.

Marijuana   A mild hallucinogen that produces a "high" often characterized by feelings of euphoria, a sense of well-being, and swings in mood from gaiety to relaxation; may also cause feelings of anxiety and paranoia.

Mean Arithmetical average calculated by dividing a sum of values by the total number of cases.

Means-end analysis A heuristic strategy that aims to reduce the discrepancy between the current situation and the desired goal at a number of intermediate points.

Median Point that divides a set of scores in half.

Meditation Any of the various methods of concentration, reflection, or focusing of thoughts undertaken to suppress the activity of the sympathetic nervous system.

Medulla Structure in the hindbrain that controls essential life support functions including breathing, heart rate and blood pressure.

Memory The ability to remember the things that we have experienced, imagined, and learned.

Menarche First menstrual period.

Menopause The time in a woman's life when menstruation ceases.

Mental representations Mental images or symbols (such as words) used to think about or remember an object, a person, or an event.

Mental retardation Condition of significantly subaverage intelligence combined with deficiencies in adaptive behavior.

Mental set The tendency to perceive and to approach problems in certain ways.

Meta-analysis A statistical procedure for combining the results of several studies so the strength, consistency, and direction of the effect can be estimated.

Midbrain Region between the hindbrain and the forebrain; it is important for hearing and sight, and it is one of several places in the brain where pain is registered.

Midlife crisis A time when adults discover they no longer feel fulfilled in their jobs or personal lives and attempt to make a decisive shift in career or lifestyle.

Midlife transition According to Levinson, a process whereby adults assess the past and formulate new goals for the future.

Minnesota Multiphasic Personality Inventory (MMPI-2) The most widely used objective personality test, originally intended for psychiatric diagnosis.

Mirror neurons Specialized neurons that respond when we observe others perform a behavior or express an emotion.

Mnemonics Techniques that make material easier to remember.

Mnemonists People with highly developed memory skills.

Mode Point at which the largest number of scores occurs.

Modeling A behavior therapy in which the person learns desired behaviors by watching others perform those behaviors.

Monaural cues Cues to sound location that require just one ear.

Monocular cues Visual cues requiring the use of one eye.

Mood disorders Disturbances in mood or prolonged emotional state.

Morphemes The smallest meaningful units of speech, such as simple words, prefixes, and suffixes.

Motion parallax Monocular distance cue in which objects closer than the point of visual focus seem to move in the direction opposite to the viewer's moving head, and objects beyond the focus point appear to move in the same direction as the viewer's head.

Motive Specific need or desire, such as hunger, thirst, or achievement, that prompts goal-directed behavior.

Motor (or efferent) neurons Neurons that carry messages from the spinal cord or brain to the muscles and glands.

Muscle dysmorphia A disorder generally seen in young men involving an obsessive concern with muscle size.

Myelin sheath White fatty covering found on some axons.

Narcissistic personality disorder Personality disorder in which the person has an exaggerated sense of self-importance and needs constant admiration.

Narcolepsy Hereditary sleep disorder characterized by sudden nodding off during the day and sudden loss of muscle tone following moments of emotional excitement.

Natural selection The mechanism proposed by Darwin in his theory of evolution, which states that organisms best adapted to their environment tend to survive, transmitting their genetic characteristics to succeeding generations, whereas organisms with less adaptive characteristics tend to vanish from the earth.

Naturalistic observation Research method involving the systematic study of animal or human behavior in natural settings rather than in the laboratory.

Negative reinforcers Events whose reduction or termination increases the likelihood that ongoing behavior will recur.

NEO-PI-R An objective personality test designed to assess the Big Five personality traits.

Neonates Newborn babies.

Nerve (or tract) Group of axons bundled together.

Neural impulse (or action potential) The firing of a nerve cell.

Neural plasticity The ability of the brain to change in response to experience.

Neurofeedback A biofeedback technique that monitors brain waves with the use of an EEG to teach people to gain voluntary control over their brain wave activity.

Neurogenesis The growth of new neurons.

Neural network a group of neurons that are functionally connected.

Neurons Individual cells that are the smallest unit of the nervous system.

Neuroscience The study of the brain and the nervous system.

Neurosurgery Brain surgery performed to change a person's behavior and emotional state; a biological therapy rarely used today.

Neurotransmitters Chemicals released by the synaptic vesicles that travel across the synaptic space and affect adjacent neurons.

Night terrors Frightening, often terrifying dreams that occur during NREM sleep from which a person is difficult to awaken and doesn't remember the content.

Nightmares Frightening dreams that occur during REM sleep and are remembered.

Nominal scale A set of categories for classifying objects.

Non-REM (NREM) sleep Non-rapid-eye-movement stages of sleep that alternate with REM stages during the sleep cycle.

Non-shared environment The unique aspects of the environment that are experienced differently by siblings, even though they are reared in the same family.

Norm A shared idea or expectation about how to behave.

Normal curve Hypothetical bell-shaped distribution curve that occurs when a normal distribution is plotted as a frequency polygon.

Obedience Change of behavior in response to a command from another person, typically an authority figure.

Object permanence The concept that things continue to exist even when they are out of sight.

Objective performance appraisal Method of performance appraisal based on quantitative measurement of the amount of work done.

Objective tests Personality tests that are administered and scored in a standard way.

Observational (or vicarious) learning Learning by observing other people's behavior.

Observer bias Expectations or biases of the observer that might distort or influence his or her interpretation of what was actually observed.

Obsessive–compulsive disorder (OCD) An anxiety related disorder in which a person feels driven to think disturbing thoughts or to perform senseless rituals.

Occipital lobe Part of the cerebrum that receives and interprets visual information.

Oedipus complex and Electra complex According to Freud, a child's sexual attachment to the parent of the opposite sex and jealousy toward the parent of the same sex; generally occurs in the phallic stage.

Olfactory bulb The smell center in the brain.

On-the-job training Teaching employees a new job by actually performing the job.

Operant (or instrumental) conditioning The type of learning in which behaviors are emitted (in the presence of specific stimuli) to earn rewards or avoid punishments.

Operant behaviors Behaviors designed to operate on the environment in a way that will gain something desired or avoid something unpleasant.

Opiates Drugs, such as opium and heroin, derived from the opium poppy, that dull the senses and induce feelings of euphoria, well-being, and relaxation. Synthetic drugs resembling opium derivatives are also classified as opiates.

Opponent-process theory Theory of color vision that holds that three sets of color receptors (yellow–blue, red–green, black–white) respond to determine the color you experience.

Optic chiasm The point near the base of the brain where some fibers in the optic nerve from each eye cross to the other side of the brain.

Optic nerve The bundle of axons of ganglion cells that carries neural messages from each eye to the brain.

Oral stage First stage in Freud's theory of personality development, in which the infant's erotic feelings center on the mouth, lips, and tongue.

Ordinal scale Scale indicating order or relative position of items according to some criterion.

Organ of Corti Structure on the surface of the basilar membrane that contains the receptor cells for hearing.

Organizational justice Degree to which employees perceive fairness in the workplace.

Organizational psychology Subfield of industrial/organizational psychology that focuses on the organization as a whole, rather than on the individuals who work within it.

Orgasmic disorders Inability to reach orgasm in a person able to experience sexual desire and maintain arousal.

Oval window Membrane across the opening between the middle ear and inner ear that conducts vibrations to the cochlea.

Overtones Tones that result from sound waves that are multiples of the basic tone; primary determinant of timbre.

Pancreas Organ lying between the stomach and small intestine; it secretes insulin and glucagon to regulate blood-sugar levels.

Panic disorder An anxiety disorder characterized by recurrent panic attacks in which the person suddenly experiences intense fear or terror without any reasonable cause.

Paranoid personality disorder Personality disorder in which the person is inappropriately suspicious and mistrustful of others.

Paraphilias Use of unconventional objects or situations to achieve sexual arousal.

Parasympathetic division Branch of the autonomic nervous system; it calms and relaxes the body.

Parathyroids Four tiny glands embedded in the thyroid.

Parietal lobe Part of the cerebrum that receives sensory information from throughout the body.

Participants Individuals whose reactions or responses are observed in an experiment.

Pedophilic disorder Desire to have sexual relations with children as the preferred or exclusive method of achieving sexual excitement.

Peer group A network of same-aged friends and acquaintances who give one another emotional and social support.

Perception The brain's interpretation of sensory information so as to give it meaning.

Perceptual constancy A tendency to perceive objects as stable and unchanging despite changes in sensory stimulation.

Performance appraisal systems Formal methods used to assess the quantity and quality of work contributed by each individual within an organization.

Performance standards In Bandura's theory, standards that people develop to rate the adequacy of their own behavior in a variety of situations.

Performance tests Intelligence tests that minimize the use of language.

Peripheral nervous system (PNS) Division of the nervous system that connects the central nervous system to the rest of the body.

Persistent depressive disorder A depressive disorder where the symptoms are generally less severe than for major depressive disorder, but are present most days and persist for at least 2 years.

Persona According to Jung, our public self; the mask we wear to represent ourselves to others.

Personal unconscious In Jung's theory of personality, one of the two levels of the unconscious; it contains the individual's repressed thoughts, forgotten experiences, and undeveloped ideas.

Personality An individual's unique pattern of thoughts, feelings, and behaviors that persists over time and across situations.

Personality disorders Disorders in which inflexible and maladaptive ways of thinking and behaving learned early in life cause distress to the person or conflicts with others.

Personality traits Dimensions or characteristics on which people differ in distinctive ways.

Personnel selection The process of selecting from a pool of job applicants those who will be hired to perform a job.

Phallic stage Third stage in Freud's theory of personality development, in which erotic feelings center on the genitals.

Phenotype The characteristics of an organism; determined by both genetics and experience.

Pheromones Chemicals that communicate information to other organisms through smell.

Phi phenomenon Apparent movement caused by flashing lights in sequence, as on theater marquees.

Phonemes The basic sounds that make up any language.

Pineal gland A gland located roughly in the center of the brain that appears to regulate activity levels over the course of a day.

Pitch Auditory experience corresponding primarily to frequency of sound vibrations, resulting in a higher or lower tone.

Pituitary gland Gland located on the underside of the brain; it produces the largest number of the body's hormones.

Place theory Theory that pitch is determined by the location of greatest vibration on the basilar membrane.

Placebo   Chemically inactive substance used for comparison with active drugs in experiments on the effects of drugs.

Placebo effect   Pain relief that occurs when a person believes a pill or procedure will reduce pain. The actual cause of the relief seems to come from endorphins.

Pleasure principle   According to Freud, the way in which the id seeks immediate gratification of an instinct.

Polarization   (as applied to group decision making) Shift in attitudes by members of a group toward more extreme positions than the ones held before group discussion.

Polarization   (as applied to neurons) The condition of a neuron when the inside is negatively charged relative to the outside; for example, when the neuron is at rest.

Polygenic inheritance   Process by which several genes interact to produce a certain trait; responsible for our most important traits.

Pons   Structure in the midbrain that regulates sleep and wake cycles.

Positive psychology   An emerging field of psychology that focuses on positive experiences, including subjective well-being, self-determination, the relationship between positive emotions and physical health, and the factors that allow individuals, communities, and societies to flourish.

Positive reinforcers   Events whose presence increases the likelihood that ongoing behavior will recur.

Posttraumatic growth (PTG)   Positive personal growth that may follow an extremely stressful event.

Posttraumatic stress disorder (PTSD)   Psychological disorder characterized by episodes of anxiety, sleeplessness, and nightmares resulting from some disturbing past event.

Prefrontal cortex   The forward most region of the frontal lobe involved in impulse control, judgment, and conscious awareness.

Prejudice   An unfair, intolerant, or unfavorable attitude toward a group of people.

Premature ejaculation   Inability of man to inhibit orgasm as long as desired.

Prenatal development   Development from conception to birth.

Preoperational stage   In Piaget's theory, the stage of cognitive development between 2 and 7 years of age in which the individual becomes able to use mental representations and language to describe, remember, and reason about the world, though only in an egocentric fashion.

Preparedness   A biological readiness to learn certain associations because of their survival advantages.

Pressure   A feeling that one must speed up, intensify, or change the direction of one's behavior or live up to a higher standard of performance.

Primacy effect   The fact that early information about someone weighs more heavily than later information in influencing one's impression of that person.

Primary drives   Unlearned drives, such as hunger, that are based on a physiological state.

Primary motor cortex   The section of the frontal lobe responsible for voluntary movement.

Primary prevention   Techniques and programs to improve the social environment so that new cases of mental disorders do not develop.

Primary reinforcers   Reinforcers that are rewarding in themselves, such as food, water, or sex.

Primary somatosensory cortex   Area of the parietal lobe where messages from the sense receptors are registered.

Principles of conservation   The concept that the quantity of a substance is not altered by reversible changes in its appearance.

Proactive interference   The process by which information already in memory interferes with new information.

Problem representation   The first step in solving a problem; it involves interpreting or defining the problem.

Procedural memories   The portion of long-term memory that stores information relating to skills, habits, and other perceptual-motor tasks.

Projection   Attributing one's repressed motives, feelings, or wishes to others.

Projective tests   Personality tests, such as the Rorschach inkblot test, consisting of ambiguous or unstructured material.

Prototype (or model)   According to Rosch, a mental model containing the most typical features of a concept.

Proximity   How close two people live to each other.

Psychoactive drugs   Chemical substances that change moods and perceptions.

Psychoanalysis   The theory of personality Freud developed, as well as the form of therapy he invented.

Psychoanalytic model   View that psychological disorders result from unconscious internal conflicts.

Psychobiology   The area of psychology that focuses on the biological foundations of behavior and mental processes.

Psychodynamic theories   Personality theories contending that behavior results from psychological factors that interact within the individual, often outside conscious awareness.

Psychology   The scientific study of behavior and mental processes.

Psychoneuroimmunology (PNI)   A new field that studies the interaction between stress on the one hand and immune, endocrine, and nervous system activity on the other.

Psychosomatic illness   A real physical illness that is largely caused by psychological factors such as stress and anxiety.

Psychostimulant   Drugs that increase ability to focus attention in people with ADHD.

Psychotherapy   The use of psychological techniques to treat personality and behavior disorders.

Psychotic (psychosis)   Behavior characterized by a loss of touch with reality.

Puberty   The onset of sexual maturation, with accompanying physical development.

Punishers   Stimuli that follows a behavior and decreases the likelihood that the behavior will be repeated.

Punishment   Any event whose presence decreases the likelihood that ongoing behavior will recur.

Pupil   A small opening in the iris through which light enters the eye.

Race   A subpopulation of a species, defined according to an identifiable characteristic (that is, geographic location, skin color, hair texture, genes, facial features, and so forth).

Racism   Prejudice and discrimination directed at a particular racial group.

Random sample   Sample in which each potential participant has an equal chance of being selected.

Range   Difference between the largest and smallest measurements in a distribution.

Rapid-eye movement (REM) or paradoxical sleep   Sleep stage characterized by rapid-eye movements and increased dreaming.

Ratio scale   Scale with equal distances between the points or values and with a true zero.

Rational–emotive therapy (RET)   A directive cognitive therapy based on the idea that clients' psychological distress is caused by irrational and self-defeating beliefs and that the therapist's job is to challenge such dysfunctional beliefs.

Reaction formation   Expression of exaggerated ideas and emotions that are the opposite of one's repressed beliefs or feelings.

Reality principle   According to Freud, the way in which the ego seeks to satisfy instinctual demands safely and effectively in the real world.

Receptor cell   A specialized cell that responds to a particular type of energy.

Receptor sites   Locations on a receptor neuron into which a specific neurotransmitter fits like a key into a lock.

Recessive gene   Member of a gene pair that can control the appearance of a certain trait only if it is paired with another recessive gene.

Regression   Reverting to childlike behavior and defenses.

Reinforcement theory   Theory that work behavior that is followed by positive outcomes will be maintained and repeated.

Reinforcers   A stimuli that follows a behavior and increases the likelihood that the behavior will be repeated.

Reliability   Ability of a test to produce consistent and stable scores.

Representative sample   Sample carefully chosen so that the characteristics of the participants correspond closely to the characteristics of the larger population.

Representativeness   A heuristic by which a new situation is judged on the basis of its resemblance to a stereotypical model.

Repression   Excluding uncomfortable thoughts, feelings, and desires from consciousness.

Response generalization   Giving a response that is somewhat different from the response originally learned to that stimulus.

Resting potential   Electrical charge across a neuron membrane resulting from more positive ions concentrated on the outside and more negative ions on the inside.

Reticular formation (RF)   Network of neurons in the hindbrain, the midbrain, and part of the forebrain, whose primary function is to alert and arouse the higher parts of the brain.

Retina   The lining of the eye containing receptor cells that are sensitive to light.

Retinal disparity   Binocular distance cue based on the difference between the images cast on the two retinas when both eyes are focused on the same object.

Retroactive interference   The process by which new information interferes with information already in memory.

Retrograde amnesia   The inability to recall events preceding an accident or injury, but without loss of earlier memory.

Risky shift   Greater willingness of a group than an individual to take substantial risks.

Rods   Receptor cells in the retina responsible for night vision and perception of brightness.

Rorschach test   A projective test composed of ambiguous inkblots; the way people interpret the blots is thought to reveal aspects of their personality.

Rote rehearsal   Retaining information in memory simply by repeating it over and over.

Sample   A subgroup of a population.

Saturation   The vividness or richness of a hue.

Scatter plot   Diagram showing the association between scores on two variables.

Schedule of reinforcement   In operant conditioning, the rule for determining when and how often reinforcers will be delivered.

Schema   (skee-mah; plural: schemata) A set of beliefs or expectations about something that is based on past experience.

Schizoid personality disorder   Personality disorder in which a person is withdrawn and lacks feelings for others.

Schizophrenic spectrum disorders   Severe disorders in which there are disturbances of thoughts, communications, and emotions, including delusions and hallucinations.

Scientific method   An approach to knowledge that relies on collecting data, generating a theory to explain the data, producing testable hypotheses based on the theory, and testing those hypotheses empirically.

Secondary drives   Learned drives, such as ambition, that are not based on a physiological state.

Secondary prevention   Programs to identify groups that are at high risk for mental disorders and to detect maladaptive behavior in these groups and treat it promptly.

Secondary reinforcers   Reinforcers whose value is acquired through association with other primary or secondary reinforcers.

Selection studies   Studies that estimate the heritability of a trait by breeding animals with other animals that have the same trait.

Self-actualizing tendency   According to Rogers, the drive of human beings to fulfill their self-concepts, or the images they have of themselves.

Self-efficacy   According to Bandura, the expectancy that one's efforts will be successful.

Self-fulfilling prophecy   The process in which a person's expectation about another elicits behavior from the second person that confirms the expectation.

Self-monitoring   The tendency for an individual to observe the situation for cues about how to react.

Semantic memories   The portion of long-term memory that stores general facts and information.

Sensation   The experience of sensory stimulation.

Sensory (or afferent) neurons   Neurons that carry messages from sense organs to the spinal cord or brain.

Sensory registers   Entry points for raw information from the senses.

Sensory-motor stage   In Piaget's theory, the stage of cognitive development between birth and 2 years of age in which the individual develops object permanence and acquires the ability to form mental representations.

Serial position effect   The finding that when asked to recall a list of unrelated items, performance is better for the items at the beginning and end of the list.

Set point theory   A theory that our bodies are genetically predisposed to maintaining a certain weight by changing our metabolic rate and activity level in response to caloric intake.

Sex-typed behavior   Socially prescribed ways of behaving that differ for boys and girls.

Sexual desire disorders   Disorders in which the person lacks sexual interest or has an active distaste for sex.

Sexual dysfunction   Loss or impairment of the ordinary physical responses of sexual function for at least six months.

Sexual harassment   Soliciting sexual favors in exchange for favorable treatment, or creating a hostile work environment.

Sexual masochism   Inability to enjoy sex without accompanying emotional or physical pain.

Sexual orientation   Refers to the direction of one's sexual interest toward members of the same sex, the other sex, or both sexes.

Sexual response cycle   The typical sequence of events, including excitement, plateau, orgasm, and resolution, characterizing sexual response in males and females.

Sexual sadism   Obtaining sexual gratification from humiliating or physically harming a sex partner.

Shadowing   Monocular cue to distance and depth based on the fact that shadows often appear on the parts of objects that are more distant.

Shape constancy   A tendency to see an object as the same shape no matter what angle it is viewed from.

Shaping   Reinforcing successive approximations to a desired behavior.

Short-term memory (STM)   Working memory; briefly stores and processes selected information from the sensory registers.

Short-term psychodynamic therapy   Insight therapy that is time limited and focused on trying to help clients correct the immediate problems in their lives.

Significance   Probability that results obtained were due to chance.

Signs   Stereotyped communications about an animal's current state.

Sixteen Personality Factor Questionnaire   Objective personality test created by Cattell that provides scores on the 16 traits he identified.

Size constancy   The perception of an object as the same size regardless of the distance from which it is viewed.

Skinner box   A box often used in operant conditioning of animals; it limits the available responses and thus increases the likelihood that the desired response will occur.

Social cognition   Knowledge and understanding concerning the social world and the people in it (including oneself).

Social influence   The process by which others individually or collectively affect one's perceptions, attitudes, and actions.

Social learning theorists   Psychologists whose view of learning emphasizes the ability to learn by observing a model or receiving instructions, without firsthand experience by the learner.

Social neuroscience   The application of brain imaging and other neuroscience methods to social psychology.

Social anxiety disorder   Anxiety disorders characterized by excessive, inappropriate fears connected with social situations or performances in front of other people.

Social psychology   The scientific study of the ways in which the thoughts, feelings, and behaviors of one individual are influenced by the real, imagined, or inferred behavior or characteristics of other people.

Socialization   Process by which children learn the behaviors and attitudes appropriate to their family and culture.

Somatic nervous system   The part of the peripheral nervous system that carries messages from the senses to the central nervous system and between the central nervous system and the skeletal muscles.

Somatic symptom disorder   Disorder characterized by recurrent vague somatic complaints without a physical cause.

Somatic symptom and related disorders   Disorders in which there is an apparent physical illness for which there is no organic basis.

Sound   A psychological experience created by the brain in response to changes in air pressure that are received by the auditory system.

Sound waves   Changes in pressure caused when molecules of air or fluid collide with one another and then move apart again.

Specific phobia   Anxiety disorder characterized by an intense, paralyzing fear of something.

Spinal cord   Complex cable of neurons that runs down the spine, connecting the brain to most of the rest of the body.

Split-half reliability   A method of determining test reliability by dividing the test into two parts and checking the agreement of scores on both parts.

Spontaneous recovery   The reappearance of an extinguished response after the passage of time, without training.

Standard deviation   Statistical measure of variability in a group of scores or other values.

Statistics   A branch of mathematics that psychologists use to organize and analyze data.

Stereoscopic vision   Combination of two retinal images to give a three-dimensional perceptual experience.

Stereotype   A set of characteristics presumed to be shared by all members of a social category.

Stimulants   Drugs, including amphetamines and cocaine, that stimulate the sympathetic nervous system and produce feelings of optimism and boundless energy.

Stimulus control   Control of conditioned responses by cues or stimuli in the environment.

Stimulus discrimination   Learning to respond to only one stimulus and to inhibit the response to all other stimuli.

Stimulus generalization   The transfer of a learned response to different but similar stimuli.

Stimulus motives   Unlearned motives, such as curiosity or contact, that prompt us to explore or change the world around us.

Strain studies   Studies of the heritability of behavioral traits using animals that have been inbred to produce strains that are genetically similar to one another.

Stranger anxiety   Fear of unfamiliar people which usually emerges around 7 months, reaching its peak at 12 months and declining during the second year.

Stress   A state of psychological tension or strain.

Stress-inoculation therapy   A type of cognitive therapy that trains clients to cope with stressful situations by learning a more useful pattern of self-talk.

Stressor   Any environmental demand that creates a state of tension or threat and requires change or adaptation.

Stroboscopic motion   Apparent movement that results from flashing a series of still pictures in rapid succession, as in a motion picture.

Structuralism   School of psychology that stresses the basic units of experience and the combinations in which they occur.

Subgoals   Intermediate, more manageable goals used in one heuristic strategy to make it easier to reach the final goal.

Subjective performance appraisal   Performance appraisal that relies on judgments about the quality of an employee's work.

Sublimation   Redirecting repressed motives and feelings into more socially acceptable channels.

Substance abuse   A pattern of drug use that diminishes the ability to fulfill responsibilities at home, work, or school that results in repeated use of a drug in dangerous situations or that leads to legal difficulties related to drug use.

Substance dependence   A pattern of compulsive drug taking that results in tolerance, withdrawal symptoms, or other specific symptoms for at least a year.

Subtractive color mixing   The process of mixing pigments, each of which absorbs some wavelengths of light and reflects others.

Superego   According to Freud, the social and parental standards the individual has internalized; the conscience and the ego ideal.

Suprachiasmatic nucleus (SCN)   A cluster of neurons in the hypothalamus that receives input from the retina regarding light and dark cycles and is involved in regulating the biological clock.

Survey research   Research technique in which questionnaires or interviews are administered to a selected group of people.

Sympathetic division   Branch of the autonomic nervous system; it prepares the body for quick action in an emergency.

Synapse   Area composed of the axon terminal of one neuron, the synaptic space, and the dendrite or cell body of the next neuron.

Synaptic space (or synaptic cleft)   Tiny gap between the axon terminal of one neuron and the dendrites or cell body of the next neuron.

Synaptic vesicles   Tiny sacs in a terminal button that release chemicals into the synapse.

Systematic desensitization   A behavioral technique for reducing a person's fear and anxiety by gradually associating a new response (relaxation) with stimuli that have been causing the fear and anxiety.

Systems approach   View that biological, psychological, and social risk factors combine to produce psychological disorders. Also known as the biopsychosocial model of psychological disorders.

Taste buds   Structures on the tongue that contain the receptor cells for taste.

Temperament   Characteristic patterns of emotional reactions and emotional self-regulation.

Temporal lobe   Part of the cerebral hemisphere that helps regulate hearing, balance and equilibrium, and certain emotions and motivations.

Teratogens   Toxic substances such as alcohol or nicotine that cross the placenta and may result in birth defects.

Terminal button (or synaptic knob)   Structure at the end of an axon terminal branch.

Tertiary prevention   Programs to help people adjust to community life after release from a mental hospital.

Testosterone   The primary male sex hormone.

Texture gradient   Monocular cue to distance and depth based on the fact that objects seen at greater distances appear to be smoother and less textured.

Thalamus   Forebrain region that relays and translates incoming messages from the sense receptors, except those for smell.

Thematic Apperception Test (TAT)   A projective test composed of ambiguous pictures about which a person is asked to write a complete story.

Theory   Systematic explanation of a phenomenon; it organizes known facts, allows us to predict new facts, and permits us to exercise a degree of control over the phenomenon.

Theory of multiple intelligences   Howard Gardner's theory that there is not one intelligence, but rather many intelligences, each of which is relatively independent of the others.

Threshold of excitation   The level an impulse must exceed to cause a neuron to fire.

Thyroid gland   Endocrine gland located below the voice box; it produces the hormone thyroxin.

Timbre   The quality or texture of sound; caused by overtones.

Tip-of-the-tongue phenomenon (or TOT)   Knowing a word, but not being able to immediately recall it.

Token economy   An operant conditioning therapy in which people earn tokens (reinforcers) for desired behaviors and exchange them for desired items or privileges.

Transduction   The conversion of physical energy into coded neural signals.

Transference   The client's carrying over to the analyst feelings held toward childhood authority figures.

Transvestic fetishism   Wearing the clothes of the opposite sex to achieve sexual gratification.

Triarchic theory of intelligence   Sternberg's theory that intelligence involves mental skills (analytical intelligence), insight and creative adaptability (creative intelligence), and environmental responsiveness (practical intelligence).

Trichromatic (or three-color) theory   The theory of color vision that holds that all color perception derives from three different color receptors in the retina (usually red, green, and blue receptors).

Twin studies   Studies of identical and fraternal twins to determine the relative influence of heredity and environment on human behavior.

Unconditional positive regard   In Rogers's theory, the full acceptance and love of another person regardless of his or her behavior.

Unconditioned response (UR)   A response that takes place in an organism whenever an unconditioned stimulus occurs.

Unconditioned stimulus (US)   A stimulus that invariably causes an organism to respond in a specific way.

Unconscious   In Freud's theory, all the ideas, thoughts, and feelings of which we are not and normally cannot become aware.

Vaginismus   Involuntary muscle spasms in the outer part of the vagina that make intercourse impossible.

Validity   Ability of a test to measure what it has been designed to measure.

Variable-interval schedule   A reinforcement schedule in which the correct response is reinforced after varying lengths of time following the last reinforcement.

Variable-ratio schedule   A reinforcement schedule in which a varying number of correct responses must occur before reinforcement is presented.

Vestibular senses   The senses of equilibrium and body position in space.

Vestibule training   Teaching employees new techniques and behaviors in a simulated workplace.

Vicarious reinforcement (or punishment)   Reinforcement or punishment experienced by models that affects the willingness of others to perform the behaviors they learned by observing those models.

Visual acuity   The ability to distinguish fine details visually.

Volley principle   Refinement of frequency theory; it suggests that receptors in the ear fire in sequence, with one group responding, then a second, then a third, and so on, so that the complete pattern of firing corresponds to the frequency of the sound wave.

Voyeurism   Desire to watch others having sexual relations or to spy on nude people.

Waking consciousness   Mental state that encompasses the thoughts, feelings, and perceptions that occur when we are awake and reasonably alert.

Wavelengths   The different energies represented in the electromagnetic spectrum.

Weber's law   The principle that the jnd for any given sense is a constant fraction or proportion of the stimulation being judged.

Wechsler Adult Intelligence Scale—Fourth Edition (WAIS-IV)   An individual intelligence test developed especially for adults; measures both verbal and performance abilities.

Wechsler Intelligence Scale for Children—Fourth Edition (WISC-IV)   An individual intelligence test developed especially for school-aged children; measures verbal and performance abilities and also yields an overall IQ score.

Withdrawal   Avoiding a situation when other forms of coping are not practical.

Working backward   A heuristic strategy in which one works backward from the desired goal to the given conditions.

Yerkes–Dodson law   States that there is an optimal level of arousal for the best performance of any task; the more complex the task, the lower the level of arousal that can be tolerated before performance deteriorates.

References

Aaker, D. A., & Bruzzone, D. E. (1985). Causes of irritation in advertising. *Journal of Marketing, 49*, 47–57.

Abbass, A. A., Joffres, M. R., & Ogrodniczuk, J. S. (2008). A naturalistic study of intensive short-term dynamic psychotherapy trial therapy. *Brief Treatment and Crisis Intervention, 8*, 164–170.

Abraham, W. C., & Williams, J. M. (2008). LTP maintenance and its protein synthesis-dependence. *Neurobiology of Learning and Memory, 89*, 260–268.

Accreditation Council for Graduate Medical Education. (2003). *The ACGME's approach to limit resident duty hours: The common standards and activities to promote adherence.* Retrieved from http://www.acgme.org/acWebsite/duty Hours/dh_dhSummary.pdf

Acharya, N., & Joshi, S. (2011). Achievement motivation and parental support to adolescents. *Journal of the Indian Academy of Applied Psychology, 37*, 132–139.

Achter, J. A., Lubinski, D., & Benbow, C. P. (1996). Multipotentiality among the intellectually gifted: "It was never there and already it's vanishing." *Journal of Counseling Psychology, 43*, 65–76.

Ackerman, D. (1995). *A natural history of the senses.* New York, NY: Vintage.

Acredolo, L. P., & Hake, J. L. (1982). Infant perception. In B. B. Wolman (Ed.), *Handbook of developmental psychology* (pp. 244–283). Englewood Cliffs, NJ: Prentice Hall.

Addis, M. E., & Mahalik, J. R. (2003). Men, masculinity, and the contexts of help seeking. *American Psychologist, 58*, 5–14.

Addolorato, G., Leggio, L., Abenavoli, L., & Gasbarrini, G. (2005). Neurobio-chemical and clinical aspects of craving in alcohol addiction: A review. *Addictive Behaviors, 30*, 1209–1224.

Adolphs, R. (2006). Perception and emotion. How we recognize facial expressions. *Current Directions in Psychological Science, 15*, 222–226.

Adolphs, R. (2008). Fear, faces, and the human amygdala. *Current Opinion in Neurobiology, 18*, 166–172.

Adolphs, R., & Tranel, D. (2003). Amygdala damage impairs emotion recognition from scenes only when they contain facial expressions. *Neuropsychologia, 41*, 1281–1289.

Adolphs, R., Baron-Cohen, S., & Tranel, D. (2002). Impaired recognition of social emotions following amygdala damage. *Journal of Cognitive Neuroscience, 14*, 1264–1274.

Adolphs, R., Tranel, D., Damasio, H., & Damasio, A. (1994). Impaired recognition of emotion in facial expressions following bilateral damage to the human amygdala. *Nature, 372*, 669–672.

Adorno, T. W., Frenkel-Brunswick, E., Levinson, D. J., & Sanford, R. N. (1950). *The authoritarian personality.* New York, NY: Harper & Row.

Aeschleman, S. R., Rosen, C. C., & Williams, M. R. (2003). The effect of non-contingent negative and positive reinforcement operations on the acquisition of superstitious behaviors. *Behavioural Processes, 61*, 37–45.

AhYun, K. (2002). Similarity and attraction. In M. Allen, R. W. Preiss, B. M. Gayle, & N. A. Burrell (Eds.), *Interpersonal communication research: Advances through meta-analysis* (pp. 145–167). Mahwah, NJ: Erlbaum.

Ainsworth, M. D. S. (1977). Attachment theory and its utility in cross cultural research. In P. H. Leiderman, S. Tulkin, & A. Rosenfeld (Eds.), *Culture and infancy: Variations in the human experience* (pp. 49–67). New York, NY: Academic Press.

Ajzen, I., & Cote, N. (2008). Attitudes and the prediction of behavior. In W. D. Crano & R. Prislin (Eds.), *Attitudes and attitude change* (pp. 289–311). New York, NY: Psychology Press.

Alexander, C. N., Robinson, P., & Rainforth, M. (1994). Treating and preventing alcohol, nicotine, and drug abuse through Transcendental Meditation: A review and statistical meta-analysis. *Alcoholism Treatment Quarterly, 11*(1–2), 13–87.

Ali, A. (2008). Sadness revealed: Insights on women's depression. *Psychology of Women Quarterly, 32*, 108–109.

Alia-Klein, N., Goldstein, R. Z., Kriplani, A., Logan, J., Tomasi, D., Williams, B., . . . Fowler, J. S. (2008). Brain monoamine oxidase A activity predicts trait aggression. *The Journal of Neuroscience, 28*, 5099–5104.

Allen, R. S., Haley, W. E., Roff, L. L., Schmid, B., & Bergman, E. J. (2006). Responding to the needs of caregivers near the end of life: Enhancing benefits and minimizing burdens. In J. L. Werth, Jr. & D. Blevins (Eds.), *Psychosocial issues near the end of life: A resource for professional care providers* (pp. 183–201). Washington, DC: American Psychological Association.

Allen, S. (2008). Procedural memory consolidation in musicians. *Dissertation Abstracts International Section A, 68*, 2714. Retrieved from EBSCOhost.

Alliger, G. M., & Janak, E. A. (1989). Kirkpatrick's levels of training criteria: Thirty years later. *Personnel Psychology, 42*, 331–342.

Allport, G. W. (1954). *The nature of prejudice.* New York, NY: Anchor.

Allport, G. W., & Odbert, H. S. (1936). Trait-names: A psycholexical study. *Psychological Monographs, 47*(1, Whole No. 211).

Almeida, D. M. (2005). Resilience and vulnerability to daily stressors assessed via diary methods. *Current Directions in Psychological Science, 14*, 64–68.

Almer, E. (2000, April 22). On-line therapy: An arm's-length approach. *New York Times*, pp. A1, A11.

Almgren, G., Guest, A., Immerwahr, G., & Spittel, M. (2002). Joblessness, family disruption, and violent death in Chicago, 1970–90. *Social Forces, 76*, 1465–1493.

Alonso, P., Gratacòs, M., Menchón, J. M., Segalàs, C., González, J. R., Labad, J., . . . Estivill, X. (2008). Genetic susceptibility to obsessive-compulsive hoarding: The contribution of neurotrophic tyrosine kinase receptor type 3 gene. *Genes, Brain & Behavior, 7*, 778–785.

Altabe, M. N., & Thompson, J. K. (1994). Body image. In V. A. Ramachandran (Ed.), *Encyclopedia of human behavior* (Vol. 1, pp. 407–414). San Diego, CA: Academic Press.

Altemeyer, B. (2004). Highly dominating, highly authoritarian personalities. *Journal of Social Psychology, 144*, 421–447.

Alzheimer's Association. (2006). *Statistics about Alzheimer's disease.* Retrieved from http://www.alz.org/AboutAD/statistics.asp

Amaral, D. G., Schumann, C., & Nordahl, C. (2008). Neuroanatomy of autism. *Trends in Neurosciences, 31*, 137–145.

Amedi, A., Merabet, L. B., Bermpohl, F., & Pascual-Leone, A. (2005). The occipital cortex in the blind: Lessons about plasticity and vision. *Current Directions in Psychological Science, 14*, 306–311.

Amen, D. G., Stubblefield, M., Carmichael, B., & Thisted, R. (1996). Brain SPECT findings and aggressiveness. *Annals of Clinical Psychiatry, 8*, 129–137.

American Academy of Pediatrics. (1999, August 2). *AAP discourages television for very young children.* Press release.

American Academy of Pediatrics. (2007). *TV and your family.* Retrieved from http://www.aap.org/publiced/BR_TV.htm

American Heart Association. (2009). *Overweight in children.* Retrieved from http://www.americanheart.org/presenter.jhtml?identifier=4670

American Psychiatric Association (APA). (1994). *Diagnostic and statistical manual of mental disorders* (4th ed.). Washington, DC: Author.

American Psychiatric Association (APA). (2013). *Diagnostic and statistical manual of mental disorders (5th ed.), (DSM-5).* Arlington, VA: Author.

American Psychological Association. (2000, November). Facts & figures. *Monitor on Psychology, 31*(11), 10.

American Psychological Association. (2005). *New definition: Hypnosis.* Retrieved from http://www.apa.org/divisions/div30/define_hypnosis.html

American Psychological Association. (2006). *Briefing sheet: Women and depression.* Washington, DC: Public Policy Office, American Psychological Association. Retrieved from http://www.apa.org/ppo/issues/pwomenanddepress.html

American Psychological Association. (2007). Reports of the Association: Guidelines for psychological practice with girls and women. *American Psychologist, 62*, 949–979.

American Psychological Association. (2008, June). Psychology is the fourth most popular undergraduate major. *Monitor on Psychology, 39*(6), 11.

American Psychological Association. (2010). *Ethical Principles of Psychologists and Code of Conduct.* Retrieved from http://www.apa.org/ethics/code/index.aspx

American Psychological Association. (2010). *Guidelines for Ethical Conduct in the Care and Use of Animals.* Retrieved from http://www.apa.org/science/leadership/care/animal-guide-2010.pdf

American Psychological Association. (2011a). *Just the facts about sexual orientation and youth: Efforts to change sexual orientation through therapy.* Retrieved from http://www.apa.org/pi/lgbt/resources/just-the-facts.aspx

American Psychological Association. (2011b). Membership statistics March 2011. Retrieved from http://memforms.apa.org/apa/cli/mbdirsearch/memstat.cfm

Andersen, B. L., Kiecolt-Glaser, J. K., & Glaser, R. (1994). A biobehavioral model of cancer stress and disease course. *American Psychologist, 49,* 389–404.

Anderson, C. A., Gentile, D. A., & Buckley, K. E. (2007). *Violent video game effects on children and adolescents: Theory, research, and public policy.* New York, NY: Oxford University Press.

Anderson, C. A., Berkowitz, L., Donnerstein, E., Huesmann, L. R., Johnson, J. D., Linz, D., . . . Wartella, E. (2003). The influence of media violence on youth. *Psychological Science in the Public Interest, 4,* 81–110.

Anderson, C. A., Shibuya, A., Ihori, N., Swing, E. L., Bushman, B. J., Sakamoto, A., . . . Saleem, M. (2010). Violent video game effects on aggression, empathy, and prosocial behavior in Eastern and Western countries: A meta-analytic review. *Psychological Bulletin, 136,* 151–173.

Anderson, D. R. (1998). Educational television is not an oxymoron. *Annals of Public Policy Research, 557,* 24–38.

Anderson, D. R., Huston, A. C., Wright, J. C., & Collins, P. A. (1998). Initial findings on the long term impact of *Sesame Street* and educational television for children: The Recontact Study. In R. Noll & M. Price (Eds.), *A communications cornucopia: Markle Foundation essays on information policy* (pp. 279–296). Washington, DC: Brookings Institution.

Anderson, R. I., Varlinskaya, E. I., & Spear, L. P. (2010). Ethanol-induced conditioned taste aversion in male Sprague-Dawley rats: Impact of age and stress. *Alcoholism: Clinical and Experimental Research, 34,* 2106–2115.

Anderson, S. E. [Sarah], Dallal, G. E., & Must, A. (2003). Relative weight and race influence average age at menarche: Results from two nationally representative surveys of US girls studied 25 years apart. *Pediatrics, 111,* 844–850.

Anderson, S. W. [Shawanda], & Booker, M. B. (2006). Cognitive behavioral therapy versus psychosurgery for refractory obsessive-compulsive disorder. *Journal of Neuropsychiatry & Clinical Neurosciences, 18,* 129.

Ang, R. P., & Woo, A. (2003). Influence of sensation seeking on boys' psychosocial adjustment. *North American Journal of Psychology, 5,* 121–136.

Angus, J. (2011). Autism spectrum disorders: Current thinking on etiology and diagnosis. In A. M. Bursztyn (Ed.), *Childhood psychological disorders: Current controversies* (pp. 71–85). Santa Barbara, CA: Praeger/ABC-CLIO.

Annesi, J. J. (2005). Changes in depressed mood associated with 10 weeks of moderate cardiovascular exercise in formerly sedentary adults. *Psychological Reports, 96,* 855–862.

Antoni, M. H. (2003). Stress management and psychoneuroimmunology in HIV Infection. *CNS Spectrums, 8,* 40–51.

Antoniello, D., Kluger, B. M., Sahlein, D. H., & Heilman, K. M. (2010). Phantom limb after stroke: An underreported phenomenon. *Cortex, 46,* 1114.

Aranow, E., Weiss, K. A., & Reznikoff, M. (2001). *A practical guide to the Thematic Apperception Test: The TAT in clinical practice.* Philadelphia, PA: Brunner-Routledge.

Archer, J. (2009). Does sexual selection explain human sex differences? *Behavioral and Brain Sciences, 32,* 249–311.

Aries, E. (2006). Sex differences in interaction: A reexamination. In K. Dindia & D. J. Canary (Eds.), *Sex differences and similarities in communication* (2nd ed., pp. 21–36). Mahwah, NJ: Erlbaum.

Arnedt, J. T., Owens, J., Crouch, M., Stahl, J., & Carskadon, M. A. (2005). Neurobehavioral performance of residents after heavy night call vs. after alcohol ingestion. *JAMA: Journal of the American Medical Association, 294,* 1025–1033.

Arnett, J. J. (1999). Adolescent storm and stress, reconsidered. *American Psychologist, 54,* 317–326.

Arnett, J. J. (2008). The neglected 95%: Why American psychology needs to become less American. *American Psychologist, 63,* 602–614.

Arria, A. M., Caldeira, K. M., Kasperski, S. J., Vincent, K. B., Griffiths, R. R., & O'Grady, K. E. (2011). Energy drink consumption and increased risk for alcohol dependence. *Alcoholism: Clinical and Experimental Research, 35,* 365–375.

Arsenio, W. F. (2004). The stability of young children's physical aggression: Relations with child care, gender, and aggression subtypes. *Monographs of the Society for Research in Child Development, 69,* 130–143.

Ary, D. V., Duncan, T. E., Duncan, S. C., & Hops, H. (1999). Adolescent problem behavior: The influence of parents and peers. *Behaviour Research and Therapy, 37,* 217–230.

Asch, S. E. (1951). Effects of group pressure upon the modification and distortion of judgments. In H. Guetzkow (Ed.), *Groups, leadership, and men* (pp. 295–303). Pittsburgh, PA: Carnegie Press.

Asch, S. E. (1956). Studies of independence and conformity: I. A minority of one against a unanimous majority. *Psychological Monographs, 70*(9, Whole No. 416).

Asendorpf, J. B., & Van-Aken, M. A. G. (2003). Validity of big five personality judgements in childhood: A 9 year longitudinal study. *European Journal of Personality, 17,* 1–17.

Ashley, R. (1975, October 17). The other side of LSD. *New York Times Magazine,* pp. 40ff.

Aspinwall, L. G., & Taylor, S. E. (1997). A stitch in time: Self-regulation and proactive coping. *Psychological Bulletin, 121,* 417–436.

Asrican, B. (2007). Plasticity at excitatory hippocampal synapses and CaMKII as a molecular memory molecule. *Dissertation Abstracts International: Section B: The Sciences and Engineering, 68,* 1456.

Astur, R. S., Taylor, L. B., Marnelak, A. N., Philpott, L., & Sutherland, R. J. (2002). Humans with hippocampus damage display severe spatial memory impairments in a virtual Morris water task. *Behavioural Brain Research, 132,* 77–84.

Atchley, R. C. (1982). Retirement as a social institution. *Annual Review of Sociology, 8,* 263–287.

Aust, U., & Huber, L. (2006). Picture–object recognition in pigeons: Evidence of representational insight in a visual categorization task using a complementary information procedure. *Journal of Experimental Psychology: Animal Behavior Processes, 32,* 190–195.

Auyeung, B., Baron-Cohen, S., Ashwin, E., Knickmeyer, R., Taylor, K., Hackett, G., & Hines, M. (2009). Fetal testosterone predicts sexually differentiated childhood behavior in girls and in boys. *Psychological Science, 20,* 144–148.

Ayan, S. (2009, April/May). Laughing matters. *Scientific American Mind, 20*(2), 24–31.

Ayas, N. T., White, D. P., Manson, J. E., Stampfer, M. J., Speizer, F. E., Malhotra, A., & Hu, F. B. (2003). A prospective study of sleep duration and coronary heart disease in women. *Archives of Internal Medicine, 163,* 205–209.

Ayman, R., Chemers, M. M., & Fiedler, F. E. (2007). The contingency model of leadership effectiveness: Its levels of analysis. In R. P. Vecchio (Ed.), *Leadership: Understanding the dynamics of power and influence in organizations* (2nd ed., pp. 335–360). South Bend, IN: University of Notre Dame Press.

Azar, B. (1999, March). "Decade of Behavior" moves forward. *APA Monitor, 30*(3), 16.

Back, M. D., & Egloff, B. (2009). Discussion on 'personality psychology as a truly behavioral science' by R. Michael Furr: Yes we can! A plea for direct behavioural observation in personality research. *European Journal of Personality, 23,* 403–408.

Back-Madruga, C., Boone, K. B., Chang, L., Grob, C. S., Lee, A., Nations, H., & Poland, R. E. (2003). Neuropsychological effects of 3, 4-methylenedioxymethamphetamine (MDMA or Ecstasy) in recreational users. *Clinical Neuropsychologist, 17,* 446–459.

Baddeley, A. D. (1986). *Working memory.* New York, NY: Clarendon.

Baddeley, A. D. (2002). Is working memory still working? *European Psychologist, 7,* 85–97.

Baddeley, R., & Attewell, D. (2009). The relationship between language and the environment: Information theory shows why we have only three lightness terms. *Psychological Science, 20,* 1100–1107.

Badner, J. A. (2003). The genetics of bipolar disorder. In B. Geller & M. P. DelBello (Eds.), *Bipolar disorder in childhood and early adolescence* (pp. 247–254). New York, NY: Guilford Press.

Badr, L. K., & Abdallah, B. (2001). Physical attractiveness of premature infants affects outcome at discharge from the NICU. *Infant Behavior and Development, 24,* 129–133.

Baer, J. (2008). Commentary: Divergent thinking tests have problems, but this is not the solution. *Psychology of Aesthetics, Creativity, and the Arts, 2,* 89–92.

Bagby, R. M., & Marshall, M. B. (2005). Assessing response bias with the MCMI modifying indices. In R. J. Craig (Ed.), *New directions in interpreting the Millon™ Clinical Multiaxial Inventory-III (MCMI-III™)* (pp. 227–247). Hoboken, NJ: Wiley.

Bagby, R. M., Sellbom, M., Costa, P. T., & Widiger, T. A. (2008). Predicting Diagnostic and Statistical Manual of Mental Disorders-IV personality disorders with the five-factor model of personality and the personality psychopathology five. *Personality and Mental Health, 2,* 55–69.

Bagemihl, B. (2000). *Biological exuberance: Animal homosexuality and natural diversity.* New York, NY: St. Martin's Press.

Bailey, A. (2006). Long-term retention of olfactory discrimination learning set in rats. *The Psychological Record, 56*, 219–231.

Baillargeon, R. (1994). How do infants learn about the physical world? *Current Directions in Psychological Science, 3*, 133–140.

Bajbouj, M., Lang, U. E., Niehaus, L., Hellen, F. E., Heuser, I., & Neu, P. (2006). Effects of right unilateral electroconvulsive therapy on motor cortical excitability in depressive patients. *Journal of Psychiatric Research, 40*, 322–327.

Baker, A., & Dawe, S. (2005). Amphetamine use and co-occurring psychological problems: Review of the literature and implications for treatment. *Australian Psychologist, 40*, 88–95.

Balcetis, E., & Dunning, D. (2007). Cognitive dissonance and the perception of natural environments. *Psychological Science, 18*, 917–921.

Balcetis, E., Dunning, D., & Miller, R. L. (2008). Do collectivists know themselves better than individualists? Cross-cultural studies of the holier than thou phenomenon. *Journal of Personality and Social Psychology, 95*, 1252–1267.

Balfour, M. E. (2004). Sexual behavior causes activation and functional alterations of mesolimbic systems: Neurobiology of motivation and reward. *Dissertation Abstracts International: Section B: The Sciences and Engineering, 64*, 4789.

Ball, D. (2004). Genetic approaches to alcohol dependence. *British Journal of Psychiatry, 185*, 449–451.

Balschun, D., Moechars, D., Callaerts-Vegh, Z., Vermaercke, B., Van Acker, N., Andries, L., & D'Hooge, R. (2010). Vesicular glutamate transporter VGLUT1 has a role in hippocampal long-term potentiation and spatial reversal learning. *Cerebral Cortex, 20*, 684–693.

Bamberg, S., & Moser, G. (2007). Twenty years after Hines, Hungerford, & Tomera: A new meta-analysis of psycho-social determinants of pro-environment behavior. *Journal of Environmental Psychology, 27*, 14–25.

Banaji, M. R., & Hardin, C. D. (1996). Automatic stereotyping. *Psychological Science, 7*, 136–141.

Bandstra, E. S., Morrow, C. E., Mansoor, E., & Accornero, V. H. (2010). Prenatal drug exposure: Infant and toddler outcomes. *Journal of Addictive Diseases, 29*, 245–258.

Bandura, A. (1965). Influence of models' reinforcement contingencies on the acquisition of imitative responses. *Journal of Personality and Social Psychology, 1*, 589–595.

Bandura, A. (1977). *Social learning theory*. Englewood Cliffs, NJ: Prentice Hall.

Bandura, A. (1997). *Self-efficacy: The exercise of control*. New York, NY: Freeman.

Bandura, A. (2004). Model of causality in social learning theory. In A. Freeman, M. J. Mahoney, P. DeVito, & D. Martin (Eds.), *Cognition and psychotherapy* (2nd ed., pp. 25–44). New York, NY: Springer.

Bandura, A., & Locke, E. A. (2003). Negative self-efficacy and goal effects revisited. *Journal of Applied Psychology, 8*, 87–99.

Bandura, A., Blanchard, E. B., & Ritter, B. (1969). Relative efficacy of desensitization and modeling approaches for inducing behavioral, affective, and attitudinal changes. *Journal of Personality and Social Psychology, 13*, 173–199.

Barbaree, H. E., & Seto, M. C. (1997). Pedophilia: Assessment and treatment. In D. R. Laws & W. T. O'Donohue (Eds.), *Sexual Deviance: Theory, assessment and treatment* (pp. 175–193). New York, NY: Guilford Press.

Barber, B. L., Stone, M. R., Hunt, J. E., & Eccles, J. S. (2005). Benefits of activity participation: The roles of identity affirmation and peer group norm sharing. In J. L. Mahoney, R. W. Larson, & J. S. Eccles (Eds.), *Organized activities as contexts of development: Extracurricular activities, after-school and community programs* (pp. 185–210). Mahwah, NJ: Erlbaum.

Bard, K. A., Todd, B. K., Bernier, C., Love, J., & Leavens, D. A. (2006). Self-awareness in human and chimpanzee infants: What is measured and what is meant by the mark and mirror test? *Infancy, 9*, 191–219.

Barel, E., Van IJzendoorn, M. H., Sagi-Schwartz, A., & Bakermans-Kranenburg, M. J. (2010). Surviving the Holocaust: A meta-analysis of the long-term sequelae of a genocide. *Psychological Bulletin, 136*, 677–698.

Barinaga, M. (2000). Asilomar revisited: Lessons for today. *Science, 287*, 1584–1585.

Barnett, J. E., & Scheetz, K. (2003). Technological advances and telehealth: Ethics, law, and the practice of psychotherapy. *Psychotherapy: Theory, Research, Practice, Training, 40*, 86–93.

Barnett, K. J. (2008). Colour knowledge: The role of the right hemisphere in colour processing and object colour knowledge. *Laterality: Asymmetries of Body, Brain and Cognition, 13*, 456–467.

Barnett, M. A. (2008). Economic disadvantage in complex family systems: Expansion of family stress models. *Clinical Child and Family Psychology Review, 11*, 145–161.

Barnett, W. S. (1998). Long-term effects on cognitive development and school success. In W. S. Barnett & S. S. Boocock (Eds.), *Early care and education for children in poverty: Promises, programs, and long-term results* (pp. 11–44). Albany: State University of New York Press.

Barrett, L. F. (2009). The future of psychology: Connecting mind to brain. *Perspectives on Psychological Science, 4*, 326–339.

Barrett, L. F., & Wager, T. D. (2006). The structure of emotion: Evidence from neuroimaging studies. *Current Directions in Psychological Science, 15*, 79–83.

Barrick, M. R., & Mount, M. K. (1991). The Big Five personality dimensions and job performance: A meta-analysis. *Personnel Psychology, 44*, 1–26.

Barrick, M. R., Mount, M. K., & Judge, T. A. (2001). Personality and performance at the beginning of the new millennium: What do we know and where do we go next? *International Journal of Selection and Assessment, 9*, 9–30.

Barron, F. (1963). *Creativity and psychological health*. Princeton, NJ: Van Nostrand.

Barry, H. III (2007). Corporal punishment and other formative experiences associated with violent crimes. *Journal of Psychohistory, 35*, 71–81.

Bartlett, F. C. (1932). *Remembering: A study in experimental and social psychology*. New York, NY: Macmillan.

Bartoshuk, L. (2009, December). Spicing up psychological science. *APS Observer, 22*, pp. 3, 46.

Basow, S. A. (2010). Changes in psychology of women and psychology of gender textbooks (1975–2010). *Sex Roles, 62*, 151–152.

Batson, C. D. (2006). 'Not all self-interest after all': Economics of empathy-induced altruism. In D. De Cremer, M. Zeelenberg, & J. K. Murnighan (Eds.), *Social psychology and economics* (pp. 281–299). Mahwah, NJ: Erlbaum.

Batson, C. D. (2011). *Altruism in humans*. New York, NY: Oxford University Press.

Batson, C. D., Ahmad, N., Lishner, D. A., & Tsang, J.-A. (2002). Empathy and altruism. In C. R. Snyder & S. J. Lopez (Eds.), *Handbook of positive psychology* (pp. 485–498). New York, NY: Oxford University Press.

Battro, A. M. (2006). *The story of Nico: Half a brain is enough*. Cambridge, England: Cambridge University Press.

Bauer, P. J. (1996). What do infants recall of their lives? Memory for specific events by one- to two-year-olds. *American Psychologist, 51*, 29–41.

Bauer, P. J. (2008). Toward a neuro-developmental account of the development of declarative memory. *Developmental Psychobiology, 50*, 19–31.

Bauer, P. J., Burch, M. M., Scholin, S. E., & Güler, O. E. (2007). Using cue words to investigate the distribution of autobiographical memories in childhood. *Psychological Science, 18*, 910–916.

Baumeister, A. A., & Baumeister, A. A. (2000). Mental retardation: Causes and effects. In M. Hersen & R. T. Ammerman (Eds.), *Advanced abnormal child psychology* (2nd. ed.) (pp. 327–355). Mahwah, NJ: Erlbaum.

Bauminger, N., Finzi-Dottan, R., Chason, S., & Har-Even, D. (2008). Intimacy in adolescent friendship: The roles of attachment, coherence, and self-disclosure. *Journal of Social and Personal Relationships, 25*, 409–428.

Baumrind, D. (1972). Socialization and instrumental competence in young children. In W. W. Hartup (Ed.), *The young child: Reviews of research* (Vol. 2, pp. 202–224). Washington, DC: National Association for the Education of Young Children.

Baumrind, D. (1991). Parenting styles and adolescent development. In J. Brooks-Gunn, R. Lerner, & A. C. Petersen (Eds.), *The encyclopedia of adolescence* (Vol. 2, pp. 746–758). New York, NY: Garland.

Baumrind, D. (1996). The discipline controversy revisited. *Family Relations: Journal of Applied Family and Child Studies, 45*, 405–414.

Beasley, M., Thompson, T., & Davidson, J. (2003). Resilience in response to life stress: The effects of coping style and cognitive hardiness. *Personality and Individual Differences, 34*, 77–95.

Beck, A. T. (1967). *Depression: Clinical, experimental and theoretical aspects*. New York, NY: Harper (Hoeber).

Beck, A. T. (1976). *Cognitive therapy and emotional disorders*. New York, NY: International Universities Press.

Beck, A. T. (1984). Cognition and therapy. *Archives of General Psychiatry, 41*, 1112–1114.

Beck, H. P., Levinson, S., & Irons, G. (2009). Finding Little Albert: A journey to John B. Watson's infant laboratory. *American Psychologist, 64*, 605–614.

Beebe, D. W., Rose, D., & Amin, R. (2010). Attention, learning, and arousal of experimentally sleep-restricted adolescents in a simulated classroom. *Journal of Adolescent Health, 47*, 523–525.

Beilock, S. L. (2008). Math performance in stressful situations. *Current Directions in Psychological Science, 17*, 339–343.

Bekinschtein, P., Cammarota, M., Katche, C., Slipczuk, L., Rossato, J. I., Goldin, A., . . . Medina, J. H. (2008). BDNF is essential to promote persistence of long-term memory storage. *PNAS Proceedings of the National Academy of Sciences of the United States of America, 105*, 2711–2716.

Belin, P. (2008, August/September). Monkeys hear voices. *Scientific American Mind, 19*(4), 14–15.

Bellman, S., Forster, N., Still, L., & Cooper, C. L. (2003). Gender differences in the use of social support as a moderator of occupational stress. *Stress and Health: Journal of the International Society for the Investigation of Stress, 19*, 45–58.

Belsky, J. (2006). Early child care and early child development: Major findings of the NICHD Study of Early Child Care. *European Journal of Developmental Psychology, 3*, 95–110.

Bem, S. L. (1989). Genital knowledge and gender constancy in preschool children. *Child Development, 60*, 649–662.

Ben-Zur, H. (2008). Personal resources of mastery–optimism, and communal support beliefs, as predictors of posttraumatic stress in uprooted Israelis. *Anxiety, Stress & Coping: An International Journal, 21*, 295–307.

Benjamin, L. T., Jr. (2000). The psychology laboratory at the turn of the 20th century. *American Psychologist, 55*, 318–321.

Bensley, D. A., Crowe, D. S., Bernhardt, P., Buckner, C., & Allman, A. L. (2010). Teaching and assessing critical thinking skills for argument analysis in psychology. *Teaching of Psychology, 37*, 91–96.

Bennett, K. K., & Elliott, M. (2005). Pessimistic explanatory style and cardiac health: What is the relation and the mechanism that links them? *Basic and Applied Social Psychology, 27*, 239–248.

Bennett, M. D., Jr., & Miller, D. B. (2006). An exploratory study of the Urban Hassles Index: A contextually relevant measure of chronic multidimensional urban stressors. *Research on Social Work Practice, 16*, 305–314.

Benton, D., & Roberts, G. (1988). Effect of vitamin and mineral supplementation on intelligence of a sample of schoolchildren. *Lancet, 1*, 140–143.

Benton, T. R., Ross, D. F., Bradshaw, E., Thomas, W. M., & Bradshaw, G. S. (2006). Eyewitness memory is still not common sense: Comparing jurors, judges and law enforcement to eyewitness experts. *Applied Cognitive Psychology, 20*, 115–129.

Beran, M. J. (2008). Monkeys (*Macaca mulatta* and *Cebus apella*) track, enumerate, and compare multiple sets of moving items. *Journal of Experimental Psychology: Animal Behavior Processes, 34*, 63–74.

Berg, R. C. (2008). Barebacking among MSM Internet users. *AIDS and Behavior, 12*, 822–833.

Berg, S. J., & Wynne-Edwards, K. E. (2001). Changes in testosterone, cortisol, estradiol levels in men becoming fathers. *Mayo Clinic Proceedings, 76*, 582–592.

Bergeron, N., & Schneider, B. H. (2005). Explaining cross-national differences in peer-directed aggression: A quantitative synthesis. *Aggressive Behavior, 31*, 116–137.

Berglund, H., Lindström, P., & Savic, I. (2006). Brain response to putative pheromones in lesbian women. *PNAS Proceedings of the National Academy of Sciences of the United States of America, 103*, 8269–8274.

Berkowitz, L., & Harmon-Jones, E. (2004). Toward an understanding of the determinants of anger. *Emotion, 4*, 107–130.

Bernal, M. E., & Castro, F. G. (1994). Are clinical psychologists prepared for service and research with ethnic minorities? Report of a decade of progress. *American Psychologist, 49*, 797–805.

Berns, G. S., Chappelow, J., Zink, C. F., Pagnoni, G., Martin-Skurski, M. E., & Richards, J. (2005). Neurobiological correlates of social conformity and independence during mental rotation. *Biological Psychiatry, 58*, 245–253.

Bernstein, D. M., & Loftus, E. F. (2009). How to tell if a particular memory is true or false. *Perspectives on Psychological Science, 4*, 370–374.

Bertolini, M. (2001). Central masturbatory fantasy, fetish and transitional phenomenon. In M. Bertolini & A. Giannakoulas (Eds.), *Squiggles and spaces: Revisiting the work of D. W. Winnicott* (Vol. 1, pp. 210–217). London, England: Whurr.

Bettencourt, B. A., & Miller, N. (1996). Gender differences in aggression as a function of provocation: A meta-analysis. *Psychological Bulletin, 119*, 422–447.

Bhawuk, D. P. S., & Brislin, R. W. (2000). Cross-cultural training: A review. *Applied Psychology: An International Review, 49*, 162–191.

Bhui, K., Shanahan, L., & Harding, G. (2006). Homelessness and mental illness: A literature review and a qualitative study of perceptions of the adequacy of care. *International Journal of Social Psychiatry, 52*, 152–165.

Bialystok, E., & Craik, F. I. M. (2010). Cognitive and linguistic processing in the bilingual mind. *Current Directions in Psychological Science, 19*, 19–23.

Bialystok, E., Craik, F. I. M., Green, D. W., & Gollan, T. H. (2009). Bilingual minds. *Psychological Science in the Public Interest, 10*, 89–129.

Bianchi-Demicheli, F., & Ortigue, S. (2007). Toward an understanding of the cerebral substrates of woman's orgasm. *Neuropsychologia, 45*, 2645–2659.

Biassoni, E. C., Serra, M. R., Richter, U., Joekes, S., Yacci, M. R., Carignani, J. A., . . . Franco, G. (2005). Recreational noise exposure and its effects on the hearing of adolescents. Part II: Development of hearing disorders. *International Journal of Audiology, 44*, 74–85.

Biddle, S. (2000). Exercise, emotions, and mental health. In Y. L. Hanin (Ed.), *Emotions in sport* (pp. 267–291). Champaign, IL: Human Kinetics.

Biel, A., & Thøgersen, J. (2007). Activation of social norms in social dilemmas: A review of the evidence and reflections on the implications for environmental behavior. *Journal of Economic Psychology, 28*, 93–112. doi:10.1016/j.joep.2006.03.003

Biesmeijer, J. C., & Seeley, T. D. (2005). The use of waggle dance information by honey bees throughout their foraging careers. *Behavioral Ecology and Sociobiology, 59*, 133–142.

Bike, D. H., Norcross, J. C., & Schatz, D. M. (2009). Processes and outcomes of psychotherapists' personal therapy: Replication and extension 20 years later. *Psychotherapy: Theory, Research, Practice, Training, 46*, 19–31.

Bilkey, D. K., & Clearwater, J. M. (2005). The dynamic nature of spatial encoding in the hippocampus. *Behavioral Neuroscience, 119*, 1533–1545.

Bing, N. M., Nelson, W. M., III, & Wesolowski, K. L. (2009). Comparing the effects of amount of conflict on children's adjustment following parental divorce. *Journal of Divorce & Remarriage, 50*, 159–171.

Binns, C. (2007, August/September). The hidden power of culture. *Scientific American Mind, 18*(4), 9.

Birdsong, D., & Paik, J. (2008). Second language acquisition and ultimate attainment. In B. Spolsky & F. M. Hult (Eds.), *The handbook of educational linguistics* (pp. 424–436). Malden, MA: Blackwell.

Birkenhäger, T. K., Pluijms, E. M., & Lucius, S. A. P. (2003). ECT response in delusional versus non-delusional depressed inpatients. *Journal of Affective Disorders, 74*, 191–195.

Birmingham, C. L., Su, J., Hlynsky, J. A., Goldner, E. M., & Gao, M. (2005). The mortality rate from anorexia nervosa. *International Journal of Eating Disorders, 38*, 143–146.

Black, D. W., Gunter, T., Loveless, P., Allen, J., & Sieleni, B. (2010). Antisocial personality disorder in incarcerated offenders: Psychiatric comorbidity and quality of life. *Annals of Clinical Psychiatry, 22*, 113–120.

Blanchard, E. B., Appelbaum, K. A., Radnitz, C. L., Morrill, B., Michultka, D., Kirsch, C., . . . Barron, K. D. (1990). A controlled evaluation of thermal biofeedback and thermal biofeedback combined with cognitive therapy in the treatment of vascular headache. *Journal of Consulting & Clinical Psychology, 58*, 216–224.

Blass, T. (2009). From New Haven to Santa Clara: A historical perspective on the Milgram obedience experiments. *American Psychologist, 64*, 37–45.

Blatt, S. J., Zuroff, D. C., Quinlan, D. M., & Pilkonis, P. A. (1996). Interpersonal factors in brief treatment of depression: Further analyses of the NIMH Treatment of Depression Collaborative Research Program. *Journal of Consulting and Clinical Psychology, 64*, 162–171.

Blehar, M. C., & Keita, G. P. (2003). Women and depression: A millennial perspective. *Journal of Affective Disorders, 74*, 1–4.

Bliss, T. V. P., Collingridge, G. L., & Morris R. G. M. (2004). *Long-term potentiation: Enhancing neuroscience for 30 years.* Oxford, England: Oxford University Press.

Bloom, B., & Cohen, R. A. (2006). Summary health statistics for U.S. children: National health interview survey, 2006. *Vital and Health Statistics, Series 10, No. 234.* Hyattsville, MD: Centers for Disease Control and Prevention.

Blum, J. M. (1979). *Pseudoscience and mental ability: The origins and fallacies of the IQ controversy.* New York, NY: Monthly Review Press.

Boardman, J. D., Blalock, C. L., & Pampel, F. C. (2010). Trends in the genetic influences on smoking. *Journal of Health and Social Behavior, 51*, 108–123.

Boelte, S., Uhlig, N., & Poustka, F. (2002). The savant syndrome: A review. *Zeitschrift fuer Klinische Psychologie und Psycholtherapie: Forschung und Praxis, 31*, 291–297.

Boes, A. D., Tranel, D., Anderson, S. W., & Nopoulos, P. (2008). Right anterior cingulate: A neuroanatomical correlate of aggression and defiance in boys. *Behavioral Neuroscience, 122*, 677–684.

Bogaert, A. F., & Fawcett, C. (2006). Sexual desire issues and problems. In R. D. McAnulty & M. M. Burnette (Eds.), *Sex and sexuality, Vol 2: Sexual function and dysfunction* (pp. 115–134). Westport, CT: Praeger.

Bohanna, I., Georgiou-Karistianis, N., Hannan, A. J., & Egan, G. F. (2008). Magnetic resonance imaging as an approach towards identifying neuropathological biomarkers for Huntington's disease. *Brain Research Reviews, 58,* 209–225.

Bolour, S., & Braunstein, G. (2005). Testosterone therapy in women: A review. *International Journal of Impotence Research, 17,* 399–408.

Bonanno, G. A. (2004). Loss, trauma, and human resilience: Have we underestimated the human capacity to thrive after extremely aversive events? *American Psychologist, 59,* 20–28.

Bonanno, G. A., Boerner, K., & Wortman, C. B. (2008). Trajectories of grieving. In M. S. Stroebe, R. O. Hansson, H. Schut, & W. Stroebe (Eds.), *Handbook of bereavement research and practice: Advances in theory and intervention* (pp. 287–307). Washington, DC: American Psychological Association.

Bonanno, G. A., Brewin, C. R., Kaniasty, K., & La Greca, A. M. (2010). Weighing the costs of disaster: Consequences, risks, and resilience in individuals, families, and communities. *Psychological Science in the Public Interest, 11,* 1–49.

Bonanno, G. A., Galea, S., Bucciarelli, A., & Vlahov, D. (2006). Psychological resilience after disaster: New York City in the aftermath of the September 11th terrorist attack. *Psychological Science, 17,* 181–186.

Bonanno, G. A., Wortman, C. B., & Nesse, R. M. (2004). Prospective patterns of resilience and maladjustment during widowhood. *Psychology and Aging, 19,* 260–271.

Bond, C. F., Pitre, U., & Van Leeuwen, M. D. (1991). Encoding operations and the next-in-line effect. *Personality and Social Psychology Bulletin, 17,* 435–141.

Bond, R. (2005). Group size and conformity. *Group Processes & Intergroup Relations, 8,* 331–354.

Bonham, V. L. (2001). Race, ethnicity, and pain treatment: Striving to understand the causes and solutions to the disparities in pain treatment. *Journal of Law and Medical Ethics, 29,* 52–68.

Boniecki, K. A., & Moore, S. (2003). Breaking the silence: Using a token economy to reinforce classroom participation. *Teaching of Psychology, 30,* 224–227.

Bonvillian, J. D., & Patterson, F. G. P. (1997). Sign language acquisition and the development of meaning in a lowland gorilla. In C. Mandell & A. McCabe (Eds.), *The problem of meaning: Behavioral and cognitive perspectives* (pp. 181–219). Amsterdam, Netherlands: North-Holland/Elsevier Science.

Boom, J. (2004). Commentary on: Piaget's stages: The unfinished symphony of cognitive development. *New Ideas in Psychology, 22,* 239–247.

Boom, J., Wouters, H., & Keller, M. (2007). A cross-cultural validation of stage development: A Rasch re-analysis of longitudinal socio-moral reasoning data. *Cognitive Development, 22,* 213–229.

Booth-LaForce, C., & Oxford, M. L. (2008). Trajectories of social withdrawal from grades 1 to 6: Prediction from early parenting, attachment, and temperament. *Developmental Psychology, 44,* 1298–1313.

Borkovec, T. D., & Costello, E. (1993). Efficacy of applied relaxation and cognitive-behavioral therapy in the treatment of generalized anxiety disorder. *Journal of Consulting and Clinical Psychology, 61,* 611–619.

Borman, W. C., Ilgen, D. R., & Klimoski, R. J. (Eds.). (2003). *Handbook of psychology: Vol. 12, Industrial and organizational psychology.* New York, NY: Wiley.

Bornstein, R. F. (1989). Exposure and affect: Overview and meta-analysis of research, 1968–1987. *Psychological Bulletin, 106,* 265–289.

Bornstein, R. F. (2004). Reconnecting psychoanalysis to mainstream psychology: An agenda for the 21st century. In J. Reppen, J. Tucker, & M. A. Schulman (Eds.), *Way beyond Freud: Postmodern psychoanalysis observed* (pp. 1–19). London, England: Open Gate Press.

Bornstein, R. F. (2005). Reconnecting psychoanalysis to mainstream psychology: Challenges and opportunities. *Psychoanalytic Psychology, 22,* 323–340.

Borthwick-Duffy, S. A. (2007). Adaptive behavior. In J. W. Jacobson, J. A. Mulick, & J. Rojahn (Eds.), *Handbook of intellectual and developmental disabilities* (pp. 279–293). New York, NY: Springer.

Bosacki, S. L., & Moore, C. (2004). Preschoolers' understanding of simple and complex emotions: Links with gender and language. *Sex Roles, 50,* 659–675.

Boscarino, J. A. (2008). A prospective study of PTSD and early-age heart disease mortality among Vietnam veterans: Implications for surveillance and prevention. *Psychosomatic Medicine, 70,* 668–676.

Bouchard, T. J., Jr. (1984). Twins reared together and apart: What they tell us about human diversity. In S. W. Fox (Ed.), *Individuality and determinism* (pp. 147–178). New York, NY: Plenum.

Bouchard, T. J., Jr. (1996). IQ similarity in twins reared apart: Findings and responses to critics. In R. J. Sternberg & E. Grigorenko (Eds.), *Intelligence: Heredity and environment* (pp. 126–160). New York, NY: Cambridge University Press.

Bouchard, T. J., Jr., Lykken, D. T., McGue, M., Segal, N. L., & Tellegren, A. (1990). Sources of human psychological differences: The Minnesota study of twins reared apart. *Science, 250,* 223–228.

Bouckenooghe, D., Buelens, M., Fontaine, J., & Vanderheyden, K. (2005). The prediction of stress by values and value conflict. *Journal of Psychology: Interdisciplinary and Applied, 139,* 369–382.

Boulkroune, N., Wang, L., March, A., Walker, N., & Jacob, T. J. C. (2007). Repetitive olfactory exposure to the biologically significant steroid androstadienone causes a hedonic shift and gender dimorphic changes in olfactory-evoked potentials. *Neuropsychopharmacology, 32,* 1822–1829.

Bourgois, P. (1999). Participant observation study of indirect paraphernalia sharing/HIV risk in a network of heroin injectors. Community Epidemiology Work Group Publications, National Institute on Drug Abuse (NIDA). Retrieved from http://www.drugabuse.gov/about/organization/cewg/ethno.html

Bower, B. (2003a, April 19). Words get in the way: Talk is cheap, but it can tax your memory. *Science News, 163*(16), 250–251.

Bower, B. (2003b, May 24). Repeat after me: Imitation is the sincerest form of perception. *Science News, 163*(21), 330–332.

Bower, B. (2008, March 22). Road to eureka! Insight may lie at the end of a chain of neural reactions. *Science News, 173*(12), 184–185.

Bower, G. H., & Mann, T. (1992). Improving recall by recoding interfering material at the time of recall. *Journal of Experimental Psychology: Learning, Memory, and Cognition, 18,* 1310–1320.

Bower, J. E., Moskowitz, J. T., & Epel, E. (2009). Is benefit finding good for your health? Pathways linking positive life changes after stress and physical health outcomes. *Current Directions in Psychological Science, 18,* 337–341.

Boyle, G. J. (2008). Critique of the five-factor model of personality. In G. J. Boyle, G. Matthews, & D. H. Saklofske (Eds.), *The SAGE handbook of personality theory and assessment, Vol 1: Personality theories and models* (pp. 295–312). Thousand Oaks, CA: Sage Publications, Inc.

Boysen, S. T., & Himes, G. T. (1999). Current issues and emerging theories in animal cognition. *Annual Review of Psychology, 50,* 683–705.

Bozarth, J. (2007). Unconditional positive regard. In M. Cooper, M. S. O'Hara, P. F. Schmid, & G. Wyatt (Eds.), *The handbook of person-centered psychotherapy and counseling* (pp. 182–193). New York, NY: Palgrave Macmillan.

Brackbill, R. M., Hadler, J. L., DiGrande, L., Ekenga, C. C., Farfel, M. R., Friedman, S., . . . Thorpe, L. E. (2009). Asthma and posttraumatic stress symptoms 5 to 6 years following exposure to the World Trade Center terrorist attack. *JAMA The Journal of the American Medical Association, 302,* 502–516.

Bradley, R. G., Binder, E. B., Epstein, M. P., Tang, Y., Nair, H. P, Liu, W., . . . Ressler, K. J. (2008). Influence of child abuse on adult depression: Moderation by the corticotropin-releasing hormone receptor gene. *Archives of General Psychiatry, 65,* 190–200.

Brainerd, C. J., & Reyna, V. F. (1998). When things that were never experienced are easier to "remember" than things that were. *Psychological Science, 9,* 484–489.

Brainerd, C. J., Stein, L. M., Silveira, R. A., Rohenkohl, G., & Reyna, V. F. (2008). How does negative emotion cause false memories? *Psychological Science, 19,* 919–925.

Brand, M. (2007). Cognitive profile of patients with alcoholic Korsakoff's syndrome. *International Journal on Disability and Human Development, 6,* 161–170.

Brehm, J. W. (2007). A brief history of dissonance theory. *Social and Personality Psychology Compass, 1,* 381–391.

Brehm, S. S. (2002). *Intimate relationships* (3rd ed.). New York, NY: McGraw-Hill.

Bremner, J. D., & Marmar, C. R. (Eds.). (1998). *Trauma, memory and dissociation.* Washington, DC: American Psychiatric Publishing.

Brenner, M. H. (1973). *Mental illness and the economy.* Cambridge, MA: Harvard University Press.

Bressan, R. A., & Crippa, J. A. (2005). The role of dopamine in reward and pleasure behaviour—Review of data from preclinical research. *Acta Psychiatrica Scandinavica, 111,* 14–21.

Brewer, M. B. (2008). Deprovincialization: Social identity complexity and outgroup acceptance. In U. Wagner, L. R. Tropp, G. Finchilescu, & C. Tredoux (Eds.), *Improving intergroup relations: Building on the legacy of Thomas F. Pettigrew* (pp. 160–176). Malden, MA: Blackwell.

Brewer, R. D., & Swahn, M. H. (2005). Binge drinking and violence. *JAMA: Journal of the American Medical Association, 294,* 616–617.

Brinkley, A. (1999). *American history: A survey* (10th ed.). New York, NY: McGraw-Hill.

Broadbent, D. E. (1958). *Perception and communication.* New York, NY: Pergamon.

Brobert, A. G., Wessels, H., Lamb, M. E., & Hwang, C. P. (1997). Effects of day care on the development of cognitive abilities in 8-year-olds: A longitudinal study. *Developmental Psychology, 33,* 62–69.

Brodbeck, F. C. (2008). Leadership in organizations. In N. Chmiel (Ed.), *An introduction to work and organizational psychology: A European perspective* (2nd ed., pp. 281–304). Malden, MA: Blackwell.

Brody, J. E. (2004, February 24). Age-fighting hormones put men at risk, too. *New York Times,* p. D7.

Brody, L., & Hall, J. (2000). Gender, emotion, and expression. In M. Lewis & J. Haviland-Jones (Eds.), *Handbook of emotions* (2nd ed., pp. 338–349). New York, NY: Guilford Press.

Brody, N. (2000). Intelligence. In A. Kazdin, (Ed.), *Encyclopedia of psychology* (Vol. 4, pp. 318–324). Washington, DC: American Psychological Association.

Bronfenbrenner, U. (1986). Ecology of the family as a context for human development: Research perspectives. *Developmental Psychology, 22,* 723–742.

Bronstad, P. M., Langlois, J. H., & Russell, R. (2008). Computational models of facial attractiveness judgments. *Perception, 37,* 126–142.

Bronstein, P. (2006). The family environment: Where gender role socialization begins. In J. Worell & C. D. Goodheart (Eds.), *Handbook of girls' and women's psychological health: Gender and well-being across the lifespan* (pp. 262–271). New York, NY: Oxford University Press.

Brooks-Gunn, J., & Lewis, M. (1984). The development of early visual self-recognition. *Developmental Review, 4,* 215–239.

Brosnan, S. F. (2011). An evolutionary perspective on morality. *Journal of Economic Behavior & Organization, 77,* 23–30.

Brown, A. S., & Derkits, E. J. (2010). Prenatal infection and schizophrenia: A review of epidemiologic and translational studies. *The American Journal of Psychiatry, 167,* 261–280.

Brown, I., Buell, M. K., Birkan, R., & Percy, M. (2007). Lifestyles of adults with intellectual and developmental disabilities. In I. Brown & M. Percy (Eds.), *A comprehensive guide to intellectual and developmental disabilities* (pp. 545–560). Baltimore, MD: Paul H Brookes.

Brown, L. S. (2009). *Feminist therapy.* Washington, DC: American Psychological Association.

Brown, N. R. (2005). On the prevalence of event clusters in autobiographical memory. *Social Cognition, 23,* 35–69.

Brown, P., van der Hart, O., & Graafland, M. (1999). Trauma-induced dissociative amnesia in World War I combat soldiers. II. Treatment dimensions. *Australian and New Zealand Journal of Psychiatry, 33,* 392–398.

Brown, R., & McNeill, D. (1966). The "tip of the tongue phenomenon." *Journal of Verbal Learning and Verbal Behavior, 8,* 325–337.

Brownell, P. (2009). *Gestalt therapy.* New York, NY: Springer.

Bruder, G. E., Stewart, J. W., Mercier, M. A., Agosti, V., Leite, P., Donovan, S., & Quitkin, F. M. (1997). Outcome of cognitive-behavioral therapy for depression: Relation to hemispheric dominance for verbal processing. *Journal of Abnormal Psychology, 106,* 138–144.

Bruen, P. D., McGeown, W. J., Shanks, M. F., & Venneri, A. (2008). Neuroanatomical correlates of neuropsychiatric symptoms in Alzheimer's disease. *Brain: A Journal of Neurology, 131,* 2455–2463.

Bubka, A., & Bonato, F. (2003). Optokinetic drum tilt hastens the onset of vection-induced motion sickness. *Aviation, Space, and Environmental Medicine, 74,* 315–319.

Buccino, G., & Amore, M. (2008). Mirror neurons and the understanding of behavioural symptoms in psychiatric disorders. *Current Opinion in Psychiatry, 21,* 281–285.

Buckholtz, J. W., & Meyer-Lindenberg, A. (2008). MAOA and the neurogenetic architecture of human aggression. *Trends in Neurosciences, 31,* 120–129.

Buckholtz, J. W., Callicott, J. H., Kolachana, B., Hariri, A. R., Goldberg, T. E., Genderson, M., . . . Meyer-Lindenberg, A. (2008). Genetic variation in MAOA modulates ventromedial prefrontal circuitry mediating individual differences in human personality. *Molecular Psychiatry, 13,* 313–324.

Buhle, M. J. (1998). *Feminism and its discontents: A century of struggle with psychoanalysis.* Cambridge, MA: Harvard University Press.

Bühner, M., König, C., Pick, M., & Krumm, S. (2006). Working memory dimensions as differential predictors of the speed and error aspect of multitasking performance. *Human Performance, 19,* 253–275.

Buklina, S. B. (2005). The corpus callosum, interhemisphere interactions, and the function of the right hemisphere of the brain. *Neuroscience and Behavioral Physiology, 35,* 473–480.

Bulik, C. M., Sullivan, P. F., Tozzi, F., Furberg, H., Lichtenstein, P., & Pedersen, N. L. (2006). Prevalence, heritability, and prospective risk factors for anorexia nervosa. *Archives of General Psychiatry, 63,* 305–312.

Burack, C. (1998). Feminist psychoanalysis: The uneasy intimacy of feminism and psychoanalysis. In P. Marcus & A. Rosenberg (Eds.), *Psychoanalytic versions of the human condition: Philosophies of life and their impact on practice* (pp. 392–411). New York: New York University Press.

Burgdorf, J., & Panksepp, J. (2006). The neurobiology of positive emotions. *Neuroscience and Biobehavioral Reviews, 30,* 173–187.

Burghardt, G. M. (2009). Darwin's legacy to comparative psychology and ethology. *American Psychologist, 64,* 102–110.

Bursik, K. (1998). Moving beyond gender differences: Gender role comparisons of manifest dream content. *Sex Roles, 38,* 203–214.

Burt, M. R., Aron, L. Y., Douglas, T., Valente, J., Lee, E., & Iwen, B. (1999). Homelessness: Programs and the people they serve. Retrieved from http://www.urban.org/UploadedPDF/homelessness.pdf

Bushman, B. J. (2002). Does venting anger feed or extinguish the flame? Catharsis, rumination, distraction, anger and aggressive responding. *Personality and Social Psychology Bulletin, 28,* 724–731.

Bushnell, I. W. R. (2003). Newborn face recognition. In O. Pascalis & A. Slater (Eds.), *The development of face processing in infancy and early childhood: Current perspectives* (pp. 41–53). Hauppauge, NY: Nova Science.

Buss, D. M. (1985). Human mate selection. *American Scientist, 73,* 47–51.

Buss, D. M. (2005). *The handbook of evolutionary psychology.* Hoboken, NJ: Wiley.

Buss, D. M. (2006). The evolution of love. In R. J. Sternberg & K. Weis (Eds.), *The new psychology of love* (pp. 65–86). New Haven, CT: Yale University Press.

Buss, D. M. (2009). The great struggles of life: Darwin and the emergence of evolutionary psychology. *American Psychologist, 64,* 140–148.

Butler, K. (2006, July 4). The grim neurology of teenage drinking. *The New York Times,* pp. D1, D6.

Butler, R. N., & Lewis, M. I., & Sunderland, T. (1998). *Aging and mental health: Positive psychosocial and biomedical approaches* (5th ed.). Boston, MA: Allyn & Bacon.

Byne, W. (1994, May). The biological evidence challenged. *Scientific American, 270*(5), 50–55.

Byrne-Davis, L. M. T., & Vedhara, K. (2008). Psychoneuroimmunology. *Social and Personality Psychology Compass, 2,* 751–764.

Cabeza, R., & Nyberg, L. (2000). Imaging cognition II: An empirical review of 275 PET and fMRI studies. *Journal of Cognitive Neuroscience, 12,* 1–47.

Cacioppo, J. T., & Berntson, G. G. (2005). *Social neuroscience: Key readings.* New York, NY: Psychology Press.

Cacioppo, J. T., Hawkley, L. C., Berntson, G. C., Ernst, J. M., Gibbs, A. C., Stickgold, R., & Hobson, J. A. (2002). Do lonely days invade the nights? Potential social modulation of sleep efficiency. *Psychological Science, 13,* 384–387.

Cahill, J., Barkham, M., Hardy, G., Rees, A., Shapiro, D. A., Stiles, W. B., & Macaskill, N. (2003). Outcomes of patients completing and not completing cognitive therapy for depression. *British Journal of Clinical Psychology, 42,* 133–143.

Cahill, L., & Alkire, M. T. (2003). Epinephrine enhancement of human memory consolidation: Interaction with arousal at encoding. *Neurobiology of Learning and Memory, 79,* 194–198.

Cahn, B. R., & Polich, J. (2006). Meditation states and traits: EEG, ERP, and neuroimaging studies. *Psychological Bulletin, 132,* 180–211

Cain, D. J. (2002). History, and evolution of humanistic psychotherapies. In D. J. Cain (Ed.), *Humanistic psychotherapies: Handbook of research and practice* (pp. 3–54). Washington, DC: American Psychological Association.

Cain, D. J. (2010). *Person-centered psychotherapies.* Washington, DC: American Psychological Association.

Cairns, E., & Darby, J. (1998). The conflict in Northern Ireland: Causes, consequences, and controls. *American Psychologist, 53,* 754–760.

Calhoun, L. G., & Tedeschi, R. G. (2001). Posttraumatic growth: The positive lessons of loss. In R. A. Neimeyer (Ed.), *Meaning reconstruction & the experience of loss* (pp. 157–172). Washington, DC: American Psychological Association.

Califano, J. A., Jr. (1999, August 24). White-Line Fever: What an older and wiser George W. should do. *Washington Post*, p. A17.

Cameron, J., Banko, K. M., & Pierce, W. D. (2001). Pervasive negative effects of rewards on intrinsic motivation: The myth continues. *The Behavior Analyst, 24*, 1–44.

Campbell, D. B., Li, C., Sutcliffe, J. S., Persico, A. M., & Levitt, P. (2008). Genetic evidence implicating multiple genes in the MET receptor tyrosine kinase pathway in autism spectrum disorder. *Autism, 1*, 159–168.

Camperio-Ciani A., Corna, F., & Capiluppi C. (2004). Evidence for maternally inherited factors favouring male homosexuality and promoting female fecundity. *Proceedings of the Royal Society of London B., 271*, 2217–2221.

Campitelli, G., Gobet, F., & Parker, A. (2005). Structure and stimulus familiarity: A study of memory in chess-players with functional magnetic resonance imaging. *The Spanish Journal of Psychology, 8*, 238–245.

Campo, P., Maestú, F., Capilla, A., Fernández, S., Fernández, A., & Ortiz, T. (2005). Activity in human medial temporal lobe associated with encoding process in spatial working memory revealed by magnetoencephalography. *European Journal of Neuroscience, 21*, 1741–1748.

Cannella-Malone, H., Sigafoos, J., O'Reilly, M., de la Cruz, B., Edrisinha, C., & Lancioni, G. E. (2006). Comparing video prompting to video modeling for teaching daily living skills to six adults with developmental disabilities. *Education and Training in Developmental Disabilities, 41*, 344–356.

Cannon, W. B. (1929). *Bodily changes in pain, hunger, fear, and rage* (Rev. ed.). New York, NY: D. Appleton.

Cano, G., Mochizuki, T., & Saper, C. B. (2008). Neural circuitry of stress-induced insomnia in rats. *The Journal of Neuroscience, 28*, 10167–10184.

Cao, J., Hu, J., Ye, X., Xia, Y., Haile, C. A., Kosten, T. R., & Zhang, X. (2011). Association between the 5-HTR1B gene polymorphisms and alcohol dependence in a Han Chinese population. *Brain Research, 1376*, 1–9.

Capron, C., & Duyme, M. (1989). Assessment of effects of socioeconomic status on IQ in a full cross-fostering study. *Nature, 340*, 552–554.

Carmona, F. J., Sanz, L. J., & Marín, D. (2002). Type-A behaviour pattern and coronary heart disease. *Psiquis: Revista de Psiquiatria, Psicologia Medica y Psicosomatica, 23*, 22–30.

Carr, L., Iacoboni, M., Dubeau, M.-C., Mazziotta, J. C., & Lenzi, G. L. (2005). Neural mechanisms of empathy in humans: A relay from neural systems for imitation to limbic areas. In J. T. Cacioppo & G. G. Berntson (Eds.), *Social neuroscience: Key readings* (pp. 143–152). New York, NY: Psychology Press.

Carr, M., Borkowski, J. G., & Maxwell, S. E. (1991). Motivational components of underachievement. *Developmental Psychology, 27*, 108–118.

Carré, J. M., Gilchrist, J. D., Morrissey, M. D., & McCormick, C. M. (2010). Motivational and situational factors and the relationship between testosterone dynamics and human aggression during competition. *Biological Psychology, 84*, 346–353.

Carrére, S., Mittmann, A., Woodin, E., Tabares, A., & Yoshimoto, D. (2005). Anger dysregulation, depressive symptoms, and health in married women and men. *Nursing Research, 54*, 184–192.

Carskadon, M. A., Acebo, C., & Jenni, O. G. (2004). Regulation of adolescent sleep: Implications for behavior. In D. E. Ronald & L. P. Spear (Eds.), *Adolescent brain development: Vulnerabilities and opportunities* (pp. 276–291). New York: New York Academy of Sciences.

Carskadon, M. A., & Dement, W. C. (1982). Nocturnal determinants of daytime sleepiness. *Sleep, 5*(Suppl. 2), 73–81.

Carson, R. C., & Butcher, J. N. (1992). *Abnormal psychology and modern life.* New York, NY: HarperCollins.

Carstensen, L. L. (1995). Evidence for a life-span theory of socioemotional selectivity. *Current Directions in Psychological Science, 4*, 151–156.

Carter, C. S. (2005). Biological perspectives on social attachment and bonding. In C. S. Carter, L. L. Ahnert, K. E. Grossmann, S. B. Hardy, M. E. Lamb, S. W. Porges, . . . N. N. Sachser (Eds.), *Attachment and bonding: A new synthesis* (pp. 85–100). Cambridge, MA: MIT Press.

Carter, J. A. (2006). Theoretical pluralism and technical eclecticism. In C. D. Goodheart, A. E. Kazdin, & R. J. Sternberg (Eds.), *Evidence-based psychotherapy: Where practice and research meet* (pp. 63–79). Washington, DC: American Psychological Association.

Casas, J. M. (1995). Counseling and psychotherapy with racial/ethnic minority groups in theory and practice. In B. Bongar & L. E. Beutler (Eds.), *Comprehensive handbook of psychotherapy* (pp. 311–335). New York, NY: Oxford University Press.

Casey, G. W. (2011). Comprehensive soldier fitness. *American Psychologist, 66*, 1–3.

Caspi, O., & Burleson, K. O. (2005). Methodological challenges in meditation research. *Advances in Mind-Body Medicine, 21*, 4–11.

Cassidy, J. P. (2002). The Stockholm Syndrome, battered woman syndrome and the cult personality: An integrative approach. *Dissertation Abstracts International: Section B: The Sciences and Engineering, 62*, 5366.

Castelli, L., Macrae, C. N., Zogmaister, C., & Arcuri, L. (2004). A tale of two primes: Contextual limits on stereotype activation. *Social Cognition, 22*, 233–247.

Castelli, L., Zogmaister, C., & Tomelleri, S. (2009). The transmission of racial attitudes within the family. *Developmental Psychology, 45*, 586–591.

Cattell, R. B. (1965). *The scientific analysis of personality.* Baltimore, MD: Penguin.

Cattell, R. B., & Kline, P. (1977). *The specific analysis of personality and motivation.* New York, NY: Academic Press.

Cavanaugh, J. C., & Blanchard-Fields, F. (2005). *Adult development and aging* (5th ed.). Belmont, CA: Wadsworth.

Ceci, S. J., & Williams, W. M. (1997). Schooling, intelligence, and income. *American Psychologist, 52*, 1051–1058.

Ceci, S. J., & Williams, W. M. (2010). Sex differences in math-intensive fields. *Current Directions in Psychological Science, 19*, 275–279.

Centers for Disease Control and Prevention. (1999). *Suicide deaths and rates per 100,000.* Retrieved from http://www.cdc.gov/ncipe/data/us9794/suic.htm

Centers for Disease Control and Prevention. (2006). Deaths: Final data for 2003. *National Vital Statistics Reports, 54*(13). Retrieved from http://www.cdc.gov/nchs/data/nvsr/nvsr54/nvsr54_13.pdf

Centers for Disease Control and Prevention. (2009). Trends in the prevalence of sexual behaviors. *The National Youth Risky Behavior Survey.* Retrieved from http://www.cdc.gov/HealthyYouth/yrbs/pdf/yrbs07_us_sexual_behaviors_trend.pdf

Chaiken, S., & Eagly, A. H. (1976). Communication modality as a determinant of message persuasiveness and message comprehensibility. *Journal of Personality and Social Psychology, 34*, 605–614.

Champagne, F. A. (2009, April). Beyond nature vs. nurture: Philosophical insights from molecular biology. *Observer: American Psychological Society, 22*(4), 4, 27–28.

Chandler, D. R. (2011). Proactively addressing the shortage of Blacks in psychology: Highlighting the school psychology subfield. *Journal of Black Psychology, 37*, 99–127.

Chapman, R. A. (2006). Introduction to cognitive behavior therapy and hypnosis. In R. A. Chapman (Ed.), *The clinical use of hypnosis in cognitive behavior therapy: A practitioner's casebook* (pp. 3–24). New York, NY: Springer.

Chassin, L., Flora, D. B., & King, K. M. (2004). Trajectories of alcohol and drug use and dependence from adolescence to adulthood: The effects of familial alcoholism and personality. *Journal of Abnormal Psychology, 113*, 483–498.

Chassin, L., Pitts, S. C., DeLucia, C., & Todd, M. (1999). A longitudinal study of children of alcoholics: Predicting young adult substance use disorders, anxiety, and depression. *Journal of Abnormal Psychology, 108*, 106–119.

Chatterjee, A., Thomas, A., Smith, S. E., & Aguirre, G. K. (2009). The neural response to facial attractiveness. *Neuropsychology, 23*, 135–143.

Chekroun, P., & Brauer, M. (2002). The bystander effect and social control behavior: The effect of the presence of others on people's reactions to norm violations. *European Journal of Social Psychology, 32*, 853–866.

Chen, G., & Manji, H. K. (2006). The extracellular signal-regulated kinase pathway: An emerging promising target for mood stabilizers. *Current Opinion in Psychiatry, 19*, 313–323.

Chen, H., & Jackson, T. (2008). Prevalence and sociodemographic correlates of eating disorder endorsements among adolescents and young adults from China. *European Eating Disorders Review, 16*, 375–385.

Chen, J.-Q., Moran, S., & Gardner, H. (Eds.) (2009). *Multiple intelligences around the world.* San Francisco, CA: Jossey-Bass.

Cherlin, A. J. (1992). *Marriage, divorce, remarriage.* Cambridge, MA: Harvard University Press.

Cherniss, C., & Goleman, D. (2001). *The emotionally intelligent workplace: How to select for, measure, and improve emotional intelligence in individuals, groups, and organizations.* San Francisco, CA: Jossey-Bass.

Cherry, C. (1966). *On human communication: A review, a survey, and a criticism* (2nd ed.). Cambridge, MA: MIT Press.

Chervin, R. D., Killion, J. E., Archbold, K. H., & Ruzicka, D. L. (2003). Conduct problems and symptoms of sleep disorders in children. *Journal of the American Academy of Child and Adolescent Psychiatry, 42*, 201–208.

Chin, J. (2010). Introduction to the special issue on diversity and leadership. *American Psychologist, 65*, 150–156.

Chin, J. L. (2008). Women and leadership. In F. L. Denmark & M. A. Paludi (Eds.), *Psychology of women: A handbook of issues and theories* (2nd ed., pp. 701–716). Westport, CT: Praeger.

Chiu, C., Leung, A. K., & Kwan, L. (2007). Language, cognition, and culture: Beyond the Whorfian hypothesis. In S. Kitayama & D. Cohen (Eds.), *Handbook of cultural psychology* (pp. 668–688). New York, NY: Guilford Press.

Choi, I. [Incheol], Dalal, R., Kim-Prieto, C., & Park, H. (2003). Culture and judgment of causal relevance. *Journal of Personality and Social Psychology, 84*, 46–59.

Choi, I. Y. [Irene], Allan, A. M., & Cunningham, L. A. (2005). Moderate fetal alcohol exposure impairs the neurogenic response to an enriched environment in adult mice. *Alcoholism: Clinical and Experimental Research, 29*, 2053–2062.

Choi, K. H., Higgs, B. W., Wendland, J. R., Song, J., McMahon, F. J., & Webster, M. J. (2011). Gene expression and genetic variation data implicate PCLO in bipolar disorder. *Biological Psychiatry, 69*, 353–359.

Choi, W. S., Pierce, J. P., Gilpin, E. A., Farkas, A. J., & Berry, C. C. (1997). Which adolescent experimenters progress to established smoking in the United States. *American Journal of Preventive Medicine, 13*, 385–391.

Chomsky, N. (1957). *Syntactic structures*. Oxford, England: Mouton.

Chomsky, N. (1965). *Aspects of the theory of syntax*. Cambridge, MA: MIT Press.

Chomsky, N., Place, U. T., & Schoneberger, T. (Eds.). (2000). The Chomsky–Place correspondence 1993–1994. *Analysis of Verbal Behavior, 17*, 7–38.

Chong, S.-A., Tay, J. A. M., Subramaniam, M., Pek, E., & Machin, D. (2009). Mortality rates among patients with schizophrenia and tardive dyskinesia. *Journal of Clinical Psychopharmacology, 29*, 5–8.

Chrisler, J. C., & McCreary, D. R. (Eds.) (2010). *Handbook of gender research in psychology* (Vol. 1, pp. 248–249). New York: Springer.

Christiansen, M. H., & Chater, N. (2008a). Language as shaped by the brain. *Behavioral and Brain Sciences, 31*, 489–509.

Christiansen, M. H., & Chater, N. (2008b). Brains, genes, and language evolution: A new synthesis. *Behavioral and Brain Sciences, 31*, 537–558.

Chrobot-Mason, D., & Quinones, M. A. (2002). Training for a diverse workplace. In K. Kraiger (Ed.), *Creating, implementing, and managing effective training and development* (pp. 117–159). San Francisco, CA: Jossey-Bass.

Cialdini, R. B., & Trost, M. (1998). Social influence: Social norms, conformity, and compliance. In D. Gilbert, S. T. Fiske, & G. Lindzey (Eds.), *Handbook of social psychology* (4th ed., Vol. 2, pp. 151–192). Boston, MA: McGraw-Hill.

Clapham, M. M. (2004). The convergent validity of the Torrance Tests of Creative Thinking and Creativity Interest Inventories. *Educational and Psychological Measurement, 64*, 828–841.

Clark, D. A., & Beck, A. T. (2010). Cognitive theory and therapy of anxiety and depression: Convergence with neurobiological findings. *Trends in Cognitive Sciences, 14*, 418–424.

Clark, J. C. (2009, October). Improving care for people with serious mental illness. *Monitor on Psychology, 40*(10), 45–47.

Clay, R. A. (1997, July). Do hearing devices impair deaf children? *APA Monitor, 28*(7), 1.

Clay, R. A. (1999, May). "Lean production" may also be a lean toward injuries. *APA Monitor, 30*(5), 26.

Clay, R. A. (2009, February). Mini-multitaskers. *Monitor on Psychology, 40*, 38.

Clay, R. A. (2009, November). Repairing psychology's leaky pipeline. *Monitor on Psychology, 40*(11), 57–58.

Clay, R. A. (2011, January). Stressed in America. *Monitor on Psychology, 42*(1), 60.

Cobos, P., Sánchez, M., Pérez, N., & Vila, J. (2004). Effects of spinal cord injuries on the subjective component of emotions. *Cognition and Emotion, 18*, 281–287.

Cochran, S. V., & Rabinowitz, F. E. (2003). Gender-sensitive recommendations for assessment and treatment of depression in men. *Professional Psychology: Research and Practice, 34*, 132–140.

Cochrane, L., & Quester, P. (2005). Fear in advertising: The influence of consumers' product involvement and culture. *Journal of International Consumer Marketing, 17*, 7–32.

Cohen, D. A., Freitas, C., Tormos, J., Oberman, L., Eldaief, M., & Pascual-Leone, A. (2010). Enhancing plasticity through repeated rTMS sessions: The benefits of a night of sleep. *Clinical Neurophysiology, 121*, 2159–2164.

Cohen, L. J., & Galynker, I. I. (2002). Clinical features of pedophilia and implications for treatment. *Journal of Psychiatric Practice, 8*, 276–289.

Cohen, P. J. (2009). Medical marijuana: The conflict between scientific evidence and political ideology. Part one of two. *Journal of Pain & Palliative Care Pharmacotherapy, 23*, 4–25.

Cohen, S. (1996). Psychological stress, immunity, and upper respiratory infections. *Current Directions in Psychological Science, 5*, 86–90.

Cohen, S., Doyle, W. J., Turner, R. B., Alper, C. M., & Skoner, D. P. (2003a). Emotional styles and susceptibility to the common cold. *Psychosomatic Medicine, 65*, 652–657.

Cohen, S., Doyle, W. J., Turner, R. B., Alper, C. M., & Skoner, D. P. (2003b). Sociability and susceptibility to the common cold. *Psychological Science, 14*, 389–396.

Cohen, S., Frank, E., Doyle, W. J., Skoner, D. P., Rabin, B. S., & Gwaltney, J. M., Jr. (1998). Types of stressors that increase susceptibility to the common cold in healthy adults. *Health Psychology, 17*, 214–223.

Cohen, S., Hamrick, N., Rodriguez, M. S., Feldman, P. J., Rabin, B. S., & Manuck, S. B. (2002). Reactivity and vulnerability to stress-associated risk for upper respiratory illness. *Psychosomatic Medicine, 64*, 302–310.

Cohen, S., & Herbert, T. B. (1996). Health psychology: Psychological factors and physical disease from the perspective of human psychoneuroimmunology. *Annual Review of Psychology, 47*, 113–142.

Cohen, S., Tyrrell, D. A., & Smith, A. P. (1991). Psychological stress and susceptibility to the common cold. *The New England Journal of Medicine, 325*, 606–612.

Coleman, J., Glaros, A., & Morris, C. G. (1987). *Contemporary psychology and effective behavior* (6th ed.). Glenview, IL: Scott Foresman.

Coleman, L. J., & Cross, T. L. (2001). *Gifted: Is it a state of being or an application of abilities?* Waco, TX: Prufrock Press.

Coley, R. L., & Chase-Lansdale, L. (1998). Adolescent pregnancy and parenthood: Recent evidence and future directions. *American Psychologist, 53*, 152–166.

Collaer, M. L., & Hines, M. (1995). Human behavioral sex differences: A role for gonadal hormones during early development? *Psychological Bulletin, 118*, 55–107.

Collett, T. S., & Graham, P. (2004). Animal navigation: Path integration, visual landmarks and cognitive maps. *Current Biology, 14*, R475–R477.

Collins, F. S. (2010). *The language of life: DNA and the revolution in personalized medicine*. New York, NY: Harper Collins.

Colquitt, J. A., Conlon, D. E., Wesson, M. J., Porter, C. O., & Ng, K. Y. (2001). Justice at the millennium: A meta-analytic review of 25 years of organizational justice research. *Journal of Applied Psychology, 86*, 425–445.

Comaty, J. E., Stasio, M., & Advokat, C. (2001). Analysis of outcome variables of a token economy system in a state psychiatric hospital: A program evaluation. *Research in Developmental Disabilities, 22*, 233–253.

Comstock, E. J. (2011). The end of drugging children: Toward the genealogy of the ADHD subject. *Journal of the History of the Behavioral Sciences, 47*, 44–69.

Confer, J. C., Easton, J. A., Fleischman, D. S., Goetz, C. D., Lewis, D. M. G., Perilloux, C., & Buss, D. M. (2010). Evolutionary psychology: Controversies, questions, prospects, and limitations. *American Psychologist, 65*, 110–126.

Construction Equipment. (2006). Train operators with a PC-based simulator. *Construction Equipment, 10*, 23.

Conte, J. M., & Jacobs, R. R. (2003). Validity evidence linking polychronicity and Big Five personality dimensions to absence, lateness, and supervisory performance ratings. *Human Performance, 16*, 107–129.

Conte, J. M., & Gintoft, J. N. (2005). Polychronicity, Big Five personality dimensions, and sales performance. *Human Performance, 18*, 427–444.

Contrada, R. J., Idler, E. L., Goyal, T. M., Cather, C., Rafalson, L., & Drause, T. J. (2004). Why not find out whether religious beliefs predict surgical outcomes? If they do, why not find out why? Reply to Freedland (2004). *Health Psychology, 23*, 243–246.

Contreras, M., Ceric, F., & Torrealba, F. (2007). Inactivation of the interoceptive insula disrupts drug craving and malaise induced by lithium. *Science, 318*, 655–658.

Conway, M. A. [Martin]. (1996). Failures of autobiographical remembering. In D. J. Hermann, C. McEvoy, C. Hertzog, P. Hertel, & M. K. Johnson (Eds.), *Basic and applied memory research: Theory in context* (pp. 294–312). Mahwah, NJ: Erlbaum.

Conway, M. [Michael], & Dubé, L. (2002). Humor in persuasion on threatening topics: Effectiveness is a function of audience sex role orientation. *Personality and Social Psychology Bulletin, 28*, 863–873.

Cook, V. D. (2006). An investigation of the construct validity of the big five construct of emotional stability in relation to job performance, job satisfaction, and career satisfaction. *Dissertation Abstracts International, 66*, 5128. Retrieved from EBSCOhost.

Cooke, C. A. (2004). Young people's attitudes towards guns in America, Great Britain and Western Australia. *Aggressive Behavior, 30*, 93–104.

Cooke, L. J., Chambers, L. C., Añez, E. V., Croker, H. A., Boniface, D., Yeomans, M. R., & Wardle, J. (2011). Eating for pleasure or profit: The effect of incentives on children's enjoyment of vegetables. *Psychological Science, 22*, 190–196.

Cooper, J., Mirabile, R., & Scher, S. J. (2005). Actions and attitudes: The theory of cognitive dissonance. In T. C. Brock & M. C. Green (Eds.), *Persuasion: Psychological insights and perspectives* (2nd ed., pp. 63–79). Thousand Oaks, CA: Sage.

Corales, T. A. (2005). *Focus on posttraumatic stress disorder research*. Hauppauge, NY: Nova Science.

Cornelis, I., & Van Hiel, A. (2006). The impact of cognitive styles on authoritarianism based conservatism and racism. *Basic and Applied Social Psychology, 28,* 37–50.

Cornelius, R. R. (1996). *The science of emotion: Research and tradition in the psychology of emotions*. Upper Saddle River, NJ: Prentice Hall.

Cosgrove, L., & Riddle, B. (2004). Gender bias and sex distribution of mental disorders in the *DSM-IV-TR*. In P. J. Caplan & L. Cosgrove (Eds.), *Bias in psychiatric diagnosis* (pp. 127–140). Lanham, MD: Jason Aronson.

Cosmides, L., & Tooby, J. (2000). Evolutionary psychology and the emotions. In M. Lewis & J. M. Haviland-Jones (Eds.), *Handbook of Emotions* (2nd ed., pp. 91–115). New York, NY: Guilford Press.

Costa, P. T., Jr., & McCrae, R. R. (1992). *Revised NEO Personality Inventory (NEO-PI-R) and NEO Five-Factor Inventory (NEO-FFI) professional manual*. Odessa, FL: Psychological Assessment Resources.

Costa, P. T., Jr., & McCrae, R. R. (2006). Trait and factor theories. In J. C. Thomas, D. L. Segal, L. Daniel, & M. Hersen (Eds.), *Comprehensive handbook of personality and psychopathology, Vol. 1: Personality and everyday functioning* (pp. 96–114). Hoboken, NJ: Wiley.

Côté, J. E. (2006). Emerging adulthood as an institutionalized moratorium: Risks and benefits to identity formation. In J. J. Arnett & J. L. Tanner (Eds.), *Emerging adults in America: Coming of age in the 21st century* (pp. 85–116). Washington, DC: American Psychological Association.

Courage, M. L., & Howe, M. L. (2002). From infant to child: The dynamics of cognitive change in the second year of life. *Psychological Bulletin, 128,* 250–277.

Cousins, N. (1981). *Anatomy of an illness as perceived by the patient*. New York, NY: Bantam.

Cowan, N., & Chen, Z. (2009). How chunks form in long-term memory and affect short-term memory limits. In A. Thorn & M. Page (Eds.), *Interactions between short-term and long-term memory in the verbal domain* (pp. 86–107). New York, NY: Psychology Press.

Cowan, N., Elliott, E. M., Saults, J. S., Morey, C. C., Mattox, S., Hismjatullina, A., & Conway, A. R. A. (2005). On the capacity of attention: Its estimation and its role in working memory and cognitive aptitudes. *Cognitive Psychology, 51,* 42–100.

Cox, J. J., Reimann, F., Nicholas, A. K., Thornton, G., Roberts, E., Springell, K., . . . Woods, C. G. (2006). An SCN9A channelopathy causes congenital inability to experience pain. *Nature, 444,* 894–898.

Coyne, J. C., & Whiffen, V. E. (1995). Issues in personality as diathesis for depression: The case of sociotropy-dependency and autonomy-self-criticism. *Psychological Bulletin, 118,* 358–378.

Craik, F. I. M. (2002). Levels of processing: Past, present . . . and future? *Memory, 10,* 305–318.

Craik, F. I. M., & Lockhart, R. S. (1972). Levels of processing: A framework for memory research. *Journal of Verbal Learning and Verbal Behavior, 11,* 671–684.

Craik, F. I. M., Moroz, T. M., Moscovitch, M., Stuss, D. T., Winocur, G., Tulving, E., & Kapur, S. (1999). In search of the self: A positron emission tomography study. *Psychological Science, 10,* 26–34.

Cramer, P. (2000). Defense mechanisms in psychology today: Further processes for adaptation. *American Psychologist, 55,* 637–646.

Cramond, B., & Kim, K. H. (2008). The role of creativity tools and measures in assessing potential and growth. In J. L. VanTassel-Baska (Ed.), *Alternative assessments with gifted and talented students* (pp. 203–225). Waco, TX: Prufrock Press.

Craske, M. G. (2003). *Origins of phobias and anxiety disorders: Why more women than men?* Oxford, England: Elsevier.

Craske, M. G. (2009). *Cognitive-behavioral therapy*. Washington, DC: American Psychological Association.

Crawford, N. (2002, June). Employees' longer working hours linked to family conflict, stress-related health problems. *Monitor on Psychology, 33*(6), 17.

Creed, P. A., & Klisch, J. (2005). Future outlook and financial strain: Testing the personal agency and latent deprivation models of unemployment and wellbeing. *Journal of Occupational Health Psychology, 10,* 251–260.

Crinion, J. T., Lambon-Ralph, M. A., & Warburton, E. A. (2003). Temporal lobe regions engaged during normal speech comprehension. *Brain: A Journal of Neurology, 126,* 1193–1201.

Crisp, R. J. (2010). Introduction. In R. J. Crisp (Ed.), *The psychology of social and cultural diversity* (pp. 1–8). Hoboken, NJ: Wiley-Blackwell.

Criswell, E. (2003). A challenge to humanistic psychology in the 21st century. *Journal of Humanistic Psychology, 43,* 42–52.

Crooks, R., & Baur, K. (2002). *Our sexuality* (8th ed.). Belmont, CA: Wadsworth.

Cross, M. R. (2003). The relationship between trauma history, daily hassles, and physical symptoms. *Dissertation Abstracts International: Section B: The Sciences and Engineering, 63,* 4364.

Crosscope-Happel, C. (2005). Male anorexia nervosa: An exploratory study. *Dissertation Abstracts International: Section A: Humanities and Social Sciences, 65,* 4472.

Crovitz, H. F., & Schiffman, H. (1974). Frequency of episodic memories as a function of their age. *Bulletin of the Psychonomic Society, 4,* 517–518.

Crowther, J. H., Kichler, J. C., Shewood, N. E., & Kuhnert, M. E. (2002). The role of familial factors in bulimia nervosa. *Eating Disorders: The Journal of Treatment & Prevention, 10,* 141–151.

Csikszentmihalyi, M., Rathunde, K. R., Whalen, S., & Wong, M. (1993). *Talented teenagers: The roots of success and failure*. New York, NY: Cambridge University Press.

Cuadrado, I., Morales, J., Recio, P., & Howard, V. (2008). Women's access to managerial positions: An experimental study of leadership styles and gender. *The Spanish Journal of Psychology, 11,* 55–65.

Cubelli, R., & Della Sala, S. (2008). Flashbulb memories: Special but not iconic. *Cortex, 44,* 908–909.

Culbertson, F. M. (1997). Depression and gender: An international review. *American Psychologist, 52,* 25–31.

Cunningham, W. A., Johnson, M. K., Raye, C. L., Gatenby, J. C., & Gore, J. C. (2004). Separable neural components in the processing of black and white faces. *Psychological Science, 15,* 806–813.

Cunningham, W. A., & Zelazo, P. (2007). Attitudes and evaluations: A social cognitive neuroscience perspective. *Trends in Cognitive Sciences, 11,* 97–104.

Currenti, S. A. (2010). Understanding and determining the etiology of autism. *Cellular and Molecular Neurobiology, 30,* 161–171.

Curtin, J. S. (2004). *Suicide in Japan: Part Eleven—Comparing international rates of suicide*. Japanese Institute of Global Communications. Retrieved from http://www.glocom.org/special_topics/social_trends/20040818_trends_s79/index.html

Cusin, C., Evans, K. C., Carpenter, L. L., Greenberg, B. D., Malone, D. A., Jr., Eskandar, E., & Dougherty, D. D. (2010). Deep brain stimulation for treatment resistant depression: The role of the ventral capsule/ventral striatum. *Psychiatric Annals, 40,* 477–484.

Cutler, D. M. (2001). The reduction in disability among the elderly. *PNAS Proceedings of the National Academy of Sciences of the United States of America, 98,* 6546–6547.

Cutler, W. B., Friedmann, E., & McCoy, N. L. (1998). Pheromonal influences on sociosexual behavior in men. *Archives of Sexual Behavior, 27,* 1–13.

D'Argembeau, A., & Mathy, A. (2011). Tracking the construction of episodic future thoughts. *Journal of Experimental Psychology: General, 140,* 258–271.

D'Silva, M. U., Grant-Harrington, N., Palmgreen, P., Donohew, L., & Pugzles-Lorch, E. (2001). Drug use prevention for the high sensation seeker: The role of alternative activities. *Substance Use and Misuse, 36,* 373–385.

Dabbs, J. M., Jr., Carr, T. S., Frady, R. L., & Riad, J. K. (1995). Testosterone, crime, and misbehavior among 692 male prison inmates. *Personality and Individual Differences, 19,* 627–633.

Dahl, D. W., Frankenberger, K. D., & Manchanda, R. V. (2003). Does it pay to shock? Reactions to shocking and nonshocking advertising content among university students. *Journal of Advertising Research, 43,* 268–280.

Dal Cin, S., Gibson, B., Zanna, M. P., Shumate, R., & Fong, G. T. (2007). Smoking in movies, implicit associations of smoking with the self, and intentions to smoke. *Psychological Science, 18,* 559–563.

Dalbert, C. (2001). *The justice motive as a personal resource: Dealing with challenges and critical life events*. New York, NY: Kluwer Academic/Plenum.

Dalley, J. W., Fryer, T. D., Brichard, L., Robinson, E. S. J., Theobald, D. E. H., Lääne, K., . . . Robbins, T. W. (2007). Nucleus accumbens D2/3 receptors predict trait impulsivity and cocaine reinforcement. *Science, 315,* 1267–1270.

Dalton, P. (2002). Olfaction. In H. Pashler & S. Yantis (Eds.), *Stevens' handbook of experimental psychology* (3rd ed., Vol. 1, pp. 691–746). Hoboken, NJ: John Wiley & Sons.

Dalton, P., Doolittle, N., & Breslin, P. A. S. (2002). Gender-specific induction of enhanced sensitivity to odors. *Nature Neuroscience, 5,* 199–200.

Damasio, A. R. (2010). *Self comes to mind: Constructing the conscious brain*. NY: Pantheon/Random House.

Damasio, A. R., & Anderson, S. W. (2003). The frontal lobes. In K. M. Heilman & E. Valenstein (Eds.), *Clinical neuropsychology* (4th ed., pp. 404–446). New York, NY: Oxford University Press.

Damasio, H., Grabowski, T. F. R., Galaburda, A. M., & Damasio, A. R. (2005). The return of Phineas Gage: Clues about the brain from the skull of a famous patient. In J. T. Cacioppo & G. G. Berntson (Eds.), *Social neuroscience: Key readings* (pp. 21–28). New York, NY: Psychology Press.

Damasio, H., Grabowski, T. J., Tranel, D., Hichawa, R. D., & Damasio, A. R. (1996). A neural basis for lexical retrieval. *Nature, 380*, 499–505.

Damisch, L., Stoberock, B., & Mussweiler, T. (2010). Keep your fingers crossed! How superstition improves performance. *Psychological Science, 21*, 1014–1020.

Dang-Vu, T., Schabus, M., Desseilles, M., Schwartz, S., & Maquet, P. (2007). Neuroimaging of REM sleep and dreaming. In D. Barrett & P. McNamara, (Eds.), *The new science of dreaming: Volume 1. Biological aspects* (pp. 95–113). Westport, CT: Praeger Publishers/Greenwood Publishing Group.

Darcangelo, S., Hollings, A., & Paladino, G. (2008). Fetishism: Assessment and treatment. In D. R. Laws & W. T. O'Donohue (Eds.), *Sexual deviance: Theory, assessment, and treatment* (2nd ed., pp. 119–130). New York, NY: Guilford Press.

Darwin, C. R. (1859). *On the origin of species*. London, England: John Murray.

Darwin, C. R.. (1965). *The expression of emotions in man and animals*. Chicago: University of Chicago Press. (Original work published 1872).

Davidson, K. (2008). *Cognitive therapy for personality disorders: A guide for clinicians* (2nd ed.). New York, NY: Routledge.

Davidson, R. J. (1992). Emotion and affective style: Hemispheric substrates. *Psychological Science, 3*, 39–43.

Davidson, R. J., Jackson, D. C., & Kalin, N. H. (2000). Emotion, plasticity, context, and regulation: Perspectives from affective neuroscience. *Psychological Bulletin, 126*, 890–909.

Davidson, R. J., Kabat-Zinn, J., Schumacher, J., Rosenkranz, M., Muller, D., Santorelli, S. F., ... Sheridan, J. F. (2003). Alterations in brain and immune function produced by mindfulness meditation. *Psychosomatic Medicine, 65*, 564–570.

Davidson, R. J., Putnam, K. M., & Larson, C. L. (2000). Dysfunction in the neural circuitry of emotion regulation—A possible prelude to violence. *Science, 289*, 591–594.

Davies, M., Stankov, L., & Roberts, R. D. (1998). Emotional intelligence: In search of an elusive construct. *Journal of Personality and Social Psychology, 75*, 989–1015.

Davies, R. (2009). Review of adolescent substance abuse: Psychiatric comorbidity and high-risk behaviors. *American Journal of Psychiatry, 166*, 117–117.

Davis, C. G., Wortman, C. B., Lehman, D. R., & Silver, R. C. (2000). Searching for meaning in loss: Are clinical assumptions correct? *Death Studies, 24*, 497–540.

Davis, O. S. P., Haworth, C. M. A., & Plomin, R. (2009). Dramatic increase in heritability of cognitive development from early to middle childhood: An 8-year longitudinal study of 8,700 pairs of twins. *Psychological Science, 20*, 1301–1308.

Dawson, M., Soulières, I., Gernsbacher, M. A., & Mottron, L. (2007). The level and nature of autistic intelligence. *Psychological Science, 18*, 657–662.

Day, N. L., Leech, S. L., & Goldschmidt, L. (2011). The effects of prenatal marijuana exposure on delinquent behaviors are mediated by measures of neurocognitive functioning. *Neurotoxicology and Teratology, 33*, 129–136.

De la Fuente, M. (2002). Effects of antioxidants on the immune system aging. *European Journal of Clinical Nutrition, 56*(Suppl. 3), S5–8.

de Maat, S., de Jonghe, F., Schoevers, R., & Dekker, J. (2009). The effectiveness of long-term psychoanalytic therapy: A systematic review of empirical studies. *Harvard Review of Psychiatry, 17*, 1–23.

de Vries, M., Holland, R. W., Chenier, T., Starr, M. J., & Winkielman, P. (2010). Happiness cools the warm glow of familiarity: Psychophysiological evidence that mood modulates the familiarity-affect link. *Psychological Science, 21*, 321–328.

de Waal, F. (2007). *Primates and philosophers: How morality evolved*. Princeton, NJ: Princeton University Press.

de-l'Etoile, S. K. (2002). The effect of musical mood induction procedure on mood state-dependent word retrieval. *Journal of Music Therapy, 39*, 145–160.

Dean, J. W., Jr., & Evans, J. R. (1994). *Total quality: Management, organization, and strategy*. St. Paul, MN: West.

DeAngelis, T. (2002, June). How do mind–body interventions affect breast cancer? *Monitor on Psychology, 33*(6), 51–53.

Deary, I. J., Johnson, W., & Houlihan, L. (2009). Genetic foundations of human intelligence. *Human Genetics, 126*, 215–232.

Deary, I. J., Penke, L., & Johnson, W. (2010). The neuroscience of human intelligence differences. *Nature Reviews Neuroscience, 11*, 201–211.

Deary, I. J., Weiss, A., & Batty, G. D. (2010). Intelligence, personality and health outcomes. *Psychological Science in the Public Interest, 11*, 53–80.

deCharms, R. C., Maeda, F., Glover, G. H., Ludlow, D., Pauly, J. M., Soneji, D., ... Mackey, S. C. (2005). Control over brain activation and pain learned by using real-time functional MRI. *PNAS Proceedings of the National Academy of Sciences of the United States of America, 102*, 18626–18631.

Deci, E. L., Koestner, R., & Ryan, R. M. (2001). Extrinsic rewards and intrinsic motivation in education: Reconsidered once again. *Review of Educational Research, 71*, 1–27.

Deci, E. L., & Ryan, R. M. (2008). Facilitating optimal motivation and psychological well-being across life's domains. *Canadian Psychology, 49*, 14–23.

Degenhardt, L., Bucello, C., Mathers, B., Briegleb, C., Ali, H., Hickman, M., & McLaren, J. (2011). Mortality among regular or dependent users of heroin and other opioids: A systematic review and meta-analysis of cohort studies. *Addiction, 106*, 32–51.

Dell, P. F. (2006). A new model of dissociative identity disorder. *Psychiatric Clinics of North America, 29*, 1–26.

Dell'Osso, M. C. (2003). A historical discussion of the neuropsychological correlates in dissociative identity disorder. *Dissertation Abstracts International: Section B: The Sciences and Engineering, 63*, 5510.

Della Sala, S. (2011). Cognition and the cerebellum. Cortex: *A Journal Devoted to the Study of the Nervous System and Behavior, 47*, 1. doi:10.1016/j.cortex.2010.05.010

Demorest, S. M., Morrison, S. J., Stambaugh, L. A., Beken, M., Richards, T. L., & Johnson, C. (2010). An fMRI investigation of the cultural specificity of music memory. *Social Cognitive and Affective Neuroscience, 5*, 282–291.

Demyttenaere, K., & Jaspers, L. (2008). Bupropion and SSRI-induced side effects. *Journal of Psychopharmacology, 22*, 792–804.

Dennerstein, L., Dudley, E., & Guthrie, J. (2002). Empty nest or revolving door? A prospective study of women's quality of life in midlife during the phase of children leaving and re-entering the home. *Psychological Medicine, 32*, 545–550.

Denollet, J. (2005). DS14: Standard assessment of negative affectivity, social inhibition, and Type D personality. *Psychosomatic Medicine, 67*, 89–97.

Denson, N. (2008). Do curricular and co-curricular diversity activities influence racial bias? A meta-analysis. *Dissertation Abstracts International Section A: Humanities and Social Sciences, 68*, 2840.

DePaulo, B. M., Lindsay, J. J., Malone, B. E., Muhlenbruck, L., Charlton, K., & Cooper, H. (2003). Cues to deception. *Psychological Bulletin, 129*, 74–118.

Depue, B. E., Burgess, G. C., Willcutt, E. G., Ruzic, L. L., & Banich, M. T. (2010). Inhibitory control of memory retrieval and motor processing associated with the right lateral prefrontal cortex: Evidence from deficits in individuals with adhd. *Neuropsychologia, 48*, 3909–3917. doi:10.1016/j.neuropsychologia.2010.09.013

DeRamus, B. (2000, August 26). Lax reaction to killing shows how numb many have become. *Detroit News*. Retrieved from http://detnews.com/2000/features/0008/26/c01–110895.htm

Desrumaux, P., De Bosscher, S., & Léoni, V. (2009). Effects of facial attractiveness, gender, and competence of applicants on job recruitment. *Swiss Journal of Psychology/Schweizerische Zeitschrift für Psychologie/Revue Suisse de Psychologie, 68*, 33–42.

DeSteno, D., & Braverman, J. (2002). Emotion and persuasion: Thoughts on the role of emotional intelligence. In L. F. Barrett & P. Salovey (Eds.), *The wisdom in feeling: Psychological processes in emotional intelligence* (pp. 191–210). New York, NY: Guilford Press.

DeWall, C. N., & Baumeister, R. F. (2007). From terror to joy: Automatic tuning to positive affective information following mortality salience. *Psychological Science, 18*, 984–990.

DeYoung, C. G., Hirsh, J. B., Shane, M. S., Papademetris, X., Rajeevan, N., & Gray, J. R. (2010). Testing predictions from personality neuroscience: Brain structure and the big five. *Psychological Science, 21*, 820–828.

DeYoung, R. (2005). Contingency theories of leadership. In N. Borkowski (Ed.), *Organizational behavior in health care* (pp. 187–208). Boston, MA: Jones & Bartlett.

Diala, C., Muntaner, C., Walrath, C., Nickerson, K. J., LaVeist, T. A., & Leaf, P. J. (2000). Racial differences in attitudes toward professional mental health care and in the use of services. *American Journal of Orthopsychiatry, 70*, 455–464.

Diano, S., Farr, S. A., Benoit, S. C., McNay, E. C., da Silva, I., Horvath, B., ... Horvath, T. L. (2006). Ghrelin controls hippocampal spine synapse density and memory performance. *Nature Neuroscience, 9*, 381–388.

Dickins, T. E. (2008). Humane intelligence. *Journal of Evolutionary Psychology, 6*, 85–88.

Diehm, R., & Armatas, C. (2004). Surfing: An avenue for socially acceptable risk-taking, satisfying needs for sensation seeking and experience seeking. *Personality and Individual Differences, 36*, 663–677.

Dietrich, A., & Kanso, R. (2010). A review of EEG, ERP, and neuroimaging studies of creativity and insight. *Psychological Bulletin, 136*, 822–848.

DiFranza, J. R., Savageau, J. A., Fletcher, K., O'Loughlin, J., Pbert, L., Ockene, J. K., . . . Wellman, R. J. (2007). Symptoms of tobacco dependence after brief intermittent use. *Archives of Pediatrics and Adolescent Medicine, 161*, 704–710.

Dijksterhuis, A., Aarts, H., & Smith, P. K. (2005). The power of the subliminal: On subliminal persuasion and other potential applications. In R. R. Hassin, J. S. Uleman, & J. A. Bargh (Eds.), *The new unconscious* (pp. 77–106). New York, NY: Oxford University Press.

Dill, K. E., Gentile, D. A., Richter, W. A., & Dill, J. C. (2005). Violence, sex, race, and age in popular video games: A content analysis. In E. Cole & J. H. Daniel (Eds.), *Featuring females: Feminist analyses of the media* (pp. 115–130). Washington, DC: American Psychological Association.

Dillard, J. P., & Anderson, J. W. (2004). The role of fear in persuasion. *Psychology & Marketing, 21*, 909–926.

Dillaway, H., & Paré, E. (2008). Locating mothers: How cultural debates about stay-at-home versus working mothers define women and home. *Journal of Family Issues, 29*, 437–464.

Din, F. S., & Calao, J. (2001). The effects of playing educational video games on kindergarten achievement. *Child Study Journal, 31*, 95–102.

Dingfelder, S. F. (2007, April). Introduction to science. *Monitor on Psychology, 38*(4), 24–25.

Dion, K. L. (2003). Prejudice, racism, and discrimination. In T. Millon & M. Lerner (Eds.), *Handbook of psychology: Vol. 5, Personality and social psychology* (pp. 507–536). Hoboken, NJ: Wiley.

Dixon, J. F., & Hokin, L. E. (1998). Lithium acutely inhibits and chronically up-regulates and stabilizes glutamate uptake by presynaptic nerve endings in mouse cerebral cortex. *PNAS Proceedings of the National Academy of Sciences of the United States of America, 95*, 8363–8368.

Dobson, J. L. (2004). The relationship of personal and contextual differences to grief distress and personal growth. *Dissertation Abstracts International: Section B: The Sciences and Engineering, 64*, 4611.

Docherty, S. J., Davis, O. P., Kovas, Y. Y., Meaburn, E. L., Dale, P. S., Petrill, S. A., & Plomin, R. R. (2010). A genome-wide association study identifies multiple loci associated with mathematics ability and disability. *Genes, Brain & Behavior, 9*, 234–247.

Doherty, W. J., & McDaniel, S. H. (2009). *Family therapy.* Washington, DC: American Psychological Association.

Dohrenwend, B. P., Turner, J. B., Turse, N. A., Adams, B. G., Koenen, K. C., & Marshall, R. (2007). Continuing controversy over the psychological risks of Vietnam for U.S. veterans. *Journal of Traumatic Stress, 20*, 449–465.

Domhoff, G. W. (2003). A critique of traditional dream theories. In G. W. Domhoff (Ed.), *The scientific study of dreams: Neural networks, cognitive development, and content analysis* (pp. 135–170). Washington, DC: American Psychological Association.

Domhoff, G. W. (2005). The content of dreams: Methodologic and theoretical implications. In M. H. Kryger, T. Roth, & W. C. Dement (Eds.), *Principles and Practice of Sleep Medicine* (4th ed., pp. 522–534). Philadelphia, PA: Saunders.

Domhoff, G. W. (2010). Dream content is continuous with waking thought, based on preoccupations, concerns, and interests. *Sleep Medicine Clinics, 5*, 203–215.

Domhoff, G. W., & Schneider, A. (2008). Similarities and differences in dream content at the cross-cultural, gender, and individual levels. *Consciousness and Cognition: An International Journal, 17*, 1257–1265.

Donatelle, R. J. (2004). *Access to health* (8th ed.). Englewood Cliffs, NJ: Prentice Hall.

Donley, M. P., Schulkin, J., & Rosen, J. B. (2005). Glucocorticoid receptor antagonism in the basolateral amygdala and ventral hippocampus interferes with long-term memory of contextual fear. *Behavioural Brain Research, 164*, 197–205.

Donovan, J. J. (2002). Work motivation. In N. Anderson, D. S. Ones, H. K. Sinangil, & C. Viswesvaran (Eds.), *Handbook of industrial, work and organizational psychology, Volume 2: Organizational psychology* (pp. 53–76). Thousand Oaks, CA: Sage.

Doré, R., Wagner, S., Doré, I., & Brunet, J.-P. (2002). From mainstreaming to inclusion: A transformation of service delivery. In R. L. Schalock, P. C. Baker, & M. D. Croser (Eds.), *Embarking on a new century: Mental retardation at the end of the 20th century* (pp. 185–201). Washington, DC: American Association on Mental Retardation.

Doty, R. L. (1989). Influence of age and age-related diseases on olfactory function. *Annals of the New York Academy of Sciences, 561*, 76–86.

Doty, R. L. (2001). Olfaction. *Annual Review of Psychology, 52*, 423–452.

Doty, R. L. (2006). Smelling and tasting problems. In F. E. Bloom, M. F. Beal, & D. J. Kupfer (Eds.), *The Dana guide to brain health* (pp. 347–351). New York, NY: Dana Press.

Dougall, A. L., & Baum, A. (2004). Psychoneuroimmunology and trauma. In P. P. Schnurr & B. L. Green (Eds.), *Trauma and health: Physical health consequences of exposure to extreme stress* (pp. 129–155). Washington, DC: American Psychological Association.

Dozois, D. J. A., Frewen, P. A., & Covin, R. (2006). Cognitive theories. In J. C. Thomas, D. L. Segal, & M. Hersen (Eds.), *Comprehensive handbook of personality and psychopathology, Vol. 1: Personality and everyday functioning* (pp. 173–191). Hoboken, NJ: Wiley.

Driscoll, E. V. (2008, June/July). Bisexual species. *Scientific American Mind, 19*(3), 68–73.

Druskat, V. U., Sala, F., & Mount, G. (2006). *Linking emotional intelligence and performance at work: Current research evidence with individuals and groups.* Mahwah, NJ: Erlbaum.

Dubner, R., & Gold, M. (1998, December). *The neurobiology of pain.* Paper presented at the National Academy of Sciences colloquium, Irvine, CA.

Duchek, J. M., Balota, D. A., Storandt, M., & Larsen, R. (2007). The power of personality in discriminating between healthy aging and early-stage Alzheimer's disease. *The Journals of Gerontology: Series B: Psychological Sciences and Social Sciences, 6B*, 353–361.

Duckworth, A. L., Steen, T. A., & Seligman, M. E. P. (2005). Positive psychology in clinical practice. *Annual Review of Clinical Psychology, 1*, 629–651.

Dudai, Y. (2004). The neurosciences: The danger that we will think that we have understood it all. In D. Rees & S. Rose (Eds.), *The new brain sciences: Perils and prospects* (pp. 167–180). New York, NY: Cambridge University Press.

Duesenberg, D. (2006). ADHD: Diagnosis and current treatment options to improve functional outcomes. In T. K. Parthasarathy (Ed.), *An introduction to auditory processing disorders in children* (pp. 187–201). Mahwah, NJ: Erlbaum.

Duke, N., Resnick, M. D., & Borowsky, I. W. (2005). Adolescent firearm violence: Position paper of the Society for Adolescent Medicine. *Journal of Adolescent Health, 37*, 171–174.

Dunn, W. S., Mount, M. K., & Barrick, M. R. (1995). Relative importance of personality and general mental ability in managers' judgments of applicant qualifications. *Journal of Applied Psychology, 80*, 500–509.

Dunkel Schetter, C. (2009). Stress processes in pregnancy and preterm birth. *Current Directions in Psychological Science, 18*, 205–209.

Dunkel Schetter, C., & Glynn, L. M. (2011). Stress in pregnancy: Empirical evidence and theoretical issues to guide interdisciplinary research. In R. J. Contrado & A. Baum (Eds.), *The handbook of stress science: Biology, psychology, and health* (pp. 321–347). New York, NY: Springer.

Durex Global Sex Survey (2005). Retrieved from http://www.durex.com/cm/gss2005result.pdf

Durmer, J. S., & Dinges, D. F. (2005). Neurocognitive consequences of sleep deprivation. *Seminars in Neurology, 25*, 117–129.

Dwyer, K. (2006). Maternal and paternal parenting and girls' and boys' attachment security in middle childhood. *Dissertation Abstracts International: Section B: The Sciences and Engineering, 66*, 6948.

Eachus, P. (2004). Using the brief sensation seeking scale (BSSS) to predict holiday preferences. *Personality and Individual Differences, 36*, 141–153.

Eagly, A. H. (2003). The rise of female leaders. *Zeitschrift-fur-Sozialpsychologie, 34*, 123–132.

Eagly, A. H., & Carli, L. L. (1981). Sex of researchers and sex-typed communications as determinants of sex differences in influenceability: A meta-analysis of social influence studies. *Psychological Bulletin, 90*, 1–20.

Eagly, A. H., Johannesen-Schmidt, M. C., & van-Engen, M. L. (2003). Transformational, transactional, and laissez-faire leadership styles: A meta analysis comparing women and men. *Psychological Bulletin, 129*, 569–591.

Eagly, A. H., & Steffen, V. J. (1986). Gender and aggressive behavior: A meta-analytic review of the social psychological literature. *Psychological Bulletin, 100*, 309–330.

Eastwick, P. W., Finkel, E. J., Mochon, D., & Ariely, D. (2007). Selective versus unselective romantic desire: Not all reciprocity is created equal. *Psychological Science, 18,* 317–319.

Eberhard, J., Lindström, E., & Levander, S. (2006). Tardive dyskinesia and antipsychotics: A 5-year longitudinal study of frequency, correlates and course. *International Clinical Psychopharmacology, 21,* 35–42.

Ebster, C., & Neumayr, B. (2008). Applying the door-in-the-face compliance technique to retailing. *The International Review of Retail, Distribution and Consumer Research, 18,* 121–128.

Eccles, J. S., Midgley, C., Wigfield, A., Buchanan, C. M., Reuman, D., Flanagan, C., & MacIver, D. M. (1993). Development during adolescence: The impact of stage-environment fit on young adolescents' experiences in school and families. *American Psychologist: Special Issue: Adolescence, 48,* 90–101.

Edelman, S., Lemon, J., Bell, D. R., & Kidman, A. D. (1999). Effects of group CBT on the survival time of patients with metastatic breast cancer. *Psycho-Oncology, 8,* 474–481.

Edelstein, R. S., Luten, T. L., Ekman, P., & Goodman, G. S. (2006). Detecting lies in children and adults. *Law and Human Behavior, 30,* 1–10.

Edery, H. G., & Nachson, I. (2004). Distinctiveness in flashbulb memory: Comparative analysis of five terrorist attacks. *Memory, 12,* 147–157.

Edgette, J. H., & Rowan, T. (2003). *Winning the mind game: Using hypnosis in sport psychology.* Williston, VT: Crown House.

Edwards, R. R., Campbell, C., Jamison, R. N., & Wiech, K. (2009). The neurobiological underpinnings of coping with pain. *Current Directions in Psychological Science, 18,* 237–241.

Egger, J. I. M., Delsing, P. A. M., & DeMey, H. R. A. (2003). Differential diagnosis using the MMPI-2: Goldberg's index revisited. *European Psychiatry, 18,* 409–411.

Ehigie, B. O., & Shenge, N. A. (2000). Psychological strategies in managing television commercial efficacy. *IFE Psychologia: An International Journal, 9,* 115–122.

Ehrenfeld, T. (2011). Reflections on mirror neurons. *Observer: American Psychological Society, 24,* 11–13.

Eichenbaum, H., & Fortin, N. (2003). Episodic memory and the hippocampus: It's about time. *Current Directions in Psychological Science, 12,* 53–57.

Eisenberg, N., & Lennon, R. (1983). Sex differences in empathy and related capacities. *Psychological Bulletin, 94,* 100–131.

Eisenberger, R., & Cameron, J. (1996). Detrimental effects of reward. *American Psychologist, 51,* 1153–1166.

Eisenberger, R., & Rhoades, L. (2001). Incremental effects of reward on creativity. *Journal of Personality and Social Psychology, 81,* 728–741.

Eisenberger, R., Rhoades, L., & Cameron, J. (1999). Does pay for performance increase or decrease perceived self-determination and intrinsic motivation? *Journal of Personality and Social Psychology, 77,* 1026–1040.

Ekman, P. (2003). *Emotions revealed: Recognizing faces and feelings to improve communication and emotional life.* New York, NY: Holt.

Ekman, P., & Friesen, W. V. (1971). Constants across cultures in the face and emotion. *Journal of Personality and Social Psychology, 17,* 124–129.

Ekman, P., & Friesen, W. V. (1975). *Unmasking the face.* Englewood Cliffs, NJ: Prentice Hall.

Ekman, P., Friesen, W. V., & Ellsworth, P. (1972). *Emotion in the human face.* Elmsford, NY: Pergamon.

Ekman, P., & O'Sullivan, M. (1991). Who can catch a liar? *American Psychologist, 46,* 913–920.

Ekman, P., Sorenson, E. R., & Friesen, W. V. (1969). Pancultural elements in facial displays of emotion. *Science, 164,* 86–88.

El-Ad, B., & Lavie, P. (2005). Effect of sleep apnea on cognition and mood. *International Review of Psychiatry, 17,* 277–282.

Eldar-Avidan, D., Haj-Yahia, M. M., & Greenbaum, C. W. (2008). Money matters: Young adults' perception of the economic consequences of their parents' divorce. *Journal of Family and Economic Issues, 29,* 74–85.

Eley, T. C., Lichtenstein, P., & Stevenson, J. (1999). Sex differences in the etiology of aggressive and nonaggressive antisocial behavior: Results from two twin studies. *Child Development, 70,* 155–168.

Eley, T. C., & Stevenson, J. (1999). Exploring the covariation between anxiety and depression symptoms: A genetic analysis of the effects of age and sex. *Journal of Child Psychology & Psychiatry & Allied Disciplines, 40,* 1273–1282.

Elfenbein, H. A., & Ambady, N. (2002). On the universality and cultural specificity of emotion recognition: A meta-analysis. *Psychological Bulletin, 128,* 203–235.

Elfenbein, H. A., & Ambady, N. (2003). Universals and cultural differences in recognizing emotions. *Current Directions in Psychological Science, 12,* 159–164.

Elliot, A. J., Maier, M. A., Moller, A. C., Friedman, R., & Meinhardt, J. (2007). Color and psychological functioning: The effect of red on performance attainment. *Journal of Experimental Psychology: General, 136,* 154–168.

Ellis, A. (1973). *Humanistic psychotherapy: The rational emotive approach.* New York, NY: Julian.

Ellis, A. (2001). *Overcoming destructive beliefs, feelings, and behaviors: New directions for Rational Emotive Behavior Therapy.* Amherst, NY: Prometheus.

Ellis, A., & Harper, R. A. (1975). *A new guide to rational living.* North Hollywood, CA: Wilshire.

Ellis, A., & MacLaren, C. (1998). *Rational emotive behavior therapy: A therapist's guide.* San Luis Obispo, CA: Impact.

Ellis, L., & Coontz, P. D. (1990). Androgens, brain functioning, and criminality: The neurohormonal foundations of antisociality. In L. Ellis & H. Hoffman (Eds.), *Crime in biological, social, and moral contexts* (pp. 36–49). New York, NY: Praeger.

Ellis, L., Robb, B., & Burke, D. (2005). Sexual orientation in United States and Canadian college students. *Archives of Sexual Behavior, 34,* 569–581.

Elloy, D. F., & Mackie, B. (2002). Overload and work-family conflict among Australian dual-career families: Moderating effects of support. *Psychological Reports, 91,* 907–913.

Elwood, L. S., Hahn, K. S., Olatunji, B. O., & Williams, N. L. (2009). Cognitive vulnerabilities to the development of PTSD: A review of four vulnerabilities and the proposal of an integrative vulnerability model. *Clinical Psychology Review, 29,* 87–100.

Emack, J., Kostaki, A., Walker, C.-D., & Matthews, S. G. (2008). Chronic maternal stress affects growth, behaviour and hypothalamo-pituitary-adrenal function in juvenile offspring. *Hormones and Behavior, 54,* 514–520.

Emamian, S., Naghdi, N., Sepehri, H., Jahanshahi, M., Sadeghi, Y., & Choopani, S. (2010). Learning impairment caused by intra-CA1 microinjection of testosterone increases the number of astrocytes. *Behavioural Brain Research, 208,* 30–37.

Engemann, K. M., & Owyang, M. T. (2006, April). Social changes lead married women into labor force. *The Regional Economist,* 10–11.

Enticott, P. G., Johnston, P. J., Herring, S. E., Hoy, K. E., & Fitzgerald, P. B. (2008). Mirror neuron activation is associated with facial emotion processing. *Neuropsychologia, 46,* 2851–2854.

Epel, E. S., Lin, J., Wilhelm, F. H., Wolkowitz, O. M., Cawthon, R., Adler, N. E., . . . Blackburn, E. H. (2006). Cell aging in relation to stress arousal and cardiovascular disease risk factors. *Psychoneuroendocrinology, 31,* 277–287.

Epstein, N. B. (2004). Cognitive-behavioral therapy with couples: Theoretical and empirical status. In R. L. Leahy (Ed.), *Contemporary cognitive therapy: Theory, research, and practice* (pp. 367–388). New York, NY: Guilford Press.

Epstude, K., & Roese, N. J. (2008). The functional theory of counterfactual thinking. *Personality and Social Psychology Review, 12,* 168–192.

Erdley, C. A., & D'Agostino, P. R. (1988). Cognitive and affective components of automatic priming effects. *Journal of Personality and Social Psychology, 54,* 741–747.

Erickson, K. I., Voss, M. W., Prakash, R. S., Basak, C., Szabo, A., Chaddock, L., . . . Kramer, A. F. (2011). Exercise training increases size of hippocampus and improves memory. *PNAS Proceedings of the National Academy of Sciences of the United States of America, 108,* 3017–3022.

Erickson, R. J. (2005). Why emotion work matters: Sex, gender, and the division of household labor. *Journal of Marriage and Family, 67,* 337–351.

Erikson, E. H. (1968). *Identity: Youth in crisis.* New York, NY: Norton.

Eriksson, U. K., Pedersen, N. L., Reynolds, C. A., Hong, M., Prince, J. A., Gatz, M., . . . Bennet, A. M. (2011). Associations of gene sequence variation and serum levels of C-reactive protein and interleukin-6 with Alzheimer's disease and dementia. *Journal of Alzheimer's Disease, 23,* 361–369.

Ermer, E., Cosmides, L., & Tooby, J. (2007). Functional specialization and the adaptationist program. In S. W. Gangestad & J. A. Simpson (Eds.), *The evolution of mind: Fundamental questions and controversies* (pp. 153–160). New York, NY: Guilford Press.

Ermer, E., Cosmides, L., & Tooby, J. (2008). Relative status regulates risky decision making about resources in men: Evidence for the co-evolution of motivation and cognition. *Evolution and Human Behavior, 29,* 106–118.

Esler, M., Schwarz, R., & Alvarenga, M. (2008). Mental stress is a cause of cardiovascular diseases: From scepticism to certainty. *Stress and Health: Journal of the International Society for the Investigation of Stress, 24,* 175–180.

Esterman, M., & Yantis, S. (2010). Perceptual expectation evokes category-selective cortical activity. *Cerebral Cortex, 20,* 1245–1253.

Esterson, A. (2002). The myth of Freud's ostracism by the medical community in 1896–1905: Jeffrey Masson's assault on truth. *History of Psychology, 5,* 115–134.

Etter, J.-F. (2009). Dependence on the nicotine gum in former smokers. *Addictive Behaviors, 34,* 246–251.

Ey, D. (2010). Body dissatisfaction and self-esteem in males: Relationships with muscle dysmorphia. *Dissertation Abstracts International, 71,* 2010. Retrieved from EBSCOhost.

Eysenck, H. J. (1947). *Dimensions of personality.* London, England: Routledge.

Eysenck, H. J. (1976). *The measurement of personality.* Baltimore, MD: University Park Press.

Fadiga, L., Fogassi, L., Pavesi, G., & Rizzolatti, G. (1995). Motor facilitation during action observation: A magnetic stimulation study. *Journal of Neurophysiology, 73,* 2608–2611.

Fagan, P. J., Lehne, G., Strand, J. G., & Berlin, F. S. (2005). Paraphilias. In G. O. Beck & J. Holmes (Eds.), *Oxford textbook of psychotherapy* (pp. 213–225). New York, NY: Oxford University Press.

Fagot, B. I. (1994). Parenting. In V. A. Ramachandran (Ed.), *Encyclopedia of human behavior* (Vol. 3, pp. 411–419). San Diego, CA: Academic Press.

Fairbrother, N., & Rachman, S. (2006). PTSD in victims of sexual assault: Test of a major component of the Ehlers-Clark theory. *Journal of Behavior Therapy and Experimental Psychiatry, 37,* 74–93.

Fairburn, C. G., Cooper, Z., Shafran, R., & Wilson, G. T. (2008). Eating disorders: A transdiagnostic protocol. In D. H. Barlow (Ed.), *Clinical handbook of psychological disorders: A step-by-step treatment manual* (4th ed., pp. 578–614). New York, NY: Guilford Press.

Fals-Stewart, W., & Lam, W. K. K. (2008). Brief behavioral couples therapy for drug abuse: A randomized clinical trial examining clinical efficacy and cost-effectiveness. *Families, Systems, & Health, 26,* 377–392.

Fantz, R. L., Fagan, J. F., & Miranda, S. B. (1975). Early visual selectivity. In L. B. Cohen & P. Salapatek (Eds.), *Infant perception: From sensation to cognition* (Vol. 1, pp. 249–345). New York, NY: Academic Press.

Faraut, B., Boudjeltia, K., Dyzma, M., Rousseau, A., David, E., Stenuit, P., & Kerkhofs, M. (2011). Benefits of napping and an extended duration of recovery sleep on alertness and immune cells after acute sleep restriction. *Brain, Behavior, and Immunity, 25,* 16–24.

Farberman, R. K. (2011, April). Bridging the multicultural gap. *Monitor on Psychology, 42*(4), 66–68.

Farr, W. (2008). The effects of video modeling on leisure time activities for learners with severe special needs. *Dissertation Abstracts International Section A: Humanities and Social Sciences, 69,* 564.

Farris, C., Treat, T. A., Viken, R. J., & McFall, R. M. (2008). Perceptual mechanisms that characterize gender differences in decoding women's sexual intent. *Psychological Science, 19,* 348–354.

Farroni, T., Massaccesi, S., Pividori, D., & Johnson, M. H. (2004). Gaze following in newborns. *Infancy, 5,* 39–60.

Farroni, T., Menon, E., Rigato, S., & Johnson, M. H. (2007). The perception of facial expressions in newborns. *European Journal of Developmental Psychology, 4,* 2–13.

Fatima, I., & Suhail, K. (2010). Belief in a just world and subjective well-being: Mothers of normal and Down syndrome children. *International Journal of Psychology, 45,* 461–468.

Faulconbridge, L. H. (2008). Ghrelin and neuropeptide Y: Actions and interactions within the neuroanatomically distributed system for the control of feeding behavior. *Dissertation Abstracts International, 68,* 4294. Retrieved from EBSCOhost.

Faure, A., Reynolds, S. M., Richard, J. M., & Berridge, K. C. (2008). Mesolimbic dopamine in desire and dread: Enabling motivation to be generated by localized glutamate disruptions in nucleus accumbens. *The Journal of Neuroscience, 28,* 7184–7192.

Fava, G. A., & Sonino, N. (2007). The biopsychosocial model thirty years later. *Psychotherapy and Psychosomatics, 77,* 1–2.

Federal Bureau of Investigation, (2009). Crime in the United States: Violent crime. Retrieved from http://www2.fbi.gov/ucr/cius2009/offenses/violent_crime/index.html

Feeney, B. C., & Cassidy, J. (2003). Reconstructive memory related to adolescent-parent conflict interactions: The influence of attachment-related representations on immediate perceptions and changes in perceptions over time. *Journal of Personality and Social Psychology, 85,* 945–955.

Fehr, B. (1994). Prototype-based assessment of laypeople's views of love. *Personal Relationships, 1,* 309–331.

Feinauer, L., Hilton, H. G., & Callahan, E. H. (2003). Hardiness as a moderator of shame associated with childhood sexual abuse. *American Journal of Family Therapy, 31,* 65–78.

Feinson, M. C. (1986). Aging widows and widowers: Are there mental health differences? *International Journal of Aging and Human Development, 23,* 244–255.

Feinstein, J. S., Adolphs, R., Damasio, A., & Tranel, D. (2010). The human amygdala and the induction and experience of fear. *Current Biology, 21,* 34–38.

Fendrich, D. W., & Arengo, R. (2004). The influence of string length and repetition on chunking of digit strings. *Psychological Research, 68,* 216–223.

Feshbach, S., & Weiner, B. (1982). *Personality.* Lexington, MA: Heath.

Festinger, L. (1957). *A theory of cognitive dissonance.* Evanston, IL: Row, Peterson.

ffytche, D. H., & Zeki, S. (2011). The primary visual cortex, and feedback to it, are not necessary for conscious vision. *Brain: A Journal of Neurology, 134,* 247–257.

Fiedler, F. E. (1967). *A theory of leadership effectiveness.* New York, NY: McGraw-Hill.

Fiedler, F. E. (1993). The leadership situation and the black box contingency theories. In M. Chemers & R. Ayman (Eds.), *Leadership theory and research: Perspective and directions* (pp. 1–28). San Diego, CA: Academic Press.

Fiedler, F. E. (2002). The curious role of cognitive resources in leadership. In R. E. Riggio & S. E. Murphy (Eds.), *Multiple intelligences and leadership. LEA's organization and management series* (pp. 91–104). Mahwah, NJ: Erlbaum.

Fiedler, K. (2008). Language: A toolbox for sharing and influencing social reality. *Perspectives on Psychological Science, 3,* 36–47.

Fingerman, K. L., & Charles, S. T. (2010). It takes two to tango: Why older people have the best relationships. *Current Directions in Psychological Science, 19,* 172–176.

Finn, P. R., Sharkansky, E. J., Brandt, K. M., & Turcotte, N. (2000). The effects of familial risk, personality, and expectancies on alcohol use and abuse. *Journal of Abnormal Psychology, 109,* 122–133.

Fiore, S. M., & Schooler, J. W. (2002). How did you get here from there? Verbal overshadowing of spatial mental models. *Applied Cognitive Psychology, 16,* 897–910.

Fischer, A. H., Rodriguez-Mosquera, P. M., van-Vianen, A. E. M., & Manstead, A. S. R. (2004). Gender and culture differences in emotion. *Emotion, 4,* 87–94.

Fischer, P., Krueger, J. I., Greitemeyer, T., Vogrincic, C., Kastenmüller, A., Frey, D., . . . Kainbacher, M. (2011). The bystander-effect: A meta-analytic review on bystander intervention in dangerous and non-dangerous emergencies. *Psychological Bulletin, 137,* 517–537. doi:10.1037/a0023304

Fischhoff, B., & Downs, J. (1997). Accentuate the relevant. *Psychological Science, 8,* 154–158.

Fisher, S., & Greenberg, R. P. (1985). *The scientific credibility of Freud's theories and therapy.* New York, NY: Columbia University Press.

Fishman, N. (2005, June 13). Risky business: Making hiring decisions without background checks can lead to costly mistakes. *Nation's Restaurant News, 13,* 12. Retrieved from http://findarticles.com/p/articles/mi_m3190/is_24_39/ai_n14697040

Fiske, S. T. (1995). Social cognition. In A. Tesser (Ed.), *Advanced social psychology* (pp. 149–194). New York, NY: McGraw-Hill.

Fiske, S. T., & Taylor, S. E. (1991). *Social cognition* (2nd ed.). New York, NY: McGraw-Hill.

Fitch, W. T., Hauser, M. D., & Chomsky, N. (2005). The evolution of the language faculty: Clarifications and implications. *Cognition, 97,* 179–210.

Fitzgerald, P. J. (2008). A neurotransmitter system theory of sexual orientation. *Journal of Sexual Medicine, 5,* 746–748.

Fitzgerald, S. (1999, October 11). "Brain exercise" under scrutiny to aid attention deficit. *Charlotte Observer,* p. 12E.

Flavell, J. H. (1999). Cognitive development: Children's knowledge about the mind. *Annual Review of Psychology, 50,* 21–45.

Flavell, J. H., Miller, P. H., & Miller, S. A. (2002). *Cognitive development* (4th ed.). Upper Saddle River, NJ: Prentice Hall.

Flege, J. E., Munro, M. J., & MacKay, I. R. A. (1995). Factors affecting strength of perceived foreign accent in a second language. *Journal of the Acoustical Society of America, 97,* 3125–3134.

Flieller, A. (1999). Comparison of the development of formal thought in adolescent cohorts aged 10–15 years. *Developmental Psychology, 35,* 1048–1058.

Flor, H., Nikolajsen, L., & Jensen, T. S. (2006). Phantom limb pain: A case of maladaptive CNS plasticity? *Nature Reviews Neuroscience, 7,* 873–881.

Flynn, J. R. (1984). The mean IQ of Americans: Massive gains 1932 to 1978. *Psychological Bulletin, 95*, 29–51.

Flynn, J. R. (1987). Massive IQ gains in 14 nations: What IQ tests really measure. *Psychological Bulletin, 101*, 171–191.

Flynn, J. R. (1999). Searching for justice: The discovery of IQ gains over time. *American Psychologist, 54*, 5–20.

Flynn, J. R. (2007). *What is intelligence? Beyond the Flynn effect.* New York, NY: Cambridge University Press.

Fogassi, L. (2011). The mirror neuron system: How cognitive functions emerge from motor organization. *Journal of Economic Behavior & Organization, 77*, 66–75.

Foley, D. L., Neale, M. C., & Kendler, K. S. (2000). Does intra-uterine growth discordance predict differential risk for adult psychiatric disorder in a population-based sample of monozygotic twins? *Psychiatric Genetics, 10*, 1–8.

Forrest, D. (2002). Mesmer. *International Journal of Clinical and Experimental Hypnosis, 50*, 295–308.

Forsman, M., Lichtenstein, P., Andershed, H., & Larsson, H. (2008). Genetic effects explain the stability of psychopathic personality from mid- to late adolescence. *Journal of Abnormal Psychology, 117*, 606–617.

Forstmeier, S., & Maercker, A. (2008). Motivational reserve: Lifetime motivational abilities contribute to cognitive and emotional health in old age. *Psychology and Aging, 23*, 886–899.

Forthun, L. F., Montgomery, M. J., & Bell, N. J. (2006). Identity formation in a relational context: A person-centered analysis of troubled youth. *Identity, 6*, 141–167.

Foundry Management and Technology. (2006). Fire extinguisher training simulator. *Foundry Management and Technology, 1334*, 22.

Fox, N. A., Hane, A. A., & Pine, D. S. (2007). Plasticity for affective neurocircuitry: How the environment affects gene expression. *Current Directions in Psychological Science, 16*, 1–5.

Fox, R. E., DeLeon, P. H., Newman, R., Sammons, M. T., Dunivin, D. L., & Baker, D. C. (2009). Prescriptive authority and psychology: A status report. *American Psychologist, 64*, 257–268.

Foxcroft, D. R., Ireland, D., Lister, S. D. J., Lowe, G., & Breen, R. (2003). Longer-term primary prevention for alcohol misuse in young people: A systematic review. *Addiction, 98*, 397–411.

Frank, M. G. (2006). Research methods in detecting deception research. In J. A. Harrigan, R. Rosenthal, & K. R. Scherer (Eds.), *The new handbook of methods in nonverbal behavior research* (pp. 341–368). New York, NY: Oxford University Press.

Fraser, J. S., & Solovey, A. D. (2007). Couples therapy. In J. S. Fraser & A. D. Solovey (Eds.), *Second-order change in psychotherapy: The golden thread that unifies effective treatments* (pp. 191–221). Washington, DC: American Psychological Association.

Frayling, T. M., Timpson, N. J., Weedon, M. N., Zeggini, E., Freathy, R. M., Lindgren, C. M., . . . McCarthy, M. I. (2007). A common variant in the *FTO* gene is associated with Body Mass Index and predisposes to childhood and adult obesity. *Science, 316*, 889–894.

Fredrickson, P., Boules, M., Lin, S. C., & Richelson, E. (2005). Neurobiologic basis of nicotine addiction and psychostimulant abuse: A role for neurotensin? *Psychiatric Clinics of North America, 28*, 737–751.

Freedland, K. E. (2004). Religious beliefs shorten hospital stays? Psychology works in mysterious ways: Comment on Contrada et al. (2004). *Health Psychology, 23*, 239–242.

Freedman, J. L., & Fraser, S. C. (1966). Compliance without pressure: The foot-in-the-door technique. *Journal of Personality and Social Psychology, 4*, 195–202.

Freud, S. (1900). The interpretation of dreams. In J. Strachey (Ed.), *The standard edition of the complete psychological works of Sigmund Freud* (Vol. 5). London, England: Hogarth.

Friedman, B. J. (2000). An historical review of the life and works of an important man: Leon Festinger. *Dissertation Abstracts International: Section B: The Sciences and Engineering, 61*, 2816.

Friedman, H. S. (2002). *Health Psychology* (2nd ed.). Upper Saddle River, NJ: Prentice Hall.

Friedman, M., Breall, W. S., Goodwin, M. L., Sparagon, B. J., Ghandour, G., & Fleischmann, N. (1996). Effect of Type A behavioral counseling on frequency of episodes of silent myocardial ischemia in coronary patients. *American Heart Journal, 132*, 933–937.

Friedman, M., & Rosenman, R. H. (1959). Association of specific overt behavior patterns with blood and cardiovascular findings: Blood cholesterol level, blood clotting time, incidence of arcus senilis and clinical coronary artery disease. *JAMA: Journal of the American Medical Association, 169*, 1286–1296.

Frijda, N. H., Markam, S., & Sato, K. (1995). Emotions and emotion words. In J. A. Russell, J.-M. Fernàndez-Dols, A. S. R. Manstead, & J. C. Wellenkamp (Eds.), *Everyday conceptions of emotion: An introduction to the psychology, anthropology and linguistics of emotion* (pp. 121–143). New York, NY: Kluwer Academic/Plenum.

Fu, Q., Heath, A. C., Bucholz, K. K., Nelson, E., Goldberg, J., Lyons, M. J., . . . Eisen, S. A. (2002). Shared genetic risk of major depression, alcohol dependence, and marijuana dependence: Contribution of antisocial personality disorder in men. *Archives of General Psychiatry, 59*, 1125–1132.

Fuchs, T., Birbaumer, N., Lutzenberger, W., Gruzelier, J. H., & Kaiser, J. (2003). Neurofeedback treatment for attention-deficit/hyperactivity disorder in children: A comparison with methylphenidate. *Applied Psychophysiology and Biofeedback, 28*, 1–12.

Funder, D. C. (1995). On the accuracy of personality judgment: A realistic approach. *Psychological Review, 102*, 652–670.

Fung, K., Andermann, L., Zaretsky, A., & Lo, H.-T. (2008). An integrative approach to cultural competence in the psychiatric curriculum. *Academic Psychiatry, 32*, 272–282.

Funnell, M. G. (2010). The interpreting hemispheres. In P. A. Reuter-Lorenz, K. Baynes, G. R. Mangun, & E. A. Phelps (Eds.), *The cognitive neuroscience of mind: A tribute to Michael S. Gazzaniga* (pp. 73–86). Cambridge, MA: MIT Press.

Furnham, A., & Bachtiar, V. (2008). Personality and intelligence as predictors of creativity. *Personality and Individual Differences, 45*, 613–617.

Furnham, A., Batey, M., Anand, K., & Manfield, J. (2008). Personality, hypomania, intelligence and creativity. *Personality and Individual Differences, 44*, 1060–1069.

Furstenberg, F. F., Jr., Brooks-Gunn, J., & Chase-Lansdale, L. (1989). Teenaged pregnancy and childbearing. *American Psychologist, 44*, 313–320.

Gabbard, G. O. (2005). Mind, brain, and personality disorders. *American Journal of Psychiatry, 162*, 648–655.

Gabrieli, J. D. E. (1998). Cognitive neuroscience of human memory. *Annual Review of Psychology, 49*, 87–115.

Gades, N. M., Jacobson, D. J., McGree, M. E., St. Sauver, J. L., Lieber, M. M., Nehra, A., . . . Jacobsen, S. J. (2008). The associations between serum sex hormones, erectile function, and sex drive: The Olmsted County Study of urinary symptoms and health status among men. *Journal of Sexual Medicine, 5*, 2209–2220.

Gaertner, L., Sedikides, C., & Chang, K. (2008). On pancultural self-enhancement: Well-adjusted Taiwanese self-enhance on personally valued traits. *Journal of Cross-Cultural Psychology, 39*, 463–477.

Gaertner, S. L., & Dovidio, J. F. (2008). Addressing contemporary racism: The common ingroup identity model. In C. Willis-Esqueda (Ed.), *Motivational aspects of prejudice and racism* (pp. 111–133). New York, NY: Springer Science + Business Media.

Gage, F. H. (2000). Mammalian neural stem cells. *Science, 287*, 1433–1438.

Galambos, N. L., & Leadbeater, B. J. (2002). Transitions in adolescent research. In W. W. Hartup & R. K. Silbereisen (Eds.), *Growing points in developmental science: An introduction* (pp. 287–306). Philadelphia, PA: Psychology Press.

Galambos, N. L., Barker, E. T., & Almeida, D. M. (2003). Parents do matter: Trajectories of change in externalizing and internalizing problems in early adolescence. *Child Development, 74*, 578–594.

Galanter, M., Hayden, F., Castañeda, R., & Franco, H. (2005). Group therapy, self-help groups, and network therapy. In R. J. Frances, S. I. Miller, & A. H. Mack (Eds.), *Clinical textbook of addictive disorders* (3rd ed., pp. 502–527). New York, NY: Guilford Press.

Galef, B. G., Jr., Dudley, K. E., & Whiskin, E. E. (2008). Social learning of food preferences in 'dissatisfied' and 'uncertain' Norway rats. *Animal Behaviour, 75*, 631–637.

Galef, B. G., Jr., & Whiskin, E. E. (2004). Effects of environmental stability and demonstrator age on social learning of food preferences by young Norway rats. *Animal Behaviour, 68*, 897–902.

Gallo, L. C., de los Monteros, K. E., & Shivpuri, S. (2009). Socioeconomic status and health: What is the role of reserve capacity? *Current Directions in Psychological Science, 18*, 269–274.

Gallup, G. G., Jr. (1985). Do minds exist in species other than our own? *Neuroscience and Biobehavioral Reviews, 9*, 631–641.

Gallup, G. G., Jr. (1998). Self-awareness and the evolution of social intelligence. *Behavioural Processes, 42,* 239–247.

Gandhi, N., Depauw, K. P., Dolny, D. G., & Freson, T. (2002). Effect of an exercise program on quality of life of women with fibromyalgia. *Women and Therapy, 25,* 91–103.

Ganis, G., Rosenfeld, J., Meixner, J., Kievit, R. A., & Schendan, H. E. (2011). Lying in the scanner: Covert countermeasures disrupt deception detection by functional magnetic resonance imaging. *NeuroImage, 55,* 312–319.

Garavan, H. (2010). Insula and drug cravings. *Brain Structure & Function, 214,* 593–601.

Garbarino, J. (1999). *Lost boys: Why our sons turn violent and how we can save them.* New York, NY: Free Press.

Garber, H., & Heber, R. (1982). Modification of predicted cognitive development in high risk children through early intervention. In D. K. Detterman & R. J. Sternberg (Eds.), *How and how much can intelligence be increased?* (pp. 121–137). Norwood, NJ: Ablex.

Garnefski, N., Kraaij, V., Schroevers, M. J., & Somsen, G. A. (2008). Post-traumatic growth after a myocardial infarction: A matter of personality, psychological health, or cognitive coping? *Journal of Clinical Psychology in Medical Settings, 15,* 270–277.

Garner, D. M., & Magana, C. (2006). Cognitive vulnerability to anorexia nervosa. In L. B. Alloy & J. H. Riskind (Eds.), *Cognitive vulnerability to emotional disorders* (pp. 365–403). Mahwah, NJ: Erlbaum.

Garnets, L. K. (2002). Sexual orientation in perspective. *Cultural Diversity and Ethnic Minority Psychology, 8,* 115–129.

Gatewood, R. D., & Field, H. S. (1998). *Human resource selection.* Fort Worth, TX: Harcourt.

Gathchel, R. J., & Oordt, M. S. (2003). Insomnia. In R. J. Gathchel & M. S. Oordt (Eds.), *Clinical health psychology and primary care: Practical advice and clinical guidance for successful collaboration* (pp. 135–148). Washington, DC: American Psychological Association.

Gaugler, B. B., Rosenthal, D. B., Thornton, G. C., & Bentson, C. (1987). Metaanalysis of assessment center validity. *Journal of Applied Psychology, 72,* 493–511.

Gazzaniga, M. S. (2005). Forty-five years of split-brain research and still going strong. *Nature Reviews Neuroscience, 6,* 653–659.

Gazzaniga, M. S. (2008). *Human: The science behind what makes us unique.* New York, NY: Ecco/HarperCollins.

Gehrman, P. R., & Harb, G. C. (2010). Treatment of nightmares in the context of posttraumatic stress disorder. *Journal of Clinical Psychology, 66,* 1185–1194.

Gelernter, J., & Stein, M. B. (2009). Heritability and genetics of anxiety disorders. In M. M. Antony & M. B. Stein (Eds.), *Oxford handbook of anxiety and related disorders* (pp. 87–96). New York, NY: Oxford University Press.

George, L. K. (2001). The social psychology of health. In R. H. Binstock & L. K. George (Eds.), *Handbook of the psychology of aging* (5th ed., pp. 213–237). San Diego, CA: Academic Press.

George, R. M., & Lee, B. J. (1997). Abuse and neglect of the children. In R. A. Maynard (Ed.), *Kids having kids: Economic costs and social consequences of teen pregnancy* (pp. 205–230). Washington, DC: Urban Institute Press.

George, S., Rogers, R. D., & Duka, T. (2005). The acute effect of alcohol on decision making in social drinkers. *Psychopharmacology, 182,* 160–169.

Georgieva, L., Dimitrova, A., Ivanov, D., Nikolov, I., Williams, N. M., Grozeva, D., ... O'Donovan, M. C. (2008). Support for neuregulin 1 as a susceptibility gene for bipolar disorder and schizophrenia. *Biological Psychiatry, 64,* 419–427.

Geraerts, E., Lindsay, D., Merckelbach, H., Jelicic, M., Raymaekers, L., Arnold, M. M., & Schooler, J. W. (2009). Cognitive mechanisms underlying recovered-memory experiences of childhood sexual abuse. *Psychological Science, 20,* 92–98.

Geraerts, E., Raymaekers, L., & Merckelbach, H. (2008). Recovered memories of childhood sexual abuse: Current findings and their legal implications. *Legal and Criminological Psychology, 13,* 165–176.

Geraerts, E., Raymaekers, L., & Merckelbach, H. (2010). Mechanisms underlying recovered memories. In G. M. Davies & D. B. Wright (Eds.), *Current issues in applied memory research* (pp. 101–118). New York, NY: Psychology Press.

Germain, V., Marchand, A., Bouchard, S., Drouin, M.-S., & Guay, S. (2009). Effectiveness of cognitive behavioural therapy administered by videoconference for posttraumatic stress disorder. *Cognitive Behaviour Therapy, 38,* 42–53.

Gershoff, E. T., & Bitensky, S. H. (2007). The case against corporal punishment of children: Converging evidence from social science research and international human rights law and implications for U.S. public policy. *Psychology, Public Policy, and Law, 13,* 231–272.

Gershon, S., & Soares, J. C. (1997). Current therapeutic profile of lithium. *Archives of General Psychiatry, 54,* 16–20.

Getzels, J. W., & Jackson, P. (1962). *Creativity and intelligence.* New York, NY: Wiley.

Ghahramanlou-Holloway, M., Brown, G. K., & Beck, A. T. (2008). Suicide. In M. A. Whisman (Ed.), *Adapting cognitive therapy for depression: Managing complexity and comorbidity* (pp. 159–184). New York, NY: Guilford Press.

Ghuman, J. K., Arnold, L. E., & Anthony, B. J. (2008). Psychopharmacological and other treatments in preschool children with attention-deficit/hyperactivity disorder: Current evidence and practice. *Journal of Child and Adolescent Psychopharmacology, 18,* 413–447.

Giancola, P. R., Josephs, R. A., Parrott, D. J., & Duke, A. A. (2010). Alcohol myopia revisited: Clarifying aggression and other acts of disinhibition through a distorted lens. *Perspectives on Psychological Science, 5,* 265–278.

Gibbs, J. C., Basinger, K. S., Grime, R. L., & Snarey, J. R. (2007). Moral judgment development across cultures: Revisiting Kohlberg's universality claims. *Developmental Review, 27,* 443–500.

Gibson, C. J., & Gruen, J. R. (2008). The human lexinome: Genes of language and reading. *Journal of Communication Disorders, 41,* 409–420.

Gibson, R. L., & Mitchell, M. (2003). *Introduction to counseling and guidance* (6th ed.). Upper Saddle River, NJ: Prentice Hall.

Giese-Davis, J., Koopman, C., Butler, L. D., Classen, C., Cordova, M., Fobair, P., ... Spiegel, D. (2002). Change in emotion-regulation strategy for women with metastic breast cancer following supportive-expressive group therapy. *Journal of Consulting and Clinical Psychology, 70,* 916–925.

Gifford, R. (2011). The dragons of inaction: Psychological barriers that limit climate change mitigation and adaptation. *American Psychologist, 66,* 290–302.

Gila, A., Castro, J., & Cesena, J. (2005). Anorexia nervosa in male adolescents: Body image, eating attitudes and psychological traits. *Journal of Adolescent Health, 36,* 221–226.

Gilbert, S. P., & Weaver, C. C. (2010). Sleep quality and academic performance in university students: A wake-up call for college psychologists. *Journal of College Student Psychotherapy, 24,* 295–306.

Gillespie, C. F., & Nemeroff, C. B. (2007). Corticotropin-releasing factor and the psychobiology of early-life stress. *Current Directions in Psychological Science, 16,* 85–89.

Gilligan, C. (1982). *In a different voice: Psychological theory and women's development.* Cambridge, MA: Harvard University Press.

Gilligan, C. (1992, August). *Joining the resistance: Girls' development in adolescence.* Paper presented at the meeting of the American Psychological Association, Montreal, Canada.

Gilman, S. L. (2001). Karen Horney, M. D., 1885–1952. *American Journal of Psychiatry, 158,* 1205.

Gimpel, G. A., Collett, B. R., Veeder, M. A., Gifford, J. A., Sneddon, P., Bushman, B., ... Odell, J. D. (2005). Effects of stimulant medication on cognitive performance of children with ADHD. *Clinical Pediatrics, 44,* 405–411.

Gladstone, G. L., Parker, G. B., Mitchell, P. B., Wilhelm, K. A., & Malhi, G. S. (2005). Relationship between self-reported childhood behavioral inhibition and lifetime anxiety disorders in a clinical sample. *Depression and Anxiety, 22,* 103–113.

Glassbrenner, D., Carra, J. S., & Nichols, J. (2004). Recent estimates of safety belt use. *Journal of Safety Research, 35,* 237–244.

Glassop, L. I. (2002). The organizational benefits of teams. *Human Relations, 55,* 225–250.

Gleaves, D. H., Miller, K. J., Williams, T. L., & Summers, S. A. (2000). Eating disorders: An overview. In K. J. Miller & J. S. Mizes (Eds.), *Comparative treatments for eating disorders* (pp. 1–49). New York, NY: Springer.

Gleaves, D. H., Smith, S. M., Butler, L. D., Spiegel, D., & Kihlstrom, J. (2010). Are the recovered memories of psychological trauma valid? In B. Slife (Ed.), *Clashing views on psychological issues* (16th ed., pp. 218–247). New York, NY: McGraw-Hill/Dushkin.

Gnambs, T., Appel, M., & Batinic, B. (2010). Color red in web-based knowledge testing. *Computers in Human Behavior, 26,* 1625–1631.

Gnanadesikan, M., Freeman, M. P., & Gelenberg, A. J. (2003). Alternatives to lithium and divalproex in the maintenance treatment of bipolar disorder. *Bipolar Disorders, 5,* 203–216.

Gobl, C., & Chasaide, A. N. (2003). The role of voice quality in communicating emotion, mood, and attitude. *Speech Communication, 40,* 189–212.

Goddard, A. W., Mason, G. F., Rothman, D. L., Behar, K. L., Petroff, O. A. C., & Krystal, J. H. (2004). Family psychopathology and magnitude of reductions in occipital cortex GABA levels in panic disorder. *Neuropsychopharmacology, 29,* 639–640.

Goh, J. O., Chee, M. W., Tan, J. C., Venkatraman, V., Hebrank, A., Leshikar, E. D., . . . Park, D. C. (2007). Age and culture modulate object processing and object-scene binding in the ventral visual area. *Cognitive, Affective, & Behavioral Neuroscience, 7*, 44–52.

Gold, P. E. (2003). Acetylcholine modulation of neural systems involved in learning and memory. *Neurobiology of Learning and Memory, 80*, 194–210.

Goldberg, E. (2009). *The new executive brain: Frontal lobes in a complex world.* NY: Oxford University Press.

Goldey, K. L., & van Anders, S. M. (2010). Sexy thoughts: Effects of sexual cognitions on testosterone, cortisol, and arousal in women. *Hormones and Behavior, 59*, 754–764. doi:10.1016/j.yhbeh.2010.12.005

Goldin-Meadow, S. (2003). *The resilience of language: What gesture creation in deaf children can tell us about how all children learn language.* New York, NY: Psychology Press.

Goldman-Mellor, S. J., Saxton, K. B., & Catalano, R. C. (2010). Economic contraction and mental health: A review of the evidence, 1990–2009. *International Journal of Mental Health, 39*(2), 6–31.

Goldney, R. D. (2003). Deinstitutionalization and suicide. *Crisis, 24*, 39–40.

Goldstein, G. (2004). Abstract reasoning and problem solving in adults. In G. Goldstein, S. R. Beers, & M. Hersen (Eds.), *Comprehensive handbook of psychological assessment, Vol. 1: Intellectual and neuropsychological assessment* (pp. 293–308). Hoboken, NJ: Wiley.

Goldstein, I. L., & Ford, J. K. (2002). *Training in organizations* (4th ed.). Belmont, CA: Wadsworth.

Goldstein, N. J., Cialdini, R. B., & Griskevicius, V. (2008). A room with a viewpoint: Using social norms to motivate environmental conservation in hotels. *Journal of Consumer Research, 35*, 472–482.

Goldston, D. B., Molock, S. D., Whitbeck, L. B., Murakami, J. L., Zayas, L. H., & Hall, G. C. N, (2008). Cultural considerations in adolescent suicide prevention and psychosocial treatment. *American Psychologist, 63*, 14–31.

Goleman, D. (1997). *Emotional intelligence.* New York, NY: Bantam.

Golimbet, V. E., Alfimova, M. V., Gritsenko, I. K., & Ebstein, R. P. (2007). Relationship between dopamine system genes and extraversion and novelty seeking. *Neuroscience and Behavioral Physiology, 37*, 601–606.

Golinkoff, R. M., & Hirsh-Pasek, K. (2006). Baby wordsmith: From associationist to social sophisticate. *Current Directions in Psychological Science, 15*, 30–33.

Gonsalkorale, W. M., Miller, V., Afzal, A., & Whorwell, P. J. (2003). Long term benefits of hypnotherapy for irritable bowel syndrome. *Gut, 52*, 1623–9.

Goode, E. (2000, March 14). Human nature: born or made? *New York Times*, pp. F1, F9.

Goodwin, P. J., Leszcz, M., Ennis, M., Koopmans, J., Vincent, L., Guther, H., . . . Hunter, J. (2001). The effect of group psychosocial support on survival in metastatic breast cancer. *The New England Journal of Medicine, 345*, 1719–1726.

Gooren, L. (2008). Recent perspectives on the age-related decline of testosterone. *Journal of Men's Health & Gender, 5*, 86–93.

Gopnik, A. (2009). *The philosophical baby.* New York, NY: Farrar, Straus and Giroux.

Gorchoff, S. M., John, O. P., & Helson, R. (2008). Contextualizing change in marital satisfaction during middle age: An 18-year longitudinal study. *Psychological Science, 19*, 1194–1200.

Gordis, E. (1996). Alcohol research: At the cutting edge. *Archives of General Psychiatry, 53*, 199–201.

Gordon, D., & Bidar-Sielaff, S. (2006). Cultural aspects of pain management, 2nd edition. Fast Facts and Concepts, #78. Retrieved from http://www.eperc.mcw.edu/fastfact/ff_078.htm

Gosling, S. D., & John, O. P. (1999). Personality dimensions in nonhuman animals: A cross-species review. *Current Directions in Psychological Science, 8*, 69–75.

Gottesman, I. I. (1991). *Schizophrenia genesis: The origins of madness.* New York, NY: Freeman.

Gottesman, I. I., & Hanson, D. R. (2005). Human development: Biological and genetic processes. *Annual Review of Psychology, 56*, 263–286.

Gottfredson, L. (2009). Logical fallacies used to dismiss the evidence on intelligence testing. In R. P. Phelps (Ed.), *Correcting fallacies about educational and psychological testing* (pp. 11–65). Washington, DC: American Psychological Association.

Gottschall, J. (2008). The "beauty myth" is no myth: Emphasis on male-female attractiveness in world folktales. *Human Nature, 19*, 174–188.

Goudriaan, A. E., Lapauw, B., Ruige, J., Feyen, E., Kaufman, J., Brand, M., & Vingerhoets, G. (2010). The influence of high-normal testosterone levels on risk-taking in healthy males in a 1-week letrozole administration study. *Psychoneuroendocrinology, 35*, 1416–1421.

Gougoux, F., Lepore, F., Lassonde, M., Voss, P., Zatorre, R. J., & Belin, P. (2004). Pitch discrimination in the early blind. *Nature, 430*, 309.

Gougoux, F., Zatorre, R. J., Lassonde, M., Voss, P., & Lepore, F. (2005). A functional neuroimaging study of sound localization: Visual cortex activity predicts performance in early-blind individuals. *PLoS Biology, 3*, 324–333.

Gouzoulis-Mayfrank, E., Daumann, J., Tuchtenhagen, F., Pelz, S., Becker, S., Kunert, H. J., . . . Sass, H. (2000). Impaired cognitive performance in drug free users of recreational Ecstasy (MDMA). *Journal of Neurology, Neurosurgery and Psychiatry, 68*, 719–725.

Gradisar, M., Terrill, G., Johnston, A., & Douglas, P. (2008). Adolescent sleep and working memory performance. *Sleep and Biological Rhythms, 6*, 146–154.

Graham, S. (1992). Most of the subjects were white and middle class. *American Psychologist, 47*, 629–639.

Grandchamp, N., & Schenk, F. (2006). Adaptive changes in a radial maze task: Efficient selection of baited arms with reduced foraging in senescent hooded rats. *Behavioural Brain Research, 168*, 161–166.

Grandjean, E. M., & Aubry, J.-M. (2009). Lithium: Updated human knowledge using an evidence-based approach: Part I: Clinical efficacy in bipolar disorder. *CNS Drugs, 23*, 225–240.

Granek, J. A., Gorbet, D. J., & Sergio, L. E. (2010). Extensive video-game experience alters cortical networks for complex visuomotor transformations. *Cortex, 46*, 1165–1177.

Gray, J. R., Braver, T. S., & Raichle, M. E. (2002). Integration of emotion and cognition in the lateral prefrontal cortex. *PNAS Proceedings of the National Academy of Sciences of the United States of America, 99*, 4115–4120.

Gray, P. (2008, October). The value of psychology 101 in liberal arts education: A psychocentric theory of the university. *Observer: American Psychological Society, 21*(9), 29–32.

Gray, P. B., Kahlenberg, S. M., Barrett, E. S., Lipson, S. F., & Ellison, P. T. (2002). Marriage and fatherhood are associated with lower testosterone in males. *Evolution and Human Behavior, 23*, 193–201.

Greek, R., & Greek, J. (2010). Is the use of sentient animals in basic research justifiable? *Philosophy, Ethics, and Humanities in Medicine 2010, 5*, 14.

Greely, H. T. (2007). Knowing sin: Making sure good science doesn't go bad. In C. A. Read (Ed.), *Cerebrum 2007: Emerging ideas in brain science* (pp. 85–94). Washington, DC: Dana Press.

Greene, J., & Haidt, J. (2002). How (and where) does moral judgment work? *Trends in Cognitive Sciences, 6*, 517–523.

Greene, S. M., Anderson, E. R., Doyle, E. A., & Riedelbach, H. (2006). Divorce. In G. G. Bear & K. M. Minke (Eds.), *Children's needs III: Development, prevention, and intervention* (pp. 745–757). Washington, DC: National Association of School Psychologists.

Greenfield, P. M. (1998). The cultural evolution of IQ. In U. Neisser (Ed.), *The rising curve: Long-term gains in IQ and related measures* (pp. 81–123). Washington, DC: American Psychological Association.

Greenglass, E. R. (2002). Proactive coping and quality of life management. In E. Frydenber (Ed.), *Beyond coping: Meeting goals, visions, and challenges* (pp. 37–62). New York, NY: Oxford University Press.

Greenwald, A. G., Spangenberg, E. R., Pratkanis, A. R., & Eskenazi, J. (1991). Double-blind tests of subliminal self-help audiotapes. *Psychological Science, 2*, 119–122.

Gregory, R. L. (1970). *The intelligent eye.* London, England: Weidenfeld.

Grensing-Pophal, L. (2005). Job rotation. *Credit Union Management, 28*, 50–53.

Griffin, A. M., & Langlois, J. H. (2006). Stereotype directionality and attractiveness stereotyping: Is beauty good or is ugly bad? *Social Cognition, 24*, 187–206.

Griffin, J. A., Umstattd, M., & Usdan, S. L. (2010). Alcohol use and high-risk sexual behavior among collegiate women: A review of research on alcohol myopia theory. *Journal of American College Health, 58*, 523–532.

Griffiths, M. D., & Dancaster, I. (1995). The effect of Type A personality on physiological arousal while playing computer games. *Addictive Behaviors, 120*, 543–548.

Griskevicius, V., Goldstein, N. J., Mortensen, C. R., Cialdini, R. B., & Kenrick, D. T. (2006). Going along versus going alone: When fundamental motives facilitate strategic (non)conformity. *Journal of Personality and Social Psychology, 91*, 281–294.

Grossman, J. B., & Tierney, J. P. (1998). Does mentoring work? An impact study of the Big Brothers Big Sisters program. *Evaluation Review, 22*, 403–426.

Groth-Marnat, G. (2009). *Handbook of Psychological Assessment* (5th ed.). New York, NY: Wiley.

Gruber, H. E., & Wallace, D. B. (2001). Creative work: The case of Charles Darwin. *American Psychologist, 56*, 346–349.

Gruber, S. A., Silveri, M. M., Dahlgren, M., & Yurgelun-Todd, D. (2011). Why so impulsive? White matter alterations are associated with impulsivity in chronic marijuana smokers. *Experimental and Clinical Psychopharmacology, 19*, 231–242. doi:10.1037/a0023034

Grunwald, I. S., Borod, J. C., Obler, L. K., Erhan, H. M., Pick, L. H., Welkowitz, J., ... Whalen, J. (1999). The effects of age and gender on the perception of lexical emotion. *Applied Neuropsychology, 6*, 226–238.

Gruzelier, J. (2005). Altered states of consciousness and hypnosis in the twenty-first century: Comment. *Contemporary Hypnosis, 22*, 1–7.

Guéguen, N., Pascual, A., & Dagot, L. (2002). Low-ball and compliance to a request: An application in a field setting. *Psychological Reports, 91*, 81–84.

Guenther, V. K., Schaefer, P., Holzner, B. J., & Kemmler, G. W. (2003). Long-term improvements in cognitive performance through computer-assisted cognitive training: A pilot study in a residential home for older people. *Aging and Mental Health, 7*, 200–206.

Guitton, M. J., Klin, Y., & Dudai, Y. (2008). Taste-dependent sociophobia: When food and company do not mix. *Behavioural Brain Research, 191*, 148–152.

Guohua, R., & Jiliang, L. (2005). The advance in correlation research between Big Five personality dimensions and job performance. *Psychological Science* (China), *28*, 406–408.

Gur, R. E. (2011). Neuropsychiatric aspects of schizophrenia. *CNS Neuroscience & Therapeutics, 17*, 45–51.

Gurman, A. S., & Kniskern, D. P. (Eds.). (1991). *Handbook of family therapy* (Vol. 2). Philadelphia, PA: Brunner/Mazel.

Gurpegui, M., Jurado, D., Luna, J. D., Fernández-Molina, C., Moreno-Abril, O., & Gálvez, R. (2007). Personality traits associated with caffeine intake and smoking. *Progress in Neuro-Psychopharmacology & Biological Psychiatry, 31*, 997–1005.

Gurwitch, R. H., Sitterle, K. A., Young, B. H., & Pfefferbaum, B. (2002). The aftermath of terrorism. In A. M. La Greca & W. K. Silverman (Eds.), *Helping children cope with disasters and terrorism* (pp. 327–357). Washington, DC: American Psychological Association.

Guðmundsdóttir, D. (2011). Positive psychology and public health. In R. Biswas-Diener (Ed.), *Positive psychology as social change* (pp. 109–122). New York: Springer Science + Business Media.

Guthrie, M. L., & Bates, L. W. (2003). Sex education sources and attitudes toward sexual precautions across a decade. *Psychological Reports, 92*, 581–592.

Guthrie, R. (1976). *Even the rat was white*. New York, NY: Harper.

Gutiérrez, I. T. (2010, Summer). Death and culture: Views on death from across the border. *Psychology Times, 1*, 4.

Gutteling, B. M., de Weerth, C., Willemsen-Swinkels, S. H. N., Huizink, A. C., Mulder, E. J. H., Visser, G. H. A., ... Buitelaar, J. K. (2005). The effects of prenatal stress on temperament and problem behavior of 27-month-old toddlers. *European Child & Adolescent Psychiatry, 14*, 41–51.

Guyer, A. E., Monk, C. S., McClure-Tone, E. B., Nelson, E. E., Roberson-Nay, R., Adler, A. D., ... Ernst, M. (2008). A developmental examination of amygdala response to facial expressions. *Journal of Cognitive Neuroscience, 20*, 1565–1582.

Haber, R. N. (1969, April). Eidetic images. *Scientific American, 220*(4), 36–44.

Haberstick, B. C., Zeiger, J. S., Corley, R. P., Hopfer, C. J., Stallings, M. C., Rhee, S., & Hewitt, J. K. (2011). Common and drug-specific genetic influences on subjective effects to alcohol, tobacco and marijuana use. *Addiction, 106*, 215–224.

Haenschel, C., & Linden, D. (2011). Exploring intermediate phenotypes with EEG: Working memory dysfunction in schizophrenia. *Behavioural Brain Research, 216*, 481–495.

Hagemann, N., Strauss, B., & Leiβing, J. (2008). When the referee sees red.... *Psychological Science, 19*, 769–771.

Haghighi, F., Bach-Mizrachi, H., Huang, Y. Y., Arango, V., Shi, S., Dwork, A. J., ... Mann, J. J. (2008). Genetic architecture of the human tryptophan hydroxylase 2 gene: Existence of neural isoforms and relevance for major depression. *Molecular Psychiatry, 13*, 813–820.

Haile, C. N., Kosten, T. A., & Kosten, T. R. (2008). Pharmacogenetic treatments for drug addiction: Alcohol and opiates. *American Journal of Drug and Alcohol Abuse, 34*, 355–381.

Halbreich, U., & Karkun, S. (2006). Cross-cultural and social diversity of prevalence of postpartum depression and depressive symptoms. *Journal of Affective Disorders, 91*, 97–111.

Hall, G. S. (1904). *Adolescence: Its psychology and its relations to physiology, anthropology, sex, crime, religion and education* (Vol. 1). New York, NY: Appleton-Century-Crofts.

Hall, J. A., Bernieri, F. J., & Carney, D. R. (2006). Nonverbal behavior and interpersonal sensitivity. In J. A. Harrigan, R. Rosenthal, & K. R. Scherer (Eds.), *The new handbook of methods in nonverbal behavior research* (pp. 237–281). New York, NY: Oxford University Press.

Hall, J. A., & Matsumoto, D. (2004). Gender differences in judgments of multiple emotions from facial expressions. *Emotion, 4*, 201–206.

Hall, W. G., Arnold, H. M., & Myers, K. P. (2000). The acquisition of an appetite. *Psychological Science, 11*, 101–105.

Halpern, D. F. (2007). Science, sex, and good sense: Why women are underrepresented in some areas of science and math. In S. J. Ceci & W. M. Williams (Eds.), *Why aren't more women in science: Top researchers debate the evidence* (pp. 121–130). Washington, DC: American Psychological Association.

Halpern, D. F. (1992). *Sex differences in cognitive abilities* (2nd ed.). Mahwah, NJ: Erlbaum.

Halpern, D. F., Benbow, C. P., Geary, D. C., Gur, R. C., Hyde, J. S., & Gernsbacher, M. A. (2007). The science of sex differences in science and mathematics. *Psychological Science in the Public Interest, 8*, 1–51.

Hamberger, M. J., & Seidel, W. T. (2003). Auditory and visual naming tests: Normative and patient data for accuracy, response time, and tip-of-the-tongue. *Journal of the International Neuropsychological Society, 9*, 479–489.

Hamblin, D. L., Croft, R. J., Wood, A. W., Stough, C., & Spong, J. (2008). The sensitivity of human event-related potentials and reaction time to mobile phone emitted electromagnetic fields. *Bioelectromagnetics, 27*, 265–273.

Hamdan-Mansour, A. M., Puskar, K., & Bandak, A. G. (2009). Effectiveness of cognitive-behavioral therapy on depressive symptomatology, stress and coping strategies among Jordanian university students. *Issues in Mental Health Nursing, 30*, 188–196.

Hamilton, J. (2008, October 16). Multitasking in the car: Just like drunken driving. *NPR: Morning Edition*. Retrieved from http://www.npr.org/templates/story/story.php?storyId=95702512

Hamilton, S. P., Slager, S. L., de Leon, A. B., Heiman, G. A., Klein, D. F., Hodge, S. E., ... Knowles, J. A. (2004). Evidence for genetic linkage between a polymorphism in the Adenosine 2A receptor and panic disorder. *Neuropsychopharmacology, 29*, 558–565.

Hammack, P. L. (2005). The life course development of human sexual orientation: An integrative paradigm. *Human Development, 48*, 267–290.

Hammack, P. L., Robinson, W. L., Crawford, I., & Li, S. T. (2004). Poverty and depressed mood among urban African-American adolescents: A family stress perspective. *Journal of Child and Family Studies, 13*, 309–323.

Hane, A. A., Cheah, C., Rubin, K. H., & Fox, N. A. (2008). The role of maternal behavior in the relation between shyness and social reticence in early childhood and social withdrawal in middle childhood. *Social Development, 17*, 795–811.

Haney, M., Hart, C. L., Vosburg, S. K., Nasser, J., Bennett, A., Zubaran, C., & Foltin, R. W. (2004). Marijuana withdrawal in humans: Effects of oral THC or divalproex. *Neuropsychopharmacology, 29*, 158–170.

Hanna, F. J. (2002). *Therapy with difficult clients: Using the precursors model to awaken change*. Washington, DC: American Psychological Association.

Hansen, F., & Christensen, S. R. (2007). *Emotions, advertising & consumer choice*. Copenhagen, Denmark: Business School Press.

Hantouche, E., Angst, J., & Azorin, J. (2010). Explained factors of suicide attempts in major depression. *Journal of Affective Disorders, 127*, 305–308.

Harlow, H. F. (1949). The formation of learning sets. *Psychological Review, 56*, 51–65.

Harlow, H. F. (1958). The nature of love. *American Psychologist, 13*, 673–685.

Harlow, H. F., & Zimmerman, R. R. (1959). Affectional responses in the infant monkey. *Science, 130*, 421–432.

Harms, W. (2006). Gender equality leads to better sex lives among people 40 and over. Retrieved from http://www.eurekalert.org/pub_releases/2006-04/uoc-gel041406.php

Haro, R., & Drucker-Colín, R. (2004). A two-year study on the effects of nicotine and its withdrawal on mood and sleep. *Pharmacopsychiatry, 37*, 221–227.

Harreé, R. (2000). Piaget's "sociological studies." *New Ideas in Psychology, 18*, 135–138.

Harris, J. C. [James]. (2003). Pinel delivering the insane. *Archives of General Psychiatry, 60,* 552.

Harris, J. R. [Judith]. (1998). *The nurture assumption: Why children turn out the way they do.* New York, NY: Free Press.

Harris, M., & Rosenthal, R. (1985). Mediation of the interpersonal expectancy effect: A taxonomy of expectancy situations. In P. Blanck (Ed.), *Interpersonal expectations: Theory, research, and application* (pp. 350–378). New York, NY: Cambridge University Press.

Harris, S. K., Sherritt, L., Van Hook, S., Wechsler, H., & Knight, J. R. (2010). Alcohol policy enforcement and changes in student drinking rates in a statewide public college system: A follow-up study. *Substance Abuse Treatment, Prevention, and Policy, 5,* 18. doi:10.1186/1747-597X-5-18

Harrison, L. J., Manocha, R., & Rubia, K. (2004). Sahaja yoga meditation as a family treatment programme for children with attention deficit-hyperactivity disorder. *Clinical Child Psychology and Psychiatry, 9,* 479–497.

Harvey, R. J. (1991). Job analysis. In M. D. Dunnette & L. M. Hough (Eds.), *Handbook of industrial and organizational psychology* (2nd ed., Vol. 2, pp. 71–163). Palo Alto, CA: Consulting Psychologists Press.

Hashimoto, R., Okada, T., Kato, T., Kosuga, A., Tatsumi, M., Kamijima, K., & Kunugi, H. (2005). The breakpoint cluster region gene on chromosome 22q11 is associated with bipolar disorder. *Biological Psychiatry, 57,* 1097–1102.

Hasin, D. S., Stinson, F. S., Ogburn, E., & Grant, B. F. (2007). Prevalence, correlates, disability, and comorbidity of DSM-IV alcohol abuse and dependence in the United States. *Archives of General Psychiatry, 64,* 830–842.

Haskell, I. O. (2003). Explaining regional variation in rates of aggression: Are differences accounted for by the southern culture of violence? *Dissertation Abstracts International: Section B: The Sciences and Engineering, 64,* 463.

Haslam, S. A., Jetten, J., Postmes, T., & Haslam, C. (2009). Social identity, health, and well-being: An emerging agenda for applied psychology. *Applied Psychology: An International Review, 58,* 1–23.

Hatzenbuehler, M. L. (2009). How does sexual minority stigma "get under the skin"? A psychological mediation framework. *Psychological Bulletin, 135,* 707–730.

Hayashi, K., Ohta, S., Kawakami, Y., & Toda, M. (2009). Activation of dendritic-like cells and neural stem/progenitor cells in injured spinal cord by GM-CSF. *Neuroscience Research, 64,* 96–103.

Hayes, R. D., Dennerstein, L., Bennett, C. M., & Fairley, C. K. (2008). What is the "true" prevalence of female sexual dysfunctions and does the way we assess these conditions have an impact? *Journal of Sexual Medicine, 5,* 777–787.

Haykin, S., & Chen, Z. (2006). The cocktail party problem. *Neural Computation, 17,* 1875–1902.

Hayne, H. (2004). Infant memory development: Implications for childhood amnesia. *Developmental Review, 24,* 33–73.

Hays, P. A. (2008). How to help best: Culturally responsive therapy. In P. A. Hays (Ed.), *Addressing cultural complexities in practice: Assessment, diagnosis, and therapy* (2nd ed., pp. 175–201). Washington, DC: American Psychological Association.

Hayslip, B., Jr., & Peveto, C. A. (2005). *Cultural changes in attitudes toward death, dying, and bereavement.* New York, NY: Springer.

Hazel, M. T. (2005). Visualization and systematic desensitization: Interventions for habituating and sensitizing patterns of public speaking anxiety. *Dissertation Abstracts International Section A: Humanities and Social Sciences, 66,* 30.

Hazlett-Stevens, H., Pruitt, L. D., & Collins, A. (2009). Phenomenology of generalized anxiety disorder. In M. M. Antony & M. B. Stein (Eds.), *Oxford handbook of anxiety and related disorders* (pp. 47–55). New York, NY: Oxford University Press.

Heath, K. M., & Gant, L. M. (2005). Evolution, culture, and the processes of learning and memory. *International Journal of Cognitive Technology, 10,* 12–14.

Heatherton, T. F., & Sargent, J. D. (2009). Does watching smoking in movies promote teenage smoking? *Current Directions in Psychological Science, 18,* 63–67.

Hebb, D. O. (1955). Drives and the CNS (conceptual nervous system). *Psychological Review, 62,* 243–254.

Hebebrand, J., & Hinney, A. (2009). Environmental and genetic risk factors in obesity. *Child and Adolescent Psychiatric Clinics of North America, 18,* 83–94.

Heber, R., Garber, H., Harrington, S., & Hoffman, C. (1972). *Rehabilitation of families at risk for mental retardation.* Madison: University of Wisconsin, Rehabilitation Research and Training Center in Mental Retardation.

Heckel, R. V., & Shumaker, D. M. (2001). *Children who murder: A psychological perspective.* Westport, CT: Praeger.

Heider, F. (1958). *The psychology of interpersonal relations.* New York, NY: Wiley.

Heine, S. J., & Norenzayan, A. (2006). Toward a psychological science for a cultural species. *Perspectives on Psychological Science, 1,* 251–269.

Heinrichs, M., Wagner, D., Schoch, W., Soravia, L. M., Hellhammer, D. H., & Ehlert, U. (2005). Predicting posttraumatic stress symptoms from pretraumatic risk factors: A 2-year prospective follow-up study in firefighters. *American Journal of Psychiatry, 162,* 2276–2286.

Heinzel, A., Bermpohl, F., Niese, R., Pfennig, A., Pascual-Leone, A., Schlaug, G., & Northoff, G. (2005). How do we modulate our emotions? Parametric fMRI reveals cortical midline structures as regions specifically involved in the processing of emotional valences. *Cognitive Brain Research, 25,* 348–358.

Helder, S. G., & Collier, D. A. (2011). The genetics of eating disorders. In R. H. Adan & W. H. Kaye (Eds.), *Behavioral neurobiology of eating disorders* (pp. 157–175). New York, NY: Springer-Verlag Publishing.

Helgesen, S. (1998). *Everyday revolutionaries: Working women and the transformation of American life.* New York, NY: Doubleday.

Hendrick, C., & Hendrick, S. S. (2003). Romantic love: Measuring Cupid's arrow. In S. J. Lopez & C. R. Snyder (Eds.), *Positive psychological assessment: A handbook of models and measures* (pp. 235–249). Washington, DC: American Psychological Association.

Hendricks, J. C., & Sehgal, A. (2004). Why a fly? Using *Drosophila* to understand the genetics of circadian rhythms and sleep. *Journal of Sleep and Sleep Disorders Research, 27,* 334–342.

Henig, R. M. (2004, October 17). Something's off. *New York Times Magazine,* p. 110.

Henig, R. M. (2009, October 4). The anxious mind. *New York Times Magazine,* 30–37, 44, 62, 64.

Henkel, L. A., Franklin, N., & Johnson, M. K. (2000). Cross-modal source monitoring confusions between perceived and imagined events. *Journal of Experimental Psychology: Learning, Memory, & Cognition, 26,* 321–335.

Hennessy, D. A., Jakubowski, R., & Benedetti, A. (2005). The influence of the actor-observer bias on attributions of other drivers. In D. A. Hennessy & D. L. Wiesenthal (Eds.), *Contemporary issues in road user behavior and traffic safety* (pp. 13–20). Hauppauge, NY: Nova Science.

Henningsen, D. D., Henningsen, M. L. M., & Eden, J. (2006). Examining the symptoms of groupthink and retrospective sensemaking. *Small Group Research, 37,* 36–64.

Henry, J. A., Alexander, C. A., & Sener, E. K. (1995). Relative mortality from overdose of antidepressants. *British Medical Journal, 310,* 221–224.

Henry, P. J., Reyna, C., & Weiner, B. (2004). Hate welfare but help the poor: How the attributional content of stereotypes explains the paradox of reactions to the destitute in America. *Journal of Applied Social Psychology, 34,* 34–58.

Herbenick, D., Reece, M., Schick, V., Sanders, S. A., Dodge, B., & Fortenberry, J. D. (2010). Sexual behavior in the United States: Results from a national probability sample of men and women ages 14–94. *The Journal of Sexual Medicine, 7*(Suppl. 5), 255–265.

Herman, L. M., Uyeyama, R. K., & Pack, A. A. (2008). Bottlenose dolphins understand relationships between concepts. *Behavioral and Brain Sciences, 31,* 139–140.

Hermann, B., Seidenberg, M., Sears, L., Hansen, R., Bayless, K., Rutecki, P., & Dow, C. (2004). Cerebellar atrophy in temporal lobe epilepsy affects procedural memory. *Neurology, 63,* 2129–2131.

Herrmann, E., Hernández-Lloreda, M. V., Call, J., Haer, B., & Tomasello, M. (2010). The structure of individual differences in the cognitive abilities of children and chimpanzees. *Psychological Science, 21,* 102–110.

Hernandez, T. M., Aldridge, M. A., & Bower, T. G. R. (2000). Structural and experiential factors in newborns' preference for speech sounds. *Developmental Science, 3,* 46–49.

Hernandez-Reif, M., Diego, M., & Field, T. (2007). Preterm infants show reduced stress behaviors and activity after 5 days of massage therapy. *Infant Behavior & Development, 30,* 557–561.

Herpertz-Dahlmann, B. (2009). Adolescent eating disorders: Definitions, symptomatology, epidemiology and comorbidity. *Child and Adolescent Psychiatric Clinics of North America, 18,* 31–47.

Herpertz-Dahlmann, B., & Salbach-Andrae, H. (2009). Overview of treatment modalities in adolescent anorexia nervosa. *Child and Adolescent Psychiatric Clinics of North America, 18,* 131–145.

Hersher, L. (Ed.). (1970). *Four psychotherapies.* New York, NY: Appleton-Century-Crofts.

Hertenstein, M. J., Holmes, R., McCullough, M., & Keltner, D. (2009). The communication of emotion via touch. *Emotion, 9*, 566–573.

Hertzog, C., Kramer, A. F., Wilson, R. S., & Lindenberger, U. (2009). Enrichment effects on adult cognitive development. *Psychological Science in the Public Interest, 9*, 1–65.

Herzog, H. A. (2005). Dealing with the animal research controversy. In C. K. Akins, S. Panicker, & C. L. Cunningham (Eds.), *Laboratory animals in research and teaching: Ethics, care, and methods* (pp. 9–29). Washington, DC: American Psychological Association.

Heschl, A., & Burkart, J. (2006). A new mark test for mirror self-recognition in non-human primates. *Primates, 47*, 187–198.

Hess, U., & Thibault, P. (2009). Darwin and emotional expression. *American Psychologist, 64*, 120–128.

Hilgard, E. R., Hilgard, J. R., & Kaufmann, W. (1983). *Hypnosis in the relief of pain* (2nd ed.). Los Altos, CA: Kaufmann.

Hill, C. E. (Ed.). (2004). *Dream work in therapy: Facilitating exploration, insight, and action.* Washington, DC: American Psychological Association.

Hill, C. E., Liu, J., Spangler, P., Sim, W., & Schottenbauer, M. (2008). Working with dreams in psychotherapy: What do psychoanalytic therapists report that they do? *Psychoanalytic Psychology, 25*, 565–573.

Hill, C. E., Zack, J. S., Wonnell, T. L., Hoffman, M. A., Rochlen, A. B., Goldberg, J. L., . . . Hess, S. (2000). Structured brief therapy with a focus on dreams or loss for clients with troubling dreams and recent loss. *Journal of Counseling Psychology, 47*, 90–101.

Hill, J. (2003). Early identification of individuals at risk for antisocial personality disorder. *British Journal of Psychiatry, 182*(Suppl. 44), s11–s14.

Hines, A. R., & Paulson, S. E. (2007). Parents' and teachers' perceptions of adolescent storm and stress: Relations with parenting and teaching styles. *Family Therapy, 34*, 63–80.

Hines, M. (2004). *Brain gender.* New York, NY: Oxford University Press.

Hines, M. (2010). Sex-related variation in human behavior and the brain. *Trends in Cognitive Sciences, 14*, 448–456.

Hingson, R., Heeren, T., Winter, M., & Wechsler, H. (2005). Magnitude of alcohol-related mortality and morbidity among U.S. college students ages 18–24: Changes from 1998 to 2001. *Annual Review of Public Health 26*, 259–279.

Hoelzle, J. B., & Meyer, G. J. (2008). The factor structure of the MMPI-2 Restructured Clinical (RC) Scales. *Journal of Personality Assessment, 90*, 443–455.

Hofer, J., & Chasiotis, A. (2004). Methodological considerations of applying a TAT-type picture-story test in cross-cultural research. *Journal of Cross Cultural Psychology, 35*, 224–241.

Hoffman, E. (2008). Maslow in retrospect: Editorial board member assessments. *Journal of Humanistic Psychology, 48*, 456–457.

Hoffman, H. S., & DePaulo, P. (1977). Behavioral control by an imprinting stimulus. *American Scientist, 65*, 58–66.

Hoffrage, U., & Pohl, R. F. (2003). Research on hindsight bias: A rich past, a productive present, and a challenging future. *Memory, 11*, 329–335.

Hofmann, S. G., Moscovitch, D. A., & Heinrichs, N. (2004). Evolutionary mechanisms of fear and anxiety. In P. Gilbert (Ed.), *Evolutionary theory and cognitive therapy* (pp. 119–136). New York, NY: Springer.

Hogan, J., & Holland, B. (2003). Using theory to evaluate personality and job-performance relations: A socioanalytic perspective. *Journal of Applied Psychology, 88*, 100–112.

Hogan, R., Hogan, J., & Roberts, B. W. (1996). Personality measurement and employment decisions: Questions and answers. *American Psychologist, 51*, 469–477.

Hollins, M. (2010). Somesthetic senses. *Annual Review of Psychology, 61*, 243–271.

Holmbeck, G. N. (1994). Adolescence. In V. A. Ramachandran (Ed.), *Encyclopedia of human behavior* (Vol. 1, pp. 17–28). San Diego, CA: Academic Press.

Holmberg, D., & Blair, K. L. (2009). Sexual desire, communication, satisfaction, and preferences of men and women in same-sex versus mixed-sex relationships. *Journal of Sex Research, 46*, 57–66.

Hopkins, W. D., & Cantalupo, C. (2008). Theoretical speculations on the evolutionary origins of hemispheric specialization. *Current Directions in Psychological Science, 17*, 233–237.

Hopkins, W. D., Phillips, K. A., Bania, A., Calcutt, S. E., Gardner, M., Russell, J., & Schapiro, S. J. (2011). Hand preferences for coordinated bimanual actions in 777 great apes: Implications for the evolution of handedness in Hominins. *Journal of Human Evolution, 60*, 605–611.

Horner, V., & Whiten, A. (2005). Imitation and emulation switching in chimpanzees (*Pan troglodytes*) and children (*Homo sapiens*). *Animal Cognition, 8*, 164–181.

Horney, K. (1937). *The neurotic personality of our time.* New York, NY: Norton.

Horstmann, G. (2003). What do facial expressions convey: Feeling states, behavioral intentions, or action requests? *Emotion, 3*, 150–166.

Hosoda, M., Stone, R. E., & Coats, G. (2003). The effects of physical attractiveness on job-related outcomes: A meta-analysis of experimental studies. *Personnel Psychology, 56*, 431–462.

Howe, M. L. (2003). Memories from the cradle. *Current Directions in Psychological Science, 12*, 62–65.

Howland, J., Rohsenow, D. J., Calise, T., MacKillop, J., & Metrik, J. (2011). Caffeinated alcoholic beverages: An emerging public health problem. *American Journal of Preventive Medicine, 40*, 268–271.

Howland, R. H. (2008). Neurosurgical approaches to therapeutic brain stimulation for treatment-resistant depression. *Journal of Psychosocial Nursing and Mental Health Services, 46*, 15–19.

Huang, Y., Yao, S., Huang, R., Guo, R., & Yang, X. (2008). Type D personality as a risk factor in patients with coronary heart disease. *Chinese Journal of Clinical Psychology, 16*, 305–308.

Huas, C. C., Caille, A. A., Godart, N. N., Foulon, C. C., Pham⊠Scottez, A. A., Divac, S. S., . . . Falissard, B. B. (2011). Factors predictive of ten⊠year mortality in severe anorexia nervosa patients. *Acta Psychiatrica Scandinavica, 123*, 62–70.

Hudson, J. A., & Sheffield, E. G. (1998). Deja vu all over again: Effects of reenactment on toddlers' event memory. *Child Development, 69*, 51–67.

Huebner, A. M., Garrod, A., & Snarey, J. (1990). *Moral development in Tibetan Buddhist monks: A cross-cultural study of adolescents and young adults in Nepal.* Paper presented at the meeting of the Society for Research in Adolescence, Atlanta, GA.

Huesmann, L. R. (2007). The impact of electronic media violence: Scientific theory and research. *Journal of Adolescent Health, 41*, S6–S13.

Huffman, C. J., Matthews, T. D., & Gagne, P. E. (2001). The role of part-set cuing in the recall of chess positions: Influence of chunking in memory. *North American Journal of Psychology, 3*, 535–542.

Hughes, J. M. [Julie]. (2009). African American and European American adolescents' attitudes toward affirmative action and school desegregation. *Dissertation Abstracts International: Section B: The Sciences and Engineering, 69*, 5076.

Hughes, J. R. [John]. (2006). A general review of recent reports on homosexuality and lesbianism. *Sexuality and Disability, 24*, 195–205.

Huizink, A. C., Robles, de M., Pascale, G., Mulder, E. J. H., Visser, G. H. A., & Buitelaar, J. K. (2002). Psychological measures of prenatal stress as predictors of infant temperament. *Journal of the American Academy of Child and Adolescent Psychiatry, 41*, 1078–1085.

Hulin, C. L., & Judge, T. A. (2003). Job attitudes. In W. C. Borman, D. R. Ilgen, & R. J. Klimoski (Eds.), *Handbook of psychology: Vol. 12, Industrial and organizational psychology* (pp. 255–276). Hoboken, NJ: Wiley.

Hunt, E., & Carlson, J. (2007). Considerations relating to the study of group differences in intelligence. *Perspectives on Psychological Science, 2*, 194–213.

Hunt, R. R., & Ellis, H. (2003). *Fundamentals of cognitive psychology.* New York, NY: McGraw-Hill.

Hunter, C. L., Goodie, J. L., Oordt, M. S., & Dobmeyer, A. C. (2009). Sexual dysfunctions. In C. L. Hunter, J. L. Goodie, M. S. Oordt, & A. C. Dobmeyer (Eds.), *Integrated behavioral health in primary care: Step-by-step guidance for assessment and intervention* (pp. 195–211). Washington, DC: American Psychological Association.

Hussong, A. M. (2003). Further refining the stress-coping model of alcohol involvement. *Addictive Behaviors, 28*, 1515–1522.

Hutsler, J. J. (2003). The specialized structure of human language cortex: Pyramidal cell size asymmetries within auditory and language-associated regions of the temporal lobes. *Brain and Language, 86*, 226–242.

Huttenlocher, P. R. (2002a). Morphometric study of human cerebral cortex development. In M. H. Johnson, Y. Munakata, & R. O. Gilmore (Eds.), *Brain development and cognition: A reader* (2nd ed., pp. 117–128). Malden, MA: Blackwell.

Hyde, J. S. (1984). Children's understanding of sexist language. *Developmental Psychology, 20*, 697–706.

Hyde, J. S. (1986). Gender differences in aggression. In J. S. Hyde, & M. C. Linn (Eds.), *The psychology of gender differences: Advances through meta-analysis* (pp. 51–66). Baltimore, MD: Johns Hopkins University Press.

Hyde, J. S. (2005). The gender similarities hypothesis. *American Psychologist, 60,* 581–592.

Hyde, J. S., & Mezulis, A. H. (2002). Gender difference research: Issues and critique. In J. Worrell (Ed.), *Encyclopedia of women and gender: Sex similarities and differences and the impact of society on gender* (Vol. 1, pp. 551–559). San Diego, CA: Academic Press.

Hyman, I. E., Husband, T. H., & Billings, F. J. (1995). False memories of childhood experiences. *Applied Cognitive Psychology, 9,* 181–197.

Impens, A. J. (2005). Bereavement related mortality among older adults. *Dissertation Abstracts International: Section B: The Sciences and Engineering, 66,* 846.

Imrie, R. (1999, September 3). $850,000 awarded in repressed-memory case. *Charlotte Observer,* p. 8A.

Inciardi, J. A., & Harrison, L. D. (1998). *Heroin in the age of crack cocaine.* Thousand Oaks, CA: Sage.

Insel, T. R., & Wang, P. S. (2010). Rethinking mental illness. *JAMA: Journal of the American Medical Association, 303,* 1970–1971.

Irwin, M. (2002). Psychoneuroimmunology of depression: Clinical implications. *Brain, Behavior and Immunity, 16,* 1–16.

Irwin, M. (2008). Human psychoneuroimmunology: 20 years of discovery. *Brain, Behavior, and Immunity, 22,* 129–139.

Ito, K. (2002). Additivity of heuristic and systematic processing persuasion: Effects of source credibility, argument quality, and issue involvement. *Japanese Journal of Experimental Social Psychology, 41,* 137–146.

Ito, M., Baumer, S., Bittanti, M., boyd, d., Cody, R., Herr-Stephenson, B., . . . Tripp, L. (2009). *Hanging out, messing around, geeking out: Living and learning with new media.* Cambridge, MA: MIT Press.

Ito, M., Horst, H., Bittanti, M., boyd, d., Herr-Stephenson, B., Lange, P. G., . . . Tripp, L. (2008). Living and learning with new media: Summary of findings from the Digital Youth Project. Retrieved from http://www.macfound.org/atf/cf/%7BB0386CE3-8B29-4162-8098-E466FB856794%7D/DML_ETHNOG_WHITEPAPER.PDF

Iwamasa, G. Y., & Smith, S. K. (1996). Ethnic diversity in behavioral psychology: A review of the literature. *Behavioral Modification, 20,* 45–59.

Izaki, Y., Takita, M., & Akema, T. (2008). Specific role of the posterior dorsal hippocampus-prefrontal cortex in short-term working memory. *European Journal of Neuroscience, 27,* 3029–3034.

Izard, C. E. (1971). *The face of emotion.* New York, NY: Appleton-Century-Crofts.

Izard, C. E. (1980). Cross-cultural perspectives on emotion and emotion communication. In H. C. Triandis & W. J. Lonner (Eds.), *Handbook of cross-cultural psychology* (Vol. 3, pp. 185–220). Boston, MA: Allyn & Bacon.

Izard, V., Dehaene-Lambertz, G., & Dehaene, S. (2008). Distinct cerebral pathways for object identity and number in human infants. *PLoS Biology, 6,* e11. doi:10.1371/ journal.pbio.0060011

Jack, R. E., Caldara, R., & Schyns, P. G. (2011). Internal representations reveal cultural diversity in expectations of facial expressions of emotion. *Journal of Experimental Psychology: General, 141,* 1–7. doi:10.1037/a0023463

Jaakkola, K., Fellner, W., Erb, L., Rodriguez, M., & Guarino, E. (2005). Understanding of the concept of numerically "less" by bottlenose dolphins (*Tursiops truncatus*). *Journal of Comparative Psychology, 119,* 296–303.

Jackson, D. C., Mueller, C. J., Dolski, I., Dalton, K. M., Nitschke, J. B., Urry, H. L., . . . Davidson, R. J. (2003). Now you feel it, now you don't: Frontal brain electrical asymmetry and individual differences in emotion regulation. *Psychological Science, 14,* 612–617.

Jackson, J. S., Knight, K. M., & Rafferty, J. A. (2010). Race and unhealthy behaviors: Chronic stress, the HPA axis, and physical and mental health disparities over the life course. *American Journal of Public Health, 100,* 933–939.

Jackson, L. A., Hunter, J. E., & Hodge, C. N. (1995). Physical attractiveness and intellectual competence: A meta-analytic review. *Social Psychology Quarterly, 58,* 108–122.

Jackson, O. (2004). Episodic memory in the brain: Association, recognition, and prediction. *Dissertation Abstracts International: Section B: The Sciences and Engineering, 64,* 4647.

Jacobs, N., van Os, J., Derom, C., & Thiery, E. (2008). Heritability of intelligence. *Twin Research and Human Genetics, 10*(Suppl), 11–14.

Jacobson, N. S., & Christensen, A. (1996). Studying the effectiveness of psychotherapy: How well can clinical trials do the job? *American Psychologist, 51,* 1031–1039.

Jain, S., & Posavac, S. S. (2001). Prepurchase attribute verifiability, source credibility, and persuasion. *Journal of Consumer Psychology, 11,* 169–180.

James, L., & Nahl, D. (2000). *Road rage and aggressive driving: Steering clear of highway warfare.* Amherst, NY: Prometheus.

James, W. (1890). *The principles of psychology.* New York, NY: Holt.

Jamison, R. N., & Virts, K. L. (1990). The influence of family support on chronic pain. *Behaviour Research and Therapy, 28,* 283–287.

Jäncke, L., Brunner, B., & Esslen, M. (2008). Brain activation during fast driving in a driving simulator: The role of the lateral prefrontal cortex. *Neuroreport: For Rapid Communication of Neuroscience Research, 19,* 1127–1130.

Jang, K. L., Livesley, W. J., Angleitner, A., Riemann, R., & Vernon, P. A. (2002). Genetic and environmental influences on the convariance of facets defining the domains of the five-factor model of personality. *Personality and Individual Differences, 33,* 83–101.

Jang, K. L., Livesley, W. J., & Vernon, P. A. (1996). Heritability of the Big Five personality dimensions and their facets: A twin study. *Journal of Personality, 64,* 577–591.

Janis, I. L. (1982). *Groupthink: Psychological studies of policy decisions and fiascoes* (2nd ed.). Boston, MA: Houghton Mifflin.

Janis, I. L. (1989). *Crucial decisions: Leadership in policymaking and crisis management.* New York, NY: Free Press.

Janofsky, M. (1994, December 13). Survey reports more drug use by teenagers. *New York Times,* p. A1.

Janos, P. M., & Robinson, N. M. (1985). Psychosocial development in intellectually gifted children. In F. D. Horowitz & M. O'Brien (Eds.), *Gifted and talented: Developmental perspectives* (pp. 149–195). Washington, DC: American Psychological Association.

Jansen, P. G. W., & Stoop, B. A. M. (2001). The dynamics of assessment center validity: Results of a 7-year study. *Journal of Applied Psychology, 86,* 741–753.

Janssen, S. M. J., Chessa, A. G., & Murre, J. M. J. (2005). The reminiscence bump in autobiographical memory: Effects of age, gender, education, and culture. *Memory, 13,* 658–668.

Järvinen-Pasley, A., Bellugi, U., Reilly, J., Mills, D. L., Galaburda, A., Reiss, A. L., & Korenberg, J. R. (2008). Defining the social phenotype in Williams syndrome: A model for linking gene, the brain, and behavior. *Development and Psychopathology, 20,* 1–35.

Jawahar, I. M. (2001). Attitudes, self-monitoring, and appraisal behaviors. *Journal of Applied Psychology, 86,* 875–883.

Jaycox, L. H., Zoellner, L., & Foa, E. B. (2002). Cognitive-behavior therapy for PTSD in rape survivors. *Journal of Clinical Psychology, 58,* 891–906.

Jehna, M. M., Neuper, C. C., Ischebeck, A. A., Loitfelder, M. M., Ropele, S. S., Langkammer, C. C., . . . Enzinger, C. C. (2011). The functional correlates of face perception and recognition of emotional facial expressions as evidenced by fmri. *Brain Research, 1393,* 73–83. doi:10.1016/j.brainres.2011.04.007

Jemmott, J. B., III, Jemmott, L. S., Fong, G. T., & McCaffree, K. (2002). Reducing HIC risk-associated sexual behavior among African-American adolescents: Testing the generality of intervention effects. *American Journal of Community Psychology, 27,* 161–187.

Jetten, J., Haslam, C., & Haslam, S. A. (2011). *The social cure: Identity, health, and well-being.* Hove, England: Psychology Press.

Jex, S. M., Adams, G. A., & Bachrach, D. G. (2003). The impact of situational constraints, role stressors, and commitment on employee altruism. *Journal of Occupational Health Psychology, 8,* 171–180.

Ji, D., & Wilson, M. A. (2007). Coordinated memory replay in the visual cortex and hippocampus during sleep. *Nature Neuroscience, 10,* 100–107.

Johnson, C. (2003). Procedural memory and skill acquisition. In A. F. Healy & R. W. Proctor (Eds.), *Handbook of Psychology: Vol. 4, Experimental Psychology* (pp. 499–523). New York, NY: Wiley.

Johnson, C. (2002). Obesity, weight management, and self-esteem. In T. A. Wadden & A. J. Stunkard, *Handbook of obesity treatment* (pp. 480–493). New York, NY: Guilford Press.

Johnson, H., & Thompson, A. (2008). The development and maintenance of posttraumatic stress disorder (PTSD) in civilian adult survivors of war trauma and torture: A review. *Clinical Psychology Review, 28,* 36–47.

Johnson, J. L., Kalaw, C., Lovato, C. Y., Baillie, L., & Chambers, N. A. (2004). Crossing the line: Adolescents' experiences of controlling their tobacco use. *Qualitative Health Research, 14,* 1276–1291.

Johnson, S. L. [Sharon]. (2003). *Therapist's guide to substance abuse intervention.* San Diego, CA: Academic Press.

Johnson, S. M. [Susan]. (2003). Couples therapy research: Status and directions. In G. P. Sholevar (Ed.), *Textbook of family and couples therapy: Clinical applications* (pp. 797–814). Washington, DC: American Psychiatric Publishing.

Johnson, W., Bouchard, T. J., Jr., Segal, N. L., & Samuel, J. (2005). General intelligence and reading performance in adults: Is the genetic factor structure the same as for children? *Personality and Individual Differences, 38,* 1413–1428.

Johnson, W., & Krueger, R. F. (2004). Genetic and environmental structure of adjectives describing the domains of the Big Five model of personality: A nationwide US twin study. *Journal of Research in Personality, 38,* 448–472.

Johnston, C., & Ohan, J. L. (2005). The importance of parental attributions in families of children with attention-deficit/hyperactivity and disruptive behavior disorders. *Clinical Child and Family Psychology Review, 8,* 167–182.

Jones, C. J., & Meredith, W. (2000). Developmental paths of psychological health from early adolescence to later adulthood. *Psychology & Aging, 15,* 351–360.

Jones, M. C. (1924). Elimination of children's fears. *Journal of Experimental Psychology, 7,* 381–390.

Jones, S. R., & Fernyhough, C. (2007). A new look at the neural diathesis–stress model of schizophrenia: The primacy of social-evaluative and uncontrollable situations. *Schizophrenia Bulletin, 33,* 1171–1177.

Joseph, J. (2001). Is crime in the genes? A critical review of twin and adoption studies of criminality and antisocial behavior. *Journal of Mind and Behavior, 22,* 179–218.

Joseph, J. E., Liu, X., Jiang, Y., Lynam, D., & Kelly, T. H. (2009). Neural correlates of emotional reactivity in sensation seeking. *Psychological Science, 20,* 215–223.

Joseph, S., Linley, P. A., & Maltby, J. (2006). Editorial: Positive psychology, religion, and spirituality. *Mental Health, Religion & Culture, 9,* 209–212.

Jost, J. T., & Sidanius, J. (2004). The authoritarian personality and the organization of attitudes. In R. Brown (Ed.), *Political psychology: Key readings* (pp. 39–68). New York, NY: Psychology Press.

Juckel, G., Uhl, I., Padberg, F., Brüne, M., & Winter, C. (2009). Psychosurgery and deep brain stimulation as ultima ratio treatment for refractory depression. *European Archives of Psychiatry and Clinical Neuroscience, 259,* 1–7.

Judge, T. A., & Bono, J. E. (2000). Five-factor model of personality and transformational leadership. *Journal of Applied Psychology, 85,* 751–765.

Judge, T. A., Thoresen, C. J., Bono, J. E., & Patton, G. K. (2001). The job satisfaction–job performance relationship: A qualitative and quantitative review. *Psychological Bulletin, 127,* 376–407.

Juliano, L. M., & Griffiths, R. R. (2004). A critical review of caffeine withdrawal: Empirical validation of symptoms and signs, incidence, severity, and associated features. *Psychopharmacology, 176,* 1–29.

Julius, M., Harburg, E., Cottington, E. M., & Johnson, E. H. (1986). Anger-coping types, blood pressure, and all-cause mortality: A follow-up in Tecumseh, Michigan (1971–1983). *American Journal of Epidemiology, 124,* 220–233.

Juncos-Rabadán, O., Facal, D., Rodríguez, M., & Pereiro, A. X. (2010). Lexical knowledge and lexical retrieval in ageing: Insights from a tip-of-the-tongue (TOT) study. *Language and Cognitive Processes, 25,* 1301–1334.

Jung, H. (2006). Assessing the influence of cultural values on consumer susceptibility to social pressure for conformity: Self-image enhancing motivations vs. information searching motivation. In L. R. Kahle & C. H. Kim (Eds.), *Creating images and the psychology of marketing communication* (pp. 309–329). Mahwah, NJ: Erlbaum.

Jussim, L., Robustelli, S. L., & Cain, T. R. (2009). Teacher expectations and self-fulfilling prophecies. In K. R. Wenzel & A. Wigfield (Eds.), *Handbook of motivation at school* (pp. 349–380). New York, NY: Routledge/Taylor & Francis Group.

Kabat-Zinn, J. (2006). *Coming to our senses: Healing ourselves and the world through mindfulness.* New York, NY: Hyperion.

Kagan, J. (2008). In defense of qualitative changes in development. *Child Development, 79,* 1606–1624.

Kagan, J., & Snidman, N. (2004). *The long shadow of temperament.* Cambridge, MA: Belknap Press/Harvard University Press.

Kaiser, R. B., Hogan, R., & Craig, S. B. (2008). Leadership and the fate of organizations. *American Psychologist, 63,* 96–110.

Kaiser, S., & Sachser, N. (2009). Effects of prenatal social stress on offspring development. *Current Directions in Psychological Science, 18,* 118–121.

Kalat, J. W. (2001). *Biological psychology* (7th ed.). Belmont, CA: Wadsworth/Thomson Learning.

Kamin, L. J. (1969). Selective association and conditioning. In N. J. Mackintosh & W. K. Honig (Eds.), *Fundamental issues in associative learning* (pp. 42–64). Halifax, Nova Scotia: Dalhousie University Press.

Kaminski, M. (1999). *The team concept: A worker-centered alternative to lean production.* Washington, DC: American Psychological Association Public Interest Directorate. Retrieved from http://www.apa.org/pi/wpo/niosh/abstract22.html

Kanaya, T. (2004). Age differences in IQ trends: Unpacking the Flynn effect. *Dissertation Abstracts International: Section B: The Sciences and Engineering, 65,* 1051.

Kandel, E. R. (2001). The molecular biology of memory storage: A dialogue between genes and synapses. *Science, 294,* 1030–1038.

Karg, K., Burmeister, M., Shedden, K., & Sen, S. (2011). The serotonin transporter promoter variant (5-HTTLPR), stress, and depression meta-analysis revisited: Evidence of genetic moderation. *Archives of General Psychiatry, 68,* 444–454. doi: 10.1001/archgenpsychiatry.2010.189

Karakashian, L. M., Walter, M. I., Christopher, A. N., & Lucas, T. (2006). Fear of negative evaluation affects helping behavior: The bystander effect revisited. *North American Journal of Psychology, 8,* 13–32.

Karmiloff-Smith, A. (2002). Elementary, my dear Watson, the clue is in the genes. Or is it? *The Psychologist, 15,* 608–611.

Karpicke, J. D., & Blunt, J. R. (2011). Retrieval practice produces more learning than elaborate studying with concept mapping. *Science, 331,* 772–775.

Kashdan, T. B., & Fincham, F. D. (2002). "Facilitating creativity by regulating curiosity": Comment. *American Psychologist, 57,* 373–374.

Kashdan, T. B., Julian, T., Merritt, K., & Uswatte, G. (2006). Social anxiety and posttraumatic stress in combat veterans: Relations to well-being and character strengths. *Behaviour Research and Therapy, 44,* 561–583.

Kashdan, T. B., & Silvia, P. J. (2009). Curiosity and interest: The benefits of thriving on novelty and challenge. In S. J. Lopez & C. R. Snyder (Eds.), *Oxford handbook of positive psychology* (2nd ed., pp. 367–374). New York, NY: Oxford University Press.

Kashima, Y., & Triandis, H. C. (1986). The self-serving bias in attributions as a coping strategy: A cross-cultural study. *Journal of Cross-Cultural Psychology, 17,* 83–98.

Kaslow, N. J., Clark, A. G., & Sirian, L. M. (2008). Childhood depression. In R. J. Morris & T. R. Kratochwill (Eds.), *The practice of child therapy* (4th ed., pp. 29–92). Mahwah, NJ: Erlbaum.

Kasper, J. D., Ensminger, M. E., Green, K. M., Fothergill, K. E., Juon, H.-S., Robertson, J., & Thorpe, R. J. (2008). Effects of poverty and family stress over three decades on the functional status of older African American women. *The Journals of Gerontology: Series B: Psychological Sciences and Social Sciences, 63B,* S201–S210.

Kass, S. (1999, September). Employees perceive women as better managers than men, finds five-year study. *APA Monitor, 30*(8) p. 6.

Kathuria, S., Gaetani, S., Fegley, D., Valiño, F., Duranti, A., Tontini, A., . . . Piomelli, D. (2003). Modulation of anxiety through blockade of anadamide hydrolysis. *Nature Medicine, 9,* 76–81.

Katrios, T. (2009). The contemporary relevance of Freud's work. *Hellenic Journal of Psychology, 6,* 14–25.

Katz, S. (2003). Physical appearance: The importance of being beautiful. In J. M. Henslin (Ed.), *Down to earth sociology: Introductory readings* (12th ed., pp. 313–320). New York, NY: Free Press.

Kavale, K. A. (2002). Mainstreaming to full inclusion: From orthogenesis to pathogenesis of an idea. *International Journal of Disability, Development and Education, 49,* 201–214.

Kazdin, A. E. (2009). Psychological science's contributions to a sustainable environment: Extending our reach to a grand challenge of society. *American Psychologist, 64,* 339–356.

Keel, P. K., Heatherton, T. F., Dorer, D. J., Joiner, T. E., & Zalta, A. K. (2006). Point prevalence of bulimia nervosa in 1982, 1992, and 2002. *Psychological Medicine, 36,* 119–127.

Keitner, G. I., Archambault, R., Ryan, C. E., & Miller, I. W. (2003). Family therapy and chronic depression. *Journal of Clinical Psychology, 59,* 873–884.

Kelemen, W. L., & Creeley, C. E. (2003). State-dependent memory effects using caffeine and placebo do not extend to metamemory. *Journal of General Psychology, 130,* 70–86.

Keller, M. B., McCullough, J. P., Klein, D. N., Arnow, B., Dunner, D. L., Gelenberg, A. J., . . . Zajecka, A. (2000). A comparison of Nefazodone, the cognitive behavioral-analysis system of psychotherapy, and their combination for the treatment of chronic depression. *The New England Journal of Medicine, 342,* 1462–1470.

Keller, R. T. (2006). Transformational leadership, initiating structure, and substitutes for leadership: A longitudinal study of research and development project team performance. *Journal of Applied Psychology, 91,* 202–210.

Kelley, H. H. (1967). Attribution theory in social psychology. In D. Levine (Ed.), *Nebraska Symposium on Motivation* (Vol. 15, pp. 192–238). Lincoln: University of Nebraska Press.

Kelley, H. H. (1973). The process of causal attribution. *American Psychologist, 28,* 107–128.

Kempt, H. (2000). Culture assimilator training for students with limited English proficiency at the University of Mississippi intensive English program. *Dissertation Abstracts International Section A: Humanities and Social Sciences, 60,* 2773.

Kendall-Tackett, K. (2010). *The psychoneuroimmunology of chronic disease: Exploring the links between inflammation, stress, and illness.* Washington, DC: American Psychological Association.

Kendall-Tackett, K. A. (2001). *The hidden feelings of motherhood: Coping with stress, depression, and burnout.* Oakland, CA: New Harbinger.

Kerr, A. L., & Swain, R. A. (2011). Rapid cellular genesis and apoptosis: Effects of exercise in the adult rat. *Behavioral Neuroscience, 125,* 1–9.

Keshavan, M. S., Tandon, R., Boutros, N. N., & Nasrallah, H. A. (2008). Schizophrenia, "just the facts": What we know in 2008: Part 3: Neurobiology. *Schizophrenia Research, 106,* 89–107.

Kessler, R. C., Adler, L., Barkley, R., Biederman, J., Conners, C. K., Demler, O., . . . Zaslavsky, A. M. (2006). The prevalence and correlates of adult ADHD in the United States: Results from the National Comorbidity Survey Replication. *American Journal of Psychiatry, 163,* 716–723.

Kessler, R. C., Berglund, P., Demler, O., Jin, R., Koretz, D., Merikangas, K. R., . . . Wang, P. S. (2003). The epidemiology of major depressive disorder: Results from the National Comorbidity Survey Replication (NCS-R). *JAMA: Journal of the American Medical Association, 289,* 3095–3105.

Kessler, R. C., Chiu, W. T., Demler, O., & Walters, E. E. (2005). Prevalence, severity, and comorbidity of 12-month DSM-IV disorders in the National Comorbidity Survey replication. *Archives of General Psychiatry, 62,* pp. 617–627.

Kessler, R. C., Price, R. H., & Wortman, C. B. (1985). Social factors in psychopathology: Stress, social support, and coping processes. *Annual Review of Psychology, 36,* 531–572.

Khalyfa, A., Serpero, L. D., Kheirandish-Gozal, L., Capdevila, O., & Gozal, D. (2011). TNF-α gene polymorphisms and excessive daytime sleepiness in pediatric obstructive sleep apnea. *The Journal of Pediatrics, 158,* 81–86.

Kidron, C. A. (2008). Review of psychic trauma: Dynamics, symptoms and treatment. *Transcultural Psychiatry, 45,* 342–347.

Kiecolt-Glaser, J. K., & Glaser, R. (2002). Depression and immune function: Central pathways to morbidity and mortality. *Journal of Psychosomatic Research, 53,* 873–876.

Kiesler, C. A. (1982). Public and professional myths about mental hospitalization: An empirical reassessment of policy-related beliefs. *American Psychologist, 37,* 1323–1339.

Kiesler, C. A., & Simpkins, C. G. (1993). *The unnoticed majority in psychiatric inpatient care.* New York, NY: Plenum.

Kihara, T., & Shimohama, S. (2004). Alzheimer's disease and acetylcholine receptors. *Acta Neurobiologiae Experimentalis, 64,* 99–105.

Kihlström, J. F. (2005). Is hypnosis an altered state of consciousness or what? Comment. *Contemporary Hypnosis, 22,* 34–38.

Killgore, W. D. S., Rosso, H. M., Gruber, S. A., & Yurgelun-Todd, D. A. (2009). Amygdala volume and verbal memory performance in schizophrenia and bipolar disorder. *Cognitive and Behavioral Neurology, 22,* 28–37.

Kilpatrick, D. G., Acierno, R., Saunders, B., Resnick, H. S., Best, C. L., & Schnurr, P. P. (2000). Risk factors for adolescent substance abuse and dependence: Data from a national sample. *Journal of Consulting & Clinical Psychology, 68,* 19–30.

Kim, H. S., Sherman, D. K., & Taylor, S. E. (2008). Culture and social support. *American Psychologist, 63,* 518–526

Kim, K. H. (2008). Meta-analyses of the relationship of creative achievement to both IQ and divergent thinking test scores. *Journal of Creative Behavior, 42,* 106–130.

Kim, T. J. (2011). Insights on telehealth and virtual reality. In N. A. Dewan, A. Naakesh, J. S. Luo, & N. M. Lorenzi (Eds.), *Information technology essentials for behavioral health clinicians* (pp. 65–75). New York, NY: Springer-Verlag.

King, J. E., Weiss, A., & Farmer, K. H. (2005). A chimpanzee (*Pan troglodytes*) analogue of cross-national generalization of personality structure: Zoological parks and an African sanctuary. *Journal of Personality, 73,* 389–410.

Kingstone, A., Enns, J. T., Mangun, G. R., & Gazzaniga, M. S. (1995). Right-hemisphere memory superiority: Studies of a split-brain patient. *Psychological Science, 6,* 118–121.

Kinney, T. (2008). Task and individual characteristics as predictors of performance in a job-relevant multi-tasking environment. *Dissertation Abstracts International: Section B: The Sciences and Engineering, 68,* 7011.

Kinsley, C., & Lambert, K. G. (2006, January). The maternal brain. *Scientific American, 294*(1), 72–79.

Kirilly, E., Benko, A., Ferrington, L., Ando, R. D., Kelly, P. A. T., & Bagdy, G. (2006). Acute and long-term effects of a single dose of MDMA on aggression in Dark Agouti rats. *International Journal of Neuropsychopharmacology, 9,* 63–76.

Kirsch, I., Montgomery, G., & Sapirstein, G. (1995). Hypnosis as an adjunct to cognitive behavioral psychotherapy: A meta analysis. *Journal of Consulting and Clinical Psychology, 63,* 214–220.

Kirschenbaum, H., & Jourdan, A. (2005). The current status of Carl Rogers and the person-centered approach. *Psychotherapy: Theory, Research, Practice, Training, 42,* 37–51.

Kisilevsky, B. S., Hains, S. M. J., Lee, K., Xie, X., Huang, H., Ye, H. H., . . . Wang, Z. (2003). Effects of experience on fetal voice recognition. *Psychological Science, 14,* 220–224.

Kisley, M. A., Wood, S., & Burrows, C. L. (2007). Looking at the sunny side of life: Age-related change in an event-related potential measure of the negativity bias. *Psychological Science, 18,* 838–843.

Kiss, S. (2001). The formation of the object concept during ontogeny. *Pszichológia: Az MTA Pszichológiai Intézetenek folyóirata, 21,* 249–267.

Kitayama, S., Duffy, S., Kawamura, T., & Larsen, J. T. (2003). Perceiving an object and its context in different cultures: A cultural look at New Look. *Psychological Science, 14,* 201–206.

Kleim, J. A., Vij, K., Ballard, D. H., & Greenough, W. T. (1997). Learning-dependent synaptic modifications in the cerebellar cortex of the adult rat persist for at least four weeks. *The Journal of Neuroscience, 17,* 717–721.

Klein, G. S. (1951). The personal world through perception. In R. R. Blake & G. V. Ramsey (Eds.), *Perception: An approach to personality* (pp. 328–355). New York, NY: Ronald Press.

Klein, O., Snyder, M., & Livingston, R. W. (2004). Prejudice on the stage: Self-monitoring and the public expression of group attitudes. *British Journal of Social Psychology, 43,* 299–314.

Kline, K. (2008, August). Nature and nurture as allies. *Observer: Association for Psychological Science, 21*(7). Retrieved from http://www.psychologicalscience. org/observer/getArticle.cfm?id=2374

Kling, K. C., Hyde, J. S., Showers, C. J., & Buswell, B. N. (1999). Gender differences in self-esteem: A meta-analysis. *Psychological Bulletin, 125,* 470–500.

Kluger, J. (2010, August 16). Inside the minds of animals. *Time,* 36–43.

Knecht, S., Dräger, B., Deppe, M., Bobe, L., Lohmann, H., & Flöel, A., . . . Hennigsen, H. (2000). Handedness and hemispheric language dominance in healthy humans. *Brain: A Journal of Neurology, 123,* 2512–2518.

Knickmeyer, R. C., Wheelwright, S., Taylor, K., Raggatt, P., Hackett, G., & Baron-Cohen, S. (2005). Gender-typed play and amniotic testosterone. *Developmental Psychology, 41,* 517–528.

Knierim, J. J. (2007, June/July). The matrix in your head. *Scientific American Mind, 18*(3), 43–49.

Knight, G. P., Fabes, R. A., & Higgins, D. A. (1996). Concerns about drawing causal inferences from meta-analyses: An example in the study of gender differences in aggression. *Psychological Bulletin, 119,* 410–421.

Kobasa, S. C. (1979). Stressful life events, personality, and health: An inquiry into hardiness. *Journal of Personality and Social Psychology, 37,* 1–11.

Kobayashi, H. (2007). Mimicry as social glue: Spontaneous mimicry in autism spectrum disorder. *Japanese Psychological Review, 50,* 89–95.

Koenig, H. G., McCullough, M. E., & Larson, D. B. (2000). *Handbook of religion and health.* New York, NY: Oxford University Press.

Kohlberg, L. (1969). Stage and sequence: The cognitive–developmental approach to socialization. In D. A. Goslin (Ed.), *Handbook of socialization theory and research* (pp. 347–480). Chicago, IL: Rand McNally.

Kohlberg, L. (1979). *The meaning and measurement of moral development* (Clark Lectures). Worcester, MA: Clark University Press.

Kohlberg, L. (1981). *The philosophy of moral development* (Vol. 1). San Francisco, CA: Harper & Row.

Kohn, A. (1993). *Punished by rewards.* Boston, MA: Houghton Mifflin.

Kokaia, Z., & Lindvall, O. (2003). Neurogenesis after ischaemic brain insults. *Current Opinion in Neurobiology, 13,* 127–132.

Kolb, B., Gibb, R., & Robinson, T. E. (2003). Brain plasticity and behavior. *Current Directions in Psychological Science, 12*, 1–5.

Komaki, J. L. (2003). Reinforcement theory at work: Enhancing and explaining what employees do. In L. W. Porter, G. A. Bigley, & R. M Steers (Eds.), *Motivation and work behavior* (7th ed., pp. 95–112). Boston, MA: McGraw-Hill Irwin.

Komarraju, M., Karau, S. J., & Schmeck, R. R. (2009). Role of the big five personality traits in predicting college students' academic motivation and achievement. *Learning and Individual Differences, 19*, 47–52.

Komiya, N., Good, G. E., & Sherrod, N. B. (2000). Emotional openness as a predictor of college students' attitudes toward seeking psychological help. *Journal of Counseling Psychology, 47*, 138–143.

Kong, J., Gollub, R. L., Rosman, I. S., Webb, J. M., Vangel, M. G., Kirsch, I., & Kaptchuk, T. J. (2006). Brain activity associated with expectancy-enhanced placebo analgesia as measured by Functional Magnetic Resonance Imaging. *The Journal of Neuroscience, 26*, 381–388.

Konishi, Y. (2010). Making working mothers: The unhappy marriage of neoliberalism and feminism in contemporary Japan. *Dissertation Abstracts International: Section A. Humanities and Social Sciences, 71*, 2118.

Konrad, K., Neufang, S., Hanisch, C., Fink, G. R., & Herpertz-Dahlmann, B. (2006). Dysfunctional attentional networks in children with attention deficit/hyperactivity disorder: Evidence from an event-related functional magnetic resonance imaging study. *Biological Psychiatry, 59*, 643–651.

Kontula, O., & Haavio-Mannila, E. (2009). The impact of aging on human sexual activity and sexual desire. *Journal of Sex Research, 46*, 46–56.

Koopman, C., Ismailji, T., Holmes, D., Classen, C. C., Palesh, O., & Wales, T. (2005). The effects of expressive writing on pain, depression and posttraumatic stress disorder symptoms in survivors of intimate partner violence. *Journal of Health Psychology, 10*, 211–221.

Koordeman, R., Anschutz, D. J., van Baaren, R. B., & Engels, R. E. (2010). Exposure to soda commercials affects sugar-sweetened soda consumption in young women. An observational experimental study. *Appetite, 54*, 619–622. doi:10.1016/j.appet.2010.03.008

Kop, W. J. (2005). Psychological interventions in patients with coronary heart disease. In L. C. James & R. A. Folen (Eds.), *The primary care consultant: The next frontier for psychologists in hospitals and clinics* (pp. 61–81). Washington, DC: American Psychological Association.

Kopta, S. M., Howard, K. I., Lowry, J. L., & Beutler, L. E. (1994). Patterns of symptomatic recovery in psychotherapy. *Journal of Consulting and Clinical Psychology, 62*, 1009–1016.

Korol, D. L., & Gold, P. E. (2007). Modulation of learning and memory by adrenal and ovarian hormones. In R. P. Kesner & J. L. Martinez (Eds.), *Neurobiology of learning and memory* (2nd ed., pp. 243–268). San Diego, CA: Elsevier Academic Press.

Kort-Butler, L. A. (2009). Coping styles and sex differences in depressive symptoms and delinquent behavior. *Journal of Youth and Adolescence, 38*, 122–136.

Koss, M. P. (1990). Violence against women. *American Psychologist, 45*, 374–380.

Kotov, R., Gamez, W., Schmidt, F., & Watson, D. (2010). Linking "big" personality traits to anxiety, depressive, and substance use disorders: A meta-analysis. *Psychological Bulletin, 136*, 768–821.

Kotzalidis, G. D., Patrizi, B., Caltagirone, S. S., Koukopoulos, A., Savoja, V., Ruberto, G., . . . Girardi, P. (2007). The adult SSRI/SNRI withdrawal syndrome: A clinically heterogeneous entity. *Clinical Neuropsychiatry: Journal of Treatment Evaluation, 4*, 61–75.

Kounios, J., Fleck, J. I., Green, D. L., Payne, L., Stevenson, J. L., Bowden, E. M., & Jung-Beeman, M. (2008). The origins of insight in resting-state brain activity. *Neuropsychologia, 46*, 281–291.

Koyama, T., McHaffie, J. G., Laurienti, P. J., & Coghill, R. C. (2005). The subjective experience of pain: Where expectations become reality. *PNAS Proceedings of the National Academy of Sciences of the United States of America, 102*, 12950–12955.

Kramer, A. F., & Willis, S. L. (2002). Enhancing the cognitive vitality of older adults. *Current Directions in Psychological Science, 11*, 173–176.

Kraut, R., & Kiesler, S. (2003). The social impact of Internet use. *Psychological Science Agenda, 16*(4), 11–14.

Kraut, R., Kiesler, S., Boneva, B., Cummings, J. N., Helgeson, V., & Crawford, A. M. (2002). Internet paradox revisited. *Journal of Social Issues, 58*, 49–74.

Kraut, R., Patterson, M., Lundmark, V., Kiesler, S., Mukopadhyay, T., & Scherlis, W. (1998). Internet paradox: A social technology that reduces social involvement and psychological well-being? *American Psychologist, 53*, 1017–1031.

Kringelbach, M. L., & Aziz, T. Z. (2009). Deep brain stimulation: Avoiding the errors of psychosurgery. *JAMA: Journal of the American Medical Association, 301*, 1705–1707.

Kroll, J. F. (2009). The consequences of bilingualism for the mind and the brain. *Psychological Science in the Public Interest, 10*, i–ii.

Kropp, P., Siniatchkin, M., & Gerber, W.-D. (2005). On the pathophysiology of migraine—Links for "empirically based treatment" with neurofeedback. *Applied Psychophysiology and Biofeedback, 27*, 203–213.

Kruglinski, S. (2004, September 14). When vision goes, the hallucinations begin. *New York Times*, p. D7.

Krützen, M., Mann, J., Meithaus, M. R., Connor, R. C., Bejder, L., & Sherwin, W. B. (2005). Cultural transmission of tool use in bottlenose dolphins. *PNAS Proceedings of the National Academy of Sciences, 95*, 8939–8943.

Krystal, A. D., Holsinger, T., Weiner, R. D., & Coffey, C. E. (2000). Prediction of the utility of a switch from unilateral to bilateral ECT in the elderly using treatment 2 ictal EEG indices. *Journal of ECT, 16*, 327–337.

Kübler-Ross, E. (1969). *On death and dying*. New York, NY: Macmillan.

Kubzansky, L. D., Koenen, K. C., Jones, C., & Eaton, W. W. (2009). A prospective study of posttraumatic stress disorder symptoms and coronary heart disease in women. *Health Psychology, 28*, 125–130.

Kucharski, L. T., Johnsen, D., & Procell, S. (2004). The utility of the MMPI-2 infrequency psychopathology F(p) and the revised infrequency psychopathology scales in the detection of malingering. *American Journal of Forensic Psychology, 22*, 33–40.

Kudo, E., & Numazaki, M. (2003). Explicit and direct self-serving bias in Japan. Reexamination of self-serving bias for success and failure. *Journal of Cross-Cultural Psychology, 34*, 511–521.

Kuflik, A. (2008). The "future like ours" argument and human embryonic stem cell research. *Journal of Medical Ethics, 34*, 417–421.

Kugler, P. (2004). Reading psychoanalysis: Freud, Rank, Ferenczi, Groddeck. *The Journal of Analytical Psychology, 49*, 271–274.

Kuhn, D. (2009). Adolescent thinking. In R. Lerner & L. Steinberg (Eds.), *Handbook of adolescent psychology* (3rd ed., Vol. 1, pp. 152–156). New York, NY: Wiley.

Kumkale, G. T., & Albarracín, D. (2004). The sleeper effect: A meta-analytic review. *Psychological Bulletin, 130*, 143–172.

Kumra, S. (2008). Digging deeper using neuroimaging tools reveals important clues to early-onset schizophrenia. *Journal of the American Academy of Child & Adolescent Psychiatry, 47*, 1103–1104.

Kumra, S., Oberstar, J. V., Sikich, L., Findling, R. L., McClellan, J. M., Vinogradov, S., & Schulz, S. C. (2008). Efficacy and tolerability of second-generation antipsychotics in children and adolescents with schizophrenia. *Schizophrenia Bulletin, 34*, 60–71.

Kuncel, N. R., Hezlett, S. A., & Ones, D. S. (2004). Academic performance, career potential, creativity, and job performance: Can one construct predict them all? *Journal of Personality and Social Psychology, 86*, 148–161.

Kung, H. C., Hoyert, D. L., Xu, J. Q., & Murphy, S. L. (2008). Deaths: Final data for 2005. *National Vital Statistics Reports, 56*(10). Hyattsville, MD: National Center for Health Statistics.

Kunkel, D., Wilson, B. J., Linz, D., Potter, W. J., Donnerstein, E., Smith, S. L., . . . Grey, T. E. (1996). *The national television violence study*. Studio City, CA: Mediascope.

Kuratomi, G., Iwamoto, K., Bundo, M., Kusumi, I., Kato, N., Iwata, N., . . . Kato, T. (2008). Aberrant DNA methylation associated with bipolar disorder identified from discordant monozygotic twins. *Molecular Psychiatry, 13*, 429–441.

Kurdek, L. A. (2005). What do we know about gay and lesbian couples? *Current Directions in Psychological Science, 14*, pp. 251–254.

Kuroshima, H., Kuwahata, H., & Fujita, K. (2008). Learning from others' mistakes in capuchin monkeys (Cebus apella). *Animal Cognition, 11*, 599–609.

Kurtz, L. D. (2004). Support and self-help groups. In C. D. Garvin, L. M. Gutiérrez, & M. J. Galinsky (Eds.), *Handbook of social work with groups* (pp. 139–159). New York, NY: Guilford Press.

Kuseske, J. (2008). The influence of self-focused attention on satisfaction with physical appearance in relation to self-esteem in adolescents. *Dissertation Abstracts International: Section B: The Sciences and Engineering, 69*, 2654.

Kwallek, N., Soon, K., & Lewis, C. M. (2007). Work week productivity, visual complexity, and individual environmental sensitivity in three offices of different color interiors. *Color Research and Application, 32*, 130–143.

Kwon, S. M., & Oei, T. P. S. (2003). Cognitive change processes in a group cognitive behavior therapy of depression. *Journal of Behavior Therapy and Experimental Psychiatry, 34,* 73–85.

LaBar, K. S. (2007). Beyond fear: Emotional memory mechanisms in the human brain. *Current Directions in Psychological Science, 16,* 173–177.

LaBar, K. S., & Cabeza, R. (2006). Cognitive neuroscience of emotional memory. *Nature Reviews Neuroscience, 7,* 54–64.

Lachman, M. E. (2004). Development in midlife. *Annual Review of Psychology, 55,* 305–331.

Lachman, S. J. (1984, August). *Processes in visual misperception: Illusions for highly structured stimulus material.* Paper presented at the 92nd annual convention of the American Psychological Association, Toronto, Canada.

Laganà, L., & Sosa, G. (2004). Depression among ethnically diverse older women: The role of demographic and cognitive factors. *Educational Gerontology, 30,* 801–820.

Laird, J. (2003). Lesbian and gay families. In F. Walsh (Ed.), *Normal family processes: Growing diversity and complexity* (3rd ed., pp. 176–209). New York, NY: Guilford Press.

LaMalfa, G., Lassi, S., Bertelli, M., Salvini, R., & Placidi, G. F. (2004). Autism and intellectual disability: A study of prevalence on a sample of the Italian population. *Journal of Intellectual Disability Research, 48,* 262–267.

Lamb, H. R., & Weinberger, L. E. (2001). *Deinstitutionalization: Promise and problems.* San Francisco, CA: Jossey-Bass.

Lamberg, L. (1998). New drug for erectile dysfunction boon for many, "viagravation" for some. *JAMA: Medical News & Perspectives, 280,* 867–871.

Lambert, M. J., & Archer, A. (2006). Research findings on the effects of psychotherapy and their implications for practice. In C. D. Goodheart, A. E. Kazdin, & R. J. Sternberg (Eds.), *Evidence-based psychotherapy: Where practice and research meet* (pp. 111–130). Washington, DC: American Psychological Association.

Lambert, W. W., Solomon, R. L., & Watson, P. D. (1949). Reinforcement and extinction as factors in size estimation. *Journal of Experimental Psychology, 39,* 637–641.

Lampl, M., Veidhuis, J. D., & Johnson, M. L. (1992). Saltation and stasis: A model of human growth. *Science, 258,* 801–803.

Lanciano, T., Curci, A., & Semin, G. R. (2010). The emotional and reconstructive determinants of emotional memories: An experimental approach to flashbulb memory investigation. *Memory, 18,* 473–485.

Landrigan, C. P. (2005). Sliding down the bell curve: Effects of 24-hour work shifts on physicians' cognition and performance. *Sleep, 28,* 1351–1353.

Landrigan, C. P., Rothschild, J. M., Cronin, J. W., Kaushal, R., Burdick, E., Katz, J. T., . . . Czeisler, C. A. (2004). Effect of reducing interns' work hours on serious medical errors in intensive care units. *The New England Journal of Medicine, 351,* 1838–1848.

Landy, F. J. (1987). *Psychology: The science of people.* Englewood Cliffs, NJ: Prentice Hall.

Landy, F. J., & Conte, J. M. (2004). *Work in the 21st century.* New York, NY: McGraw-Hill.

Lane, H.-Y., Liu, Y.-C., Huang, C.-L., Chang, Y.-C., Wu, P.-L., Lu, C.-T., & Chang, W.-H. (2006). Risperidone-related weight gain: Genetic and nongenetic predictors. *Journal of Clinical Psychopharmacology, 26,* 128–134.

Lane, S. D., Cherek, D. R., Lieving, L. M., & Tcheremissine, O. V. (2005). Marijuana effects on human forgetting functions. *Journal of the Experimental Analysis of Behavior, 83,* 67–83.

Langlois, J. H., Ritter, J. M., Casey, R. J., & Sawin, D. B. (1995). Infant attractiveness predicts maternal behaviors and attitudes. *Developmental Psychology, 31,* 464–472.

Langosch, W., Budde, H.-G, & Linden, W. (2007). Psychological interventions for coronary heart disease: Stress management, relaxation, and Ornish groups. In J. Jordan, B. Bardé, & A. M. Zeiher (Eds.), *Contributions toward evidence-based psychocardiology: A systematic review of the literature* (pp. 231–254). Washington, DC: American Psychological Association.

Lansford, J. E. (2009). Parental divorce and children's adjustment. *Perspectives on Psychological Science, 4,* 140–152.

Lansford, J. E., & Dodge, K. A. (2008). Cultural norms for adult corporal punishment of children and societal rates of endorsement and use of violence. *Parenting: Science and Practice, 8,* 257–270.

Lanza, S. T., & Collins, L. M. (2002). Pubertal timing and the onset of substance use in females during early adolescence. *Prevention Science, 3,* 69–82.

Latané, B., & Rodin, J. (1969). A lady in distress: Inhibiting effects of friends and strangers on bystander intervention. *Journal of Experimental Social Psychology, 5,* 189–202.

Lawrence, C. J., Lott, I., & Haier, R. J. (2005). Neurobiology of autism, mental retardation, and Down syndrome: What can we learn about intelligence? In C. Stough (Ed.), *Neurobiology of exceptionality* (pp. 125–142). New York, NY: Kluwer/Plenum.

Lawrie, S. M., McIntosh, A. M., Hall, J., Owens, D. G. C., & Johnstone, E. C. (2008). Brain structure and function changes during the development of schizophrenia: The evidence from studies of subjects at increased genetic risk. *Schizophrenia Bulletin, 34,* 330–340.

Laws, E. L., Apperson, J. M., Buchert, S., & Bregman, N. J. (2010). Student evaluations of instruction: When are enduring first impressions formed? *North American Journal of Psychology, 12,* 81–92.

Layng, T. (2010). Buying green. *The Behavior Analyst, 33,* 175–177.

Lazar, S. W., Bush, G., Gollub, R. L., Fricchione, G. L., Khalsa, G., & Benson, H. (2000). Neuroreport: Functional brain mapping of the relaxation response and meditation. *For Rapid Communication of Neuroscience Research, 11,* 1581–1585.

Lazarus, R. S. (1981, July). Little hassles can be hazardous to health. *Psychology Today,* 58–62.

Lazarus, R. S. (1991). Cognition and motivation in emotion. *American Psychologist, 46,* 352–367.

Leahy, R. L. (2004). *Contemporary cognitive therapy: Theory, research, and practice.* New York, NY: Guilford Press.

Leary, C. E., Kelley, M. L., Morrow, J., & Mikulka, P. J. (2008). Parental use of physical punishment as related to family environment, psychological well-being, and personality in undergraduates. *Journal of Family Violence, 23,* 1–7.

Leary, M. R., Kowalski, R. M., Smith, L., & Phillips, S. (2003). Teasing, rejection, and violence: Case studies of the school shootings. *Aggressive Behavior, 29,* 202–214.

Leckman, J. F., Hrdy, S. B., Keverne, E. B., & Carter, C. (2006). A biobehavioral model of attachment and bonding. In R. J. Sternberg & K. Weis (Eds.), *The new psychology of love* (pp. 116–145). New Haven, CT: Yale University Press.

Lee, L., Loewenstein, G., Ariely, D., Hong, J., & Young, J. (2008). If I'm not hot, are you hot or not? Physical-attractiveness evaluations and dating preferences as a function of one's own attractiveness. *Psychological Science, 19,* 669–677.

Lehnert, G., & Zimmer, H. D. (2008). Modality and domain specific components in auditory and visual working memory tasks. *Cognitive Processing, 9,* 53–61.

Leichsenring, F. (2005). Are psychodynamic and psychoanalytic therapies effective? A review of empirical data. *International Journal of Psychoanalysis, 86,* 841–868.

Leichsenring, F., & Leibing, E. (2003). The effectiveness of psychodynamic therapy and cognitive behavior therapy in the treatment of personality disorders: A meta-analysis. *American Journal of Psychiatry, 160,* 1223–1232.

Leifer, M., Kilbane, T., & Kalick, S. (2004). Vulnerability or resilience to intergenerational sexual abuse: The role of maternal factors. *Child Maltreatment: Journal of the American Professional Society on the Abuse of Children, 9,* 78–91.

Leigh, H. (2009). A proposal for a new multiaxial model of psychiatric diagnosis: A continuum-based patient model derived from evolutionary developmental gene-environment interaction. *Psychopathology, 42,* 1–10.

Leitzell, K. (2008, February/March). Irritable? Take a nap. *Scientific American Mind, 19*(1), 10.

Lennon, M. C., & Limonic, L. (2010). Work and unemployment as stressors. In T. L. Scheid & T. N. Brown (Eds.), *A handbook for the study of mental health: Social contexts, theories, and systems* (2nd ed., pp. 213–225). New York, NY: Cambridge University Press.

Leonardo, E. D., & Hen, R. (2006). Genetics of affective and anxiety disorders. *Annual Review of Psychology, 57,* 117–137.

Lequerica, A. H., Forchheimer, M., Tate, D. G., Roller, S., & Toussaint, L. (2008). Ways of coping and perceived stress in women with spinal cord injury. *Journal of Health Psychology, 13,* 348–354.

Lerman, C., Caporaso, N. E., Audrain, J., Main, D., Bowman, E. D., Lockshin, B., . . . Shields, P. G. (1999). Evidence suggesting the role of specific genetic factors in cigarette smoking. *Health Psychology, 18,* 14–20.

Lerman, H. (1996). *Pigeonholing women's misery: A history and critical analysis of the psychodiagnosis of women in the twentieth century.* New York, NY: Basic Books.

Lerner, M. [Marc], & Wigal, T. (2008). Long-term safety of stimulant medications used to treat children with ADHD. *Journal of Psychosocial Nursing & Mental Health Services, 46,* 39–48.

Lerner, M. J. [Melvyn]. (1980). *The belief in a just world: A fundamental delusion.* New York, NY: Plenum.

Leschied, A. W., & Cummings, A. L. (2002). Youth violence: An overview of predictors, counseling interventions, and future directions. *Canadian Journal of Counseling, 36,* 256–264.

Lester, P. B., McBride, S., Bliese, P. D., & Adler, A. B. (2011). Bringing science to bear: An empirical assessment of the comprehensive soldier fitness program. *American Psychologist, 66,* 77–81.

Leuner, K., & Müller, W. E. (2006). The complexity of the dopaminergic synapses and their modulation by antipsychotics. *Pharmacopsychiatry, 39*(Suppl. 1), S15–20.

Leutwyler-Ozelli, K. (2007, September). This is your brain on food. *Scientific American, 297*(3), 84–85.

Leuzinger-Bohleber, M. (Ed.), Engels, E. (Ed.), & Tsiantis, J. (Ed.). (2008). *The Janus face of prenatal diagnostics: A European study bridging ethics, psychoanalysis, and medicine.* London, England: Karnac Books.

Lev-Wiesel, R. (2008). Child sexual abuse: A critical review of intervention and treatment modalities. *Children and Youth Services Review, 30,* 665–673.

LeVay, S. (1991). A difference in hypothalamic structure between heterosexual and homosexual men. *Science, 253,* 1034–1038.

LeVay, S. (2011). *Gay, straight, and the reason why: The science of sexual orientation.* New York, NY: Oxford University Press.

LeVay, S., & Hamer, D. H. (1994, May). Evidence for a biological influence in male homosexuality. *Scientific American, 270*(5), 44–49.

Levin, B. E. (2010). Developmental gene × environment interactions affecting systems regulating energy homeostasis and obesity. *Frontiers in Neuroendocrinology, 31,* 270–283.

Levin, F. R., McDowell, D., Evans, S. M., Nunes, E., Akerele, E., Donovan, S., & Vosburg, S. K. (2004). Pharmacotherapy for marijuana dependence: A double-blind, placebo-controlled pilot study of divalproex sodium. *American Journal on Addictions, 13,* 21–32.

Levin, J. S., & Vanderpool, H. Y. (1989). Is religion therapeutically significant for hypertension? *Social Science and Medicine, 29,* 69–78.

Levine, C. (2003). Introduction: Structure, development, and identity formation. *Identity, 3,* 191–195.

Levine, E. L., Sistrunk, F., McNutt, K. J., & Gael, S. (1988). Exploring job analysis systems in selected organizations: A description of process and outcomes. *Journal of Business and Psychology, 3,* 3–21.

Levine, S. B. (2006). The PDE-5 inhibitors and psychiatry. *Journal of Psychiatric Practice, 12,* 46–49.

Levinson, D. J. (1978). *The seasons of a man's life.* New York, NY: Knopf.

Levinson, D. J. (1986). A conception of adult development. *American Psychologist, 41,* 3–13.

Levinson, D. J. (1987). *The seasons of a woman's life.* New York, NY: Knopf.

Levy, B. R. (2009). Stereotype embodiment: A psychosocial approach to aging. *Current Directions in Psychological Science, 18,* 332–336.

Levy, B. R., Zonderman, A. B., Slade, M. D., & Ferrucci, L. (2009). Age stereotypes held earlier in life predict cardiovascular events later in life. *Psychological Science, 20,* 296–298.

Levy, J., & Pashler, H. (2008). Task prioritisation in multitasking during driving: Opportunity to abort a concurrent task does not insulate braking responses from dual-task slowing. *Applied Cognitive Psychology, 22,* 507–525.

Levy, J., Pashler, H., & Boer, E. (2006). Central interference in driving: Is there any stopping the psychological refractory period? *Psychological Science, 17,* 228–235.

Levy, T. M., & Orlans, M. (2004). Attachment disorder, antisocial personality, and violence. *Annals of the American Psychotherapy Association, 7,* 18–23.

Lewin, K. A. (1935). *A dynamic theory of personality* (K. E. Zener & D. K. Adams, trans.). New York, NY: McGraw-Hill.

Lewin, T. (1994, May 18). Boys are more comfortable with sex than girls are, survey finds. *New York Times,* p. A10.

Lewin, T. (1995, May 30). The decay of families is global study says. *New York Times,* p. A5.

Lewis, I., Watson, B., & White, K. (2008). An examination of message-relevant affect in road safety messages: Should road safety advertisements aim to make us feel good or bad? *Transportation Research Part F: Traffic Psychology and Behaviour, 11,* 403–417.

Leyro, T. M., Zvolensky, M. J., & Bernstein, A. (2010). Distress tolerance and psychopathological symptoms and disorders: A review of the empirical literature among adults. *Psychological Bulletin, 136,* 576–600.

Li, S.-C., Schmiedek, F., Huxhold, O., Röcke, C., Smith, J., & Lindenberger, U. (2008). Working memory plasticity in old age: Practice gain, transfer, and maintenance. *Psychology and Aging, 23,* 731–742.

Li, Y., & Hou, Y. (2005). Burnout, stress and depression. *Psychological Science* (China), *28,* 972–974.

Li, Y., Johnson, E. J., & Zaval, L. (2011). Local warming: Daily temperature change influences belief in global warming. *Psychological Science, 22,* 454–459.

Lichtenstein, P., Yip, B. H., Björk, C., Pawitan, Y., Cannon, T. D., Sullivan, P. F., & Hultman, C. M. (2009). Common genetic determinants of schizophrenia and bipolar disorder in Swedish families: A population-based study. *Lancet, 373,* 234–239.

Liddle, H. A., & Rowe, C. L. (2002). Multidimensional family therapy for adolescent drug abuse: Making the case for a developmental-contextual, family-based intervention. In D. W. Brook & H. I. Spitz (Eds.), *The group therapy of substance abuse* (pp. 275–291). New York, NY: Haworth.

Liggett, D. R. (2000). *Sport hypnosis.* Champaign, IL: Human Kinetics.

Lightdale, J. R., & Prentice, D. A. (1994). Rethinking sex differences in aggression: Aggressive behavior in the absence of social roles. *Personality and Social Psychology Bulletin, 20,* 34–44.

Lilienfeld, S. O., & Arkowitz, H. (2008, February/March). Uncovering "Brainscams." *Scientific American Mind, 19*(1), 80–81.

Lilienfeld, S. O., & Lynn, S. J. (2003). Dissociative identity disorder: Multiple personalities, multiple controversies. In S. O. Lilienfeld & S. J. Lynn (Eds.), *Science and pseudoscience in clinical psychology* (pp. 109–142). New York, NY: Guilford Press.

Lin, C., Lane, H., & Tsai, G. E. (2011). Glutamate signaling in the pathophysiology and therapy of schizophrenia. *Pharmacology, Biochemistry and Behavior.* Advance online publication. doi:10.1016/j.pbb.2011.03.023

Lin, L., & Reid, K. (2009). The relationship between media exposure and antifat attitudes: The role of dysfunctional appearance beliefs. *Body Image, 6,* 52–55.

Lindau, S. T., Schumm, L. P., Laumann, E. O., Levinson, W., O'Muircheartaigh, C. A., & Waite, L. J. (2007). A study of sexuality and health among older adults in the United States. *New England Journal of Medicine, 357,* 762–775.

Lindberg, S. M., Hyde, J. S., Petersen, J. L., & Linn, M. C. (2010). New trends in gender and mathematics performance: A meta-analysis. *Psychological Bulletin, 136,* 1123–1135.

Lindsay, D. S., & Read, J. D. (2006). *Memory and society: Psychological perspectives.* New York, NY: Psychology Press.

Lipina, T. V., Kaidanovich-Beilin, O., Patel, S., Wang, M., Clapcote, S. J., Liu, F., & Roder, J. C. (2011). Genetic and pharmacological evidence for schizophrenia-related Disc1 interaction with GSK-3. *Synapse, 65,* 234–248.

Lipman, S. (1991). *Laughter in Hell: The use of humor during the Holocaust.* Northvale, NJ: Aronson.

Lippa, R. R. (2005). *Gender, nature, and nurture* (2nd ed.). Mahwah, NJ: Erlbaum.

Lipsky, S., Field, C. A., Caetano, R., & Larkin, G. L. (2005). Posttraumatic stress disorder symptomatology and comorbid depressive symptoms among abused women referred from emergency department care. *Violence and Victims, 20,* 645–659.

Liu, I.-C., Blacker, D. L., Xu, R., Fitzmaurice, G., Tsuang, M. T., & Lyons, M. J. (2004). Genetic and environmental contributions to age of onset of alcohol dependence symptoms in male twins. *Addiction, 99,* 1403–1409.

Liu, J. H., & Latane, B. (1998). Extremitization of attitudes: Does thought-and-discussion-induced polarization cumulate? *Basic and Applied Social Psychology, 20,* 103–110.

LoBue, V., & DeLoache, J. S. (2008). Detecting the snake in the grass: Attention to fear-relevant stimuli by adults and young children. *Psychological Science, 19,* 284–289.

LoBue, V., Rakison, D. H., & DeLoache, J. S. (2010). Threat perception across the life span: Evidence for multiple converging pathways. *Current Directions in Psychological Science, 19,* 375–379.

Locke, E. A., & Latham, G. P. (2002). Building a practically useful theory of goal setting and task motivation: A 35-year odyssey. *American Psychologist, 57,* 705–717.

Loftus, E. F., Garry, M., & Hayne, H. (2008). Repressed and recovered memory. In E. Borgida & S. T. Fiske (Eds.), *Beyond common sense: Psychological science in the courtroom* (pp. 177–194). Malden, MA: Blackwell.

Loftus, E. F., & Palmer, J. C. (1974). Reconstruction of automobile destruction: An example of the interaction between language and memory. *Journal of Verbal Learning and Verbal Behavior, 13,* 585–589.

Loftus, E. F., & Pickrell, J. E. (1995). The formation of false memories. *Psychiatric Annals, 25,* 720–725.

Logue, A. W. (2000). Self-control and health behavior. In W. K. Bickel & R. E. Vuchinich (Eds.), *Reframing health behavior change with behavioral economics* (pp. 167–192). Mahwah, NJ: Erlbaum.

Lonsdorf, E. V. (2005). Sex differences in the development of termite-fishing skills in wild chimpanzees (*Pan troglodytes schweinfurthii*) of Gombe National Park, Tanzania. *Animal Behaviour, 70,* 673–683.

López, S. R., & Guarnaccia, P. J. J. (2000). Cultural psychopathology: Uncovering the social world of mental illness. *Annual Review of Psychology, 51,* 571–598.

Lorenz, K. (1935). Der Kumpan in der Umwelt des Vogels. *Journal of Ornithology, 83,* 137–213, 289–413.

Lorenzo, G. L., Biesanz, J. C., & Human, L. J. (2010). What is beautiful is good and more accurately understood: Physical attractiveness and accuracy in first impressions of personality. *Psychological Science, 21,* 1777–1782.

Losh, M., Sullivan, P. F., Trembath, D., & Piven, J. (2008). Current developments in the genetics of autism: From phenome to genome. *Journal of Neuropathology and Experimental Neurology, 67,* 829–837.

Lovaglia, M., Mannix, E. A., Samuelson, C. D., Sell, J., & Wilson, R. K. (2005). Conflict, power, and status in groups. In M. S. Poole, & A. B. Hollingshead (Eds.), *Theories of small groups: Interdisciplinary perspectives* (pp. 139–184). Thousand Oaks, CA: Sage.

Lovibond, P. F., Siddle, D. A., & Bond, N. W. (1993). Resistance to extinction of fear-relevant stimuli: Preparedness or selective sensitization? *Journal of Experimental Psychology: General, 122,* 449–461.

Lu, Y., Christian, K., & Lu, B. (2008). BDNF: A key regulator for protein synthesis-dependent LTP and long-term memory? *Neurobiology of Learning and Memory, 89,* 312–323.

Lucas, R. E. (2005). Time does not heal all wounds: A longitudinal study of reaction and adaptation to divorce. *Psychological Science, 16,* 945–950.

Luciano, M., Wainwright, M. A., Wright, M. J., & Martin, N. G. (2006). The heritability of conscientiousness facets and their relationship to IQ and academic achievement. *Personality and Individual Differences, 40,* 1189–1199.

Lumeng, J. C., Somashekar, D., Appugliese, D., Kaciroti, N., Corwyn, R. F., & Bradley, R. H. (2007). Sleep characteristics and overweight risk at ages 9–12 years. *Pediatrics, 120,* 1020–1029.

Lundström, J. N., & Olsson, M. J. (2005). Subthreshold amounts of social odorant affect mood, but not behavior, in heterosexual women when tested by a male, but not a female, experimenter. *Biological Psychology, 70,* 197–204.

Luo, F., Florence, C. S., Quispe-Agnoli, M., Ouyang, L., & Crosby, A. E. (2011). Impact of business cycles on US suicide rates, 1928–2007. *American Journal of Public Health, 101,* 1139–1146.

Luo, Y. (2011). Cell-based therapy for stroke. *Journal of Neural Transmission, 118,* 61–74.

Luria, A. R. (1968). *The mind of a mnemonist* (L. Solotaroff, Trans.). New York, NY: Basic Books.

Luria, A. R., & Solotaroff, L. (1987). *The mind of a mnemonist: A little book about a vast memory.* Cambridge, MA: Harvard University Press.

Lyddon, W. J., & Jones, J. V. (2001). Empirically supported treatments: An introduction. In W. J. Lyddon & J. V. Jones (Eds.), *Empirically supported cognitive therapies: Current and future applications* (pp. 1–12). New York, NY: Springer.

Lykins, A. D., Meana, M., & Strauss, G. P. (2008). Sex differences in visual attention to erotic and non-erotic stimuli. *Archives of Sexual Behavior, 37,* 219–228.

Lyness, S. A. (1993). Predictors of differences between Type A and B individuals in heart rate and blood pressure reactivity. *Psychological Bulletin, 114,* 266–295.

Lynn, S. J., Fassler, O., & Knox, J. (2005). Hypnosis and the altered state debate: Something more or nothing more? Comment. *Contemporary Hypnosis, 22,* 39–45.

Lynn, S. J., & Kirsch, I. (2006a). Anxiety disorders. In S. J. Lynn & I. Kirsch (Eds.), *Essentials of clinical hypnosis: An evidence-based approach* (pp. 135–157). Washington, DC: American Psychological Association.

Lynn, S. J., & Kirsch, I. (2006b). Posttraumatic stress disorder. In S. J. Lynn, & I. Kirsch (Eds.), *Essentials of clinical hypnosis: An evidence-based approach* (pp. 159–173). Washington, DC: American Psychological Association.

Lynn, S. J., & Kirsch, I. (2006c). Questions and controversies. In S. J. Lynn, & I. Kirsch, (Eds.), *Essentials of clinical hypnosis: An evidence-based approach* (pp. 197–213). Washington, DC: American Psychological Association.

Lynn, S. J., Kirsch, I., & Rhue, J. W. (2010). An introduction to clinical hypnosis. In S. Lynn, J. W. Rhue, & I. Kirsch (Eds.), *Handbook of clinical hypnosis* (2nd ed., pp. 3–18). Washington, DC: American Psychological Association.

Lyons, M. J., True, W. R., Eisen, S. A., Goldberg, J., Meyer, J. M., Faraone, S. V., . . . Tsuang, M. T. (1995). Differential heritability of adult and juvenile antisocial traits. *Archives of General Psychiatry, 52,* 906–915.

Ma, D. J. (2004). Wedding planning: Brides' engagement stress and social support. *Dissertation Abstracts International: Section B: The Sciences and Engineering, 65,* 2101.

Maag, J. W., Swearer, S. M., & Toland, M. D. (2009). Cognitive-behavioral interventions for depression in children and adolescents: Meta-analysis, promising programs, and implications for school personnel. In M. J. Mayer, J. E. Lochman, & R. Van Acker (Eds.), *Cognitive-behavioral interventions for emotional and behavioral disorders: School-based practice* (pp. 235–265). New York, NY: Guilford Press.

Macavei, B. (2005). The role of irrational beliefs in the rational emotive behavior theory of depression. *Journal of Cognitive and Behavioral Psychotherapies, 5,* 73–81.

Maccoby, E. E. (1998). *The two sexes: Growing up apart, coming together.* Cambridge, MA: Belknap.

Mack, A. (2003). Inattentional blindness: Looking without seeing. *Current Directions in Psychological Science, 12,* 180–184.

Mackavey, W. R., Malley, J. E., & Stewart, A. J. (1991). Remembering autobiographically consequential experiences: Content analysis of psychologists' accounts of their lives. *Psychology and Aging, 6,* 50–59.

MacKenzie, G., & Donaldson, D. I. (2009). Examining the neural basis of episodic memory: ERP evidence that faces are recollected differently from names. *Neuropsychologia, 47,* 2756–2765.

Mackey, S. (2005). The strain in pain lies mainly in the brain. Retrieved from http://paincenter.stanford.edu/research

MacWhinney, B. (2005). Language evolution and human development. In B. J. Ellis & D. F. Bjorklund (Eds.), *Origins of the social mind: Evolutionary psychology and child development* (pp. 383–410). New York, NY: Guilford Press.

Maddi, S. R. (2008). The courage and strategies of hardiness as helpful in growing despite major, disruptive stresses. *American Psychologist, 63,* 563–564.

Maddi, S. R. (1989). *Personality theories: A comparative approach* (5th ed.). Homewood, IL: Dorsey.

Maio, G. R., & Olson, J. M. (1998). Values as truisms: Evidence and implications. *Journal of Personality and Social Psychology, 74,* 294–311.

Majid, H., & Hirshkowitz, M. (2010). Therapeutics of narcolepsy. *Sleep Medicine Clinics, 5,* 659–673.

Mallimson, K. (2006). Survivor guilt and posttraumatic stress disorder 18 months after September 11, 2001: Influences of prior trauma, exposure to the event, and bereavement. *Dissertation Abstracts International: Section B: The Sciences and Engineering, 66,* 5096.

Malott, R. W. (2010). I'll save the world from global warming—tomorrow: Using procrastination management to combat global warming. *The Behavior Analyst, 33,* 179–180.

Malterer, M. B., Glass, S. J., & Newman, J. P. (2008). Psychopathy and trait emotional intelligence. *Personality and Individual Differences, 44,* 735–745.

Manber, R., Kraemer, H. C., Arnow, B. A., Trivedi, M. H., Rush, A. J., Thase, M. E., . . . Keller, M. E. (2008). Faster remission of chronic depression with combined psychotherapy and medication than with each therapy alone. *Journal of Consulting and Clinical Psychology, 76,* 459–467.

Mandeville-Norden, R., & Beech, A. R. (2009). Development of a psychometric typology of child molesters: Implications for treatment. *Journal of Interpersonal Violence, 24,* 307–325.

Manger, T. A., & Motta, R. W. (2005). The impact of an exercise program on posttraumatic stress disorder, anxiety, and depression. *International Journal of Emergency Mental Health, 7,* 49–57.

Mann, K., Ackermann, K., Croissant, B., Mundle, G., Nakovics, H., & Diehl, A. (2005). Neuroimaging of gender differences in alcohol dependence: Are women more vulnerable? *Alcoholism: Clinical and Experimental Research, 29,* 896–901.

Mann, R. E., Zhao, J., Stoduto, G., Adlaf, E. M., Smart, R. G., & Donovan, J. E. (2007). Road rage and collision involvement. *American Journal of Health Behavior, 31,* 384–391.

Mann, T., Tomiyama, A. J., Westling, E., Lew, A.-M., Samuels, B., & Chatman, J. (2007). Medicare's search for effective obesity treatments: Diets are not the answer. *American Psychologist, 62,* 220–233.

Manns, J. R., Hopkins, R. O., & Squire, L. R. (2003). Semantic memory and the human hippocampus. *Neuron, 38,* 127–133.

Manto, M. U., & Jacquy, J. (2002). Alcohol toxicity in the cerebellum: Clinical aspects. In M. U. Manto & M. Pandolfo (Eds.), *The cerebellum and its disorders* (pp. 336–341). New York, NY: Cambridge University Press.

Manton, K. G., & Gu, X. (2001). Changes in the prevalence of chronic disability in the United States black and nonblack population above age 65 from 1982 to 1999. *PNAS Proceedings of the National Academy of Sciences of the United States of America, 98,* 6354–6359.

Maquet, P., Laureys, S., Peigneux, P., Fuchs, S., Petiau, C., Phillips, C., . . . Cleeremans, A. (2000). Experience-dependent changes in cerebral activation during human REM sleep. *Nature: Neuroscience, 3,* 831–836.

Marcia, J. E. (2002). Identity and psychosocial development in adulthood. *Identity, 2,* 7–28.

Marcia, J. E. (1980). Identity in adolescence. In J. Adelson (Ed.), *Handbook of adolescent psychology* (pp. 159–187). New York, NY: Wiley.

Mark, G., Gudith, D., & Klocke, U. (2008). The cost of interrupted work: More speed and stress. Presented at the Annual Computer Human Interaction (CHI) Conference, Florence, Italy (April 5–10). Retrieved from http://www.ics.uci.edu/~gmark/chi08-mark.pdf

Markel, H. (2003, September 2). Lack of sleep takes its toll on student psyches. *New York Times,* p. D6.

Markon, K. E., Krueger, R. F., Bouchard, T. J., Jr., & Gottesman, I. I. (2002). Normal and abnormal personality traits: Evidence for genetic and environmental relationships in the Minnesota Study of Twins Reared Apart. *Journal of Personality, 70,* 661–693.

Marsh, A. A., & Blair, R. J. R. (2008). Deficits in facial affect recognition among antisocial populations: A meta-analysis. *Neuroscience & Biobehavioral Reviews, 32,* 454–465.

Marshall, M. B., De Fruyt, F., Rolland, J.-P., & Bagby, R. M. (2005). Socially desirable responding and the factorial stability of the NEO PI-R. *Psychological Assessment, 17,* 379–384.

Marshall, J. R. (2011). Ultimate causes and the evolution of altruism. *Behavioral Ecology and Sociobiology, 65,* 503–512.

Martin, L. A., Ashwood, P., Braunschweig, D., Cabanlit, M., Van de Water, J., & Amaral, D. G. (2008). Stereotypies and hyperactivity in rhesus monkeys exposed to IgG from mothers of children with autism. *Brain, Behavior, and Immunity, 22,* 806–816.

Martin, R. A. (2002). Is laughter the best medicine? Humor, laughter, and physical health. *Current Directions in Psychological Science, 11,* 216–220.

Martin, S., (2001, June). Substance abuse is nation's No. 1 health problem, but there is hope. *Monitor on Psychology, 32*(5), 10.

Martins, I. P., Caeiro, L., & Ferro, J. M. (2007). Right versus left hemisphere syndromes. In O. Godefroy & J. Bogousslavsk (Eds), *The behavioral and cognitive neurology of stroke* (pp. 617–636). New York, NY: Cambridge University Press.

Martire, K. A., & Kemp, R. I. (2011). Can experts help jurors to evaluate eyewitness evidence? A review of eyewitness expert effects. *Legal and Criminological Psychology, 16,* 24–36.

Martens, U., Leuthold, H., & Schweinberger, S. R. (2010). On the temporal organization of facial identity and expression analysis: Inferences from event-related brain potentials. *Cognitive, Affective & Behavioral Neuroscience, 10,* 505–522.

Marui, T. T., Funatogawa, I. I., Koishi, S. S., Yamamoto, K. K., Matsumoto, H. H., Hashimoto, O. O., . . . Kato, N. N. (2011). The NADH-ubiquinone oxidoreductase 1 alpha subcomplex 5 (NDUFA5) gene variants are associated with autism. *Acta Psychiatrica Scandinavica, 123,* 118–124.

Maslach, C., & Leiter, M. P. (1997). *The truth about burnout.* San Francisco, CA: Jossey-Bass.

Masling, J. (2002). How do I score thee? Let me count the ways. Or some different methods of categorizing Rorschach responses. *Journal of Personality Assessment, 79,* 399–421.

Maslow, A. H. (1954). *Motivation and personality.* New York, NY: Harper & Row.

Mason, M. F., & Morris, M. W. (2010). Culture, attribution and automaticity: A social cognitive neuroscience view. *Social Cognitive and Affective Neuroscience, 5,* 292–306.

Master, S. L., Eisenberger, N. I., Taylor, S. E., Naliboff, B. D., Shirinyan, D., & Lieberman, M. D. (2009). A picture's worth: Partner photographs reduce experimentally induced pain. *Psychological Science, 20,* 1316–1318.

Masters, K. S. (2008). Mechanisms in the relation between religion and health with emphasis on cardiovascular reactivity to stress. *Research in the Social Scientific Study of Religion, 19,* 91–115.

Masters, W. H., & Johnson, V. E. (1966). *Human sexual response.* Boston, MA: Little, Brown.

Masters, W. H., & Johnson, V. E. (1970). *Human sexual inadequacy.* Boston, MA: Little, Brown.

Matre, D., Casey, K. L., & Knardahl, S. (2006). Placebo-induced changes in spinal cord pain processing. *The Journal of Neuroscience, 26,* 559–563.

Matsumoto, D. (2000). *Culture and psychology: People around the world* (2nd ed.). Belmont, CA: Wadsworth/Thomson.

Matsumoto, D., Olide, A., Schug, J., Willingham, B., & Callan, M. (2009). Cross-cultural judgments of spontaneous facial expressions of emotion. *Journal of Nonverbal Behavior, 33,* 213–238.

Matsumoto, D., & Willingham, B. (2009). Spontaneous facial expressions of emotion of congenitally and noncongenitally blind individuals. *Journal of Personality and Social Psychology, 96,* 1–10.

Matsumoto, D., Yoo, S., & Chung, J. (2010). The expression of anger across cultures. In M. Potegal, G. Stemmler, & C. Spielberger (Eds.), *International handbook of anger: Constituent and concomitant biological, psychological, and social processes* (pp. 125–137). New York, NY: Springer.

Matthews, G., & Campbell, S. E. (2010). Dynamic relationships between stress states and working memory. *Cognition and Emotion, 24,* 357–373.

Maunsell, E., Brisson, J., Mondor, M., Verreault, R., & Deschenes, L. (2001). Stressful life events and survival after breast cancer. *Psychosomatic Medicine, 63,* 306–315.

Mayo Foundation for Medical Education and Research. (2005). *Alzheimer's disease: Prevention.* Retrieved from http://www.mayoclinic.com/health/alzheimers-disease/DS00161/DSECTION_8

Mays, V. M., Bullock, M., Rosenzweig, M. R., & Wessells, M. (1998). Ethnic conflict: Global challenges and psychological perspectives. *American Psychologist, 53,* 737–742.

Mazzeo, S. E., & Bulik, C. M. (2009). Environmental and genetic risk factors for eating disorders: What the clinician needs to know. *Child and Adolescent Psychiatric Clinics of North America, 18,* 67–82.

Mazzoni, G. A. L., & Memon, A. (2003). Imagination can create false autobiographical memories. *Psychological Science, 14,* 186–188.

McAdams, D. P., & Olson, B. D. (2010). Personality development: Continuity and change over the life course. *Annual Review of Psychology, 61,* 517–542.

McBee, C. H. (2005). Fetal alcohol syndrome and other drug use during pregnancy. *Journal of Applied Rehabilitation Counseling, 36,* 43–44.

McBurney, D. H., & Collings, V. B. (1984). *Introduction to sensation/perception* (2nd ed.). Englewood Cliffs, NJ: Prentice Hall.

McCall, G. S., & Shields, N. (2008). Examining the evidence from small-scale societies and early prehistory and implications for modern theories of aggression and violence. *Aggression and Violent Behavior, 13,* 1–9.

McCall, M. (1997). Physical attractiveness and access to alcohol: What is beautiful does not get carded. *Journal of Applied Social Psychology, 27,* 453–462.

McCann, I. L., & Holmes, D. S. (1984). Influence of aerobic exercise on depression. *Journal of Personality and Social Psychology, 46,* 1142–1147.

McClelland, K., & Linnander, E. (2006). The role of contact and information in racial attitude change among white college students. *Sociological Inquiry, 76,* 81–115.

McClintock, M. K. (1999). Reproductive biology. Pheromones and regulation of ovulation. *Nature, 401,* 232–233.

McClure, E. B. (2000). A meta-analytic review of sex differences in facial expression processing and their development in infants, children, and adolescents. *Psychological Bulletin, 126,* 424–453.

McConnell, A. R., Rydell, R. J., Strain, L. M., & Mackie, D. M. (2008). Forming implicit and explicit attitudes toward individuals: Social group association cues. *Journal of Personality and Social Psychology, 94,* 792–807.

McCoy, N. L., & Pitino, L. (2002). Pheromonal influences on sociosexual behavior in young women. *Physiology & Behavior, 75,* 367–375.

McCrae, R. R., & Costa, P. T., Jr. (1994). The stability of personality: Observations and evaluations. *Current Directions in Psychological Science, 3,* 173–175.

McCrae, R. R., & Costa, P. T., Jr. (1997). Personality trait structure as a human universal. *American Psychologist, 52,* 509–516.

McCrae, R. R., Yamagata, S., Jang, K. L., Riemann, R., Ando, J., Ono, Y., . . . Spinath, F. M. (2008). Substance and artifact in the higher-order factors of the Big Five. *Journal of Personality and Social Psychology, 95,* 442–455.

McCrea, M. A. (2008). *Mild traumatic brain injury and postconcussion syndrome: The new evidence base for diagnosis and treatment*. Oxford, England: Oxford University Press.

McCullough, L., & Magill, M. (2009). Affect-focused short-term dynamic therapy. In R. A. Levy & J. S. Ablon (Eds.), *Handbook of evidence-based psychodynamic psychotherapy: Bridging the gap between science and practice* (pp. 249–277). Totowa, NJ: Humana Press.

McCurdy, S. A., Williams, M. L., Kilonzo, G. P., Ross, M. W., & Leshabari, M. T. (2005). Heroin and HIV risk in Dar es Salaam, Tanzania: Youth hangouts, mageto and injecting practices. *AIDS Care, 17*, S65–S76.

McDonough, I. A., & Gallo, D. A. (2008). Autobiographical elaboration reduces memory distortion: Cognitive operations and the distinctiveness heuristic. *Journal of Experimental Psychology: Learning, Memory, and Cognition, 34*, 1430–1445.

McDonough, P. (2009). TV viewing among kids at an eight-year high. Retrieved from http://blog.nielsen.com/nielsenwire/media_entertainment/tv-viewing-among-kids-at-an-eight-year-high/

McElhatton, P. R., Bateman, D. N., Evans, C., Pughe, K. R., & Thomas, S. H. L. (1999). Congenital anomalies after prenatal Ecstasy exposure. *Lancet, 354*, 1441–1442.

McFarland, L. J., Senn, L. E., & Childress, J. R. (1993). *21st century leadership: Dialogues with 100 top leaders*. Los Angeles, CA: Leadership Press.

McGuffin, P., Katz, R., Watkins, S., & Rutherford, J. (1996). A hospital-based twin register of the heritability of *DSM-IV* unipolar depression. *Archives of General Psychiatry, 53*, 129–136.

McIntosh, D. N. (2006). Spontaneous facial mimicry, liking and emotional contagion. *Polish Psychological Bulletin, 37*, 31–42.

McKellar, J., Stewart, E., & Humphreys, K. (2003). Alcoholics Anonymous involvement and positive alcohol-related outcomes: Cause, consequence, or just a correlate? A prospective 2-year study of 2,319 alcohol-dependent men. *Journal of Consulting and Clinical Psychology, 71*, 302–308.

McKenna, M. C., Zevon, M. A., Corn, B., & Rounds, J. (1999). Psychosocial factors and the development of breast cancer: A meta-analysis. *Health Psychology, 18*, 520–531.

McKim, W. A. (2007). *Drugs and behavior: An introduction to behavioral pharmacology* (6th ed.). Upper Saddle River, NJ: Prentice Hall.

McMain, S., & Pos, A. E. (2007). Advances in psychotherapy of personality disorder. A research update. *Current Psychological Reports, 9*, 46–52.

McNamara, H. J., Long, J. B., & Wike, E. L. (1956). Learning without response under two conditions of external cues. *Journal of Comparative and Physiological Psychology, 49*, 477–480.

McNaughton, B. L., Barnes, C. A., Battaglia, F., Bower, M. R., Cowen, S., Ekstrom, A., . . . Pennartz, C. M. A. (2003). Off-line reprocessing of recent memory and its role in consolidation: A progress report. In P. Maguet, C. Smith, & R. Stickgold (Eds.), *Sleep and brain plasticity* (pp. 225–246). Oxford, England: Oxford University Press.

McNeil, B. J., Pauker, S. G., Sox, H. C., Jr., & Tversky, A. (1982). On the elicitation of preferences for alternative therapies. *The New England Journal of Medicine, 306*, 1259–1262.

McNeil, D. W., & Zvolensky, M. J. (2000). Systematic desensitization. In A. E. Kazdin (Ed.), *Encyclopedia of psychology* (Vol. 7, pp. 533–535). Washington, DC: American Psychological Association.

McPherson, J. M., Smith-Lovin, L., & Cook, J. M. (2001). Birds of a feather: Homophily in social networks. *Annual Review of Sociology, 27*, 415–444.

Mcquillan, J. (2007). Predicting achievement for students from low socioeconomic backgrounds using the Wechsler Intelligence Scale for Children—Third Edition and the Universal Nonverbal Intelligence Test. *Dissertation Abstracts International Section A: Humanities and Social Sciences, 67*, 2954.

McQuown, S. C. (2010). Neural mechanisms underlying nicotine as a 'gateway' drug. *Dissertation Abstracts International, 70*, 5453. Retrieved from EBSCOhost.

Meade, C. S., McDonald, L. J., & Weiss, R. D. (2009). HIV risk behavior in opioid dependent adults seeking detoxification treatment: An exploratory comparison of heroin and oxycodone users. *The American Journal on Addictions, 18*, 289–293.

Mead, M. (1935). *Sex and temperament in three primitive societies*. New York, NY: Morrow.

Mednick, S. A. [Sarnoff]. (1962). The associative basis of creativity. *Psychological Review, 69*, 220–232.

Mednick, S. C. [Sarah], Nakayama, K., Cantero, J. L., Atienza, M., Levin, A. A., Pathak, N., & Stickgold, R. (2002). The restorative effect of naps on perceptual deterioration. *Nature Neuroscience, 5*, 677–681.

Melnyk, B. M. (2008). The latest evidence on telehealth interventions to improve patient outcomes. *Worldviews on Evidence-Based Nursing, 5*, 163–166.

Melzack, R., & Katz, J. (2004). The gate control theory: Reaching for the brain. In T. Hadjistavropoulos & K. Craig (Eds.), *Pain: Psychological perspectives* (pp. 13–34). Mahwah, NJ: Erlbaum.

Melzack, R., Israel, R., Lacroix, R., & Schultz, G. (1997). Phantom limbs in people with congenital limb deficiency or amputation in early childhood. *Brain, 120*, 1603–1620.

Mental Health America. (2009). Economic downturn taking toll on Americans' mental health: New national survey finds jobless individuals four times as likely to report serious problems. Retrieved from http://www.nmha.org/index.cfm?objectid=2A7E7943-1372-4D20-C8B93F1EEE06C70A

Merrick, J., Aspler, S., & Schwarz, G. (2005). Phenylalanine-restricted diet should be life long. A case report on long term follow-up of an adolescent with untreated phenylketonuria. *International Journal of Adolescent Medicine and Health, 15*, 165–168.

Meston, C. M., & Frohlich, M. A. (2000). The neurobiology of sexual function. *Archives of General Psychiatry, 57*, 1012–1030.

Meston, C. M., & Rellini, A. (2008). Sexual dysfunction. In W. E. Craighead, D. J. Miklowitz, & L. W. Craighead (Eds.), *Psychopathology: History, diagnosis, and empirical foundations* (pp. 544–564). Hoboken, NJ: Wiley.

Mestre, J. M., Guil, R., Lopes, P. N., Salovey, P., & Gil-Olarte, P. (2006). Emotional intelligence and social and academic adaptation to school. *Psicothema, 18*, 112–117.

Meuret, A. E., Wilhelm, F. H., & Roth, W. T. (2004). Respiratory feedback for treating panic disorder. *Journal of Clinical Psychology, 60*, 197–207.

Meyer, G. J., Finn, S. E., Eyde, L. D., Kay, G. G., Moreland, K. L., Dies, R. R., . . . Read, G. M. (2001). Psychological testing and psychological assessment: A review of evidence and issues. *American Psychologist, 56*, 128–165.

Michael, R. T., Gagnon, J. H., Laumann, E. O., & Kolata, G. (1994). *Sex in America*. Boston, MA: Little, Brown.

Middlebrooks, J. C., & Snyder, R. L. (2008). Intraneural stimulation for auditory prosthesis: Modiolar trunk and intracranial stimulation sites. *Hearing Research, 242*, 52–63.

Mieda, M., Williams, S. C., Richardson, J. A., Tanaka, K., & Yanagisawa, M. (2006). The dorsomedial hypothalamic nucleus as a putative food-entrainable circadian pacemaker. *PNAS Proceedings of the National Academy of Sciences of the United States of America, 103*, 12150–12155.

Milgram, S. (1963). Behavioral study of obedience. *Journal of Abnormal and Social Psychology, 67*, 371–378.

Milgram, S. (1974). *Obedience to authority: An experimental view*. New York, NY: Harper & Row.

Miller, J. A. (2002). Individual motivation loss in group settings: An exploratory study of the social-loafing phenomenon. *Dissertation Abstracts International: Section A: Humanities and Social Sciences, 62*, 2972.

Miller, K., Brewer, M., & Arbuckle, N. (2009). Social identity complexity: Its correlates and antecedents. *Group Processes & Intergroup Relations, 12*, 79–94.

Miller, L. K. (2005). What the savant syndrome can tell us about the nature and nurture of talent. *Journal for the Education of the Gifted, 28*, 361–373.

Miller, T. Q. [Todd], Turner, C. W., Tindale, R. S., Posavac, E. J., & Dugoni, B. L. (1991). Reasons for the trend toward null findings in research on Type A behavior. *Psychological Bulletin, 110*, 469–485.

Miller, T. W. [Thomas], Miller, J. M., Kraus, R. F., Kaak, O., Sprang, R., & Veltkamp, L. J. (2003). Telehealth: A clinical application model for rural consultation. *Consulting Psychology Journal: Practice and Research, 55*, 119–127.

Miller, W. R., & Thoresen, C. E. (2003). Spirituality, religion, and health: An emerging research field. *American Psychologist, 58*, 24–35.

Milner, B., Corkin, S., & Teuber, H. H. (1968). Further analysis of the hippocampal amnesic syndrome: 14-year follow-up study of H. M. *Neuropsychologia, 6*, 215–234.

Mindell, J. A., & Owens, J. A. (2003). *A clinical guide to pediatric sleep: Diagnosis and management of sleep problems in children and adolescents*. Philadelphia, PA: Lippincott Williams & Wilkins.

Mindell, J. A., Sadeh, A., Wiegand, B., & How, T. H. (2008, June). *Culturally-based infant and toddler sleep differences*. Paper presented at the meeting of the Associated Professional Sleep Societies, Seattle, WA.

Ming, X., Brimacombe, M., Chaaban, J., Zimmerman-Bier, B., & Wagner, G. C. (2008). Autism spectrum disorders: Concurrent clinical disorders. *Journal of Child Neurology, 23*, 6–13.

Miniño, A. M., Heron, M., & Smith, B. L. (2006). Deaths: Preliminary data for 2004. Retrieved from http://www.cdc.gov/nchs/products/pubs/pubd/hestats/prelimdeaths04/preliminarydeaths04.htm

Mirkin, M. P., Suyemoto, K. L., & Okun, B. F. (Eds.). (2005). *Psychotherapy with women: Exploring diverse contexts and identities.* New York, NY: Guilford Press.

Mischel, W. (2003). Challenging the traditional personality psychology paradigm. In R. J. Sternberg (Ed.), *Psychologists defying the crowd: Stories of those who battled the establishment and won* (pp. 139–156). Washington, DC: American Psychological Association.

Mischel, W. (2004). Toward an integrative science of the person. *Annual Review of Psychology, 55*, 1–22.

Mischel, W., & Shoda, Y. (1995). A cognitive-affective system theory of personality: Reconceptualizing situations, dispositions, dynamics, and invariance in personality structure. *Psychological Review, 102*, 246–268.

Mitka, M. (2008). Routine depression screening advised for patients with coronary heart disease. *JAMA: Journal of the American Medical Association, 300*, 2356–2357.

Miyake, N., Thompson, J., Skinbjerg, M., & Abi-Dargham, A. (2011). Presynaptic dopamine in schizophrenia. *CNS Neuroscience & Therapeutics, 17*, 104–109.

Miyamoto, Y., Nisbett, R. E., & Masuda, T. (2006). Culture and the physical environment: Holistic versus analytical perceptual affordances. *Psychological Science, 17*, 113–119.

Mlacic, B., & Goldberg, L. R. (2007). An analysis of a cross-cultural personality inventory: The IPIP Big Five factor markers in Croatia. *Journal of Personality Assessment, 88*, 168–177.

Modecki, K. (2008). Underlying processes of antisocial decisions: Adolescents versus adults. *Dissertation Abstracts International: Section B: The Sciences and Engineering, 68*, 5635.

Modesto-Lowe, V., & Fritz, E. M. (2005). The opioidergic-alcohol link: Implications for treatment. *CNS Drugs, 19*, 693–707.

Modirrousta, M., & Fellows, L. K. (2008). Medial prefrontal cortex plays a critical and selective role in "feeling of knowing" meta-memory judgments. *Neuropsychologia, 46*, 2958–2965.

Mody, R. R., & Smith, M. J. (2006). Smoking status and health-related quality of life: Findings from the 2001 Behavioral Risk Factor Surveillance System data. *American Journal of Health Promotion, 20*, 251–258.

Moffitt, T. E., Caspi, A., & Rutter, M. (2006). Measured gene-environment interactions in psychopathology: Concepts, research strategies, and implications for research, interventions, and public understanding of genetics. *Perspectives on Psychological Science, 1*, 5–26.

Mohan, J. (2006). Cardiac psychology. *Journal of the Indian Academy of Applied Psychology, 3*, 214–220.

Möller-Leimkühler, A. M. (2003). The gender gap in suicide and premature death or: Why are men so vulnerable? *European Archives of Psychiatry and Clinical Neuroscience, 253*, 1–8.

Mollica, R. F. (2000, June). Invisible wounds. *Scientific American, 282*(6), 54–57.

Monastra, V. J. (2008a). Electroencephalographic biofeedback in the treatment of ADHD. In V. J. Monastra (Ed.), *Unlocking the potential of patients with ADHD: A model for clinical practice* (pp. 147–159). Washington, DC: American Psychological Association.

Monastra, V. J. (2008b). The etiology of ADHD: A neurological perspective. In V. Monastra (Ed.), *Unlocking the potential of patients with ADHD: A model for clinical practice* (pp. 35–47). Washington, DC: American Psychological Association.

Monteiro, M. B., de França, D. X., & Rodrigues, R. (2009). The development of intergroup bias in childhood: How social norms can shape children's racial behaviours. *International Journal of Psychology, 44*, 29–39.

Montgomery, G. H., DuHamel, K. N., & Redd, W. H. (2000). A meta-analysis of hypnotically induced analgesia: How effective is hypnosis? *International Journal of Clinical & Experimental Hypnosis [Special Issue: The Status of Hypnosis as an Empirically Validated Clinical Intervention], 48*, 138–153.

Monti, M. R., & Sabbadini, A. (2005). New interpretative styles: Progress or contamination? Psychoanalysis and phenomenological psychopathology. *International Journal of Psychoanalysis, 86*, 1011–1032.

Moont, R., Pud, D., Sprecher, E., Sharvit, G., & Yarnitsky, D. (2010). 'Pain inhibits pain' mechanisms: Is pain modulation simply due to distraction? *Pain, 150*, 113–120.

Moore, C. S., Abdullah, S. L., Brown, A., Arulpragasam, A., & Crocker, S. J. (2011). How factors secreted from astrocytes impact myelin repair. *Journal of Neuroscience Research, 89*, 13–21.

Moore, D. S., & Johnson, S. P. (2008). Mental rotation in human infants. *Psychological Science, 19*, 1063–1066.

Moore, E. S., Ward, R. E., Wetherill, L. F., Rogers, J. L., Autti-Rämö, I., Fagerlund, Å., . . . Foroud, T. (2007). Unique facial features distinguish fetal alcohol syndrome patients and controls in diverse ethnic populations. *Alcoholism: Clinical and Experimental Research, 31*, 1707–1713.

Moore, J. J. (2010). Behaviorism and the stages of scientific activity. *The Behavior Analyst, 33*, 47–63.

Moore, K. A., Morrison, D. R., & Greene, A. D. (1997). Effects on the children born to adolescent mothers. In R. A. Maynard (Ed.), *Kids having kids: Economic costs and social consequences of teen pregnancy* (pp. 145–180). Washington, DC: Urban Insitute Press.

Moore, R. Y. (2007). Suprachiasmatic nucleus in sleep-wake regulation. *Sleep Medicine, 8*(Suppl 3), S27–S33.

Moran, P. (1999). The epidemiology of antisocial personality disorder. *Social Psychiatry and Psychiatric Epidemiology, 34*, 231–242.

Morgan, M. (1999). Sensory perception: Supernormal hearing in the blind? *Current Biology, 9*, R53–R54.

Mori, K., & Mori, H. (2008). Conformity among cowitnesses sharing same or different information about an event in experimental collaborative eyewitness testimony. *Perceptual and Motor Skills, 106*, 275–290.

Moriarty, T. (1975). Crime, commitment and the responsive bystander: Two field experiments. *Journal of Personality and Social Psychology, 31*, 370–376.

Moriconi, C. B. (2004). A systemic treatment program of mindfulness meditation for fibromyalgia patients and their partners. *Dissertation Abstracts International: Section B: The Sciences and Engineering, 64*, 5228.

Morling, B., & Kitayama, S. (2008). Culture and motivation. In J. Y. Shah & W. L. Gardner (Eds.), *Handbook of motivation science* (pp. 417–433). New York, NY: Guilford Press.

Morra, S., Gobbo, C., Marini, Z., & Sheese, R. (2008). *Cognitive development: Neo-Piagetian perspectives.* New York, NY: Taylor & Francis.

Morris, R. J., Kratochwill, T. R., Schoenfield, G., & Auster, E. A. (2008). Childhood fears, phobias, and related anxieties. In R. J. Morris & T. R. Kratochwill (Eds.), *The practice of child therapy* (4th ed., pp. 93–141). Mahwah, NJ: Erlbaum.

Morrison, R. G. (2005). Thinking in working memory. In K. J. Holyoak & R. G. Morrison (Eds.), *The Cambridge handbook of thinking and reasoning* (pp. 457–473). New York, NY: Cambridge University Press.

Mortimer, J. S. B., Sephton, S. E., Kimerling, R., Butler, L., Bernstein, A. S., & Spiegel, D. (2005). Chronic stress, depression and immunity in spouses of metastatic breast cancer patients. *Clinical Psychologist, 9*, 59–63.

Moser, H. W. (2004). Genetic causes of mental retardation. In S. G. Kaler & O. M. Rennert (Eds.), *Understanding and optimizing human development: From cells to patients to populations* (pp. 44–48). New York, NY: New York Academy of Sciences.

Moser, R. S., Frantz, C. E., & Brick, J. (2008). The neuropsychological consequences of alcohol and drug abuse. In J. Brick (Ed.), *Handbook of the medical consequences of alcohol and drug abuse* (2nd ed., pp. 57–96). New York, NY: Haworth.

Moskowitz, J. T., Hult, J. R., Bussolari, C., & Acree, M. (2009). What works in coping with HIV? A meta-analysis with implications for coping with serious illness. *Psychological Bulletin, 135*, 121–141.

Moulds, M. L., & Nixon, R. D. V. (2006). In vivo flooding for anxiety disorders: Proposing its utility in the treatment posttraumatic stress disorder. *Journal of Anxiety Disorders, 20*, 498–509.

Mroczek, D. K., & Kolarz, C. M. (1998). The effect of age on positive and negative affect: A developmental perspective on happiness. *Journal of Personality and Social Psychology, 75*, 1333–1349.

Mucci, A., Galderisi, S., Bucci, P., Tresca, E., Forte, A., Koenig, T., & Maj, M. (2005). Hemispheric lateralization patterns and psychotic experiences in healthy subjects. *Psychiatry Research: Neuroimaging, 139*, 141–154.

Muchinsky, P. M. (2006). *Psychology applied to work* (8th ed.). Belmont, CA: Thomson Wadsworth.

Muczyk, J. P., & Holt, D. T. (2008). Toward a cultural contingency model of leadership. *Journal of Leadership & Organizational Studies, 14*, 277–286.

Mueser, K. T. (2006). Family intervention for schizophrenia. In L. VandeCreek (Ed.), *Innovations in clinical practice: Focus on adults* (pp. 219–233). Sarasota, FL: Professional Resource Press.

Mulas, F., Capilla, A., Fernández, S., Etchepareborda, M. C., Campo, P., Maestú, F., . . . Ortiz, T. (2006). Shifting-related brain magnetic activity in attention-deficit/hyperactivity disorder. *Biological Psychiatry, 59,* 373–379.

Munsey, C. (2009, October). Operation diversity. *Monitor on Psychology, 40*(10), 72–73.

Murias, M., Swanson, J. M., & Srinivasan, R. (2007). Functional connectivity of frontal cortex in healthy and ADHD children reflected in EEG coherence. *Cerebral Cortex, 17,* 1788–1799.

Murphy, E. A., Davis, J. M., Carmichael, M. D., Gangemi, J. D., Ghaffar, A., & Mayer, E. P. (2008). Exercise stress increases susceptibility to influenza infection. *Brain, Behavior, and Immunity, 22,* 1152–1155.

Murphy, H. M., Ihekoronze, C., & Wideman, C. H. (2011). Zolpidem-induced changes in activity, metabolism, and anxiety in rats. *Pharmacology, Biochemistry and Behavior, 98,* 81–86.

Murphy, K. R., & Cleveland, J. N. (1995). *Understanding performance appraisal: Social, organizational, and goal-based perspectives.* Thousand Oaks, CA: Sage.

Murphy, S. A., (2008). The loss of a child: Sudden death and extended illness perspectives. In M. S. Stroebe, R. O. Hansson, H. Schut, & W. Stroebe, (Eds.), *Handbook of bereavement research and practice: Advances in theory and intervention* (pp. 375–395). Washington, DC: American Psychological Association.

Murray, J. P. (2008). Media violence: The effects are both real and strong. *American Behavioral Scientist, 51,* 1212–1230.

Muth, E. R., Stern, R. M., Uijtdehaage, S. H. J., & Koch, K. L. (1994). Effects of Asian ancestry on susceptibility to vection-induced motion sickness. In J. Z. Chen & R. W. McCallum (Eds.), *Electrogastrography: Principles and applications* (pp. 227–233). New York, NY: Raven.

Myers, J. E., & Sweeney T. J. (2006). *Counseling for wellness: Theory, research, and practice.* Alexandria, VA: American Counseling Association.

Naglieri, J. A., & Kaufman, J. C. (2001). Understanding intelligence, giftedness, and creativity using PASS theory. *Roeper Review, 23,* 151–156.

Nairne, J. S. (2003). Sensory and working memory. In A. F. Healy & R. W. Proctor (Eds.), *Handbook of Psychology: Vol. 4, Experimental Psychology* (pp. 423–444). New York, NY: Wiley.

Najavits, L. M. (2004). Assessment of trauma, PTSD, and substance use disorder: A practical guide. In J. Wilson & T. M. Keane (Eds.), *Assessing psychological trauma and PTSD* (2nd ed., pp. 466–491). New York, NY: Guilford Press.

Nakao, M., Kashiwagi, M., & Yano, E. (2005). Alexithymia and grief reactions in bereaved Japanese women. *Death Studies, 29,* 423–433.

Naqvi, N. H., & Bechara, A. (2009). The hidden island of addiction: The insula. *Trends in Neurosciences, 32,* 48–55.

Naqvi, N. H., Rudrauf, D., Damasio, H., & Bechara, A. (2007). Damage to the insula disrupts addiction to cigarette smoking. *Science, 315,* 531–534.

Narayanan, L., Shanker, M., & Spector, P. E. (1999). Stress in the workplace: A comparison of gender and occupations. *Journal of Organizational Behavior, 20,* 63–73.

Näslund, E., & Hellström, P. M. (2007). Appetite signaling: From gut peptides and enteric nerves to brain. *Physiology & Behavior, 92,* 256–262.

National Alliance on Mental Illness. (2003). *About mental illness: Women and depression.* Retrieved from http://www.nami.org/Template.cfm?Section_By_Illness &template_/ContentManagement/ContentDisplay.cfm&ContentID_17627

National Center on Addiction and Substance Abuse (NCADA). (2007, March). *Wasting the best and the brightest: Substance abuse at America's colleges and universities.* Washington, DC: Author.

National Clearing House on Child Abuse and Neglect. (2006). *Child Maltreatment 2004.* Retrieved from http://www.acf.hhs.gov/programs/cb/pubs/cm04/index.htm

National Head Start Association. (2008). *Up to 120,000 new jobs in worst-off U.S. communities possible from 4.3 billion boost for Head Start in economic recovery package.* Retrieved from http://www.nhsa.org/press/News_Archived/index_news_010809.htm

National Household Survey on Drug Abuse. (1998). *Summary of findings from the 1998 National Household Survey on Drug Abuse.* Retrieved from http://www.oas.samhsa.gov/NHSDA/98MF.pdf

National Institute of Mental Health. (2005). *The numbers count: Mental disorders in America.* Retrieved from http://www.nimh.nih.gov/health/publications/the-numbers-count-mental-disorders-in-america

National Institute on Aging. (2006). *The impact of Alzheimer's disease.* Retrieved from http://www.nia.nih.gov/Alzheimers/Publications/UnravelingTheMystery/ImpactOfAlzheimerIll.htm

National Institute on Alcohol Abuse and Alcoholism. (2003). *Does alcohol affect women differently?* Retrieved from http://www.niaaa.nih.gov/FAQs/General-English/FAQs16.htm

National Institute on Drug Abuse. (2004). *NIDA InfoFacts: Marijuana: Facts parents need to know.* Retrieved from http://www.nida.nih.gov/MarijBroch/Marij parentsN.html

National Institute on Drug Abuse. (2005a). *NIDA InfoFacts: Methamphetamine.* Retrieved from http://www.nida.nih.gov/Infofacts/methamphetamine.html

National Institute on Drug Abuse (2005b). *What is the scope of heroin use in the United States?* Retrieved from http://www.nida.nih.gov/ResearchReports/Heroin/heroin2.html#scope

National Institutes of Health. (2007, Summer). Placebos: Sugar, shams, therapies, or all of the above? *CAM at the NIH, XIV*(3), 1–2, 4–5.

National Institutes of Health. (n.d.). *Alcohol abuse and dependence.* Retrieved from http://ospp.od.nih.gov/pdf/alcohol_abuse.pdf

National Mental Health Association. (2006). *Suicide: Teen suicide.* Alexandria, VA: National Mental Health Association. Retrieved from http://www.nmha.org/infoctr/factsheets/82.cfm

National Sleep Foundation. (2005). *Sleepwalking.* Retrieved from http://www.sleepfoundation.org/sleeptionary/index.php?id_22

National Sleep Foundation. (2006, August). *The ABCs of back-to-school sleep schedules: The consequences of insufficient sleep.* Washington, DC: Author.

Navarro, J. F., & Maldonado, E. (2004). Effects of acute, subchronic, and intermittent MDMA ("Ecstasy") administration on agonistic interactions between male mice. *Aggressive Behavior, 30,* 71–83.

Neath, I. (1993). Contextual and distinctive processes and the serial position function. *Journal of Memory and Language, 32,* 820–840.

Neisser, U. (1982). *Memory observed: Remembering in natural contexts.* San Francisco, CA: Freeman.

Neisser, U. (1998). Introduction: Rising test scores and what they mean. In U. Neisser (Ed.), *The rising curve: Long-term gains in IQ and related measures* (pp. 3–22). Washington, DC: American Psychological Association.

Nekisha, E. L., Gerald, D. W, Hsiao-ye, Y., & Michael, E. H. (2005). Surveillance report #73, Apparent per capita alcohol consumption: National, State, and Regional trends, 1977–2003. *National Institute on Alcohol Abuse and Alcoholism, Division of Epidemiology and Prevention Research.* Retrieved from http://pubs.niaaa.nih.gov/publications/surveillance73/CONS03.htm#fig1

Nelson, C. A. (1999). Neural plasticity and human development. *Current Directions in Psychological Science, 8,* 42–45.

Nelson, N. W., Hoelzle, J. B., Sweet, J. J., Arbisi, P. A., & Demakis, G. J. (2010). Updated meta-analysis of the MMPI-2 Symptom Validity Scale (FBS): Verified utility in forensic practice. *The Clinical Neuropsychologist, 24,* 701–724.

Nemeroff, C. B., & Schatzberg, A. F. (2002). Pharmacological treatments for unipolar depression. In P. Nathan & J. M. Gorman (Eds.), *A guide to treatments that work* (2nd ed., pp. 212–225). New York, NY: Oxford University Press.

Nestoriuc, Y., Martin, A., Rief, W., & Andrasik, F. (2008). Biofeedback treatment for headache disorders: A comprehensive efficacy review. *Applied Psychophysiology and Biofeedback, 33,* 125–140.

Neuringer, A., & Oleson, K. C. (2010). Helping for change. *The Behavior Analyst, 33,* 181–184.

Neuschatz, J. S., Lampinen, J. M., Toglia, M. P., Payne, D. G., & Cisneros, E. (2007). False memory research: History, theory, and applied implications. In M. P. Toglia, J. Read, D. F. Ross, & R. L. Lindsay (Eds.), *The handbook of eyewitness psychology, Vol I: Memory for events* (pp. 239–260). Mahwah, NJ: Erlbaum.

Neuschatz, J. S., Preston, E. L., Burkett, A. D., Toglia, M. P., Lampinen, J. M., Neuschatz, J. S., . . . Goodsell, C. A. (2005). The effects of post-identification feedback and age on retrospective eyewitness memory. *Applied Cognitive Psychology, 19,* 435–453.

Newman, M. B., & Bakay, R. A. E. (2008). Therapeutic potentials of human embryonic stem cells in Parkinson's disease. *Neurotherapeutics, 5,* 237–251.

Newsome, W. S., & Kelly, M. (2006). Bullying behavior and school violence. In R. J. Waller (Ed.), *Fostering child & adolescent mental health in the classroom* (pp. 183–201). Thousand Oaks, CA: Sage.

Newton, T. F. (2006). Addictions. In D. Wedding & M. L. Stuber (Eds.), *Behavior & medicine* (4th ed., pp. 125–131). Ashland, OH: Hogrefe & Huber.

Nguyen-Michel, S. T., Unger, J. B., Hamilton, J., & Spruijt-Metz, D. (2006). Associations between physical activity and perceived stress/hassles in college students. *Stress and Health: Journal of the International Society for the Investigation of Stress, 22,* 179–188.

Nickerson, R. S., & Adams, M. J. (1979). Long-term memory for a common object. *Cognitive Psychology, 11,* 287–307.

Nicotine Anonymous. (2008). *Find a meeting: Easy search.* Huntington Beach, CA: Nicotine Anonymous World Services. Retrieved from https://www.nicotine-anonymous.org/standard_search.php

Nielsen, A. L., & Bonn, S. (2008). Media exposure and attitudes toward drug addiction spending, 1975–2004. *Deviant Behavior, 29,* 726–752.

Nigg, J. T. (2005). Neuropsychologic theory and findings in attentiondeficit/hyperactivity disorder: The state of the field and salient challenges for the coming decade. *Biological Psychiatry, 57,* 1424–1435.

Nisbett, R. E. (2009). *Intelligence and how to get it: Why schools and culture count.* New York, NY: Norton.

Nixon, N. L., & Doody, G. A. (2005). Official psychiatric morbidity and the incidence of schizophrenia 1881–1994. *Psychological Medicine, 35,* 1145–1153.

Nolan, J. M., Schultz, P. W., Cialdini, R. B., Goldstein, N. J., & Griskevicius, V. (2008). Normative social influence is underdetected. *Personality and Social Psychology Bulletin, 34,* 913–923.

Nolen-Hoeksema, S. (2006). The etiology of gender differences in depression. In C. M. Mazure & G. P. Keita (Eds.), *Understanding depression in women: Applying empirical research to practice and policy* (pp. 9–43). Washington, DC: American Psychological Association.

Norcross, J. C. (2002). *Psychotherapeutic relationships that work.* New York, NY: Oxford University Press.

Norton, M. C., Smith, K. R., Østbye, T., Tschanz, J. T., Corcoran, C., Schwartz, S., . . . Welsh-Bohmer, K. A. (2010). Greater risk of dementia when spouse has dementia? The Cache County Study. *Journal of the American Geriatrics Society, 58,* 895–900.

Novak, M. A. (1991, July). "Psychologists care deeply" about animals. *APA Monitor, 22*(7), 4.

Novotney, A. (2010, November.) What works to protect cognition? *Monitor on Psychology, 41(10),* 36–38.

Nowakowski, R. S., & Hayes, N. L. (2004). Quantitative analysis of fetal and adult neurogenesis: Regulation of neuron number. In M. S. Gazzaniga (Ed.), *The cognitive neurosciences* (3rd ed., pp. 149–159). Cambridge, MA: MIT Press.

Nower, L., Derevensky, J. L., & Gupta, R. (2004). The relationship of impulsivity, sensation seeking, coping, and substance use in youth gamblers. *Psychology of Additive Behaviors, 18,* 49–55.

NPR. (2008). Bad at multitasking? Blame your brain. Retrieved from http://www.npr.org/templates/story/story.php?storyId=95784052

Nurnberger, J. I., Jr., & Bierut, L. J. (2007, April). Seeking the connections: Alcoholism and our genes. *Scientific American, 296*(4), 46–53.

Nyberg, L., Marklund, P., Persson, J., Cabeza, R., Forkstam, C., Petersson, K. M., . . . Ingvar, M. (2003). Common prefrontal activations during working memory, episodic memory, and semantic memory. *Neuropsychologia, 41,* 371–377.

Nysse-Carris, K. L., Bottoms, B. L., & Salerno, J. M. (2011). Experts' and novices' abilities to detect children's high-stakes lies of omission. *Psychology, Public Policy, and Law, 17,* 76–98.

O'Connell, M. E., Boat, T., & Warner, K. E. (2009). *Preventing mental, emotional, and behavioral disorders among young people: Progress and possibilities.* Washington, DC: The National Academies Press.

O'Connor, T. G., McGuire, S., Reiss, D., Hetherington, E. M., & Plomin, R. (1998). Co-occurrence of depressive symptoms and antisocial behavior in adolescence: A common genetic liability. *Journal of Abnormal Psychology, 107,* 27–37.

O'Leary, A. (1990). Stress, emotion, and human immune function. *Psychological Bulletin, 108,* 363–382.

O'Leary, D. S., Block, R. I., Turner, B. M., Koeppel, J., Magnotta, V. A., Ponto, L. B., . . . Andreasen, N. C. (2003). Marijuana alters the human cerebellar clock. *Neuroreport: For Rapid Communication of Neuroscience Research, 14,* 1145–1151.

O'Leary, V. E., & Bhaju, J. (2006). Resilience and empowerment. In J. Worell & C. D. Goodheart (Eds.), *Handbook of girls' and women's psychological health: Gender and well-being across the life span* (pp. 157–165). New York, NY: Oxford University Press.

O'Leary, V. E., & Flanagan, E. H. (2001). Leadership. In J. Worell (Ed.), *Encyclopedia of gender* (Vol. 2, pp. 245–257). San Diego, CA: Academic Press.

Office of the Surgeon General. (2007). *The Surgeon General's call to action to prevent and decrease overweight and obesity.* Retrieved from http://www.surgeogeneral.gov/topics/obesity/calltoaction/fact_adolescents.htm

Ogrodniczuk, J. S., Piper, W. E., & Joyce, A. S. (2004). Differences in men's and women's responses to short-term group psychotherapy. *Psychotherapy Research, 14,* 231–243.

Ogrodniczuk, J. S., & Staats, H. (2002). Psychotherapy and gender: Do men and women require different treatments? *Zeitschrift fuer Psychosomatische Medizin und Psychotherapie, 48,* 270–285.

Öhman, A. (2010). Post-traumatic fear memories: Analysing a case study of a sexual assault. In L. Bäckman & L. Nyberg (Eds.), *Memory, aging and the brain: A Festschrift in honour of Lars-Göran Nilsson* (pp. 211–228). New York, NY: Psychology Press.

Ohring, R., Graber, J. A., & Brooks-Gunn, J. (2002). Girls' recurrent and concurrent body dissatisfaction: Correlates and consequences over 8 years. *International Journal of Eating Disorders, 31,* 404–415.

Okazaki, S. (2009). Impact of racism on ethnic minority mental health. *Perspectives on Psychological Science, 4,* 103–107.

Oken, B. S., & Salinsky, M. C. (2007). Sleeping and driving: Not a safe dual-task. *Clinical Neurophysiology, 118,* 1899–1900.

Olivardia, R. (2007). Body image and muscularity. In J. E. Grant & M. N. Potenza (Eds.), *Textbook of men's mental health* (pp. 307–324). Arlington, VA: American Psychiatric Publishing.

Olney, J. W., Wozniak, D. F., Farber, N. B., Jevtovic-Todorovic, V., & Bittigau, I. C. (2002). The enigma of fetal alcohol neurotoxicity. *Annals of Medicine, 34,* 109–119.

Olson, M. V., & Varki, A. (2003). Sequencing the chimpanzee genome: insights into human evolution and disease. *Nature Review Genetics, 4,* 20–8.

Olszewski, P. K., Cedernaes, J., Olsson, F., Levine, A. S., & Schiöth, H. B. (2008). Analysis of the network of feeding neuroregulators using the Allen Brain Atlas. *Neuroscience & Biobehavioral Reviews, 32,* 945–956.

Olszewski, P. K., Schiöth, H. B., & Levine, A. S. (2008). Ghrelin in the CNS: From hunger to a rewarding and memorable meal? *Brain Research Reviews, 58,* 160–170.

Oltmanns, T. F., & Emery, R. E. (1998). *Abnormal psychology* (2nd ed.). Upper Saddle River, NJ: Prentice Hall.

Oltmanns, T. F., & Emery, R. E. (2006). *Abnormal psychology* (5th ed.). Upper Saddle River, NJ: Prentice Hall.

Olszewski-Kubilius, P. (2003). Gifted education programs and procedures. In W. M. Reynolds & G. E. Miller (Eds.), *Handbook of psychology: Vol. 7, Educational psychology* (pp. 487–510). New York, NY: Wiley.

Orengo, C., Kunik, M. E., Molinari, V., Wristers, K., & Yudofsky, S. C. (2002). Do testosterone levels relate to aggression in elderly men with dementia? *The Journal of Neuropsychiatry and Clinical Neurosciences, 14,* 161–166.

Orlinsky, D. E., & Howard, K. I. (1994). Unity and diversity among psychotherapies: A comparative perspective. In B. Bonger & L. E. Beutler (Eds.), *Foundations of psychotherapy: Theory, research, and practice* (pp. 3–23). New York, NY: Basic Books.

Ornish, D., Scherwitz, L. W., Billings, J. H., Gould, K. L., Merritt, T. A., Sparler, S., . . . Brand, R. J. (1998). Intensive lifestyle changes for reversal of coronary heart disease. *JAMA: Journal of the American Medical Association, 280,* 2001–2007.

Orzeł-Gryglewska, J. (2010). Consequences of sleep deprivation. *International Journal of Occupational Medicine and Environmental Health, 23,* 95–114.

Ostroff, C., & Ford, J. K. (1989). Assessing training needs: Critical levels of analysis. In I. L. Goldstein & Associates (Eds.), *Training and development in organizations* (pp. 25–62). San Francisco, CA: Jossey-Bass.

Ousley, L., Cordero, E. D., & White, S. (2008). Eating disorders and body image of undergraduate men. *Journal of American College Health, 56,* 617–621.

Overholser, J. C. (2003). Rational–emotive therapy: An interview with Albert Ellis. *Journal of Contemporary Psychotherapy, 33,* 187–204.

Overmier, J. B. (2002). On learned helplessness. *Integrative Physiological and Behavioral Science, 37,* 4–8.

Ozer, E. J., Best, S. R., Lipsey, T. L., & Weiss, D. S. (2003). Predictors of posttraumatic stress disorder and symptoms in adults: A meta-analysis. *Psychological Bulletin, 2003,* 52–73.

Pace, T. W., Negi, L., Adame, D. D., Cole, S. P., Sivilli, T. I., Brown, T. D., & Raison, C. L. (2009). Effect of compassion meditation on neuroendocrine, innate immune and behavioral responses to psychosocial stress. *Psychoneuroendocrinology, 34,* 87–98.

Padhi, K. (2005). Pain and psychological approaches to its management—The gate control theory of pain. *Social Science International, 21,* 121–130.

Paivio, A. (2007). *Mind and its evolution: A dual coding theoretical approach.* Mahwah, NJ: Erlbaum.

Paley, B., & O'Connor, M. J. (2007). Neurocognitive and neurobehavioral impairments in individuals with fetal alcohol spectrum disorders: Recognition and assessment. *International Journal on Disability and Human Development, 6,* 127–142.

Palmer, J. K., & Loveland, J. M. (2008). The influence of group discussion on performance judgments: Rating accuracy, contrast effects, and halo. *Journal of Psychology: Interdisciplinary and Applied, 142,* 117–130.

Palmer, S., Davidson, K., Tyrer, P., Gumley, A., Tata, P., Norrie, J., . . . Seivewright, H. (2006). The cost-effectiveness of cognitive behavior therapy for borderline personality disorder. Results from the BOSCOT trial. *Journal of Personality Disorders, 20,* 466–481.

Palomares, N. A. (2004). Gender schematicity, gender identity salience, and gender-linked language use. *Human Communication Research, 30,* 556–588.

Pan, Y., Wang, K., & Aragam, N. (2011). NTM and NR3C2 polymorphisms influencing intelligence: Family-based association studies. *Progress in Neuro-Psychopharmacology & Biological Psychiatry, 35,* 154–160.

Pankow, L. J., & Solotoroff, J. M. (2007). Biological aspects and theories of aging. In J. A. Blackburn & C. N. Dulmus (Eds.), *Handbook of gerontology: Evidence-based approaches to theory, practice, and policy* (pp. 19–56). Hoboken, NJ: Wiley.

Park, C. L., Edmondson, D., Fenster, J. R., & Blank, T. O. (2008). Meaning making and psychological adjustment following cancer: The mediating roles of growth, life meaning, and restored just-world beliefs. *Journal of Consulting and Clinical Psychology, 76,* 863–875.

Park, D., & Huang, C-M. (2010). Culture wires the brain: A cognitive neuroscience perspective. *Perspectives on Psychological Science, 5,* 391–400.

Parks, J. B., & Roberton, M. A. (2004). Explaining age and gender effects on attitudes toward sexist language. *Journal of Language and Social Psychology, 24,* 401–411.

Parslow, R. A., Jorm, A. F., & Christensen, H. (2006). Associations of pretrauma attributes and trauma exposure with screening positive for PTSD: Analysis of a community-based study of 2085 young adults. *Psychological Medicine, 36,* 387–395.

Partridge, T. (2010). Infant EEG asymmetry differentiates between attractive and unattractive faces. *Dissertation Abstracts International, 70.* Retrieved from EBSCOhost.

Pascoe, E. A., & Richman, L. S. (2009). Perceived discrimination and health: A meta-analytic review. *Psychological Bulletin, 135,* 531–554.

Patrick, C. J. (1994). Emotion and psychopathy: Startling new insights. *Psychophysiology, 31,* 319–330.

Patterson, C. J. (2009). Lesbian and gay parents and their children: A social science perspective. In D. A. Hope (Ed.), *Contemporary perspectives on lesbian, gay, and bisexual identities* (pp. 141–182). New York, NY: Springer Science + Business Media.

Patterson, C. J. (1995). Families of the baby boom: Parents' division of labor and children's adjustment. [Special issue: *Sexual orientation and human development*]. *Developmental Psychology, 31,* 115–123.

Patterson, C. J. (2000). Family relationships of lesbians and gay men. *Journal of Marriage and the Family, 62,* 1052–1069.

Patterson, D. R. (2010). *Clinical hypnosis for pain control.* Washington, DC: American Psychological Association.

Patterson, D. R., & Jensen, M. P. (2003). Hypnosis and clinical pain. *Psychological Bulletin, 129,* 495–521.

Patterson, F. G. (1981). *The education of Koko.* New York, NY: Holt.

Patton, P. (2008, December 1). One world, many minds. *Scientific American Mind, 19*(6), 72–79.

Patton, W., & Goddard, R. (2006). Coping with stress in the Australian job network: Gender differences. *Journal of Employment Counseling, 43,* 135–144.

Paulík, K. (2001). Hardiness, optimism, self-confidence and occupational stress among university teachers. *Studia Psychologica, 43,* 91–100.

Paunonen, S. V. (2003). Big Five factors of personality and replicated predictions of behavior. *Journal of Personality and Social Psychology, 84,* 411–422.

Paunovic, N., & Oest, L. G. (2001). Cognitive behavior therapy versus exposure therapy in the treatment of PTSD in refugees. *Behaviour Research and Therapy, 39,* 1183–1197.

Pavlov, I. P. (1927). *Conditional reflexes* (G. V. Anrep, Trans.). London, England: Oxford University Press.

Payne, J. D., Jackson, E. D., Ryan, L., Hoscheidt, S., Jacobs, W. J., & Nadel, L. (2006). The impact of stress on neutral and emotional aspects of episodic memory. *Memory, 14,* 1–16.

Payne, J. D., & Kensinger, E. A. (2010). Sleep's role in the consolidation of emotional episodic memories. *Current Directions in Psychological Science, 19,* 290–295.

Payne, J. D., & Nadel, L. (2004). Sleep, dreams, and memory consolidation: The role of the stress hormone cortisol. *Learning & Memory, 11,* 671–678.

Pechnick, R. N., & Ungerleider, J. T. (2004). Hallucinogens. In M. Galanter & D. Herbert (Eds.), *The American Psychiatric Publishing textbook of substance abuse treatment* (3rd ed., pp. 199–209). Washington, DC: American Psychiatric Publishing.

Pedersen, P. B., & Carey, J. C. (2003). *Multicultural counseling in schools* (2nd ed.). Boston, MA: Allyn & Bacon.

Pedersen, S. L., & McCarthy, D. M. (2008). Person-environment transactions in youth drinking and driving. *Psychology of Addictive Behaviors, 22,* 340–348.

Pederson, D. (2002). Political violence, ethnic conflict, and contemporary wars: Broad implications for health and social well-being. *Social Science and Medicine, 55,* 175–190.

Pegna, A. J., Caldara-Schnetzer, A.-S., & Khateb, A. (2008). Visual search for facial expressions of emotion is less affected in simultanagnosia. *Cortex, 44,* 46–53.

Pegna, A. J., Khateb, A., Lazeyras, F., & Seghier, M. L. (2005). Discriminating emotional faces without primary visual cortices involves the right amygdala. *Nature Neuroscience, 8,* 24–25.

Peigneux, P., Laureys, S., Fuchs, S., Collette, F., Perrin, F., Reggers, J., . . . Maquet, P. (2004). Are spatial memories strengthened in the human hippocampus during slow wave sleep? *Neuron, 44,* 535–545.

Pennebaker, J. W., & Chung, C. K. (2007). Expressive writing, emotional upheavals, and health. In H. S. Friedman & R. C. Silver (Eds.), *Foundations of health psychology* (pp. 263–284). New York, NY: Oxford University Press.

Penner, J., Rupsingh, R., Smith, M., Wells, J. L., Borrie, M. J., & Bartha, R. (2010). Increased glutamate in the hippocampus after galantamine treatment for Alzheimer disease. *Progress in Neuro-Psychopharmacology & Biological Psychiatry, 34,* 104–110.

Peplau, L. A. (2003). Human sexuality: How do men and women differ? *Current Directions in Psychological Science, 12,* 37–40.

Peplau, L. A., & Beals, K. P. (2004). The family lives of lesbians and gay men. In A. L. Vangelisti (Ed.), *Handbook of family communication* (pp. 233–248). Mahwah, NJ: Erlbaum.

Pepperberg, I. M. (2007). Grey parrots do not always "parrot": The roles of imitation and phonological awareness in the creation of new labels from existing vocalizations. *Language Sciences, 29,* 1–13.

Pepperberg, I. M. (2000). *The Alex studies: Cognitive and communicative abilities of grey parrots.* Cambridge, MA: Harvard University Press.

Perez, M. F., Ford, K. A., Goussakov, I., Stutzmann, G. E., & Hu, X. (2011). Repeated cocaine exposure decreases dopamine D_2-like receptor modulation of Ca^{2+} homeostasis in rat nucleus accumbens neurons. *Synapse, 65,* 168–180.

Perloff, R. M. (2003). *The dynamics of persuasion: Communication and attitudes in the 21st century* (2nd ed.). Mahwah, NJ: Erlbaum.

Perls, F. S. (1969). *Gestalt theory verbatim.* Lafayette, CA: People Press.

Perrig-Chiello, P., Hutchison, S., & Hoepflinger, F. (2008). Role involvement and well-being in middle-aged women. *Women & Health, 48,* 303–323.

Perry, J., Silvera, D., Rosenvinge, J. H., & Holte, A. (2002). Are oral, obsessive, and hysterical personality traits related to disturbed eating patterns? A general population study of 6,313 men and women. *Journal of Personality Assessment, 78,* 405–416.

Persky, H. (1978). Plasma testosterone level and sexual behavior of couples. *Archives of Sexual Behavior, 7,* 157–173.

Pert, C. B., & Snyder, S. H. (1973). The opiate receptor: Demonstration in nervous tissue. *Science, 179,* 1011–1014.

Petersen, J. L., & Hyde, J. (2010). A meta-analytic review of research on gender differences in sexuality, 1993–2007. *Psychological Bulletin, 136,* 21–38.

Petersen, J. L., & Hyde, J. (2011). Gender differences in sexual attitudes and behaviors: A review of meta-analytic results and large datasets. *Journal of Sex Research, 48,* 149–165.

Peterson, C. (2000). The future of optimism. *American Psychologist, 55,* 44–55.

Peterson, C., & Bossio, L. M. (1989). Learned helplessness. In R. C. Curtis (Ed.), *Self-defeating behaviors: Experimental research, clinical impressions, and practical implications* (pp. 235–257). New York, NY: Plenum.

Peterson, C., Vaillant, G. E., & Seligman, M. E. P. (1988). Explanatory style as a risk factor for illness. *Cognitive Therapy and Research, 12,* 119–132.

Peterson, L. R., & Peterson, M. J. (1959). Short-term retention of individual verbal items. *Journal of Experimental Psychology, 58,* 193–198.

Petkov, C. I., Kayser, C., Steudel, T., Whittingstall, K., Augath, M., & Logothetis, N. K. (2008). A voice region in the monkey brain. *Nature Neuroscience, 11,* 367–374.

Pettit, J. W., & Joiner, T. E. (2006). Interpersonal conflict avoidance. In J. W. Pettit & J. T. Joiner (Eds.), *Chronic depression: Interpersonal sources, therapeutic solutions* (pp. 73–84). Washington, DC: American Psychological Association.

Petty, R. E., & Cacioppo, J. T. (1986a). The elaboration likelihood model of persuasion. In L. Berkowitz (Ed.), *Advances in experimental social psychology* (Vol. 19, pp. 123–205). Orlando, FL: Academic Press.

Petty, R. E., & Cacioppo, J. T. (1986b). *Communication and persuasion: Central and peripheral routes to attitude change.* New York, NY: Springer-Verlag.

Pew Research Center. (2010). *The decline of marriage and rise of new families.* Retrieved from http://pewsocialtrends.org/files/2010/11/pew-social-trends-2010-families.pdf

Pew Research Center for the People and the Press. (2002, September 5). *One year later: New Yorkers more troubled, Washingtonians more on edge.* Retrieved from http://people-press.org/reports/display.php3?PageID_632

Pew Research Center for the People and the Press. (2005). *Huge racial divide over Katrina and its consequences.* Retrieved from http://people-press.org/reports/pdf/255.pdf

Pezdek, K. (2007). Expert testimony on eyewitness memory and identification. In M. Costanzo, D. Krauss, & K. Pezdek (Eds.), *Expert psychological testimony for the courts* (pp. 99–117). Mahwah, NJ: Erlbaum.

Phelps, C., Bennett, P., & Brain, K. (2008). Understanding emotional responses to breast/ovarian cancer genetic risk assessment: An applied test of a cognitive theory of emotion. *Psychology, Health & Medicine, 13,* 545–558.

Phelps, J. A., Davis, J. O., & Schartz, K. M. (1997). Nature, nurture, and twin research strategies. *Current Directions in Psychological Science, 6,* 117–121.

Phinney, J. S. (2008). Ethnic identity exploration in emerging adulthood. In D. L. Browning (Ed.), *Adolescent identities: A collection of readings* (pp. 47–66). New York, NY: The Analytic Press.

Piaget, J. (1967). *Six psychological studies.* New York, NY: Random House.

Piaget, J. (1969). The intellectual development of the adolescent. In G. Caplan & S. Lebovici (Eds.), *Adolescence: Psychosocial perspectives* (pp. 22–26). New York, NY: Basic Books.

Piefke, M., Weiss, P. H., Markowitsch, H. J., & Fink, G. R. (2005). Gender differences in the functional neuroanatomy of emotional episodic autobiographical memory. *Human Brain Mapping, 24,* 313–324.

Pietrzak, R. H., & Petry, N. M. (2005). Antisocial personality disorder is associated with increased severity of gambling, medical, drug and psychiatric problems among treatment-seeking pathological gamblers. *Addiction, 100,* 1183–1193.

Pihl, R. O. (2010). Mental disorders are brain disorders: You think? *Canadian Psychology/Psychologie canadienne, 51,* 40–49.

Pinker, S. (1999). *Words and rules: The ingredients of language.* New York, NY: Basic Books.

Pinker, S. (2004). Clarifying the logical problem of language acquisition. *Journal of Child Language, 31,* 949–953.

Pinker, S. (2007). Language as an adaptation by natural selection. *Acta Psychologica Sinica, 39,* 431–438.

Pinker, S., & Jackendoff, R. (2005). The faculty of language: What's special about it? *Cognition, 95,* 201–236.

Piomelli, D. (2001). Cannabinoid activity curtails cocaine craving. *Nature Medicine, 7,* 1099–1100.

Pirkle, E. C., & Richter, L. (2006). Personality, attitudinal and behavioral risk profiles of young female binge drinkers and smokers. *Journal of Adolescent Health, 38,* 44–54.

Pizzighello, S., & Bressan, P. (2008). Auditory attention causes visual inattentional blindness. *Perception, 37,* 859–866.

Plomin, R. (1997). Identifying genes for cognitive abilities and disabilities. In R. J. Sternberg & E. L. Grigorenko (Eds.), *Intelligence: Heredity and environment* (pp. 89–104). New York, NY: Cambridge University Press.

Plomin, R., & Rende, R. (1991). Human behavioral genetics. *Annual Review of Psychology, 42,* 161–190.

Plutchik, R. (1980). *Emotion: A psychoevolutionary synthesis.* New York, NY: Harper & Row.

Pogarsky, G., & Piquero, A. R. (2003). Can punishment encourage offending? Investigating the "resetting" effect. *Journal of Research in Crime and Delinquency, 40,* 95–120.

Pogue-Geile, M. F., & Yokley, J. L. (2010). Current research on the genetic contributors to schizophrenia. *Current Directions in Psychological Science, 19,* 214–219.

Pole, N., Neylan, T. C., Otte, C., Henn-Hasse, C., Metzler, T. J, & Marmar, C. R. (2009). Prospective prediction of posttraumatic stress disorder symptoms using fear potentiated auditory startle responses. *Biological Psychiatry, 65,* 235–240.

Pollack, M. H., & Simon, N. M. (2009). Pharmacotherapy for panic disorder and agoraphobia. In M. M. Antony & M. B. Stein (Eds.), *Oxford handbook of anxiety and related disorders* (pp. 295–307). New York, NY: Oxford University Press.

Pollack, W. S., & Levant, R. F. (1998). *New psychotherapy for men.* New York, NY: Wiley.

Pooley, E. (2005). Job rotation. *Canadian Business, 78,* 109.

Pope, C. G., Pope, H. G., & Menard, W. (2005). Clinical features of muscle dysmorphia among males with body dysmorphic disorder. *Body Image, 2,* 395–400.

Pope, H. G., Jr., Barry, S., Bodkin, J. A., & Hudson, J. I. (2006). "The validity of the dissociative disorders": Reply. *Psychotherapy and Psychosomatics, 76,* 59–60.

Pope, M., & Scott, J. (2003). Do clinicians understand why individuals stop taking lithium? *Journal of Affective Disorders, 74,* 287–291.

Port, C. L., Engdahl, B., & Frazier, P. (2001). A longitudinal and retrospective study of PTSD among older prisoners of war. *American Journal of Psychiatry, 158,* 1474–1479.

Pothier, P. K. T. (2002). Effect of relaxation on neuro-immune responses of persons undergoing chemotherapy. *Dissertation Abstracts International: Section B: The Sciences and Engineering, 62,* 4471.

Potter, M. C. (2009). Kynurenic acid, learning and memory: The glutamate connection. *Dissertation Abstracts International, 69,* Retrieved from EBSCOhost.

Powell, S., Rosner, R., Butollo, W., Tedeschi, R. G., & Calhoun, L. G. (2003). Posttraumatic growth after a war: A study with former refugees and displaced people in Sarajevo. *Journal of Clinical Psychology, 59,* 71–83.

Powers, M. B., & Emmelkamp, M. G. (2008). Virtual reality exposure therapy for anxiety disorders: A meta-analysis. *Journal of Anxiety Disorders, 22,* 561–569.

Preckel, F., Holling, H., & Wiese, M. (2006). Relationship of intelligence and creativity in gifted and non-gifted students: An investigation of threshold theory. *Personality and Individual Differences, 40,* 159–170.

Price, M. (2008, June). Genes matter in addiction. *Monitor on Psychology, 39*(6), 16.

Price, M. (2011, January). The risks of night work. *Monitor on Psychology, 42*(1), 39–41.

Prince, S. E., Tsukiura, T., & Cabeza, R. (2007). Distinguishing the neural correlates of episodic memory encoding and semantic memory retrieval. *Psychological Science, 18,* 144–151.

Principe, C. P., & Langlois, J. H. (2011). Faces differing in attractiveness elicit corresponding affective responses. *Cognition and Emotion, 25,* 140–148.

Pring, L., Woolf, K., & Tadic, V. (2008). Melody and pitch processing in five musical savants with congenital blindness. *Perception, 37,* 290–307.

Prinz, J. (2008). Embodied emotions. In W. G. Lycan & J. J. Prinz (Eds.), *Mind and cognition: An anthology* (3rd ed., pp. 839–849). Malden, MA: Blackwell Publishing.

Prior, H., Schwarz, A., & Güntürkün, O. (2008). Mirror-induced behavior in the magpie (Pica pica): Evidence of self-recognition. *PLoS Biology, 6:* e202. doi:10.1371/journal.pbio.0060202

Prokopcáková, A. (2004). Choice of coping strategies in the interaction: Anxiety and type of a demanding life situation (a research probe). *Studia Psychologica, 46,* 235–238.

Puma, M., Bell, S., Cook, R., & Hyde, C. (2010). *Head Start Impact Study Final Report.* Washington, DC: U.S. Department of Health and Human Services, Administration for Children and Families.

Purcell, C. E., & Arrigo, B. A. (2006). *The psychology of lust murder: Paraphilia, sexual killing, and serial homicide.* Amsterdam, Netherlands: Elsevier.

Putrevu, S. (2005). Differences in readers' response towards advertising versus publicity. *Psychological Reports, 96,* 207–212.

Pych, J. C., Chang, Q., & Colon-Rivera, C. (2005). Acetylcholine release in the hippocampus and striatum during place and response training. *Learning & Memory, 12,* 564–572.

Qiu, J., Li, H., Jou, J., Wu, Z., & Zhang, Q. (2008). Spatiotemporal cortical activation underlies mental preparation for successful riddle solving: An event-related potential study. *Experimental Brain Research, 186,* 629–634.

Quesnel, C., Savard, J., Simard, S., Ivers, H., & Morin, C. M. (2003). Efficacy of cognitive-behavioral therapy for insomnia in women treated for nonmetastatic breast cancer. *Journal of Consulting and Clinical Psychology, 71*, 189–200.

Quinn, P. C., & Liben, L. S. (2008). A sex difference in mental rotation in young infants. *Psychological Science, 19*, 1067–1070.

Rabasca, L. (2000, February). Lessons in diversity [and] helping American Indians earn psychology degrees. *Monitor on Psychology, 31*(2), 50–53.

Rabin, B. S., & Koenig, H. G. (2002). Immune, neuroendocrine, and religious measures. In H. G. Koenig & H. J. Cohen (Eds.), *The link between religion and health: Psychoneuroimmunology and the faith factor* (pp. 197–249). London, England: Oxford University Press.

RAC Foundation. (2008). The effect of text messaging on driver behaviour. Retrieved from http://www.racfoundation.org/files/textingwhiledrivingreport.pdf

Ralat, J. R. (2006). Retrospective study highlights benefits of SSRIs in PTSD. *CNS Spectrums, 11*, 166.

Raloff, J. (2007, July 7). Restoring scents: Faulty sniffers may get some help. *Science News, 172*(1), 10–11.

Ramachandran, V. S., & Rogers-Ramachandran, D. (2007, August–September). It's all done with mirrors. *Scientific American Mind, 18*(4), 16–18.

Ramadori, G., Lee, C., Bookout, A., Lee, S., Williams, K., Anderson, J., . . . Coppari, R. (2008). Brain SIRT1: Anatomical distribution and regulation by energy availability. *Journal of Neuroscience, 28*, 9989–9996.

Ramey, C. T., & Ramey, S. L. (2007). Early learning and school readiness: Can early intervention make a difference? In G. W. Ladd (Ed.), *Appraising the human developmental sciences: Essays in honor of Merrill-Palmer Quarterly* (pp. 329–350). Detroit, MI: Wayne State University Press.

Ramey, C. T., Ramey, S. L., & Lanzi, R. G. (2001). Intelligence and experience. In R. J. Sternberg & E. L. Grigorenko (Eds.), *Environmental effects on cognitive abilities* (pp. 83–115). Mahwah, NJ: Erlbaum.

Ramey, S. L. (1999). Head Start and preschool education: Toward continued improvement. *American Psychologist, 54*, 344–346.

Rasch, B., & Born, J. (2008). Reactivation and consolidation of memory during sleep. *Current Directions in Psychological Science, 17*, 188–192.

Rasch, B., Büchel, C., Gais, S., & Born, J. (2007). Odor cues during slow-wave sleep prompt declarative memory consolidation. *Science, 315*, 1426–1429.

Rathus, S. A. (2006). *Childhood and adolescence: Voyages in development.* Belmont, CA: Wadsworth.

Raven, B. H. (1998). Groupthink: Bay of Pigs and Watergate reconsidered. *Organizational Behavior and Human Decision Processes, 73*, 352–361.

Rayner, K., White, S. J., Johnson, R. L., & Liversedge, S. P. (2006). Raeding wrods with jumbled lettres. *Psychological Science, 17*, 192–193.

Redelmeier, D. A., & Tversky, A. (2004). On the belief that arthritis pain is related to the weather. In E. Shafir (Ed.), *Preference, belief, and similarity: Selected writings by Amos Tversky* (pp. 377–381). Cambridge, MA: MIT Press.

Ree, M. J., & Earles, J. A. (1992). Intelligence is the best predictor of job performance. *Current Directions in Psychological Science, 1*, 86–89.

Ree, M. J., Earles, J. A., & Teachout, M. S. (1994). Predicting job performance: Not much more than g. *Journal of Applied Psychology, 79*, 518–524.

Reed, D. C. (2008). A model of moral stages. *Journal of Moral Education, 37*, 357–376.

Reiche, E. M. V., Morimoto, H. K., & Nunes, S. O. V. (2005). Stress and depression-induced immune dysfunction: Implications for the development and progression of cancer. *International Review of Psychiatry, 17*, 515–527.

Reineke, A. (2008). The effects of heart rate variability biofeedback in reducing blood pressure for the treatment of essential hypertension. *Dissertation Abstracts International: Section B: The Sciences and Engineering, 68*(7-B), 4880.

Reis, H. T., Maniaci, M. R., Caprariello, P. A., Eastwick, P. W., & Finkel, E. J. (2011). Familiarity does indeed promote attraction in live interaction. *Journal of Personality and Social Psychology, 101*, 557–570. doi:10.1037/a0022885

Reiss, S. (2005). Extrinsic and intrinsic motivation at 30: Unresolved scientific issues. *Behavior Analyst, 28*, 1–14.

Renner, M. J., & Mackin, R. S. (1998). A life stress instrument for classroom use. *Teaching of Psychology, 25*, 46–48.

Renner, M. J., & Mackin, R. S. (2002). A life stress instrument for classroom use. In R. A. Griggs (Ed.), *Handbook for teaching introductory psychology* (Vol. 3, pp. 236–238). Mahwah, NJ: Erlbaum.

Repetti, R., Wang, S., & Saxbe, D. (2009). Bringing it all back home: How outside stressors shape families' everyday lives. *Current Directions in Psychological Science, 18*, 106–111.

Rescorla, R. A. (1966). Predictability and number of pairings in Pavlovian fear conditioning. *Psychonomic Science, 4*, 383–384.

Rescorla, R. A. (1967). Pavlovian conditioning and its proper control procedures. *Psychological Review, 74*, 71–80.

Rescorla, R. A. (1988). Pavlovian conditioning: It's not what you think. *American Psychologist, 43*, 151–160.

Ressel, V., Wilke, M., Lidzba, K., Lutzenberger, W., & Krägeloh-Mann, I. (2008). Increases in language lateralization in normal children as observed using magnetoencephalography. *Brain and Language, 106*, 167–176.

Reyna, V. F., & Titcomb, A. L. (1997). Constraints on the suggestibility of eyewitness testimony: A fuzzy-trace theory analysis. In D. G. Payne & F. G. Conrad (Eds.), *Intersections in basic and applied memory research* (pp. 27–55). Mahwah, NJ: Erlbaum.

Rhodewalt, F., & Vohs, K. D. (2005). Defensive strategies, motivation, and the self: A self-regulatory process view. In A. J. Elliot & C. S. Dweck (Eds.), *Handbook of competence and motivation* (pp. 548–565). New York, NY: Guilford Press.

Ricaurte, G. A., Yuan, J., Hatzidimitriou, G., Cord, B. J., & McCann, U. D. (2003). Severe dopaminergic neurotoxicity in primates after a common recreational dose regime of MDMA ("Ecstasy"): Retraction. *Science, 301*, 1479.

Riccio, D. C., Millin, P. M., & Gisquet-Verrier, P. (2003). Retrograde amnesia: Forgetting back. *Current Directions in Psychological Science, 12*, 41–44.

Richards, J., Encel, J., & Shute, R. (2003). The emotional and behavioural adjustment of intellectually gifted adolescents: A multidimensional, multi-informant approach. *High Ability Studies, 14*, 153–164.

Richards, T. L., & Berninger, V. W. (2008). Abnormal fMRI connectivity in children with dyslexia during a phoneme task: Before but not after treatment. *Journal of Neurolinguistics, 21*, 294–304.

Riggio, R. E. (2003). *Introduction to industrial/organizational psychology* (4th ed.). Upper Saddle River, NJ: Prentice Hall.

Ringach, D. L., & Jentsch, J. (2009). We must face the threats. *The Journal of Neuroscience, 29*, 11417–11418.

Riniolo, T. C., Johnson, K. C., Sherman, T. R., & Misso, J. A. (2006). Hot or not: Do professors perceived as physically attractive receive higher student evaluations? *Journal of General Psychology, 133*, 19–35.

Rioux, L. (2005). The well-being of aging people living in their own homes. *Journal of Environmental Psychology, 25*, 231–243.

Rizzolatti, G., Fogassi, L., & Gallese, V. (2008). Mirrors in the mind. In M. H. Imordino-Yang (Ed.), *The Jossey-Bass reader on the brain and learning* (pp. 12–19). San Francisco, CA: Jossey-Bass.

Robb, C. (2006). *This changes everything: The relational revolution in psychology.* New York, NY: Farrar, Straus and Giroux.

Roberson, D. (2010). Color in mind, culture, and language. In M. Schaller, A. Norenzayan, S. J. Heine, T. Yamagishi & T. Kameda (Eds.), *Evolution, culture, and the human mind* (pp. 167–184). New York, NY: Psychology Press.

Roberts, A. H., Kewman, D. G., Mercer, L., & Hovell, M. (1993). The power of nonspecific effects in healing: Implications for psychosocial and biological treatments. *Clinical Psychology Review, 13*, 375–391.

Roberts, B. W., & Mroczek, D. (2008). Personality trait change in adulthood. *Current Directions in Psychological Science, 17*, 31–35.

Roberts, B. W., Walton, K. E., & Viechtbauer, W. (2006). Patterns of mean-level change in personality traits across the life course: A meta-analysis of longitudinal studies. *Psychological Bulletin, 132*, 1–25.

Robins, L. N., & Regier, D. A. (1991). *Psychiatric disorders in America: The Epidemiologic Catchment Area Study.* New York, NY: Free Press.

Robinson, A., & Clinkenbeard, P. R. (1998). Giftedness: An exceptionality examined. *Annual Review of Psychology, 49*, 117–139.

Rodafinos, A., Vucevic, A., & Sideridis, G. D. (2005). The effectiveness of compliance techniques: Foot in the door versus door in the face. *Journal of Social Psychology, 145*, 237–239.

Rofé, Y. (1984). Stress and affiliation: A utility theory. *Psychological Review, 91*, 251–268.

Rofé, Y., Hoffman, M., & Lewin, I. (1985). Patient affiliation in major illness. *Psychological Medicine, 15*, 895–896.

Rogers, C. R. (1961). *On becoming a person: A therapist's view of psychotherapy.* Boston, MA: Houghton Mifflin.

Roh, S., Ahn, D. H., & Nam, J. H. (2006). Cardiomyopathy associated with clozapine. *Experimental and Clinical Psychopharmacology, 14*, 94–98.

Roncadin, C., Guger, S., Archibald, J., Barnes, M., & Dennis, M. (2004). Working memory after mild, moderate, or severe childhood closed head injury. *Developmental Neuropsychology, 25,* 21–36.

Roper, R., & Shewan, D. (2002). Compliance and eyewitness testimony: Do eyewitnesses comply with misleading "expert pressure" during investigative interviewing. *Legal and Criminological Psychology, 7,* 155–163.

Rosch, E. H. (2002). Principles of categorization. In D. J. Levitin (Ed.), *Foundations of Cognitive Psychology: Core Readings* (pp. 251–270). Cambridge, MA: MIT Press.

Rose, R. J., Viken, R. J., Dick, D. M., Bates, J. E., Pulkkinen, L., & Kaprio, J. (2003). It *does* take a village: Nonfamilial environments and children's behavior. *Psychological Science, 14,* 273–277.

Rosenfield, S., & Pottick, K. J. (2005). Power, gender, and the self: Reflections on improving mental health for males and females. In S. A. Kirk (Ed.), *Mental disorders in the social environment: Critical perspectives* (pp. 214–228). New York, NY: Columbia University Press.

Rosengren, A., Hawken, S., Ounpuu, S., Sliwa, K., Zubaid, M., Almahmeed, W. A., . . . Yusuf, S. (2004). Association of psychosocial risk factors with risk of acute myocardial infarction in 11119 cases and 13648 controls from 52 countries (the INTERHEART study): Case-control study. *Lancet, 364,* 953–962.

Rosenstein, D., & Oster, H. (2005). Differential facial responses to four basic tastes in newborns. In P. Ekman & E. Rosenberg (Eds.), *What the face reveals: Basic and applied studies of spontaneous expression using the facial action coding system (FACS)* (2nd ed., pp. 302–327). New York, NY: Oxford University Press.

Rosenthal, A. M. (2008). *Thirty-eight witnesses: The Kitty Genovese case.* New York, NY: Melville House.

Rosenthal, R. (2002). The Pygmalion effect and its mediating mechanisms. In J. Aronson (Ed.), *Improving academic achievement: Impact of psychological factors on education* (pp. 25–36). San Diego, CA: Academic Press.

Rosenthal, R. (2006). Applying psychological research on interpersonal expectations and covert communication in classrooms, clinics, corporations, and courtrooms. In S. I. Donaldson, D. E. Berger, & K. Pezdek (Eds.), *Applied psychology: New frontiers and rewarding careers* (pp. 107–118). Mahwah, NJ: Erlbaum.

Rosenzweig, M. R. (1984). Experience, memory, and the brain. *American Psychologist, 39,* 365–376.

Rosenzweig, M. R. (1996). Aspects of the search for neural mechanisms of memory. *Annual Review of Psychology, 47,* 1–32.

Rosenzweig, M. R., & Leiman, A. L. (1982). *Physiological psychology.* Lexington, MA: Heath.

Ross, C. A., Norton, G. R., & Wozney, K. (1989). Multiple personality disorder: An analysis of 236 cases. *Canadian Journal of Psychiatry, 34,* 413–418.

Ross, M., & Wang, Q. (2010). Why we remember and what we remember: Culture and autobiographical memory. *Perspectives on Psychological Science, 5,* 401–409.

Roth, B. (2004). *Separate roads to feminism: Black, chicana, and white feminist movements in America's second wave.* New York, NY: Cambridge University Press.

Roth, T. (2007). Insomnia: Definition, prevalence, etiology, and consequences. *Journal of Clinical Sleep Medicine, 3*(5), S7–S10.

Rothblum, E. D, Brand, P. A., Miller, C. T., & Oetjen, H. A. (1990). The relationship between obesity, employment discrimination, and employment-related victimization. *Journal of Vocational Behavior, 37,* 251–266.

Rotter, J. B. (1954). *Social learning and clinical psychology.* Englewood Cliffs, NJ: Prentice Hall.

Rouhana, N. N., & Bar-Tal, D. (1998). Psychological dynamics of intractable ethnonational conflicts: The Israeli-Palestinian case. *American Psychologist, 53,* 761–770.

Rowland, N. E. (2002). Thirst and water-salt appetite. In H. Pashler & R. Gallistel (Eds.), *Stevens' handbook of experimental psychology: Vol. 3, Learning, motivation, and emotion* (3rd ed., pp. 669–707). New York, NY: Wiley.

Rubin, K. H., Fredstrom, B., & Bowker, J. (2008). Future directions in friendship in childhood and early adolescence. *Social Development, 17,* 1085–1096.

Rubinstein, J. S., Meyer, D. E., & Evans, J. E. (2001). Executive control of cognitive processes in task switching. *Journal of Experimental Psychology: Human Perception and Performance, 27,* 763–797.

Ruble, D. N., Fleming, A. S., Hackel, L. S., & Stangor, C. (1988). Changes in the marital relationship during the transition to first time motherhood: Effects of violated expectations concerning division of household labor. *Journal of Personality and Social Psychology, 55,* 78–87.

Rugulies, R. (2002). Depression as a predictor for coronary heart disease: A review and meta-analysis. *American Journal of Preventive Medicine, 23,* 51–61.

Ruifang, G., & Danling, P. (2005). A review of studies on the brain plasticity. *Psychological Science, 28,* 409–411.

Rule, N. O., Moran, J. M., Freeman, J. B., Whitfield-Gabrieli, S., Gabrieli, J. E., & Ambady, N. (2010). Face value: Amygdala response reflects the validity of first impressions. *NeuroImage, 54,* 734–741. doi:10.1016/j.neuroimage.2010.07.007

Rumbaugh, D. M. (1977). *Language learning by a chimpanzee.* New York, NY: Academic Press.

Rumbaugh, D. M., & Savage-Rumbaugh, E. S. (1978). Chimpanzee language research: Status and potential. *Behavior Research Methods and Instrumentation, 10,* 119–131.

Runco, M. A. (2008). Commentary: Divergent thinking is not synonymous with creativity. *Psychology of Aesthetics, Creativity, and the Arts, 2,* 93–96.

Rushton, J. P., Bons, T. A., & Hur, Y.-M. (2008). The genetics and evolution of the general factor of personality. *Journal of Research in Personality, 42,* 1173–1185.

Russell, J. A. (1991). Culture and the categorization of emotions. *Psychological Bulletin, 110,* 426–450.

Rust, J. O., & Wallace, M. A. (2004). Adaptive Behavior Assessment System (2nd ed.). *Journal of Psychoeducational Assessment, 22,* 367–373.

Rutter, M. L. (2005). Genetic influences and autism. In F. R. Volkmar, R. Paul, A. Klin, & D. Cohen (Eds.), *Handbook of autism and pervasive developmental disorders, Vol. 1: Diagnosis, development, neurobiology, and behavior* (3rd. ed., pp. 425–452). Hoboken, NJ: Wiley.

Ryan, R. M., & Deci, E. L. (2000). Self-determination theory and the facilitation of intrinsic motivation, social development, and well-being. *American Psychologist, 55,* 68–78.

Rynes, S. L., Gerhart, B., & Parks, L. (2005). Personnel psychology: Performance evaluation and pay for performance. *Annual Review of Psychology, 56,* 571–600.

Sabanayagam, C., & Shankar, A. (2010). Sleep duration and cardiovascular disease: Results from the National Health Interview Survey. *Sleep: Journal of Sleep and Sleep Disorders Research, 33,* 1037–1042.

Sabattini, L., & Crosby, F. J. (2009). Ceilings and walls: Work-life and "family-friendly" policies. In M. Barreto, M. K. Ryan, & M. T. Schmitt (Eds.), *The glass ceiling in the 21st century: Understanding barriers to gender equality* (pp. 201–223). Washington, DC: American Psychological Association.

Sabini, J., & Silver, M. (2005). Ekman's basic emotions: Why not love and jealousy? *Cognition & Emotion, 19,* 693–712.

Sachdev, P. S., & Chen, X. (2009). Neurosurgical treatment of mood disorders: Traditional psychosurgery and the advent of deep brain stimulation. *Current Opinion in Psychiatry, 22,* 25–31.

Sacks, O. (2000). *Seeing voices: A journey into the world of the deaf.* New York, NY: Vintage.

Safdar, S., Friedlmeier, W., Matsumoto, D., Yoo, S. H., Kwantes, C. T., Kakai, H., & Shigemasu, E. (2009). Variations of emotional display rules within and across cultures: A comparison between Canada, USA, and Japan. *Canadian Journal of Behavioural Science/Revue canadienne des sciences du comportement, 41,* 1–10.

Safdar, S., & Lay, C. H. (2003). The relations of immigrant-specific and immigrant-nonspecific daily hassles to distress controlling for psychological adjustment and cultural competence. *Journal of Applied Social Psychology, 33,* 299–320.

Saha, S., Chant, D., & McGrath, J. (2008). Meta-analyses of the incidence and prevalence of schizophrenia: Conceptual and methodological issues. *International Journal of Methods in Psychiatric Research, 17,* 55–61.

Saiz, P. A., García-Portilla, M. P., Paredes, B., Arango, C., Morales, B., Alvarez, V., . . . Bobes, J. (2008). Association between the A-1438G polymorphism of the serotonin 2A receptor gene and nonimpulsive suicide attempts. *Psychiatric Genetics, 18,* 213–218.

Sakai, K. L. (2005). Language acquisition and brain development. *Science, 310,* 815–819.

Sakai, K. L., & Muto, M. (2007). Cortical plasticity for language processing in the human brain. In M.-K. Sun (Ed.), *Research in cognitive sciences* (pp. 163–173). Hauppauge, NY: Nova Science.

Salas, E., Stagl, K. C., & Burke, C. S. (2004). 25 years of team effectiveness in organizations: Research, themes, and emerging needs. In C. L. Cooper & I. T. Robertson (Eds.), *International review of industrial and organizational psychology 2004* (Vol. 19, pp. 47–91). West Sussex, England: Wiley.

Saletan, W. (2010, May 24). The ministry of truth: A mass experiment in altering political memories. Retrieved from http://www.slate.com/id/2254054/

Salgado, J. F., Moscoso, S., & Lado, M. (2003). Evidence of cross-cultural invariance of the Big Five personality dimensions in work settings. *European Journal of Personality, 1*(Suppl. 1), S67–S76.

Salovey, P. (2006). Epilogue: The agenda for future research. In V. U. Druskat, F. Sala, & G. Mount (Eds.), *Linking emotional intelligence and performance at work: Current research evidence with individuals and groups* (pp. 267–272). Mahwah, NJ: Erlbaum.

Salovey, P., Mayer, J. D., & Rosenhan, D. L. (1991). Mood behavior. In M. S. Clark (Ed.), *Review of personality and social psychology: Prosocial behavior* (Vol. 12, pp. 215–237). Newbury Park, CA: Sage.

Salovey, P., Rothman, A. J., Detweiler, J. B., & Steward, W. T. (2000). Emotional states and physical health. *American Psychologist, 55,* 110–121.

Salzman, C. D., & Fusi, S. (2010). Emotion, cognition, and mental state representation in amygdala and prefrontal cortex. *Annual Review of Neuroscience, 33,* 173–202.

Samokhvalov, A. V., Popova, S., Room, R., Ramonas, M., & Rehm, J. (2010). Disability associated with alcohol abuse and dependence. *Alcoholism: Clinical and Experimental Research, 34,* 1871–1878.

Sampson, G. (1999). *Educating Eve: The "language instinct" debate.* London, England: Cassell.

Sancaktar, I., & Demirkan, H. (2008). Spatial updating of objects after rotational and translational body movements in virtual environments. *Computers in Human Behavior, 24,* 2682–2696.

Sanders Thompson, V. L., & Alexander, H. (2006). Therapists' race and African American clients' reactions to therapy. *Psychotherapy: Theory, Research, Practice, Training, 43,* 99–110.

Sandler, I., Miles, J., Cookston, J., & Braver, S. (2008). Effects of father and mother parenting on children's mental health in high- and low-conflict divorces. *Family Court Review, 46,* 282–296.

Sankari, Z., Adeli, H., & Adeli, A. (2011). Intrahemispheric, interhemispheric, and distal EEG coherence in Alzheimer's disease. *Clinical Neurophysiology, 122,* 897–906.

Sano, D. L. (2002). Attitude similarity and marital satisfaction in long-term African American and Caucasian marriages. *Dissertation Abstracts International: Section A: Humanities and Social Sciences, 62,* 289.

Saporta, I., & Halpern, J. J. (2002). Being different can hurt: Effects of deviation from physical norms on lawyers' salaries. *Industrial Relations: A Journal of Economy and Society, 41,* 442–466.

Saretzki, G., & von Zglinicki, T. (2002). Replicative aging, telomeres, and oxidative stress. In D. Harman (Ed.), *Increasing healthy life span: Conventional measures and slowing the innate aging process* (pp. 24–29). New York, NY: New York Academy of Sciences.

Saris, W. E., & Gallhofer, I. N. (2007). *Design, evaluation, and analysis of questionnaires for survey research.* Hoboken, NJ: Wiley.

Sarpal, D., Buchsbaum, B. R., Kohn, P. D., Kippenhan, J. S., Mervis, C. B., Morris, C. A., . . . Berman, K. F. (2008). A genetic model for understanding higher order visual processing: Functional interactions of the ventral visual stream in Williams syndrome. *Cerebral Cortex, 18,* 2402–2409.

Sattler, J. M. (1992). *Assessment of children* (3rd ed.). San Diego, CA: Author.

Sattler, J. M. (2005). *Assessment of children: Behavioral and clinical applications* (5th ed.). La Mesa, CA: Author.

Savage-Rumbaugh, E. S., & Lewin, R. (1994). *Kanzi: The ape at the brink of the human mind.* New York, NY: Wiley.

Save, E., & Poucet, B. (2005). Piloting. In I. Q. Whishaw & B. Kolb (Eds.), *The behavior of the laboratory rat: A handbook with tests* (pp. 392–400). New York, NY: Oxford University Press.

Savic, I., Berglund, H., & Lindström, P. (2005). Brain response to putative pheromones in homosexual men. *PNAS Proceedings of the National Academy of Sciences of the United States of America, 102,* 7356–7361.

Savic, I., Berglund, H., & Lindström, P. (2007). Brain response to putative pheromones in homosexual men. In G. Einstein (Ed.), *Sex and the brain* (pp. 731–738). Cambridge, MA: MIT Press.

Savin-Williams, R. C. (2006). Who's gay? Does it matter? *Current Directions in Psychological Research, 15,* 40–44.

Scerbo, M. W., Bliss, J. P., Schmidt, E. A., & Thompson, S. N. (2006). The efficacy of a medical virtual reality simulator for training phlebotomy. *Human Factors, 48,* 72–84.

Schachter, S., & Singer, J. E. (1962). Cognitive, social, and physiological determinants of emotional state. *Psychological Review, 69,* 379–399.

Schachter, S., & Singer, J. E. (2001). Cognitive, social, and psychological determinants of emotional state. In G. W. Parrott (Ed.), *Emotions in social psychology: Essential readings* (pp. 76–93). Philadelphia, PA: Psychology Press.

Schacter, D. L., & Addis, D. (2009). Remembering the past to imagine the future: A cognitive neuroscience perspective. *Military Psychology, 21*(Suppl 1), S108–S112.

Schaefer, C. E., & Mattei, D. (2005). Catharsis: Effectiveness in children's aggression. *International Journal of Play Therapy, 14,* 103–109.

Schafe, G. E., & LeDoux, J. E. (2002). Emotional plasticity. In H. Pashler & R. Gallistel (Eds.), *Stevens' handbook of experimental psychology: Vol. 3, Learning, motivation, and emotion* (3rd ed., pp. 535–561). New York, NY: Wiley.

Schaie, K. W. (1984). Midlife influences upon intellectual functioning in old age. *International Journal of Behavioral Development, 7,* 463–478.

Schaie, K. W., & Willis, S. L. (2001). *Adult development and aging* (5th ed.). Upper Saddle River, NJ: Prentice Hall.

Schaie, K. W., & Zanjani, F. A. K. (2006). Intellectual development across adulthood. In C. Hoare (Ed.), *Handbook of adult development and learning* (pp. 99–122). New York, NY: Oxford University Press.

Schedlowski, M., & Pacheco-López, G. (2010). The learned immune response: Pavlov and beyond. *Brain, Behavior, and Immunity, 24,* 176–185.

Scheibel, R. S., & Levin, H. S. (2004). Working memory and the functional anatomy of the frontal lobes. *Cortex, 40,* 218–219.

Scherer, K. R., Schorr, A., & Johnstone, T. (Eds.). (2001). *Appraisal processes in emotion: Theory, methods, research.* New York, NY: Oxford University Press.

Schick, S., & Glantz, S. (2005). Scientific analysis of second-hand smoke by the tobacco industry, 1929–1972. *Nicotine & Tobacco Research, 7,* 591–612.

Schiffman, S. S. (1997). Taste and smell losses in normal aging and disease. *JAMA: Journal of the American Medical Association, 278,* 1357–1352.

Schimmack, U., & Crites, S. L., Jr. (2005). The structure of affect. In D. Albarracín, B. T. Johnson, & M. P. Zanna (Eds.), *The handbook of attitudes* (pp. 397–435). Mahwah, NJ: Erlbaum.

Schinke, S., & Schwinn, T. (2005). Gender-specific computer-based intervention for preventing drug abuse among girls. *American Journal of Drug and Alcohol Abuse, 31,* 609–616.

Schlossberg, M. K. (2004). *Retire smart, retire happy: Finding your true path in life.* Washington, DC: American Psychological Association.

Schmahl, C. G., Vermetten, E., Elzinga, B. M., & Bremmer, J. D. (2004). A positron emission tomography study of memories of childhood abuse in borderline personality disorder. *Biological Psychiatry, 55,* 759–765.

Schmid, S. M., Hallschmid, M., Jauch-Chara, K., Born, J., & Schultes, B. (2008). A single night of sleep deprivation increases ghrelin levels and feelings of hunger in normal-weight healthy men. *Journal of Sleep Research, 17,* 331–334.

Schmidt, F. L., & Hunter, J. (2004). General mental ability in the world of work: Occupational attainment and job performance. *Journal of Personality and Social Psychology, 86,* 162–173.

Schmidt, F. L., & Hunter, J. E. (1998). The validity and utility of selection methods in personnel psychology: Practical and theoretical implications of 85 years of research findings, *Psychological Bulletin, 124,* 262–274.

Schnall, S., Roper, J., & Fessler, D. T. (2010). Elevation leads to altruistic behavior. *Psychological Science, 21,* 315–320.

Schneider, B. M. (2002). Using the Big-Five personality factors in the Minnesota Multiphasic Personality Inventory, California Psychological Inventory, and Inwald Personality Inventory to predict police performance. *Dissertation Abstracts International: Section B: The Sciences and Engineering, 63,* 2098.

Schneider, J. A. (2010). From Freud's dream-work to Bion's work of dreaming: The changing conception of dreaming in psychoanalytic theory. *The International Journal of Psychoanalysis, 91,* 521–540.

Schneider, M. F., Krick, C. M., Retz, W., Hengesch, G., Retz-Junginger, P., Reith, W., & Rösler, M. (2010). Impairment of fronto-striatal and parietal cerebral networks correlates with attention deficit hyperactivity disorder (ADHD) psychopathology in adults—A functional magnetic resonance imaging (fMRI) study. *Psychiatry Research: Neuroimaging, 183,* 75–84.

Schoenthaler, S. J., Amos, S. P., Eysenck, H. J., Peritz, E., & Yudkin, J. (1991). Controlled trial of vitamin-mineral supplementation: Effects on intelligence and performance. *Personality and Individual Differences, 12,* 251–362.

Scholey, A. B., Bosworth, J. A. J., & Dimitrakaki, V. (1999). The effects of exposure to human pheromones on mood and attraction. *Proceedings of the British Psychological Society, 7,* 77.

Schooler, C. (1998). Environmental complexity and the Flynn effect. In U. Neisser (Ed.), *The rising curve: Long-term gains in IQ and related measures* (pp. 67–79). Washington, DC: American Psychological Association.

Schooler, C. (2007). Use it—and keep it, long, probably. *Perspectives on Psychological Science, 2*, 24–32.

Schredl, M., Biemelt, J., Roos, K., Dünkel, T., & Harris, N. (2008). Nightmares and stress in children. *Sleep and Hypnosis, 10*, 19–25.

Schreiber Compo, N., Evans, J. R., Carol, R. N., Kemp, D., Villalba, D., Ham, L. S., & Rose, S. (2011). Alcohol intoxication and memory for events: A snapshot of alcohol myopia in a real-world drinking scenario. *Memory, 19*, 202–210.

Schultz, D. P., & Schultz, S. E. (1998). *Psychology and work today: An introduction to industrial and organizational psychology* (7th ed.). Upper Saddle River, NJ: Prentice Hall.

Schwartz, B. [Barry]. (1989). *Psychology of learning and behavior* (3rd ed.). New York, NY: Norton.

Schwartz, B. L. [Bennett]. (2002). *Tip-of-the-tongue states: Phenomenology, mechanism, and lexical retrieval.* Mahwah, NJ: Erlbaum.

Schwartz, B. L. [Bennett]. (2010). The effects of emotion on tip-of-the-tongue states. *Psychonomic Bulletin & Review, 17*, 82–87.

Schwartz, C. E., Christopher, I. W., Shin, L. M., Kagan, J., & Rauch, S. L. (2003). Inhibited and uninhibited infants "grown up": Adult amygdalar response to novelty. *Science, 300*, 1952–1953.

Schwartz, C. E., Wright, C. I., Shin, L. M., Kagan, J., Whalen, P. J., McMullin, K. G., & Rauch, S. L. (2003). Differential amygdalar response to novel versus newly familiar neutral faces: A functional MRI probe developed for studying inhibited temperament. *Biological Psychiatry, 53*, 854–862.

Scott, J. P. R., McNaughton, L. R., & Polman, R. C. J. (2006). Effects of sleep deprivation and exercise on cognitive, motor performance and mood. *Physiology & Behavior, 87*, 396–408.

Scullin, M. K., & McDaniel, M. A. (2010). Remembering to execute a goal: Sleep on it! *Psychological Science, 21*, 1028–1035.

Sedikides, C., & Luke, M. (2008). On when self-enhancement and self-criticism function adaptively and maladaptively. In E. C. Change (Ed.), *Self-criticism and self-enhancement: Theory, research, and clinical implications* (pp. 181–198). Washington, DC: American Psychological Association.

Sedikides, C., Gaertner, L., & Toguchi, Y. (2003). Pancultural self-enhancement. *Journal of Personality and Social Psychology, 84*, 60–79.

Sedikides, C., Olsen, L., & Reis, H. T. (1993). Relationships as natural categories. *Journal of Personality and Social Psychology, 64*, 71–82.

Selarta, M., Nordström, T., Kuvaas, B., & Takemura, K. (2008). Effects of reward on self-regulation, intrinsic motivation and creativity. *Scandinavian Journal of Educational Research, 52*, 439–458.

Seligman, M. E. P. (1971). Phobias and preparedness. *Behavior Therapy, 2*, 307–320

Seligman, M. E. P. (1995). The effectiveness of psychotherapy: The *Consumer Reports* study. *American Psychologist, 50*, 965–974.

Seligman, M. E. P. (1996). Science as an ally of practice. *American Psychologist, 51*, 1072–1079.

Seligman, M. E. P., & Maier, S. F. (1967). Failure to escape traumatic shock. *Journal of Experimental Psychology, 74*, 1–9.

Seligman, M. E. P., & Schulman, P. (1986). Explanatory styles as a predictor of productivity and quitting among life insurance sales agents. *Journal of Personality and Social Psychology, 50*, 832–838.

Selye, H. (1956). *The stress of life.* New York, NY: McGraw-Hill.

Selye, H. (1976). *The stress of life* (rev. ed.). New York, NY: McGraw-Hill.

Seppa, N. (1997, June). Children's TV remains steeped in violence. *APA Monitor, 28*(6), 36.

Serretti, A., & Mandelli, L. (2008). The genetics of bipolar disorder: Genome "hot regions," genes, new potential candidates and future directions. *Molecular Psychiatry, 13*, 742–771.

Shaffer, J. B. P. (1978). *Humanistic psychology.* Upper Saddle River, NJ: Prentice Hall.

Shah, A. K., & Oppenheimer, D. M. (2009). The path of least resistance: Using easy-to-access information. *Current Directions in Psychological Science, 18*, 232–236.

Shah, K. R., Eisen, S. A., Xian, H., & Potenza, M. N. (2005). Genetic studies of pathological gambling: A review of methodology and analyses of data from the Vietnam era twin registry. *Journal of Gambling Studies, 21*, 179–203.

Shamay-Tsoory, S. G., Adler, N. N., Aharon-Peretz, J. J., Perry, D. D., & Mayseless, N. N. (2011). The origins of originality: The neural bases of creative thinking and originality. *Neuropsychologia, 49*, 178–185.

Shankman, S. A., Tenke, C. E., Bruder, G. E., Durbin, C. E., Hayden, E. P., & Klein, D. N. (2005). Low positive emotionality in young children: Association with EEG asymmetry. *Development and Psychopathology, 17*, 85–98.

Shapiro, T. F. (2002). Suggestibility in children's eyewitness testimony: Cognitive and social influences. *Dissertation Abstracts International: Section B: The Sciences and Engineering, 63*, 2086.

Shargorodsky, J., Curhan, S. G., Curhan, G. C., & Eavey, R. (2010). Change in prevalence of hearing loss in US adolescents. *JAMA: The Journal of the American Medical Association, 304*, 772–778.

Shaw, P., Bramham, J., Lawrence, E. J., Morris, R., Baron-Cohen, S., & David, A. S. (2005). Differential effects of lesions of the amygdala and prefrontal cortex on recognizing facial expressions of complex emotions. *Journal of Cognitive Neuroscience, 17*, 1410–1419.

Shawn, A. (2007). *Wish I could be there: Notes from a phobic life.* New York, NY: Viking.

Shayer, M. (2003). Not just Piaget; not just Vygotsky, and certainly not Vygotsky as an alternative to Piaget. *Learning and Instruction, 13*, 465–485.

Sheehy, R., & Horan, J. J. (2004). Effects of stress inoculation training for 1st-year law students. *International Journal of Stress Management, 11*, 41–55.

Shehryar, O. H., & Hunt, D. M. (2005). A terror management perspective on the persuasiveness of fear appeals. *Journal of Consumer Psychology, 15*, 275–287.

Shelton R. C., & Hollon, S. D. (2000). Antidepressants. In A. Kazdin (Ed.), *Encyclopedia of psychology* (Vol. 1, pp. 196–200). Washington, DC: American Psychological Association.

Sher, L. (2004). Type D personality, cortisol and cardiac disease. *Australian and New Zealand Journal of Psychiatry, 38*, 652–653.

Sheras, P. L., & Koch-Sheras, P. R. (2006). Redefining couple: Shifting the paradigm. In P. L. Sheras & P. R. Koch-Sheras (Eds.), *Couple power therapy: Building commitment, cooperation, communication, and community in relationships* (pp. 19–39). Washington, DC: American Psychological Association.

Sherva, R., Wilhelmsen, K., Pomerleau, C. S., Chasse, S. A., Rice, J. P., Snedecor, S. M., . . . Pomerleau, O. F. (2008). Association of a single nucleotide polymorphism in neuronal acetylcholine receptor subunit alpha 5 (CHRNA5) with smoking status and with 'pleasurable buzz' during early experimentation with smoking. *Addiction, 103*, 1544–1552.

Shields, B. (2006). *Down came the rain: My journey through postpartum depression.* New York, NY: Hyperion Press.

Shimamura, A. P., Berry, J. M., Mangels, J. A., Rusting, C. L., & Jurica, P. J. (1995). Memory and cognitive abilities in university professors: Evidence for successful aging. *Psychological Science, 6*, 271–277.

Shiner, R. L., Masten, A. S., & Roberts, J. M. (2003). Childhood personality foreshadows adult personality and life outcomes two decades later. *Journal of Personality, 71*, 1145–1170.

Shorter, E., & Healy, D. (2007). *Shock therapy: A history of electroconvulsive treatment in mental illness.* Piscataway, NJ: Rutgers University Press.

Shrum, L. J. (2007). Social cognition and cultivation. In D. R. Roskos-Ewoldsen & J. L. Monahan (Eds.), *Communication and social cognition: Theories and methods* (pp. 245–272). Mahwah, NJ: Erlbaum.

Shum, M. S. (1998). The role of temporal landmarks in autobiographical memory processes. *Psychological Bulletin, 124*, 423–442.

Siegal, M. (2003). Cognitive development. In A. Slater & G. Bremner (Eds.), *An introduction to developmental psychology* (pp. 189–210). Malden, MA: Blackwell.

Siegel, J. M. (2008). Do all animals sleep? *Trends in Neurosciences, 31*, 208–213.

Siegel, J. M. [Jerome]. (2005). Clues to the functions of mammalian sleep. *Nature, 437*, 1264–1271.

Siegel, J. P. [Judith]. (2007). The enduring crisis of divorce for children and their parents. In N. B. Webb (Ed.), *Play therapy with children in crisis: Individual, group, and family treatment* (3rd ed., pp. 133–151). New York, NY: Guilford Press.

Siegel, S. (2005). Drug tolerance, drug addiction, and drug anticipation. *Current Directions in Psychological Science, 14*, 296–300.

Siegert, R. J., & Ward, T. (2002). Evolutionary psychology: Origins and criticisms. *Australian Psychologist, 37*, 20–29.

Siep, N., Roefs, A., Roebroeck, A., Havermans, R., Bonte, M. L., & Jansen, A. (2009). Hunger is the best spice: An fMRI study of the effects of attention, hunger and calorie content on food reward processing in the amygdala and orbitofrontal cortex. *Behavioural Brain Research, 198*, 149–158.

Sigman, M. [Maxine], & Hassan, S. (2006). Benefits of long-term group therapy to individuals suffering schizophrenia: A prospective 7-year study. *Bulletin of the Menninger Clinic, 70*, 273–282.

Sigman, M. D. [Marian]. (2000). Determinants of intelligence: Nutrition and intelligence. In A. E. Kazdin (Ed.), *Encyclopedia of psychology* (Vol. 2, pp. 501–502). Washington, DC: American Psychological Association.

Silberg, J. L., & Bulik, C. M. (2005). The developmental association between eating disorders symptoms and symptoms of depression and anxiety in juvenile twin girls. *Journal of Child Psychology and Psychiatry, 46,* 1317–1326.

Silver, H., Goodman, C., Isakov, V., Knoll, G., & Modai, I. (2005). A doubleblind, cross-over comparison of the effects of amantadine or placebo on visuomotor and cognitive function in medicated schizophrenia patients. *International Clinical Psychopharmacology, 20,* 319–326.

Silver, M. A., & Kastner, S. (2009). Topographic maps in human frontal and parietal cortex. *Trends in Cognitive Sciences, 13,* 488–495.

Silver, S. M., Rogers, S., & Russell, M. (2008). Eye movement desensitization and reprocessing (EMDR) in the treatment of war veterans. *Journal of Clinical Psychology, 64,* 947–957.

Simcock, G., & Hayne, H. (2002). Breaking the barrier? Children fail to translate their preverbal memories into language. *Psychological Science, 13,* 225–231.

Simons, T., & Roberson, Q. (2003). Why managers should care about fairness: The effects of aggregate justice perceptions on organizational outcomes. *Journal of Applied Psychology, 88,* 432–443.

Singer, B. H., Gamelli, A. E., Fuller, C. L., Temme, S. J., Parent, J. M., & Murphy, G. G. (2011). Compensatory network changes in the dentate gyrus restore long-term potentiation following ablation of neurogenesis in young-adult mice. *Proceedings of the National Academy of Sciences (USA), 108,* 5437–5442.

Singh, S. J. B. (2002, March 19). "I was wrongly accused of being a terrorist." *The Progressive.* Retrieved from http://progressive.org/media_1611

Sinnott, J. D. (1994). Sex roles. In V. A. Ramachandran (Ed.), *Encyclopedia of human behavior* (Vol. 4, pp. 151–158). San Diego, CA: Academic Press.

Skaalvik, E. M., & Rankin, R. J. (1994). Gender differences in mathematics and verbal achievement, self-perception and motivation. *British Journal of Educational Psychology, 64,* 419–428.

Skeels, H. M. (1938). Mental development of children in foster homes. *Journal of Consulting Psychology, 2,* 33–43.

Skeels, H. M. (1942). The study of the effects of differential stimulation on mentally retarded children: A follow-up report. *American Journal of Mental Deficiencies, 46,* 340–350.

Skeels, H. M. (1966). Adult status of children with contrasting early life experiences. *Monographs of the Society for Research in Child Development, 31*(3), 1–65.

Skinner, B. F. (1948). *Science and human behavior.* New York, NY: Macmillan.

Skinner, B. F. (1953). Some contributions of an experimental analysis of behavior to psychology as a whole. *American Psychologist, 8,* 69–78.

Skinner, B. F. (1957). *Verbal behavior.* Englewood Cliffs, NJ: Prentice Hall.

Slater, A. (2000). Visual perception in the young infant. Early organization and rapid learning. In D. Muir & A. Slater (Eds.), *Infant development: Essential readings in developmental psychology* (pp. 95–116). Malden, MA: Blackwell.

Sleek, S. (1998, May). Older vets just now feeling pain of war. *APA Monitor, 29*(5), 1, 28.

Slessareva, E., & Muraven, M. (2004). Sensitivity to punishment and self-control: The mediating role of emotion. *Personality and Individual Differences, 36,* 307–319.

Slife, B. D., & Reber, J. S. (2001). Eclecticism in psychotherapy: Is it really the best substitute for traditional theories? In B. D. Slife & R. N. Williams (Eds.), *Critical issues in psychotherapy: Translating new ideas into practice* (pp. 213–233). Thousand Oaks, CA: Sage.

Sligh, A. C., Conners, F. A., & Roskos-Ewoldsen, B. (2005). Relation of creativity to fluid and crystallized intelligence. *Journal of Creative Behavior, 39,* 123–136.

Smith, B. L. (2011, January). Hypnosis today. *Monitor on Psychology, 42*(1), 51–52.

Smith, C. T., Nixon, M. R., & Nader, R. S. (2004). Posttraining increases in REM sleep intensity implicate REM sleep in memory processing and provide a biological marker of learning potential. *Learning & Memory, 11,* 714–719.

Smith, D. N. (1998). The psychocultural roots of genocide: Legitimacy and crisis in Rwanda. *American Psychologist, 53,* 743–753.

Smith, E. R., & Mackie, D. M. (2005). Aggression, hatred, and other emotions. In J. F. Dovidio, P. Glick, & L. A. Rudman (Eds.), *On the nature of prejudice: Fifty years after Allport* (pp. 361–376). Malden, MA: Blackwell.

Smith, J. E. [Joanna], Richardson, J., & Hoffman, C. (2005). Mindfulness-based stress reduction as supportive therapy in cancer care: Systematic review. *Journal of Advanced Nursing, 52,* 315–327.

Smith, J. M. [Jack]. (2006). Mobile training unit: A cost-effective live fire option. *Fire Engineering, 159,* 133–134.

Smith, K. H., & Stutts, M. A. (2003). Effects of short-term cosmetic versus long-term health fear appeals in anti-smoking advertisements on the smoking behaviour of adolescents. *Journal of Consumer Behaviour, 3,* 157–177.

Smith, P. B., & Bond, M. H. (1994). *Social psychology across cultures: Analysis and perspectives.* Boston, MA: Allyn & Bacon.

Smith, R. A. (2005). The classroom as a social psychology laboratory. *Journal of Social & Clinical Psychology, 24* [Special issue: *Dispelling the fable of "Those who can, do, and those who can't, teach": The (social and clinical) psychology of instruction*], 62–71.

Smith, S. M., Gleaves, D. H., Pierce, B. H., Williams, T. L., Gilliland, T. R., & Gerkens, D. R. (2003). Eliciting and comparing false and recovered memories: An experimental approach. *Applied Cognitive Psychology, 17,* 251–279.

Smith, W. B. (2007). Karen Horney and psychotherapy in the 21st century. *Clinical Social Work Journal, 35,* 57–66.

Smithson, H., & Mollon, J. (2006). Do masks terminate the icon? *Quarterly Journal of Experimental Psychology, 59,* 150–160.

Smyth, J. M., Hockemeyer, J. R., & Tulloch, H. (2008). Expressive writing and posttraumatic stress disorder: Effects on trauma symptoms, mood states, and cortisol reactivity. *British Journal of Health Psychology, 13,* 85–93.

Snowden, L. R., & Yamada, A.-M. (2005). Cultural differences in access to care. *Annual Review of Clinical Psychology, 1,* 143–166.

Snyder, C. R., Lopez, S. J., & Pedrotti, J. T. (2011). *Positive psychology: The scientific and practical explorations of human strengths* (2nd ed.). Thousand Oaks, CA: Sage Publications, Inc.

Snyder, M., & Swann, W. B., Jr. (1978). Behavioral confirmation in social interaction: From social perception to social reality. *Journal of Experimental Social Psychology, 14,* 148–162.

Solomon, B. C. (2004). Psychoanalysis and feminism: A personal journey. *The Annual of Psychoanalysis, 32,* 149–160.

Solomon, S., & Knafo, A. (2007). Value similarity in adolescent friendships. In T. C. Rhodes (Ed.), *Focus on adolescent behavior research* (pp. 133–155). Hauppauge, NY: Nova Science.

Sommers-Flanagan, R., Sommers-Flanagan, J., & Davis, B. (1993). What's happening on music television? A gender role content analysis. *Sex Roles, 28,* 745–754.

Sonstroem, R. J. (1997). Physical activity and self-esteem. In W. P. Morgan (Ed.), *Physical activity and mental health* (pp. 127–143). Philadelphia, PA: Taylor & Francis.

Sookoian, S., Gemma, C., Gianotti, T. F., Burgueño, A., Alvarez, A., González, C. D., & Pirola, C. J. (2007). Serotonin and serotonin transporter gene variant in rotating shift workers. *Sleep, 30,* 1049–1053.

Sorensen, R. C. (1973). *Adolescent sexuality in contemporary America.* New York, NY: World.

Soto, C. J., John, O. P., Gosling, S. D., & Potter, J. (2010). Age differences in personality traits from 10 to 65: Big five domains and facets in a large cross-sectional sample. *Journal of Personality and Social Psychology, 100,* 330–348. doi:10.1037/a0021717

Soussignan, R. (2002). Duchenne smile, emotional experience, and autonomic reactivity: A test of the facial feedback hypothesis. *Emotion, 2,* 52–74.

Soygüt, G., & Tüerkçapar, H. (2001). Assessment of interpersonal schema patterns in antisocial personality disorder: A cognitive interpersonal perspective. *Turk Psikoloji Dergisi, 16,* 55–69.

Spalding, K. L., Arner, E., Westermark, P. O., Bernard, S., Buchholz, B. A., Bergmann, O., . . . Arner, P. (2008). Dynamics of fat cell turnover in humans. *Nature, 453,* 783–787.

Speitzer, G. M., McCall, M. M., & Mahoney, J. D. (1997). Early identification of international executive potential. *Journal of Applied Psychology, 82,* 6–29.

Spence, P. R., Nelson, L. D., & Lachlan, K. A. (2010). Psychological responses and coping strategies after an urban bridge collapse. *Traumatology, 16,* 7–15. doi: 10.1177/1534765609347544

Sperling, G. (1960). The information available in brief visual presentations. *Psychological Monographs, 74,* 1–29.

Sperry, R. W. (1964, January). The great cerebral commissure. *Scientific American, 210*(1), 42–52.

Spiegel, D., & Moore, R. (1997). Imagery and hypnosis in the treatment of cancer patients. *Oncology, 11,* 1179–1189.

Spitzer, R. L., Gibbon, M., Skodol, A. E., Williams, J. B. W., & First, M. B. (2002). *DSM-IV-TR Casebook.* Washington, DC: American Psychiatric Publishing.

Stajkovic, A. D., & Luthans, F. (1997). Business ethics across cultures: A social cognitive model. *Journal of World Business, 32,* 17–34.

Stanley, M. A., Wilson, N. L., Novy, D. M., Rhoades, H. M., Wagener, P. D., Greisinger, A. J., . . . Kunik, M. E. (2009). Cognitive behavior therapy for generalized anxiety disorder among older adults in primary care: A randomized clinical trial. *JAMA: Journal of the American Medical Association, 301,* 1460–1467.

Stanley, R. O., & Burrows, G. D. (2008). Psychogenic heart disease—Stress and the heart: A historical perspective. *Stress and Health: Journal of the International Society for the Investigation of Stress, 24,* 181–187.

Stanley, T. L. (2004). The wisdom of employment testing. *Supervision, 65,* 11–13.

Steele, H. (2008). Editorial: Day care and attachment re-visited. *Attachment & Human Development, 10,* 223.

Steele, J. [James]. (2000). Handedness in past human populations: Skeletal markers. *Laterality 5,* 193–220.

Steele, J. [Jennifer]. (2003). Children's gender stereotypes about math: The role of stereotype stratification. *Journal of Applied Social Psychology, 33,* 2587–2606.

Steinberg, L. (2008). A social neuroscience perspective on adolescent risk-taking. *Developmental Review, 28,* 78–106.

Steinberg, L., Cauffman, E., Woolard, J., Graham, S., & Banich, M. (2009). Are adolescents less mature than adults?: Minors' access to abortion, the juvenile death penalty, and the alleged APA 'flip-flop.' *American Psychologist, 64,* 583–594.

Steinke, W. R. (2003). Perception and recognition of music and song following right hemisphere stroke: A case study. *Dissertation Abstracts International: Section B: The Sciences and Engineering, 63,* 4948.

Stel, M., Van Baaren, R. B., & Vonk, R. (2008). Effects of mimicking: Acting prosocially by being emotionally moved. *European Journal of Social Psychology, 38,* 965–976.

Stel, M., van Dijk, E., & Olivier, E. (2009). You want to know the truth? Then don't mimic! *Psychological Science, 20,* 693–699.

Stelmack, R. M., Knott, V., & Beauchamp, C. M. (2003). Intelligence and neural transmission time: A brain stem auditory evoked potential analysis. *Personality and Individual Differences, 34,* 97–107.

Stern, K., & McClintock, M. K. (1998). Regulation of ovulation by human pheromones. *Nature, 392,* 177.

Stern, R. M., & Koch, K. L. (1996). Motion sickness and differential susceptibility. *Current Directions in Psychological Science, 5,* 115–120.

Sternberg, R. J. (2007). A systems model of leadership: WICS. *American Psychologist, 62,* 34–42.

Sternberg, R. J. (2008). The WICS approach to leadership: Stories of leadership and the structures and processes that support them. *Leadership Quarterly, 19,* 360–371.

Sternberg, R. J. (2009). Toward a triarchic theory of intelligence. In R. J. Sternberg, J. C. Kaufman, & E. Grigorenko (Ed.), *The essential Sternberg: Essays on intelligence, psychology, and education* (pp. 33–70). New York, NY: Springer.

Sternberg, R. J., Jarvin, L., & Grigorenko, E. (2009). *Teaching for wisdom, intelligence, creativity, and success.* Thousand Oaks, CA: Corwin Press.

Stevens, W. D., & Grady, C. L. (2007). Insight into frontal lobe function from functional neuroimaging studies of episodic memory. In B. L. Miller & J. L. Cummings (Eds.), *The human frontal lobes: Functions and disorders* (2nd ed., pp. 207–226). New York, NY: Guilford Press.

Stevenson, H. W. (1992, December). Learning from Asian schools. *Scientific American, 265*(6), 70–76.

Stevenson, H. W. (1993). Why Asian students still outdistance Americans. *Educational Leadership, 50,* 63–65.

Stevenson, H. W., Chen, C., & Lee, S.-Y. (1993). Mathematics achievement of Chinese, Japanese, and American children: Ten years later. *Science, 259,* 53–58.

Stevenson, H. W., Lee, S.-Y., & Stigler, J. W. (1986). Mathematics achievment of Chinese, Japanese, and American children. *Science, 231,* 693–697.

Stewart, L. (2008). Do musicians have different brains? *Clinical Medicine, 8,* 304–308.

Stine-Morrow, E. A. L., Parisi, J. M., Morrow, D. G., & Park, D. C. (2008). The effects of an engaged lifestyle on cognitive vitality: A field experiment. *Psychology and Aging, 23,* 778–786.

Stoffregen, T. A., Faugloire, E., Yoshida, K., Flanagan, M. B., & Merhi, O. (2008). Motion sickness and postural sway in console video games. *Human Factors, 50,* 322–331.

Stokes, P. D. (2006). *Creativity from constraints: The psychology of breakthrough.* New York, NY: Springer.

Stolzenberg, R. M., & Waite, L. J. (2005). Effects of marriage, divorce, and widowhood on health. In S. M. Bianchi, L. M. Casper, & B. R. King (Eds.), *Work, family, health, and well-being* (pp. 361–377). Mahwah, NJ: Erlbaum.

Stone, A. A., Schwartz, J. E., Broderick, J. E., & Deaton, A. (2010). A snapshot of the age distribution of psychological well-being in the United States. *PNAS Proceedings of the National Academy of Sciences of the United States of America, 107,* 9985–9990.

Stoner, J. A. F. (1961). *A comparison of individual and group decisions involving risk.* Unpublished master's thesis, School of Industrial Management, MIT.

Storandt, M. (2008). Cognitive deficits in the early stages of Alzheimer's disease. *Current Directions in Psychological Science, 17,* 198–202.

Storksen, I., Roysamb, E., & Holmen, T. L. (2006). Adolescent adjustment and well-being: Effects of parental divorce and distress. *Scandinavian Journal of Psychology, 47,* 75–84.

Straton, D. (2004). Guilt and PTSD. *Australian and New Zealand Journal of Psychiatry, 38,* 269–270.

Strayer, D. L., & Drews, F. A. (2007). Multitasking in the automobile. In A. F. Dramer, D. A. Wiegmann, & A. Kirlik (Eds.), *Attention: From theory to practice* (pp. 121–133). New York, NY: Oxford University Press.

Strenger, C. (2009). Sosein: Active self-acceptance in midlife. *Journal of Humanistic Psychology, 49,* 46–65.

Strick, M., van Baaren, R. B., Holland, R. W., & van Knippenberg, A. (2009). Humor in advertisements enhances product liking by mere association. *Journal of Experimental Psychology: Applied, 15,* 35–45.

Strickland, B. R. (2000). Misassumptions, misadventures, and the misuse of psychology. *American Psychologist, 55,* 331–338.

Strollo, P. J., Jr., & Davé, N. B. (2005). Sleep apnea. In D. J. Buysse (Ed.), *Sleep disorders and psychiatry* (pp. 77–105). Washington, DC: American Psychiatric Publishing.

Subotnik, R. F., & Arnold, K. D. (1994). *Beyond Terman: Contemporary longitudinal studies of giftedness and talent.* Norwood, NJ: Ablex.

Süer, C., Dolu, N., Artis, A., Sahin, L., Yilmaz, A., & Cetin, A. (2011). The effects of long-term sleep deprivation on the long-term potentiation in the dentate gyrus and brain oxidation status in rats. *Neuroscience Research, 70,* 71–77. doi:10.1016/j.neures.2011.01.008

Suhr, J. A. (2002). Malingering, coaching, and the serial position effect. *Archives of Clinical Neuropsychology, 17,* 69–77.

Suitor, J. J., Sechrist, J., Plikuhn, M., Pardo, S. T., & Pillemer, K. (2008). Within-family differences in parent-child relations across the life course. *Current Directions in Psychological Science, 17,* 334–338.

Sullivan, M. (2004). Exaggerated pain behavior: By what standard? *Clinical Journal of Pain, 20,* 433–439.

Sumnall, H. R., Jerome, L., Doblin, R., & Mithoefer, M. C. (2004). Response to Parrott, A. C., Buchanan T., Heffernan, T. M., Scholey, A., Ling, J., & Rodgers, J. (2003): Parkinson's disorder, psychomotor problems and dopaminergic neurotoxicity in recreational Ecstasy/MDMA users. *Psychopharmacology, 167,* 449–450.

Sundet, J. M., Borren, I., & Tambs, K. (2008). The Flynn effect is partly caused by changing fertility patterns. *Intelligence, 36,* 183–191.

Sundqvist, F. (2007). The Gestalt according to the Berlin school (The crossroads between empiricism and rationalism: Part III). *Gestalt Theory, 29,* 223–241.

Sundstrom, E., DeMeuse, K. P., & Futrell, D. (1990). Work teams: Applications and effectiveness. *American Psychologist, 31,* 120–133.

Surguladze, S. A., Young, A. W., Senior, C., Brebion, G., Travis, M. J., & Phillips, M. L. (2004). Recognition accuracy and response bias to happy and sad facial expressions in patients with major depression. *Neuropsychology, 18,* 212–218.

Susman, E. J., Schmeelk, K. H., Ponirakis, A., & Gariepy, J. L. (2001). Maternal prenatal, postpartum, and concurrent stressors and temperament in 3-year-olds: A person and variable analysis. *Development and Psychopathology, 13,* 629–652.

Swim, J. K., Stern, P. C., Doherty, T. J., Clayton, S., Reser, J. P., Weber, E. U., . . . Howard, G. S. (2011). Special issue: Psychology and global climate change. *American Psychologist, 66,* 241–328.

Szekely, A. A., Balota, D. A., Duchek, J. M., Nemoda, Z. Z., Vereczkei, A. A., & Sasvari-Szekely, M. M. (2011). Genetic factors of reaction time performance: DRD4 7-repeat allele associated with slower responses. *Genes, Brain & Behavior, 10,* 129–136.

Suzuki, S. (2006). Investigation of the cognitive process in selection of stress coping behavior. *Japanese Journal of Psychology, 76,* 527–533.

Szucs, R. P., Frankel, P. S., McMahon, L. R., & Cunningham, K. A. (2005). Relationship of cocaine-induced c-Fos expression to behaviors and the role of serotonin 5-HT2A receptors in cocaine-induced c-Fos expression. *Behavioral Neuroscience, 119,* 1173–1183.

Takahashi, M., Shimizu, H., Saito, S., & Tomoyori, H. (2006). One percent ability and ninety-nine percent perspiration: A study of a Japanese memorist. *Journal of Experimental Psychology: Learning, Memory, and Cognition, 32,* 1195–1200.

Tacker, M. (2007). Family experiences of the terminal illness and death of a family member. *Dissertation Abstracts International: Section B: The Sciences and Engineering, 67,* 6773.

Talarico, J. M., & Rubin, D. C. (2003). Confidence, not consistency, characterizes flashbulb memories. *Psychological Science, 14,* 455–461.

Tamminen, J., Payne, J. D., Stickgold, R., Wamsley, E. J., & Gaskell, M. (2010). Sleep spindle activity is associated with the integration of new memories and existing knowledge. *The Journal of Neuroscience, 30,* 14356–14360.

Tang, C. Y., Eaves, E. L., Ng, J. C., Carpenter, D. M., Mai, X., Schroeder, D. H., . . . Haier, R. J. (2010). Brain networks for working memory and factors of intelligence assessed in males and females with fMRI and DTI. *Intelligence, 38,* 293–303.

Tanner, J. M. (1978). *Foetus into man: Physical growth from conception to maturity.* Cambridge, MA: Harvard University Press.

Tapert, S. F., & Schweinsburg, A. D. (2005). The human adolescent brain and alcohol use disorders. In M. Galanter (Ed.), *Recent developments in alcoholism: Volume 17. Alcohol problems in adolescents and young adults* (pp. 177–197). New York, NY: Kluwer/Plenum.

Tappan, M. B. (2006). Mediated moralities: Sociocultural approaches to moral development. In M. Killen & J. G. Smetana (Eds.), *Handbook of moral development* (pp. 351–374). Mahwah, NJ: Erlbaum.

Tarrier, N., Taylor, K., & Gooding, P. (2008). Cognitive-behavioral interventions to reduce suicide behavior: A systematic review and meta-analysis. *Behavior Modification, 32,* 77–108.

Taufiq, A. M., Fujii, S., Yamazaki, Y., Sasaki, H., Kaneko, K., Li, J., . . . Mikoshiba, K. (2005). Involvement of IP3 receptors in LTP and LTD induction in guinea pig hippocampal CA1 neurons. *Learning & Memory, 12,* 594–600.

Taylor, D. M., & Moghaddam, F. M. (1994). *Theories of intergroup relations: International social psychological perspectives.* Westport, CT: Praeger.

Taylor, P. J., Russ-Eft, D. F., & Chan, D. W. L. (2005). A meta-analytic review of behavior modeling training. *Journal of Applied Psychology, 90,* 692–709.

Taylor, S. E. (2006). Tend and befriend: Biobehavioral bases of affiliation under stress. *Current Directions in Psychological Science, 15,* 273–277.

Taylor, S. E. (2003). *Health Psychology* (5th ed.). New York, NY: McGraw-Hill.

Taylor, S. E., Klein, L. C., Lewis, B. P., Gruenewald, T. L., Gurung, R. A. R., & Updegraff, J. A. (2000). Biobehavioral responses to stress in females: Tend-and-befriend, not fight-or-flight. *Psychological Review, 107,* 411–429.

Taylor, S. E., Welch, W. T., Kim, H. S., & Sherman, D. K. (2007). Cultural differences in the impact of social support on psychological and biological stress responses. *Psychological Science, 18,* 831–837.

Teasdale, T. W., & Owen, D. R. (2005). A long-term rise and recent decline in intelligence test performance: The Flynn effect in reverse. *Personality and Individual Differences, 39,* 837–843.

Tedeschi, R. G., & Calhoun, L. G. (2008). Beyond the concept of recovery: Growth and the experience of loss. *Death Studies, 32,* 27–39.

Telerman, A., Lapter, S., Sharabi, A., Zinger, H., & Mozes, E. (2011). Induction of hippocampal neurogenesis by a tolerogenic peptide that ameliorates lupus manifestations. *Journal of Neuroimmunology, 232,* 151–157.

Terhune, D., Cardena, E., & Lindgren, M. (2011). Dissociative tendencies and individual differences in high hypnotic suggestibility. *Cognitive Neuropsychiatry, 16,* 113–135.

Terman, L. M. (1925). *Mental and physical traits of a thousand gifted children: Genetic studies of genius* (Vol. 1). Stanford, CA: Stanford University Press.

Terrace, H. S., Son, L. K., & Brannon, E. M. (2003). Serial expertise of rhesus macaques. *Psychological Science, 14,* 66–73.

Terry, W. S. (2005). Serial position effects in recall of television commercials. *Journal of General Psychology, 132,* 151–163.

Tess, A. V., & Smetana, G. W. (2009). Medical evaluation of patients undergoing electroconvulsive therapy. *The New England Journal of Medicine, 360,* 1437–1444.

Thakkar, M. M., Winston, S., & McCarley, R. W. (2003). A-sub-1 receptor and adenosinergic homeostatic regulation of sleep-wakefulness: Effects of antisense to the A-sub-1 receptor in the cholinergic basal forebrain. *The Journal of Neuroscience, 23,* 4278–4287.

Theiss, J. A., & Solomon, D. H. (2008). Parsing the mechanisms that increase relational intimacy: The effects of uncertainty amount, open communication about uncertainty, and the reduction of uncertainty. *Human Communication Research, 34,* 625–654.

Thierry, K. L., & Spence, M. J. (2002). Source-monitoring training facilitates preschoolers' eyewitness memory performance. *Developmental Psychology, 38,* 428–437.

Thierry, N., Willeit, M., Praschak-Rieder, N., Zill, P., Hornik, K., Neumeister, A., . . . Kasper, S. (2004). Serotonin transporter promoter gene polymorphic region (5-HTTLPR) and personality in female patients with seasonal affective disorder and in healthy controls. *European Neuropsychopharmacology, 14,* 53–58.

Thoman, D. B., White, P. H., Yamawaki, N., & Koishi, H. (2008). Variations of gender-math stereotype content affect women's vulnerability to stereotype threat. *Sex Roles, 58,* 702–712.

Thomas, A., & Chess, S. (1977). *Temperament and development.* New York, NY: Brunner/Mazel.

Thomas, M. S. C., & Johnson, M. H. (2008). New advances in understanding sensitive periods in brain development. *Current Directions in Psychological Science, 17,* 1–5.

Thomas, P., Alptekin, K., Gheorghe, M., Mauri, M., Olivares, J. M., & Riedel, M. (2009). Management of patients presenting with acute psychotic episodes of schizophrenia. *CNS Drugs, 23,* 193–212.

Thomas, S. G., & Kellner, C. H. (2003). Remission of major depression and obsessive-compulsive disorder after a single unilateral ECT. *Journal of ECT, 19,* 50–51.

Thompson, A. H. (2008). Younger onset of depression is associated with greater suicidal intent. *Social Psychiatry and Psychiatric Epidemiology, 43,* 538–544.

Thorne, F., Neave, N., Scholey, A., Moss, M., & Fink, B. (2002). Effects of putative male pheromones on female ratings of male attractiveness: Influence of oral contraceptives and the menstrual cycle. *Neuroendocrinology Letters, 23,* 291–297.

Thorne, F., Scholey, A. B., & Neave, N. (2000). Love is in the air? Effects of pheromones, oral contraceptive use and menstrual cycle phase on attraction. *Proceeding of the British Psychological Society, 8,* 49.

Thornton, A. (2008). Social learning about novel foods in young meerkats. *Animal Behaviour, 76,* 1411–1421.

Thornton, L. M. (2005). Stress and immunity in a longitudinal study of breast cancer patients. *Dissertation Abstracts International: Section B: The Sciences and Engineering, 66,* 2843.

Thurstone, L. L. (1938). Primary mental abilities. *Psychometric Monographs, 1.*

Tilleczek, K. C., & Hine, D. W. (2006). The meaning of smoking as health and social risk in adolescence. *Journal of Adolescence, 29,* 273–287.

Tindale, R. S., Munier, C., Wasserman, M., & Smith, C. M. (2002). Group processes and the holocaust. In L. S. Newman & R. Erber (Eds.), *Understanding genocide: The social psychology of the Holocaust* (pp. 143–161). New York, NY: Oxford University Press.

Ting, J., & Piliavin, J. A. (2000). Altruism in comparative international perspective. In J. Phillips, B. Chapman, & D. Stevens (Eds.), *Between state and market: Essays on charities law and policy in Canada* (pp. 51–105). Montreal and Kingston, Ontario, Canada: McGill-Queens University Press.

Ting, R. S.-K., & Watson, T. (2007). Is suffering good? An explorative study on the religious persecution among Chinese pastors. *Journal of Psychology & Theology, 35,* 202–210.

Tobin, J. (2007, Spring). Counting sheep and the study of sleep, from A to ZZZZZ. *Medicine at Michigan, 9*(1), 20–25.

Toft, M. D. (2003). *The geography of ethnic violence: Identity, interests, and the indivisibility of territory.* Princeton, NJ: Princeton University Press.

Tolman, E. C., & Honzik, C. H. (1930). Introduction and removal of reward, and maze performance in rats. *University of California Publications in Psychology, 4,* 257–275.

Tomasello, M., & Herrmann, E. (2010). Ape and human cognition: What's the difference? *Current Directions in Psychological Science, 19,* 3–8.

Tomer, A. (Ed.). (2000). *Death attitudes and the older adult: Theories, concepts, and applications.* Philadelphia, PA: Brunner-Routledge.

Tone, A. (2007). [Review of the book *Prozac on the couch: Prescribing gender in the era of wonder drugs,* by J. M. Metzl]. *Transcultural Psychiatry, 44,* 302–304.

Tooby, J., & Cosmides, L. (2008). The evolutionary psychology of the emotions and their relationship to internal regulatory variables. In M. Lewis, J. M. Haviland-Jones, & L. F. Barrett (Eds.), *Handbook of emotions* (3rd ed., pp. 114–137). New York, NY: Guilford Press.

Tramontana, J. (2009). *Hypnotically enhanced treatment for addictions: Alcohol abuse, drug abuse, gambling, weight control, and smoking cessation.* Norwalk, CT: Crown House Publishing Limited.

Travis, J. (2003, October 11). Visionary research: Scientists delve into the evolution of color vision in primates. *Science News, 164*(15), 234–236.

Travis, J. (2004a, February 14). Code breakers: Scientists tease out the secrets of proteins that DNA wraps around. *Science News, 165*(7), 106–107.

Travis, J. (2004b, January 17). Fear not: Scientists are learning how people can unlearn fear. *Science News, 165*(3), 42–44.

Treaster, J. B. (1994, February 1). Survey finds marijuana use is up in high schools. *New York Times,* p. A1.

Treffert, D. A., & Wallace, G. L. (2002, June). Islands of genius. *Scientific American, 286*(6), 76–85.

Trehub, S. E., Schellenberg, E., & Nakata, T. (2008). Cross-cultural perspectives on pitch memory. *Journal of Experimental Child Psychology, 100,* 40–52.

Treisman, A. M. (2004). Psychological issues in selective attention. In M. S. Gazzaniga (Ed.), *The cognitive neurosciences* (3rd ed., pp. 529–544). Cambridge, MA: MIT Press.

Treisman, A. M. (1960). Contextual cues in selective listening. *Quarterly Journal of Experimental Psychology, 12,* 242–248.

Treisman, A. M. (1964). Verbal cues, language and meaning in selective attention. *American Journal of Psychology, 77,* 206–219.

Tremblay, J., & Cohen, J. (2005). Spatial configuration and list learning of proximally cued arms by rats in the enclosed four-arm radial maze. *Learning and Behavior, 33,* 78–89.

Tremblay, R. E., Hartup, W. W., & Archer, J. (Eds.). (2005). *Developmental origins of aggression.* New York, NY: Guilford Press.

Trichopoulou, A, Costacou, T., Bamia, C., & Trichopoulos, D. (2003). Adherence to a Mediterranean diet and survival in a Greek population. *The New England Journal of Medicine, 348,* 2599–2608.

Tseng, R. J., Padgett, D. A., Dhabhar, F. S., Engler, H., & Sheridan, J. F. (2005). Stress-induced modulation of NK activity during influenza viral infection: Role of glucocorticoids and opioids. *Brain, Behavior and Immunity, 19,* 153–164.

Tsien, J. Z. (2007, July). The memory code. *Scientific American, 297*(1), 52–59.

Tsujimoto, S. (2008). The prefrontal cortex: Functional neural development during early childhood. *The Neuroscientist, 14,* 345–358.

Tsukiura, T., & Cabeza, R. (2011). Remembering beauty: Roles of orbitofrontal and hippocampal regions in successful memory encoding of attractive faces. *NeuroImage, 54,* 653–660. doi:10.1016/j.neuroimage.2010.07.046

Tsukiura, T., Sekiguchi, A., Yomogida, Y., Nakagawa, S., Shigemune, Y., Kambara, T., . . . Kawashima, R. (2011). Effects of aging on hippocampal and anterior temporal activations during successful retrieval of memory for face–name associations. *Journal of Cognitive Neuroscience, 23,* 200–213.

Tugade, M. M., & Fredrickson, B. L. (2004). Resilient individuals use positive emotions to bounce back from negative emotional experiences. *Journal of Personality and Social Psychology, 86,* 320–333.

Turati, C. (2004). Why faces are not special to newborns: An alternative account of the face preference. *Current Directions in Psychological Science, 13,* 5–8.

Turkheimer, E., Haley, A., Waldron, M., D'Onofrio, B., & Gottesman, I. I. (2003). Socioeconomic status modifies heritability of IQ in young children. *Psychological Science, 14,* 623–628.

Turkheimer, E., & Waldron, M. (2000). Nonshared environment: A theoretical, methodological, and quantitative review. *Psychological Bulletin, 126,* 78–108.

Turnbull, C. M. (1961). Observations. *American Journal of Psychology, 1,* 304–308.

Turnbull, S., Ward, A., Treasure, J., Jick, H., & Derby, L. (1996). The demand for eating disorder care. An epidemiological study using the general practice research database. *British Journal of Psychiatry, 169,* 705–712.

Turton, S., & Campbell, C. (2005). Tend and befriend versus fight or flight: Gender differences in behavioral response to stress among university students. *Journal of Applied Biobehavioral Research, 10,* 209–232.

Twenge, J. M. (2009). Change over time in obedience: The jury's still out, but it might be decreasing. *American Psychologist, 64,* 28–31.

Uchino, B. N. (2009). Understanding the links between social support and physical health. *Perspectives on Psychological Science, 4,* 236–255.

Ulmer, C., Wolman, D. M., & Johns, M. M. E. (2008). *Resident duty hours: Enhancing sleep, supervision, and safety.* Washington, DC: The National Academies Press.

United Nations Statistics Division. (2006). *Demographic Yearbook 2006.* New York, NY: United Nations.

U.S. Bureau of the Census. (2001). *The 65 years and over population.* Retrieved from http://www.census.gov/prod/2001pubs/c2kbr01-10.pdf

U.S. Bureau of the Census. (2002). *United States Department of Commerce News.* Retrieved from http://www.census.gov/Press-Release/www/2002/cb02-19.html

U.S. Bureau of the Census. (2006). *Estimated median age at first marriage, by sex: 1890 to the present.* Retrieved from http://www.census.gov/population/socdemo/hh-fam/ms2.pdf

U.S. Bureau of the Census. (2007). *Most people make only one trip down the aisle, but first marriages shorter.* Retrieved from http://www.census.gov/Press-Release/www/releases/archives/marital_status_living_arrangements/010624.html

U.S. Census Bureau. (2010). *The next four decades. The older population in the United States: 2010 to 2050.* Retrieved from http://www.census.gov/prod/2010pubs/p25-1138.pdf

U.S. Department of Labor. (2006). *Training: Apprenticeship.* Retrieved from http://www.dol.gov/dol/topic/training/apprenticeship.htm

U.S. Department of Labor. (2010a). *Labor force statistics from the current population survey: Characteristics of the employed.* Table 2. Retrieved from http://www.bls.gov/cps/cpsaat2.pdf

U.S. Department of Labor. (2010b). *Labor force statistics from the current population survey: Characteristics of the employed.* Table 8. Retrieved from http://www.bls.gov/cps/cpsaat8.pdf

U.S. Department of Labor. (2010c). *Labor force statistics from the current population survey: Characteristics of the employed.* Table 10. Retrieved from http://www.bls.gov/cps/cpsaat10.pdf

U.S. Food and Drug Administration (2010). *FDA Warning letters issued to four makers of caffeinated alcoholic beverages: These beverages present a public health concern.* Retrieved from http://www.fda.gov/NewsEvents/Newsroom/PressAnnouncements/2010/ucm234109.htm

U.S. Senate. (2004). *Report on the US Intelligence community's prewar intelligence assessments on Iraq.* Retrieved from http://www.gpoaccess.gov/serialset/creports/iraq.html

Vadasz, C., Saito, M., Gyetvai, B. M., Oros, M., Szakall, I., Kovacs, K. M., . . . Toth, R. (2007). Glutamate receptor metabotropic 7 is *cis*-regulated in the mouse brain and modulates alcohol drinking. *Genomics, 90,* 690–702.

Vaillant, G. E. (2000). Adaptive mental mechanisms: Their role in positive psychology. *American Psychologist, 55,* 89–98.

Valkenburg, P. M., & Peter, J. (2009). Social consequences of the internet for adolescents: A decade of research. *Current Directions in Psychological Science, 18,* 1–5.

Vallar, G. (2006). Memory systems: The case of phonological short-term memory. A festschrift for Cognitive Neuropsychology. *Cognitive Neuropsychology, 23,* 135–155.

van Achterberg, M. E., Rohrbaugh, R. M., & Southwick, S. M. (2001). Emergence of PTSD in trauma survivors with dementia. *Journal of Clinical Psychiatry, 62,* 206–207.

Van den Bulck, J. (2004). Media use and dreaming: The relationship among television viewing, computer game play, and nightmares or pleasant dreams. *Dreaming, 14,* 43–49.

Van den Bussche, E., Van den Noortgate, W., & Reynvoet, B. (2009). Mechanisms of masked priming: A meta-analysis. *Psychological Bulletin, 135,* 452–477.

van der Laan, L. N., de Ridder, D. D., Viergever, M. A., & Smeets, P. M. (2011). The first taste is always with the eyes: A meta-analysis on the neural correlates of processing visual food cues. *NeuroImage, 55,* 296–303.

Van Dongen, H. A., Belenky, G., & Krueger, J. M. (2011). Investigating the temporal dynamics and underlying mechanisms of cognitive fatigue. In P. L. Ackerman (Ed.), *Cognitive fatigue: Multidisciplinary perspectives on current research and future applications* (pp. 127–147). Washington, DC: American Psychological Association.

Van Eerde, W., & Thierry, H. (1996). Vroom's expectancy models and work-related criteria: A meta-analysis. *Journal of Applied Psychology, 81,* 575–586.

Van Liempt, S., Vermetten, E., Geuze, E., & Westenberg, H. (2006). Pharmacotherapeutic treatment of nightmares and insomnia in posttraumatic stress disorder: An overview of the literature. *Annals of the New York Academy of Sciences, 1071,* 502–507.

van Os, J., Rutten, B. P. F., & Poulton, R. (2008). Gene-environmental interactions in schizophrenia: Review of epidemiological findings and future directions. *Schizophrenia Bulletin, 34,* 1066–1082.

Van Praag, H., Zhao, X., & Gage, F. H. (2004). Neurogenesis in the adult mammalian brain. In M. S. Gazzaniga (Ed.), *The cognitive neurosciences* (3rd ed., pp. 127–137). Cambridge, MA: MIT Press.

Vanderwerker, L. C., & Prigerson, H. G. (2004). Social support and technological connectedness as protective factors in bereavement. *Journal of Loss & Trauma, 9,* 45–57.

Vandewater, E. A., Shim, M. S., & Caplovitz, A. G. (2004). Linking obesity and activity level with children's television and video game use. *Journal of Adolescence, 27,* 71–85.

Van-Hooff, J. C., & Golden, S. (2002). Validation of an event-related potential memory assessment procedure: Intentional learning as opposed to simple repetition. *Journal of Psychophysiology, 16*, 12–22.

Varnum, M. E. W., Grossmann, I., Kitayama, S., & Nisbett, R. E. (2010). The original of cultural differences in cognition: The social orientation hypothesis. *Current Directions in Psychological Science, 19*, 9–13.

Vauclair, J. (1996). *Animal cognition: An introduction to modern comparative psychology.* Cambridge, MA: Harvard University Press.

Vaughn, D. (1996). *The Challenger launch decision: Risky technology, culture, and deviance at NASA.* Chicago, IL: University of Chicago Press.

Vermetten, E., & Bremner, J. D. (2002). Circuits and systems in stress: II. Applications to neurobiology and treatment in posttraumatic stress disorder. *Depression and Anxiety, 16*, 14–38.

Vernon, P. A., Villani, V. C., Vickers, L. C., & Harris, J. (2008). A behavioral genetic investigation of the Dark Triad and the Big 5. *Personality and Individual Differences, 44*, 445–452.

Verona, E., Joiner, T. E., Johnson, F., & Bender, T. W. (2006). Gender specific gene-environment interactions on laboratory-assessed aggression. *Biological Psychology, 71*, 33–41.

Viding, E., Spinath, F. M., Price, T. S., Bishop, D. V. M., Dale, P. S., & Plomin, R. (2004). Genetic and environmental influence on language impairment in 4-year-old same-sex and opposite-sex twins. *Journal of Child Psychology and Psychiatry and Allied Disciplines, 45*, 315–325.

Vierbuchen, T., Ostermeier, A., Pang, Z. P., Kokubu, Y., Südhof, T. C., & Wernig, M. (2010). Direct conversion of fibroblasts to functional neurons by defined factors. *Nature, 463*, 1035–1041.

Viglione, D. J., & Taylor, N. (2003). Empirical support for interrater reliability of Rorschach comprehensive system coding. *Journal of Clinical Psychology, 59*, 111–121.

Vinkhuyzen, A. E., van der Sluis, S., & Posthuma, D. (2010). Behavioral genetics. In R. A. Carlstedt (Ed.), *Handbook of integrative clinical psychology, psychiatry, and behavioral medicine: Perspectives, practices, and research* (pp. 81–94). NY: Springer.

Vinnicombe, S., & Singh, V. (2003). Women-only management training: An essential part of women's leadership development. *Journal of Change Management, 3*, 294–306.

Völlm, B., Richardson, P., McKie, S., Reniers, R., Elliott, R., Anderson, I. M., & ... Deakin, B. (2010). Neuronal correlates and serotonergic modulation of behavioural inhibition and reward in healthy and antisocial individuals. *Journal of Psychiatric Research, 44*, 123–131.

Volpe, K. (2004, January). Taylor takes on "fight-or-flight." *APS Observer*, p. 21.

Volz, K. G., & Von Cramon, D. Y. (2008). Can neuroscience tell a story about intuition? In H. Plessner, C. Betsch, & T. Betsch (Eds), *Intuition in judgment and decision making* (pp. 71–87). Mahwah, NJ: Erlbaum.

von Hippel, W., Hawkins, C., & Narayan, S. (1994). Personality and perceptual expertise: Individual differences in perceptual identification. *Psychological Science, 5*, 401–406.

Voorspoels, W., Vanpaemel, W., & Storms, G. (2008). Exemplars and prototypes in natural language concepts: A typicality-based evaluation. *Psychonomic Bulletin & Review, 15*, 630–637.

Voss, J. L., & Paller, K. A. (2008). Brain substrates of implicit and explicit memory: The importance of concurrently acquired neural signals of both memory types. *Neuropsychologia, 46*, 3021–3029.

Votruba-Drzal, E., Coley, R. L., & Chase-Lansdale, P. L. (2004). Child care and low-income children's development: Direct and moderated effects. *Child Development, 75*, 296–312.

Vroom, V. H. (1964). *Work and motivation.* New York, NY: Wiley.

Vygotsky, L. S. (1978). *Mind in society: The development of higher mental processes.* Cambridge, MA: Harvard University Press. (Original works published 1930, 1933, and 1935.)

Wagar, B. M., & Thagard, P. (2004). Spiking Phineas Gage: A neurocomputational theory of cognitive–affective integration in decision making. *Psychological Review, 111*, 67–79.

Wagner, U., Gais, S., Haider, H., Verleger, R., & Born, J. (2004). Sleep inspires insight. *Nature, 427*, 352–355.

Wai, J., Cacchio, M., Putallaz, M., & Makel, M. C. (2010). Sex differences in the right tail of cognitive abilities: A 30 year examination. *Intelligence, 38*, 412–423.

Waite, L. J., & Joyner, K. (2001). Emotional satisfaction and physical pleasure in sexual unions: Time horizon, sexual behavior, and sexual exclusivity. *Journal of Marriage & the Family, 63*, 247–264.

Walk, R. D., & Gibson, E. J. (1961). A comparative and analytical study of visual depth perception. *Psychological Monographs*, No. 75.

Walker, E., & Tessner, K. (2008). Schizophrenia. *Perspectives on Psychological Science, 3*, 30–37.

Walker, M. P., & Stickgold, R. (2006). Sleep, memory, and plasticity. *Annual Review of Psychology, 57*, 139–166.

Walker, P., & Shaffer, M. (2007). Reducing depression among adolescents dealing with grief and loss: A program evaluation report. *Health & Social Work, 32*, 67–68.

Wall, P. D., & Melzack, R. (1996). *The challenge of pain* (2nd ed.). Harmondworth, England: Penguin.

Waller, B. M., Parr, L. A., Gothard, K. M., Burrows, A. M., & Fuglevand, A. J. (2008). Mapping the contribution of single muscles to facial movements in the rhesus macaque. *Physiology & Behavior, 95*, 93–100.

Wallerstein, J. S., Blakeslee, S., & Lewis, J. (2000). *The unexpected legacy of divorce: Twenty-five year landmark study.* New York, NY: Hyperion.

Wallner, B., & Machatschke, I. H. (2009). The evolution of violence in men: The function of central cholesterol and serotonin. *Progress in Neuro-Psychopharmacology & Biological Psychiatry, 33*, 391–397.

Wallien, M. S. C., & Cohen-Kettenis, P. T. (2008). Psychosexual outcome of gender-dysphoric children. *Journal of the American Academy of Child & Adolescent Psychiatry, 47*, 1413–1423.

Walls, A. (2008). Resilience and psychoneuroimmunology: The role of adaptive coping in immune system responses to stress. *Dissertation Abstracts International: Section B: The Sciences and Engineering, 69*, 1350.

Walters, G. D., Rogers, R., Berry, D. T. R., Miller, H. A., Duncan, S. A., McCusker, P. J., ... Granacher, R. P., Jr. (2008). Malingering as a categorical or dimensional construct: The latent structure of feigned psychopathology as measured by the SIRS and MMPI-2. *Psychological Assessment, 20*, 238–247.

Walther, E., Bless, H., Strack, F., Rackstraw, P., Wagner, D., & Werth, L. (2002). Conformity effects in memory as a function of group size, dissenters and uncertainty. *Applied Cognitive Psychology, 16*, 793–810.

Wampold, B. E. (2001). *The great psychotherapy debate: Models, methods, and findings.* Mahwah, NJ: Erlbaum.

Wampold, B. E., Mondin, G. W., Moody, M., Stich, F., Benson, K., & Ahn, H. (1997). A meta-analysis of outcome studies comparing bona fide psychotherapies: Empirically, "all must have prizes." *Psychological Bulletin, 122*, 203–215.

Wang, Q., & Ross, M. (2005). What we remember and what we tell: The effects of culture and self-priming on memory representations and narratives. *Memory, 13*, 594–606.

Wang, Y.-C. [Ying-Chieh], Chen, M.-L., Chen, C.-H., Lai, I.-C., Chen, T.-T., ... Liou, Y.-J. (2008). Neuregulin 3 genetic variations and susceptibility to schizophrenia in a Chinese population. *Biological Psychiatry, 64*, 1093–1096.

Wang, Y. C. [Claire], Colditz, G. A., & Kuntz, K. M. (2007). Forecasting the obesity epidemic in the aging U.S. population. *Obesity, 15*, 2855–2865.

Ward-Begnoche, W. L., Pasold, T. L., McNeill, V., Peck, K. D., Razzaq, S., Fry, E. M. & Young, K. L. (2009). Childhood obesity treatment literature review. In L. C. James & J. C. Linton (Eds.), *Handbook of obesity intervention for the lifespan* (pp. 1–16). New York, NY: Springer.

Warnock, J. K. (2002). Female hypoactive sexual desire disorder: Epidemiology, diagnosis and treatment. *CNS Drugs, 16*, 745–753.

Wasik, B. A., Bond, M. A., & Hindman, A. (2006). The effects of a language and literacy intervention on Head Start children and teachers. *Journal of Educational Psychology, 98*, 63–74.

Waterhouse, L. (2006). Multiple intelligences, the Mozart effect, and emotional intelligence: A critical review. *Educational Psychologist, 41*, 207–225.

Waters, A. J., Gobet, F., & Leyden, G. (2002). Visuospatial abilities of chess players. *British Journal of Psychology, 93*, 557–565.

Waters, M. (1999, October). Men and women handle negative situations differently, study suggests. *APA Monitor, 30*(9), 8.

Watson, C. J., Baghdoyan, H. A., & Lydic, R. (2010). Neuropharmacology of sleep and wakefulness. *Sleep Medicine Clinics, 5*, 513–528.

Watson, D. L. (2008). The fundamental attribution error. In L. T. Benjamin (Ed.), *Favorite activities for the teaching of psychology* (pp. 248–251). Washington, DC: American Psychological Association.

Watson, J. B. (1924). *Behaviorism*. Chicago, IL: University of Chicago Press.

Watson, J. B., & Rayner, R. (1920). Conditioned emotional reactions. *Journal of Experimental Psychology, 3*, 1–14.

Wechsler, H., Dowdall, G. W., Davenport, A., & DeJong, W. (2000). *Binge drinking on college campuses: Results of a national study*. Retrieved from www.hsph.harvard.edu/cas

Wegner, D. M., Wenzlaff, R. M., & Kozak, M. (2004). Dream rebound. *Psychological Science, 15*, 232–236.

Weinberg, M. K., Tronick, E. Z., Cohn, J. F., & Olson, K. L. (1999). Gender differences in emotional expressivity and self-regulation during early infancy. *Developmental Psychology, 35*, 175–188.

Weiner, B. (2008). Reflections on the history of attribution theory and research: People, personalities, publications, problems. *Social Psychology, 39*, 151–156.

Weiner, I. B. (2006). The Rorschach inkblot method. In R. P. Archer (Ed.), *Forensic uses of clinical assessment instruments* (pp. 181–207). Mahwah, NJ: Erlbaum.

Weingarten, S. M., & Cummings, J. L. (2001). Psychosurgery of frontal–subcortical circuits. In D. G. Lichter & J. L. Cummings (Eds.), *Frontal-subcortical circuits in psychiatric and neurological disorders* (pp. 421–435). New York, NY: Guilford Press.

Weinstein, N., & Ryan, R. M. (2010). When helping helps: Autonomous motivation for prosocial behavior and its influence on well-being for the helper and recipient. *Journal of Personality and Social Psychology, 98*, 222–244.

Weinstein, R. S., Soule, C. R., Collins, F., Cone, J., Melhorn, M., & Simantocci, K. (1991). Expectations and high school change: Teacher-researcher collaboration to prevent school failure. *American Journal of Community Psychology, 19*, 333–402.

Weinstock, M. (2008). The long-term behavioural consequences of prenatal stress. *Neuroscience & Biobehavioral Reviews, 32*, 1073–1086.

Weiss, S. J., Wilson, P., & Morrison, D. (2004). Maternal tactile stimulation and the neurodevelopment of low birth weight infants. *Infancy, 5*, 85–107.

Weisse, C. S., Foster, K. K., & Fisher, E. A. (2005). The influence of experimenter gender and race on pain reporting: Does racial or gender concordance matter? *Pain Medicine, 6*, 80–87.

Wenzel, A., Brown, G. K., & Beck, A. T. (2009). Evidence-based treatments for the prevention of suicidal acts. In A. Wenzel, G. K. Brown, & A. T. Beck (Eds.), *Cognitive therapy for suicidal patients: Scientific and clinical applications* (pp. 79–100). Washington, DC: American Psychological Association.

Werker, J. F. (1989). Becoming a native listener. *American Scientist, 77*, 54–59.

Wesley, M. J., Hanlon, C. A., & Porrino, L. J. (2011). Poor decision-making by chronic marijuana users is associated with decreased functional responsiveness to negative consequences. *Psychiatry Research: Neuroimaging, 191*, 51–59.

Westen, D. (2005). Implications of research in cognitive neuroscience for psychodynamic psychotherapy. In F. O. Gabbard, J. S. Beck, & J. Holmes (Eds.), *Oxford textbook of psychotherapy* (pp. 443–448). New York, NY: Oxford University Press.

Weston, W. W. (2005). Patient-centered medicine: A guide to the biopsychosocial model. *Families, Systems, & Health, 23* [Special issue: The Current State of the Biopsychosocial Approach], 387–392.

Westwell, M. (2007). How too many interruptions is like a "kick in the head." Oxford Research Group. Retrieved from http://www.iii-p.org/research/cxo_reports/Oxford-Interrupt-CxO-April2007.pdf

Wetzel, W., Wagner, T., & Balschun, D. (2003). REM sleep enhancement induced by different procedures improves memory retention in rats. *European Journal of Neuroscience, 18*, 2611–2617.

Whealin, J. M., & Ruzek, J. (2008). Program evaluation for organizational cultural competence in mental health practices. *Professional Psychology: Research and Practice, 39*, 320–328.

Whittle, S., Yap, M. B. H., Yücel, M., Fornito, A., Simmons, J. G., Barrett, A., . . . Allen, N. B. (2008). Prefrontal and amygdala volumes are related to adolescents' affective behaviors during parent–adolescent interactions. *PNAS Proceedings of the National Academy of Sciences of the United States of America, 105*, 3652–3657.

Whorf, B. L. (1956). *Language, thought, and reality*. New York, NY: MIT Press–Wiley.

Wichers, M., Myin-Germeys, I., Jacobs, N., Peeters, F., Kenis, G., Derom, C., . . . van Os, J. (2007). Genetic risk of depression and stress-induced negative affect in daily life. *British Journal of Psychiatry, 191*, 218–223.

Wickelgren, I. (2009, September/October). I do not feel your pain. *Scientific American Mind, 20*(4), 51–57.

Widaman, K. F. (2009). Phenylketonuria in children and mothers. *Current Directions in Psychological Science, 18*, 48–52.

Widiger, T. A., & Sankis, L. M. (2000). Adult psychopathology: Issues and controversies. *Annual Review of Psychology, 51*, 377–404.

Widner, R. L., Otani, H., & Winkelman, S. E. (2005). Tip-of-the-tongue experiences are not merely strong feeling-of-knowing experiences. *Journal of General Psychology, 132*, 392–407.

Wiens, A. N., & Menustik, C. E. (1983). Treatment outcome and patient characteristics in an aversion therapy program for alcoholism. *American Psychologist, 38*, 1089–1096.

Wilcox, S., Evenson, K. R., Aragaki, A., Wassertheil–Smoller, S., Mouton, C. P., & Loevinger, B. L. (2003). The effects of widowhood on physical and mental health, health behaviors, and health outcomes: The Women's Health Initiative. *Health Psychology, 22*, 513–522.

Wilkins, V. M. (2005). Religion, spirituality, and psychological distress in cardiovascular disease. *Dissertation Abstracts International: Section B: The Sciences and Engineering, 66*, 3430.

Williams, J. E., Paton, C. C., Siegler, I. C., Eigenbrodt, M. L., Nieto, F. J., & Tyroler, H. A. (2000). Anger proneness predicts coronary heart disease risk: Prospective analysis from the atherosclerosis risk in communities (ARIC) study. *Circulation, 101*, 2034–2039.

Williams, R. B. (2001). Hostility (and other psychological risk factors): Effects on health and the potential for successful behavioral approaches to prevention and treatment. In A. Baum, T. A. Revenson, & J. E. Singer (Eds.), *Handbook of health psychology* (pp. 661–688). Mahwah, NJ: Erlbaum.

Williams, S. (2000, April). How is telehealth being incorporated into psychology practice? *Monitor on Psychology, 31*(4), 15.

Willis, J., & Todorov, A. (2006). First impressions: Making up your mind after a 100-Ms exposure to a face. *Psychological Science, 17*, 592–598.

Willner, P., Bergman, J., & Sanger, D. (2008). Behavioural genetics and its relevance to psychiatry. *Behavioural Pharmacology, 19*, 371–373.

Willyard, C. (2011, January). Men: A growing minority. *GradPsych Magazine, 9*(1), 40.

Wilson, G. T., Grilo, C. M., & Vitousek, K. M. (2007). Psychological treatment of eating disorders. *American Psychologist, 62*, 199–216.

Wilson, R. S., Bennett, D. A., Bienias, J. L., de Leon, C. F. M., Morris, M. C., & Evans, D. A. (2003). Cognitive activity and cognitive decline in a biracial community population. *Neurology, 61*, 812–816.

Wing, H. (1969). *Conceptual learning and generalization*. Baltimore, MD: Johns Hopkins University Press.

Winner, E. (1998). *Psychological aspects of giftedness*. New York, NY: Basic Books.

Winner, E. (2000). The origins and ends of giftedness. *American Psychologist, 55*, 159–169.

Wise, D., & Rosqvist, J. (2006). Explanatory style and well-being. In J. C. Thomas, D. L. Segal, & M. Hersen (Eds.), *Comprehensive handbook of personality and psychopathology, Vol. 1: Personality and everyday functioning* (pp. 285–305). Hoboken, NJ: Wiley.

Witek-Janusek, L., Albuquerque, K., Chroniak, K. R., Chroniak, C., Durazo-Arvizu, R., & Mathews, H. L. (2008). Effect of mindfulness based stress reduction on immune function, quality of life and coping in women newly diagnosed with early stage breast cancer. *Brain, Behavior, and Immunity, 22*, 969–981.

Witkiewitz, K., Marlatt, G., & Walker, D. (2005). Mindfulness-based relapse prevention for alcohol and substance use disorders. *Journal of Cognitive Psychotherapy, 19*, 211–228.

Wolberg, L. R. (1977). *The technique of psychotherapy* (3rd ed.). New York, NY: Grune & Stratton.

Wolfson, C., Wolfson, D. B., Asgharian, M., M'Lan, C. E., Østbye, T., Rockwood, K., & Hogan, D. B. (2001). A reevaluation of the duration of survival after the onset of dementia. *The New England Journal of Medicine, 344*, 1111–1116.

Wolke, D., & Sapouna, M. (2008). Big men feeling small: Childhood bullying experience, muscle dysmorphia and other mental health problems in bodybuilders. *Psychology of Sport and Exercise, 9*, 595–604.

Wolpe, J. (1973). *The practice of behavior therapy* (2nd ed.). New York, NY: Pergamon.

Wolpe, J. (1990). *The practice of behavior therapy* (4th ed.). New York, NY: Pergamon.

Wood, J. M., Lilienfeld, S. O., Nezworski, M., Garb, H. N., Allen, K., & Wildermuth, J. L. (2010). Validity of Rorschach Inkblot scores for discriminating psychopaths from nonpsychopaths in forensic populations: A meta-analysis. *Psychological Assessment, 22*, 336–349.

Wood, W., & Quinn, J. M. (2003). Forewarned and forearmed? Two meta-analytic syntheses of forewarnings of influence appeals. *Psychological Bulletin, 129,* 119–138.

Woodhouse, S. S., Dykas, M. J., & Cassidy, J. (2009). Perceptions of secure base provision within the family. *Attachment & Human Development, 11,* 47–67.

Woods, S. C., Schwartz, M. W., Baskin, D. G., & Seeley, R. J. (2000). Food intake and the regulation of body weight. *Annual Review of Psychology, 51,* 255–277.

Woodward, A., & Needham, A. (2009). *Learning and the infant mind.* New York, NY: Oxford University Press.

Wooffitt, R. (2005). From process to practice: Language, interaction and "flash-bulb" memories. In H. te Molder, & J. Potter (Eds.), *Conversation and cognition* (pp. 203–225). New York, NY: Cambridge University Press.

The World Health Organization. (2004). *The world health report 2004: Changing history, annex table 3: Burden of disease in DALYs by cause, sex, and mortality stratum in WHO regions, estimates for 2002.* Geneva: WHO, 2004.

World Health Organization World Mental Health Survey Consortium. (2004). Prevalence, severity, and unmet need for treatment of mental disorders in the World Health Organization World Mental Health Surveys. *JAMA: Journal of the American Medical Association, 291,* 2581–2590.

Worthman, C. M., & Melby, M. K. (2002). Toward a comparative developmental ecology of human sleep. In M. A. Carskadon (Ed.), *Adolescent sleep patterns: Biological, social, and psychological influences* (pp. 69–117). New York, NY: Cambridge University Press.

Wortman, C. B., & Silver, R. C. (1989). The myths of coping with loss. *Journal of Consulting & Clinical Psychology, 57,* 349–357.

Wright, A. A., & Katz, J. S. (2007). Generalization hypothesis of abstract-concept learning: Learning strategies and related issues in *Macaca mulatta, Cebus apella,* and *Columba livia. Journal of Comparative Psychology, 121,* 387–397.

Wright, D. B., & Loftus, E. F. (2008). Eyewitness memory. In G. Cohen & M. A. Conway, (Eds.), *Memory in the real world* (3rd ed., pp. 91–105). New York, NY: Psychology Press.

Wright, D. B., Memon, A., Skagerberg, E. M., & Gabbert, F. (2009). When eyewitnesses talk. Current Directions in Psychological Science, 18, 174–178.

Wright, J. C., Anderson, D. R., Huston, A. C., Collins, P. A., Schmitt, K. L., & Linebarger, D. L. (1999). Early viewing of educational television programs: The short- and long-term effects on schooling. *Insights, 2,* 5–8.

Wright, K. (2003). Relationships with death: The terminally ill talk about dying. *Journal of Marital and Family Therapy, 29,* 439–454.

Wu, M. N., Ho, K., Crocker, A., Yue, Z., Koh, K., & Sehgal, A. (2009). The effects of caffeine on sleep in Drosophila require PKA activity, but not the adenosine receptor. *The Journal of Neuroscience, 29,* 11029–11037.

Wubbolding, R. E. (2005). The power of belonging. *International Journal of Reality Therapy, 24,* 43–44.

Yager, J. (2008). Binge eating disorder: The search for better treatments. *American Journal of Psychiatry, 165,* 4–6.

Yaggi, H. K., Concato, J., Kernan, W. N., Lichtman, J. H., Brass, L. M., & Mohsenin, V. (2005). Obstructive sleep apnea as a risk factor for stroke and death. *The New England Journal of Medicine, 353,* 2034–2041.

Yamamoto, K., & Chimbidis, M. E. (1966). Achievement, intelligence, and creative thinking in fifth grade children: A correlational study. *Merrill-Palmer Quarterly, 12,* 233–241.

Yang, Q., & Chen, F. (2001). Behavior problems in children with simple obesity. *Chinese Journal of Clinical Psychology, 9,* 273–274.

Yang, X., Bi, Y., & Feng, D. (2011). From the vascular microenvironment to neurogenesis. *Brain Research Bulletin, 84,* 1–7.

Yarkoni, T., Poldrack, R. A., Van Essen, D. C., & Wager, T. D. (2010). Cognitive neuroscience 2.0: Building a cumulative science of human brain function. *Trends in Cognitive Sciences, 14,* 489–496.

Yerkes, R., & Dodson, J. (2007). The relation of strength of stimulus to rapidity of habit-formation. In D. Smith & M. Bar-Eli (Eds.), *Essential readings in sport and exercise psychology* (pp. 13–22). Champaign, IL: Human Kinetics. (Reprinted from *Journal of Comparative Neurology and Psychology, 18,* 459–482).

Yi, H., Williams, G. D., & Dufour, M. C. (December, 2002). *Surveillance Report #61: Trends in alcohol-related fatal traffic crashes, United States, 1977-2000.* Rockville, MD: National Institute on Alcohol Abuse and Alcoholism, Division of Biometry and Epidemiology.

Yirmiya, R., & Goshen, I. (2011). Immune modulation of learning, memory, neural plasticity and neurogenesis. *Brain, Behavior, and Immunity, 25,* 181–213.

Yoo, S. H., Matsumoto, D., & LeRoux, J. A. (2006). The influence of emotion recognition and emotion regulation on intercultural adjustment. *International Journal of Intercultural Relations, 30,* 345–363.

Young, J. E., Rygh, J. L., Weinberger, A. D., & Beck, A. T. (2008). Cognitive therapy for depression. In D. H. Barlow (Ed.), *Clinical handbook of psychological disorders: A step-by-step treatment manual* (4th ed., pp. 250–305). New York, NY: Guilford Press.

Young, S. G., & Hugenberg, K. (2010). Mere social categorization modulates identification of facial expressions of emotion. *Journal of Personality and Social Psychology, 99,* 964–977. doi:10.1037/a0020400

Yu, Q., & Yuan, D.-H. (2008). The impact of the emotional intelligence of employees and their manager on the job performance of employees. *Acta Psychologica Sinica, 40,* 74–83.

Yukl, G. A. (2002). *Leadership in organizations.* Upper Saddle River, NJ: Prentice Hall.

Zadra, A., Pilon, M., & Donderi, D. C. (2006). Variety and intensity of emotions in nightmares and bad dreams. *Journal of Nervous and Mental Disease, 194,* 249–254.

Zahr, N. M., Pitel, A., Chanraud, S., & Sullivan, E. V. (2010). Contributions of studies on alcohol use disorders to understanding cerebellar function. *Neuropsychology Review, 20,* 280–289.

Zajonc, R. B. (1984). On the primacy of affect. *American Psychologist, 39,* 117–129.

Zald, D. H., Cowan, R. L., Riccardi, P., Baldwin, R. M., Ansari, M. S., Li, R., . . . Kessler, R. M. (2008). Midbrain dopamine receptor availability is inversely associated with novelty-seeking traits in humans. *The Journal of Neuroscience, 28,* 14372–14378.

Zalsman, G., & Mann, J. J. (2005). Editorial: The neurobiology of suicide in adolescents. An emerging field of research. *International Journal of Adolescent Medicine and Health, 17,* 195–196.

Zaragoza, M. S., & Mitchell, K. J. (1996). Repeated exposure to suggestion and the creation of false memories. *Psychological Science, 7,* 294–300.

Zeedyk, M. S., & Greenwood, R. M. (2008). Editor's introduction: Reflections on the work of feminist theorist Jean Baker Miller. *Feminism & Psychology, 18,* 321–325.

Zeidan, F. (2010). The effects of brief mindfulness meditation training on mood, cognitive, and cardiovascular variables. *Dissertation Abstracts International, 71.* Retrieved from EBSCOhost.

Zeng, C., & Shi, K. (2007). Relationship of big five personality with employees' job burnout. *Chinese Journal of Clinical Psychology, 15,* 614–616.

Zeskind, P. S., & Gingras, J. L. (2006). Maternal cigarette-smoking during pregnancy disrupts rhythms in fetal heart rate. *Journal of Pediatric Psychology, 31,* 5–14.

Zetterberg, H. (2008). Biomarkers reflecting different facets of Alzheimer's disease. *European Journal of Neurology, 15,* 1143–1144.

Zhai, F. (2008). Effects of Head Start on the outcomes of participants. *Dissertation Abstracts International Section A: Humanities and Social Sciences, 69,* 384.

Zigler, E., & Styfco, S. J. (2008). America's head start program: An effort for social justice. In C. Wainryb, J. G. Smetana, & E. Turiel (Eds.), *Social development, social inequalities, and social justice* (pp. 53–80). New York, NY: Taylor & Francis Group/Erlbaum.

Zimbardo, P. (2007). *The Lucifer effect: Understanding how good people turn evil.* New York, NY: Random House.

Zimmer, C. (2005, December 13). Children learn by monkey see, monkey do. Chimps don't. *New York Times,* p. D2.

Zimmerman, A. W., Connors, S. L., & Pardo-Villamizar, C. A. (2006). Neuroimmunology and neurotransmitters in autism. In R. Tuchman & I. Rapin (Eds), *Autism: A neurological disorder of early brain development* (pp. 141–159). London, England: Mac Keith Press.

Zinbarg, R. E., & Griffith, J. W. (2008). Behavior therapy. In J. L. Lebow (Ed.), *Twenty-first century psychotherapies: Contemporary approaches to theory and practice* (pp. 8–42). Hoboken, NJ: Wiley.

Zonnevylle-Bender, M. J. S., van Goozen, S. H. M., Cohen-Kettenis, P. T., van Elburg, A., de Wildt, M., Stevelmans, E., & van Engeland, H. (2004). Emotional functioning in anorexia nervosa patients: Adolescents compared to adults. *Depression and Anxiety, 19,* 35–42.

Zipursky, R. B. (2007). Imaging mental disorders in the 21st century. *The Canadian Journal of Psychiatry/La Revue canadienne de psychiatrie, 52,* 133–134.

Zubieta, J.-K., Heitzeg, M. M., Smith, Y. R., Bueller, J. A., Xu, K., Xu, Y., Koeppe, R. A., . . . Goldman, D. (2003). COMT val[158]met genotype affects μ-opioid neurotransmitter responses to a pain stressor. *Science, 299,* 1240–1243.

Zucker, K. J. (2005). Gender identity disorder in children and adolescents. *Annual Review of Clinical Psychology, 1,* 467–492.

Zuckerman, M. (2006). Sensation seeking in entertainment. In J. Bryant & P. Vorderer (Eds.), *Psychology of entertainment* (pp. 367–387). Mahwah, NJ: Erlbaum.

Zuckerman, M. (2007a). Sensation seeking. In M. Zuckerman (Ed.), *Sensation seeking and risky behavior* (pp. 3–49). Washington, DC: American Psychological Association.

Zuckerman, M. (2007b). Sensation seeking and risky driving, sports, and vocations. In M. Zuckerman (Ed.), *Sensation seeking and risky behavior* (pp. 73–106). Washington, DC: American Psychological Association.

Zur, O. (2007). Telehealth and the technology for delivering care. In O. Zur (Ed.), *Boundaries in Psychotherapy: Ethical and Clinical Explorations* (pp. 133–146). Washington, DC: American Psychological Association.

Zvolensky, M. J., Vujanovic, A. A., Bernstein, A., & Leyro, T. (2010). Distress tolerance: Theory, measurement, and relations to psychopathology. *Current Directions in Psychological Science, 19*, 406–410.

Zwettler-Otte, S. (2008). Freud's actual reception in the scientific literature. *Canadian Journal of Psychoanalysis, 16*, 23–37.

Credits

PHOTO CREDITS

FM

Front Cover: Ian Cumming/Axiom Photographic/Glow Images

CHAPTER 1

Opener: Huntstock, Inc./Alamy; 5 (T) Helga Esteb/Shutterstock.com; 5 (B) Scott Camazine & Sue Trainor/Photo Researchers, Inc.; 7 (T) The New Yorker Collection, 1999, Donald Reilly from cartoonbank.com. All Rights Reserved; 7 (BL) guatebrian/Alamy; 7 (CL) BMCL/Shutterstock.com; 7 (CR) blickwinkel/Alamy; 7 (BR) Steve Vidler/SuperStock; 9 Bob Daemmrich/The Image Works; 13 (T) Bettmann/CORBIS; 13 (B) Library of Congress; 14 Bildarchiv der Osterreichische Nationalbibliothek; 15 (T) Hulton Archive/Archive Photos/Getty Images; 15 (B) G. Paul Bishop; 16 Bettmann/CORBIS; 18 JAPANESE RED CROSS/Reuters/Landov; 19 (T) Bettmann/CORBIS; 19 (B) REUTERS/POOL New; 21 Michael Newman/PhotoEdit; 22 (T) Carol Gilligan; 22 (B) Creatas/Jupiter Images; 23 Bettmann/CORBIS; 25 Attila JANDI/Shutterstock.com; 26 Bill Anderson/Photo Researchers, Inc.; 27 Robert Brenner/PhotoEdit Inc.; 32 Wiley Miller. Distributed by Universal Press Syndicate; 34 (TL) Alexandra Milgram.

CHAPTER 2

Opener: Martin Bond/Alamy; 45 E.R. Lewis, Y.Y. Zeevi, & F.S. Werblin (1969); 48 Raphael Daniaud/Shutterstock.com; 50 s44/ZUMA Press/Newscom; 53 The divisions of the brain. Psychology: The Core , 1st edition, by Charles G. Morris and Albert A. Maisto. Copyright © 2008. Reproduced by permission of Pearson Education, Inc.; 54 PHOTOEDIT/PhotoEdit; 55 (B) Library of Congress; 61 AJPhoto/Photo Researchers, Inc.; 62 (T) Mark Herreid/Shutterstock.com; 62 (CR) Catherine Pouedras/Science Photo Library/Photo Researchers, Inc.; 62 (B) WDCN/Univ. College London / Photo Researchers, Inc.; 66 Chase Swift/Corbis; 70 (L) CNRI/Photo Researchers, Inc.; 70 (R) CNRI/Photo Researchers, Inc.; 72 Sebastian Kaulitzki/Shutterstock.com; 73 Rick Gomez/Corbis; 74 Robin Nelson/PhotoEdit; 74 Schizophrenia Genesis: The Origins of Madness by I. I. Gottesman. Copyright © 1991 by Henry Holt & Company, LLC.

CHAPTER 3

Opener: Sebastian Kaulitzki/Alamy; 82 Bob Daemmrich/The Image Works; 83 (B) Reuters/CORBIS; 85 Adapted from Hubel, 1963; 86 (T) Don Wong/Photo Researchers, Inc.; 87 (T) E. R. Lewis, Y. Y. Zeevi, & F. S. Werblin (1969); 90 (T) Pearson Education/PH College; 90 (B) Fritz Goro/Time & Life Pictures/Getty Images; 94 CICCARELLI, SAUNDRA; WHITE, J. NOLAND, PSYCHOLOGY, 3rd,©2012. Printed and Electronically reproduced by permission of Pearson Education, Inc., Upper Saddle River, New Jersey; 96 Sebastian Kaulitzki/Alamy; 97 (T) Aija Lehtonen/Shutterstock.com; 99 (T) Amaviael/Dreamstime.com; 101 Robbie Jack/Corbis; 102 (B) Fujifotos/The Image Works; 103 Steve Raymer/CORBIS; 105 Signac, Paul (1893–1935), "Saint-Tropez, in a thunderstorm." Musee de l'Annonciade, St. Tropez, France. Reunion des Musees Nationaux/Art Resource, NY. © ARS, NY.); 106 (T) The New Yorker Collection, 2000, John O'Brien from cartoonbank.com. All Rights Reserved.; 106 (B) Chris Madden/Alamy; 107 (TR) M. C. Escher's "Circle Limit IV" © 2003, Cordon Art B. V. Baarn, Holland. All rights reserved.; 110 (B) John Lindsay-Smith/Shutterstock.com; 111 GERRIG, RICHARD J.; ZIMBARDO, PHILIP G., PSYCHOLOGY AND LIFE, 19th, ©2010. Printed and Electronically reproduced by permission of PearsonEducation, Inc., Upper Saddle River, New Jersey; 112 (T) Sherab/Alamy.

CHAPTER 4

Opener: Piko/Photo Researchers, Inc.; 120 Will & Deni McIntyre/Photo Researchers, Inc.; 121 (T) Jim Arbogast/Photodisc/Getty Images; 126 Zigy Kaluzny/Stone/Getty Images; 127 Topham/The Image Works; 131 Tek Image/Photo Researchers, Inc.; 135 Stephane Bidouze/Shutterstock.com; 139 Centers for Disease Control, Office on Smoking and Health; 141 The Granger Collection, NYC; 142 (T) Getty Images; 146 Tibor Hirsch/Photo Researchers, Inc.; 148 Michael Newman/PhotoEdit.

CHAPTER 5

Opener: PRNewsFoto/The Atlantic City International Power Boat Show/AP Photos; 156 Joe Sohm/The Image Works; 157 (T) Gregory K. Scott/Photo Researchers, Inc.; 157 (B) Brent Madison/Dorling Kindersley; 160 (T) The New Yorker Collection, 1978, S. Gross from cartoonbank.com. All Rights Reserved.; 160 (B) Walter. Dawn/Photo Researchers, Inc.; 162 Meeke/Zefa Value/Corbis; 169 Elaine Davis/Shutterstock.com; 171 Tim Ridley/Dorling Kindersley; 172 Gerard Brown/Dorling Kindersley; 176 Library of Congress; 177 age fotostock/SuperStock; 178(a—l) Albert Bandura; 179 (B) Amanda Coakes and Janet Mann.

CHAPTER 6

Opener: Suzanne Long/Alamy; 186 Bonnie Kamin/PhotoEdit; 187 Kelly-Mooney Photography/Corbis; 189 (T) ENRIQUE ALONSO/EPA/Newscom; 189 (B) The New Yorker Collection, Arnie Levin from cartoonbank.com. All Rights Reserved.; 193 Stephen Webster/Corbis; 196 PhotoLink/Photodisc/Getty Images; 197 Jens Lucking/cultura/Corbis; 200 (B) H. Damasio, T. Grabowski, R. Frank, A.M. Galaburda & A.R. Damasio (1994) The return of Phineas Gage: clues about the brain from a famous patient, Science, 264, 1102–1105. Dornsife Neuroscience Imaging Center and Brain and Creativity Institute, University of Southern California; 202 The New Yorker Collection, 1998, Mick Stevens from cartoonbank.com. All Rights Reserved.; 203 Dr. Paul Thompson; 207 Alberto Loyo/Shutterstock.com; 209 Carmen Taylor/AP Photos.

CHAPTER 7

Opener: James King-Holmes/Photo Researchers, Inc.; 219 (B) The New Yorker Collection, 1994, Sam Gross from cartoonbank.com. All Rights Reserved.; 220 Reunion des Musees Nationaux/Art Resource, NY ; 221 Imagestate Media Partners Limited - Impact Photos/Alamy; 223 Michael K. Nichols/National Geographic Image Collection; 236 AYAKOVLEV.COM/Shutterstock.com; 238 Bob Daemmrich/The Image Works; 244 Jeff Greenberg/Photo Researchers, Inc.; 245 AP Photos/Greg Wahl-Stephens; 246 Yuri Arcur/Dreamstime.com; 249 Paul Conklin/PhotoEdit.

CHAPTER 8

Opener: Andrey Bandurenko/Shutterstock.com; 262 James Marshall/The Image Works; 265 (L) Stewart Cohen Pictures/Alamy; 265 (R) Camermann/The Image Works; 266 (L) AP Photos/Peter Kramer; 273 Tim Booth/Shutterstock.com; 275 (T) Allihays/Dreamstime.com; 275 (B) Harlow Primate Laboratory/University of Wisconsin; 276 AP Photos/Ben Birchall; 277 Stefan Sollfors/Alamy; 278 Catherine Ursillo/Photo Researchers, Inc.; 280 Plutchik, 1980; 281 blickwinkel/Alamy; 282 Photos by Peter DaSilva for The New York Times; 282 The New York Times, 2003/The Paul Ekman Group, LLC; 286 Zurijeta/Shutterstock; 288 The Paul Ekman Group, LLC.

CHAPTER 9

Opener: Michael Newman/PhotoEdit; 293 Paolo Vairo/ Shutterstock.com; 296 AP Photo/Anchorage Daily News, Bill Roth; 297 Martin Novak/Shutterstock; 298 Mark Richards/PhotoEdit; 303 Lew Merrim/Photo Researchers, Inc.; 306 Dorothy Littell Greco/The Image Work; 307 Jonny Cochrane/Alamy; 308 Nina Leen/Time Life Pictures/Getty Images; 310 (T) Jamie Grill/Blend Images/Alamy; 310 (B) Michael Newman/PhotoEdit; 312 (T) Harald Eisenberger/Getty Images; 312 (B) Peter Byron/Photo Researchers, Inc.; 317 The New Yorker Collection, 1997, Leo Cullum from cartoonbank.com. All Rights Reserved.; 319 Deborah Davis/PhotoEdit; 322 SW Productions/Brand X Picture/Getty Images; 324 (B) Bob Daemmrich/The Image Works; 326 Rhoda Sidney/The Image Works.

CHAPTER 10

Opener: Jacob Gregory/Shutterstock; 335 (B) The New Yorker Collection, 1992, Lee Lorenz from cartoonbank.com. All Rights Reserved.; 337 Erich Lessing/Art Resource, NY; 338 Warner Bros./Photofest; 339 (T) The New Yorker Collection, 2000, Mike Twohy from cartoonbank.com. All Rights Reserved.; 339 (C) Ron Sachs/Pool/CNP/Corbis; 339 (B) Bettmann/CORBIS; 340 (T) Library of Congress; 346 (B) The New Yorker Collection, 1986, Mischa Richter from cartoonbank.com. All Rights Reserved.; 350 (TL) Corbis; 350 (R) Paul Chinn/San Francisco Chronicle/Corbis; 356 Markus Gann/Shutterstock.com; 357 Reprinted by permission of the publishers from Henry A. Murray, Thematic Apperception Test, Cambridge, Mass.: Harvard University Press, Copyright © 1943 by the President and Fellows of Harvard College, © 1971 by Henry A. Murray.

CHAPTER 11

Opener: DAVID EULITT/MCT/Newscom; 365 Wedding Photo/Fotolia; 366 Robert Brenner/PhotoEdit; 368 Peter Rogers/Getty Images; 376 Lichtmeister/Shutterstock.com; 378 .shock/Fotolia; 382 Andrew Holbrooke/Corbis; 384 Przemek Tokar/Shutterstock.com.

CHAPTER 12

Opener: Rubberball Productions/Getty Images; 393 Stock Montage/Contributor/Getty Images; 394 Jim Cummins/Taxi/Getty Images; 407 Gardai/PA Wire URN:5210308, Press Association via AP Images; 409 Brigitte Sporrer/Corbis; 415 Monte S. Buchsbaum, M.D.; 417 BURGER/PHANIE/Photo Researchers, Inc.; 419 wavebreakmedia ltd/Shutterstock.com.

CHAPTER 13

Opener: Nancy Sheehan/PhotoEdit; 426 Bjanka Kadic/Alamy; 427 The New Yorker Collection, 1989, Danny Shanahan from cartoonbank.com. All Rights Reserved.; 428 Time & Life Pictures/Getty Images; 432 (a–i) Albert Bandura; 434 Bob Daemmrich/PhotoEdit; 436 Richard T. Nowitz/Corbis; 447 (T) Peter Turnley/CORBIS; 447 (B) Laima Druskis/Pearson Education; 448 Mark Antman/The Image Works; 450 NotarYES/Shutterstock.com; 451 Spencer Grant/PhotoEdit.

CHAPTER 14

Opener: Drx/Fotolia; 457 AP Photos/Pool, Tom Landers; 459 David Buffington/Photodisc/Getty Images; 461 PHILLIP HAYSON/PhotoLibrary; 463 Rhoda Sidney/The Image Works; 467 Corbis; 468 Monkey Business / Fotolia; 470 Marcus Bleasdale/VII Photo; 470 Patrick Barta/Corbis RF; 473 ALAN ODDIE/PhotoEdit; 476 (T) H Miller/Getty Images; 476 (B) AP Photos; 477 Tommy E Trenchard/Alamy; 479 Walter Hodges/Getty Images; 480 AP Photos

TEXT CREDITS

CHAPTER 1

4 American Psychological Association Divisions (2001) Published by the American Psychological Association; 4–5 MORRIS, CHARLES G.; MAISTO, ALBERT A., PSYCHOLOGY: THE CORE, 1st, © 2009. Printed and Electronically reproduced by permission of Pearson Education, Inc., Upper Saddle River, New Jersey; 20 Summary Report: Doctorate Recipients from US. National Research Council. Published by the American Psychological Association; 32 Mizuko Ito et al, HANGING OUT, MESSING AROUND, AND GEEKING OUT: KIDS LIVING AND LEARNING WITH NEW MEDIA, published by The MIT Press. Reprinted with permission; 34 (T) APA's Code of Ethics Published by the American Psychological Association; 34 APA's Committee on Animal Research and Ethics (CARE) Published by the American Psychological Association.

CHAPTER 2

43 Adapted from Fundamentals of Human Neuropsychology (4th ed.), by Brian Kolb and Ian Q. Whishaw. Copyright © 1980, 1985, 1990, 1996; 49 Brain changes in response to experience. Illustration from Bunji Tagawa from "Brain changes in response to experience" by M. R. Rosenzweig, E. L. Bennett, and M. C. Diamond,© 1972 by Scientific American, Inc. Adapted with permission from the Estate of Bunji Tagawa; 53 Psychology: The Core, 1st edition, by Charles G. Morris and Albert A. Maisto. Copyright © 2008. Reproduced by permission of Pearson Education, Inc.; 59 (B) The split-brain experiment. ZIMBARDO, PHILIP G.; JOHNSON, ROBERT L.; MCCANN, VIVIAN, PSYCHOLOGY: CORE CONCEPTS, 6th, © 2009. Printed and Electronically reproduced by permission of Pearson Education, Inc., Upper Saddle River, New Jersey; 63 Reprinted from Human Physiology: An Integrated Approach by A. C. Silverthorn. Copyright © 1989. Reprinted by permission of Pearson Education, Inc., Upper Saddle River, NJ; 65 Figure 15.14, p. 262, from General Biology, Revised Edition by Willis Johnson. Copyright © 1961 by Brooks/Cole, a part of Cengage Learning, Inc. Reproduced by permission. www.cengage.com/permissions.

CHAPTER 3

89 Adapted from "The Split Brain of Man," by Michael S. Gazzaniga, illustrations by Eric Mose. Copyright © 1967. Reprinted by permission of the Estate of Eric Mose; 97 (B) Drawing adapted from "The Hair Cells of the Inner Ear" by A. J. Hudspeth, illustrated by Bunji Tagawa. Copyright © 1983. Adapted with permission from the Estate of Bunji Tagawa.

CHAPTER 4

122 Adapted from p. 487 in "Medical Progress of Sleep Disorders: Recent Findings in the Diagnosis and Treatment of Disturbed Sleep" by Anthony Kales, M.D. et al., The New England Journal of Medicine, 290 (1974), 487–499. Copyright © 1974 by the Massachusetts Medical Society. All rights reserved.; 123 Reprinted p. 16 in "Ontogenetic Development of the Human Sleep-Dream Cycle" by Roffwarg et al., Science, 152 (1966). Copyright © 1966 by the American Association from the Advancement of Science. Reprinted by permission of Copyright Clearance Center on behalf of AAAS; 132 Signs of Substance Dependence. Newton's definition of clinical dependence. Published by the American Psychological Association; 133 (B) Monitoring the future: A continuing study of American Youth. http://www.monitoringthefuture.org/ data/10data/pr10t3.pdf; 136 (T) http://www.niaaa.nih.gov; 136 (B) http://www.alcoholalert.com; 138 (B) The amount of caffeine in some common preparations. Based on Get Pharmacy Advice. http://www.getpharmacyadvice.com; 140 (T) Teenage use of Ecstasy. The Monitoring the Future Study, the University of Michigan. 2010; 142 (B) Teenage use of marijuana in past years. The Monitoring the Future Study, the University of Michigan. 2010; 147 "Hypnosis typically involves an introduction to the procedure..." The Society of Psychological Hypnosis. Division 30 of the APA. Published by the American Psychological Association.

CHAPTER 5

168 (B) Examples of Reinforcement in Everyday Life (adapted) LANDY, F., PSYCHOLOGY: THE SCIENCE OF PEOPLE, 2nd, © 1987. Printed and

Electronically reproduced by permission of Pearson Education, Inc., Upper Saddle River, New Jersey; 175 Tolman & Honzik, 1930; 179 (T) Results of Bandura's study. Influence of models' reinforcement contingencies on the acquisition of imitative responses. Journal of Personality and Social Psychology, 1, 592, 1965. Published by the American Psychological Association.

CHAPTER 7

243 (T) Correlations of IQ scores and family relationships. Data from Genetics and intelligence: A review; 247–248 Definition of mental retardation. DSM-IV, APA. Published by the American Psychological Association.

CHAPTER 8

261 (B) The Yerkes–Dodson law. Psychological Review, 62, 243–254. Published by the American Psychological Association; 262 Motivation and Personality by Abraham H.Maslow. Copyright © 1970; 266 (T) Four symptoms used in the diagnosis of anorexia nervosa. APA 2000. Published by the American Psychological Association; 266 (B) Criteria for the diagnosis of Bulimia. Herpertz-Dahlmann. Published by the American Psychological Association; 267 CDC/NCHS, NHES, and NHANES; 271 Adapted from Masters & Johnson, 1966. Reprinted by permission of The Masters and Johnson Institute; 272 http://www.durex.com/cm/ gss2005result.pdf.

CHAPTER 9

300 "Regional Differences in the Synaptogenesis in the Human Cerebral Cortex" by Huttenlocher and Debholkar, Journal of Comparative Neurology, 387 (October 20, 1997) 2, pp. 167–178. Copyright © 1997; 301 (B) Body proportions at various ages. Data from Individual Patterns of Development; 315 http://www.cdc.gov/healthyyouth/sexualbehaviors; 320 (T) Marital satisfaction. Data from American Sociological Association; 325 (T) Psychological well-being across the life-span. Stone et al. Reprinted by permission of Proceedings of the National Academy of Sciences, 107, 9985–9990; 327 Data from On Death and Dying, 1953.

CHAPTER 10

335 (T) The structural relationship formed by the id, ego, and superego. Data from New Introductory Lectures on Psychoanalysis; 340 (B) Erickson's Stages of Personality Development. Data from Childhood and Society; 346 (T) (adapted) "Heritability of Facet-Level Traits in a Cross-Cultural Twin Sample". From Journal of Personality & Social Psychology. Published by the American Psychological Association.

CHAPTER 11

364 Sources of Stress in America. From Stressed in America. Published by the American Psychological Association; 383 "Invisible Wounds" by R. F. Mollica, Scientific American, June 2000. Copyright © 2000.

CHAPTER 12

391 Opening case: Jack was a very successful chemical engineer (adapted) (as submitted). Selections from pages 170, 214, 270 labeled "Jack" "Claudia" and "Jonathan" respectively. NEVID, JEFFREY S.; RATHUS, SPENCER A.; GREENE, BEVERLY, ABNORMAL PSYCHOLOGY IN A CHANGING WORLD, MEDIA AND RESEARCH UPDATE, 5th, © 2005. Printed and Electronically reproduced by permission of Pearson Education, Inc., Upper Saddle River, New Jersey; 392 From "A Tripartite Model of Mental Health and Therapeutic Outcomes with Special Reference to Negative Effects on Psychotherapy" by H. H. Strupp and S. W. Hadley, American Psychologist, 32 (1977), pp. 187–196. Copyright © 1977 by American Psychological Association.; 395 National Institute of Mental Health (2005); 398 Recognizing Depression. Data from Diagnostic and Statistical Manual of Mental Disorders, American Psychiatric Association; 400 Gender and race differences in the suicide rate across the life span. Data from CDC, http://www.cdc.gov/nchs/data/dvs/MortFinal2007_WorkTable210R.pdf; 410 Sexual dysfunction in the United States. Data from the American Medical Association, February 1999.

CHAPTER 13

426 Bjanka Kadic/Alamy; 426 Dialogue starting "Therapist: (summarizing and restating) It sounds as if you would like to let loose with me..." Wolberg, Lewis. The Technique of Psychotherapy, 3/e. Jason Aronson Inc. Reprinted with permission of Rowman & Littlefield Publishers, Inc.; 428 Dialogue between client and therapist. Hersher, Leonard. Four Psychotherapies. 1970. Reprinted by permission of Pearson Higher Education; 429 Dialogue starting "Therapist: Try to describe just what you are aware of at each moment..." SHAFFER, HUMANISTIC PSYCHOLOGY., 1st, ©1978. Printed and Electronically reproduced by permission of Pearson Education, Inc., Upper Saddle River, New Jersey; 439 Duration of therapy and improvement (adapted) From the American Psychologist Published by the American Psychological Association; 442 Major Types of Psychoactive Medications (adapted and updated) Data from Handbook of psychotherapy and behavior change.

APPENDIX B

498 Predictive Validity of Commonly Used Selection Methods. From Psychological Bulletin Published by the American Psychological Association; 501 Example of a BARS Performance Evaluation. Data from Psychology of Work Behavior.

Name Index

Subject Index

Abnormal behavior. See also
    Psychological disorders
    classification of, 396–97
    defining, 491–92
    early attitudes toward, 392–93
    prevalence of, 395
    treatment of, 393
Absenteeism, in the workplace, 346
Absolute refractory period, 46
Absolute threshold, 82, 83fig
Abu Ghraib prison scandal, 476
Academic success, 246–47
Acceptance, 280, 327
Accreditation Council for
    Graduate Medical Education
    (ACGME), 124
Acetylcholine (ACh), 46, 47tab, 49, 203
Achievement motive, 277
Action potential, 44, 45fig, 46fig
Actor–observer bias, 460–61
Actualizing tendency, 343
Acupuncture, 103
Acute stress disorder, 404
Adaptation
    dark, 87
    defined, 82
    hearing, 95
    light, 88
    sensory, 82
    skin senses, 102
    taste, 100
    visual, 87–88
Adaptive behaviors, 75–76
Addiction
    to cocaine and crack, 140–41
    defined, 132
    insula and, 57
Additive color mixing, 90–91, 90fig
Adenosine, 49, 120
Adjustment to stress, 363
Adolescence/adolescents,
    313–18, 330–31
    alcohol use by, 133, 133fig
    cognitive changes in, 315
    depression in, 317, 399
    eating disorders in, 266–67
    Ecstasy use by, 140
    fetishism in, 409
    formal-operational stage in, 303–4
    identity crisis in, 316
    identity formation in, 316
    marijuana use by, 141, 142fig, 143
    maturity of, 303–4
    mental health care for, 448–49
    moral development in, 304–5
    parent relationships, 317
    peer relationships, 316
    personality development
      in, 315–17
    physical change in, 313–14
    pregnancy in, 314–15

    problems in, 317–18
    self-esteem in, 317
    sexual activity by, 314
    sexual development in, 314–15
    sleep deprivation in, 124
    smoking by, 139, 380
    social development in, 315–17
    storm and stress view of, 316
    suicide in, 317
    violence and, 317–18
Adolescent psychology, 5
Adoption studies, 74
Adrenal cortex, 68
Adrenal glands, 67fig, 68
Adrenaline, 374
Adrenal medulla, 68
Adultery, 272
Adulthood, 331
    anxiety in, 339
    cognitive changes in, 322
    development stags, 319–23
    dual-career families, 321–22
    ending relationships, 320
    formal-operational stage in, 303–4
    menopause, 323
    midlife, 322
    parenthood, 319–20
    partnerships in, 319
    personality in, 319
    work issues, 320–22
Advertising
    antismoking ads, 139
    attention-getting, 468–69
    hunger and, 264
    subliminal messages in, 83, 83fig
Aerial perspective, 109
Afferent neurons, 42, 44tab
Affiliation motive, 278
African Americans
    life expectancy, 324
    as psychologists, 23
    psychology research and, 31
    therapist preferences, 451
Africans, racial categories, 22–23
Afterimages, 88, 91, 92fig
Aggression, 275–77
    culture and, 276–77
    defined, 276
    evolution and, 276
    frustration-aggression theory, 466
    gender and, 277
    observational learning of, 177–78
    punishment and, 163–64
    road rage, 367
    in sports, 276, 277fig
    stress and, 373
    testosterone and, 68
Aging, 323–28. See also Late adulthood
    cognitive changes and, 326
    dying, 327
    end-of-life issues, 326–27

    life expectancy, 323–24
    physical changes, 324–25
    social development and, 325–26
    stereotypes about, 324
    widowhood, 327–28
Agoraphobia, 403
Agreeableness, 345–48, 350
AIDS, 232
Air traffic controllers, 121
Al-Anon Family Groups, 438
Alarm reaction, 375
Alcohol
    abuse and addiction, 133–35
    binge drinking, 137
    caffeine and, 139
    characteristics and
      effects, 134tab
    defined, 133
    health effects, 133–35
    historic use of, 131
    per capita consumption, 136fig
    physical impacts of, 134
    prenatal development and, 295
    social costs, 133–34
    studying effects of, 133
    traffic accidents related to, 136fig
    women and, 135–36
Alcohol aversion treatment, 432
Alcoholic myopia, 135
Alcoholics Anonymous, 144, 437, 438
Alcoholism
    as a disease, 144
    genetic factors and, 143–44
    memory impairment and, 203
    self-tests for, 132
Alcohol poisoning, 134
Alex (African gray parrot), 224
Algorithms, 227
All-or-none law, 46
Alpha brain waves, 146
Altered states of consciousness, 119
Altruism, 378–79
Altruistic behavior, 478–79
Alzheimer's Association, 326
Alzheimer's disease, 46
    acetylcholine and, 203
    hippocamus and, 203
    progression of, 203fig, 326
American Academy of Pediatrics, 312
American Heart Association, 268
American Men of Science
    (Cattell), 19–20
American Psychiatric Association
    (APA), 132tab, 247, 266, 395, 438
American Psychological Association
    (APA), 19, 273, 303, 438, 450
    code of ethics, 33–35
    Committee on Animal Research
      and Ethics (CARE), 35
    divisions, 4, 6
    Office of Ethnic Minority Affairs, 23

American Psychologist, The,
    369, 481, 482
Amnesia
    childhood, 208
    retrograde, 203
Amniocentesis, 74
Amphetamines, 139–40
    characteristics and effects, 134tab
    defined, 139
    effects of, 140
    historical uses of, 139
Amplitude of sound waves, 94
Amputation, 102
Amygdala, 56tab, 57, 285
    infant temperament and, 297
    memory storage and, 200fig, 201
Amytal, 137
Anal stage, 337
Androgens, 68
Anger, 280
    in coping with death, 327
    expressing, 287
    heart disease and, 376
    as stress coping strategy, 370
    sublimation of, 372
    Type A behavior pattern
      and, 375–76
Animals
    behavior genetics and, 73
    classical conditioning in,
      153–56, 157, 181
    cognition in, 223–24
    cognitive learning in, 175, 179, 183
    color vision in, 92
    conditioned taste aversion in, 157
    contingencies in classical
      conditioning in, 167
    emotion in, 281fig
    extinction in, 170
    homosexuality in, 273, 273fig
    insight in, 175–76
    language and, 222–23, 256
    learned helplessness in, 164–65
    learning set and, 176
    maze learning in, 175
    nonverbal communication in, 285
    operant conditioning in,
      158–60, 171fig
    in psychological research, 34–35
    research ethics, 34–35
    sense of self, 224
    sense of smell, 99
    sex drive in, 270
    signs and, 223
    sleep in, 119
    tool use by, 179
Anorexia nervosa, 266–67
Anosmia, 99
Antianxiety medications, 444
Anticipation, 280
Antidepressant drugs, 49, 443